D0154589

Your Office

Microsoft® Office 365®
Excel™ 2019 Comprehensive

Series Editor **AMY KINSER**

JACOBSON | KINSER | MORIARITY | NIGHTINGALE

Vice President of Courseware Portfolio Management: Andrew Gilfillan
Executive Portfolio Manager: Samantha Lewis
Team Lead, Content Production: Laura Burgess
Content Producer: Shannon Stanton
Development Editor: Nancy Lamm
Portfolio Management Assistant: Bridget Daly
Director of Product Marketing: Brad Parkins
Director of Field Marketing: Jonathan Cottrell
Product Marketing Manager: Heather Taylor
Field Marketing Manager: Bob Nisbet
Product Marketing Assistant: Liz Bennett
Field Marketing Assistant: Derrica Moser

Senior Operations Specialist: Maura Garcia
Senior Art Director: Mary Seiner
Interior and Cover Design: Pearson CSC
Cover Photo: Courtesy of Shutterstock® Images
Senior Product Model Manager: Eric Hakanson
Manager, Digital Studio: Heather Darby
Digital Content Producer, MyLab IT: Becca Golden
Course Producer, MyLab IT: Amanda Losonsky
Digital Studio Producer: Tanika Henderson
Full-Service Project Management: Pearson CSC (Amy Kopperude)
Composition: Pearson CSC

Credits and acknowledgments borrowed from other sources and reproduced, with permission, in this textbook appear on appropriate page within text.

Microsoft and/or its respective suppliers make no representations about the suitability of the information contained in the documents and related graphics published as part of the services for any purpose. All such documents and related graphics are provided "as is" without warranty of any kind. Microsoft and/or its respective suppliers hereby disclaim all warranties and conditions with regard to this information, including all warranties and conditions of merchantability, whether express, implied or statutory, fitness for a particular purpose, title and non-infringement. In no event shall Microsoft and/or its respective suppliers be liable for any special, indirect or consequential damages or any damages whatsoever resulting from loss of use, data or profits, whether in an action of contract, negligence or other tortious action, arising out of or in connection with the use or performance of information available from the services.

The documents and related graphics contained herein could include technical inaccuracies or typographical errors. Changes are periodically added to the information herein. Microsoft and/or its respective suppliers may make improvements and/or changes in the product(s) and/or the program(s) described herein at any time.

Microsoft® and Windows® are registered trademarks of the Microsoft Corporation in the U.S.A. and other countries. This book is not sponsored or endorsed by or affiliated with the Microsoft Corporation.

Copyright © 2020 by Pearson Education, Inc., New York, NY 10013. All rights reserved. Printed in the United States of America. This publication is protected by Copyright and permission should be obtained from the publisher prior to any prohibited reproduction, storage in a retrieval system, or transmission in any form or by any means, electronic, mechanical, photocopying, recording, or likewise. For information regarding permission(s), write to: Rights and Permissions Department.

Pearson Prentice Hall™ is a trademark of Pearson Education, Inc.
Pearson® is a registered trademark of Pearson plc
Prentice Hall® is a registered trademark of Pearson Education, Inc.

Pearson Education Ltd., London
Pearson Education Singapore, Pte. Ltd
Pearson Education, Canada, Inc.
Pearson Education–Japan
Pearson Education Australia PTY, Limited

Pearson Education North Asia Ltd., Hong Kong
Pearson Educación de Mexico, S.A. de C.V.
Pearson Education Malaysia, Pte. Ltd.

Library of Congress Cataloging-in-Publication Data available upon request

ISBN-10: 0-13-539472-4
ISBN-13: 978-0-13-539472-4

Dedications

I dedicate this series to my Kinser Boyz for their unwavering love, support, and patience; to my parents and sister for their love; to my students for inspiring me; to Sam for believing in me; and to the instructors I hope this series will inspire!

Amy S. Kinser

I dedicate this book to the three most imaginative, exciting, and encouraging pages in my book of life; Paige, Emma, and Jerra!

Kristyn A. Jacobson

For my wife, Amy, and our two boys, Matt and Aidan. I cannot thank them enough for their support, love, and endless inspiration.

J. Eric Kinser

I dedicate this book to my beautiful and amazing wife, April. Without her support and understanding, this would not have been possible. Also, to my wonderful son, Patton, whose strength to overcome so many obstacles in his life inspires me to continue to do my best work.

Brant Moriarity

To my parents, who always believed in and encouraged me and have given me unconditional support, patience, and love. To my brother and my hero—may you be watching from Heaven with joy in your heart.

Jennifer Paige Nightingale

About the Authors

Amy S. Kinser, Esq., Series Editor

Amy holds a B.A. degree in Chemistry with a Business minor from Indiana University, and a J.D. from the Maurer School of Law, also at Indiana University. After working as an environmental chemist, starting her own technology consulting company, and practicing intellectual property law, she has spent the past 15 years teaching technology at the Kelley School of Business in Bloomington, Indiana. Currently, she serves as the Director of Computer Skills and Senior Lecturer at the Kelley School of Business at Indiana University. She also loves spending time with her two sons, Aidan and J. Matthew, and her husband J. Eric.

Kristyn A. Jacobson

Kristyn holds an M.S. in Education from the University of Wisconsin-La Crosse and a B.S. in Business Education from the University of Wisconsin-Eau Claire. She has been a faculty member and department chair of the Business Technology department at Madison College in Madison, Wisconsin for over 16 years. She also serves as the curriculum coordinator for Microsoft Excel beginning, intermediate, and advanced level courses for the college. As well as teaching, Kristyn enjoys providing trainings to businesses on the Microsoft Office Suite including Microsoft Project, project management, customer service, personal productivity, and time management. Prior to teaching at Madison College, she taught at a business college in Des Moines, Iowa where she helped implement their online learning program while also teaching traditional business courses.

J. Eric Kinser

Eric Kinser received his B.S. degree in Biology from Indiana University and his M.S. in Counseling and Education from the Indiana School of Education. He has worked in the medical field and in higher education as a technology and decision support specialist. He is currently a senior lecturer in the Operations and Decision Technology Department at the Kelley School of Business at Indiana University. When not teaching he enjoys experimenting with new technologies, traveling, and hiking with his family.

Brant Moriarity

Brant P. Moriarity earned a B.A. in Religious Studies/Philosophy and a M.S. in Information Systems at Indiana University. He is a Senior Lecturer at the Indiana University's Kelley School of Business, where he teaches topics such as data management and analysis, as well as the strategic use of Information Systems in business. He is also the founder of Beats Per Minute Technologies, LLC, bringing the benefits of business analytics and custom database application development to small businesses and non-profit organizations.

Jennifer Paige Nightingale

Jennifer Nightingale, associate professor at Slippery Rock University of Pennsylvania, has taught Information Systems Management since 2000. Before joining Slippery Rock University, she spent 15 years in industry with a focus in management and training. Her research expertise is in instructional technology, using technology as a teaching tool, and the impact of instructional technologies on student learning. She has earned numerous teaching and research honors and awards, holds an Ed.D. (instructional technology) and two M.S. degrees (information systems management and education) from Duquesne University, and a B.A. from the University of Pittsburgh.

Brief Contents

Contents

Acknowledgments

The *Your Office* team would like to thank the following reviewers who have invested time and energy to help shape this series from the very beginning, providing us with invaluable feedback through their comments, suggestions, and constructive criticism.

We'd like to thank all of our conscientious reviewers, including those who contributed to our previous editions:

Sven Aelterman
Troy University

Nitin Aggarwal
San Jose State University

Heather Albinger
Waukesha County Technical College

Angel Alexander
Piedmont Technical College

Melody Alexander
Ball State University

Karen Allen
Community College of Rhode Island

Maureen Allen
Elon University

Wilma Andrews
Virginia Commonwealth University

Mazhar Anik
Owens Community College

David Antol
Harford Community College

Kirk Atkinson
Western Kentucky University

Barbara Baker
Indiana Wesleyan University

Lynn Baldwin
Madison College

Kristi Berg
Minot State University

Kavuri Bharath
Old Dominion University

Ann Blackman
Parkland College

Jeanann Boyce
Montgomery College

Lynn Brooks
Tyler Junior College

Cheryl Brown
Delgado Community College
West Bank Campus

Bonnie Buchanan
Central Ohio Technical College

Peggy Burrus
Red Rocks Community College

Richard Cacace
Pensacola State College

Margo Chaney
Carroll Community College

Shanan Chappell
College of the Albemarle, North Carolina

Kuan-Chou Chen
Purdue University, Calumet

David Childress
Ashland Community and Technical College

Keh-Wen Chuang
Purdue University North Central

Suzanne Clayton
Drake University

Amy Clubb
Portland Community College

Bruce Collins
Davenport University

Linda Collins
Mesa Community College

Margaret Cooksey
Tallahassee Community College

Charmayne Cullom
University of Northern Colorado

Christy Culver
Marion Technical College

Wanda Curtsinger
Texas A&M

Juliana Cypert
Tarrant County College

Harold Davis
Southeastern Louisiana University

Jeff Davis
Jamestown Community College

Jennifer Day
Sinclair Community College

Anna Degtyareva
Mt. San Antonio College

Beth Deinert
Southeast Community College

Kathleen DeNisco
Erie Community College

Donald Dershem
Mountain View College

Sallie Dodson
Radford University

Joseph F. Domagala
Duquesne University

Bambi Edwards
Craven Community College

Elaine Emanuel
Mt. San Antonio College

Diane Endres
Ancilla College

Nancy Evans
Indiana University, Purdue University, Indianapolis

Christa Fairman
Arizona Western College

Marni Ferner
University of North Carolina, Wilmington

Paula Fisher
Central New Mexico Community College

Linda Fried
University of Colorado, Denver

Diana Friedman
Riverside Community College

Susan Fry
Boise State University

Virginia Fullwood
Texas A&M University, Commerce

Janos Fustos
Metropolitan State College of Denver

John Fyfe
University of Illinois at Chicago

Saiid Ganjalizadeh
The Catholic University of America

Randolph Garvin
Tyler Junior College

Diane Glowacki
Tarrant County College

Jerome Gonnella
Northern Kentucky University

Lorie Goodgine
Tennessee Technology Center in Paris

Connie Grimes
Morehead State University

Debbie Gross
Ohio State University

Babita Gupta
California State University, Monterey Bay

Lewis Hall
Riverside City College

Jane Hammer
Valley City State University

Marie Hartlein
Montgomery County Community College

Darren Hayes
Pace University

Paul Hayes
Eastern New Mexico University

Mary Hedberg
Johnson County Community College

Lynda Henrie
LDS Business College

Deedee Herrera
Dodge City Community College

Marilyn Hibbert
Salt Lake Community College

Jan Hime
University of Nebraska, Lincoln

Cheryl Hinds
Norfolk State University

Mary Kay Hinkson
Fox Valley Technical College

Margaret Hohly
Cerritos College

Brian Holbert
Spring Hill College

Susan Holland
Southeast Community College

Anita Hollander
University of Tennessee, Knoxville

Emily Holliday
Campbell University

Stacy Hollins
St. Louis Community College
Florissant Valley

Mike Horn
State University of New York, Geneseo

Christie Hovey
Lincoln Land Community College

Margaret Hvatum
St. Louis Community College Meramec

Jean Insinga
Middlesex Community College

Kristyn Jacobson
Madison College

Jon (Sean) Jasperson
Texas A&M University

Glen Jenewein
Kaplan University

Gina Jerry
Santa Monica College

Dana Johnson
North Dakota State University

Mary Johnson
Mt. San Antonio College

Penny Johnson
Madison College

Linda Johnsonius
Murray State University

Carla Jones
Middle Tennessee State University

Susan Jones
Utah State University

Nenad Jukic
Loyola University, Chicago

Sali Kaceli
Philadelphia Biblical University

Sue Kanda
Baker College of Auburn Hills

Robert Kansa
Macomb Community College

Susumu Kasai
Salt Lake Community College

Linda Kavanaugh
Robert Morris University

Debby Keen
University of Kentucky

Mike Kelly
Community College of Rhode Island

Melody Kiang
California State University, Long Beach

Lori Kielty
College of Central Florida

Richard Kirk
Pensacola State College

Dawn Konicek
Blackhawk Tech

John Kucharczuk
Centennial College

Anthony Lapes
Baylor University

David Largent
Ball State University

Stephen Larson
Slippery Rock University

Frank Lee
Fairmont State University

Luis Leon
The University of Tennessee at Chattanooga

Freda Leonard
Delgado Community College

Karen Leskoven
Baylor University

Julie Lewis
Baker College, Allen Park

Suhong Li
Bryant Unversity

Renee Lightner
Florida State College

John Lombardi
South University

Rhonda Lucas
Spring Hill College

Adriana Lumpkin
Midland College

Lynne Lyon
Durham College

Nicole Lytle
California State University, San Bernardino

Donna Madsen
Kirkwood Community College

Susan Maggio
Community College of Baltimore County

Michelle Mallon
Ohio State University

Kim Manning
Tallahassee Community College

Paul Martin
Harrisburg Area Community College

Cheryl Martucci
Diablo Valley College

Sebena Masline
Florida State College of Jacksonville

Sherry Massoni
Harford Community College

Lee McClain
Western Washington University

Sandra McCormack
Monroe Community College

Sue McCrory
Missouri State University

Joan McGrory
Southwest Tennessee Community College

Barbara Miller
University of Notre Dame

Pati Milligan
Baylor University

Johnette Moody
Arkansas Tech University

Michael O. Moorman
Saint Leo University

Kathleen Morris
University of Alabama

Alysse Morton
Westminster College

Elobaid Muna
University of Maryland Eastern Shore

Johnna Murray
University of Missouri - St. Louis

Leigh Mutchler
James Madison University

Jackie Myers
Sinclair Community College

Russell Myers
El Paso Community College

Bernie Negrete
Cerritos College

John Nelson
Texas Christian University

Melissa Nemeth
Indiana University, Purdue University,
Indianapolis

Jennifer Nightingale
Slippery Rock University

Kathie O'Brien
North Idaho College

Michael Ogawa
University of Hawaii

Janet Olfert
North Dakota State University

Rene Pack
Arizona Western College

Patsy Parker
Southwest Oklahoma State Unversity

Laurie Patterson
University of North Carolina, Wilmington

Alicia Pearlman
Baker College

Diane Perreault
Sierra College and California State
University, Sacramento

Theresa Phinney
Texas A&M University

Vickie Pickett
Midland College

Marcia Polanis
Forsyth Technical Community College

Rose Pollard
Southeast Community College

Stephen Pomeroy
Norwich University

Leonard Presby
William Paterson University

Donna Reavis
Delta Career Education

Eris Reddoch
Pensacola State College

James Reddoch
Pensacola State College

Michael Redmond
La Salle University

Terri Rentfro
John A. Logan College

David Reva
Kalamazoo Valley Community College

Vicki Robertson
Southwest Tennessee Community College

Jennifer Robinson
Trident Technical College

Dianne Ross
University of Louisiana at Lafayette

Ann Rowlette
Liberty University

Amy Rutledge
Oakland University

Candace Ryder
Colorado State University

Joann Segovia
Winona State University

Eileen Shifflett
James Madison University

Sandeep Shiva
Old Dominion University

Robert Sindt
Johnson County Community College

Cindi Smatt
Texas A&M University

Edward Souza
Hawaii Pacific University

Nora Spencer
Fullerton College

Alicia Stonesifer
La Salle University

Jenny Lee Svelund
University of Utah

Cheryl Sypniewski
Macomb Community College

Arta Szathmary
Bucks County Community College

Nasser Tadayon
Southern Utah University

Asela Thomason
California State University Long Beach

Nicole Thompson
Carteret Community College

Terri Tiedeman
Southeast Community College, Nebraska

Lewis Todd
Belhaven University

Barb Tollinger
Sinclair Community College

Allen Truell
Ball State University

Erhan Uskup
Houston Community College

Lucia Vanderpool
Baptist College of Health Sciences

Michelle Vlaich-Lee
Greenville Technical College

Barry Walker
Monroe Community College

Rosalyn Warren
Enterprise State Community College

Sonia Washington
Prince George's Community College

Eric Weinstein
Suffolk County Community College

Jill Weiss
Florida International University

Lorna Wells
Salt Lake Community College

Rosalie Westerberg
Clover Park Technical College

Clemetee Whaley
Southwest Tennessee Community College

Kenneth Whitten
Florida State College of Jacksonville

MaryLou Wilson
Piedmont Technical College

John Windsor
University of North Texas

Kathy Winters
University of Tennessee, Chattanooga

Nancy Woolridge
Fullerton College

Jensen Zhao
Ball State University

Martha Zimmer
University of Evansville

Molly Zimmer
University of Evansville

Mary Anne Zlotow
College of DuPage

Matthew Zullo
Wake Technical Community College

Special thanks to our content development and technical team:

Lynn Bowen
Technical Editor

Lori Damanti
Technical Editor

Elizabeth Lockley
Technical Editor

Lisa Bucki
Technical Editor

Morgan Hetzler
Technical Editor

Janet Pickard
Technical Editor

Additionally, we'd like to thank our MyLab IT team for their review and collaboration with our text authors:

LeeAnn Bates
MyLab IT content author

Jennifer Hurley
MyLab IT content author

Ralph Moore
MyLab IT content author

Becca Golden
Media Producer

Kevin Marino
MyLab IT content author

Jerri Williams
MyLab IT content author

Preface

The Your Office Series and You

Your Office is Pearson's business-focused Office applications series that teaches problem solving for business and beyond. In this edition, the *Your Office* experience focuses even more on critical thinking to help you learn to use Microsoft Office to solve problems and make decisions in the real world. With an emphasis on improving the connection with MyLab IT Grader, Mac compatibility, critical thinking, and continual updates to stay in sync with the changing Microsoft Office 365, the *Your Office* series offers you the most usable, current, and beneficial learning experience ever.

The goal of *Your Office* is to illustrate how different parts of a realistic business utilize Office applications to approach business problems and respond to business needs. You will become skilled and efficient—a master of Microsoft Excel and Access, learning how to utilize these applications as tools to help you succeed now and in the future. Through using the resources in this series, you will learn how to make Microsoft Office **Your Office**.

New to This Edition

Continual eText Updates: This edition of *Your Office* is written to Microsoft Office 365®, which has regular updates. To stay current with the software, we are committed to twice-annual updates of the eText and Content Updates document available as an instructor resource for text users.

Improved Grader Experience: Students and instructors have the best experience with *Your Office* by using the Grader projects along with the text. Our authors made it a point to improve the one-to-one nature of the Graders and cases within the book, even including a Grader Heads Up feature to alert students to potential differences between the two.

Focus on Mac: Mac usage is growing, and even outstripping PC usage at some four-year institutions. In response, new features such as Mac Troubleshooting and the new Mac appendix help ensure Mac users have a flawless experience using *Your Office*.

Prebuilt Learning Modules: Prebuilt inside MyLab IT, these make course setup a snap. The modules are based on research and instructor best practices, and can be easily customized to meet your course requirements.

Critical Thinking Modules: Prebuilt inside MyLab IT, these pair a Grader project with a Critical Thinking quiz that requires students to first complete a hands-on project, then reflect on what they did and the data or information they interacted with, to answer a series of objective Critical Thinking questions. These are offered at the chapter and business unit level for regular practice, as well as at the application level where students can earn a Critical Thinking badge.

What's New for MyLab IT Graders

Graders with WHY: All Grader project instructions now incorporate the scenario and the WHY to help students critically think and understand why they're performing the steps in the project.

Prepare Case Graders: These existing Prepare Case Graders are built to be more instructional and feature Learning Aids such as Read (eText) and Watch (video) in the Grader report to help students learn, remediate, and resubmit.

Auto-graded Critical Thinking Quizzes:

- Application Capstones that allow students to earn a Critical Thinking badge
- Chapter-level quizzes for each Problem Solve Assessment Grader project
- Business Unit-level quizzes for one Problem Solve Assessment Grader

Improved Mac Compatibility in Graders: All Graders are tested for Mac compatibility and any that can be made 100 percent Mac compatible are identified in the course. This excludes Access projects as well as any that use functionality not available in Mac Office.

Autograded Integrated Grader Projects: Based on discipline-specific integrated projects, covering Word, Excel, PowerPoint, and Access in various combinations.

Final Solution Image: Included with Grader student downloads, a final output image allows students to visualize what their solution should look like.

The *Your Office* Series and MyLab IT

The *Your Office* series has offered instructors a real-world, problem-solving approach to teaching Microsoft Office since 2011. With a hallmark realistic global business scenario that introduces students to the Painted Paradise Resort & Spa throughout multiple applications, students get a real-world sense of how Office is used in an organization. With an emphasis on critical thinking and problem solving, students learn valuable skills about not just how to use Microsoft Office tools, but also when and how best to apply them to solving business problems. In this edition, the pairing of the text with MyLab IT Graders, Critical Thinking modules, and Resources as a fully complementary program allows students and instructors to get the very most out of their use of the *Your Office* series.

To maximize student results, we recommend pairing the text content with MyLab IT, which is the teaching and learning platform that empowers you to reach every student. By combining trusted author content with digital tools and a flexible platform, MyLab IT personalizes the learning experience and improves results for each student. MyLab IT delivers trusted content through easy-to-use prebuilt Learning modules that promote effective learning. Through an authentic learning experience, students become proficient in Microsoft Office and become sharp critical thinkers, developing essential skills employers seek.

Solving Teaching and Learning Challenges

Practice and feedback: What do I do when I get stuck or need more practice?

MyLab IT features **Integrated Learning Aids** within the Grader reports, allowing students to choose to Read (via the eText), Watch (via an author-created hands-on video), or Practice (via a guided simulation) whenever they get stuck. MyLab IT offers **Grader project reports** for coaching, remediation, and defensible grading. Score Card Detail allows you to easily see where students were scored correctly or incorrectly, pointing out how many points were deducted on each step. The Live Comments report allows you and the students to see the actual files the student submitted with markups/comments on what they missed.

Application, motivation, and employability skills: Why am I taking this course and will this help me get a job?

Students want to know that what they're doing in this class is setting them up for their ultimate goal—to get a job. With an emphasis on **employability skills** like critical thinking and other soft skills, **digital badges** to prove student proficiency in Microsoft skills as well as critical thinking, and **MOS certification practice materials** in MyLab IT, the *Your Office* series is putting students on the path to differentiate themselves in the job market, find a job that values their skills, and land that job when they leave school.

Application: How do I get students to apply what they've learned in a meaningful way?

The *Your Office* series and MyLab IT offer instructors the ability to provide students with authentic formative and summative assessments. The **Grader projects** allow students to gain real-world context as they work live in the application, applying both an understanding of how and why to perform certain skills to complete a project. New **Critical Thinking quizzes** require students to demonstrate their understanding of why, by answering questions that force them to analyze and interpret the project they worked on to answer a series of objective questions. The hallmark **Global Business scenario** woven through all chapters and applications requires students to apply their knowledge in a realistic way to a series of cases focused on the same company.

Ease of use: I need a course solution that is easy to use for both myself and my students.

MyLab IT 2019 is the easiest and most accessible in its history. With new **prebuilt learning modules** and **Critical Thinking modules,** course setup is simple! The inclusion of new features such as a helpful **AI chatbot** and **in-product Appcues** that walk both students and instructors through key workflows helps ensure everyone gets up to speed quickly. **LMS integration capabilities** allow users to seamless access to MyLab IT with single sign-on, grade sync, and asset-level deep linking. Continuing a focus on accessibility, MyLab IT includes an **integrated accessibility toolbar** with translation feature for students with disabilities, as well as a **virtual keyboard** that allows students to complete keyboard actions entirely on screen for those who choose to use simulations. And with an enhanced focus on **Mac compatibility** with even more Mac compatible Grader projects, the *Your Office* series makes it easy to deliver a course to students using both PCs and Macs.

Developing Employability Skills

High-demand Office skills are taught to help students gain these skills and prepare for the Microsoft Office Certification exams (MOS). The MOS objectives are covered throughout the content, and an MOS Objective appendix provides clear mapping of where to find each objective. Practice exams in the form of Graders and simulations are available in MyLab IT.

Digital badges are available for students in introductory and advanced Microsoft Excel and Access. This digital credential is issued to students upon successful completion (90%+ score) of an Application Capstone Badging Grader project. MyLab IT badges provide verified evidence that learners have demonstrated specific skills and competencies using Microsoft Office tools in a real project and help distinguish students within the job pool. Badges are issued through the Acclaim system and can be placed into a

LinkedIn ePortfolio, posted on social media (Facebook, Twitter), and/or included in a resume. Badges include relevant tags that allow students to be discoverable by potential employers, as well as search for jobs for which they are qualified.

"The badge is a way for employers to actually verify that a potential employee is actually somewhat fluent with Excel.

—Bunker Hill Community College Student

The new **Critical Thinking badge** in MyLab IT for 2019 provides verified evidence that learners have demonstrated the ability to not only complete a real project, but also analyze and problem solve using Microsoft Office applications. Students prove this by completing an objective quiz that requires them to critically think about the project, interpret data, and explain why they performed the actions they did in the project. Critical Thinking is a hot button issue at many institutions and is highly sought after in job candidates, allowing students with the Critical Thinking badge to stand out and prove their skills.

Soft Skills videos are included in MyLab IT for educators who want to emphasize key employability skills such as accepting criticism and being coachable, customer service, and resume and cover letter best practices.

Key Features

The **Outcomes focus** allows students and instructors to focus on higher-level learning goals and how those can be achieved through particular objectives and skills.

- **Outcomes** are written at the course level and the business unit level.
- **Chapter Objectives list** identifies the learning objectives to be achieved as students work through the chapter. Page numbers are included for easy reference. These are revisited in the Concepts Check at the end of the chapter.
- **MOS Certification Guide** for instructors and students directs anyone interested in prepping for the MOS exam to the specific series resources to find all content required for the test.

Business Application Icons

Customer Service

Finance & Accounting

General Business

Human Resources

Information Technology

Production & Operations

Sales & Marketing

Research & Development

Real World Interview Video

Blue Box Videos

Soft Skills

The **real-world focus** reminds students that what they are learning is practical and useful the minute they leave the classroom.

- **Real World Success** features in the chapter opener share anecdotes from real former students, describing how knowledge of Office has helped them be successful in their lives.
- **Real World Advice boxes** offer notes on best practices for general use of important Office skills. The goal is to advise students as a manager might in a future job.
- **Business Application icons** appear with every case in the text and clearly identify which business application students are being exposed to (finance, marketing, operations, and so on).
- **Real World Interview Video icons** appear with the Real World Success story in the business unit. Each interview features a real businessperson discussing how he or she actually uses the skills in the chapter on a day-to-day basis.

Features for active learning help students learn by doing and immerse them in the business world using Microsoft Office.

- **Blue boxes** represent the hands-on portion of the chapter and help students quickly identify what steps they need to take to complete the chapter Prepare Case. This material is easily distinguishable from explanatory text by the blue-shaded background.
- **Starting and ending files** appear before every case in the text. Starting files identify exactly which student data files are needed to complete each case. Ending files are provided to show students the naming conventions they should use when saving their files. Each file icon is color coded by application.
- **Side Note** conveys a brief tip or piece of information aligned visually with a step in the chapter, quickly providing key information to students completing that particular step.
- **Consider This** offers critical thinking questions and topics for discussion, set apart as a boxed feature, allowing students to step back from the project and think about the application of what they are learning and how these concepts might be used in the future.
- **Soft Skills icons** appear with other boxed features and identify specific places where students are being exposed to lessons on soft skills.

Study aids help students review and retain the material so they can recall it at a moment's notice.

- **Quick Reference boxes** summarize generic or alternative instructions on how to accomplish a task. This feature enables students to quickly find important skills.
- **Concept Check** review questions, which appear at the end of the chapter, require students to demonstrate their understanding of the objectives.
- **Visual Summary** offers a review of the objectives learned in the chapter using images from the completed solution file, mapped to the chapter objectives with callouts and page references, so students can easily find the section of text to refer to for a refresher.
- **MyLab IT™ icons** identify which cases from the book match those in MyLab IT.™
- **Blue Box Video icons** appear with each Active Text box and identify the brief video, demonstrating how students should complete that portion of the Prepare Case.

MyLab IT Grader

Extensive cases allow students to progress from a basic understanding of Office through to proficiency.

- **Chapters all conclude with Practice, Problem Solve, and Perform Cases** to allow full mastery at the chapter level. Alternative versions of these cases are available in Instructor Resources.
- **Business Unit Capstones all include More Practice, Problem Solve, and Perform Cases** that require students to synthesize objectives from the two previous chapters to extend their mastery of the content. Alternative versions of these cases are available in Instructor Resources.
- **More Grader Projects** are offered with this edition, including Prepare cases as well as Problem Solve cases at both the chapter and business unit capstone levels.

Resources

Instructor Teaching Resources

Supplements available to instructors at www.pearsonhighered.com	Features of the Supplement
Instructor's Manual	Available for each chapter and includes: • List of all Chapter Resources, File Names, and Where to Find • Chapter Overview • Class Run-Down • Key Terms • Discussion Questions • Teaching Notes • Additional Web Resources • Cases with File Names • Solutions to Concepts Check Questions

AACSB and Business Application Mapping	A mapping spreadsheet to help you identify content to emphasize key AACSB requirements or focus on key business applications. The spreadsheet lists all features and cases in every chapter that:
	• Demonstrate AACSB Learning Standards including:
	  • Multicultural and diversity understanding
	  • Reflective thinking skills
	  • Communication abilities
	  • Use of information technology
	  • Analytical thinking skills
	  • Ethical understanding and reasoning
	• Identifies the business area/application used, including:
	  • Sales & Marketing
	  • Information Technology
	  • General Business
	  • Human Resources
	  • Finance & Accounting
	  • Production & Operations

Solutions Files, Annotated Solution Files, Scorecards	• Available for all cases with definitive solutions • Annotated Solution Files in PDF feature callouts to enable easy grading • Scorecards to allow for easy scoring for hand-grading all cases with definitive solutions, with all adding up to 100 points and points being divided by step
Rubrics	For Perform Cases without a definitive solution. Available in Microsoft Word format, enabling instructors to customize the assignments for their classes
Test Bank	Approximately 75–100 total questions per chapter, made up of multiple-choice, true/false, and matching. Questions include these annotations: • Correct Answer • Difficulty level • Learning objective Alternative versions of the Test Bank are available for the following LMS: Blackboard CE/Vista, Blackboard, Desire2Learn, Moodle, Sakai, and Canvas

Supplements available to instructors at www.pearsonhighered.com	Features of the Supplement
Computerized TestGen	TestGen allows instructors to: • Customize, save, and generate classroom tests • Edit, add, or delete questions from the Test Item Files • Analyze test results • Organize a database of tests and student results
PowerPoint Presentations	PowerPoints for each chapter cover key topics, feature key images from the text, and include detailed speaker notes in addition to the slide content. PowerPoints meet accessibility standards for students with disabilities. Features include, but are not limited to: • Keyboard and Screen Reader access • Alternative text for images • High-color contrast between background and foreground colors
Scripted Lectures	• A lecture guide that provides the actions and language to help demonstrate skills from the chapter • Follows the activity similar to the Prepare Case but with an alternative scenario and data files
Prepared Exams	• An optional hands-on project that can be used to assess students' ability to perform the skills from each chapter, each business unit, or across all chapters in an application • Each Prepared Exam folder includes the needed data files, instruction file, solution, annotated solution, and scorecard
Additional Problem Solve Cases	• Additional Problem Solve cases that allow instructors to swap out cases from semester to semester, available at the chapter and business unit level • Each additional case folder includes the needed data files, instruction file, solution, annotated solution, and scorecard
Outcome & Objective Maps	• Available for each chapter to help you determine what to assign • Includes every case and identifies which outcomes, objectives, and skills are included from the chapter
MOS Mapping, MOS Online Appendix	• Based on the Office 2019 MOS Objectives • Includes a full mapping of where each objective is covered in the materials • For any content not covered in the textbook, additional material is available in the online appendix document
Transition Guide	A detailed spreadsheet that provides a clear mapping of content from *Your Office Microsoft Office 2016* to *Your Office Microsoft Office 365, 2019* Edition
Content Updates Guide	A living document that features any changes in content based on Microsoft Office 365 changes as well as any errata
Sample Syllabus	Syllabus templates set up for 8-week, 12-week, and 16-week courses
Answer Keys for Concept Checks	Answer keys for each objective question type from each chapter
Answer Keys and Guide for Critical Thinking Quizzes	Answer keys for each Critical Thinking objective quiz from each chapter, business unit, and application

Student Resources

Supplements available to students at www.pearsonhighered.com/youroffice	Features of the Supplement
Student Data Files	All data files needed for the following cases, organized by chapter: • Prepare Case • Practice Case • Problem Solve Case • Perform Case
MOS Certification Material	• Based on the Office 2019 MOS Objectives • Includes a full mapping of where each objective is covered in the materials • For any content not covered in the textbook, additional material is available in the online appendix document
Video supplements available to students within MyLab IT for *Your Office*	**Features of the Videos**
Blue Box Videos	• Screen capture videos following the action in the blue boxes • Available both as one continuous video to cover the entire Prepare Case as well as in individual videos per blue box
Real World Interview Videos	• Live action videos interviewing real business professionals about how they use Microsoft Office to be successful in their careers. One per chapter • Complement the Real World Success feature in each Business Unit
Soft Skills Videos	A video library available in MyLab IT that focuses on a variety of soft skills topics such as interview skills, accepting criticism, and being coachable, resume tips, customer service, and so on

Welcome to the Team!

Welcome to your new office at Painted Paradise Resort & Spa, where we specialize in painting perfect getaways. As the Chief Technology Officer, I am excited to have staff dedicated to the Microsoft Office integration between all the areas of the resort. Our team is passionate about our paradise, and I hope you find this to be your dream position here!

Painted Paradise is a resort and spa in New Mexico catering to business people, romantics, families, and anyone who just needs to get away. Inside our resort are many distinct areas. Many of these areas operate as businesses in their own right but must integrate with the other areas of the resort. The main areas of the resort are as follows.

- The **Hotel** is overseen by our Chief Executive Officer, William Mattingly, and is at the core of our business. The hotel offers a variety of accommodations, ranging from individual rooms to a grand villa suite. Further, the hotel offers packages including spa, golf, and special events.

  Room rates vary according to size, season, demand, and discount. The hotel has discounts for typical groups, such as AARP. The hotel also has a loyalty program where guests can earn free nights based on frequency of visits. Guests may charge anything from the resort to the room.

- **Red Bluff Golf Course** is a private world-class golf course and pro shop. The golf course has services such as golf lessons from the famous golf pro John Schilling and playing packages. Also, the golf course attracts local residents. This requires variety in pricing schemes to accommodate both local and hotel guests. The pro shop sells many retail items online.

  The golf course can also be reserved for special events and tournaments. These special events can be in conjunction with a wedding, conference, meetings, or other events covered by the event planning and catering area of the resort.

- **Turquoise Oasis Spa** is a full-service spa. Spa services include haircuts, pedicures, massages, facials, body wraps, waxing, and various other spa services—typical to exotic. Further, the spa offers private consultation, weight training (in the fitness center), a water bar, meditation areas, and steam rooms. Spa services are offered both in the spa and in the resort guest's room.

  Turquoise Oasis Spa uses top-of-the-line products and some house-brand products. The retail side offers products ranging from candles to age-defying home treatments. These products can also be purchased online. Many of the hotel guests who fall in love with the house-brand soaps, lotions, candles, and other items appreciate being able to buy more at any time.

  The spa offers a multitude of packages including special hotel room packages that include spa treatments. Local residents also use the spa. So, the spa guests are not limited to hotel guests. Thus, the packages also include pricing attractive to the local community.

3355 Hemmingway Circle • Santa Fe, New Mexico 89566

- **Painted Treasures Gift Shop** has an array of items available for purchase, from toiletries to clothes to presents for loved ones back home including a healthy section of kids' toys for traveling business people. The gift shop sells a small sampling from the spa, golf course pro shop, and local New Mexico culture. The gift shop also has a small section of snacks and drinks. The gift shop has numerous part-time employees including students from the local college.

- The **Event Planning & Catering** area is central to attracting customers to the resort. From weddings to conferences, the resort is a popular destination. The resort has a substantial number of staff dedicated to planning, coordinating, setting up, catering, and maintaining these events. The resort has several facilities that can accommodate large groups. Packages and prices vary by size, room, and other services such as catering. Further, the Event Planning & Catering team works closely with local vendors for floral decorations, photography, and other event or wedding typical needs. However, all catering must go through the resort (no outside catering permitted). Lastly, the resort stocks several choices of decorations, table arrangements, and centerpieces. These range from professional, simple, themed, and luxurious.

- **Indigo5** and the **Silver Moon Lounge**, a world-class restaurant and lounge that is overseen by the well-known Chef Robin Sanchez. The cuisine is balanced and modern. From steaks to pasta to local southwestern meals, Indigo5 attracts local patrons in addition to resort guests. While the catering function is separate from the restaurant—though menu items may be shared—the restaurant does support all room service for the resort. The resort also has smaller food venues onsite such as the Terra Cotta Brew coffee shop in the lobby.

Currently, these areas are using Office to various degrees. In some areas, paper and pencil are still used for most business functions. Others have been lucky enough to have some technology savvy team members start Microsoft Office Solutions.

Using your skills, I am confident that you can help us integrate and use Microsoft Office on a whole new level! I hope you are excited to call Painted Paradise Resort & Spa *Your Office*.

Looking forward to working with you more closely!

Aidan Matthews
Aidan Matthews
Chief Technology Officer

Dear Students,

If you want an edge over the competition, make it personal. Whether you love sports, travel, the stock market, or ballet, your passion is personal to you. Capitalizing on your passion leads to success. You live in a global marketplace, and your competition is global. The honors students in China exceed the total number of students in North America. Skills can help set you apart, but passion will make you stand above. *Your Office* is the tool to harness your passion's true potential.

In prior generations, personalization in a professional setting was discouraged. You had a "work" life and a "home" life. As the Series Editor, I write to you about the vision for *Your Office* from my laptop, on my couch, in the middle of the night when inspiration struck me. My classroom and living room are my office. Life has changed from generations before us.

So, let's get personal. My degrees are not in technology, but chemistry and law. I helped put myself through school by working full time in various jobs, including a successful technology consulting business that continues today. My generation did not grow up with computers, but I did. My father was a network administrator for the military. So, I was learning to program in Basic before anyone had played Nintendo's *Duck Hunt* or *Tetris*. Technology has always been one of my passions from a young age. In fact, I now tell my husband: Don't buy me jewelry for my birthday, buy me the latest gadget on the market!

In my first law position, I was known as the Office guru to the extent that no one gave me a law assignment for the first two months. Once I submitted the assignment, my supervisor remarked, "Wow, you don't just know how to leverage technology, but you really know the law, too." I can tell you novel-sized stories from countless prior students in countless industries who gained an edge from using Office as a tool. Bringing technology to your passion makes you well rounded and a cut above the rest, no matter the industry or position.

I am most passionate about teaching, in particular teaching technology. I come from many generations of teachers, including my mother who is a kindergarten teacher. For more than 12 years, I have found my dream job passing on my passion for teaching, technology, law, science, music, and life in general at the Kelley School of Business at Indiana University. I have tried to pass on the key to engaging passion to my students. I have helped them see what differentiates them from all the other bright students vying for the same jobs.

Microsoft Office is a tool. All of your competition will have learned Microsoft Office to some degree or another. Some will have learned it to an advanced level. Knowing Microsoft Office is important, but it is also fundamental. Without it, you will not be considered for a position.

Today, you step into your first of many future roles bringing Microsoft Office to your dream job working for Painted Paradise Resort & Spa. You will delve into the business side of the resort and learn how to use *Your Office* to maximum benefit.

Don't let the context of a business fool you. If you don't think of yourself as a business person, you have no need to worry. Whether you realize it or not, everything is business. If you want to be a nurse, you are entering the health care industry. If you want to be a football player in the NFL, you are entering the business of sports as entertainment. In fact, if you want to be a stay-at-home parent, you are entering the business of a family household where *Your Office* still gives you an advantage. For example, you will be able to prepare a budget in Excel and analyze what you need to do to afford a trip to Disney World!

At Painted Paradise Resort & Spa, you will learn how to make Office yours through four learning levels designed to maximize your understanding. You will Prepare, Practice, and Problem Solve your tasks. Then, you will astound when you Perform your new talents. You will be challenged through Consider This questions and gain insight through Real World Advice.

There is something more. You want success in what you are passionate about in your life. It is personal for you. In this position at Painted Paradise Resort & Spa, you will gain your personal competitive advantage that will stay with you for the rest of your life—*Your Office*.

Sincerely,

Amy Kinser

Series Editor

Common Features of Microsoft Office

Chapter 1 UNDERSTANDING THE COMMON FEATURES OF MICROSOFT OFFICE

MyLab IT Grader

Sales & Marketing

General Business

Prepare Case

Painted Paradise Resort & Spa Employee Training Preparation

The gift shop at the Painted Paradise Resort & Spa has an array of items available for purchase, from toiletries and clothes to souvenirs for loved ones back home. There are numerous part-time employees, including students from the local college. The gift shop frequently holds training luncheons for new employees. Your first assignment will be to prepare two documents for a meeting with your manager, Susan Brock: a starting file for meeting minutes and an Excel budget. To complete this task, you need to understand and work with the common features in the Microsoft Office suite.

Mentatdgt/Shutterstock

Student data files needed:

 Blank Word document

 cf01ch01Budget.xlsx

 cf01ch01Logo.jpg

You will save your files as:

 cf01ch01Minutes_LastFirst.docx

 cf01ch01Budget_LastFirst.xlsx

 cf01ch01Budget_LastFirst.pdf

Working with the Office Interface

When you walk into a grocery store, you usually know what you are going to find and that items are likely to be in approximately the same location, regardless of which store you are visiting. The first items you usually see are the fresh fruits and vegetables, while the frozen foods are typically near the end of the store. This similarity among stores creates a comfortable and welcoming experience for the shopper, even if the shopper has never been in that particular store. The brands may be different, but the food types are the same. Canned corn is canned corn.

Microsoft Office was designed to create that same level of familiarity and comfort with its ribbons, features, and functions. Each application has an appearance or user interface that is similar to the appearance or interface of the other applications. The interface for Microsoft Office 2019 has the default being a colorful appearance. The look is minimalist; even the ribbon is hidden by default—unless a setting from a prior version of Office carries into your Office 2019 installation. In this section, you will learn to navigate and use the Microsoft Office interface.

Understand the Office Suite and Applications

Microsoft Office 2019 is a suite of productivity applications or programs that are available for purchase separately or as a package. The exact applications available depend on the package installed. Office 2019 is available in greater variety and flexibility than ever before.

QUICK REFERENCE	Programs in Office 2019

- **Microsoft Word** is a word-processing program. This application can be used to create, edit, and format **documents** such as letters, memos, reports, brochures, resumes, and flyers.
- **Microsoft Excel** is a **spreadsheet** program—a two-dimensional grid that can be used to model quantitative data and perform accurate and rapid calculations with results ranging from simple budgets to financial and statistical analyses.
- **Microsoft PowerPoint** is a **presentation** program—an oral performance aid that uses slides or a stand-alone presentation such as those at kiosks.
- **Microsoft OneNote** is a planner and note-taking program.
- **Microsoft Outlook** is an email, contact, and information management program.
- **Microsoft Access** is known as a **relational database**—or three-dimensional database software—because it connects data in separate tables, allowing you to make the most efficient storage of your data.
- **Microsoft Publisher** is a desktop publishing program that offers professional tools and templates to help communicate a message easily in a variety of publication types, saving time and money while creating a polished and finished look.
- **Microsoft Skype for Business**—formerly known as Lync—is a unified communication platform.

With Office 2019 and Windows 10, Microsoft has embraced the concept of flexible versions for multiple platforms such as Windows Phone, iPads, Android devices, and even a web browser. Different versions of Office have different levels of functionality, but Microsoft has tried to keep the universal user interface as similar as possible. Microsoft Office 2019 will only run on Windows 10 or higher version.

Microsoft Office 2019 is available in several different suite packages from home to enterprise. This book is written with Microsoft Office 365 ProPlus—some packages do not contain the database program Access. Furthermore, most schools have special educational pricing and versions. You should consult your instructor or institution for further information.

For non-educational consumers, Office 2019 is available in two main pricing schemes. You can purchase Office 2019 the traditional way from a retailer for a one-time fee. Microsoft has announced that Office 2019 will be the last time it offers a one-time-fee version. It also has shortened the support period for the one-time-fee version. With the one-time-fee version, you can install the software on exactly one computer. Alternatively, Office 2019 can be purchased by subscription for a yearly or monthly fee. This version is called Office 365. It is the same product as Office 2019, but it comes with more frequent updates, feature updates in addition to the security updates, the ability to be installed on more than one computer, more OneDrive storage space, free minutes in Skype, and several other additional perks. At the time of this writing, the Office 365 version is competitively priced to be less expensive for most people despite the monthly or yearly fee. For the latest in pricing and options, you can visit http://office.microsoft.com.

REAL WORLD ADVICE   **Help, I Have a Mac!**

Traditionally, Office has been available in different versions for Windows and Macs with different functionality, such as the absence of the Access program in the Mac versions. Instead of using the Mac version of Office, two other popular options exist for using Office on a Mac: virtualization and dual boot.

Virtualization of Office on a Mac uses software that mimics Windows in order to run Office. In any major search engine, search for "PC virtualization on Mac" and you will find many software options for emulating a PC on a Mac. While many virtualization programs promise to mimic entirely, there can be some—usually minor—differences.

Dual boot is the ability to choose the operating system on startup. **Bootcamp** is the Mac software that allows the user to decide which operating system—Mac operating system or Windows—to run. When the computer is turned on, the user is given the choice of operating system. Thus, the user can run the Windows version of Office under the Windows operating system.

You should consult your instructor about the policy in your course. Policies on the usage of the Mac operating system vary greatly from course to course and from school to school.

Typically, using Office requires you to have a free Microsoft account. If you are working in a computer lab or enterprise version of Windows 10, you may not need to sign into a Microsoft account to run Office or Windows 10. If you are running Office on a personal computer, you will need to have a Microsoft account. You can create the account when you install Windows 10. If you do not have an account, you need to sign up for one at https://signup.live.com and follow the on-screen instructions. Your first name, last name, and profile image for your Microsoft account will appear in various screens of Windows and Microsoft Office.

Start, Save, and Manipulate Office Applications and Use the Office Ribbon

Each Office application has its own specific application Start screen. From the **application Start screen**, you can select a blank document, workbook, presentation, database, or one of many application-specific templates. Files that have already been created can also be opened from this screen. When existing files are double-clicked from a File Explorer window, the Start screen is not needed and does not open.

Opening Microsoft Word and the Start Screen

Once you start working with these applications, you can have more than one application or more than one instance of the same application open at a time. This means that you can open one file in Word in one window and also open another file in Word in a different window. In this exercise, you will start Microsoft Word so you can create a beginning file for meeting minutes.

 **CF01.01**

SIDE NOTE
Windows Button
Instead of clicking ⊞
you can also press 🏁
on your keyboard.

SIDE NOTE
Windows 10
Office 2019 will not run on
previous versions of Win-
dows. It must be installed
on Windows 10 or greater.

To Open Microsoft Word and Use the Start Screen

a. Click ⊞ and type Word The search results display. Verify the first result is Word, and then press Enter. Pressing Enter automatically selects the first search result. Microsoft Word opens to the Word Start screen.

> **Troubleshooting**
> If Word is not the first option, you will need to select Word from the search results.

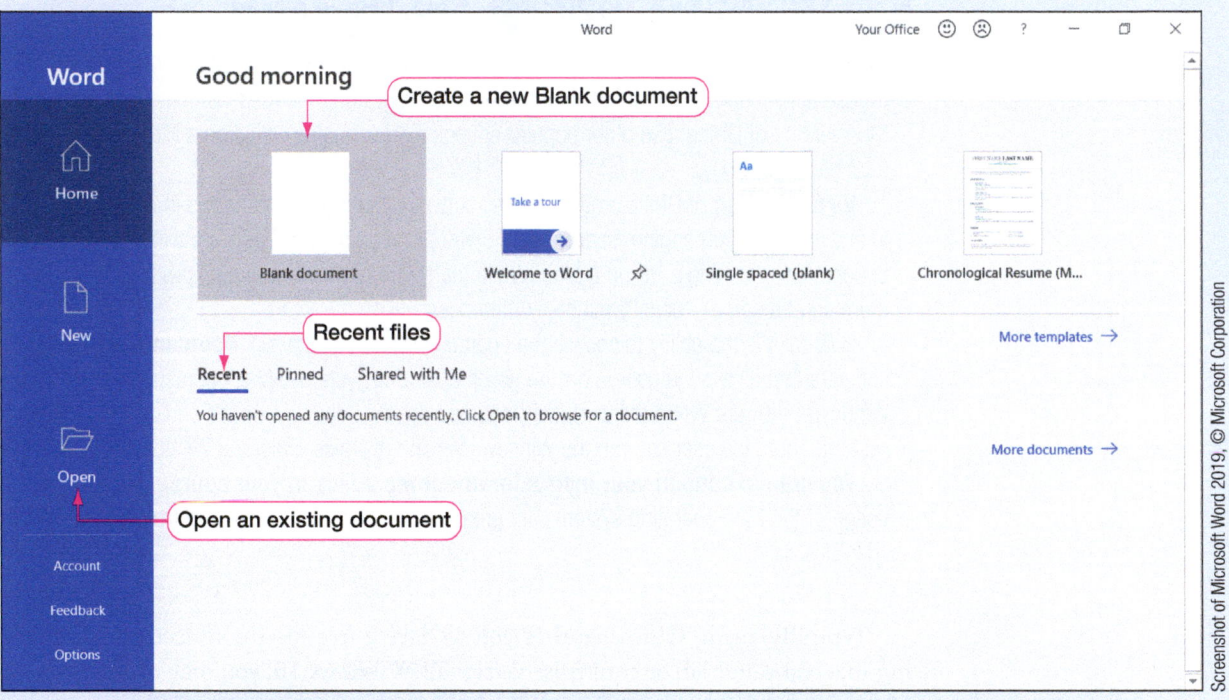

Figure 1 Word Start screen

MAC COMPATIBILITY
Start Screen on a Mac
If you are using a Mac, your screen will look a little different. In most places, even if the Mac screen looks a little different, the same options are still there. This book will point out major, not small screen, differences. All differences are current at the time this book is published. The Mac version could change over time, making these differences no longer correct.

b. Click **Blank document**. A new Word document opens.

Notice the words Document1 – Word appear on the title bar. This means that the document has not been saved yet. The insertion point is at the beginning of the document.

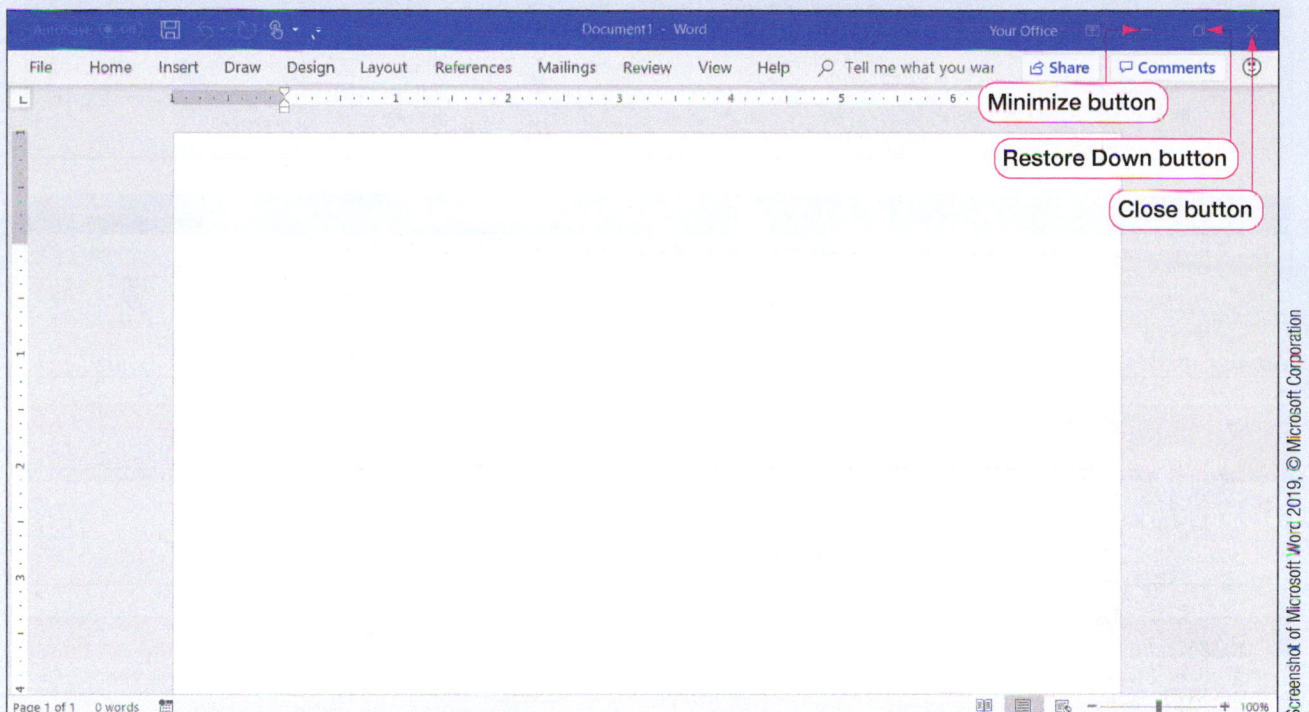

Minimize button

Restore Down button

Close button

Screenshot of Microsoft Word 2019, © Microsoft Corporation

Figure 2   New Word document

Using the Ribbon and Ribbon Display Options

Office has a consistent design and layout that help to make its programs familiar and comfortable to the user. Once you learn to use one Office 2019 program, you can use many of those skills when working with other Office programs. The **ribbon** is the row of tabs across the top of the application window. The ribbon display changes according to the screen resolution of your monitor. The figures in this text are set to a screen resolution of 1366×768. When open, the ribbons look like Figure 3.

The ribbon for each Office application has two tabs in common: the File tab and the Home tab. The File tab is the first tab on the ribbon and is used for file management needs such as saving and printing. The Home tab is the second tab and contains the commands for the most frequently performed activities, such as copying, cutting, and pasting. The commands on these tabs may differ from program to program. Other tabs are program specific, such as the Formulas tab in Excel, the Design tab in Word and PowerPoint, and the Database Tools tab in Access. The ribbon is further subdivided into **groups**—logical groupings of related commands.

By default, the ribbon is hidden. This allows you more room to work with your document rather than having the ribbon take up screen space with buttons and tools. However, hiding the ribbon makes it harder to perform tasks while learning Office. To open the ribbon, you need to pin it open. All directions and figures in this book will assume that the ribbon is pinned open.

Touch mode switches Office into a version that makes a touch screen easy to use. The Touch Mode button ⬚ on the **Quick Access Toolbar** can help you easily switch between mouse and touch modes. If your device has a touch screen, Office may automatically put your ribbon in touch mode.

COMMON FEATURES

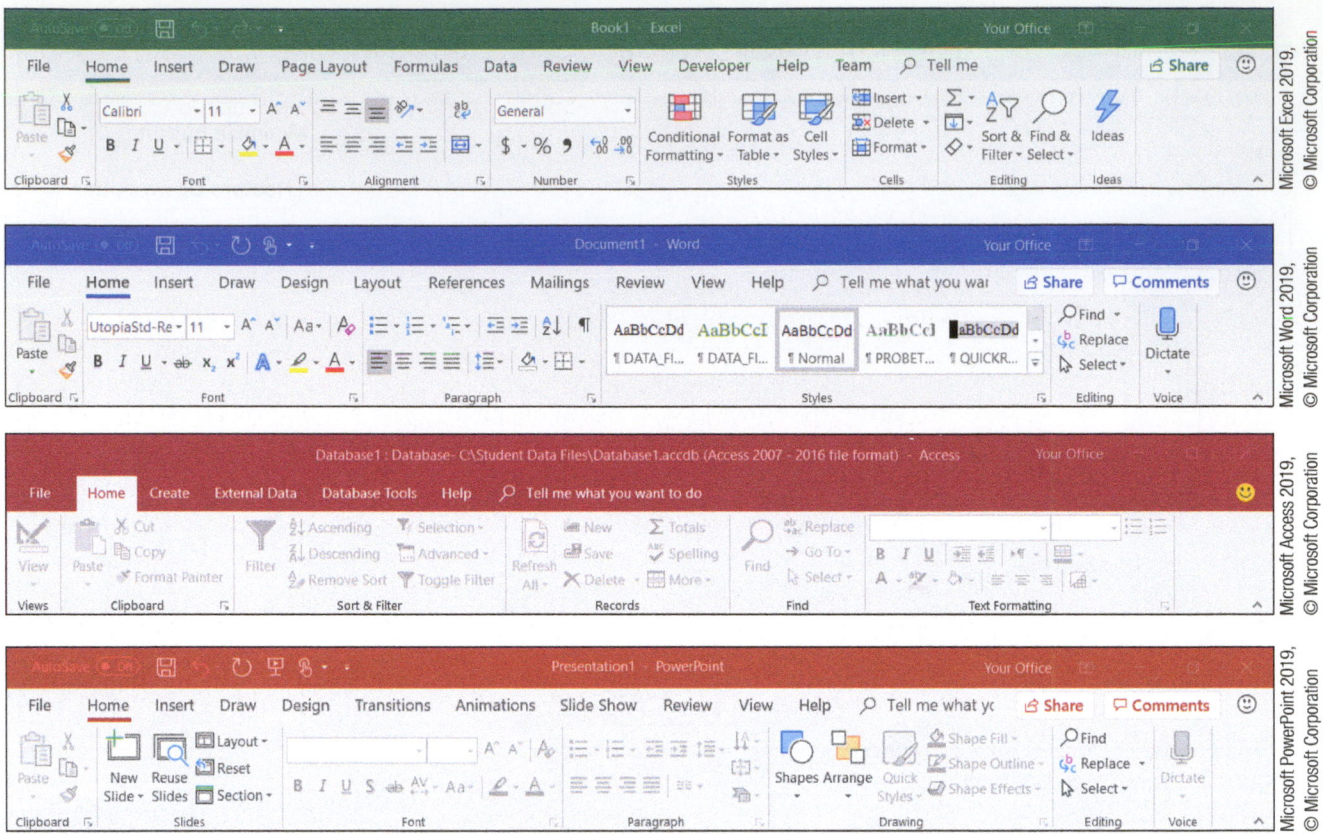

Figure 3   Ribbons of Excel, Word, Access, and PowerPoint

Microsoft Excel 2019, © Microsoft Corporation

Microsoft Word 2019, © Microsoft Corporation

Microsoft Access 2019, © Microsoft Corporation

Microsoft PowerPoint 2019, © Microsoft Corporation

One feature common to all the application ribbons is the four buttons that appear in the top-right corner of an application title bar as shown in Table 1.

Button	Keyboard Shortcut	Action
Ribbon Display Options ⊡	Ctrl + F1 (toggles between collapsing and showing the ribbon)	Auto-hide Ribbon, Show Tabs, and Show Tabs and Commands.
Minimize —	Alt + SpaceBar	Hides a window so it is visible only on the taskbar.
Restore Down ⧉ **or Maximize** ☐	Alt + SpaceBar	When the window is at its maximum size, the button will restore the window to a previous, smaller size. When a window is in the Restore Down mode, the button expands the window to its full size.
Close ☒	Alt + F4	Closes a file; also exits the program if no other files are open for that program.

Table 1   Top-right ribbon buttons

In this exercise, you will pin the ribbon open so that you can see all the tabs and commands. You will also add a title to the document.

CF01.02

To Pin the Ribbon Open and Switch between Mouse and Touch Mode

SIDE NOTE
Pin the Ribbon Open
You can also use the keyboard shortcut of Ctrl+F1. You can also click a tab and In the lower-right corner of the ribbon, click Pin the ribbon.

a. In the top-right corner, click **Ribbon Display Options** and then click **Show Tabs and Commands**. The ribbon opens with the Home tab selected.

Troubleshooting

Your ribbon may seem to have condensed or expanded buttons and groups. The most common causes are different screen resolution, auto-detecting touch mode, or a smaller program window. Because the ribbon changes to accommodate the size of the window or screen, buttons can appear as icons without labels, and a group can be condensed into a button that must be clicked to display the group options. So, do not worry! All the same features are on the ribbon and in the same general area.

All the figures in this book use a screen resolution of **1366 × 768**. Setting your computer to that resolution, if it is available, will minimize this issue. In Windows 10, you can find the screen resolution by right-clicking the desktop, clicking Display settings, and clicking Advanced display settings.

Save button | Touch/Mouse Mode on the Quick Access Toolbar | Title bar name for unsaved documents | Ribbon Display Options

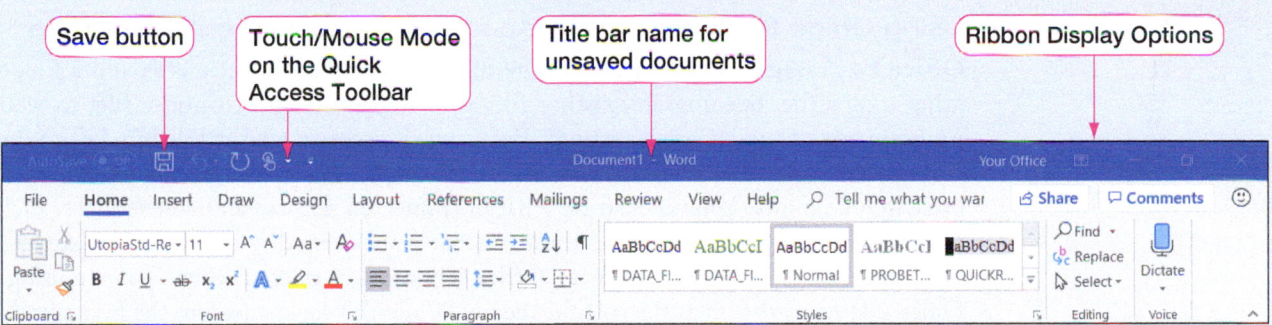

Figure 4 Word with ribbon pinned open

Screenshot of Microsoft Word 2019, © Microsoft Corporation

b. On the Quick Access Toolbar in the top-left corner, click Customize the Quick Access Toolbar and then click **Touch/Mouse Mode**. This adds the Touch/Mouse Mode icon to the Quick Access Toolbar. Click **Touch/Mouse Mode** and then click **Touch**. If your ribbon does not change, you were already in Touch mode—and you most likely have a device with a touch screen.

Troubleshooting

Touch/Mouse Mode is a toggle. So, if Touch/Mouse Mode was already checked, clicking it again turns it off.

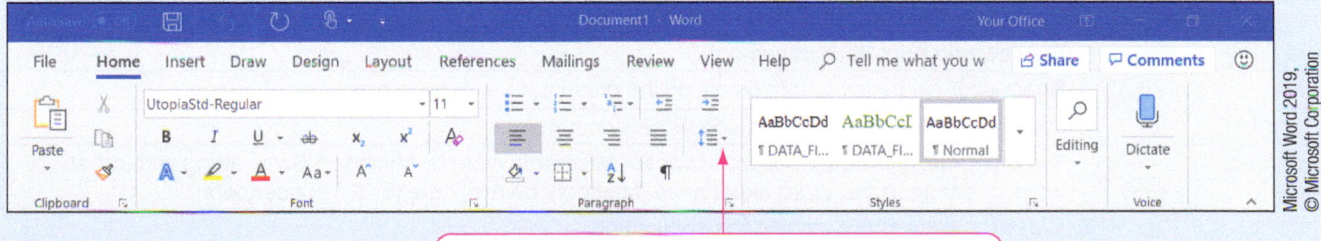

Buttons and commands larger and more spaced out

Microsoft Word 2019, © Microsoft Corporation

Figure 5 Word ribbon in Touch mode

SIDE NOTE
Customize the Quick Access Toolbar
You can customize the Quick Access Toolbar for favorite or frequently used commands such as Quick Print, Spelling & Grammar, or New.

c. All the figures in this text were made in mouse mode. On the Quick Access Toolbar in the upper left, click **Touch/Mouse Mode** 🔲. Then click **Mouse** to ensure that you are in mouse mode.

d. With your insertion point still at the beginning of the document, type
Meeting Minutes – Budget Meeting

CONSIDER THIS | **Advantages of a Common Interface**

The ribbon provides a common user interface. This common interface can help you learn additional applications quickly. What elements have you noticed that are common? What elements have you noticed that are different? Of the elements that are different, how are they still presented in a common way?

Using Office Backstage, Your Account, and Document Properties

Office Backstage provides access to the file-level commands, such as saving a file, creating a new file, opening an existing file, printing a file, and closing a file, as well as program options and account settings. Backstage is accessed via the File tab. Office Backstage includes an area called Account. This enables you to log into your Microsoft account or switch accounts. You can also see a list of connected services and add services, such as LinkedIn and Skype. Table 2 lists the areas that you can modify in Office Backstage.

Under Account, you can see what **Office Theme**—or color scheme—you are using. In Office 2019, the default is the colorful theme. While this looks modern, the best theme for accessibility for people with vision impairments or color blindness is the White theme. For this reason, all of the figures in this book were made with the White theme after this next exercise.

Under Account, you can also see your **Office Background**—an artistic design in the upper right area of the title bar. Again for accessibility reasons, all the figures in this text were made with No Background. In this exercise, you will look at Backstage for your meeting minutes starting document.

Area	Description
Info	Adding properties, protecting, inspecting, and managing a document.
New	Creating a new blank or template-based document.
Open	Opening a file from your computer, recent documents list, or OneDrive account.
Save	Save your file to your computer or OneDrive account.
Save As	Save your file with a new name, as a new file type, or to a different location. Only shows if the file has never been saved.
Save as Adobe PDF	Save your file in Adobe PDF format. May not be present in all versions of Word.
Print	Preview and print your document.
Share	Share your file by invitation, email, online presentation, or blog post.
Export	Change the file type or create a PDF/XPS document.
Transform	Turns on Intelligent Services that connect Microsoft Word to Microsoft Sway along with other ways to enhance the Word experience. May only be available to 365 subscribers.
Close	Close the file without closing the application.
Account	User and product information, including connected services.
Options	Launches the Application Options dialog box with many options, including advanced options.

Table 2 Office Backstage

 **CF01.03**

To Use Backstage to Set Account Settings and View Document Properties

a. Click the **File** tab and then, in the left pane, click **Info**.

Notice the file properties on the right side of the window. Because you have not saved yet, most of the properties are blank. The properties will appear once the file has been saved.

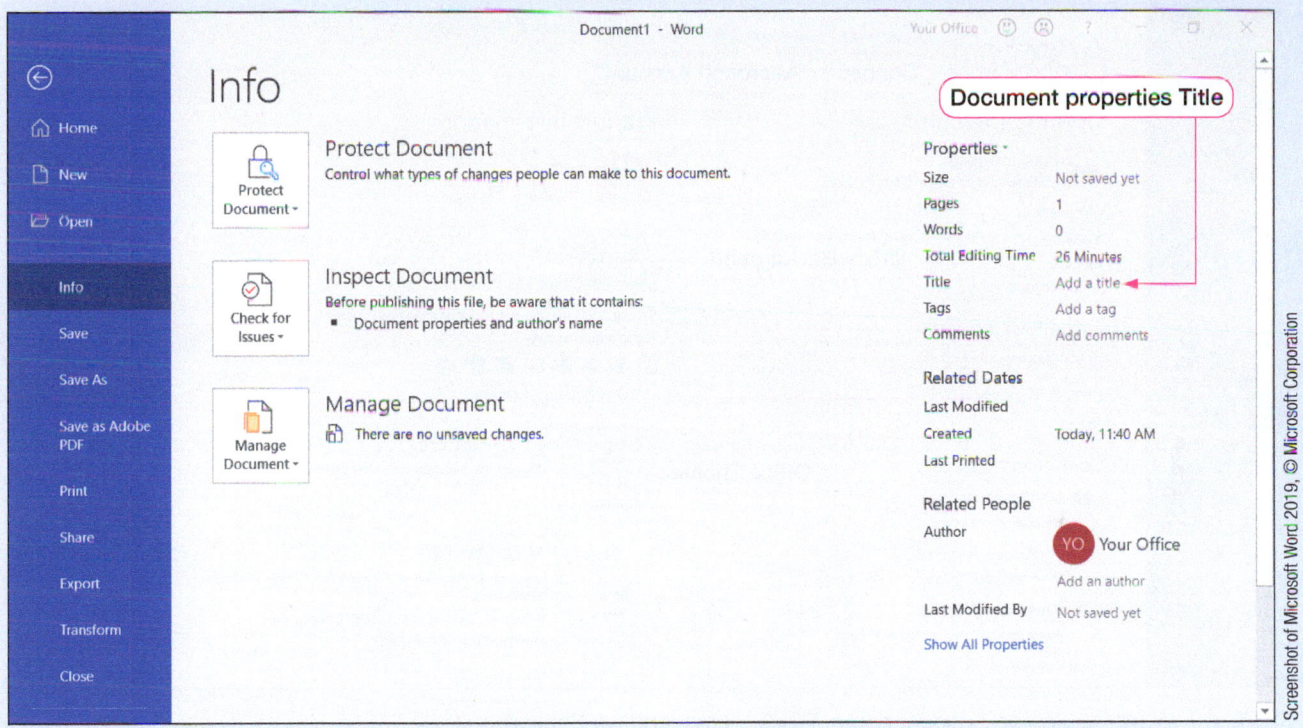

Figure 6 Word Backstage, Info page

b. In the properties, click **Add a title**, and then type Budget Meeting Minutes LastFirst using your last and first name.

> ### Mac Troubleshooting
>
> On a Mac, to set the title property, point to the menu bar to display the File menu and click Properties. Click the Summary tab and enter the title in the Title box. To change the Office theme, on the menu bar, click Word, and then click Preferences, click General, and then under Personalize, select Classic, which is most like the Windows White theme.

c. In the left pane, click **Account**.

If your Microsoft account is already connected, you will see your information and links to access and modify your account. If it is not connected, you will see an option to sign in. In a computer lab, you may see something entirely different, depending on your administrator's setup. If desired and needed, you can sign in to your account now.

Notice that you can also check for updates and see your version of Office. As Microsoft is updated in between new versions of Office, your version may change the way the interface works slightly from these instructions. This chapter is written for Version 1810. The Office 2019 versions used in this book are between 1808-1810. Because Microsoft has a rolling release, the version number will change over time.

d. If you would like your screen to match the figures in this text, ensure that the **Office Background** is set to **No Background** and the **Office Theme** is set to **White**. Leave Backstage open for the next exercise.

The best theme for accessibility for people with vision impairments or color blindness is the White theme and No Background. For this reason, from this point forward all figures in this book were made with the White theme.

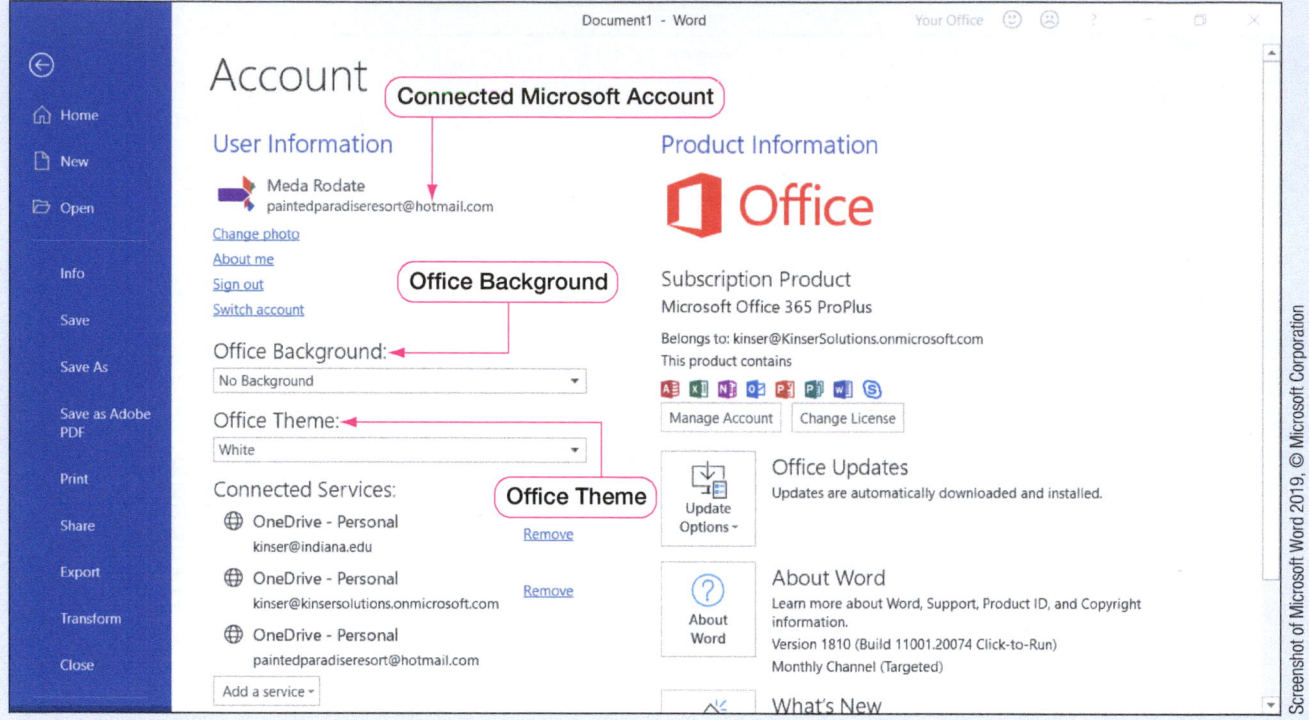

Figure 7   Word Backstage Account name, White theme, and No Background

Saving a New Document to the Local OneDrive That Syncs to the Cloud

While you are working on an Office file, whether creating a new file or modifying an existing file, your work is stored in the temporary memory on your computer, not on the hard drive or your USB flash drive. Any work that you do will be lost if you exit the program, turn off the computer, or experience a power failure or computer crash without you or the program's automatic save function saving your work. To prevent losing your work, you need to save your work and remember to do so frequently—at least every 10 minutes or after adding several changes. That saves you from having to re-create any work you did after the last save.

You can save files to the hard drive, which is located inside the computer; to an external drive, such as a USB flash drive; to a network storage device; or to One-Drive or another cloud storage service. Office has an **AutoSave** and **AutoRecovery** feature that will attempt to recover any changes made to a document since your last save if something goes wrong, but this should never be relied upon as a substitute for saving your work manually. Also, AutoSave will keep a version history of your document.

Traditionally, for file storage, files are saved locally on a hard drive or an external storage device such as a USB drive. **A USB drive** is a small, portable storage device—popular for moving files back and forth between a lab, office, and/or home computer. However, USB drives are easily lost, and file versions and backups are usually maintained manually, potentially causing versioning problems.

With Windows 10 and Office 2019, cloud file storage technologies are easier to use than ever. **OneDrive**—Microsoft's cloud storage solution—is fully integrated into File Explorer and Backstage. **Cloud computing** is computing resources, either hardware or software, on remote servers being used by a local computer over the internet. Apps exist for all of your devices, even Apple and Android devices, that connect to your files on the cloud. Other cloud storage systems also exist, such as Dropbox, Google Drive, and Box.

When you edit a file, your computer or device automatically updates the file in the online storage location. All of the other computers and devices check the online storage for changes and update as needed. Thus, when saving your file, you automatically place a copy online and in all of your synced computers. This creates an online backup if your computer crashes. Additionally, there is no USB drive to lose. File versioning problems are also minimized—in fact, OneDrive by default keeps all versions of your file for you, just in case. Once all applications have been properly set up, you have your files everywhere you want them and shared with exactly who needs them without having multiple copies of files around or emailing attachments.

REAL WORLD ADVICE	Not All Terms of Service Are the Same

Terms of service for online cloud storage services vary. Some services require you to waive your rights to file content. You really should read the terms of service before signing up for any online service. If you do not, you may not "own" your own files.

Your school's computer lab may or may not be integrated with cloud storage. In this case, you can always log into the cloud storage via a web browser and upload your files. For OneDrive, the URL is http://onedrive.live.com. If you are unsure about your school's computers, ask your instructor.

REAL WORLD ADVICE	Backing Up to the Cloud

Best practice still dictates bringing files to important meetings on a physical drive such as a USB drive as backup. Cloud technologies are dependent on an internet connection. Suppose you show up for a presentation and cannot get to your files because of a poor internet connection. Your presentation is likely to be a disaster.

The Save, Save As, and Save a Copy options in Office Backstage give you direct access to OneDrive, which you can access with your Microsoft account—except Access, which requires you to save locally. With Windows 10, you have a local folder that is directly accessible from the File Explorer and automatically syncs with OneDrive. Thus, you can sync Access files in the local syncing OneDrive folder.

When you save a file, you must provide a name. A file name includes the name you specify and a **file extension**—a few letters that come after the period in the name—assigned by the Office program to indicate the file type. The file extension may or may not be visible, depending on your computer settings. You can check your computer's setting in the File Explorer window on the View tab in the Show/Hide group. The check box for File name extensions should be checked to see file extensions, as shown in Figure 8. Each Office program adds a period and a file extension after the file name to identify the program in which that file was created. Table 3 shows the common default file extensions for Office.

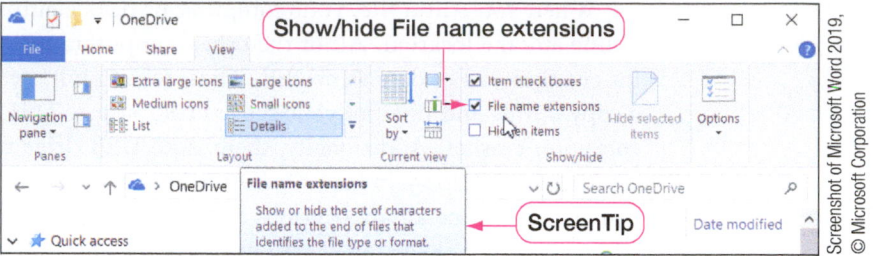

Figure 8   File Explorer extension setting

Application	Extension
Microsoft Word 2019	.docx
Microsoft Excel 2019	.xlsx
Microsoft PowerPoint 2019	.pptx
Microsoft Access 2019	.accdb

Table 3   Office 2019 default file extensions

Name your file with a descriptive name that accurately reflects the content of the document, workbook, presentation, or database, such as "January 2017 Budget" or "012017 Minutes". The descriptive name can include uppercase and lowercase letters, numbers, hyphens, spaces, and some special characters—excluding ? " / | < > * : —in any combination.

A file exists on your local machine at a **file path**—the physical location of the file starting with a letter that represents the drive and separating folders with a "\". This could be to your hard drive, usually the C:\ drive. Or it could be a USB drive that could be any letter of the alphabet, such as G:\. Assuming your main hard drive is C:\, the OneDrive location on your local computer is C:\Users\username\OneDrive—where username is the username you logged in with. Thus, if you put a file called Meeting.docx in your local OneDrive—and not in a subfolder—the file path combined with the file name would be C:\Users\username\OneDrive\Meeting.docx.

The file path and name combined can include a maximum of 255 characters including the extension. Even though Windows 10 can handle a long file name, some systems cannot. Thus, shorter names can prevent complications in transferring files between different systems.

In this exercise, you will save the meeting minutes document to OneDrive or the location where you are saving your files.

 **CF01.04**

To Save a Document to the Local OneDrive Folder That Syncs to the Cloud

SIDE NOTE
Saving a File
To save in OneDrive, you must be signed in. You can also save to This PC or Add a Place.

a. If necessary, return to Backstage by clicking the **File** tab. Then, on the left pane, click **Save As**.

Notice there is an option for Save and Save As. Save saves a file to the location in which it already exists with the same name. Because this is a new, never saved file, Save and Save As work the same. You will work with an existing file to understand the difference later in this chapter.

> **Grader Heads Up**
> You will not turn this Word file in for MyLab IT Grader.

> **Mac Troubleshooting**
> On a Mac, display the menu bar, click File and then click Save As. If you installed the OneDrive app, you should see OneDrive listed as a location. To save on your Mac, click the On My Mac button and specify a file name and a folder location.

b. Click **This PC**. You may see a folder icon that links to Documents. You will also see recent locations, potentially your OneDrive. If you see OneDrive here, you can click it. You can also click Browse to open the Save As dialog box.

c. If you are logged into your Microsoft account, double-click **OneDrive**. If you want to navigate to a subfolder in your OneDrive, do so now.

If you are saving your files to a different location, double-click **This PC**. In the Save As dialog box, navigate to the location where you are saving your project files.

d. In the Save As dialog box in the File name box, change the name to cf01ch01Minutes_LastFirst using your last and first name. Click **Save**.

Notice the Save as type. This determines the file type and extension. In Word, the default is .docx.

> **Troubleshooting**
> You are not connected to OneDrive! If this is your PC, log into your Microsoft account as directed in the previous exercise. If you cannot do that, such as in a computer lab, double-click **This PC** or **Browse** and navigate to a location where you would like to store your files.
>
> You can store the files on the desktop and then upload them at http://onedrive.live.com when you are finished. If you do this, make sure all files are closed before you upload them.
>
> Alternatively, you can save the files to a USB drive or other location of your choosing.

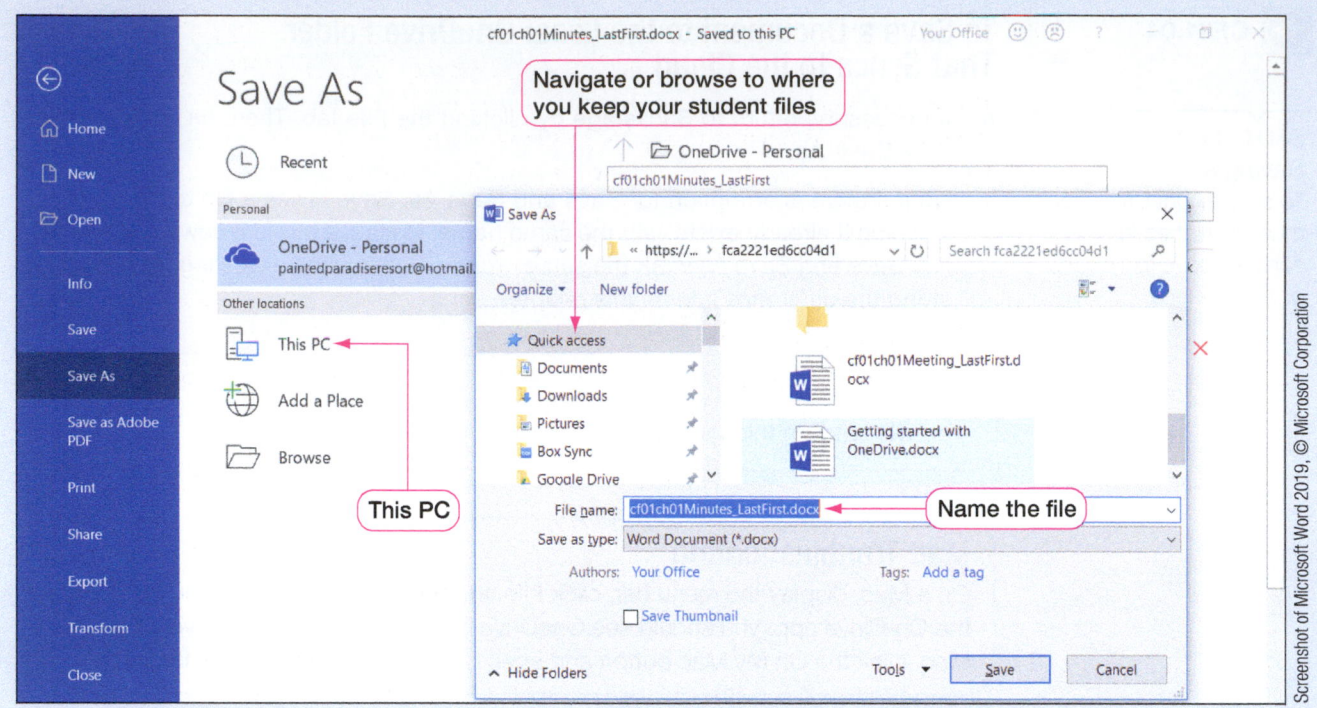

Figure 9 Word Save As

e. Click **Minimize** ⬜. Then on the taskbar, click **File Explorer** 🗂.

f. In the left Navigation pane, click **OneDrive** or otherwise navigate to where you saved your file. In the file list, verify that your file is there. If you do not see the .docx file extension on the end, then on the View tab, click to select the check box for File name extensions.

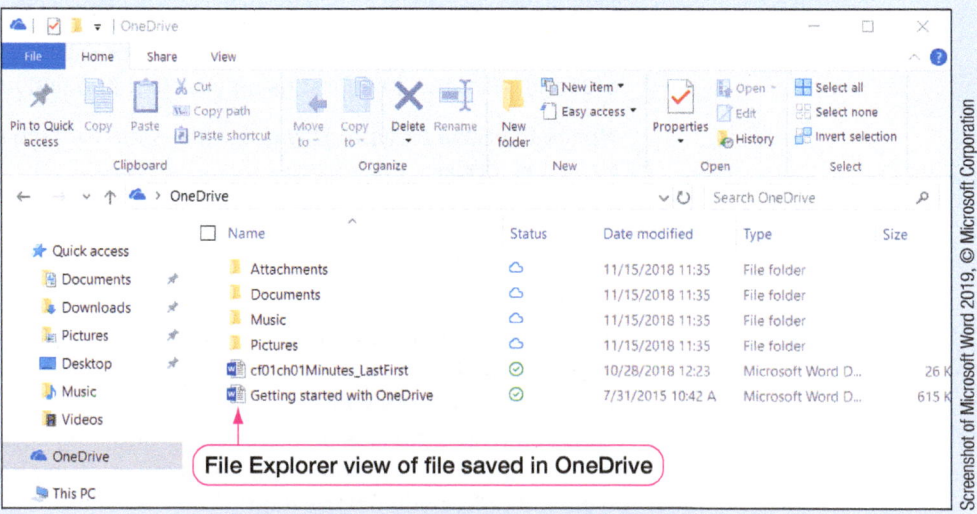

Figure 10 Word file in File Explorer

g. In the top-right corner of File Explorer, click **Close** ⊠.

h. On the taskbar, point to the **Word icon** until you see the Live Preview of your file. Click the **Live Preview** to maximize your file again.

Closing a File, Reopening from the Recent Documents List, and Exiting an Application

When you are ready to close a file, you can click the Close command in Office Backstage. If the file you close is the only file that's open for that particular program, the program window remains open with no file in the window. You can also close a file by using the Close button ☒ in the top-right corner of the window to exit the window. If you exit the window, it will close both the file and the program. Exiting programs when you are finished with them helps to save system resources and keeps your Windows desktop and taskbar uncluttered. It also prevents data from being accidentally lost. Importantly, files must be closed before being uploaded to the web, copied to a new location, or attached to an email; otherwise you risk corrupting the file.

Office's **roaming settings** are a group of settings that offer easy remotely synced user-specific data that affect the Office experience. Across logins, these settings remain the same. When signing into Office, the user will experience Office the same way, whether on a desktop, a laptop, or a mobile device.

Roaming settings include the Most Recently Used (MRU) list, Documents and Places, MRU Templates, Office Personalization, Custom Dictionary, List of Connected Services, Word Resume Reading Position, OneNote—custom name a notebook view, and in PowerPoint the Last Viewed Slide.

As a part of roaming settings, Office keeps a list of your most recently modified files in the **Most Recently Used list**. As the list grows, older files are removed to make room for more recently modified files. You can pin a frequently used file to always remain at the top of the list. To clear the recent files, right-click any file in the recent files list and select the option to clear unpinned files. In this exercise, you will close the meeting minutes and reopen it from the most recently used list; then you will close the file and Word.

 **CF01.05**

To Close a File and Exit an Application

a. Verify that you saved your file properly in the previous exercise and know the location to which you saved the file.

b. Click the **File** tab, and then click **Close**. The file closes, but Word remains open.

c. Click the **File** tab, and then click **Open**. On the right, you should see your file in the Most Recently Used list organized by last saved date—labeled Today, Yesterday, Last Week, or Older.

d. Click **cf01ch01Minutes_LastFirst**. Your file opens from the originally saved location.

e. Click **Close** ☒. Because this was the only open document, the document closes and Word exits.

> ### Grader Heads Up
> For the purposes of this chapter, you will not turn this Word document in to MyLab IT Grader. You will turn in the Excel Spreadsheet that you will start in the next exercise.

Opening an Existing File in Microsoft Excel and Then Saving as Another Name

You create a new file when you open a blank document, workbook, presentation, or database. If you want to work on a previously created file, you must first open it. When you open a file, it copies the file from the file's storage location to the computer's temporary memory and displays it on the screen. When you save a file, it updates the storage location with the changes. Until then, the file exists only in your computer's memory. If you want to open a second file while one is open, the keyboard shortcut of pressing [Ctrl] and then pressing [O] will display the Open tab of Office Backstage. Using the keyboard shortcut of [Ctrl]+[F12] will launch the Open dialog box without taking you to Office Backstage.

Many times, you will open a file that already exists rather than starting a new file. You can open the program and then open the file. You also can double-click a file in File Explorer, and the file will open in the associated program. When you have an existing file open, the Save command saves the file to the current location with the same name. If you want to change the name of a file or save it to a different location, you will need to use the Save As command. This allows you to specify the save options. When you use Save As, it allows you to select any location and give the file a new name.

An Excel file is referred to as a **workbook**. Each Excel workbook can contain many different worksheets. Each sheet has rows represented by numbers and columns represented by letters of the alphabet. The intersection of any row and column is a **cell**. For example, cell B2 refers to the cell where column B and row 2 intersect. The **active cell** is the currently selected cell. In a new worksheet, the active cell is the first cell of the first row, cell A1.

When you open files that you downloaded from the Internet, accessed from a shared network, or received as an attachment in email, the file usually opens in a read-only format called **Protected View**. In Protected View, the file contents can be seen and read, but you cannot edit, save, or print the contents until you enable editing. If you see the information bar right under the ribbon and you trust the source of the file, simply click the Enable Editing button on the information bar.

REAL WORLD ADVICE   **Sharing Files between Office Versions**

Different Office versions are not always compatible with one another. The general rule is that files created in an older version can always be opened in a newer version but not the other way around—an Office 2019 file is not easily opened in earlier versions of Office. Sharing files with Office 2003 users is a concern because different file extensions were used. For example, .doc was used for Word files instead of docx, .xls instead of .xlsx for Excel, and so on.

It is possible to save the Office 2019 files in a previous file format. To save in one of these formats, use the Save As or Save a Copy command, and click the 97-2003 file format. If the file is already in the format of a previous version of Office, it will open in Office 2019 and be saved with the same format in which it was created. However, if a file is saved with the extension of a previous version, it may lose anything created with newer features.

If you have not already done so, you need to download the files for this text at www.pearsonhighered.com/youroffice. On a personal computer, you may prefer to use the Windows Start menu to open the program, but in a computer lab or on an unfamiliar computer, the search method may be preferable. In this exercise, you will search for and open Microsoft Excel, open an existing file and save it with another name. Susan Brock has already started a budget for the training lunches that she asked you to finish before your meeting with her.

 **CF01.06**

To Open an Existing File

a. Click ⊞ and type Excel Click the **Excel** search result. The Excel Start screen opens.

b. Click **Open Other Workbooks** in the left pane, and then click **Browse**. Navigate through the folder structure to the location of your student data files, and then double-click **cf01ch01Budget**.

 The budget previously started by Susan Brock opens in Excel.

c. If necessary, click Enable Editing. If you needed to click Enable Editing, your file opened in Protected View.

d. Click the **File** tab, click **Save As**, and then double-click **This PC**. In the Save As dialog box, navigate to the location where you are saving your project files, and then change the file name to cf01ch01Budget_LastFirst using your last and first name. Click **Save** 💾.

> ### Grader Heads Up
> The file naming for MyLab IT Grader is different than the book. For example, this workbook would be **Excel_Ch01_Prepare_Budget** with your last name automatically added to the beginning of the file name. Thus, there is no need to save your file with LastFirst at the end of the file.

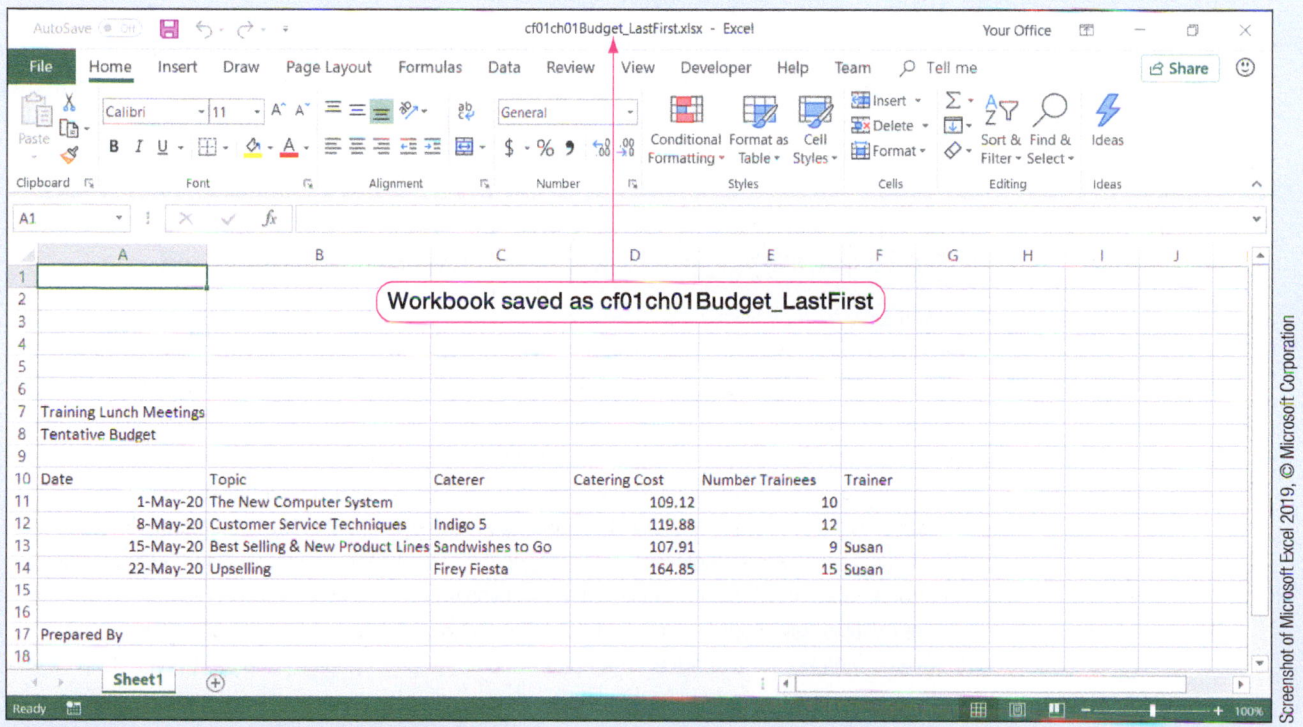

Figure 11 Beginning the Budget spreadsheet

e. If you do not see the ribbon, press Ctrl + F1. The ribbon is pinned open so that you can see all of the commands.

Troubleshooting

You pressed the keyboard shortcut, but nothing happened or something else happened. Are you working on a laptop? If so, then you may need to hold down the [fn] key as well. The function keys on a laptop are generally assigned to other things, such as volume. You can change these key assignments, but they are specific to the device—you may need to search the web to find out how to change them on yours.

Zooming, Scrolling, and Navigating with Keyboard Shortcuts

To get a closer look at the content within the program, you can zoom in. Alternatively, if you would like to see more of the contents, you can zoom out. Keep in mind that the zoom level affects only your view of the document on the screen and does not affect the printed output of the document. It is similar to using a magnifying glass on a page of a book to make the words look bigger—the print on the page is still be the same size. Therefore, do not confuse the zoom level with how big the text will print—it affects only your view of the document on the screen.

On the right side of the status bar in the lower right corner is a slide control that permits zooming in Excel from 10% to 400%. The minus and plus buttons provide an easy method to change the view size, or you can drag the Zoom Slider. When zoom is used, text is sometimes shifted off the viewing screen. Depending on the program and the zoom level, you might see the vertical or horizontal scroll bars or both scroll bars, which can be used to adjust what is displayed in the window. The scroll bars have arrows that can be clicked to shift the workspace in small increments in a specific direction and a scroll box that can be dragged to move a work space in larger increments. Touch screens allow you to zoom in and out by using pinch and stretch gestures. In addition to zooming and scrolling, you can navigate the file using keyboard shortcuts.

REAL WORLD ADVICE	Using Keyboard Shortcuts and KeyTips

Keyboard shortcuts—keyboard equivalents of software commands—are extremely useful, and some are universal to all Windows programs. They allow you to keep your hands on the keyboard instead of reaching for the mouse—increasing efficiency and saving time. Some companies have even taken the mouse away from their interns to force them to use keyboard shortcuts. Keyboard shortcuts are also very useful for accessibility and people with vision impairments.

Pressing [Alt] will toggle the display of **KeyTips**—or keyboard shortcuts—for items on the ribbon and Quick Access Toolbar. After displaying the KeyTips, you can press the corresponding letter or number to request the action from the keyboard.

For multiple-key shortcuts, you hold down the first key listed and press the second key once. Some common keyboard shortcuts are listed below.

[Ctrl]+[C]	Copy the selected item.
[Ctrl]+[X]	Cut the selected item.
[Ctrl]+[V]	Paste a copied or cut item.
[Ctrl]+[A]	Select all the items in a document, all the cells in a worksheet, or window.
[Ctrl]+[B]	Bold selected text.

Ctrl + Z	Undo an action.
Ctrl + Home	Move to the top of the document or make cell A1 the active cell in Excel.
Ctrl + End	Move to the end of the document or select the farthest cell containing data to the right and bottom of an Excel worksheet.

In this exercise, you will zoom in and out on the agenda document and navigate it with keyboard shortcuts.

 **CF01.07**

To Zoom

a. Click cell **A1** to make it the active cell.

b. On the Excel status bar, drag the **Zoom Slider** ⟷ to the right until it reaches **400%**. The worksheet is enlarged to its largest size. This makes the text appear larger.

c. On the Excel status bar, click **400%**.

Notice that this percentage is the Zoom level button that opens the Zoom dialog box. This dialog box provides options for custom and preset settings.

SIDE NOTE

Methods for Zooming
Several ways exist to zoom Office applications: Zoom Slider, View tab in the Zoom group, Ctrl and a mouse wheel, and touch gestures.

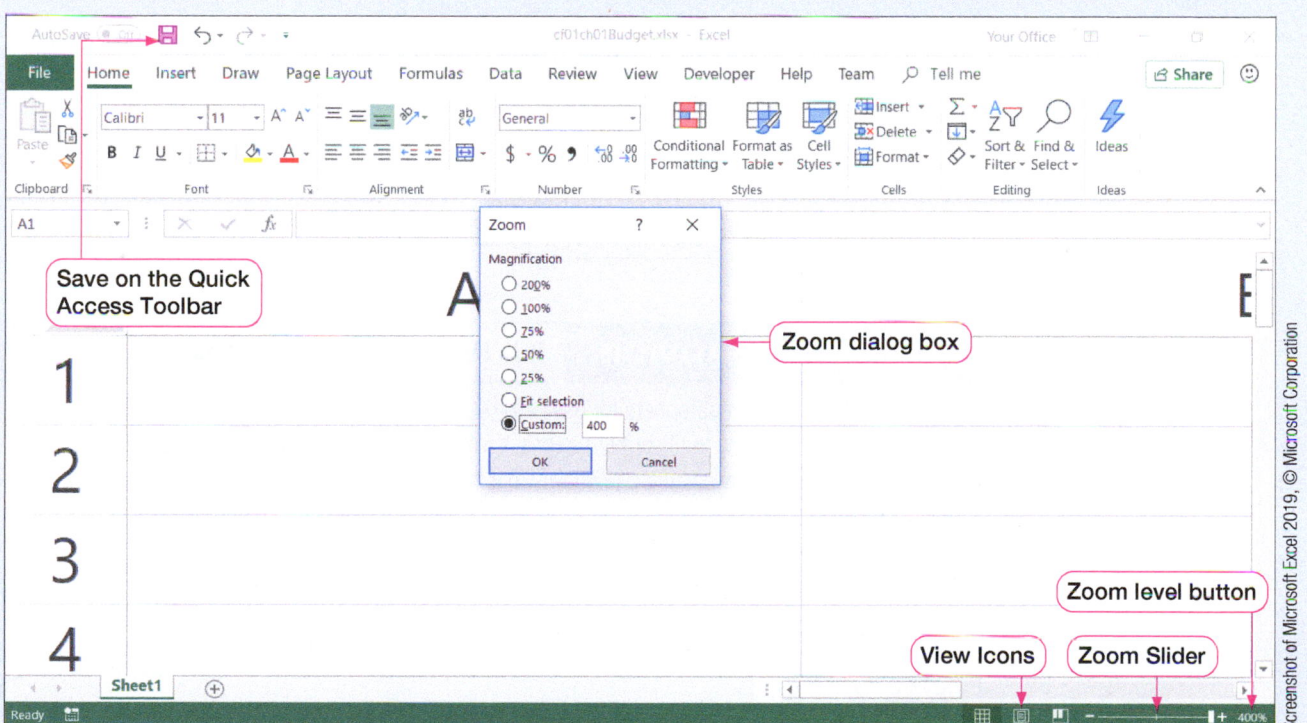

Figure 12 Zoom controls and dialog box

SIDE NOTE

Long Worksheets
When you are scrolling in long worksheets, it is fastest to right-click the scroll box in the scroll bar and select your desired option.

d. Click **100%**, and then click **OK**. The worksheet returns to the original 100%.

e. If needed, right-click the scroll box in the scroll bar. Then select Top to return to the beginning of the worksheet.

Using the Quick Access Toolbar to Save a Currently Open File

In addition to Office Backstage, Office provides several ways to save a file. To quickly save a file, simply click Save 🔖 on the Quick Access Toolbar or use the keyboard short-cut Ctrl+S. The Quick Access Toolbar is the series of small icons in the top-left corner of the title bar that can be customized to display commonly used commands.

When this method is used, the program simply saves the file to its current location with the same name. Once you save a file the first time, the simple shortcut methods to save any changes to the file work fine to update the existing file—as long as you do not need to change the file name or location with the Save As command. In this exercise, you will save your file to its current location with the same name as previously given.

 **CF01.08**

SIDE NOTE
Save Keyboard Shortcut
You can also save with the keyboard shortcut of Ctrl+S.

To Save an Existing File with the Quick Access Toolbar

a. In the top-left corner in the Quick Access Toolbar, click **Save** 🔖.

The file is now saved to the same location and with the same name you designated earlier in this chapter. Although you have not made changes since the document was last saved, best practice is to save your files frequently.

Manipulate, Correct, and Format Content in Excel

A personal brand is important in business. If a person dresses poorly, colleagues may assume that this person's work is poor as well. In the business world, everything a person does influences the way colleagues and superiors view that person, including the content and formatting of the files he or she produces. Thus, understanding appropriate content and formatting is very important—it is a direct reflection of you as a professional.

REAL WORLD ADVICE	It Is Not the Place for Jokes!	

Jokes are rarely, if ever, appropriate for business documents and files. Consider a job applicant who lists, as the last thing in his or her résumé, "Will work for food"—this has actually happened. The job applicant may have wanted to convey that he or she had a good sense of humor. But in reality, the message shows that the job applicant did not understand that humor was inappropriate in this situation or he or she did not take getting the job seriously.

 CONSIDER THIS | **Consider Your Personal Brand**

Have you thought about your personal brand? Are you the creative person? Are you the efficient person? Describe your brand. Give an example of how you were influenced positively or negatively by the way another person presented themselves or their work.

Checking Spelling

Checking spelling is a must—and it is easy in Office. There are no excuses for spell-ing mistakes. Everyone makes typos, but that is no excuse for poor spelling. Further, you need to understand your audience and purpose before using jargon, acronyms, text abbreviations, or other informal language. Using informal language in a business chat in Skype is appropriate. However, in a business budget, formal language is expected.

While checking for spelling is easy, Excel does not underline words in red that are misspelled like Word and PowerPoint do. Thus, it is important to remember to run the spell checker. You will find more spelling mistakes in Excel documents because people depend on the red underlining—and Excel does not do that!

In this exercise, you will correct a spelling mistake.

 **CF01.09**

To Correct Spelling

a. If needed, click cell **A1** to make it the active cell. Best practice is to always start at the top of a spreadsheet. Click the **Review** tab, and then in the Proofing group, click **Spelling**.

b. The Spelling dialog box appears. It first identifies Sandwishes as a misspelled word. You know that is the correct spelling of a local sandwich shop. Click **Ignore Once**.

c. The Spelling dialog box next identifies that Firey is the incorrect spelling for the word Fiery. Click **Change** to correct the spelling.

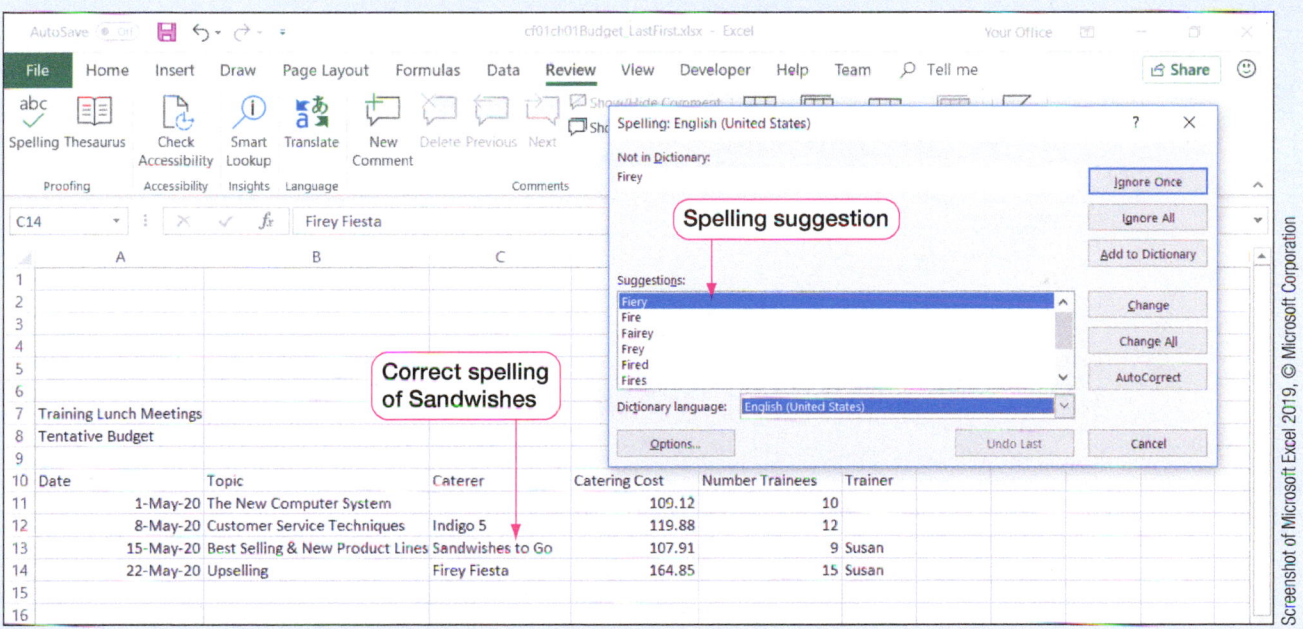

Figure 13 Correcting spelling in Excel with the Spelling dialog box

d. Click **OK** to the message informing you that the spell check is complete. Notice, the corrected cell C14 is now the active cell.

e. **Save** the workbook.

Entering, Copying, and Pasting Text

As you add content, you will inevitably find an occasion when copying and pasting the text will save you time. Of course, someone looking at the end product will have no way of knowing what you typed by hand and what you copied and pasted. In many instances, copy and paste not only will save you time but also will increase accuracy—assuming that you do not copy a mistake! Susan just recently figured out that Carlos would run the first two trainings and asked you to add him. In this exercise, you will enter Carlos' name. Along the way, you will copy and paste to enter text as efficiently as possible.

 **CF01.10**

To Enter, Copy, and Paste Text

a. Carlos will teach the first two trainings. Click cell **F11** to make it the active cell and type Carlos Press Ctrl+Enter.

   Pressing Ctrl+Enter enters the value into the cell and keeps that cell as the active cell.

b. With cell F11 as the active cell, press Ctrl+C. This copies the text to a virtual clipboard to use anytime you want, even multiple times, until the clipboard content is replaced with something else. The moving cell border indicates the cell was copied.

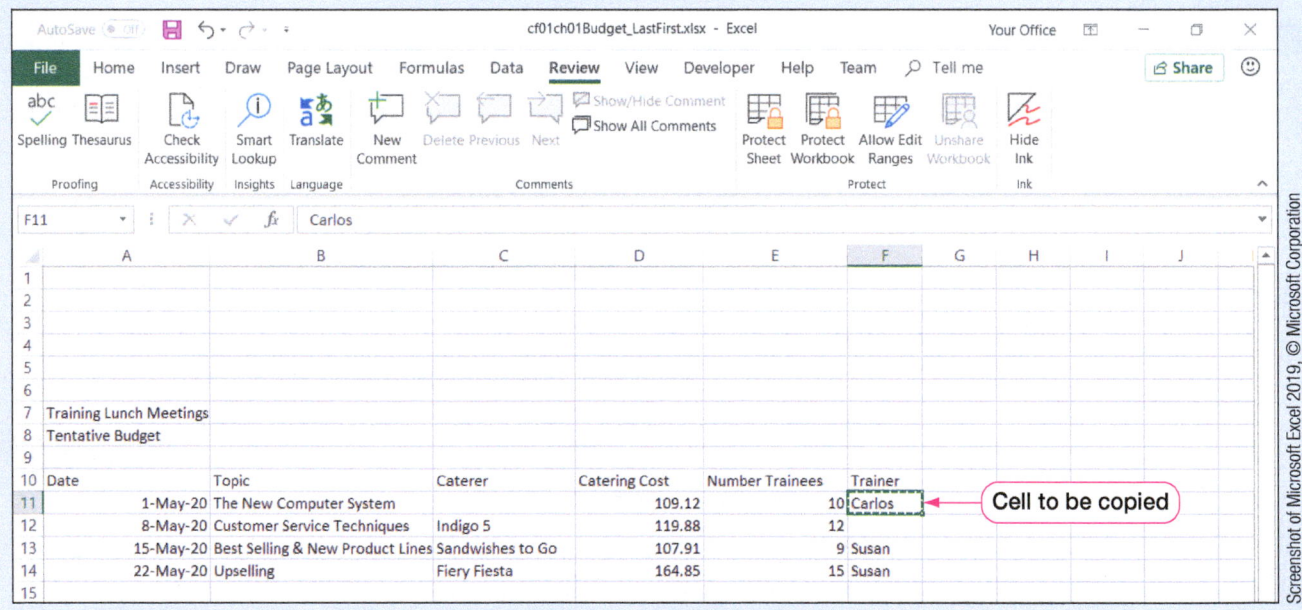

Figure 14 Active Cell with border indicating it was copied to the clipboard

Screenshot of Microsoft Excel 2019, © Microsoft Corporation

SIDE NOTE
Copy without Formatting
To copy, press Ctrl+C, including formatting. On the ribbon you can choose to copy values only by clicking on the arrow under Paste.

c. Click cell **F12** to make it the active cell. Press Ctrl+V to paste Carlos into cell F12.

d. Press Esc to empty the clipboard. The moving border is removed.

7	Training Lunch Meetings					
8	Tentative Budget					
9						
10	Date	Topic	Caterer	Catering Cost	Number Trainees	Trainer
11	1-May-20	The New Computer System		109.12	10	Carlos
12	8-May-20	Customer Service Techniques	Indigo 5	119.88	12	Carlos
13	15-May-20	Best Selling & New Product Lines	Sandwishes to Go	107.91	9	Susan
14	22-May-20	Upselling	Fiery Fiesta	164.85	15	Susan
15						

Carlos copied and pasted

Figure 15 Carlos entered as a trainer

Screenshot of Microsoft Excel 2019, © Microsoft Corporation

e. Click cell **A18**. Enter **Last** using your last name.

> ### Grader Heads Up
> If you are using MyLab IT Grader, please enter **Smith** into cell A18 as a fictitious student last name instead of your own name.

f. Save  the workbook.

Using Undo to Correct a Mistake

Everyone makes a typo from time to time, and you are going to make mistakes that you need to undo. The easiest way to do that is through the Undo and Redo buttons in the Quick Access Toolbar or with Keyboard shortcuts. In this exercise, you will add some data to your budget, undo it, and then correct it.

▶ **CF01.11**

SIDE NOTE
Quick Access
You can also use the Undo and Redo buttons on the Quick Access toolbar.

SIDE NOTE
Redo
If you undo too many steps, you can Redo with the Quick Access toolbar or Ctrl+Y.

To Use Undo and Redo

a. Click cell **C11** to make it the active cell. Type **Indigo5** and press Enter. You were out of ideas on whom to book for the first training meeting. So, you listed the restaurant at the resort.

b. A coworker just mentioned a new caterer called New World Catering. Press Ctrl+Z to undo the Indigo5 entry. Notice cell C11 becomes the active cell again.

c. With cell C11 as the active cell, type **New World Catering** and then press Enter.

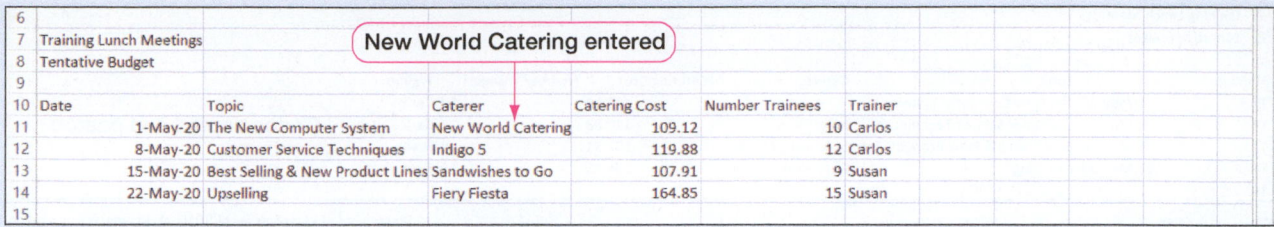

6						
7	Training Lunch Meetings					
8	Tentative Budget					
9						
10	Date	Topic	Caterer	Catering Cost	Number Trainees	Trainer
11	1-May-20	The New Computer System	New World Catering	109.12	10	Carlos
12	8-May-20	Customer Service Techniques	Indigo 5	119.88	12	Carlos
13	15-May-20	Best Selling & New Product Lines	Sandwishes to Go	107.91	9	Susan
14	22-May-20	Upselling	Fiery Fiesta	164.85	15	Susan
15						

Figure 16 New World Catering added

Screenshot of Microsoft Excel 2019, © Microsoft Corporation

    d. **Save**  the workbook.

Finding and Replacing Text

Sometimes, you may not know where certain text is in a document. Or you may need to replace text with something different. You can use Find and Replace on the ribbon rather than manually looking for text and changing it. If you click Find, it opens the Find and Replace dialog box. A dialog box is a window that provides options. Susan recently told you she is scheduled to be out of town for the weeks she is scheduled as a trainer. In this exercise, you will find the word "Susan" and replace it with her replacement Taylor.

REAL WORLD ADVICE	What to "Find" in a Find and Replace?

Be careful what you look for in a find and replace. If you are not careful, you can end up replacing items that should not have been replaced. If this ever happens, remember the Undo command!

▶ **CF01.12**

SIDE NOTE
Be Careful with Replace All
When using Replace All, be very careful. It is easy to unintentionally change text that should not have been changed.

To Use Find and Replace

a. Click the **Home** tab, and then in the Editing group, click **Find & Select** and then click **Replace**. The Find and Replace dialog box opens.

> **Mac Troubleshooting**
> Point above the ribbon to display the menu bar. Cl ick Edit, point to Find, and then select Replace. The following steps b–f are exactly the same on a Mac.

b. Click in the **Find what** box, and type Susan

c. Click in the **Replace with** box, and type Taylor

d. Click **Find Next**. The first instance of the words is selected in the worksheet. Both instances need to be replaced.

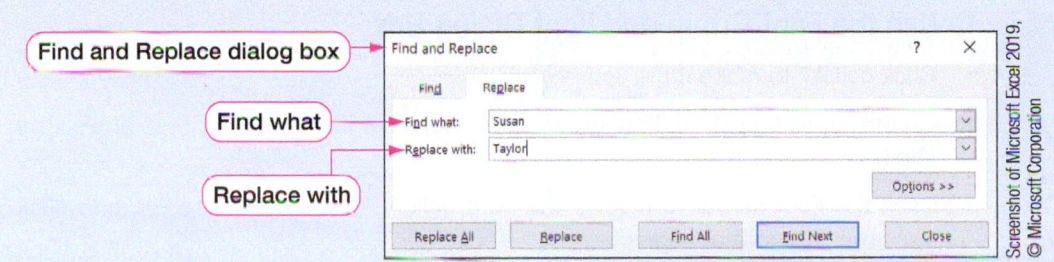

Figure 17 Find and Replace dialog box

e. Click **Replace All**. Both instances are updated, and a message box appears. Click **OK**, and click **Close** to close the Find and Replace dialog box.

f. Press Ctrl+Home to make cell A1 the active cell.

g. **Save** 🖫 the workbook.

Using the Font Group and the Font Dialog Box

One of the most commonly used groups on the ribbon is the Font group. A **font** is the way the letters in words look, including the size, weight, and style. In the Font group, you can change many attributes of the text, including color, size, alignment, type of font, and common emphasis.

Clicking a command will produce an action. For example, the Font group on the Home tab includes buttons for bold and italic. Clicking any of these buttons will produce an intended action. So if you have selected text to which you want to apply bold formatting, simply click the Bold button, and bold formatting is applied to the selected text.

Some buttons are **toggle buttons**—one click turns the feature on and a second click turns the feature off. When a feature is toggled on, the button remains highlighted. Clicking toggles the setting on and off. Bold is an example of a toggle button.

Some buttons have two parts: a button that accesses the most commonly used setting or command and an arrow that opens additional options. A **gallery** is a set of menu options that appears when you click the arrow next to a button. A normal arrow will bring up the options or enable you to scroll through the options. If there is a More arrow ⏷, it brings up all of the options.

For example, on the Home tab, in the Font group, the Font Color button 🅰 includes a gallery of the different colors that are available for fonts. If you click the button, the default is to apply the last color used, which is displayed on the icon. To access the gallery for other color options, click the arrow next to the Font Color button.

Some commands open other menus. These commands expand to a list of options when the arrow next to the list is selected. Whenever you see an arrow next to a button, this is an indicator that more options are available. Then you can select the option from the list that you want.

Some ribbon groups include a diagonal arrow in the bottom-right corner of the group, called a **Dialog Box Launcher** 🗖, which opens a corresponding dialog box. Click the Dialog Box Launcher to open a dialog box related to the group. It often provides access to more precise or less frequently used commands along with the commands that are offered on the ribbon; thus, using a dialog box offers the ability to apply many related options at the same time and from one location.

In this exercise, you will change the formatting of the font to be more appropriate.

 **CF01.13**

To Use the Font Group and Font Dialog Box

a. Click cell **A7** to make it the active cell.

b. On the Home tab, in the Font group, click **Increase Font Size** A^ three times. The title is now larger.

c. Click the Font **arrow** to display the Font gallery. Scroll down the list, and click **Verdana**. The font changes.

d. On the Home tab, in the Font group, click the Font Color arrow A ▾. Under Standard Colors, select **Blue**.

e. On the Home tab, in the Font group, click **Bold** B.

f. Click cell **A8** to make it the active cell.

g. On the Home tab, in the Font group, click the Font Size 10 ▾ arrow. Click **12**. The font increases in size to 12 points.

h. On the Home tab, in the Font group, click the **Dialog Box Launcher** ⌐. The Format Cells dialog box opens. Under Font style, click **Italic**.

MAC COMPATIBILITY
Dialog Box Launchers
A Mac does not have dialog box launchers. You can usually find the same options by right-clicking. On a Mac, a right-click is performed by a Ctrl + click. See the Mac Appendix for a listing of different various keyboard differences on a Mac.

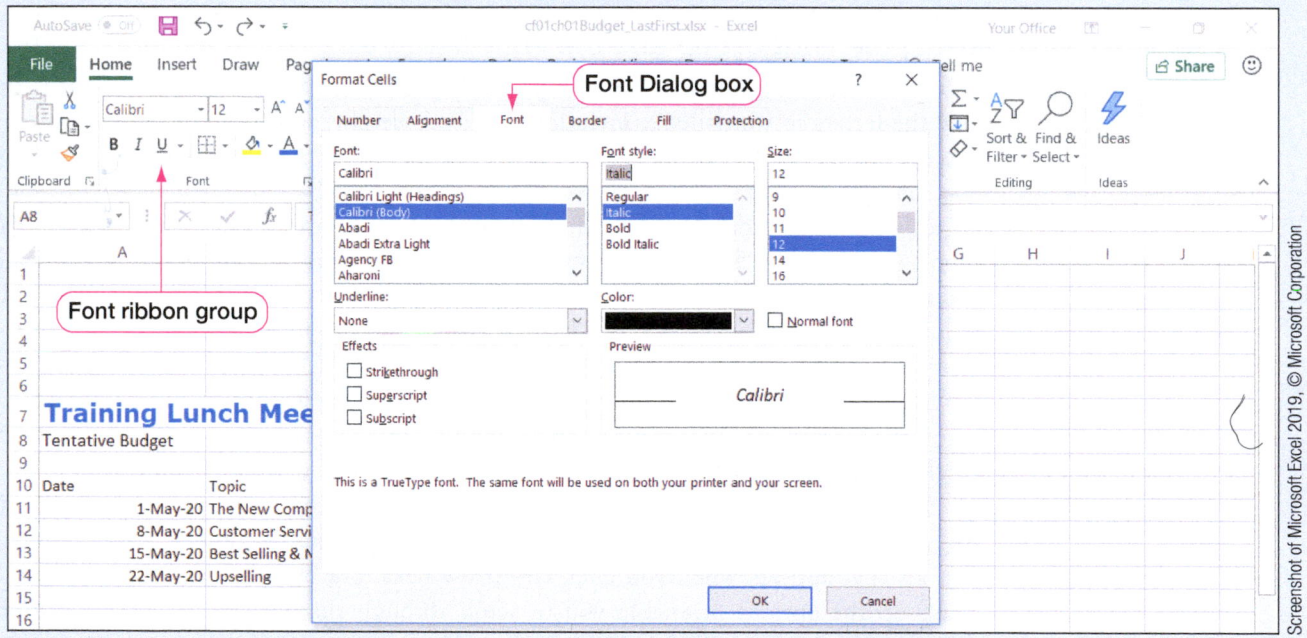

Figure 18 Format Cells dialog box

i. Click **OK**. The dialog box closes.

j. **Save** 🖫 the workbook.

Using the Style Gallery with Live Preview

Live Preview lets you see the effects of menu selections on your document file or selected item before making a commitment to a particular choice. The menu or grid shows samples of the available options. Not all additional options under arrows have Live Preview. Using Live Preview, you can experiment with settings before making a final choice.

Predefined styles are a type of preset formatting. Styles can also be customized. So, if you later decide that a style should be in a larger font size, you change the style, and it changes every instance of that style in your document. Finally, for the purpose of this chapter, styles help you apply aesthetically pleasing formatting very quickly—and can also be helpful for users with vision color impairments.

In this exercise, you will add a style to the gift shop budget.

To Use the Styles Gallery and Live Preview

SIDE NOTE
Live Preview
Live Preview shows how formatting looks before you apply it. This feature is available for many of the galleries.

a. Click cell **A17** to make it the active cell.

b. On the Home tab, in the Styles group, click **More** ▾. Point to the option for Output. Notice, the worksheet shows the Live Preview. If you move your mouse over other style options, the worksheet will change accordingly.

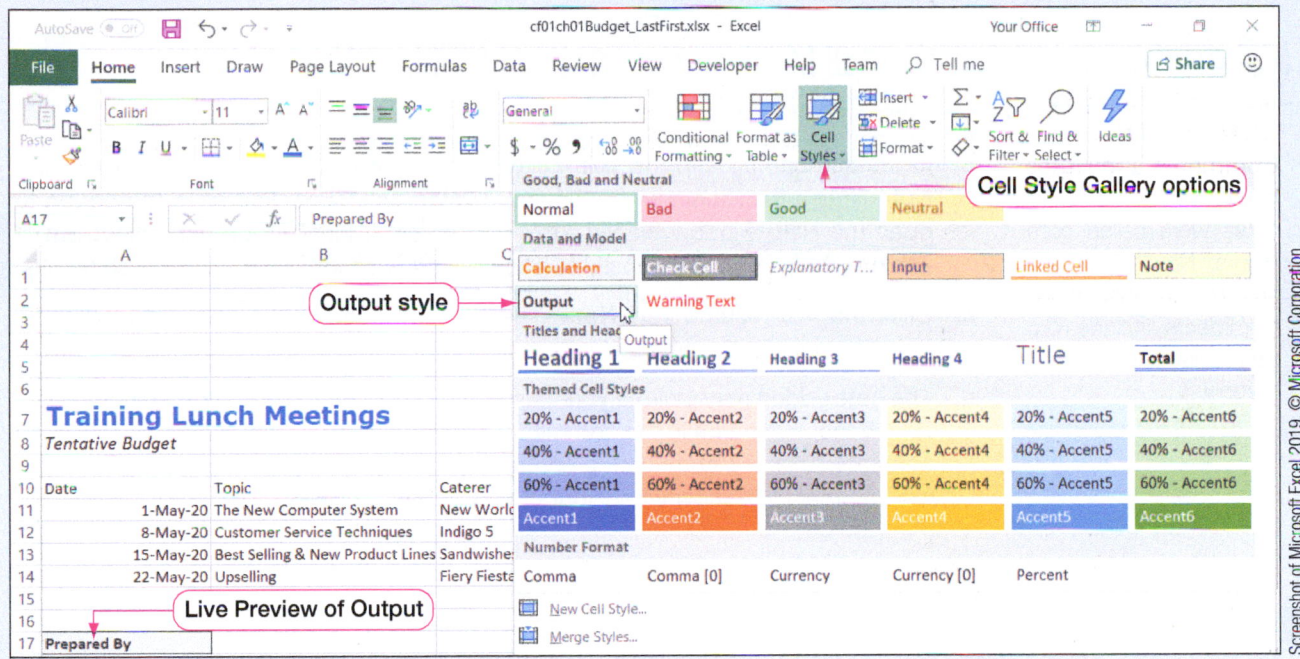

Figure 19 Styles Live Preview

SIDE NOTE
Closing a Gallery
Press [Esc] to close a gallery without making a selection. Alternatively, you can click outside the gallery menu.

c. Click **Output**. The Output style is now applied to that cell.

d. **Save** 🖫 the workbook.

Inserting a Note and Total Using the Tell me what you want to do Box

All of the applications have a **Tell me what you want to do** box in the title bar—"Tell me" for short. This tool is particularly useful when you do not know where a specific command is located on the ribbon. This tool will not just take you to help on that item—though it does provide options for that as well. It actually performs the action for you. Although the Tell me feature is not currently connected to Cortana or speech recognition, it is easy to see that as a potential feature upgrade in the future.

Under the Tell me what you want to do search results, you also have an option for a Smart Lookup. With Smart Lookup, you can open search results and do research without leaving the application. Instead, it brings up the results in the Insights pane.

A note allows you to leave a note for another person to read. Notes provide great internal documentation to explain your spreadsheet. You also want to include a total cost for the catering. You will learn more about notes and functions in a later chapter and will use only basic ones in this exercise. The Tell me feature is great for using and finding features you do not know a lot about. In prior versions of Excel, notes were called comments. Now, comments are different than notes. Comments include profile images and the ability to reply.

In this exercise, you will use this tool to add a note and a total cost for the catering. You need to add a note to remind yourself about getting a price for New World Catering.

 CF01.15

SIDE NOTE

Comments and Notes

In prior versions of Excel, notes were called comments. Now, comments are different than notes. Comments include profile images and the ability to reply.

To Use Tell Me to Insert a Note and Total

a. Click on **D11** to make it the active cell.

b. In the title bar, click in the **Tell me what you want to do …** box and type Add Note Notice that command options are listed first. Next, you have the option to open the Help window on the topic you entered. Finally, you can select Smart Lookup, which opens the Insights pane on the right with Bing web search results.

c. Click the first result **Insert Note**. The note is added to the cell and places the insertion point in the note.

d. The note added may include your name, the computer's name, or something else. Delete the user name in the comment and type Call to find real cost as this is an estimate After the comment is entered, a red triangle will appear in the cell and the comment will show when your mouse is hovered over the cell.

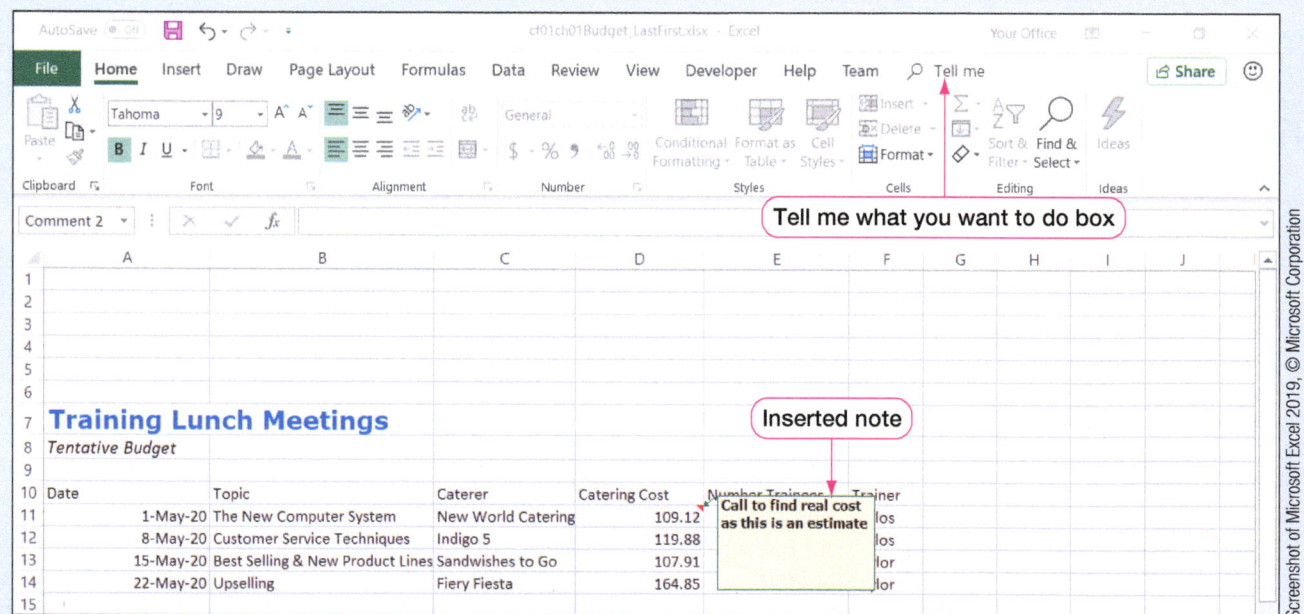

Figure 20 Inserted note in Excel

e. Click cell **D15** to make it the active cell.

f. In the title bar, click in the **Tell me what you want to do …** box, type Sum and then click the first result **AutoSum**. Press Enter to get the total cost for the catering.

g. **Save** 🖫 the workbook. If you need to take a break before finishing this chapter, now is a good time.

REAL WORLD ADVICE	Saving Files

Most programs have an added safeguard or warning dialog box to remind you to save if you attempt to close a file without saving your changes first. Despite that warning, best practice dictates that you save files before closing them or exiting a program. If you select the wrong option on the warning by accident, you will lose work. Remembering to save before you close prevents this kind of accident.

Best practice also dictates saving often. The more often you save, the less work you can lose in the event of an unexpected closing of the application. Pressing Ctrl+S takes only a few seconds. Train yourself now to use this keyboard shortcut regularly and often. If you do, it will become second nature and save you from losing work in the future!

Formatting, Finding Help, and Printing in Office

The accuracy and quality of your content are the most important aspect of your documents. However, even the most high-quality, accurate document is much harder to use if it is formatted poorly causing confusion for anyone who looks at it. After accuracy, clarity of your document to others—and even yourself—is extremely important. It is much more than just making a document look "pretty."

For example, imagine a table of numbers. The title says "2020 Sales," and the numbers in the table do not have any dollar signs. What does that mean? Are the numbers the total quantities sold—known as sales volume? However, the word "sales" often means dollar amounts. Did someone forget the dollar signs and these numbers really show how much was sold in dollars before costs are removed—known as sales revenue? This example highlights how a simple format issue could confuse users and cause poor decision making. Do a search on the web for "Excel mistakes costing companies big money" and you will find numerous examples.

In this section, you will learn how to appropriately format your budget, how to print a copy, and how to find help.

Format Using Various Office Methods

Too much formatting is just as bad as too little. You need to be aware of accessibility for vision-impaired individuals—discussed in depth later in this text. Styles in Office provide nice options for users who don't have an artistic eye. Remember, less can be more. However, lack of formatting can lead to incorrect conclusions. For example, suppose there is a number labeled Sales in Excel. Without a clearer title or currency formatting, how does a user know whether that is sales in dollars or in quantity sold?

Earlier in the chapter, you started formatting your budget. Now, you are ready to refine your budget in Excel.

Using Excel to Enter Content, Apply Bold, and Apply a Fill Color

As was discussed earlier in the chapter, Office uses a common interface for all the applications. This does not mean an identical interface. While some things are the same, how they are applied or how they work may be slightly different. For example, in Excel, if you select the cell, the formatting options apply to the entire cell—not just part of the text inside a cell. By contrast, in Word, you select precisely the words for which to change the font color. To make only a single word a different color in Excel, you must select the specific text you want inside the cell first. Some formatting must be applied to the entire cell, such as number formats—Currency, Text, and Date, among others. When exploring features that are common to the Office applications, you need to experience how a feature can be slightly different or very different in an application-specific way.

In this exercise, you will add content to the budget, apply bold to some cells, and apply different background color to others.

 **CF01.16**

To Use the Bold Button and the Fill Color Button

a. If you took a break, open the **cf01ch01Budget_LastFirst** workbook.

b. Click cell **A10** to make it the active cell. On the Home tab, in the Font group, click **Bold** [B]. The button applies bold to cell A10, and the Bold button is highlighted.

c. With A10 active, on the Home tab, in the Font group, click the **Fill Color arrow** [▼]. The color options appear. Under Theme Colors, point to the colors to find Blue, Accent 1, Lighter 80%. At the writing of this text, that is the second color down in the fifth column. Click **Blue, Accent 1, Lighter 80%**.

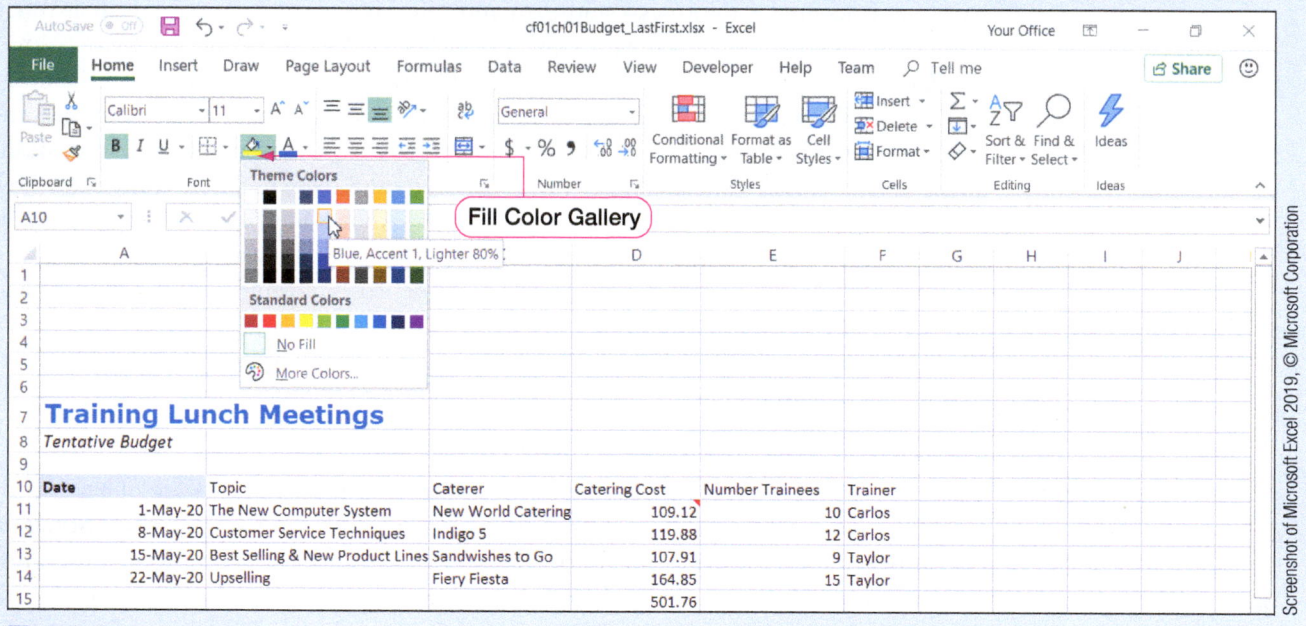

Figure 21 Fill color

d. **Save** [💾] the workbook.

Opening an Excel Dialog Box

Excel has dialog boxes, just like Word. The Format Cells dialog box is probably the most used dialog box in Excel, as it allows you to specify many things. Most important, it allows you to specify the type of data in the cell, such as Currency or Text. Because spreadsheets use many calculations, specifying the type of data is very important.

In this exercise, you will use a dialog box to format some of the cells in the budget you are beginning for your manager, Susan Brock.

 **CF01.17**

To Use the Dialog Box Launcher to Format a Number

a. Click cell **D11** to make it the active cell and then press $\boxed{\text{Shift}}$+$\boxed{\text{Ctrl}}$+$\boxed{\downarrow}$. Notice that cells D11 through D15 are now selected. This keyboard shortcut will select cells below until it reaches an empty cell. You can also select multiple cells by clicking and dragging.

b. With cells D11 through D15 selected, on Home tab, in the Number group, click the **Dialog Box Launcher** ⬚. The Format Cells dialog box opens to the Number tab.

c. On the left side, under Category, click **Currency**.

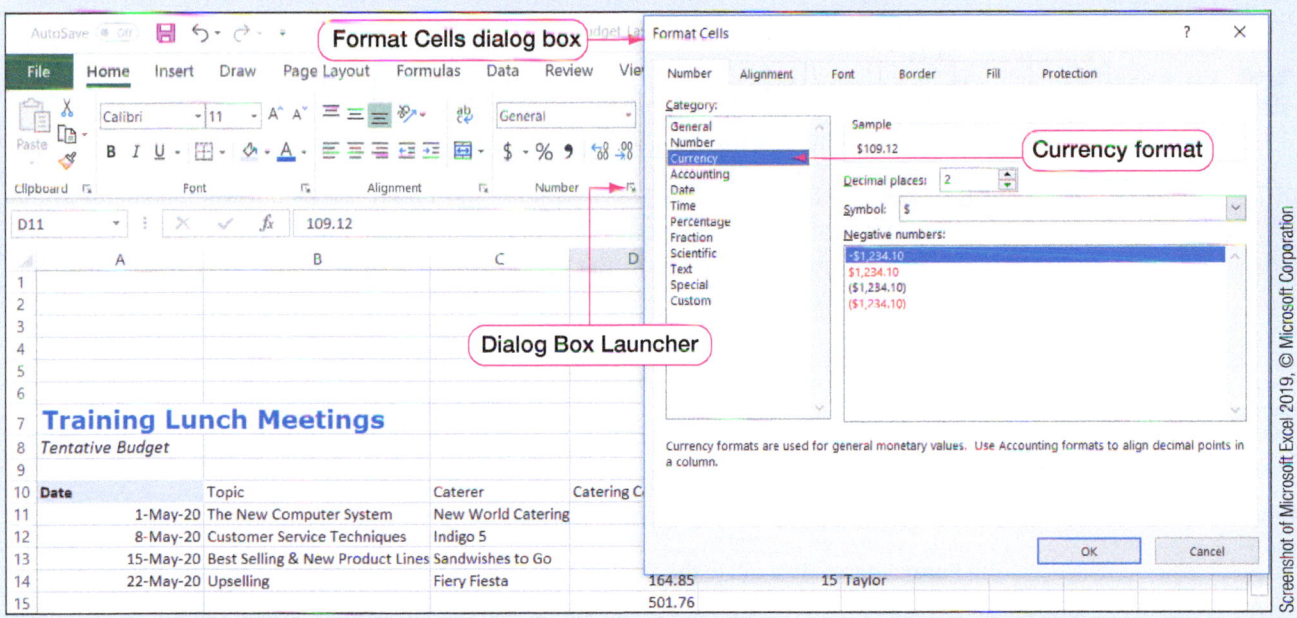

Figure 22 Format Cells dialog box, Number tab

d. Click **OK**. The cells now show a dollar sign before the number. Notice that the default of two decimals is applied.

e. **Save** 🖫 the workbook.

Inserting Images and Using Contextual Tools to Resize

In Word, Excel, PowerPoint, and Publisher, you can insert pictures from a file, a screen shot, or various online sources. The online options include inserting images within the Office Online Pictures collection, via a Bing search, or from your own OneDrive. Be careful when you insert Online Pictures—you must ensure that you have the right to use the image you selected for the purpose you want.

The term "contextual tools" refers to tools that appear only when needed for specific tasks. Some tabs, toolbars, and menus are displayed as you work and appear only if a particular object is selected. Because these tools become available only as you need them, the workspace remains less cluttered.

A **contextual tab** contains commands related to selected objects so that you can manipulate, edit, and format the objects. Examples of objects that can be selected to display contextual tabs include a table, a picture, a shape, or a chart. A contextual tab appears to the right of the standard ribbon tabs. The contextual tab disappears when you click somewhere outside the selected object—in the file—to deselect the object. In some instances, contextual tabs can also appear as you switch views.

In this exercise, you will insert a Painted Treasures Gift Shop logo into the budget you are beginning for your manager, Susan Brock. This budget will become a part of Susan's larger budget that she must present to the CEO of Painted Paradise in an internal memo once a year. Logos are an excellent way to brand both internal and external communications.

 **CF01.18**

To Insert an Image and Use the Contextual Tab to Resize

a. Press Ctrl + Home to make cell A1—the beginning of this worksheet—the active cell.

b. Click the **Insert** tab, click **Illustrations**, and then click **Pictures**. Navigate to the location of your student data files, click **cf01ch01Logo.jpg**, and then click **Insert**. The image is inserted, and the Picture Tools contextual tab displays. Notice the image is too big and needs to be resized.

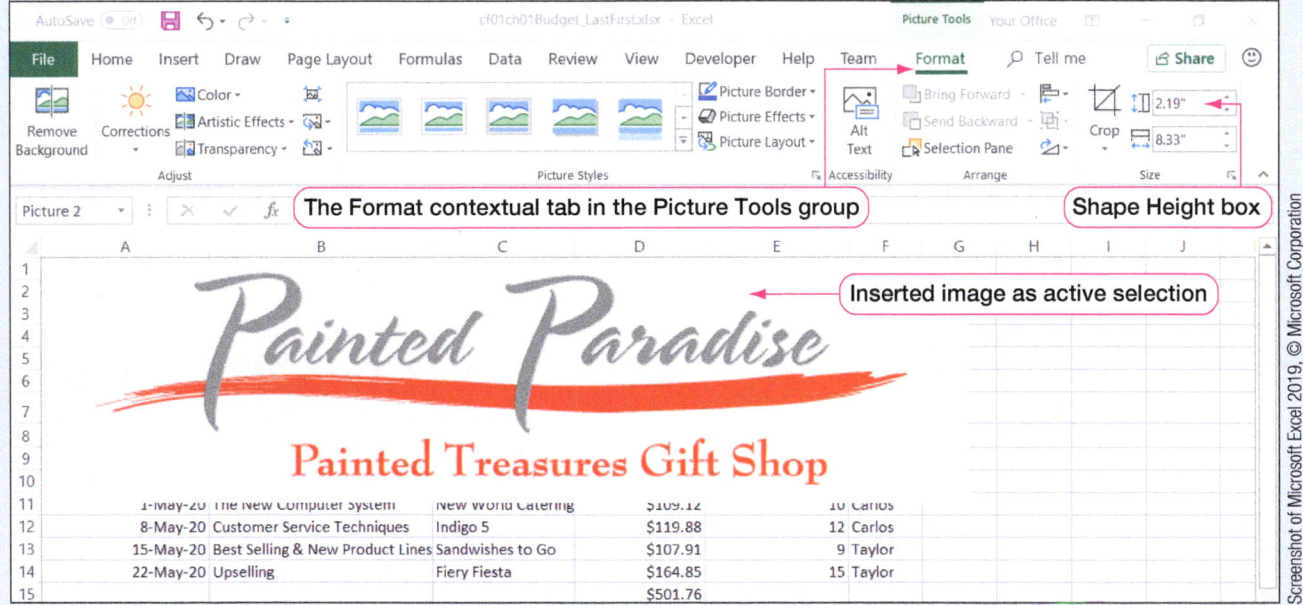

Figure 23   Picture Tools Format contextual tab

c. Under Picture Tools, on the Format tab, in the Size group, click in the **Shape Height** box. Then type **1** and press Enter. The image now fits the spreadsheet more appropriately.

d. Click cell **A7**. The contextual tab disappears because the image is no longer selected.

e. **Save** 🖫 the workbook.

COMMON FEATURES

<table>
<tr><td>REAL WORLD ADVICE</td><td>What Is Creative Commons, and Why Should You Care?</td></tr>
</table>

Office used to provide clip art pictures that were free to use. Office 2019 instead searches web sources for images. By default, it will find images that have Creative Commons licenses. These are images for which the copyright owner has chosen to allow anyone to use the image without commercial compensation. However, it is up to *you* to make sure that image really is free to use. You must read the specific license for that image to be sure your use is acceptable—otherwise, you could be sued for copyright infringement. When you insert the image, the source URL will be listed on the bottom. Click the link to open the source URL. From there, it may or may not be easy to find the license that is specific to that URL. When in doubt, do not use the file, or contact the owner before using.

Formatting Using the Mini Toolbar

The **Mini toolbar** appears after text has been selected and contains buttons for the most commonly used formatting commands, such as font, font size, font color, bold, and italic. The Mini toolbar button commands vary for each Office program. The toolbar disappears if you move the pointer away from the toolbar, press a key, or click the workspace. All the commands on the Mini toolbar are available on the ribbon; however, the Mini toolbar offers quicker access to common commands, because you do not have to move the mouse pointer far away from the selected text for these commands.

In this exercise, you will edit some of the cells in your budget with the Mini toolbar.

To Use the Mini Toolbar to Make the Text Italic

a. Double-click cell **A18** to place the insertion point in the cell. Double-clicking a cell enables you to enter edit mode for the cell text.

b. Double-click cell **A18** again to select the text. The Mini toolbar appears, coming into view directly above the selected text. If you move the pointer off the cell, the Mini toolbar becomes transparent or disappears entirely. If you don't move it too far away, you can move the pointer back over the Mini toolbar, and it becomes completely visible again. If it doesn't reappear, double-click on the text again.

Troubleshooting

If you are having a problem with the Mini toolbar disappearing, you may have inadvertently moved the mouse pointer to another part of the document. If you need to redisplay the Mini toolbar, right-click the selected text, and the Mini toolbar will appear along with a shortcut menu. Once you have selected an option on the Mini toolbar, the shortcut menu will disappear and the Mini toolbar will remain while in use—or repeat the prior two steps and then make sure the pointer stays over the toolbar.

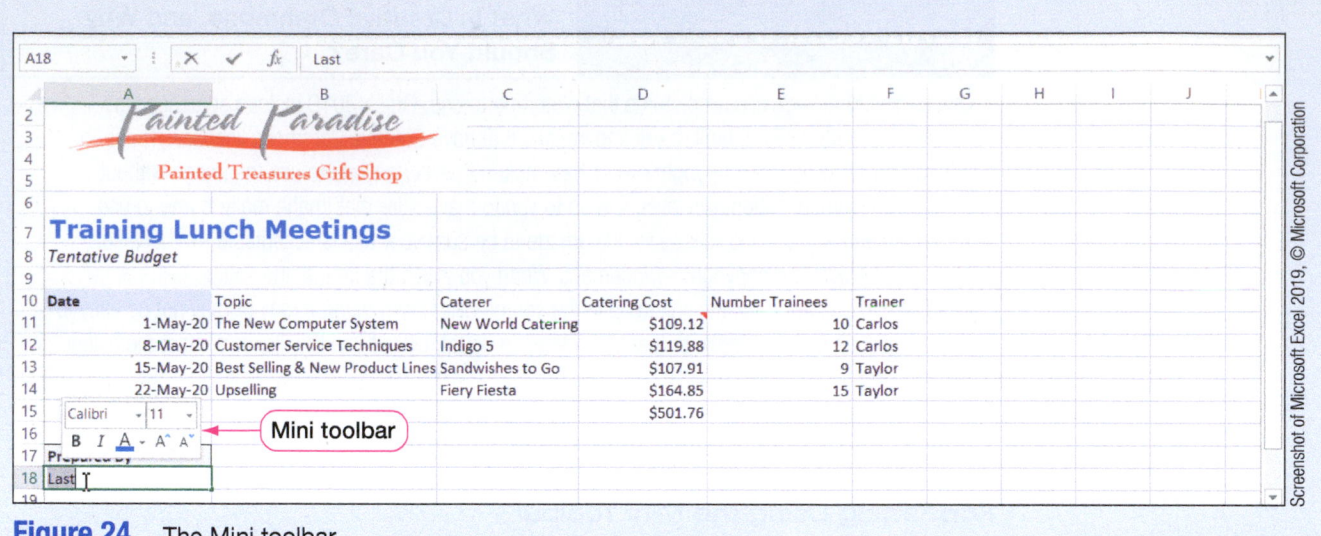

Figure 24 The Mini toolbar

Screenshot of Microsoft Excel 2019, © Microsoft Corporation

MAC COMPATIBILITY

Mini Toolbar

A Mini toolbar does not exist on a Mac. You can use the Home tab to apply these same settings.

c. On the Mini toolbar, click **Italic** I and then press `Enter`.

d. **Save**  the workbook.

The Mini toolbar is particularly helpful with the touch interface. When Office recognizes that you are using touch instead of a mouse or digitizer pen, it displays a Mini toolbar that is larger and designed to work with fingers more easily. An example of a touch Mini toolbar in Excel Touch mode is shown in Figure 25.

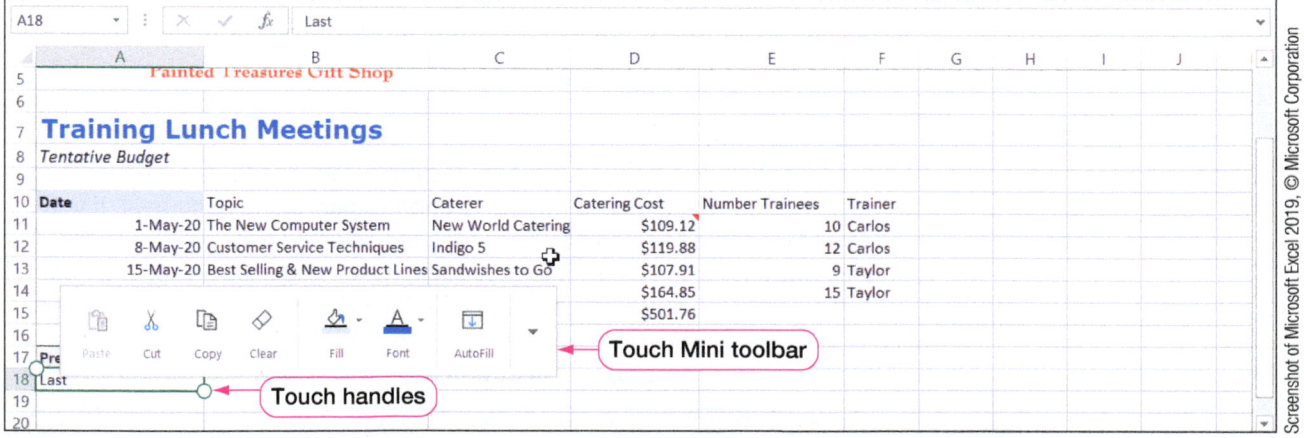

Figure 25 The Mini toolbar in Touch mode and selecting with a finger instead of a mouse

Screenshot of Microsoft Excel 2019, © Microsoft Corporation

Opening Shortcut Menus and Format Painter

A **shortcut menu** is a list of commands related to a selection that appears when you right-click—click the right mouse button. Shortcut menus are also context sensitive and enable you to quickly access commands that are most likely to be needed in the context of the task being performed. This means that you can access popular commands without using the ribbon. Included are commands that perform actions, commands that open dialog boxes, and galleries of options that provide a Live Preview. The Mini toolbar also opens with the shortcut menu when you right-click. If you click a button on the Mini toolbar, the shortcut menu closes, and the Mini toolbar remains open, allowing you to continue formatting your selection.

The **Format Painter**  allows you to copy a format and apply it to other selections. This allows you to format in one place and quickly apply the same formatting elsewhere. If you click the Format Painter button once, Format Painter will turn off after you use it just once. If you double-click the Format Painter, it leaves Format Painter active until you click the Format Painter button again or press Esc; leaving Format Painter active allows you to apply the formatting to multiple locations.

In this exercise, you will add some additional information to the budget you are beginning for your manager. You will also edit some of the cells using a shortcut menu and copy the format using Format Painter.

▶ **CF01.20**

To Use a Shortcut Menu and Format Painter

a. Click cell **A11**. Press Shift + Ctrl + ↓. Cells A11 through A14 are selected.

b. Right-click cell **A11** to display the shortcut menu.

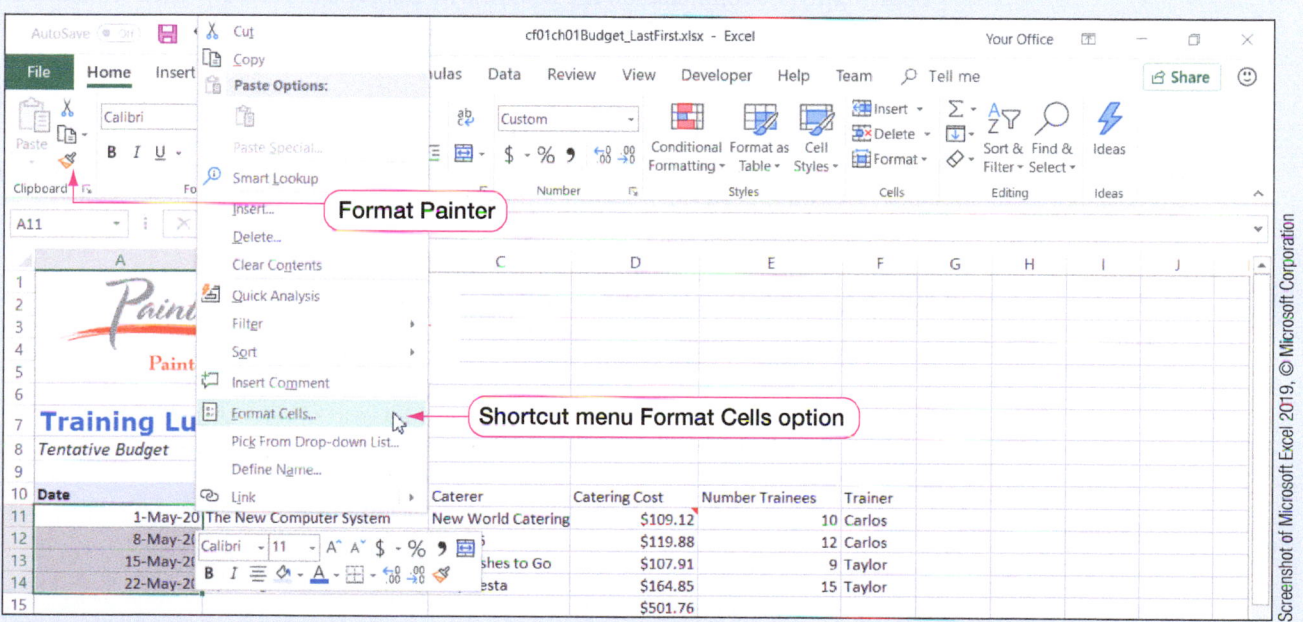

Figure 26   The shortcut menu

c. Click **Format Cells**.

d. In the Format Cells dialog box, under Category, click **Date** and then click **OK**. The date in cell A11 is now displayed as 5/1/2020.

SIDE NOTE
Single-Click the Format Painter
If you single-click the Format Painter , it will only allow you to copy the format to one cell. Double-clicking allows you to apply the formatting to more than one cell.

e. Click cell **A10** to make it the active cell. On the Home tab, in the Clipboard group, double-click **Format Painter** . Your mouse pointer now appears with a paint-brush next to it .

f. Click cells **B10**, **C10**, **D10**, **E10**, and **F10**. Notice that the cells are now formatted with bold and a blue background like cell A10.

g. Press Esc and the Format Painter is turned off. You can also turn off the Format Painter by clicking the button on the ribbon again.

h. **Save** the workbook.

Find Help, Print, and Share in Office

Office **Help** can give you additional information about a feature or steps for how to perform a new task. Your ability to find and use Help can greatly increase your Office proficiency and save you time from seeking outside assistance. Office has several levels of help, from a searchable search window to more directed help such as ScreenTips.

The Help pane provides detailed information on a multitude of topics, as well as access to templates, training videos installed on your computer, and content available on Office.com—the website maintained by Microsoft that provides access to the latest information and additional Help resources. To access the contents at Office.com, you must have access to the Internet from the computer. If there is no Internet access, only the files installed on the computer will be displayed in the Help pane. The easiest way to access Help is through pressing F1—in some of the programs. If available, this will take you directly to an article about what is actively selected.

Pointing to any command on the ribbon will display a **ScreenTip** with screen text to indicate more information. You may have seen these while working earlier in the chapter. They are very useful to learn what the command on the button will do.

Using the Help Pane and ScreenTips

In this exercise, you will view a ScreenTip, learn how to insert a footer using Excel Help, and then add a footer to the meeting minutes.

To Access Office Help and Insert a Footer

CF01.21

a. With your Excel budget open, press F1. The Excel Help pane opens.

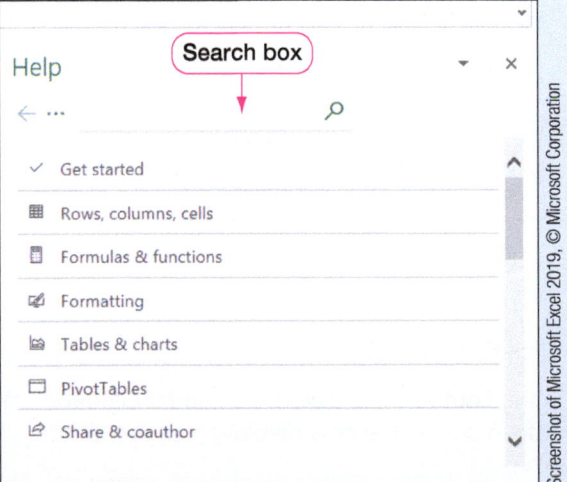

Figure 27   The Excel Help pane

SIDE NOTE
ScreenTip and F1
If a topic for a ScreenTip does not exist in Help, the window will open to the starting search page.

b. In the search box, type add a footer and then press Enter. Then click **the first link** and read about how to add a footer. When you are done, click **Close** ✕ to close the Help pane.

c. Click the **Page Layout** tab, and then, in the Page Setup group, point to Print Titles. Notice the ScreenTip with a link for Tell me more. If you clicked on Tell me more, it would take you to the Help window specifically for Print Titles.

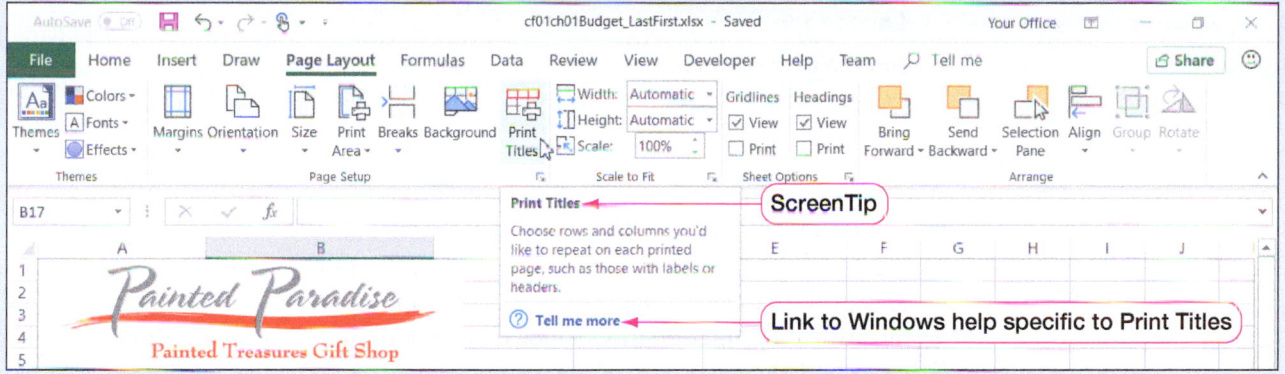

Figure 28 ScreenTip

Screenshot of Microsoft Excel 2019, © Microsoft Corporation

d. In the Page Setup group, point to the Page Setup Dialog Box Launcher ⌐. Notice the ScreenTip, this time without the Tell me more option. Click the **Page Setup Dialog Box Launcher** ⌐.

e. Click the **Header/Footer** tab, and then click **Custom Footer** to display the Footer dialog box.

f. Click in the **Left** section and type First Last using your first and last name.

> **Grader Heads Up**
>
> If using MyLab IT Grader, enter Julie Smith representing a fictitious student instead of your name.

g. Click in the **Center** section and then click **Insert File Name** 🗎.

h. Click in the **Right** section and then type InstructorLast using your instructor's last name.

> **Grader Heads Up**
>
> If using MyLab IT Grader, enter Thompson representing a fictitious instructor last name instead of your instructor's last name.

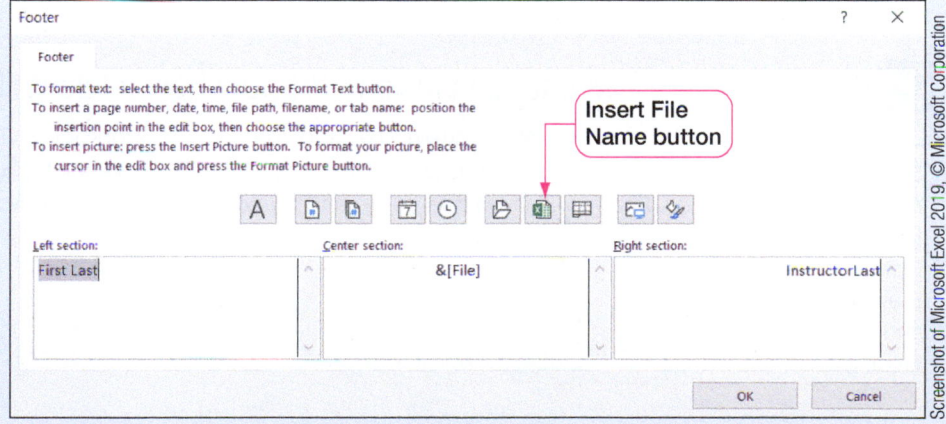

Figure 29 The Footer dialog box

Screenshot of Microsoft Excel 2019, © Microsoft Corporation

i.   Click **OK**, and then click **OK** again. The footer is inserted. In Normal view, you will not see the footer. You will see the footer in the next exercise.

Notice, you now see a dotted line between column D and E. This is where the page will break and part of the worksheet does not fit on the page. To fix this, you need to change the orientation.

j.   On the Page Layout tab, in the Page Setup group, click **Orientation** and then click **Landscape**.

k.   Save  the workbook.

Accessing the Share Pane

In Office, many options exist for sharing files. There are times when you will need a paper copy—also known as a hard copy—of an Office document, spreadsheet, or presentation. When a printed version is not needed, a digital copy will save paper and costs. Office provides many ways to share your document. You can use traditional ways of sharing by printing or exporting a PDF. From the Share link in Office, you can invite other people to share the document, and you can specify whether others are allowed to edit the document if the file is saved to OneDrive. From Office Backstage, the document can be emailed to others, transformed into an online presentation, or posted to a blog.

New in Excel 2019, you can share your file while it is open in Excel. In the top-right corner of the Excel window, next to your account image, click Share. This will open the Share task pane. From there, you can add a person, choose whether he or she can edit or just view the file, and even give a personal message. In addition, new with Office 2019, you and those you share with can all be editing the document in real time. You will be able to see the changes being made to the document while you are also making changes. To do this, you must have the file saved in your OneDrive and be logged into your Microsoft account.

Changing Views

In each of the Office applications, there are different ways to view the file. For example, in Word, you can view in Read Mode, as a Web Layout, Outline, or Draft. In Excel, it is particularly important to change your view to Page Break Preview before attempting to print a file. This view shows you where the page breaks will happen and, if needed, allows you to modify them. Also, Page Layout view will allow you to view any headers and footers before printing. In this exercise, you will change to Page Break Preview and the Page Layout view to ensure that everything will fit on one page.

CF01.22

SIDE NOTE
Adjusting Page Breaks
From Page Break Preview you can click and drag to adjust page break lines.

To Change Views to Preview How a File Will Print

a.   Click the **View** tab, and then, in the Workbook Views group, click **Page Break Preview**. Excel zooms to 60% and shows each page with blue lines. The budget will fit on one page, and no adjustments are needed.

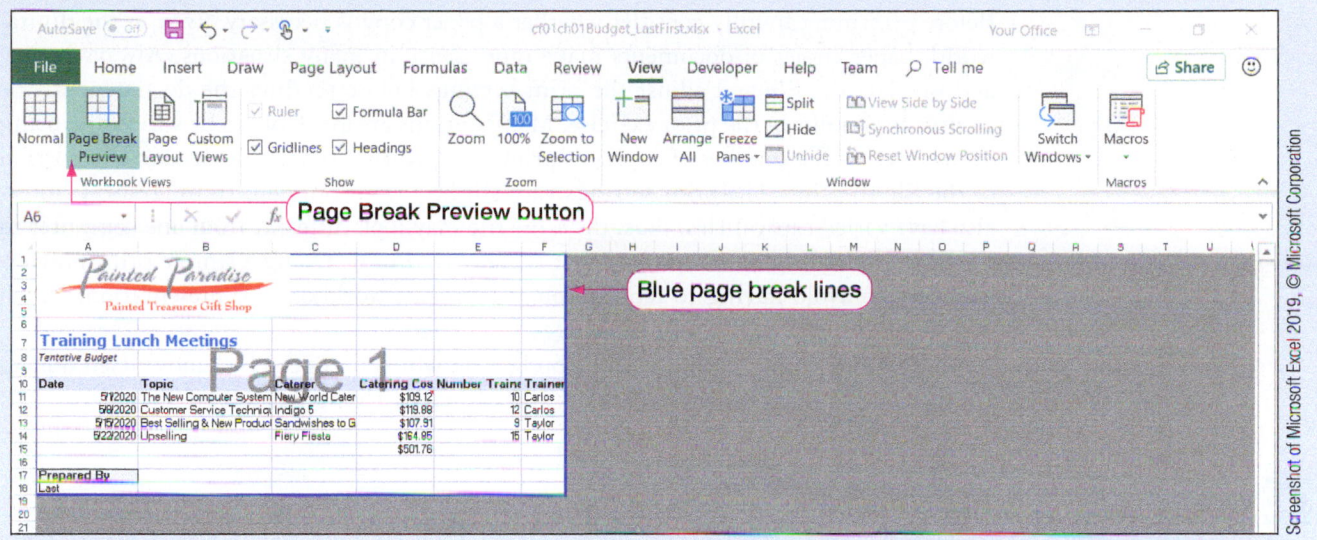

Figure 30 Page Break Preview

b. On the View tab, in the Workbook Views group, click **Page Layout**. Scroll down and verify that the footer you created in a prior exercise looks correct.

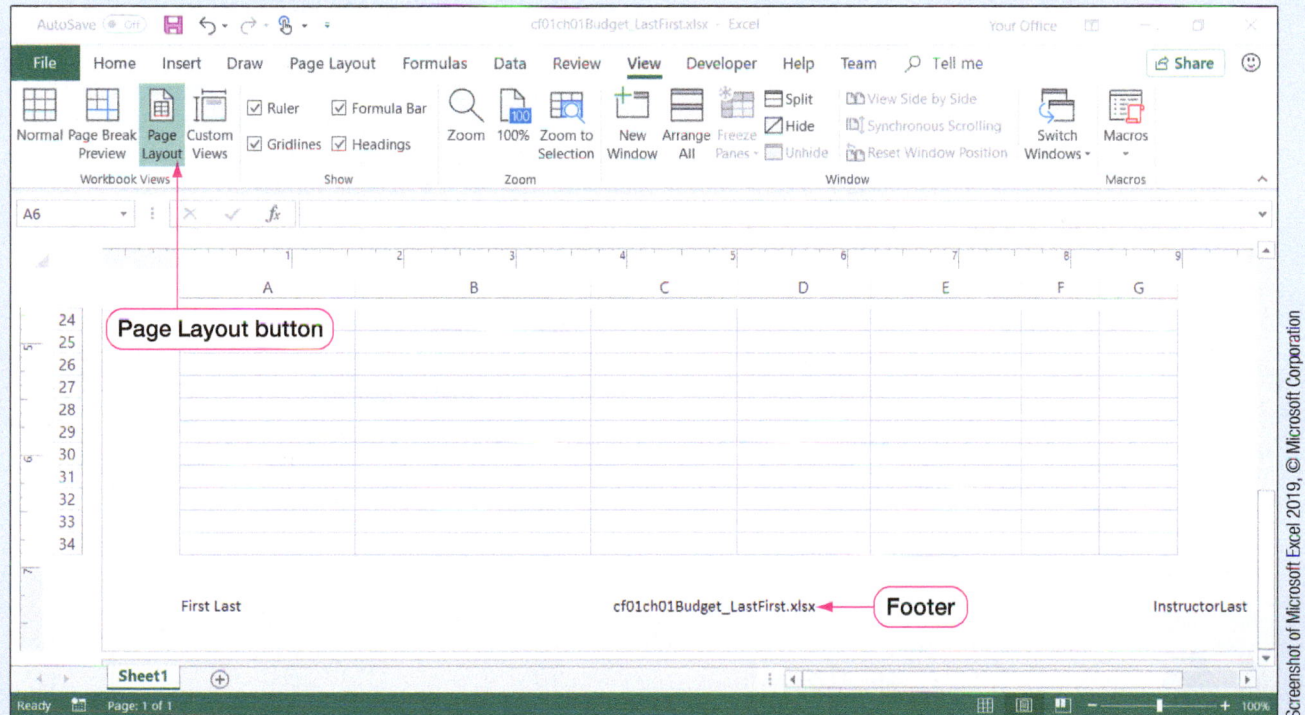

Figure 31 Page Layout view

c. In the Workbook Views group, click **Normal** to return to the normal Excel view. Press [Ctrl]+[Home] to make cell A1 the active cell.

d. **Save** 💾 the workbook.

Printing a File

Before printing, carefully consider whether a paper copy is necessary. Even in the digital world, paper copies of documents make more sense in many situations. Always review and preview the file and adjust the print settings before sending the document to the printer as you did in the prior exercise. Many options are available to fit various printing needs, such as the number of copies to print, the printing device to use, and the portion of the file to print. The print settings vary slightly from program to program. Printers also have varied capabilities; thus, the same file may look different from one computer to the next, depending on the printer that is connected to it. Doing a simple print preview will help to avoid having to reprint your document, workbook, or presentation, which requires additional paper, ink, and energy resources.

In this exercise, you will print the budget on which notes can be handwritten during the meeting so that you can update the spreadsheet with more detail later.

 **CF01.23**

To Print a File

a. In Excel, click the **File** tab to open Office Backstage.

> **Grader Heads Up**
> You will not need to turn in a paper copy for MyLab IT Grader. Consult your instructor to see if you should actually print the budget.

b. Click **Print**. The Print settings and Print Preview appear. Verify that the Copies box displays **1**.

c. Verify that the correct printer—as directed by your instructor—appears in the Printer box. Choices may vary depending on the computer you are using. If the correct printer is not displayed, click the Printer arrow, and then click to choose the correct or preferred printer from the list of available printers.

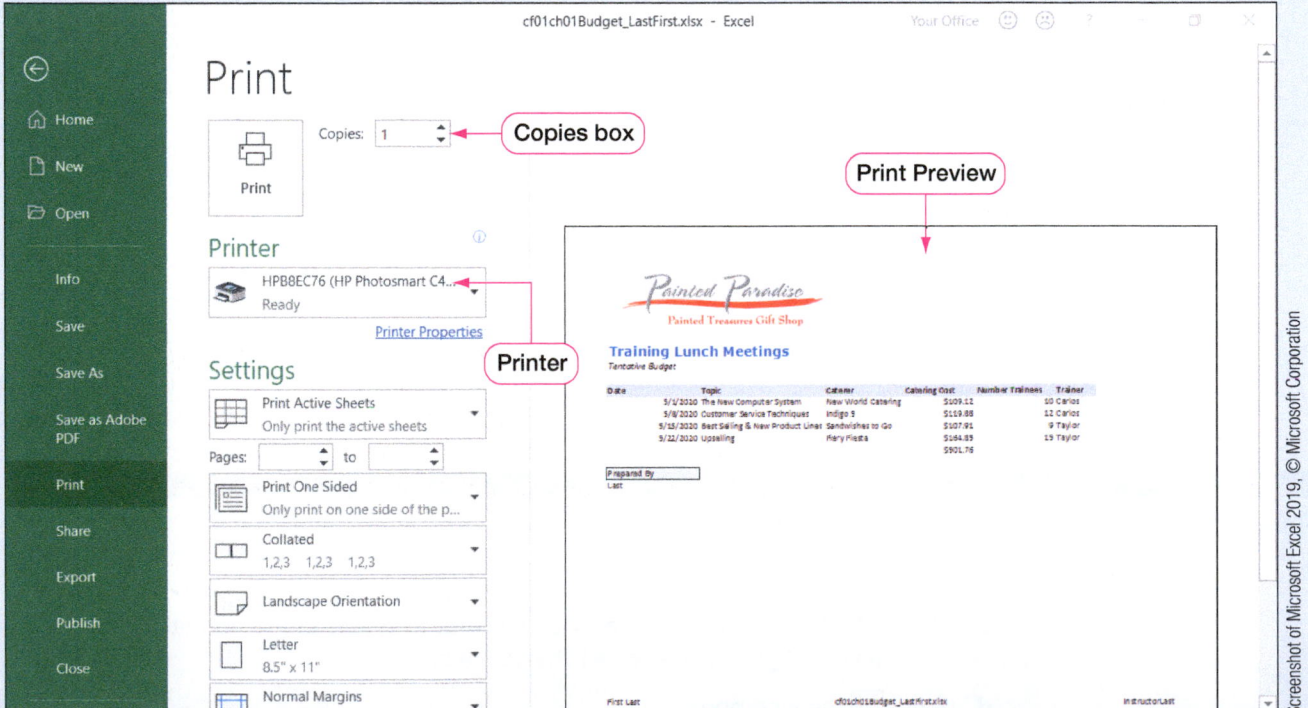

Figure 32 Backstage Print

d. If your instructor asks you to print the document, click **Print**.

Exporting a PDF

When you want to give someone else a document, consider whether an electronic version of the file is better than a printed copy. A **Portable Document Format (PDF)** file is a type of file that ensures that the document will look the same on someone else's computer. For example, different computers may have different fonts installed. A PDF maintains the fonts used in the original document. Even if the computer on which the file is being viewed does not have the same fonts as the computer that was used to create the file, the viewer will see the correct font. PDFs are a common file format used in business to share documents because of the readily available free readers. In Word, you can edit a PDF. Also, in Windows 10, the default PDF reader is now the new Edge browser. You can still install the Adobe reader program and set it as the default if you prefer.

In this exercise, you will export a PDF of the budget document so you can email a copy to your colleagues who are also attending the meeting.

 CF01.24

MAC COMPATIBILITY

Printing to PDF on a Mac

Point above the Excel window to display the menu. Click File and then click Print. In the Print dialog box, in the lower-left corner, click the PDF arrow and select Save as PDF. In the dialog box, accept the file name in the Save As box, in the Where box choose the location to which you want to save the file, and click Save.

To Create a PDF File

a. If you are not already in Office Backstage, click the **File** tab. Click **Export**, and then click **Create PDF/XPS**.

> **Grader Heads Up**
> You will not need to turn in a PDF for MyLab IT Grader. Consult your instructor to see if you need to turn it in.

b. Navigate to the location where your student files are stored. Verify that the file name selected is **cf01ch01Budget_LastFirst.pdf**. Notice settings in the Publish as PDF or XPS dialog box for optimizing for publishing online versus printing. Because your colleague will print this document, the default setting of Standard is appropriate.

c. Click **Publish**. Close the **PDF** file. If the PDF opens in the default reader, then close the reader.

d. **Save** 🖫 the workbook and click **Close** ☒ to close this file and exit Excel. Submit your files as directed by your instructor.

> **SS** **CONSIDER THIS** | **Sending or Sharing Files Electronically**
>
> Sending an electronic file can be easier and cheaper than sending a printed copy to someone. Sharing a file also saves on email quotas. What should you consider when deciding the type of file to send? When you send an application-specific file, such as a Word or Excel file, what happens if the recipient does not have the relevant Office application installed? When you send a PDF, how easy is it for a recipient to edit a document? How does the file type affect the quality of a recipient's printout?

Insert Office Add-ins

To enhance the features of Office, you can install **Add-ins for Office** from Microsoft's Office Store. These Add-ins run in the side pane to provide extra features such as web search, dictionary, and maps. There are different Add-ins for the different Office programs. You must be signed into Office with your Microsoft account to take advantage of them.

QUICK REFERENCE	Installing Add-ins for Office

1. Open up any Office application in which you want to use apps.

2. Click the Insert tab, and then in the Add-ins group, select the My Add-ins arrow. Select See All from the list.

3. The Office Add-ins window appears, showing all the apps you have installed in your Microsoft account under My Add-ins. If you see the app you want, select the app, and then click Add.

4. If you do not see the app you want, click the Store link.

5. Search for the add-in you want, and then follow the steps online to install the add-in in your account. You may have to sign into your Microsoft account.

6. Once the add-in has been installed, return to the Office application and repeat steps 2 and 3.

Concept Check

1. Which Microsoft application would you use to create a budget? p. 2

2. What are the advantages of using OneDrive instead of a USB flash drive? p. 10

3. What is the difference between Save and Save As? p. 8

4. How do you pin the ribbon open? Explain what can be done in Office Backstage. p. 6

5. Explain a way to copy and paste. What advantages are there to knowing keyboard shortcuts? p. 18

6. What is the Tell me what you want to do feature, and how is it different from Help? p. 27

7. Describe three different ways to apply bold to text. p. 30

8. What is a contextual tab? p. 32

9. Describe ways to obtain help in Office 2019. p. 36

10. How could you share a newsletter with all the members of your business fraternity without printing the document? p. 41

11. What are Add-ins for Office? p. 41

Key Terms

Active cell   p. 16
Application Start screen   p. 3
Add-ins for Office   p. 42
AutoRecovery   p. 10
AutoSave   p. 10
Bootcamp   p. 3
Cell   p. 16
Close   p. 6
Cloud computing   p. 11
Contextual tab   p. 32
Dialog Box Launcher   p. 25
Document   p. 2
File extension   p. 11
File path   p. 12
Font   p. 25
Format Painter   p. 35

Gallery   p. 25
Groups   p. 5
Help   p. 36
Keyboard shortcut   p. 18
KeyTip   p. 18
Live Preview   p. 26
Maximize   p. 6
Mini toolbar   p. 33
Minimize   p. 6
Most Recently Used list   p. 15
Office Background   p. 8
Office Backstage   p. 8
Office Theme   p. 8
OneDrive   p. 11
Portable Document Format
   (PDF)   p. 41

Presentation   p. 2
Protected View   p. 16
Quick Access Toolbar   p. 5
Relational database   p. 2
Restore Down   p. 6
Ribbon   p. 5
Ribbon Display Options   p. 6
Roaming settings   p. 15
ScreenTip   p. 36
Shortcut menu   p. 35
Spreadsheet   p. 2
Tell me what you want to do   p. 27
Toggle button   p. 25
USB drive   p. 10
Virtualization   p. 3
Workbook   p. 16

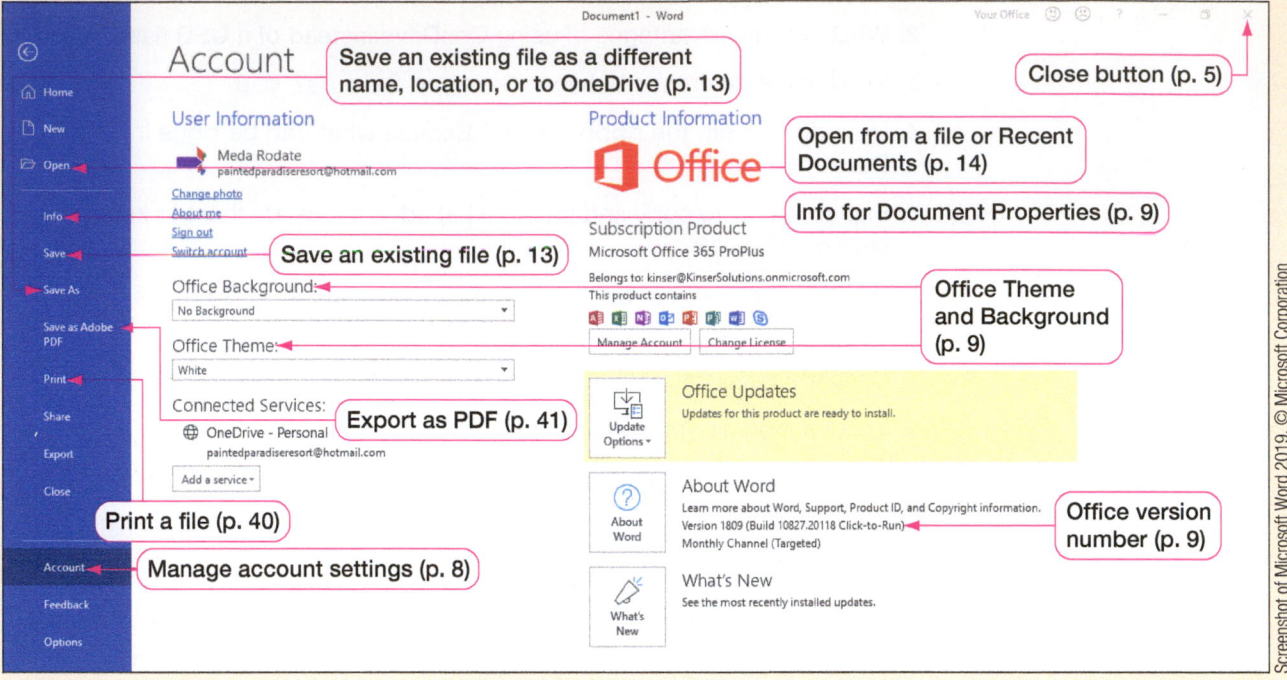

Figure 33

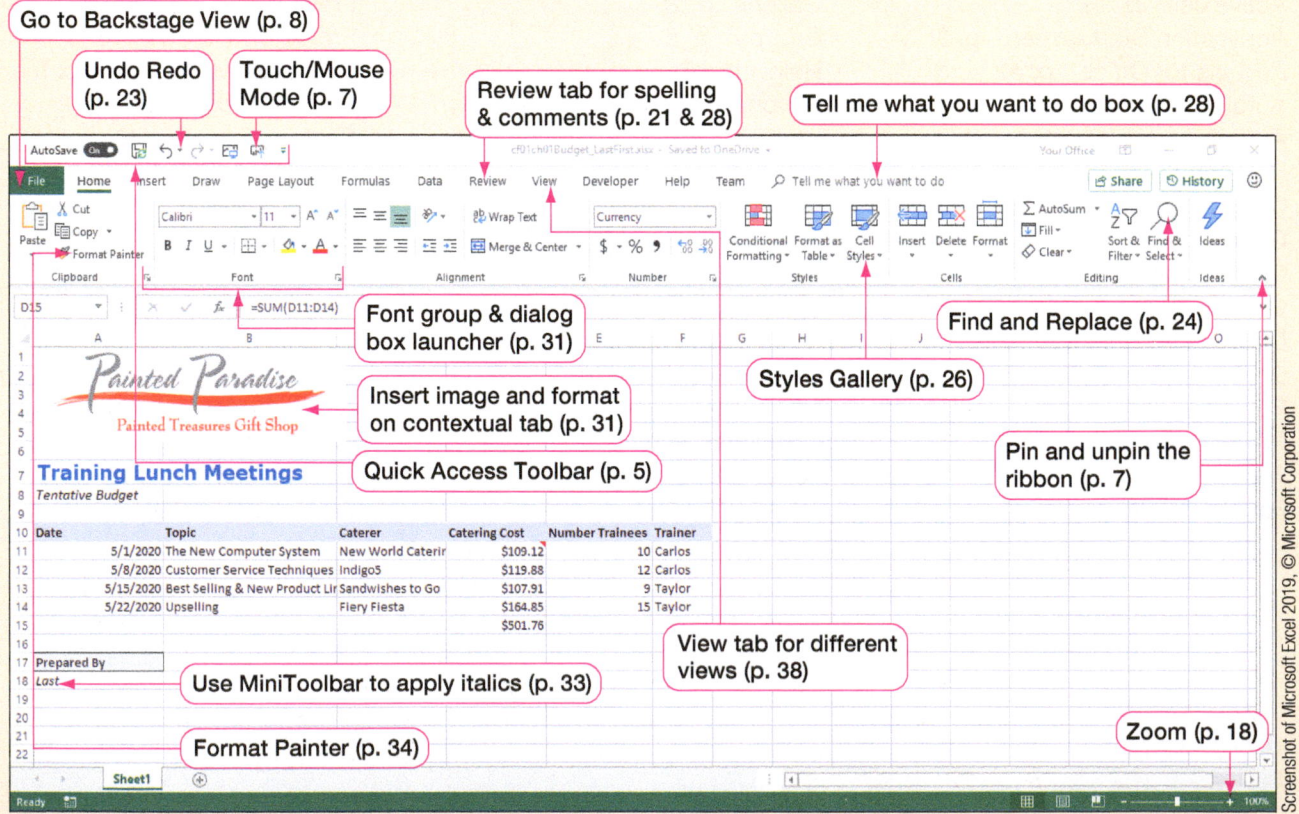

Figure 34

Practice 1

Student data files needed:

cf01ch01Inventory.xlsx

cf01ch01Logo.jpg

You will save your file as:

cf01ch01Inventory_LastFirst.xlsx

Formatting and Inventory List

Human
Resources

Susan Brock, the manager of the gift shop, is working on a list of inventory and quantity in stock. She needs it to do a physical inventory check/audit. During the audit an employee counts how many items are on a shelf to see if it matches the number in the computer system.

a. Open the Excel file **cf01ch01Inventory** and save your file as cf01ch01Inventory _LastFirst using your first and last name. Enable Editing if necessary.

b. Click cell **A1**. Click the **Insert** tab, and then in the Illustrations group, click **Pictures**. Browse to where you are keeping your student files and select **cf01ch01Logo.jpg**, and then click **Insert**.

c. On the Picture Tools Format tab. in the Size group, set the Height to 0.6 inches.

d. The T-shirts are not listed properly. The T-shirts should be listed as LS T-shirts—LS is the brand. On the Home tab, in the Editing group, click **Find & Select** and then click **Replace**. In the Find what box, type T-shirts in the Replace with box, type **LS T-shirts**. Click **Replace All**, click **OK**, and then click **Close**.

e. One of the items is omitted from the list. Select cells A14 and B14. Press Ctrl+C. Click cell **A49**. Press Ctrl+V.

f. Modify cell **A49** to be Stuffed animal – cat Click cell **C49**, type 32 and then press Enter. Click cell **D49**, type 11 and then press Enter.

g. Click cell **C1**. On the Home tab, in the Styles group, click **More** ⏷ and then click **Title**.

h. Click cell **A5**. On the Home Tab, in the Alignment group, click **Align Right** ☰. In the Font group, click **Bold**. Click the **Fill Color arrow** and select **Orange, Accent 2, Lighter 80%**. Click the **Font Size arrow**. Click **12**.

i. Click cell **B5** and type First Last using your first and last name. Press Ctrl+Enter. On the Home tab, in the Font group, click **Italic**. Click the **Font Size arrow**. Click **12**.

j. Click cell **A7**. On the Home tab in the Font group, click **Bold**. Click the **Fill Color arrow** and select **Orange, Accent 2, Lighter 80%**. Click the **Border arrow** ⊞▾ and then select **Outside Borders**.

k. With cell A7 still the active cell, on the Home tab, in the Clipboard group, double-click **Format Painter**. Click cells **B7**, **C7**, **D7**, **E7**, and **F7**. Press Esc.

l. Click cell **D8**. Then, press Shift+Ctrl+↓. On the Home tab, in the Number group, click the **Dialog Box Launcher**. In the Format Cells dialog box, on the Number tab, under Category, click **Accounting** and then **OK**.

m. Click the **Page Layout** tab, and in the Page Setup group, click the **Dialog Box Launcher**. Click the **Header/Footer** tab and then click **Custom Footer**. Click in the left section and type First Last using your first and last name. Click in the **Center** section and click **Insert File Name**. Click in the **Right** section and type InstructorLast using your instructor's last name. Click OK twice.

n. **Save** the workbook, exit Excel, and then submit your file as directed by your instructor.

MyLab IT Grader

Student data files needed:

 cf01ch01Coffee.xlsx

cf01ch01Coffee.jpg

You will save your file as:

 cf01ch01Coffee_LastFirst.xlsx

Finance & Accounting

Roasted 4U

You are an intern at the local coffeehouse, Roasted 4U, which processes its own coffee beans. They offer a service where customers can sign up to get a bag of freshly roasted coffee beans every week, every other week, or monthly. As the intern, you have been asked to help them create a better social media presence. You have already created various social media accounts. Now, you want to connect with the customers. The owner gave you a spreadsheet list of current customers. You will format this spreadsheet. You will also add a space to research their social media accounts and try to connect with past customers on social media. While they have a coffee shop, the owner wants you to concentrate on the subscription customers who get freshly roasted beans on a regular basis.

a. Open the Excel file **cf01ch01Coffee.xlsx**. Save your file as cf01ch01Coffee_LastFirst using your last and first name.

b. In cell **A1**, insert the image **cf01ch01Coffee.jpg**. Change the height of the image to 2.2 inches.

c. Set the cell style for cell **C1** to **Title**.

d. Change cell **C2** to **12 pt** font size, **Bold**, and **Italic**.

e. Apply **Bold** to cell **C4**.

f. In cell C5, enter Micah Ratliff as a fictitious student name.

g. Check the spelling to correct all spelling errors. Assume all customer names are spelled correctly.

h. Someone entered this data for those who receive a bag of coffee twice a month as "Twice a Month" when it should have been **Bi-Weekly** according to Roasted 4U's website. Find all instances and replace it to the correct wording.

i. Format the cells from G13 through G49 as **Accounting**.

j. Change the formatting for cell C13 through C49 to **Short Date**. Thus, the date in C13 should look like 7/11/2020.

k. Change cell A12 to be **Bold**, **outside borders**, and a fill color of **Green, Accent 6, Lighter 40%**.

l. Use the Format Painter to apply the formatting in cell A12 to **B12**, **C12**, **D12**, **E12**, **F12**, **G12**, **H12**, and **I12**.

m. In cell F50 enter the text Total Monthly Make cell F50 be **bold** with a fill color of **Green, Accent 6, Lighter 40%**.

n. Using the Tell me box, in cell **G50**, enter the sum of cells G13 through G49. Format cell G50 to be a fill color of **Green, Accent 6, Lighter 40%**.

o. Add a custom footer with Micah Ratliff in the left section, **file name** in the center, and Roasted 4U on the right. If needed, return to Normal view.

p. Change the print orientation to Landscape.

q. Save the workbook and click **Close** to close this file and exit Excel. Submit your file as directed by your instructor.

Critical Thinking

These directions told you how to format the workbook. Do you have any suggestions for improvements or anything that might be problematic? Do you think the spreadsheet looks professional? You may suggest changes that you have not learned how to make yet. Submit your answer as directed by your instructor.

Perform 1: Perform in Your Career

Student data file needed: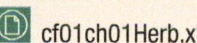

cf01ch01Herb.xlsx

You will save your file as: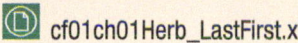

cf01ch01Herb_LastFirst.xlsx

General
Business

Harry's Herbs

You are interning for a local nursery. One of the employees, Harry, specializes in herbs. Every year, he offers herb classes as a fundraiser for the local homeless shelter. Another intern began to create a spreadsheet but was unexpectedly unavailable to finish it. Your supervisor has asked you to help get the spreadsheet ready for the classes.

a. Open the Excel file **cf01ch01Herb**. Save your file as cf01ch01Herb_LastFirst using your last and first name.

b. Change the worksheet headings to differentiate them from the data.

c. Format any data to appropriately indicate the type of data, such as money having a format that represents money.

d. With consistent formatting, give organization to the workbook.

e. Spell check the workbook and correct any spelling errors.

f. Add any other formatting that will make this spreadsheet look more professional or have more clarity. Do not change any of the content (beyond spelling errors) or move cells.

g. Add a custom footer that contains First Last, using your first and last name, in the Left section and the File Name in the Right section. Do not worry if the file will not print on a single page.

h. Save the workbook, and close Excel. Submit your file as directed by your instructor.

Perform 2: Perform in Your Life

Student data files needed:

Blank Word document

cf01ch01Dinner.xlsx

You will save your file as:

cf01ch01Critique_LastFirst.docx

Human
Resources

Finance &
Accounting

Improving the Appearance of Vintage Clothing's Spreadsheet

Your boss at a local vintage clothing store has asked you to review a spreadsheet—made by a prior employee—and make suggestions on what to do to improve the appearance of the spreadsheet. The spreadsheet is to outline the budget for a dinner for a customer appreciation event. Examine the file cf01ch01Dinner. Then do the following.

a. Open a new blank document in Word, and then save the file as cf01ch01Critique_LastFirst using your last and first name.

b. For things you know how to do, list five items that you would change in the spreadsheet and why.

c. For things you do not know how to do such as adding a logo, border, or chart, list at least two items that you would change in the spreadsheet and why.

d. Discuss any content that you think should be added to the spreadsheet—even if you don't know what that content is. For example, you could discuss additional information about the event.

e. Add a footer with First Last, using your first and last name, and the file name.

f. Exit Word, and then submit your file as directed by your instructor.

Excel Business Unit 1

Understanding the Fundamentals

Data is vital to businesses to help them determine their profits or their losses, their place in a competitive market, and/or their ability to branch into new markets. Businesses use Excel to structure and process data to create information to help in the decision-making process. To use Excel effectively, you need to plan, structure, and format workbooks appropriately. This business unit will introduce you to the fundamentals of creating and working with an Excel workbook.

Learning Outcome 1

Use Excel to enter text, number, date, and time data to create efficient, effective worksheets.

REAL WORLD SUCCESS

"My family has operated the same farm for four generations. When I graduated from college, I decided to become the first woman to run the family farm. I now track all of our production inputs and outputs using Excel. The high-quality information I produce with Excel has made our farm more efficient and more profitable. Farming is a business, and a successful business requires intelligence in handling information as much as, or more than, it requires intelligence in any other critical business activity."

– Leah, graduate

Learning Outcome 2

Use Excel to effectively communicate information using functions and worksheet formatting.

REAL WORLD SUCCESS

"I worked in an insurance agency while I was in college. Part of my job was to administer marketing strategies. Every month, we received data from our parent company that identified prospective clients. I used Excel to calculate a ranking so I could contact prospects with the highest potential value first. Agency performance was significantly improved as a result and I received a regional award for efficiency improvement."

– Mike, alumnus and insurance agent

Microsoft Excel

OBJECTIVES

1. Understand spreadsheet terminology and components   p. 51

2. Navigate worksheets and workbooks   p. 53

3. Document your work   p. 57

4. Enter and edit data   p. 59

5. Work with cells and cell ranges   p. 62

6. Adjust columns and rows   p. 69

7. Manipulate worksheets and workbooks   p. 75

8. Preview, print, and export workbooks   p. 84

Chapter 1 CREATE, NAVIGATE, WORK WITH, AND PRINT WORKSHEETS

Prepare Case

MyLab IT Grader

Finance & Accounting

Red Bluff Golf Course & Pro Shop
Golf Cart Purchase Analysis

The Painted Paradise Resort & Spa has a world-class golf course and pro shop. The Red Bluff Golf Course & Pro Shop makes golf carts available to its members for a fee. Recently, the resort has been running out of carts due to wear and tear. The time has come for the club to add more golf carts to its fleet. Club manager, Barry Cheney, wants to use Microsoft Excel to analyze the purchase of golf carts by model, price, and financing parameters.

Karamysh/Shutterstock

Student data file needed:

 e01ch01GolfCartAnalysis.xlsx

You will save your files as:

 e01ch01GolfCartAnaylsis_LastFirst.xlsx

 e01ch01GolfCartAnalysis_LastFirst.pdf

 e01ch01Mowers_LastFirst.xlsx

Getting Started with Excel

Data plays an integral part in supporting business. Without data, businesses cannot determine their effectiveness in the market, or their profit or loss performance. In addition, as businesses grow and change, the types of data collected by a business are among the few things that remain relatively static over time. Jobs change, products change, and businesses grow, shrink, or evolve into different lines of business—even into different organizations—based on customer and market demands. However, the types of data that businesses gather and analyze are relatively constant. Much of the same information is required about customers, vendors, products, services, materials, transactions, and so on regardless of the type of business or its stage of growth. Data tracking typically expands as new data is made available and deemed necessary for business purposes or as new technologies easily capture data that was prohibitive to track in the past. Many things may change, but the type of information remains the same.

Data requires processing—categorizing, summarizing, counting, averaging, statistical analysis, and formatting for effective communication—to reveal information that the data itself cannot tell you. With an application such as Excel, it is possible to structure data and to process it in a manner that creates information for decision-making purposes.

Understand Spreadsheet Terminology and Components

Excel is a spreadsheet program that can be used to manage, analyze, and share information. With the help of Excel, you can reveal underlying trends, calculate values, make predictions, make recommendations, and display or share information with large or small amounts of data.

To learn the efficient and effective utilization of Excel, you must know the terminology and components of a spreadsheet. If you are unsure where something is located or how Excel is functioning, you can use the Excel Help feature. You can access Excel Help by pressing the F1 key or by typing your question into the *Tell me what you want to do …* or by clicking the Help tab on the ribbon.

What Is a Spreadsheet?

Excel is a spreadsheet application. A **spreadsheet** is a collection of data that is organized in a row and column format. The intersection of each row and column is called a **cell**. A **row** is a horizontal set of cells that encompasses all the columns in a worksheet. A **column** is a vertical set of cells that encompasses all the rows in a worksheet. Each cell can contain text, numbers, formulas, and/or functions. A **formula** is a mathematical equation that produces a result and may contain numbers, operators, text, and/or functions. A **function** is a built-in program that performs a task such as calculating a sum or average. Both formulas and functions must always start with the equal sign (=). In Excel, a single spreadsheet is referred to as a **worksheet**, which is a grid of columns and rows in which data is entered.

From balancing an accounting ledger to creating a financial report, many business documents use Excel spreadsheets. Excel spreadsheets are designed to support analyzing business data, representing data through charts, and modeling real world situations.

Spreadsheets are also commonly used to perform what-if analysis. **What-if analysis** allows one to examine the outcome of the changes to values in a worksheet. In what-if analysis, you change values in spreadsheet cells to investigate the effects on calculated values of interest.

Spreadsheets are used for much more than what-if analysis, however. A spreadsheet can be used as a basic collection of data in which each row is a record and each column is a field in the record. A **record** is all of the categories of data that pertain to one person, place, thing, event, or idea and are formatted as a row in a worksheet. A **field** is an item of information in a worksheet column that is associated with something of interest. Spreadsheets can be built to act as a simple accounting system. Businesses often use spreadsheets to analyze complex financial statements and information. Excel can calculate statistical values such as mean, variance, and standard deviation. Excel can even be used for advanced statistical models such as forecasting and regression analysis. Spreadsheet applications "excel" at calculations of almost any kind.

What Is a Workbook?

Excel files are known as workbooks. A **workbook** is a file that contains one or more worksheets. In Microsoft Excel 2019, workbooks have a file extension of .xlsx. By default, a new, blank workbook contains one worksheet, identified by a tab at the bottom of the Excel window titled Sheet1. As additional worksheets are added, each is given a default name. For example, two new worksheets would be given the names Sheet2 and Sheet3. The **active worksheet** is the worksheet that is visible in the Excel application window and is denoted by a white tab—unless a tab color has been applied—with bold letters and a thick bottom border. Worksheets that are not active are denoted by gray tabs—unless tab colors have been applied—with normal letters. The number of worksheets that can be contained in a workbook is determined by the amount of available memory.

Once a workbook has been created, any changes to it will need to be saved. The Save command can accomplish this task; however, Save As is useful for saving a copy of a file with a new name. Save As is also useful for creating a backup of a file or for creating a copy of a workbook when you want to use that workbook as the starting point for another workbook.

In this exercise, to get started on the golf cart analysis, you will open a workbook that club manager Barry Cheney has prepared for you and then will save the workbook with a new name.

E01.00

MAC COMPATIBILITY
Opening a Workbook
To open a workbook, use the Menu bar. Click **On my Mac** and browse to the file location.

SIDE NOTE
Office Updates
Depending on your exact Office version, you may see Open or Open Other Workbooks.

SIDE NOTE
Pin the Ribbon
If your ribbon is collapsed, pin your ribbon open. Click the Home tab. In the lower-right corner of the ribbon, click Pin the ribbon ⊟.

To Start Excel and Open, Save, and Rename a Workbook

a. Click the **Windows button** ⊞ in the lower-left corner of your screen, type **exc** and then click **Excel** in the search results.

b. Click the **File** tab, click **Open**, and then click **Browse**. Navigate to the location where you are storing your data files, then double-click **e01ch01GolfCartAnalysis**. If a Security Warning message displays, click the **Enable Editing** button.

   A workbook opens providing data to analyze the purchase of golf carts by model, price, and financing.

c. Click the **File** tab, click **Save As**, and then double-click **This PC**. In the Save As dialog box, navigate to the location where you are saving your project files, and then change the file name to **e01ch01GolfCartAnalysis_LastFirst** using your last and first name. Click **Save**.

CONSIDER THIS | **Excel Can Store a Vast Amount of Data**

There are 1,048,576 rows × 16,384 columns = 17,179,869,184 cells in an Excel 2019 worksheet. With so much capacity, it can be tempting to use Excel as a database. What other Office application would be better for storing vast amounts of data?

REAL WORLD ADVICE | **AutoRecover and Quick Save**

Computers are not perfect. While life's imperfections often make things interesting, they are also an opportunity for Murphy's Law: Anything that can go wrong, will go wrong. However, never fear, AutoRecover and Quick Save are here!

Excel automatically saves your work every 10 minutes, but you can change that interval. Click the File tab, click Options, and then click Save. In the Excel Options dialog box, change the value in the Save AutoRecover information every box. The saved copies of your work are called AutoRecover files. If your computer shuts down unexpectedly, Office will recognize that the file you were working on was not closed properly and will give you the option of opening the most recent AutoRecover file.

The [Ctrl]+[S] shortcut quickly saves your file to the same location as the last save. Whenever you make a significant change to your file, save it immediately using the quick save keyboard shortcut.

QUICK REFERENCE | **Back Up Your Workbook!**

It is a good idea to back up your workbook when you are about to make significant changes to it, when those changes have been made, and/or when you have finished working for the moment.

To make a backup of your workbook, do the following.

1. Click the File tab, click Save As, and then click Browse.

2. In the Save As dialog box, navigate to the location where you are saving your files. In the File name box, type the name of your file, such as YourFile_yyyy-mm-dd, where yyyy-mm-dd is today's date. Click Save.

If possible, best practice is to store backup files on an entirely different drive, such as a USB drive, or to a cloud service such as OneDrive.

Save As not only saves a copy of your file but also changes the file Excel has open. YourFile_yyyy-mm-dd will be the open file, and the title bar at the top of the Excel application window will display the new file name. Click Close and open your original file again before continuing your work.

Navigate Worksheets and Workbooks

Workbooks often contain more than a single worksheet. Sometimes the worksheets are related to each other, such as monthly sales data. Other times, worksheets may be separate from the rest of the data and used only to document the workbook's worksheet(s). To effectively develop and use workbooks and worksheets, you must be able to navigate within worksheets and between worksheets in a workbook.

Navigating Between Worksheets

Workbooks may contain more than one worksheet. The worksheet tabs are located on the bottom left side of the Excel window. Each tab represents a single worksheet in the workbook.

The active worksheet, the worksheet that is visible, is readily identifiable because the background color of its worksheet tab is white and it has a thick bottom border. To make a different worksheet active, click its worksheet tab. When you open a workbook that you have not worked with before, it is a best practice to spend some time familiarizing yourself with its worksheets.

You may have noticed that the golf cart analysis workbook you have opened contains four worksheets. In this exercise, you will navigate between worksheets to familiarize yourself with their contents.

 **E01.01**

To Change the Active Worksheet

a. In the lower-left corner of the worksheet, click the **GolfCartPurchases** worksheet to make it the active worksheet. This worksheet is the start of a purchase analysis for the purchase of additional golf carts for the Red Bluff Golf Course & Pro Shop fleet of golf carts.

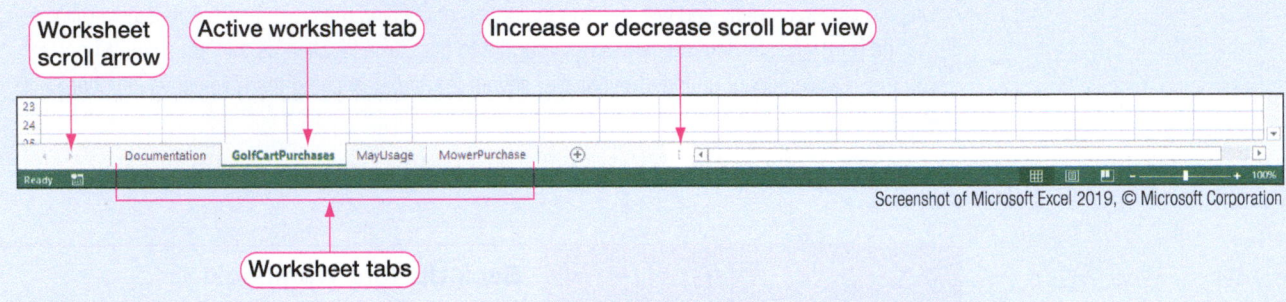

Screenshot of Microsoft Excel 2019, © Microsoft Corporation

Figure 1   Change the active worksheet

SIDE NOTE
Naming Worksheets
It is best practice to not use spaces when naming worksheet tabs. Consider using capitalization if your worksheet names contain more than one word.

b. Click the **MayUsage** worksheet. This worksheet is an analysis of golf cart usage for the month of May that Barry Cheney developed to assess whether the number of carts in the current fleet is optimal.

c. Click the **MowerPurchase** worksheet. This worksheet is an analysis of the five different types of mowers available for purchase.

d. Click the **Documentation** worksheet. You may need to scroll left using the worksheet scroll arrows to see the Documentation worksheet. This worksheet is used to document the contents of the workbook. Documentation is an important component of a well-structured workbook.

e. Save 🖫 the workbook.

MAC COMPATIBILITY
Delete and Backspace
Use fn + Delete for the Delete and Backspace keys to function like a PC.

> **Troubleshooting**
> All the figures in this text were taken at a monitor resolution of 1366 × 768. Higher or lower resolution will affect the way Excel displays ribbon options.

Once Excel is open, it is important to recognize the components of the worksheet window so that you can effectively use a workbook and navigate within a worksheet. As Figure 2 shows, the worksheet window has many components. With Microsoft Office updates, the ribbon may have updates not included in Figure 2.

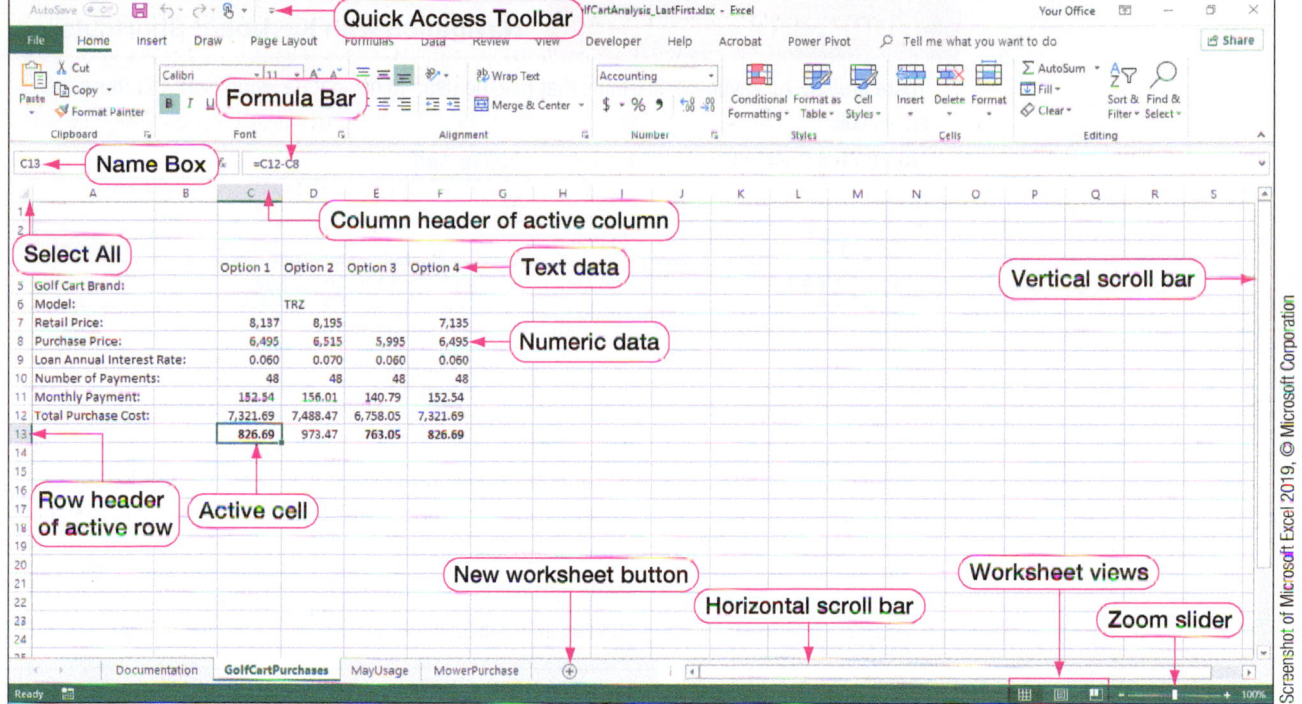

Figure 2 The worksheet window

Navigating within Worksheets

Whether a worksheet is small or extremely large, navigation from one cell to another is necessary to enter or edit numbers, formulas, functions, or text. Navigation requires an understanding of how Excel handles rows, columns, and cells.

Each row is identified by a number in ascending sequence from top to bottom. Each column is identified by a letter in ascending sequence from left to right. Each cell has a default name called a cell reference. A **cell reference** refers to a cell or range of cells within a formula or function instead of a value. The cell reference is a combination of its column letter and row number. For example, the intersection of column A and row 1 has a cell reference of A1, and the intersection of column D and row 20 is cell D20.

Navigating in a small worksheet is simple: Point to the cell and click to make it the active cell. The **active cell** is the recipient of an action, such as a clicking, typing, entering a calculation, or pasting. When a cell becomes the active cell, the border around it changes to a thick, green line. Only the active cell can have data entered into it. Any data you enter via the keyboard is placed into the active cell. Worksheet navigation is simply defined as moving the location of the active cell. The **formula bar** is a toolbar at the top of the Excel spreadsheet window that can be used to enter, edit, or copy text, data, or formulas.

When a part of a worksheet is out of view, it may be because the worksheet is too large to be displayed completely in the visible application window. In this case, use the vertical and horizontal scroll bars to bring other parts of the document into view. The vertical scroll bar is on the right side of the application window, and the horizontal scroll bar is at the bottom right of the application window. It is important to note that scrolling does not move the active cell; it only changes your view in the worksheet.

A **keyboard shortcut** is a keyboard equivalent for a software command that allows you to keep your hands on the keyboard instead of reaching for the mouse to make ribbon selections. Keyboard shortcuts allow rapid navigation in a worksheet without having to use the mouse. It is considered best practice to learn and use keyboard shortcuts whenever possible.

There are several keyboard shortcuts that may be used to navigate a worksheet and move the active cell.

Keyboard Shortcuts	Moves the Active Cell
Enter	Down one row
Shift + Enter	Up one row
→ ← ↓ ↑	One cell in the direction of the arrow key
Home	To column A of the current row
Ctrl + Home	To column A, row 1 (cell A1)
Ctrl + End	To the last cell, highest number row and far right column, that contains information
End + → , End + ←	To the last cell containing data in the arrow direction before an empty cell if the first cell in the direction of the arrow beyond the active cell contains data
End + ↓ , End + ↑	To the next cell in the arrow direction that contains information if the first cell in the direction of the arrow beyond the active cell is empty
PgUp	Up one screen
PgDn	Down one screen
Alt + PgUp	Left one screen
Alt + PgDn	Right one screen
Ctrl + PgUp	One worksheet left
Ctrl + PgDn	One worksheet right
Tab	One column right
Shift + Tab	One column left

For large worksheets, Go To allows rapid navigation. Although the worksheet you are currently working with is not large, knowledge of how to use the Go To dialog box to navigate directly to any cell in the worksheet by specifying a cell reference is a skill that you may find useful.

In this exercise, you will learn to navigate within a worksheet.

 E01.02

MAC COMPATIBILITY
No Home Key
To make cell A1 the active cell, press fn + Ctrl + ←.

SIDE NOTE
Alternate Method
Instead of pressing Ctrl + Enter to finish a cell entry, you can use the Enter button ✔ on the formula bar.

To Navigate within a Worksheet

a. Click the **GolfCartPurchases** worksheet, and then press Ctrl + Home to make A1 the active cell. Press the ↓ six times, and then press → four times. The active cell should be **E7**.

b. Type **6742** and then press Ctrl + Enter to keep cell E7 active.

c. Click cell **D5**. Type **Easy Go** and then press Enter.

Notice that the active cell is now D6. Pressing Enter moved the active cell down one row.

d. On the Home tab, in the Editing group, click **Find & Select**, and then click **Go To**. The Go To dialog box appears. Click in the Reference box, and type **D13**

Mac Troubleshooting

There is no Find & Select option on the Home tab. To Go To on a Mac, click the Edit menu, point to Find, and then click Go To.

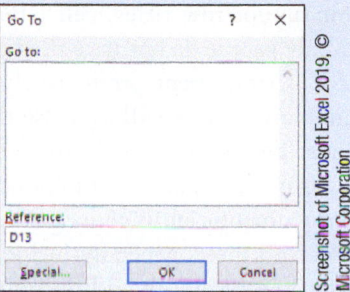

Screenshot of Microsoft Excel 2019, © Microsoft Corporation

MAC COMPATIBILITY

Displaying Groups

To display groups, click the Excel menu, click Preferences, click View, and select the Group Titles check box.

SIDE NOTE

Alternate Method

The name box to the left of the formula bar can also be used as a Go To command. Type the cell reference in the Name Box and press Enter.

SIDE NOTE

Alternate Method

You can also press Ctrl+B to bold a cell.

Figure 3 Go To dialog box

e. Click **OK**. The active cell is now D13. On the Home tab, in the Font group, click B to apply Bold to the cell.

f. Press Home. This takes you to column A of the row with the active cell. The active cell should be A13. Type **Total Interest Cost:** and then press Tab. Cell B13 is now the active cell.

g. Press Ctrl+Home to return the active cell to A1.

> **Troubleshooting**
>
> The active cell is repositioned by using the mouse or keyboard. Even experienced users often scroll through a worksheet and press an arrow key only to find themselves returned to the active cell where they began scrolling.

h. Save 💾 the workbook.

Touch Devices

If you have a device such as a tablet PC with a touch screen, you can control Excel 2019 using your finger. The commands on the ribbon and in shortcut menus are the same, but Excel recognizes when you have touched the screen and enables touch mode. In **touch mode**, the ribbon and shortcut menus are enlarged to make selecting commands with your fingertip easier. Figure 4 shows the Excel interface in touch mode. With Microsoft Office updates, the ribbon may have updates not included in Figure 4.

Touch mode   Ribbon in Touch mode

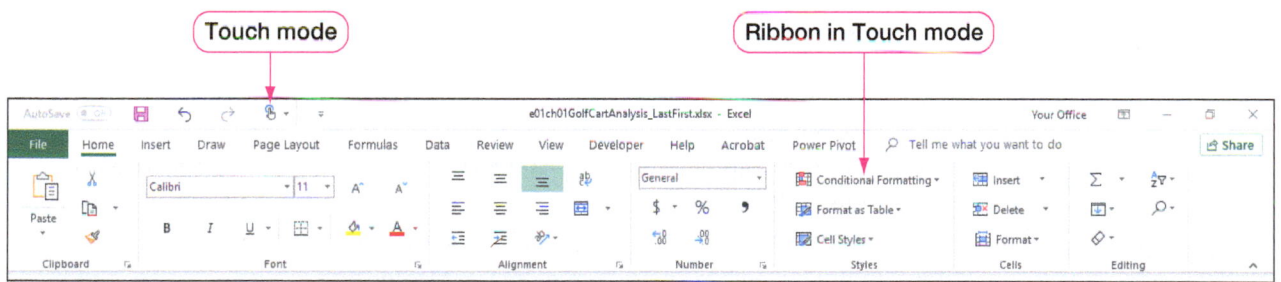

Screenshot of Microsoft Excel 2019, © Microsoft Corporation

Figure 4 Touch mode in Excel 2019

Document Your Work

Workbooks may be used by people who did not develop them. Even if a workbook will never be used by anyone other than its builder, best practice dictates that you document a workbook and its worksheets.

Documentation is vital to ensure that a workbook remains usable. A well-documented workbook is much easier to use and maintain, particularly for a user who did not develop the workbook. You may use a workbook on a regular basis, you may even have developed it, but over time you may forget how the workbook operates.

Documentation takes several forms, such as descriptive file and worksheet names, worksheet titles, column and/or row titles, cell labels, cell notes, or a dedicated documentation worksheet. Many people do not take the time to document adequately because they do not think that it is time spent productively. Some do not think it is necessary because they do not think anyone else will ever use the workbook. However, for a workbook to be useful, it must be accurate, easily understood, flexible, efficient, and documented. While accuracy is most important, an undocumented workbook can later create inaccurate data. Where documentation is concerned, more is more.

While documentation worksheets generally include documentation for an entire workbook, notes can be created specifically to add documentation to a worksheet and address individual fields, calculations, and so on and are included as content in an individual cell.

Using Notes to Document a Workbook

A cell **note** is a text box, like a sticky note, that is attached to a cell in a worksheet in which you can enter information or give instructions. In this exercise, you will insert notes into a worksheet to document a workbook.

 **E01.03**

SIDE NOTE
Office Updates
Depending on your exact version of Office, you may also see the Comments group on the Review tab. Comments are used for threaded discussions in a workbook.

To Document a Workbook Using Notes

a. Click the **MayUsage** worksheet, and notice the notes indicators in the upper-right corners of several cells in row 7. The triangle indicates the existence of a note. Point to cell B7. The note that appears defines the number of carts available.

To familiarize yourself with the worksheet, review the other notes in row 7.

Figure 5   Insert a cell note

SIDE NOTE
Delete or Edit a Note
To delete or Edit a note, right-click or select the cell which contains the note.

Screenshot of Microsoft Excel 2019, © Microsoft Corporation

b. Click the **GolfCartPurchases** worksheet. Click cell **A9**, and then click the **Review** tab.

c. In the Notes group, click the **Notes** button, and then click **New Note**.

d. In the Notes box, select the text user name and the colon that is automatically inserted into the note. Press [Delete] to delete the text.

e. In the Notes box, type Annual Interest Rate: press [SpaceBar] once, and then type Annual rate of interest in decimal or percentage format.

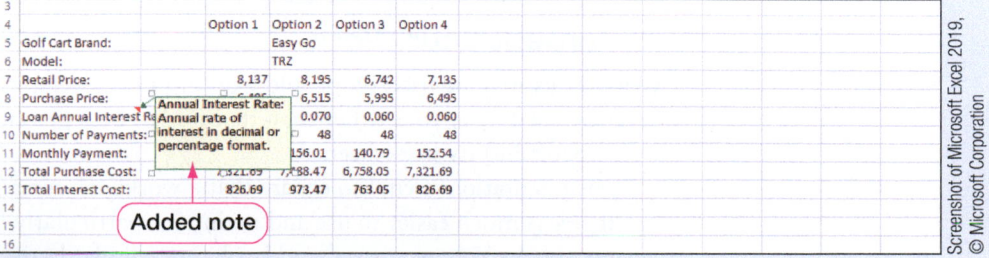

Figure 6   Documenting a worksheet using a note

f. Click cell **A1** to exit the note. Cell A9 now has a triangle in the top-right corner to indicate the presence of a cell note.

g. **Save** the workbook.

Using a Worksheet for Documentation

A well-structured worksheet will have descriptive titles, column headings, and cell labels. However, a separate documentation worksheet includes information that is not generally specified in a worksheet, such as authorship, modification dates, modification history, or specific information that should be noted. Documentation worksheets go beyond the file properties that are automatically stored by Excel when a workbook is saved. For example, a documentation worksheet could include the indication of cell note or an explanation of calculations being performed, which could assist the user of the workbook.

In this exercise, you will update the documentation worksheet to include your name as well as the addition of the cell note you added previously.

 **E01.04**

To Document a Workbook Using a Documentation Worksheet

a. Click the **Documentation** worksheet. You may have to scroll left in the worksheet tabs. Click cell **A8**, and then type 6/01/2022 and then press Tab.

b. In cell **B8**, type your name in Firstname Lastname format. Press Tab. In cell **C8**, type Added a note to a key heading on the GolfCartPurchases worksheet and then press Enter.

c. **Save** the workbook.

REAL WORLD ADVICE	Failing to Plan Is Planning to Fail

Winston Churchill said, "He who fails to plan, plans to fail." The first step in building a worksheet should be planning. There are several questions that you should consider before you begin entering information.

- What is the objective of the worksheet? Is it to solve a problem? Is it to analyze data and recommend a course of action? Is it to summarize data and present usable information? Is it to store information for use by another application?

- Do you have all the data necessary to build this worksheet?

- What information does your worksheet need to generate?

- How should the information in your worksheet be presented? Who is the audience? What form will best present the worksheet information?

Plan your work before you begin. The time spent planning will save you time when creating the worksheet(s), and the result will be of higher quality.

Enter and Edit Data

In building and maintaining worksheets, the ability to enter, edit, and format data is fundamental. As data is entered via the keyboard, the data appears simultaneously in the active cell and in the formula bar. Figure 7 shows the result when a cell is double-clicked to place the insertion point into cell contents. Pressing the F2 key also will place the insertion point into the cell contents. If you click in the formula bar, the insertion point is displayed in the formula bar.

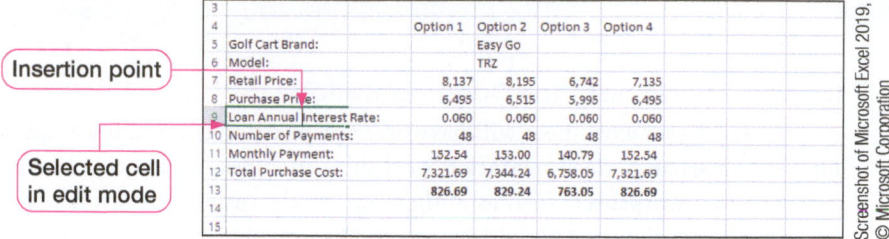

Figure 7   Editing data in a cell

Using Text, Number, Date, and Time Data in Cells

Cell entries can consist of text data or numerical data. **Text data** consists of any combination of printable characters, including letters, numbers, and special characters available on any standard keyboard. By default, text data is left-aligned in a cell.

Numeric data consists of numbers (0–9) in any form not combined with letters and special characters such as the period (decimal) and/or hyphen (to indicate negative values). Technically, special characters such as the dollar sign ($) or comma (,) are not considered numeric. They are displayed only for contextual and readability purposes and are not stored as part of a numeric cell value. By default, numeric data is right-aligned in a cell.

In Excel, date data and time data are special forms of numeric data. **Date data** is data recognized by Excel as a date. Data formatted as a date takes the form of a serial number, with the number 1 representing January 1, 1900. **Time data** is data recognized by Excel as representing time. Time data is represented as a decimal value where .1 is 144 minutes, .01 is 14.4 minutes, and so on. Information entered in a recognized date and/or time format will be converted automatically to an Excel date and/or time value. If Excel recognizes a value as a date/time, it will right-align the entry. If you enter a date or time that is not recognized, Excel treats the information as text and left-aligns it in the cell.

Table 1 includes examples of valid dates and times that can be entered into Excel and how they will be displayed by default.

Enter	Excel Displays	Enter	Excel Displays
December 21, 2022	21-Dec-22	1:00 p	1:00 PM
21 Dec 2022	21-Dec-22	1 a	1:00 AM
Dec 21, 2022	21-Dec-22	13:00	13:00

Table 1   Date and time entries and how Excel displays dates

The GolfCartPurchases worksheet not only contains text, numbers, and date information, it also contains formulas and functions. Although you will not learn about formulas and functions until the next chapter, it is important to note that they appear throughout the Golf Cart Analysis workbook. A formula performs a mathematical calculation (or calculations) using data in the worksheet to calculate new values, as in cell D12 of the GolfCartPurchases worksheet. A function is a built-in program that performs operations against data and returns a value, as in cell D11 of the GolfCart-Purchases worksheet.

After reviewing the GolfCartPurchases worksheet, you think that the worksheet is missing an appropriate title which will help define its contents. In this exercise, you will add worksheet titles and edit existing information.

SIDE NOTE
Use Undo History
If you need to undo a change after other changes have been made, click the Undo arrow on the Quick Access Toolbar.

SIDE NOTE
Keyboard Shortcut for Undo
Ctrl + Z is a fast and efficient method of performing an Undo ⤾.

To Enter Information into a Worksheet

a. Click the **GolfCartPurchases** worksheet, click cell **A2**, type Red Bluff Golf Course & Pro Shop and then press Enter.

Notice the active cell is cell A3 and Excel displays the text as left-aligned.

b. In cell **A3**, type Golf Cart Purchase Analysis and then press Enter.

c. In cell **A4**, type 06/01/2022 and then press Enter. Notice that Excel displays the date as 6/1/2022 and right-aligned.

d. Click cell **G4**, type Option 5 and then press Enter. Notice that the text in cell G4 is left-aligned.

e. Note the value in cell D12 of 7,488.47. Click cell **D9**, type .06 and then press Enter.

Notice that the monthly payment in cell D11 changes to 7,344.24. The values in cells D11, D12, and D13 are automatically recalculated because those cells contain formulas. You will learn how to create formulas in Chapter 2.

> **Troubleshooting**
>
> If the monthly payment is larger than it should be, you may have entered .6. That is actually 60% for calculation purposes. You must enter the percentage 6% or enter .06, the decimal equivalent of 6%.

f. **Save** 🖫 the workbook.

Wrapping Text and Line Breaks

By default, Excel places all information in a single line in a cell. Text that is too long to fit in a cell is displayed over adjoining cells to the right unless those cells also contain information. If adjoining cells contain information, lengthy text from cells to the left is not fully displayed.

Text truncation can be avoided by changing the alignment of a cell to wrap words or by placing a hard return—two or more lines of text in one cell—into text to force wrapping at a particular location.

In this exercise, you will wrap text in a cell.

SIDE NOTE
View Contents of the Formula Bar
To view more lines of text in the formula bar, you could expand the formula bar by clicking the down arrow on the right-hand side of the formula bar.

To Wrap Text in a Cell

a. Click cell **A3**, and then click in the formula bar immediately to the right of the word Cart. Press Delete to remove the space between Cart and Purchase, and then press Alt + Enter to insert a line break, often referred to as a hard return.

> **Troubleshooting**
>
> If the "t" on the word Cart was deleted, you may have pressed the Backspace key instead of the Delete key. Press the Undo ⤾ key on the Quick Access Toolbar and repeat step a.

b. Press Ctrl + Enter to complete the entry. Notice how only the words before the hard return are visible on the formula bar.

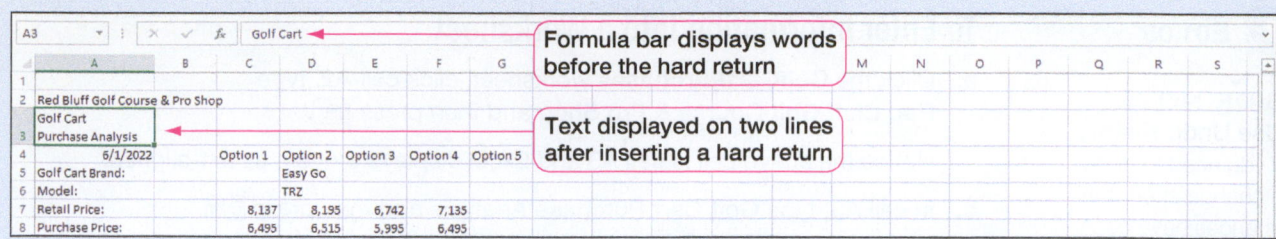

Figure 8   Insert a hard return to control text wrap location

Screenshot of Microsoft Excel 2019, © Microsoft Corporation

    c. Click the **Documentation** worksheet, and then click cell **C8**. Notice how the contents of cell C8 appear to be displayed over cell D8. Click cell **D8**, and then view the formula bar. It should be blank.

    d. Click cell **C8** again. Click the **Home** tab, and in the Alignment group, click **Wrap Text**. The vertical size of row 8 is increased to display all content within the boundaries of cell C8.

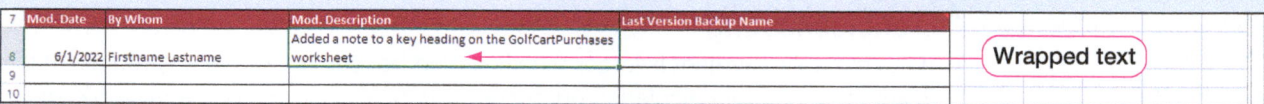

Figure 9   Wrap text in a cell

Screenshot of Microsoft Excel 2019, © Microsoft Corporation

    e. Save the workbook.

Work with Cells and Cell Ranges

Part of what makes a worksheet an efficient tool is the ability to perform actions that affect many cells at once. Knowing how to work with cells and cell ranges is an important part of maximizing your efficiency. **Cell range** refers to the cells in the worksheet that have been selected. A cell range can reference a single cell, several contiguous cells, or noncontiguous cells. A **contiguous cell range** consists of multiple selected cells, all directly adjacent to one another. For example, A1:A10. When you read a range such as A1:A10, the colon stands for "through." A **noncontiguous cell range** consists of multiple selected cells with at least one cell not directly adjacent to other cells.

Cutting, Copying, and Pasting

Copy and paste operations copy everything in a cell, including formatting. Cut and paste operations move everything in a cell, including formatting. However, by using Paste Options and Paste Special, you can control exactly what is placed into the destination cells. A **destination cell** is the location cell to be modified by a move or paste operation. When you copy or cut data in Excel, the data is placed in the Clipboard. The **Clipboard** is a temporary storage location where information that was cut or copied is stored until you paste or clear the information.

In this exercise, you will make changes to the GolfCartPurchases worksheet by using the cut, copy, and paste commands in Excel.

 **E01.07**

To Cut, Copy, and Paste Cells

a. Click the **GolfCartPurchases** worksheet, and then click cell **D5**. On the Home tab, in the Clipboard group, notice that the Paste ▢ option is light gray in color, meaning it is unavailable.

> ### Troubleshooting
>
> If the Paste option is not grayed out on your screen, you could have another application open in which you have been copying information and therefore information remains on the Clipboard. To clear the Clipboard, click the Clipboard launcher, click Clear All in the Clipboard pane, and then close the Clipboard pane.

SIDE NOTE
Keyboard Shortcuts
The keyboard shortcut for Cut is Ctrl+X; the shortcut for Paste is Ctrl+V; the shortcut for Copy is Ctrl+C.

b. In the Clipboard group, click **Cut** ✂. The solid border around cell D5 changes to a moving dashed border.

c. Click cell **C5**.

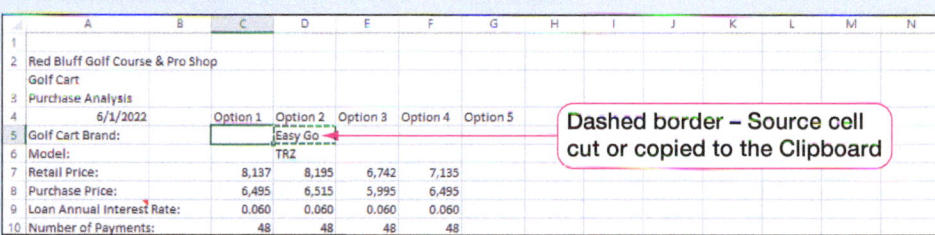

Figure 10 Cut, copy, and paste

d. In the Clipboard group, click **Paste** ▢.

e. Click cell **D6**, and then, in the Clipboard group, click **Copy** ▤. The solid border around cell D6 changes to a moving dashed border. Click cell **C6**, and then, in the Clipboard group, click **Paste** ▢.

f. Press Esc to remove the dashed border from around cell D6. This also clears the Clipboard.

Notice that once the Clipboard has been cleared by pressing Esc, Paste ▢ becomes unavailable again.

g. **Save** ▢ the workbook.

Selecting Cell Ranges

By using the mouse, multiple cells can be selected simultaneously. Selected cells can be contiguous to each other, or they can be noncontiguous. Once multiple cells have been selected, they can be affected by actions such as clear, delete, copy, paste, formatting, and many others while offering the convenience of performing the desired task only once for the selected cells.

In this exercise, you will select, copy, and paste to contiguous and noncontiguous selections.

E01.08

SIDE NOTE
Select a Cell Range
[Shift] can be used in combination with other navigation keys and/or the mouse to select a contiguous range of cells.

SIDE NOTE
Select Noncontiguous Cell Range
[Ctrl] can be used in combination with other navigation keys and/or the mouse to select noncontiguous cell ranges.

To Select, Copy, and Paste to Contiguous and Noncontiguous Selections

a. On the GolfCartPurchases worksheet, click cell **C5**. Press [Shift]+[↓]. The active cell border expands to include cells **C5:C6**.

b. Press [Ctrl]+[C] to copy the selected cells to the Clipboard. Click cell **E5**, and then press [Ctrl]+[V] to paste the Clipboard contents to the selected cell.

c. Click cell **D5**, press and hold [Ctrl], click cell **F5**, and then click cell **G5**.

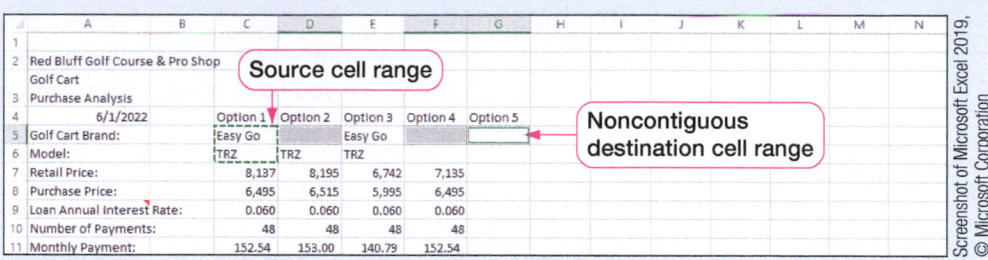

Figure 11   Selecting a noncontiguous cell range

d. Press [Ctrl]+[V], and then press [Esc] to clear the Clipboard.

Troubleshooting

If nothing was pasted when you pressed [Ctrl]+[V], it could be that you canceled the copy command by clicking another cell or command. Retry by selecting C5:C6, pressing [Ctrl]+[C], and then repeating step c.

---

e. **Save** 🖫 the workbook.

QUICK REFERENCE   **Selecting Cell Ranges**

There are several ways to select a contiguous range of cells.

- Expand the active cell by dragging the mouse.
- Select the first cell in the range, press [Shift], and click the last cell in the desired range.

A contiguous range of rows or columns can be selected in the following ways.

- Click a row or column header. Drag the mouse pointer across the headers to select contiguous rows or columns.
- Click a row or column header, press [Shift], and then click the header of the last row or column you wish to select.

Once a cell or contiguous range of cells has been selected, you can add noncontiguous cells and ranges by pressing [Ctrl] and using any of the above methods for selecting ranges that do not involve [Shift].

Dragging and Dropping

As worksheets are designed, built, and modified, it is often necessary to move information from one cell or range of cells to another. One of the most efficient ways to do this is called "drag and drop." Dragging and dropping cells or cell ranges has a similar result to cutting and pasting cells or cell ranges. In this exercise, you will drag and drop cells to reorganize a worksheet.

CHAPTER 1

Screenshot of Microsoft Excel 2019, © Microsoft Corporation

To Drag and Drop Cells

SIDE NOTE
Drag and Drop
A ghost range, also referred to as a destination range, and a destination range Screen-Tip are displayed as a pointer is moved to show exactly where the moved cells will be placed.

a. On the GolfCartPurchases worksheet, click cell **A2**, and when the pointer changes to [⊕], drag to select cell range **A2:A4**.

b. Point to the border of the selected range. The mouse pointer changes to a move pointer [⇖].

c. Click and hold the left mouse button, and then drag the selected cells up one row to cell range **A1:A3**.

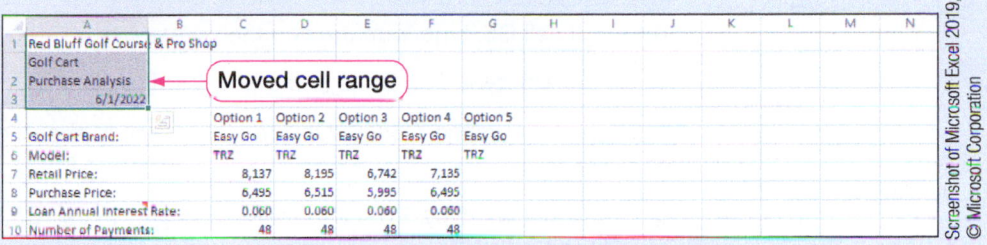

Figure 12   Moved cell range

d. Drop the dragged cells by releasing the mouse button.

e. Select cell range **F7:F13**. Move the mouse pointer until it is over the border of the selected range in column F. The mouse pointer changes to a move pointer [⇖]. Press and hold Ctrl. The move pointer [⇖] changes to a copy pointer [⇖]. Drag the selected range until the ghost range is directly to the right of column F, over cell range **G7:G13**. Release the mouse button, and then release Ctrl.

   Cell range F7:F13 has been copied to cell range G7:G13.

f. **Save** [💾] the workbook.

QUICK REFERENCE	Moving Cells

Moving cells may cause formulas to quit working properly. After moving a cell or range of cells, always double-click any formulas to ensure that they still reference the appropriate cells.

Modifying Cell Information

Copying and pasting content from one range of cells to another range or ranges is a highly efficient way to reuse parts of a worksheet. The range you just copied into column G contains information that is calculated by using formulas in the cell range G11:G13. However, once you have duplicated a cell or cell range, it is usually necessary to change some content.

If only part of the content is to change, a cell can be placed into edit mode. In edit mode, the active cell will contain an insertion point. Double-click the cell to enter edit mode and use arrow keys or click to position the insertion point at the desired location. Cells can also be edited by using the formula bar.

If all the cell content is to be replaced, click the cell once to make it the active cell, and then begin entering the new content. All cell content will be replaced when you begin typing to enter the new content for the selected cell.

In this exercise, you want to correct the GolfCartPurchases worksheet to reflect the correct golf cart brands and prices.

 **E01.10**

To Modify Worksheet Contents

a. On the GolfCartPurchases worksheet, click cell **D6**, type **Freedom RXV** and then press →.

Notice that the entire contents of the cell are replaced with the new text.

SIDE NOTE
Alternate Method
Press the F2 key to place a cell in edit mode.

b. Double-click cell **E6**, press Home to go to the left margin of the cell, type **Freedom** and then press SpaceBar once so the formula bar displays Freedom TRZ. Press Tab.

c. In cell **F6**, type **Freedom RXV** and then press Tab.

d. Click cell **G5**, type **Yamaha** and then press Enter.

e. In cell **G6**, type **The Drive** and then press Enter.

f. Select cell range **C6:G6**. On the Home tab, in the Alignment group, click **Wrap Text**,

g. Click cell **G7**, type **9164** and then press Enter. In cell **G8**, type **7748** and then press Ctrl+Enter.

If you recall, the Monthly Payment, Total Purchase Cost, and Total Interest Cost were recalculated because these cells contain formulas.

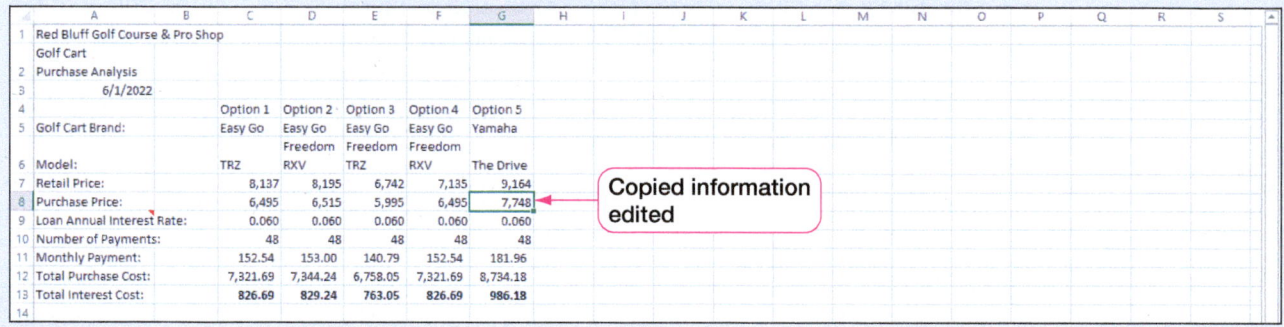

Figure 13 Modified worksheet

Screenshot of Microsoft Excel 2019, © Microsoft Corporation

h. **Save** the workbook.

Inserting and Deleting Cells, Clearing Cells, and Cell Ranges

It is sometimes necessary to insert or delete cells to make a worksheet easier to read or to improve its appearance. Inserting or deleting cells is not the same as inserting or deleting entire rows or column. If you insert a cell in a worksheet where data already exists, Excel will adjust the current data by shifting cells down or to the right. If you delete a cell in a worksheet where data already exists, Excel will shift cells up or to the left.

Worksheet data can either be cleared or deleted; there is a difference. Clearing contents from a cell does not change the location of other cells in the worksheet. Deleting a cell shifts surrounding cells in a direction determined from a prompt. When you are editing a string of characters in a cell, pressing Delete works exactly as you would expect. When you are not in edit mode, pressing Delete clears content but does not delete the cell or cells.

You want to change the appearance of the golf cart purchase analysis worksheet. In this exercise, you will insert and delete cells.

To Insert, Delete, or Clear Cells and Cell Ranges in a Worksheet

a. On the GolfCartPurchases worksheet, click cell **B5**. On the Home tab, in the Cells group, click **Delete** .

Notice that the brand headings in row 5 moved to the left one cell.

> ### Troubleshooting
> If nothing happened, you may have pressed the Delete button on the keyboard. Click the Delete button in the Cells group. If you click the Delete arrow, you can then click Delete Cells in the list.

b. Click cell **B4**. On the Home tab, in the Cells group, click the **Delete** arrow, and then click **Delete Cells**. The Delete dialog box opens.

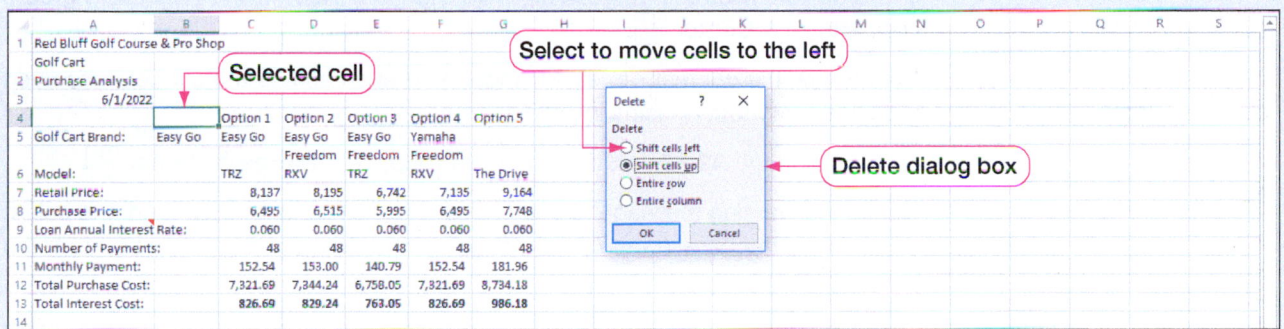

Screenshot of Microsoft Excel 2019, © Microsoft Corporation

Figure 14   Delete dialog box for deleting cells

c. In the Delete dialog box, click **Shift cells left**, and then click **OK**.

d. Select cell range **B6:B13**. Right-click the selection, and then select **Delete** from the shortcut menu. Verify **Shift cells left** is selected, and then click **OK**. The remaining cell values in rows 6:13 moved left one cell.

e. Click cell **B5**, and then, in the Cells group, click **Insert** .

Notice how the contents of column B shifted down a row and no longer align appropriately with the labels in column A. You will undo this change.

f. Click **Undo** on the Quick Access Toolbar in the upper left corner of the Excel window to undo the last action.

g. In cell **B5**, press Delete . Notice how the content of cell B5 is cleared but the cell is not deleted. Click **Undo** .

h. **Save** the workbook.

Merging & Centering versus Centering Across Selection

The titles in the golf cart analysis worksheet are in cells A1:A3. Although they contain the correct information to communicate the purpose of the golf cart analysis worksheet, that information might be better presented with some formatting improvements.

Titles that identify the general purpose of a worksheet are often at the top and centered above worksheet content. Clicking the Center button in the Alignment group on the Home tab will center contents only within the active cell. However, the **Merge & Center** feature combines selected cells into a single cell and then centers the text within that single cell. Merge & Center can be applied to horizontal or vertical cell ranges. Content in the left and/or top cell of the selected range is centered; all other data in the selected range is deleted.

If more than one row of cells need to be centered, another option is to use the Center Across Selection command. Center Across Selection removes the borders between cells such that a selected range looks like a single cell, but the original cells remain, the borders between them are hidden, and the content is centered across the cells. Center Across Selection can only be applied horizontally. Additionally, Center Across Selection will never replace the data in the other cells.

In this exercise, you will center the headings in rows 1:3 to improve the appearance of the golf cart purchase analysis worksheet.

 **E01.12**

To Merge & Center and Center Headings Across Selection

a. On the GolfCartPurchases worksheet, press Ctrl+Home to return to cell **A1**. Click and drag to select cell range **A1:F1**. On the Home tab, in the Alignment group, click **Merge & Center**.

   Notice how the content of cell A1 appears to span across the six columns even though the content remains in cell A1.

b. Select cell range **A2:F3**. In the Alignment group, click **Merge & Center** .

   Notice the warning message. If you Merge & Center data in more than one cell at a time, only the data in the upper left cell of the selected range will be kept; the rest will be lost.

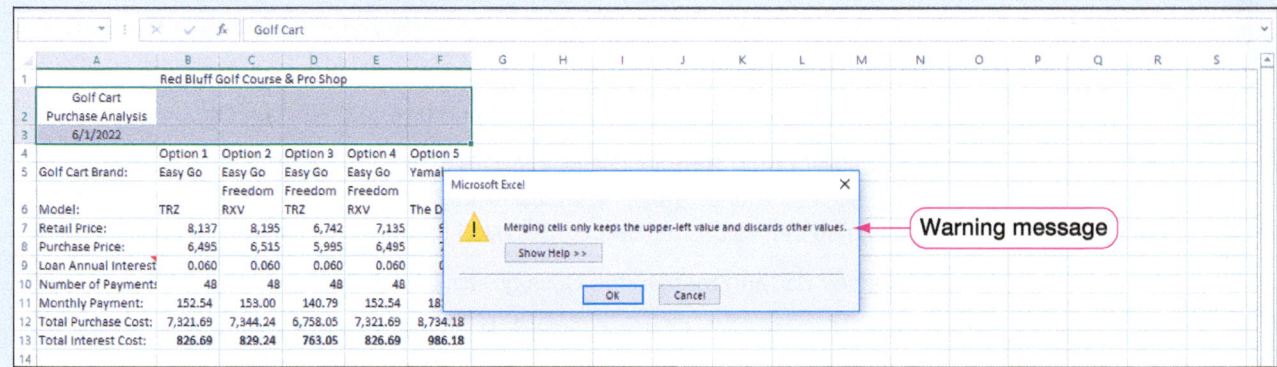

Figure 15 Merge and center a range containing multiple values

Screenshot of Microsoft Excel 2019, © Microsoft Corporation

c. Click **Cancel**. You do not want to lose the data in cell A3.

> **Troubleshooting**
> If you clicked OK instead of Cancel, press Ctrl+Z to undo the last change.

d. With cell range A2:F3 still selected, on the Home tab, in the Alignment group, click the **Alignment Dialog Box Launcher**. This opens the Format Cells dialog box.

e. With the Alignment tab selected, click the **Horizontal** arrow, and then click **Center Across Selection**.

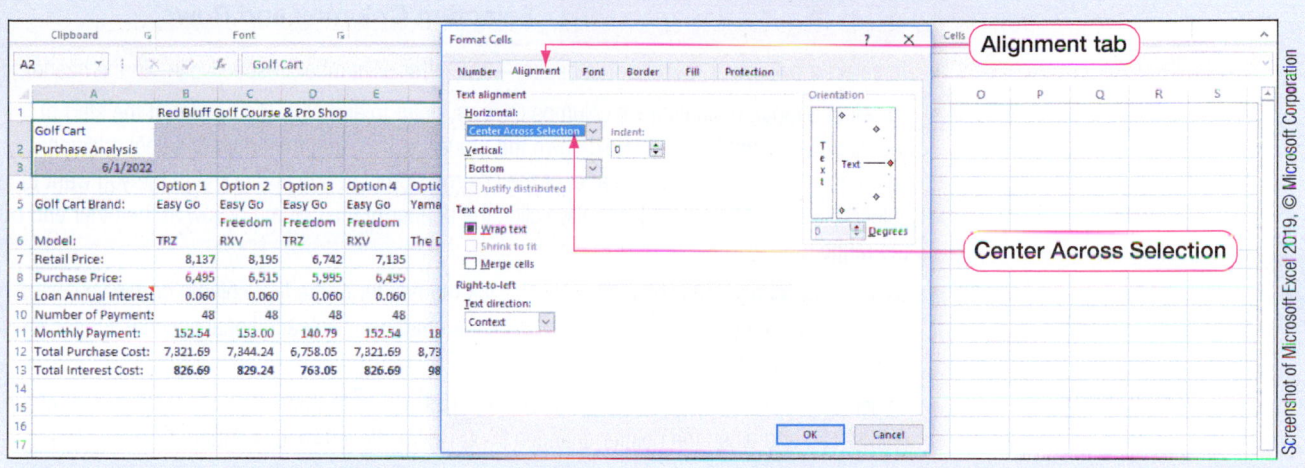

Figure 16 Center Across Selection

f. Click **OK**. Cell A2 content is centered across cell range A2:F2, and cell A3 content is centered across cell range A3:F3.

g. **Save** the workbook.

CONSIDER THIS | **Merge & Center and Cell Range Selection**

Try this: Try to select cell range A1:D13. Try to select cell range A1:B9. Now select cell range A2:F13.

Merge & Center creates a single cell that can cause problems if you want to select a range of cells that includes only part of the merged cell range. Center Across Selection does not cause this problem.

Some Excel users think that Merge & Center should never be used. Do you agree?

Adjust Columns and Rows

Any worksheet created has default column widths and row heights. As you build, refine, and modify a worksheet, it is often necessary to add and/or delete columns and rows or to change column widths and/or row heights for formatting and content purposes. Fortunately, Excel makes these activities easy to accomplish.

Selecting Contiguous and Noncontiguous Columns and Rows

To manipulate columns and rows, you must first indicate which of each you wish to affect by your actions. As with cells and cell ranges, you can select entire columns, entire rows, multiple columns, and multiple rows. You can select noncontiguous columns and rows, and you can even select multiple columns and multiple rows at the same time.

QUICK REFERENCE | **Selecting Columns and Rows**

- To select a column or row click the header—the letter or number, respectively—in the header.

- To select a range of contiguous columns or rows, point to and click the header at the start of the range you want to select. Hold down the mouse button, and then drag to select additional columns or rows, or click the header of the column or row at one end of the range you want to select, press and hold [Shift], and then click the header of the column or row at the other end of the range.

- To select noncontiguous columns or rows, click the header of the first column or row you want to select. Press and hold [Ctrl], and then click the headers of any additional columns and/or rows you want to select.

- To select all cells in a worksheet, point to the Select All ◤ button in the upper-left corner of the worksheet, and when the pointer changes to ⊕, click the left mouse button. Click any cell to cancel the selection.

Inserting and Deleting Columns or Rows

It is sometimes necessary to insert or remove rows or columns in a worksheet. The user may need to add or delete data, or perhaps it is necessary to refine the white space in a worksheet to improve its readability. **White space** refers to blank areas of a worksheet that do not contain data or documentation—regardless of the actual color. The blank space gives a document visual structure and creates a sense of order in the mind of the worksheet user.

A selected range is defined as a contiguous set of cells, columns, or rows that are all part of a single contiguous selection. However, how you select cells, columns, and rows determines whether they are a single contiguous range or are considered separate individual selections.

If you click column C, press and hold [Shift], and then click column E, you have created a contiguous selection of columns C:E. All three columns are highlighted as a group. But if you click column C, press and hold [Ctrl], click column D, and then click column E, you have just selected three individual columns—three individual selections. In this situation, Excel treats columns C, D, and E as noncontiguous columns—there is a white border highlighted between the columns. Whether columns or rows are contiguous or noncontiguous influences how actions such as Insert are applied to a worksheet.

You want to make the golf cart analysis worksheet easier to read and to use by refining the white space. There is also a need to add some white space to the GolfCartPurchases worksheet because the columns and rows of information for the different golf carts are too close together. One way to add white space is to insert blank columns or blank rows to not only separate the data but also add visual interest to the worksheet. In this exercise, you will insert and delete sheet columns and rows to adjust the white space in a worksheet.

 **E01.13**

To Insert or Delete Columns and Rows

a. On the GolfCartPurchases worksheet, click cell **A4**. On the Home tab, in the Cells group, click the **Insert** arrow, and then click **Insert Sheet Rows**.

Excel inserts a row above the active cell location and moves all cells in row 4 and below down one row; row 4 is now a blank row.

b. Right-click the **row header** for row **8**.

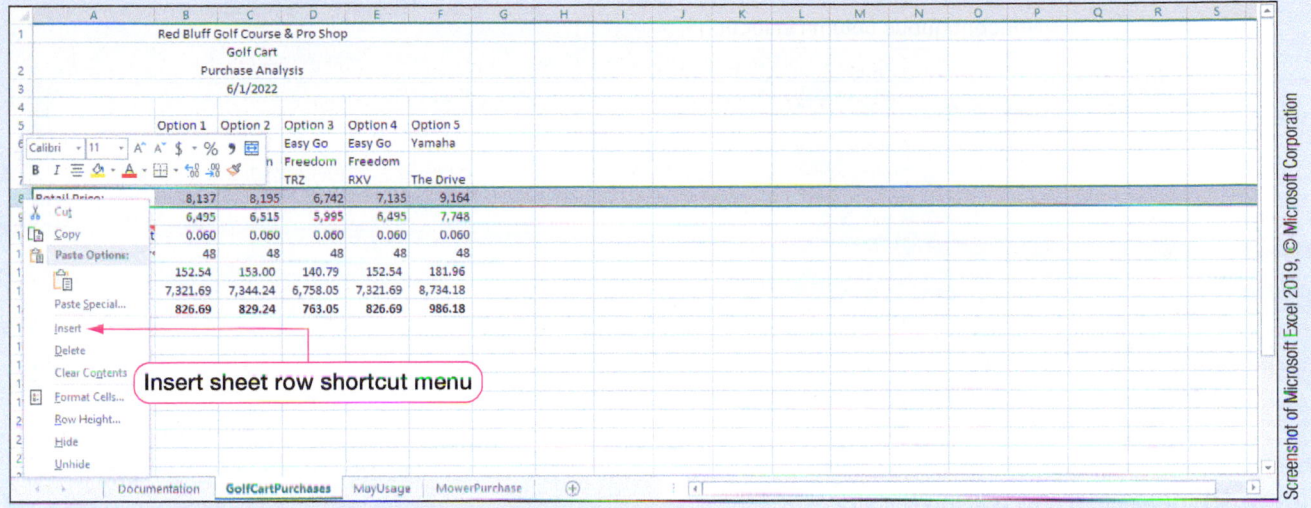

Insert sheet row shortcut menu

Figure 17   Inserting a sheet row by row header

c.   Select **Insert** on the shortcut menu. Excel inserts a row above row 8 and moves all cells in row 8 and below down one row; row 8 is now a blank row.

d.   Select cell range **A11:A12**. In the Cells group, click the **Insert** arrow, and then click **Insert Sheet Rows**. Excel inserts a row for each row in the selected range; in this case two blank rows are inserted.

> **Troubleshooting**
>
> If you clicked the Insert ▦ button in the Cells group instead of the Insert arrow, Excel will default to inserting extra cells only, instead of a row. Press Ctrl+Z to undo the last change, and then repeat step d.

SIDE NOTE
Alternate Method
To delete a sheet row, you can also right-click a row header, and select Delete from the shortcut menu.

e.   Select the row headers for rows **15:16**, and in the Cells group, click **Insert** ▦.

Inserting two rows above and below rows 13 and 14 appears to be too much. Often, you cannot tell until you try, but the worksheet might look better if a couple of the rows of white space were removed.

f.   Click the header for row **11**, press Ctrl, and then click the header for row **15**. In the Cells group, select **Delete** ▦.

SIDE NOTE
Alternate Method
To add or delete a column, right-click the column header, and select Insert or Delete from the shortcut menu.

g.   Click the header for column **C** to select column C, and then, in the Cells group, select **Insert** ▦. A new column is added to the left of the selected column.

h.   Click the header for column **E**, press and hold Ctrl, and then select column **F** and column **G** by clicking on each column header individually.

Notice the white line between the columns. This is not a selected range of columns; it is three individually selected columns.

Screenshot of Microsoft Excel 2019, © Microsoft Corporation

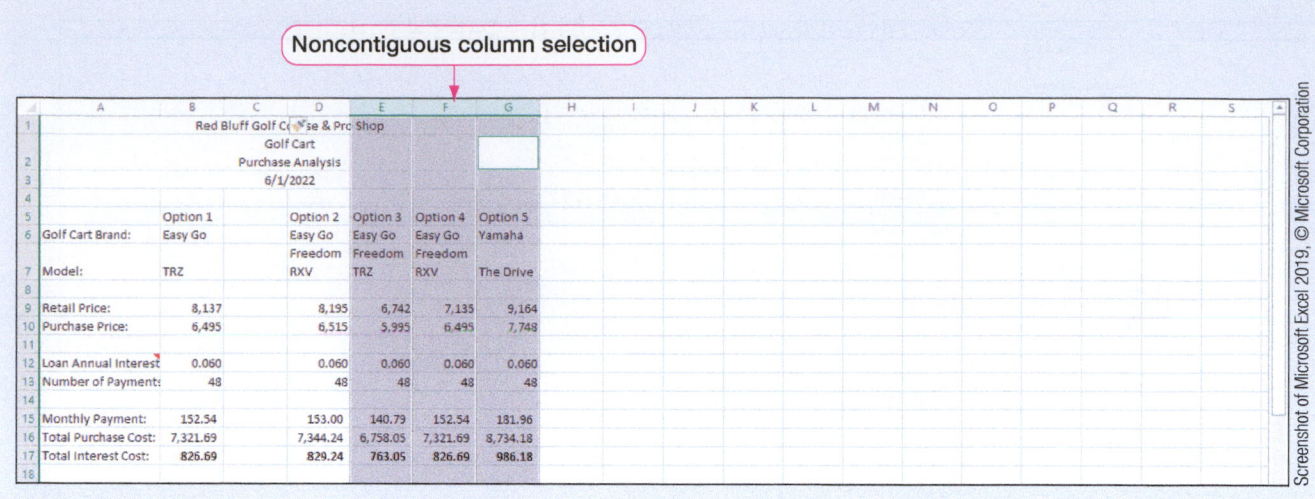

Figure 18 Selecting noncontiguous columns

Screenshot of Microsoft Excel 2019, © Microsoft Corporation

SIDE NOTE

Selecting Several Rows or Columns Using Shift

Click the header of the first row or column, press Shift, and then click the last row or column.

i. In the Cells group, click **Insert** 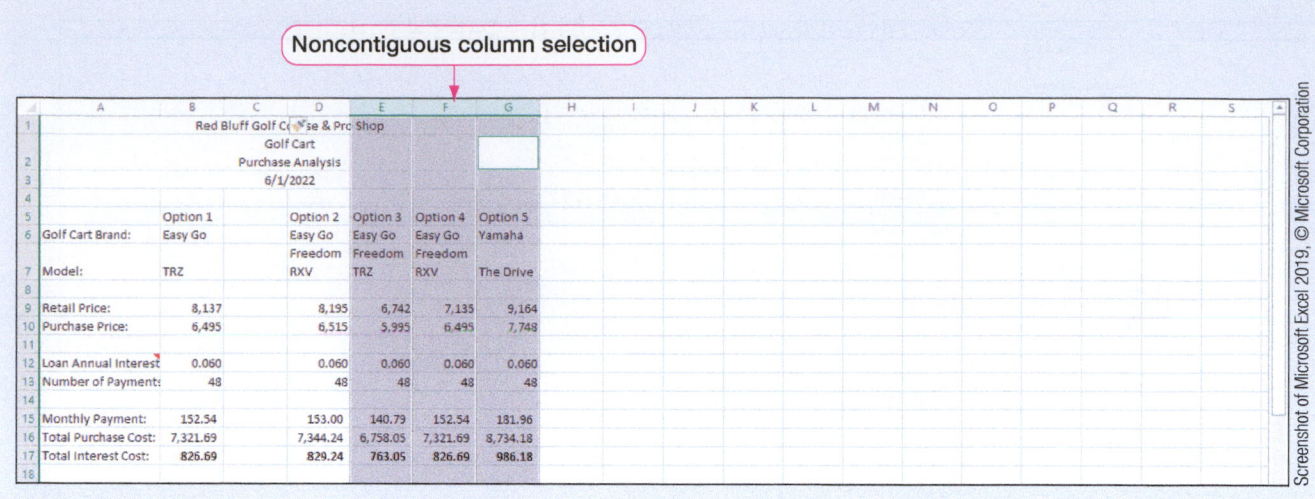.

A column has been inserted to the left of each selected column because columns E, F, and G were selected as noncontiguous individual columns.

> **Troubleshooting**
>
> If you now have three blank columns to the left of column H, you selected columns E:G as a contiguous selection. Press Ctrl+Z to Undo, and repeat steps h and i.

Notice also that the merged and centered cells in rows 1:3 expanded to include the inserted columns. This ensures that the content in rows 1:3 remains centered over the columns that were in the original merged range.

j. **Save** the workbook.

Adjusting Column Width and Row Height

You have inserted columns and rows to add additional white space, but there is still a need to refine the amount of white space in the worksheet. At this point, there is too much white space; the information is spread too far apart.

Column width and row height often need to be adjusted for a couple of reasons. One reason is to reduce the amount of white space a blank column or row represents in a worksheet; the other is to allow the content of cells in a row or column to be displayed properly. Column width is defined in characters. The default width is 8.43 characters. The maximum width of a column is 255 characters. Row height is defined in points. A point is approximately 1/72 of an inch (0.035 cm). The default row height in Excel is 15 points, or approximately 1/6 of an inch (0.4 cm). A row can be up to 409 points in height (about 5.4 inches).

In this exercise, you will manually adjust column width and row height to improve the appearance of a worksheet.

 **E01.14**

To Manually Adjust Column Width and Row Height

a. On the GolfCartPurchases worksheet, select the header for column **C**, press and hold Ctrl, and then select columns **E**, **G**, and **I**.

b. In the Cells group, click **Format** ⊞. In the Cell Size list, click **Column Width**, and then, in the Column Width dialog box, type **2**

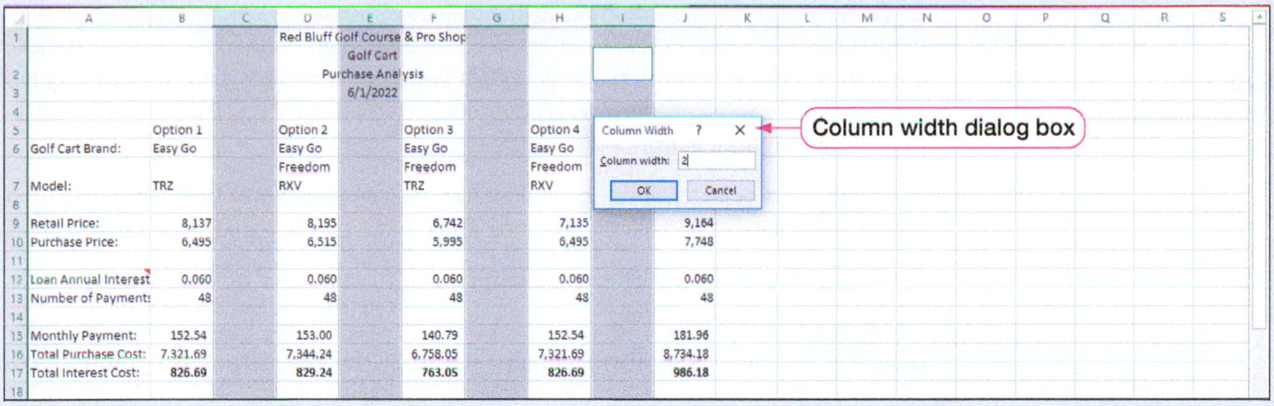

Figure 19   Column Width dialog box

Screenshot of Microsoft Excel 2019, © Microsoft Corporation

SIDE NOTE
Alternate Method
To adjust column width, you can also right-click the selected columns, select Column Width from the menu, enter the desired column width, and click OK.

SIDE NOTE
Alternate Method
To adjust row height, you can also right-click the selected rows, select Row Height from the menu, enter the desired row height, and click OK.

c. Click **OK**. By changing the column width, there is less white space between the columns.

d. Click the row **4** header, press and hold Ctrl, and then select headers for rows **8, 11,** and **14.**

e. In the Cells group, click **Format** ⊞, and then, in the Cell Size list, click **Row Height**. In the Row Height dialog box, type **10** and then click **OK.**

f. **Save** 🖫 the workbook.

Changing Column Widths Using AutoFit

By using the AutoFit feature, column width and row height can be adjusted automatically based on the width and height of selected content. AutoFit adjusts the width of columns and the height of rows to allow selected content to fit. Care is required in adjusting column widths so that data in unselected cells is not truncated or improperly displayed.

In this exercise, you will use AutoFit to adjust column width to change the appearance of a worksheet.

 **E01.15**

To Use AutoFit to Adjust Column Width

SIDE NOTE
AutoFit Row Height
AutoFit Row Height works in the same manner as AutoFit Column Width.

SIDE NOTE
Alternate Method
If you see number (#) signs in columns, point to the line between two column headers. When the mouse pointer changes to [+], double-click.

a. On the GolfCartPurchases worksheet, click cell **A7**, press and hold Ctrl, and then select cells **B7**, **D7**, **F7**, **H7**, and **J7**.

b. On the Home tab, in the Cells group, click **Format** 🔳, and in the Cell Size list, click **AutoFit Column Width**.

Because AutoFit sizes columns to the selected content, which in this case was individual cells, column B is too narrow to display most of its numeric information, so now the information is displayed as a series of number signs (#). Notice also that column A is too narrow to display the content of most of the cells in range A6:A17, so content is truncated on the right.

c. Select column A by clicking the column **A** header, press and hold Ctrl, and then select the column headers for columns **B**, **D**, **F**, **H**, and **J**.

d. In the Cells group, click **Format** 🔳. In the Cell Size list, click **AutoFit Column Width**.

Because columns were selected instead of individual cells, the columns are automatically adjusted to the widest content in the column, resulting in no number signs.

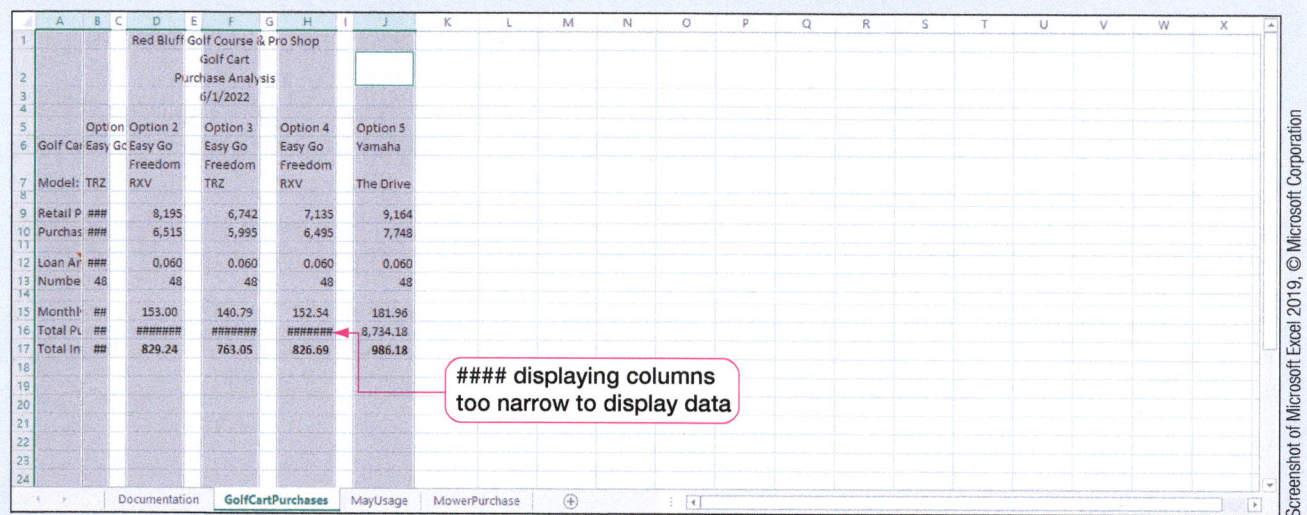

displaying columns too narrow to display data

Screenshot of Microsoft Excel 2019, © Microsoft Corporation

Figure 20 AutoFit Column Width results for selected cells

e. Column width can also be set manually. Column A could be a little wider than was set by AutoFit Column Width. Click cell **A1** to deselect the columns. Point to the border between column A and column B. The pointer should change to [+]. Click and hold the left mouse button. Drag the mouse to the right until column A has a width of **26.00 (187 pixels)**.

Notice the column width ScreenTip.

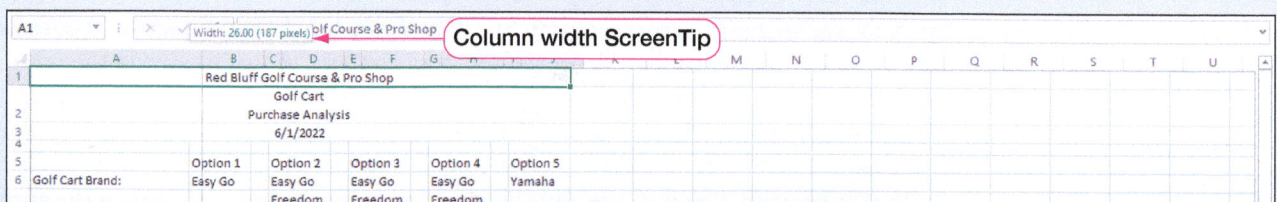

Column width ScreenTip

Figure 21 Manually adjust column width

Screenshot of Microsoft Excel 2019, © Microsoft Corporation

SIDE NOTE
Column Pixels
The number of pixels corresponding to a width of 26.00 may vary based on your monitor's screen resolution.

f. Release the left mouse button.

g. **Save** 💾 the workbook.

h. If you need to take a break before finishing this chapter, now is a good time.

REAL WORLD ADVICE	**Quick Ways to Adjust Column Width and Row Height**

You can quickly adjust column width and row height using any of the following methods.

1. Point to the line between two column headers. The mouse pointer will change to ⟷.
2. Click and hold the left mouse button, and move the mouse left or right to adjust the width of the column to the left of the pointer or double-click to use the AutoFit feature.

The same procedure can be used to adjust row height.

1. Point to the line between two row headers; the pointer will change to ⥮.
2. Click and hold the left mouse button, and then move the mouse up or down to adjust the height of the row above the pointer or double-click to use the AutoFit feature.

If multiple columns or rows are selected, adjusting the width or height for one selected column or row adjusts the width or height for all.

Working with and Printing Workbooks and Worksheets

Worksheets must often be printed for discussion at meetings, for distribution in venues where paper is the most effective medium, or to send digitally in a printed file format. Excel has a lot of built-in functionality that makes printed worksheets easy to read and understand. Further, as workbooks grow to include multiple worksheets and evolve to require maintenance, it is necessary to be able to create new worksheets, copy worksheets, delete worksheets, and reorder worksheets.

Manipulate Worksheets and Workbooks

Worksheets can be added to a workbook, deleted from a workbook, moved or copied within a workbook, or moved or copied to other workbooks. Worksheet names are displayed on each sheet's tab at the bottom of the application window, just above the status bar (see Figure 22). The white worksheet tab identifies the active worksheet. Gray worksheet tabs identify inactive worksheets.

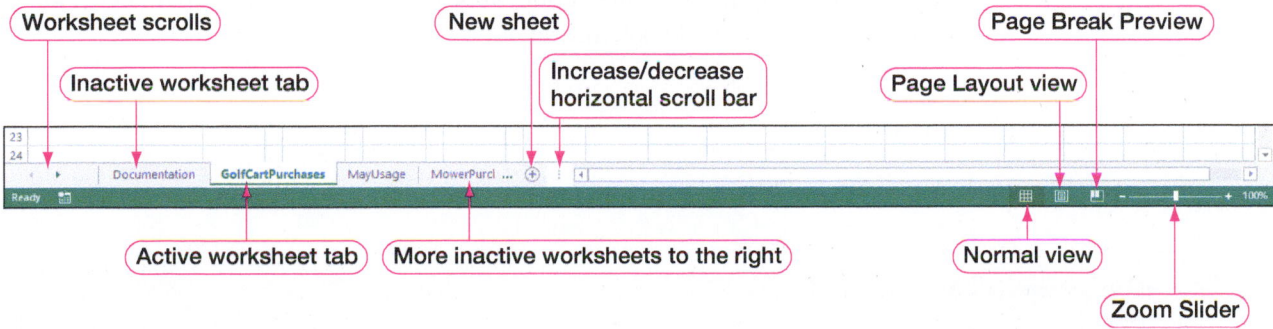

Figure 22   Worksheet tabs and controls

Screenshot of Microsoft Excel 2019, © Microsoft Corporation

When a workbook contains many worksheets or when the worksheets have very long names, some worksheet tabs may not be visible in the application window. To bring tabs that are not visible into view, use the worksheet tab scrolling buttons to the left of the worksheet tabs.

Creating a New Workbook

When you first open Excel, you can click Blank workbook to create a new, blank workbook. However, sometimes you may wish to create a blank workbook when Excel is already open. This can be accomplished on the File tab in Backstage view.

Barry Cheney used the golf cart analysis as an example to create an analysis of lawn mowers he is considering for purchase. The MowerPurchase worksheet is in the GolfCartAnalysis workbook. Barry wants to present the mower analysis at an upcoming staff meeting. Therefore, he asked you to create a separate workbook for the mower analysis.

In this exercise, you will create a new workbook and move or copy the appropriate worksheets to the new workbook.

 **E01.16**

To Create a Blank Workbook

> ### Grader Heads Up
> In the MyLab IT Grader, you will not be creating a Mowers workbook and therefore will not be completing the steps in blue box E01.16.

a. If you took a break, open the **e01ch01GolfCartAnalysis_LastFirst** workbook. Click the **File** tab to access Backstage view, and then click **New**.

b. Click **Blank workbook**. You will leave Backstage view and see the new blank workbook. You now have two files open in Excel.

c. Click the **File** tab, click **Save**, and under Save As, click **Browse**. In the Save As dialog box, navigate to the location where you are saving your files. In the File name box, type e01ch01Mowers_LastFirst using your last and first name.

d. Click **Save**. You have now created a new, blank workbook.

Moving and Copying Worksheets between Workbooks

Well-developed worksheets are often used as the starting point for new worksheets. Excel makes it easy to copy worksheets from one workbook to another.

Barry has asked you to create a separate workbook for the mower analysis. In this exercise, to save yourself some time, you have decided to move the MowerPurchase worksheet and copy the Documentation worksheet from the GolfCartAnalysis workbook to the new Mowers workbook instead of recreating them.

 **E01.17**

To Move or Copy a Worksheet to Another Workbook

Grader Heads Up

In the MyLab IT Grader, you will not be creating a Mowers workbook and therefore will not be completing the steps in blue box E01.17.

MAC COMPATIBILITY

Selecting a Workbook
The [Ctrl]+[Tab] command is not available on a Mac. Instead, click the Window menu to select the other workbook.

a. Press [Ctrl]+[Tab] to make **e01ch01GolfCartAnalysis_LastFirst** the active workbook.

Troubleshooting

If [Ctrl]+[Tab] did not make e01ch01GolfCartAnalysis_LastFirst the active workbook, there are two possible explanations. One is that you have more than two workbooks open. If that is the case, you need to press [Ctrl]+[Tab] more than once to cycle through open workbooks until e01ch01GolfCartAnalysis_LastFirst is active. The other possibility is that you closed e01ch01GolfCartAnalysis_LastFirst. In this case, you will need to open the file, at which time it will be the active workbook. These keystroke commands will not work on a Mac.

b. Right-click the **MowerPurchase** worksheet, and then select **Move or Copy** in the shortcut menu.

c. In the Move or Copy dialog box, click the **To book** arrow, and then click **e01ch01Mowers_LastFirst**. Leave Sheet1 selected in the Before sheet section.

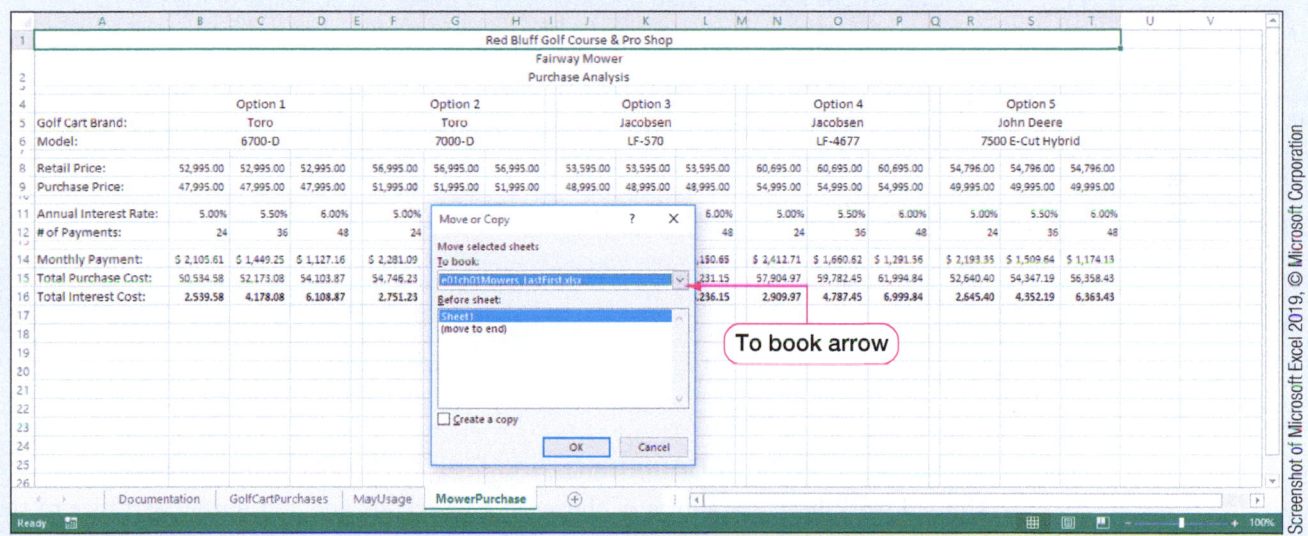

Figure 23 Move or Copy dialog box

d. Click **OK**. The MowerPurchase worksheet is moved to the e01ch01Mowers_LastFirst workbook, which is now the active workbook.

e. Press [Ctrl]+[Tab] to make **e01ch01GolfCartAnalysis_LastFirst** the active workbook.

f. If necessary, scroll to the left to view the Documentation worksheet. Right-click the **Documentation** worksheet, and then select **Move or Copy** in the shortcut menu. In the Move or Copy dialog box, click the **To book** arrow, and then click **e01ch01Mowers_LastFirst**. In the Before sheet box, click **Sheet1**, and click to select the **Create a copy** check box.

CHAPTER 1

Screenshot of Microsoft Excel 2019, © Microsoft Corporation

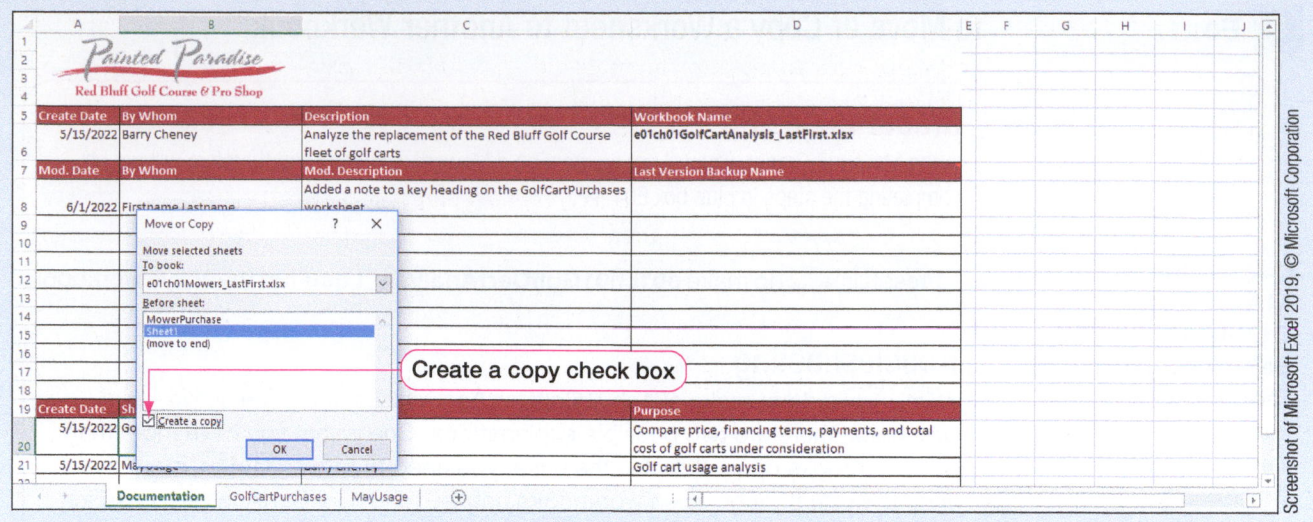

Figure 24 Copy a worksheet to another workbook

Screenshot of Microsoft Excel 2019, © Microsoft Corporation

SIDE NOTE
Copying a Worksheet
Worksheets can also be copied by right-clicking the worksheet tab, select Move or Copy, and then select and selecting Create a copy from the Move or Copy dialog box.

MAC COMPATIBILITY
The Ctrl + Tab command is not available on a Mac. Instead, click the Window menu to select the other workbook.

g. Click **OK**. The Documentation worksheet is copied to the e01ch01Mowers_LastFirst workbook, which is now the active workbook.

h. On the **Documentation** worksheet of the **e01ch01Mowers_LastFirst** workbook, select cell range **A20:D21**, press and hold Ctrl, and then select cell **C8**. On the Home tab, in the Editing Group, click the **Clear** arrow, and then select **Clear Contents**.

i. Select cell range **A22:D22**. Press Ctrl + X to cut the contents of the cell range. Click in cell **A20**, and then press Ctrl + V to paste the contents of the cell range.

j. Double-click cell **C6**. Position the insertion point after the word **carts**, delete **fleet of golf carts**, type fairway mowers and then press Enter. Click **Save** 🖫.

k. Press Ctrl + Tab to make **e01ch01GolfCartAnalysis_LastFirst** the active workbook. In the Documentation worksheet, select cell range **A22:D22**, and then press Delete.

l. **Save** 🖫 the workbook.

Deleting, Inserting, Renaming, and Coloring Worksheet Tabs

Unused worksheets are a form of clutter in a workbook and add unnecessary size to the stored workbook file, so it is best practice to delete any unused sheets in a workbook. Do so with caution, however, because deleting a worksheet removes it from a workbook. This action cannot be undone. Inserted worksheets are by default given a name such as "Sheet2" in which the number is one larger than the last number used for a worksheet name. An inserted worksheet is automatically the active worksheet. To insert a worksheet, move to the right of the list of worksheet tabs, and click New sheet ⊕. In Excel 2019, new worksheets are always inserted to the right of the active worksheet.

The default worksheet names are not particularly descriptive and do nothing to help document the contents or purpose of a worksheet. Worksheets can be renamed in two ways: by double-clicking the worksheet tab and typing a descriptive name or by right-clicking the worksheet tab and then clicking Rename on the shortcut menu. Worksheet names can be up to 31 characters long. Worksheet tabs can also be colored to add interest or for visual separation of the worksheets.

Now that you have created a separate workbook for the mower purchase analysis, Barry wants you to prepare a worksheet in the golf cart purchase analysis to extend the golf cart usage analysis to the month of June. He has asked you to create a new worksheet and to use the May usage analysis as a starting point. You just need to create the worksheet and get it ready for Barry to enter the data later. First, you should remove any unnecessary worksheets from the mower analysis workbook.

In this exercise, you will delete, insert, rename, and color worksheet tabs.

 **E01.18**

To Delete, Insert, Rename, and Color Worksheet Tabs

> ### Grader Heads Up
> In the MyLab IT Grader, you will not be creating a Mowers workbook and therefore will not be completing steps a and b.

SIDE NOTE

Be Careful—There Is No Undo!

Workbook and worksheet manipulation, such as deleting a worksheet, cannot be undone.

a. Press Ctrl+Tab to make **e01ch01Mowers_LastFirst** the active workbook.

b. Right-click the **Sheet1** worksheet, and then select **Delete** in the shortcut menu. Click **Save** 💾.

c. Now prepare a new golf cart usage analysis worksheet for June. Press Ctrl+Tab to make **e01ch01GolfCartAnalysis_LastFirst** the active workbook.

d. Click the **MayUsage** worksheet.

e. Click **New sheet** ⊕ to the right of the worksheet tabs. A new Sheet1 worksheet is inserted to the right of the MayUsage worksheet.

f. Double-click the **Sheet1** worksheet, type **JuneUsage** and then press Enter.

g. Right-click the **JuneUsage** worksheet, and then point to **Tab Color**.

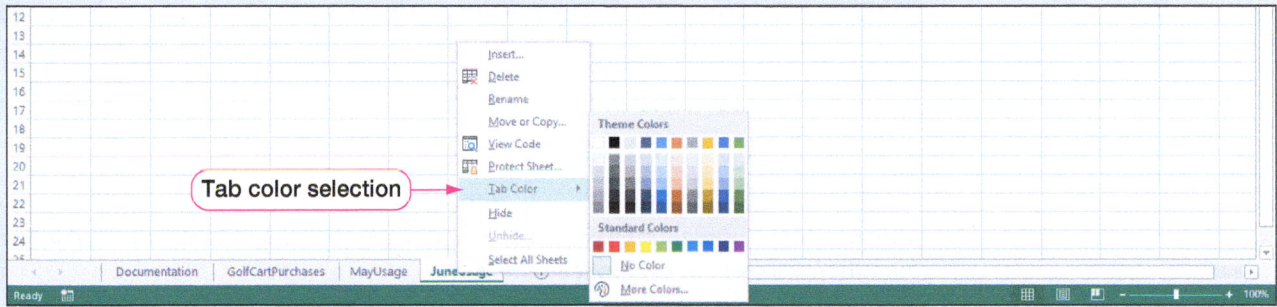

Figure 25   Worksheet tab color

Screenshot of Microsoft Excel 2019, © Microsoft Corporation

h. Select **Blue, Accent 1** in the top row, fifth column.

i. Right-click the **MayUsage** worksheet, point to **Tab Color**, and then select **Orange, Accent 2** in the top row, sixth column.

j. **Save** 💾 the workbook.

Using Series (Auto Fill)

The Auto Fill feature is a powerful way to minimize the effort required to enter certain types of data. **Auto Fill** copies information from one cell or a series in contiguous cells into contiguous cells. Auto Fill is a smart copy that will try to guess how you want values or formulas changed as you copy. Sometimes, Auto Fill will save significant time by changing the contents correctly. Other times, Auto Fill changes the contents in a way you did not intend. When that happens, Auto Fill Options makes options available that may be helpful.

To engage the Auto Fill feature, drag the fill handle in the direction in which you wish to expand the active cell. The **fill handle** is a feature in Excel that allows the user to extend—fill—a series of numbers, dates, or text to a desired number of cells. It is the small green square in the bottom right corner of the active cell. When you point to and drag the fill handle, the mouse pointer is a thin black plus sign +.

To make the JuneUsage worksheet ready for data entry, in this exercise you will copy and then clear some of the May data. You will also generate date information for June.

 E01.19

SIDE NOTE
Alternate Method
To select all the data in a worksheet, you can also use the Select All button ◤ above the Row 1 header.

To Quickly Generate Data Using Auto Fill

a. On the MayUsage worksheet, press Ctrl+Home to make cell **A1** the active cell, and then press Ctrl+A to select the entire worksheet.

b. Press Ctrl+C to copy the contents of the MayUsage worksheet.

c. Click the **JuneUsage** worksheet, press Ctrl+Home to ensure that cell **A1** is the active cell, and then press Ctrl+V to paste the contents from the **MayUsage** worksheet.

d. Click cell **A8**. If necessary, scroll down until you can see cell **A38**. Press and hold Shift, and then click cell **A38**. Cell range A8:A38 should be selected. Press Delete.

e. June contains one less day than May. Therefore, you need to delete one row of the daily data. Right-click the header for row **8**, and then click **Delete** in the shortcut menu.

f. Double-click cell **A6**, delete the word **May**, and then type June

g. Click cell **A8**. Type 06/01/2022 and then press Ctrl+Enter.

h. Click and hold the **fill handle**. When the point turns into +, drag the fill handle down until the border around the cell range expands to include cell range **A9:A37**, and then release the left mouse button.

    Notice that the date is incremented by one day in each cell from top to bottom. Also notice the Auto Fill Options button to the right of cell A37.

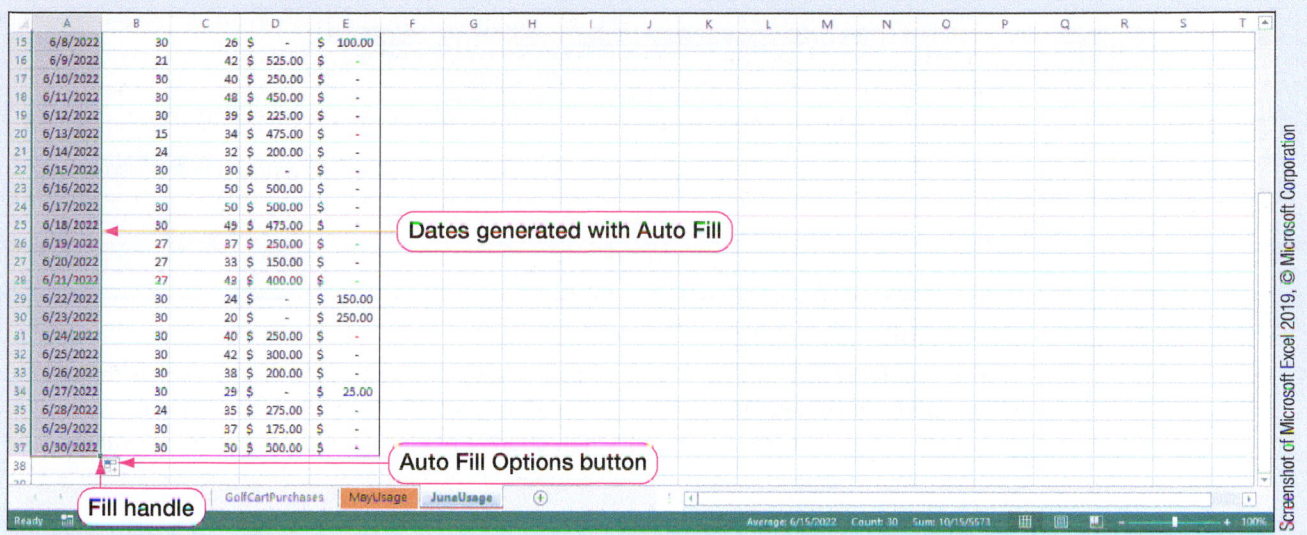

Figure 26 Generate data using Auto Fill

i. Click the **Auto Fill Options** button.

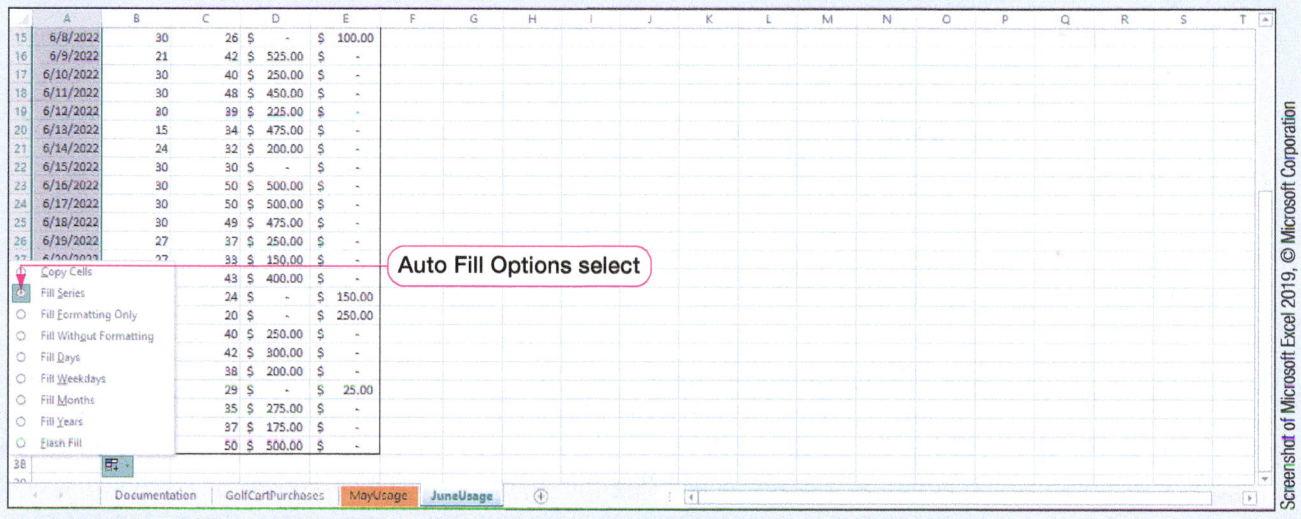

Figure 27 Auto Fill Options menu

j. Click **Fill Without Formatting** so the border of cell A37 does not disappear. Press Home to deselect the Auto Fill range.

k. Select cell range **C8:C37**, and then press Delete to clear the May golf cart demand from the JuneUsage worksheet.

l. If necessary, scroll to the left, and then click the **Documentation** worksheet. Click cell **A22**, and type **6/01/2022** and then press Tab. Type **JuneUsage** and then press Tab. Type **your name** in Firstname Lastname format, press Tab, and then type **G**.

Because you entered text, Excel examines other contiguous cells that contain content in the same column and uses the AutoComplete feature, which completes the entry with other cell contents that begin with "G."

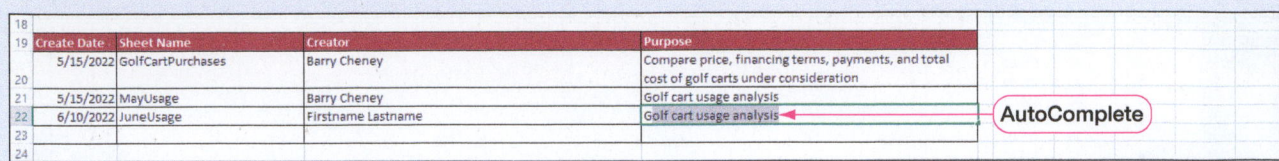

	Create Date	Sheet Name	Creator	Purpose	
18					
19	5/15/2022	GolfCartPurchases	Barry Cheney	Compare price, financing terms, payments, and total cost of golf carts under consideration	
20					
21	5/15/2022	MayUsage	Barry Cheney	Golf cart usage analysis	
22	6/10/2022	JuneUsage	Firstname Lastname	Golf cart usage analysis	← AutoComplete
23					
24					

Screenshot of Microsoft Excel 2019, © Microsoft Corporation

Figure 28   AutoComplete

Troubleshooting

If you didn't see the AutoComplete feature after typing a G, the AutoComplete feature may be disabled. To enable the AutoComplete feature, click the File tab, select Options, select Advanced, and then check Enable AutoComplete for cell values.

Mac Troubleshooting

Click Excel on the menu bar. Click Preferences, click AutoComplete, and then check desired options.

---

m. Press Enter to accept the AutoComplete suggestion.

n. Save 💾 the workbook.

Moving or Copying a Worksheet

The order of worksheets in a workbook can be changed by reordering the worksheet tabs. To move a worksheet, make the worksheet you wish to move the active worksheet by clicking on its tab. Click and hold the worksheet tab, drag the worksheet tab to its new location, and drop it by releasing the mouse button. As a worksheet is dragged, a small black triangle will appear between worksheet tabs. This indicates the location where the worksheet will be inserted when the mouse button is released.

If a new worksheet needs to be created that will be similar to another worksheet in the workbook, the worksheet can be copied to save time. To copy a worksheet within a workbook, after clicking on the worksheet tab, press and hold Ctrl, and drag a copy of the worksheet to a new location.

In the GolfCartAnalysis workbook, the Documentation worksheet is the first worksheet tab on the far left. Red Bluff Golf Course & Pro Shop standards require the Documentation worksheet to be the far right or last worksheet in a workbook. In this exercise, you will move and copy worksheets.

 **E01.20**

To Move and Copy a Worksheet

a. On the e01ch01GolfCartAnalysis_LastFirst workbook, click and hold the **Documentation** worksheet. The mouse pointer will change to the Move Worksheet pointer. Drag the mouse to the right until appears to the right of the JuneUsage worksheet.

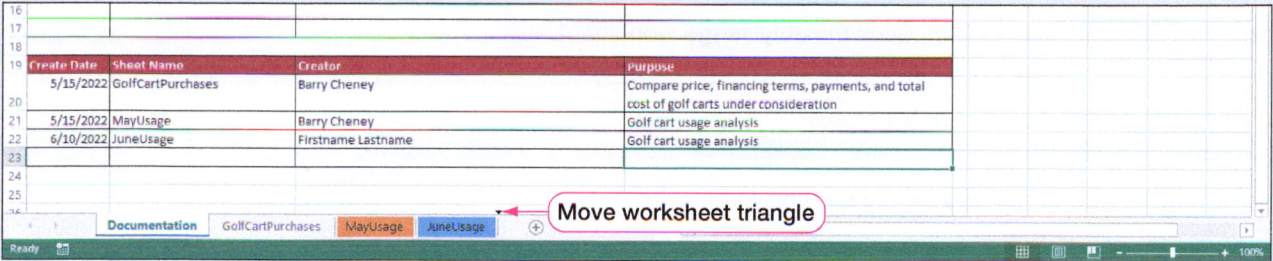

Figure 29   Move a worksheet

Screenshot of Microsoft Excel 2019, © Microsoft Corporation

SIDE NOTE
Navigating between Worksheets
Press Ctrl+PgUp to go to the prior worksheet. Press Ctrl+PgDn to go to the next worksheet.

b. Release the mouse button. The Documentation sheet is now the last worksheet on the right.

Barry has decided that he wants the most recent golf cart usage analysis to be first (leftmost) in the sequence of worksheets. You need to move the JuneUsage worksheet to the left of the MayUsage worksheet.

c. Click and hold the **JuneUsage** worksheet, drag to the left of MayUsage, and then release the mouse button. The worksheets are now in the following order from left to right: GolfCartPurchases, JuneUsage, MayUsage, and Documentation.

Barry also wants you to create a JulyUsage worksheet. He has decided that three months of usage data will help him better determine the number of carts to purchase. Rather than creating a new worksheet and then copying a range of cells from another worksheet, this time you will copy the MayUsage worksheet in its entirety to a new worksheet.

d. Click and hold the **MayUsage** worksheet, and then press and hold Ctrl. The mouse pointer will change from the Move Worksheet pointer to the Copy Worksheet pointer. Move the mouse to the left until appears to the left of the June-Usage worksheet. Release the mouse button, and then release the Ctrl key.

e. A copy of the MayUsage worksheet has been created, named "MayUsage (2)". Double-click the **MayUsage (2)** worksheet, type JulyUsage and then press Enter.

f. Right-click the **JulyUsage** worksheet, point to **Tab Color**, and then select **Gold, Accent 4**, in the top row, eighth column.

g. Double-click cell **A6**, delete the word **May**, and then type July

h. Click cell **A8**. Type 07/01/2022 and then press Ctrl+Enter.

i. Double-click the **fill handle** to fill the dates in the cell range A9:A38. Scroll, if necessary, to see row 38. Click the **Auto Fill Options**, and then select **Fill Without Formatting**.

j. Select cell range **C8:C38**, and then press Delete to clear the May golf cart demand from the JulyUsage worksheet. Press Ctrl+Home.

k. Click the **Documentation** worksheet, click cell **A23**, and then type 6/01/2022 Press Tab, type JulyUsage and then press Tab. Type your name in Firstname Lastname format, press Tab, and then type G and then press Enter to use Auto Complete to fill in the remainder of the text.

l. Click the **JulyUsage** worksheet.

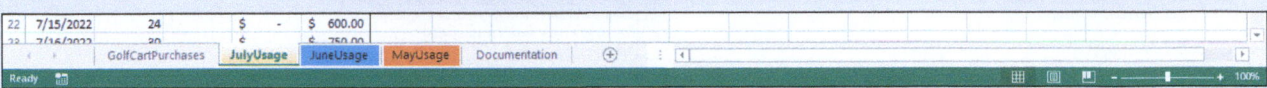

Figure 30 Worksheet tabs moved and copied

Screenshot of Microsoft Excel 2019, © Microsoft Corporation

m. **Save** 💾 the workbook.

Preview, Print, and Export Workbooks

Excel has a great deal of flexibility built into its printing functionality. To appropriately present your work in printed form, it is important that you understand how to take advantage of Excel's previewing, printing, and exporting features.

Using Worksheet Views

In the bottom-right corner of the application window are three icons that control the worksheet view. **Normal view** ⊞ is the default view in Excel and what is most commonly used when building and editing a worksheet. Only the cells in the worksheet are visible; print-specific features such as margins, headers, footers, and page breaks are not displayed.

Page Layout view ▣ shows page margins, print headers and footers, and page breaks. It presents you with a reasonable preview of how a worksheet will print on paper.

Page Break Preview ⊡ does not show page margins, headers, or footers, but it allows you to manually adjust the location of page breaks. This is particularly helpful when you would like to force a page break after a set of summary values and/or between data categories and force part of a worksheet to print on a new page.

Excel places a default page break wherever it is necessary to split content between pages. If the size of content changes, the location of a default break can change. A hard page break remains in its defined location until you move it. Changes in content size have no effect on the location of a hard page break.

In this exercise, you will switch between worksheet views and adjust page breaks.

To Switch between Worksheet Views and Adjust Page Breaks

> ### Grader Heads Up
>
> In the MyLab IT Grader, you will not be creating the Mowers workbook and therefore will not be completing the steps in blue box E01.21.

a. Select the **e01ch01Mowers_LastFirst** workbook, and click the **MowerPurchase** worksheet.

b. Click the **File** tab, and then click **Print**.

Notice that the worksheet does not print on a single page, nor does information break across pages correctly.

c. Press $\boxed{\text{Esc}}$ to leave Backstage view, and then click **Page Break Preview** 🖿 on the status bar.

Only the part of the worksheet that will print is displayed. A dashed blue border indicates where printing will break from one page to another.

d. If necessary, use the **Zoom Slider** to decrease the zoom level to make the pages as large as possible so that all data displays in the application window.

Now move the default page break, because it divides Option 3 between two pages.

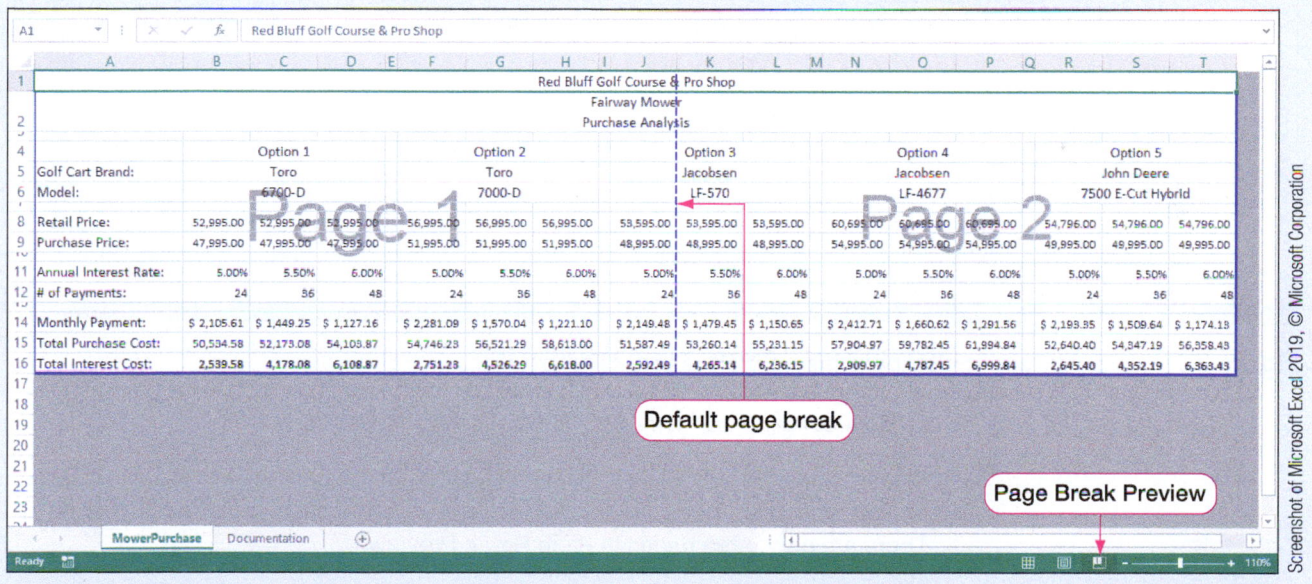

Figure 31 Page Break Preview

Screenshot of Microsoft Excel 2019, © Microsoft Corporation

e. Move the mouse pointer over the vertical dashed line between columns **J** and **K** to display the Vertical Page Break pointer ↔. Click and drag to move the page break between columns **I** and **J**.

Notice that the page break changes to a solid blue line. By moving the page break, you changed it from the default break to a hard page break. Now you need to insert a new page break so that Option 5 will print on a separate page.

f. On the ribbon, click the **Page Layout** tab. Be sure you do not click Page Layout on the status bar.

g. Click cell **R2**. In the Page Setup group, click **Breaks**, and then select **Insert Page Break**.

Two page breaks are inserted: a horizontal page break above the active cell and a vertical page break to the left of the active cell. You want only the vertical page break between columns Q and R. There are currently six pages in Page Break Preview.

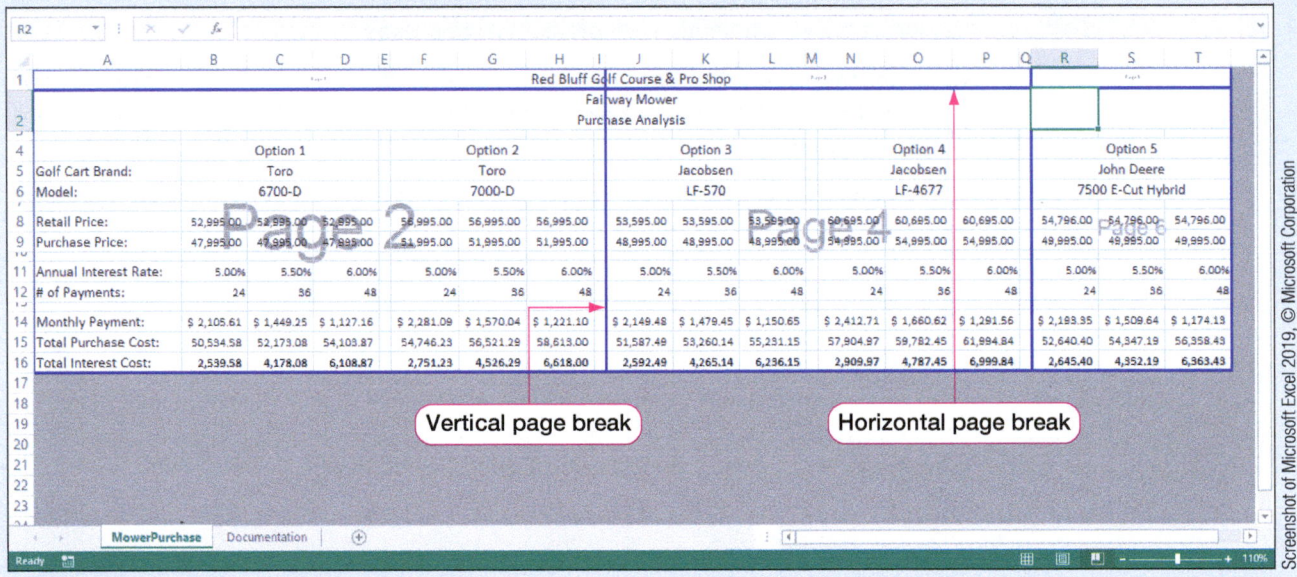

Figure 32 Horizontal and vertical page breaks in Page Break Preview

h. Point to the horizontal page break, and the mouse pointer will change to ↕. Drag the horizontal page break off the bottom or top of the print area to remove it. There should now be a page break after column I and a page break after column Q. There are now three pages in Page Break Preview.

Notice that the titles in rows 1:2 are split between two pages. You need to remove them from the print area.

i. Point to the top border, and the mouse pointer will change to the Horizontal Page Break pointer ↕. Click and hold the left mouse button, and then move the top border down until it is between rows **2** and **3**.

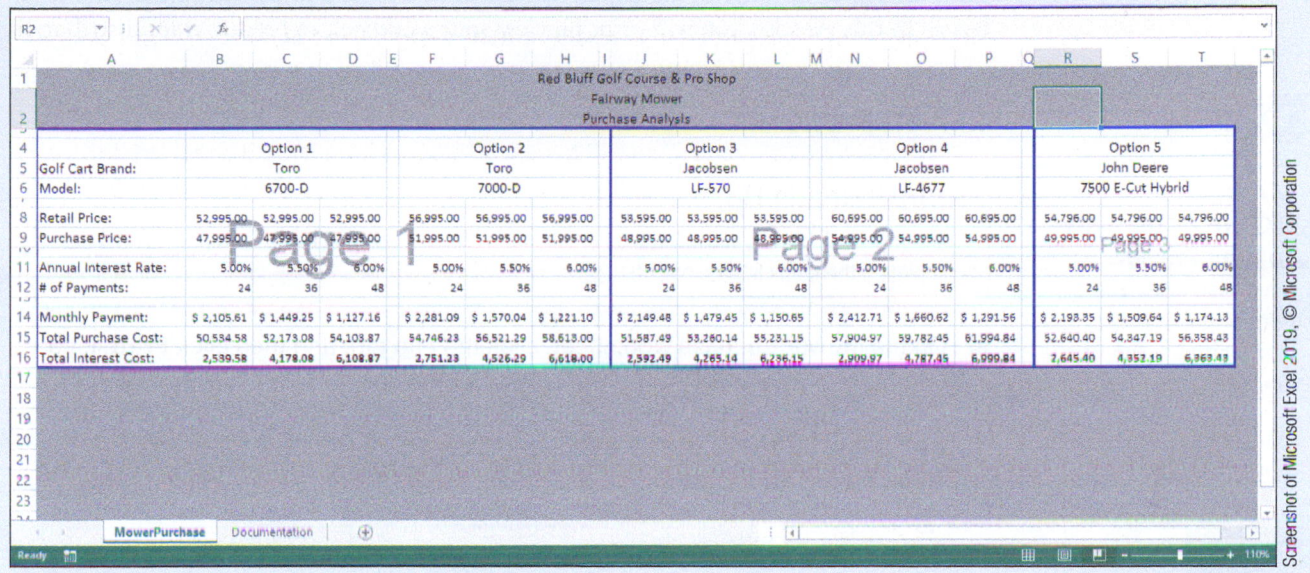

Figure 33 Page Break Preview with edited print area

j. Click **Page Layout** 🔲 on the status bar, and then press Ctrl + Home. Page Layout view displays the worksheet with print margins. A thin border shows which part(s) of the worksheet will be printed on a page and shows the location of the header.

k. Click **Normal** ⊞ on the status bar. The thin lines between rows 2 and 3, between rows 16 and 17, between columns I and J, and between columns Q and R show the print area and the locations of page breaks.

l. **Save** 💾 the workbook.

QUICK REFERENCE	Switching among Worksheet Views

On the right side of the status bar, do the following.

- Click ⊞ for Normal view.
- Click 🔲 for Page Layout view.
- Click 🔳 for Page Break Preview.

Using Print Preview and Printer Selection

Print Preview is the Backstage view of how a document, workbook, presentation, table, or other object will appear when printed. You can use the scroll bar on the right or the page navigation arrows on the bottom to view additional pages if your worksheet requires more than one page to print.

More than one print device can be made available to a computer. Always pay attention to the printer name before printing and be sure to select the device you want to use. The default printer is selected automatically and is usually acceptable. When a different printer is required, click the Printer Status arrow to see a list of available devices.

Printing a worksheet is as simple as clicking the Print button on the Print tab in Backstage view. If you want to print more than one copy, change the number in the Copies box to the right of the Print button. The copy count can be increased or decreased by clicking the arrows or by clicking in the Copies box and entering the number of copies from the keyboard. In this exercise, you will print preview your workbook to prepare it for distribution.

 **E01.22**

To Print Preview

MAC COMPATIBILITY
To Print Preview
On a Mac, click File, Print on the Menu Bar, and then click the Show details button.

> ### Grader Heads Up
> In the MyLab IT Grader, you will not be creating the Mowers workbook and therefore will not be completing the steps in blue box E01.22

a. On the MowerPurchase worksheet, click the **File** tab, and then click **Print**. If your computer has access to a printer, the Printer box displays the default printer. Click the **Printer Status** arrow to determine what print devices are available on your network. The right pane displays a preview of what will print.

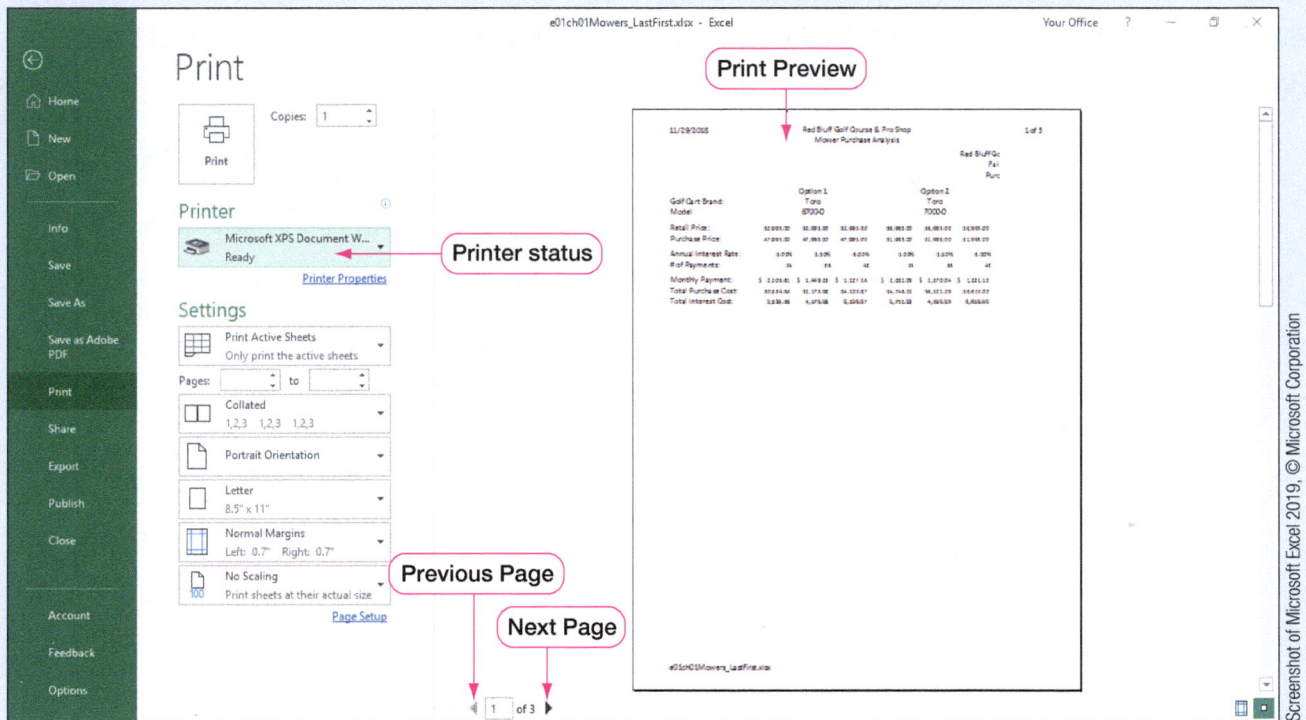

Figure 34 Print Preview and the Printer list

SIDE NOTE
To Print Preview
You can click the Previous Page button ◀ to go back a page.

> ### Troubleshooting
> The list of devices displayed in the Printer list is determined by your installation and may be different than the printer displaying in Figure 34.

b. Click the **Next Page** button ▶ to view page 2, and then click the **Next Page** button ▶ to view page 3.

Notice that pages 2 and 3 do not have any row headings. None of the pages have a page title. There is more to be done before this worksheet is ready for printing.

c. Press Esc to leave Backstage view.

d. **Save** 🖫 the workbook.

SIDE NOTE
Alternate Method
You can also click the Excel Back button ⊙ to exit Backstage view.

Using Print Titles

When a worksheet is too large to print on a single page, it is often difficult to keep track of what information is being viewed from one page to another. Headers, such as those in column A of the Mowers worksheet, are printed only on the first page.

Print titles can be included on each printed page so every column and/or row is labeled and easily identified from one page to another. Because you set page breaks between cart categories, you should print at least one column on each page that identifies cell contents in each row. In this exercise, you will specify print titles to prepare the worksheet to print.

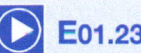 **E01.23**

To Specify Print Titles

> ### Grader Heads Up
>
> In the MyLab IT Grader, you will not be creating the Mowers workbook and therefore will not be completing the steps in blue box E01.23

a. On the MowerPurchase worksheet, on the **Page Layout** tab, in the Page Setup group, click **Print Titles**. The Page Setup dialog box is displayed.

b. On the **Sheet** tab of the Page Setup dialog box, under Print titles, in the Columns to repeat at left box, type **A:A**

The Print Titles feature requires the specification of a range, even when only a single column will be printed—thus the need to enter column A as A:A.

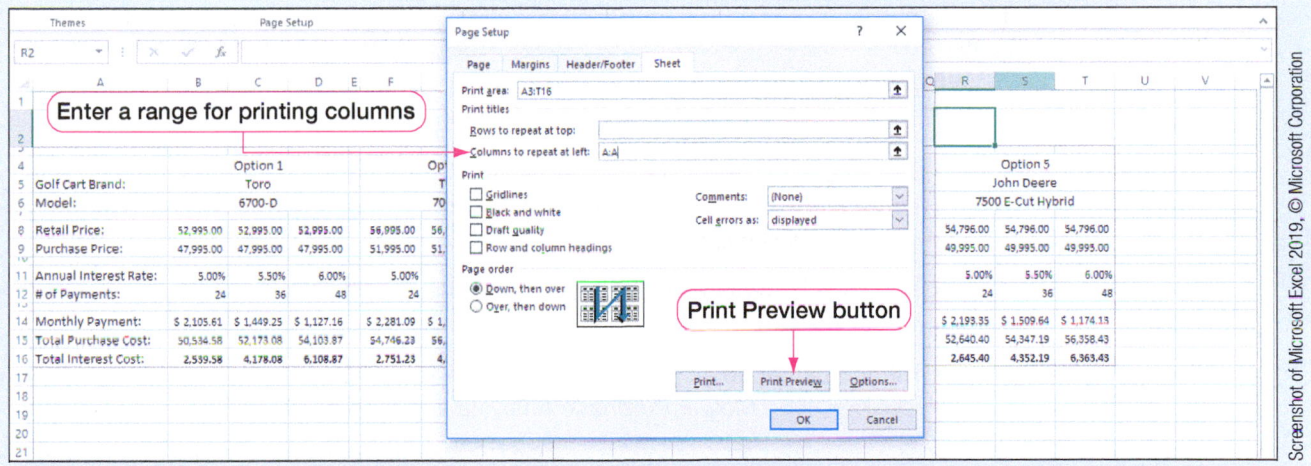

Figure 35   Sheet tab in the Page Setup dialog box for creating print titles

c. Click **Print Preview**. In the Print Preview pane, click ▶ to view page 2, and then click ▶ again to view page 3.

d. Notice that pages 2 and 3 now have the column A row headings. Press Esc to exit Backstage view.

e. **Save** 💾 the workbook.

Adding Headers and Footers

There are often items of information that should be included on a printed document that are not necessary in a worksheet. These items might include the following.

- Print date
- Print time
- Company name
- Page number
- Total number of pages
- File name and location

Headers place information at the top of each printed page. Footers place information at the bottom of each printed page. Headers and footers are divided into three sections: left, center, and right. Information can be placed in any combination of the sections. You may include information in either the header or the footer or both, as deemed necessary. In this exercise, you will add a header and a footer to prepare the worksheet to print.

 **E01.24**

To Add a Header and a Footer

> ### Grader Heads Up
> In the MyLab IT Grader, you will not be creating the Mowers workbook and therefore will not be completing the steps in blue box E01.24.

a. On the MowerPurchase worksheet, press Ctrl + Home to make A1 the active cell.

b. Click **Page Layout** on the status bar. If necessary, use the Zoom Slider to adjust zoom to 100%.

c. Click **Add header** in the top margin of Page Layout view. The Design tab for Header & Footer Tools will appear on the ribbon. If necessary, click the **Header & Footer Tools Design** tab.

d. Click the **left section** of the header, and then, in the Header & Footer Elements group, click **Current Date**.

e. Click the center section of the header, type Red Bluff Golf Course && Pro Shop Press Enter, type Mower Purchase Analysis and then press Tab.

The ampersand (&) performs a special function in headers and footers. It indicates the start of a field name. To display "&" in the print header, it must be entered twice.

f. In the right section of the header, on the Design tab, in the Header & Footer Elements group, click **Page Number**, press SpaceBar to add a space, type of and then press the SpaceBar to add a space.

g. In the Header & Footer Elements group, click **Number of Pages**.

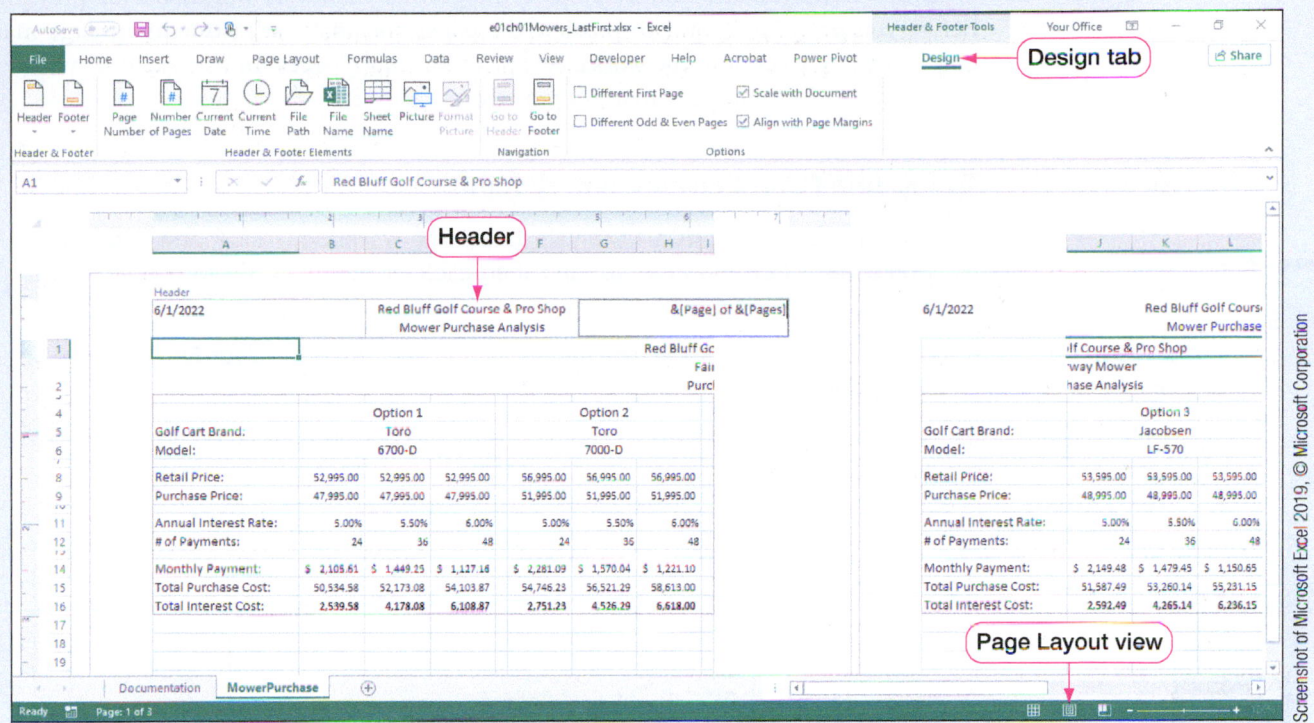

Figure 36 Page Layout view with header information added

h. On the Design tab, in the Navigation group, click **Go to Footer**.

i. Click the **left section** of the footer, and then, on the Design tab, in the Header & Footer Elements group, click **File Name**. Select any cell in the worksheet, press Ctrl + Home, and then, on the status bar, click **Normal** ▦.

j. Click the **File** tab, and then click **Print**. In the Print Preview pane, scroll through the pages to see that the header and footer are added to every page.

k. If your computer is attached to a printer, the default printer is displayed. If you want to print to a different printer, click the Printer arrow next to the printer name, and then select the desired printer from the list. If requested by your instructor, click Print. If you are not instructed to print, press Esc.

l. **Save** 🖫 and then **Close** ✕ the **e01ch01Mowers_LastFirst** workbook.

Changing Page Margins and Scaling

Page margins are the white space at the edges of the printed page. Normal margins for Excel are 0.7 inch on the left and right sides of the page, 0.75 inch on the top and bottom of the page, and 0.3 inch for the header and footer if included.

Margins can be changed to suit conventions or standards for an organization, to better position information on the page, or to avoid a page break at the last column or line of a worksheet.

It is not uncommon for worksheets to be too large to print on a single page or to be so small that they appear lost in the top left corner of the page. Scaling changes the size of the print font to allow more of a worksheet to be printed on a page or for a worksheet to be printed larger and use more page space. A printed worksheet that has been scaled to fit a sheet of paper generally looks more professional and is easier to read and understand than a worksheet that is printed on two pages that uses only a small part of the second page.

Barry Cheney wants you to prepare the golf cart analysis workbook for printing. Before you print, you want to preview the pages and make adjustments in page margins or scaling to be sure the worksheets print on single pages. In this exercise, you will change the scaling and page margins of three worksheets.

 **E01.25**

MAC COMPATIBILITY
Scaling
Click the File menu, select Print, and click Show Details. The only option will be Scale to fit—pages wide by pages tall.

To Change Page Margins and Scaling

a. On the **e01ch01GolfCartAnalysis_LastFirst** workbook, click the **MayUsage** worksheet. Click the **File** tab, and then click **Print**. You want to ensure that all rows always fit on one page.

b. Under Settings, click the **Scaling** arrow, the last setting. Select **Fit All Rows on One Page**.

c. Click the **Margins** arrow, just above the Scaling setting, and then, in the Margins list, select **Wide**.

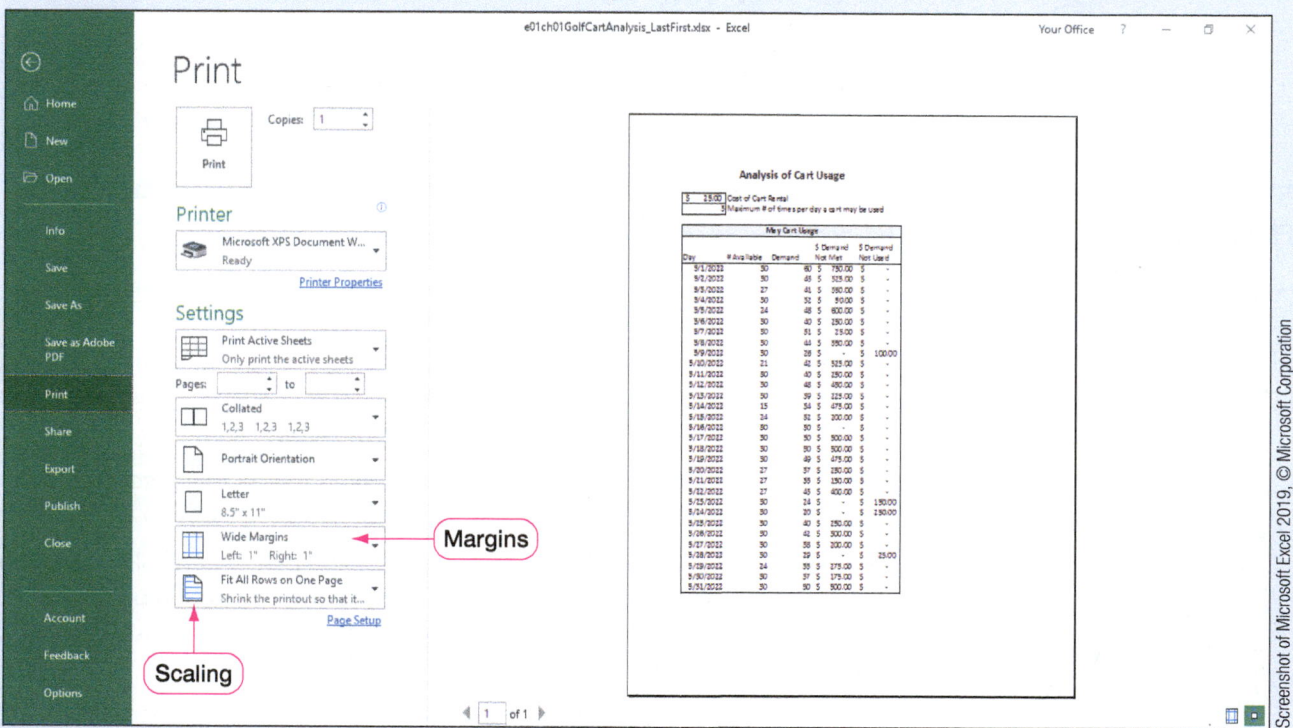

Figure 37   Print Preview with scaling control and narrow margins

d. Repeat steps b and c for the **JuneUsage** and **JulyUsage** worksheets. Press Esc to exit Backstage view.

e. Click the **GolfCartPurchases** worksheet, and then click the **Insert** tab. In the Text group, click **Header & Footer**. On the Design tab, in the Navigation group, click **Go to Footer**. If necessary, click in the center footer. In the Header & Footer Elements group, click **File Name**. Click cell **A1** to exit the footer, and then on the status bar, click **Normal**.

f. **Save** the workbook.

Changing Page Orientation and Print Range

Worksheets can be oriented to print on paper in one of two ways: portrait or landscape. **Landscape orientation** indicates that the page is wider than it is tall. Landscape orientation is generally used when a worksheet has too many columns to print well on a single page in portrait orientation. **Portrait orientation** indicates that the page is taller than it is wide.

Scaling the worksheet to fit all columns on a single page can work in portrait orientation, but if scaling makes the data too small to be readable, landscape orientation is an option.

Print range defines what part of a workbook will be printed. The default is Print Active Sheets. This is often adequate, but you can also choose to print only a selected range of cells or to print the entire workbook.

Barry Cheney does not like the last printout you produced of the Documentation worksheet; the print is too small. He suggests changing the page orientation to landscape.

In this exercise, you will change the page orientation of a worksheet.

 E01.26

SIDE NOTE
Alternate Method
To change the page orientation, click the Page Layout tab, and in the Page Setup group, click the Orientation button.

To Change Page Orientation and Print Range

a. Click the **Documentation** worksheet. Click the **File** tab, and then click **Print**.

b. Click the **Orientation** arrow—fourth from the bottom under Settings—and then select **Landscape Orientation**.

c. Click the **Print Range** arrow—the first selection under Settings—and then select **Print Entire Workbook**. Notice that five pages will print.

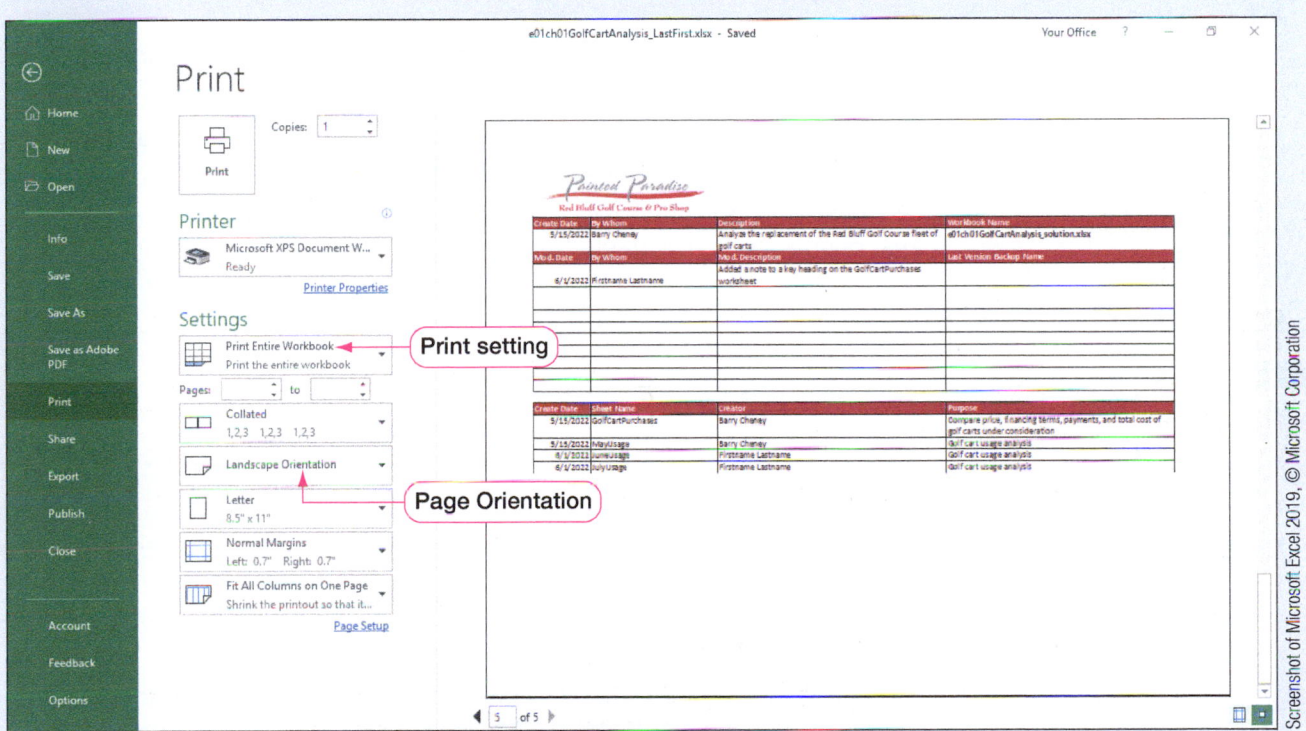

Figure 38   Print Preview with page orientation and print range

d. Scroll through the pages to preview how the workbook would print. Click **Print** only if requested by your instructor, or press Esc to exit Backstage view.

e. **Save** the workbook.

Exporting a Workbook to PDF

Portable Document Format (PDF), which was developed by Adobe Systems in 1993, is a file type that preserves most formatting attributes of a source document regardless of the software in which the document was created. PDF preserves exactly the original "look and feel" of a document but allows the document to be viewed in many different applications. Exporting to PDF is a great way to document your worksheets. One way to distribute a worksheet or workbook in a manner that allows it to be read by anyone with a free PDF reader application is to export the worksheet or entire workbook to PDF.

Now that you have the e01ch01GolfCartAnalysis_LastFirst workbook prepared for distribution, Barry wants a PDF version.

In this exercise, you will export the workbook to PDF.

 **E01.27**

To Export a Workbook to PDF

> ### Grader Heads Up
> The MyLab IT Grader version of this project does not include creating a PDF and therefore will not complete the steps in blue box E01.27

a. On the e01ch01GolfCartAnalysis_LastFirst workbook, click the **File** tab, and then click **Export**.

b. Click **Create PDF/XPS Document**, and then in the right pane under Create a PDF/XPS Document, click the **Create PDF/XPS** button.

c. In the Publish as PDF or XPS dialog box, click **Options**. In the Options dialog box, under Publish what, click **Entire workbook**.

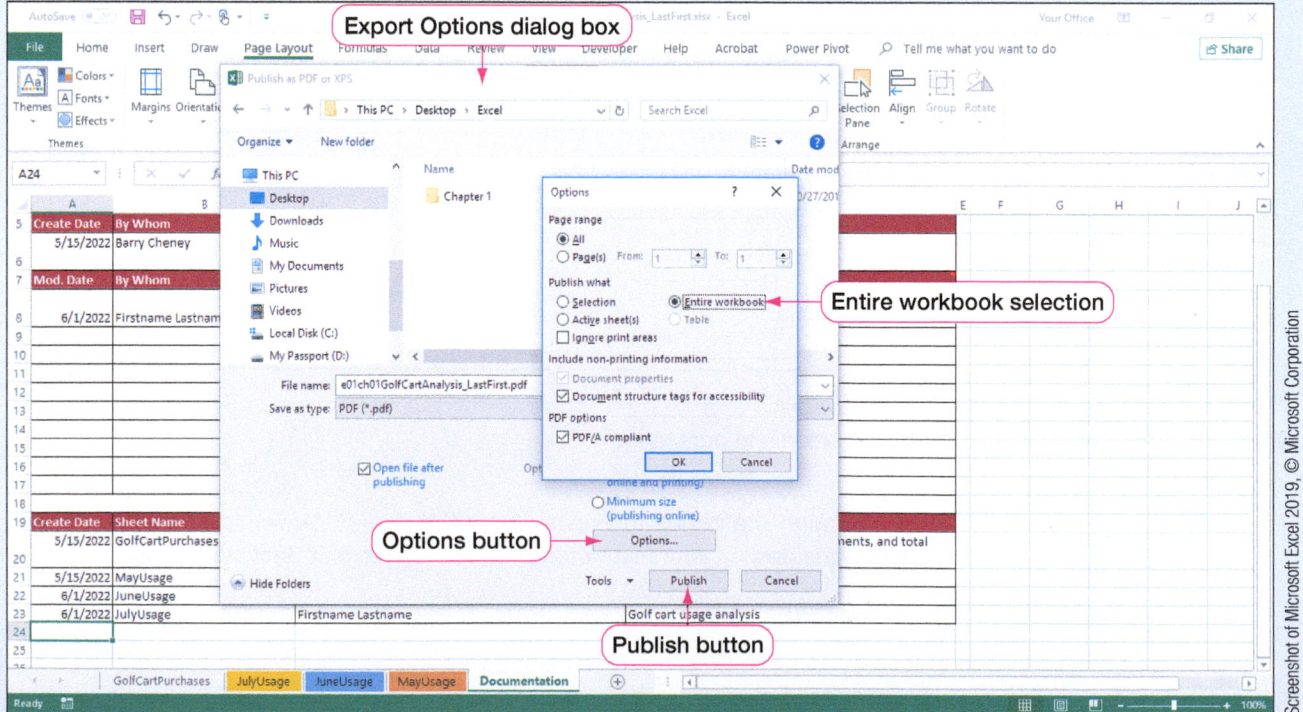

Figure 39   Export Options dialog box

> ## Mac Troubleshooting
> Point above the Excel window to display the menu bar. Click File and then click Print. In the lower-left corner of the dialog box, click the PDF arrow and then click Save as PDF. In the next dialog box, accept the file name in the Save As box. In the Where box, choose the location to save the file, and then click Save. The PDF opens in the default PDF reader. (The Mac version does not offer options for optimizing for publishing online versus printing. Also the dialog boxes do not have titles on them as they do on a PC.)

MAC COMPATIBILITY

Creating a PDF

To create a PDF on a Mac, click File, Print, and at the bottom of the dialog box, select PDF.

d. Click **OK**. In the Publish as PDF or XPS dialog box, be sure **Open file after publishing** is checked.

e. Navigate to where you are saving your Excel files, verify the file name listed in the File name box to be **e01ch01GolfCartAnalysis_LastFirst** using your last and first name, and then click **Publish**.

f. Once the PDF file has been created, it may be opened in the Windows 10 default browser, Edge.

> ## Troubleshooting
> Your PDF file may not open in Edge if a different PDF reader, such as Adobe Reader, is installed as the default PDF file reader. If the PDF file displays in a different reader, close the reader and skip step g.

g. Right-click anywhere on the screen. A menu bar will appear at the bottom of the screen. Click **More**.

h. Click **Close** to close the PDF file.

i. **Save** ⊟ the workbook, exit Excel, and then submit your files as directed by your instructor.

1. Explain the following terms for a reader who is not familiar with Excel.

   • Worksheet p. 51

   • Workbook p. 52

   • Cell p. 51

   • Row p. 51

   • Column p. 51

   • Cell range p. 62

2. How do you quickly navigate to the last row in a worksheet that contains data? What happens when you press End in Excel? How do you move from one worksheet to another in Excel using shortcut keys? What purpose does the Go To dialog box serve? How do you access the Go To dialog box? p. 53-57

3. Why is documentation important? Why do many people not properly document their workbooks? What are the possible costs associated with inadequate documentation? p. 57

4. What happens if you select a cell that contains important data, type Your Office and then press Enter? How does the outcome change if you first double-click a cell that contains important data, type Your Office and then press Enter? p. 59

5. How do you select noncontiguous cells? Is the ability to select noncontiguous cells important to the effective use of Excel? If yes, why? If no, why make use of noncontiguous cell selection? p. 64

6. Describe two ways in which columns and rows can be inserted and deleted. p. 70

7. How do you reorder worksheets in a workbook? p. 82

8. Explain the purpose of print titles, page headers, and page footers and describe when you would use them. What are page orientation and scaling, and how can they be used in tandem to allow you to efficiently print a professional-looking worksheet? p. 89-92

Key Terms

Active cell p. 55
Active worksheet p. 52
Auto Fill p. 80
Cell p. 51
Cell range p. 62
Cell reference p. 55
Clipboard p. 62
Column p. 51
Contiguous cell range p. 62
Date data p. 60
Destination cell p. 62
Field p. 51
Fill handle p. 80
Formula p. 51

Formula bar p. 55
Function p. 51
Keyboard shortcut p. 55
Landscape orientation p. 92
Merge & Center p. 67
Noncontiguous cell range p. 62
Note p. 58
Normal view p. 84
Numeric data p. 60
Page Break Preview p. 84
Page Layout view p. 84
Portable Document
    Format (PDF) p. 94
Portrait orientation p. 92

Print Preview p. 87
Record p. 51
Row p. 51
Spreadsheet p. 51
Text data p. 60
Time data p. 60
Touch mode p. 57
What-if analysis p. 51
White space p. 70
Workbook p. 52
Worksheet p. 51

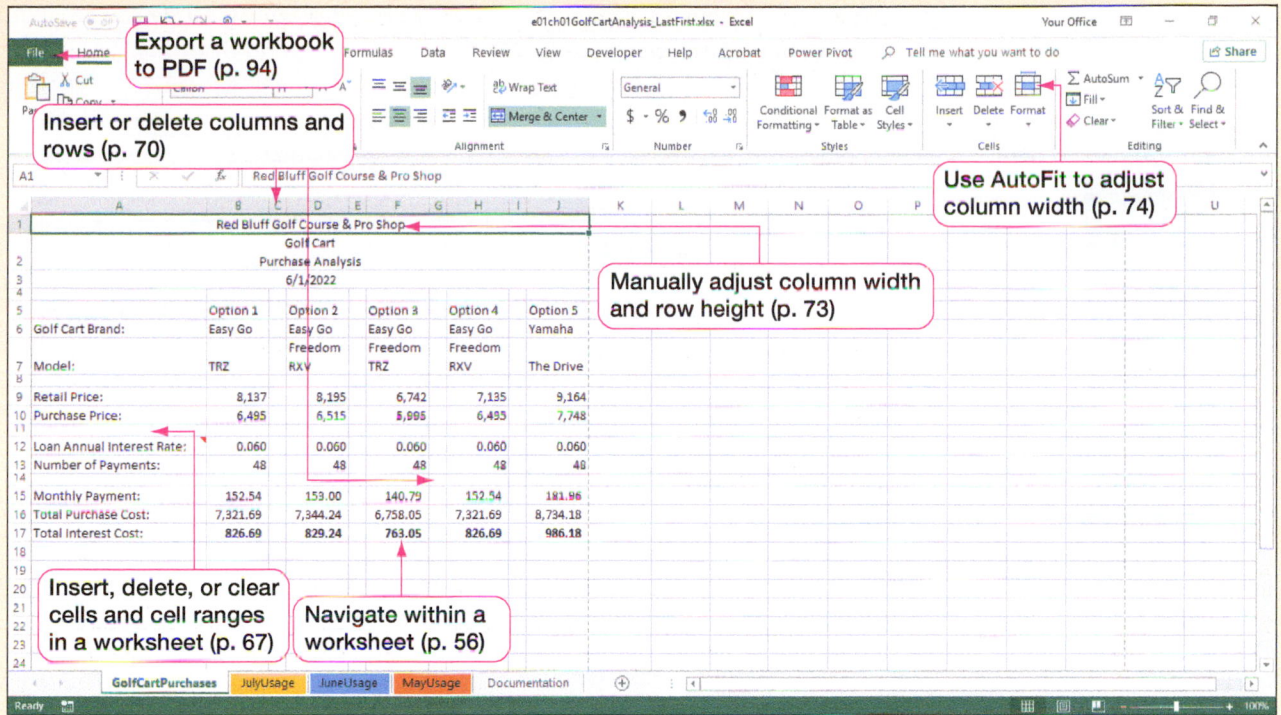

Figure 40

Screenshot of Microsoft Excel 2019, © Microsoft Corporation

- Export a workbook to PDF (p. 94)
- Insert or delete columns and rows (p. 70)
- Use AutoFit to adjust column width (p. 74)
- Manually adjust column width and row height (p. 73)
- Insert, delete, or clear cells and cell ranges in a worksheet (p. 67)
- Navigate within a worksheet (p. 56)

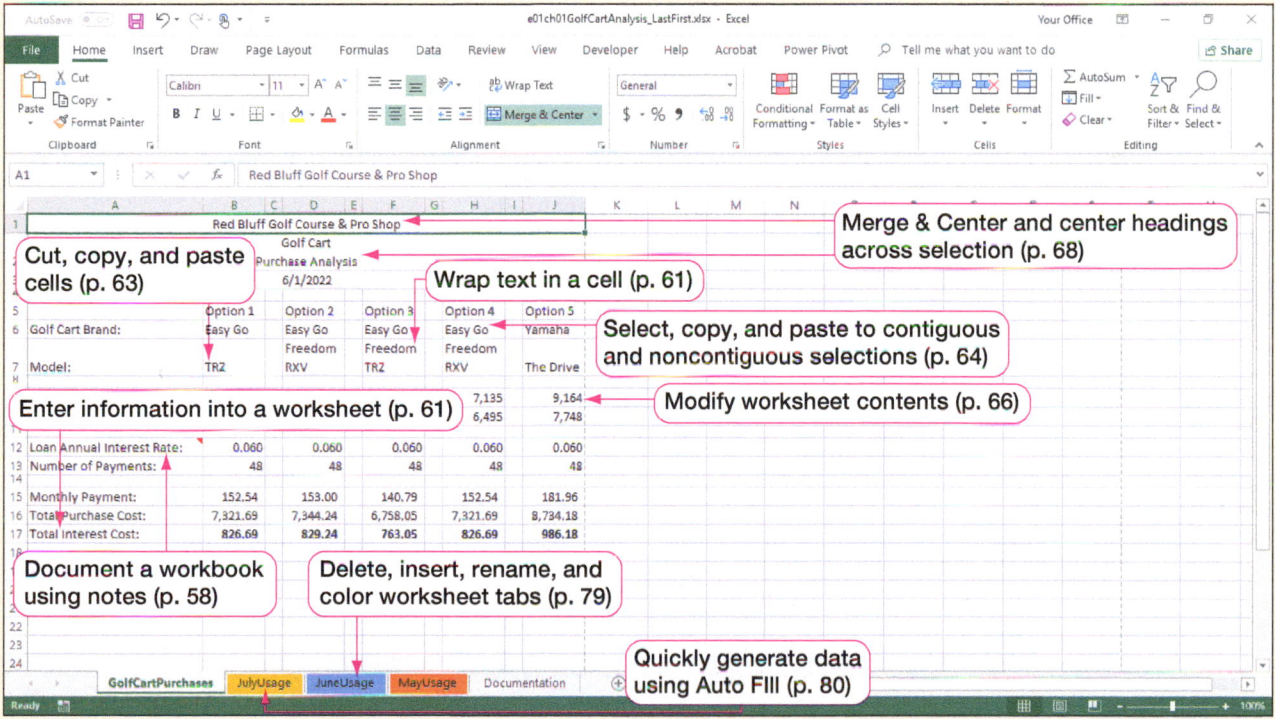

Figure 41

Screenshot of Microsoft Excel 2019, © Microsoft Corporation

- Cut, copy, and paste cells (p. 63)
- Wrap text in a cell (p. 61)
- Merge & Center and center headings across selection (p. 68)
- Select, copy, and paste to contiguous and noncontiguous selections (p. 64)
- Enter information into a worksheet (p. 61)
- Modify worksheet contents (p. 66)
- Document a workbook using notes (p. 58)
- Delete, insert, rename, and color worksheet tabs (p. 79)
- Quickly generate data using Auto Fill (p. 80)

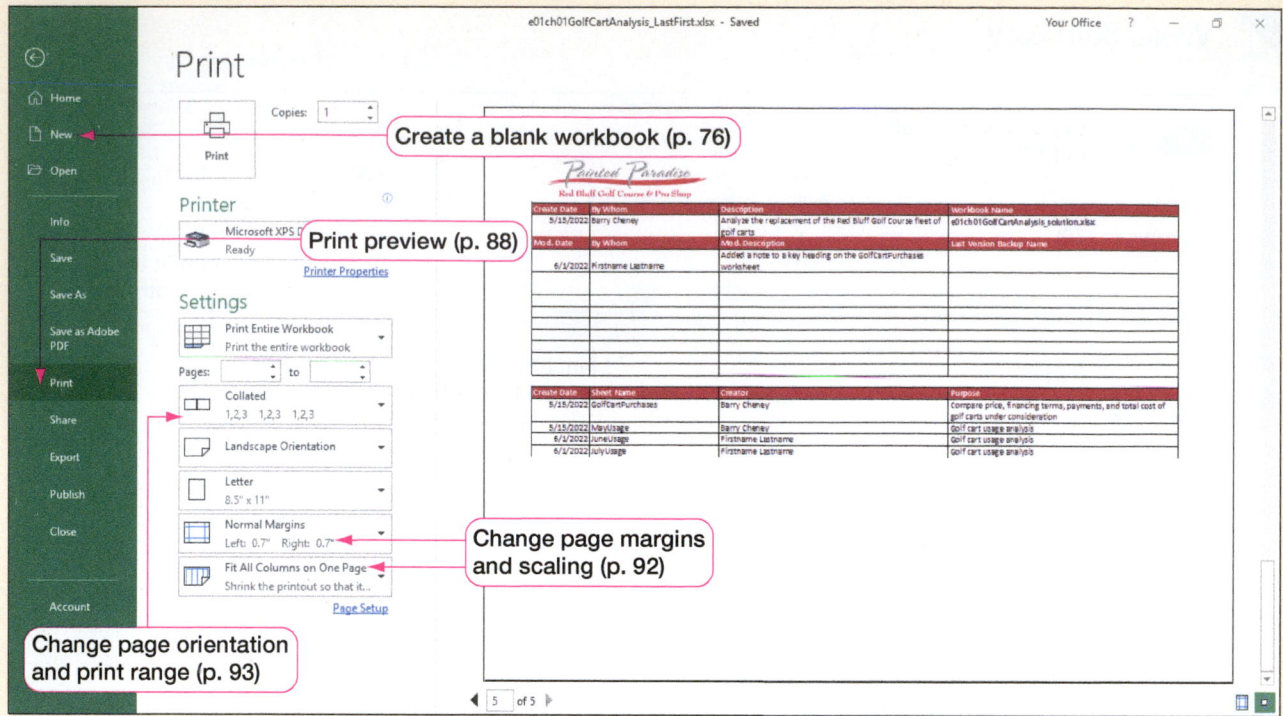

Figure 42

Screenshot of Microsoft Excel 2019, © Microsoft Corporation

Annotations in Figure 42:
- Create a blank workbook (p. 76)
- Print preview (p. 88)
- Change page margins and scaling (p. 92)
- Change page orientation and print range (p. 93)

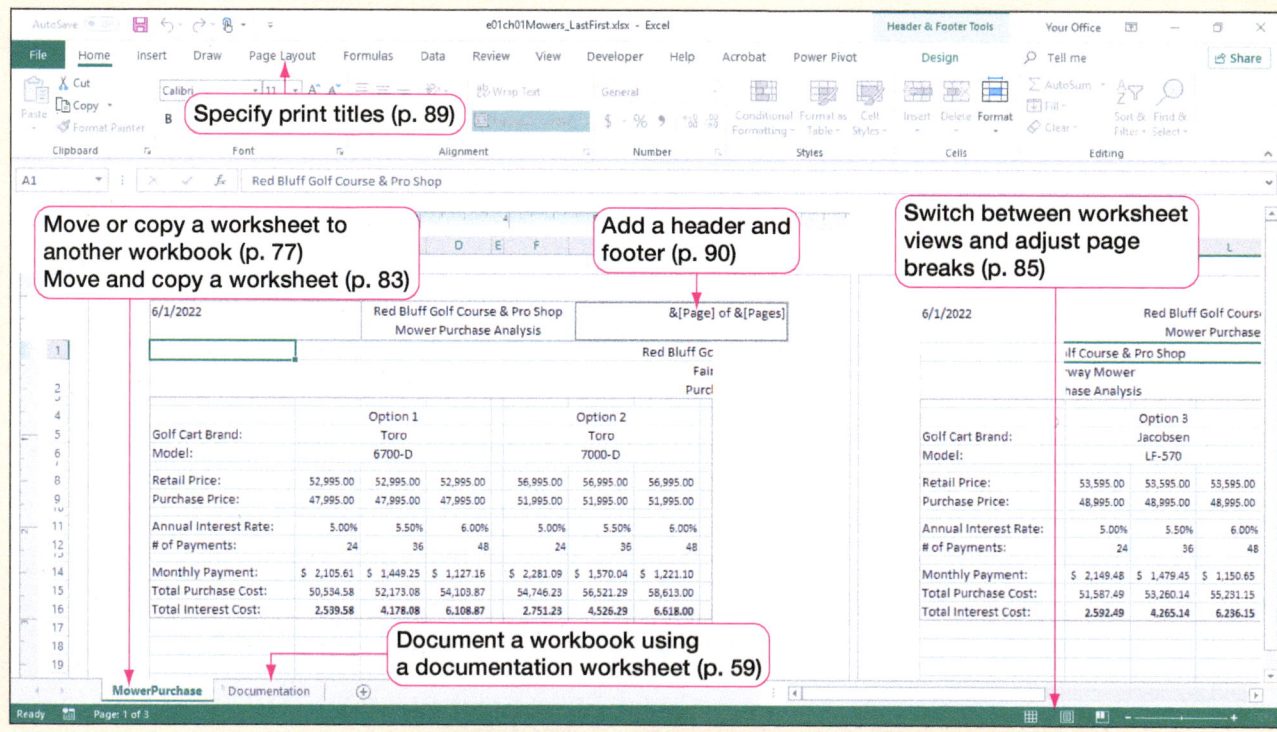

Figure 43

Screenshot of Microsoft Excel 2019, © Microsoft Corporation

Annotations in Figure 43:
- Specify print titles (p. 89)
- Move or copy a worksheet to another workbook (p. 77) / Move and copy a worksheet (p. 83)
- Add a header and footer (p. 90)
- Switch between worksheet views and adjust page breaks (p. 85)
- Document a workbook using a documentation worksheet (p. 59)

Student data file needed:

 e01ch01WeddingPlanner.xlsx

You will save your files as:

 e01ch01WeddingPlanner_LastFirst.xlsx

 e01ch01WeddingPlanner_LastFirst.pdf

 e01ch01PreferredPartners_LastFirst.xlsx

Sales & Marketing

Painted Paradise Resort & Spa Wedding Planning Worksheet

Weddings are becoming an important part of the Painted Paradise Resort & Spa business, so Patti Rochelle started a worksheet to improve the wedding-planning process for her staff. Last year, the resort hosted three weddings per week, on average, and it has done as many as six in a weekend. The worksheet Patti wants you to finish will allow for changes in pricing to be immediately reflected in the planning process.

You have been given a workbook that includes product/service categories, prices, and an initial worksheet structure to help standardize the process and pricing of weddings. You will build a worksheet that calculates the price of a wedding and doubles as a checklist to use as weddings are set up, to ensure that subcontractors, such as DJs, are reserved in a timely fashion and that all contracted services are delivered.

a. Start Excel, click **Open** in the left pane, and then double-click **This PC**. Navigate through the folder structure to the location of your student data files, and then double-click **e01ch01WeddingPlanner**. If a Security Warning message displays, click the **Enable Editing** button.

b. Click the **File** tab, click **Save As**, and then double-click **This PC**. In the Save As dialog box, navigate to the location where you are saving your project files, and then change the file name to e01ch01WeddingPlanner_LastFirst using your last and first name. Click **Save**.

c. To delete a blank worksheet, right-click the **Sheet2** worksheet, and then select **Delete**.

d. Click the **File** tab, click **New**, and then click **Blank workbook**. Save the workbook to the location where you are storing your data files as e01ch01PreferredPartners_LastFirst using your last and first name. Press Ctrl + Tab to return to the **e01ch01WeddingPlanner** workbook.

e. To move the Sheet4 worksheet to the e01ch01PreferredPartners workbook, right-click **Sheet4**, and then select **Move or Copy**. Click the **To book:** arrow, select **e01ch01PreferredPartners_LastFirst**, and then click **OK**.

f. On the e01ch01PreferredPartners_LastFirst workbook, double-click the **Sheet4** worksheet, and then type Partners to rename the worksheet. Press Enter. Press Ctrl + Tab to return to the **e01ch01WeddingPlanner_LastFirst** workbook.

g. On the **e01ch01WeddingPlanner_LastFirst** workbook, double-click the **Sheet1** worksheet, type Documentation and then press Enter.

h. Right-click the **Documentation** worksheet, and then select **Move or Copy**. Click the **To book:** arrow, select **e01ch01PreferredPartners**, and then click **(move to end)**. Click **Create a copy**, and then click **OK**. Click **Save**, and then close the e01ch01PreferredPartners workbook.

i. On the **e01ch01WeddingPlanner_LastFirst** workbook, double-click the **Sheet3** worksheet, type WeddingPlanner and then press Enter. Right-click the **WeddingPlanner** sheet, point to **Tab Color**, and then select **Purple**.

j. Click the **Documentation** worksheet, click in cell **B20**, type WeddingPlanner and then press Ctrl + Home.

k. Click the **WeddingPlanner** worksheet, and then type the information into the indicated cells as follows.

Data Item	Cell	Value
Wedding Date	B2	7/23/2022
Start Time	D2	3 p
End Time	D3	4 p
Reception Start Time	G2	6 p
Reception End Time	G3	12 a
Total Hours	B5	8
Reception Hours	D5	6
Estimated Guests	B7	325
Piano Player (Hours)	C28	1
String Quartet (Hours)	C29	2
DJ (Hours)	C32	4

l. Click cell **E2**. Point to the border of the active cell, and when the mouse pointer changes, click and hold the left mouse button, drag cell E2 to cell **G7**, and then release the mouse button.

m. Select cell range **F2:G3**, press ⌃Ctrl+X, click cell **H7**, and then press ⌃Ctrl+V.

n. Select cell range **C2:D3**, and then point to the border of the selected range. When the mouse pointer changes to a move pointer, click and hold the left mouse button, and then drag to cell **H4**. Release the mouse button.

o. Select cell range **A2:B2**, press ⌃Ctrl+X, and then click cell **G3** to make it the active cell. Press ⌃Ctrl+V.

p. Select columns **G:I**. On the Home tab, in the Cells group, click the **Format** arrow, and then click **AutoFit Column Width**.

q. Select columns **B:C**, and in the Cells group, click **Format**, and then click **Column Width**. Type **17** in the Column Width box, and then click **OK**.

r. Click the header for column **E**, and then right-click and select **Delete** from the shortcut menu to delete the column. Right-click column **E**, select **Column Width**, type **2** in the Column Width box, and then click **OK**.

s. Press ⌃Ctrl+Home. Select cell range **A1:H1,** and then on the Home tab, in the Alignment group, click **Merge & Center**.

t. Right-click the header for row **1**, select **Row Height**, type **20** in the Row Height box, and then click **OK**.

u. Select cell range **B9:C9**, and then on the Home tab, in the Alignment group, click **Merge & Center**.

v. Select cell range **B34:C34**. On the Home tab, in the Alignment group, click the **Alignment Dialog Box Launcher** ⌐. With the Alignment tab selected, click the **Horizontal** arrow, and then click **Center Across Selection**.

w. Click cell **A9**. On the Home tab, in the Cells group, click the **Insert** arrow, and then click **Insert Sheet Rows** to insert a row.

x. Click **Page Layout view** on the status bar, scroll to the bottom of the worksheet, and click in the left section of the **Add footer**. If necessary, under Header & Footer Tools, click the **Design** tab. In the Header & Footer Elements group, click **File Name**, and then click a cell in the worksheet. Press ⌃Ctrl+Home, and then click **Normal** on the status bar.

y. Click the **Documentation** worksheet. Repeat step x to insert the **File Name** code in the left footer of the Documentation worksheet.

z. Click cell **A8**, and then type today's date in mm/dd/yyyy format. Click cell **B8**, and then type your name in Firstname Lastname format. Click cell **C8**, and then type Completed Ms. Rochelle's initial work; reorganized worksheet to function better as a checklist and then press Ctrl+Enter. In cell **C8**, on the Home tab, in the Alignment group, click **Wrap Text**.

aa. Click and hold the **Documentation** worksheet, and then drag to the right to move the Documentation worksheet to the right of the **WeddingPlanner** worksheet to make it the last worksheet.

bb. On the **Documentation** worksheet, click the **File** tab, and then click **Print**. Click the **Next Page** button to view page 2.

cc. Click the **Orientation** arrow, and then select **Landscape Orientation**. Click the **Scaling** arrow, and then select **Fit All Columns on One Page**. Press Esc to exit Backstage view.

dd. Click the **WeddingPlanner** worksheet, click the **File** tab, and then click **Print**. Click the **Scaling** arrow, and then select **Fit All Columns on One Page**.

ee. Click **Export**, click **Create PDF/XPS Document**, and then click **Create PDF/XPS**. Click **Options**. In the Options dialog box, under Publish what, click **Entire workbook**, and then click **OK**. Navigate to the folder where you are saving your files. In the File name box, type e01ch01WeddingPlanner_LastFirst using your last and first name. Verify **Open file after publishing** is checked, and then click **Publish**. View the pages, and then close the PDF.

ff. Click **Save**, close Excel, and then submit your files as directed by your instructor.

Problem Solve 1

MyLab IT Grader

Student data file needed:

 e01ch01Athletics.xlsx

You will save your files as:

 e01ch01Athletics_LastFirst.xlsx

 e01ch01GolfCartAnalysis_LastFirst.pdf

All Sports Athletics Inventory

General Business

Darin Learn recently opened a small sporting goods store next to the local community college. He wants to use Excel to track supply inventory, the total cost of inventory, and items on back order. Darin has created a workbook containing a list of the products in inventory, a list of items on back order, and a documentation worksheet. You have been asked to enhance the appearance of the worksheets, edit content, insert notes, and improve overall formatting, making the information easier to review and analyze.

a. Open the Excel file, **e01ch01Athletics**. Save your file as e01ch01Athletics_LastFirst using your last and first name.

b. Rename Sheet1 as Inventory and then rename Sheet2 as BackOrders

c. On the **Inventory** worksheet, in cell **A23**, insert the note 4-pack

d. In cell **A17**, edit the contents to read Inventory

e. Wrap the text in the following cell ranges: **B4:L4**, **B10:L10**, **B17:D17**, and **B25:D25**.

f. In cell **A25**, using the Alt and Enter keys, insert a hard return between **Miscellaneous Items**. Remove the space between the two words before inserting a hard return.

g. Insert a column to the left of column **E**. Insert a column to the left of column **J**. Change the width of columns **E** and **J** to 5

h. Copy the formula in cell **D18** through cell **D23**. Copy the formula in cell **D26** through cell **D28**.

i. Drag and drop the contents in the cell range **A25:D28** to cell range **F17:I20**.

j. Merge and center the contents in cell **A1** through the cell range **A1:N1**.

k. Delete row **3**, and then change the color of the **Inventory** worksheet to **Red**.

l. Change the width of the worksheet columns as follows:

Columns **A**, **F**, and **K** to 17

Columns **B**, **C**, **G**, **H**, **L**, and **M** to 8

Columns **D**, **I** and **N** to 10

m. On the **BackOrders** worksheet, apply **Center Across Selection** to cell range **A1:D2**.

n. In cell **C6**, enter Date Ordered as 12/15/22 In cell **D6**, enter the Date to be Received as 12/29/22

o. Select cell range **C6:D6**. Use the fill handle to copy the cell range through **C8:D8**. Use the Auto Fill Options button to copy the dates, not fill the series.

p. Delete **Sheet3**.

q. In Page Layout view, insert the **File Name** code into the left footer of all worksheets in the workbook. Return all worksheets to **Normal** view.

r. On the **Documentation** worksheet, in cell **A8**, type today's date In cell **B8**, type your name in Firstname Lastname format. In cell **C8**, type Formatted Inventory worksheet and in cell **C9**, type Updated the BackOrders worksheet In cell **B20**, type Inventory In cell **B21**, type BackOrders

s. On the **Inventory** and **Documentation** worksheets, set orientation to **Landscape**, and set scaling to **Fit All Columns on One Page**.

Grader Heads Up
In the MyLab IT Grader version of this project, you will not create a PDF.

---

t. Export the entire workbook to PDF. Save the PDF file as e01ch01Athletics_LastFirst

u. Save the workbook, exit Excel, and then submit your files as directed by your instructor.

Critical Thinking

In a business office, workbooks are often shared with team members. Shared workbooks may be edited by more than one person. What are two ways changes to a workbook can be documented?

Perform 1: Perform in Your Career

Student data file needed:

 e01ch01Relocation.xlsx

You will save your files as:

 e01ch01Relocation_LastFirst.xlsx

 e01ch01Relocation_LastFirst.pdf

Relocation

General Business

You accepted a promotion within your company. Now you must put your home up for sale and relocate to another state. Your best friend, Timothy Sweffel, has helped you by creating a workbook with information on recent home sales in your town and surrounding towns. You want to format the data to make it easier to read and print so you can examine the data and determine how to price your home appropriately for a quick sale.

a. Open the Excel file, **e01ch01Relocation**. Save your file as e01ch01Relocation_LastFirst using your last and first name.

b. Rename Sheet1 Homes

c. Rename Sheet2 Features

d. Change the color of the Documentation worksheet to Blue, Accent 1.

e. On the Homes worksheet, wrap the text of cell range A3:O3.

f. On the Features worksheet, wrap the text of cell range A1:G1.

g. Modify the column widths on both worksheets using AutoFit Column Width so that the contents display completely and no column heading names are split incorrectly.

h. On the Features worksheet, insert a row above row 1. In cell A1, type Additional Features

i. Merge and center the data in row 1 across cell range A1:G1.

j. On the Homes worksheet, in cell A1, type Home Sales Comparison

k. Merge and center cell A1 across cell range A1:N1. Change the height of row 1 to 24

l. Change the height of row 2 to 9

m. Insert a column to the left of column C. Change the width of column C to 3

n. In cell G3, add the comment Neighborhoods within 15 miles

o. Add a footer on all worksheets that displays the Page Number in the center of the footer and the File Name in the left footer.

p. On the Homes worksheet, apply a Landscape orientation. Scale to Fit All Columns on One Page. Set rows 1:3 to print on the top of each page.

q. Move the Documentation worksheet to be the last worksheet on the right. Update the Documentation sheet according to your instructor's directions.

r. Export the entire workbook to a PDF using the name e01ch01Relocation_LastFirst Close the PDF.

s. Save the workbook, exit Excel, and then submit your files as directed by your instructor.

Microsoft Excel

Chapter 2 FORMATS, FUNCTIONS, AND FORMULAS

MyLab IT Grader

Finance & Accounting

Prepare Case

Red Bluff Golf Course & Pro Shop Sales Analysis

The Red Bluff Golf Course & Pro Shop sells products ranging from golf clubs and accessories to clothing displaying the club logo. In addition, the pro shop collects fees for rounds of golf and services such as lessons from golf pro John Schilling.

Manager Aleeta Herriott needs to track pro shop sales by category on a day-by-day basis. Sales, at least to some extent, reflect traffic in the pro shop and can be used to help determine staffing requirements on different days of the week. In addition, summary sales data can be compared to inventory investments to determine whether the product mix is optimal, given the demands of the clientele.

Each item or service at the time of sale is recorded in the pro shop point-of-sale (POS) system. At the end of each day, the POS system produces a cash register report with categorized sales for the day. This is the data source of each day's sales for the worksheet. Aleeta has created an initial layout for a sales analysis workbook, but she needs you to finish it.

Sirtravelalot/Shutterstock

Student data files needed:

 e01ch02WeeklySales.xlsx

 e01ch02red_bluff.jpg

You will save your files as:

 e01ch02WeeklySales_LastFirst.xlsx

 e01ch02WeeklySalesFormulas_LastFirst.pdf

Worksheet Formatting

To be of value, information must be communicated effectively. Effective communication of information generally requires the information is formatted in a manner that aids in proper interpretation and understanding.

Some of the most revolutionary ideas in history were initially recorded on a handy scrap of paper, a yellow legal pad, a tape recorder—even a paper napkin. Communication of those ideas generally required that they were presented in a different medium and formatted in a manner that aided other people's understanding. The content may not have changed, but the format of the presentation is important. People are more receptive to well-formatted information because it is easier to understand and to absorb. While accuracy of information is of the utmost importance, of what use is accurate data that is misunderstood? In this section, you will manipulate a worksheet by formatting numbers, aligning and rotating text, changing cell fill color and borders, using built-in cell and table styles, and applying workbook themes.

Format Cells, Cell Ranges, and Worksheets

There are several ways to present information. If different technologies, media, and audiences are considered, a list of more than 50 ways to present information would be easy to produce. The list could include varied communication methods such as books, speeches, websites, tweets, RSS feeds, and bumper stickers. However, an analysis of such a list would reveal generic communication methodologies.

- Oral
- Written narrative
- Tabular
- Graphical

Excel is an application specifically designed to present information in tabular and graphical formats. **Tabular format** is the presentation of text and numbers in tables—essentially organized in labeled columns and numbered rows. **Graphical format** is the presentation of information in charts, graphs, and pictures. Excel facilitates the graphical presentation of information via charts and graphs based on the tabular information in worksheets.

E02.00

SIDE NOTE
Office Updates
Depending on your exact Office version, you may see Open or Open Other Workbooks.

To Get Started

a. Start Excel, click **Open** in the left pane, and then double-click **This PC**. Navigate through the folder structure to the location of your student data files, and then double-click **e01ch02WeeklySales**. If a Security Warning message displays, click the **Enable Editing** button.

b. Click the **File** tab, click **Save As**, and then double-click **This PC**. In the Save As dialog box, navigate to the location where you are saving your project files, and then change the file name to **e01ch02WeeklySales_LastFirst** using your last and first name. Click **Save**.

Number Formatting

Through number formatting, context can be given to numbers, reducing the need for text labeling, such as for date and/or time values. Most of the world's currencies can be represented in Excel through number formatting. Financial numbers, scientific numbers, percentages, dates, times, and so on all have special formatting requirements and can be properly displayed in a worksheet. The ability to manipulate and properly display many different types of numeric information is a feature that makes Excel an incredibly powerful and ubiquitously popular application.

Numbers can be formatted in many ways in Excel. The most common formats are shown in Table 1.

Format Name	Ribbon	Number Format List	Keyboard Shortcut	Example
Accounting	$ ▾	(icon)		$ (1,234.00)
Comma*	,		Ctrl + Shift + !	(1,234.00)
Currency		(icon)		−1,234.00
			Ctrl + Shift + $	($1,234.00)
General		123	Ctrl + Shift + ~	−1234
Number		General ▾		−1234.00
Percentage	%	%	Ctrl + Shift + %	−7.00%
Short Date		(icon)		6/28/2022
			Ctrl + Shift + #	28-Jun-22
Time		(icon)		6:00:00 PM
			Ctrl + Shift + @	6:00 PM

*Comma format is the Accounting format without a currency symbol.

Table 1   Common number formats

Your manager, Aleeta Herriott, has asked you to format the WeeklySales worksheet so the data is easier to understand. You think using simple Excel formatting such as the Accounting Number Format, Currency Format, Comma Style, Percent Style, and Decimals will make the worksheet more readable. In this exercise, you will format numbers on the WeeklySales worksheet.

 **E02.01**

SIDE NOTE
Pin the Ribbon
If your ribbon is collapsed, pin your ribbon open. Click the Home tab, and then, in the lower right-hand corner of the ribbon, click Pin the ribbon ⊟.

SIDE NOTE
Accounting Number Format
The Accounting Number Format also formats a cell with a comma at the thousand place and two decimal places.

To Format Numbers

a. On the WeeklySales worksheet, select cell range **B6:H6**. Click the Home tab, and then, in the Number group, click **Accounting Number Format** $ ▾. The top row of numbers is often formatted with a currency symbol to indicate that subsequent values are currency as well.

> **Troubleshooting**
> If any of the cells you just formatted display a series of number signs (#), select the cell(s), and in the Cells group, click Format ⊞, and then, under Cell Size, click AutoFit Column Width.

b. Select cell range **B7:H8**, and then on the Home tab, in the Number group, click **Comma Style** ,.

c. Select cell range **C29:C30**, press and hold Ctrl, click cell **C33**, and then select cell range **C36:C38**. On the Home tab, in the Number group, click **Percent Style** %, and then, in the Number group, click **Increase Decimal** once.

SIDE NOTE

Comma Style

The Comma Style is simply the Accounting Number Format without a monetary symbol.

d. Click cell **C31**, press Ctrl, and then click **C34**. In the Number group, click the **Number Format** arrow General , and then select **More Number Formats**. The Format Cells dialog box is displayed. If necessary, click the **Number** tab. Under Category, select **Currency**.

e. Double-click the Decimal places box, and type **0**

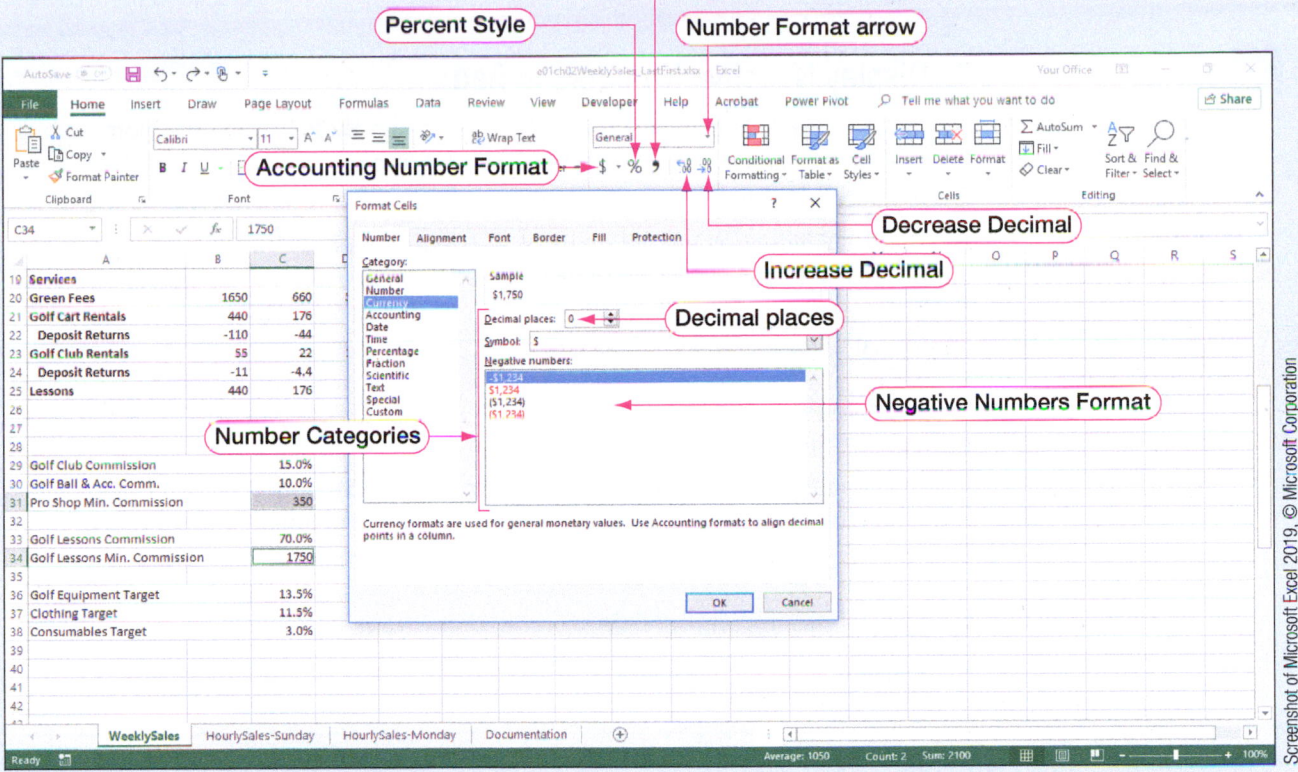

Figure 1   Number Format options

f. Click **OK**, and then **Save** 💾 the workbook.

REAL WORLD ADVICE   **Accounting Number Format versus Currency Number Format**

The Accounting and Currency number formats are both intended for monetary values.
The Accounting format has the following characteristics.

- Negative numbers are enclosed in parentheses.
- The currency symbol is aligned to the left side of the cell.
- Zero values are displayed as a long dash (—) aligned at the decimal position.
- The decimal place is aligned.

The Currency format has the following characteristics.

- Negative numbers can be identified with a dash (-) or parentheses or displayed in red. The red color option can be combined with parentheses as well.
- The currency symbol is placed directly left of the value.
- Zero values are displayed as 0 with zeroes in each decimal place.

It is important to understand the differences so you can make intelligent formatting decisions. For appearance purposes, best practice is to try to use only the currency *or* only the accounting format in the same table or with numbers that are next to one another.

Displaying Negative Values and Color

Negative numbers often require more than parentheses or a hyphen to call attention to the fact that a value is less than zero. The phrase *in the red* is often used to describe financial values that are less than zero, so, not surprisingly, Excel makes it very easy to display negative numbers in a red font color.

To draw attention to negative numbers, in this exercise you will format the worksheet to display negative numbers in red.

 E02.02

SIDE NOTE

Alternate Method
To launch the Format Cells dialog box, you can also right-click the number(s) you wish to format and select Format Cells from the menu.

To Display Negative Numbers in Red

a. On the WeeklySales worksheet, select cell range **B20:H22**. On the Home tab, in the Number group, click the **Number Format** arrow General , and then select **More Number Formats**.

b. Under Category, select **Number**. If necessary, type a 2 in the Decimal places box. Click to select **Use 1000 Separator (,)**. Under Negative numbers, select the **red negative number format** (1,234.10), and then click **OK**. You will change the format of rows 23:25 in a later exercise.

> **Troubleshooting**
> If the negative numbers in B20:H22 are not displayed in red, you didn't select the correct negative number format. Press Ctrl+Z, and repeat steps a and b.

c. Save 💾 the workbook.

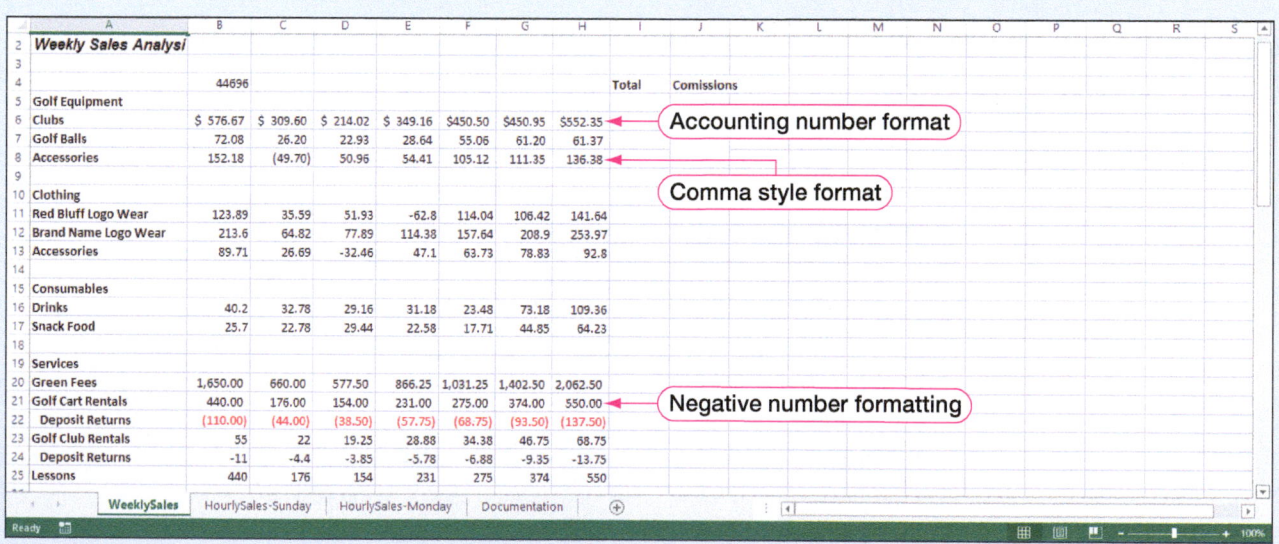

Figure 2 Formatted numbers

SS **CONSIDER THIS** | **Accessibility and Color Blindness**

Approximately 8% to 12% of men of European descent are color-blind. This does not mean they cannot see any color, but for about 99% of them, it means they have trouble distinguishing between reds and greens. How should this information affect the way you format your worksheets?

Formatting Date and Time

Excel stores a date and time as a number in which the digits to the left of the decimal place are the number of complete days since January 1, 1900, inclusive. The right side of the decimal place is the decimal portion of the current day, which represents the current time. This date system allows Excel to use dates in calculations. For example, if you add 7 to today's date, the result is the date one week in the future.

While this is useful for computer systems and applications such as Excel, people have not been taught to interpret time in this manner, so unformatted date and time values—those displayed in General format—mean little or nothing to us. Date and time formatting allows Excel date and time values to be displayed in a fashion that allows human interpretation. A heading that identifies a column as date values gives context to the information, but in the case of date information, without proper formatting, it is for the most part unusable by the reader.

In this exercise, you will format cells with date and time formats.

 **E02.03**

To Format a Cell or Cell Range as a Date or Time

a. On the WeeklySales worksheet, click cell **B4**; this is an unformatted date in Excel. On the Home tab, and in the Number group, click the **Number Format** arrow [General ▾], and then select **Short Date**. Using the fill handle, drag to the right until the border around the active cell expands to include cell range **B4:H4**. The date in cell B4 has been incremented by one day in each of the cells in C4:H4.

Notice the series of number (#) signs in F4:H4. This indicates the columns are not wide enough to display the data.

	A	B	C	D	E	F	G	H	I	J	K	L	M	N	O	P	Q	R	S
2	Weekly Sales Analysi																		
3																			
4		5/15/2022	5/16/2022	5/17/2022	5/18/2022	########	########	########	Total		Comissions				#### displayed due to column width				
5	Golf Equipment																		
6	Clubs	$ 576.67	$ 309.60	$ 214.02	$ 349.16	$450.50	$450.95	$552.35											
7	Golf Balls	72.08	26.20	22.93	28.64	55.06	61.20	61.37											
8	Accessories	152.18	(49.70)	50.96	54.41	105.12	111.35	136.38											
9																			
10	Clothing																		
11	Red Bluff Logo Wear	123.89	35.59	51.93	-62.8	114.04	106.42	141.64											
12	Brand Name Logo Wear	213.6	64.82	77.89	114.38	157.64	208.9	253.97											
13	Accessories	89.71	26.69	-32.46	47.1	63.73	78.83	92.8											
14																			
15	Consumables																		
16	Drinks	40.2	32.78	29.16	31.18	23.48	73.18	109.36											
17	Snack Food	25.7	22.78	29.44	22.58	17.71	44.85	64.23											
18																			
19	Services																		
20	Green Fees	1,650.00	660.00	577.50	866.25	1,031.25	1,402.50	2,062.50											
21	Golf Cart Rentals	440.00	176.00	154.00	231.00	275.00	374.00	550.00											
22	Deposit Returns	(110.00)	(44.00)	(38.50)	(57.75)	(68.75)	(93.50)	(137.50)											
23	Golf Club Rentals	55	22	19.25	28.88	34.38	46.75	68.75											

Figure 3 Display #### for column width

b. Select columns **F:H**. On the Home tab, in the Cells group, click **Format** ⊞, and then select **AutoFit Column Width**. Next you want to format numbers to appropriately reflect time.

c. Click the **HourlySales-Sunday** worksheet. Select cell range **A6:A7**. In the Number group, click the **Number Format** arrow [General ▾].

Notice the Time format includes hours, minutes, and seconds. You have no need to display seconds, so you need to use the Format Cells dialog box to access additional time formats.

d. Select **More Number Formats**. Under Category, select **Time**. In the Type box, select **1:30 PM**.

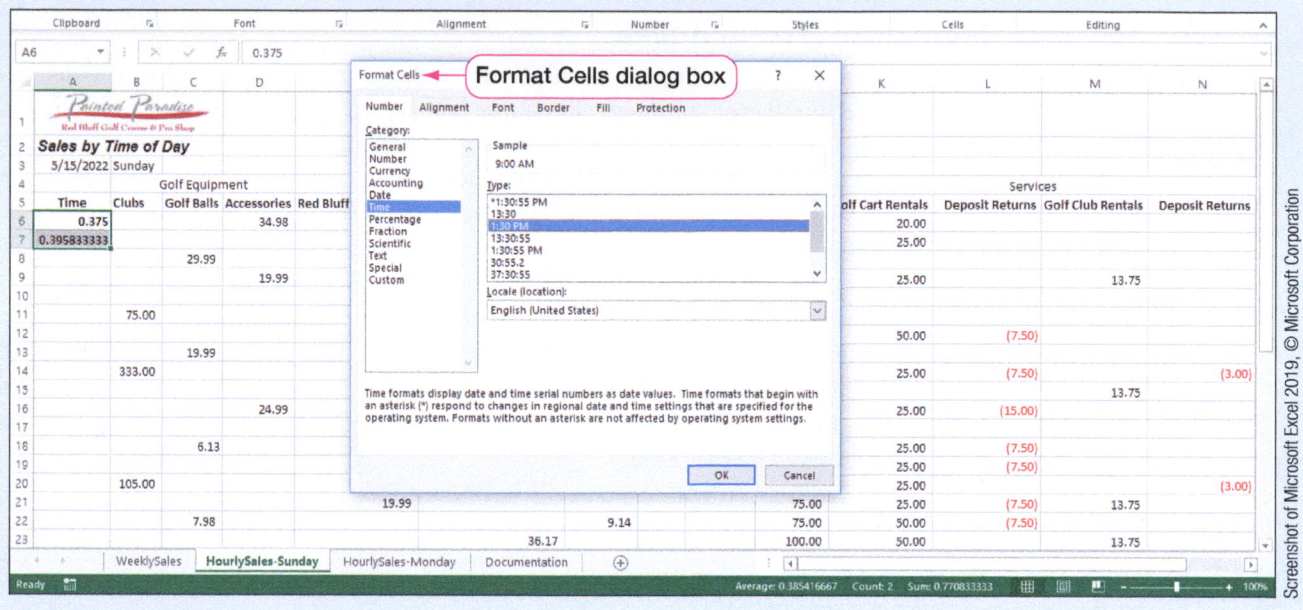

Figure 4 Format Cells dialog box

e. Click **OK**. With A6:A7 still selected, click and hold the **fill handle**, and then drag the fill handle to copy cells through cell **A28**.

The series in cell range A6:A7 has been expanded through cell A28. Note each cell is incremented by 30 minutes from the cell above. The 30-minute increment was determined by the time difference between cells A6 and A7. That is why you selected two cells before using AutoFill in cell range A6:A28.

f. **Save** the workbook.

CONSIDER THIS | **Time Values**

Excel stores time values as decimal portions of one day as follows.

- 1 = 1 day = 1,440 minutes
- .1 = 144 minutes = 2:24 AM
- .01 = 14.4 minutes = 12:14:24 AM

For this system to work in conjunction with date values, 0 and 1 are displayed as equivalent time values: 12:00:00 AM. However once a time value increases to 1, the date is incremented by 1 day and time reverts to 0. Would you be able to adapt if your digital watch or cell phone showed time the way Excel stores it? Would there be any advantages if time were displayed and handled in this format? What about date values?

Aligning Cell Content

Cell alignment allows cell content to be left-aligned, centered, and right-aligned on the horizontal axis, as well as top-aligned, middle-aligned, and bottom-aligned on the vertical axis. Certain cell formats are aligned left or right by **default**—a setting that is automatically in place unless you specify otherwise. Number formats are right-aligned, including date and time formats. Text formatting aligns cell contents to the left by default. For the most part, horizontal alignment changes will be made to alphabetic content such as titles, headings, and labels.

To improve the appearance of the data labels, in this exercise you will align text on the WeeklySales worksheet.

E02.04

To Align Text

a. Click the **WeeklySales** worksheet, and select cell range **A5:A25**.

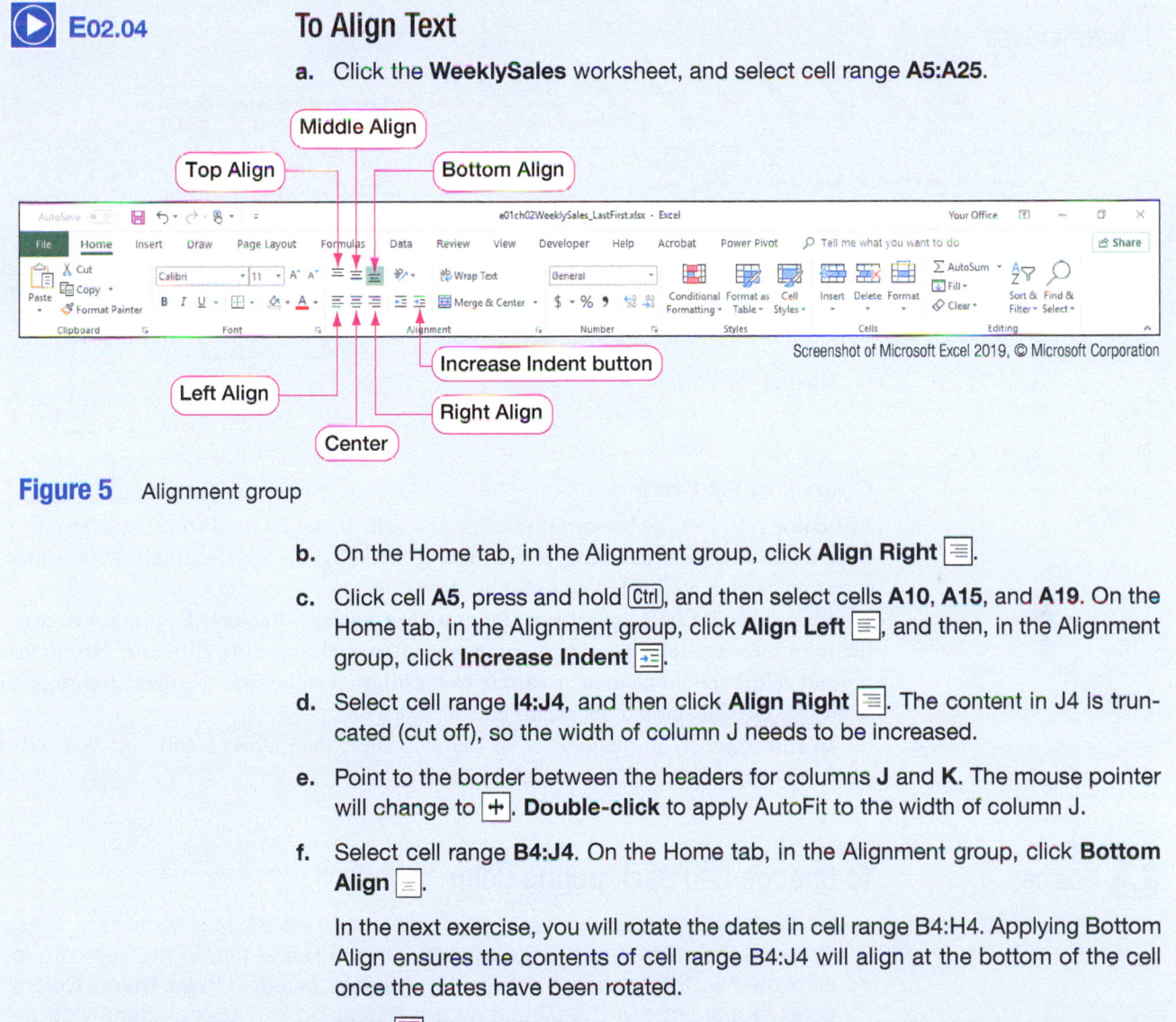

Figure 5 Alignment group

b. On the Home tab, in the Alignment group, click **Align Right** ▤.

c. Click cell **A5**, press and hold Ctrl, and then select cells **A10**, **A15**, and **A19**. On the Home tab, in the Alignment group, click **Align Left** ▤, and then, in the Alignment group, click **Increase Indent** ▤.

d. Select cell range **I4:J4**, and then click **Align Right** ▤. The content in J4 is truncated (cut off), so the width of column J needs to be increased.

e. Point to the border between the headers for columns **J** and **K**. The mouse pointer will change to ╋. **Double-click** to apply AutoFit to the width of column J.

f. Select cell range **B4:J4**. On the Home tab, in the Alignment group, click **Bottom Align** ▤.

   In the next exercise, you will rotate the dates in cell range B4:H4. Applying Bottom Align ensures the contents of cell range B4:J4 will align at the bottom of the cell once the dates have been rotated.

g. **Save** 🖫 the workbook.

Setting Content Orientation

Sometimes it is helpful to display information at an angle or even vertically rather than in the standard horizontal left to right orientation. This is particularly true for tabular information. When you are formatting charts and graphs, rotating textual content can be very helpful in presenting information in a space-efficient yet readable manner.

You think the dates on the WeeklySales worksheet appear too close to one another. In this exercise, you will rotate text on the WeeklySales worksheet.

 **E02.05**

To Rotate Text

a. On the WeeklySales worksheet, select cell range **B4:J4** if necessary.

b. On the Home tab, in the Alignment group, click **Orientation** .

c. Select **Angle Counterclockwise**.

d. On the Home tab, in the Alignment group, click **Center** , and then, in the Font group, click **Bold** .

Figure 6 Orientation list

Screenshot of Microsoft Excel 2019, © Microsoft Corporation

e. Save the workbook.

Changing Fill Color

Fill color refers to the background color of a cell. It can be used to categorize information, to band rows or columns as a means of assisting the reader to follow information across or down a worksheet, or to highlight values.

It is generally best practice to use muted or pastel fill colors. Bright colors are difficult to view for long periods of time and often make reading difficult. Bright background colors should be used sparingly to highlight a value that requires attention, such as a value outside normal operating parameters.

In this exercise, to make some of the worksheet data labels stand out, you will fill cells and cell ranges with background color.

 **E02.06**

To Change Cell Background Color

a. On the WeeklySales worksheet, select the cell range **B4:J4** if necessary. Press Ctrl, and then select cell range **A5:A25**. On the Home tab, in the Font group, click the **Fill Color** arrow to display the color palette. Under Theme Colors, point to any color in the palette, and a ScreenTip will appear identifying the color name.

b. Select **Gold, Accent 4, Lighter 40%** (eighth column, fourth row).

c. Click cell **A4**. Click **Fill Color** .

Notice that the fill color applied in step b is now applied to A4 without having to click the Fill Color arrow.

d. Click cell **A9**, press Ctrl, and then select cells **A14** and **A18**. On the Home tab, in the Font group, click the **Fill Color** arrow , and then select **No Fill**.

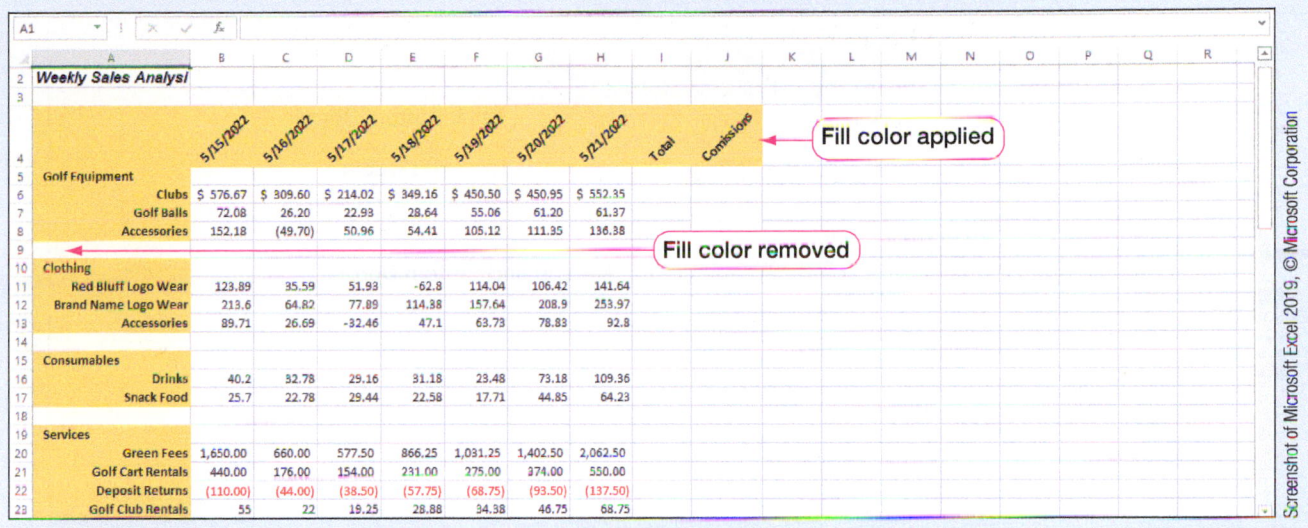

Figure 7 Theme colors

    e. **Save**  the workbook.

Adding Cell Borders

In the previous exercise, you changed the background color in a range of cells. When the background color is changed for a range of contiguous cells, cell borders are no longer visible. If it would be preferable to have visible cell borders, cell borders can be formatted to make them visible.

    In this exercise, on the WeeklySales worksheet, you want to have the worksheet total rows identified, so you have decided to format the cells using borders.

E02.07

SIDE NOTE

Hide the Ribbon

Double-click the Home tab to hide the ribbon and see more of your worksheet. Double-click the Home tab again to unhide the ribbon.

To Format Cell Borders

a. On the WeeklySales worksheet, select cell range **B4:J4**, press Ctrl, and then select cell range **A5:A25**.

b. On the Home tab, in the Font group, click the **Borders** arrow.

> **Troubleshooting**
>
> The Borders button may look different in your Excel application window than it does when referenced in this text; this is because the Borders button in the Font group of the Home tab displays the last border setting applied.

c. In the Borders list, select **All Borders**.

d. Click cell **A5**, press Ctrl, and then select cells **A10**, **A15**, and **A19**. On the Home tab, in the Font group, click the **Borders** arrow, and then, in the Borders list, select **Thick Bottom Border**.

e. Click cell **J9**, click the **Borders** arrow, and then select **Top and Double Bottom Border**.

f. Select cell range **B9:I9**, press Ctrl, and then select cell ranges **B14:I14**, **B18:I18**, and **B26:I26**. Click the **Borders** arrow, and then select **Top and Bottom Border**.

g. Select cell range **B27:I27**, click the Borders arrow, and then select **Bottom Double Border**.

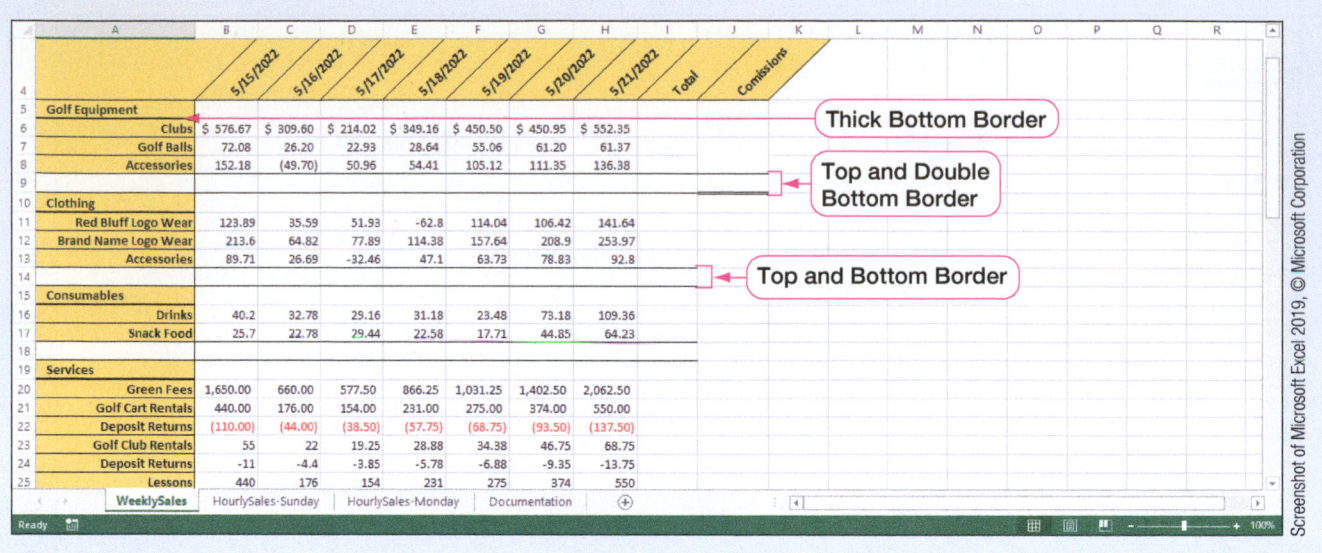

Figure 8 Borders list

h. **Save** 💾 the workbook.

Screenshot of Microsoft Excel 2019, © Microsoft Corporation

REAL WORLD ADVICE | **Formatting—Less Is More**

Too much formatting results in a worksheet that is difficult to look at, is difficult to read, and conveys a sense that the designer lacked a plan. Here are some formatting guidelines.

- Format for a reason, not just for appearances.

- Use at most three fonts in a worksheet. Use each font for a purpose, such as to differentiate titles.

- Use color only to assist in readability, categorization, or identification purposes. For example, use organization colors for titles, use bright colors to highlight small details, and use background colors for categorization.

- Background colors should be pale, pastel colors. Bright background colors are tiring for the reader and can become painful to look at after a while.

- Special characters such as the dollar sign ($) should be applied only as necessary. A dollar sign in the first value of a column of numbers is often sufficient to identify its values as monetary. Then format subtotals and totals with a dollar sign to differentiate them.

Copying Formats

Formatting a cell can consist of several steps involving fonts, colors, sizes, borders, alignment, and so on. You gain a significant efficiency advantage by reusing your work. Once a cell has been formatted properly, you can apply the formatting properties to other cells. Copying formats from one cell to another saves a great deal of time.

Format Painter 🖌 is a tool that enables a copy of the format of objects, such as text or pictures, to other objects. To use the Format Painter, simply select the cell that is the source of the format you want to copy, click the Format Painter in the Clipboard group on the Home tab, and then select the cell or range of cells you want to "paint" with the source cell's formatting. To paint a format to more than one nonadjacent cell, you can double-click Format Painter and then select nonadjacent cells. Once you have finished applying the format to nonadjacent cells, press ESC or click the Format Painter again to toggle off the feature.

In this exercise, to save time formatting the WeeklySales worksheet, you will use the Format Painter to copy formats.

 E02.08

SIDE NOTE
How to Use the Format Painter Multiple Times
Double-click the Format Painter, and it will remain active until you click it again or press Esc.

To Use the Format Painter to Copy Formats

a. On the WeeklySales worksheet, click cell **B22**, and then, on the Home tab, in the Clipboard group, click **Format Painter**. The mouse pointer will change to. Select cell range **B23:H25**.

b. Click cell **B6**, double-click **Format Painter**, and then select cell range **B11:H11**. Select cell range **B16:H16**, select cell range **B20:H20**, and then click Format Painter to toggle it off.

c. On the Home tab, in the Cell group, click **Format**, and then select **AutoFit Column Width**.

d. **Save** the workbook.

Using Paste Options/Paste Special

When a cell is copied to the Clipboard, there is much more than a simple value ready to be pasted to another location. Formats, formulas, and values are all copied and can be selectively pasted to other locations in a workbook.

Different paste options are shown in Table 2. Although there are a large number of paste options, most worksheet activities require only a few of these options. Paste, Paste Formatting, and Paste Values will accomplish most of what you will need to do. The various paste options are additive, in that you can first paste a value to a copied cell and then paste the format from the copied cell, after which you could paste the formula from the copied cell.

Button	Function	Pastes
	Paste	All content from the Clipboard to a cell
	Formatting	Only the formatting from the Clipboard to a cell
	Values	Only the value from the Clipboard to a cell
	Formulas	Only the formula from the Clipboard to a cell
	Paste Link	A link (e.g., =A25) to the source cell from the Clipboard to a cell
	Transpose	A range of cells to a new range of cells with columns and rows switched

Table 2 Paste options

In this exercise, you will use the Paste Options to copy formats in the WeeklySales worksheet.

 E02.09

To Use Paste Options to Copy Formats

a. On the WeeklySales worksheet, click cell **B7**. On the Home tab, in the Clipboard group, click **Copy** to copy cell B7 to the Clipboard. Select cell range **B12:H13**, press Ctrl, and then select cell range **B17:H17**.

b. Right-click the selected range. The shortcut menu is displayed, which includes options that are determined by the context of the object that is the focus of the right-click.

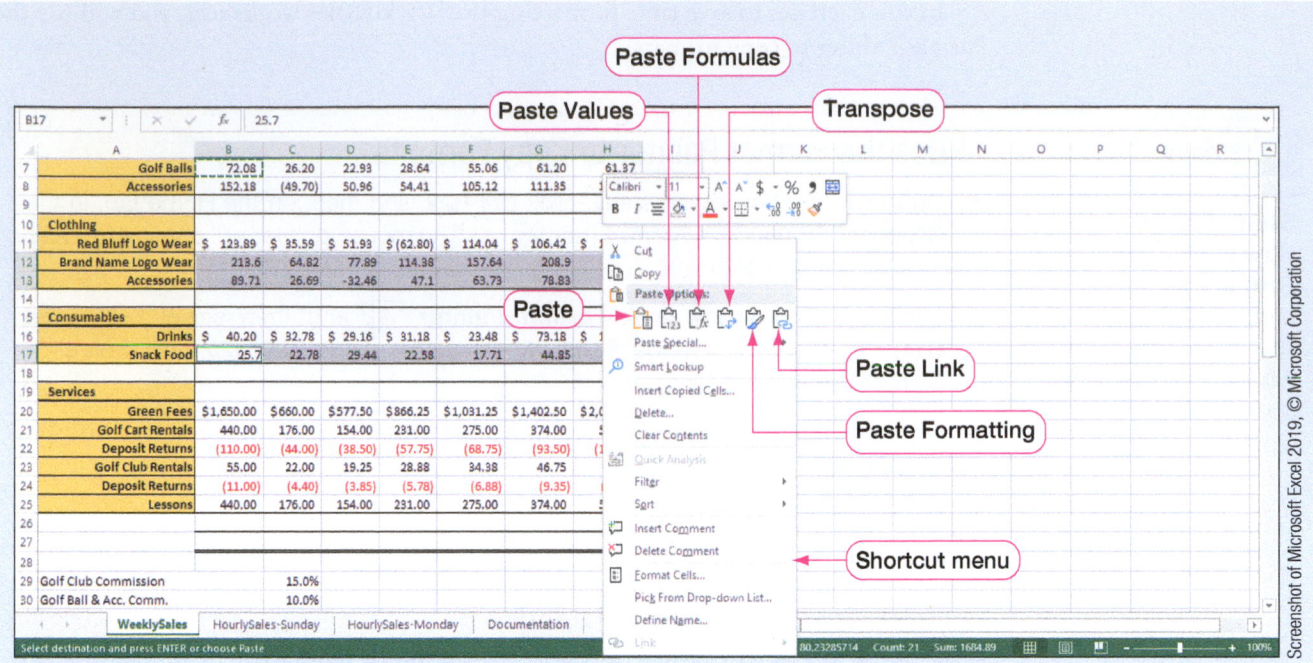

Figure 9 Paste Options menu

MAC SIDE NOTE
Paste Options
Control+click to display
the shortcut menu and
click Paste Special.

c. Point to each button on the Paste Options menu and notice what happens in the selected cell range.

d. On the Paste Options menu, click **Formatting** 📝, and then press ⎋ to clear the Clipboard.

e. **Save** 💾 the workbook.

Checking the Spelling of a Worksheet

Not only should worksheets be professionally formatted, they should also contain correct spelling. Even professionally formatted worksheets can be confusing if they contain misspelled words or phrases. Unlike other Microsoft applications such as Word, Outlook, or PowerPoint, by default Microsoft Excel does not automatically check for misspelled text. Also, Excel does not have a grammar checker, as Word, Outlook, and PowerPoint do.

If a single cell is selected, Excel begins checking the spelling from the active cell. Excel checks spelling only on the active worksheet, not the entire workbook, but it will spell check the entire worksheet, including any comments, page headers, footers, and charts. If you have a range of cells selected, Excel will check spelling only on the range of cells, not the entire worksheet. There are several ways to check the spelling of a worksheet. On the Review tab, in the Proofing group, click the Spelling button. For easy reference, the Spelling 🔤 command can be added to the Quick Access Toolbar.

In this exercise, you will check the spelling on the WeeklySales worksheet.

 **E02.10**

SIDE NOTE
AutoCorrect
You can use the Excel AutoCorrect feature to correct typos or add words to the dictionary. Select File, Options, Proofing, and AutoCorrect Options.

To Check Spelling

a. On the WeeklySales worksheet, press Ctrl + Home to make **A1** the active cell.

b. Click the **Review** tab, and then in the Proofing group, click **Spelling**.

c. The first spelling error was found, and the Spelling dialog box is displayed.

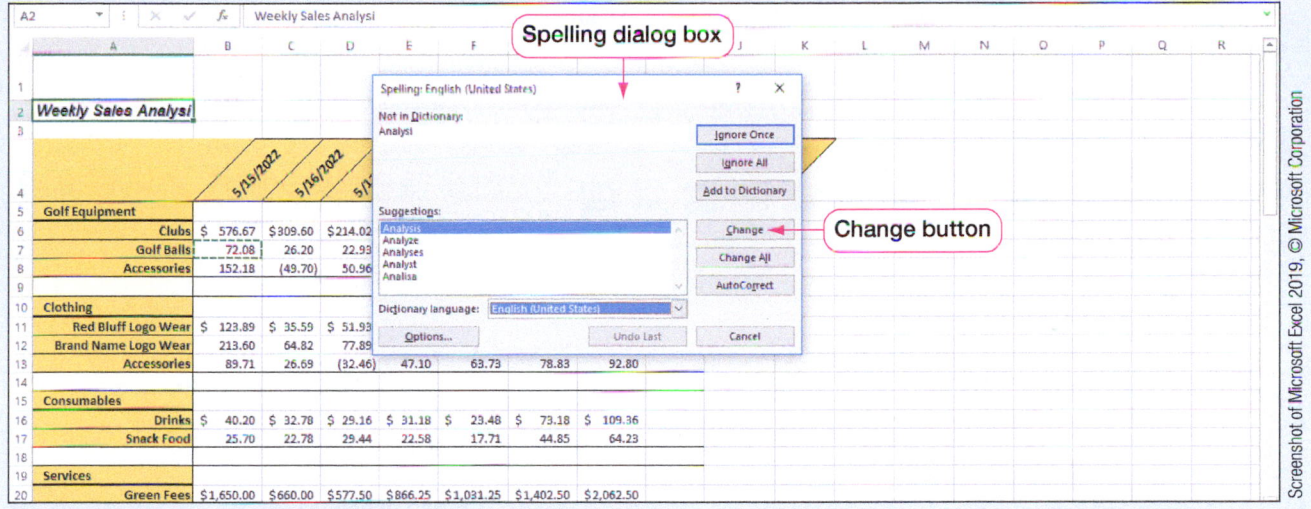

Figure 10   Spelling dialog box

SIDE NOTE
Quick Access Spelling
To add the Spelling button to the Quick Access Toolbar, click the Customize Quick Access Toolbar arrow, and select Spelling.

d. Verify **Analysis** is selected in the Suggestions box, and then click **Change**.

e. A second spelling error was found. Verify **Commissions** is selected in the Suggestions box, and then click **Change**. There were only two spelling errors on this worksheet; therefore, the spell check is finished.

f. Click **OK**, and then **Save** 🖫 the workbook.

SIDE NOTE
Alternate Method
You can also press the F7 key to begin to spell check a worksheet.

Inserting a Picture

Adding pictures to a worksheet can add visual interest and can also help with the branding of your company. Painted Paradise Resort & Spa has logos for each of its core businesses. All documents must include the appropriate logo whenever possible. Excel allows images, such as logos, to be inserted into a worksheet. Images are not contained in a cell, as data is, but can be sized to fit cell borders by using the Snap to Grid feature.

In this exercise, you will insert an image into a worksheet.

 **E02.11**

MAC SIDE NOTE
Inserting Pictures
Click Pictures, then choose Picture from File. Use the Picture Format tab.

To Insert an Image into a Worksheet

a. On the WeeklySales worksheet, click cell **A1**.

b. Click the **Insert** tab, and then, in the Illustrations group, click **Pictures**. In the Insert Picture dialog box, navigate to the location where your student data files are stored, click **e01ch02red_bluff.jpg**, and then click **Insert**.

c. Click the **Picture Tools Format** tab if necessary, and then, in the Arrange group, click **Align Objects**. If Snap to Grid is not selected—it does not have a border around it as shown around View Gridlines—then select **Snap to Grid**.

Figure 11 Insert a picture and toggle on Snap to Grid

d. Click and hold the right horizontal sizing handle, and then drag the edge of the logo to the left until it snaps to the border between columns **B** and **C**. Click and hold the bottom vertical sizing handle, and then drag the bottom edge of the logo up until it snaps to the border between rows **1** and **2**. Click cell **B6** to deselect the picture.

e. **Save** the workbook.

Using Built-In Cell Styles

Built-in cell styles are predefined and named combinations of cell and content formatting properties that can be applied to a cell or range of cells to define several formatting properties at once. A built-in cell style can set the font, font size and color, number format, background color, borders, and alignment with just a few clicks of the mouse. Built-in cell styles allow for rapid, consistent, and accurate changes to the appearance of a workbook with very little effort.

To change the appearance of the HourlySales-Sunday worksheet, in this exercise you will apply built-in cell styles on the HourlySales-Sunday worksheet.

 **E02.12**

To Apply Built-In Cell Styles

a. Click the **HourlySales-Sunday** worksheet, and then click the **Home** tab.

b. Click cell **B4**, press Ctrl, and then select cell **H4**.

c. On the Home tab, in the Styles group, click **Cell Styles** 🗔. The Cell Styles gallery appears.

> ### Troubleshooting
> If you do not see the Cell Styles button 🗔, it may be that your screen has a different resolution and the Cell Styles button has been expanded.

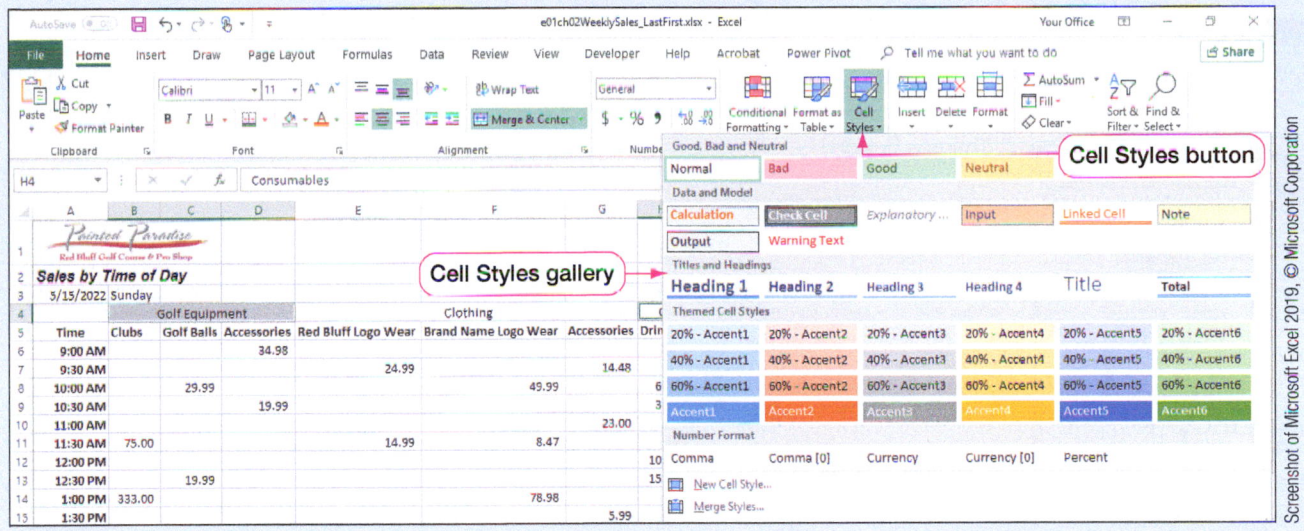

Figure 12 Cell Styles gallery

Screenshot of Microsoft Excel 2019, © Microsoft Corporation

> **SIDE NOTE**
>
> **Multiple Styles Can Be Applied to One Cell**
>
> The final appearance of the cell is determined by the order in which styles are applied.

d. Under Themed Cell Styles, click **20% - Accent1**.

e. Click cell **E4**, press Ctrl, and then select cell **J4**. In the Styles group, click **Cell Styles**, and then select **40% - Accent1**.

f. Select cell range **A3:B3**, press Ctrl, select cell range **B4:O5**, and then select **A5:A33**.

g. On the Home tab, in the Styles group, click **Cell Styles**, and then, under Titles and Headings, select **Heading 4**. Click cell **B6**.

Notice in cell range B4:O4, the Accent1 cell background colors have not changed.

h. Select cell range **B29:O29**, and on the Home tab, in the Styles group, click **Cell Styles**, and then, under Titles and Headings, select **Total**.

i. Press Ctrl+Home, and then click **Save** 🗔.

Changing Themes

A **theme** is a collection of fonts, styles, colors, and effects associated with a theme name that enables you to create professional, color-coordinated documents quickly. The default theme—the theme that is automatically applied unless you specify otherwise—is the Office theme.

Changing the assigned theme is a way to very quickly change the appearance of the worksheets in your workbook. When a different workbook theme is applied, the built-in cell styles in the Styles group on the Home tab change to reflect the new workbook theme. Applying a workbook theme ensures a consistent, well-designed look throughout your workbook.

In this exercise, to ensure all the worksheets in the WeeklySales workbook have the same formatting features, you will apply a theme to the workbook.

 **E02.13**

To Change the Workbook Theme

a. On the HourlySales-Sunday worksheet, click the **Page Layout** tab, and then, in the Themes group, click **Themes**. The Themes gallery is displayed.

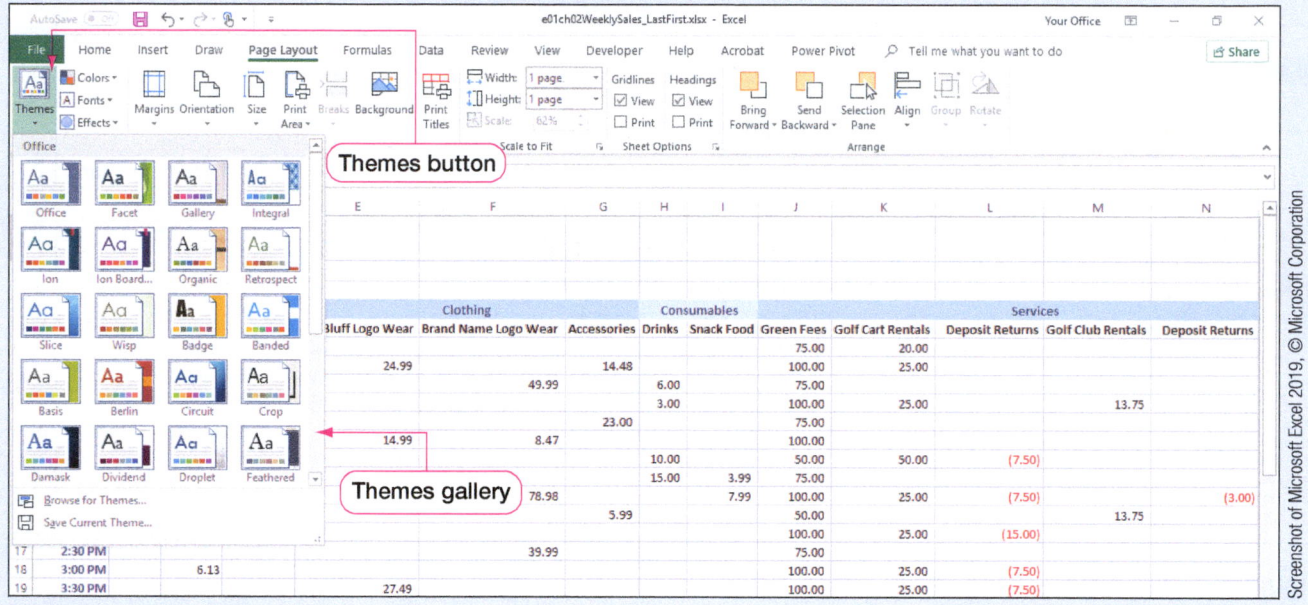

Figure 13 Themes gallery

b. Scroll down, and then select the **Parallax** built-in theme.

Note you may need to click a cell before the font name changes. Any cell that was assigned a cell style now reflects the corresponding cell style in the Parallax theme. For example, click the Home tab, and see that the default font has changed to Corbel.

c. Click the **HourlySales-Monday** worksheet. Note the Parallax theme has been applied to this worksheet as well as the HourlySales-Sunday worksheet.

d. On the Page Layout tab in the Themes group, click **Themes**, and then select the **Headlines** theme.

Note that themes affect the entire workbook. A theme cannot be selectively applied to individual worksheets in a workbook.

e. Click the **WeeklySales** worksheet, and then click the **Home** tab.

Notice the background colors that were set by using cell formatting are also affected by the new workbook theme. Also notice for any cell in which a font was not explicitly set, the font has changed to Corbel.

f. **Save** 💾 the workbook.

g. If you need to take a break before finishing this chapter, now is a good time.

REAL WORLD ADVICE

Formatting Does Not Change the Data Value, but Formatting Can Make Information More Valuable

Formatting affects how information is displayed and understood. It does not change the value stored in a cell. Special formatting characters such as the dollar sign ($) and comma (,) are not stored with values, but they make financial values easier to read and to understand. Formatting helps to turn data into information.

The next time you are adding formatting to a worksheet, ask yourself, "Does this formatting make my worksheet easier to understand?" or "Does this formatting add value in other ways?" such as confirming your organizational identity or its look and feel. If the answer to both questions is "No," maybe you should reconsider.

Remember formatting does not change a data value, but it certainly can add information value. If formatting does not add value, it is likely unnecessary and may detract from the overall value of your worksheet. Consider your formatting decisions carefully.

Creating Information for Decision Making

In Excel, new information is most often produced using formulas and functions to make calculations against data in the workbook. Often, the objective is to improve decision making by providing additional information. In this section, you will manipulate data using functions and formulas, and you will add information using conditional formatting to highlight or categorize information based on problem-specific parameters.

Create Information with Formulas

A **formula** performs mathematical calculations using information in the active worksheet and other worksheets to calculate new values; formulas can contain cell references, constants, functions, and mathematical operators. Formulas in Excel have a very specific syntax. In Excel, formulas always begin with an equal sign (=). Formulas can contain references to specific cells that contain information; a **constant**, which is a number that never changes, such as a number that is typed into a cell; **mathematical operators** such as ( ), +, −, *, /, and ^; and functions. Cells that contain formulas can be treated like any other worksheet cell. They can be referenced, edited, formatted, copied, and pasted.

A **cell reference** refers to a particular cell or range of cells within a formula or function instead of a value. If a formula contains a cell reference, the cell reference in the formula changes when the formula is copied and then pasted into a new location. The new cell reference reflects a new location relative to the old location. This is called a relative cell reference. In a **relative cell reference**, the default reference in a formula to a cell address will automatically adjust when the formula is copied or extended to other cells; the cell being referenced changes relative to the placement of the formula.

For example, as shown in Figure 14, when a formula is copied one column to the right, the cell references in the formula change to reflect the new cell destination. Consequently, the reference to cell A1 changes to cell B1 and the reference to cell B2 changes to cell C2 when the formula is copied one column to the right. Note that the column and row numbers of the cells that contain the formulas are not shown in Figure 14. The active cell address does not matter in relative addressing. All that matters is the relative shift in columns and rows from source to destination and the cell references in the formula.

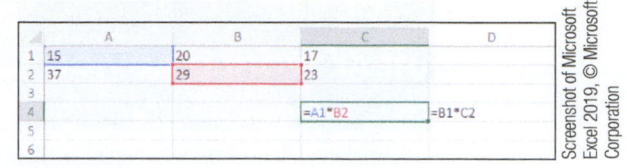

Screenshot of Microsoft Excel 2019, © Microsoft Corporation

Figure 14 Relative referencing when copying a formula

Relative cell references allow you to reuse formulas in a well-designed worksheet. You can enter a formula once and use it many times without having to reenter it in each location and change the cell references. Simply copy the formula and paste it to a new location.

Further, relative references adjust formulas to ensure correctness when the structure of the worksheet changes. If a column is inserted to the left of a cell referenced in a formula or a row is inserted above a cell referenced in a formula, the cells referenced by the formula will be adjusted to ensure the formula still references the same relative locations.

Using Operators

Excel formulas are constructed by using basic mathematical operators very similar to those used in everyday mathematics and the same as those used in most programming languages. Table 3 contains the mathematical operators recognized in Excel.

Operation	Operator	Example	Formula Entered in Current Cell
Addition	+	=B4+B5	Assign the sum of B4 and B5 to the current cell.
Subtraction	-	=B5-B4	Assign the difference of B4 and B5 to the current cell.
Multiplication	*	=B5*3.14	Assign B5 multiplied by 3.14 to the current cell.
Division	/	=B5/B4	Assign the result of dividing B5 by B4 to the current cell.
Exponentiation	^	=B4^2	Assign the square of B4 to the current cell.

Table 3 Mathematical operators in Excel

Applying Order of Operations

The **order of operations** is the order in which Excel processes calculations in a formula that contains more than one operator. Mathematical operations execute in a specific order, which can be remembered by using the mnemonic PEMDAS.

- (P) Parentheses
- (E) Exponentiation
- (M) Multiplication or (D) Division
- (A) Addition or (S) Subtraction

Excel scans a formula from left to right while performing calculations using the above order of operation rules. Thus, you can control which part of a calculation is performed first by enclosing parts of a formula in parentheses. Portions of a formula enclosed in parentheses are evaluated first, following the previously listed order. Table 4 contains some examples of the effect of order of operations on formula results.

Formula	Result	Formula	Result
=4-2*5^2	-46	=(5+5)*4/2-3*6	2
=(4-2)*5^2	50	=(5+5)*4/(2-3)*6	-240
=5+5*4/2-3*6	-3	=(5+5)*4/(2-3*6)	-2.5

Table 4   Order of operations

The WeeklySales workbook is designed to analyze sales by category such as golf equipment, clothing, and so on. Aleeta Herriott wants to know the total of each category by date.

In this exercise, you will calculate the total of the golf equipment sales by creating a simple addition formula.

To Calculate Total Sales Using a Formula

a. If you took a break, open the **e01ch02WeeklySales_LastFirst** workbook, and, if necessary, navigate to the **WeeklySales** worksheet.

b. Click cell **B9**.

c. Type **=** and then click cell **B6**. Type **+** and then click cell **B7**. Type **+** and then click cell **B8**.

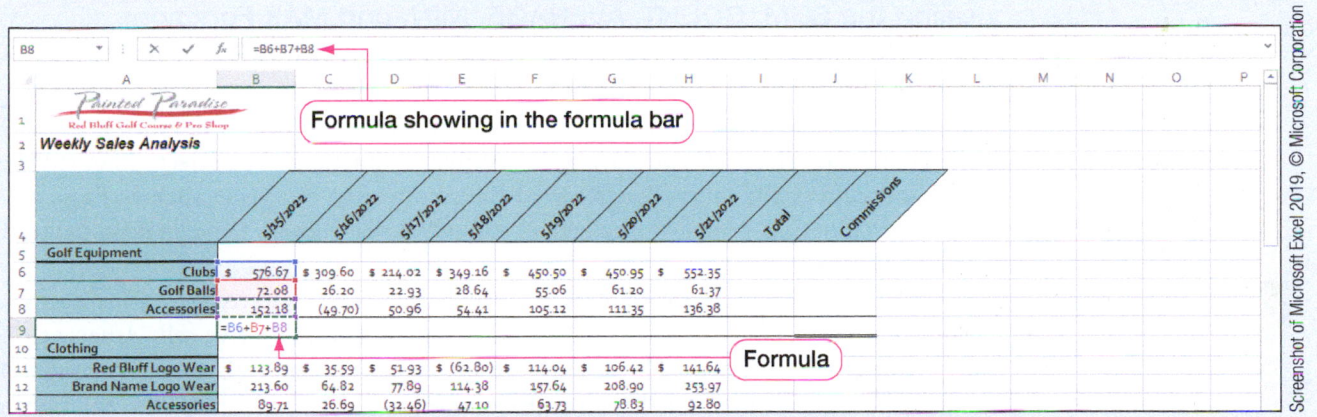

Figure 15   Entering a formula in a cell

Screenshot of Microsoft Excel 2019, © Microsoft Corporation

SIDE NOTE

Copying a Formula and Not Changing Relative References

Select the formula in the formula bar, click Copy, press Esc, select the new cell location, and then click Paste.

d. Press Ctrl+Enter.

Notice the result of the formula appears in cell B9 but the formula appears in the formula bar.

e. With cell B9 still selected, press and hold the **fill handle** and drag through cell range **C9:H9**.

f. Click cell **H9**. Review the formula in the formula bar. Notice how the cell references in the formula changed relative to where the formula was copied. The formula in H9 is =H6+H7+H8.

g. **Save** the workbook.

Create Information with Functions

Functions are one of Excel's most powerful features. A **function** is a built-in program that performs operations on data. Function syntax takes the following form:

function name (argument 1, ..., argument n)

where "function name" is the name of the function and arguments inside the parentheses are the values the function requires. **Arguments** are variables or values the function requires to calculate a solution. Different functions require different arguments. Arguments can be entered as letters, numbers, cell references, cell ranges, or other functions. Some functions do not require any arguments at all. There are more than 400 built-in functions in Excel. **Built-in functions** can be categorized as financial, statistical, mathematical, date and time, text, and several others.

Part of what makes functions so useful is the use of cell references as arguments. Cell references refer to a cell or range of cells within a formula or function instead of a value. Cell references enable you to use information from a cell or cell range in a function. Recall that a cell reference is the combination of a cell's column and row addresses. When a function that includes a cell reference as an argument is copied, the cell reference is changed to reflect the copied location relative to the original location. For example, suppose a function in cell B26 calculates the sum of cells B1:B25; if you copy the function from cell B26 to cell C26, the function in cell C26 will automatically be changed to sum C1:C25—the copied function will be relatively adjusted one column to the right.

Using the SUM, COUNT, AVERAGE, MIN, and MAX Functions

Of the more than 400 functions built into Excel, commonly used functions such as SUM, COUNT, AVERAGE, MIN, and MAX are readily available via the AutoSum ∑ AutoSum ▾ button in the Function Library group on the Formulas tab or in the Editing group on the Home tab. There are two ways to use AutoSum functions. You select either the **destination cell(s)**, the cell(s) that received the result of an operation such as Paste or an AutoSum function, or the **source cell(s)**, the cell(s) that contain the data supplied to the function.

When you invoke AutoSum with the destination cell(s) selected, Excel inspects your worksheet and automatically includes a range adjacent to the active cell. Adjacent cells above the active cell are used by default. If there are no adjacent cells above, then adjacent cells to the left are used for the range. Excel does not inspect cell ranges to the right or below the active cell.

If a column of source cells is selected, if the cell at the bottom of the selected range does not contain data, the bottom cell is treated as the destination cell. If a row of source cells is selected, if the far right cell in the selected range does not contain data, the far right cell is treated as the destination cell. If the bottom or far right cell contains data, the next open cell is used as the destination cell. Table 5 contains examples of the different ways in which data can be included in a function.

Type of Data	Function
Numbers	=SUM(1,3,5,7,11,13)
Cell range	=SUM(B3:B25)
List of noncontiguous cells	=SUM(B3,B9,C5,D14)
Column or columns	=COUNT(J:J) or =AVERAGE(J:L)
Row or rows	=MIN(9:9) or =MAX(9:11)
Combination	=MIN(B3,B9:B15,C12/100,D:E)

Table 5 Function variations

Using the SUM Function by Selecting Destination Cells

The **SUM function** is a commonly used function that adds all numeric information in a specified range, list of numbers, list of cells, or any combination. In this exercise, you will generate new information in the WeeklySales worksheet by selecting destination cells and inserting the SUM function.

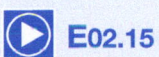 **E02.15**

To Use the SUM Function by Selecting Destination Cells

a. Click cell **B14**. On the Home tab, in the Editing group, click **AutoSum** ![AutoSum]. Excel inspects the cells above B14 and suggests that you want to sum range B11:B13 by surrounding it with a dashed, moving border.

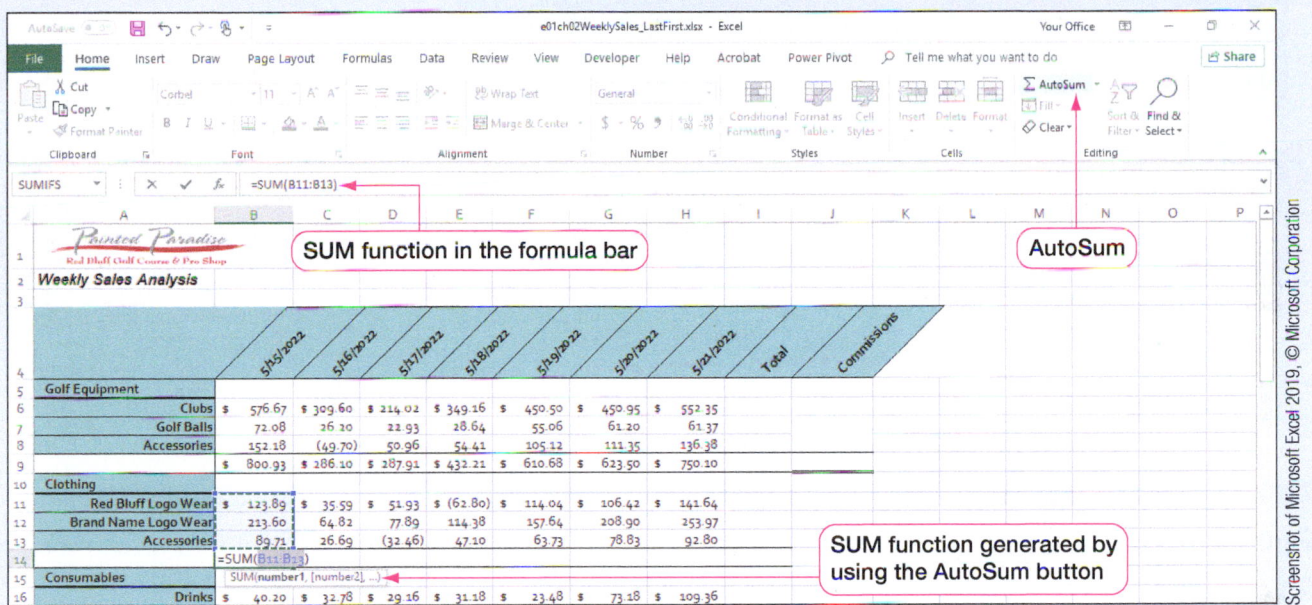

Figure 16 AutoSum range

SIDE NOTE

Double-Click AutoSum

If you are sure Excel will predict the correct range, double-click the AutoSum button ![AutoSum].

SIDE NOTE

SUM Shortcut

SUM can be quickly invoked by pressing Alt + =.

b. Because the suggested range is correct, press Ctrl + Enter. Notice the Accounting Number Format is automatically applied to cell B14. Drag the fill handle to copy the formula through cell range **C14:H14**.

c. Click cell **H14**. Review the formula on the formula bar. Notice how the cell references in the formula changed relative to where the formula was copied.

d. Select the cell range **B18:H18**, press and hold Ctrl, and then select cell ranges **B26:H26, I6:I9, I11:I14, I16:I18,** and **I20:I26**. Click **AutoSum** ![AutoSum].

Notice how formatting was automatically applied to the cell ranges.

e. On the Home tab, in the Cells group, click **Format** ![icon], and then select **AutoFit Column Width**.

AutoSum will operate on noncontiguous cell ranges as well, but it must be handled a little differently. To calculate the total sales for each day, you must sum the category totals.

f. Click cell **B27**, and then click **AutoSum** [∑ AutoSum ▾]. AutoSum recognizes that cell B26 contains a SUM function and selects only B26 as the predicted range. Press and hold Ctrl, select cells **B18**, **B14**, and **B9**; and then click **AutoSum** [∑ AutoSum ▾] again.

g. Drag the fill handle to copy the formula in cell **B27** through cell range **C27:I27**. If any of the cells display a series of number signs (#), select the column header, in the Cells group, click **Format** [⊞], and then select **AutoFit Column Width**.

h. Press Ctrl+Home. **Save** [💾] the workbook.

	A	B	C	D	E	F	G	H	I	J	K
		5/15/2022	5/16/2022	5/17/2022	5/18/2022	5/19/2022	5/20/2022	5/21/2022	Total	Commissions	
5	Golf Equipment										
6	Clubs	$ 576.67	$ 309.60	$ 214.02	$ 349.16	$ 450.50	$ 450.95	$ 552.35	$ 2,903.25		
7	Golf Balls	72.08	26.20	22.93	28.64	55.06	61.10	61.37	$ 327.48		
8	Accessories	152.18	(49.70)	50.96	54.41	105.12	111.35	136.38	$ 560.70		
9		$ 800.93	$ 286.10	$ 287.91	$ 432.21	$ 610.68	$ 623.50	$ 750.10	$ 3,791.43		
10	Clothing										
11	Red Bluff Logo Wear	$ 123.89	35.59	51.93	(62.80)	114.04	106.42	141.64	$ 510.71		
12	Brand Name Logo Wear	213.60	64.82	77.89	114.38	157.64	208.90	253.97	$ 1,091.20		
13	Accessories	89.71	26.69	(32.46)	47.10	63.73	78.83	92.80	$ 366.40		
14		$ 427.20	$ 127.10	$ 97.36	$ 98.68	$ 335.41	$ 394.15	$ 488.41	$ 1,968.31		
15	Consumables										
16	Drinks	$ 40.20	$ 32.78	$ 29.16	$ 31.18	$ 23.48	$ 73.18	$ 109.36	$ 339.34		
17	Snack Food	25.70	22.78	29.44	22.58	17.71	44.85	64.23	$ 227.29		
18		$ 65.90	$ 55.56	$ 58.60	$ 53.76	$ 41.19	$ 118.03	$ 173.59	$ 566.63		
19	Services										
20	Green Fees	$ 1,650.00	$ 660.00	$ 577.50	$ 866.25	$ 1,031.25	$ 1,402.50	$ 2,061.50	$ 8,250.00		
21	Golf Cart Rentals	440.00	176.00	154.00	231.00	275.00	374.00	550.00	$ 2,200.00		
22	Deposit Returns	(110.00)	(44.00)	(38.50)	(57.75)	(68.75)	(93.50)	(137.50)	$ (550.00)		
23	Golf Club Rentals	55.00	22.00	19.25	28.88	34.38	46.75	68.75	$ 275.01		
24	Deposit Returns	(11.00)	(4.40)	(3.85)	(5.78)	(6.88)	(9.35)	(13.75)	$ (55.01)		
25	Lessons	440.00	176.00	154.00	231.00	275.00	374.00	550.00	$ 2,200.00		
26		$ 2,464.00	$ 985.60	$ 862.40	$ 1,293.60	$ 1,540.00	$ 2,094.40	$ 3,080.00	$ 12,320.00		
27		$ 3,758.03	$ 1,454.36	$ 1,306.27	$ 1,878.25	$ 2,527.28	$ 3,230.08	$ 4,492.10	$ 18,646.37		

WeeklySales HourlySales-Sunday HourlySales-Monday Documentation

Screenshot of Microsoft Excel 2019, © Microsoft Corporation

Figure 17 Calculating totals using the SUM function

Golf pro John Schilling is paid a commission on golf lessons. He earns 70% of all lesson fees received by the pro shop. Pro shop manager Aleeta Herriott oversees all golf club sales. She receives a 15% commission on all sales of clubs and a 10% commission on golf balls and accessories.

In this exercise, you will create a formula to calculate the total commissions for golf equipment and lessons.

 **E02.16**

SIDE NOTE
Alternate Method
To enter the formula in J25, type =I25*C33, and then press Enter.

To Calculate Commissions Using Formulas

a. On the WeeklySales worksheet, click cell **J25**. You will calculate the commissions John Schilling earned on golf lessons. The total revenue from golf lessons for the week is in cell I25, and the commission paid for golf lessons is in cell C33.

b. Type **=** click **I25**. Excel puts the cell reference to cell I25 into the formula. Type ***** click **C33**. Excel puts the cell reference to cell C33 into the formula.

c. Press Ctrl+Enter. The formula in cell J25 multiplies I25 and C33 for a result of $1,540.00. AutoFit the column width as necessary.

Next, you need to calculate the commissions that Aleeta Herriott earned selling golf clubs in the Pro Shop by multiplying the total golf club sales for the weekly by the commission percentage on golf club sales.

d. Click cell **J6**. Type = click cell **I6**, type * click cell **C29**, and then press Enter. The formula multiplies cell I6* C29 for a result of $435.49.

Next, you need to calculate the commission earned on Pro Shop accessories by multiplying the sum of golf ball and accessory sales for the week by the appropriate commission.

SIDE NOTE
Alternate Method
To enter the formula in J7, type =(I7+I8)*C30, and then press Enter.

e. Click cell **J7**. This cell has been merged. Type =(click **I7**. Type + and then click **I8**. Type)* click **C30**, and then press Enter.

You added the parentheses to ensure cells I7 and I8 are added before they are multiplied by cell C30. Next you need to sum Aleeta Herriott's commissions.

f. Click cell **J9**, and then double-click the **AutoSum** button Σ AutoSum ▾ .

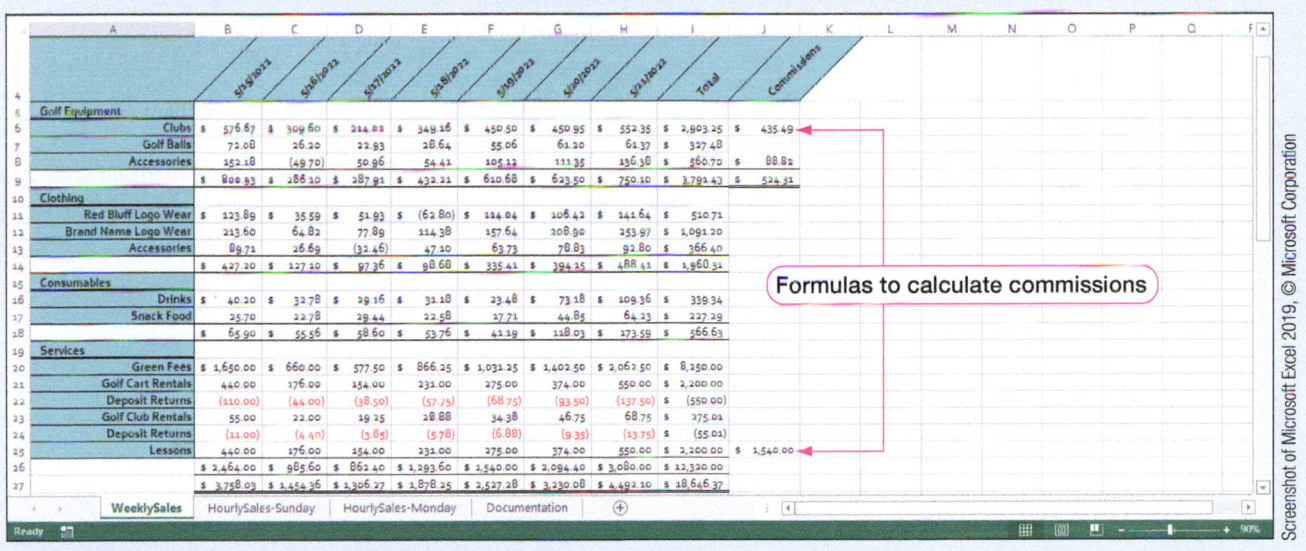

Figure 18   Calculating commissions with formulas

g. **Save** 💾 the workbook.

> ## Troubleshooting
> Excel allows you to copy formulas from one location to another and adjusts cell references to ensure calculation accuracy. This is not necessarily true when a formula is moved from one location to another, however. If you move a formula by dragging it from one location to another, cell references do not change. Be sure you double-check a formula after you move it to ensure it is still producing a correct result.

REAL WORLD ADVICE   **An Alternative to Typing Cell References**

An alternative—and more accurate—method of typing cell references into a formula is to type only the operators and then select the cells from the worksheet. The steps to enter the daily sales total in the WeeklySales worksheet would be as follows.

1. Select cell B27.
2. Type =.
3. Click cell B9, and then type **+**.
4. Click cell B14, and then type **+**.
5. Click cell B18, and then type **+**.
6. Click cell B26, and then press Enter.

This method of building formulas is much less error prone than typing cell references.

Using the SUM Function by Selecting Source Cells

Inserting a function using AutoSum after selecting source cells works particularly well when the source range does not contain contiguous data, as in the HourlySales-Sunday worksheet. In the next exercise, you will generate new information in the HourlySales-Sunday worksheet by selecting source cells and inserting a SUM function using the AutoSum button.

E02.17

To Use the SUM Function by Selecting Source Cells

a. Click the **HourlySales-Sunday** worksheet.

b. Select cell range **B29:B6**. If you start your selection with the cell where you wish to insert the SUM function, then when the function is inserted, you will see it in the formula bar.

c. On the Home tab, in the Editing group, click the **AutoSum** button [Σ AutoSum ▾] to insert a SUM function.

Because the bottom cell in the selected range did not contain data, the SUM function is placed into cell B29.

d. Select cell range **C6:O29**. You have included a row of empty cells below your destination range. In this case, you are selecting both the source and destination cells. Click the **AutoSum** button [Σ AutoSum ▾].

e. Click cell **B6** to deselect the selected range, and then **Save** [💾] the workbook.

Using COUNT and AVERAGE

The **AVERAGE function** returns the average (mean) from a specified range of cells. The sum of all numeric values in the range is calculated and then divided by the count of numbers in the range. Essentially the AVERAGE function is SUM/COUNT. COUNT and AVERAGE can be inserted in any manner by which the SUM function can be inserted. The **COUNT function** returns the number of cells in a cell range that contain numbers. It can be used to generate information such as the number of sales in a period by counting invoice numbers, the number of items in inventory, and so on.

In this exercise, you will calculate averages and counts for the HourlySales-Sunday worksheet and take advantage of the AutoSum feature that places results in the first open cell following a selected destination range.

 **E02.18**

To Use the COUNT and AVERAGE Functions

a. On the HourlySales-Sunday worksheet, select cell range **B6:O28**. On the Home tab, in the Editing group, click the **AutoSum** arrow Σ AutoSum ▾.

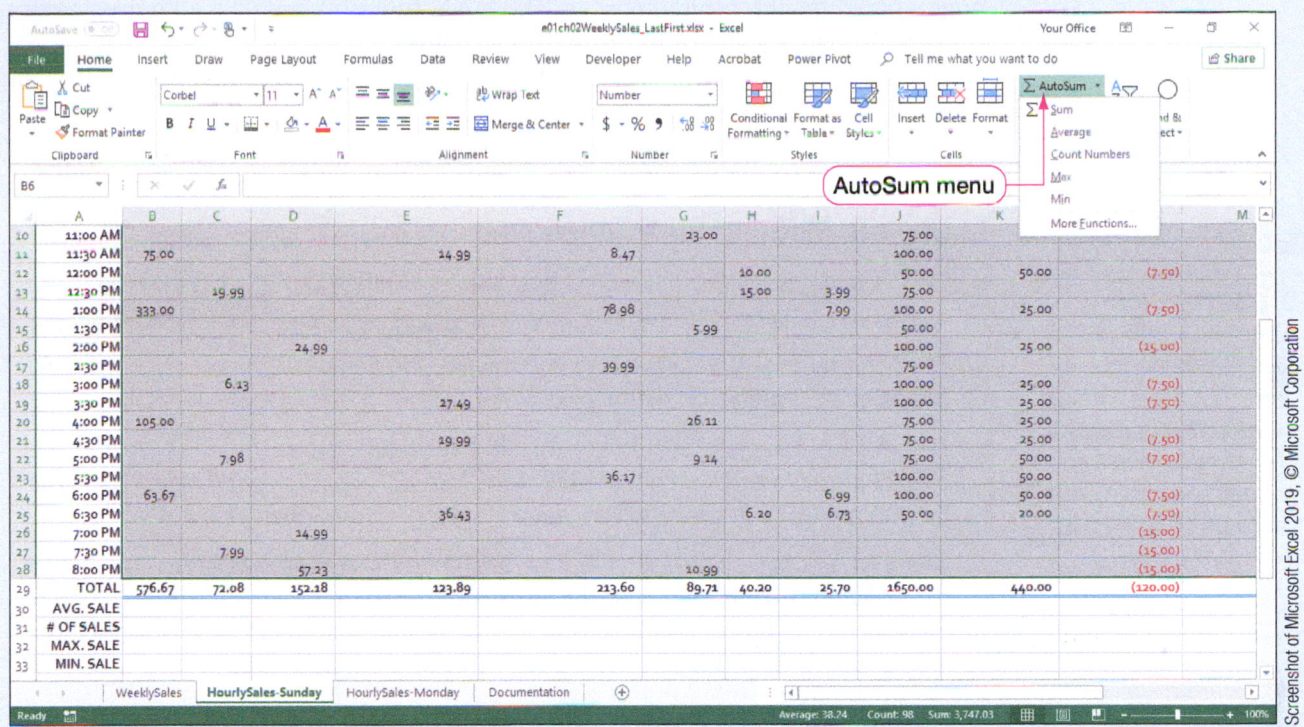

Figure 19 AutoSum arrow selection

Screenshot of Microsoft Excel 2019, © Microsoft Corporation

SIDE NOTE

Alternate Method

Type **=AVER** A list of available functions beginning with AVER will appear. Double-click AVERAGE from the list of available functions.

b. Select **Average**.

Notice Excel expanded the selected range to include row 29 but inserted the AVERAGE functions into row 30, the first available empty cells below the selected destination range. Click cell O30. Also notice the AVERAGE function in cell O30 does not include row 29; it includes the rows specified in the originally selected range.

c. Select cell range **B6:O28**, in the Editing group, click the **AutoSum** arrow Σ AutoSum ▾, and then select **Count Numbers**.

Once again, AutoSum expanded the selected range to include row 29, but this time it inserted the COUNT functions into row 31, the first available empty cells below the selected destination range.

d. **Save** 💾 the workbook.

Using MIN and MAX

An average gives you an incomplete picture. If your instructor states that the average score on the exam is 75%, you do not have any information about the actual score distribution. Everyone in the class may have gotten a C with a low of 71% and a high of 79%. Conversely, no one may have gotten a C; it may be that half the class got an A and half got an F. Both situations could result in a 75% average but with very different distributions. You should never rely on the average without looking at additional statistics that help to complete the picture. While many statistics exist to do this, the minimum value and the maximum value provide at least a little more insight into the distribution of data by defining the extremes. The **MIN function** examines all numeric values in a specified range and returns the minimum value. The **MAX function** examines all numeric values in a specified range and returns the maximum value.

In this exercise, you will use the MIN and MAX functions to find the smallest and largest values in a range of cells.

 E02.19

SIDE NOTE
Alternate Method

Type **=MAX** and then press Tab. Excel will insert the beginning parenthesis of the function and then you can select the cells or cell range.

To Use the MIN and MAX Functions

a. On the HourlySales-Sunday worksheet, select cell range **B6:O28**. On the Home tab, in the Editing group, click the AutoSum arrow ⎸∑ AutoSum ▾⎹, and then select **Max**.

The MAX functions were inserted into row 32, the first available empty row below the selected destination range.

b. Rather than selecting cell range B6:O28 over again, press Shift + ↑ to remove row 29 from the selected range. Cell range B6:O28 should now be selected. In the Editing group, click the AutoSum arrow ⎸∑ AutoSum ▾⎹, and then select **Min**.

The MIN functions were inserted into row 33, the first available empty row below the selected destination range. The functions inserted into the HourlySales-Sunday worksheet can be used to calculate the same values in the HourlySales-Monday worksheet. They simply need to be copied between worksheets.

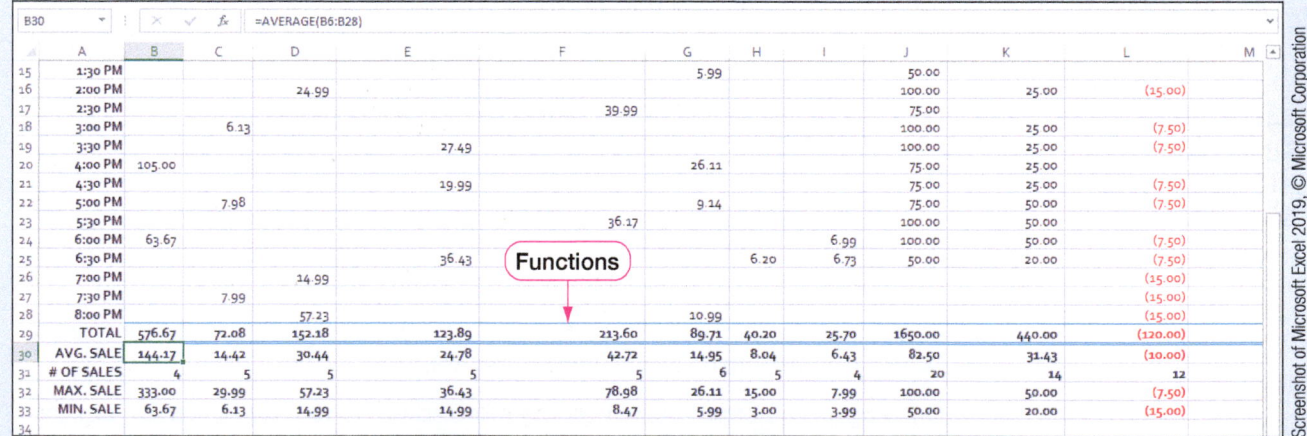

Figure 20 Completed worksheet using functions

c. Click the header for row **29**, press and hold Shift, and then click the header for row **33**. In the Clipboard group, click **Copy**.

d. Click the **HourlySales-Monday** worksheet, click cell **A29**, and then, in the Clipboard group, click **Paste**.

The functions in rows 29:33 in the HourlySales-Sunday worksheet have been copied to the same locations in the HourlySales-Monday worksheet. Notice how the formulas were copied from the HourlySales-Sunday worksheet, not the values.

e. **Save**  the workbook.

Use Conditional Formatting to Assist in Decision Making

As was discussed previously, one of the primary purposes of information analysis in Excel worksheets is to assist in decision making. People are often influenced by the format in which information is presented. Worksheets can be very large—thousands of rows and dozens of columns of information. The number of calculated items can be daunting to analyze, digest, and interpret. To the extent to which Excel can be used to assist the decision maker in understanding information, decision-making speed and quality should improve. **Conditional formatting** allows the specification of rules that apply formatting to a cell as determined by the rule outcome. It is a way to dynamically change the visual presentation of information in a manner that adds information to the worksheet.

Highlighting Values in a Range with Conditional Formatting

Conditional formatting can aid the decision maker by changing the way information is displayed based on rules specific to the problem the worksheet is designed to address. Conditional formatting can be used to highlight information by changing cell fill color, font color, font style, font size, border, and number format and by adding visual cues such as scales and icons. Conditional formatting will apply formatting based on the actual values in the cells.

In the next exercise, you will apply conditional formatting to highlight the sales figures in each category.

E02.20

MAC SIDE NOTE
Conditional Formatting
Use the Format only top or bottom ranked values.

To Use Conditional Formatting to Highlight Sales Figures

a. Click the **WeeklySales** worksheet, and then select cell range **B9:H9**. On the Home tab, and in the Styles group, click **Conditional Formatting** ⊞. Point to **Top/Bottom Rules**, and then select **Top 10 Items**. In the Top 10 Items dialog box, in the Format cells that rank in the TOP box, double-click **10**, and then type **1**

b. Click the **with arrow**, select **Green Fill with Dark Green Text**.

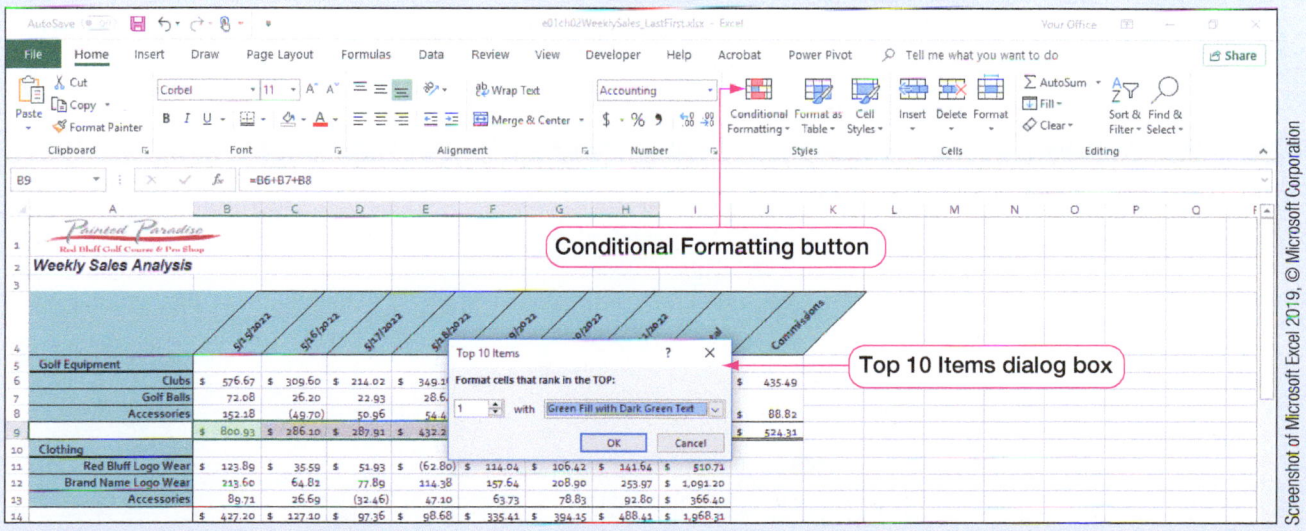

Figure 21 Top 10 Items dialog box

SIDE NOTE
Want Negative Numbers in Blue?
In the with box, click Custom Format, click Color, and choose a different color for negative numbers.

c. Click **OK**.

d. With cell range **B9:H9** still selected, on the Home tab, in the Styles group, click **Conditional Formatting** 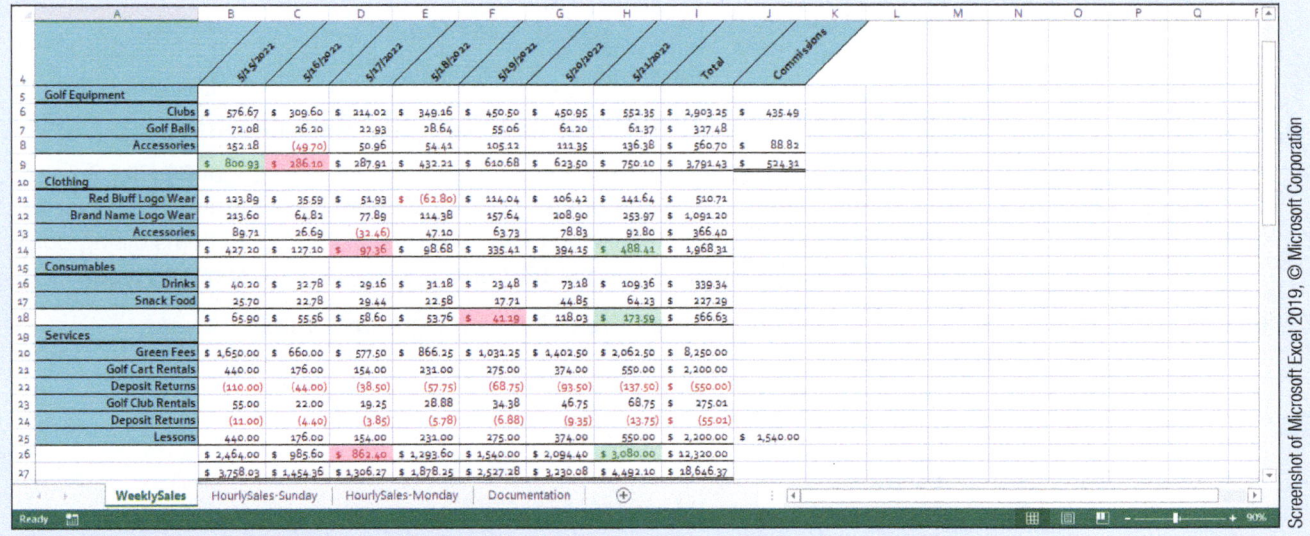, point to **Top/Bottom Rules**, and then select **Bottom 10 Items**. In the Bottom 10 Items dialog box, in the Format cells that rank in the BOTTOM box, double-click **10**, and then type **1**

e. Click **OK** to accept the **Light Red Fill with Dark Red Text**.

Now you can copy the formatting you just added to B9:H9 to the other category totals and to the overall totals in the WeeklySales worksheet.

f. With cell range **B9:H9** still selected, on the Home tab, in the Clipboard group, double-click **Format Painter**. Select cell ranges **B14:H14**, **B18:H18**, and **B26:H26**. Click **Format Painter** to turn off the Format Painter.

Recall that Accounting Number Format does not include the option to display negative numbers in red—notice cell C8. This can be accomplished with conditional formatting.

g. Select cell range **B6:I27**. On the Home tab, in the Styles group, click **Conditional Formatting**, point to **Highlight Cells Rules**, and then click **Less Than**. In the Format cells that are LESS THAN box, type **0**

h. Click the with box arrow, and select **Red Text**. Click **OK**.

i. **Save** the workbook.

Figure 22 Data with conditional formatting

Applying Conditional Formatting to Assess Benchmarks Using Icon Sets

Conditional formatting can also be used to highlight whether a value satisfies criteria such as a benchmark. The staff in the pro shop is guaranteed a minimum commission amount—stored in cells C31 and C34. The resort management prefers that a staff member's commissions exceed the minimum. You can use conditional formatting to clearly identify whether Aleeta Herriott's commissions in the pro shop and John Schilling's commissions for lessons exceed the contractual minimum.

In this exercise, you will use conditional formatting with icon sets to highlight above-minimum commissions.

 E02.21

To Use Conditional Formatting with Icon Sets to Highlight Above-Minimum Commissions

a. On the WeeklySales worksheet, click cell **J9**. On the Home tab, in the Styles group, click **Conditional Formatting**, point to **Icon Sets**, and then select **More Rules**. In the New Formatting Rule dialog box, under Select a Rule Type, make sure **Format all cells based on their values** is selected.

b. Under Edit the Rule Description, click the **Icon Style arrow**, and then select the first item in the list, **3 Arrows (Colored)**—you will have to scroll up.

c. Under Icon, next to the **yellow arrow** icon, click the arrow, and then select the **red down arrow** for the middle Icon box; the Icon Style box will change to Custom. In the bottom Icon box, next to the red arrow icon, click the arrow, select **No Cell Icon**, and then select **Number** in both **Type** boxes.

d. Double-click in the top **Value** box, and then press ⌴Delete⌴. Click the **Collapse** button, select cell **C31**—the minimum commission for the Pro Shop manager—and then click the **Expand** button.

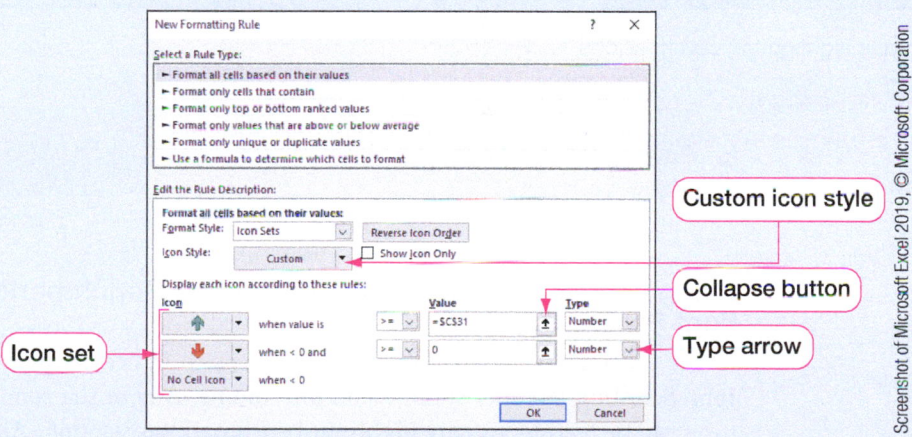

Figure 23 Conditional Formatting icon sets

Screenshot of Microsoft Excel 2019, © Microsoft Corporation

e. Click **OK**. Now you can use the conditional format you just created for the golf lessons commission in cell J25.

f. With cell **J9** selected, click **Format Painter** 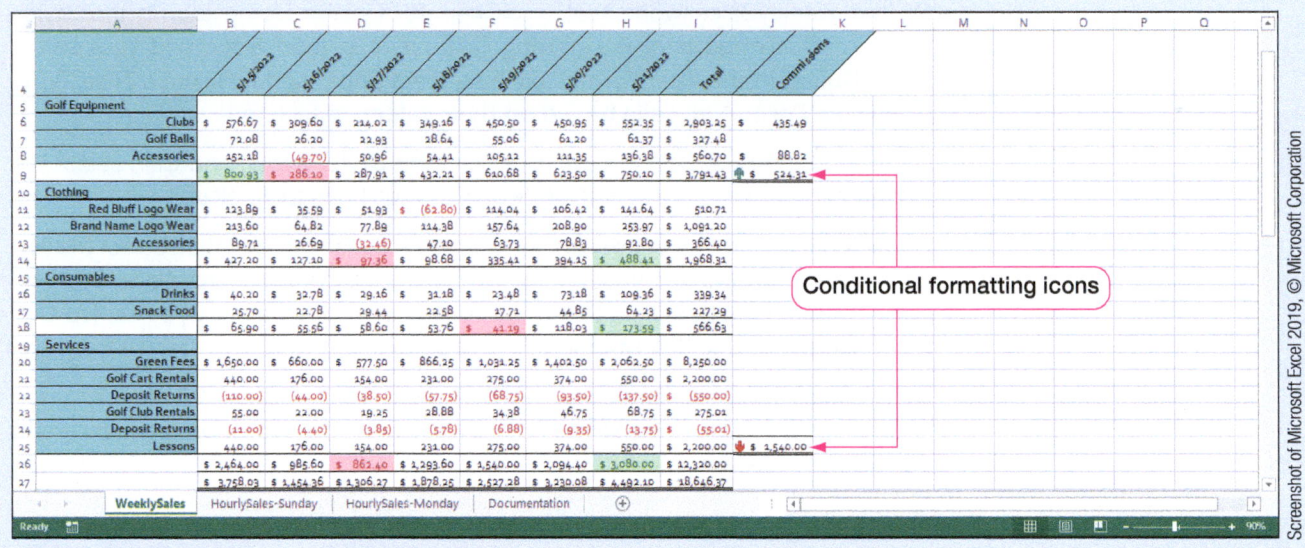, and then click cell **J25** to paste formatting, including conditional formatting.

g. With **J25** still selected, on the Home tab in the Styles group, click **Conditional Formatting** , and then select **Manage Rules**. The Conditional Formatting Rules Manager dialog box is displayed.

h. In the Conditional Formatting Rules Manager dialog box, click **Edit Rule**. In the Edit Formatting Rule dialog box, under Display each icon according to these rules, double-click the top **Value** box.

i. Click the **Collapse** button in the top Value box. Click cell **C34**—the minimum commission for the golf pro—and then click the **Expand** button .

j. Click **OK**, and then click **OK**. AutoFit the column width of column **J**.

Figure 24 Icons highlighting commissions

k. **Save** the workbook.

Using Conditional Formatting to Assess Benchmarks Using Font Formatting

In the previous exercise, you used arrow icons to indicate whether Aleeta Herriott and John Schilling had met commission minimums. Any of the conditional formatting features can be used to visually highlight benchmark satisfaction. Aleeta has used historical sales data to identify a proportion of weekly sales that is a minimum goal (benchmark) for each product category.

In this exercise, you will format weekly sales totals to be displayed in a bold and green font if they meet or exceed benchmarks.

 **E02.22**

To Use Conditional Formatting to Highlight Sales That Meet or Exceed Benchmarks

a. On the **WeeklySales** worksheet, click cell **I9**. On the Home tab, in the Styles group, click **Conditional Formatting**. Point to **Highlight Cells Rules**, and then select **More Rules**. In the New Formatting Rule dialog box, under Select a Rule Type, select **Use a formula to determine which cells to format**.

b. In the Format values where this formula is true box, type =I9/I27>=C36 (golf equipment percentage of total sales compared to the golf equipment target percentage of sales).

When using a formula to determine which cells to format, the conditional format always starts with an equal sign, which is followed by a conditional test. If that condition is TRUE then the formatting is applied. If the condition is FALSE, then it will not apply the formatting.

c. Click **Format**. In the Format Cells dialog box, on the Font tab, in the Font style box, select **Bold**, and then click the **Color** arrow. Under Standard Colors, select **Green**. Click **OK**.

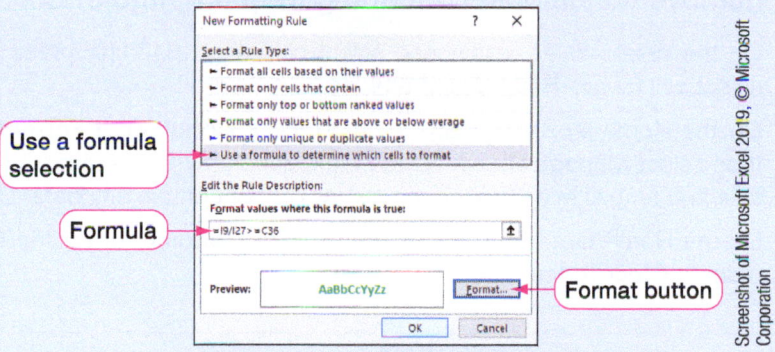

Use a formula selection

Formula

Format button

Screenshot of Microsoft Excel 2019, © Microsoft Corporation

Figure 25   Conditional Formatting using a formula

d. Click **OK**. If necessary, AutoFit Column Width on cell I9.

e. Click cell **I14**. On the Home tab, in the Styles group, click **Conditional Formatting**. Point to **Highlight Cells Rules**, and then select **More Rules**. In the New Formatting Rule dialog box, under Select a Rule Type, select **Use a formula to determine which cells to format**. Type =I14/I27>=C37 Click **Format**. On the Font tab, in the Font style box, click **Bold**, and then click the **Color** arrow. Under Standard Colors, select **Green**. Click **OK** two times.

f. Click cell **I18**. In the Styles group, click **Conditional Formatting**. Point to **Highlight Cells Rules**, and then select **More Rules**. In the New Formatting Rule dialog box, under Select a Rule Type, select **Use a formula to determine which cells to format**. Type =I18/I27>=C38

Click **Format**. On the Font tab, in the Font style box, click **Bold**, and then click the **Color** arrow. Under Standard Colors, select **Green**. Click **OK** two times.

g. **Save** the workbook.

Removing Conditional Formatting

Once conditional formatting has been applied to a cell or range of cells, it may be necessary to remove the conditional formatting without affecting other cell formatting or cell contents. Conditional formatting can be removed from a selected cell or cell range, and it can be removed from the entire sheet, depending on which option is chosen.

When you applied the conditional formatting to cell range B6:I27 to display negative numbers in red regardless of the number format, several cells that did not contain data were also conditionally formatted. Although applying conditional formatting to a large range of cells all at once is efficient, applying it to cells that do not contain data in the current design may cause unforeseen problems as the worksheet is modified in the future. You need to remove the conditional formatting in the empty cells.

 CONSIDER THIS | **How Might You Use Conditional Formatting?**

Can you think of ways you could use conditional formatting in worksheets to aid in making personal decisions? Could you use conditional formatting as an aid in tracking your stock portfolio? Monthly budget and expenses? Checking account?

In this exercise, you will remove the conditional formatting in the empty cells.

▶ E02.23

To Remove Conditional Formatting from a Range of Cells

SIDE NOTE
Alternate Method
To remove conditional formatting, click Conditional Formatting, select Manage Rules, click Delete Rule.

a. On the WeeklySales worksheet, select cell range **B10:I10**, press Ctrl, and then select cell ranges **B15:I15** and **B19:I19**.

b. On the Home tab, in the Styles group, click **Conditional Formatting** 📊, and then select **Manage Rules**. Notice the Cell Value < 0 rule that was applied to the selected ranges even though the ranges do not contain any data. Click **Close**.

c. On the Home tab, in the Styles group, click **Conditional Formatting**, and then point to **Clear Rules**.

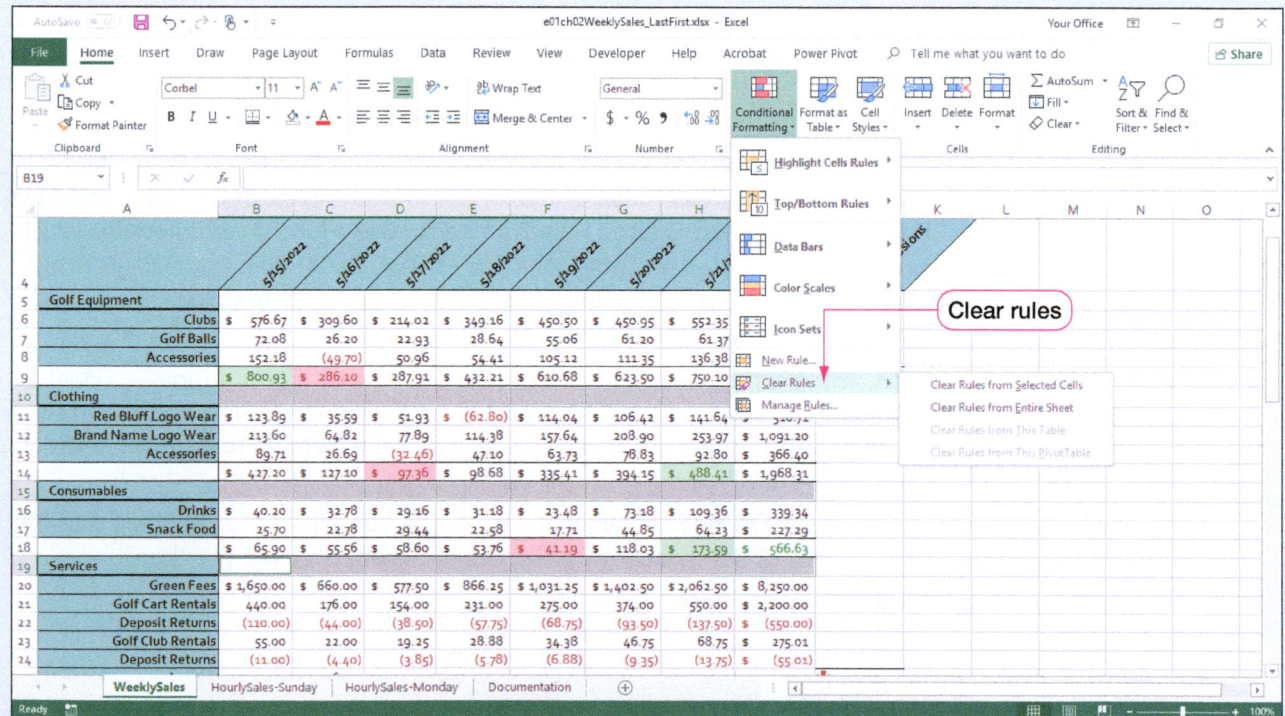

Figure 26 Remove Conditional Formatting

d. Select **Clear Rules from Selected Cells**.

e. **Save** 💾 the workbook.

Hide Information in a Worksheet

A worksheet can contain information that may not be necessary, or even desirable, to display. For example, detailed information used to calculate totals might be hidden until such time that the person using the worksheet would like to see it.

Hiding information in a worksheet is relatively simple. Entire worksheet rows and columns can be hidden. Simply select the rows and/or columns to be hidden by clicking on the row or column heading. Point to the selected row or column heading(s), right-click, and then select Hide on the displayed shortcut menu.

Gridlines are very helpful in visualizing and navigating a workbook during development, but some users feel gridlines clutter a worksheet. Gridlines can be "hidden" simply by unchecking the Gridlines box in the Show group on the View tab.

Hiding Worksheet Rows

In the WeeklySales worksheet, rows 29:38 contain parameters that are used to calculate commissions, to identify minimum commission levels, and to specify sales percentage benchmarks for golf equipment, clothing, and consumables. Once the WeeklySales worksheet has been fully developed, there is little need to have this data visible. In fact, having this kind of data visible can be problematic in that a user could inadvertently or intentionally change the data and cause the worksheet to display incorrect information.

In this exercise, you will hide rows 29:38 from view in the WeeklySales worksheet.

E02.24

SIDE NOTE
Alternate Method
You can also click and drag to select rows 29:38.

To Hide Rows in a Worksheet

a. On the WeeklySales worksheet, click the heading for row **29**, press and hold `Shift`, and then click the heading for row **38**.

b. Right-click anywhere in the selected rows.

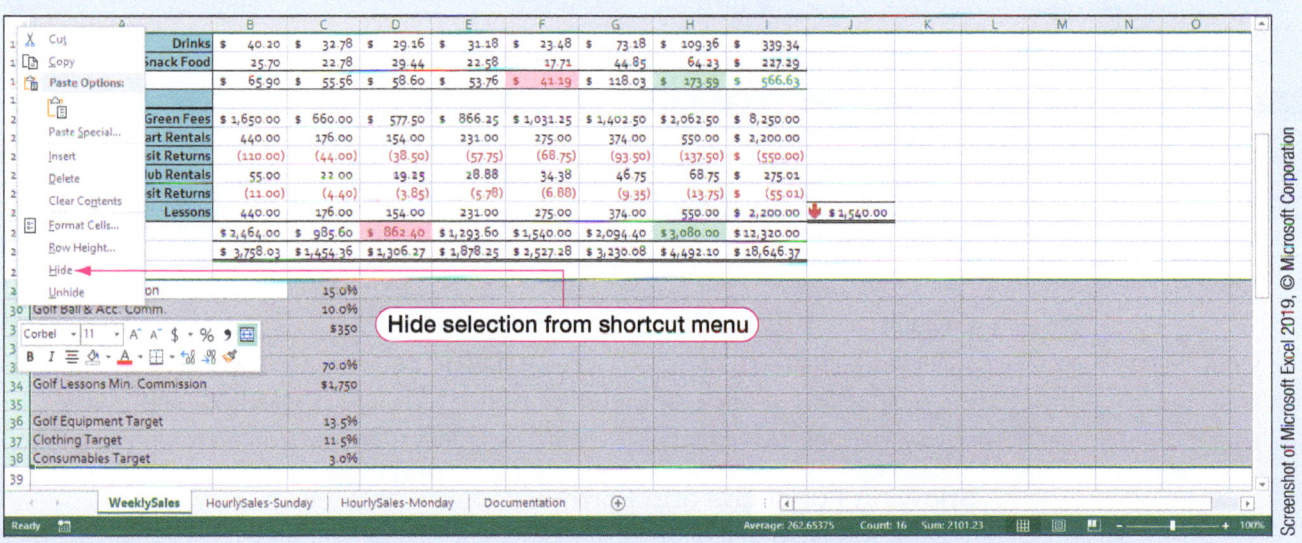

Figure 27 Shortcut menu

c. Select **Hide** on the shortcut menu, and then press `Ctrl`+`Home`.

d. **Save** the workbook.

Hiding Worksheet Gridlines

Gridlines, the vertical and horizontal lines on a worksheet that help define a cell's boundaries, are helpful, but they are not always necessary to use in a workbook. The gridlines you see when creating a workbook are not printed unless you select the Print option to print the gridlines. This print option is available even if the gridlines are hidden in the workbook. They assist in identifying cells in manipulating a worksheet. Once a worksheet is complete, some people think gridlines detract from a worksheet's professional appearance.

In this exercise, you will turn off, or hide, gridlines in the WeeklySales worksheet.

E02.25 | To Hide Gridlines in a Worksheet

a. On the WeeklySales worksheet, click the **View** tab, and then, in the Show group, click to deselect the **Gridlines** check box and turn the gridlines off.

Notice the worksheet now has a white background. To many users, this is more visually appealing than a worksheet in which gridlines are visible.

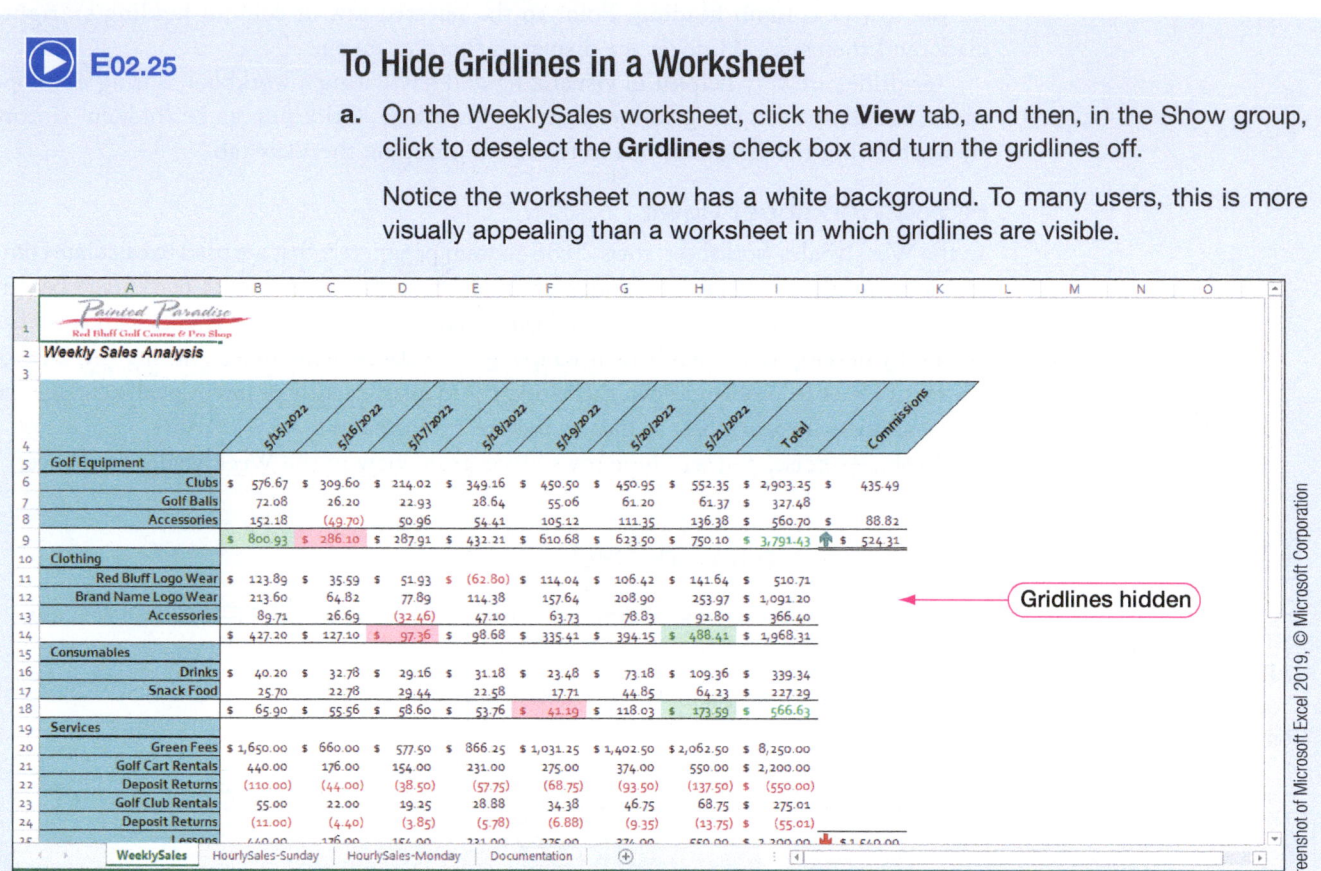

Figure 28 Worksheet without gridlines

b. **Save** the workbook.

Document Functions and Formulas

An important part of building a good worksheet is documentation. Aleeta Herriott included the standard documentation worksheet in the WeeklySales workbook and updated it to reflect what she had accomplished before assigning completion of the workbook to you.

Showing Functions and Formulas

What is displayed in a cell that contains a function or a formula is the calculated result. The function or formula that generated the displayed value is visible only one cell at a time by selecting a cell and then looking at the formula bar. When the Show Formulas feature is turned on, the calculated results are hidden and functions and formulas are shown in the cells instead, whenever applicable.

Show Formulas is very helpful in understanding how a worksheet is structured. It is an essential aid in correcting errors or updating the function of a worksheet. A worksheet that has Show Formulas turned on can be printed and/or exported for documentation purposes.

In this exercise, you will view worksheet formulas and export a formulas worksheet to a PDF.

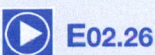 **E02.26**

To View Worksheet Formulas and Export to PDF

a. On the WeeklySales worksheet, click the **Formulas** tab, and then, in the Formula Auditing group, select **Show Formulas** 🔣.

Cells now display formulas rather than values. Notice that Show Formulas also displays cell data without number formatting—the conditional formatting will still appear.

b. Use the **Zoom Slider** [− ▬▬▬▮▬▬ +] on the status bar to move the zoom level so you can view the entire worksheet on your monitor.

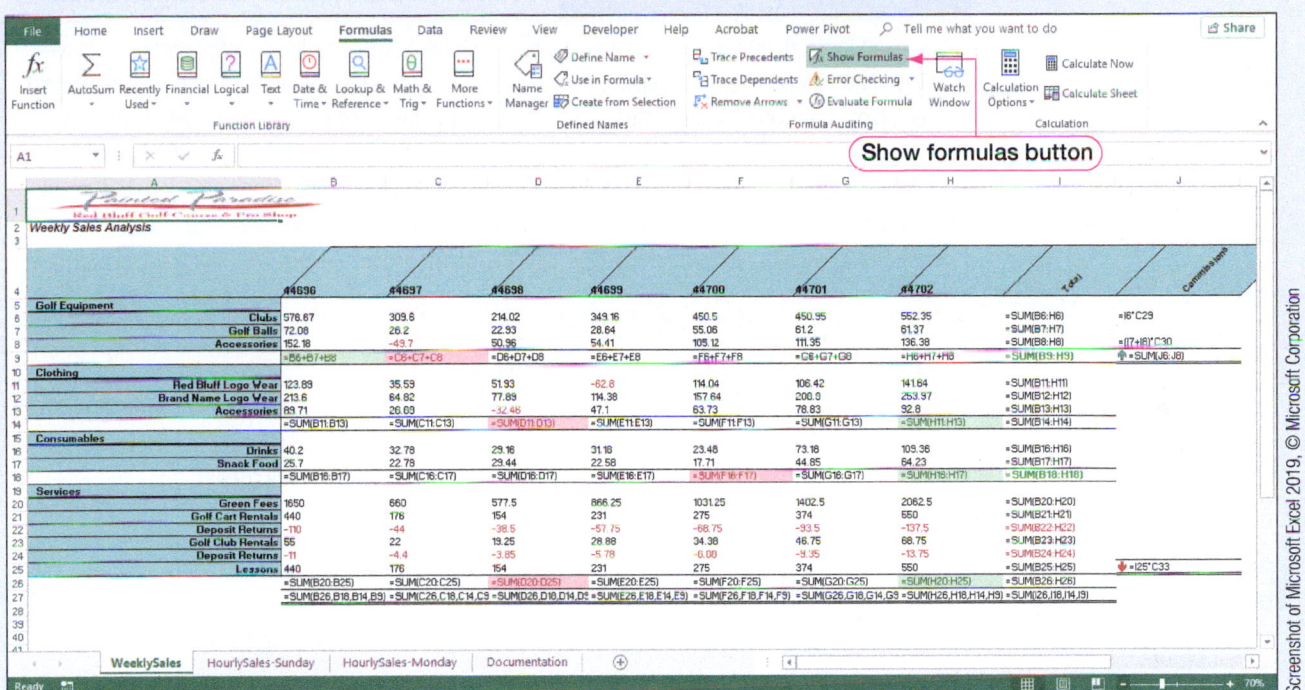

Figure 29 Show formulas

c. Click the **Page Layout** tab, and then, in the Scale to Fit group, click the **Width** arrow, and then select **1 page**. This will scale your worksheet to print in the width of a single page.

d. In the Scale to Fit group, click the **Height** arrow, and then select **1 page**. This will scale your document to print in the height of a single page.

e. In the **Page Setup** group, click **Orientation**, and then select **Landscape**.

f. Repeat steps c–d for all remaining worksheets.

> **Grader Heads Up**
>
> The MyLab IT Grader version of this project does not include the creation of the PDF document.

g. Click the **File** tab to enter Backstage view, and then click **Export**. Click **Create PDF/XPS Document**, and then click the **Create PDF/XPS** button. In the Publish as PDF or XPS dialog box, double-click the **File name** box, and then type e01ch02WeeklySalesFormulas_LastFirst using your last and first name. Make sure **Open file after publishing** is checked. Click **Publish**.

h. The WeeklySales worksheet with Show Formulas turned on is displayed as a PDF document in Reader. Close Reader.

i. Click the **Formulas** tab, and then click **Show Formulas** ⟨ⓕₓ⟩ to toggle off Show Formulas and return to the default Normal view.

j. Use the Zoom Slider ⟨—————▮————＋⟩ on the status bar to set the zoom to 100%.

k. **Save** ⟨💾⟩ the workbook.

REAL WORLD ADVICE **Print Formula View for Documentation**

You need to document your workbooks. As the worksheets you develop become more complex—using more functions and formulas—the need for documentation increases. Once your worksheet is complete, one vital documentation step is to print the formulas of your worksheet. If anything ever goes wrong with your worksheet in the future, the formulas printout may be the fastest way to fix it. Remember that an environmentally friendly documentation option can be to print to Portable Document Format (PDF). A PDF preserves exactly the original "look and feel" of a document but allows its viewing in many different applications.

Updating Existing Documentation

You have made some significant and very important improvements to the WeeklySales workbook. You must document the updates that require identification or explanation. In this exercise, you will update the existing documentation worksheet.

 **E02.27**

To Update Existing Documentation

a. Click the **Documentation** worksheet, and then complete the following.

- Click cell **A8**, type 6/01/2022 in mm/dd/yyyy format, and then press ⟨Tab⟩.

- In cell **B8**, type your name in Firstname Lastname format, and then press ⟨Tab⟩.

- In cell **C8**, type Green background for high sales and then press ⟨Enter⟩.

- Click cell **C9**, type Red background for low sales and then press ⟨Enter⟩.

b. Add the **File Name** code to the left page footer on all worksheets.

c. Click the **WeeklySales** worksheet. Click the **File** tab, and then click **Print**. Under Settings, click the Print Active Sheets arrow, and then click **Print Entire Workbook**. If requested by your instructor, click **Print**.

d. **Save** ⟨💾⟩ the workbook, exit Excel, and then submit your files as directed by your instructor.

REAL WORLD ADVICE **The Power and Risk of "Machine Decision Making"**

Never forget that tools such as Excel are decision-making aids, not decision makers. Certainly, there are highly structured situations, such as a product mix problem, that can be programmed into a worksheet in Excel such that the result is the decision. Excel is also used for the analysis of information in less highly structured problems. In addition, not all factors in a decision can typically be quantified and programmed into a worksheet.

Computers make calculations; people make decisions.

Concept Check

1. Why should you format data in Excel? How might you format data for a person who is color-blind? pp. 103, 107

2. What are the different functions made available via the AutoSum button? What does each function calculate? p. 122

3. What character precedes all formulas and functions in Excel? What purpose do parentheses serve in Excel formulas? p. 119

4. What is conditional formatting? How can conditional formatting assist in decision making? p. 128

5. List two reasons why it might be necessary to hide rows or columns of information in a worksheet. p. 133

6. Why might you choose to print the formulas of a worksheet? Why is PDF good for saving documentation? p. 134

Key Terms

Argument   p. 124
AVERAGE function   p. 128
Built-in cell style   p. 118
Built-in function   p. 124
Cell alignment   p. 111
Cell reference   p. 121
Conditional formatting   p. 131
Constant   p. 121
COUNT function   p. 128

Default   p. 111
Destination cell(s)   p. 124
Fill color   p. 112
Format Painter   p. 114
Formula   p. 121
Function   p. 124
Graphical format   p. 105
Gridlines   p. 137
Mathematical operator   p. 121

MAX function   p. 130
MIN function   p. 130
Order of operations   p. 122
Relative cell reference   p. 121
Source cell(s)   p. 124
SUM function   p. 125
Tabular format   p. 105
Theme   p. 119

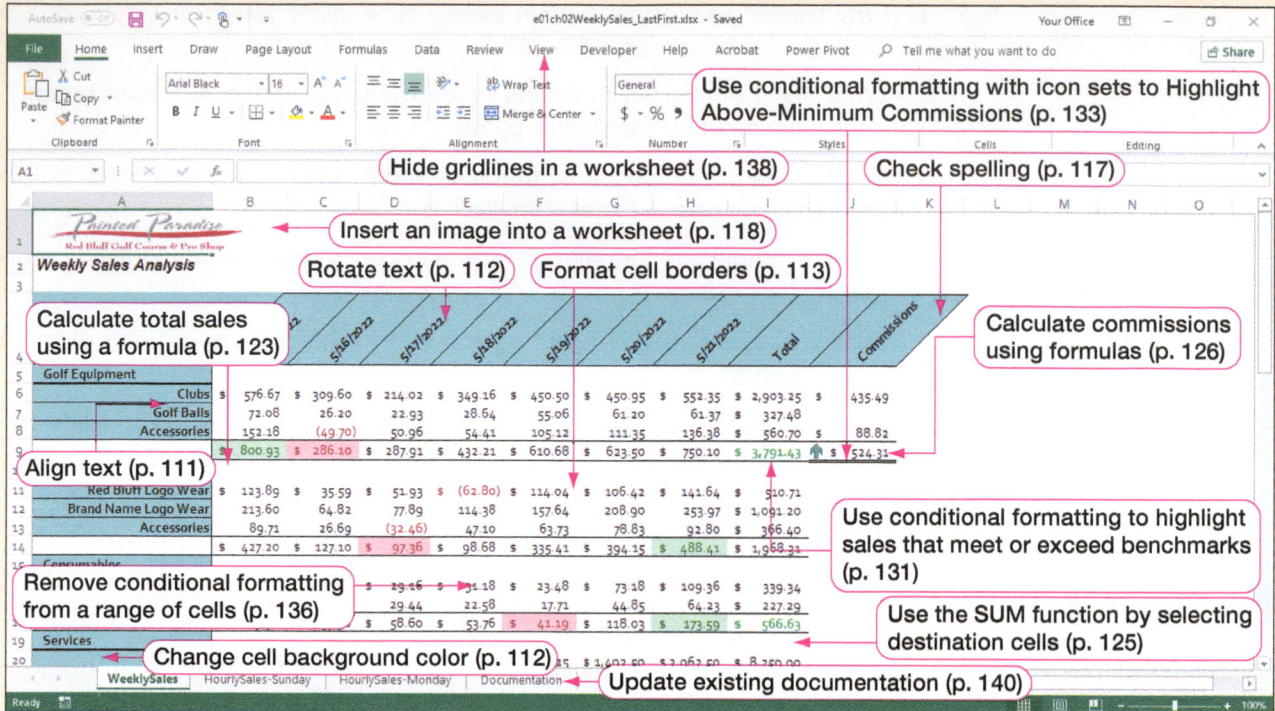

Figure 30

Screenshot of Microsoft Excel 2019, © Microsoft Corporation

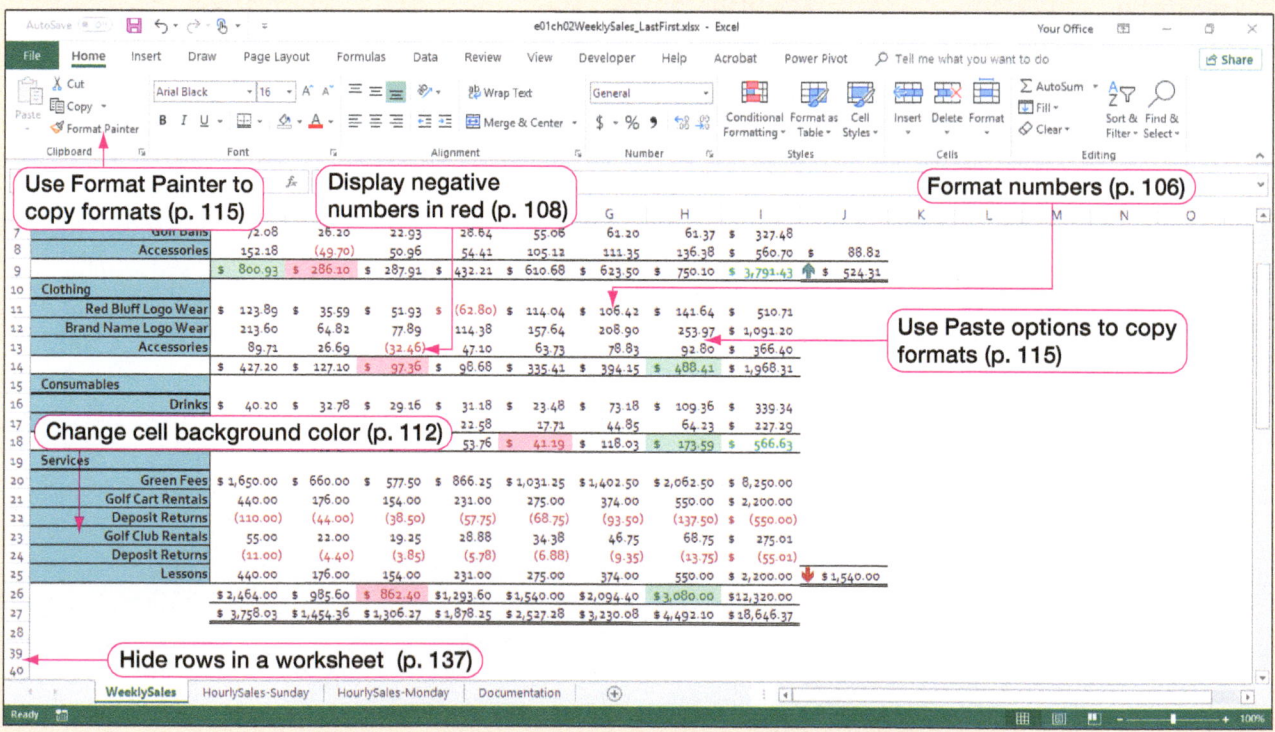

Figure 31

Screenshot of Microsoft Excel 2019, © Microsoft Corporation

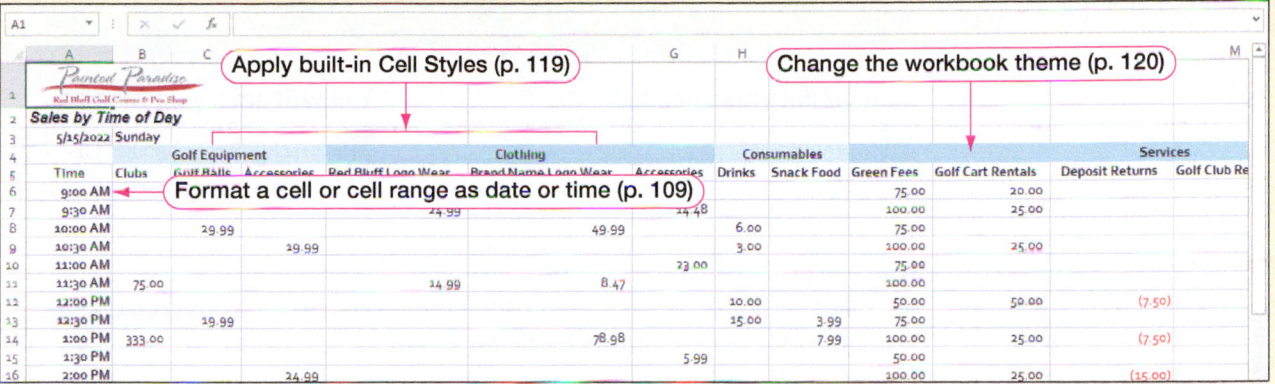

Figure 32

Screenshot of Microsoft Excel 2019, © Microsoft Corporation

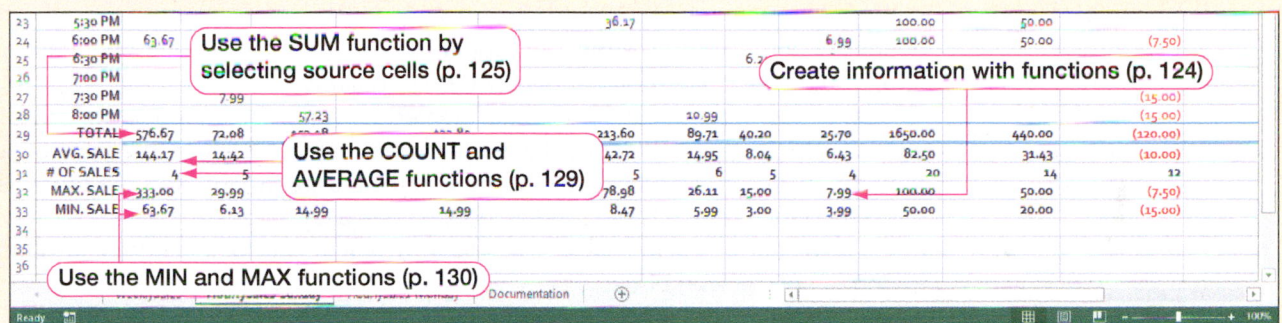

Figure 33

Screenshot of Microsoft Excel 2019, © Microsoft Corporation

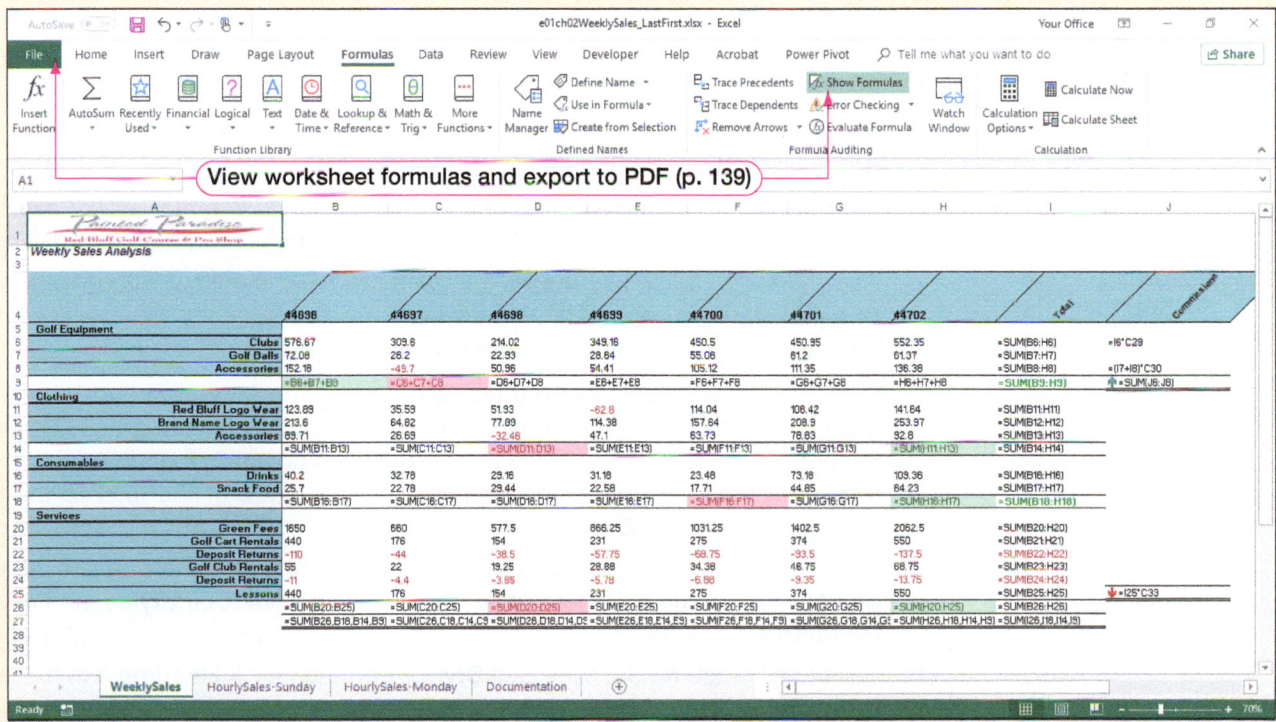

Figure 34

Screenshot of Microsoft Excel 2019, © Microsoft Corporation

Student data files needed:

 e01ch02SpaSchedule.xlsx

 e01ch02turquoise_oasis.jpg

You will save your files as:

e01ch02SpaSchedule_LastFirst.xlsx

e01ch02SpaSchedule_LastFirst.pdf

Spa Schedule

Production & Operations

Irene Kai, another manager at the Turquoise Oasis Spa, has exported sales data from a database program into an Excel spreadsheet to facilitate the analysis of services received by a client during a visit to the spa. This spreadsheet is in the initial development stages, but the intention is to keep track of the treatments performed on an individual client during the client's stay at the resort, the therapist who performed each service, and the treatments that seem most popular. This will allow the staff to review spa usage in a visually appealing layout, notice trends in treatment choices, and improve the scheduling of a therapist. In the future, it might lead to the mailing of special promotions to regular or repeat customers, a reevaluation of pricing, or the addition or deletion of treatments based on popularity.

Irene has imported the data and created a workbook that will consist of three worksheets. One worksheet contains the clients' names, a list of the dates of service, the type of treatment administered, the cost of the treatment, and the therapist who performed that service. A second worksheet has a list of spa therapists and the days of the week and times that each is available. The third worksheet contains information to document the workbook.

a. Open Excel, click **Open** in the left pane, and then double-click **This PC**. Navigate through the folder structure to the location of your student data files, and then double-click **e01ch02SpaSchedule**. If a Security Warning message displays, click the **Enable Editing** button.

b. Click the **File** tab, click **Save As**, and then double-click **This PC**. In the Save As dialog box, navigate to the location where you are saving your project files, and then change the file name to e01ch02SpaSchedule_LastFirst using your last and first name. Click **Save**.

c. On the **ScheduleByDate** worksheet, click the **Page Layout** tab. In the Themes group, click **Themes**, and then select **Ion** from the gallery.

d. Click cell **A1**. Click the **Home** tab, and then, in the Cells group, click **Format**, and then click **Row Height**. Type 60 in the Row height box, and then click **OK**.

e. Click cell **E1**. Click the **Insert** tab, and then, in the Illustrations group, click **Pictures**. Navigate to the location where your student data files are stored, click **e01ch02turquoise_oasis.jpg**, and then click **Insert**.

f. Click the **Picture Tools Format** tab, and then, in the Arrange group, click **Align**. If necessary, select **Snap to Grid**. Click the right horizontal sizing handle and snap the right edge of the logo to the border between columns **F** and **G**. Click the bottom vertical sizing handle and snap the bottom edge of the logo to the border between rows **1** and **2**.

g. Select the cell range **A2:J2**. Click the **Home** tab, and then, in the Alignment group, click **Merge & Center**. In the Styles group, click **Cell Styles**, and then click **Heading 4** in the gallery.

h. Select cell range **A4:J4**, click **Cell Styles**, and then click **Heading 3** in the gallery.

i. Click cell **A2**, and then, in the Clipboard group, click **Copy**. Right-click cell **A26**, and then, in the Paste Options shortcut menu, select **Formatting**. On the Home tab, in the Alignment group, click **Align Left**.

j. Click cell **A6**. On the Home tab, in the Number group, click the **General Number Format**, and then select **Short Date**. With cell A6 still selected, in the Clipboard group, click **Format Painter**, and then select cell range **A7:A23**.

k. Select cell range **I6:I23**. In the Number group, click the **Number Format** arrow, and then select **Currency**. In the Number group, click **Decrease Decimal** two times.

l. Select cell range **C6:C23**. Click the **Number Format** arrow, and then select **More Number Formats**. In the Type box, select **1:30 PM**, and then click **OK**.

m. Click cell **J10**. On the Home tab, in the Editing group, Click **AutoSum**, select the cell range **I6:I9**, and then press ⏎. Click cell **J13**. On the Home tab, in the Editing group, click **AutoSum**, select the cell range **I11:I12**, and then press ⏎. Click cell **J18**. Click **AutoSum**, select cell range **I14:I17**, and then press ⏎. Click cell **J21**. Click **AutoSum**, select cell range **I19:I20**, and then press ⏎. Click cell **J24**. Click **AutoSum**, select cell range **I22:I23**, and then press ⏎.

n. Click cell **C28**, type **=MAX(** Click cell **J10**, press and hold Ctrl. Click cells **J13**, **J18**, **J21**, and **J24**. Press Ctrl + ⏎. Click cell **J24**, click the **Format Painter**, and then click cell **C28**.

o. Select cell **J10**, press and hold Ctrl, and then select cells **J13**, **J18**, **J21**, and **J24**. On the Home tab, in the Styles group, click **Conditional Formatting**, point to **Highlight Cells Rules**, and then select **Greater Than**. Type **=C$29** in the Format cells that are GREATER THAN box. Click the **with** arrow, and then select **Green Fill with Dark Green Text**, then click **OK**.

p. Right-click the header for row **5**, and then click **Hide** to hide the row.

q. Click cell **I25**, and then type Total and then press Ctrl + ⏎. On the Home tab, in the Alignment group, click **Align Right**.

r. Click cell **J25**. On the Home tab, in the Editing group, click the **AutoSum** button. Click cell **J10**, and then press and hold the Ctrl key. Click cells **J13**, **J18**, **J21**, **J24**, and then press Ctrl + ⏎.

s. In cell **J25**, on the Home tab, in the Styles group, click **Cell Styles** and then select the **Total** style.

t. Select cell range **A28:C29**. On the Home tab, in the Font group, click the **Border** arrow, and then select **Thick Outside Borders**. With A28:C29 still selected, on the Home tab, in the Font group, click the **Fill** arrow and then select **White, Background 1, Darker 5%**.

u. Click the **TherapistSchedule** worksheet. Select cell **C8**, type Monday and then press Ctrl + ⏎. Click and hold the **fill handle**, and then fill the cell contents through cell range **C9:C14**. With cell range C8:C14 still selected, press Ctrl + C. Click cell **C16**, press and hold Ctrl, and then click cell **C24**. Press Ctrl + V. Press Esc to clear the Clipboard.

v. Select cell range **A6:D6**. On the Home tab, in the Styles group, click the **Cell Styles** button, and then select **20% - Accent5** from the gallery. In the Font group, click **Bold**.

w. Select cell range **A8:A14**. Press Ctrl, and then select cell ranges **B8:B14**, **A16:A22**, **B16:B22**, **A24:A30**, and **B24:B30**. On the Home tab, in the Alignment group, click **Merge & Center**. In the Alignment group, click **Orientation**, and then select **Vertical Text**. In the Alignment group, click **Middle Align**. In the Font group, click **Bold**. Select columns **A:B**. In the Cells group, click **Format**, and select **AutoFit Column Width**.

x. Click the **Documentation** worksheet. Click cell **A8**, insert today's date and then press Tab. In cell **B8**, type your name in the Firstname Lastname format, and then press Tab. In cell **C8**, type Calculated daily totals Press ⏎. In cell **C9**, type Determined maximum day's sales Press ⏎. In cell **C10**, type Formatted daily sales totals that met target with green text Press ⏎, and then press Ctrl + Home.

y. Click the **ScheduleByDate** worksheet. On the Page Layout tab, in the Page Setup group, click **Orientation**, and then select **Landscape**. In the Scale to Fit group, click the **Width** arrow, and then select **1 page**.

z. On the ScheduleByDate worksheet, click the **View** tab. In the Show group, click to deselect **Gridlines** to remove the gridlines.

aa. Click the **Review** tab, in the Proofing group, click **Spelling** to check the spelling of the entire worksheet. Ignore proper names when completing the spell check.

bb. Add a footer to all worksheets. Click the **Insert** tab, in the Text group, click **Header & Footer**. On the Design tab, in the Navigation group, click **Go to Footer**. Click in the center footer. On the Design tab, in the Header & Footer Elements group, click **File Name** to insert the file name in the center footer on all worksheets. Click any cell out of the footer, and then on the taskbar click **Normal View** to return all worksheets to Normal view.

cc. Click the **File** tab, click **Export**, and then, under Create a PDF/XPS Document, click **Create PDF/XPS**. Be sure Open file after publishing is not checked. Click **Options**. In the Options dialog box, under Publish what, click **Entire workbook**, and then click **OK**. Navigate to the folder where you are saving your files. In the File name box, type **e01ch02SpaSchedule_LastFirst** using your last and first name, and then click **Publish**.

dd. **Save** the workbook, exit Excel, and then submit your files as directed by your instructor.

Problem Solve 1

 MyLab IT Grader

Student data file needed:

 e01ch02BooksInventory.xlsx

You will save your files as:

 e01ch02BooksInventory_LastFirst.xlsx

e01ch02BooksInventory_LastFirst.pdf

Human Resources

Accounting & Finance

Store Inventory

Roger Harding, the manager of Thunder City Bookstore, wants to improve the appearance of the workbook created to review the store inventory. Roger has a workbook started with the Inventory, Promotions, and Documentation worksheets already created. This project will require you to use your Excel skills to improve Roger's workbook. Some of the actions needed include enhancing the appearance of the worksheets by applying a theme, using built-in cell styles, rotating labels, changing a worksheet theme, formatting a section of a worksheet as a table, and using and printing functions and formulas.

a. Open the Excel file, **e01ch02BooksInventory**. Save your file as **e01ch02BooksInventory_LastFirst** using your last and first name.

b. Change the workbook theme to **Mesh**.

c. On the **Inventory** worksheet, in cell **D4**, enter the label Inventory Cost In cell **E4**, enter the label Total

d. In cell **D6**, enter a formula to calculate the total cost of inventory for **gym shorts**. The inventory cost is calculated by the price per unit times the quantity in stock. If necessary, format the result as **Currency** with two decimal places. Copy the formula entered in cell D6 to the cell range **D7:D39**. Then delete the contents of cells **D10**, **D15**, **D20**, **D25**, **D26**, **D33**, and **D34**.

e. In cell **E10**, enter a function to calculate the total cost of all gym shorts in inventory in the cell range **D6:D9**. In cell **E15**, enter a function to calculate the total cost of all sweatpants in inventory. In cell **E20**, enter a function to calculate the total cost of all T-shirts in inventory. In cell **E25**, enter a function to calculate the total cost of all sweatshirts in inventory. In cell **E33**, enter a function to calculate the total cost of all school supplies in inventory. In cell **E40**, enter a function to calculate the total cost of all miscellaneous items in inventory.

f. Select cell ranges **A10:E10, A15:E15, A20:E20, A25:E25, A33:E33**, and **A40:E40**. Apply **Tan, Accent 3, Lighter 40%** fill color.

g. Merge and center cell range **A1:E1**. Apply the **Title** cell style to the selected range, and then change the fill color to **Tan, Accent 3, Lighter 40%**.

h. Merge and center cell range **A2:E2**. Apply the **Heading 2** cell style.

i. In cell **B45**, enter a function to display the average price per unit of clothing items only. It is okay to include blank cells in the cell range.

j. In cell **B46**, enter a function to display the highest price per unit of any item in inventory. It is okay to include blank cells in the cell range.

k. In cell **B47**, enter a function to display the lowest price per unit of any item in inventory. It is okay to include blank cells in the cell range.

l. In cell range **D6:D39**, apply conditional formatting on the Inventory Costs in column D to highlight any inventory cost that is greater than **$500.00** to appear **Green Fill with Dark Green Text**. Clear the conditional format from cells **D10, D15, D20, D25:D26, D33:D34**.

m. Change the column width of column **A** to 35 and columns **B:E** to 10

n. Hide rows **42:43**.

o. In cell **D41**, type Grand Total and then right align the text.

p. In cell **E41**, create a function to add the noncontiguous cell of **E10, E15, E20, E25, E33**, and **E40**.

q. Hide the gridlines on the Inventory worksheet.

r. Select cell range **A4:E4**, apply **Bold**, and **Italic**. Apply a **Thick Bottom Border**. Change the orientation of the text in this range to **Angle Counterclockwise**. Apply **Middle Align**.

s. In the Inventory worksheet, in the center position, add the header Open Daily from 10 AM to 8 PM Return the worksheet to **Normal** view.

t. On the **Promotions** worksheet, change the format for cell **B5** to **Long Date** format. Use the Format Painter to apply the format in cell B5 to cell ranges **B6:B8** and **C5:C8**.

u. Apply the **Heading 2** cell style to cells **A4:D4**.

v. Create a copy of the Inventory worksheet and name the new worksheet Formulas Display the formulas on the Formulas worksheet. Move the Formulas worksheet to the right of the Promotions worksheet.

w. On the **Documentation** worksheet:

   • In cells **A8** and **A22**, type 10/16/2022

   • In cells **B8** and **C22**, type your name in Firstname Lastname format.

   • In cell **C8**, type Added formulas and formatting to the Inventory worksheet

   • In cell **C9**, type Added a Formulas worksheet

   • In cell **B22**, type Formulas

x. Add the **File Name** code to the center footer on all worksheets. Return all worksheets to Normal view.

Grader Heads Up
In the MyLab IT Grader, you will not be creating a PDF.

y. Spell check the entire workbook.

z. Scale all worksheets for Height and Width to fit to **1 page**. Set the page orientation of the Promotions, Formulas, and Documentation worksheet to **Landscape** orientation.

aa. Export the Inventory worksheet to PDF. Name the PDF file **e01ch02BooksInventory_LastFirst** Close the PDF file.

bb. Save the workbook, exit Excel, and then submit your files as directed by your instructor.

Critical Thinking Conditional formatting was used to identify high inventory costs. How else could conditional formatting be used in this workbook?

Perform 1: Perform in Your Career

Student data file needed:

 e01ch02Plants.xlsx

You will save your files as:

 e01ch02Plants_LastFirst.xlsx

 e01ch02Plants_LastFirst.pdf

Sales & Marketing

Fundraising Summary

You are the executive director of the Women's Center. You just held the yearly month-long fundraiser for the center, an annual plant sale. Now you need to summarize the data and look for sales trends.

a. Open the Excel file, **e01ch02Plants.xlsx**. Save your file as **e01ch02Plants_LastFirst.xlsx** using your last and first name.

b. The Cost (C) column records what the Women's Center paid for the herbs. The Price column (D) records the herb's selling price at the plant sale. Format the values in the Cost and Price columns using the Accounting Number Format, 2 decimal places.

c. In cell F1, enter the label Total Cost

d. In cell F2, enter a formula to calculate the Total Cost in the F column for each of the herbs. Fill the formula down column F.

e. In cell G1, enter the label Total Revenue

f. In cell G2, enter a formula to calculate the Total Revenue in column G for each of the herbs. Fill the formula down column G.

g. In cell H1, enter the label Profit

h. In cell H2, enter a formula to calculate the profit from the sale of each of the herbs in the H column. Profit is the difference between Total Revenue and Total Cost.

i. Adjust the column width of columns F:H so the data in each column is visible.

j. Use conditional formatting to format the top five profit generators using a Green Fill with Dark Green Text. Highlight the bottom five profit generators using a Light Red Fill with Dark Red Text.

k. The profit shown for the 8-inch Mints seems high to you. When you investigate, you discover that 162 plants were sold, not 1062. Make the correction.

l. Name the worksheet **HerbSalesReport**

m. Insert two rows above row 1. Merge and center A1:H1. Enter the title **Annual Plant Sale** in cell A1. Apply the Title style, and then apply bold to the title.

n. Using a function, in row 31 calculate the overall Total Cost, Total Revenue, and Profit.

o. In cell B33, use a function to determine the total herb count.

p. In cell E33, use a function to determine the largest herb Quantity on hand.

q. Place a Thick Outside Border on cell ranges A33:B33 and D33:E33.

r. Apply Bold to cells A33 and D33. Wrap the text in cell D33.

s. Hide row 2 and remove the gridlines.

t. Apply Accent5 cell style to cell range A3:H3. Apply a Thick Bottom Border to cell range A3:H3.

u. Add the File Name code to the left footer on all worksheets. Prepare all worksheets for printing. Each worksheet should print on one page.

v. Spell check the entire workbook.

w. Update the Documentation sheet as requested by your instructor.

x. Export the HerbSalesReport worksheet to a PDF named **e01ch02Plants_LastFirst**

y. Save your workbook, exit Excel, and then submit your files as directed by your instructor.

Excel Business Unit 1 **CAPSTONE**

Understanding the Fundamentals

This business unit had two outcomes:

Learning Outcome 1:
Use Excel to enter text, number, date, and time data to create efficient, effective worksheets.

Learning Outcome 2:
Use Excel to effectively communicate information using functions and worksheet formatting.

In Business Unit 1 Capstone, students will demonstrate competency in these outcomes through a series of business problems at various levels from guided practice, problem solving an existing spreadsheet, and performing to create new spreadsheets.

More Practice 1

Student data files needed:

e01BeverageSales.xlsx

e01Indigo5.jpg

You will save your files as:

e01BeverageSales_LastFirst.xlsx

e01BeverageSales_LastFirst.pdf

Beverage Sales and Inventory Analysis

Production & Operations

Finance & Accounting

The Painted Paradise Resort & Spa offers a wide assortment of beverages through the Indigo5 restaurant and bar. The resort must track the inventory levels of these beverages as well as the sales and costs associated with each item. Restaurant manager Alberto Dimas has asked you to analyze the inventory and sales data found in the worksheet. There are four categories of beverages: beer, wine, soda, and water. You also have three inventory figures: Starting, Delivered, and Ending. You will work with a beverage sales workbook to generate an analysis of beverage sales in which you identify units sold of each beverage, cost of goods sold, revenue, profit, profit margin, and appropriate totals.

a. Open **Excel**, click **Open** in the left pane, and then double-click **This PC**. Navigate through the folder structure to the location of your student data files, and then double-click **e01BeverageSales**. If a Security Warning message displays, click the **Enable Editing** button.

b. Click the **File** tab, click **Save As**, and then double-click **This PC**. In the Save As dialog box, navigate to the location where you are saving your project files, and then change the file name to e01BeverageSales_LastFirst using your last and first name. Click **Save**.

c. On the **BeverageSales** worksheet, select cell range **C2:K2**, and then on the Home tab, in the Alignment group, click **Merge & Center** for the selected range. On the Home tab, in the Styles group, click **Cell Styles**, and then select the **Title** style.

d. Select cell range **C3:K3**, and then click **Merge & Center** for the selected range. Apply the **Heading 4** cell style to the selected range.

e. Insert a hard return by pressing [Alt]+[Enter] between the words as directed—be sure to remove any spaces between the words before pressing [Alt]+[Enter].

   • In cell **C6**, insert a hard return between **Starting** and **Inventory**.

   • In cell **D6**, insert a hard return between **Inventory** and **Delivered**.

   • In cell **E6**, insert a hard return between **Ending** and **Inventory**.

f. Enter the following calculations.

- Click cell **F7**. Calculate Units Sold by adding Starting Inventory to Inventory Delivered and then subtracting Ending Inventory. Type = click cell **C7**, type + click cell **D7,** type - and then click cell **E7.** Press Ctrl+Enter. Press Ctrl+C to copy the contents of cell F7. Highlight cell ranges **F8:F12**, **F15:F18**, **F21:F25**, and **F28:F29**. Right-click any of the highlighted cells, and then select **Paste Formulas** from the gallery. If any cells contain a series of number signs (#), select the column. On the Home tab, in the Cells group, click **Format**, and then click **AutoFit Column Width**.

- Click cell **H7**. Calculate Cost of Goods Sold by multiplying Units Sold by Cost Per Unit. Type = click cell **F7**, type * and then click cell **G7**. Press Ctrl+Enter, and then copy the formula in cell H7 to cell ranges **H8:H12**, **H15:H18**, **H21:H25**, and **H28:H29**. If any cells contain a series of number signs (#), select the column, and then on the Home tab, in the Cells group, click the **Format** button, and then select **AutoFit Column Width**.

- Click cell **J7**. Calculate Revenue as Units Sold multiplied by Sale Price Per Unit. Type = click cell **F7**, type * and then click cell **I7**. Press Ctrl+Enter, and then copy the formula in cell J7 to cell ranges **J8:J12**, **J15:J18**, **J21:J25**, and **J28:J29**. If any cells contain a series of number signs (#), select the column, and then apply **AutoFit Column Width**.

- Click cell **K7**. Calculate Profit Margin as (Revenue - Cost of Goods Sold)/Revenue. Type =(click cell **J7**, type - click cell **H7**, type)/ and then click cell **J7**. Press Ctrl+Enter, and then copy the formula in cell K7 to cell ranges **K8:K12**, **K15:K18**, **K21:K25**, and **K28:K29**.

g. Select cell ranges **C13:F13**, **C19:F19**, **C26:F26**, **C30:F30**, and cells **H13**, **J13**, **H19**, **J19**, **H26**, **J26**, **H30**, **J30**. On the Home tab, in the Editing group, click **AutoSum**.

h. Click cell **C31**. Calculate the total number of items in Starting Inventory for all categories combined by using the SUM() function. Type =SUM(C13,C19,C26,C30) and then using the fill handle, copy cell C31 to cell range **D31:F31** as well as cells **H31** and **J31**. If any cells contain a series of number signs (#), select the cells, and then apply **AutoFit Column Width**.

i. Make the following formatting changes.

- Format the row height of row 6 to 32

- Select cell range **C6:K6** along with cells **B13**, **B19**, **B26**, **B30**, and **B31**. On the Home tab, in the Alignment group, click **Align Right**.

- Select cell ranges **C13:K13**, **C19:K19**, **C26:K26**, and **C30:K30**. On the Home tab, in the Font group, click the **Border** button, and then select **Top and Bottom Border**.

- Select cell range **C31:K31**, and then add a **Bottom Double Border** to the selected range.

j. Select cell range **C7:F31**. On the Home tab, in the Number group, click the **Number Format** arrow, and then select **More Number Formats**. On the Number tab, select **Number** if necessary, select **Use 1000 Separator** (,), and then change the Decimal places to 0

k. Select cell range **G7:J31**, and then format the selected range as **Number** with a comma separator and **two** decimal places.

l. Copy cell **K12**, and then, on the Home tab, in the Clipboard group, click **Paste** to paste the formulas into cells **K13**, **K19**, **K26**, **K30**, and **K31**. Select cell range **K7:K31**. On the Home tab, in the Number group, click **Percent Style**, and then click **Increase Decimal** twice.

m. Select cells **H13**, **J13**, **H19**, **J19**, **H26**, **J26**, **H30**, **J30**, **H31**, and **J31**. On the Home tab, in the Number group, click the **Number Format** arrow, and then click **Currency**. If any cells contain a series of number signs (#), select the cells, and then apply **AutoFit Column Width**.

n. Select cell range **F7:F12**. On the Home tab, in the Styles group, click **Conditional Formatting**. Point to **Top/Bottom Rules** and then select **Top 10 Items**. Change the number of ranked items to **1** and then select **Green Fill with Dark Green Text**.

o. Click cell **F12**, and then on the Home tab, in the Clipboard group, click **Copy**. Select cell range **J7:J12**. Right-click the selected cell range, and then under **Paste Options**, click **Paste Formatting**. Continue pasting conditional formatting as follows.

- Select cell range **F15:F18**, right-click the selection, and then click **Paste Formatting**.
- Select cell range **J15:J18**, right-click the selection, and then click **Paste Formatting**.
- Select cell range **F21:F25**, right-click the selection, and then click **Paste Formatting**.
- Select cell range **J21:J25**, right-click the selection, and then click **Paste Formatting**.
- Select cell range **F28:F29**, right-click the selection, and then click **Paste Formatting**.
- Select cell range **J28:J29**, right-click the selection, and then click **Paste Formatting**.

p. Select cell range **J7:J12**, press Ctrl, and then select cell ranges **J15:J18**, **J21:J25**, and **J28:J29**. Click **Increase Decimal** two times.

q. Select cell range **A6:K6**, press Ctrl, and then click cells **A14**, **A20**, and **A27**. On the Home tab, in the Styles group, click **Cell Styles**, and then, under Themed Cell Styles, apply **Accent6** to the selected cells. With the cells still selected, press Ctrl and then select cell ranges **B13:K13**, **B19:K19**, **B26:K26**, and **B30:K31**. Click **Bold**.

r. Delete row **4**.

s. Click the **Page Layout** tab. In the Themes group, click **Themes**, and then click **Organic** to change the workbook theme. Click the **Home** tab. Select columns **A:K**, and then in the Cells group, click the **Format** button and select **AutoFit Column Width**. Click the **Page Layout** tab, and in the Page Setup group, click **Orientation**. Select **Landscape**. In the Scale to Fit group, change the Width to **1 page**, and then press Ctrl+Home.

t. Click the **Insert** tab, and then in the Illustrations group, click **Pictures**. Navigate to the location of your student data files, and then click **e01Indigo5**. Click **Insert**. On the **Picture Tools Format** tab, in the Arrange group, click **Align**, and then click **Snap to Grid**. Drag the round resizing handle on the right side of the logo left until the right border is between columns **B** and **C**. Drag the round resizing handle on the bottom of the logo up until the bottom border is between rows **4** and **5**.

u. Click the **Documentation** worksheet, click cell **A8**, and then enter today's date In cell **B8**, type your name in the Firstname Lastname format. In cell **C8**, type Formatted BeverageSales worksheet and then press Enter. Press Ctrl+Home.

v. On the **Insert** tab, in the Text group, click **Header & Footer**. In the Navigation group, click **Go to Footer**, and then click the **File Name** code in the left footer. Click cell **C1**, and then click **Normal** view.

w. Click the **File** tab, click **Export**, and then under Create a PDF/XPS Document, click **Create PDF/XPS**. Be sure Open file after publishing is not checked. Click **Options**. In the Options dialog box, under Publish what, click **Entire workbook**, and then click **OK**. Navigate to the folder where you are saving your files. In the File name box, verify **e01BeverageSales_LastFirst** is the file name, and then click **Publish**.

> **Mac Troubleshooting**
> If using a Mac, on the File menu, click Save As, and in the Save As dialog box, under File Format, select PDF.

x. Save the workbook, exit Excel, and then submit your files as directed by your instructor.

Problem Solve 1

MyLab IT Grader

Student data files needed:

e01HotelDiscount.xlsx

e01PaintedParadise.jpg

You will save your files as:

e01HotelDiscount_LastFirst.xlsx

e01HotelDiscount_LastFirst.pdf

Finance & Accounting

General Business

Guest Discount Services

The Painted Paradise Resort & Spa has 700 rooms. The resort gives discounts to guests who meet certain conditions. First, the Paradise discount, a 10% discount applicable to all products and services at the resort, is offered to guests who opt into the resort's rewards program. The second, the Paramount discount, is a 15% discount for hotel rooms and services offered to groups who book a block of 40 rooms or more. Finally, the Complimentary discount, is a free room discount which may be given to customers at the discretion of the resort management. The resort's management would like to get an idea of how much revenue is lost to discounts on Friday and Saturday nights, the busiest nights of the week.

a. Open the Excel file, **e01HotelDiscount**. Save your file as e01HotelDiscount_LastFirst using your last and first name.

b. Format cell **A2** and **A7** with the **Heading 4** cell style. Merge and center cell **A2** to cell range **A2:G2**. Merge and center cell **A7** to cell range **A7:G7**. Format cell range **B3:G3** with the **Heading 3** cell style. Format cell ranges **A4:A5** and **A8:A10** with the font color **Blue** and apply **Bold**. Format cell ranges **B8:G10** as **Percent** style with **one decimal** place.

c. In cell **B26**, enter a formula to calculate Gross Sales for One Double room for Friday night by multiplying the sum of B14:B17 by the Standard Rate in cell B5.

d. In cell **B27**, calculate the discount total for the Paradise Club for One Double room for Friday night by multiplying the Standard Rate in B5 by the Discount rate in B8 and then by the number of Paradise Club rooms rented in B15.

e. In cell **B28**, calculate the Group discount total. Multiply the Standard Rate for One Double room in B5 by the Group Discount in B9 by the number of Group Discount rooms rented for Friday night in B16.

f. In cell **B29**, calculate the Comp discount total. Multiply the Standard Rate for One Double room in cell **B5** by the Comp Discount in cell **B10** and then by the number of Comp Discount rooms rented for Friday night in cell **B17**. Using the fill handle, copy the cell range **B26:B29** through cell range **C26:G29**.

g. In cell **B30**, enter a function to total the Friday net sales of cell range **B26:B29**. In cell **B31**, subtract the Net Sales from the **Gross Sales** to calculate the total discount. Copy cell range **B30:B31** through cell range **C30:G31**.

h. In cell **B34**, enter a formula to calculate Gross Sales for One Double room for Saturday night by multiplying the sum of cell range **B19:B22** by the Standard Rate in cell **B5**.

i. In cell **B35**, enter a formula to calculate the Paradise Club discount total for One Double rooms for Saturday night by multiplying the Paradise Club discount rate by the Standard Rate and then by the number of Paradise Club rooms rented in **B20**.

j. In cell **B36**, enter a formula to calculate a Group discount total for One Double rooms for Saturday night. Multiply the Standard Rate by the number of Group One Double rooms rented Saturday night and then by the Group discount.

k. In cell **B37**, enter a formula to calculate Comp discount total for One Double rooms for Saturday night. Multiply the Standard Rate for the One Double room by the One Double Comp discount and then by the number of Comp One Double rooms sold Saturday night. Using the fill handle, copy cell range **B34:B37** to cell range **C34:G37**.

l. In cell **B38**, enter a function to total the Saturday net sales of cell range **B34:B37**. In cell **B39**, subtract the Net Sales from the **Gross Sales** to calculate the total discount. Copy cell range **B38:B39** through cell range **C38:G39**.

m. In cell **B43**, calculate the Paradise Club discounts for Friday and Saturday night for One Double rooms by adding the Friday Paradise Club discounts to the Saturday Paradise Club discounts.

n. Use the fill handle to copy cell **B43** to cell range **B44:B45**. Copy cell range **B43:B45** to cell range **C43:G45**.

o. In cell **B46**, enter a function to calculate the total discounts for Friday and Saturday sales. Use the fill handle to copy the formula through cell **G46**.

p. In cell ranges **H26:H31**, **H34:H39**, and **H43:H46**, enter a function to total each row.

q. Format cell ranges **B26:G29**, **B34:G37**, and **B43:G45** as **Number**. Negative numbers should be displayed in **black** and within **parentheses**. Make sure that **two decimal places** are displayed and that **Use 1000 Separator (,)** is checked.

r. Format cell ranges **B30:H31**, **H26:H29**, **B38:H39**, **H34:H37**, **B46:H46**, and **H43:H45** with Accounting Number Format.

s. Bold cell ranges **B31:H31**, **B39:H39**, and **B46:H46**.

t. Center align cell ranges **B25:H25**, **B33:H33**, and **B42:H42**.

u. Change the width of column **A** to 15 Change the width of columns **B:H** to 13

v. Set the height of row **1** to 40 In cell **C1**, insert the picture **e01PaintedParadise.jpg**. Format the picture to **Snap to Grid**. Resize the picture to fit so the left border is between columns **C** and **D**, the right border is between columns **F** and **G**, and the bottom is between rows **1** and **2**.

w. Change the workbook theme to **Integral**. Hide the **gridlines** on the **HotelDiscounts** worksheet and change the color of the worksheet. Change the color of the worksheet tab to **Blue**.

x. Change the discount rate in cell range **B8:G8** to -.10 Change the discount rate in cell range **B9:G9** to -.15

y. In cell **A8**, add a cell note Rate Increased from 9% to 10% Depending on your version of Microsoft Office, you may not see the Note feature. In this case, enter a cell comment.

z. In cell **A9**, add a cell note Rate Increased from 10% to 15%

aa. Scale the page **Width** to **1 page**.

bb. On the **Documentation** worksheet, change the page orientation to **Landscape** and scale the page **Width** to **1 page**.

cc. In cell **A8**, enter today's date In cell **B8**, type your name in the Firstname Lastname format. In cell **C8**, enter Created formulas to determine total amount of discounts offered

dd. Delete the **Specials** worksheet. Insert the **File Name** code in the center footer of the remaining worksheets. Check the **HotelDiscounts** worksheet for spelling. Ignore the suggestion to change Qty in cell A4 if necessary.

Grader Heads Up
The MyLab IT Grader version of this project does not include the creation of a PDF.

---

ee. Publish the entire workbook as a PDF named e01HotelDiscount_LastFirst

ff. Save the workbook, exit Excel, and submit your files as directed by your instructor.

Critical Thinking

After completing the hotel discount analysis workbook, what decision could be made about offering discounts to your hotel guests?

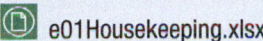
Problem Solve 2

MyLab IT Grader

Student data file needed:

 e01Housekeeping.xlsx

You will save your files as:

 e01Housekeeping_LastFirst.xlsx

e01Housekeeping_LastFirst.pdf

Productions & Operations

Housekeeping Analysis

The Painted Paradise Resort & Spa takes great pride in the efficiency of its housekeeping staff. The housekeeping staff at the Painted Paradise Resort & Spa is expected to properly clean a hotel room in an average of 25 minutes and never more than 30 minutes. Management is interested in how long it takes to begin cleaning rooms after guests check out. This is referred to as lag time—time when a room cannot be rented. The Painted Paradise Resort & Spa wants guests to be able to check in early at no charge if there is a room available. By keeping lag time to a minimum, room availability is maximized.

a. Open the Excel file, **e01Housekeeping**. Save your file as e01Housekeeping_LastFirst using your last and first name.

b. On the **HousekeepingAnalysis** worksheet, in cell range **C8:F8**, wrap the text. In cell **B8**, remove the space between Checkout and Time, and then enter a hard return.

c. Right-align cell range **A24:A29**. Move cell range **A24:A29** to **B24:B29**.

d. Merge and center cell ranges **B7:D7**, **C22:D22**, and **E22:F22**.

e. Right-align cells **A3:A5**, **A8**, **C3**, and cell range **E3:E4**. Center align cell ranges **B8:F8** and **C23:F23**.

f. In cells **A2**, **B7**, and **C22**, apply the **40% - Accent2** cell style. In cell **E22**, apply the **60% - Accent2** cell style.

g. In cell **A2**, apply the **Heading 2** cell style. In cells **B7**, **C22**, **E22**, and **A8:H8**, apply the **Heading 3** cell style. In cell ranges **A3:A5**, **E3:E4**, **C23:F23**, and cell **C3**, apply the **Heading 4** cell style.

h. Adjust the column width for the following columns:
   - Column **A** to 18
   - Columns **B:F** to 12
   - Column **G** to 20
   - Column **H** to 10

i. In cell **E9**, calculate the lag time by subtracting the checkout time from the room clean start time. Copy the formula to cell range **E10:E20**.

j. In cell **F9**, calculate the room clean duration by subtracting the room clean start from the room clean end. Copy the formula to cell range **F10:F20**.

k. In cells **D24** and **F24**, enter a function to calculate the total room cleaning lag time and room cleaning duration.

l. In cells **D25** and **F25**, enter a function to calculate the average room cleaning lag time and room cleaning duration.

m. In cells **D26** and **F26**, enter a function to calculate the minimum room cleaning lag time and room cleaning duration.

n. In cells **D27** and **F27**, enter a function to calculate the maximum room cleaning lag time and room cleaning duration.

o. In cell **C29**, enter a function to count the number of maintenance issues reported in H9:H20. Format cell C29 as **Number** with 0 decimal places.

p. Apply conditional formatting to the cell range **E9:E20** so the room with the longest lag time is formatted with **Light Red Fill with Dark Red Text**. Apply conditional formatting to the cell range **F9:F20** so the room with the longest duration time is formatted with **Light Red Fill with Dark Red Text**.

q. Apply the **Berlin** theme. Turn off worksheet **gridlines** on the **HousekeepingAnalysis** worksheet. Change the color of the worksheet tab to **Light Blue**.

r. In cell **E20**, enter the cell note Too much lag time

s. Set the Orientation to **Landscape**, and then scale the page Width to **1 page**.

t. Delete the **CleaningSupplies** worksheet. Insert the **File Name** code in the left footer of the remaining worksheets. Spellcheck the workbook.

u. On the **Documentation** worksheet, in cell **A8**, enter today's date In cell **B8**, type your name in the Firstname Lastname format. In cell **C8**, type Entered formulas to determine room cleaning lag and clean times

v. Move the **Documentation** worksheet to the right of the **HousekeepingAnalysis** worksheet.

> ## Grader Heads Up
> The MyLab IT Grader version of this project does not include the creation of a PDF.

w. Export the entire workbook to a PDF named e01Housekeeping_LastFirst

x. Save the workbook, exit Excel, and submit your files as directed by your instructor.

Perform 1: Perform in Your Life

Student data file needed:

 e01Grading.xlsx

You will save your file as:

 e01Grading_LastFirst.xlsx

Grade Analysis

Information Technology

Most students are concerned about grades and want to have some means of easily tracking grades, analyzing their performance, and calculating their current grade in every class. You will create a grade analysis workbook to assist you with tracking, calculating, and analyzing your performance in your classes.

a. Open the Excel file, **e01Grading**. Save your file as e01Grading_LastFirst using your last and first name. Rename Sheet1 with a name appropriate for this exercise.

b. A grading scale of 90-80-70-60 was entered in the worksheet. If necessary, adjust the grading scale as desired. Classes and class assignments have been entered into the workbook. Adjust to your classes and class assignments as desired.

c. Include the following calculations:
   • Using a function, calculate the total possible points for each class.
   • Using a function, calculate your total score for each class.
   • Using a formula, calculate the percentage earned on each assignment for each class.
   • Using a formula, calculate the total percentage earned in each class.

d. In cell E46, using a formula, calculate the average total percentage earned in all classes.

e. In cell E47, using a formula, calculate the lowest total percentage earned in all classes.

f. You are striving for an A in each course. Apply conditional formatting to the total percentage earned in each course based on the grading scale. For example, when 90% or greater is earned, a format is applied. When less than 90% is earned, a different format is applied.

g. Format the worksheet appropriately. Rename and color the worksheet tab containing your grade data.

h. Include a completed and well-structured Documentation worksheet.

i. Insert the File Name code in the left footer of all worksheets. Check the spelling of both worksheets.

j. Modify any page settings to ensure that each of your worksheets will print on a single page. Specify portrait or landscape orientation as is appropriate to maximize readability.

k. Apply a workbook theme. Delete any blank rows within the range A1:A47.

l. Save the workbook, exit Excel, and then submit your file as directed by your instructor.

Perform 2: How Others Perform

Student data file needed:

 e01ProjectBilling.xlsx

You will save your file as:

e01ProjectBilling_LastFirst.xlsx

Project Management Billing

Finance & Accounting

John Smart works with you at the Excellent Consulting Company. Each week, consultants are required to track how much time they spend on each project. A worksheet is used to track the date, start time, end time, project code, description of work performed, and number of billable hours completed. At the bottom of the worksheet, the hours spent on each project are summarized so clients can be billed. In your role as an internal auditor, you have been asked to double-check a tracking sheet each week. By random selection, you need to check Mr. Smith's tracking worksheet this week. Make sure his numbers are accurate, and ensure that his worksheet is set up to minimize errors. His worksheet is also in need of formatting for appearance and clarity.

a. Open the Excel file, **e01ProjectBilling**. Save your file as e01ProjectBilling_LastFirst using your last and first name.

b. The data in F7:I21 was entered into the cells and not calculated. You want to replace this data with formulas. In each cell that has a value in cell range F7:I21, subtract Start Time from End Time and multiply the difference by 24.

c. Calculate totals for each day's work in column J.

d. Examine client totals in row 22, and then correct any problems with the formulas.

e. Apply formatting, such as cell styles or bold, to improve the appearance of the worksheet.

f. Apply any data formatting that will make the data easier to interpret. Add a workbook theme to enhance the appearance of your workbook.

g. Ensure all column widths are adjusted appropriately.

h. Delete any blank worksheets.

i. Add workbook documentation as directed by your instructor. Add cell notes as you feel necessary.

j. Insert the File Name code in the left footer on all worksheets in the workbook.

k. Modify any page settings to ensure that each of the worksheets will print on a single page. Specify portrait or landscape orientation as is appropriate to maximize readability.

l. Save the workbook, exit Excel, and then submit your file as directed by your instructor.

Student data file needed: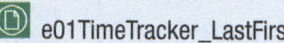

Blank Excel workbook

You will save your file as:

e01TimeTracker_LastFirst.xlsx

Finance & Accounting

Human Resources

Personal Time Tracking

You have started working as a computer programmer with BetaWerks Software Corporation. The company requires you to track the time that you spend doing different things during the day each week. This helps the company to determine how many of your hours are billable to customers. You have several different projects to work on as well as a few training sessions throughout the week. The company pays for one 15-minute coffee break and a one-hour lunch each day. Any additional time is considered personal time.

a. Start Excel, and then open a blank workbook. Save your file as **e01TimeTracker_LastFirst** using your last and first name. Rename Sheet1 with a name appropriate to this exercise.

b. Create a worksheet to track your time for the company this week. The following requirements must be met.

- The worksheet should identify the first day of the work week with a title such as Week of mm/dd/yyyy.

- Your time must be broken down by project/client and weekdays.

- Time not billable to a project should be classified as Unbillable.

- Unbillable time should be broken into at least two categories: Breaks and Work.

c. Set up your worksheet so you can easily calculate the amount of time you spent working on each account, in meetings, in training, and on breaks according to the following information.

- Monday, you spent two hours in a meeting with your development team. You will bill this to the BetaWerks Software company as unbillable hours. After the meeting, you took a 20-minute coffee break. After your break, you spent two hours and 15 minutes working on your project for Garske Advising. After a one-hour lunch, you attended a two-hour training and development meeting. Before heading home for the day, you spent two hours working on the ISBC Distributing project.

- Tuesday morning, you spent four hours on the Klemisch Kompany project. To help break up the morning, you took a 20-minute coffee break at 10:00. You had time for only a 30-minute lunch because you had to get back to the office for a team-building activity. The activity lasted 40 minutes. To finish the day, you spent four hours working on the Garske Advising assignment.

- Wednesday morning, you spent two hours each on the Garske Advising and Klemisch Kompany projects. Lunch was a quick 30 minutes because you had a conference call with Mr. Atkinson from ISBC at 1 p.m. The conference call took one hour, and then you spent an additional three hours working on the ISBC project.

- Thursday, the day started with a 30-minute update with your supervisor. Following the meeting, you were able to spend two hours on the ISBC project. After a 15-minute coffee break, you started on a new project for K&M Worldwide for 90 minutes. You took a 45-minute lunch break; then spent two and a half hours on the Klemisch Kompany project and one and a half hours on your work for L&H United.

- Friday started with a two-hour training and development session about a new software package that BetaWerks is starting to implement, followed by a 15-minute coffee break. After your coffee break, you were able to squeeze in two more hours for L&H United before taking a one-hour lunch. After lunch, you put in four hours on the Klemisch Kompany project before finally going home for the week.

d. BetaWerks bills your time spent on each account according to the following rates.

Klemisch Kompany	$275
Garske Advising	$250
ISBC Distributing	$225
K&M Worldwide	$175
L&H United	$200

e. Your salary is $100,000/year with benefits. Given two weeks of vacation, you cost BetaWerks $2,000 in salary and benefits per week.

f. Include in your worksheet a calculation of your profit/loss to BetaWerks for the week.

g. Be sure to document your worksheet using a separate Documentation worksheet, comments, and instructions.

h. Modify any page settings to ensure that each of your worksheets will print on a single page. Specify portrait or landscape orientation as is appropriate to maximize readability.

i. Insert the File Name code in the left footer of all worksheets.

j. Save the workbook, exit Excel, and then submit your file as directed by your instructor.

Perform 4: Perform in Your Team

Student data file needed:

 Blank Excel workbook

You will save your file as:

 e01CheckRegister_TeamName.xlsx

Check Register

Finance & Accounting

You volunteer time with a local nonprofit, the Mayville Community Theatre. Because of your business background, the board of directors has asked you to serve as the new treasurer and to track all the monetary transactions for the group.

a. Select one team member to set up the document by completing steps b through e. Then continue with step f.

b. Open your browser, and then navigate to either https://www.onedrive.live.com, https://www.drive.google.com, or any other instructor-assigned location. Be sure all members of the team have an account on the chosen system, such as Microsoft or Google.

c. Create a new workbook, and then save it as e01CheckRegister_TeamName Replace Name with the number assigned to your team by your instructor.

d. Rename Sheet1 as CheckRegister-TeamName Replace Name with the number of your team.

e. Share the worksheet with the other members of your team. Make sure that each team member has the appropriate permission to edit the document.

f. Hold a team meeting and plan. Lay out on paper the worksheet you are going to build, discuss the requirements of each of the remaining steps, and then divide the remaining steps (steps g through n) among team members. Note that the steps should be completed in order, so as each team member completes his or her steps, he or she should notify the entire team, not just the team member responsible for the next step.

g. Create the Check Register worksheet to track receipts and expenditures that should be assigned to one of the following categories:

- Costumes
- Marketing
- Operating and Maintenance
- Scripts and Royalties
- Set Construction
- Deposit.

Also track the following for each receipt or expenditure: the date, amount of payment, check/reference number, recipient, and item description.

h. Enter the following receipts and expenditures under the appropriate category.

Date	Item	Paid To	Check or Ref. #	Amount
11/1/2022	Starting Balance	N/A		$1793.08
11/2/2022	Royalties for "The Cubicle"	Office Publishing Company	95201	–$400.00
11/2/2022	Scripts for "The Cubicle"	Office Publishing Company	95211	–$250.00
11/5/2022	Building Maintenance—Ticket Office	Fix It Palace	95212	–$187.92
11/8/2022	Patron Donation	N/A	53339	$1,000.00
11/12/2022	Costumes for "The Cubicle"	Jane's Fabrics	95213	–$350.00
11/21/2022	Building Materials for set construction of "The Cubicle"	Fix It Palace	95214	–$430.00
11/30/2022	TV and Radio ads for "The Cubicle"	AdSpace	95215	–$229.18
11/30/2022	General Theater Operating Expenses—November	The Electric Co-op, City Water Works	95216	–$149.98
12/15/2022	Ticket Revenue from "The Cubicle"	N/A	59431	$1,115.50
12/31/2022	General Theater Operating Expenses—December	The Electric Co-op, City Water Works	95217	–$195.13

i. Money is deposited periodically into the checking account. Include a column to track deposits.

j. Finally, include a column to track the running balance. This should be updated any time money is deposited into or withdrawn from the account.

k. If the running account balance drops below $1,000, there should be a conditional formatting alert for any balance figure below the threshold.

l. Document the check register using a separate Documentation worksheet.

m. Modify any page settings to ensure that each of your worksheets will print on a single page. Specify portrait or landscape orientation as is appropriate to maximize readability.

n. Insert the File Name code in the left footer on all worksheets in the workbook. Include a list of the names of the students in your team in the right section of the footer.

o. Save the workbook, exit Excel, and then submit your file as directed by your instructor.

Excel Business Unit 2

Conducting Business Analysis

Businesses must manage and analyze data daily. This can be a difficult feat for any business employee. However, Excel can help you organize data, making that data easier to manage, update, and analyze. You can also use Excel to report or present information to internal and external customers, company stakeholders, or your supervisor. This business unit will introduce you to the importance of using Excel for business analysis.

Learning Outcome 1

Use Excel to create formulas and functions to perform calculations, analyze data, solve problems, and help in making wise business decisions.

REAL WORLD SUCCESS

"The skills I have learned through Excel have become incredibly valuable in my everyday life. I recently worked at a private golf course and was asked to create an inventory workbook to track beverage cart sales. This would allow the golf course to forecast demand and predict the amount of starting inventory we needed to maintain. In addition, we needed to use functions that would be user-friendly for the beverage cart employees. At the end of the day, the beverage cart employees would count to see how many items from the set amount of inventory were missing and input the numbers into the Excel workbook. Then Excel would compute the amount of sales the beverage cart employee would need to turn in. The remaining amount would equal the tips the employee had earned. The use of Excel functions helped the golf course to track not only its inventory but also its profits."

– Miri, alumnus

Learning Outcome 2

Use Excel to create a variety of detailed charts appropriate to the data that will visually represent and analyze the data.

REAL WORLD SUCCESS

"In my internship, I used a combo chart to analyze inventory trends over time, presenting inventory buildup or shrinkage on one axis and production levels on another. I was able to use this visual representation to better understand supply chain coordination throughout a quarter, providing my superiors with data to improve our operating efficiency. By combining these charts with charts presenting demand variance, our company was able to pinpoint sources of inventory buildup and higher operating costs."

– Steven, alumnus

Microsoft Excel

Chapter 3 CELL REFERENCES, NAMED RANGES, AND FUNCTIONS

MyLab IT Grader

Sales & Marketing

Finance & Accounting

Prepare Case

Painted Paradise Resort & Spa Wedding Planning

Clint Keller and Addison Ryan have just booked a wedding at Painted Paradise Resort & Spa. When requested by a couple, the Turquoise Oasis Spa coordinates a variety of events including spa visits, golf massages, and gift baskets made up of various spa products. Given the frequency of wedding events at the Turquoise Oasis Spa, Meda Rodate has asked for your assistance in modifying an Excel workbook that can be used and reused to plan and analyze these events in the future.

In The Light Photography/Shutterstock

Student data file needed:

 e02ch03Wedding.xlsx

You will save your file as:

 e02ch03Wedding_LastFirst.xlsx

Referencing Cells and Named Ranges

The value of Excel expands as you move from using the spreadsheet for displaying data to analyzing data in order to make informed decisions. As the complexity of a spreadsheet increases, techniques that promote effective and efficient development of the spreadsheet become of utmost importance. Integrating cell references within formulas and working with functions are common methods used in developing effective spreadsheets. These skills will become the foundation for more advanced skills.

A **cell reference** refers to a cell or range of cells within a formula or function instead of a value. A cell reference contains two parts: a column reference, which is the alphabetic portion that comes first, and a row reference, which is the numeric portion that comes last. For example, cell reference B4 refers to the intersection of column B and row 4. When a formula is created, you can simply use values, such as =5*5. However, writing a formula without cell references is limiting. Formulas with cell references are substantially more powerful. For example, the formula =B4*C4, where cells B4 and C4 contain values to be used in the calculation, allows the formula to reference a cell (or cell range) rather than a value (or values). This means that when data changes in an individual cell, any formulas that reference the cell are automatically recalculated.

A **named range** is a group of cells that have been given a name. The name can then be used within a formula or function. In this section, you will use cell referencing and named ranges to build a worksheet model for planning events at the Turquoise Oasis Spa.

Understand the Types of Cell References

There are three types of cell referencing: relative, absolute, and mixed. A **relative cell reference** is the default cell reference that changes automatically when the formula or function is copied to another location. The change in the cell reference will reflect the number of rows and/or columns from which the cell was copied relative to its original location. Relative cell references are the default in Excel. An **absolute cell reference** is the exact address of a cell when both the column and the row need to remain constant regardless of the position of the cell when the formula is copied to other cells. When an absolute cell reference is used, a cell reference does not change if a formula or function is copied to another location. An absolute cell reference is specified by placing a dollar sign ($) in front of both the column letter(s) and the row number(s). For example, to make B4 an absolute reference, you would specify $B$4. A **mixed cell reference** is a combination of relative and absolute cell references. In a mixed cell reference, the column or row portion of the reference is absolute, and the corresponding row or column is relative. For example, $B4 is a mixed reference in which the column is absolute and the row is relative. B$4 is a mixed reference in which the column is relative and the row is absolute. In essence, the dollar sign ($) sign locks down the letter or number it precedes so the letter or number will not change when copied.

QUICK REFERENCE	Types of Cell Referencing

Below are examples of the types of cell referencing for cell A5.

1. Relative cell referencing: =A5+B5
2. Absolute cell referencing: =$A$5+B5
3. Mixed cell referencing: =$A5+B5 (cell reference to column A is absolute, cell reference to row 5 is relative)
4. Mixed cell referencing: =A$5+B5 (cell reference to column A is relative, cell reference to row 5 is absolute)

Cell referencing is a useful feature when formulas need to be copied across ranges in a spreadsheet. When you create a spreadsheet and develop a formula that will not be copied elsewhere, absolute cell referencing and mixed cell referencing are not necessary. However, data arranged in a table may require a formula to perform calculations on each row, or record. Excel allows this process to be completed quickly and easily by using cell referencing. The formula can be constructed once and then quickly copied across a range of cells.

REAL WORLD ADVICE | **Creating Dynamic Workbooks**

The use of cell references in formulas helps to make spreadsheets in Excel extremely powerful. By using a cell reference to refer to a value in a formula, you can make your spreadsheet flexible. In other words, using cell references makes your spreadsheet easier to use and more efficient. If something about your business changes and requires an update to a value in your spreadsheet, you need only make the update in one place.

Opening the Starting File

Meda Rodate would like for the Turquoise Oasis Spa to become more efficient in planning for wedding events. She has asked for your help in designing an Excel workbook to accomplish this goal. You will begin in this exercise by opening the wedding planning workbook and organizing the number and pricing of spa gift baskets by creating common Excel functions using various types of cell referencing.

E03.00

SIDE NOTE
Office Updates
Depending on your exact Office version, you may see Open or Open Other Workbooks.

SIDE NOTE
Pin the Ribbon
If your ribbon is collapsed, pin your ribbon open. Click the Home tab. In the lower-right corner of the ribbon, click Pin the ribbon ⊟.

To Open the Wedding Workbook

a. Start Excel, click **Open** in the left pane, and then double-click **This PC**. Navigate through the folder structure to the location of your student data files, and then double-click **e02ch03Wedding**. If a Security Warning message displays, click **Enable Editing**.

b. Click the **File** tab, click **Save As**, and then double-click **This PC**. In the Save As dialog box, navigate to the location where you are saving your project files. Change the file name to **e02ch03Wedding_LastFirst** using your last and first name. Click **Save**.

Using Relative Cell Referencing

Relative cell referencing (as shown in Figure 1) is the default reference type in constructing formulas in Excel. Remember that relative cell referencing changes the cell references in a formula if it is copied or otherwise moved to another location. This includes the use of copy and paste or the AutoFill feature to copy a formula to another location. If a formula is copied to the right or left, the column references will change in the formula. If a formula is copied up or down, the row references will change in the formula.

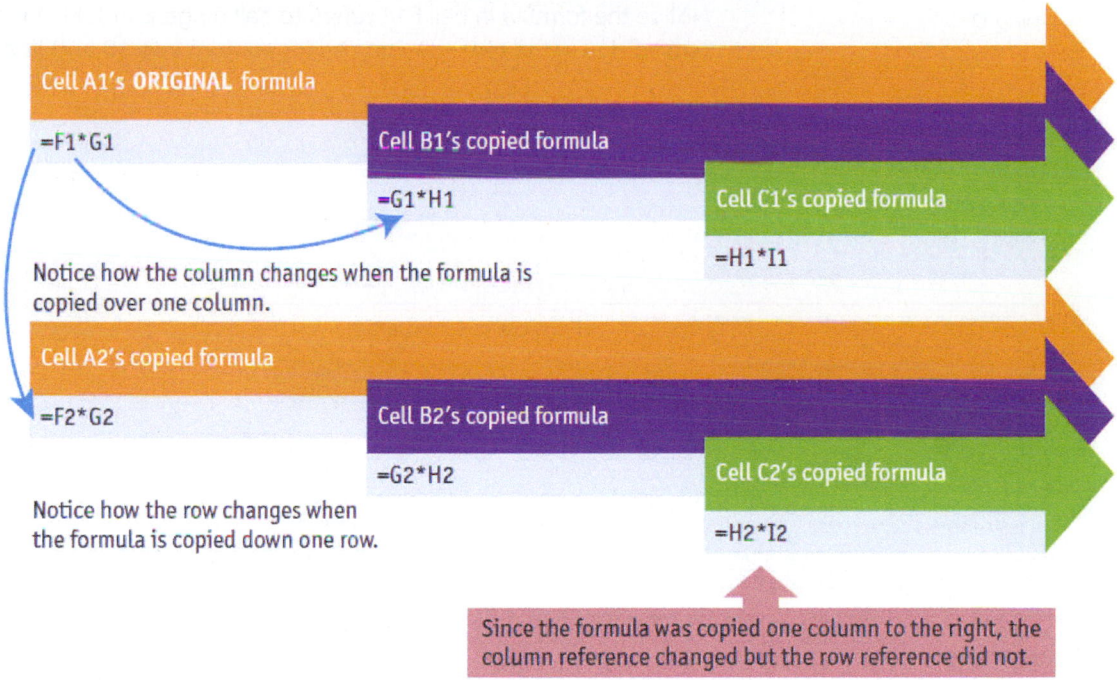

Cell A1's **ORIGINAL** formula

=F1*G1

Cell B1's copied formula

=G1*H1

Cell C1's copied formula

=H1*I1

Notice how the column changes when the formula is copied over one column.

Cell A2's copied formula

=F2*G2

Cell B2's copied formula

=G2*H2

Cell C2's copied formula

=H2*I2

Notice how the row changes when the formula is copied down one row.

Since the formula was copied one column to the right, the column reference changed but the row reference did not.

Figure 1   Understanding cell referencing

Relative cell referencing is useful in situations in which the same calculation is needed in multiple cells but the location of the data needed for the calculation changes relative to the position of the calculation cell. The GiftBaskets worksheet in the Wedding workbook contains a list of individual items that are included in the different types of gift baskets offered at the Turquoise Oasis Spa. The worksheet contains the prices for individual items in the baskets, the number of each item in the basket, and the prices of each basket.

The Turquoise Oasis Spa allows wedding parties to specify up to three different kinds of custom gift baskets. Each gift basket can contain up to four different items in each basket. The workbook has been set up such that cells with a blue fill need to be changed from one event to another. In this exercise, you will use relative cell referencing to display the total number of items in each type of gift basket.

 **E03.01**

SIDE NOTE
Using AutoFill
You can also use AutoFill with a formula in a vertical range by selecting the range, pressing Ctrl, and typing **D**

SIDE NOTE
Viewing Formulas
You can view your formulas by pressing Ctrl+~.

To Use Relative Cell Referencing

a. Click the **GiftBaskets** worksheet if necessary, and then click cell **F9**.

b. On the Home tab, in the Editing group, click **AutoSum** ∑, and then press Ctrl+Enter.

c. Double-click the **fill handle** on the bottom right corner of cell F9 to copy the formula through cell F11.

Notice the formula in cell F11 refers to cell range B11:E11. Since the formula was copied down, the row reference changed from 9 to 10 and finally to 11.

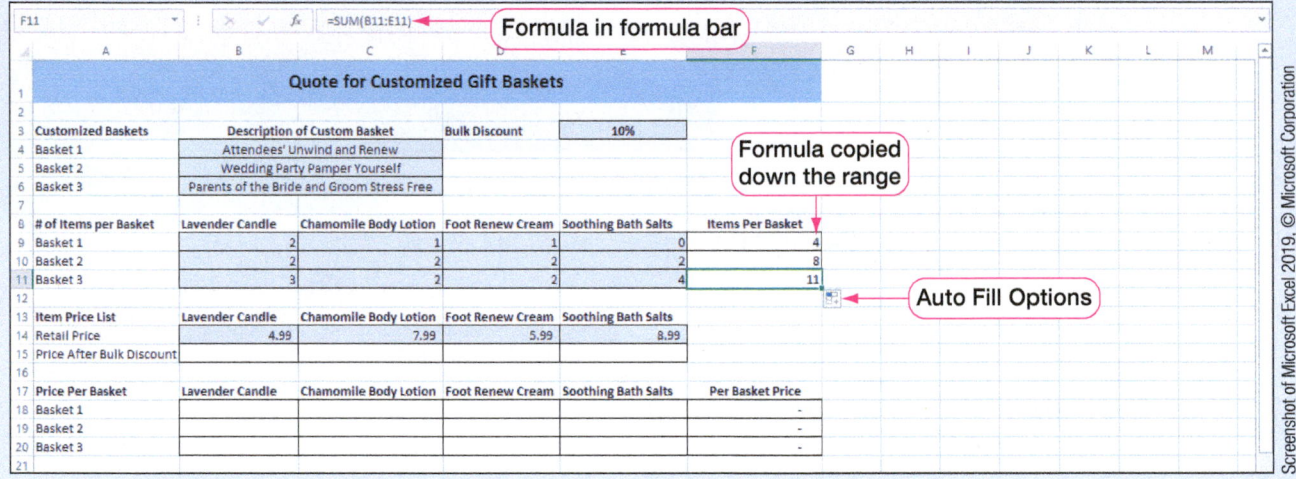

Figure 2   Relative cell referencing

d. **Save** 🖫 the workbook.

Using Absolute Cell Referencing

Absolute cell referencing (as shown in Figure 3) is useful when a formula needs to be copied and the reference to one or more cells within the formula must not change as the formula is copied. Thus, the column and row address of a referenced cell remains constant regardless of the position of the cell when the formula is copied to other cells.

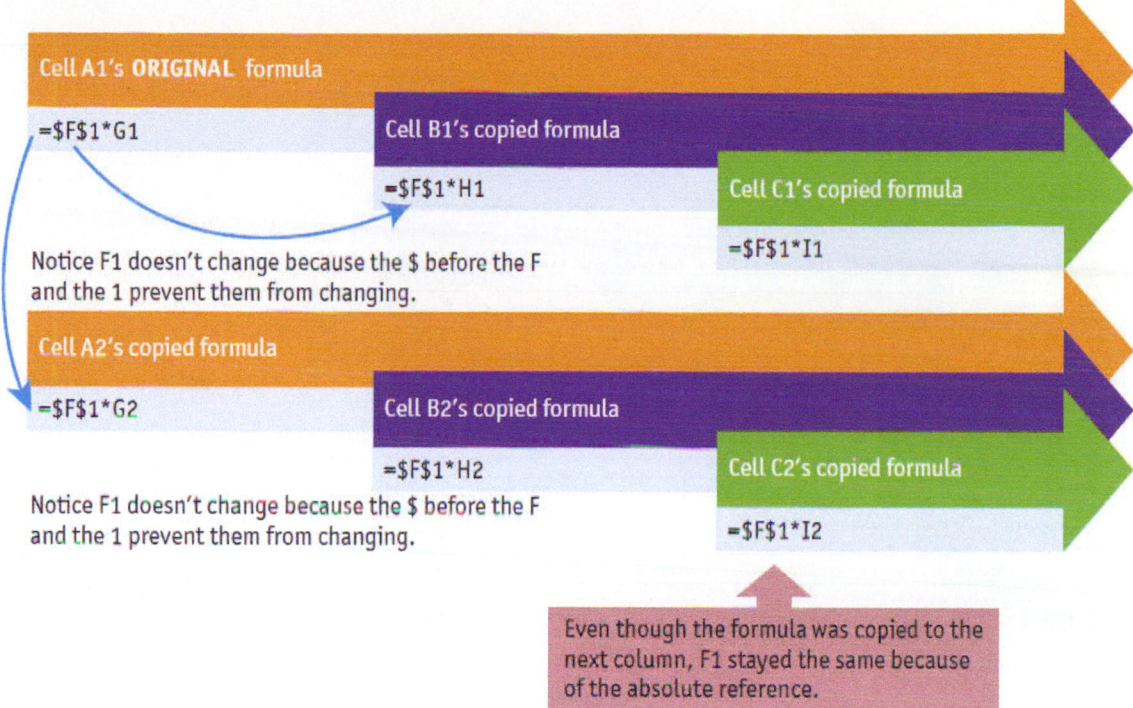

Figure 3 Understanding absolute cell referencing

Meda has decided to offer a bulk percentage discount on all gift baskets purchased for this event because of the large number being ordered. In this exercise, you will edit the GiftBaskets worksheet in cell range B15:E15 to include formulas that contain an absolute reference to the bulk discount.

 **E03.02**

SIDE NOTE
Using F4 Key
An alternative to typing the dollar signs is to press F4 after typing or selecting the cell reference.

SIDE NOTE
Alternate Method
You can also use AutoFill with a formula in a horizontal range by selecting the range, pressing Ctrl, and typing **R**

To Use Absolute Cell Referencing

a. On the GiftBaskets worksheet, click cell **B15**.

b. Type **=B14-(B14*$E$3)** and then click Enter ✓ to the left of the Insert Function button *fx* on the formula bar.

c. Click the **fill handle** and drag to copy the cell through cell **E15**.

Notice that the formula in cell E15 refers to cell E3. The dollar signs in front of the column letter and row number force Excel to keep the same cell reference as the formula is copied.

Also, notice that the dollar sign before row 3 is not required, because the formula was not copied to a different row. However, no matter where this formula is copied to on the worksheet, the calculation should always use cell E3. Thus, common practice is to put dollar signs before the column and row, making the cell reference absolute.

| E15 | : × ✓ fx | =E14-(E14*$E$3) | | | | | **Formula with absolute reference** | | | | | |

| | A | B | C | D | E | F | G | H | I | J | K | L | M |

Quote for Customized Gift Baskets

3	Customized Baskets	Description of Custom Basket		Bulk Discount	10%			
4	Basket 1	Attendees' Unwind and Renew						
5	Basket 2	Wedding Party Pamper Yourself						
6	Basket 3	Parents of the Bride and Groom Stress Free						
8	# of Items per Basket	Lavender Candle	Chamomile Body Lotion	Foot Renew Cream	Soothing Bath Salts		Items Per Basket	
9	Basket 1	2	1	1	0		4	
10	Basket 2	2	2	2	2		8	
11	Basket 3	3	2	2	4		11	
13	Item Price List	Lavender Candle	Chamomile Body Lotion	Foot Renew Cream	Soothing Bath Salts			
14	Retail Price	4.99	7.99	5.99	8.99		**Formula copied across range**	
15	Price After Bulk Discount	4.49	7.19	5.39	8.09			
17	Price Per Basket	Lavender Candle	Chamomile Body Lotion	Foot Renew Cream	Soothing Bath Salts		Per Basket Price	
18	Basket 1						-	
19	Basket 2						-	
20	Basket 3						-	
22	Basket Orders	Baskets Requested	Basket Subtotals					
23	Basket 1	50	$ -			Total Baskets in Order	10	

< ► | GiftBaskets | WeddingSummary | SpaServices | WeddingFinancing | Commission | SalesAnalysi ... ⊕

Screenshot of Microsoft Excel 2019, © Microsoft Corporation

Figure 4 Absolute cell referencing

> **d. Save** 💾 the workbook.

Using Mixed Cell Referencing

Mixed cell references can be very useful in the development of spreadsheets. Mixed cell references refer to referencing a cell within the formula where part of the cell address is preceded by a dollar sign to lock—either the column letter or the row value—as an absolute reference. This will leave the other part of the cell as relatively referenced when the formula is copied to new cells. Figure 5 shows a representation of how mixed cell referencing works.

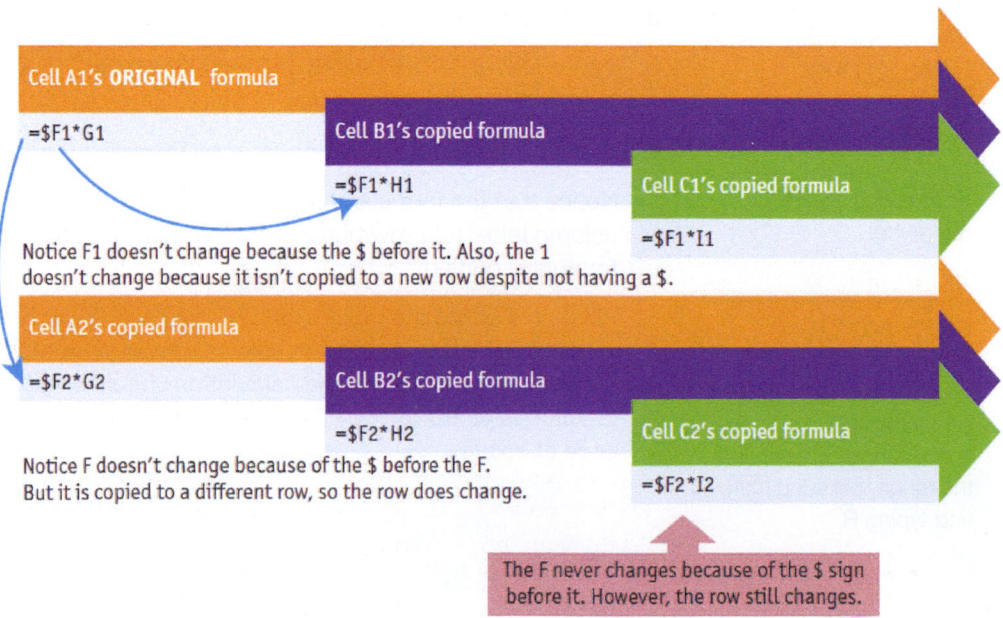

Figure 5 Understanding mixed cell referencing

REAL WORLD ADVICE | **Layout of a Spreadsheet Model**

Think of a spreadsheet model as an interactive report. Some of the data is static and may not change often, if ever. Some of the data, as in the wedding planning workbook, will need to change with each use of the spreadsheet. It can be helpful to color-code cells so anyone using the spreadsheet can easily see which cells require a change and which should be left alone. For example, in the Wedding workbook, cells with a blue fill are cells that need to be updated from one event to another.

If you need to verify that the formula has the correct relative and absolute referencing after it has been copied or moved into other cells within the spreadsheet, a quick and easy verification method is to examine one of the cells in edit mode. Best practice dictates following these steps.

1. Double-click a cell containing the formula to enter edit mode.
2. In edit mode, notice that the color-coded borders around cells match the cell address references in the formula. Using the color-coding as a guide, verify that the cells are referenced correctly.
3. If the referencing is incorrect, notice which cells are not referenced correctly.
4. Edit the cell references, and then, if necessary, recopy the corrected formula.
5. Always recheck the formula again to see whether your correction worked when it was copied into other cells or cell ranges.

To exit out of edit mode, press [Esc] to return to the original formula.

Repeat this process as needed. Instead of typing the dollar signs within your cell references, [F4] can be used to change the type of cell referencing. If the insertion point is placed within a cell reference in your formula, press [F4] one time, and Excel will insert dollar signs in front of both the row reference and the column reference. If you press [F4] again, Excel places a dollar sign in front of the row number only. If you press [F4] a third time, Excel places a dollar sign in front of the column reference and removes the dollar sign from the row reference. Pressing [F4] a fourth time returns the cell to a relative reference.

QUICK REFERENCE | **Using [F4]**

[F4] can be used to change the type of cell referencing.

1. Press [F4] one time to place a dollar sign in front of both the column and row values (absolute reference).
2. Press [F4] a second time to place a dollar sign in front of the row value only (mixed reference).
3. Press [F4] a third time to place a dollar sign in front of the column value only (mixed reference).
4. Press [F4] a fourth time to remove all dollar sign characters (relative reference).

Meda has asked you to update the cell range B18:E20 to include formulas that calculate the price of individual items included in each basket type. In this exercise, you will do so, using mixed cell referencing.

 **E03.03**

SIDE NOTE

Alternate Method

You can click the Enter button ✓ to the left of the Insert Function button f_x on the Formula Bar for the same result as Ctrl+Enter.

To Use Mixed Cell Referencing

a. On the GiftBaskets worksheet, click cell **B18**.

b. Type **=B9*B$15** and then press Ctrl+Enter.

c. Double-click the **fill handle** in cell B18 to copy the formula through cell **B20**.

Notice that the formula in cell B20 still refers to cell B15. The dollar sign in front of the row heading forces Excel to use row 15 as the referenced row no matter where the formula is copied to. However, the column will change as the formula is copied to the left or right in the worksheet.

d. With cell range B18:B20 still selected, click the **fill handle** on cell **B20**, and then drag to the right to copy the formulas through cell range **C18:E20**.

Notice that as the formulas are copied, column B changes, while the row reference to row 15 remains unchanged as the formula is copied to the range.

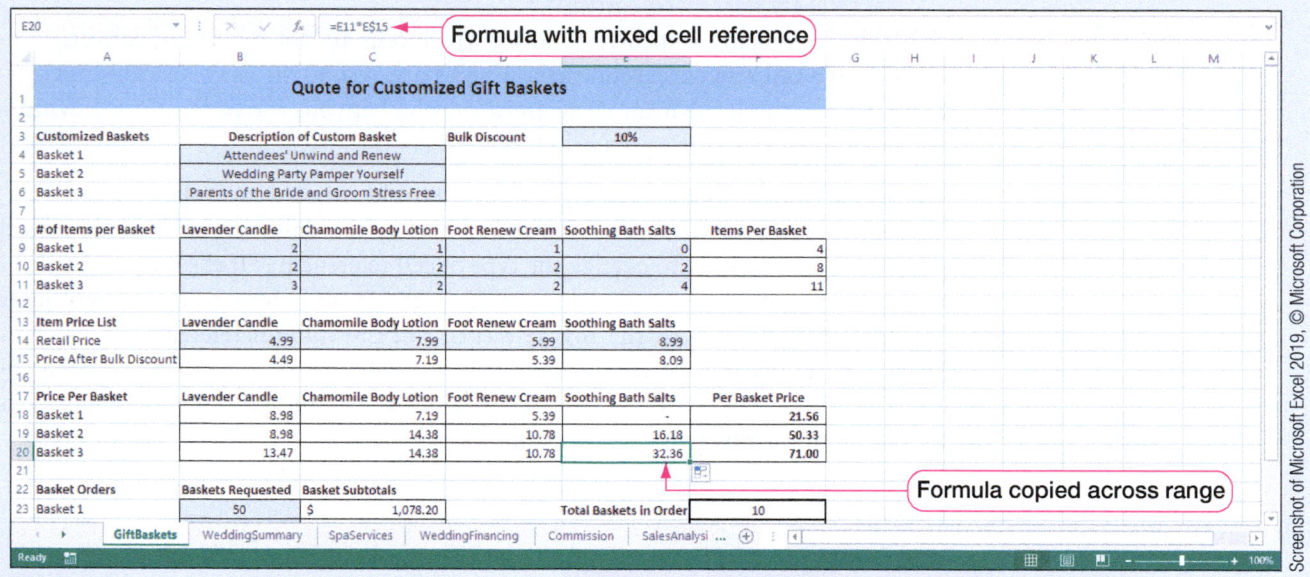

Figure 6   Mixed cell referencing

e. Click cell **E14**, type **9.99** and then press Enter.

Notice that the values in cell range E19:E20 have been updated. For reference, E20 previously displayed 32.36; now it displays 35.96.

f. **Save** 💾 the workbook.

S₅ CONSIDER THIS | **Cell Referencing**

In cell B18 of the GiftBaskets worksheet, the formula uses mixed cell referencing by referring to cell B$15. Would there have been a different result if absolute referencing ($B$15) had been used? Would there have been a different result if relative referencing (B15) had been used? Why would these options be incorrect?

REAL WORLD ADVICE | **Building for Scalability**

When you develop a spreadsheet, you should consider the potential for the model to expand. A good spreadsheet model allows the user to add more data as needed. Instead of assuming that current conditions will never change, your spreadsheet should be built to accommodate growth. While developing the model, you may consider using hypothetical data so you can see how the model will look when it has real data.

QUICK REFERENCE | **Understanding Referencing Based on Copy Destination**

Cell references in a formula can change when copied. To understand where to put a dollar sign, you must understand how the cell references will change when copied. Excel determines what to change by the original location and the copy destination. Remember that the dollar sign locks down the letter (column) or number (row) it precedes so it will not change.

Original Location	Copy Destination	Column Becomes	Row Becomes	Considerations
A1	Formula will not be copied.	N/A	N/A	Cell referencing is irrelevant. Example: A1
A1	A5	The column reference will not change (stays column A).	The row reference will change by 4 rows to row 5.	Adding a dollar sign before the column is irrelevant. Add a dollar sign before the row if the row should not change. Example: A$1
A1	C1	The column reference will change by 2 columns to column C.	The row reference will not change (row 1).	Add a dollar sign before the column if the column should not change. Adding a dollar sign before the row is irrelevant. Example: $A1
A1	C5	The column reference will change by 2 columns to column C.	The row reference will change by 4 rows to row 5.	Because both the column and row references will change, add a dollar sign before any references that should not change. Example: $A$1

Create Named Ranges

Once you are comfortable working with formulas and cells, there is a natural progression to using named ranges and functions. As has been mentioned, a named range is a group of cells that have been given a name that can then be used within a formula or function. Named ranges are an extension of cell references and provide a quick alternative for commonly used cell references or ranges.

Spreadsheet formulas that use cell references, such as =C5*C6, may be easy to interpret when they are simple. However, as the size and complexity of the workbook increase, so do the difficulty and time needed to incorporate cell references in formulas. This is especially the case with workbooks that use multiple worksheets. The use of named ranges enables a developer to quickly develop formulas that make sense. It also increases the readability of formulas to other individuals who are using the same workbook. For example, the formula =SUM(BasketSubtotals) is much easier to interpret than =SUM(C23:C25). Also, named ranges create absolute referencing when used in a formula. You can quickly understand the formula if it is written with assigned names you designate.

Creating Named Ranges Using the Name Box

Named ranges are easy to create as you develop a spreadsheet. A **named range** is a cell or group of cells that have been given a name, other than the default column and row cell address reference, that can then be used within a formula or function. Most named ranges are groups of cells used within multiple formulas. A simple way to name a range is to select the range and use the Name Box to create the name. This allows for a custom name to be given to the range. In naming ranges, a descriptive name should be used for the range being named. Named ranges do have some restrictions on the types of characters that can be used. Named ranges cannot start with a number and cannot contain spaces, and the name cannot resemble a cell reference.

QUICK REFERENCE	Conventions for Naming Ranges

Below is a list of conditions that must be met when creating named ranges.

1. Names for ranges must start with a letter, an underscore (_), or a backslash (\ ).

2. Create names that provide specific meaning to the range being named.

3. Spaces cannot be used in creating a named range. Instead, use an underscore or a hyphen character, or capitalize the first letter of each word (e.g., HairStyles).

4. Do not use combinations of letters and numbers that resemble cell references.

In this exercise, you will create a named range using the Name Box. This named range can then be used in future calculations as an absolute cell reference.

 **E03.04**

SIDE NOTE
Expand the Name Box
When using named ranges, you may want to increase the size of the Name Box by dragging the right edge of the Name Box.

To Create a Named Range Using the Name Box

a. On the GiftBaskets worksheet, select cell range **C23:C25**.

b. Click in the **Name Box** to select the existing text. Type BasketSubtotals and then press Enter to create a new named range. Notice that when cell range C23:C25 is selected, the text BasketSubtotals is displayed in the Name Box.

Screenshot of Microsoft Excel 2019, © Microsoft Corporation

E03.05

SIDE NOTE
Selecting a Range

Click the Name Box arrow to display a list of all named ranges in a workbook. Click any named range in the Name Box to select that range in a worksheet.

Troubleshooting

If you click outside of the Name Box before pressing [Enter], the named range will not be created.

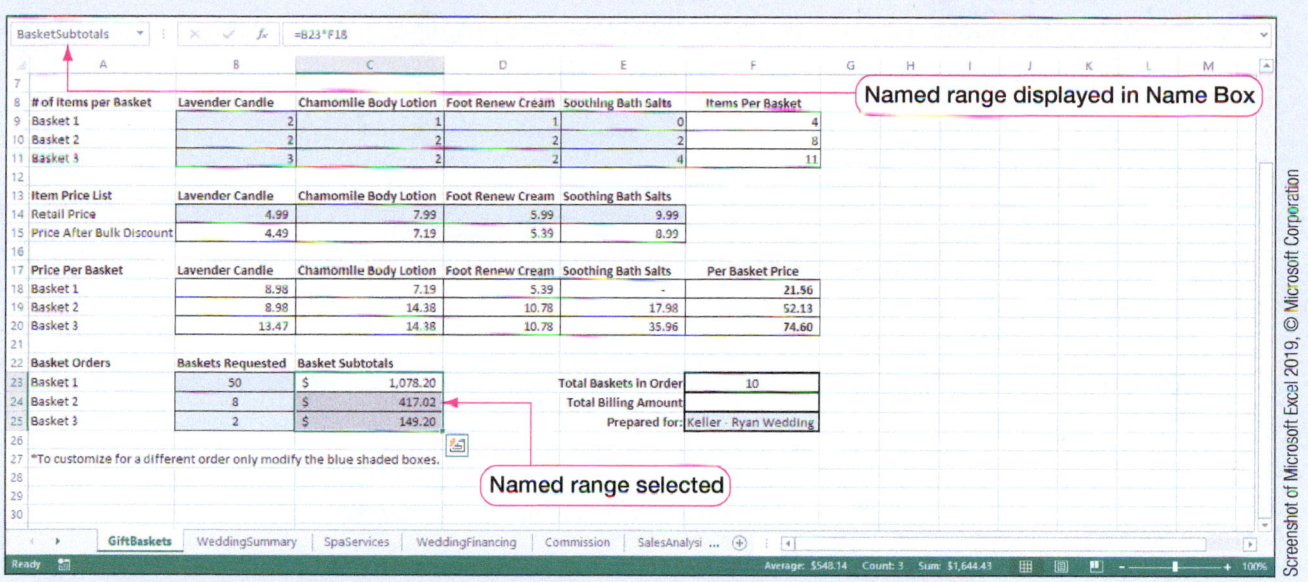

Named range displayed in Name Box

Named range selected

Figure 7 Name range applied to cell range C23:C25

c. **Save**  the workbook.

Modifying Named Ranges

If a named range has been created incorrectly, it can be redefined by selecting the correct data and naming the range again. The **Name Manager** can be used to create, edit, delete, or troubleshoot named ranges in a workbook. Alternatively, the Name Manager can be used to modify an existing range or to view a list of already defined ranges.

Currently, the range BasketsRequested includes only gift basket options 2 and 3. In this exercise, you will modify the named range that was previously created in the workbook to include all basket options.

SIDE NOTE
Office Updates

Depending on your exact Office version, you may see a Comments button to the right of the Share button in the upper-right corner of the screen. The Comment box may appear different if you use the Comments button.

To Modify a Named Range

a. On the GiftBaskets worksheet, click the **Name Box** arrow, and then click **BasketsRequested**.

Notice that the cell range selected is B24:B26. This is the incorrect range. The correct cell range is B23:B25.

b. Click the **Formulas** tab, and then, in the Defined Names group, click **Name Manager**.

Mac Troubleshooting

On the Formulas tab, click the Define Name arrow, and then click Define Name in the Names in workbook box, and make the necessary changes.

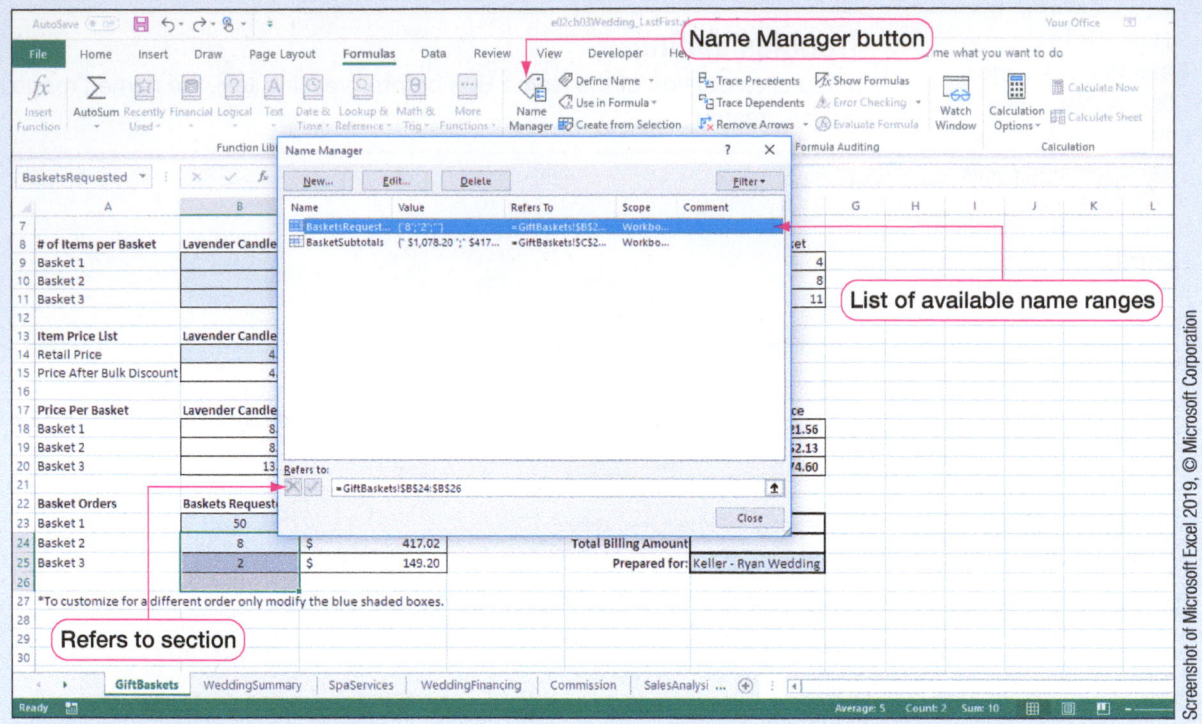

Figure 8 Name Manager dialog box

SIDE NOTE

Alternate Method

Instead of typing, click and drag to select cell range B23:B25.

c. From the displayed list of names, click **BasketsRequested**, and then, in the Refers to section in the box, select the text **$B$24:$B$26**.

d. Type **$B$23:$B$25** click **Close**, and then click **Yes** to accept the changes to the named range.

e. Click the **Name Box** arrow, and then click **BasketsRequested**. Notice that the correct cell range, B23:B25, is now selected.

f. **Save** 🖫 the workbook.

Using Named Ranges

Using named ranges in place of cell references is a simple process. Instead of typing in the cells that you want to use in a formula, you can type the range name you have created. Excel will begin to recognize the name you are typing and offer to automatically complete the name for you. Another method of using named ranges is to use the Paste Name feature in Excel. While typing a formula, you can press F3 to view a list of named ranges in the workbook and then insert it into the formula you are constructing. A third way of using named ranges is the Use in Formula button in the Defined Names group of the Formulas tab. When typing a formula, click the Use in Formula arrow and select an available range name.

QUICK REFERENCE   **Using Range Names in Formulas**

- Type the range name when entering a formula.
- While typing a formula, press F3 to view and select a range name.
- While typing a formula, click the Formulas tab, and then, in the Defined Names group, click Use in Formula to view and select a range name.

Meda has requested that the worksheet display the total amount that the wedding party is to be billed for the gift baskets being made. In this exercise, you will use a named range to create a calculation to display the total price of the requested gift baskets in the worksheet.

E03.06

To Use Named Ranges in a Formula

SIDE NOTE
Alternate Method
After typing **=SUM(** press the F3 key, double-click **BasketSubtotals**, and then press Ctrl+Enter.

a. On the GiftBaskets worksheet, click cell **F24**.

b. Type **=SUM(B**

Notice that a list of functions and named ranges beginning with the letter "B" appear in a list. The named ranges appear with a ⊞ next to the name of the range. The functions have ⨍ to the left of the function name.

c. Type **ask**

Notice the two range names that appear in the list.

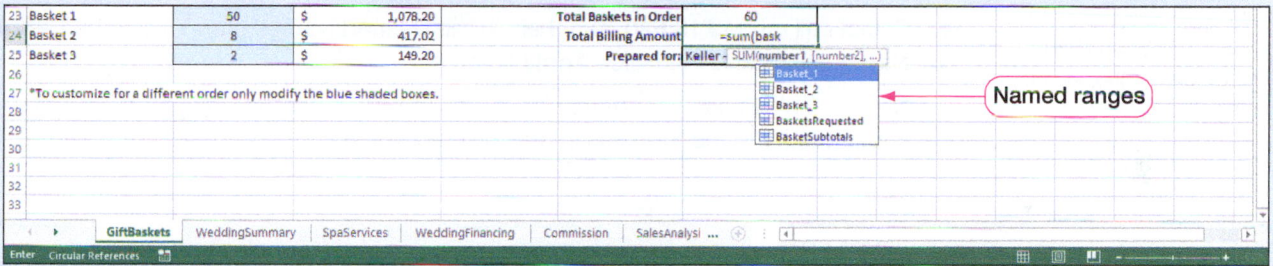

Figure 9 List of functions

Screenshot of Microsoft Excel 2019, © Microsoft Corporation

d. Press ↓, and then press Tab to select the BasketSubtotals named range. Press Ctrl+Enter to complete the formula for a result of $1,644.43.

e. **Save** 💾 the workbook.

Creating Named Ranges from Selections

At times, your worksheet's data will be organized in such a way that the names for your ranges exist in a cell in the form of a heading for each row or each column in the data set. Rather than selecting each row or column separately, which is a time-consuming process, you can use the Create from Selection method.

The Create from Selection method produces multiple named ranges from the headings in rows, columns, or both from the data set. The key element is to realize that the names for the ranges need to exist in a cell adjacent to the data range. Most commonly, these names are row or column headers that make for very convenient names for each row or column of data.

Meda has asked you to create named ranges for the item subtotals for each type of gift basket. In this exercise, you will create the named ranges. You will then apply them to the formulas in cell range F18:F20.

E03.07

To Create Named Ranges and Apply the Names to Formulas

a. On the GiftBaskets worksheet, select cell range **A18:E20**.

b. On the Formulas tab, in the Defined Names group, click **Create from Selection**. The Create Names from Selection dialog box opens.

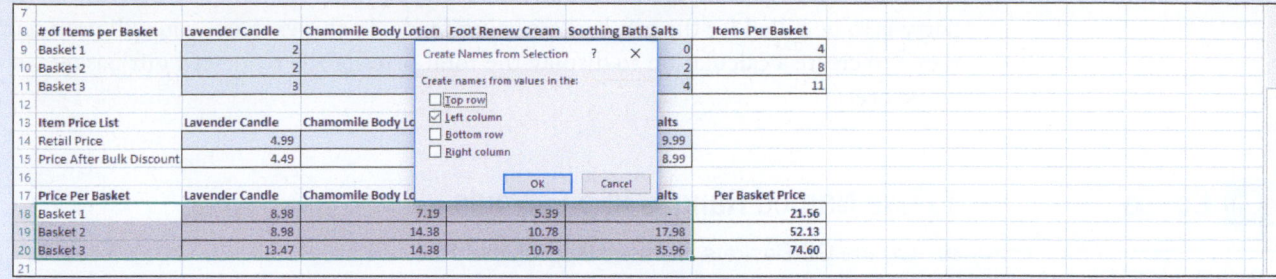

Figure 10 Create Names from Selection dialog box

Screenshot of Microsoft Excel 2019, © Microsoft Corporation

SIDE NOTE
Alternate Method
After you have selected the range of data you wish to name, the keyboard short-cut Ctrl + Shift + F3 will create a single named range or multiple named ranges from the selection.

c. Confirm that the **Left column** check box is selected, and then click **OK**.

d. Select cell range **B18:E18**.

Notice that the Name Box displays the name Basket_1. In creating the named range, Excel replaced all space characters in the name with underscore characters. Cell ranges B19:E19 and B20:E20 will appear similarly.

e. Select cell range **F18:F20**, and then, in the Defined Names group, click the **Define Name** arrow, and then click **Apply Names**.

Notice that Excel has detected three potential named ranges that can be substituted into the formulas in the selected range.

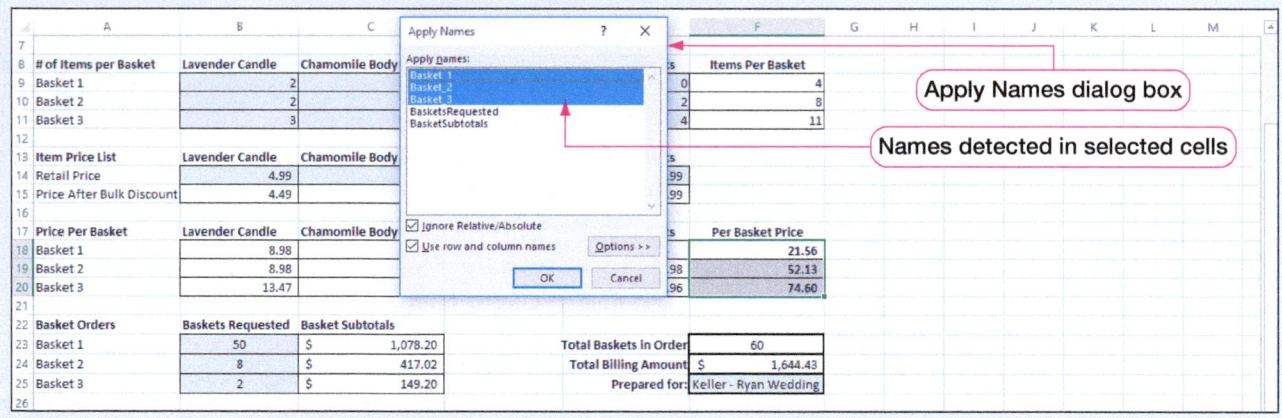

Figure 11 Apply Names dialog box

Screenshot of Microsoft Excel 2019, © Microsoft Corporation

f. Click **OK**.

Notice in the Formula Bar that the formula in cell F18 is now =SUM(Basket_1).

g. **Save** the workbook. If you need to take a break before finishing this chapter, now is a good time.

REAL WORLD ADVICE **When to Use Named Ranges**

Like any useful feature, named ranges can be overused. Named ranges make it easy to understand formulas and can be used to select a range of cells quickly. However, you must invest time and effort to create and use the named ranges. Named ranges have the most value when sets of data are used in multiple formulas or when other users need to understand the construction of the spreadsheet. Not every cell or range in your workbook needs to be a named range. If you need a formula to copy across a range of cells with the references remaining relative, named ranges are not the best option. You should do a mental cost-benefit analysis to ensure it is worth the time and effort. Your decision on when to use named ranges will become easier with practice and experience.

Understanding Functions

A function is a built-in formula that performs operations against data based on a set of inputs. Excel uses functions to calculate output on the basis of the input provided. Functions can be simple, such as using the SUM function you learned in Chapter 2, which totals the contents of the cells in a range. Functions can also be more complex. For example, calculating a monthly loan payment is accomplished by providing various arguments: the loan amount, number of payments, and interest rate. An **argument** is a variable or value the function requires to calculate a solution. As long as you have the correct inputs, Excel will perform the calculation for the function. Some functions do not require arguments. In this section, you will use common business functions to continue building the worksheet to be used for planning events at the Turquoise Oasis Spa.

Create and Structure Functions

Functions are composed of several elements and need to be structured in a particular order. In discussing functions, you need to be aware of the syntax of an Excel function. The **syntax** is the structure and order of the function and the arguments needed for Excel to run a function. If you understand the syntax of a function, you can easily learn how to use new functions quickly. The syntax for a function is represented in Figure 12.

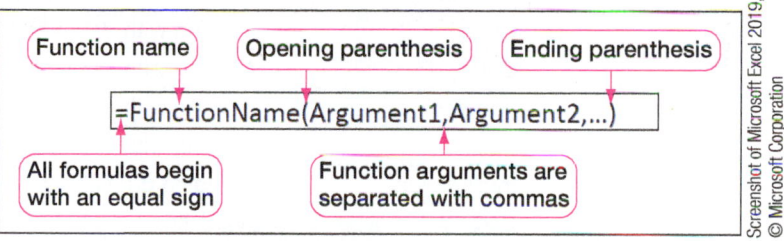

Figure 12 Syntax of a function

The FunctionName is any function that is in the Excel library. Examples are SUM, AVERAGE, and TODAY. With all functions, a pair of parentheses () are required after the FunctionName that may contain arguments associated with the function. Functions such as SUM() have one or more arguments that are required. If the required argument or arguments are not supplied, an error will occur. Some functions, such as TODAY(), do not have any arguments. These functions do not need any inputs to be able to generate output. The TODAY() function uses the clock on the computer to return the current date. Even though no arguments are needed, the () parentheses are always included, which helps Excel understand that a function is being used.

Arguments can be either required or optional. The required arguments always come before any optional arguments. Arguments are separated by commas. Optional arguments are identified by square brackets [ ] around the argument name. You never type the square brackets into the actual construction of the function; they are used only to inform you that the argument is optional.

For example, the syntax for the SUM function is

=SUM(number1, [number2], …)

The first argument is required; the SUM function must have a number, cell, or range to begin the calculation. The second argument—a second cell or range—is optional. Notice that the second argument uses square brackets to identify that it is optional. The periods after the second argument indicate that one or more arguments can be added as needed. The SUM function can hold up to 255 arguments.

Arguments, like variables in a math equation, need to be appropriate values that are suitable for the function. With Excel, the acceptable values can take six common forms, including other functions, as shown in Table 1.

Form of Input	Example	Explanation
Numeric value	5	Type the value
Cell reference	C5	Type the cell or range of cells
Named range	SALES	Type the name of the cell range
Text string	"Bonus"	Type the text with quotation marks so Excel will recognize it as a text string rather than a named range
Function	SUM(C5:C19)	Type a function using the correct syntax of the function name, pair of parentheses, and any arguments
Formula	(C5+D5)/100	Type the formula using correct mathematical formula structure

Table 1 Function argument formats

Functions are typically categorized for easy access. The primary categories are shown in Table 2. Functions can be found on the Formulas tab under these categorical names. They can also be searched to find the usage and syntax of functions that are unfamiliar.

Category	Description
Compatibility	A set of functions that are compatible with older versions of Excel
Cube	Working with data and filtering, similar to pivot tables
Date & Time	Working with serial date and time values
Engineering	Working with engineering formulas and calculations
Financial	Working with common financial formulas
Information	Providing data about cell content within a worksheet
Logical	Evaluating expressions or conditions as being either true or false
Lookup & Reference	Working with indexing and retrieving information from data sets
Math & Trig	Working with mathematics
Text	Working with text strings
Statistical	Working with common statistical calculations
Web	Working with URL, XML, and web services connections

Table 2 Function categories

Use Math and Statistical Functions

At the most fundamental level, spreadsheets are used to perform calculations. These calculations may result in loan payments, GPA calculations, profit margins, or even age calculations. Excel has a large array of functions available for simple and complex mathematical functions. There are functions available to sum, count, perform algebra or trigonometry, and create a wide range of statistical calculations.

Using Math and Trig Functions

The math and trigonometry functions are useful for various numerical manipulations. For example, there are several functions that round data in a cell or calculation. The **ABS function** returns the absolute value of the number analyzed by the function. A cell or calculation resulting in the number –4 would be returned as 4 by the ABS function. The **INT function** rounds down any decimal values associated with a number to the nearest whole integer. The **ROUND function** is important when you want to round a number to a specific number of digits. The ROUND function can round values to the left or right of the decimal in a number. For example, using the ROUND function, you could change the number 115.89 to 116 by rounding to the ones place. You could also display

120 by rounding to the integer value to the tens place. While ROUND will round to the nearest digit, ROUNDDOWN and ROUNDUP can be used to force the rounding in a particular direction.

When a function is used to round data, the result of that function is used in future calculations. This is different from formatting a cell to a specific number of decimal places, as formatting does not change the underlying data. Commonly used math functions are shown in Table 3.

Function	Usage
ABS(number)	Returns the absolute value of a number
INT(number)	Rounds a number down to the nearest integer
RAND( )	Returns a random number from 0 to less than 1
RANDBETWEEN(bottom,top)	Returns a random integer between the numbers you specify
ROUND(number,num_digits)	Rounds a number to a specified number of digits
ROUNDDOWN(number,num_digits)	Rounds a number down to a specified number of digits
ROUNDUP(number,num_digits)	Rounds a number up to a specified number of digits

Table 3 Commonly used math functions

There are two common methods for creating functions: by using the Function Arguments dialog box and by typing the function in the cell. The **Function Arguments dialog box** provides additional information and previews results of the function being constructed. When you are first developing the skills for using functions in Excel, the Function Arguments dialog box can be very valuable. As you gain more experience with functions, you will depend less on the Function Arguments dialog box, particularly when nesting multiple functions together.

Meda has received some historical data on wedding events that she would like to have summarized. In planning new events, referring to this historical data will be helpful. The data contains four items of interest.

1. The number of days spent by wedding parties at the Painted Paradise Resort & Spa. Previously, the value was calculated by using decimal values based on check-in and checkout times. Meda would like this data to be in integers, or whole numbers of days. Because wedding parties receive a late checkout time, these values would need to be rounded down to the nearest whole number.

2. The value of merchandise that was returned after the wedding took place—the price in the column represents the money refunded to customers for the merchandise. The system used at the spa erroneously allowed employees to enter some of this data as either negative or positive values. In the new system, this data must be displayed as positive values.

3. Data displaying the amount spent in total by each wedding party at the Turquoise Oasis Spa. The average of this column has been calculated in cell C1 of the WeddingSummary worksheet. Currently, the average is formatted to display too many decimal places. However, the actual value of the cell has many more than two decimals. Meda plans to use this average in subsequent calculations. Formatting the cell to two decimals will not change the value of the cell. Thus, the value needs to be rounded to two decimals.

4. Data indicating whether the bridal party from the wedding is a member of the spa. The system used by the spa indicates a 1 for spa members and a null (missing or no value) for nonmembers. When this data was imported into Excel, the result for nonmembers was the text "Null".

In this exercise, you will summarize these data items using the INT and ABS functions.

To Use the INT and ABS Functions

a. If you took a break, open the **e02ch03Wedding_LastFirst** workbook, click the **WeddingSummary** worksheet, and then click cell **C7**.

E03.08

SIDE NOTE
Alternate Method
Instead of typing B7 in the Function Arguments dialog box, you can click cell B7. The cell reference will be supplied automatically.

b. To the left of the formula bar, click **Insert Function** f_x. Click the **Or select a category** arrow, and then select **Math & Trig**.

c. In the Select a function box, scroll down, click **INT**, and then click **OK**.

d. In the Function Arguments dialog box, in the Number box, type **B7** and notice that to the right of the Number box, you see the value currently in cell B7. In the lower left corner of the dialog box, the Formula result will display a preview of the result of the INT function.

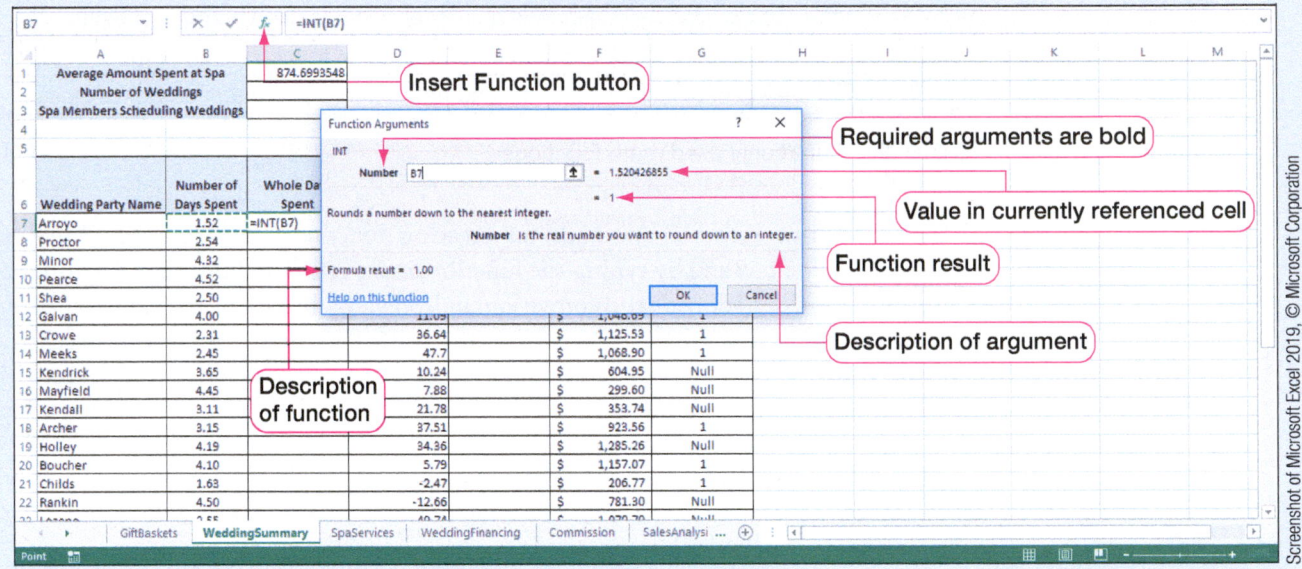

Figure 13 Function Arguments dialog box

e. Click **OK**, and then double-click the **fill handle** to copy cell C7 through cell **C37**.

Notice that the values in column B have now been rounded down to the nearest whole number. Illustratively, the value of cell C22 is 4.00 even though the value in cell B22 is 4.50. Because all the values are now whole days without a decimal value, the format for C7:C37 should have decimals decreased to zero decimals.

f. With cell range C7:C37 selected, click the **Home** tab, and then, in the Number group, click **Decrease Decimal** twice.

g. Click cell **E7**, and then click **Insert Function** f_x. If necessary, click the **Or select a category** arrow, and then verify that **Math & Trig** is selected.

h. In the Select a function box, click **ABS**, and then click **OK**.

SIDE NOTE
Function Help
Click the Help on this function link in the lower left of the Function Arguments dialog box to open Excel Help for the function being used.

i. In the Function Arguments dialog box, in the Number box, type **D7** and then click **OK**. Double-click the **fill handle** to copy cell E7 through cell **E37**. All values in column E now appear as positive numbers.

j. **Save** the workbook.

SS **CONSIDER THIS** | **Exploring Functions**

Use the Insert Function button to the left of the formula bar to find a function with which you are not familiar. Read the description for the function in the Insert Function dialog box. Use Microsoft Help or the Internet to learn more about the function, and share your findings with another person. Did you have any trouble understanding the function? Is the Insert Function button a useful tool for exploring new functions?

Inserting a Function Using Formulas

Formula AutoComplete can help you construct formulas without using the Function Arguments dialog box. This is accomplished by typing the equal sign and typing the function name directly into the cell. Excel will still provide guidance if you use this method. Additionally, as needed, you can always enter the Function Arguments dialog box to get more assistance.

When you initially type in the beginning of a function name, the Formula AutoComplete listing of functions will be shown, from which you can select the appropriate function. Formula AutoComplete will provide a list of functions and named ranges that match the text after the equal sign. The list will automatically reflect changes as you type in more letters. Excel will even display a short description of the function when the function name is highlighted. As the function names appear, you can use ⬆, ⬇, ➡, ⬅, or the mouse to move through the listing. To select a function, press [Tab] or double-click the selected function.

Once the function is selected, the arguments will be listed in a movable tag, called a ScreenTip, to provide guidance in completing the function. The argument you are currently editing will be displayed in bold. If you have entered some of the arguments, you can click the argument in the ScreenTip, and Excel will relocate the insertion point to that argument.

In this exercise, you will insert the ROUND function, using Formula AutoComplete.

 E03.09

SIDE NOTE
Alternate Method
You can also edit a cell by pressing the [F2] key.

To Insert a Function Using Formula AutoComplete

a. On the WeddingSummary worksheet, double-click cell **C1** to begin editing the function.

b. Click after the equal sign to place the insertion point before the AVERAGE function. Type round(to begin the new function.

Notice how the Formula AutoComplete suggested possible functions while you typed "round". Uppercase text and lowercase text are equivalent when typing function names. Also, notice that the number argument is shown in bold to indicate that this is the argument being edited.

ABS	▾	:	×	✓	fx	=round(AVERAGE(F7:F37)

	A	B	C	D	E	F	G	H	I	J	K	L	M
1	Average Amount Spent at Spa		=round(AVERAGE(F7:F37) ←			ScreenTip showing the function being used							
2	Number of Weddings		ROUND(number, num_digits)										
3	Spa Members Scheduling Weddings					Current argument is bold							
4													
5													
6	Wedding Party Name	Number of Days Spent	Whole Days Spent	Returned Merchandise	Value of Returned Merchandise	Amount Spent at Spa	Spa Member						
7	Arroyo	1.52	1	-37.34	37.34	$ 1,215.63	1						
8	Proctor	2.54	2	41.12	41.12	$ 720.60	1						
9	Minor	4.32	4	-12.7	12.7	$ 455.78	1						
10	Pearce	4.52	4	13.97	13.97	$ 1,309.51	Null						
11	Shea	2.50	2	18.53	18.53	$ 1,345.57	1						
12	Galvan	4.00	4	11.09	11.09	$ 1,046.69	1						
13	Crowe	2.31	2	36.64	36.64	$ 1,125.53	1						
14	Meeks	2.45	2	47.7	47.7	$ 1,068.90	1						
15	Kendrick	3.65	3	10.24	10.24	$ 604.95	Null						
16	Mayfield	4.45	4	7.88	7.88	$ 299.60	Null						
17	Kendall	3.11	3	21.78	21.78	$ 353.74	Null						

Figure 14 ScreenTip showing ROUND function

Screenshot of Microsoft Excel 2019. © Microsoft Corporation

SIDE NOTE
Formula AutoComplete

To reduce typing and possible errors, you can use the arrow keys or the mouse to select functions from the Formula AutoComplete list.

c. Click after the ending parenthesis for the AVERAGE function, type **,**—a comma—and then notice in the ScreenTip that the num_digits argument of the ROUND function is in bold.

d. Type **2)** to complete the num_digits argument. This will round the result of the AVERAGE function to two decimal places. Press Ctrl+Enter.

Notice that the value in cell C1 is now $874.70, rounded to two decimal places. It is important to know that if you had formatted cell C1 to display only two decimal places, the cell would also show $874.70 on the screen. However, formatting does not change the value. So even though the cell would show $874.70, the cell value used in subsequent mathematical calculations would still be $874.6993548. If you increase the number of decimals for cell C1 after using the ROUND function, you will see that the cell value is changed to $874.700000.

e. On the Home tab, in the Number group, click **Accounting Number Format**.

f. **Save** 🖫 the workbook. On the Home tab, in the Number group, click Accounting Number Format.

REAL WORLD ADVICE | **Rounding versus Formatting**

Formatting text as currency will only give the appearance of true rounding. Any calculations using a cell formatted as currency but containing extra decimal places will include all decimal places in the calculation. Using the ROUND function will eliminate extra decimal places. Thus, future calculations will use the value displayed as a result of the ROUND function.

Using Statistical Functions

Similar to mathematical functions, statistical functions, as shown in Table 4, handle common statistical calculations such as averages, minimums, and maximums. Statistical functions are extremely useful for business analysis, as they aggregate and compare data. Common descriptive statistics are used to describe the data. The average, median, and mode are common descriptive statistics that help describe the nature of a data set. They help understand and predict future data.

Statistical Functions	Usage
AVERAGE(number1,[number2],...)	Returns the average from a set of numbers
COUNT(value1,[value2],...)	Counts the number of cells in a range that contain numbers
COUNTA(value1,[value2],...)	Counts the number of cells in a range that are not empty
COUNTBLANK(range)	Counts the number of empty cells in a range
MEDIAN(number1,[number2],...)	Returns the number in the middle of a set of numbers
MAX(number1,[number2],...)	Returns the largest number from a set of numbers
MIN(number1,[number2],...)	Returns the smallest number from a set of numbers
MODE.SNGL(number1,[number2],...)	Returns the value that occurs most often within a set

Table 4 Commonly used statistical functions

The **COUNTA function** is a useful function for counting the number of cells within a range that contain any type of data. Using COUNTA is a great method to count the number of records in a data set that may include numbers and letters. This is different from the COUNT function. The COUNT function returns the number of cells in a range of cells that contain numeric data.

On the WeddingSummary worksheet, column G contains a list indicating whether the bridal party were members of the spa. When the data was imported into Excel, the system used by the spa marked members with the number one. Nonmembers were marked with the text "Null". Meda has asked you to find the number of weddings held at the spa as well the number of members who have scheduled weddings. In this exercise, you will find this data using statistical functions.

 E03.10

To Use the COUNTA function

SIDE NOTE

Creating Formulas

When creating formulas, to avoid typing mistakes, you can use your mouse to click and drag a cell or a range of cells.

SIDE NOTE

Alternate Method

To count numbers, on the Home tab, in the Editing group, click the AutoSum arrow, and then click Count Numbers.

a. On the WeddingSummary worksheet, click cell **C2**. Click the **Formulas** tab, in the Function Library group, click **More Functions**, point to **Statistical,** and then click **COUNTA**. For Value1 type **A7:A37** and then click **OK**.

The COUNTA function counts all the cells that contain any value in the range A7:A37 to display the 31 wedding parties represented in the data.

b. Click cell **C3**, type **=COUNT(G7:G37)** and then press Ctrl+Enter.

The COUNT function counts all the cells that contain numbers only in the range G7:G37 to display 17 spa members scheduled weddings.

c. **Save** 🖫 the workbook.

| C1 | | | fx | =ROUND(AVERAGE(F7:F37),2) | | | | | |

	A	B	C	D	E	F	G	H
1	Average Amount Spent at Spa		$ 874.70					
2	Number of Weddings		31					
3	Spa Members Scheduling Weddings		17					
4								
5								
6	Wedding Party Name	Number of Days Spent	Whole Days Spent	Returned Merchandise	Value of Returned Merchandise	Amount Spent at Spa	Spa Member	
7	Arroyo	1.52	1	-37.34	37.34	$ 1,215.63	1	
8	Proctor	2.54	2	41.12	41.12	$ 720.60	1	
9	Minor	4.32	4	-12.7	12.7	$ 455.78	1	
10	Pearce	4.52	4	13.97	13.97	$ 1,309.51	Null	
11	Shea	2.50	2	18.53	18.53	$ 1,345.57	1	
12	Galvan	4.00	4	11.09	11.09	$ 1,046.69	1	
13	Crowe	2.31	2	36.64	36.64	$ 1,125.53	1	
14	Meeks	2.45	2	47.7	47.7	$ 1,068.90	1	
15	Kendrick	3.65	3	10.24	10.24	$ 604.95	Null	
16	Mayfield	4.45	4	7.88	7.88	$ 299.60	Null	
17	Kendall	3.11	3	21.78	21.78	$ 353.74	Null	
18	Archer	3.15	3	37.51	37.51	$ 923.56	1	

Figure 15 Statistical functions

Screenshot of Microsoft Excel 2019, © Microsoft Corporation

Use Date and Time Functions

Date and time functions are useful for entering the current day and time into a worksheet as well as for calculating the intervals between dates. This category of functions is based on a serial date system in which each day is represented sequentially from a starting point. In Microsoft applications, that standard is 1/1/1900, which has a serial number of 1. Thus, dates before January 1, 1900, will not be recognized by the system. Interestingly, when Apple initially made its starting point, it began in 1904. Excel settings can be changed to use the Apple starting point, but it is generally accepted practice to keep the default setting of 1/1/1900 as the starting point. Using two different starting points for dates in Excel spreadsheets can cause significant problems. Common date and time functions are shown in Table 5.

Function	Usage
DATE(year,month,day)	Returns the number that represents the date in Microsoft Excel date-time code
DATEDIF(date1,date2,interval)	Returns the time unit specified between two dates, including the two dates (inclusive)
DAY(serial_number)	Returns the day of the month, a number from 1 to 31
MONTH(serial_number)	Returns the month, a number from 1 to 12
NETWORKDAYS(start_date,end_date,[holidays])	Returns the number of whole workdays between two dates, inclusive; does not count weekends and can skip holidays that are listed
TODAY()	Returns the computer system date
WEEKDAY(serial_number, [return_type])	Returns a number from 1 to 7 representing the day of the week. Can be set to return 0–6 or 1–7
WEEKNUM(serial_number, [return_type])	Returns the week number in the year, which week of the year the date occurs
YEAR(serial_number)	Returns the year of a date, an integer in the range 1900–9999

Table 5 Common date functions

> **CONSIDER THIS** | **Dates in Microsoft Applications**
>
> Do you suppose the same Microsoft employees developed Access, Excel, Word, and PowerPoint? Is it possible that even within a company, there may have been differences in the starting date? Does Access use the same 1/1/1900 for its date starting point? See if you can find out.

Using Date and Time Functions

Because Excel tracks time by the number of days that have occurred since 1/1/1900, time is represented by the decimal portion of this number. The decimal is based on the number of minutes in a day (24*60=1440). Thus, a 0.1 decimal is equal to 144 minutes. A full date and time value—such as 5/14/2022 8:35 AM—would appear as 44695.35763. There are 44695 days between 1/1/1900 and 5/14/2022. The time of 8:35 AM is represented by the .35763 portion of the number.

The TODAY and NOW functions are two common functions for inserting the current date into a spreadsheet. There is a difference between these functions. The key difference is that the **TODAY function** inserts the current date into a cell, while the **NOW function** inserts the current date and time into a cell. If you think about it, the TODAY function works only with integer representation of days, while the NOW function uses decimals to include the time in addition to the day. Both functions can be formatted to show just the date, and you can work with time calculations that mix the two functions. Common time functions are listed in Table 6.

Function	Usage
HOUR(serial_number)	Returns the hour in a time value, from 0 to 23
MINUTE(serial_number)	Returns the minute in a time value, from 0 to 59
SECOND(serial_number)	Returns the number of seconds in a time value, from 0 to 59
NOW()	Returns the computer system date and time

Table 6 Common time functions

REAL WORLD ADVICE | **NOW versus TODAY**

Be careful when using NOW versus TODAY, especially when doing date calculations. Both functions use a serial number, counting from 1/1/1900. But the NOW function also includes decimals for the time of day, while TODAY works with integer serial numbers. At noon on 5/14/2022, the NOW function has the value of 44695.5, while the TODAY function has a value of 44695.0. If you are using these date functions inside another function, this could change the result if you are comparing a date the user provided. The TODAY function should be used if a user will be inserting the date into Excel by hand so the hand-typed value will be compared or used in a calculation with the function, eliminating the decimal issue.

DATEDIF function is a useful date function because it enables you to calculate the time between two dates. The function can return the time unit as days, months, or years. However, while all the other functions are listed and can be found in Excel, neither Help nor the Function Library offers any information about the DATEDIF function. You will not find any information on the DATEDIF function unless you search the Microsoft site. Because no information exists on it within Excel, this is one function that you must hand type and do the research to understand the syntax. Nonetheless, DATEDIF is one of the more useful date functions.

The syntax of the function is

=DATEDIF(date1,date2,interval)

The first argument is the starting date in time—the older date—and the second argument is the ending date in time—the newer, more recent date. It may be helpful to remember that time lines are usually depicted as moving from left to right, just as they would be listed in the DATEDIF function. The third argument is the interval that should be used, such as the number of months or days between the two dates. The interval is expressed as a text value and therefore must be surrounded by quotes for correct syntax. The viable interval options are shown in Table 7.

Interval	Description
"D"	Returns the number of complete days between the dates
"M"	Returns the number of complete months between the dates
"Y"	Returns the number of complete years between the dates
"MD"	Returns the difference between days in two dates, ignoring months and years
"YM"	Returns the difference between months in two dates, ignoring days and years
"YD"	Returns the difference between days in two dates, ignoring years

Table 7   Unit value options for DATEDIF

The options "D", "M", and "Y" are commonly used to calculate differences between dates. For example, using "Y" for the Interval argument is common practice for calculating an age. The options "YM", "YD", and "MD" are not as commonly used because they ignore certain aspects of the date structure. For example, using "YM" for the Interval argument with the dates 7/1/2021 and 9/12/2022 will result in a value of 2. This is because the "YM" unit value ignores the years in the two dates and calculates only the number of whole months between July (7) and September (9). Using "M" in the Interval argument will result in the value 14, the more commonly expected result.

Meda has asked for your help in completing an analysis of customers in the Keller-Ryan wedding party who have requested spa services. She would like the current date to appear in cell B1 of the spreadsheet and the current age of customers to appear in column D. In this exercise, you will use common date functions to complete the analysis.

 **E03.11**

To Use Date and Time Functions

a. Click the **SpaServices** worksheet tab, and then click cell **B1**.

b. Type **=TODAY()** and then press Ctrl + Enter.

Notice that cell B1 now displays the current date. Each time the worksheet is opened or when a cell is edited, the current date will be updated and displayed in cell B1. Because the time of day is not relevant here, the TODAY function is preferred over the NOW function.

SIDE NOTE
Alternate Method
You could also use the TODAY function in the formula in place of the absolute reference to B1. For example, the formula could be =DATEDIF(C5, TODAY(),"Y").

c. Click cell **D5**, type **=DATEDIF(C5,$B$1,"Y")** and then press Ctrl + Enter.

In this formula, C5 is the start date, $B$1 is the end date, and the "Y" stands for years. Using an absolute reference to cell B1 will allow you to copy the formula down a range. Because the interval is set to year, the result is that the age of the guest is always current in this calculation.

> ### Troubleshooting
> No ScreenTip will appear when you type the DATEDIF function. If the DATEDIF function returns a #NUM! error, the most likely problem is mixing up the order of the two dates within the function. The first date should be the earliest date, and the second date should be the most recent one. The other common error is actually typing in a date as the argument. Typing 12/3/2022 will be interpreted as division instead of a date. The value must be either in serial date format or typed inside of quotation marks.

d. Double-click the **fill handle** to copy cell D5 through cell **D22**. The current ages of all guests are now displayed in column D.

e. **Save** the workbook.

 CONSIDER THIS | **Calculating Days**

Do you really need to use the DATEDIF function to calculate the difference between days—the "D" unit? In what other way could you calculate the difference? What would that formula look like?

Use Text Functions

Excel is frequently used to bring data together from multiple different locations and/or systems, including text data. Many times, the data is inconsistent from one source to another. For example, one workbook could list names as First Name Last Name—Olivia Garcia—and the next may list names as Last Name, First Name—Garcia, Olivia. In situations like this, knowing how to alter text data is extremely valuable and can save a lot of time.

There are many reasons why text data in a cell may need to be altered. Names in a cell may need to be separated or combined. Several pieces of data may be stored in a single cell but need to be separated into many columns of data for easier analysis. Excel contains a wide array of functions and features that allow for the manipulation of text data. Some newer features in Excel are optimized for touch screen devices. This makes it easier to manipulate data when using Excel on a mobile device such as a tablet computer.

Using Text Functions

A **text function** is a function that manages, manipulates, and formats text data. Text functions can be used to change the appearance of data, such as displaying text in all lowercase letters. They can also be used to cleanse text. **Cleansing text** involves removing unwanted characters, rearranging data in a cell, or correcting erroneous data.

Data stored as text is commonly referred to as a string. Text functions can change the way data is viewed, cut a string of text into multiple pieces, or combine multiple pieces of text together into one string of text. While most text functions can be used individually, they become increasingly powerful when nested together to transform text. Common text functions are defined in Table 8.

Function	Usage
CONCAT(text1,text2,…)	Joins text1, text2,…,textn together into a single string value.
FIND(find_text,within_text,[start_num])	Finds find_text in within_text. The search begins at start_num (start_num defaults to 1) and is case sensitive. The starting position of find_text is returned. If the find_text is not present, an error will be returned.
LEFT(text,[num_chars])	Returns a string num_chars long from the left side of text. Num_chars defaults to 1.
LEN(text)	Returns a number that represents the number of characters.
MID(text,start_num,num_chars)	Returns a string extracted from text beginning in position start_num that is num_chars long.
RIGHT(text,[num_chars])	Returns a string num_chars long from the right side of text. Num_chars defaults to 1.
TRIM(text)	Returns text with any leading, trailing, or extra spaces between words removed.
UPPER(text)	Returns text with all characters in uppercase.
PROPER(text)	Returns text with only the first letter in each word in uppercase. All other letters will return in lowercase.
SEARCH(find_text,within_text,[start_num])	Finds find_text in within_text. The search begins at start_num (start_num defaults to 1) and is case insensitive. The starting position of find_text is returned. If the find_text is not present, an error will be returned.
TEXT(value,format_text)	Returns a number value as a string with the format specified in format_text.

Table 8   Common text functions

Meda has asked for your help in converting the guest names in column A from all uppercase to the proper format with the first letter of the first and last name capitalized, and the rest of the letters lowercased. In this exercise, you will use a text function to correct a capitalization issue on the SpaServices worksheet.

 E03.12

SIDE NOTE
Alternate Method
Instead of using the Collapse and Expand buttons when selecting cells, just click the cell or range of cells for that box.

To Use Text Functions

a. On the SpaServices worksheet, click cell **B5**.

b. On the Formulas tab, in the Function Library group, click **Text**, and then select **Proper**.

c. In the Text box, click **Collapse** [⬆], click cell **A5**, click **Expand** [⬇], and then click **OK**.

Notice how the name in cell B5 is now in the proper case format.

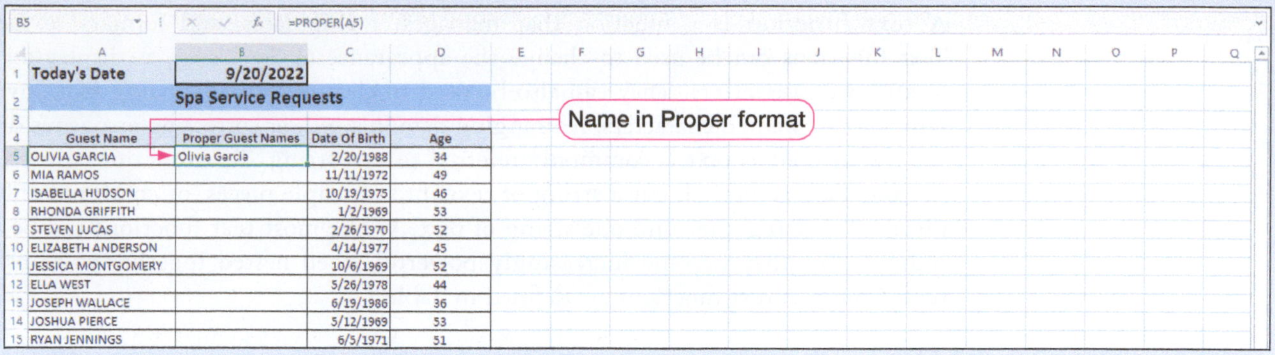

Figure 16 TEXT Function

Screenshot of Microsoft Excel 2019, © Microsoft Corporation

d. Double-click the **fill handle** to copy the formula through cell **B22**.

e. Save ▣ the workbook.

Use Lookup and Financial Functions

Excel has many functions available to help businesses make decisions. These decisions may include calculating payments on a loan or returning data from a table based upon a specific value in a worksheet. The ability to combine these processes in more complex tasks is even more powerful. For example, a lookup function can retrieve an interest rate from a table of data to be used in a subsequent loan calculation. As with other functions, lookup and reference functions can be very effective when combined with financial functions.

Using Lookup and Reference Functions

Lookup and reference functions look up matching values in a table of data. Lookup and reference functions can be used for simple matches or complex retrieval tasks. This can be as simple as retrieving a value from a vertical or horizontal list or as complex as finding the value of a cell within a table of data at a given row and column intersection.

The **VLOOKUP function** matches a provided value in a table of data and returns a value from a subsequent column. The VLOOKUP lets you search for specific information in your spreadsheet. For example, if you have a list of products with part numbers, you could search for the part number of a specific item. The "V" signifies that the function matches the provided value vertically in the first column of the table of data. The syntax of a VLOOKUP function is

=VLOOKUP(lookup_value, table_array, col_index_num, [range_lookup])

- The lookup_value argument is the data you are looking up. It can be any text, any number, or a reference to a cell that contains data.

- The table_array argument is a range in a spreadsheet where you are looking up data. The range can be a single column of cells or multiple columns of cells.

- The col_index_num is the column number of the corresponding value that will be returned.

- The optional range_lookup argument allows the VLOOKUP to perform an approximate or exact match. The range_lookup argument is TRUE for an approximate match. To get an exact match, the range_lookup argument should be set to FALSE.

The Turquoise Oasis Spa has recently partnered with a local bank to offer financing to customers who are booking large, costly events. Booking spa services is usually one of the last things guests will do. Thus, some guests will book fewer services than they desire because of budget concerns. The spa is hoping that offering a financing package and discounts for large events will increase revenue. As part of the workbook you are building for the spa,

Meda has asked that you finish the WeddingFinancing worksheet that she started. This worksheet contains cells to enter information about guest weddings being planned. The worksheet already has cells prepared for entering the cost of the event, the down payment supplied by the guest, the annual interest rate, and the term of the loan in years. You have been asked to complete this worksheet so that when a wedding is scheduled, the guest will understand the financing plan options and whether they qualify for a discount.

In this exercise, you will use a lookup function to return the discount that the spa will provide based on the total cost of the wedding event being planned.

 **E03.13**

SIDE NOTE
Lookup Table Array
Notice the values in the table array (E4:F8) are listed in ascending order; otherwise, the correct value may not be returned.

SIDE NOTE
Table Array Text
Uppercase text and low-ercase text are equivalent in lookup table arrays.

To Use the VLOOKUP Function

a. Click the **WeddingFinancing** worksheet tab, and then click cell **B7**.

b. On the Formulas tab, in the Function Library group, click **Lookup & Reference**, and then click **VLOOKUP**. The Function Arguments dialog box is now open.

c. In the Lookup_value text box, type **B3** as the lookup value to match on the list of discounts, and then press Tab.

d. In the Table_array text box, type **E4:F8** and then press Tab.

e. In the Col_index_num text box, type **2** and then press Tab.

f. In the Range_lookup text box, type true

The VLOOKUP matches the value in cell B3 to the cell range E4:E8. When a match is found, the corresponding row value from column F—column 2 from the table array—will be returned. By placing TRUE as the range_lookup argument, the VLOOKUP will perform an approximate match; true is the default setting for this function. This means that an event costing $37,000 will return a 5.0% discount.

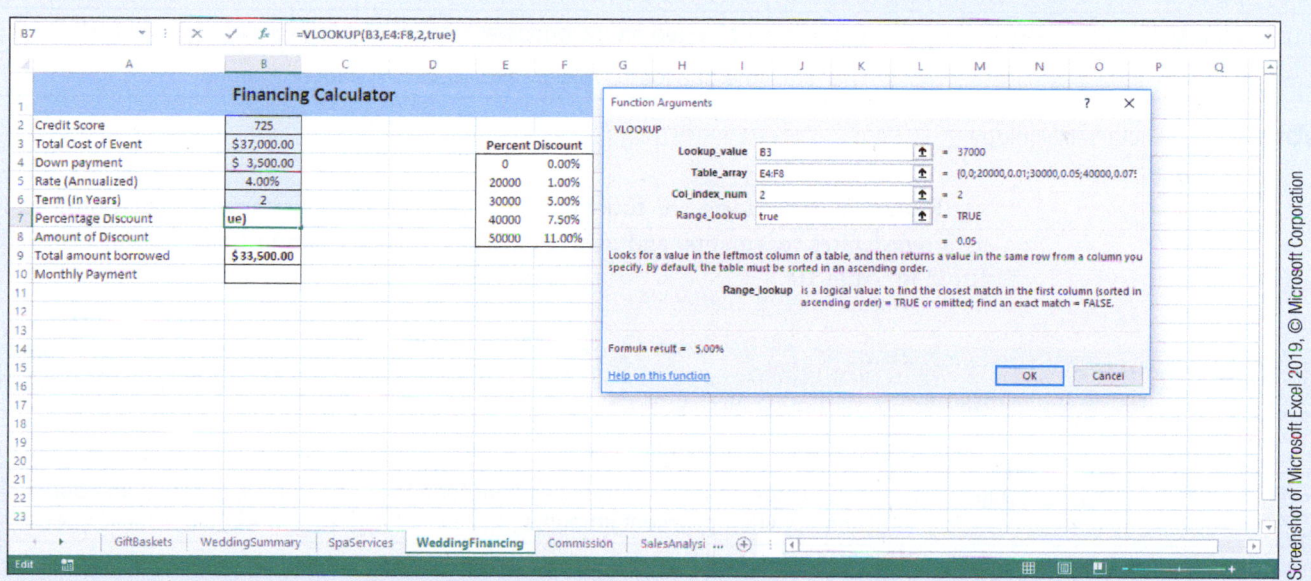

Figure 17 VLOOKUP Function Arguments dialog box

g. Click **OK** to complete the VLOOKUP function and get a result of 5.00%.

> **Troubleshooting**
> If the VLOOKUP function returns a #N/A error, check to make sure the range_lookup argument is TRUE. Using FALSE for the argument will force the VLOOKUP into an exact match. Since $37,000 is not listed in E4:E8, an error will be returned.

h. **Save** the workbook.

| REAL WORLD ADVICE | Approximate and Exact Matches |

If the range_lookup argument is left blank, it will default to TRUE for an approximate match. If the range_lookup should be FALSE but is mistakenly left blank, an incorrect result will be returned.

Using Financial Functions

Having a foundational knowledge of financial terms is an important element of succeeding in both your personal life and your professional life. Some common financial terms that you will see and hear or possibly use in an Excel spreadsheet are shown in Table 9.

Financial Term	Definition
APR	The annual percentage rate; an interest rate expressed in an annual equivalent
Compound interest	The interest charged on both the principal and the interest that accumulates on a loan
Interest payment	The amount of a payment that goes toward paying the interest accrued
NPV	The net present value of future investments
Period	The time period of payments, such as making payments monthly
Principal payment	The amount of a payment that goes toward reducing the principal amount
Principal value	The original amount borrowed or loaned
PV	Present value—the original value of the loan
Rate (and APR)	The interest rate per period of a loan or an investment
Simple interest	The interest charged on the principal amount of a loan only
Term	The total time of a loan, typically expressed in years or months

Table 9 Financial terminology

Financial functions are functions used for common financial calculations, such as interest rates, payments, and analyzing loans. Some common financial functions are listed in Table 10.

Financial Function	Definition
PMT(rate,nper,pv,[fv],[type])	Calculates periodic payment for a loan based on a constant interest rate and constant payment amounts
IPMT(rate,per, nper,pv,[fv],[type])	Calculates periodic interest payment for a loan based on a constant interest rate and constant payment amounts
PPMT(rate,per,nper,pv,[fv],[type])	Calculates periodic principal payment for a loan based on a constant interest rate and constant payment amounts
NPV(rate,value1,[value2]...)	Calculates the net present value based on a discount interest rate, a series of future payments, and future income

Table 10 Common financial functions

A common and useful financial function is the PMT function. The **PMT function** determines the periodic payment for a loan based upon constant payments and interest rate. The PMT function by default returns a negative value because the function is calculating a payment to be made. Within the financial and accounting industry, an outflow of cash is considered a negative value. In other words, this function assumes that you are making a payment—taking money out of your pocket to give to someone else. Because some people may be confused by seeing the value as negative, the value can be made positive by simply inserting a negative sign before the function or the present value.

The syntax of the PMT function is

=PMT(rate,nper,pv,[fv],[type])

The first argument is the rate, which is the periodic interest rate. It is important to remember that the interest rate must be for each period. Most loans are discussed in terms of annual percentage rate (APR), while the period would be a shorter time period such as quarterly or monthly. The APR would need to be divided by 12 to get an equivalent monthly interest rate.

The second argument is nper, which is the number of periods or total number of payments that will be made for the loan. Again, many loans are discussed in years, while the payments would be monthly. Therefore, you will often need to determine the total number of periodic payments with a calculation.

The third required argument is PV, which is the present value of an investment or loan—the amount borrowed that needs to be paid back. The last two arguments are optional. The FV argument is the future value attained after the last payment is made. If this argument is left blank, the PMT function assumes FV to be zero. The type argument indicates when a payment is due. If it is left blank, the PMT function assumes that payments are due at the end of a period; if the type argument is supplied, payments are assumed to be due at the beginning of a period.

In this exercise, you will calculate the monthly payment for the customer for the event being planned, using the PMT function.

Use Logical Functions and Troubleshoot Functions

In constructing a spreadsheet, the need will often arise to evaluate criteria in a range of cells and to make a decision based on those criteria. Excel contains functions that can evaluate a wide range of criteria and return customized results. For example, a comparison

---

 **E03.14**

SIDE NOTE
Unit Conversions
Be careful when converting the arguments of the PMT function. Monthly payments are converted by using 12; quarterly payments are converted by using 4.

SIDE NOTE
Alternate Method
The negative sign can be inserted before the present value reference to display the result of the payment function as a positive number.

To Use the PMT Function

a. On the WeddingFinancing worksheet, click cell **B10**.

b. On the Formulas tab, in the Function Library group, click **Financial**, and then select **PMT**.

c. For Rate, type B5/12

    Because the interest rate in cell B5 is annual, you need to divide by 12 to get the interest rate per payment—in this case, monthly.

d. For Nper, type B6*12

    Because the term of the loan is in years, you will need to multiply the term by 12 to get the total number of payments—in this case, months—in the loan.

e. For Pv, type B9 and then click **OK**.

    As was mentioned previously, the PMT function is calculated by default as a negative value and therefore the result of ($1,454.73) will appear in red. Adding the negative sign before the PMT function will display the result as a positive number.

f. In cell **B10**, press the F2 key. Click to the right of the equal sign, type the – (the minus sign), and then press Enter.

    The original loan amount was $37,000. Cell B9 takes the original amount in B3, subtracts the down payment supplied in cell B4, and subtracts the amount of the discount in cell B8—which will be calculated in the next exercise.

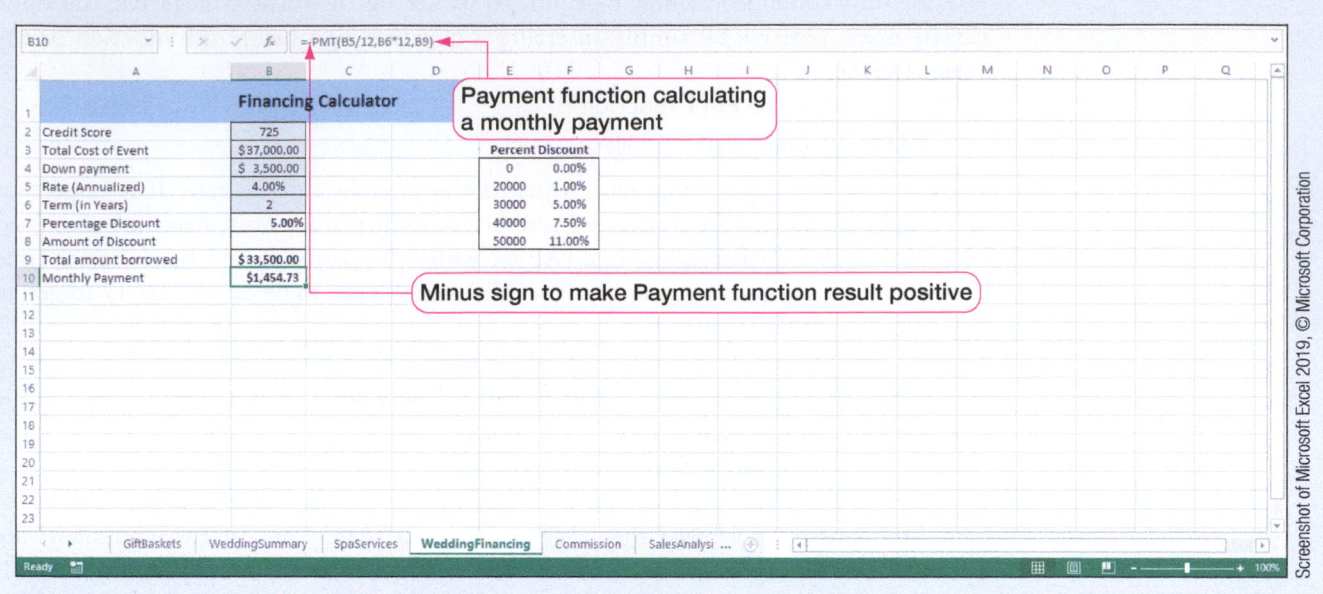

Figure 18   PMT function used to calculate a monthly payment

g. Save 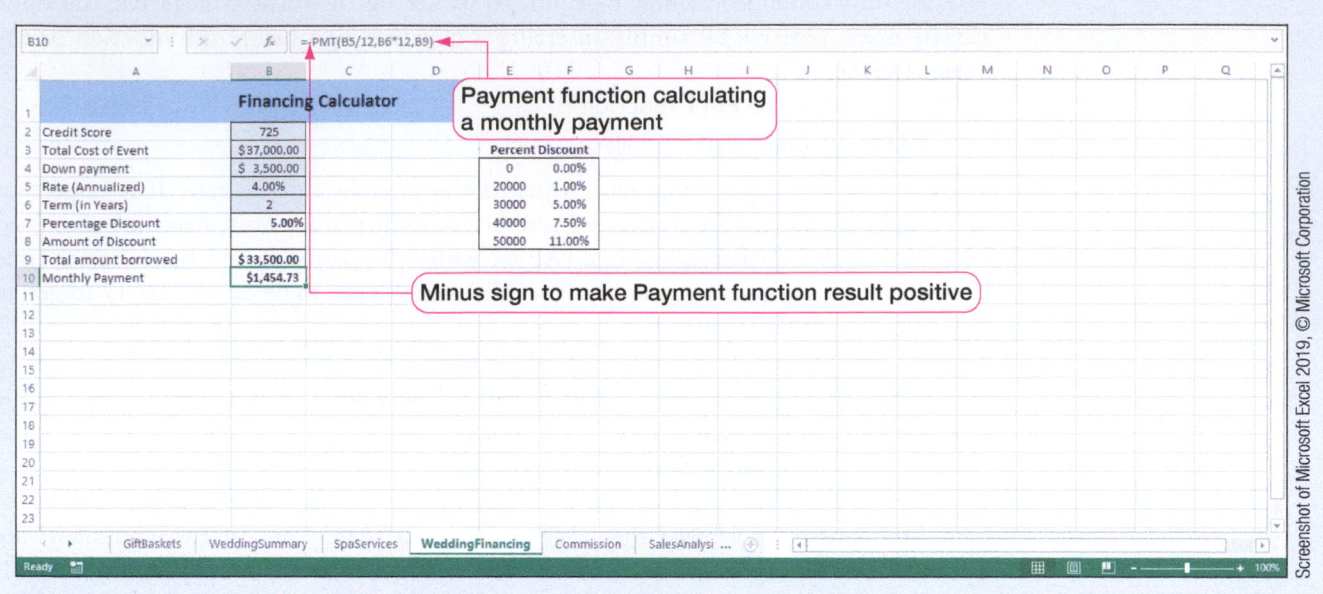 the workbook.

of two cells to see whether their values are the same may result in a cell displaying TRUE, a customized text response, or even performing another calculation. As the formulas become more complicated, errors may occur in the spreadsheet. Understanding some basic spreadsheet troubleshooting techniques can help you to easily correct these errors.

Using Logical Functions

Logical functions return a result based upon evaluating whether a logical test is true or false. For example, the statement "The sky is blue" is a declaration that can be evaluated as true. If the statement was "Is the sky blue?" the response would be a yes/no instead of true/false. So all logical functions are structured around the concept of declaring a position or statement that Excel will evaluate and return as True or False.

The best way to think of a declaration is to think of using comparison symbols such as the =, >, <, or >= symbols as shown in Table 11. When you set up a statement of X > Y, Excel can evaluate that comparison as true or false.

Comparison Operator Symbol	Example	Declarative Clause
<	A < B	A is less than B
>	A > B	A is greater than B
=	A = B	A is equal to B
<=	A <= B	A is less than or equal to B
>=	A >= B	A is greater than or equal to B
<>	A <> B	A does not equal B

Table 11   Comparison operators

The IF function is the most commonly used logical function. The **IF function** will return one of two values depending upon whether the supplied logical test being evaluated is true or false. The syntax of the IF function is

=IF(logical_test,[value_if_true],[value_if_false])

The first argument is the logical_test, the statement you want to evaluate as TRUE or FALSE. Excel will then evaluate it as either true or false. The second argument is the result you want to display in the cell if the expression is evaluated as true. The third argument is the result you want to display in the cell if the expression is evaluated as false.

Notice that only the logical_test argument is required. The last two arguments are optional. If you leave them out, Excel will automatically return TRUE or FALSE as the result of the function. However, it is much more common and expected that you will supply something for all three arguments. If you consider the context, logical statement, and results of the IF function, the structure begins to fall into place.

SS CONSIDER THIS | **Variations in Constructing Formulas**

In Excel, a formula can be written in many ways. Some are more efficient than others. At a minimum, every IF statement can be written in two ways. Why? Provide an example for each way.

To encourage couples getting married to use the resort for all their wedding services, the Painted Paradise Resort & Spa will offer a discount. The discount rate was determined by the total cost of the event. If the total cost of the event is greater than or equal to $20,000 then the cost of the event is multiplied by the discount rate or else the result will be zero.

In this exercise, you will use the IF function to evaluate whether the total cost of the event is enough to be eligible for a discount.

 **E03.15**

To Use the IF Function

a. On the WeddingFinancing worksheet, click cell **B8**.

b. On the Formulas tab, in the Function Library group, click **Logical**, and then click **IF** to begin the IF function and enter the Logical_test argument.

   If the total cost of the event is greater than or equal to $20,000, then the guest will earn a discount based on the discount percentage calculated in cell B7.

c. With the insertion point in the Logical_test box, type **B3>=20000** for the logical_test argument. Press [Tab] to enter the Value_if_true argument.

   If the logical test result is true, then the total cost of the event should be multiplied by the discount.

d. Type **B3*B7** and then press [Tab] to enter the Value_if_false argument.

   If the logical test result is not true (false), then the total cost of amount of discount should be 0.

e. Type **0**

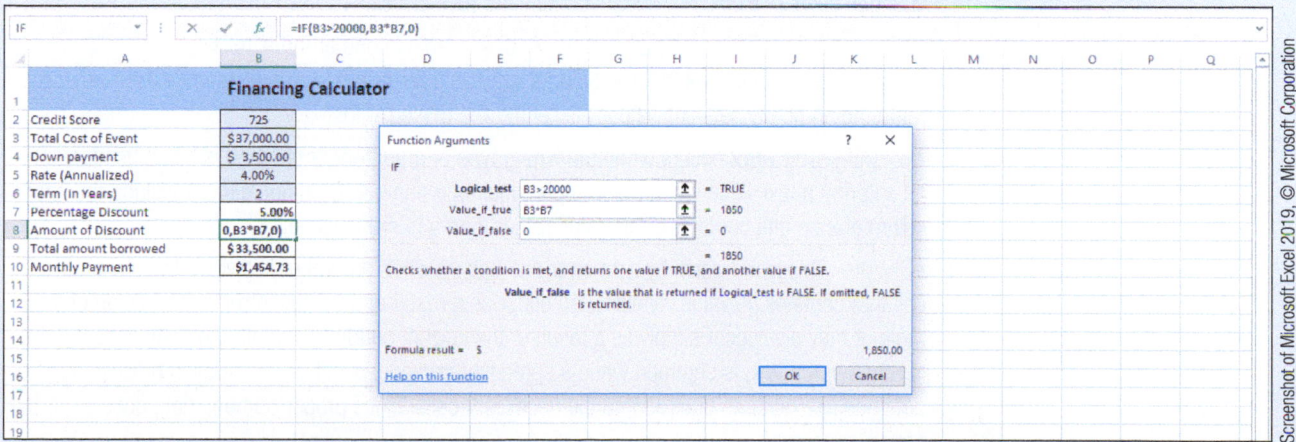

Figure 19 IF Function Arguments dialog box

f. Click **OK**.

   Notice that because the value in B3 is greater than or equal to $20,000, the result of $1,850 is calculated.

g. Click in cell **B3**, type 19000 and then press Enter. Notice the result of cell B8 changed to blank ($0.00).

h. Click **Undo**.

i. **Save** the workbook.

Troubleshooting

Logical functions dramatically increase the value of a spreadsheet. However, on the path to learning how to use functions, and even as an experienced spreadsheet user, you will still make typing errors during the development of functions. Excel does an excellent job of incorporating clues to help you determine where you have gone astray with a function.

CONSIDER THIS | What IF There Are Three Options?

An IF statement can handle just two results: true and false. Are most real world situations that simple? How could you use an IF statement if there are more than two results? It is possible!

When you make a mistake with a function that prevents Excel from returning a viable result, Excel will provide an error message. While these may seem cryptic initially, they can be interpreted. Typically, an error message will be prefaced with a number symbol (#). Examples are #VALUE!, #N/A, #NAME?, or #REF!. Over time, you will learn to recognize common issues that would cause these error messages.

QUICK REFERENCE | Common Error Messages

- #NAME?—This error indicates that text in a formula is not recognized. Excel treats unrecognized text as a named range that does not exist. This is often the result of missing quotes around a text string or mistyping the function or range name.
- #REF!—This error indicates a reference that Excel cannot find. This is often the result of changes such as a deleted worksheet, column, row, or cell.
- #N/A—This error indicates that a value is not available in one or more cells specified. Common causes occur in functions that try to find a value in a list but the value does not exist. Rather than returning an empty set—no value—Excel returns this error instead.
- #VALUE!—This error occurs when the wrong type of argument or operand is being used, such as entering a text value when the formula requires a number. Common causes include the wrong cell reference that contains a text value rather than a numeric value.
- #DIV/0!—This is a division by zero error and occurs when a number is divided by zero or by a cell that contains no value. While it can occur as a result of an actual error in the design of a formula, it may also occur simply as a result of the current conditions within the spreadsheet data. In other words, this is common when a spreadsheet model is still in the creation process and data has not yet been entered into the necessary cells. Once proper numeric data does exist, the error disappears.

There are numerous ways to troubleshoot erroneous functions in Excel. When you encounter an error, you can quickly check the cell references and arguments of the function by double-clicking the cell to edit the function. This is beneficial because while a function is being edited, Excel will outline any cells or ranges included in the function and display the ScreenTip for the function. You can also press the F2 key to place a cell in edit mode. Auditing options are available in the Formula Auditing group of the Formulas tab as well.

CHAPTER 3

QUICK REFERENCE	Troubleshooting Cells with Error Messages or Incorrect Results

- Double-click a cell to enter edit mode of the cell.
- Press the F2 key to enter edit mode of a cell.
- In the Formula Auditing group of the Formulas tab, select Error Checking-Trace Error.

On the Commission worksheet, Meda has set up a quick analysis that rewards the employee who schedules the event with a commission on the total cost of the event. The commission earned is then added to the base event pay for the employee. The base event pay is contingent upon the employee level. After setting up the worksheet, Meda noticed an error in one of the cells. Additionally, the table located in the Commission worksheet states that managers have a base event pay of $1,250. However, the value shown for the manager in the worksheet is only $750. In this exercise, you will troubleshoot the problem.

 E03.16

To Troubleshoot a Function

a. Click the **Commission** worksheet tab, and then click cell **B4**.

Notice the #N/A error being returned by the VLOOKUP function in the cell. Recall that this error commonly occurs because a value cannot be found on a list.

b. Click the **Error Message** button ⚠ next to cell B4. Notice the error message states that a value is not available.

> **MAC COMPATIBILITY**
> **Error Message Button**
> On a Mac, there is no Error Message button.

c. Click cell **B4** again, and then press F2 to edit the formula.

Notice the outlines around the cells that are part of the VLOOKUP function. From this view, you can verify that cell B3 is correctly referenced as the lookup value. Cell range E4:F8 is correctly referenced as the table array. The column index number will return a value from column F if a value is found in column E.

Notice that the range_lookup argument is set to FALSE. This means that the lookup is performing an exact match. Because $17,000 does not occur in the range E4:E8, the VLOOKUP will return a #N/A error.

d. Place the insertion point at the end of the range_lookup argument, and then delete the text FALSE. Type **TRUE** and then press Ctrl+Enter to fix the formula. Notice that the value 5.00% now appears in cell B4.

e. Double-click cell **B8** to edit the formula.

Notice that the range_lookup argument is set to TRUE. This means that the lookup is performing an approximate match and is returning the incorrect base event pay rate.

f. Place the insertion point at the end of the range_lookup argument, and then delete the text TRUE. Type **FALSE** and then press Ctrl+Enter to fix the formula. Notice that the value $1,250 now appears in cell B8.

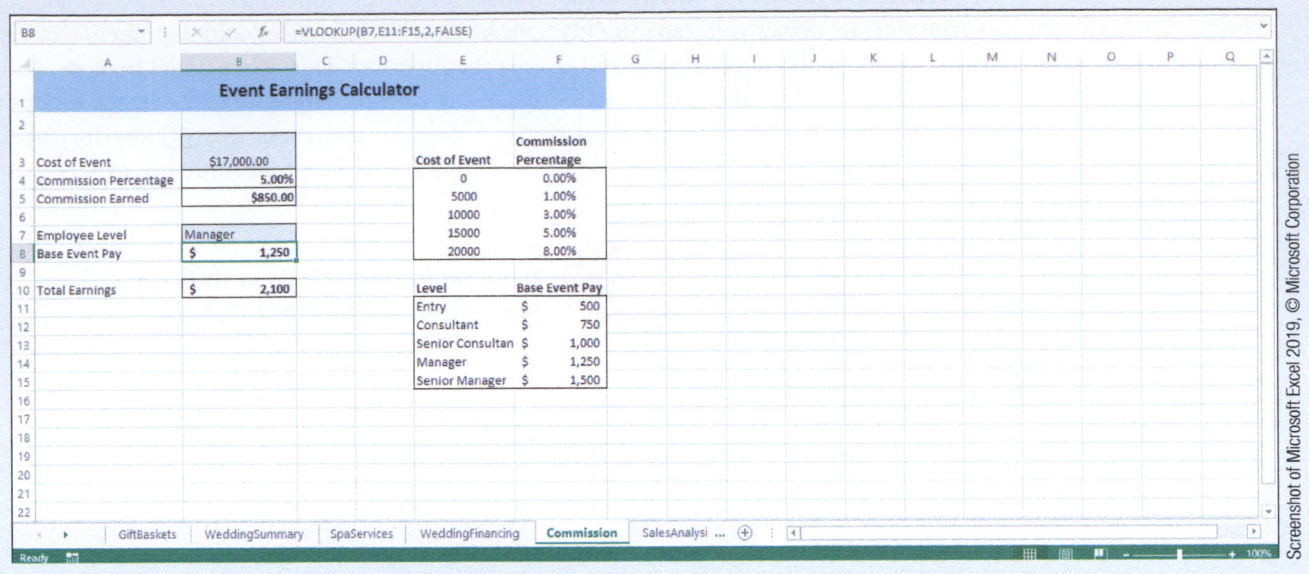

Figure 20 Worksheet with IF functions corrected

g. Save the workbook. If you need a break, now is a good time.

REAL WORLD ADVICE | **Function Construction Guidelines**

As you develop a spreadsheet, follow these guidelines for creating formulas and functions.

- Use parentheses for grouping operations in calculations to get the correct order. However, do not overuse parentheses, as this quickly adds to the complexity of the formula. For example, use =SUM(Sales) instead of =(SUM(Sales)).

- When inserting numbers into a function, use formatting such as 10000. Do not enter 10,000, with a comma. In Excel, the comma is a formatting element and is used to separate arguments. Best practice for functions and formulas dictates entering the 10000 value in a cell and then using the cell address in the formula.

- Insert currency as 4.34 instead of $4.34 to avoid confusion with relative and absolute cell referencing. Then format the cell that will contain the result as Accounting or Currency. Best practice for functions and formulas dictates entering the 4.34 value in a cell and then using the cell address in the formula.

- Enter percentages as decimals, such as .04. Then format the number as a percentage.

- Logical conditions have three parts: two components to compare and the comparison sign. Do not type >5 when there is no value to evaluate as being greater than 5.

- Use the negative sign, as in −333, to indicate negative numbers in formulas, rather than (333).

- Always put quotation marks around text unless it is a named range. Numeric values do not require quotation marks unless the number will be used in a textual context and not for a mathematical calculation. An example of numbers in a textual context would be a zip code or telephone number.

- Avoid unneeded spaces in formulas. Excel will allow a function such as =SUM(A2:A10). Best practice dictates typing the function as =SUM(A2:A10) with no extra spaces.

Use Conditional Aggregate Functions

Excel recognizes the need for having statistical functions that can calculate a subset of data that meets the specified criteria. There is a set of common functions that have been merged with the logical functions, including the COUNT and AVERAGE functions. They have been set to handle both a single criterion and multiple criteria for filtering.

Using the COUNTIF Function

The **COUNTIF function** counts the number of cells that meet specified criteria. The syntax for the COUNTIF function is

=COUNTIF(range, criteria)

The COUNTIF function has two arguments: range and criteria. The range is the cells that will be counted, and the criteria is the logical statement that will determine which cells to count within the formula cell range. For example, if there was a range of data in which the cells contained the data "Handicapped Golfer" or "Scratch Golfer" and the criterion was "Scratch Golfer", the function would count every occurrence in the cell range where the cell data content (criterion) equals "Scratch Golfer".

Meda wants to know the total number of wedding parties who spent four days at the resort. In this exercise, you will create a COUNTIF function.

 **E03.17**

To Create a COUNTIF Function

a. If you took a break, open the **e02ch03Wedding_LastFirst** workbook, and then click the **SalesAnalysis** worksheet.

b. Click cell **B3**. On the Formulas tab, in the Function Library group, click the **More Functions** arrow, and then point to **Statistical**. Scroll if necessary, and then select **COUNTIF**.

c. For the Range, click **Collapse** ⬆, select cell range **B7:B37**, and then click **Expand** ⬇. Press Tab.

d. For the Criteria, click **Collapse** ⬆, select cell **A3**, and then click **Expand** ⬇.

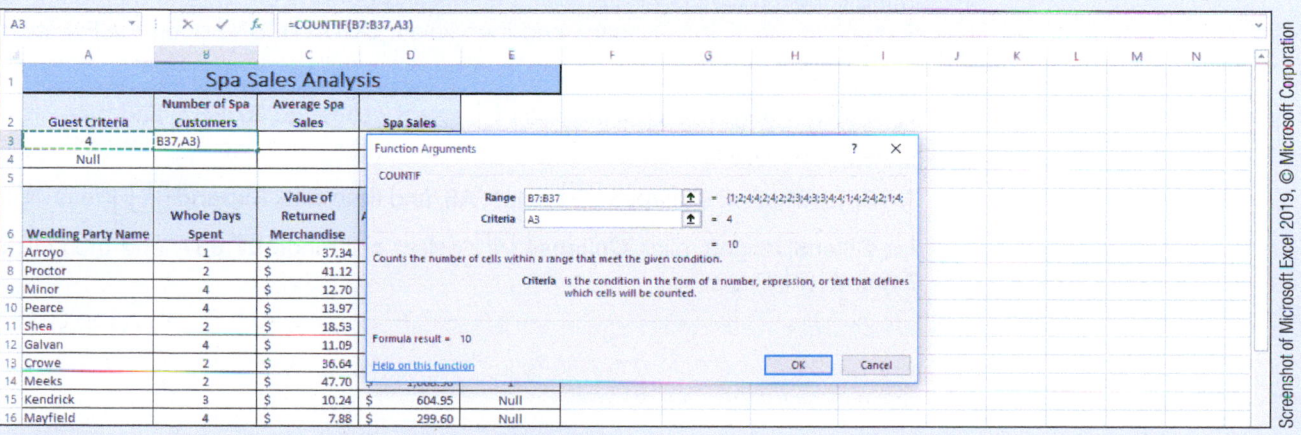

Figure 21 COUNTIF Function Arguments dialog box

e. Click **OK**.

f. **Save** 🖫 the workbook.

REAL WORLD ADVICE | **Testing Your Functions**

In the real world, you will check for errors as you develop a workbook, looking for numbers that do not make sense or seem out of line. Try testing data to ensure that formulas work the way you expect them to. It may be that an issue is caused by cells being referenced in a formula rather than by the formula itself. Develop techniques, such as using formula auditing and testing a range of data, to ensure that calculations are correct.

Using the COUNTIFS Function

The **COUNTIFS function** allows for multiple criteria in multiple ranges to be evaluated and counted. The syntax for the COUNTIFS function is

=COUNTIFS(criteria_range1, criteria1, [criteria_range2, criteria2],…)

There is no distinction between a criteria_range argument found in COUNTIFS and a range argument used in COUNTIF. When counting, it simply counts the cells that meet the criteria; thus, the range of cells to count and the criteria_range are the same range. However, in using multiple criteria, all criteria ranges must have the same shape—the same number of rows and same number of columns. Then the cells within the multiple ranges are compared and all criteria must evaluate to TRUE to be counted.

In the previous exercise, you counted the total number of wedding parties who spent four full days at the resort. Meda also wants to know the total number of wedding parties who spent four days at the resort who are non-spa (Null) members. Two criteria must match for a count to occur. The two ranges that will be checked will be the Whole Days Spent and the Spa Member fields. If both are true for their criteria, that pair will be counted.

In this exercise, you will create a COUNTIFS function.

 **E03.18**

To Create a COUNTIFS Function

a. On the SalesAnalysis worksheet, click cell **B4**, and then click the **Formulas** tab. In the Function Library group, click the **More Functions** arrow, and then point to **Statistical**. Scroll if necessary, and then select **COUNTIFS** to open the Function Arguments dialog box.

b. For Criteria_range1, click **Collapse** ⬆, select cell range **B7:B37**, and then click **Expand** ⬇. Press Tab.

c. For Criteria1, click **Collapse** ⬆, select **A3**, and then click **Expand** ⬇. Press Tab.

d. For Criteria_range2, click **Collapse** ⬆, select cell range **E7:E37**, and then click **Expand** ⬇. Press Tab.

e. For Criteria2, click **Collapse** [↑], select **A4**, and then click **Expand** [↓].

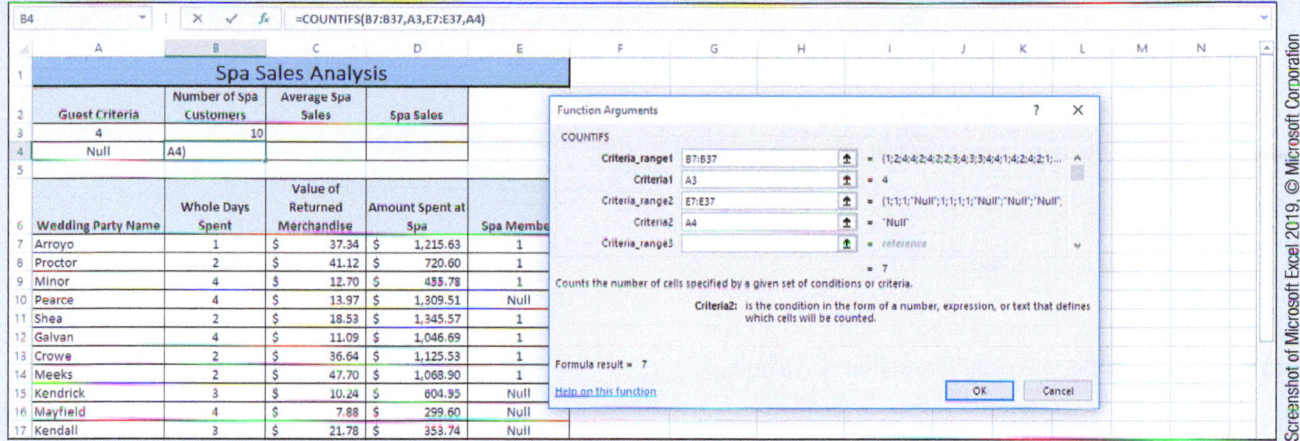

Figure 22 COUNTIFS Function Arguments dialog box

f. Click **OK**, and then **Save** [H] the workbook.

Using the AVERAGEIF Function

The **AVERAGEIF function** averages the cells that meet the specified criteria. This differs from the AVERAGE function, which averages the data in the selected cells. The AVERAGEIF function has three arguments, two required and one optional. The syntax for the AVERAGEIF function is

=AVERAGEIF(range, criteria, [average_range])

If the [average_range] argument is omitted, Excel assumes that the same range specified in the range argument will be used for filtering the data and for averaging. With the AVERAGEIF function, the third argument is required only if one range of data is being averaged based on criteria of a second range.

Meda wants to know the average amount spent at the spa for parties who spent 4 whole days in the resort.

In this exercise, you will create an AVERAGEIF function.

 **E03.19**

To Create an AVERAGEIF Function

a. On the SalesAnalysis worksheet, click cell **C3**. On the Formulas tab, in the Function Library group, click the **More Functions** arrow, and then point to **Statistical**. Scroll if necessary, and then select **AVERAGEIF** to open the Function Arguments dialog box.

b. For Range, click **Collapse** [↑], select cell range **B7:B37**, and then click **Expand** [↓]. Press Tab.

c. For Criteria, click **Collapse** [↑], select **A3**, and then click **Expand** [↓]. Press Tab.

d. For Average_range, click **Collapse** [↑], select cell range **D7:D37**, and then click **Expand** [↓].

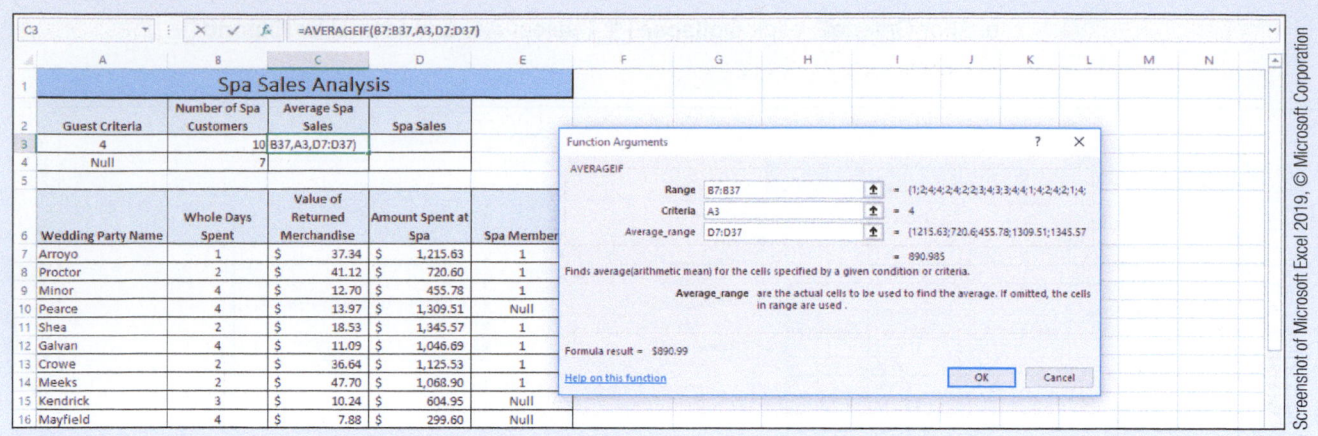

Figure 23 AVERAGEIF Function Arguments dialog box

    e. Click **OK**, and then **Save**  the workbook.

Using the AVERAGEIFS Function

The **AVERAGEIFS function** averages a range of data, selecting data to average based on criteria specified. The AVERAGEIFS function expands on the AVERAGEIF function, allowing multiple criteria to determine the subset of data. However, it is important to note that the order of the arguments changes. The syntax for the AVERAGIFS function is

=AVERAGEIFS(average_range, criteria_range1, criteria1, [criteria_range2, criteria2], ...)

    The average range is moved to become the first argument on the assumption that different ranges would be used for determining the filtered subset of data. After the average range, there are pairs of criteria ranges and criteria. In this fashion, multiple criteria can be used to filter the data to be averaged. Like the COUNTIFS function, the two ranges must be the same shape, having the same number of rows and columns. With the AVERAGEIFS function, all ranges must be the same size, although they do not have to be adjacent or even on the same worksheet.

    Meda wants to determine if there is a significant difference between the average amount spent at the spa and the average amount spent at the spa for non-spa (Null) members. To gather this information, you will need to create a formula based on two sets of criteria.

    In this exercise, you will create an AVERAGEIFS function.

▶ E03.20

To Create an AVERAGEIFS Function

    a. On the SalesAnalysis worksheet, click cell **C4**.

    b. On the Formulas tab, in the Function Library group, click the **More Functions** arrow, and then point to **Statistical**. Scroll if necessary, and then select **AVERAGEIFS** to open the Function Arguments dialog box.

    c. For Average_range, click **Collapse** ⬆, select cell range **D7:D37**, and then click **Expand** ⬇. Press ⇥ Tab.

    d. For Criteria_range1, click **Collapse** ⬆, select cell range **B7:B37**, and then click **Expand** ⬇. Press ⇥ Tab.

    e. For Criteria1, click **Collapse** ⬆, select **A3**, and then click **Expand** ⬇.

f. For Criteria_range2, click **Collapse** ⬆, select cell range **E7:E37**, and then click **Expand** ⬇. Press Tab.

g. For Criteria2, click **Collapse** ⬆, select **A4**, and then click **Expand** ⬇.

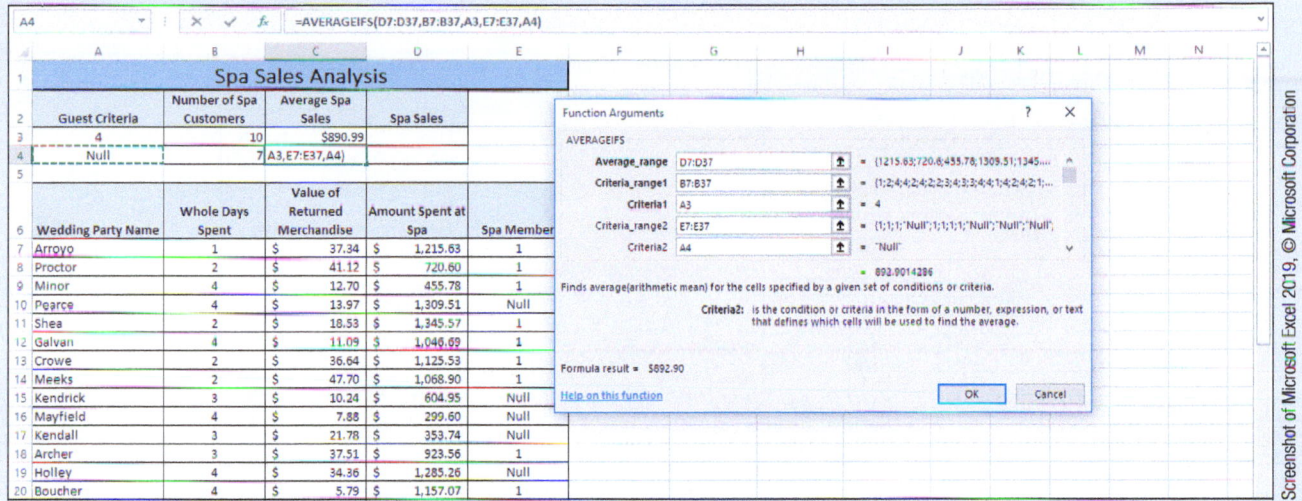

Figure 24 AVERAGEIFS Function Arguments dialog box

h. Click **OK**, and then **Save** 🖫 the workbook.

Use Conditional Math Functions

A conditional math function is a function that will calculate only when specified conditions are met. The conditional math functions include the SUMIF and SUMIFS functions.

Using the SUMIF Function

The **SUMIF function** sums cells that meet specified criteria. The syntax for the SUMIF function is

=SUMIF(range, criteria, [sum_range])

For the SUMIF function, because only one criteria is allowed, the first argument is the range associated with the criteria. The second argument is the criteria itself, which will determine which values are summed. The third argument, [sum_range], is optional because you can set the criteria on the actual sum range. If the [sum_range] argument is omitted, the default is to assume that the range and the sum_range are the same. However, a great feature with this function is that the criteria can be set on one range, such as the payment type, while the function sums a second range, such as the payment amount.

Meda wants to know the total amount spent at the spa if the guest spent four days at the resort.

In this exercise, you will create a SUMIF function.

 **E03.21**

To Create a SUMIF Function

a. On the SalesAnalysis worksheet, click cell **D3**. On the Formulas tab, in the Function Library group, click the **Math & Trig** arrow, and then scroll to select **SUMIF**.

b. For Range, click **Collapse** ⬆, select cell range **B7:B37**, and then click **Expand** ⬇. Press Tab.

c. For Criteria, click **Collapse** [↑], select **A3**, and then click **Expand** [↓]. Press [Tab].

d. For Sum_range, click **Collapse** [↑], select cell range **D7:D37**, and then click **Expand** [↓].

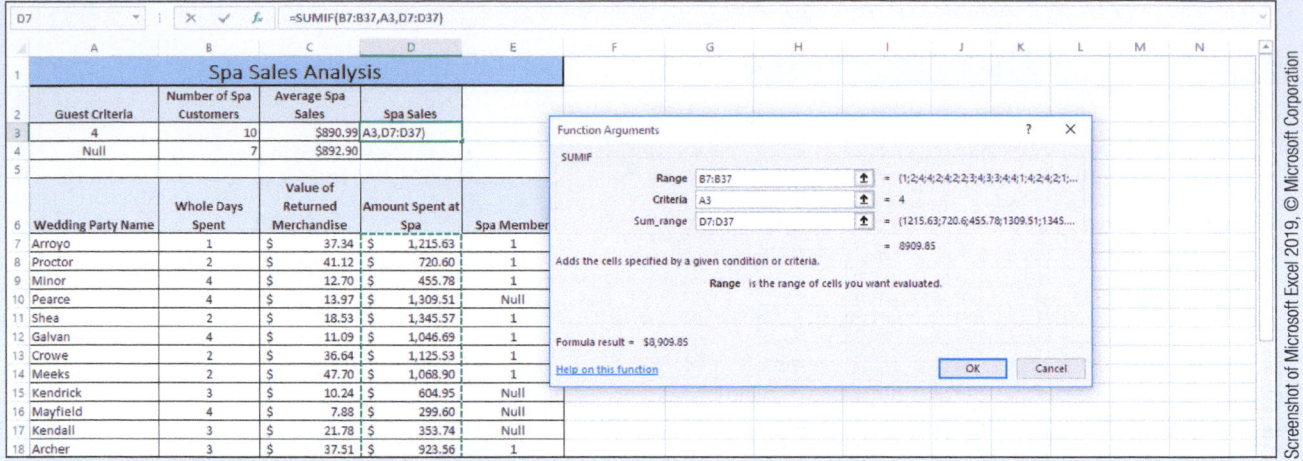

Figure 25   SUMIF Function Arguments dialog box

e. Click **OK**, and then **Save** [💾] the workbook.

Using the SUMIFS Function

The **SUMIFS function** sums a range of data, selecting data to total based on the multiple criteria specified. With the SUMIFS function, it is assumed that multiple criteria would be set, thus having a sum_range different from at least one criteria_range. Thus, the order is changed to have the sum_range first, then add criteria_range and criteria for each constraint or filter. The syntax for the SUMIFS function is

=SUMIFS(sum_range, criteria_range1, criteria1, [criteria_range2, criteria2], …)

The structure for the arguments is the same as that in the AVERAGEIFS function. The criteria ranges must match the sum_range in shape. If there are multiple criteria, the cells are evaluated for each criterion with a result of TRUE to be used in the subset of data.

Finally, Meda Rodate wants to know the total spa sales if four whole days were spent at the spa and the guests were non-spa (Null) members. To gather this information, you will need to create a formula based on two sets of criteria.

In this exercise, you will create a SUMIFS function.

 **E03.22**

To Create a SUMIFS Function

a. On the SalesAnalysis worksheet, click cell **D4**.

b. On the Formulas tab, in the Function Library group, click the **Math & Trig** arrow, and then scroll to select **SUMIFS**.

c. For Sum_range, click **Collapse** [↑], select cell range **D7:D37**, and then click **Expand** [↓]. Press [Tab].

d. For Criteria_range1, click **Collapse** ⬆, select cell range **B7:B37**, and then click **Expand** ⬇. Press Tab.

e. For Criteria1, click **Collapse** ⬆, select **A3**, and then click **Expand** ⬇.

f. For Criteria_range2, click **Collapse** ⬆, select cell range **E7:E37**, and then click **Expand** ⬇. Press Tab.

g. For Criteria2, click **Collapse** ⬆, select **A4**, and then click **Expand** ⬇.

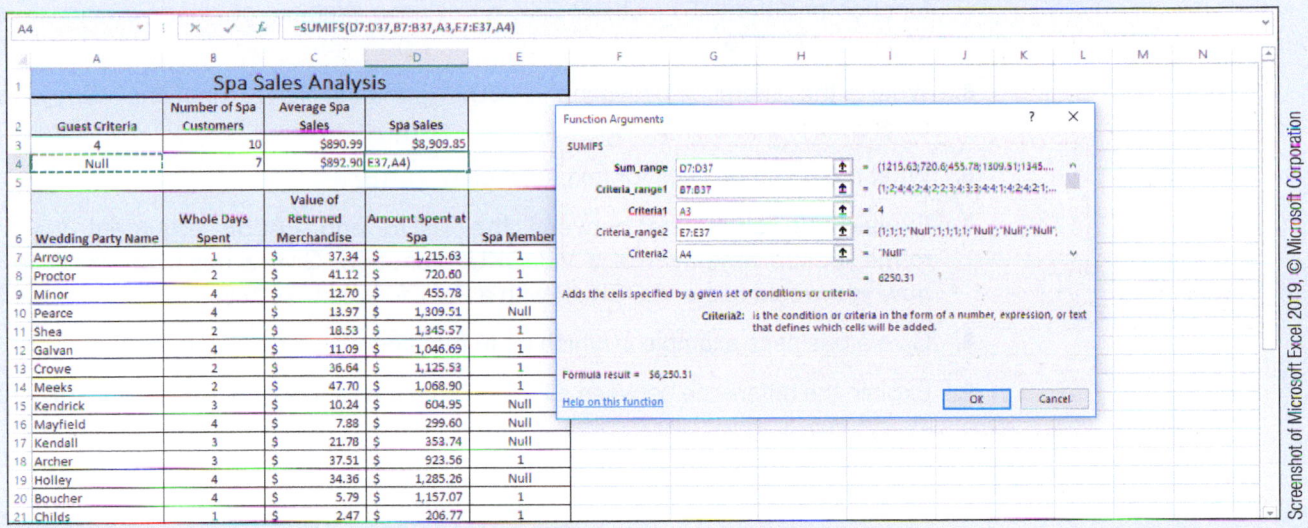

Figure 26   SUMIFS Function Arguments dialog box

h. Click **OK**.

i. Complete the Documentation worksheet according to your instructor's directions.

j. **Save** 🖫 the workbook, exit Excel, and then submit your file as directed by your instructor.

CONSIDER THIS | **Using the SUMIF Function versus the SUMIFS Function**

The SUMIF and SUMIFS functions are very similar in what they accomplish. Could you simply use the SUMIFS function all the time and become comfortable with its format? Could any situation that would use SUMIF be written by using SUMIFS?

Concept Check

1. Explain the three different types of cell referencing. p. 163

2. Why are named ranges useful? What limitations are there in creating the names for ranges? p. 172

3. Why is the syntax of an Excel function important? How can you distinguish between required and optional portions of a function? p. 177

4. In the math and statistical functions, what are the differences between the ROUND function and the INT function? Give a business example of when you would use each. p. 178–179

5. What is the difference between the TODAY() and the NOW() functions? Why is this difference important? p. 184

6. What are common uses for text functions? p. 187

7. Explain the difference between the TRUE and FALSE argument for the range_lookup argument of a VLOOKUP function. Give a business example of how you would use a VLOOKUP with a PMT function. p. 188

8. Give a business example in which an IF function would be useful. p. 192–193

9. Explain the difference between a COUNTIF and a COUNTIFS function. p. 197–198

Key Terms

ABS function   p. 178
Absolute cell reference   p. 163
Argument   p. 177
AVERAGEIF function   p. 199
AVERAGEIFS function   p. 200
Cell reference   p. 163
Cleansing text   p. 187
COUNTA function   p. 182
COUNTIF function   p. 197
COUNTIFS function   p. 198
Date and time functions   p. 183

DATEDIF function   p. 185
Financial functions   p. 190
Function Arguments dialog box   p. 179
IF function   p. 192
INT function   p. 178
Logical functions   p. 192
Lookup and reference functions   p. 188
Mixed cell reference   p. 163
Name Manager   p. 173

Named range   p. 172
NOW function   p. 184
PMT function   p. 190
Relative cell reference   p. 163
ROUND function   p. 178
SUMIF function   p. 201
SUMIFS function   p. 202
Syntax   p. 177
Text functions   p. 187
TODAY function   p. 184
VLOOKUP function   p. 188

Visual Summary

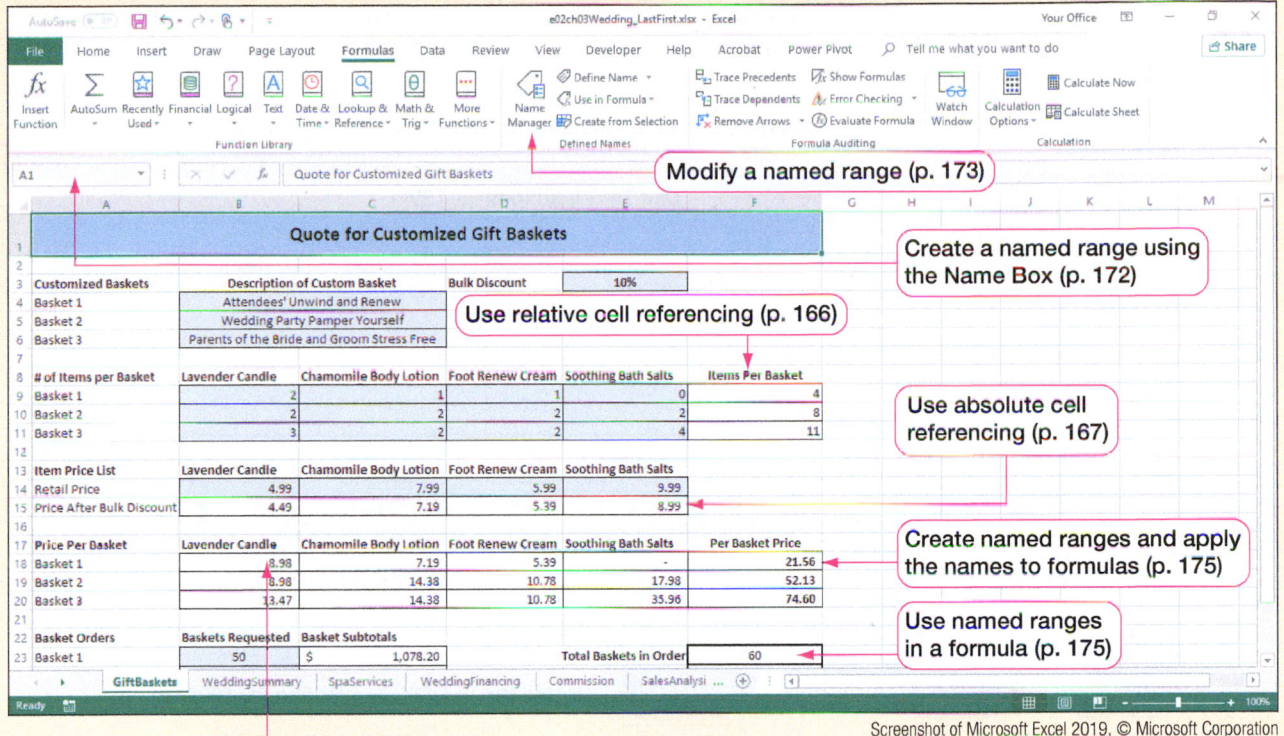

Modify a named range (p. 173)

Create a named range using the Name Box (p. 172)

Use relative cell referencing (p. 166)

Use absolute cell referencing (p. 167)

Create named ranges and apply the names to formulas (p. 175)

Use named ranges in a formula (p. 175)

Use mixed cell referencing (p. 170)

Screenshot of Microsoft Excel 2019, © Microsoft Corporation

Figure 27

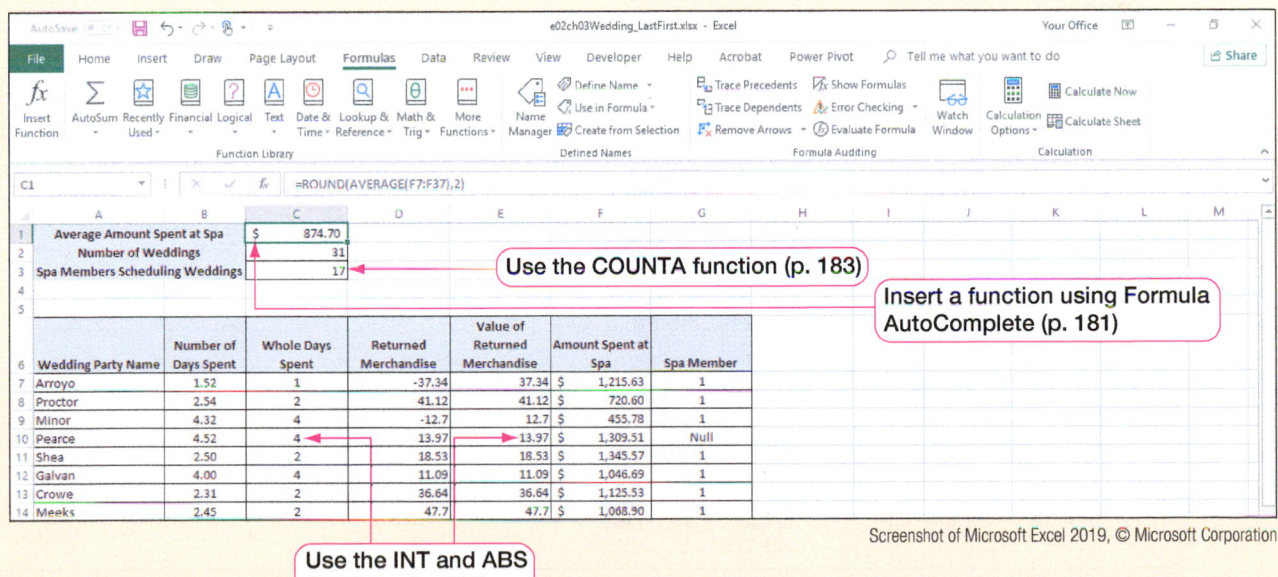

Use the COUNTA function (p. 183)

Insert a function using Formula AutoComplete (p. 181)

Use the INT and ABS functions (p. 180)

Screenshot of Microsoft Excel 2019, © Microsoft Corporation

Figure 28

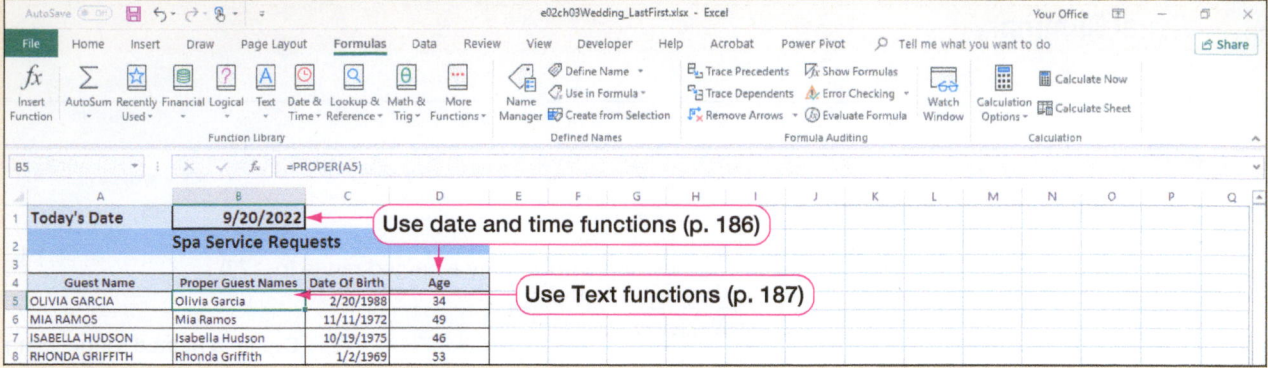

Figure 29 Screenshot of Microsoft Excel 2019, © Microsoft Corporation

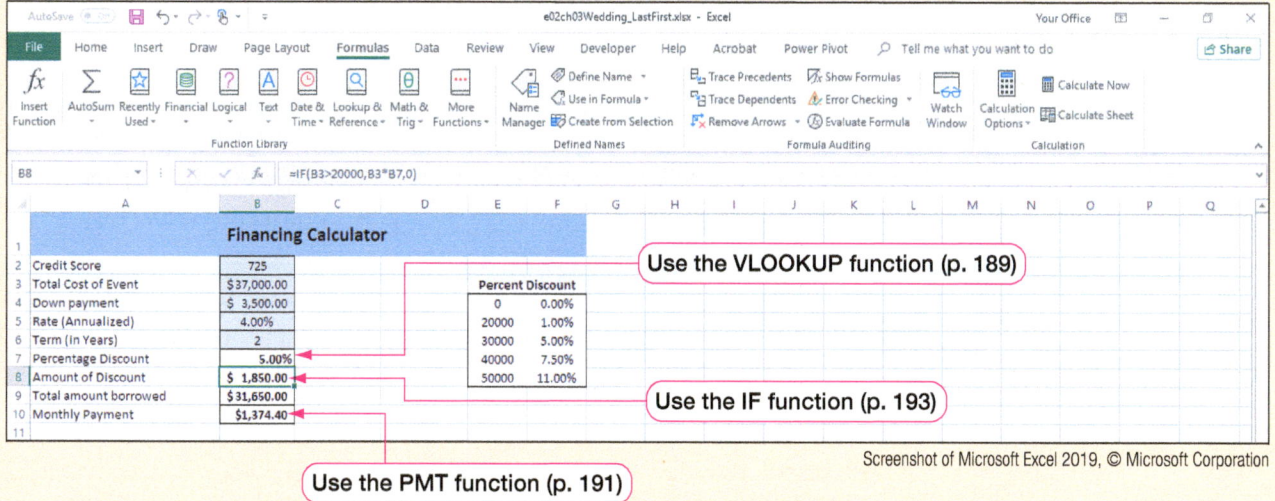

Figure 30 Screenshot of Microsoft Excel 2019, © Microsoft Corporation

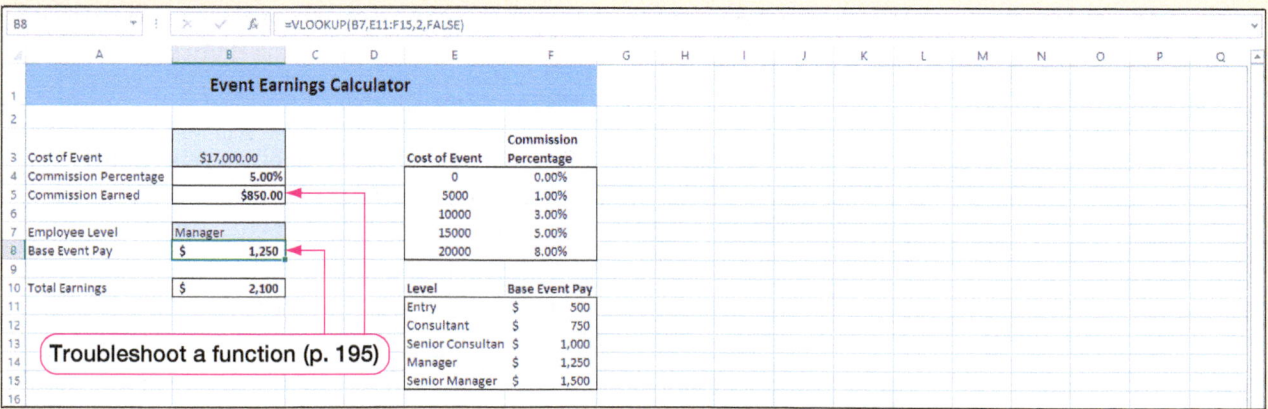

Figure 31 Screenshot of Microsoft Excel 2019, © Microsoft Corporation

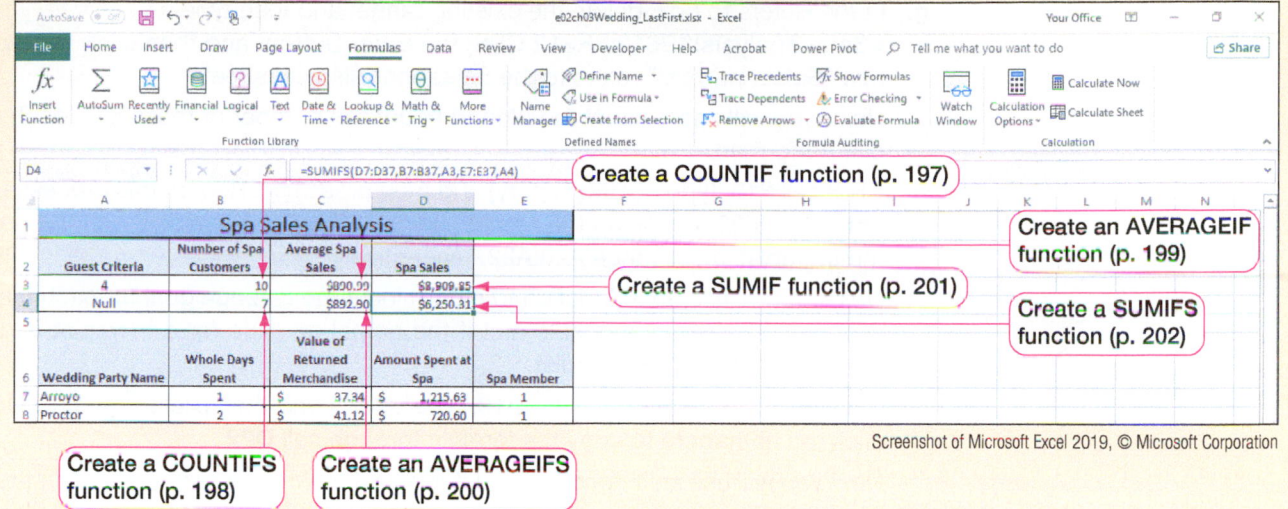

Create a COUNTIF function (p. 197)

Create an AVERAGEIF function (p. 199)

Create a SUMIF function (p. 201)

Create a SUMIFS function (p. 202)

Create a COUNTIFS function (p. 198)

Create an AVERAGEIFS function (p. 200)

Screenshot of Microsoft Excel 2019, © Microsoft Corporation

Figure 32

Practice 1

Student data file needed:

e02ch03Bonus.xlsx

You will save your file as:

e02ch03Bonus_LastFirst.xlsx

Human Resources

Finance & Accounting

Massage Therapist Bonus Workbook

Meda Rodate has been constructing a workbook that will enable her to analyze the goals for massage therapists. The massage therapists earn commissions. Meda has asked that you make some modifications to the workbook that she began to facilitate her analysis. She wants you to rank the therapists based on their commission rate. She also wants to count the number of repeat massages and analyze how many therapists met both revenue and massages goals.

a. Start Excel, click **Open** in the left pane, and then double-click **This PC**. Navigate through the folder structure to the location of your student data files, and then double-click **e02ch03Bonus**. If a Security Warning message displays, click the **Enable Editing** button.

b. Click the **File** tab, click **Save As**, and then double-click **This PC**. In the Save As dialog box, navigate to the location where you are saving your project files, and then change the file name to e02ch03Bonus_LastFirst using your last and first name. Click **Save**.

c. On the SalesAnalysis worksheet, in cell B2, type =TODAY() and then press Enter.

d. Click cell **B4**, type =B3 and then press F4 twice to create the mixed cell reference **B$3**. Type *A4 and then press F4 three times to create the mixed cell reference **$A4**. Press Ctrl+Enter.

e. In cell **B4**, double-click the **fill handle** to copy the formula through cell **B8**. With the cell range B4:B8 still selected, click the **fill handle**, and then drag to the right to copy the formulas to cell range **B4:K8**.

f. Click the **Formulas** tab, and then, in the Defined Names group, click **Name Manager**. Note the named ranges within the workbook. Click **Christy** in the list of named ranges in the workbook.

> ### Mac Troubleshooting
> If using a Mac, there is no Name Manager. Click Define Name instead of Name Manager.

g. In the Refers to box, delete the existing range, and then type =SalesAnalysis!$B$12:$K$12 Click the Enter button, and then click **Close**. The text "SalesAnalysis!" refers to the SalesAnalysis worksheet.

Next, you will use a count function to count the number of massages each therapist performed.

h. Click cell **F19**, type =SUM(Christy) and then press Enter. Repeat this process for cell range F20:F22, replacing the named range in the SUM function with the name of the therapist in cell range A20:A22, respectively.

Next you will use an IF function to determine if the revenue goal for each therapist was met. The revenue goal is met if the actual revenue for a therapist is greater than the goal for that therapist.

i. Click cell **D19**, type =IF(C19>=B19,"Yes","No") and then press Ctrl+Enter. Double-click the **fill handle** to copy the formula through cell **D22**.

Next you will use an IF function to determine if the massage goal for each therapist was met. The massage goal is met if the actual number of massages for a therapist is greater than the goal for that therapist.

j. Click cell **G19**, type =IF(F19>=E19,"Yes","No") and then press Ctrl+Enter. Double-click the **fill handle** to copy the formula through cell **G22**.

k. Select cell range I35:J38. Click in the Name Box, and then type Commissions to create the named range.

Next you will use a VLOOKUP function to determine each therapist's commission rank by looking up the commission percentage in cell B25 from the lookup table Commissions and then assign the ranking in column 2.

l. Click cell **C25**, type =VLOOKUP(B25,Commissions,2) and then press Ctrl+Enter.

m. With C25 still active, double click the **fill handle** to copy the formula through cell **C28**.

Next, you want to count the number of repeat massages.

n. Click cell **C35**. On the Formulas tab, in the Function Library group, click **More Functions**, point to **Statistical**, and then click **COUNTIF**.

o. For Range, click the **Collapse** button, select the cell range **B12:K15**, and then click the **Expand** button. With cell range B12:K15 selected, press the F4 key to make the range absolute. Press Tab, type B35 for the criteria, and then click **OK**.

p. With C35 still selected, double-click the **fill handle** to copy the formula through **C39**.

You were also asked to analyze how many therapists met both goals of revenue and massages or didn't meet both goals.

q. Click cell **G35**. On the Formulas tab, in the Function Library group, click **More Functions**, point to **Statistical**, and then click **COUNTIFS**.

r. For the Criteria_range1, click the **Collapse** button, select the cell range **D19:D22**, and then click the **Expand** button. With D19:D22 selected, press the F4 key to make the range absolute. Press Tab, type E35 for the criteria, and then press Tab.

s. For the Criteria_range2, click the **Collapse** button, select the cell range **G19:G22**, and then click the **Expand** button. With G19:G22 selected, press the F4 key to make the range absolute. Press Tab, type F35 for the criteria, and then click **OK**.

t. In cell G35, double-click the **fill handle** to copy the formula through cell **G38**.

Finally, you are asked to determine the monthly payment of the purchase of a new massage table. The interest rate will depend on the amount borrowed.

u. Click the **Financing** worksheet, and then click cell **B6**. On the Formulas tab, in the Function Library group, click **Lookup & Reference**, and then click **VLOOKUP**. Type B5 and then press Tab. Type D4:E8 and then press Tab. Type 2 and then click **OK**.

v. Click cell **B8**. On the Formulas tab, in the Function Library group, click **Financial**, and then click **PMT**. Type B6/12 and then press Tab. Type B7*12 and then press Tab. Type B5 and then click **OK**.

w. You notice the payment is displaying as a negative number, but you want it to display as a positive number. In cell B8, press F2 to enter into Edit mode. Click to the right of the equal sign and type – (minus) and then press Enter.

x. Click the **Insert** tab, and in the Text group, click **Header & Footer**. On the Design tab, in the Navigation group, click **Go to Footer**. Click in the left footer and then, on the Design tab, click the **File Name** code.

y. Click any cell on the spreadsheet to move out of the footer, and then press Ctrl+Home. Click the **View** tab, and then in the Workbook Views group, click **Normal**.

z. Click the **Documentation** worksheet. Click cell **A8**, and then type in today's date Click cell **B8**, and then type your name in the Firstname Lastname format. Complete the remainder of the Documentation worksheet according to your instructor's directions.

aa. Save the workbook, exit Excel, and then submit your file as directed by your instructor.

Problem Solve 1

MyLab IT Grader

Student data file needed:
 e02ch03Renovations.xlsx

You will save your file as:
e02ch03Renovations _LastFirst.xlsx

Finance & Accounting

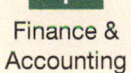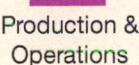
Production & Operations

Painted Paradise Resort & Spa Scenario

Lesa Martin, a member of the support/coordination staff for the conference center at Painted Paradise Resort & Spa, has created a worksheet to keep track of the renovations being made to the three rooms that are used for conferences and the two technology centers that are used for computer-based presentations and interactive sessions. The technology centers are equipped with workstations, are networked, and have Internet accessibility. This spreadsheet is simple and designed only for Lesa and her associates to keep a handle on the renovation progress and estimate the increase in capacity and revenue that might occur because of the renovations. Lesa also wants you to analyze the banquet room sales and usage for the month of January.

a. Open the Excel file, **e02ch03Renovations**. Save your file as e02ch03Renovations_LastFirst using your last and first name.

b. On the **Renovations** worksheet, in cell **D6**, enter a DATEDIF function based on the renovations started and renovations completed dates to determine the length in days of the expected renovation for The Musica Room.

c. Copy this formula through cell **D10**.

d. In cell **G6**, enter a formula to determine the room capacity that The Musica Room will hold based on the original capacity in cell F6 and the increase in capacity percentage in cell B13. Use absolute references where necessary.

e. Copy this formula through cell **G10**.

f. Modify the named range **IncreaseInRevenue** to reference cell **B14** not B15.

g. In cell **I6**, using the named range in cell B14, enter a formula to determine the projected increase in revenue for The Musica Room based on the revenue figure in cell H6 and the increase in revenue percentage in cell B14.

h. Copy this formula through cell **I10**.

i. In cell **B20**, enter a function that will calculate the monthly payment for the loan amount in cell B17, based on the Annualized Rate in B18, and the number of years in the Term in cell B19. Display the monthly payment as a positive value.

j. Assign the named range RoomClassification to cell range **A23:B26**.

k. In cell **J6**, using a lookup function, enter a formula to determine the projected room classification based on the projected quarterly revenue after renovations in cell I6. Use the named range RoomClassification when entering this formula.

l. Copy this formula through cell **J10**.

m. On the **RoomAnalysis** worksheet, in cell **G7**, determine the total charges for The Musica Room by using a SUMIF function. Use absolute references where appropriate. Copy this formula through cell **G11**.

n. In cell **G16**, determine the total count of The Musica Room usage by using a COUNTIF function. Use absolute references where appropriate. Copy this formula through cell **G20**.

o. Add the **File Name** code in the left footer of the **Renovations** sheet. Return to Normal view if necessary.

p. On the **Documentation** worksheet in cell **A8**, type today's date In cell **B8**, type your name in the Firstname Lastname format. Complete the remainder of the Documentation worksheet according to your instructor's directions.

q. Save the workbook, exit Excel, and then submit your file as directed by your instructor.

 Critical Thinking

The Renovations workbook contains named ranges. What are the benefits of using named ranges in formulas?

Not all workbooks benefit from naming cells or ranges of cells. Can you explain a scenario in which it would not be wise to use names or named ranges?

 Perform 1: Perform in Your Life

Student data file needed:	You will save your file as:
e02ch03RealEstate.xlsx	e02ch03RealEstate_LastFirst.xlsx

Real Estate Workbook

Finance & Accounting

You are interning at Schalow Real Estate. Your supervisor has asked you to add formulas to the Real Estate workbook so that she can analyze it and look for trends. She asks that you create new columns as directed. Format all currency spreadsheet values using the Currency Number Format, and display two decimal places. Fill all formulas and functions through the appropriate rows.

a. Open the **e02ch03RealEstate** Excel file. Save your file as e02ch03RealEstate_LastFirst using your last and first name.

b. On the Sold worksheet, create a column named Price/SqFt in column N, and then create a formula to calculate the price per square foot based on the square footage and the price sold.

c. Create a column named Down PMT and then create a formula that will calculate a down payment of 20% of the sold price.

d. Create a column named Days on MKT and then create a formula to calculate the number of days each property was on the market.

e. Create a column named Monthly Payment Create a formula to calculate the monthly mortgage payment for each property. With a mixed reference, use the interest rate found in cell V2. With a mixed reference, use the term in cell W2. Deduct the down payment from the sold price to calculate the amount financed. Edit the function to display positive numbers.

f. Create a column named Monthly Taxes Each development has a different tax rate. Use a lookup function to look up the Development ID from the Sold worksheet, and determine that development's Tax Rate from the Development worksheet. Then, to determine the actual tax, multiply the tax rate by the sold price, and divide the tax by 12. This will determine the amount to save each month to pay the taxes at the end of the year (Monthly Tax).

To reference a lookup table on a different worksheet, click on the worksheet tab that contains the lookup table, select the range, type a comma (,), and then click the original worksheet tab.

g. Create a column named Monthly Insurance The cost to insure homes is different in different neighborhoods. Use a lookup function to look up the Development ID and determine that development's Insurance Rates from the Development worksheet. Then multiply the insurance rate by the sold price, and divide by 12 to determine the monthly payment.

h. Create a column named Total Payment Add the monthly tax and insurance to the monthly payment to determine how much the homeowner needs to live in the newly purchased home.

i. Ensure that your columns are sufficiently wide to display their content fully. Wrap the text in the header rows on each worksheet as necessary. Format the workbook professionally.

j. On the Documentation worksheet in cell A8, type today's date In cell B8, type your name in the Firstname Lastname format. Complete the remainder of the Documentation worksheet according to your instructor's directions.

k. Add the File Name code to the left footer on all sheets.

l. Save the workbook, exit Excel, and then submit your file as directed by your instructor.

Microsoft Excel

Sales & Marketing

MyLab IT Grader

OBJECTIVES

1. Explore chart types, layouts, and styles p. 213

2. Explore the position of charts p. 217

3. Understand different chart types p. 218

4. Change chart data and styles for presentations p. 228

5. Edit and format charts to add emphasis p. 236

6. Use sparklines and data bars to emphasize data p. 245

7. Recognize and correct confusing charts p. 247

Prepare Case

Turquoise Oasis Spa Sales Reports

The Turquoise Oasis Spa managers, Irene Kai and Meda Rodate, are pleased with your work and would like to see you continue to improve the spa spreadsheets. They want to use charts to learn more about the spa. Meda has given you a workbook with some data and would like you to create various charts that accurately display the data. Visualizing the data with charts will provide knowledge about the spa for decision-making purposes.

Gtranquillity/Shutterstock

Student data files needed:

 e02ch04SpaSales.xlsx

 e02ch04TurquoiseOasis.jpg

You will save your file as:

 e02ch04SpaSales_LastFirst.xlsx

Designing a Chart

With Excel, you can organize data so it has context and meaning. **Data visualization** is the graphical presentation of data with a focus on qualitative understanding. It is central to finding trends and supporting business decisions. Modern data visualization can involve beautiful and elegant charts that include movement and convey information in real time. Charts are at the heart of data visualization. Charts enlighten you as you compare and contrast data and examine how it changes over time. Learning how to work with charts means not only knowing how to create them, but also realizing that each type of chart can discover or emphasize different knowledge.

While it may seem simple to create a pie chart or a bar chart, there are many considerations in creating charts. Like a picture, a chart can be worth a thousand words. However, different people may interpret a chart differently if it is not well developed. A well-developed chart should provide context for the information without overshadowing key points. Finally, it is easy to confuse people with the choice and layout of a chart. A chart should use accurate and complete data. The objective should be to provide a focused, clear message. In today's data-rich world, many interpretations or messages can be extracted from the data. Businesses have three primary objectives in charting: data analysis, hypothesis testing, and persuasion.

In data analysis, the Excel chart is used to manipulate the data to try to evaluate and prioritize all the interpretations or messages. There may be a need to create multiple charts, using a variety of data sources, layouts, and designs as data is interpreted.

Ideas or hypotheses may be made about the data. Charts can visually support or refute hypotheses. For example, maybe you have the impression that a certain salesperson performs better than the other salespeople. You could support or refute your hypothesis by charting their sales data.

If you have a position you want the data to support visually, you could consider using an Excel chart to help persuade your audience of your position. You will need to select a specific and appropriate chart layout, use the necessary data, and design a chart that conveys your message clearly and unambiguously. Further, you have an ethical obligation to represent the data accurately. Misrepresenting data can result in lawsuits or termination of employment.

Regardless of the objective, even a small set of data allows you to create a variety of charts, each offering a different understanding of the data. In this chapter, you will start with understanding the concepts for creating a chart in Excel and understanding which type of chart will depict the information in the best, most efficient manner.

Explore Chart Types, Layouts, and Styles

When you decide to represent data visually, you need to make some initial decisions about the basic design of the chart. These initial decisions include the location of the chart, the type of chart, the general layout and style, and what data you will be using. These elements can be set initially and modified later. Best practice dictates that you first consider and develop the basic design of the chart.

Regardless of the location or type of chart, the process of creating a chart starts with the organization of the data on the spreadsheet. The typical structure is to have labels across the top of the data, along the left side of the data, or both. While the labels do not have to be directly next to the data, this position helps in selecting data and making your chart. The data may have been brought in from an external data source, such as Access. The data may need to be filtered, calculated, or reorganized before a chart is created. Keep in mind that not all data is organized in a way that allows for the creation of charts.

When you are ready to create a chart, select the cells that contain both the label headings and the data. People rarely create a perfect chart the first time. You might start a chart, work with it for a while, and then realize that a different chart type would better convey the information. Fortunately, Excel provides ample flexibility in designing charts. Thus, if you change your mind, you can modify the chart or simply start over.

Opening the Starting File

In this exercise, you will review a pie chart that displays the use of portable massage tables by different therapists at the Turquoise Oasis Spa.

E04.00

SIDE NOTE
Office Updates
Depending on your exact Office version, you may see Open or Open Other Workbooks.

SIDE NOTE
Pin the Ribbon
If your ribbon is collapsed, pin your ribbon open. Click the Home tab. In the lower-right corner of the ribbon, click Pin the ribbon.

SIDE NOTE
Screen Size
Not all screen sizes are the same. If you cannot see all of a tab's groups, you may need to click a arrow to make a button visible.

To Open the SpaSales Workbook

a. Start Excel, click **Open** in the left pane, and then click **This PC**. Navigate through the folder structure to the location of your student data files, and then click **e02ch04SpaSales**. The workbook containing sales data for the Turquoise Oasis Spa opens. If necessary, click **Enable Editing**.

b. Click the **File** tab, and then click **Save As**, and then click **This PC**. In the Save As dialog box, navigate to the location where you are saving your project files, and then change the file name to e02ch04SpaSales_LastFirst using your last and first name. Click **Save**.

c. On the TableUse worksheet, click the **Insert** tab, and then in the Text group, click **Header & Footer**.

d. On the Header & Footer Tools Design tab, in the Navigation group, click **Go to Footer**. If necessary, click the center section of the footer, and then, in the Header & Footer Elements group, click **File Name**.

e. Click any cell on the worksheet to move out of the footer, press Ctrl+Home, and then, on the status bar, click **Normal**.

f. Click **Save**.

Modifying an Existing Chart

A chart is an object in Excel. Clicking on the chart will allow you to modify aspects of the chart or even change the type of chart. When you click an existing chart, you are activating the chart area. The border of the chart will be highlighted, while the middle of the sides and the corners of the chart will have selection handles, which can be used to resize the chart. The chart border can also be used to move the entire chart to a new location within the spreadsheet. When a chart is selected, the Chart Tools contextual tab will appear on the ribbon. To the right of the chart, the Chart Formatting control will appear as three buttons that provide quick access to common functions such as chart elements, chart styles, and filtering of chart data.

When a chart is selected by clicking on the chart, the data used in creating the chart will be highlighted in the worksheet, offering a visual clue of the associated data. In the TableUse worksheet, you will see a pie chart describing the use of massage tables by individual therapists at the spa. When the chart is selected, a purple border surrounds the data that represents the legend labels. The range with a blue border is the data that represents the data series for the pie slices. A **data series** is a group of related data values to be charted. A **data point** is an individual data value in a data series. A chart may contain multiple data series or a single data series.

REAL WORLD ADVICE First Impressions

First Impressions are important with charts. You want the audience to receive the correct message during the initial moments. An audience that is distracted by the look and feel of the chart may stop looking for the message in the chart or extend the chaotic personality of the chart to the personality of the presenter. Thus, the chart can become a reflection on you and your company.

To quickly identify the value of the data series, Meda Rodate has asked you to modify the existing pie chart on the TableUse worksheet by adding data labels, which you will do in this exercise. Because you will be modifying a pie chart, Meda prefers the addition of percentage labels over the value labels for each data series. She has also asked you to change the chart style to improve its appearance.

In this exercise, you will modify an existing chart.

 E04.01

SIDE NOTE
Alternate Method
Any action completed in the Chart Formatting control can also be completed on the Chart Tools contextual tab on the ribbon.

To Modify an Existing Chart

a. On the **TableUse** worksheet, notice the pie chart located to the right of the data on this worksheet. Click the **chart border** of the chart to select the chart and display the Chart Tools contextual tabs on the ribbon.

   The Chart Tools contextual tabs will only be visible when the chart is selected. When the chart is deselected, the contextual tabs will disappear.

b. To the right of the chart, click **Chart Elements** ⊞, and then click to select **Data Labels**. This will display the number of times each therapist used a portable massage table in the corresponding slice of the pie chart.

> ### Mac Troubleshooting
> To complete this step on a Mac, click the Chart Design tab, and then click Add Chart Element in the Chart Layouts group. Before you do this, you must point to Data Labels.

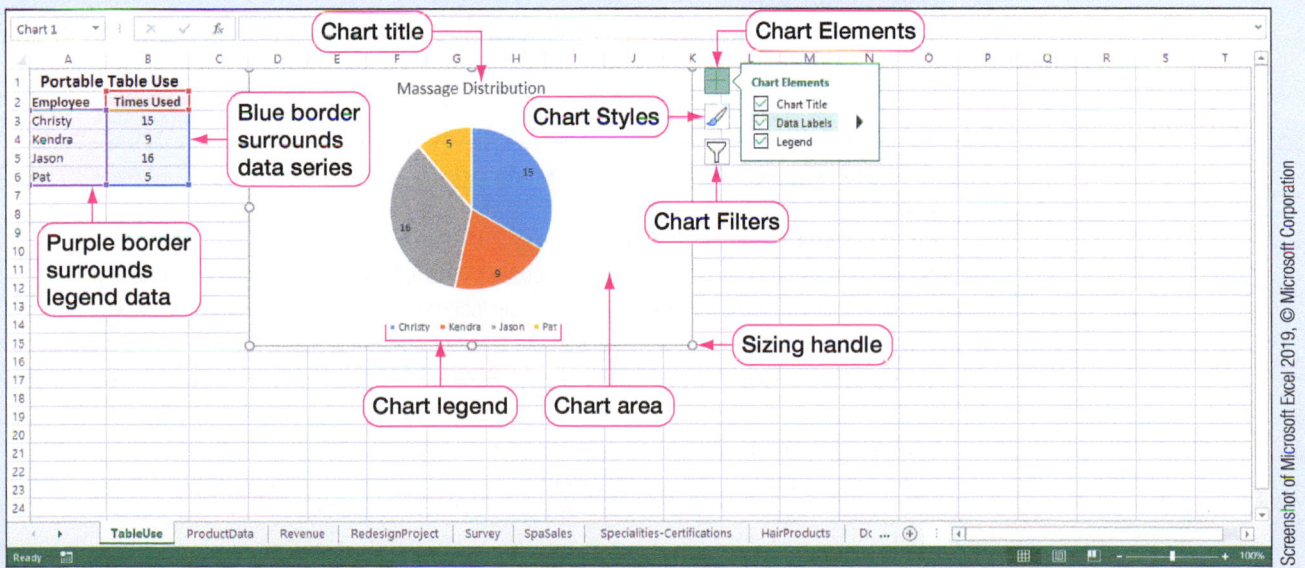

Figure 1 Selected pie chart

SIDE NOTE
**Point to See
Icon Information**
When you are presented
with a set of icons, point
to an icon. A Screen-
Tip will appear offering
descriptive information.

c. Click the arrow to the right of **Data Labels**, and then select **More Options**. This will open the Format Data Labels pane.

d. Under Label Options, expand if necessary, click to select **Percentage**, and then click to deselect **Value**.

e. In the Format Data Labels pane on the right side of the screen, click **Close** ☒.

f. Click the **chart border** of the pie chart, click **Chart Styles** 🖌, and then scroll down and point to Style 3. Notice that the chart changes to display a Live Preview of the style.

> ### Mac Troubleshooting
> On a Mac, click Style 3 in the Chart Styles group on the Chart Design tab.

g. Click **Style 3**, and then click **Chart Styles** 🖌 to close the control. The chart now displays the percentage of portable table use for each massage therapist at the spa.

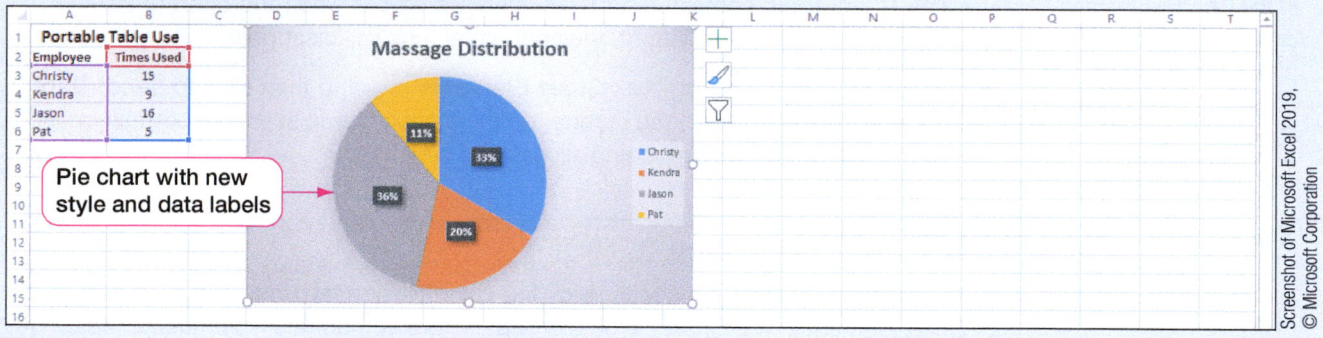

Figure 2   Modified chart

h. **Save** 💾 the workbook.

> **CONSIDER THIS** | **Misleading Charts**
>
> Charts are supposed to frame information. However, charts in newspapers, online articles, and magazines sometimes lead the viewer to an incorrect assumption or conclusion. Look for a chart that is misleading. Discuss the context and possible incorrect conclusions that could be drawn from the chart, and consider the ethical aspect for the creator of the chart.

QUICK REFERENCE | **Working with Chart Objects**

It is possible to navigate through a chart using some of these guidelines.

- Click the chart border to activate the Chart Tools contextual tabs.
- Click chart objects to select individual chart components.
- Click outside a chart object or press Esc to deselect an object.
- On the Chart Tools contextual tabs, on the Format tab, in the Current Selection group, use the Chart Elements box to select specific chart objects.
- Use border corner handles to resize selected objects.
- Click a chart object and drag to move the chart object.

Explore the Position of Charts

When designing a chart, consider the chart location, as this might affect the flexibility of moving and resizing your chart components. There are two general locations for a chart: either within an existing worksheet as an embedded chart or on a separate worksheet, referred to as a chart sheet. An **embedded chart** exists as an object located on the same worksheet with the data. The pie chart you just adjusted is an embedded chart. A **chart sheet** is a special worksheet that is dedicated to displaying chart objects.

Placing Charts on a Chart Sheet

A chart sheet is a worksheet that contains only a chart object. The familiar cell grid is replaced with the actual chart. Having the chart on a separate chart sheet can make it easier to isolate and print on a page. Chart sheets are also useful when you want to create a set of charts and easily navigate between them by worksheet names rather than by looking for them on various worksheets. Because of the nature of chart sheets, the data associated with the chart will be on a different worksheet.

Irene has mentioned that she would like to use this pie chart in future presentations and would like to be able to easily isolate and print the chart. To facilitate this, in this exercise, you will move the chart to a chart sheet.

 E04.02

SIDE NOTE
Alternate Method
To move a chart to a chart sheet, you can also right-click the chart and select Move Chart from the shortcut menu.

SIDE NOTE
Cutting and Pasting a Chart
You can move a chart to another sheet by cutting and pasting the chart. This does not create a chart sheet; rather, it creates an embedded chart on a new sheet.

To Move a Chart to a Chart Sheet

a. On the **TableUse** worksheet, click the **chart border** of the pie chart.

b. On the Chart Tools Design tab, in the Location group, click **Move Chart**.

c. In the Move Chart dialog box, click **New sheet**, and then type DistributionChart Click **OK**.

Notice that you now have a new chart sheet tab in your workbook. By default, the new sheet is placed to the left of the current sheet. This chart sheet is exclusively for the chart and will not have the normal worksheet appearance. Note that Pat's percentage of table usage is 11%.

d. Click the **TableUse** worksheet. In cell **B6**, type 7 and then press Enter.

e. Click the **DistributionChart** worksheet. Note that Pat's percentage of table usage is now 15%. Excel charts are automatically updated when the chart's data source is changed, even if the chart is on a separate chart sheet.

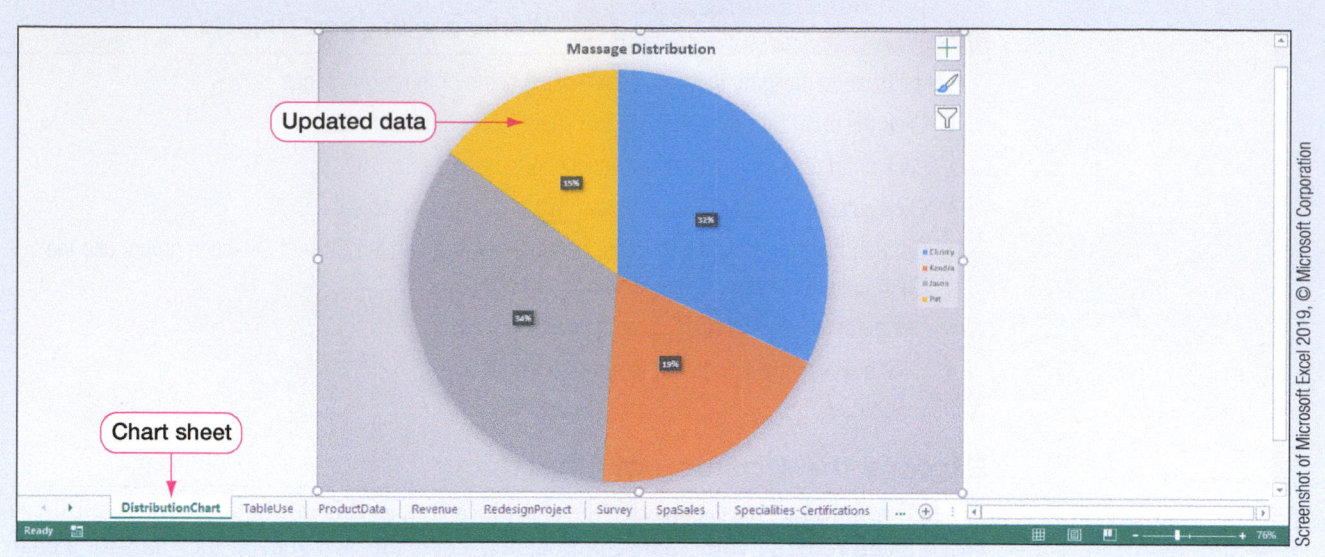

Figure 3 Chart sheet with modified data

    f. **Save** 🔲 the workbook.

Understand Different Chart Types

In creating a chart, it is important to choose the correct type of chart to use. Each chart type conveys information in a particular way. The chart type sets the tone for the basic format of the data and what kind of data is included. Thus, it helps if you become familiar with the types of charts that are commonly used for business decision making and for presentations. Always consider which type is appropriate for the message you are trying to convey.

Excel 2019 has several features that allow you to quickly analyze data. A few of these are the Quick Analysis tool, the Recommended Charts feature, and Ideas feature. The **Quick Analysis** tool is a contextual tool that appears when you select data in a worksheet and offers single-click access to formatting, charts, formulas, PivotTables, and sparklines. The Recommended Charts feature is located on the Insert tab in the Charts group. The **Recommended Charts** feature quickly analyzes a selection in a worksheet and recommends chart types that best fit the data. The **Ideas** feature is a feature in Excel that analyzes data with visual summaries, patterns, and trends. The Ideas feature, on the Home tab, works best when your data is formatted as an Excel Table with a header row.

Creating Column Charts

Column charts are used to compare data across categories and show change, sometimes over time. They are useful for comparing data sets that are categorized, such as departments, product categories, or survey results. Column charts are also useful for showing categories over time where each column represents a unit of time. Column charts are good for comparisons either individually, in groups, or stacked. Column chart data can easily allow for grouping of data, so comparisons of the groups can occur.

To aid in the analysis of the data, Irene Kai would like the data on the ProductData worksheet to be organized and presented in an effective graphical manner. Specifically, she would like to compare the total number of massages given over an eight-week period. In this exercise you will create a chart in an existing worksheet.

 **E04.03**

SIDE NOTE
Axis Labels
When creating a chart, be sure to select the appropriate data labels as well as the data. Failure to do so may produce an incomplete and confusing chart.

To Create a Column Chart

a. Click the **ProductData** worksheet, and then select cell range **A2:B12** as the data to use for creating a chart. Notice that once the data is selected, the Quick Analysis tool is displayed below and to the right of cell B12.

b. Click **Quick Analysis** [icon], and then click **Charts** [icon].

> ### Mac Troubleshooting
> Quick Analysis tool is not available on a Mac. Instead, click the Insert tab, click Recommended Charts, and then click Clustered Column.

c. Point to the **Clustered Column** chart suggestion. Notice that a Live Preview of the chart is displayed.

> ### Troubleshooting
> If Live Preview is not displaying, it may be that your taskbar is in triple height. Try changing your taskbar to double or single height. Move the pointer over the border of the taskbar until it turns into a double arrow, click and drag the border to the height or width size you desire, and then release.

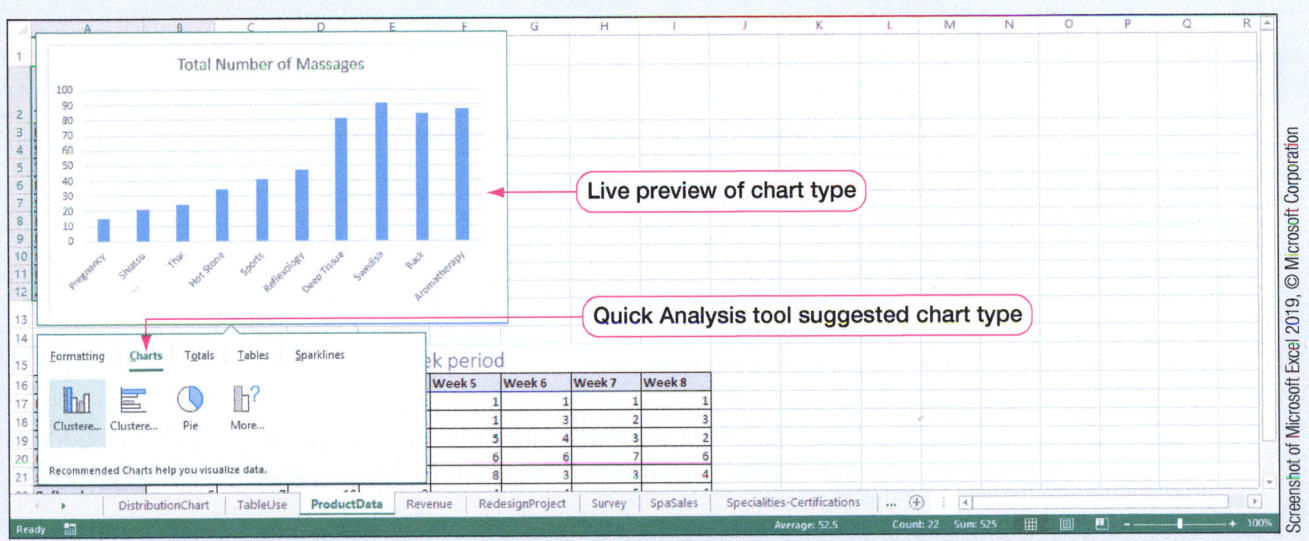

Figure 4 Quick Analysis tool with a suggested chart

SIDE NOTE
Resizing a chart
You can resize a chart by clicking and dragging a sizing handle. Be careful not to click the corners or middle areas of the chart border if you want only to move a chart.

d. Click **Clustered Column** to insert the chart into the worksheet.

Notice that the embedded chart appears on the currently active worksheet and shows colored borders surrounding the associated data linked to the chart. This chart displays the total number provided of each type of massage offered by the spa.

e. Click the **chart border** if necessary to select the chart. Click the **Chart Tools Design** tab, and then in the Location group, click **Move Chart**.

f. In the Move Chart dialog box, click **New sheet**, type TotalMassagesChart and then click **OK**.

g. Save the workbook.

Creating Pie Charts

A **pie chart** displays a comparison of each value to a total. It is commonly used for depicting the relationships of the parts to the whole, such as comparing staff performance within a department or comparing the number of transactions of each product category over time.

For a pie chart, you need two data series: the labels and a set of corresponding values. This is similar to the data selection made in the TableUse sheet to indicate the percentage of times each person used the portable massage table. Note that the data can be described as a percentage of the whole, as in the chart.

The questions you have will influence what textual data you will include in any chart. If you are exploring a usage fee for each time a table is used, then having the percentage would indicate which therapist is contributing the most fees, and the actual numbers may not be a crucial element. When you create a chart, examine it to see whether it answers your questions.

In this exercise, you will create a simple pie chart that shows the proportion of total revenue each of four different massage types earned for the spa in the month of June.

▶ E04.04

SIDE NOTE
Resizing a chart
When resizing a chart, consider pressing Alt and then dragging the sizing handle to snap the chart to a cell.

To Create a Pie Chart

a. Click the **Revenue** worksheet, and then select cell range **A1:E2**.

b. Click **Quick Analysis**, click **Charts**, and then click **Pie**.

> **Mac Troubleshooting**
> On a Mac, click the Insert tab, click Recommended Charts, and then click Pie.

c. Click and hold the **chart border** of the embedded pie chart, and then drag to move the chart to the top-left corner of cell **I3**. This will place the chart to the right of the data set.

d. Point to the **bottom-right corner** of the chart until the pointer changes to ⤡, and then drag to resize the chart so the bottom-right corner is over cell **O16**. The chart displays the proportion of revenue generated by each massage type.

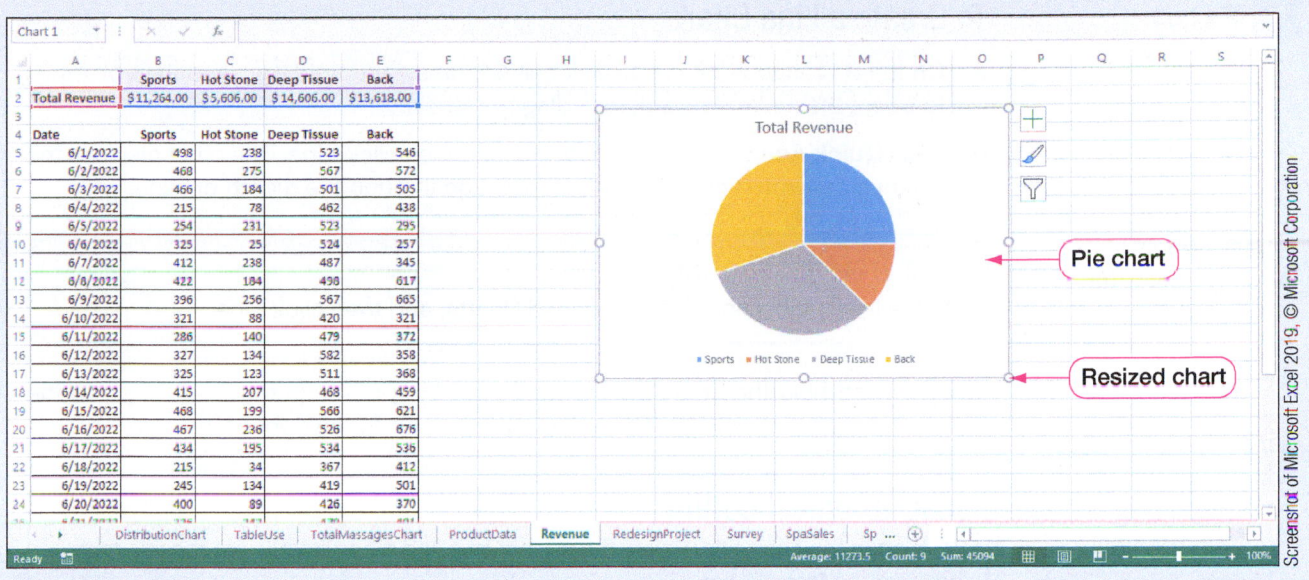

Figure 5 Pie chart

e. **Save** 🔲 the workbook.

Even though all the data is used to show every massage type, you do not have to use all the data. If the goal is to examine the data and extract a portion of the information, such as the fact that several massage types have low or high average ratings, it may be better to show only a few massage types rather than including too much information. Showing a subset of massage types may help to emphasize particular ratings.

In determining how to proceed once the data has been initially examined, start developing hypotheses and questions. For example, it may be that hot stone massages are too new and need to be marketed more, as they currently represent a small portion of revenues. Develop questions, and then use the data to determine the validity of the questions and make strategic decisions.

Creating Line Charts

Line charts help to convey change in data over time. They are great for exploring how data in a business, such as sales or production, changes over time. Line charts help people to interpret why the data is changing and to make decisions about how to proceed. For example, in examining a heart rate on an electrocardiogram, a doctor is looking at data over time to see what has been happening. The doctor wants to determine if there are issues, and then make decisions about whether the patient should go home, be given medications, or have surgery.

To create a line chart, you need to have at least one set of labels and at least one set of corresponding data. It is possible to have multiple data series, each series representing a line on the chart. You have been provided data that lists revenue generated by four different types of massages. The data is organized by day throughout the month of June.

In this exercise, you will create a line chart displaying daily revenue by massage type in June. Irene would like each day to appear as a point on the line that is created and each massage type to be a separate line on the chart.

 **E04.05**

To Create a Line Chart

a. On the **Revenue** worksheet, click cell **A4**, press and hold [Ctrl], and then press [A] to select the entire data set, including the labels.

b. Click **Quick Analysis** [icon], click **Charts**, and then click **Line**. The chart displays the revenue generated by each type of massage through the month of June.

> ### Mac Troubleshooting
> On the Insert tab, click Recommended Charts, and then click Line.

c. Click and hold the **chart border**, and then drag to move the chart to place the top-left corner in cell **I20**. This will place the chart to the right of the data set.

> ### Mac Troubleshooting
> To change the chart title, delete the current text and type directly into the title text box, not the formula bar.

d. Point to the **bottom-right corner** of the chart until the pointer changes to [icon], and then drag to resize the chart so the bottom-right corner is over cell **O34**.

e. Click the **Chart Tools Format** tab. In the Current Selection group, click the **Chart Elements** arrow, and then click **Chart Title** to select the chart title placeholder. Type June Revenue by Massage Type and then press [Enter].

SIDE NOTE
Adding Chart Title
When you select the Chart Title border and then begin typing the chart title, the title will appear in the formula bar and not update until you press [Enter].

SIDE NOTE
Alternate Method
Click the Chart Title border, select the text within the placeholder, and then begin typing the chart title.

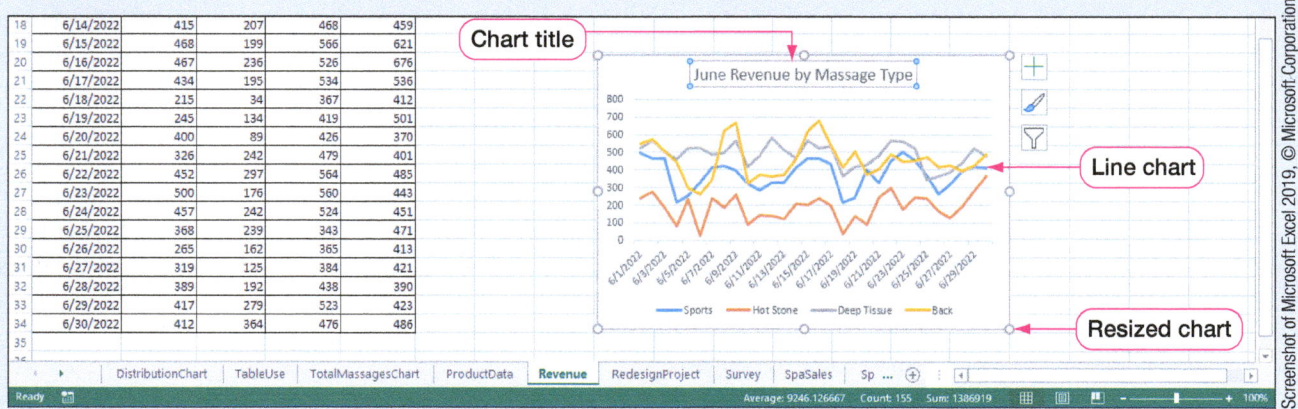

Figure 6 Line chart

> ### Troubleshooting
> If you end up with a chart that looks dramatically different from what you would expect, check the colored borders around the linked data set. It is very common to select all the data in a table when the intention was to select just part of the data. If too much data was selected, you can delete the selected chart by pressing Delete and then try recreating the chart with the appropriate data. Alternatively, you could select the corner of a colored link data border and drag the border to adjust the set of data. The blue border data is displayed in the chart. When that border is adjusted, the associated label data is automatically adjusted accordingly. The chart is also automatically adjusted so changes can be immediately seen.

f. **Save** [icon] the workbook.

Creating Bar Charts

Bar charts display data horizontally and are used for comparison among individual items. They are useful for working with categorical data. Bar charts are like column charts except the bars are horizontal representations of the data rather than vertical. Like column charts, bar charts can depict a single piece of data, can be grouped data series, and can be stacked.

Stacked bar charts can be useful when you want to see how the individual parts add up to create the entire length of each bar. A stacked bar chart can display changes over time for products or services. Stacked charts should be considered when the sum of the data values is as important as the individual items.

In this exercise, you will create a stacked bar chart that will assist Meda and Irene to visualize the status of a project to redesign the massage therapy rooms.

 E04.06

SIDE NOTE
Selecting Nonadjacent Columns
To select nonadjacent columns when creating a chart, you must first select the first column of data, then press and hold the Ctrl key, and then select the second column of data.

To Create a Stacked Bar Chart

a. Click the **RedesignProject** worksheet.

b. Select cell range **A3:A8**, press and hold the Ctrl key, and then select cell range **C3:D8**.

   Notice that because you did not select a consecutive range of cells, the Quick Analysis option is not present. Therefore, you will have to use the Insert tab to create the chart.

c. Click the **Insert** tab, and then in the Charts group, click **Recommended Charts**.

d. Click **Stacked Bar**, the second selection on the Recommended Charts tab of the Insert Chart dialog box, and then click **OK**.

e. Position the chart so the top-left corner is over cell **A10**.

f. Click the **Chart Title** border, type *Project Redesign Status* and then press Enter.

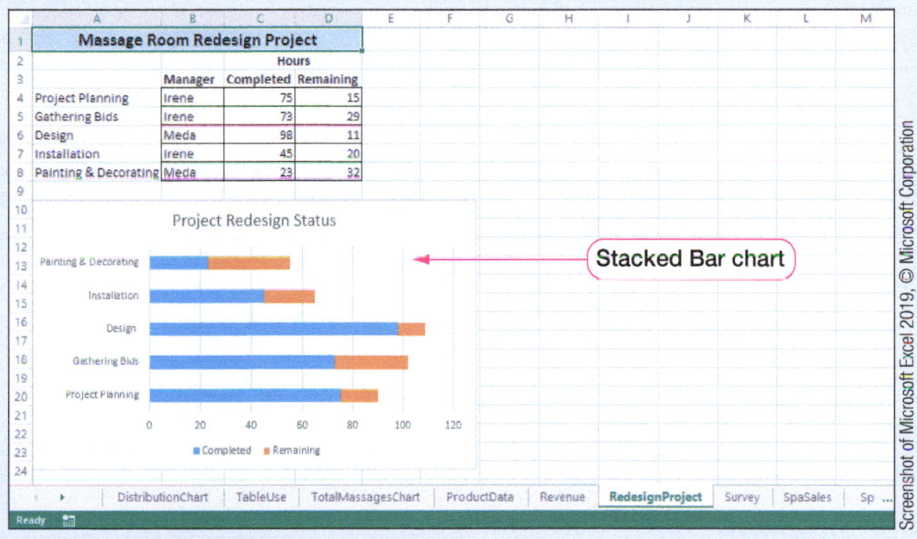

Figure 7   Stacked bar chart

g. **Save** the workbook.

The stacked bar chart helps Irene and Meda to determine the status of the redesign phases. The chart shows which phases are nearly complete and which phases still need more time to complete. They can use the information to determine whether they need to assign more resources to a phase, such as painting and decorating, to be sure it gets completed in the desired time.

Creating Scatter Charts

A **Scatter chart**, also called XY (Scatter), is a chart that conveys the relationship between two numeric variables. This type of chart is very common as a statistical tool depicting the correlation between the two variables. The standard format is to have the x-axis (horizontal) data in the left column and the y-axis (vertical) data in the right column(s).

Irene and Meda have data from a survey showing the requested temperature of the room used for massages and the age of the customer. This data may reveal important information about what temperature is typically requested by customers in different age groups. In this exercise, you will create a scatter chart of the requested temperatures of rooms and ages of customers.

 **E04.07**

To Create a Scatter Chart

a. Click the **Survey** worksheet, and then select cell range **B53:A2**. This will include the data and labels for Age and Temp.

b. Click **Quick Analysis** 📊, click **Charts**, and then click **Scatter**.

> **Mac Troubleshooting**
>
> On a Mac, click the Insert tab, click Recommended Charts, and then click Scatter.

c. Click the chart border, and then drag to move it to the right of the data so the top-left corner is over cell **E2**.

The default scale of the chart does not bring out any trends in the data. Adjusting the scaling of the y-axis will help to display any trends. You will adjust the scale of the y-axis later in this chapter.

d. Click the **Chart Title** border, type Age and Desired Room Temperature and then press Enter. This chart shows the relationship between increasing age and temperatures requested for massages.

> **Troubleshooting**
>
> If you double-clicked or clicked inside the Chart Title placeholder instead of clicking the Chart Title border, pressing Enter will add an extra line of text. Press Backspace to delete the extra line of text.

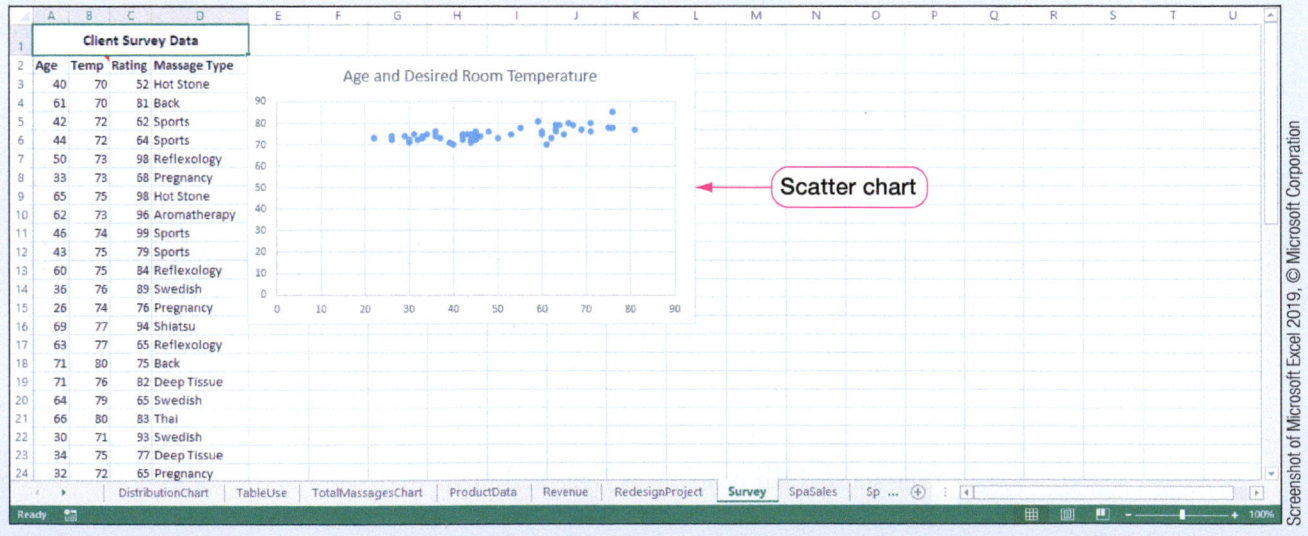

Figure 8 Scatter chart

e. **Save** 💾 the workbook.

Creating Area Charts

An **area chart** is a variation of a stacked line chart that emphasizes the magnitude of change over time and visually depicts a trend. The area chart stacks a set of data series and colors each area that is created. This type of chart provides a nice visual presentation because each colored layer changes, by growing or shrinking as it moves across time periods. With an area chart, the horizontal x-axis is typically a time sequence. The area chart could also use categories instead of time on the horizontal x-axis, where each layer again is showing the individual contribution to the area; thus, it is a quantitative chart that shows growth or change in totals.

Irene has asked you to create a chart to further understand the differences in the types of massages given over the past eight weeks at the spa. She is particularly interested in Pregnancy, Shiatsu, Thai, and Hot Stone massages. In this exercise, you will create an area chart for this purpose.

 **E04.08**

To Create an Area Chart

a. Click the **ProductData** worksheet, and then select cell range **A16:I20**.

b. Click **Quick Analysis** 🖼, click **Charts**, and then click **Stacked Area**. Notice that there are two chart choices for stacked charts. You will select the second for Stacked Area.

> **Mac Troubleshooting**
>
> On a Mac, click the Insert tab, click Recommended Charts, and then click Stacked Area.

c. Click the **Chart Title** border, type Massage Types Over 8 Week Period and then press Enter.

d. Click the **chart border**, and then drag to move the chart so the top-left corner is over cell **D2**.

e. With the chart border still selected, point to the **bottom-right corner** of the chart, and then drag to resize the chart so the bottom-right corner of the chart is over **I12**.

This chart shows the total number of massages offered for each of the past eight weeks with emphasis placed on four different massage types.

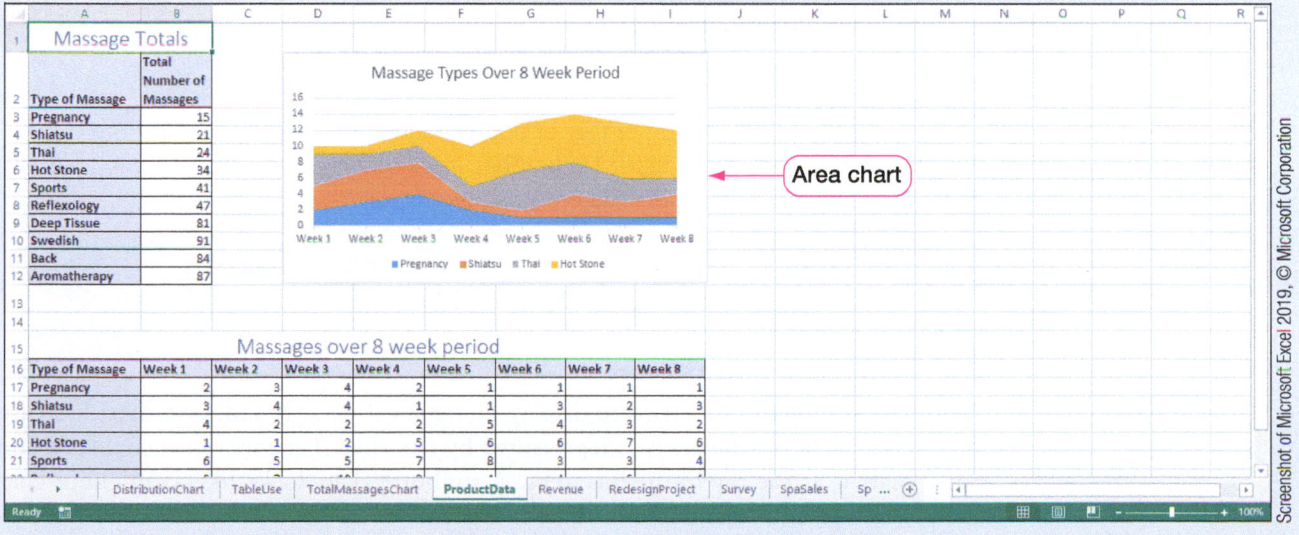

Figure 9 Area chart

f. **Save** 🖫 the workbook.

Creating Combination Charts

A **combination chart** displays two different types of data by using multiple chart types in a single chart object. Combination charts can enhance the understanding of data when the scale of data being charted varies greatly. For example, consider monitoring the number of items sold in the spa to customers over a 12-month span of time. To fully comprehend the data, it would be helpful to explore both the number of items sold and the profit from items sold. However, a single item may cost hundreds of dollars. This makes creating a chart to compare these two pieces of data difficult. In prior versions of Excel, creating a combination chart was a difficult and time-consuming process. In Excel 2019, combination charts are a standard chart type.

Meda has asked you to analyze the quantities of spa products sold from the prior year's sales and compare the result to the profits over the same time span. Currently, only data from January to November is available. In this exercise, you will create a chart to which the December data can be added when it becomes available.

 **E04.09**

To Create a Combination Chart

a. Click the **SpaSales** worksheet, and then select cell range **A2:C13**.

b. Click the **Insert** tab, in the Charts group, click **Insert Combo Chart** , and then click **Clustered Column - Line on Secondary Axis**.

c. Click the **Chart Title** border, type Profit by Quantity Sold and then press Enter.

d. Click the **chart border**, and then drag to move the chart so the top-left corner is over cell **E1**.

Figure 10 Combination chart

This chart compares the number of spa products sold and the profit from products sold in the same chart. Notice that in January, the profit for items sold is lower than might be expected from the quantity sold.

e. **Save** the workbook.

Creating a Sunburst Chart

A **Sunburst chart** can be used to display hierarchical data. A sunburst chart has rings and each level of the hierarchy is represented by one ring. The innermost circle of a sunburst chart is at the top of the hierarchy. A sunburst chart looks like a doughnut chart except a doughnut chart does not show hierarchical data. The outer rings of a sunburst chart relate to the inner rings.

Meda has asked you to create a chart which will display the types of massages each therapist performs as well as any ranking associated with each therapist. Therapists can earn a level 1–4 ranking by taking certification courses. The higher the level of certification, the more a therapist can charge for services.

In this exercise, you will create a chart to display the type of massages each massage therapist is capable of performing as well as any certification levels held.

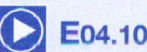 **E04.10**

To Create a Sunburst Chart

> **Grader Heads Up**
> The MyLab IT Grader version of this project does not include the creation of a Sunburst chart.

a. Click the **Specialties-Certifications** worksheet.

b. Select the cell range **A4:C44**, press and hold Ctrl, and then select cell range **H4:H44**.

c. Click the **Insert** tab, and in the Charts group, click **Insert Hierarchy Chart**, and then click **Sunburst**.

d. On the Chart Tools Design tab, click **Move Chart**.

e. Select **New Sheet**, type TherapistChart and then click **OK**.

f. Click the **Chart Title** border, type Therapist Massage Types and Certifications and then press Enter.

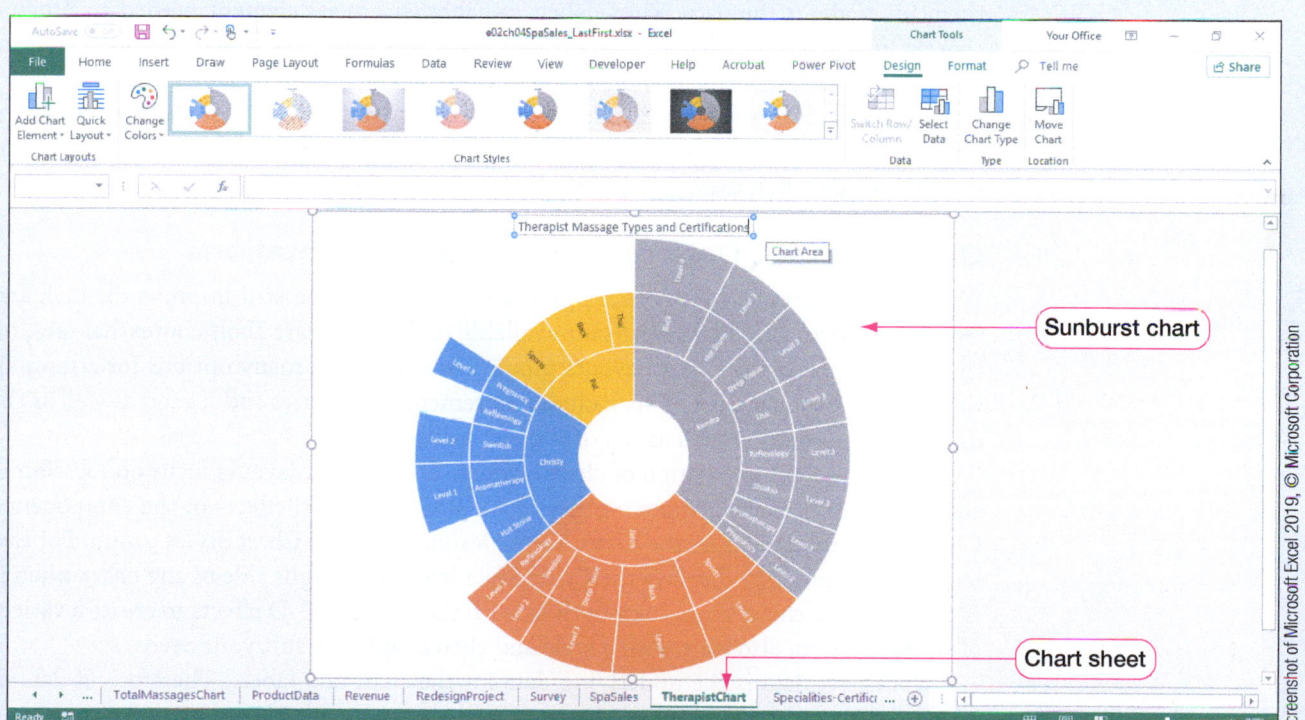

Figure 11 Sunburst chart

This chart shows the therapists' names in the inner circle, the massages they offer in the middle circle, and then any certifications held in the outer circle.

g. **Save** the workbook.

h. If you need to take a break before finishing this chapter, now is a good time.

QUICK REFERENCE	Chart Selection Guidelines

- **Pie** Used for comparing the relationship of parts to a whole
- **Line** Shows changes within a data series; often used with time on the x-axis
- **Column** Compares data vertically; can incorporate a time element and groups
- **Bar** Compares data horizontally; stacked bar can show progress or growth
- **Scatter** Used for correlations, exploring the relationship between two variables
- **Area** Used to highlight areas showing growth over time or for categories; a variation of a line chart
- **Combination** Used to display two different types of data in a single chart
- **Sunburst** Used to display hierarchical data

Exploring Chart Layouts

As you have seen, a chart can help to answer questions and may even generate more questions. This can help in moving toward the understanding of information, which can also lead to better decision making. Creating these initial charts to explore data is quick and efficient and informs the user.

When a chart is presented to other people, the context of the chart is of utmost importance. When context is not provided to the audience, your audience must try to guess the context. You need to provide meaning. Providing context means providing textual guidance to the audience. The audience will see the chart, but you need to inform them more about the data. Thus, labels are another crucial element needed to provide context in charts. The labels include the chart title and axes titles, legend, and data labels. All these elements should work cohesively to complete a picture of what the chart is trying to convey to the audience. In this section, you will change the appearance of charts by altering their layout and color patterns. You will also modify chart titles and the titles of the chart axes.

Change Chart Data and Styles for Presentations

While the default chart settings are pleasant visually, you can still improve the look and feel of the chart. The chart layouts are available under the Chart Tools contextual tabs, on the Design tab, in the Chart Layouts group. Excel provides many options for arranging the components on a chart. This includes placement of the titles and legend as well as the display of information such as the data point values.

Chart styles are a variation of chart layouts. Where chart layouts focus on location of components, styles focus more on the color coordination and effects of the components. Chart styles are located on the Chart Tools Design tab in the Chart Styles group. For easier access, Excel 2019 displays the Chart Style icon to the right side of any chart when it is selected. The choices mix color options with shadows and 3-D effects to create a variety of styles. You can also start with a style and then adapt it to suit your needs.

Worksheet data is the underlying data for the chart and labels. Therefore, if data or labels change on the worksheet, the chart will also change because charts are connected to data in the worksheet. There can be many reasons for needing to modify data. For example, there might be a data entry error that needs to be corrected, or an employee might have changed her or his last name.

Not only can you modify a chart by modifying the worksheet data it was created from, you can also modify how the chart is displaying the data. For example, if the data needs to be swapped between the data points and the axis data, you can use the Data group to switch rows and columns or select new data for a chart.

Changing the Data and Appearance of a Chart

Because charts in Excel are connected to data on the worksheet, changes to the data are automatically reflected in the chart. This is extremely useful if you have a model that is using some calculations that are then used in a chart. You can do a what-if analysis by changing data in a worksheet; the corresponding changes will appear on the chart.

Charts may need to be modified when the amount of data being charted needs to be changed. For example, a chart might have too much information included, making it difficult to get a clear picture. Conversely, a chart may need to be modified as new data becomes available. If the new data is adjacent to the existing data, it is a simple process to expand the existing data series. This is achieved by resizing the borders around the data series after activating the chart.

Irene has just provided you with the December data for quantity and profit for the spa. She has also mentioned that there is an error in the quantity in January sales. In this exercise, you will add the December data to the SpaSales worksheet, adjust the combination chart accordingly, and correct the January data. You will also modify the appearance of the chart.

 E04.11

To Modify the Layout and Data in an Existing Chart

a. If you took a break, open the **e02ch04SpaSales_LastFirst** workbook and, if needed, click the **SpaSales** worksheet. Click cell **A14**.

b. Type December and then press Tab. Type 178 and then press Tab. Type 1901 and then press Ctrl+Enter.

c. Click the **chart area** portion of the chart. Click the sizing handle on the bottom edge between cells **A13** and **B13**, and then drag the sizing handle down one row so the cell range **A2:C14** is now being charted. The chart will now include the quantity sold and profits for the month of December.

d. On the Chart Tools Design tab, in the Type group, click **Change Chart Type**.

e. Near the bottom of the Change Chart Type dialog box, next to the Profit series, click the **Chart Type** arrow. Select **Area**.

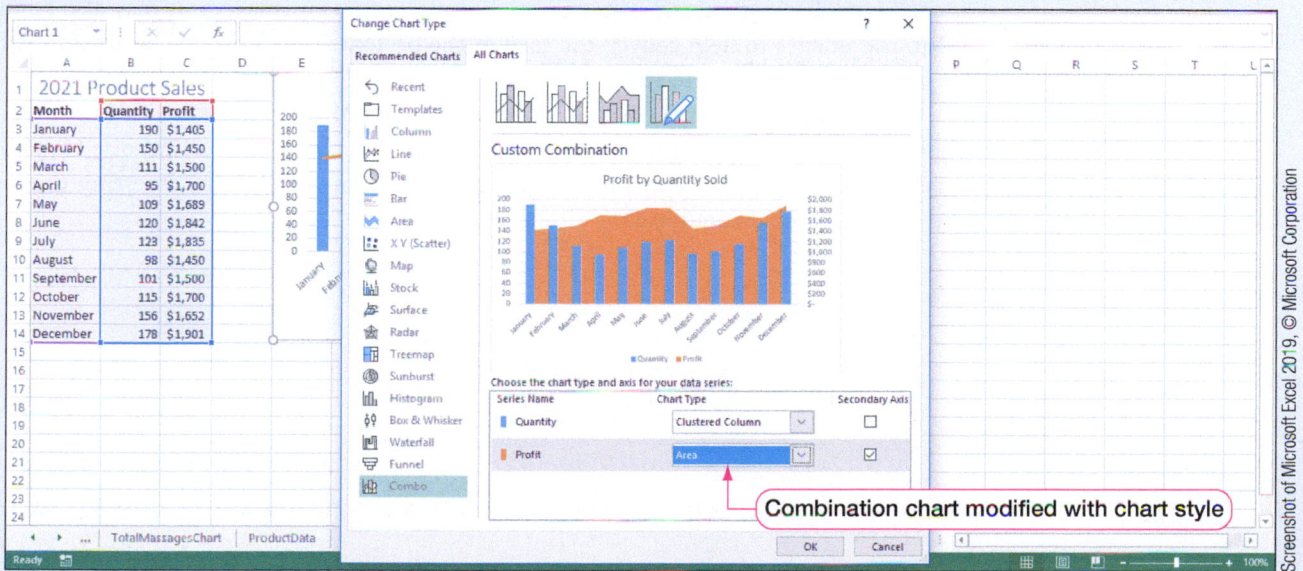

Combination chart modified with chart style

Figure 12 Modified combination chart

MAC COMPATIBILITY

Chart styles on a Mac

There is no Chart Styles button on a Mac. Instead, you must select the Chart Design tab, and then, in the Chart Styles group, click More.

f.   Click **OK**.

g.   To the right of the chart, click **Chart Styles** 🖌, scroll down, and then click **Style 6**. Click **Chart Styles** 🖌 to close the style gallery.

h.   On the Chart Tools Design tab, in the Chart Layouts group, click **Quick Layout**. In the displayed gallery, click **Layout 9**.

Notice that the new layout added labels for the x-axis and y-axis on the chart. These axis titles will be revised at a later point.

i.   On the worksheet, click cell **B6**, enter **122** and then press Tab. Notice that the combination chart reflects the new value.

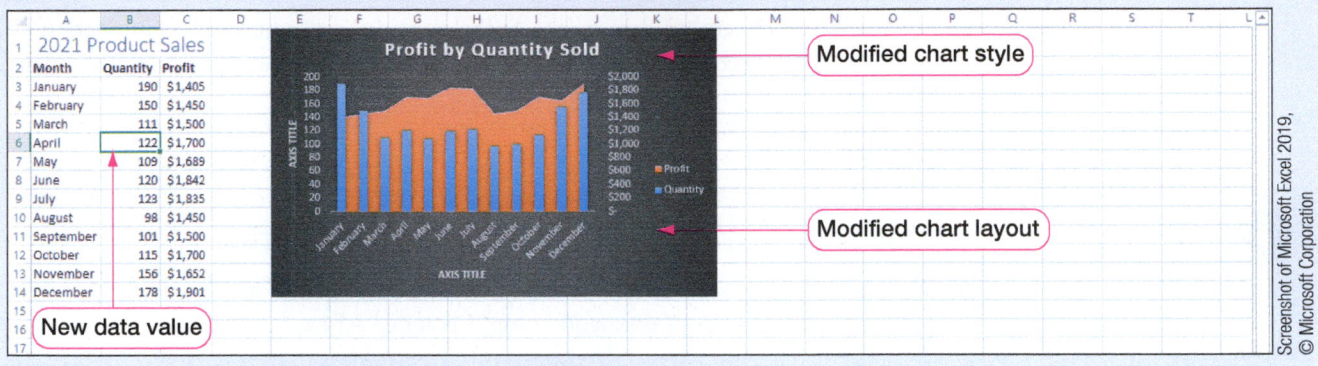

Figure 13   Combination chart with new value displayed

j.   **Save** 🖫 the workbook.

Inserting Objects

If you work for a company, it can be useful to insert the company logo into any chart that is used outside the company. After all, marketing occurs everywhere. It may also be useful to use images to help convey the tone of the presentation. This can be accomplished by inserting an image into the chart.

Irene mentioned that she would be using the TotalMassagesChart sheet in the workbook in a variety of presentations and would like it to contain the Turquoise Oasis Spa logo. In this exercise, you will modify the appearance of the chart by inserting the logo and a shape object containing the title of the chart.

 **E04.12**

To Insert Objects into a Chart

a. Click the **TotalMassagesChart** worksheet.

b. Click the **Insert** tab, click **Illustrations**, and then click **Pictures**. In the left pane of the Insert Picture dialog box, navigate to the location where you store your student data files, and then click **e02ch04TurquoiseOasis**. Click **Insert**.

c. On the **Picture Tools Format** tab, in the Size group, click the **Shape Height** 🔲 box. Clear any existing text, type **0.9** and then press Enter.

d. Click in the **Chart Area**. Click the **Chart Tools Design** tab, and then in the Chart Layouts group, click **Quick Layout**. In the gallery that appears, click **Layout 4**.

   Notice that the new layout added labels for the x-axis—columns—on the chart.

e. Click any one of the **columns** in the chart—do not double-click. Click the **Chart Tools Format** tab, and in the Shape Styles group, click **More** 🔽, and then click **Gradient Fill — Gold, Accent 4, No Outline** in the last row, fifth column.

f. Click the **Insert** tab, click **Illustrations**, and then click **Shapes** 🔲. In the displayed gallery, in the Rectangles group, click **Rectangle: Rounded Corners**—the second option. Click below the Turquoise Oasis Spa logo to place the rectangle. Type Total number of massage services by type

g. On the Drawing Tools Format tab, in the Size group, click the **Shape Height** 🔲, box type **0.8** and then press Enter. In the **Shape Width** 🔲 box, type **2.3** and then press Enter.

h. In the Shape Styles group, click **More** 🔽, and then select **Gradient Fill — Gold, Accent 4, No Outline** last row, fifth column.

i. Select the border of the rectangle. On the Home tab, in the Font group, click the **Font Size** arrow 10 ▾, and then select **14**. With the text still selected, in the Font group, click the Font Color arrow 🅰▾ and then select **Black, Text 1**.

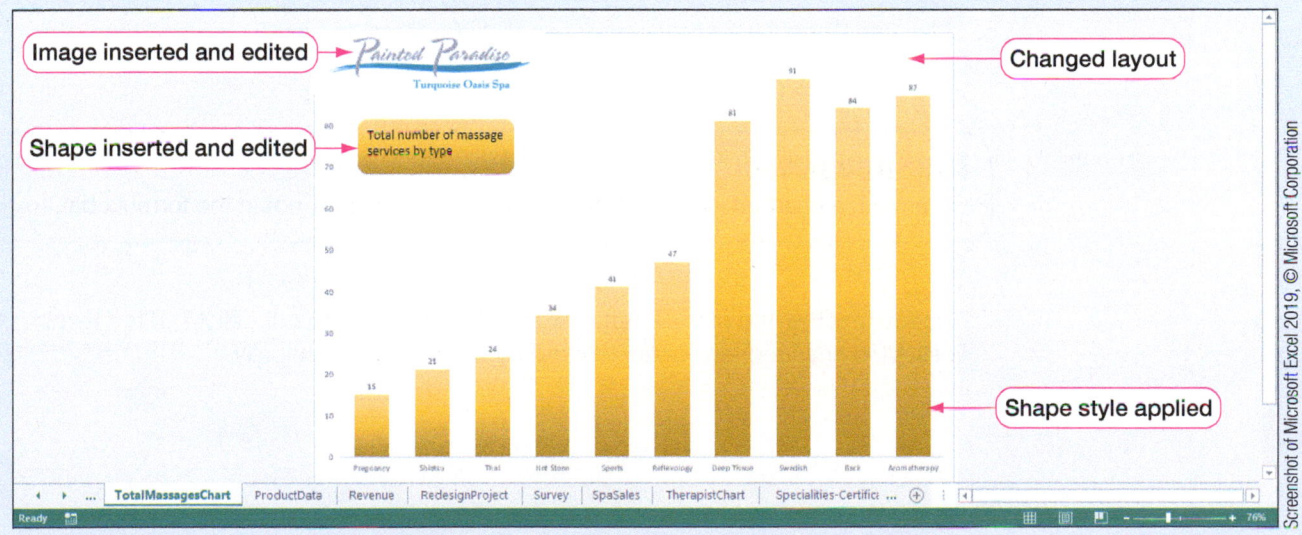

Figure 14 Chart with inserted picture and shape

j. **Save** 💾 the workbook.

QUICK REFERENCE	Formatting Options for Chart Objects

Below are chart format options and their descriptions.

- **Number**   Format data as currency, date, time, and so on.
- **Fill**   Fill the background of a element with a color, picture, or pattern.
- **Shape Outline**   Set the color and thickness of the chart border.
- **Shape Effects**   Add shadowing, reflections, glow, soft edges, bevel and 3-D rotations to chart elements.
- **Alignment**   Align text direction for a component, such as left, top, vertical, or horizontal.

Exploring Titles for the Chart and Axes

Chart and axes titles are added easily under the Chart Tools Format tab or with the Chart Elements button that appears on the right side of charts in Excel 2019. Chart titles can be added within the chart, or they can reference cells on the spreadsheet for easy updating.

In this exercise, you will edit the title of the stacked bar chart on the Redesign-Project worksheet to match the text in cell A1. You will also clarify the horizontal and vertical axis labels on the combination chart in the SpaSales worksheet.

 **E04.13**

To Modify Chart Titles and Axis Labels

a. Click the **RedesignProject** worksheet, and then click the **chart border** of the stacked bar chart.

b. Click the **Chart Title** border, and then click the **formula bar**. Type **=** and then click cell **A1**. Press Enter.

> **Mac Troubleshooting**
> On a Mac, a chart title can be typed in the Title object box, not in the formula bar.

Notice that the title of the chart now matches the contents of cell A1. If the text in cell A1 is changed, the Chart Title will be updated automatically.

CHAPTER 4

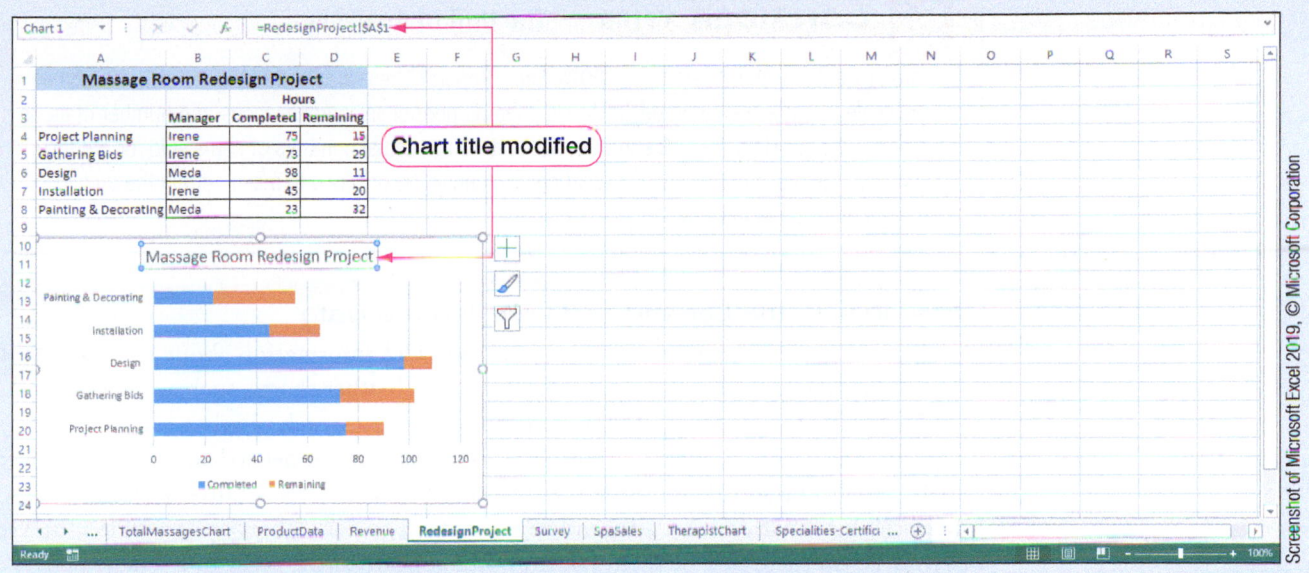

Figure 15 Chart with modified title

c. Click the **SpaSales** worksheet, and then click the **chart border** of the combination chart. Click the **Horizontal (Category) Axis Title** box, and then press Delete.

d. Click the **Vertical (Value) Axis Title** box, type Quantity and then press Enter.

e. On the Chart Tools Design tab, in the Chart Layouts group, click **Add Chart Element**.

f. Point to **Axis Titles**, and then select **Secondary Vertical**. Type Profit and then press Enter.

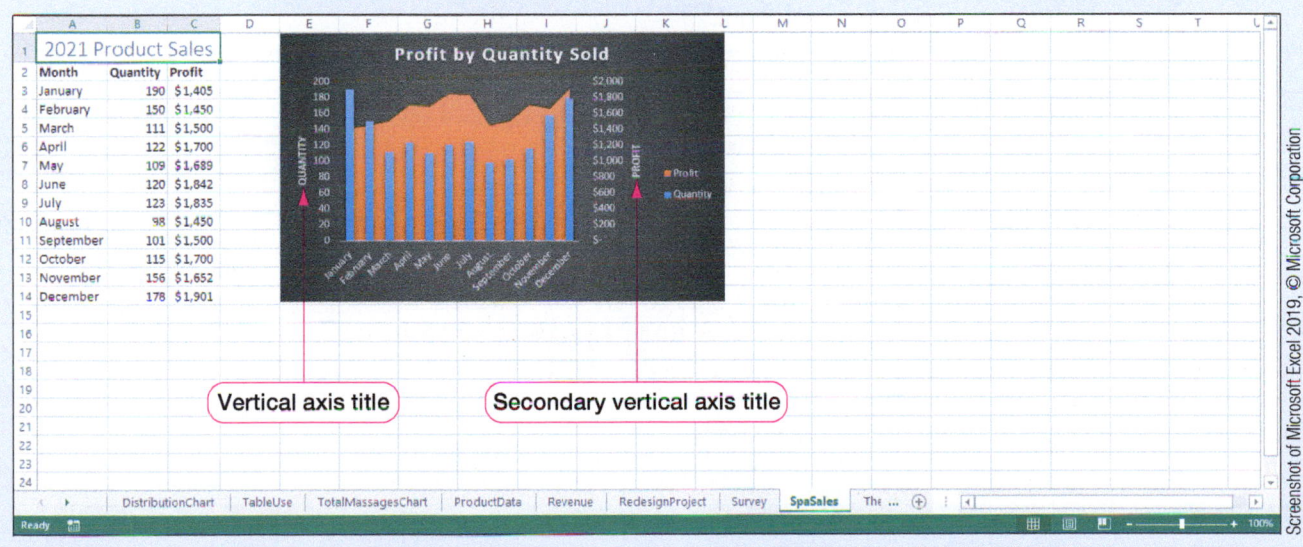

Figure 16 Chart with modified axis labels

g. **Save** the workbook.

CONSIDER THIS | **The Unit of Analysis**

You are presented with a Chart Titled "2022 Sales Report." The x-axis is showing 20, 30, 40, and so on for the scale. What is the report depicting? Is it the number of sales transactions, the number of items sold, or the revenue for 2022? Are the 20, 30, and 40 the actual numbers of items sold, or are they quantities in hundreds or thousands? What context should be provided to make certain the audience knows the meaning of the chart?

Working with the Legend and Labeling the Data

The **legend** is an index within a chart that provides information about the data. With some charts, the legend is added automatically. With other charts, such as pie charts, it is possible to incorporate the same information on or beside each pie slice as labels.

When the parts are labeled on the chart, the legend is not needed and can be removed. Labels can also be added alongside the data on the chart. This is quite informative, as it moves the information from a legend to the data. The data labels can be added, moved, or removed on the Chart Elements button that appears to the right of a selected chart or on the Chart Tools Design tab.

In this exercise, you will modify the revenue charts to make them more visually appealing.

To Work with Legends and Data Labels

a. Click the **Revenue** worksheet, and then click the **chart border** of the line chart.

b. To the right of the chart, click **Chart Elements** ⊞, point to Legend, click the **Legend** arrow, and then click **Right**. This moves the legend to the right side of the chart. Click **Chart Elements** ⊞ again to close it.

> **Mac Troubleshooting**
> On a Mac, click the Chart Design tab, click Add Chart Element, point to Legend, and then select Right.

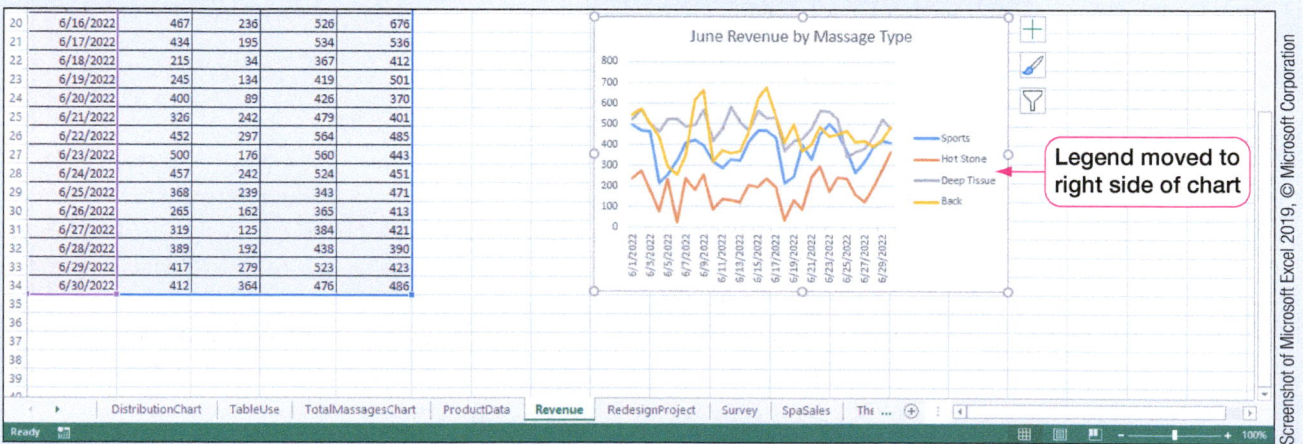

Figure 17 Line chart with legend moved

c. Scroll up if necessary, and then click the **chart border** of the pie chart. To the right of the chart, click **Chart Elements** ⊞, and then click the **Data Labels** check box. Click the arrow next to Data Labels, and then select **Data Callout**.

Notice how the legend is no longer necessary.

MAC COMPATIBILITY

Removing the Legend on a Mac

To remove a legend on a Mac, click the Chart Design tab, and in the Chart Layouts group, click Add Chart Element, point to the Legend, and then select None.

Mac Troubleshooting

For a Mac, click Add Chart Element on the Chart Design tab, point to Data Labels, and then select Data Callout.

d. Click **Legend** to clear the check box. This will remove the legend from the pie chart.

e. Click **Chart Elements** ⊞ again to close the gallery.

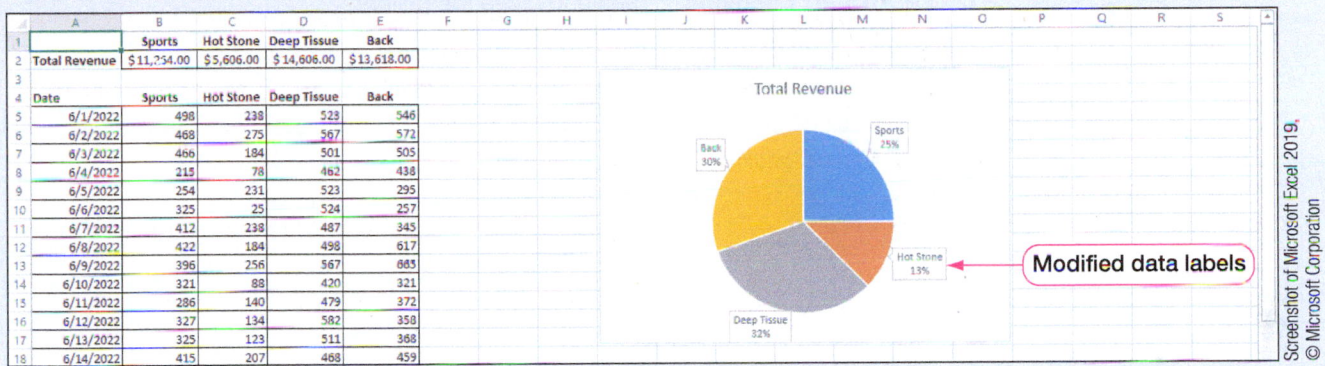

Figure 18 Pie chart with modified legend and data labels

f. **Save** 🖫 the workbook.

Troubleshooting

Adding and removing chart elements may alter the position of other elements of your chart. You may need to reposition existing or new elements in the chart to clarify the meaning of the chart.

Changing Gridlines

Chart gridlines are the lines that go across charts to help gauge the size of the bars, columns, or data lines. In Excel, the default is to display the major gridlines (the gridlines at the designated label values) and not to display the minor gridlines (the gridlines between the label values). If the chart is a line or column chart, Excel puts in the horizontal major gridlines; if it is a bar chart, Excel puts in vertical major gridlines. The default is a good starting point, but personal preferences can dictate which lines to display. The Format Major Gridlines pane allows for the customization of gridlines in a chart.

In this exercise, you will customize the gridlines in your revenue chart.

 **E04.15**

To Modify Gridlines on a Chart

MAC COMPATIBILITY

Modifying Gridlines on a Mac

To modify gridlines on a Mac, click the Chart Design tab, and in the Chart Layouts group, click Add Chart Element, point to Gridlines and then select Primary Major Vertical.

Grader Heads Up

The MyLab IT Grader version of this project does not include the addition of the primary vertical gridlines.

a. On the Revenue worksheet, click the **chart border** of the line chart.

b. To the right of the chart, click **Chart Elements** ⊞, point to Gridlines, click the **Gridlines** arrow, and then select **Primary Major Vertical**.

c. Click **Chart Elements** ⊞ again to close the gallery.

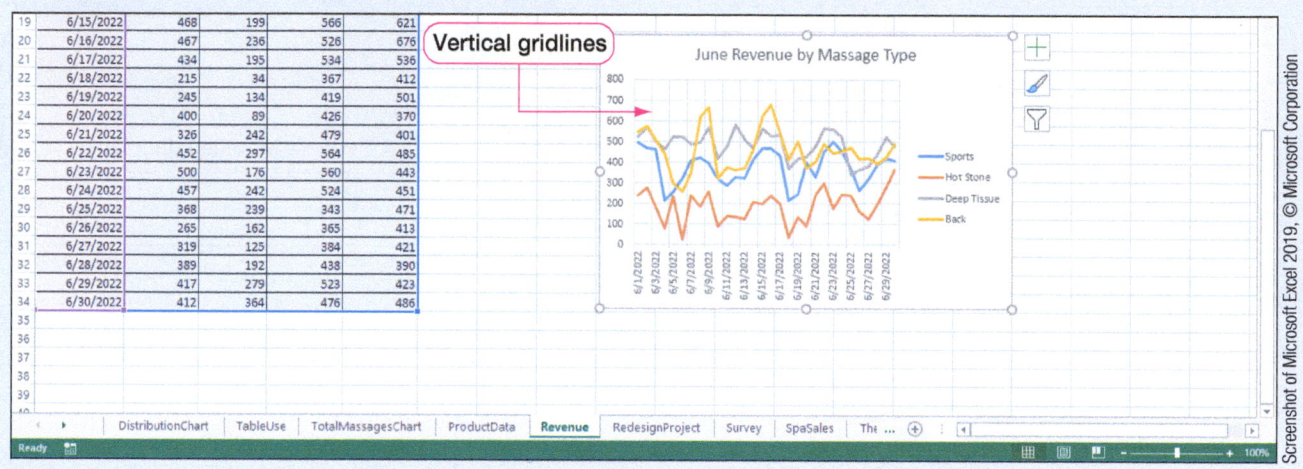

Figure 19 Line chart with modified chart gridlines

d. **Save** 🖫 the workbook.

Edit and Format Charts to Add Emphasis

In formatting a chart, it is important to have a plan in mind as to the overall layout and look and feel. With a well-thought-out plan, it will be easy to apply the desired adjustments to the elements with regard to position, color, and emphasis. Typically, you can either create a unique layout or modify one of Excel's many layouts. Either way, being able to make formatting changes is easy and a very useful, powerful way to convey information. In this section, you will explore various ways to format a chart.

Adding Color to Chart Objects

Working some color into charts can be helpful from a marketing perspective. Excel offers options that allow changing the fill color as well as the border color. Chart colors can be added to match a company's color scheme or to highlight certain important aspects of the data. Remember, however, that while it is possible to add value to charts with color, it is also possible to overdo it.

Irene has mentioned to you that she will be using the pie chart on the Revenue worksheet in a presentation. In this exercise, you will enhance the visual appeal of the chart before her presentation.

 **E04.16**

To Change the Coloring of a Chart

a. On the Revenue worksheet, click the **chart border** of the pie chart.

b. On the Chart Tools Design tab, in the Chart Styles group, click **Change Colors**, and then, in the gallery that appears, click **Colorful Palette 4** (the fourth option).

c. Click the **Chart Tools Format** tab, in the Shape Styles group, click **Shape Fill**, and then click **Gold, Accent 4, Lighter 60%**.

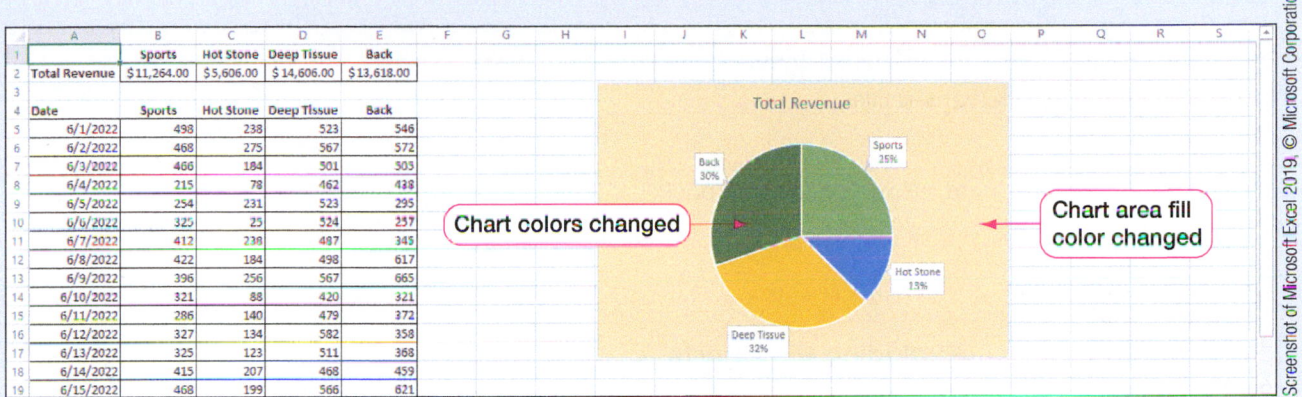

Figure 20   Pie chart with color added

d. Save  the workbook.

Working with Text

Whether the text is in a shape, title, legend, or axis scale, you can change the formatting of text and the backgrounds of the text objects in charts. The text can be formatted as WordArt, and shapes can be modified to common Shape Styles.

Irene has decided that the pie chart you modified with a new color scheme now has a title that is too difficult to read. In this exercise, you will increase the font size and apply bold to the font in the Chart Title box to address this problem.

E04.17

To Format Text within a Chart

a. On the Revenue worksheet, if necessary, click the **chart border** of the pie chart.

b. Click the **chart title**, click the **Home** tab, and then in the Font group, click **Bold** B. In the Font group, click the **Font Size** 10 arrow, and then select **16**.

c. With the chart title still selected, click the **Chart Tools Format** tab, and then in the WordArt Styles group, click **More** to expand the WordArt gallery. Select **Pattern Fill: White; Dark Upward Diagonal Stripe; Shadow** in the first column, fourth row.

Screenshot of Microsoft Excel 2019, © Microsoft Corporation

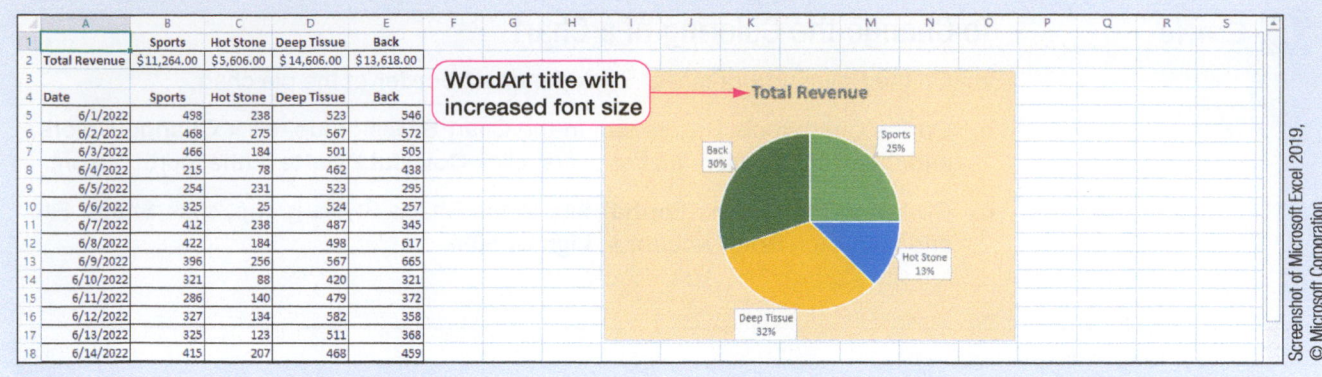

Figure 21   Pie chart with WordArt title

        d. Save  the workbook.

Exploding Pie Charts

The traditional pie chart is a pie with all the slices together. Preset options offer a pie chart with a slice pulled slightly away from the main pie, or you can manually move a slice outward, creating an exploded pie chart. This technique allows for highlighting a particular piece of the pie.

     As part of her presentation, Irene wants to emphasize the hot stone massage type because it represents the least amount of revenue in the data series. In this exercise, you will create visual emphasis by exploding the slice of the pie chart representing the revenue percentage of hot stone massages.

E04.18

To Create an Exploding Pie Chart

a. On the Revenue worksheet, if necessary, click the **chart border** of the pie chart.

b. Click anywhere inside the pie. Notice that the entire pie is selected.

c. Click the **Hot Stone** slice of the pie to select just that data point.

     Notice that only the Hot Stone slice is now selected.

d. Drag the **Hot Stone** data slice slightly to the right. The Hot Stone slice is now pulled away, or exploded, from the rest of the pie to show emphasis.

e. Double-click the exploded pie element to open the Format Data Point pane. If necessary, click **Series Option** ▥. Under Series Options, in the Point Explosion box, type **20** to change the value to 20%.

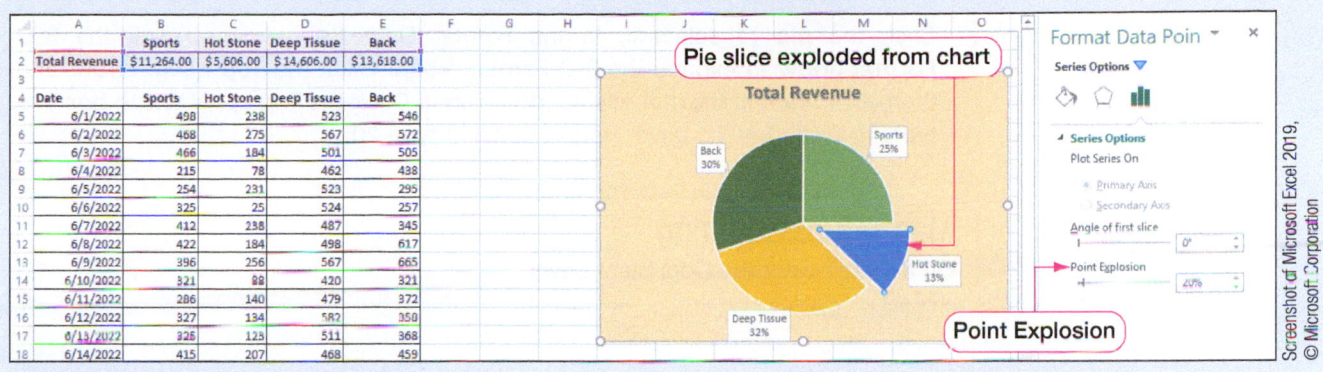

Figure 22 Exploded pie chart

f. Close the Format Data Point pane.

g. Save  the workbook.

Changing 3-D Charts and Rotation of Charts

The 3-D effect and rotation of a chart are effects that should be used conservatively. They can be done well, or they can be overused, resulting in a chart that goes overboard and distracts from the intended message. You can choose the 3-D effect when starting to develop a chart, or you can apply the effect after creating the chart. Additionally, options are available to rotate the 3-D effect, giving the chart a crisp, distinctive look. The 3-D format can be applied to a variety of objects. The 3-D Rotation setting is intended for the chart area only.

In this exercise, you will use the 3-D effect and rotation to enhance the pie chart showing the total revenue by massage type.

▶ E04.19

To Change the Chart Type to 3-D

a. On the Revenue worksheet, if necessary, click the **chart border** of the pie chart.

b. Click the **Chart Tools Design** tab, and then, in the Type group, click **Change Chart Type**.

c. In the Change Chart Type dialog box, if necessary, click the **All Charts** tab. In the left pane, click **Pie**, click **3-D Pie**, and then click **OK**.

d. Double-click the **chart area** to open the Format Chart Area pane. Click **Effects** ⬠, and then click the **3-D Rotation** arrow to expand the 3-D Rotation group.

e. Click in the box for **Y Rotation**, delete the existing value, and then type **50** Click in the box for **Perspective**, delete the existing value, and then type **35** and then press Enter.

> ### Grader Heads Up
> In MyLab IT Grader version of this project does not include adding a Top bevel.

f. Click the **pie** to select it. In the Format Data Series pane, click the **3-D Format** arrow to expand the 3-D Format group. Click the **Top bevel** arrow, and then click **Slant** in the first row, fourth column. Click the Top bevel **Width** box and type 40 Click the Top bevel **Height** box and type 20

> **Mac Troubleshooting**
> On a Mac, select the Cool Slant bevel.

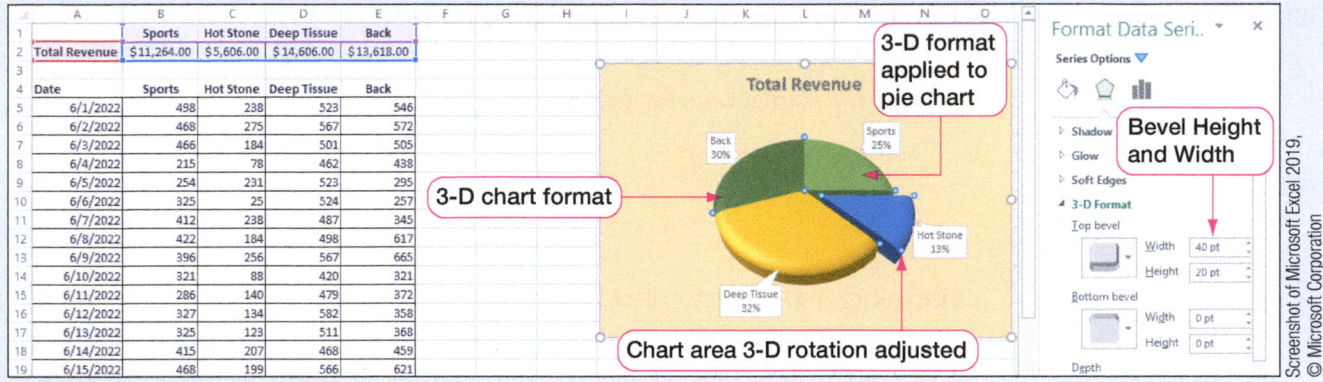

Figure 23 Pie chart with 3-D formatting

On the Format Data Series pane, click **Close** ☒.

g. **Save** 🖫 the workbook.

Modifying Axes

The horizontal x-axis and vertical y-axis scales are automatically created through a mathematical algorithm within Excel. However, sometimes the scale needs to be modified, as you have already seen. For example, when the scale of numbers is large, a significant gap can exist from 0 to the first data point. In this case, you can modify the scale to start at a more appropriate number instead of 0, which is the default minimum value for Excel. When you need to compare two or more charts, the scales must be consistent. Any time you put charts side by side, you also need to make sure your x-axis and y-axis scales are the same. Otherwise, your audience may not notice the difference and may make incorrect assumptions or decisions. The axis data may also be too crowded, making it difficult to read. In this situation, you would be able to modify the layout of the scale by adjusting the alignment of the data. The data on the axis can be vertical, horizontal, or even placed at an angle.

The Format Axis pane is used to manually set the axis options for consistency between a set of charts. Under the Axis Options, the default Excel scale minimum and maximum values are set automatically based on the data. This setting can be changed to allow for customized minimum and maximum values to be applied to the chart. If the source data for the chart is changed, the scale will remain fixed and will not automatically be updated; therefore, any fixed values may also need to be re-evaluated as source data changes.

In this exercise, you will change the minimum value of a chart.

 **E04.20**

SIDE NOTE
Deleting Chart Elements
A chart element can be easily removed by selecting the element and pressing Delete.

To Modify a Chart Axis

a. Click the **RedesignProject** worksheet, and then click the **chart border** of the stacked bar chart.

b. Double-click the **horizontal axis** for corresponding hours completed and hours remaining. This will open the Format Axis pane on the right side of the window.

c. In the Format Axis pane, click **Axis Options** ▷. Click the **Axis Options** arrow to expand the Axis Options group, and then click in the **Bounds** box for **Minimum**.

d. In the Minimum box, delete the existing value, type **20** and then press Enter.

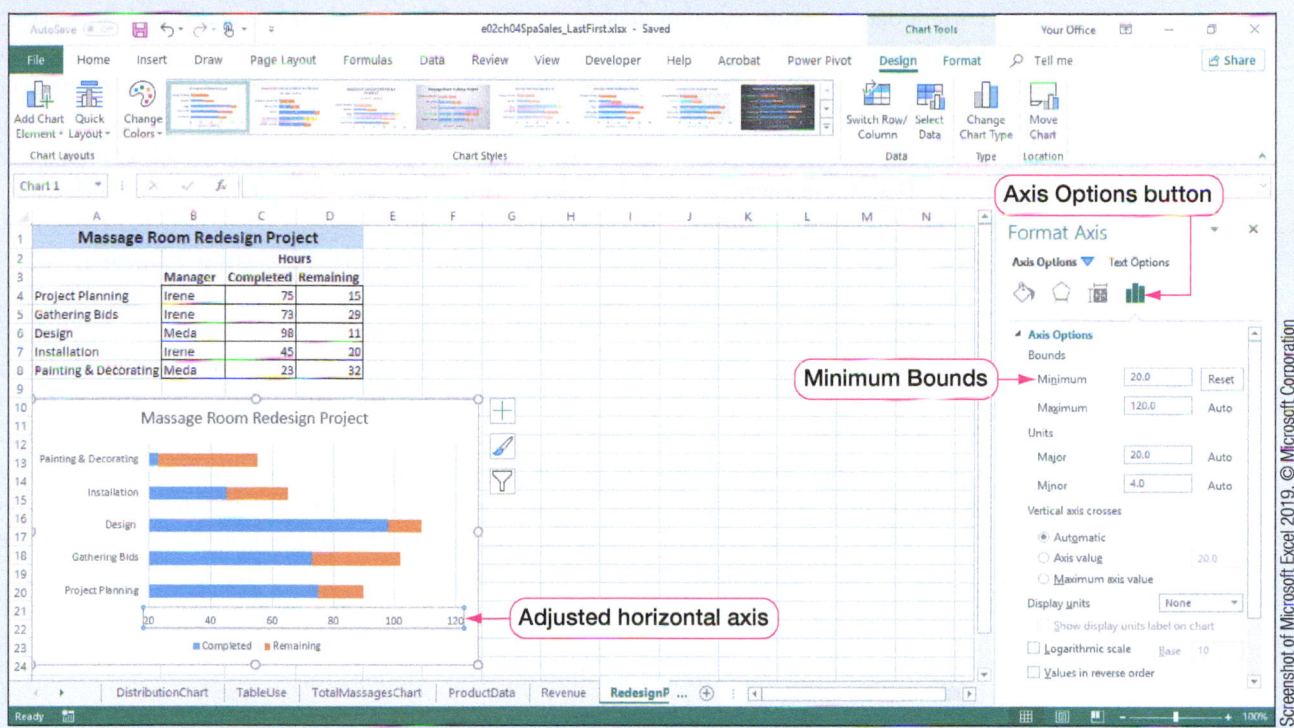

Figure 24 Stacked bar chart with modified chart axis

e. Click the **Survey** worksheet, and then select the scatter chart. Double-click the **vertical axis** corresponding to the temperature requested.

f. If necessary, in the Format Axis pane, click **Axis Options** ▷. Click the **Axis Options** arrow to expand the Axis Options group, and then click in the Bounds box for **Minimum**.

g. Select the existing number, type **65** and then press Enter.

Notice that the resulting scatter plot has a slight upward trend as the age of the customer increases. This knowledge may lead to decisions that help provide better customer service. You will learn more about modifying axes later in this chapter.

h. On the Format Axis pane, click **Close** ☒.

> **Troubleshooting**
>
> If the value you type in any of the Axis Options boxes does not work for your chart, click the Reset button to the right of the box to change the value back to the chart default.

i. **Save** 🖫 the workbook.

Analyzing with Trendlines

A common analysis tool to use within a chart is the trendline. A **trendline** is a line that uses current data to show a trend or general direction of the data. However, data can have a variety of patterns. For scatter plots that explore how two variables interact, a linear trend may be seen. If data fluctuates or varies a great deal, it may be more desirable to use a moving average trendline. Instead of creating a straight line based on all the current data, the moving average trendline uses the average of small subsets of data to set short trend segments over time. The moving average trendline will curve and adjust as the data moves up or down.

The trend or pattern of the data may suggest or predict what will happen in the future. For linear trends, the predicted data can be charted by using a linear trendline added to a scatter chart and the current trend of the data.

Adding a trendline for the scatter chart on the Survey worksheet data may help to confirm the hypothesis that older customers desire a warmer room than younger customers. This may lead the staff to adjust the room temperature before a customer arrives. The staff could predict the desired temperature based on the age of the customer. This could help to improve customer satisfaction. The spa may also want to consider other demographics or characteristics of the customers that allow for providing a customized and personalized service that will build customer loyalty and repeat business. It is easier to retain existing customers than find new ones.

The scatter chart on the Survey worksheet shows that as the age of the customer increases, so does the temperature of the room they request. In this exercise, you will add a trendline to this chart to further illustrate this relationship.

 E04.21

MAC COMPATIBILITY
Adding a Trendline on a Mac
To add a Trendline on a Mac, in the Chart Layouts group click Add Chart Element, point to Trendline, and then select More Trendline Options.

SIDE NOTE
Types of Trendlines
The type of trendline you apply to your chart will depend on your chart's data. You can fine-tune trendline settings in the Format Trendline pane.

To Insert a Trendline

a. On the **Survey** worksheet, click the **chart border** of the scatter chart if necessary.

b. To the right of the chart, click **Chart Elements** ⊞, and then click to select **Trendline**.

c. Click the **Trendline** arrow, and then click **More Options**. In the Format Trendline pane, click **Fill & Line** 🖎.

d. Click the **Color** arrow, and then select **Orange** from the Standard Colors.

e. Click the **Dash type** arrow, and then click **Solid** (the first option).

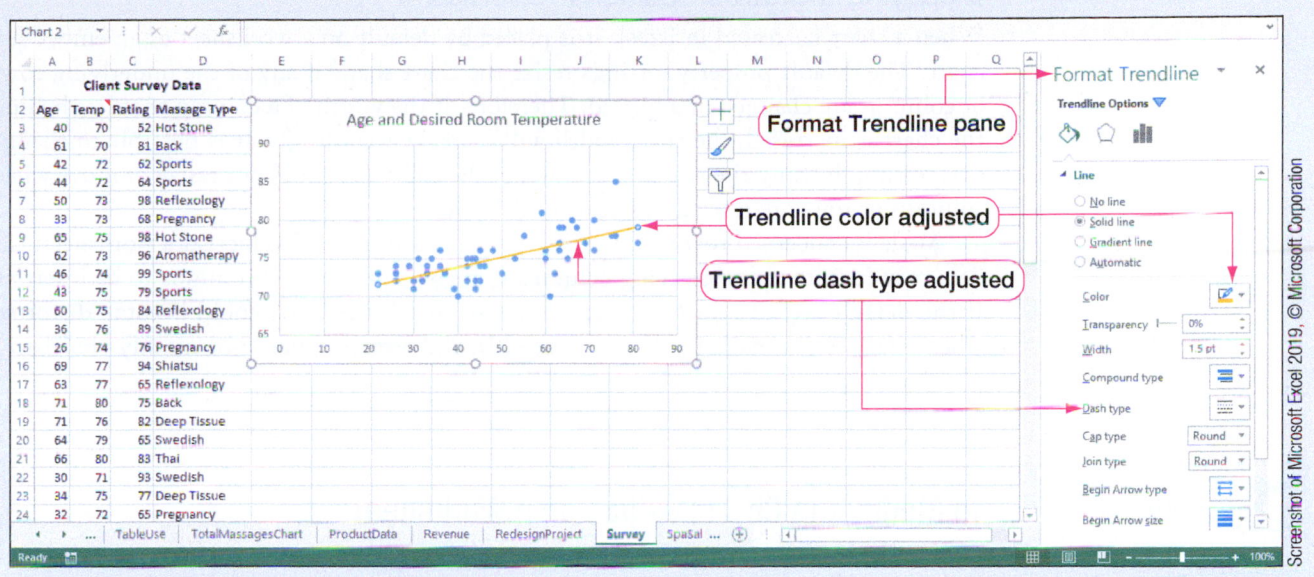

Figure 25 Scatter chart with trendline added

    f. In the Format Trendline pane, click **Close** ☒.

    g. Save 🖫 the workbook.

QUICK REFERENCE	Chart Trendlines

The following types of trendlines are available within Excel.

- **Linear**   Adds or sets a linear trendline for the selected chart series
- **Exponential**   Adds or sets an exponential trendline for the selected chart series
- **Linear Forecast**   Adds or sets a linear trendline with a two-period forecast for the selected chart series
- **Two-Period Moving Average**   Adds or sets a two-period moving average trendline for the selected chart series

---

REAL WORLD ADVICE	The Timing of Trends

Trends show patterns over time. In analyzing hourly sales at a restaurant, it becomes important to look at more than one day's worth of hourly sales to obtain a better understanding of the trend. Charting multiple days reveals any trends and consistent patterns. For example, maybe the chart shows that on Friday and Saturday, hourly sales are consistently higher than sales on other days of the week. This would suggest a need for scheduling more people to work on Fridays and Saturdays. If only one day had been charted or even just one week, the overall weekly trends may have been missed or interpreted incorrectly.

Modifying a Chart's Position Properties

When a chart is created in Excel, it is placed by default on a worksheet as an embedded chart. The default property settings resize the chart shape if any of the underlying rows or columns are changed or adjusted. Therefore, if the width of a column that lies behind the chart is increased, the chart width will increase accordingly. It is possible to change this setting, locking the size and position of the chart so it does not resize or move when columns or rows are resized, inserted, or deleted.

Meda is concerned that if additional data is added to the ProductData worksheet, the data may require the underlying columns to be widened or new columns to be inserted. If the default settings on the chart are not adjusted, the chart could become distorted when changes are made to the worksheet. In this exercise, you will modify the chart's position properties.

 **E04.22**

To Modify the Chart Position on a Worksheet

> **Grader Heads Up**
>
> The MyLab IT Grader version of this project does not include adjusting the size and properties of the area chart.

a. Click the **ProductData** worksheet, right-click the **chart border** of the area chart, and then select **Format Chart Area**. This will open the Format Chart Area pane.

b. In the Format Chart Area pane, click **Size & Properties** 🖽, and then click the **Properties** arrow to expand the Properties group.

c. Click **Move but don't size with cells**.

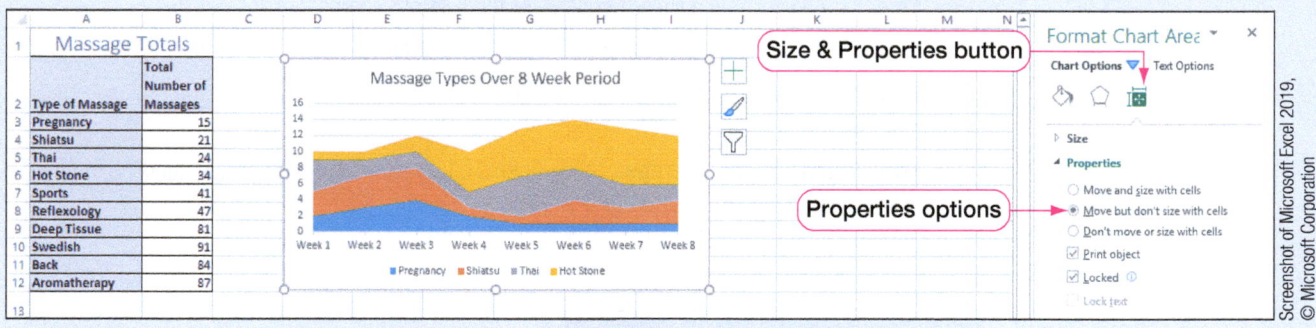

Figure 26   Format Chart Area task pane

d. In the Format Chart Area pane, click **Close** ☒.

e. **Save** 🖫 the workbook. If you need to take a break, now is a good time.

The chart size will not be resized if the width or height of the columns or rows underneath are changed or adjusted, but the chart will move along with the cells beneath the chart. From here, you can easily move the chart by dragging the border, or you can resize the chart by clicking and dragging the sizing handles.

Using Charts Effectively

The effectiveness of a chart depends on the chart type, the layout, and the formatting of the data. Charts should provide clarity and expand the viewer's understanding of the data. Charts used in a presentation should support the ideas you want to convey. The charts should highlight key components about an issue or topic being addressed in the presentation. In this section, you will use sparklines and data bars to emphasize data. You will also recognize and correct confusing charts.

Use Sparklines and Data Bars to Emphasize Data

The same data can be viewed through various perspectives, emphasizing different parts of the information. Charts typically do three things.

- Support or refute assertions
- Clarify information
- Help the audience understand trends

Sparklines and data bars are tools in Excel that can accomplish these three goals.

Emphasizing Data

As with any set of data, you can reasonably expect to find multiple ideas that could be emphasized in a chart. Typically, in a business setting, one to three key issues might be chosen for discussion. The idea is to eliminate any extraneous data from the chart that does not pertain to the issues being emphasized. Common methods can be employed to emphasize the idea in the chart. When using a single chart, highlight a particular data set within the chart to help focus attention to a key point. Depending on the chart type, the emphasis may be depicted differently, as shown in Table 1.

Single Chart Types	Common Emphasis Methods
Pie chart	Explode a pie slice
Bar/column	Use an emphasizing color on the bar/column
Line	Use line color, weight, and marker size
Scatter	Add a trendline

Table 1 Emphasis methods for single chart types

Exploring Sparklines

Sparklines are small charts embedded into cells on a spreadsheet, providing a way to graphically summarize a row or column of data in a single cell with a miniature chart. Sparklines are used to facilitate quick analysis of trends. A sparkline can be used within a worksheet to give an immediate visual trend analysis, and it adjusts as the source data changes. The sparkline can graphically depict the data over time through either a line chart or a bar chart that accumulates the data. Sparklines can also depict data points in the series as a win/loss chart. The default setting is for values above 0 to be a win while values below 0 are a loss. This value can be modified under the Format tab by using the Sparkline Axis button.

Irene and Meda would like to better examine sales of hair products at the spa. They have collected some data for you to analyze from the last eight weeks. In this exercise you will add sparklines adjacent to the data to emphasize the trend in products over time.

E04.23

SIDE NOTE
Alternate Method
Sparklines can also be inserted to the right of data by using the Quick Analysis tool.

To Insert Sparklines

a. If you took a break, open the **e02ch04SpaSales_LastFirst** workbook, and then click the **HairProducts** worksheet. Select cell range **A3:A7**.

b. Click the **Insert** tab, and then in the Sparklines group, click **Line**. In the Create Sparklines dialog box, in the Data Range box, type **C3:N7** and then click **OK**.

c. On the Sparkline Tools Design tab, in the Style group, click **More**, and then select **Blue, Sparkline Style Accent 1, Darker 25%** (First column, second row).

The sparklines show the changes in hair products sold over the 12 months represented by the data. Notice that sales of the For Men products were steady until month 7, when they spiked, then came back down in month 9, and then spiked again in month 11. This is very easy to visualize with sparklines next to the data.

d. With cell range A3:A7 still selected, on the Sparkline Tools Design tab, in the Style group, click the **Marker Color** arrow. Point to **High Point**, and then select **under Standard Colors**. Click cell **A1** to deselect the sparklines.

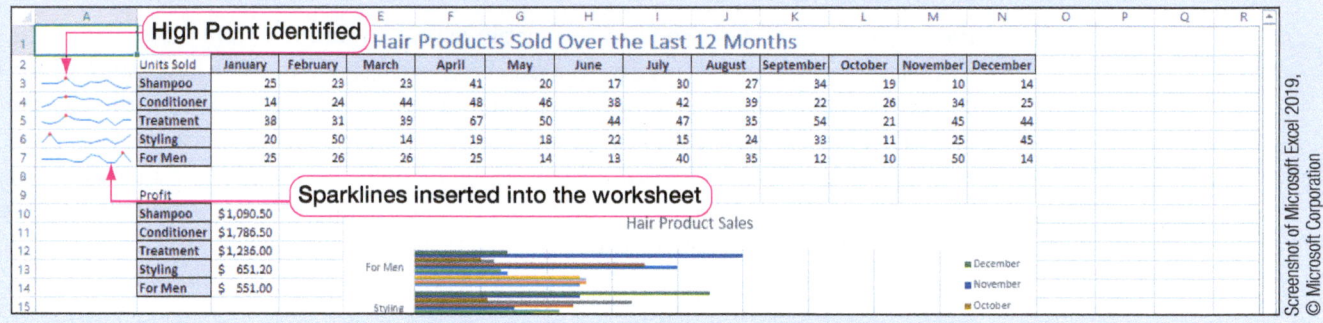

Figure 27 Sparklines applied to data

e. Save the workbook.

QUICK REFERENCE	**Working with Sparklines**

Using the following process will help in the development of sparklines.

- Select any cell within the added sparklines to display the Sparkline Tools contextual tabs.
- Ungroup sparklines using the Ungroup button on the Sparkline Tools Design tab.
- Group sparklines again using the Group button on the Design tab.
- Change colors and styles using the options available in the Style group.
- Choose to show high or low points using the options in the Show group.

Inserting Data Bars

Data bars are graphic components that are overlaid onto data in worksheet cells. The graphic component is added to a cell and interprets a set of data in a range in which the bar and, if necessary, the bar color are adjusted to help a spreadsheet user gain a quick understanding of the data. Data bars can be applied as a one-color solid fill or as a gradient fill from left to right as the numerical value gets bigger. Data bars are components of the Conditional Formatting feature. This technique can be employed with scores, ratings, or other data for which the user would want to do a visual inspection to see a relative scale on the data.

Irene and Meda have requested one more enhancement to the hair products analysis you have already begun. They would like a small visual cue added to a list of profits by hair product type. In this exercise, you will add data bars to the profits of all hair products sold at the spa over the past 12 months to emphasize which products were profitable and which were not profitable.

 **E04.24**

SIDE NOTE
Alternate Method
Data bars can also be inserted from the Quick Analysis tool. The default color is blue if you are using this method.

To Insert Data Bars

a. On the HairProducts worksheet, select cell range **C10:C14**.

b. Click the **Home** tab. In the Styles group, click **Conditional Formatting** ▦, and then point to **Data Bars**. Under Gradient Fill, click **Blue Data Bar** (first column, first row). The inserted data bars clearly show that Conditioner is the highest-grossing product, while For Men is the lowest-grossing product.

c. Click cell **A1** to deselect the data bars.

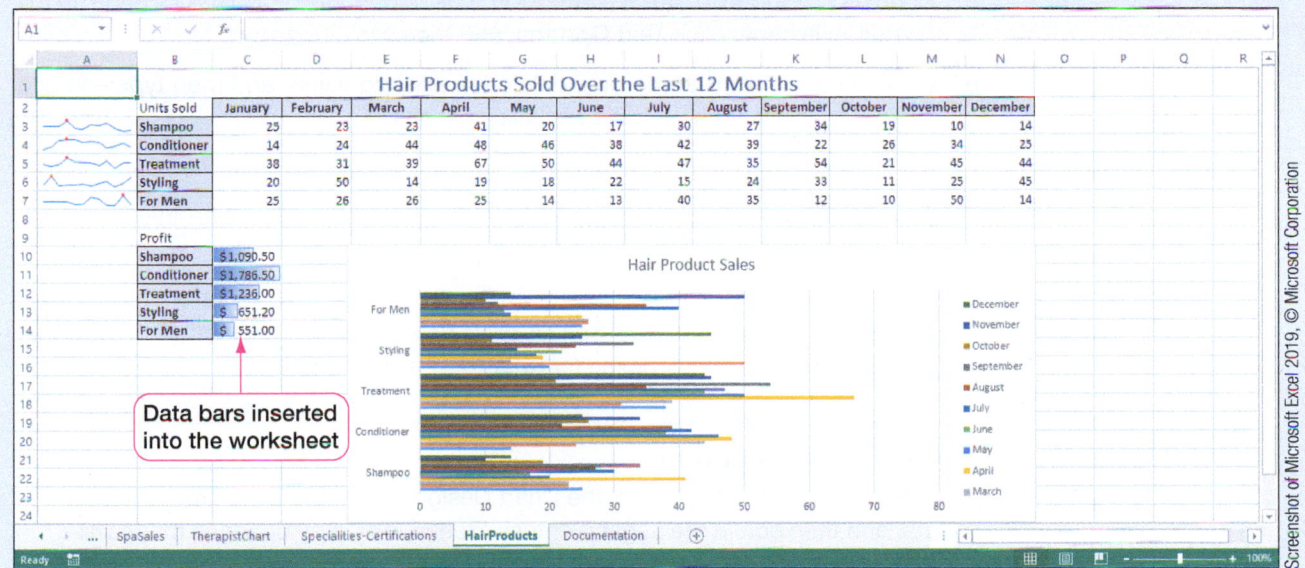

Figure 28   Data bars added to profit data

d. **Save** 💾 the workbook.

Recognize and Correct Confusing Charts

The process of working with and creating visually appealing charts with clear messages involves recognizing when you have a confusing chart. It is possible to have too much information or ambiguous information. This could include missing labels or legends, or there might be textual information on a chart that is not clear. Additionally, a common error is to use the incorrect chart type in analyzing data.

Correcting a Confusing Chart

Irene has pointed out that on the HairProducts sheet, a clustered bar chart was created that is difficult to interpret. The chart is based on the same data from which you created sparklines. Irene would like to be able to use the chart to compare different lines of product. The chart that was created shows the number of units sold as the bars, each product having a different bar for each month in the data. In this exercise, you will correct the chart so that it provides a meaningful representation of the data.

 E04.25

SIDE NOTE
Suggested Charts
Depending on your data, Excel may suggest a chart with the x-axis and y-axis already switched, saving you a step.

To Correct a Confusing Chart

a. On the **HairProducts** worksheet, click the **chart border** of the clustered bar chart.

Notice that this chart is showing time as a bar chart. Earlier in this chapter, you learned that a line chart is better for trends over time.

b. Click the **Chart Tools Design** tab, and then in the Type group, click **Change Chart Type**. In the Change Chart Type dialog box, on the All Charts tab, click **Line**, and then click **OK**.

c. In the Data group, click **Switch Row/Column**. Because the data being charted is time sensitive, the time element should be shown on the x-axis.

d. Double-click the **Horizontal (Category) Axis** to open the Format Axis pane. In the Format Axis pane, click **Text Options**, and then click **Textbox** 🔠.

e. Click in the **Custom angle** box, delete the existing value, and then type **–40** and press Enter. In the Format Axis pane, click **Close** ☒.

f. Click the **Chart Title** border, and then type **=** Click cell **B1**, and then press Enter.

Too many items on a chart can make a chart confusing, as with this line chart. Filtering a chart can improve the chart's readability.

g. Click the **chart border** of the line chart. To the right of the chart, click **Chart Filters** ▽, and then, under Series, click **Select All** to deselect all the product options. Click the check boxes for **Shampoo** and **Conditioner**.

> **Mac Troubleshooting**
> To filter a chart on a Mac, click the Chart Design tab, in the Data group Select Data, and then edit in the Legend entries (Series) box. Any changes made will break links to the source data on the worksheet.

> **Troubleshooting**
> If the Chart Elements, Chart Styles, and Chart Filters buttons do not automatically appear to the right of the selected chart, use the horizontal scroll bar to create more space to the right of the selected chart. The buttons will appear only if there is enough space beside the chart.

h. Click **Apply** at the bottom of the Chart Filters gallery, and then click **Chart Filters** ▽ again to close the gallery. Notice that the lines for these two products do not show similar trends, as might be expected.

> **Troubleshooting**
> If you cannot see the Apply button on your screen, you may need to close the dialog box, move the worksheet up, and try the steps again.

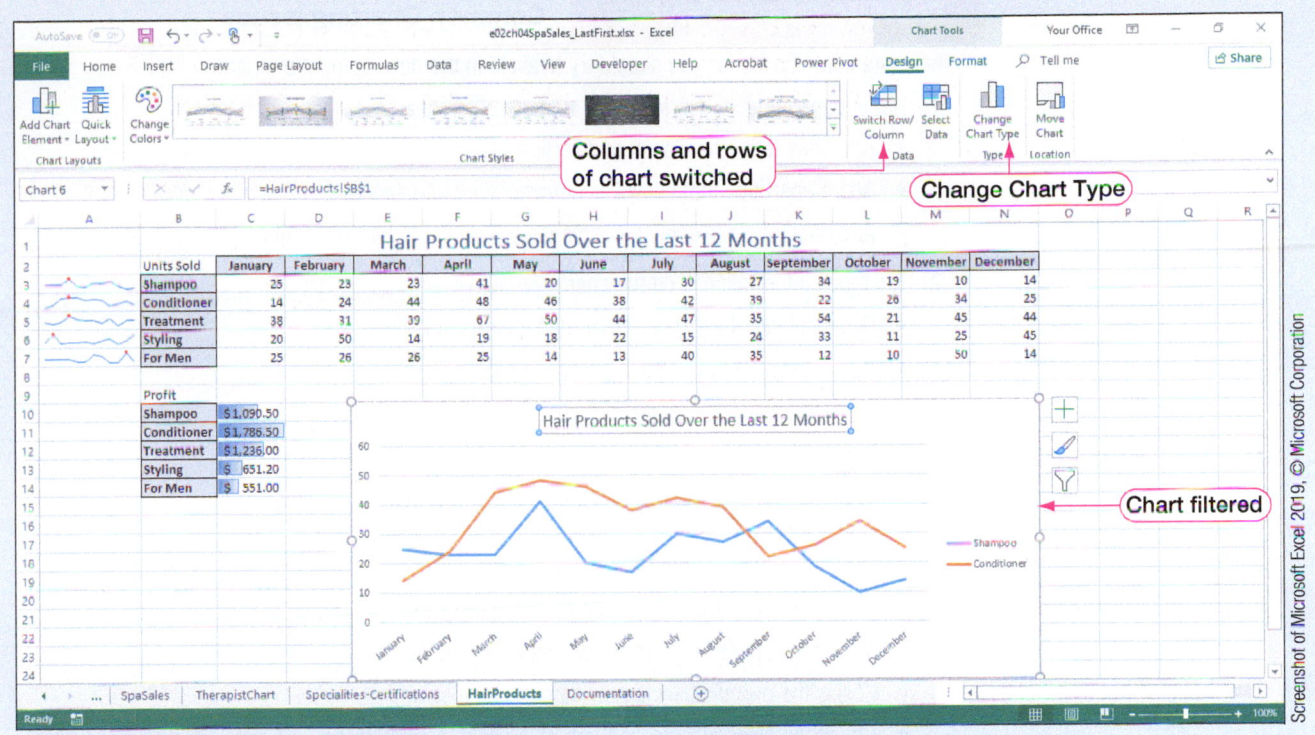

Figure 29 Filtered Line chart

> **Troubleshooting**
>
> If you click the chart to see the source data associated with the chart and see only some of the data selected with a blue border, you might have clicked a chart component by mistake instead of the full chart area. To get the data set associated with the entire chart, under Chart Tools, click the Format tab. In the Current Selection group, change the Chart Element to Chart Area. Data associated with the selected component will be highlighted with a colored border.

i. **Save** 💾 the workbook.

Preparing to Print a Chart

Printing a chart uses essentially the same process as printing a worksheet. When printing a chart sheet, select the chart sheet, go through the normal printing process, and adjust print options as you would for a worksheet. The chart will be a full-page display. If the chart is on a regular worksheet, it will be printed if you choose to print everything on the worksheet. In this case, the chart will be the size you developed on the worksheet. This is convenient when you want to print some tables or other data along with the chart. Finally, if you want to print just the chart on the worksheet, select the chart first, then choose the Print Selected Chart print option to print only the current chart.

Another useful technique in exploring data through charts is the ability to create static copies of the chart that can be used to compare with later versions. You can, in essence, take a picture of a chart that will not retain the underlying data. In this manner, subsequent versions of the chart can be made into images for comparisons. The process of creating a picture of the chart is to select the chart, copy it, then use the Paste Special option and paste it as a picture. When you paste as a picture, there are multiple picture format options, such as a PNG, JPEG, or GIF files.

QUICK REFERENCE | Common Charting Issues

These are common issues you should try to avoid in the development of charts.

1. Not enough context; users do not understand the chart.
   - Add titles to the horizontal and vertical axes.
   - Add a chart title that conveys context of time and scope.
   - Add data labels to show percentages or values of chart elements.

2. Too much information is on the chart.
   - Use a subset of the data rather than all the data.
   - Summarize the data so it is consolidated.

3. Incorrect chart type is used.
   - Choose a more appropriate type of chart, such as a line chart for trends.

4. Chart has issues with readability.
   - Check the color scheme to ensure that the text is readable.
   - Check font characteristics such as font type or font size.
   - Move data labels and remove excess information.
   - Resize the overall chart to provide more area to work.
   - Check the color scheme and formatting so it is professional and does not hide chart information or text.
   - Information or labeling is misleading.
   - Check the scaling to ensure that it is appropriate and labeled with the correct units.
   - Consider the following wording: Does "Sales" mean the number of transactions or the total revenue?

In this exercise, you will print the HairProducts chart.

To Print a Chart

a. On the **HairProducts** worksheet, click the **chart border** of the line chart.

b. Click the **File** tab, and then click **Print**. Notice that under Settings, the option for Print Selected Chart is selected by default. Also notice that only the chart is displayed in the preview pane. This is because you had the chart selected, not a cell within the worksheet.

c. Click the **Portrait Orientation** arrow, and then select **Landscape Orientation**.

d. Verify that the correct printer—as directed by your instructor—appears in the Printer box. Choices may vary depending on the computer you are using. If the correct printer is not displayed, click the Printer arrow, and then click to choose the correct or preferred printer from the list of available printers. If your instructor asks you to print the document, click **Print**.

e. Complete the Documentation worksheet as directed by your instructor.

f. **Save** the workbook, and then exit Excel. Submit your file as directed by your instructor.

Concept Check

1. What are some important items to consider in choosing the design and layout of a chart? p. 213

2. What are the two possible locations for a chart in Excel? Why would you choose one over the other? p. 217

3. Compare the purpose of a column chart and a pie chart. Give an example of a scenario in which you would use the two different types of charts. When would you create a combination chart to display worksheet data? p. 218–220

4. Why is it important to add elements and styles to charts such as titles, legends, and labels? p. 228–229

5. List two possible ways to add emphasis to an existing chart. p. 245

6. How are sparklines and data bars different from other chart objects in Excel? What are they commonly used for? p. 245–246

7. What are common mistakes that can be made in designing charts? Why is it important to correct these mistakes in existing charts? p. 247–248

Key Terms

Area chart   p. 225
Bar chart   p. 223
Chart gridlines   p. 235
Chart sheet   p. 217
Column chart   p. 218
Combination chart   p. 226
Data bar   p. 246
Data point   p. 214
Data series   p. 214
Data visualization   p. 213
Embedded chart   p. 217
Ideas   p. 218
Legend   p. 234
Line chart   p. 221
Pie chart   p. 220
Quick Analysis   p. 218
Recommended Charts   p. 219
Scatter chart   p. 224
Sparkline   p. 245
Stacked bar chart   p. 223
Sunburst chart   p. 226
Trendline   p. 242

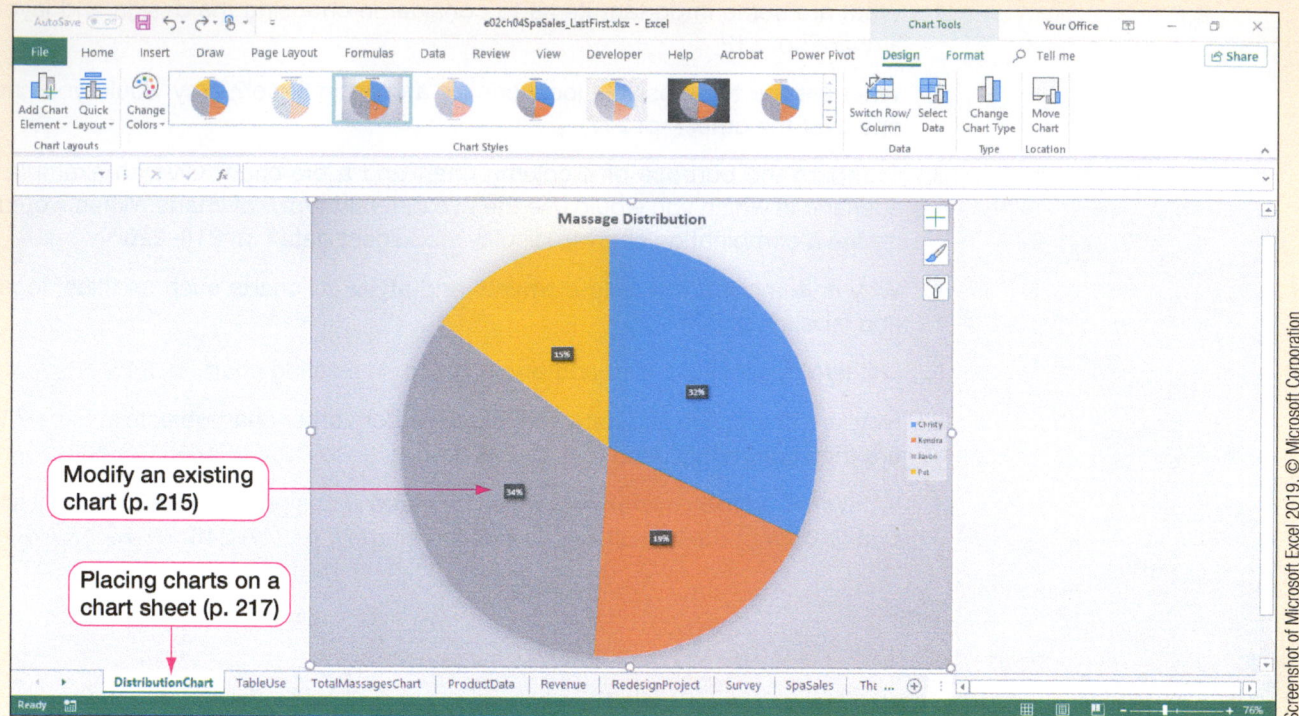

Figure 30

Figure 31

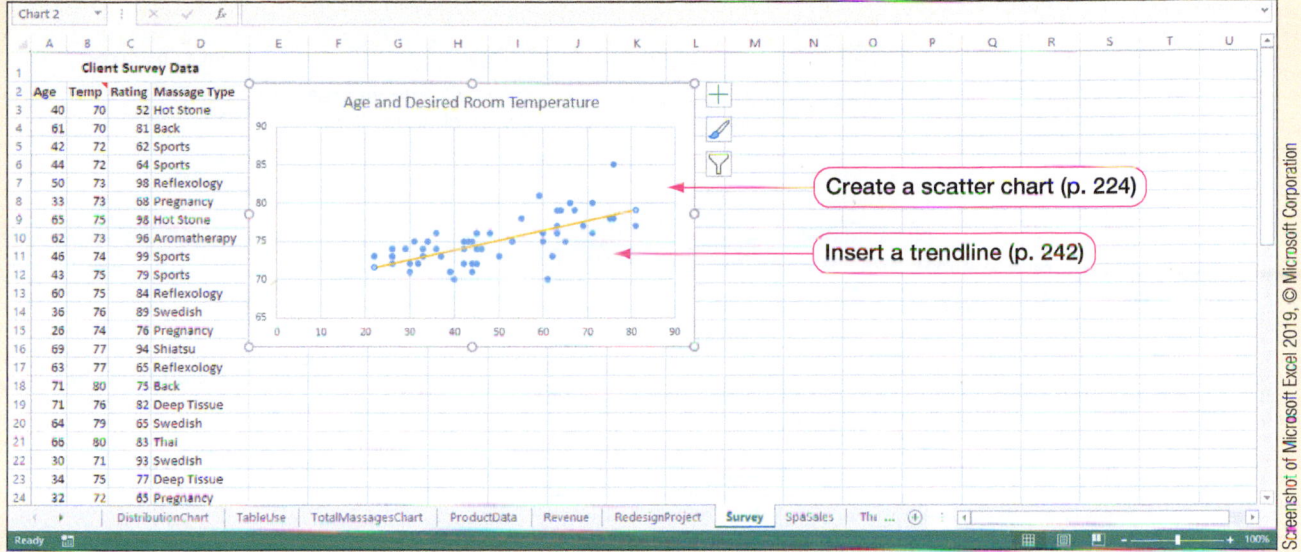

Figure 32

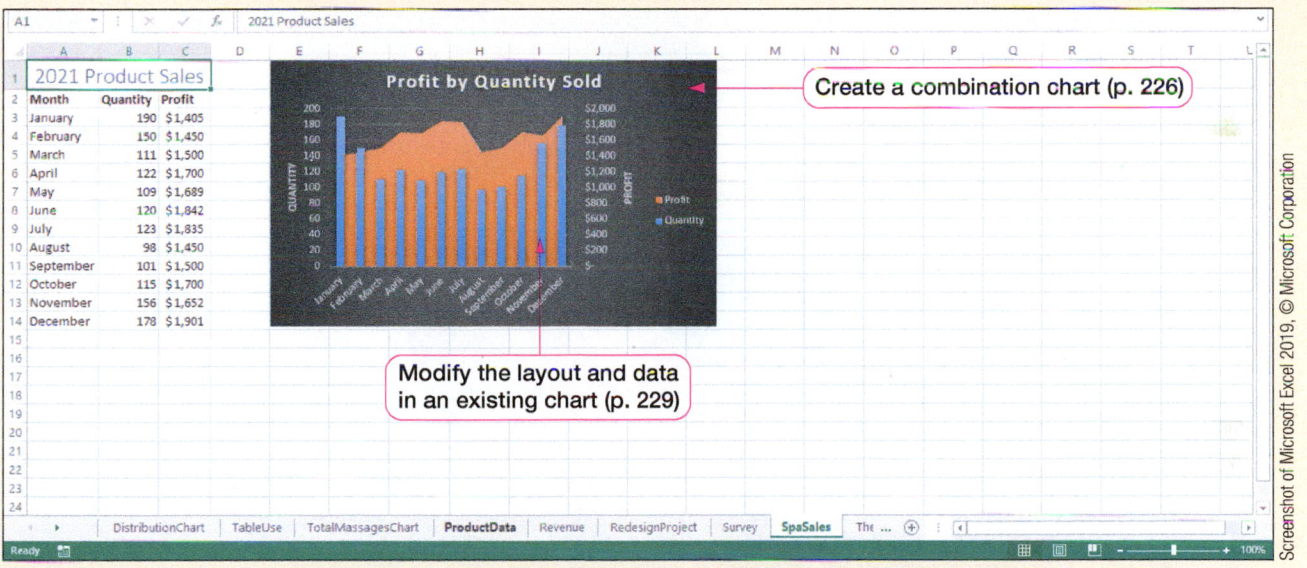

Figure 33

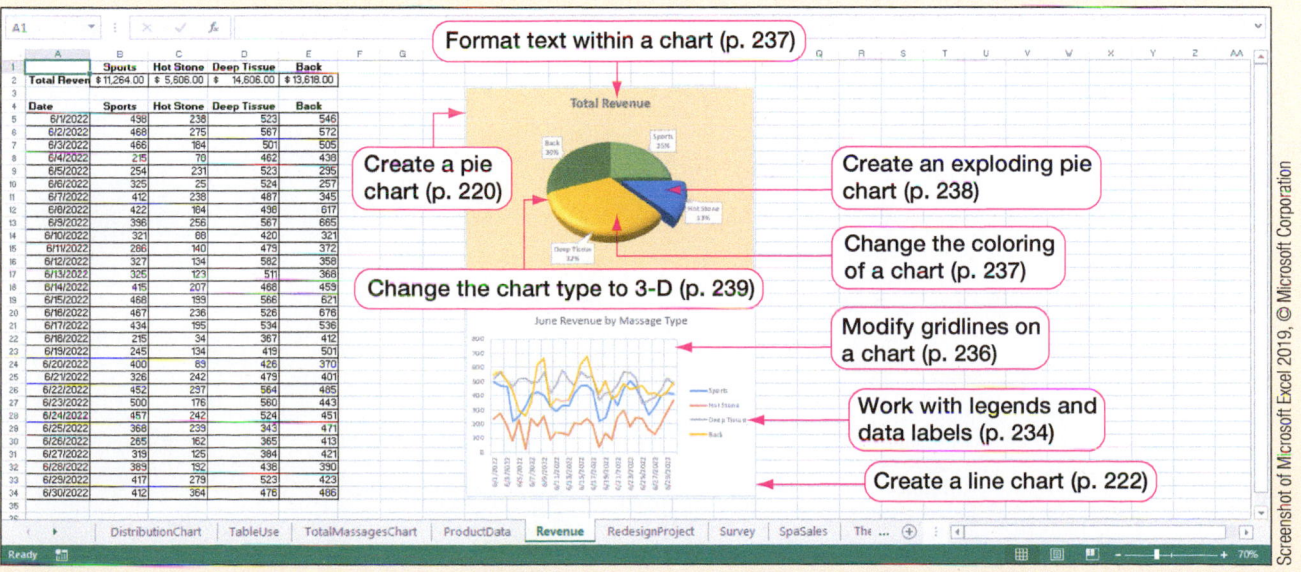

Figure 34

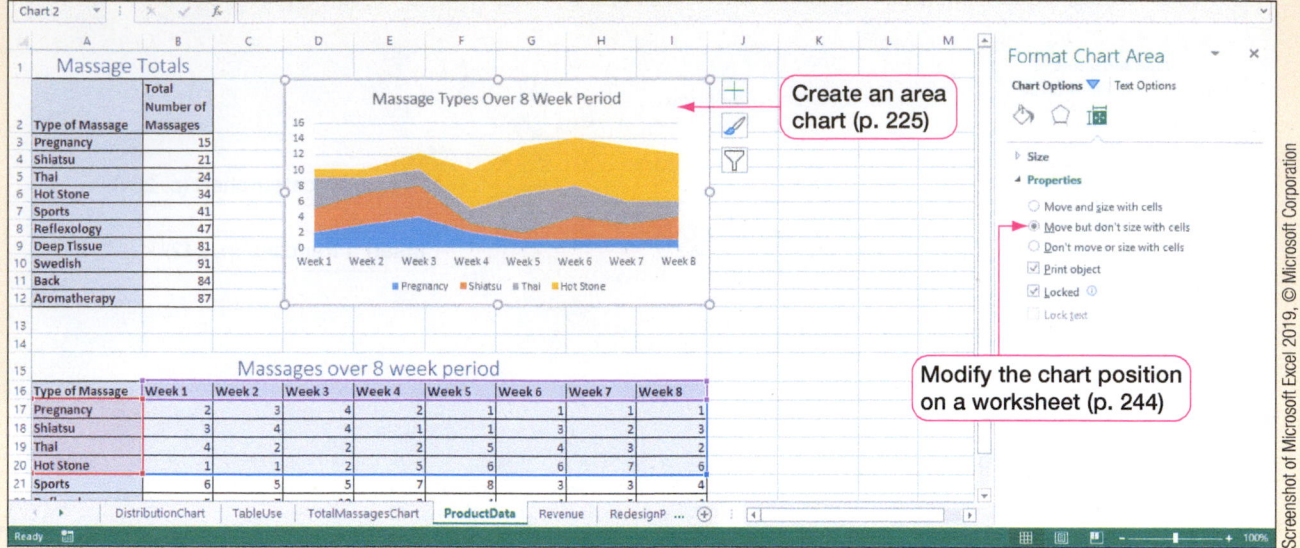

Figure 35

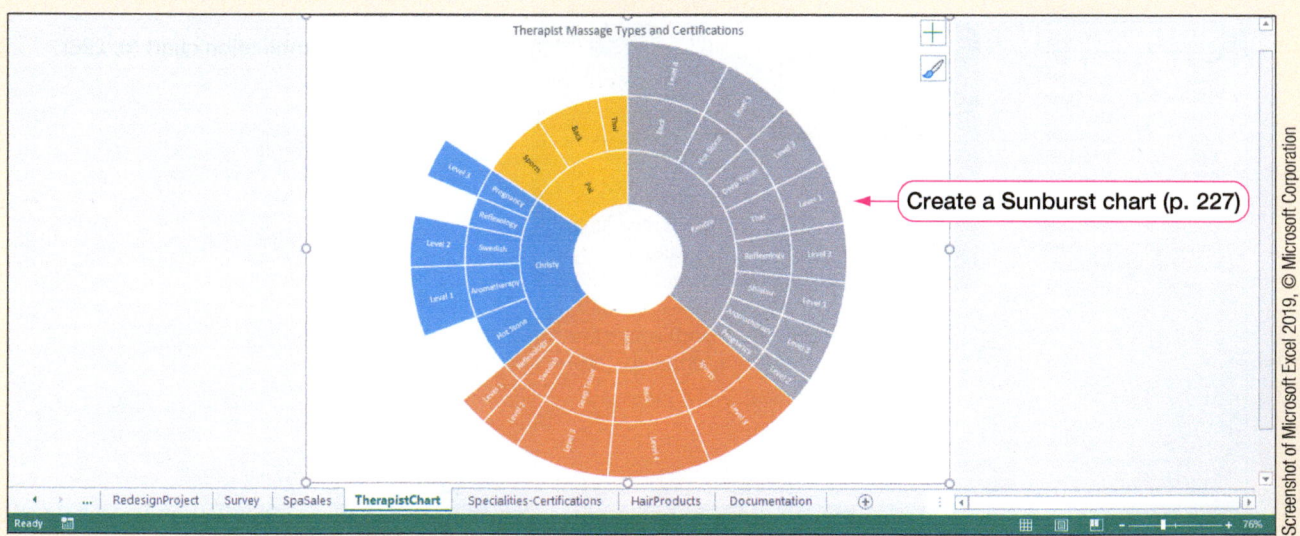

Figure 36

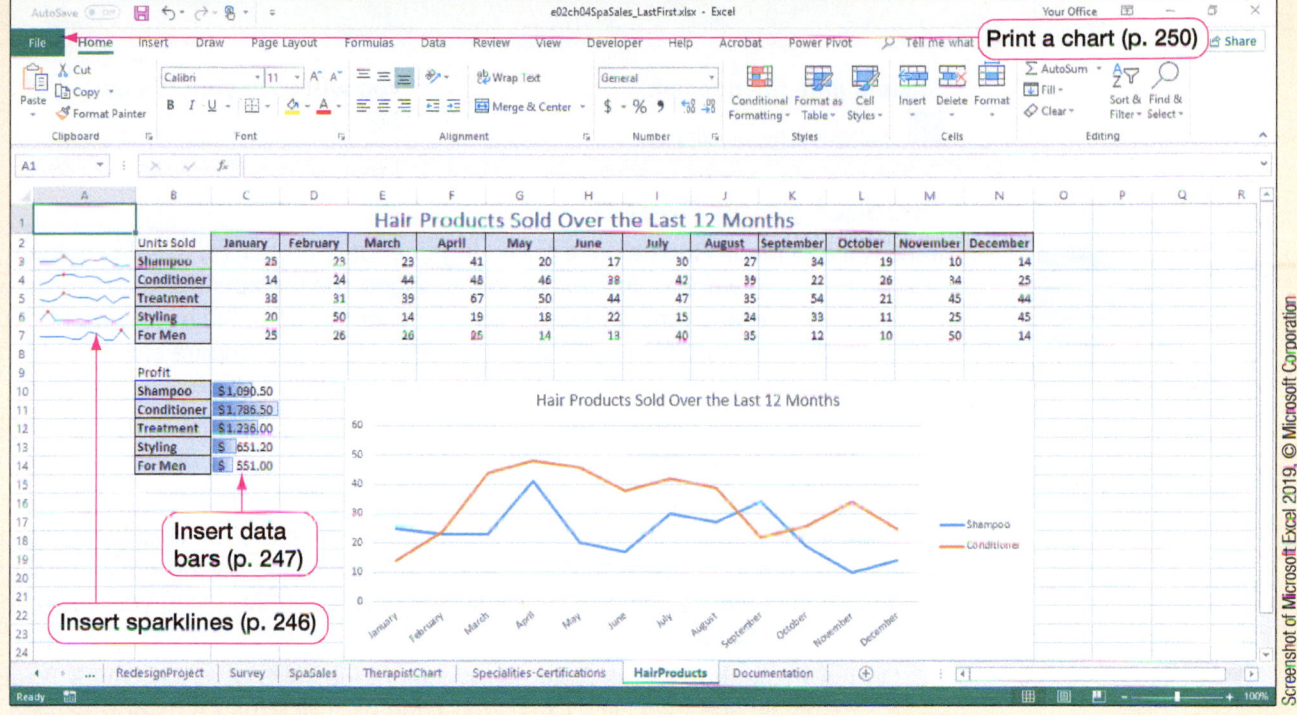

Figure 37

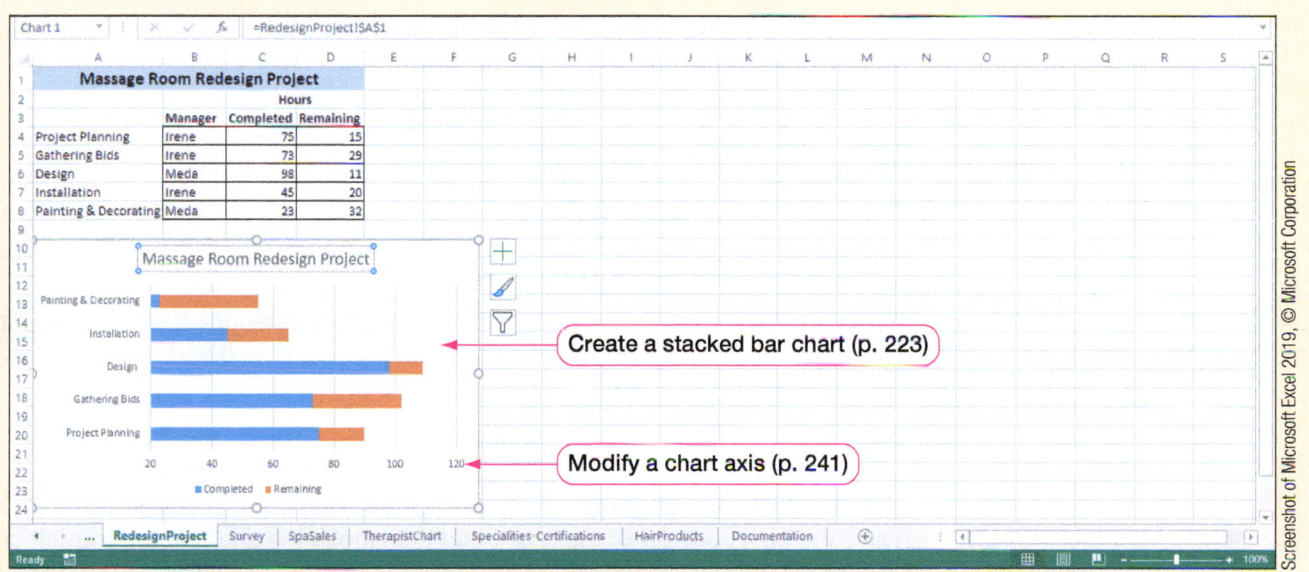

Figure 38

Student data file needed:

 e02ch04Summary.xlsx

You will save your file as:

 e02ch04Summary_LastFirst.xlsx

Sales & Marketing

Product Sales Report

Irene Kai and Meda Rodate have pulled together data pertaining to sales made by the spa's massage therapists. In addition to massages, the therapists should promote skin care, health care, and other products. With the monthly data, the managers want a few charts developed that will enable them to look at trends, compare sales, and provide feedback to the therapists. You are to help them create the charts.

a. Start Excel, click **Open** in the left pane, and then double-click **This PC**. Navigate through the folder structure to the location of your student data files, and then click **e02ch04Summary**. If necessary, click **Enable Editing**.

b. Click the **File** tab, then click **Save As**, and then double-click **This PC**. In the Save As dialog box, navigate to the location where you are saving your project files, and change the file name to e02ch04Summary_LastFirst using your last and first name. Click **Save**.

c. On the **Projections** worksheet, select cell range **A4:B12**. Click **Quick Analysis**, click **Charts**, and then click **Clustered Column**. Click the **chart border**, and then move the chart so the top-left corner is over cell **D4**. Adjust the size of the chart so the bottom-right corner is over cell **J15**.

d. Click the **Chart Title** border, type = Click cell **A1**, and then press Enter.

e. To the right of the chart, click **Chart Styles**, and then click **Style 9** from the list. Click **Chart Styles** again to close the gallery.

f. Double-click the **chart area** to open the Format Chart Area pane. Click the **Size & Properties** button. If necessary, expand the **Properties** category, and then select **Move but don't size with cells**.

g. Click the **Vertical (Value) Axis** to open the Format Axis pane. Click **Axis Options**. In the Axis Options Bounds, click in the **Minimum** box, clear the existing text, and then type 100 and then press Enter.

h. In the Format Axis pane, scroll down to the Number category. If necessary, expand the **Number** category, and then in **Decimal places**, type 0 and then press Enter.

i. **Close** the Format Axis pane.

j. Click the **Transactions** worksheet tab. Select cell range **B4:J4**, press and hold Ctrl, and then select cell range **B9:J9**. On the Insert tab, in the Charts group, click the **Insert Pie or Doughnut Chart** arrow. Click **Pie**, the first option under 2-D Pie. Click the **chart border** of the chart, and then move the chart so the top-left corner is over cell **C11**.

k. Click the **Chart Title** border, type Total Transactions by Therapist and then press Enter.

l. To the right of the chart, click **Chart Elements**. Click the **Data Labels** arrow, and then click **More Options**. In the Format Data Labels pane, under Label Options, under Label Contains, click to select **Percentage**. Click **Value** to deselect that label. Under Label Position, select **Outside End**. Close the Format Data Labels pane.

m. To the right of the chart, click **Chart Elements**. Click the **Legend** arrow, and then click **Right**. Click **Chart Elements** again to close the gallery.

n. Click the **Pie** chart, being careful not to click the label text. Click once again on the **orange pie slice** that has the associated label 6%. Drag the slice slightly to the right so it is exploded from the rest of the pie.

o. Double-click the **exploded pie** element to open the Format Data Point pane. If necessary, click the **Series Option** button. In the Series Options, type 25% if necessary to change the Point Explosion box to 20%. **Close** the Format Data Point pane.

p. To the right of the chart, click the **Chart Filters** button. Click **Select All** to clear the categories. Click **Irene**, **Meda**, **Christy**, and **Kendra**, and then click **Apply**. Click Chart Filters again to close it.

q. On the Chart Tools Design tab, click **Change Chart Type**. Select **3-D Pie**, and then click **OK**.

r. On the Chart Tools Format tab, in the Current Selection group, click the **Chart Elements** arrow, select **Plot Area**, and then double-click the plot area to open the Format Plot Area pane. Click the **Effects** button, and then click to expand the **3-D Rotation** category. Select the Y Rotation, type 40 and then press ⏎. **Close** the Format Plot Area pane.

s. With the Pie chart still selected, on the Chart Tools Design tab, in the Location group, click **Move Chart**. Click **New sheet**, type PieChart and then click **OK**.

t. On the PieChart sheet, click any one of the **data labels** to select all the data labels. Click the **Home** tab, and then in the Font group, select **20**. Click the **chart title** border, and then on the Home tab, in the Font group, select **20**. Select the **Legend**, and then on the Home tab, in the Font group, select **20**.

u. Click the **chart title** border, and then click the **Chart Tools Format** tab. In the WordArt Styles group, click the **Fill: Orange, Accent color 2; Outline: Orange, Accent color 2** (top row, third column) to format the chart title.

v. Click the **Revenue** worksheet, and then select the Area chart. On the Chart Tools Design tab, click **Change Chart Type**. In the Change Chart Type dialog box, select **Column**, and then click **OK** to select the default Clustered Column chart. On the Chart Tools Design tab, click **Switch Row/Column**.

w. Select the cell range **B9:J9**. Click the **Insert** tab, and then, in the Sparklines group, click **Line** to add sparklines to the worksheet. In the Data Range box, type B5:J8 and then click **OK**. On the Sparkline Tools Design tab, in the Style group, click the **Marker Color** arrow, point to **High Point**, and then click **Red**. Click any cell outside of the sparklines to deselect the sparklines.

x. On the **Revenue** worksheet, select cell range **K5:K8**. Click the **Home** tab, and then in the Styles group, click **Conditional Formatting**, point to **Data Bar**, and then under Gradient Fill, select **Blue Data Bar**.

y. Complete the Documentation worksheet according to your instructor's directions.

z. Save the workbook, close Excel, and then submit your file as directed by your instructor.

MyLab IT Grader

Student data file needed:

 e02ch04Advertising.xlsx

You will save your file as:

e02ch04Advertising_LastFirst.xlsx

Finance & Accounting

Sales & Marketing

Advertising

The marketing manager of the Painted Paradise Golf Resort & Spa, Timothy Smith, has created a spreadsheet of the first six months (first two quarters) of advertising expenses for the various amenities of the resort. He is planning to display the data at the next Board of Directors meeting and wants to create a few charts to make the figures easier to view and the presentation more visually appealing.

a. Open the Excel file, **e02ch04Advertising**. Save your file as e02ch04Advertising_ LastFirst using your last and first name.

b. On the AdvertisingCosts worksheet, create a **Line chart** of the data for the total spent on advertising each month from January through June. The primary Horizontal (Category) Axis should be the months of the year, and the Vertical (value) Axis should be the total spent on advertising each month.

c. Change the chart title of the line chart to Total Advertising Expenses per Month

d. Change the Vertical Axis minimum to 26000 and then change the chart style to **Style 12**.

e. Move the line chart to a **chart sheet**, and then name the sheet AdvertisingMonthlyTotals

f. On the AdvertisingCosts worksheet, create a 3-D Pie chart of the amenities and their six-month totals in cell range **A16:B22**. Reposition the chart so the left corner of the chart is in cell **C14**. Resize the chart so the bottom-right corner is in cell **H29**.

g. On the 3-D pie chart, insert the title Semi-Annual Advertising Costs and then apply **Style 8** to the chart.

h. Change the colors of the chart to **Colorful Palette 2**.

i. Add **Data Callout** as data labels to the 3-D pie chart. Include the **category name** and **percentage** in the data labels.

j. On the 3-D pie chart, explode the segment of the chart that was allocated the smallest amount of advertising funds, Exercise Facility, to 25%

k. Adjust the 3-D Rotation of the pie chart to the following:

- X rotation of 20
- Y Rotation of 40
- Perspective of 10

Grader Heads Up

In the MyLab IT Grader version of this project, a top bevel will not be added.

l. Modify the 3-D Format of the pie chart Top bevel to **Round**.

m. In cell range **H5:H11**, add **Column sparklines** that chart the advertising expense by amenity type over the months January to June. Apply the style **Dark Blue, Sparkline Style Accent 5, Darker 50%**.

n. In the cell range **B16:B22**, apply a **Gradient Fill Blue Data Bar**.

o. Create a Clustered Column chart from cell range **A4:G11**. Move the chart to a chart sheet named MonthlyExpenses

p. Change the chart title to Monthly Expenses for January - June

q. Filter the chart so only the **Exercise Facility, Banquet Facilities,** and **Technology Facilities** are showing.

r. Apply **Style 8** to the clustered column chart. Change the colors of the chart to **Monochromatic Palette 5.**

s. Update the Documentation worksheet according to your instructor's directions.

t. Save the workbook, close Excel, and then submit your file as directed by your instructor.

Critical Thinking On the pie chart, you added percentages as data labels. Why are percentage data labels often added to a pie chart?

Perform 1: Perform in Your Career

Student data file needed:

 e02ch04Homes.xlsx

You will save your file as:

 e02ch04Homes_LastFirst.xlsx

Research & Development

Real Estate

You are interning at Schalow Real Estate Company. Your supervisor wants to know why some houses sell quickly and others take more time. She asks you to create charts from data to help her analyze and look for sales trends.

a. Open the Excel file **e02ch04Homes**. Save your file as e02ch04Homes_LastFirst using your last and first name.

b. On the PropertiesSold worksheet, create a line chart showing the number of days on the market over time. Plot the days on the market on the y-axis and the sold date on the x-axis.

c. Add a linear trendline to your chart. Change the trend line Dash type to Solid.

d. Format the chart using an appropriate style, and position it below the data in the approximate cell range A40:F54. Add the Primary Vertical Gridlines to the chart.

e. Create a line chart that shows how the price per square foot of the sold properties has changed over time.

f. Add a linear trendline to your chart. Change the trend line Dash type to Solid.

g. Format the chart using a style of your choice, and position it below the data in the approximate cell range H40:N54. Add the Primary Vertical Gridlines to the chart.

h. On the Summary worksheet, the first group of data in cell range A2:D11 describes homes sold in all developments. Use that data to create three charts using a style of your choice, and show the following on the three different charts.

- The Average Number of Days on Market by Development
- The Average Percent of List Price by Development
- The Average of Sold Price by Development

i. Create a new worksheet in your workbook. Name the new worksheet Charts

j. Move the three charts showing averages by development to the Charts worksheet. Position them in the approximate cell ranges A1:I15, A17:I31, and A33:I47.

k. On the Summary worksheet, in cell A38, type your last name

l. Create a chart that shows the average number of days it took a home to sell by salesperson.

m. Format this chart using the same style used for the other three charts. Position the chart on the Charts worksheet in the approximate cell range K1:R15.

n. Complete the Documentation worksheet according to your instructor's directions.

o. Save the workbook, close Excel, and submit your file as directed by your instructor.

Conducting Business Analysis

This business unit had two outcomes:

Learning Outcome 1:

Use Excel to create formulas and functions to perform calculations, analyze data, solve problems, and help in making wise business decisions.

Learning Outcome 2:

Use Excel to create a variety of detailed charts appropriate to the data that will visually represent and analyze the data.

In Business Unit 2 Capstone, students will demonstrate competence in these outcomes through a series of business problems at various levels from guided practice to problem solving an existing spreadsheet and creating new spreadsheets.

More Practice 1

Student data file needed:

 e02Sales.xlsx

You will save your file as:

e02Sales_LastFirst.xlsx

Sales & Marketing

Finance & Accounting

Restaurant Marketing Analysis

The accounting system at the Indigo5 Restaurant tracks data daily that can be used for analysis to gauge its performance and determine any needed changes. The restaurant is considering entering into a long-term agreement with a poultry company and getting a new refrigeration unit to store the chicken. If Indigo5 enters the agreement, the poultry company agrees to give Indigo5 a substantial discount for a specified period. Management would like to stimulate sales for the lowest-revenue-producing chicken item and any chicken items that do not meet a sale performance threshold. To accomplish this, some of the savings will be passed on to the guests by having these chicken items put on special at a lower price.

a. Open **Excel**, click **Open** in the left pane, and then double-click **This PC**. Navigate through the folder structure to the location of your student data files, and then double-click **e02Sales**. If a Security Warning message displays, click **Enable Editing**.

b. Click the **File** tab, click **Save As**, and then double-click **This PC**. In the Save As dialog box, navigate to the location where you are saving your project files, and then change the file name to e02Sales_LastFirst using your last and first name. Click **Save**.

c. On the ChickenSales worksheet, click cell **D2**. Enter the formula =TODAY() and then press Enter.

Notice the data on the worksheet. The cell range A13:E18 contains four months of actual sales quantities for each menu item. The cell range A22:E27 contains the sales projections that Indigo5 made for the same four months before the start of each month.

d. Click cell **B4**. On the Home tab, in the Editing group, click **AutoSum**, select cell range B22:E22, and then press Ctrl + Enter. In cell **B4**, double-click the **fill handle** to fill the formula through B4:B9. The range now returns the total quantity projection over the four months for each item.

e. Format cell range **B4:B9** with comma style, zero decimal places.

f. Click cell **C4**. On the Home tab, in the Editing group, click **AutoSum**, select cell range **B13:E13**, and then press [Ctrl]+[Enter]. In cell **C4**, double-click the **fill handle** to fill the formula through C4:C9. The range now returns the total quantity of actual sales over the four months for each item.

g. Format cell range **C4:C9** with comma style, zero decimal places.

h. Click cell **D4**, On the Home tab, in the Editing group, click the AutoSum arrow, select **Average**, and then select cell range **B13:E13**. Press [Ctrl]+[Enter]. In cell **D4**, double-click the **fill handle** to fill the formula through D4:D9. The range now returns the average monthly quantity for actual sales over the four months for each item.

i. Format cell range **D4:D9** with comma style, two decimal places.

j. Now you need to determine the price for each item to use in revenue calculations. Notice that a list of menu prices is in cells A30:B44. Select cell range **A30:B44**. Click the **Name Box**, type Prices and then press [Enter]. The price listing is now named Prices to use in later calculations.

k. Now you want to assign the price of each item by looking up the item and exactly matching the item name in the Prices list. Click cell **E4**, enter the formula =VLOOKUP(A4,Prices,2,FALSE) and then press [Ctrl]+[Enter]. Be sure to use the range name **Prices** in the formula. In cell **E4**, double-click the **fill handle** to fill the formula through **E4:E9**.

l. To determine the total revenue for each item, click cell **F4**, enter the formula =E4*C4 and then press [Ctrl]+[Enter]. In cell **F4**, double-click the **fill handle** to fill the formula through **F4:F9**.

m. Now you need to determine whether the item fell short of the sales projection or exceeded it. Click cell **G4**, enter the formula =ROUND(C4/B4,2) and then press [Ctrl]+[Enter]. In cell **G4**, double-click the **fill handle** to fill cell range **G4:G9**.

n. The range now returns a projection percentage. An item that fell short of the sales projection will be under 100%. An item that exceeded the sales projection will be over 100%.

o. Now you need to determine what item has the highest revenue. Click cell **H4**, enter the formula =IF(F4=MAX($F$4:$F$9),"Best Item","") and then press [Ctrl]+[Enter]. In cell **H4**, double-click the **fill handle** to fill the formula through **H4:H9**.

p. The range now returns a blank for all items except the one with the highest sales revenue, which returns Best Item.

q. Next you need to determine which items to put on sale to stimulate sales. An item should be put on sale if its % of Projection is less than the Sale Threshold in cell L4. Click cell **I4**, and then click the **Formulas** tab. In the Formulas tab, in the Function Library group, click Logical, and then select **IF**.

- For the logical test, type G4<$L$4
- For the Value if true, "Put on Sale"
- For the Value if false, type "" and then click **OK**.
- In cell **I4**, double-click the **fill handle** to fill the formula through cell range **I4:I9**.

The range now returns Put on Sale for two items: the items with a % of Projection less than 95%. All other items return a blank.

r. You also need to know how many days the sale will last based on dates given by the poultry company. Click cell **L7**, type =DATEDIF(L5,L6,"D") and then press [Ctrl]+[Enter].

s. Select cell range **B13:E18**. Click the **Insert** tab, and then, in the Sparklines group, click **Line**. Select the location cell range **F13:F18**, and then click **OK**. Click the **Sparkline Tools Design** tab, and then, in the Show group, click the **Markers** check box.

t. To represent the data, you want to create a chart comparing the percentage of all sales each item represents. Select cell range **A3:A9**. Press and hold Ctrl, and then select cell range **F3:F9**.

- Click the **Insert** tab, and then, in the Charts group, click the **Insert Pie or Doughnut Chart** button. Select the first option for a Pie Chart.
- Click the **chart border**, and then drag to move the chart so the top left corner is over the top left corner of cell **H11**. Click on the right resizing handle, and then drag the right chart border to move the bottom-right corner to cell **O25**.
- On the **Chart Tools Design** tab, in the Chart Styles group, select **Style 11**.
- Click the **chart title border**, type Chicken Sales Revenue and then press Enter. On the Home tab, in the Font group, decrease the font size of the title text to **14**. Click cell **D1** to deselect the chart.

u. Then you want to count how many items will be on sale next. Click cell **O4**. Click the **Formulas** tab. In the Function Library group, click the **More Functions** button, point to **Statistical**, and then click **COUNTIF**. For the range, type I4:I9 and then press Tab. For the Criteria, type N4 and then click **OK**.

You need to look at loan options for the new refrigeration unit by looking at a quarterly payment as it varies for different numbers of payments (or terms in years) and the annual interest rate.

v. Click the **PoultryLoan** worksheet tab. Indigo5 would like to make quarterly payments (four payments per year). Click cell **C12**, enter the formula =-PMT($B12/4,C$11*4,$C$6) and then press Ctrl+Enter.

w. In cell **C12**, double-click the **fill handle** to fill the formula through cell range **C12:C14**. With C12:C14 selected, drag the **fill handle** to column **E** to fill through cell range **C12:E14**.

Notice that the mixed cell addressing of the dollar sign before the B will make the B stay the same rather than changing when copied, and the same holds true for the dollar sign before the 11. Notice that, when copied, the formula will always contain $C$6, because it has an absolute reference of a dollar sign before both the column and the row.

x. Indigo5 would like to use the option that keeps the payment under $2,000, has the shortest term, and has the lowest interest rate. Click cell **E13**, and then click the **Bold** button to indicate that option as the best.

y. Click the **ChickenSales** worksheet tab. Click the **Page Layout** tab, and then, in the Page Setup group, click the **Page Setup Dialog Box Launcher**. Click the **Header/Footer** tab. Click **Custom Footer**, then click the **Insert File Name** button to place the file name in the left section of the footer. Click **OK** twice. Repeat this step for the **PoultryLoan** worksheet.

> ### Mac Troubleshooting
> On a Mac, click the Page Layout tab, and in the Page Setup group, click the Page Setup button to open the Page Setup dialog box.

z. Complete the remainder of the **Documentation** worksheet according to your instructor's directions.

aa. **Save** the workbook, close Excel, and then submit your file as directed by your instructor.

MyLab IT Grader

Student data file needed:
e02Advertise.xlsx

You will save your file as:
e02Advertise_LastFirst.xlsx

Marketing

Sales & Marketing

Advertising Review

The Painted Paradise Resort & Spa has been investing in advertising using different media. When guests check in, the employee asks them how they heard about Painted Paradise Resort & Spa. Based on the customer's response, the employee then notes in the system either magazine, radio, television, Internet, word of mouth, or other. Because almost every guest is asked, the number of guests surveyed represents a significant portion of the actual guests. The past year's data is located on the GuestData worksheet. Every time a guest answers the question by mentioning an advertising source, it is considered a guest result. Ideally, the resort wants to purchase advertising at a low cost but then see as many guest results from that advertising as possible.

Every year, upper management sets the advertising budget before the beginning of the fiscal year, July 1. For the coming year, upper management has given you a larger television budget because of a new video marketing campaign. Also, the advertising contracts get negotiated every year, because the media vendors require a one-year commitment. The contracts are negotiated after the budget has been set. You will develop charts for an upcoming presentation that will discuss a marketing strategy, potential changes to the budget given the new media prices, anticipated monthly guest results, and the prospect of hiring a marketing consulting company with a high retainer that would require a loan.

a. Open the Excel file, **e02Advertise**. Save your file as e02Advertise_LastFirst using your last and first name.

b. On the **GuestData** worksheet, in cell **H2**, add a COUNTA function to determine the number of months listed in cell range A6:A17.

c. In cell **J2**, add a DATEDIF function to calculate the survey duration in years using the 2021 and 2022 Fiscal Start date.

d. Select cell range **L6:M17**, and then name the range Season

e. In cell range **C6:C17**, add a VLOOKUP that will look up the value in the corresponding cell in column b and then return the exact season match of Low, Mid, or High based on the value in column B. Use the named range, Season, in the formula.

f. To count the number of months in the Low season in cell **B22**, enter a COUNTIF function that counts the number of seasons in the cell range **C6:C17** that meet the criteria in cell **A22**. Use appropriate absolute referencing to copy the formula through cell **B24**.

g. To total the number of guests surveyed by season in cell **E22**, enter a SUMIF function that sums the total surveyed in cell range **J6:J17** if it meets the criteria in cell **D22**. Use appropriate absolute referencing to copy the formula through cell **E24**.

h. In cell range **D19:J19**, calculate the averages for each column with a rounded (not formatted) value to zero decimal places.

i. For later use, create the following named ranges.

Cell	Name
D19	AvgMagazine
E19	AvgRadio
F19	AvgTelevision
G19	AvgInternet

j. On the **AdvertisingPlan** worksheet, an analysis of past Guest Results and the new budget have been started. First, you need to finish out the past year analysis. In cell **F2**, enter a function that will return the current date.

k. Enter the following formulas in the cells identified in the left column.

Cell	Name
D6	=AvgMagazine
D7	=AvgRadio
D8	=AvgTelevision
D9*	=AvgInternet

* Note that these are monthly averages. Thus, all calculations on this worksheet are estimates based on the monthly average.

l. In cell range **E6:E9**, calculate the monthly Amount Spent by multiplying the Cost Per Ad and the Ads Placed.

m. In cell range **F6:F9**, calculate the Cost per Guest Result by dividing the Amount Spent by the Past Guest Results.

n. In cell range **C10:E10**, calculate the appropriate totals for each column.

o. On the **AdvertisingPlan** worksheet, you need to finish out the new budget year analysis. In cell range **I6:I9**, calculate the Number of Ads that can be purchased based on the New Budget divided by the New Cost Per Ad. A partial ad cannot be purchased, so you need to create a formula that will round the number down to the nearest integer.

p. In cell range **J6:J9**, calculate the monthly Amount to Spend by multiplying the New Cost Per Ad and the Ads to Place.

q. In cell range **G10:J10**, calculate the appropriate totals for each column. If necessary, change the format for cell I10 to general.

r. In cell range **K6:K9**, add a formula that will return the value of Increase if the Ads to Place is equal to zero. Any other result should return the value of Decrease

This column now indicates the media types for which the resort may want to consider an increase or decrease in the Ads to Place.

s. In cell range **L6:L9**, calculate the Anticipated Guest Results by dividing the Amount to Spend by the Cost per Guest Result in column F. The resulting value should be rounded (not formatted) to zero decimals.

t. In cell **L10**, calculate the total for the Anticipated Guest Results.

u. In cell **L11**, calculate the number of anticipated guest results compared to the past by subtracting the Past Guest Results total in cell D10 from the Anticipated Guest Results total in cell L10. A positive number indicates an anticipated increase in Guest Results. A negative number would indicate an anticipated decrease in Guest Results.

v. On the AdvertisingPlan worksheet, you need to make two charts for your presentation. Based on the data in cell ranges **A5:A9**, **D5:D9**, and **L5:L9**, add a 3-D Clustered Column chart to compare the past guest results to the anticipated guest results based on the new monthly advertising.

   • Under Chart Styles, select chart **Style 3**. Then change the title to Past vs. Anticipated Guest Results

   • Add data labels to the chart.

   • Move and resize the chart so the top left corner is in cell **A13** and the bottom right corner is in cell **L32**.

w. Create an additional chart based on the data in cell ranges **A5:A9**, **D5:D9**, and **E5:E9**, add a **Clustered Column - Line on Secondary Axis Combo** chart.

   • Move this chart to a chart sheet named GuestResultsBySpending

   • Under Chart Styles, select chart **Style 5**.

- Change the title to **Advertising Amount Spent by Past Guest Results**
- Set the chart title to **18** pt font size, set the value axis data label to **12** pt font size, and set all legend text to **12** pt font size.

x. On the **MarketingConsultants** worksheet, a monthly loan payment analysis has been started. The resort is considering hiring marketing consultants. However, they require a large up-front retainer fee. The resort would need to take out a loan to cover the cost. The resort needs an analysis of the loan payment by varying interest rates and down payment amount. Think carefully about how to use mixed and absolute cell referencing. In cell **D10**, add a PMT function using the following arguments.

- Calculate the monthly rate from the annual rate in cell **C10**.
- Calculate the number of monthly payments from the term in years in cell **B5**.
- Calculate the present value of the loan by the retainer amount in cell **B4** less the monthly payment in cell **D9**.
- Adjust the formula so the result is positive.

y. Complete the **Documentation** worksheet according to your instructor's directions. Insert the **File Name** code in the left footer section on all worksheets in the workbook.

z. **Save** the workbook, exit Excel, and submit your file as directed by your instructor.

Critical Thinking

When calculating the payment for the three potential loans, you were asked to have the function return a positive value. Why is it often practiced to return a positive value of a loan payment? Identify at least two ways to make a payment function return a positive value.

Problem Solve 2

MyLab IT Grader

Student data file needed:

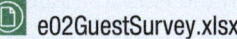 e02GuestSurvey.xlsx

You will save your file as:

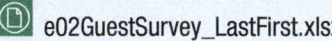 e02GuestSurvey_LastFirst.xlsx

Guest Survey Analysis

Customer Service

Painted Paradise Resort & Spa periodically surveys guests prior to departure. You have been asked to assist with the analysis of survey data. To assist you, a sample of ten surveys has been taken and formatted in a worksheet. The SurveyData worksheet contains a set of recent customer survey data for the 16 questions on the survey. Guests answer the questions on a scale of 1–5: 1 representing Very Unsatisfied, 5 representing Very Satisfied. If a guest indicates that the question is N/A (Not Applicable) for his stay (for example, the guest did not utilize the service), no value is entered. Guests also indicated if they wished to be contacted for future specials. You analyze the amount spent daily by guests who are interested in future specials and likely returning to the resort.

a. Open the Excel file, **e02GuestSurvey**. Save your file as e02GuestSurvey_LastFirst using your last and first name.

b. On the **SurveyData** worksheet, in cell **M6**, enter a COUNT function that returns the number of guests who answered the question. Use mixed referencing so you can copy the formula through cell **M21**.

c. To quickly visualize the ratings for each question, insert **Sparklines** with the **Line** type in cell range **N6:N21**. Cell range **C6:L21** are the source cells for the Sparklines. Identify the Sparkline **High Point**. Increase the width of column N to **20**

d. Next you want to create an area to be able to analyze each survey question's data separately, so a criteria section is created in cell range A23:L23. To extract information from the data based on question number, you decide to assign a range name to use in this lookup formula. Assign the range name SurveyRange to cell range **A6:L21**.

e. In cell **A24**, type 07H

f. In cell **B24**, enter a lookup function that looks up the value of cell **A24**, from the range named **SurveyRange** to supply the question found in column **2**. The result should be an exact match. Use the appropriate mixed reference for the lookup value.

g. In cell **C24**, enter a lookup function that looks up the value of cell **A24**, from the range named **SurveyRange**, to supply the score found in column **3**. Use absolute or mixed referencing where appropriate. Copy the formula in cell **C24** through **L24**. Edit the formulas in **D24:L24** to reflect the correct column index number.

h. In cell **M24**, calculate the average of the results in cell range **C24:L24**.

i. In cell **N24**, you want to determine if the question average score is satisfactory or needs attention by using a logical function. If the average score is greater than or equal to 4, the value of Satisfactory should be returned. If the score is not greater than or equal to 4, then a value of Needs Attention should be returned.

j. To visually analyze each question's rating, insert an **Area** chart using source cell range **B24:L24**. Add the following elements to the Area chart:

- Change the chart color to **Monochromatic Palette 4**.
- Change the chart style to **Style 4**.
- Move the upper-left corner of the Area chart to cell **B26**.
- Add a vertical axis title named Guest Rating
- Add a horizontal axis title named Guest Number
- Change the Bounds Maximum to 5 and, if necessary, the Units Major to 1
- Test the criteria area and chart by changing the value in cell **A24** to 01H

> ### Mac Troubleshooting
> On a Mac, the Area chart is found at the bottom of the Line chart gallery.

k. In cell **Q6**, count the number of guest responses in cell range **C6:L21** if the guests responded to a question with a rating of 5, the highest rating. Use absolute referencing where appropriate. Copy the formula through cell **Q10**.

l. On the **GuestData** worksheet, in cell **B2**, enter a formula to change the guest's name in cell A2 to the proper case. Copy the formula through cell **B11**.

m. In cell **B14**, total the daily amount spent by guests if they have an interest in future specials (C2:C11) as indicated by the criteria in cell **A14**.

n. Complete the **Documentation** worksheet according to your instructor's direction.

o. Save the workbook, exit Excel, and submit your file as directed by your instructor.

Perform 1: Perform in Your Life

Student data file needed:

📄 e02JobHunt.xlsx

You will save your file as:

📄 e02JobHunt_LastFirst.xlsx

Your Ideal Career Start

Human Resources

Even if this is your first semester, you have probably already begun to think about the type of job or career you want. Further, when you are spending long hours studying, it can be fun to imagine the new car you might buy after your ideal career starts following graduation. For this project, assume you are graduating this semester. In this project, you need to find currently available jobs and establish criteria to help you pick your most desired position. Then you will find the ideal new car to purchase, but your new position's salary must allow you to afford the monthly payment.

a. Open the Excel file, **e02JobHunt**. Save your file as *e02JobHunt_LastFirst* using your last and first name. Keep the workbook professional, but feel free to optionally add elements such as a picture of your ideal career start or new car.

b. Go to the Internet and find five or more jobs that interest you. You can select data from multiple websites or just one website (from the same website will be easiest). Search for jobs that you may apply for after graduation. Copy and paste that data into the JobData worksheet. Feel free to add columns, move columns, or rename columns to fit your data and style needs.

c. On the JobData worksheet, in cell A1, add an appropriate title for your career goals.

d. In cell B3, indicate the website you used to find the job posting (e.g., Monster.com or Indeed.com).

e. In cell B4, indicate the date you gathered the information.

f. In the center header of your worksheet, insert your full name.

g. Starting in row 7, complete the columns of data listed on the table below. You can gather more data than is listed below if it is relevant to picking the ideal job for you. At a minimum, you must have the following.

Data (no extra characters in or around the data)	Description
Company Name	Full name as you would address a letter to the company.
Job Title	Full job title, which needs to be descriptive of the position. For example, "Entry Level" is not a sufficient title. "Application Support Analyst — Entry Level" is a sufficient title.
State	State in which the position is located. State should be in a column by itself, not in combination with the city or address.
Salary	Try not to mix pay types. For example, if you are looking for a salaried position, choose all salaried positions.

h. Add headers, comments, and/or notes to make clear to your instructor what Excel steps you took to get to the final job data.

i. Format the JobData worksheet as needed.

j. On the JobAnalysis worksheet, copy data from the JobData sheet that you intend to use to help you determine which position(s) to apply for. In cell A1, enter an appropriate worksheet title, and then paste the data from the JobData sheet beginning in row 3.

k. In column D, enter an IF statement to indicate whether a job is in a state you find desirable based on criteria you determine to be important—for example, a specific state in which you wish to live.

l. In cell range A16:A18, fill in salary data to establish pay range categories for Below Expected, Expected, and Above Expected based on your personal job expectations.

m. Give the salary table data in cell range A16:B18 an appropriate range name.

n. In cell F3, use a lookup function to determine the category for the position you are evaluating. Use the table range name in the formula. Copy the formula through cell F7.

o. In cell G3, enter a function to determine whether you will apply for the job. You will apply for the job if the desirable state is equal to Yes. Copy the formula through cell G7.

p. Format the JobAnalysis worksheet as needed.

q. On the MyNewCar worksheet, in cell range B2:B7, enter data for the ideal car you wish to purchase. In cell range B13:B15, enter three current interest rates for the type of car you wish to purchase. In cell range C12:E12, enter possible terms of the loan in years for the type of car you wish to purchase. You may use the examples provided or enter your desired data.

r. In cell range C13:E15, calculate the monthly payment for your ideal car using the three different interest rates and three different terms of loans.

s. In cell B17, input the monthly gross salary by referencing the salary from your most desired job on the JobAnalysis worksheet.

t. You need to be able to afford the car you pick. The amount you will be able to afford will vary greatly depending on individual circumstances, such as marital status, credit card debt, and homeowner status. For the purposes of this project, the car you pick cannot have a monthly payment greater than 10% of your gross salary for your Most Desired job. In cell range C22:E24, determine the percentage of your monthly salary the loan payment would represent.

u. Use a conditional format to indicate feasible loan options. If none of the loan options are under 10%, you will have to do one or a combination of the following: pick a new car, increase your down payment, extend your term, or find a lower interest rate.

v. Format the MyNewCar worksheet as needed.

w. Build at least one meaningful chart on either the JobAnalysis or MyNewCar worksheet. Include at least a one-sentence explanation near the chart explaining the chart's significance.

x. Complete the Documentation worksheet according to your instructor's directions.

y. Save the workbook, exit Excel, and submit your file as directed by your instructor.

Perform 2: Perform in Your Career

Student data file needed:

 e02Investment.xlsx

You will save your file as:

 e02Investment_LastFirst.xlsx

Investment Portfolios

Finance & Accounting

You have started working as an investment intern for a financial company that helps clients invest in the stock market. Your manager, Roger Hedding, gives you a spreadsheet detailing some periodic investments in Nobel Energy, Inc. (NBL) made by one of the clients. The client would like a report and charts on the NBL investment and the stock's performance. Your manager has asked you to finish this report.

a. Open the Excel file, **e02Investment**. Save your file as e02Investment_LastFirst using your last and first name.

b. On the NBLInvestment worksheet, in column F, starting in row 21, your manager has already entered a formula to calculate total value. Update the formula to return a value of only two decimals. (Hint: Do not format to 2 decimal places.)

c. In column G, starting in the second row, cell G22, enter a formula to sum up the quarterly investments as of the date in column A to provide a cumulative total. For example, cell G22 should return the sum of the Quarterly investments on 1/2/2020 and 4/1/2020. Next, cell G23 should return the sum of the Quarterly investments on 4/1/2020 and 7/1/2020.

d. In column H, calculate the Total Growth. The total growth is the Total Value minus the Total Investment. A result of a negative value means that the investment shrank instead of growing.

e. In column I, calculate the Total Growth %. The Total Growth % is the Total Growth divided by the Total Investment.

f. In cell J21, type 0 In cell J22, calculate the Quarterly Growth. The Quarterly Growth is the Total Growth minus the Total Growth from the previous quarter. Copy the formula through cell J33.

g. In column K, calculate the Quarterly Growth %. The Quarterly Growth % is the Quarterly Growth divided by the Total Investment.

h. Assign the range name Rank to the lookup table in cell range M3:N7.

i. In column L, using a lookup function, calculate the Quarterly Rank based on the Rank table.

j. In column M, using a logical function, determine the Portfolio Status Recommendation. The Portfolio Status is "Good" if the Quarterly Rank is A+. Otherwise, the Portfolio Status will return a value of "Consider Diversifying".

k. Create a combo chart for Total Portfolio Performance that displays the Total Value, Total Investment, and Total Growth over time. (Hint: You will need to show a secondary axis for Total Growth.) Apply a chart style. Position the chart above the data in row 20.

l. Create a combo chart for Quarterly Performance that displays the Quarterly Growth and the Quarterly Growth % over time. (Hint: You will need to show a secondary axis for Quarterly Total Growth %.) Apply a chart style. Position the chart above the data. You may need to change the Label Position to Low.

m. Complete the Documentation worksheet according to your instructor's directions. Insert the File Name code in the left footer on all worksheets in the workbook.

n. Save the workbook, exit Excel, and then submit your file as directed by your instructor.

Perform 3: Perform in Your Team

Student data file needed:

 e02Paintball.xlsx

You will save your file as:

 e02Paintball_TeamName.xlsx

Paintball Facility Expansion

Productions & Operations

You work for Splat Paintball Range, a popular outdoor paintball facility near a metropolitan area. The range is open Wednesdays through Sundays from the first of April until the end of October every year. With the popularity of the sport of paintball rising and the facility's inability to accommodate the number of paintball party bookings being requested, Splat Paintball Range is considering an expansion of its paintball range. You have been assigned to a team to help with the analysis for an expansion of the range area and overall capacity. Your manager, Juanita Trilling, needs help looking at past sales, sales trends, and loan options. Located in the upper Midwest of the United States, Splat Paintball Range has typical Midwest weather. Therefore, part of the facility's marketing strategy is to offer discounted season passes in the colder months if the temperature is 60 degrees or below. The following is a description of the data Juanita has provided to you.

Date	Description
Month	The first day of the month for the data in that row.
Passes Sold	The number of paid players and season pass holders who entered the paintball range that month. Attendance does not reflect the time spent on the range. If a player leaves the range and returns, the player is counted only once.
Ticket Sales	All ticket sales that month, including single-day and season passes. If a player buys a season pass in April, the sale is accounted for only in April, yet the player can play throughout the remaining months of that season.
Other Sales	All other revenue besides ticket sales. This is primarily equipment rental and paintballs.
Avg High Temp (Degrees)	The average high temperature for the park that month.

a. Select one team member to set up the document by completing steps b through d.

b. Open your browser, and navigate to https://www.onedrive.live.com, https://www.drive.google.com, or any other instructor-assigned location. Be sure all members of the team have an account on the chosen system, such as a Microsoft or Google account.

c. Open the Excel file, e02Paintball. Save your file as e02Paintball_TeamName replacing TeamName with the name assigned to your team by your instructor.

d. Share the spreadsheet with the other members of your team. Make sure each team member has the appropriate permission to edit the document.

e. Hold a team meeting to discuss the requirements of the remaining steps. As a team, make an action plan to assign individual and team work and set deadlines for each step.

f. The Sales worksheet includes data about past revenue—earned income before any costs. The data on the Sales worksheet could be analyzed in several ways. As a team, determine possible range names that can be used in creating formulas for the Sales worksheet.

g. In cell E4, add a field labeled Total Sales In column E, calculate the total sales for each month using range names if appropriate.

h. In cell F4, add a field labeled Average Sales per Pass Sold In column F, calculate the average sales per pass sold for each month.

i. In cell J4, add a field labeled Discount Passes? In column J, determine whether Splat will offer discount passes based on the facility's marketing strategy.

j. In cell A12, add a field labeled Totals In the cell range B12:E12, enter a function to calculate the totals.

k. In cell A13, add a field labeled Averages In the cell range B13:E13, enter a function or formula to calculate the averages.

l. In cell G4, add a field labeled % of Total Sales In column G, using a mixed or absolute reference, calculate each month's percent of the total sales.

m. Add any other calculations your team feels are relevant for analyzing Splat's past revenue.

n. As a team, format the worksheet in a professional manner. Adjust column width and row height as appropriate. Apply cell formatting as necessary for data interpretation.

o. Each team member should independently create and format one or two charts about the data on this worksheet.

p. With a focus on displaying sales peaks and trends, the team should meet to decide which three to five charts to include in the final file.

q. On the Loan worksheet, you will find the basic information about two loan options to finance Splat's range expansion. In cells B8 and C8, calculate the Monthly Payment amount for the two loan options for the range expansion. Splat is considering only terms of three or five years. Edit the formula to return a positive value.

r. In cells B12 and C12, calculate the Total Loan Payments for the two loan options.

s. In cell B13, identify which loan is preferred for Splat's expansion project. The loan is preferred if the total loan payment is the lower of the two.

t. Add any other calculations your team feels are relevant to determining the best loan for Splat.

u. As a team, format the worksheet in a professional manner, applying an appropriate theme and cell styles. Adjust column width and row height as appropriate. Apply cell formatting as necessary for data interpretation.

v. Fill out the TeamComments worksheet as directed by your instructor.

w. Complete the Documentation worksheet according to your instructor's directions. At the minimum, include enough detail to identify which parts of the worksheets or workbook each team member completed.

x. Insert the File Name code in the left footer on all worksheets in the workbook. In a custom header section, include the names of the students in your team, spreading the names evenly across each of the three header sections: left section, center section, and right section.

y. Save the workbook, exit Excel, and submit your file as directed by your instructor.

Perform 4: How Others Perform

Student data file needed:

 e02Sport.xlsx

You will save your file as:

 e02Sport_LastFirst.xlsx

Sports Facility Operations

Productions & Operations

You have recently been hired as an account representative in the business office of Sports Plus, a fitness facility. Your supervisor, Tim Kerr, has requested that you finish an already-started Excel workbook file that identifies the expenses of the sports facility and projects by quarter for the current year. Beyond performing calculations for total expenses by expense category and per quarter, you are expected to create and format a series of professional-looking charts that will assist in the interpretation of the workbook data. The spreadsheet data and visual charts will not only be included in an annual report but also be presented to the board of directors of the company.

You have also been asked to look at the sales of the specific exercise classes for the year and determine which courses should continue to be offered at the facility the following year and which courses should no longer be offered. Finally, you have been asked to predict what percentage increase in the cost of classes would be needed to reach the total sales goal of $40,000.

a. Open the Excel file, **e02Sport**. Save your file as e02Sport_LastFirst using your last and first name.

b. Rename Sheet1 Expenses

c. On the Expenses worksheet, in cell D6, adjust the existing formula by taking Last Year's Avg Qtr and multiplying it by the Target Factor for Increases for Qtr 1. Use mixed referencing when correcting this formula. Copy the formula through cell G14.

d. Check to be sure the SUM function and cell range are correct in cell H6, in which you are calculating the Total for Rent for the current year only (Qtr 1–Qtr 4), and then copy the formula through cell H14.

e. Correct the SUM function in cell D16, and then fill the corrected function across through column G.

f. For cell range D19:D21, use functions to perform calculations for Qtr1 through Qtr4. Copy the formulas in cell range D19:D21 through column G.

g. Apply formatting to improve the appearance of the worksheet as necessary. Apply any data formatting that will make the data easier to interpret.

h. Create a chart to display each expense category and expense amounts for each quarter. Reposition the chart below the worksheet data beginning in cell A24. Resize the chart so the bottom left corner is in cell D38. Format the chart and add a descriptive title that represents the information displayed in the chart.

i. Create a chart to display the expense categories and total expenses for the current year. Add percentages as data labels. Reposition the chart below the worksheet data beginning in row 24. Resize the chart so the bottom left corner of the chart is in cell H38. Format the chart and add a descriptive chart title.

j. In cell range I6:I14, insert column Sparklines using the data for Qtr1:Qtr4.

k. Modify the page settings to ensure your worksheet will print on a single page. Specify page orientation as is appropriate to maximize readability.

l. Rename Sheet2 SalesData The SalesData worksheet contains sales information for exercise classes offered at the facility.

m. On the SalesData worksheet, in column D, create a formula to calculate the sales total for adult classes and youth classes.

n. Calculate the totals of Yearly Sessions Sold and Sales Total for both adult and youth classes.

o. Calculate the total sales of the exercise classes for the fitness facility.

p. Assign the range name Rank to cell range I3:J6.

q. In column E, to determine exercise class ranking for both the adult and youth classes, enter a lookup function using the Rank table.

r. To determine if you will discontinue offering classes, you will create a function that will return a value of No if the class rank is Bronze or else will return a value of Yes. Only classes with a ranking of Silver, Gold, or Platinum will be continued the following year.

s. Rename Sheet3 SalesGoal

t. On the SalesGoal worksheet, you have been asked to predict how much to raise the cost of classes to reach the total sales goal of $40,000. You will increase all classes by the same percentage. In cell C3, type =SalesData!C3*(1+$D$22) Copy the formula through cell D8.

u. In cell C12, enter a formula similar to cell C3 using the correct cell references. Copy the formula through cell C18. Because the results on the SalesData worksheet indicated that the low-selling courses should be discontinued, change the yearly sessions sold for Racquetball in cell B15 to 0

v. Through trial and error, determine the recommended percentage of increase in the cost per class session in cell D22 to reach the 2022 sales goal of at least $40,000.

w. Complete the Documentation worksheet according to your instructor's directions. Insert the file name in the left footer section on all worksheets in the workbook.

x. Save the workbook, exit Excel, and submit your file as directed by your instructor.

Integrating Complex Functions into Business Analysis

Analyzing data can be vital to your decision-making process, either on the job or for personal use. Excel includes several logical and retrieval functions that help you more easily analyze large amounts of data. Excel also has built-in tools, like tables, PivotTables, Advanced Filters, and more to make exploring large amounts of data easy. This business unit will introduce you to the importance of using Excel's complex retrieval functions for business analysis as well as various tools and functions for exploring large datasets.

Learning Outcome 1

Use Excel logical and retrieval functions to analyze data in support of decision-making.

REAL WORLD SUCCESS

"During the summer after my sophomore year, I obtained an internship with a top technology consulting firm. Several students from other local colleges worked with me. One day, three of the interns, including me, were assigned to work on a project. Our manager asked us if anyone knew how to create a VLOOKUP in Excel. I was the only one who did!"

– Raheem, current student

Learning Outcome 2

Use Excel tables, database functions, PivotTables, and PivotCharts to quickly summarize and analyze large amounts of data.

REAL WORLD SUCCESS

"My instructor taught my class how to work with large amounts of data and explained that we will need to use these skills when we enter the work force. I never imagined that as a marketing analyst I would be working with so much data and that I would have to use the skills my instructor taught. PivotTables have become a way of life for me. I could never have been able to make sense of all the data I collect had it not been for PivotTables and PivotCharts. Thank goodness I learned how to work with these data analysis tools!"

– Vanessa, recent graduate

Microsoft Excel

Chapter 5 COMPLEX LOGICAL AND RETRIEVAL FUNCTIONS

MyLab IT Grader

Finance & Accounting

Production & Operations

Prepare Case

Red Bluff Golf Course & Pro Shop Sales Analysis

The Red Bluff Golf Course & Pro Shop generates revenue through its golfers, golfer services, and pro shop sales. Aleeta Herriott, the pro shop manager, receives revenue data on a weekly basis. She would like help developing an Excel workbook that she can use to analyze various elements of the pro shop's transactions, as well as employee performance, customer rewards, and shipping costs. She has a workbook started with some sample data and a framework for the type of the analysis she needs and wants you to continue to develop the workbook. This workbook will help Aleeta make informed decisions about the business.

Tony Bowler/Shutterstock

Student data file needed:

e03ch05ProShopSales.xlsx

You will save your file as:

e03ch05ProShopSales_LastFirst.xlsx

Integrating Logical Functions

Making decisions, whether they are personal or business driven, involves evaluation and choices. Golfers use logic as they play, evaluating the scene—distance to the green; wind speed and direction; obstacles such as water features, sand traps, or trees; and terrain, including grass height and elevation—as it changes with every shot. For instance, a golfer who is 300 yards away from the green and has an unobstructed shot might choose a different club than if she is in a sand trap and 20 feet from the hole. Similarly, business success depends on the ability to choose whether to buy or lease, build or buy from a supplier, or advertise in a magazine, online, or on television. Being able to evaluate conditions and apply logic in choosing the best option is the foundation of logical functions. Excel includes 11 different functions that belong to the logical category. A **logical function** determines whether a particular expression is true or false. The most commonly used logical function is the IF function. The **IF function** allows you to specify one outcome if the expression is true and another outcome if the expression is false. Logical functions enable evaluation and choices to be integrated into a worksheet. Other common logical functions include AND, OR, and NOT. Another logical function, IFERROR, is a special function that is discussed at the end of this chapter.

The foundation of a logical function is a logical expression or logical test. A **logical test** is an expression with comparison operators that can be evaluated as either true or false. It is also known as a logical expression. For example, the logical expression "the distance to the green is more than 300 yards" compares the actual distance to 300 yards. The test—determining whether the ball is lying more than or less than 300 yards away from the green—will help to determine which club will be chosen.

Logical operators, as listed in Table 1, are mathematical comparison operators used to create logical tests.

Operator	Description	TRUE	FALSE
$<$	Less than	$5<7$	$10<3$
$>$	Greater than	$10>3$	$3>10$
$\leq$	Less than or equal to	$5\leq5$	$5\leq4$
$\geq$	Greater than or equal to	$6\geq5$	$3\geq10$
$\neq$	Not equal to	$2\neq4$	$2\neq2$

Table 1 Logical operators

Preview the Workbook

Another staff member started developing the workbook that Aleeta has requested to assist her with decision making. The workbook includes a random sample of transactions as well as other worksheets where the necessary analysis has been set up but not yet completed. You will begin by taking a few moments to look over the workbook to ensure you understand the data and the breadth of the analysis you have been asked to conduct.

Opening the Starting File

In this exercise, you will open a workbook and then save the workbook with a new name.

E05.00

SIDE NOTE
Office Updates
Depending on your exact Office version, you may see Open or Open Other Workbooks.

To Open the Starting File

a. Start **Excel**, click **Open** in the left pane, and then double-click **This PC**. Navigate through the folder structure to the location of your student data files, and then double-click **e03ch05ProShopSales**. If a Security Warning message displays, click the **Enable Editing** button.

b. Click the **File** tab, click **Save As**, and then double-click **This PC**. In the Save As dialog box, navigate to the location where you are saving your project files, and then change the file name to **e03ch05ProShopSales_LastFirst** using your last and first name. Click **Save**.

There are several different worksheets in the ProShopSales workbook. The Transactions worksheet contains a random sample of transactions that recently took place. There is room on this worksheet for a few additional transactions, and it could easily be expanded if necessary. It may appear as though the analysis has already been completed on this worksheet; however, a closer look reveals that all the values have been manually calculated and then typed into the worksheet. You will replace these manual calculations with your own analysis using various formulas and functions. This workbook contains other worksheets for developing additional analyses about employees, customers, and shipping costs.

Aleeta would like you to analyze the monthly Red Bluff Golf Course & Pro Shop sales data to transform the data into information that she can use to make sound business decisions. Being able to address the following questions may provide insight into how she can increase sales, reduce costs, incentivize employees, or provide better customer service.

- What is the net revenue for each transaction?
- How much revenue do we lose to discounts and coupons?
- Are employees meeting or exceeding their sales goals?
- How much are we spending on incentives for our employees?
- Are we rewarding our highest value customers?
- What if we implement a rewards program instead of coupons and other discounts?

 CONSIDER THIS | **How Would These Questions Help Any Business?**

Aleeta's questions are not unique to Red Bluff. Any business that wants to generate revenue would ask questions like these. Based on the analysis, Aleeta might create a marketing strategy to increase sales or ask the human resource department to provide sales training to all employees. How would these help management make decisions? What might management surmise from the answers to the questions Aleeta needs to consider?

Exploring the data, finding the answers to questions, and developing knowledge from the Red Bluff Golf Course & Pro Shop information will help management to gain and maintain a competitive advantage. **A competitive advantage** is the strategic advantage that a business has over its competition. Attaining a competitive advantage strengthens a business and positions it better within the business environment. Aleeta hopes that developing the worksheets properly will help with decision making.

CONSIDER THIS | **Can You Identify a Business That Has a Competitive Advantage?**

Think about businesses you visit or ads you see on TV. When you go to McDonald's, do you think about Burger King or Wendy's? What makes you choose one over another? In 2011, Wendy's became the second most popular fast-food hamburger restaurant, surpassing Burger King, which had held the position for 40 years. How did Wendy's do this? How does McDonald's keep its first-place position? How much money do these companies spend to maintain or gain a competitive advantage?

Use IF Functions

The IF function, the most commonly used logical function in Excel, returns one of two values depending on whether the supplied logical test being evaluated is true or false. The logical test evaluates a logical condition, or statement, and can involve either values or other functions. The IF function has three arguments

=IF(logical_test, [value_if_true], [value_if_false])

Suppose you want a list of all golf club members who have a handicap—a method used to level the playing field for golfers of different skill levels—at or below 0. A golfer who has a handicap of 0 or below is known as a scratch golfer. An IF function could be created that would check the handicap and return the words "Scratch Golfer" if the handicap is less than or equal to 0 or "Handicapped Golfer" if the handicap is greater than 0. For example, an IF function could be

=IF(C5<=0,"Scratch Golfer","Handicapped Golfer")

In this formula, C5<=0 is the logical test; the value_if_true is "Scratch Golfer", and the value_if_false is "Handicapped Golfer". In other words, the user would see "Scratch Golfer" if the value in C5 is less than or equal to 0; otherwise, "Handicapped Golfer" would be displayed in the cell containing the formula. When using words—referred to as a text string—in formulas such as the IF function, you must enter the words in quotation marks.

One of the easiest ways to begin working with IF functions is to use a decision tree. A **decision tree** is a diagramming tool that allows you to break down potential decisions in a logical, structured format. By using the decision tree, you can take a problem or decision and break down the potential possibilities. Consider the previous example. If the formula =IF(C5<=0,"Scratch Golfer","Handicapped Golfer") were inserted into a decision tree, it would be diagrammed with three labeled branches in black, the values for each argument in blue, and finished with the IF function syntax in red, as shown in Figure 1.

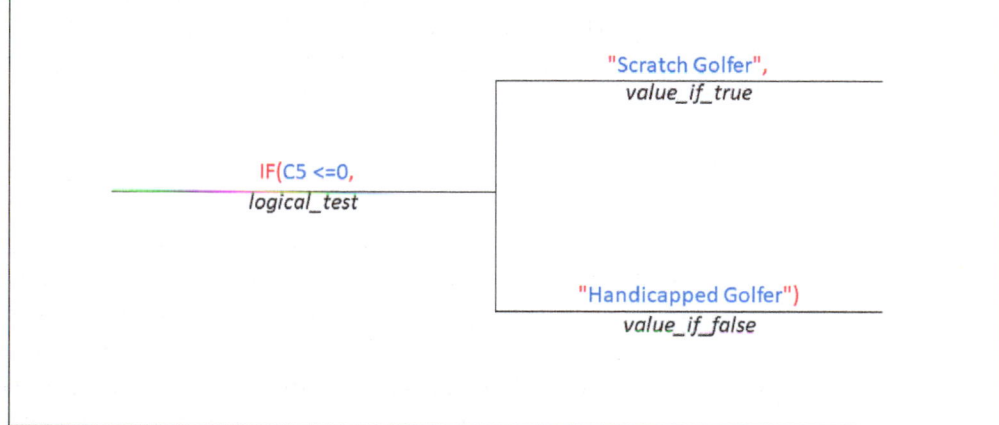

Figure 1   Decision tree

A decision tree helps to keep your thoughts organized as you work through writing your formula. Complete the following steps to create your decision tree.

1. Draw and label the three branches.

2. Determine and write the logical test argument.

3. Determine and write the [value_if_true] argument.

4. Determine and write the [value_if_false] argument.

5. Fill in the IF function syntax.

6. Type your formula into Excel.

Constructing an IF Function

Employees at the Red Bluff Golf Course & Pro Shop can become certified golf trainers if they complete 50 or more hours of training. In the EmployeeAnalysis worksheet, Aleeta would like a column that will indicate which of her employees are certified. If the employee has completed at least 50 hours of training, she wants the word "Certified" to display. Otherwise the words "Not Certified" should be displayed. You will also determine which transactions will get a 7% member discount on their order.

In this exercise, you will create logical IF functions.

 E05.01

SIDE NOTE
Pin the Ribbon

If your ribbon is collapsed, pin your ribbon open. Click the Home tab. In the lower-right corner of the ribbon, click Pin the ribbon ⊡.

SIDE NOTE
Capitalization

Functions in hands-on sections will be entered in uppercase letters. However, function names and cell references are not case sensitive.

To Construct an IF Function

a. Click the **EmployeeAnalysis** worksheet. Click cell **D5**, type **=IF** and then press [Tab] to open the function.

b. For the logical_test, click cell **C5** and then type **>=50,**

c. For the value_if_true argument, type **"Certified",**

d. For the value_if_false argument, type **"Not Certified"**

e. Type **)** to close the function and then press [Ctrl]+[Enter].

This IF function checks if the hours of training completed in cell C5 is greater than or equal to 50. Because Ramal Hample has completed 65 hours, it returns the word "Certified". If Ramal had completed fewer than 50 hours, it would return "Not Certified".

f. With cell D5 still selected, use the **fill handle** to copy the formula down through cell **D9**.

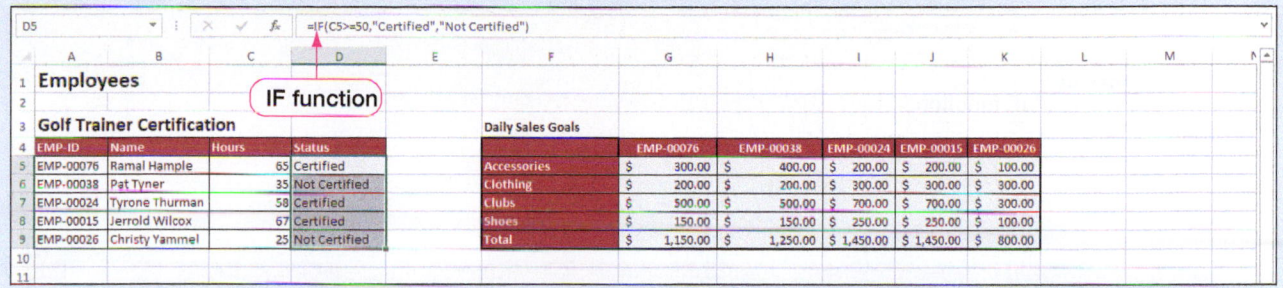

Figure 2 Certified IF function

Screenshot of Microsoft Excel 2019, © Microsoft Corporation

Next, you will determine if a customer qualifies for a 7% discount on their pro shop purchase. If the customer is a member, they get the discount; otherwise they don't.

g. Click the **Transactions** worksheet and then click cell **I10**.

h. Type **=IF**, and then press Tab to open the function.

i. For the logical_test argument, click cell **F10** and then type **="Yes",**

j. For the value_if_true argument, type **0.07,**

k. For the value_if_false argument, type **""**

l. Type **)** to close the function and then press Ctrl+Enter.

This IF function checks if the ClubMember? value in cell F10 is equal to "Yes". If so, .07 is returned. Otherwise an empty set, indicated by double quotes with nothing in between (""), will be returned. Because the first transaction is from a customer who is not a member, an empty set is returned.

SIDE NOTE

Checking the Logic

All calculations should be checked for valid logic. It is possible to have no error messages, but the logic may still provide an invalid solution.

> **Troubleshooting**
>
> If you see an error after you press Ctrl+Enter, ensure that you entered all necessary quotation marks. Additionally, ensure that you typed quotation marks and did not type two apostrophes.

m. With cell **I10** still selected, use the **fill handle** to copy the formula down through cell **I30**.

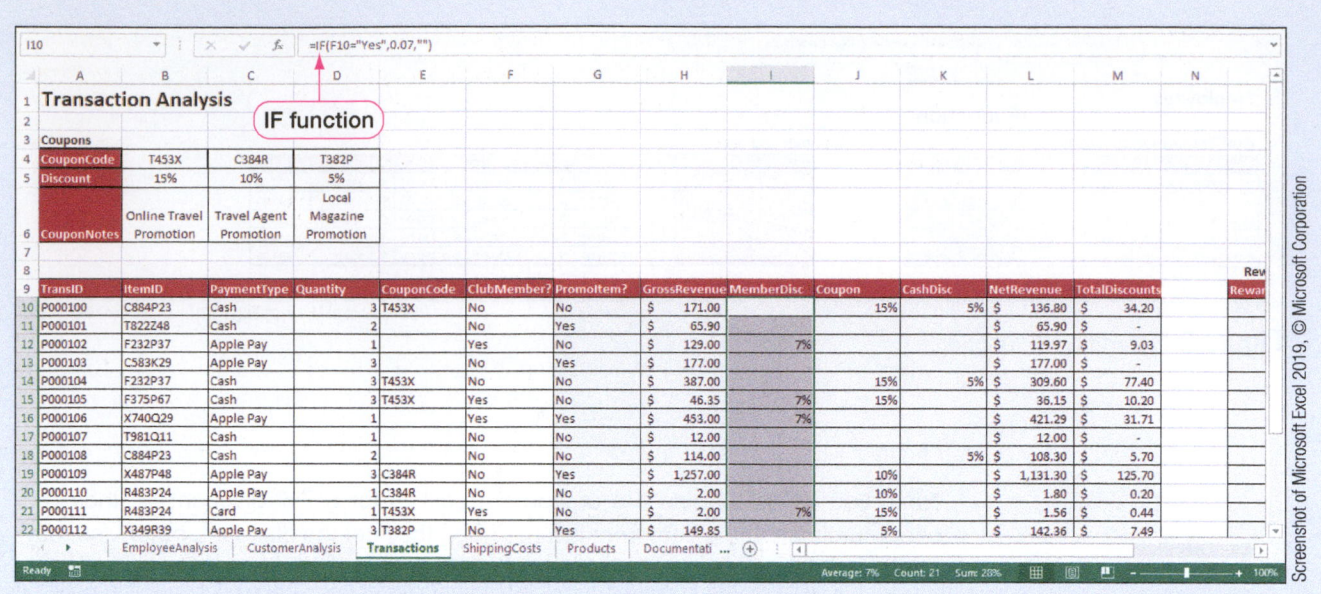

Figure 3 Membership discount IF function

> **n. Save** 🖫 the workbook.

Integrate Basic Conjunction Functions into IF Functions

IF functions are one of the most popular logical functions, but they do have their limitations. One limitation is that the IF function only allows for one logical test. Many scenarios require two or more logical tests. For example, a customer must pay in cash and spend more than $100 to receive a 5% cash discount. Because an IF function only supports one logical test, it cannot determine cash discounts by itself. Conjunction functions allow evaluation of multiple logical tests and enable linking or joining of functions or formulas. The conjunction functions within Excel are AND, OR, and NOT.

- The **AND function** returns TRUE if *all* logical tests supplied are true; otherwise, it returns FALSE.
- The **OR function** returns TRUE if at least one of the logical tests supplied is true; otherwise, if all logical tests are false, it returns FALSE.
- The **NOT function** returns the reverse of the logical value to which the logical test evaluates. For example, if the logical expression evaluates to TRUE, the function will return FALSE. It is used when there are many options that fit the desired criteria and only one option that does not fit the criteria. This function will be addressed later in the chapter.

It is important to realize that the syntax for these functions is similar to any other function: The arguments are parenthetical following the function name. A user might think the syntax would be something like

   Cash AND >100

However, the correct syntax is

   AND(logical1,[logical2],…)

   OR(logical1,[logical2],…)

   NOT(logical1)

Using the AND Function

At least one logical test must be included, and additional logical test arguments are optional for the AND function. For example, students who want to be eligible for a university scholarship must have an ACT score of 30 or more *and* a high school GPA of 3.5 or better. Using named ranges to evaluate whether a student achieved these goals, the AND function would be written as

> AND(ACT>=30,GPA>=3.5)

Both conditions must be met to display TRUE.

Like the outcomes of the IF function, the outcomes of either TRUE or FALSE are not valuable to a manager. Generally, conjunction functions are nested within other functions, such as an IF function. An AND function could be used in an IF statement:

> IF(AND(ACT>=30,GPA>=3.5),"Eligible","Not Eligible")

In this case, the ACT>=30 is the first logical argument, and the GPA>=3.5 is the second logical argument.

The logic for evaluating an AND function with two logical tests—AND(Logical Test 'A',Logical Test 'B')—is shown in Table 2 in a logical truth table. When the AND function is nested in the logical test argument of an IF function, both logical tests need to be evaluated as TRUE for the [value_if_true] argument to be returned. If either test evaluates to FALSE, then the AND function will return a FALSE for the logical test. Of the four possible outcomes, only one would return a value of TRUE.

Logical Test 'A'	Logical Test 'B'	Result of the AND Function
TRUE	TRUE	TRUE
TRUE	FALSE	FALSE
FALSE	TRUE	FALSE
FALSE	FALSE	FALSE

Table 2   AND logical truth table

Aleeta wants you to determine which of the transactions qualify to receive a cash discount of 5%. For a customer to qualify for this discount, the payment type must be cash and the gross revenue must be more than $100. Because there are two conditions that lead to the results and both must be true, an AND function can be used within the logical test for the IF function.

In this exercise, you will use the AND function within an IF function.

 **E05.02**

To Use the AND Function within an IF Function

a. On the Transactions worksheet, click cell **K10**.

b. Type **=IF** and then press Tab to open the function.

c. For the logical_test argument, type **AND**, and then press Tab to insert the AND function.

d. For the logical1 argument inside the AND function, click cell **C10**, and then type **="Cash",**

e. For the logical2 argument inside the AND function, click cell **H10** and then type **>100**

f. Type **),** to close the AND function and move on to the value_if_true argument.

g. For the value_if_true argument, type **0.05,**

h. For the value_if_false argument, type **""**

i. Type **)** to close the function and then press Ctrl+Enter.

Both logical tests in the AND function must be evaluated to TRUE for the AND to return a TRUE. When this happens, the [value_if_true] argument—0.05—is displayed, or the [value_if_false] argument—an empty set—is executed.

j. With cell K10 still selected, use the **fill handle** to copy the formula down through cell **K30**.

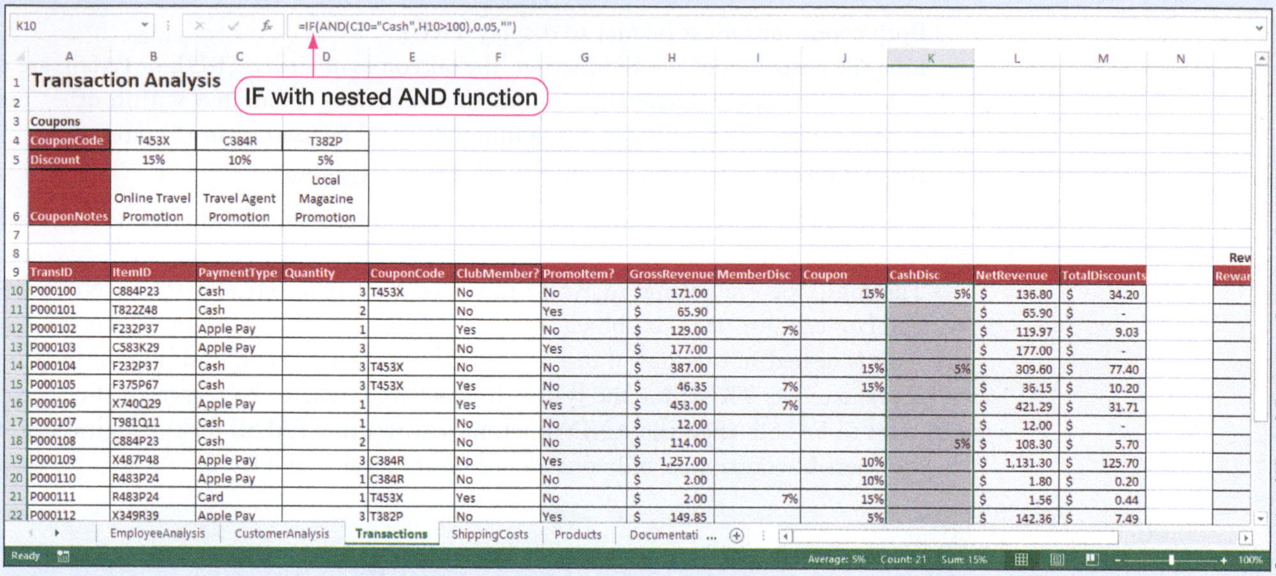

Figure 4 Cash discount – AND function nested in an IF function

k. Save 💾 the workbook.

Using the OR Function

The OR function works in the same way as the AND function except that the logical evaluation of the arguments is different. Where the AND function requires all arguments to be TRUE, the OR function requires only one of the arguments to be evaluated as TRUE. Thus, the OR function with two logical tests—OR(Logical Test 'A', Logical Test 'B')—as depicted in the logical truth table in Table 3 shows that three of the four combinations would return a result of TRUE.

Logical Test 'A'	Logical Test 'B'	Result of the OR Function
TRUE	TRUE	TRUE
TRUE	FALSE	TRUE
FALSE	TRUE	TRUE
FALSE	FALSE	FALSE

Table 3 OR logical truth table

Aleeta wants to determine which of the customers on the CustomerAnalysis worksheet are considered "high-value" and which ones are considered "low-value." High-value customers are those who have purchased more than 12 items or have spent $1,000 or more. The CustomerAnalysis worksheet contains the total sales volume and total sales revenue for each customer in columns D and E. Because there are two different ways a customer can be considered high-value, an OR function will be used in conjunction with an IF function to evaluate each customer.

In this exercise, you will use the OR function within the IF function.

To Use the OR Function within an IF Function

a. Click the **CustomerAnalysis** worksheet, and then click cell **F4**.

b. Type **=IF** and then press ⌷Tab⌷ to insert the function.

c. For the logical_test argument, type **OR** and then press ⌷Tab⌷ to insert the OR function inside the IF function.

d. For the logical1 argument inside the OR function, click cell **D4** and then type **>12,**

e. For the logical2 argument inside the OR function, click cell **E4**, and then type **>=1000**

f. Type **),** to close the OR function and move on to the value_if_true argument.

g. For the value_if_true argument, type **"High",** For the value_if_false argument type **"Low"**

h. Type **)** to close the function and then press ⌷Ctrl⌷+⌷Enter⌷.

Because neither of the logical tests return true for the first customer, the value_if_false, "Low" is returned.

i. With cell F4 still selected, use the **fill handle** to copy the formula down through cell **F16**.

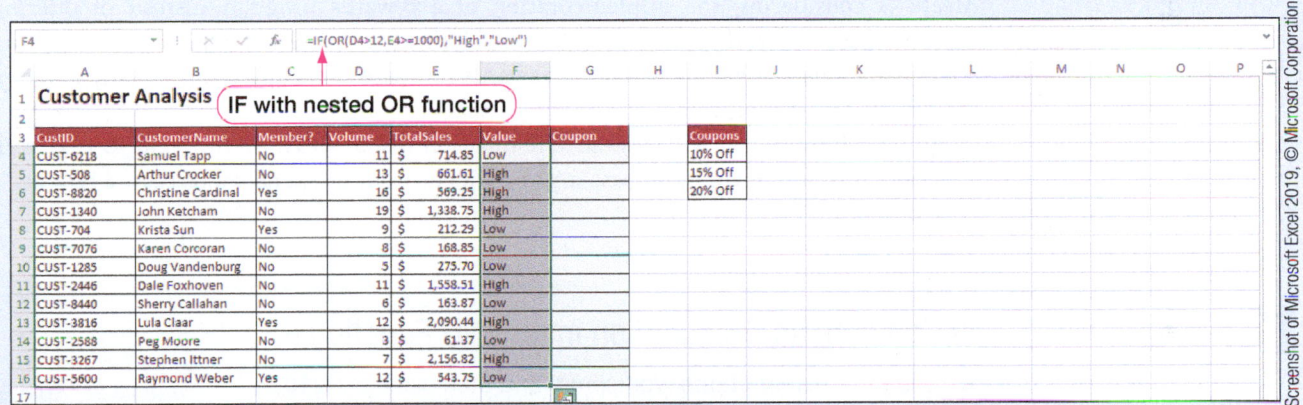

Figure 5 Customer Value – OR function nested in an IF function

j. **Save** 🖫 the workbook.

Integrate Complex Conjunction Functions into IF Functions

There are other situations in which it becomes necessary to combine the OR and AND functions to solve for more complex business logic. This could include an OR function inside an AND function or an AND function inside an OR function. The order in which you nest the logical functions together has to do with the actual business logic being emulated. Take the following scenario about a potential rewards program for the pro shop:

A customer will receive a 10% discount on their entire purchase if they are a member and if they either purchase a promotional item or spend more than $100; otherwise they receive a 0% discount. This only rewards a member who also meets at least one of the other two conditions. There are various methods that can help you comprehend the business logic of a problem like this. One method is to create a T-chart that lays out the logic for the entire IF function, including logical tests and outcomes. A **T-chart** is a common method for dividing up the logic into outcomes and conditions. See Figure 6 for an example of a T-chart used to explain the logic of the scenario described above.

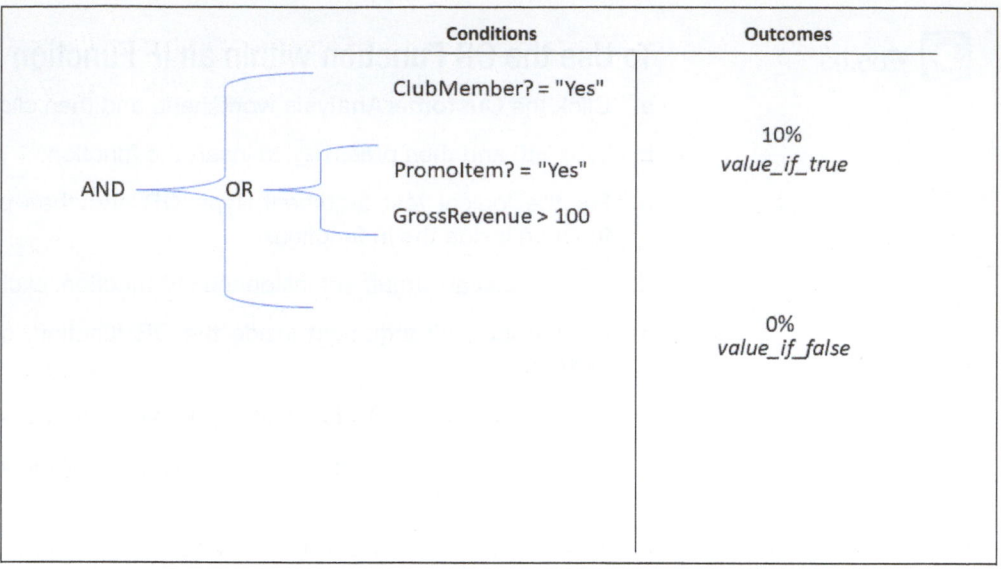

Figure 6 T-Chart – an IF function with an OR function inside an AND function

Combining an OR Function in an AND Function

Aleeta is considering the implementation of a rewards program instead of offering separate discounts and coupons. She is considering two different approaches to issuing rewards and would like to see how the rewards compare to the discounts already given in the sample transaction data.

In this exercise you will nest an OR function inside an AND function so that club members who also either purchase a promotional item or spend more than $100 get a 10% discount.

 **E05.04**

To Combine an OR Function in an AND Function

a. Click the **Transactions** worksheet, and then click cell **O10**.

b. Type **=IF** and then press ⎡Tab⎤ to insert the function.

c. Type **AND** and then press ⎡Tab⎤ to nest the function as the logical_test argument of the IF function.

d. For the logical1 argument, click cell **F10** and then type **="Yes"** This logical test ensures that only members are potentially eligible for the reward discount.

e. Type a comma **,** to move on to the logical2 argument and then type **OR** and press ⎡Tab⎤ to nest the function as the logical2 argument of the AND function.

f. For the logical1 argument of the OR function, click cell **G10** and then type **="Yes"**

g. Type a comma **,** to move onto the logical2 argument of the OR function.

h. For the logical2 argument of the OR function, click cell **H10** and then type **>100**

i. Type **))** to close both the OR function and the AND function, then type **,** to move on to the value_if_true argument.

j. For the value_if_true argument, type **0.10** and then type a comma **,** to move on to the value_if_false argument.

k. For the value_if_false argument, type **""** and then type **)** to close the IF function. Press ⎡Ctrl⎤+⎡Enter⎤.

l. Format cell **O10** as a **Percentage** with **0** decimal places.

m. With cell **O10** still selected, use the **fill handle** to copy the formula down through cell **O30**.

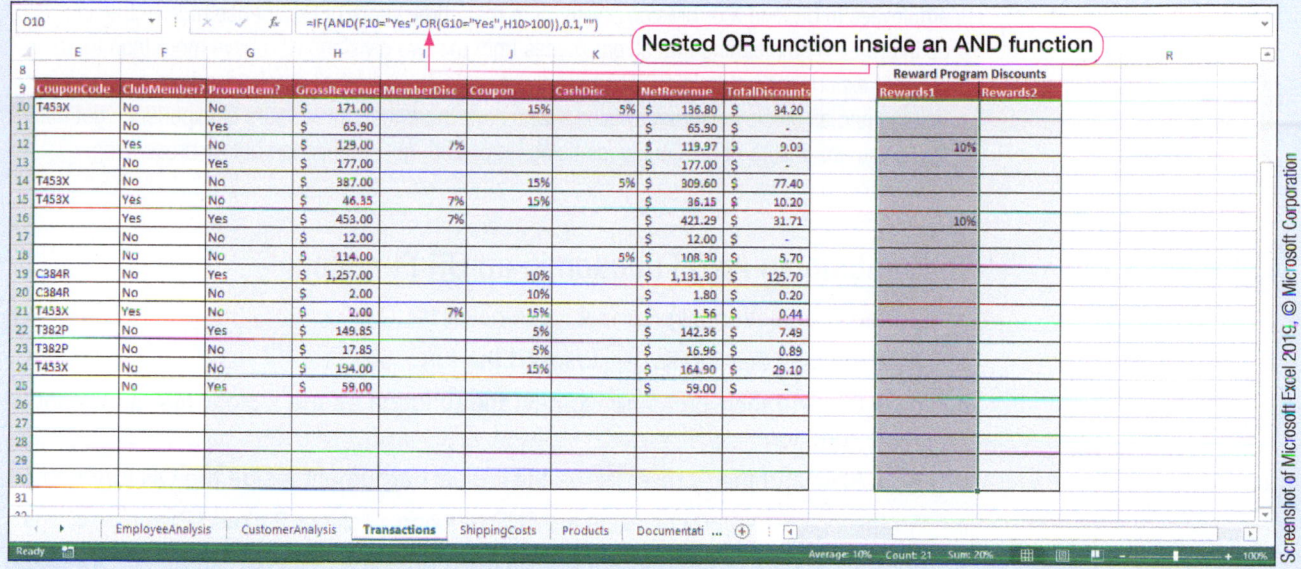

Figure 7 Rewards1 – OR function inside an AND function

> ### Troubleshooting
>
> Be careful with closing parentheses and commas as you begin nesting functions to solve more complex problems. The ScreenTip that appears below the function serves as a guide for building the formula. Every function opened must be closed when appropriate and commas are used to move from one argument to the next.

n. Save 🖫 the workbook.

Combining an AND Function in an OR Function

Aleeta is considering offering reward incentives to non-members as well. In this exercise, you will nest an AND function inside an OR function so that either club members who spend more than $200 or any non-member who purchases a promotional item get a 10% discount. Before you begin, consider the logic necessary in Figure 8.

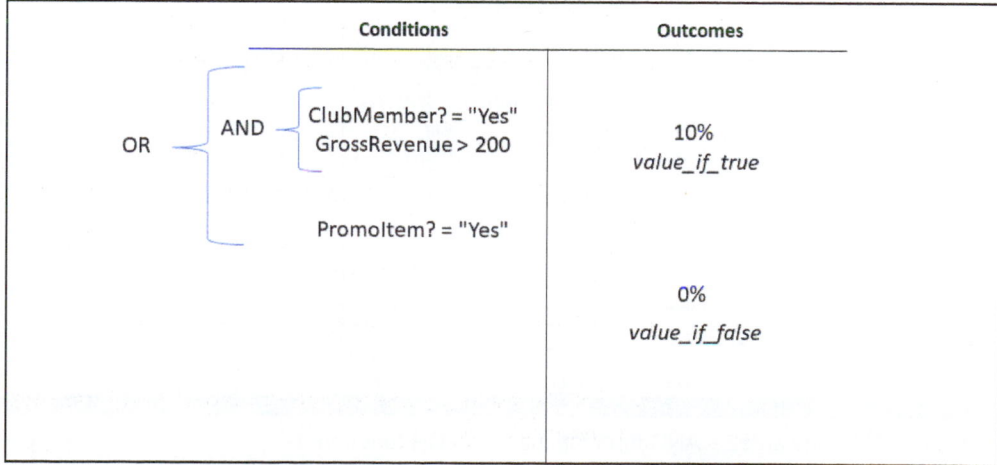

Figure 8 Necessary logic for nesting an AND function inside an OR function

REAL WORLD ADVICE

Working with Complex AND and OR Conditions

In the real world, you will want to confirm complex conditions. For example, the statement "All employees in division X or division Y with more than three years of experience receive training" can be interpreted as meaning that all employees from the two divisions who have more than three years of experience get training. Alternatively, it could mean that all employees from division X get training and all employees from division Y who have more than three years of experience get training. If you are unsure of the conditions being requested, get clarification before proceeding.

 **E05.05**

To Combine an AND Function in an OR Function

a. On the Transactions worksheet, click cell **P10**.

b. Type **=IF** and then press Tab to insert the function.

c. Type **OR** and then press Tab to nest the function as the logical_test argument of the IF function.

d. Type **AND** and then press Tab as the logical1 argument inside the OR function.

e. For the logical1 argument inside the AND function, click cell **F10** and then type **="Yes",**

f. For the logical2 argument of the AND function, click cell **H10**, and then type **>200**

g. Type **)** to close the AND function and make note that the ScreenTip shows that the AND function fulfills the logical1 argument of the OR function.

h. Type a comma **,** to move on to the logical2 argument of the OR function, click cell **G10**, and then type **="Yes"**

i. Type **)** to close the OR function and then type a comma **,** to move on to the value_if_true argument of the IF function.

j. Type **0.10** for the value_if_true and then type a comma **,** to move on to the value_if_false argument.

k. Type **""** for the value_if_false argument, type **)** to close the IF function, and then press Ctrl+Enter.

l. Format cell **P10** as a **Percentage** with **0** decimal places.

m. With cell P10 still selected, use the **fill handle** to copy the formula down through cell **P30**.

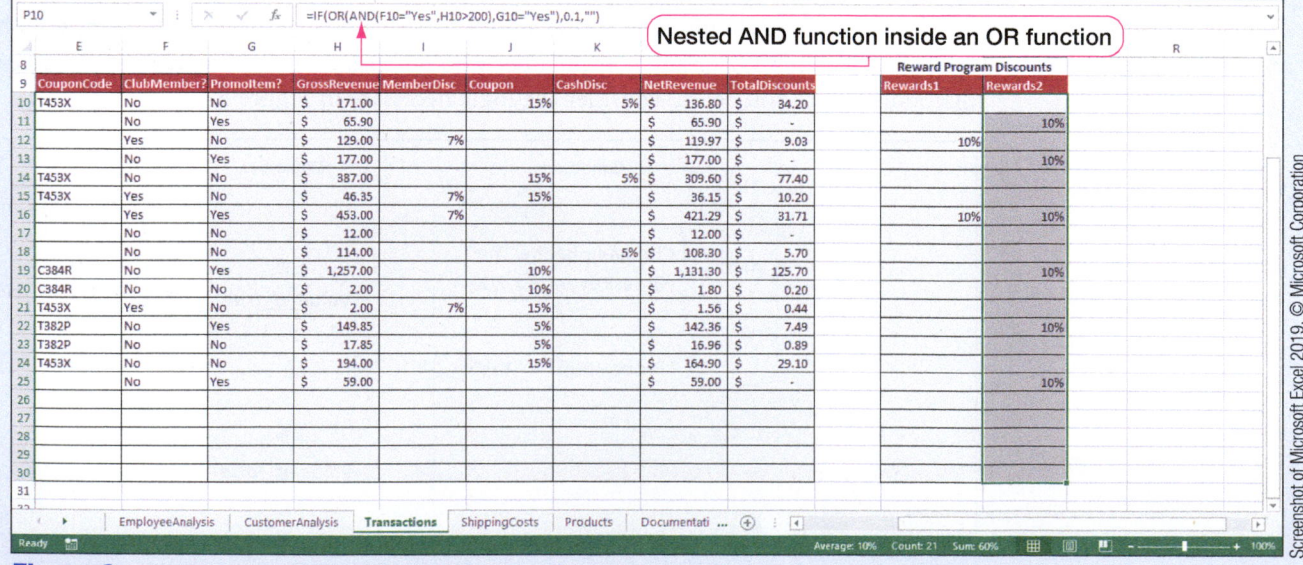

Figure 9 Rewards2 – AND function inside an OR function

n. **Save** 💾 the workbook.

Build Nested IF Functions

As discussed earlier, there are limitations with the IF function. In addition to only supporting one logical test, the IF function only allows for two outcomes. But what happens if you have more than two possible outcomes? The **IFS function** is new to Excel 2019 and allows you to test up to 127 different conditions, specifying a value if true for each with the option to also specify a default value to return if none of the conditions returns true. The syntax of the IFS function is:

=IFS(logical_test1, value_if_true1,[logical_test2, value_if_true2]…[logical_test127, value_if_true127])

To specify a default outcome, you can type TRUE as your final logical_test argument and the default outcome as that logical test's value_if_true. If none of the other conditions are met, the corresponding value will be returned. This is important to consider because if none of the conditions specified are met, the function will return #N/A.

Using the IFS Function

Aleeta has recently had a new point of sale (POS) system installed at the pro shop, and training has begun on how to use the new system to take advantage of all the new features. She would like to determine which employees are to be considered an expert, proficient, or a beginner with the new POS system based on the number of hours of training each of them have completed.

The requirements for each classification are provided in Table 4.

Classification	Greater than or equal to	Less than
Expert	40	
Proficient	25	40
Beginner	0	25

Table 4 POS classifications

Creating a number line of the business requirements like the one shown in Figure 10 can be helpful in visualizing the logic.

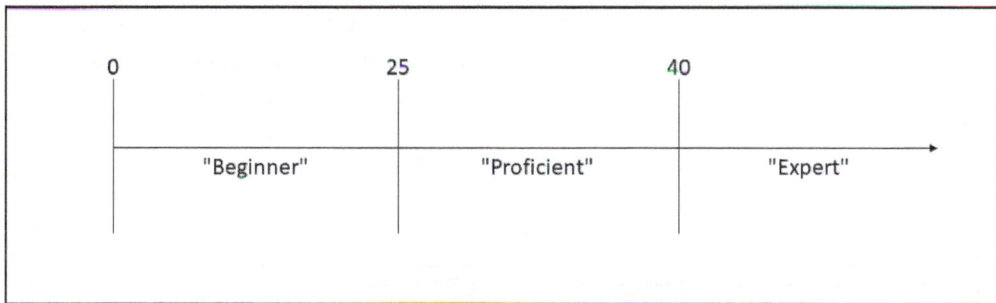

Figure 10 IFS number line

When building the IFS function where the conditions are based on numbers, you can start at either end of the number line and work your way through all the conditions. However, you must be careful that the values used in the logical tests do not overlap other values unless those values have already been used in previous logical tests. For example, you cannot start with:

=IFS(HoursOfTraining>=0,"Beginner"…

because logical_test1 would also include every other possible number for the hours of training.

However, if you started with:

=IFS(HoursOfTraining<25,"Beginner"…

then the next [logical_test2, value_if_true2] argument could be:

HoursOfTraining <40, "Proficient"...

This is because once a logical test has been defined, those values are ignored in later logical tests. So, the second logical test would only include values that are less than 40 but not values less than 25 as those values were already taken care of with the first logical test. In this scenario, because the only other values to consider are greater than or equal to 40 hours, the [logical_test3, value_if_true3] argument can be:

TRUE, "Expert"

In this exercise, you will use the IFS function to evaluate each of the employee's training hours completed and determine if they are an expert, proficient, or a beginner.

 **E05.06**

To Use the IFS Function

a. Click the **EmployeeAnalysis** worksheet and then click cell **D14**.

b. Type **=IFS** and then press Tab to insert the function.

c. For the logical_test1 argument, click cell **C14** and then type **>=40,**

d. For the value_if_true1 argument, type **"Expert",**

e. For the logical_test2 argument, click cell **C14** and then type **>=25,**

f. For the value_if_true2 argument, type **"Proficient",**

g. For the logical_test3 argument, type **TRUE,**

   The TRUE is necessary to set a default value if none of the other conditions are true.

h. For the value_if_true3 argument type **"Beginner"** and then type **)** to close the IFS function. Press Ctrl+Enter.

i. With D14 still selected, use the **fill handle** to copy the formula down through cell **D18**.

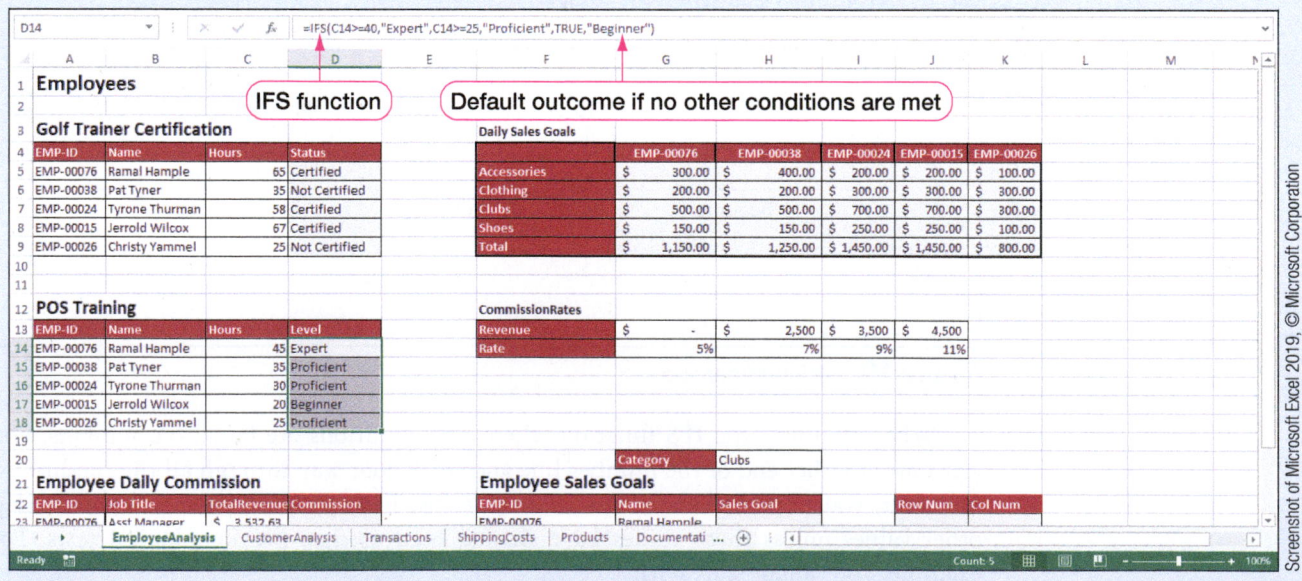

Figure 11 POS proficiency – IFS function

j. **Save** the workbook.

REAL WORLD ADVICE | Building Flexibility into Worksheets

While it is sometimes acceptable to enter the values for your logical tests directly in the formula, it is not necessarily best practice. To support decision making, it is better to build the worksheet for flexibility. It is easier to change a worksheet cell value than it is to search formulas to find the number you need to update. Whenever possible, use a cell reference in a formula instead of the values.

Building Nested IF Functions

Many organizations do not update to the latest version of software upon its release. Because the IFS function is new to Excel, it is very important that similar problems requiring more than two outcomes can still be solved. To solve these problems without the IFS function, you must use a nested IF function. A **nested IF function** uses IF functions as arguments within another IF function and increases the number of logical outcomes that can be expressed.

Nested IF functions may seem more complicated than using the IFS function, but one advantage they have over IFS is that they are often easier to read, especially if any of the logical tests require the use of the AND or OR functions. Aleeta would like to reward her customers with a coupon to celebrate customer appreciation week at the Red Bluff Golf Club & Pro Shop based on the following:

- If a customer is a club member and has been deemed a high-value customer based on their last transaction, she would like them to get 20% off.
- If they aren't a member but are still deemed a high-value customer, she would like them to get 15% off.
- All other customers will receive a 10% off coupon.

When working with nested IF functions, you can easily determine how many IF functions you need by subtracting 1 from the total number of outcomes. Because this scenario has three possible outcomes, you will need to nest two IF functions together. A T-chart, like the one in Figure 12, is extremely helpful to envision the logic necessary to solve complex problems like this one.

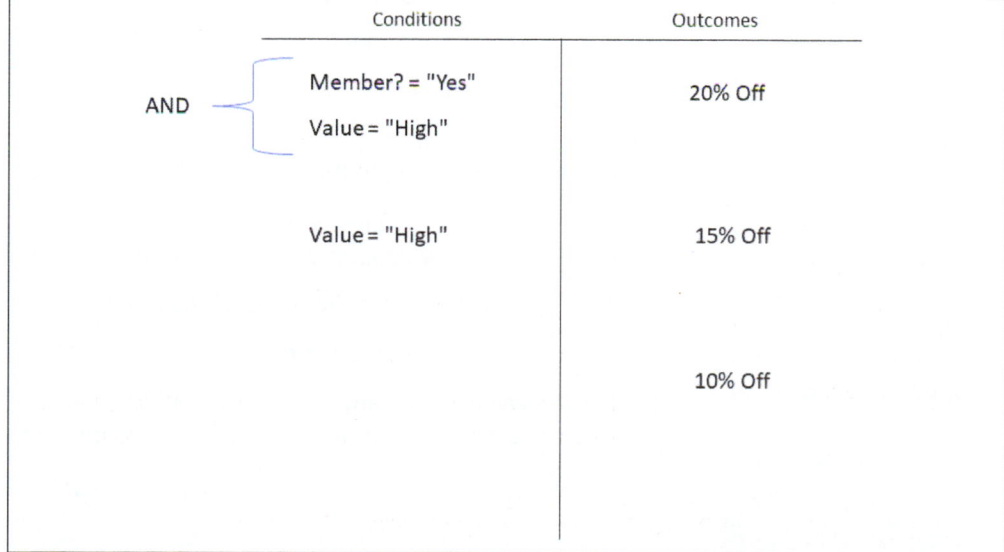

Figure 12 T-chart for customer coupons

QUICK REFERENCE | Easy Tricks for a Nested IF Function

There are two important items to note in writing nested IF functions.

- First, consider the number of outcomes. The number of IF functions needed is always one less than the number of outcomes. For example, if you had five possible outcomes of Very Cold, Cold, Warm, Hot, and Very Hot, you immediately know that you will need to nest four IF functions, three of which are nested inside the main IF function.

- Second, the number of parentheses needed to close your functions at the end of your formula is always the same number as the number of IF functions you used. In the previous example, in which you use two IF functions, you know immediately that you will need two closing parentheses at the end of your formula. Keep in mind that this would not include any parentheses that may be needed in the final [value_if_false] argument.

REAL WORLD ADVICE | Older Versions of Excel

Although more and more organizations are subscribing to Office 365, many still use older versions of Excel and therefore will not have access to the IFS function. IF functions are so common in analysis that it is important you know how to solve problems by nesting IF functions when IFS is not available.

In this exercise, you will write a nested IF function to determine which of three coupons each customer should receive for customer appreciation week.

 E05.07

SIDE NOTE
Nested IF Functions
It is important to note that the IFS function is brand new to Excel, and therefore many organizations may not have access to the function.

SIDE NOTE
Pairing Parentheses
Each function needs a pair of parentheses. Excel color codes each parenthesis to indicate which parentheses are paired.

To Build Nested IF Functions

a. Click the **CustomerAnalysis** worksheet and then click cell **G4**.

b. Type =IF and then press [Tab] to insert the function.

c. Type AND and then press [Tab] to insert the function as the logical_test argument of the IF.

d. For the logical1 argument, click cell **C4** and then type ="Yes",

e. For the logical2 argument, click cell **F4** and then type ="High"

f. Type), to close the AND function and move on to the value_if_true argument.

g. Click cell **I6**, press [F4] to make it an absolute cell reference, and then type a comma , to move on to the value_if_false argument.

By referencing cell I6 instead of just typing "20% off", Aleeta has the flexibility to easily change the coupon values without having to edit the formula.

h. Type IF and then press [Tab] to insert the function as the value_if_false argument.

i. For the logical_test argument, click cell **F4** and then type ="High",

j. For the value_if_true argument, click cell **I5**, press [F4] to make it an absolute cell reference, and then type a comma , to move on to the value_if_false argument.

k. For the value_if_false argument, click cell **I4**, press F4 to make it an absolute cell reference, and then type)) to close both IF functions.

> **Troubleshooting**
>
> If you are unable to click cell I4 because the formula has overlapped, you can either type the cell address or click cell I3 and use the down arrow key on the keyboard to navigate to I4.

l. Press Ctrl+Enter and with G4 still selected, use the **fill handle** to copy the formula down to cell **G16**.

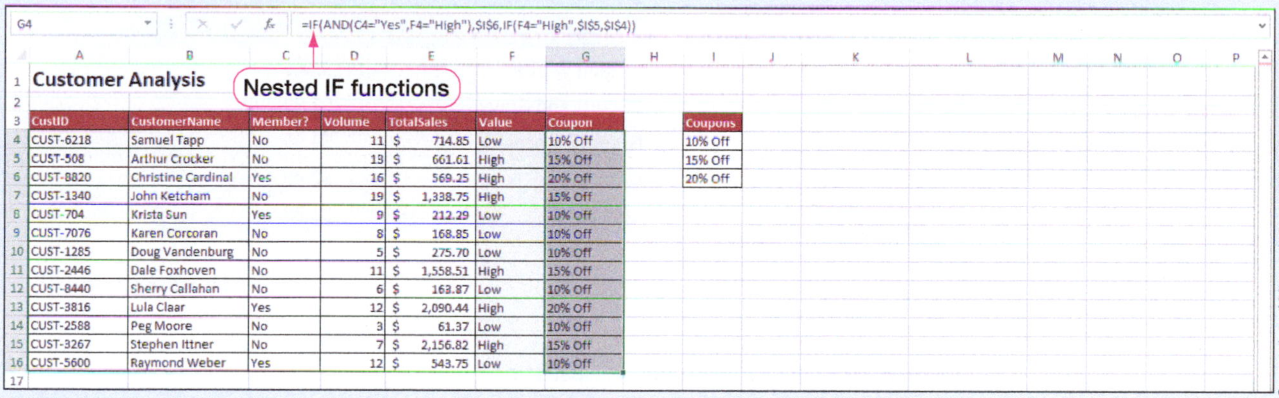

Screenshot of Microsoft Excel 2019, © Microsoft Corporation

Figure 13 Nested IF functions

m. **Save** the workbook.

n. If you need to take a break before finishing this chapter, now is a good time.

Retrieving Data Using Lookup and Reference Functions

It is extremely useful to be able to look for and retrieve specific data when working with data sets. For example, you may have exam scores and you need to convert the numerical score into a letter grade. Within a business, when conducting analysis on transactions, you may want to retrieve details about an item sold from a table containing the product information. In both cases, you want to search for or look up a value and then retrieve some corresponding information. A variety of functions exist for this type of data analysis. In this section, you will create functions that can take a value from your analysis, look for it in a separate dataset, and retrieve corresponding information about that value.

Explore LOOKUP Functions

There are two LOOKUP functions—VLOOKUP and HLOOKUP—you can use to look up a value and then, using that value as a reference, return data that is associated with that value. LOOKUP functions are extremely valuable when working with tables in which the data is in rows or columns. LOOKUP functions are also valuable when you need to retrieve values that are in another location within your workbook.

Using the VLOOKUP Function

The **VLOOKUP function** takes a value, referred to as a lookup value, looks for it in the leftmost column of a table of data, and then returns a value from the same row but in a different column. The "V" in VLOOKUP stands for vertical, and it can only retrieve values from a table when the table is arranged in vertical columns and the lookup value is located in a column to the left of the value you want to retrieve.

One way to think about how the VLOOKUP function works is to imagine a menu at your favorite restaurant. The menu items may be located along the left side of the page and the prices on the right. Once you locate the desired menu item in the left column, you can find the price, in the same row as the item, in the other column. See Figure 14 for an illustration of how the VLOOKUP function works.

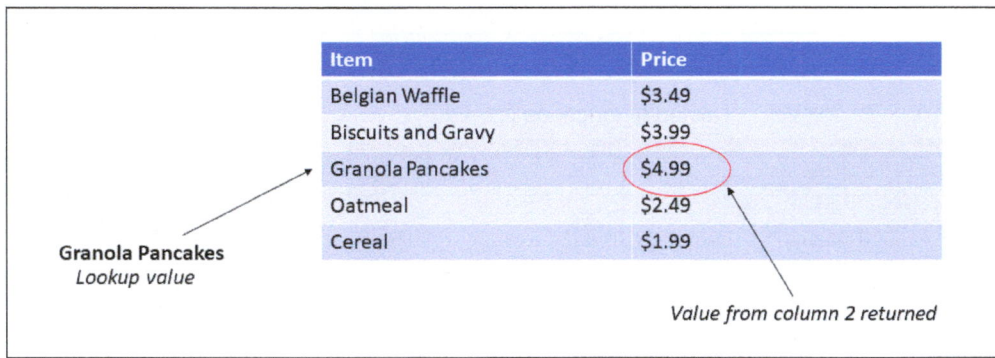

Figure 14   VLOOKUP function illustration

The **VLOOKUP** is the more commonly used **LOOKUP** function. It has four arguments, three of which are required; the other is optional. The syntax for the **VLOOKUP** function is

=VLOOKUP(lookup_value, table_array, col_index_number, [range_lookup])

- lookup_value: the value to be found in the leftmost column of table of data
- table_array: the table of data; can be a range of cells or a named range
- col_index_num: the number of the column that contains the value you want to return
- range_lookup: TRUE if the leftmost column contains a range of numbers and you want to find an approximate match to the lookup value; FALSE if you want an exact match to the lookup value. Optional—defaults to TRUE if omitted.

The sample data on the Transactions worksheet include the ItemID of each product purchased along with the quantity sold. However, the price and other information about each item are stored in the Product List table on the Products worksheet. To calculate the revenue that each transaction generates for the pro shop, the price of each item needs to be retrieved from the table. To think of this in the context of the VLOOKUP function, consider each of the arguments.

- lookup_value: ItemID
- table_array: Product List
- col_index_num: the number of the column containing the price (counting from left to right)
- range_lookup: FALSE for an exact match

In this exercise, you will use the VLOOKUP function to retrieve the price for each item sold and then multiply the price by quantity to calculate the gross revenue from each transaction.

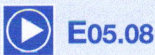 **E05.08**

To Use the VLOOKUP Function

a. If you took a break, open the **e03ch05ProShopSales_LastFirst** workbook, and then click the **Products** worksheet.

b. Examine the data and structure in the table. The left column of the table contains the ItemID of each product, followed by Description, Category, and Retail Price. A named range, Product_List, has been created so that you can more easily reference the table from another worksheet.

c. Click the **Transactions** worksheet. Click cell **H10**, type **=VLOOKUP** and then press Tab to insert the function, replacing the static value.

d. Click cell **B10** for the lookup_value argument and then type a comma , to move to the table_array argument.

SIDE NOTE
Forget the Name?
If you don't recall the name of the named range, try pressing the F3 key to bring up a list of all named ranges in the workbook from which to choose.

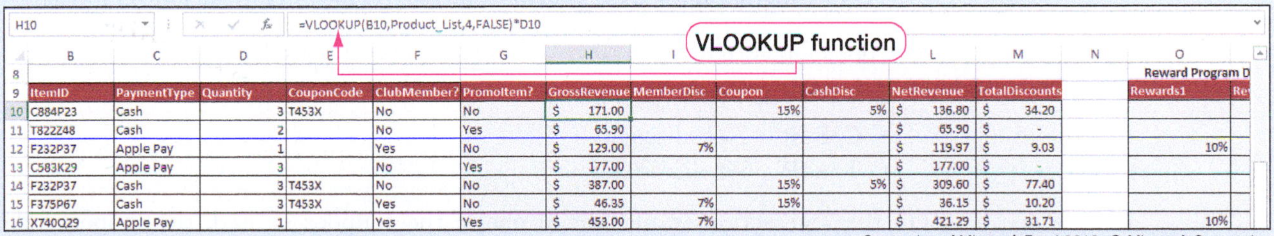

e. Type **Product_** and then press Tab to insert the Product_List named range for the table_array argument.

The VLOOKUP function will look for the ItemID value in cell B10 in the leftmost column of the Product_List named range.

f. Type a comma , to move to the col_index_num argument. Type **4** because the value retail price you want to return for the item is in the fourth column of the table.

g. Type a comma , to move to the range_lookup argument. Press ↓ to select the **False - Exact match** value and then press Tab to insert the value into the function. Because the values in the leftmost column of the Product_List named range are not ranges of numbers, you want the function to find an exact match to the ItemID.

h. Type **)** to close the function and then press Ctrl+Enter. The VLOOKUP should return the retail price of $57.00 for ItemID, C884P23.

i. Press F2 to edit the formula. Type ***** and then click cell **D10** to multiply the retail price returned by the function by the quantity sold. Press Ctrl+Enter.

| H10 | | | fx | =VLOOKUP(B10,Product_List,4,FALSE)*D10 | | | | VLOOKUP function | | | | | | |

	B	C	D	E	F	G	H	I	J	K	L	M	N	O
8														Reward Program D
9	ItemID	PaymentType	Quantity	CouponCode	ClubMember?	PromoItem?	GrossRevenue	MemberDisc	Coupon	CashDisc	NetRevenue	TotalDiscounts		Rewards1	Re
10	C884P23	Cash	3	T453X	No	No	$ 171.00		15%	5%	$ 136.80	$ 34.20		
11	T822Z48	Cash	2		No	Yes	$ 65.90				$ 65.90	$ -		
12	F232P37	Apple Pay	1		Yes	No	$ 129.00	7%			$ 119.97	$ 9.03		10%
13	C583K29	Apple Pay	3		No	Yes	$ 177.00				$ 177.00	$ -		
14	F232P37	Cash	3	T453X	No	No	$ 387.00		15%	5%	$ 309.60	$ 77.40		
15	F375P67	Cash	3	T453X	Yes	No	$ 46.35	7%	15%		$ 36.15	$ 10.20		
16	X740Q29	Apple Pay	1		Yes	Yes	$ 453.00	7%			$ 421.29	$ 31.71		10%

Screenshot of Microsoft Excel 2019, © Microsoft Corporation

Figure 15 Gross revenue – VLOOKUP function

j. With cell **H10** still selected, use the **fill handle** to copy the formula down through cell **H30**.

Note that the function returns a #N/A error for all cells below row 25. This is because there are no ItemIDs to look up. Consequently, the formula in the Cash-Disc column also returns the error in cells below 25. These errors will be addressed later in the chapter.

k. Save 🔲 the workbook.

REAL WORLD ADVICE	The VLOOKUP Function in Business

Businesses use LOOKUP functions on a regular basis because they have a tremendous amount of data stored in multiple workbooks. Employers will expect you to be comfortable with LOOKUP functions when you seek employment. An interviewer may even ask you whether you know how to work with them.

Using the HLOOKUP Function

The HLOOKUP function works in the same manner as the VLOOKUP function—helping you to retrieve values located in another location—but is used when the table of data is structured horizontally in rows. The **HLOOKUP function** takes a value, looks for it in the topmost row of a table of data, and then returns a value from the same column but in a different row. The "H" in HLOOKUP stands for horizontal and it can only retrieve values from a table when the table is arranged in horizontal rows and the lookup value is located in a row above the value you want to retrieve.

=HLOOKUP(lookup_value, table_array, row_index_number, [range_lookup])

- lookup_value: the value to be found in the topmost row of a table of data
- table_array: the table of data; can be a range of cells or a named range
- row_index_num: the number of the row that contains the value you want to return
- range_lookup: TRUE if the topmost row contains a range of numbers and you want to find an approximate match to the lookup value; FALSE if you want an exact match to the lookup value. Optional – defaults to TRUE if omitted.

The pro shop currently has three different coupons in circulation:

- T453X—15% discount
- C384R—10% discount
- T382P—5% discount

On the Transactions worksheet, if one of the coupons is used, the coupon code is recorded. Aleeta would like to be able to retrieve the discount amount from the table in order to eventually calculate the net revenue for each transaction. Figure 16 illustrates how an HLOOKUP can retrieve the discount value from a table.

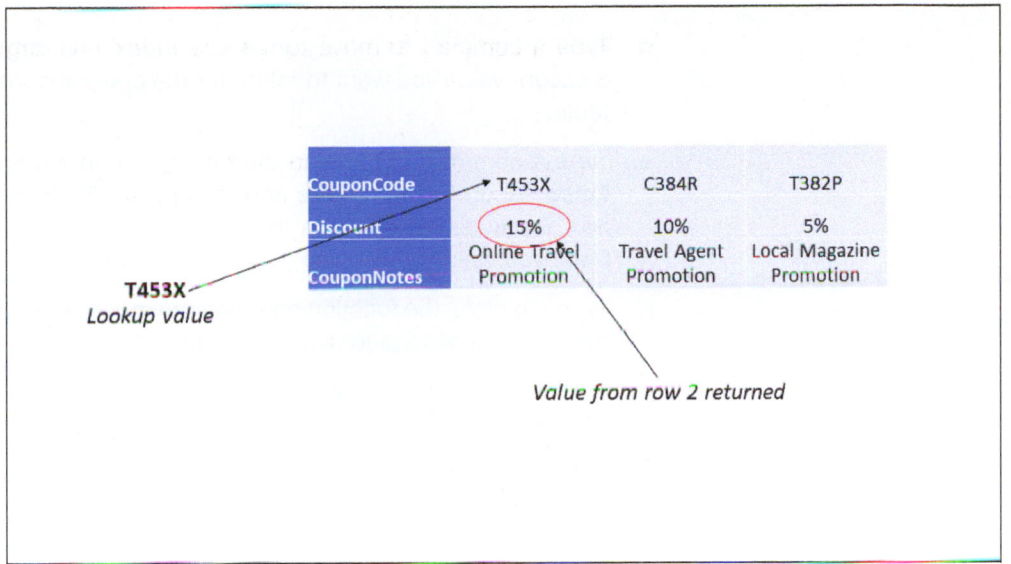

Figure 16 HLOOKUP function illustration

To think of this in the context of the HLOOKUP function, consider each of the arguments.

- lookup_value: CouponCode
- table_array: Coupon Table
- row_index_num: the number of the row containing the discount (counting from top to bottom)
- range_lookup: FALSE for an exact match

In this exercise, you will create an HLOOKUP function to retrieve the discount amount for each coupon.

 **E05.09**

To Use the HLOOKUP Function

a. On the Transactions worksheet, click cell **J10**, type **=HLOOKUP** and then press [Tab] to insert the function, replacing the static value.

b. Click cell **E10** for the lookup_value argument and then type **,** to move to the table_array argument.

c. Select the cell range **B4:D6** and then press [F4] to make it an absolute cell reference for the table_array argument.

The HLOOKUP function will look for the CouponCode value in cell E10 in the topmost row of the $B$4:$D$6 range.

d. Type a comma **,** to move to the row_index_num argument. Type **2** because the discount value you want to return for the coupon code is in the second row of the table.

e. Type a comma **,** to move to the range_lookup argument. Press ↓ to select the **False – Exact match** value and then press [Tab] to insert the value into the function. Because the values in the topmost row of the table are not ranges of numbers, you want the function to find an exact match to the CouponCode.

f. Type **)** to close the function and then press [Ctrl]+[Enter]. The HLOOKUP should return the discount of 15% for CouponCode T453X.

g. With cell **J10** still selected, use the **fill handle** to copy the formula down through cell **J30**.

Note that the function returns a #N/A error for many of the records. This is because there are no CouponCodes to look up. These errors will also be addressed later in the chapter.

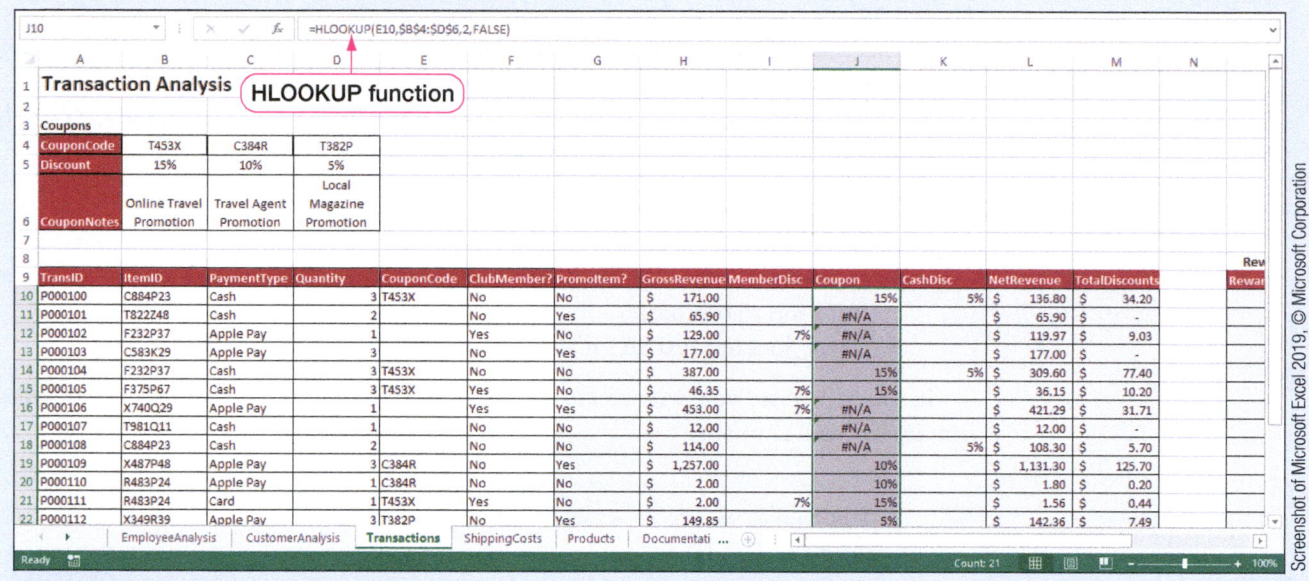

Figure 17   Coupon – HLOOKUP function

h. Save 💾 the workbook.

CONSIDER THIS | **Using LOOKUPs or Nested IFs**

Take the situation of converting coupon codes to discount amounts. Could you create an IFS function that would accomplish the same task? What logical issues would lead you to use a LOOKUP versus a nested IF? Which one would be more efficient?

Combining a LOOKUP with an IF Function

Employees of the pro shop earn a commission each day. The commission rate ranges from 5% to 11% depending on how much revenue the employee generates on any given day. Assistant managers only earn commission if they generate $4,000 or more in revenue, and then they earn a flat 10% of their sales. The best approach to a problem like this is to break it down and build the solution piece by piece.

Figure 18 is a T-chart of the logic part of the IF function needed.

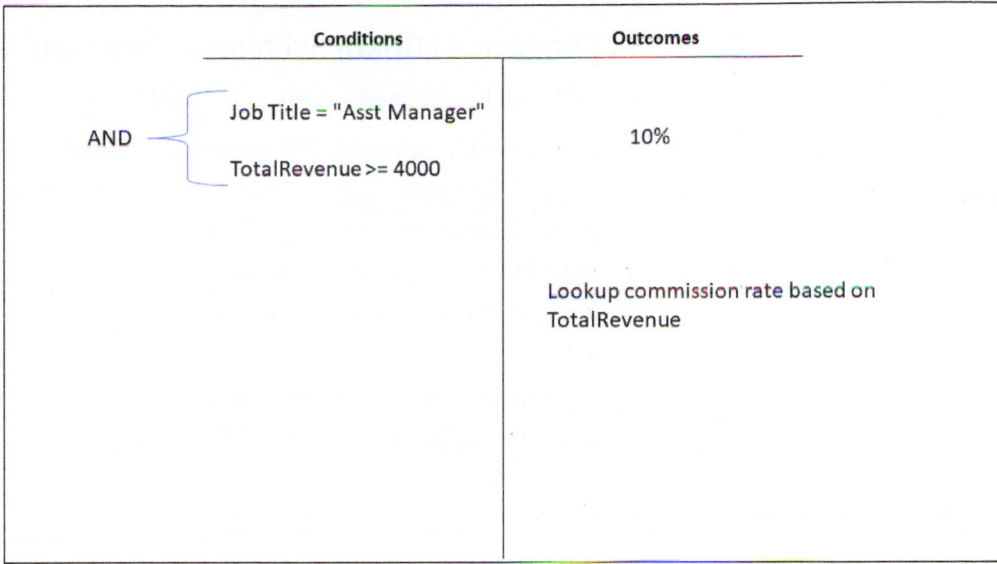

Figure 18 T-Chart for Employee Commission

Figure 19 illustrates how the HLOOKUP function can retrieve the commission rate for the value_if_false argument of the IF.

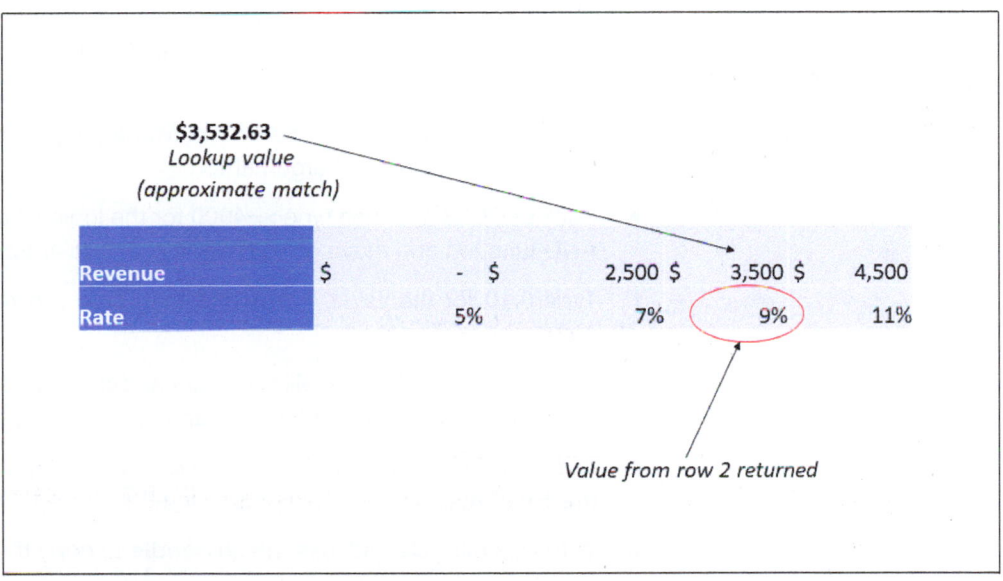

Figure 19 HLOOKUP for commission rates

In this exercise, you will combine an HLOOKUP function with an IF function.

 **E05.10**

To Combine a LOOKUP with an IF Function

a. Click the **EmployeeAnalysis** worksheet.

b. Click cell **D23**, type **=HLOOKUP** and then press Tab to insert the function.

c. Click cell **C23** for the lookup_value argument and then type a comma , to move to the table_array argument.

d. Select the cell range **G13:J14** and then press F4 to make it an absolute cell reference for the table_array argument.

   The HLOOKUP function will look for the TotalRevenue value in cell C23 in the topmost row of the $G$13:$J$14 range.

e. Type a comma , to move to the row_index_num argument. Type 2 because the commission rate you want to return for the coupon code is in the second row of the table.

f. Type a comma , to move to the range_lookup argument. Press Tab to select the **True - Approximate match** value into the function. Because the values in the topmost row of the table are ranges of numbers, you want the function to find an approximate match to the TotalRevenue amount.

SIDE NOTE
Optional Argument
The range_lookup argument defaults to TRUE if omitted.

g. Type) to close the function and then press Ctrl+Enter. The HLOOKUP should return the commission rate of .09 for a TotalRevenue amount of $3,532.63 because it is at least $3,500 but still less than $4,500.

h. Press F2 to edit the formula. Click before the HLOOKUP, type IF, and then press Tab to insert the function.

i. Type AND and then press Tab to insert the AND function for the logical_test argument.

j. Click cell **B23** and then type ="Asst Manager", for the logical1 argument and to move on to the logical2 argument.

k. Click cell **C23** and then type >=4000 for the logical2 argument. Type), to close the AND function and move on to the value_if_true argument.

l. Type 0.10 for the value_if_true and then type , to move on to the value_if_false argument.

m. Because the HLOOKUP will be what happens if the logical test is FALSE, click at the end of the HLOOKUP function and type) to close the IF.

n. At the end of the nested function, type * C23 to multiply the commission rate by the TotalRevenue, and then press Ctrl+Enter.

o. With D23 still selected, use the **fill handle** to copy the formula down through **D27**.

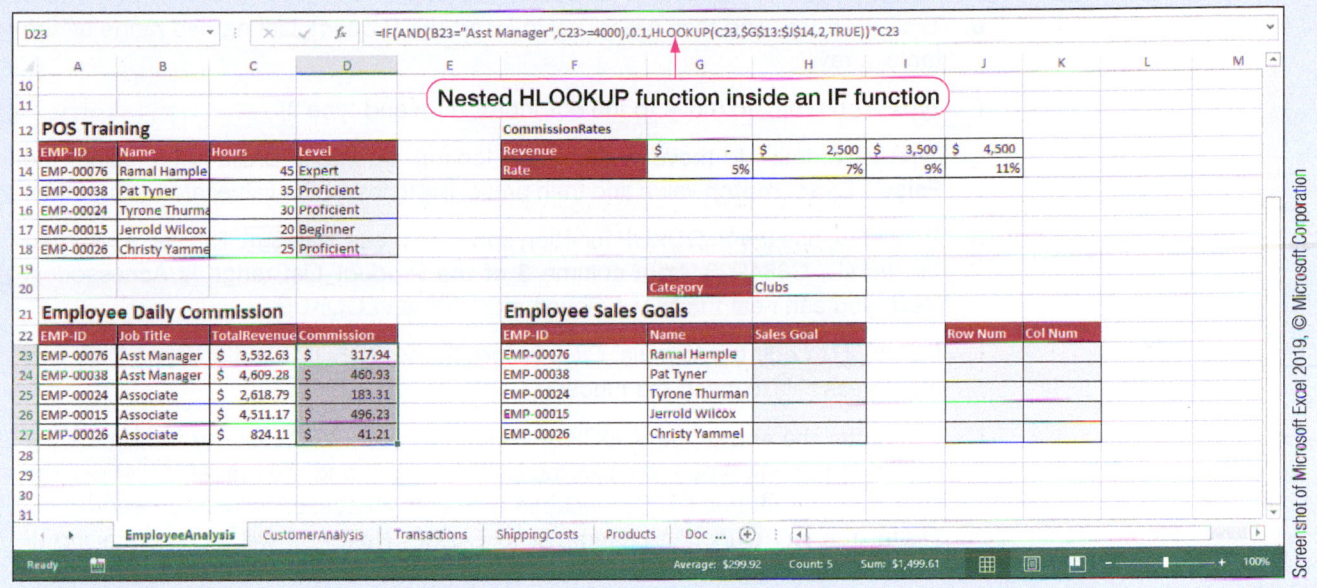

Screenshot of Microsoft Excel 2019, © Microsoft Corporation

Figure 20   HLOOKUP inside an IF function

p. **Save**  the workbook.

Combining a VLOOKUP with the IF and NOT Logical Functions

Aleeta has decided to promote all the products at the pro shop that are not accessories. She would like you to come up with a formula that will indicate, with a "Yes" or "No," which items are promotional. This is challenging, in part, because the category to which an item belongs is in the Product_List table on a different worksheet than the transactions. The category for each item will need to be retrieved from the table first.

Once you master the LOOKUP functions, you will find that you can use the values retrieved in various calculations and functions. The NOT function allows creation of logical statements in which it creates the opposite or reverse result of its argument. It evaluates to TRUE or FALSE. If the logical test is TRUE, then FALSE is returned. If the logical test is FALSE, then TRUE is returned. This is particularly useful when there are many values that would result in a TRUE and only one that would return a FALSE. In the case of products that are not part of the accessories category, you could use NOT(Category = "Accessories"). In this example, if the category for an item were Accessories, that is TRUE, and the result of the NOT function would be FALSE. If the category were Clubs, then Clubs = Accessories is FALSE, so the NOT function returns TRUE, or not false.

In this exercise, you will combine a VLOOKUP with other logical functions to return "Yes" if the product category is not accessories and "No" if it is an accessory.

E05.11   To Combine a VLOOKUP with the IF and NOT Logical Functions

a. A problem like this is best solved by breaking it down and building the formula in pieces. You will begin by retrieving the Category for each item on the Transactions worksheet. Click the **Products** worksheet and observe that column 3 contains the Category value.

b. Click the **Transactions** worksheet and then click cell **G10**.

c. Type **=VLOOKUP** and then press `Tab` to insert the function, replacing the static value.

d. Click cell **B10** for the lookup_value and then type **,** to move to the table_array argument.

e. Type Product_ and then press Tab to insert the Product_List named range as the table_array.

f. Type a comma , to move to the col_index_num and type 3.

g. Type a comma , to move to the range_lookup argument, press ↓ to select the **False – Exact match** value and then press Tab to insert the value into the function.

h. Type) to close the VLOOKUP function and then press Ctrl+Enter. The value returned for ItemID, C884P23, from column 3 of the Product_List range is Accessories. Next, you can nest the NOT function around the VLOOKUP.

i. Press F2 to edit the formula. Click before the VLOOKUP function, type NOT and then press Tab to insert the function.

j. Click after the end of the VLOOKUP function, type ="Accessories" to define the logical argument, type) to close the NOT function, and then press Ctrl+Enter. The NOT function returns FALSE because although "Accessories" = "Accessories" is TRUE, the NOT function changes it to FALSE. Next you will incorporate the IF function around the NOT function.

k. Press F2 to edit the formula. Click before the NOT function, type IF, and then press Tab to insert the function.

l. Because the NOT function serves as the logical_test, click after the end of the NOT function and type a comma , to move to the value_if_true argument.

m. Type "Yes" for the value_if_true, type , to move to the value_if_false argument, and then type "No"

n. Type) to close the IF function and then press Ctrl+Enter. Because the value in cell G10 was FALSE, the value_if_false, No, is returned.

With cell G10 still selected, use the **fill handle** to copy the formula down through **G30**. Note that the function returns a #N/A error for all cells below row 25. This is because there are no ItemIDs to look up. These errors will be addressed later in the chapter.

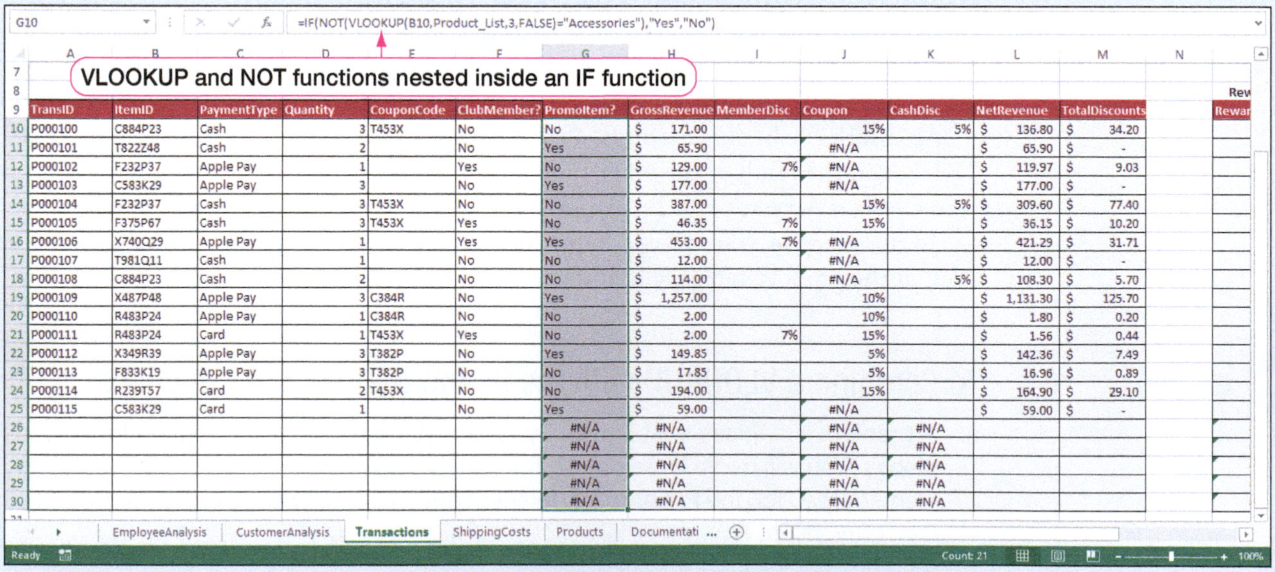

	A	B	C	D	E	F	G	H	I	J	K	L	M	N
G10				fx	=IF(NOT(VLOOKUP(B10,Product_List,3,FALSE)="Accessories"),"Yes","No")								
7		VLOOKUP and NOT functions nested inside an IF function												
8														Rev
9	TransID	ItemID	PaymentType	Quantity	CouponCode	ClubMember?	PromoItem?	GrossRevenue	MemberDisc	Coupon	CashDisc	NetRevenue	TotalDiscounts	Rewar
10	P000100	C884P23	Cash	3	T453X	No	No	$ 171.00		15%	5%	$ 136.80	$ 34.20	
11	P000101	T822Z48	Cash	2		No	Yes	$ 65.90		#N/A		$ 65.90	$ -	
12	P000102	F232P37	Apple Pay	1		Yes	No	$ 129.00	7%	#N/A		$ 119.97	$ 9.03	
13	P000103	C583K29	Apple Pay	3		No	Yes	$ 177.00		#N/A		$ 177.00	$ -	
14	P000104	F232P37	Cash	3	T453X	No	No	$ 387.00		15%	5%	$ 309.60	$ 77.40	
15	P000105	F375P67	Cash	3	T453X	Yes	No	$ 46.35	7%	15%		$ 36.15	$ 10.20	
16	P000106	X740Q29	Apple Pay	1		Yes	Yes	$ 453.00	7%	#N/A		$ 421.29	$ 31.71	
17	P000107	T981Q11	Cash	1		No	No	$ 12.00		#N/A		$ 12.00	$ -	
18	P000108	C884P23	Cash	2		No	No	$ 114.00		#N/A	5%	$ 108.30	$ 5.70	
19	P000109	X487P48	Apple Pay	3	C384R	No	Yes	$ 1,257.00		10%		$ 1,131.30	$ 125.70	
20	P000110	R483P24	Apple Pay	1	C384R	No	No	$ 2.00		10%		$ 1.80	$ 0.20	
21	P000111	R483P24	Card	1	T453X	Yes	No	$ 2.00	7%	15%		$ 1.56	$ 0.44	
22	P000112	X349R39	Apple Pay	3	T382P	No	Yes	$ 149.85		5%		$ 142.36	$ 7.49	
23	P000113	F833K19	Apple Pay	3	T382P	No	No	$ 17.85		5%		$ 16.96	$ 0.89	
24	P000114	R239T57	Card	2	T453X	No	No	$ 194.00		15%		$ 164.90	$ 29.10	
25	P000115	C583K29	Card	1		No	Yes	$ 59.00		#N/A		$ 59.00	$ -	
26							#N/A	#N/A		#N/A	#N/A			
27							#N/A	#N/A		#N/A	#N/A			
28							#N/A	#N/A		#N/A	#N/A			
29							#N/A	#N/A		#N/A	#N/A			
30							#N/A	#N/A		#N/A	#N/A			

EmployeeAnalysis   CustomerAnalysis   **Transactions**   ShippingCosts   Products   Documentati …

Ready   Count 21   100%

Figure 21   PromoItem – VLOOKUP with IF and NOT functions

o. **Save** 💾 the workbook.

Screenshot of Microsoft Excel 2019, © Microsoft Corporation

Retrieve Data Using MATCH, INDEX, and INDIRECT Functions

VLOOKUP and HLOOKUP search the first column or row of data and "look" to the right or down to retrieve a value. What if you wanted to find the name of the person with the phone number (412) 555-8767 in the phone book? Would that be easy to do? Unfortunately, the task is difficult because a traditional phone book is organized by name, not by phone number.

To overcome this limitation in the VLOOKUP and HLOOKUP functions, the INDEX and MATCH functions work to accomplish the same type of process. The primary difference is that these two functions together overcome the limitation of data arrangement. With the INDEX and MATCH functions, you have the added flexibility of multiple data ranges that can be located throughout the worksheet. The ability to use INDEX and MATCH together is a powerful capability within Excel. Several benefits of using the INDEX and MATCH functions in Excel are as follows.

- INDEX and MATCH allow for data to be retrieved from any direction.
- Columns can be added or deleted in a table array without breaking the formula.
- VLOOKUP values are limited in size (255 characters), but with the INDEX and MATCH, there is no limit to the lookup value size.

Using the INDEX and MATCH Function

The **INDEX function** has two different sets of arguments. The first set of arguments uses an array and returns a value from the array at the intersection of a specified row number and column number. The second set of arguments uses a reference and returns a reference to specified cells. The more common set of arguments, which will be discussed here, is with the array that returns a value. The syntax for the INDEX function is

=INDEX(array, row_num, [column_num])

- array: the range of cells that contain the data you wish to be able to retrieve
- row_num: the row number of the value to be returned
- column_num: the column number of the value to be returned

Examine Figure 22, which contains the daily sales goals for each employee by product category.

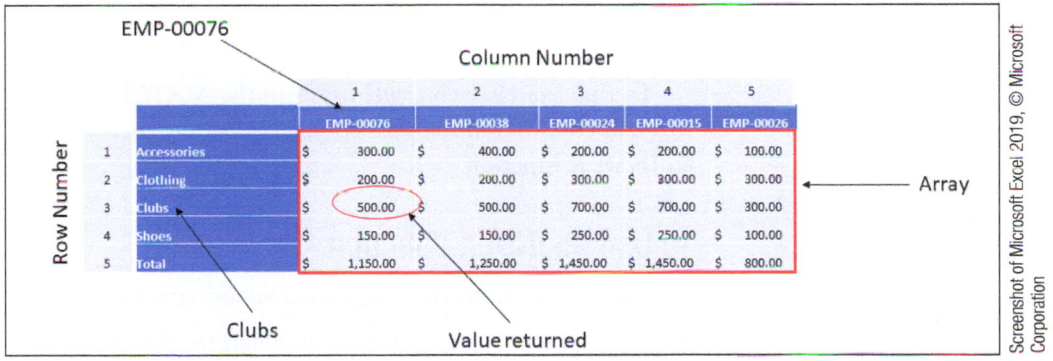

Figure 22   INDEX function illustration

If you wish to return employee EMP-00076's sales goal for the "Clubs" product category, the value to be returned would be in row 3, column 1. Having the row and column numbers manually entered means that it would be very difficult to retrieve a different employee's sales goal from a different product category. This is where the MATCH function comes into play.

The MATCH function may seem obscure and not very valuable by itself; however, it becomes extremely useful when used to create dynamic row or column numbers inside LOOKUP or INDEX functions. Unlike LOOKUP functions that return a value from a table, the **MATCH function** returns a number that represents the position where a value is located within a range. The syntax for the MATCH function is

=MATCH(lookup_value, lookup_array, [match_type])

- lookup_value: the value to be located in a column or row
- lookup_array: a contiguous range of cells where the lookup_value is to be located (must be 1 column or 1 row only)
- match_type: Three possible values; 1 – Less than, 0 – Exact match, –1 – Greater than. Optional – defaults to 1 if omitted

A [match_type] value of 0 is used for an exact match, a 1 returns a match for the largest value that is less than or equal to the lookup_value (values in lookup_array must be numbers sorted in ascending order), and a –1 finds the smallest value that is greater than or equal to the lookup_value (values in lookup_array must be numbers sorted in descending order).

The exact match will return the row where the first occurrence of the match resides. This means that if there are multiple occurrences of a value, Excel will return the first one it finds, from the top, and will not find subsequent values.

The match_type of 1 will find the location of the value that is closest to the value but not greater than the value. The –1 value will return the position of the value that is closest to the lookup_value but not less than the lookup_value.

In Figure 22, the sales goal amount for the "Clubs" category was in row 3. Consider the arguments of the MATCH function in this context.

- lookup_value: Clubs
- lookup_array: the range of cells containing product categories, starting with Accessories
- match_type: 0 – Exact match because you want to find "Clubs" in the lookup_array

Because "Clubs" is located three cells down from the first cell of the lookup_array, the MATCH function would return 3.

All the various sales goals for EMP-00076 were in column 1. Consider the arguments of the MATCH function in this context.

- lookup_value: EMP-00076
- lookup_array: the range of cells containing the Employee IDs, starting with the first one
- match_type: 0 – Exact match because you want to find "EMP-00076" in the lookup_array

Because "EMP-00076" is located in the first cell of the lookup_array, the MATCH function would return 1.

In this exercise, you will first use the MATCH functions to return the appropriate row and column numbers for the desired value; then you will incorporate those values in an INDEX function.

 E05.12

To Use an INDEX Function

a. Click the **EmployeeAnalysis** worksheet and then click cell **J23**.

b. Type **=MATCH** and press [Tab] to insert the function.

c. Because this MATCH function is to return the row number of the product category, click cell **H20** and press [F4] to make it an absolute cell reference for the lookup_value.

d. Type a comma **,** to move on to the lookup_array argument, select the cell range **F5:F9**, and then press [F4] to make it an absolute cell reference.

e. Type a comma **,** to move on to the match_type argument, press [↓] to select the **0 - Exact match** value, and then press [Tab] to insert it into the function.

f. Type **)** to close the MATCH function and then press [Ctrl]+[Enter]. Because the lookup value, Clubs, is located three cells from the top of the lookup_array, the function returns a 3. This number will change when the product category in cell H20 changes.

g. With J23 still selected, use the **fill handle** to copy the formula down through J27.

h. Click cell **K23**, type **=MATCH** and then press Tab to insert the function.

i. Because this MATCH function is to return the column number of each Employee, click cell **F23** for the lookup_value. This should be a relative cell reference so that it will follow the formula down when it is copied.

j. Type a comma **,** to move on to the lookup_array argument, select the cell range **G4:K4**, and then press F4 to make it an absolute cell reference.

k. Type a comma **,** to move on to the match_type argument, press ↓ to select the **0 - Exact match** value, and then press Tab to insert it into the function. Because the values in the lookup_array are not a sorted range of numbers, you want the function to find an exact match to the "EMP-00076".

l. Type **)** to close the MATCH function and then press Ctrl+Enter. Because the lookup value, EMP-00076, is located in the first cell on the left of the lookup_array, the function returns a 1.

m. With K23 still selected, use the **fill handle** to copy the formula down through **K27**.

Now that you have the row and column number for each employee's Club sales goal, you can incorporate these MATCH functions into an INDEX function.

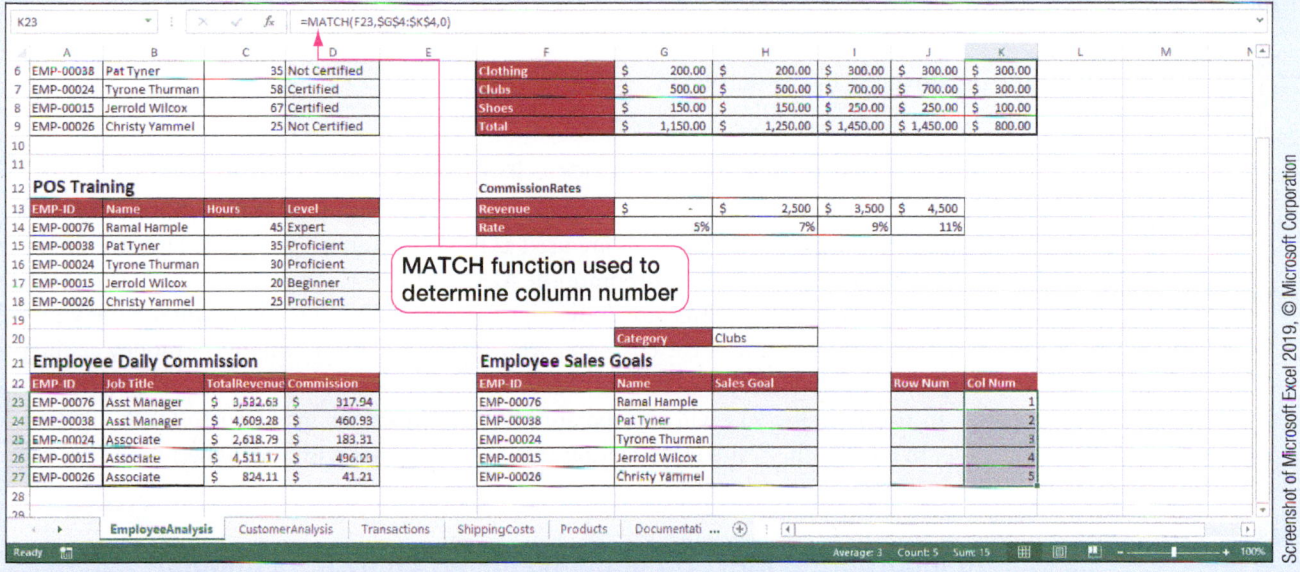

Figure 23 MATCH functions used for row and column numbers

n. Click cell **H23**, type **=INDEX** and then press Tab to insert the function.

o. The array argument should include all of the values you would like the function to be able to return, in this case it is all of the sales goal values. Select **G5:K9** and then press F4 to make it an absolute cell reference.

p. Type a comma **,** to move on to the row_num argument and then click cell **J23**.

q. Type a comma **,** to move on to the column_num argument and then click cell **K23**.

r. Type **)** to close the INDEX function and then press Ctrl+Enter. The INDEX function returns the value in row 3, column 1; 500.

s. Format the value as **Accounting** and with cell H23 still selected, use the **fill handle** to copy the formula down through **H27**.

t. Test that the function works by changing the value in cell **H20** to **Accessories** by using the list. Notice how the row numbers change to 1 in J23:J27 when the category changed to Accessories.

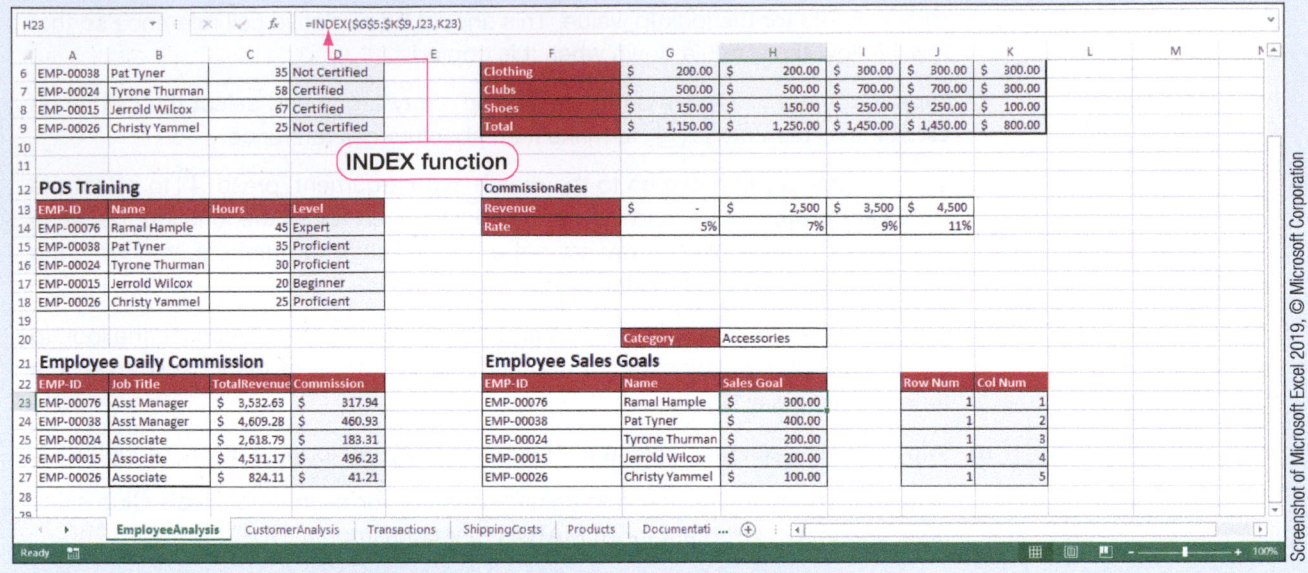

Figure 24 Daily sales goals—INDEX and MATCH functions

u. Save  the workbook.

Incorporating MATCH Functions inside an INDEX Function

Separating the MATCH functions from the INDEX function makes it easier to understand how the MATCH functions are used as row and column numbers. However, most of the time you will want to incorporate the MATCH functions directly inside the INDEX function. Aleeta would like to know the CustomerID, CustomerName, SalesVolume, and TotalSales amount of the customer who spends the most amount of money at the pro shop over a particular period of time.

In this exercise, you will incorporate MATCH functions inside an INDEX function in order to retrieve the desired information about the customer with the highest total sales value.

E05.13

To Incorporate MATCH Functions Inside an INDEX Function

a. Click the **CustomerAnalysis** worksheet and then click cell **B20**.

b. Type **=MAX** and then press ⏽Tab⏽ to insert the function. The customer information you want to retrieve from the table above is the one with the highest TotalSales value. The MAX function will return which value is the largest.

c. Select cells **E4:E16**, press ⏽F4⏽ to make it an absolute cell reference, type **)** to close the MAX function, and then press ⏽Ctrl⏽+⏽Enter⏽. The largest value in the range is $2,156.82, which is in the row for Stephen Ittner. The MATCH function can look for the maximum value in the TotalSales column and the number it returns will be the row number.

d. Press ⏽F2⏽ to edit the formula. Click before the MAX function, type **MATCH**, and then press ⏽Tab⏽ to insert the function.

e. The value the MAX function returns becomes the lookup_value of the MATCH function. Click after the MAX function and type a comma **,** to move on to the lookup_array argument.

f. Select cells **E4:E16**, press [F4] to make it an absolute cell reference, and then type a comma **,** to move on to the match_type argument.

g. Press [↓] to select the **0 - Exact match** value, and then press [Tab] to insert it into the function.

h. Type **)** to close the MATCH function and then press [Ctrl]+[Enter]. The value returned appears to be $12.00 but remember what the MATCH function does. The number 12 has nothing to do with money. Rather, it is how many cells down from E4 where the function found the maximum value of $2,156.82, the row number.

i. Press [F2] to edit the formula. Click before the MATCH function, type **INDEX** and then press [Tab] to insert the function.

j. Select **A4:G16** as the array, press [F4] to make it an absolute cell reference, and then type **,** to move on to the row_num argument. The value returned by the MATCH function, 12, is the row number.

k. Click after the MATCH function and type a comma **,** to move on to the column_num argument. The column that contains the CustomerID is 1, but in order to be able to copy this formula down and retrieve the value from columns 2, 4, and 5 as well, you need to use another MATCH function.

l. Type **MATCH** and then press [Tab] to insert the function.

m. Click **A20** for the lookup_value, type a comma **,** select **A3:G3** for the lookup_array, and then press [F4] to make it an absolute cell reference.

n. Type a comma **,** to move on to the match_type argument, press [↓] to select the **0 - Exact match** value, and then press [Tab] to insert it into the function. This MATCH function is looking for an exact match to CustID in the cell range A3:G3 and will return a 1. The 1 is the column number that contains the Customer ID.

o. Type **))** to close the MATCH and INDEX functions and then press [Ctrl]+[Enter]. The value returned from the table is from the cell where row 12 and column 1 of the table intersect.

p. With cell B20 still selected, use the **fill handle** to copy the formula down through **B23**.

q. Select cells **B20:B22**. The Accounting format applied to these cells is inappropriate for their values. Format the values as **General**.

SIDE NOTE
Size of Arrays
In order for MATCH functions to return the correct row and column numbers, all of the arrays need to be the same height, if vertical, or same width if horizontal.

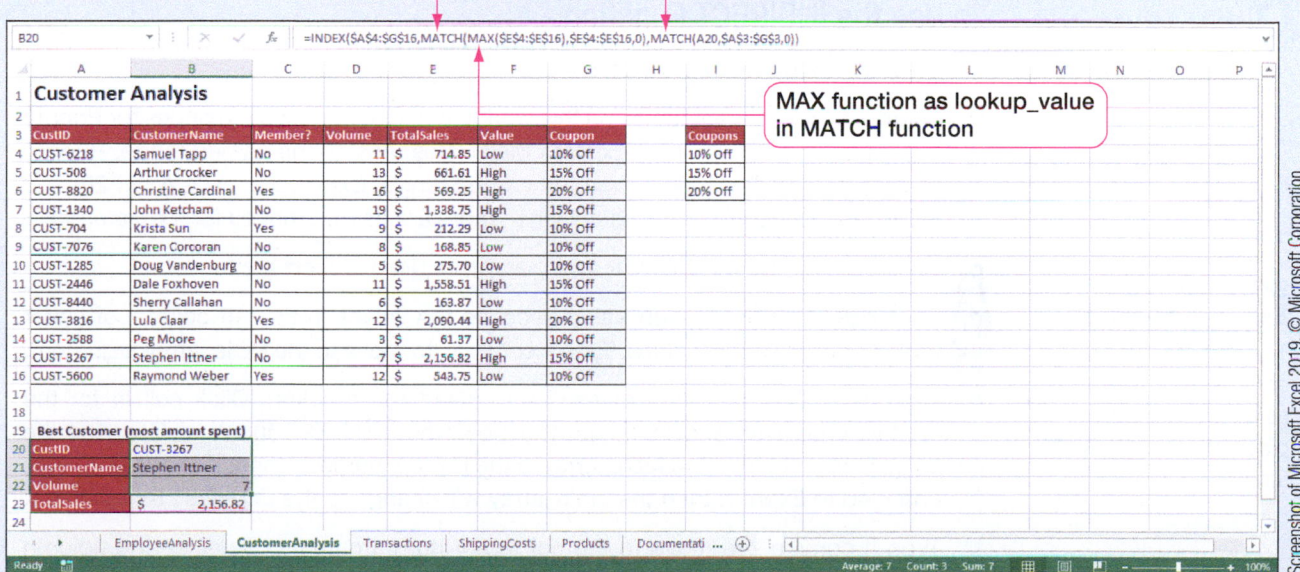

Figure 25 Integrated INDEX and MATCH functions

r. **Save** 💾 the workbook.

Screenshot of Microsoft Excel 2019, © Microsoft Corporation

Using the INDIRECT Function

The **INDIRECT function** is another reference function that can be used to add flexibility to a worksheet. One way the INDIRECT function can add value is that it can change a text string within a cell to a reference to a named range of the same name as the text string. For example, if a company offers Priority and Express shipping to their customers, there can be two different tables, each given an appropriate named range, and a cell indicating the desired shipping method can be referenced in the INDIRECT function to refer to the appropriate table.

The syntax for the INDIRECT function is
=INDIRECT(ref_text, [A1])

- ref_text: most commonly a cell reference that contains a text string where a named range exists with the same name
- [A1]: optional and defaults to TRUE if omitted. Indicates that the type of cell reference is an A1-style instead of the less common, R1C1-style.

The optional INDIRECT argument will not be a concern for the average user. The function defaults to the A1 reference method if the A1 argument is omitted, which merely refers to the **A1 reference style** for cell references. If letters appear for the column headings, the reference style for Excel is currently A1. In this mode, cells are referenced by using a letter for the column and a number for the row.

The alternative method is referred to as the **R1C1 reference style**. With R1C1 style, if numbers appear for the column headings, the reference style for Excel is currently R1C1. For example, if a value is in the third row and fourth column, the cell reference would be R3C4. Excel allows you to set the R1C1 reference style check box as a default option under Formulas within the Excel Options dialog box. Whichever reference style mode Excel is in, all cell references typed in formulas must be in that reference style form—A1 or R1C1. If not, an error will be produced. The A1 reference style is the easiest to use in Excel and is the default method.

The pro shop offers two shipping options for its customers: Priority and Express. The cost for shipping depends on the method chosen, the shipping destination's zone, and the weight of the package. In this exercise, you will incorporate the INDIRECT function to create a dynamic VLOOKUP in order to retrieve the shipping costs from one of two shipping tables.

 E05.14

To Use the INDIRECT Function

a. Click the **ShippingCosts** worksheet.

b. There are two different tables on this worksheet; one contains the prices for Priority Mail rates and the other for Express Mail Rates. Assign the named range, Priority to cells **A5:F10** and then assign the named range, Express to cells **A15:F20**. The INDIRECT function is most useful when there are named ranges for it to reference.

c. Click cell **I7**, type **=VLOOKUP** and then press Tab to insert the function.

d. Click cell **I5** for the lookup_value because the values in the left column of either table contains weight values. Type a comma , to move to the table_array argument.

e. Type **INDIRECT** and then press Tab to insert the function. Click cell **I4** for the ref_text argument, and then type) to close the INDIRECT function. Because the value in I4 is Priority, the table_array is the Priority named range. If the value in I4 is changed to Express then the table_array will change to the Express named range.

f. Type a comma , to move to the col_index_num argument. Because the column will be different depending on the Zone, a MATCH function is necessary. Type **MATCH** and then press Tab to insert the function.

SIDE NOTE
Alternate Method
The INDEX function could also be used here as it can be used in place of either LOOKUP function.

g. Click cell **I6** for the lookup_value, type a comma **,** to move on to the lookup_array, and then select **A4:F4**. It is important that the lookup_array be the same width as the table_array argument so A4 is included.

h. Type a comma **,** to move to the match_type argument, press ⬇ to select the **0 - Exact match** value, and then press Tab to insert it into the function. Type **)** to close the MATCH function which will return a 3 for Zone 2. Because the top row of each of the shipping tables, A4:F4 and A14:F14, contain the same values, the MATCH function will return the correct column number for either table.

i. Because the weight of a package could be in between any of the weight values in the left column, you need it to be an approximate match. Type **)** to close the function and then press Ctrl + Enter. Because the range_lookup argument was omitted, it will default to TRUE – Approximate match.

j. With cell I7 still selected, format the value as **Currency**.

k. Test the flexibility of the VLOOKUP function by using the list in cell **I4** to change the method to **Express**.

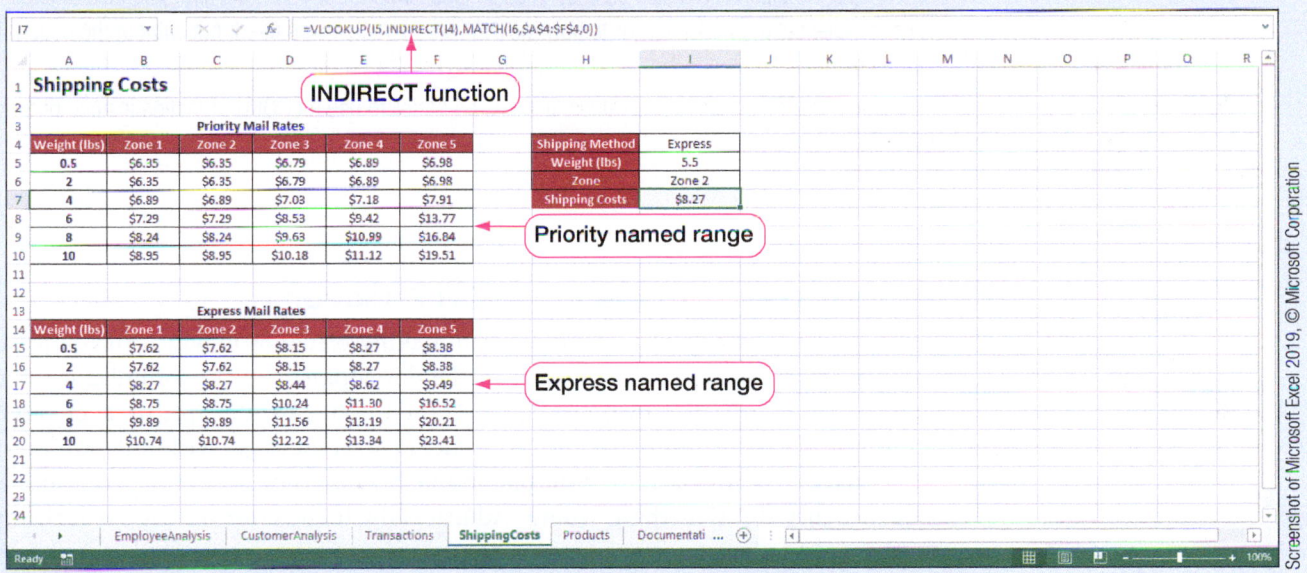

Figure 26 Shipping costs – Using the INDIRECT function inside a VLOOKUP function

l. **Save** 🖫 the workbook.

QUICK REFERENCE | **New to Excel: The SWITCH Function**

The SWITCH function evaluates one value against a list of values and returns the result corresponding to the first matching value. If there is no match, then an optional default value is returned. If no default value is specified and there is no match, then the function returns the #N/A error. It works similarly to the IFS and LOOKUP functions; however, the SWITCH function has an argument for a default value which can be quite useful.

The syntax of the SWITCH function is:

SWITCH(expression, value1, result1, [default or value2, result2], …)

The expression argument can be any type of data; a number, text, Boolean, or a cell reference that contains any of these types.

Example uses:

Use SWITCH where the expression argument is a numerical value that represents a day of the week and if that day is 1 or 7, the corresponding weekend day is returned as the result. Any other value could return the default value of "Weekday"

e.g., =SWITCH(1, 1, "Sunday", 7, "Saturday", "Weekday")

The SWITCH function could also be used in conjunction with a LOOKUP function to be able to choose from multiple table_arrays, similar to how the INDIRECT function was used, but without the need for named ranges.

If you have more than just a few values, it would be better to use a LOOKUP function instead of the SWITCH function.

Handle Errors with the IFERROR Function

Because logical functions are used in decision-making scenarios in which flexibility and scalability are desirable, there are times in the development of the formulas when the functions may return error messages. Because there could be multiple users of varying skills, it is important to minimize the occurrence of error messages within the workbook. Error messages tend to make users uncomfortable because they believe the error message means that they did something wrong. Additionally, if the error message is legitimate and other calculations reference those cells, the errors will carry forward into the next formula, compounding the problem.

The solution is to be aware of when errors may occur—such as dividing by 0 or because you are referencing an empty cell—and create functions in a way that eliminates the error message from being viewed. During development, it is possible to anticipate and handle errors within the formula if you consider the values to be used and the possible answers.

REAL WORLD ADVICE | Using a Blank or a Zero to Hide an Error

Does it matter what you put in for a result or outcome for an IF statement? What are the implications when you use "" versus a zero? When a calculation refers to a cell where you have used a blank, created with the double quotes, the result will be a #VALUE! error or #DIV/0! error. The calculation will not be able to compute the blank as a numerical value. Conversely, if you enter a zero for a value so that it is numerical, then that number would be used in aggregate functions. This could cause miscalculation of an average. Consider how the result will be used. If it is not going to be used in later calculations, then using the blank is a viable solution. Otherwise, you may need to enter a zero. In cells in a range containing a zero, an alternative is to use a calculation formula that allows you to filter data on the basis of certain criteria. For example, if you need to average your results that contain cells with a zero, you can use the AVERAGEIF and average only the numbers that are greater than zero.

Using the IFERROR Function to Eliminate Errors

The **IFERROR function** is used to detect an error and display something more user-friendly than the error message. With the IFERROR function, it is possible to evaluate whether an error will occur and replace one of Excel's default error messages with another value that you specify; otherwise, the formula result will be returned. The syntax for the IFERROR function is

=IFERROR(value, value_if_error)

The first argument—value—is the formula that is going to be checked for existing errors. If the value works and a valid output exists, that formula result will be returned. However, if the value returns any error message, such as #N/A or #DIV/0!, then the value_if_error value will be returned.

When examining the Transactions worksheet, you will see error messages showing up within the range in two different contexts. First, when there are not any transaction records, error messages exist throughout. Second, in a few columns, error messages occur even when there are transactions. The #N/A is not only distracting, it is confusing to users because they may believe that there are calculation errors when in actuality the errors are valid errors.

In the process of checking the values and eliminating errors, it is best to start with formulas that are simple and do not reference other cells that have formulas. For example, if an error exists in a formula in cell A1, that error will create an error in any other formula that references A1. For the Transactions data, it also makes sense to first correct fields in which the error message occurs only where data does not exist. In checking the formulas, it appears that fields such as PromoItem?, GrossRevenue, Coupon, and CashDisc have errors only when cells are empty. A simple way to eliminate this type of error is to leave the cell blank if an error message occurs.

In this exercise, you will eliminate errors with the IFERROR function.

E05.15

To Use the IFERROR Function to Eliminate Errors

a. Click the **Transactions** worksheet, and then click cell **G10**. Press F2 to edit the formula, click before the IF function, type **IFERROR** and then press Tab to insert the function.

b. Click at the end of the IF function, type a comma , to move to the value_if_error argument. Type **""** so that a blank is returned instead of any errors, type **)** to close the function, and then press Ctrl+Enter.

c. With cell G10 still selected, use the **fill handle** to copy the revised formula down through **G30**. Notice that all the #N/A error values are now blanks.

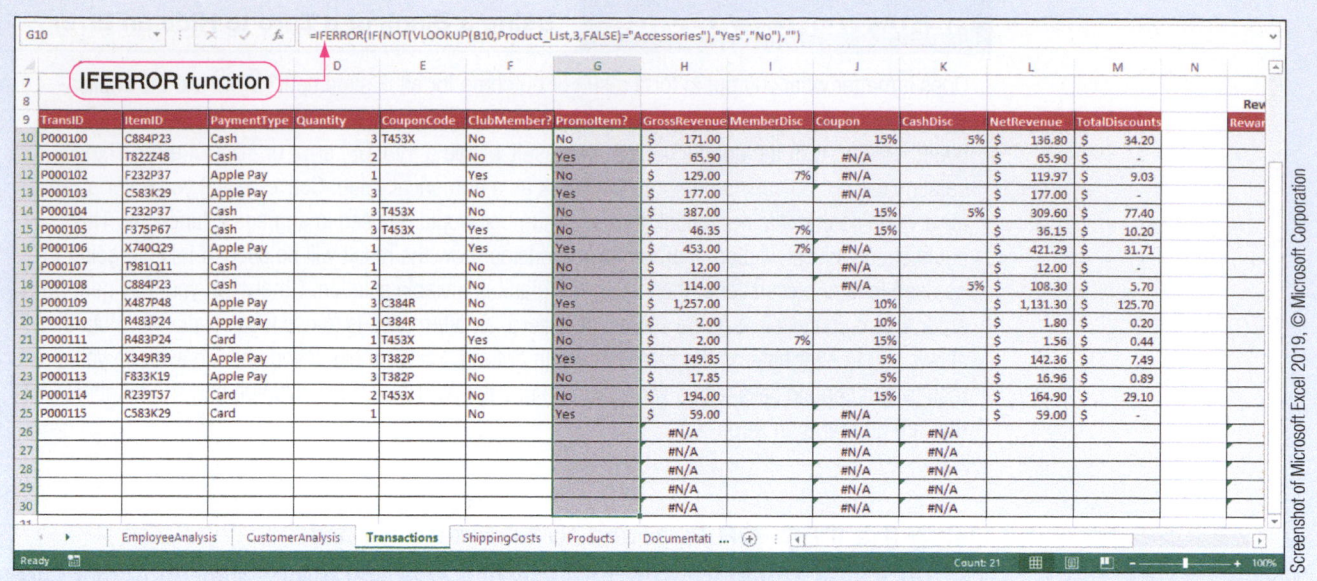

Figure 27 PromoItem? – IFERROR function

SIDE NOTE

Alternates to IFERROR

Excel also includes an IFNA function that works just like the IFERROR but only for #N/A errors. For errors caused by blank cells, an IF function with a logical test of cell value <> "" could also work.

d. Click cell **H10**. Press ⌨F2 to edit the formula, click before the VLOOKUP function, type **IFERROR** and then press ⌨Tab to insert the function.

e. Click after the reference to D10 in the formula, type a comma **,** to move to the value_if_error argument, type **""** so that a blank is returned instead of any errors, type **)** to close the function, and then press ⌨Ctrl+⌨Enter.

f. With cell H10 still selected, use the **fill handle** to copy the revised formula down through **H30**. Notice that all the #N/A error values are now blanks.

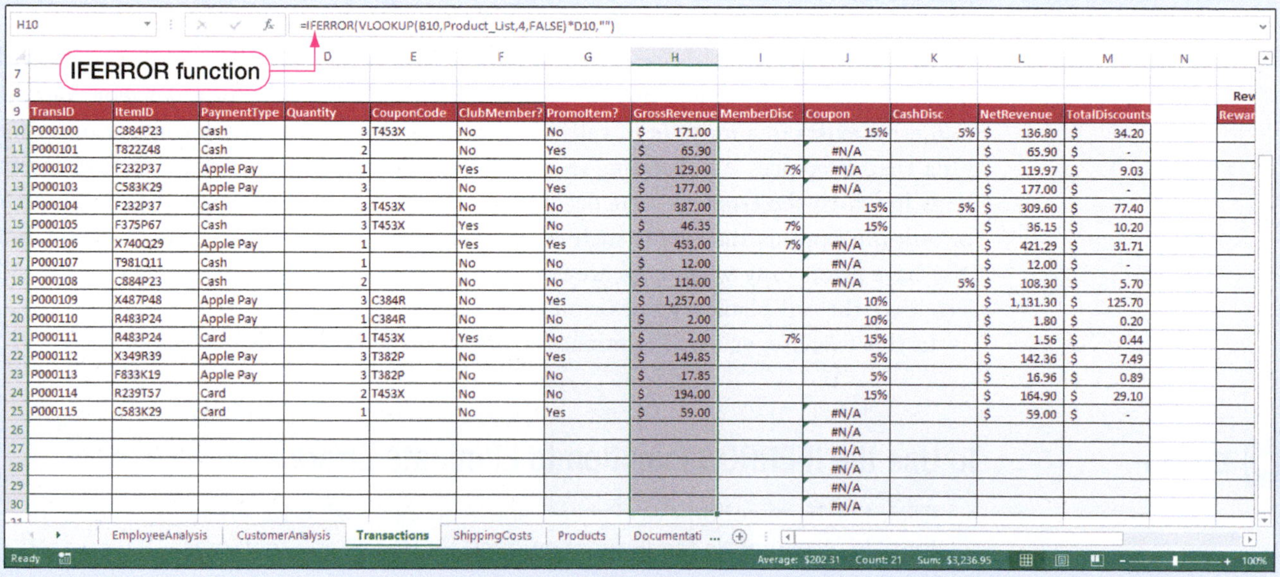

Figure 28 GrossRevenue – IFERROR function

g. Click cell **J10**. Press ⌨F2 to edit the formula, click before the HLOOKUP function, type **IFERROR** and then press ⌨Tab to insert the function.

h. Click after the HLOOKUP function, type a comma **,** to move to the value_if_error argument, type **""** so that a blank is returned instead of any errors, type **)** to close the function, and then press ⌨Ctrl+⌨Enter.

i. With cell **J10** still selected, use the **fill handle** to copy the revised formula down through **J30**. Notice that all the #N/A error values are now blanks.

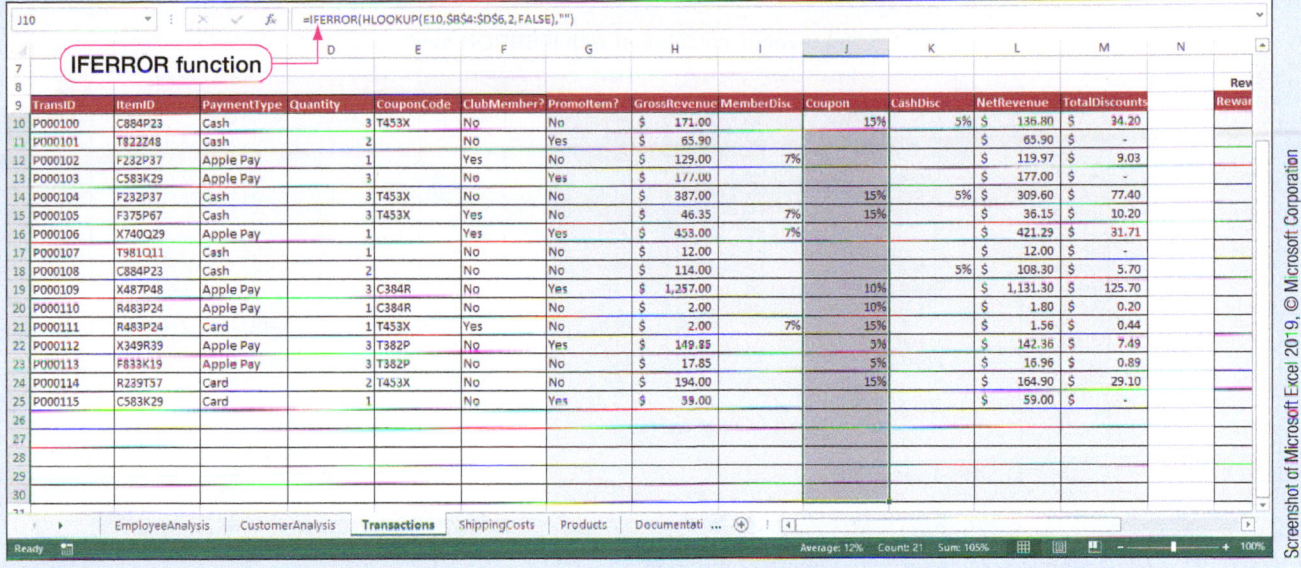

Figure 29 Coupon – IFERROR function

j. **Save** 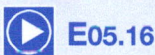 the workbook.

Anticipating and Eliminating Errors

Aleeta needs to be able to calculate the net revenue amount for each transaction as well as the total amount of discounts. Because some of the values needed to make these calculations contain blanks (""), an IFERROR function will be necessary so that the calculations do not return errors.

In this exercise, you will create calculations for NetRevenue and TotalDiscounts, incorporating the IFERROR function to prevent errors from displaying.

E05.16 | To Anticipate and Eliminate Errors

a. On the Transactions worksheet, click cell **L10**. Type **=** and then click **H10** to reference the GrossRevenue amount.

b. To calculate the net revenue, you will multiply the GrossRevenue by 1 – the sum of all discounts. Type *** (1-SUM** and then press **Tab** to insert the SUM function.

c. Select cells **I10:K10** as the range, type **))** to close the SUM function and the outer parenthesis used to control the order of operations and then press **Ctrl**+**Enter**.

d. With L10 still selected, use the **fill handle** to copy the formula down through **L30**. Notice that the #VALUE error is returned for all records missing a GrossRevenue amount.

e. Click cell **L10** again and then press **F2** to edit the formula. Click before the reference to H10, type **IFERROR** and then press **Tab** to insert the function.

f. Click after the two closing parentheses, type a comma **,** to move on to the value_if_false argument, and then type **""** so that a blank will appear instead of an error. Type **)** to close the IFERROR function and then press **Ctrl**+**Enter**.

g. With **L10** still selected, use the **fill handle** to copy the revised formula down through L**30**.

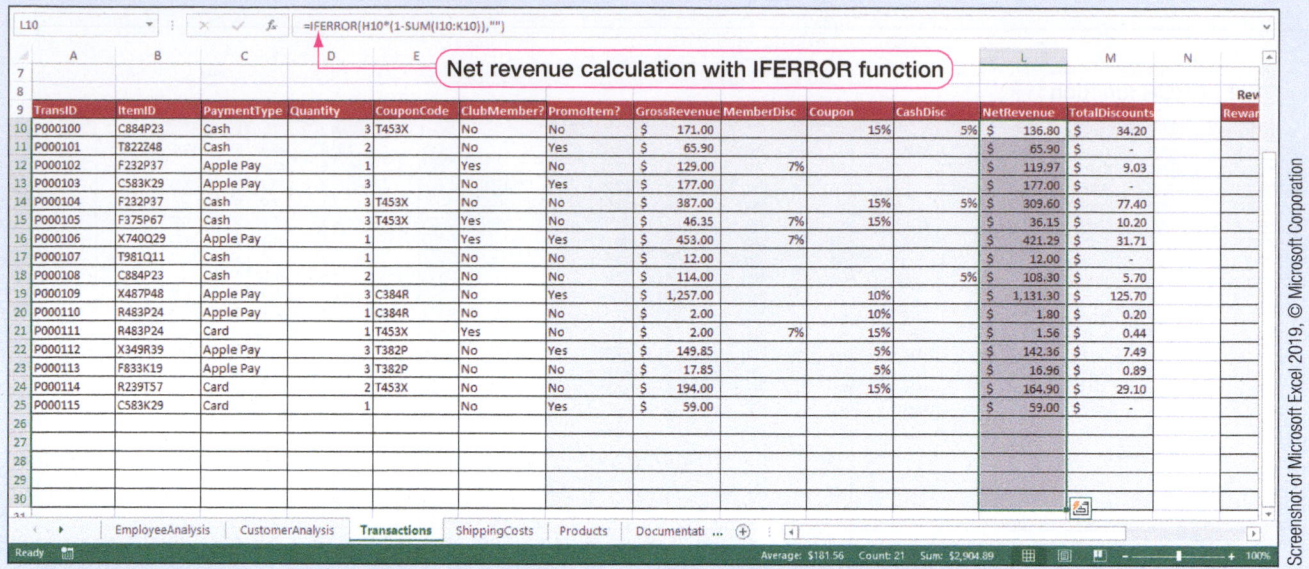

Figure 30 NetRevenue calculation with IFERROR function

h. Click cell **M10**. This column will calculate the total discounts by subtracting the net revenue from the gross revenue. However, because there are blank values that will cause errors, you will start with the IFERROR function.

i. Type **=IFERROR** and then press Tab to insert the function. Click cell **H10**, type - and then click **L10**.

j. Type a comma **,** to move to the value_if_error argument. Type **""** and then type **)** to close the IFERROR function.

k. Press Ctrl+Enter and with M10 still selected, use the **fill handle** to copy the formula down through **M30**.

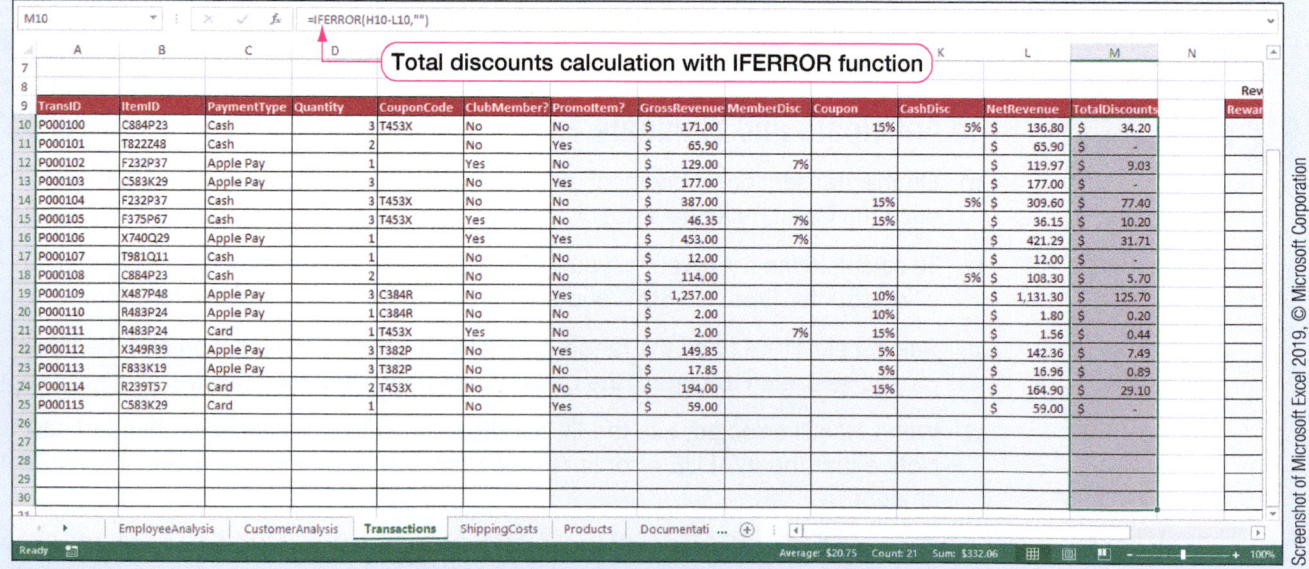

Figure 31 TotalDiscounts calculation with IFERROR function

l. Complete the **Documentation** worksheet as directed by your instructor.

m. **Save** 💾 the workbook, exit Excel, and then submit your file as directed by your instructor.

Concept Check

1. Provide an example of how an in-depth analysis of data may lead to a competitive advantage. p. 278

2. Describe three types of data inputs that can be used for arguments within an IF function. p. 279

3. Explain how a decision tree can help you write a nested IF function. p. 279

4. Explain how the limitation that an IF function only allows for one logical test can be overcome. p. 282

5. Develop a T-chart for the following situation: The result $5,000 is displayed for an employee who has been with the company for 5 years or more and has generated at least $20,000 in revenue or has been with the company for 3 years or more and has generated at least $15,000 in revenue. Otherwise, the result displayed is $0.00. p. 291

6. Provide examples of when you would use the TRUE/FALSE options for the fourth argument in a VLOOKUP. p. 294

7. What is the primary advantage of using the MATCH and INDEX combination rather than a VLOOKUP function? p. 303

8. What benefit is there to using the IFERROR function when it increases the complexity of the formulas? p. 311

Key Terms

A1 reference style   p. 308
AND function   p. 282
Competitive advantage   p. 278
Decision tree   p. 279
HLOOKUP function   p. 296
IF function   p. 277
IFERROR function   p. 311

IFS function   p. 289
INDEX function   p. 303
INDIRECT function   p. 308
Logical function   p. 277
Logical operator   p. 277
Logical test   p. 277
MATCH function   p. 303

Nested IF function   p. 291
NOT function   p. 282
OR function   p. 282
R1C1 reference style   p. 308
T-chart   p. 285
VLOOKUP function   p. 294

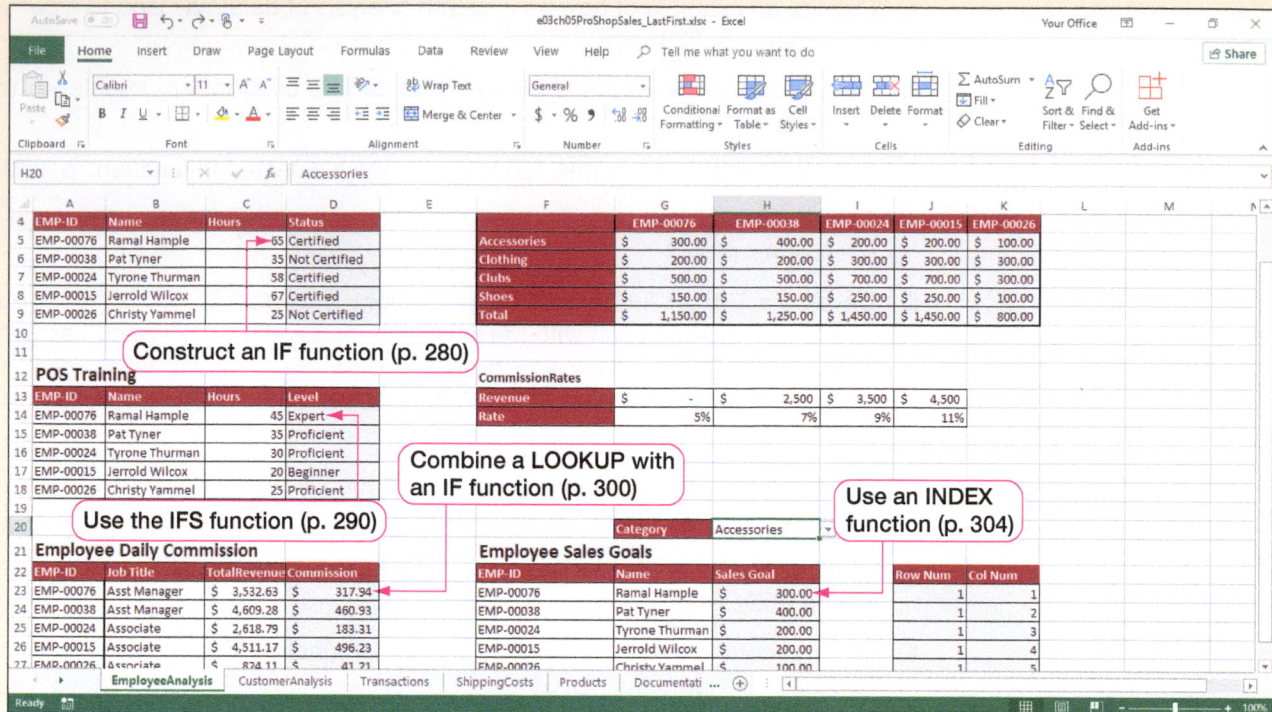

Figure 32

Screenshot of Microsoft Excel 2019, © Microsoft Corporation

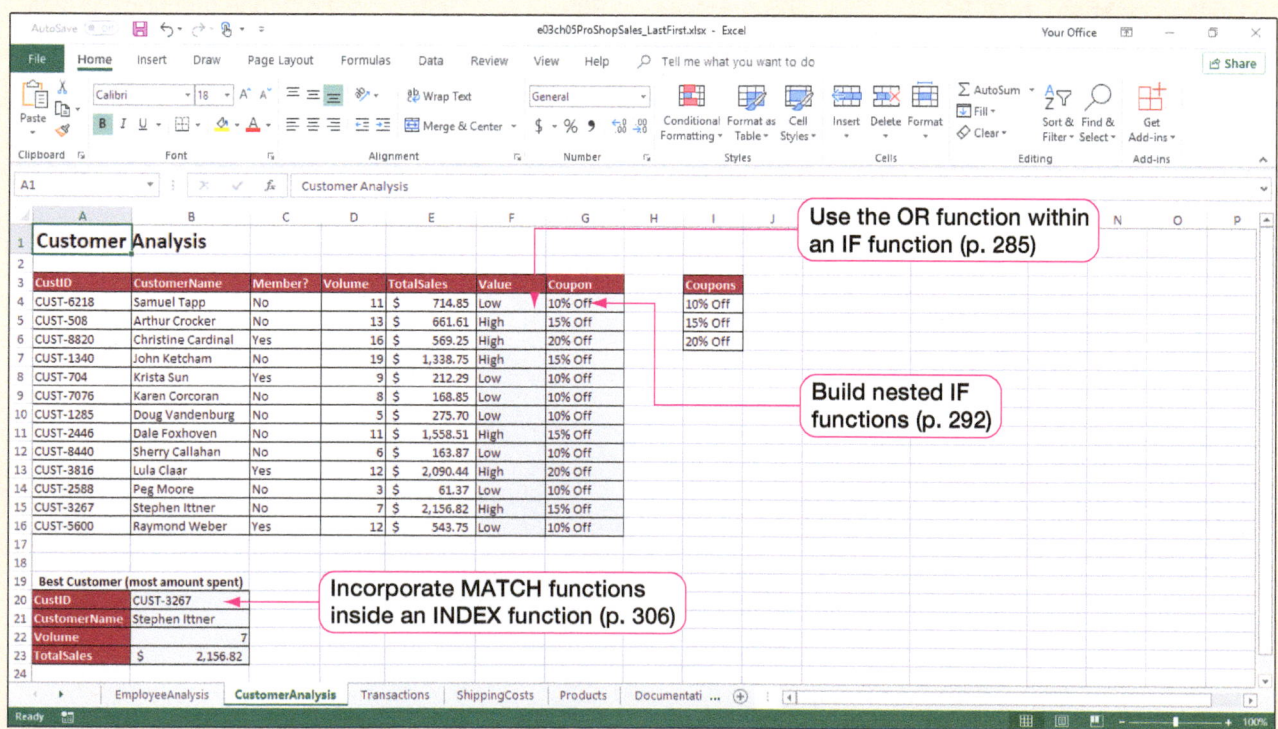

Figure 33

Screenshot of Microsoft Excel 2019, © Microsoft Corporation

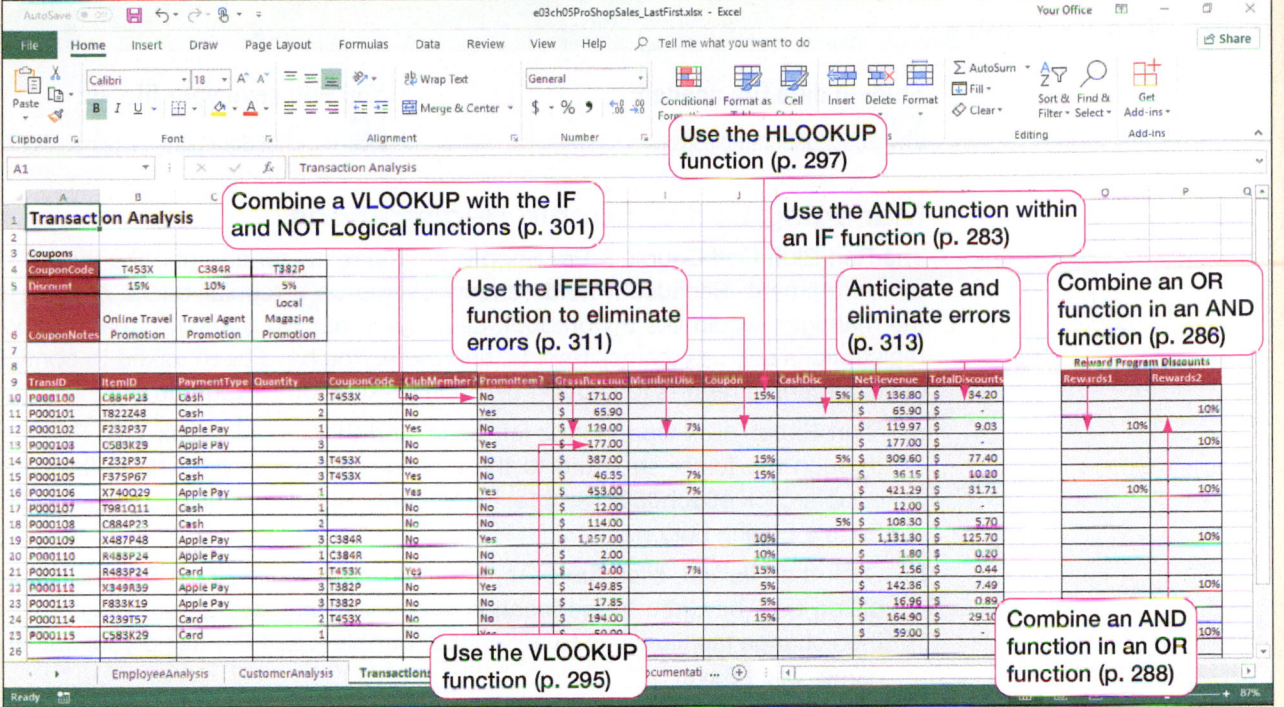

Figure 34

Screenshot of Microsoft Excel 2019, © Microsoft Corporation

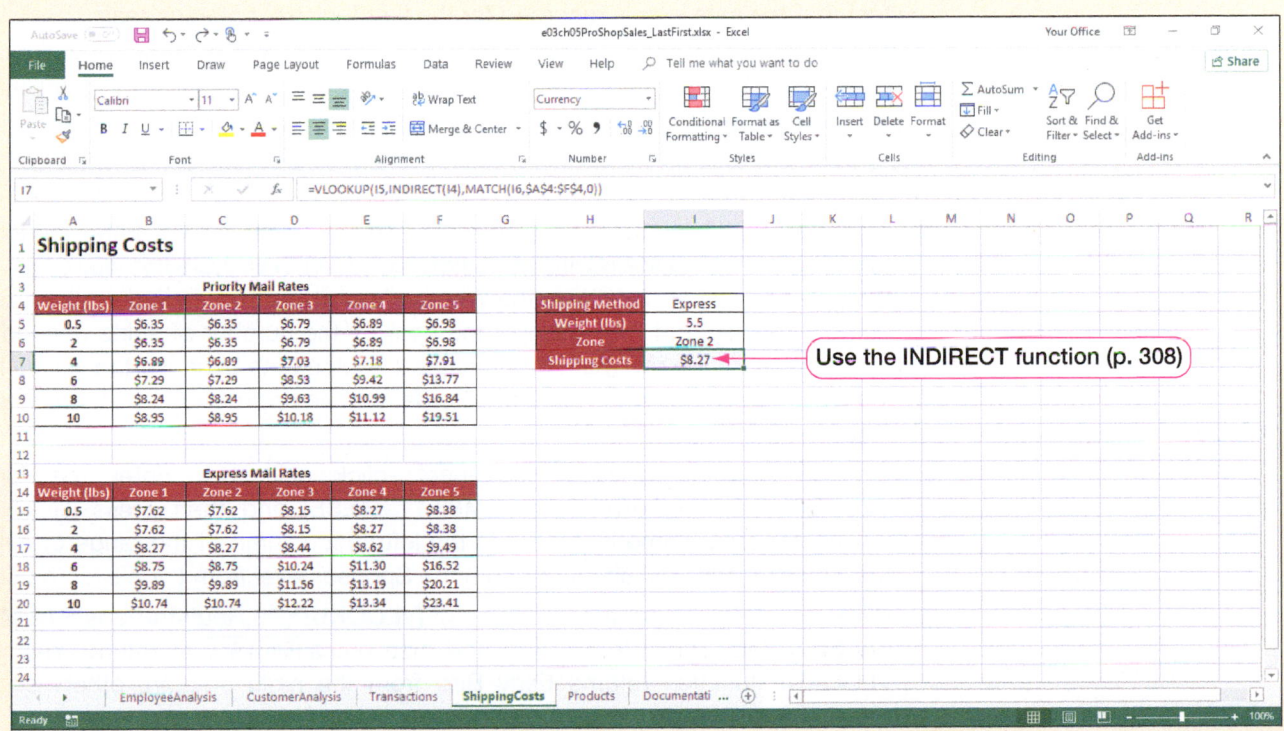

Figure 35

Screenshot of Microsoft Excel 2019, © Microsoft Corporation

Student data file needed:

 e03ch05Scramble.xlsx

You will save your file as:

 e03ch05Scramble_LastFirst.xlsx

Managing Golf Scramble Registrations

Production & Operations

The Red Bluff Golf Course & Pro Shop is getting ready for another charity golf scramble tournament. Because it holds charity events on a regular basis, Aleeta Herriott, the manager, would like a workbook developed that will track information about the registrations such as teams, T-shirts, and more. You have been asked to continue the development of reports to support decision making for the tournament.

a. Start **Excel**, click **Open** in the left pane, and then double-click **This PC**. Navigate through the folder structure to the location of your student data files, and then double-click **e03ch05Scramble**. If a Security Warning message displays, click the Enable Editing button.

b. Click the **File** tab, click **Save As**, and then double-click **This PC**. In the Save As dialog box, navigate to the location where you are saving your project files, and then change the file name to e03ch05Scramble_LastFirst using your last and first name. Click **Save**.

c. Click the **Registrations** worksheet and then click cell **L12**. The entry fee that a team pays determines their sponsorship level. In cell L12, enter the formula =IFERROR(HLOOKUP(K12,$F$3:$H$4,2,TRUE),"") and then press Ctrl+Enter to lookup the amount of the entry fee in the cell range F3:H4 on the same worksheet to retrieve the correct sponsor level. Copy the formula down to **L83**. The IFERROR function will hide any #N/A values returned for missing entry fee values due to the fact that the data is only recorded for the first registrant of each team.

d. On the Registrations worksheet, click cell **M12**. To create a level playing field, there is a maximum score per hole based on a player's handicap. Enter the formula =IF(B12="","",VLOOKUP(H12,$A$4:$C$8,3,TRUE)) and then press Ctrl+Enter. Copy the formula down to **M83**. The MaxScore/Hole will be calculated only if there is a player name.

e. Click the **RegistrationReport** worksheet and then click cell **B5**. Enter the formula =INDEX($I$4:$M$6,MATCH(B4,$H$4:$H$6,1),MATCH(B3,$I$3:$M$3,0))*B4 and then press Ctrl+Enter to retrieve the Wholesale cost per shirt based on the size and number needed and then multiply the cost by the number of shirts needed. The match_type for the row_num argument is 1 – Less than because the values in the lookup_array are sorted in ascending order and an approximate match is needed. Copy the formula over to **F5**.

f. On the RegistrationReport worksheet, click cell **B11**. Enter the formula =VLOOKUP(B9,Registrations!B12:M83,11,FALSE) and then press Ctrl+Enter to lookup the team name in cell B9 in the leftmost column of the range of cells on the Registrations worksheet to return the Sponsor level from the eleventh column.

g. Click cell **B12**. Enter the formula =IF(VLOOKUP(B9,Registrations!B12:M83,9, FALSE)="Early Bird","Yes","No") and then press Ctrl+Enter to return "Yes" if the VLOOKUP function returns Early Bird from the ninth column, otherwise "No" should be returned.

h. Each team is assigned to either flight A, B, or C based on the average handicap of the team. Click cell **B13**. Enter the formula =IFS(B10<=I10,J10,B10<=I11,J11, TRUE,J12) and then press Ctrl+Enter to determine which flight the team is assigned.

i. Bonus mulligans can be awarded to a team if they meet the criteria. Click cell **B15** and enter the formula =IF(OR(AND(B12="Yes",B14>=6),B14>=8),2,0)+VLOOKUP(B11,L10:M13,2,FALSE) to determine the number of bonus mulligans, if any, the team has earned.

j. Click the **Documentation** worksheet. Click cell **A8**, and then type today's date Click cell **B8**, and then type your name in the Firstname_Lastname format. Complete the remainder of the Documentation worksheet according to your instructor's directions.

k. **Save** the workbook, exit Excel, and then submit your file as directed by your instructor.

Problem Solve 1

MyLab IT Grader

Student data file needed:

 e03ch05ResourceCenter.xlsx

You will save your file as:

 e03ch05ResourceCenter_LastFirst.xlsx

Production & Operations

First Resource Events

First Resource is a company that connects other companies to various resources. It hosts many events to promote the benefits of becoming a member. The manager needs your help developing a workbook consisting of various analyses to better help manage the company's events. The workbook will allow the manager to make decisions with regard to event registration fees, promoting events with a low registration number, and more!

a. Open the Excel file, **e03ch05ResourceCenter**. Save your file as e03ch05ResourceCenter_LastFirst using your last and first name.

b. On the **EventDetails** worksheet, create an EventDetails named range for cells **A4:D9**.

c. On the **ClientRegistration** worksheet, in cell **I11** enter a VLOOKUP function to retrieve the registration fee from the **EventDetails** named range for the EventID in cell **G11**. Multiply the value retrieved by the number of guests in cell **H11**. Incorporate an IFERROR function to return a blank value if the VLOOKUP function returns an error. Format the value as **Accounting** and copy the formula down through **I34**.

d. Attendees who are also board members receive a discount off the registration fees. The discount amount varies based on the type of event. In cell **J11** enter a formula that will return the discount amount if the registrant is a board member and return a blank value ("") if they are not.

- Use a VLOOKUP function to retrieve the EventType from the **EventDetails** named range.

- Use an INDEX function, with the cell range **A5:B8** on the ClientRegistration worksheet as the array and the result of the VLOOKUP as the lookup_value for the MATCH function needed for the row_num argument.

- Use an IF function so that the discount only applies to board members.

- Format the result as **Percentage** with **0** decimal places.

- Copy the formula down through **J34**.

e. First Resource is offering a 5% discount off registration fees for all EventTypes except for Survey/Study. In cell **K11** enter a formula that will return 0.05 if the event is NOT a Survey/Study, otherwise return a blank value ("").

- Use a VLOOKUP function to return the EventType from the EventDetails named range.

- Use a NOT function so that any event type other than Survey/Study will return TRUE.

- Use an IF function to return 0.05 for the value_if_true and "" for the value_if_false.
- Incorporate an IFERROR function to return a blank value if the VLOOKUP function returns an error.
- Format the result as **Percentage** with **0** decimal places.
- Copy the formula down through **K34**.

f. First Resource also offers a 3% discount off registration fees if the registrant meets certain criteria. In cell **L11**, enter an IF function that will return 0.03 if the following criteria are met, otherwise return a blank value ("")

- If the registrant is a board member and had 3 or more people in the party OR the registrant has a total of 5 or more in their party.

Format the result as **Percentage** with **0** decimal places and copy the formula down through **L34**.

g. In cell **M11**, enter a formula that will calculate the total amount due after discounts have been applied. Incorporate an IFERROR function to return a blank value if the formula returns an error. Format the result as **Accounting** and copy the formula down through **M34**.

h. On the **EventAnalysis** worksheet, in cell **D4**, enter a formula that will return Goal_Met if the number of registrants for the event meets or exceeds the goal for that event outlined in the cell range **G4:H9**, otherwise return Promote_Event. Copy the formula down through **D9**.

i. First Resource offers a bonus to the coordinator for each event. The bonus amount is based on the event type and the number of registrants. In addition, there are different amounts awarded if the registration goal has been met or not. Create a Goal_Met named range for cells **H14:L17** and a Promote_Event named range for cells **H21:L24**.

j. In cell **E4** enter an INDEX function that incorporates the INDIRECT function for the array argument to retrieve the bonus amount the event coordinator will receive. Format the result as **Accounting** and copy the formula down through **E9**.

k. Complete the **Documentation** worksheet according to your instructor's directions.

l. Save the workbook, exit Excel, and then submit your file as directed by your instructor.

Perform 1: Perform in Your Life

Student data file needed:

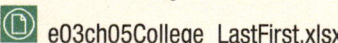 e03ch05College.xlsx

You will save your file as:

e03ch05College_LastFirst.xlsx

Research & Development

Choosing a College

You live in Lebanon, Kansas, which is the geographic center of the United States. You are looking for a college that will be near your home or near your relatives in Illinois. By doing a little research online at various websites, you have been able to obtain some information about the colleges in your area that you plan on using to rate the colleges and choose the best one for you.

a. Open the Excel file, **e03ch05College**. Save your file as e03ch05College_LastFirst using your last and first name.

b. In the area above the data, create a table, arranged horizontally, that can be used in a HLOOKUP function to retrieve a point value based on the distance (in miles) the school is from your home. For example, if the school is within 100 miles from home, you may want to assign high point value if you wish to stay close to home. Assign an appropriate named range to the table.

c. Also, in the area above the data, create a table, arranged vertically, that can be used in a VLOOKUP function to retrieve a point value based on the cost of tuition. For example, if the cost of attendance is under $10,000, you may want to assign a high point value if you're paying for it yourself. Assign an appropriate named range to the table.

d. On the **SchoolData** worksheet, create named ranges for each of the columns using the Create from Selection option and use the top for the names.

e. In cell **M10**, use appropriate functions that will return the point value from the table you created based on the resident cost of attendance if the college is in Kansas (KS). If the college is outside Kansas, return the point value from the vertical table based on the non-resident cost of attendance. If there is no cost of attendance in the table, the formula should return something besides an error.

f. In cell **N10**, use an appropriate function to return the point value from the table you created based on the distance (in miles).

g. In cell **O10**, enter a formula that will return a high point value if the Fresh Satis (Freshman Satisfaction) and Grad Rate (Graduation Rate) are both greater than 50%. Return a lower point value if both conditions are not met.

h. In cell **P10**, enter a formula that will return a high point value if the Size of the school is less than 1,000 or the school meets the financial needs of its students more than 50% of the time. If neither condition is met, return a lower value.

i. In cell **Q10**, enter a formula to total the number of points the school has earned (columns M through P).

j. Fill the formulas from the cell range M10:Q10 to row 50.

k. Somewhere on the spreadsheet, enter a function that will return the largest Points value from column Q. Add an appropriate label so that it is clear what the value represents.

l. Somewhere on the spreadsheet retrieve the name of the school that received the most points using the INDEX and MATCH functions. To allow you to quickly change from the name of the college to any other attribute, you should use an INDIRECT function. Add appropriate labels to each cell so that it is clear what the value represents.

m. Update the Documentation worksheet according to your instructor's directions.

n. Save the workbook, exit Excel, and then submit your file as directed by your instructor.

Microsoft Excel

Chapter 6 INTEGRATING COMPLEX FUNCTIONS INTO BUSINESS ANALYSIS

Prepare Case

MyLab IT Grader

Sales & Marketing

Golf Course & Pro Shop Marketing Strategies

Barry Cheney and Aleeta Herriott, managers of the Red Bluff Golf Course & Pro Shop, would like to develop marketing strategies for increasing golf course and pro shop patronage. They have requested data about the golf course's activity and pro shop sales over the past several years. They need to be able to work with the data to understand the current patronage, such as where the patrons were from, the tee time, what kind of items they purchased, how much money they spent, and so forth. Exploring the data is key in determining the marketing strategy because it helps them learn about customer preferences. After analyzing the data, Barry and Aleeta will present their ideas to the board of directors.

Monkey Business Images/Shutterstock

Student data files needed:

 e03ch06GolfData.xlsx

 e03ch06SalesAnalysis.xlsx

You will save your files as:

 e03ch06GolfData_LastFirst.xlsx

 e03ch06SalesAnalysis_LastFirst.xlsx

Organizing Data with Tables

While Excel can analyze large amounts of data, users can sometimes be overwhelmed by the volume of data that needs to be evaluated. Information overload can quickly set in as it becomes difficult to track the data across many rows and columns. However, using tools contained in Excel can help you understand the data more easily. For example, viewing data in tables allows you to examine the data in an organized manner. By organizing data, you can easily make decisions based on your analysis. In this section, you will work with a small amount of sample data, organize it by converting the data to a table, and then use various tools, methods, and functions to analyze the data.

Work with Data and Information in Tables

Barry Cheney, the golf course manager, wants to analyze data collected over the years. Daily transactions from the past ten years exist within the Red Bluff Golf Course & Pro Shop's database. However, Barry has requested a random sample of the data in order to develop the initial analysis. The database administrator was able to run a query on the database and provide a set of data to explore.

Opening the Starting File

To work with data in tables, you first need to open a workbook. In this exercise, you will open the GolfData workbook.

E06.00

SIDE NOTE
Office Updates
Depending on your exact Office version, you may see Open or Open Other Workbooks.

To Open the Starting File

a. Start **Excel**, click **Open** in the left pane, and then double-click **This PC**. Navigate through the folder structure to the location of your student data files, and then click **e03ch06GolfData**. If a Security Warning message displays, click the **Enable Editing** button.

b. Click the **File** tab, click **Save As**, and then double-click **This PC**. In the Save As dialog box, navigate to the location where you are saving your project files, and then change the file name to e03ch06GolfData_LastFirst, using your last and first name, and then click **Save**.

 CONSIDER THIS | **Is Data Really That Important?**

Data is a valuable asset to any organization. However, remember that it is what one does with the data that creates value, not the data itself. Think about the daily decisions you make. For example, think about the last time you went out to lunch. You probably considered location, menu, and price—all of which are data. What else might you consider before choosing where to eat lunch? What data do you use to make other decisions throughout the day? The value you experience with where you ate lunch came from the decision you made based on the data, not the data itself.

Organizing Raw Data with Tables

Regardless of the career you choose, the need to work with data is common. **Raw data** are considered to be elements or raw facts—numeric or text—that may or may not have meaning or relevance. For example, data such as "blue" or "brown" are raw data without context and therefore of minimal value to anyone. **Information**, however, is data that has context, meaning, and relevance and therefore is valuable to a user. The value is determined by the user and may vary from one user to another. Thus, information is created by users when they organize, interpret, and present data in a meaningful context.

   Data sets are named collections of related information that are composed of separate elements—the data. If a set of data are not organized, it is difficult to determine the context and transform the data into information. The user is informed by understanding the method by which the data have been gathered and organized and the purpose of doing so. For example, the raw data "blue" and "brown" by themselves may not have any significance. Knowing that these data were collected from a set of subjects in the context of studying the eye color of men and women allows information to be created. By having information, a user can determine whether one eye color is more prevalent in males.

Excel is an excellent tool for manipulating data. It can be used to transform data into information, which can lead to good decision making. Organizing the data by using an Excel table is a good first step toward creating and evaluating information effectively.

In working with data, care should be taken to protect its integrity. This includes keeping a backup of the original data so if errors occur, it is possible to return to the original data and start over. Whenever possible, check your data for completeness and accuracy. Also, strive to organize data within the workbook in a meaningful and efficient manner that allows for new data to be added as needed. Finally, it is best to keep sets of data separated. Avoid using cells immediately surrounding the sets of data. This will minimize the possibility of mistakenly assuming that the content in the adjacent cells is part of the main data set. When possible, keep related data on one worksheet while reporting and analyzing the data on another worksheet.

REAL WORLD ADVICE | Back Up Your Work

You hope you will never need to use your backup, but in reality, someday you may mess up, lose, or destroy your data. Make a habit of creating backups of your work. This can include quick back-ups, such as backup worksheets, as done with the files in this chapter. But you should also back up the entire file on a regular basis, such as every day or after major revisions. Keep backup files in a different physical location than the originals, such as with a backup service or on a company site.

While the data may already be arranged in a spreadsheet, an Excel table establishes the data as more than a simple collection or range of raw facts presented in rows and columns. An Excel **table** typically contains related data organized into rows and columns that have been formatted as a table, using Excel's table tools help to provide context to the user by organizing the data in a meaningful way. Data can be converted to an Excel table that offers additional capability, allowing the user to manipulate the data and to generate information and value for a variety of needs.

In this exercise, you will create an Excel table for the data on the GolfData worksheet.

 E06.01

SIDE NOTE
Pin the Ribbon

If your ribbon is collapsed, pin your ribbon open. Click the Home tab. In the lower-right corner of the ribbon, click Pin the ribbon ⊡.

SIDE NOTE
Alternate Methods

A table can also be created by clicking a cell in the data set and then press Ctrl+T. Tables can also be created by using the Format as Table options in the Styles group on the Home tab.

To Organize Raw Data with Tables

a. Click the **GolfData** worksheet and click cell **A9** or any other cell within the range of data.

b. Click the **Insert** tab, and then, in the Tables group, click **Table**. The Create Table dialog box opens.

c. In the **Where is the data for your table?** field, verify that the range **$A$9:$H$39** is selected, and then verify that the **My table has headers** check box is checked. Excel automatically assumes that when a table is inserted on a worksheet with data, you want to include all the data located in a contiguous range. Excel also determined that the values in the top row of the range are different from the values below and therefore assumed that they were headers.

Troubleshooting
If Excel fails to guess the correct range selection, you can either adjust the range by typing in the correct range or drag to select the correct range.

SIDE NOTE
Table Names
Because of the way that Excel is configured, table names cannot include spaces.

d. Click **OK**, and then click cell **A9**. An Excel table was created with banded rows. Additionally, the Table Tools Design contextual tab appears on the ribbon, containing all the options available for working with a table.

e. If necessary, click the **Design** tab. In the Properties group, on the left, click inside the Table Name box. Replace **Table1** with GolfData and then press Enter.

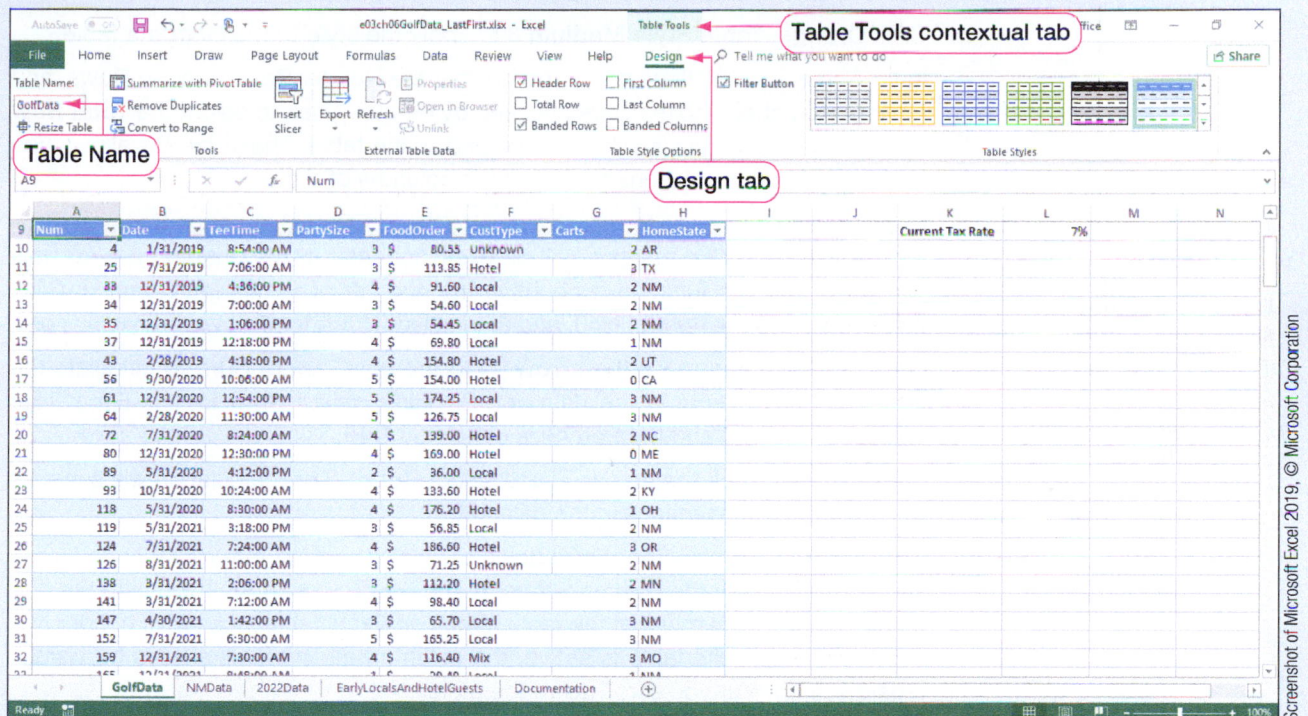

Figure 1 Excel table

f. **Save** the workbook.

Exploring Various Table Features

A table defaults to a table style that has banded rows, making it easier to read data across rows. There are options to change the applied style for banded rows—and/or columns—with alternating colors. As new rows of data are added, the table range expands, including the table formatting. Like rows, new columns are automatically formatted and added to the table. Additional benefits of creating an Excel table to organize raw data can be immediately realized.

- Data in any column can be easily sorted in ascending or descending order.
- Data in any column can be easily filtered so that you only see the data you want to see.
- The column names are always visible no matter how far down you scroll in the spreadsheet.
- Totals can easily be added for each column, such as sum, average, count, and more.

In this exercise, you will explore various table features.

 **E06.02**

To Explore Various Table Features

a. On the Design tab, click **More** ⊟ in the Table Styles group to view all available predefined table styles. The predefined table styles are arranged within three categories, Light, Medium, and Dark. Pointing to a table style will display a Live Preview of how the style will affect the table. If no predefined style meets your needs, you can create custom styles as well.

b. Click **Orange, Table Style Medium 3** to apply the style to the GolfData table.

c. In the Table Style Options group, notice that the Header Row, Banded Rows, and Filter Button check boxes were checked by default. Click to select the **Total Row** check box. A new row is added to the end of the table. The Total row allows you to easily create calculations for any of the columns of data.

SIDE NOTE
Column Letters Become Column Names
If you no longer see Column Letters, look for the HomeState column name to locate the appropriate cell in row 40.

d. Click cell **H40** and in the formula bar, notice the SUBTOTAL function that was automatically added. This function will be explained later in the chapter, but for now just know that this function is counting the number of values in column H. Click the **arrow** ⊟ to the right of H40, and then select **None** to remove the calculation.

e. Click cell **G40**, and using the **arrow** ⊟ to the right, select **Sum** to calculate the total number of Carts in the data set. Similarly, select **Sum** for the FoodOrder column in cell **E40** and the PartySize column in **D40**.

f. Click cell **B40**, click the **arrow** ⊟ and select **Count**. This calculation will serve as the number of transactions in the data set.

g. With cell B40 still selected, scroll down the worksheet so that row 9 is no longer visible. Notice how the column letters, A–H have now been replaced with the column headings from row 9 of the table. When an Excel table includes a header row and a cell inside the table is active, the column headings will always be visible, regardless how far you scroll down the table.

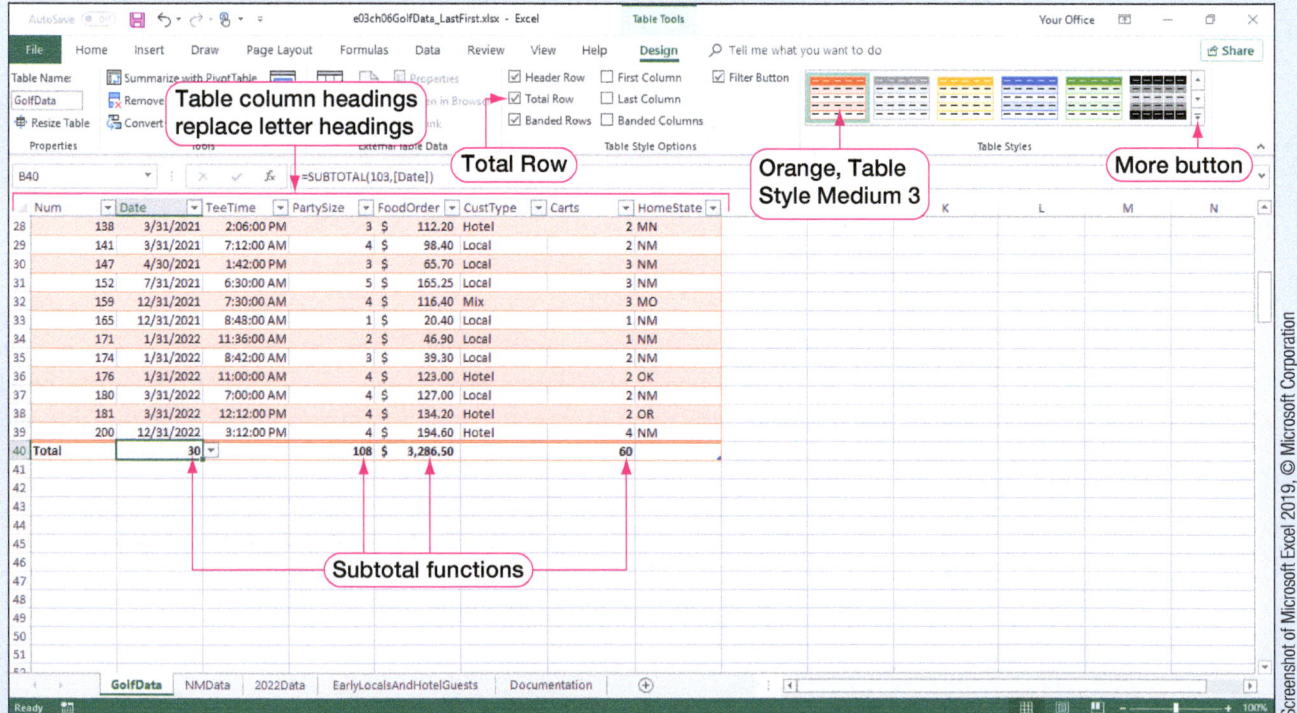

Figure 2 Excel table with Total row and table style

h. **Save** 💾 the workbook.

Creating a Structured Reference in a Table

When new columns and rows are added to an Excel table, the table will extend to include them automatically. Formatting and formula references automatically adjust as well. You can use a structured reference in an Excel table to make the formula easier to understand. A **structured reference** is a formula that refers to table columns by names that were generated when the table was created. Structured references can be useful because table data ranges may change. If they do, the cell references for the structured reference will adjust automatically.

In this exercise, you will create a structured reference in an Excel table.

 **E06.03**

To Create a Structured Reference in a Table

a. On the GolfData worksheet, click cell **I9**, type **Tax** and then press Enter.

Notice that Excel automatically applied the formatting to the newly added table cells to match the rest of the table.

b. In cell **I10**, type **=** click cell **L9** and then press F4 to make it an absolute cell reference. Type ***** click cell **E10**, and then press Enter.

Notice that [@FoodOrder] is inserted into the formula when cell E10 was clicked. Excel uses a structured reference rather than a regular cell reference. It inserted [@FoodOrder] instead of E10 because it automatically sets ranges within the table that will adjust as columns or rows are added or deleted. The table also automatically copies the formula down the entire column, similar to applying Auto Fill.

> **Troubleshooting**
>
> If your table did not automatically update, Excel may be configured to not update data tables automatically. Click the Formulas tab, and in the Calculation group, click the Calculation Options arrow, and then select Automatic.

c. Point to just above the Tax column heading until your mouse pointer changes to a downward black arrow, click to select the entire Tax column, and then apply the **Accounting** number format.

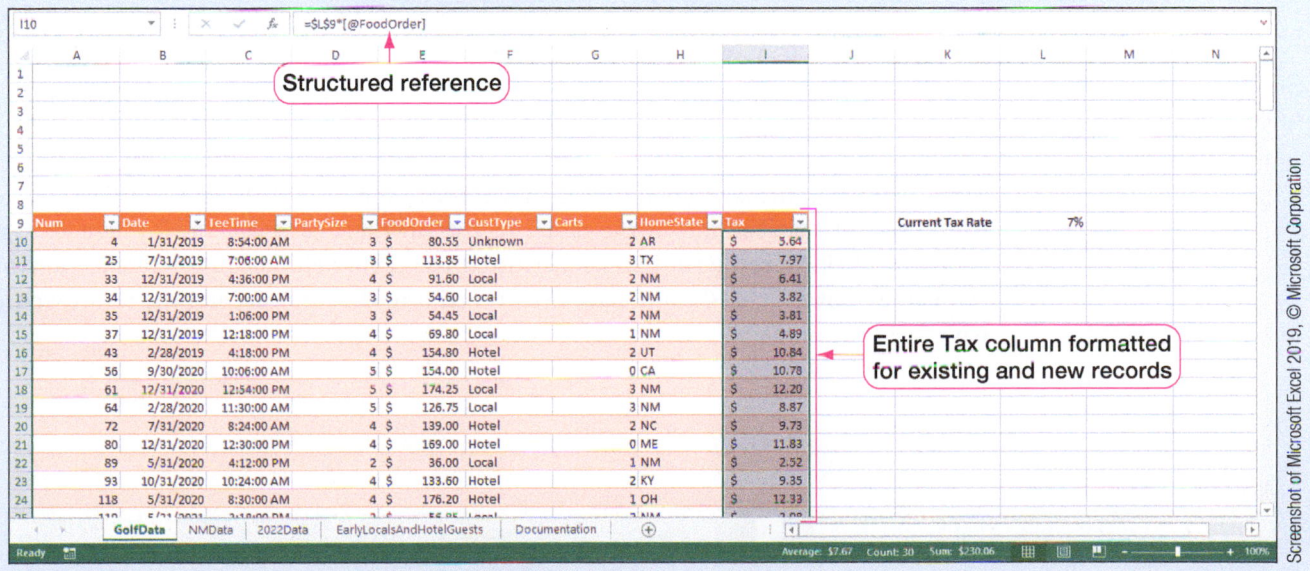

Figure 3 Selecting and formatting a Table column

d. Click cell **I39** and press Tab to add a new row to the table.

Using the following data, add a new row in row 40, pressing Tab after each entry to move to the next field. Notice that the banded color formatting appears as soon as data is initially entered and that the Tax field is copied down automatically because it is a calculation.

Num	201
Date	12/31/2022
TeeTime	8:30 AM
PartySize	4
FoodOrder	104.80
CustType	Hotel
Carts	2
HomeState	WI

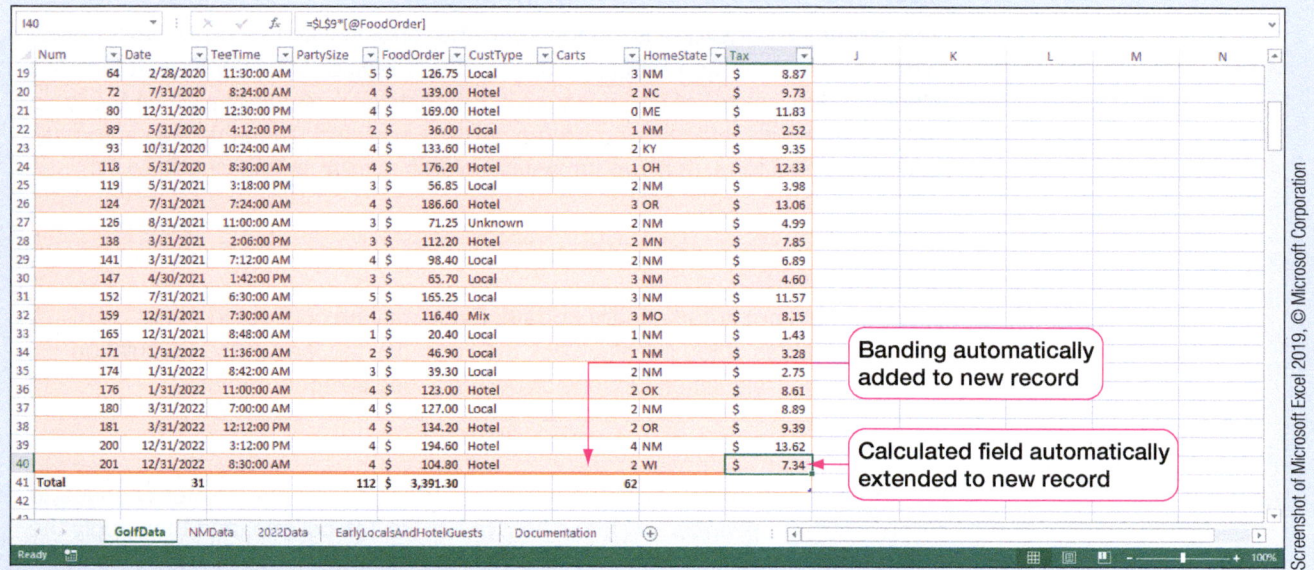

Figure 4 Adding a new row to an Excel table

e. Save the workbook.

When a formula is created in a cell of a new column, it will automatically be copied to the rest of that column in the table. In the previous exercise, a cell reference was added by clicking cell E10. Excel substituted the table field heading reference for the cell name. However, E10 could have been typed into the formula, and the result would have been the same.

It is also possible to remove the Excel table structure as well as the extra functionality. When the table is converted back to a range of data by using the **Convert to Range** option—located on the Table Tools Design tab, in the Tools group—the formatting remains, but the functionality of tables, such as adding new columns or rows, will no longer automatically be added or updated to the named ranges, and formulas would need to be manually copied down a column.

REAL WORLD ADVICE	Developing Questions for Data Analysis

It is vital to have an understanding of the company data so relevant questions can be explored. The managers could find the average size of the golf parties, but this does not provide much value. However, it may be useful to know whether larger groups tend to order more food per person than smaller groups do. Based on the answer, a marketing strategy could be developed and implemented. Always consider the value of the question.

Use Filters and the SUBTOTAL Function in Tables

The Total row, when added to an Excel table, uses the SUBTOTAL function to aggregate the data in a column. The user selects from a variety of predefined options, and then the function is inserted. To **aggregate** data means to consolidate or summarize the data, similar to the way an executive summary consolidates and summarizes a project or a report. Functions such as SUM or AVERAGE aggregate an entire set of data. However, when a set of data is filtered to show a subset of the entire data set, it would be useful to be able to aggregate the subset of data instead of the entire set of data. This is impossible to conduct with standard functions, as they will run calculations on the data regardless of whether the records—or rows—are hidden or displayed. Thus, the applied data filters have no impact on standard functions.

The **SUBTOTAL function** is specific to the filtering mechanism and will run calculations only on the data that is in the subset when a filter is applied; it can return 11 different values. Any records that are in filtered rows will not be used in the calculation of the SUBTOTAL function. The SUBTOTAL function has two arguments. The first argument requires a function number to indicate which aggregate function to apply, such as SUM, AVERAGE, or COUNT. The second argument specifies one or more ranges to be aggregated. The syntax of the SUBTOTAL function is as follows

=SUBTOTAL(function_num, ref1, [ref2],...)

The function_num argument informs Excel which function to use on the subset of records. When you are typing this function, a list will appear to help if you are not familiar with which argument number to use. There are two sets of function numbers, 1–11 and 101–111, as shown in Table 1. The first set, 1–11, will return result values for rows that are visible and rows that have been hidden by using the Hide Rows command. The second set, 101–111, will ignore rows that have been formatted to be hidden, again by using the Hide Rows command; thus, it returns a value of visible rows only. Keep in mind that the SUBTOTAL function ignores any rows not included when a filter is applied, no matter which function_num value you use. Thus, the difference between these two sets of argument values comes into importance only when you use the Hide Rows command, and it is of no importance when applied to filtered data.

Function_Num (includes hidden values)	Function_Num (ignores hidden values)	Function
1	101	AVERAGE
2	102	COUNT
3	103	COUNTA
4	104	MAX
5	105	MIN
6	106	PRODUCT
7	107	STDEV.S
8	108	STDEV.P
9	109	SUM
10	110	VAR.S
11	111	VAR.P

Table 1 Subtotal function list

 CONSIDER THIS | **Selecting a Function Number from the List**

The purpose of analyzing data is to aid in decision making. Perhaps you wanted to use all the data, including the hidden rows. What would happen if you chose a function number—function_num—that does not include hidden values? How would it affect your decision making?

REAL WORLD ADVICE | **Hiding Rows and Filtering**

It is unusual to use the Hide Rows feature when filtering, and this is not a recommended practice. Any time filters are removed, any hidden rows will become unhidden. It becomes complicated to try to work with both filtering data and hiding rows. All records should be visible when you are filtering. Any records that should not be used in the SUBTOTAL calculations should be excluded by using the filtering process.

Using Filters in a Table

A data set used in business may be large and contain numerous fields. It is useful to gain an understanding of the data by looking at subsets of data rather than the entire set at one time. Filtering data sets is useful and makes it possible to view specific data. Filtering is also useful for selecting and copying a subset of data to move to a new worksheet. **Filtering** is a process of showing only the records that meet specified criteria in a data set. Filtering enables a user to examine and analyze, if desired, a subset of records.

Filters can be applied either to a range of data or to an Excel table. For a range of data, a filter can be set by clicking the Filter button in the Sort & Filter group on the Data tab. When applying a filter to a data range, be sure the active cell is within the range to help ensure that the correct data range is selected. However, if an Excel table has been created, the range will be established on the basis of the initial creation process, decreasing the chance for error. Additionally, the filter is a standard part of the Excel table, eliminating the need to apply a filter feature to the data set.

The filter feature adds an arrow to each column heading, which offer menus with filtering options to select the criteria for each field as well as sorting options. By selecting criteria for a certain field heading, any records that do not meet the criteria will be hidden until the filter criterion is removed. The filters can be added, modified, and cleared as needed. Additionally, various filtering criteria can be applied using multiple fields.

Thus, it would be possible to filter for a specific party size and on the number of golf carts used within the GolfData table.

Filtering data allows for the exploration of the data. For example, Barry Cheney may want to determine how many golf parties of more than three listed New Mexico as their home state. For this example, Barry would filter for parties containing more than three people, which would exclude any parties that contained a number less than 3. Then the data would be explored further by filtering the records based on the home state. The golf parties with more than three people who have a home state of NM would then be displayed and available for easy analysis.

 **E06.04**

To Use Filters in a Table

a. On the GolfData worksheet, click the **PartySize** filter arrow ⏷. Notice the sorting options at the top of the menu and the check boxes at the bottom, allowing filters on specific values derived from the column.

b. Point to **Number Filters** and select **Greater Than...**

c. In the Custom AutoFilter dialog box, click in the box next to **is greater than**, if necessary, and type 3

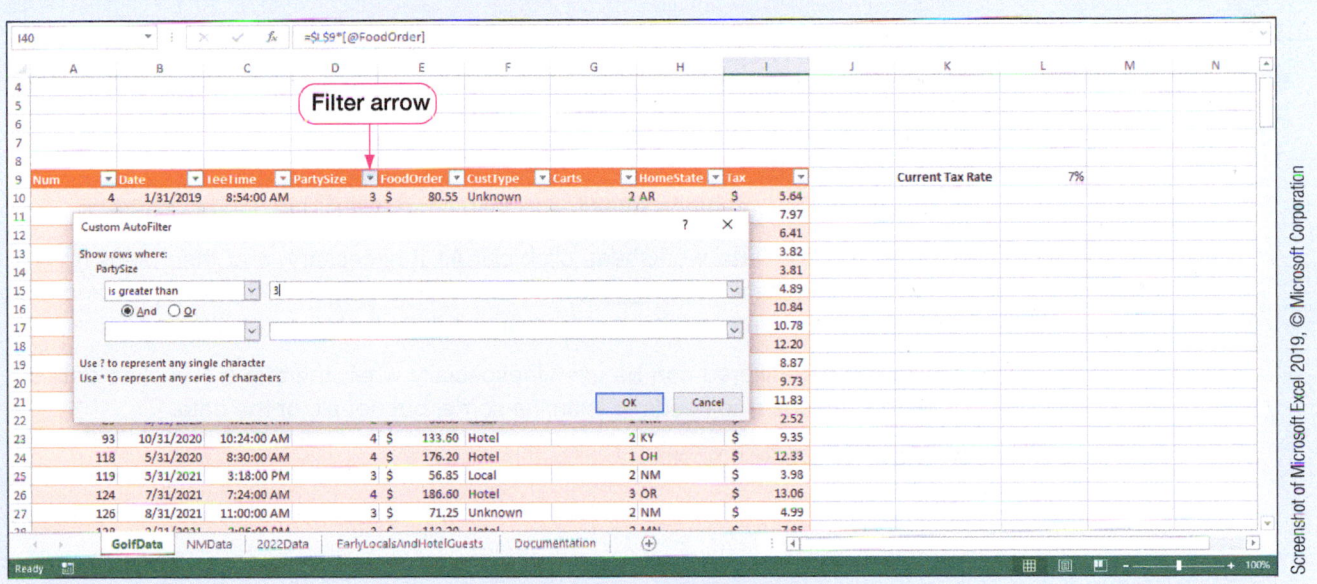

Figure 5 PartySize Custom AutoFilter dialog box

Screenshot of Microsoft Excel 2019, © Microsoft Corporation

SIDE NOTE
One Filter per Worksheet
Filtering can be applied to only one data set per worksheet. Multiple data sets that need to be filtered should be placed on separate worksheets.

d. Click **OK** and the table will only display the records where the PartySize is greater than 3. Notice the Filter icon 🔽 that appears on top of the arrow. This serves as a visual cue that the field has a filter applied.

e. Click the **HomeState** filter arrow ⏷, click inside the Search box, and then type NM The list of states available for filters changes to display only the state of NM. Click **OK** to apply the HomeState filter.

The table now only displays data that meets both criteria of having more than three people in the party and a home state of NM. Also, notice that the values in the Total row have changed. The use of the SUBTOTAL function, allows for the selected calculations to only work on data that are visible. In other words, the records hidden as a result of the filter(s) are ignored.

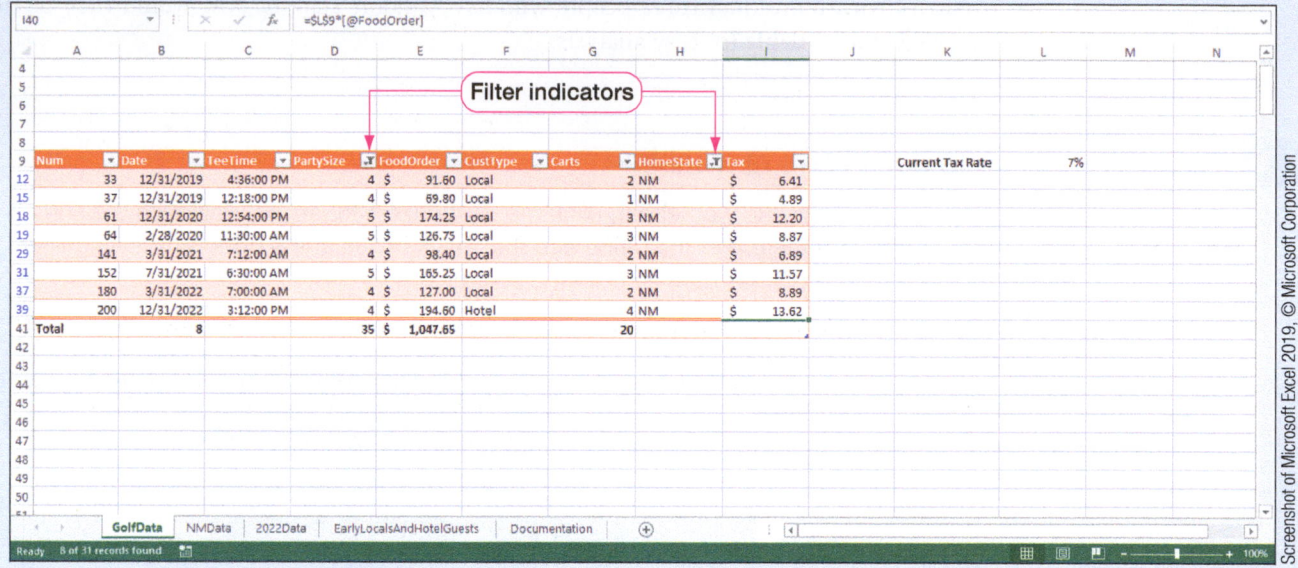

Figure 6 Data filtered on PartySize and HomeState

f. Select the filtered range **A9:I41**, and then press Ctrl+C to copy the data.

g. Click the **NMData** worksheet, click cell **A1** if necessary, and then press Ctrl+V to paste the data. Press Esc to clear the copied data from the clipboard and then adjust the column widths as necessary so that all data are visible.

Having data filtered can be useful, especially when there is a complete data set and someone else needs to examine some, but not all, of the data.

h. **Save** 💾 the workbook.

Filtering hides the rows of data that do not fit the selected criteria. In this case, both criteria must be true for the rows to be displayed. It is easy to remove, or clear, filters and apply other filters. The **standard filter** displays the values in the field that can be toggled on and off through the use of check boxes. If the check boxes are not able to provide a filter for the desired criteria, there are options above the check boxes that are specific for the type of data contained in the field. For example, the options available for fields with numeric values will differ from the options available if the field data contains date or text values.

Clearing and Changing Filters

There are times when you have several filters to apply or the current filter is not providing the output needed to answer your question. Then clearing and changing the filters becomes an important task.

In this exercise, you will clear and change filters in the table to only show records from 2022.

 E06.05

SIDE NOTE
Alternate Method
To quickly remove all filters applied to a table, click the Data tab, and in the Sort & Filter group, click Clear.

To Clear and Change Filters

a. Click the **GolfData** worksheet, click the **PartySize** filter arrow in cell D9, and then click **Clear Filter From "PartySize"**. The hidden records with a party size of less than 3 are now visible again.

b. Click the **HomeState** filter arrow in cell H9, and then click **Clear Filter From "HomeState"**. The hidden records with home states other than NM are now visible again.

c. Click the **Date** filter arrow in cell B9. Notice that it has a listing of years with plus signs. Click the **plus sign** + beside 2022. The filter options expand to months, and if needed, individual days could be shown and selected.

d. Point to **Date Filters** and notice that the options available are specific for dates. Select **Between** to display the Custom AutoFilter dialog box.

e. Click in the box next to **is after or equal to**, if necessary type **1/1/2022** and then, in the box next to "is before or equal to," type **12/31/2022**

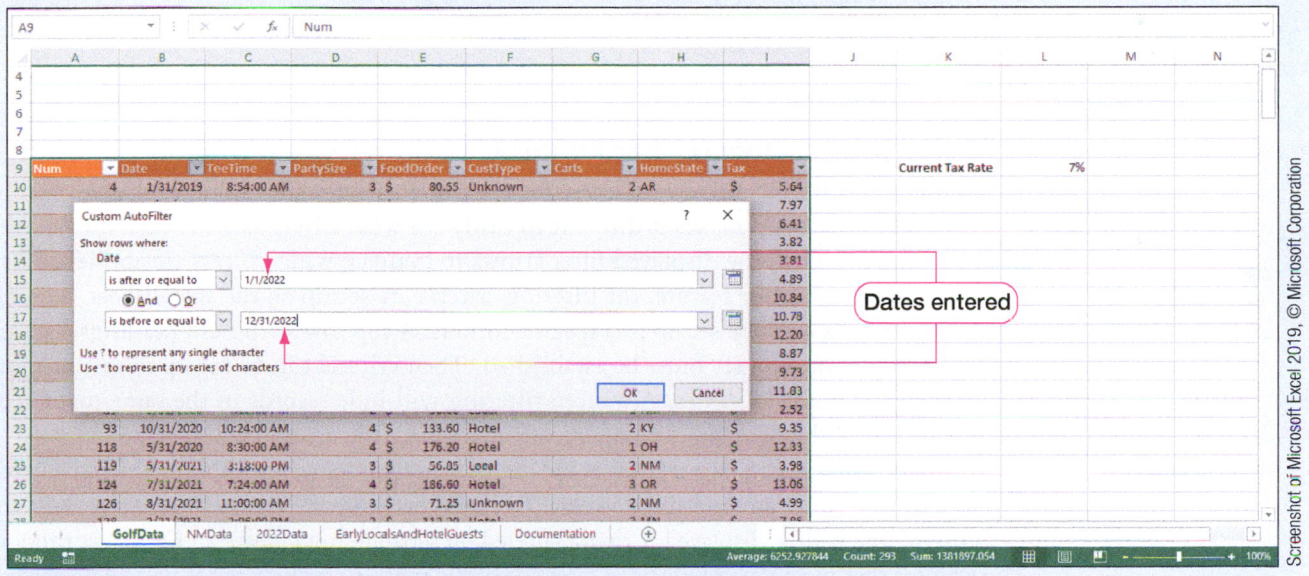

Figure 7 Custom AutoFilter dialog box—2022 dates

f. Click **OK**. The table now only displays data for transactions that took place in 2022.

g. Point to the **Date** filter arrow in cell B9 to display a ScreenTip indicating the details of the filter.

h. Select the filtered range **A9:I41**, and then press Ctrl+C to copy the data.

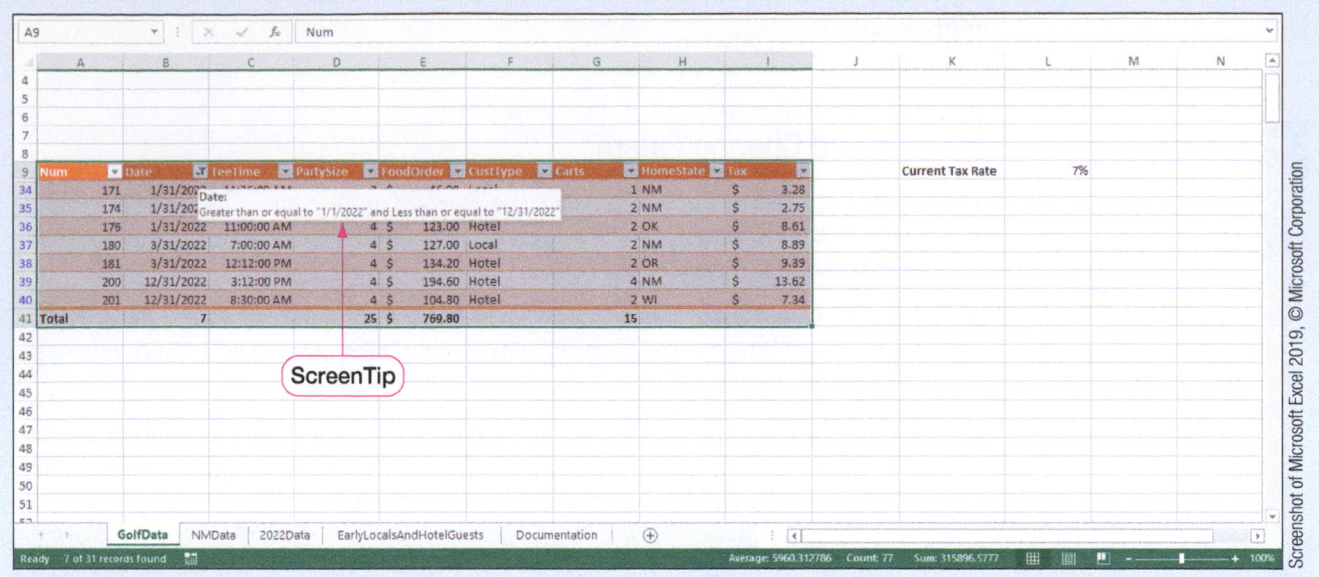

Figure 8 Filtered data for 2022

i. Click the **2022Data** worksheet, click cell **A1** if necessary, and then press `Ctrl`+`V` to paste the data. Press `Esc` to clear the copied data from the clipboard and then adjust the column widths as necessary so that all data are visible.

j. **Save** 🖫 the workbook.

Using the Advanced Filter Feature

While the filtering feature is great for spur-of-the-moment exploration of data, the filtering mechanism makes it difficult to easily see what filters exist. A user would need to point to or click the displayed filter arrows to evaluate which filters are applied. With the **Advanced Filter** feature, the filtering criteria are set up on the spreadsheet. The filtering criteria must be set up in a specific format. A top row with field headings that are identical to the data set must be established. Then criteria can be set up in one or more cells below the field names. Advanced filtering will hide records in the same manner as the filters on the data set, but only records matching the criteria will be displayed.

Once the criteria area has been set up, the Advanced Filter can be applied. Criteria entered on one row create an And filter criteria. Records that meet all the specified criteria in the criteria row will be displayed. Criteria entered on separate rows create an Or filter criterion. Records that meet the criteria on at least one of the rows in a criteria range will be displayed.

When specifying the criteria for which records you want to see, there are specific ways in which they must be typed as shown in Table 2.

What is typed as the criterion	How Excel interprets the criterion
3000	Equal to 3000
Ca	Starts with "Ca"
="=Ca"	Equal to "Ca"
>3	Greater than 3
>=40	Greater than or equal to 40
<5	Less than 5
>=22	Greater than or equal to 22
1/1/2022	Equal to 1/1/2022
>2/15/2022	Greater than 2/15/2022

Table 2 Examples of criteria for use in Advanced Filters

In this exercise, you will insert some additional rows above the GolfData table and create an advanced filter.

 **E06.06**

To Use the Advanced Filter Feature

a. Click the **GolfData** worksheet. Click the **Data** tab and in the Sort & Filter group, click **Clear** ⬚ to remove all of the filters applied to the table.

b. Select the range **A9:I9**, press Ctrl+C to copy the range, click **A1**, and then press Ctrl+V to paste the range. Press Esc to clear the copied data from the clipboard.

This row contains the field names that could potentially be used for setting criteria in the table below.

c. Click cell **F2**, type Hotel and then press Ctrl+Enter.

The second row and below could be used for the criteria for particular fields. In this case, there is only one criterion set: the customer type of Hotel. With this arrangement, the advanced filter is ready to be created and will find the records that meet the criterion entered in the data criteria range.

d. Click cell **A9**. On the Data tab, in the Sort & Filter group, click **Advanced** to display the Advanced Filter dialog box.

e. Verify that the range $A$9:$I$41 is in the List range box.

f. Click in the **Criteria range** box, and then select **A1:I2**. Verify that the Filter the list, in-place option is selected.

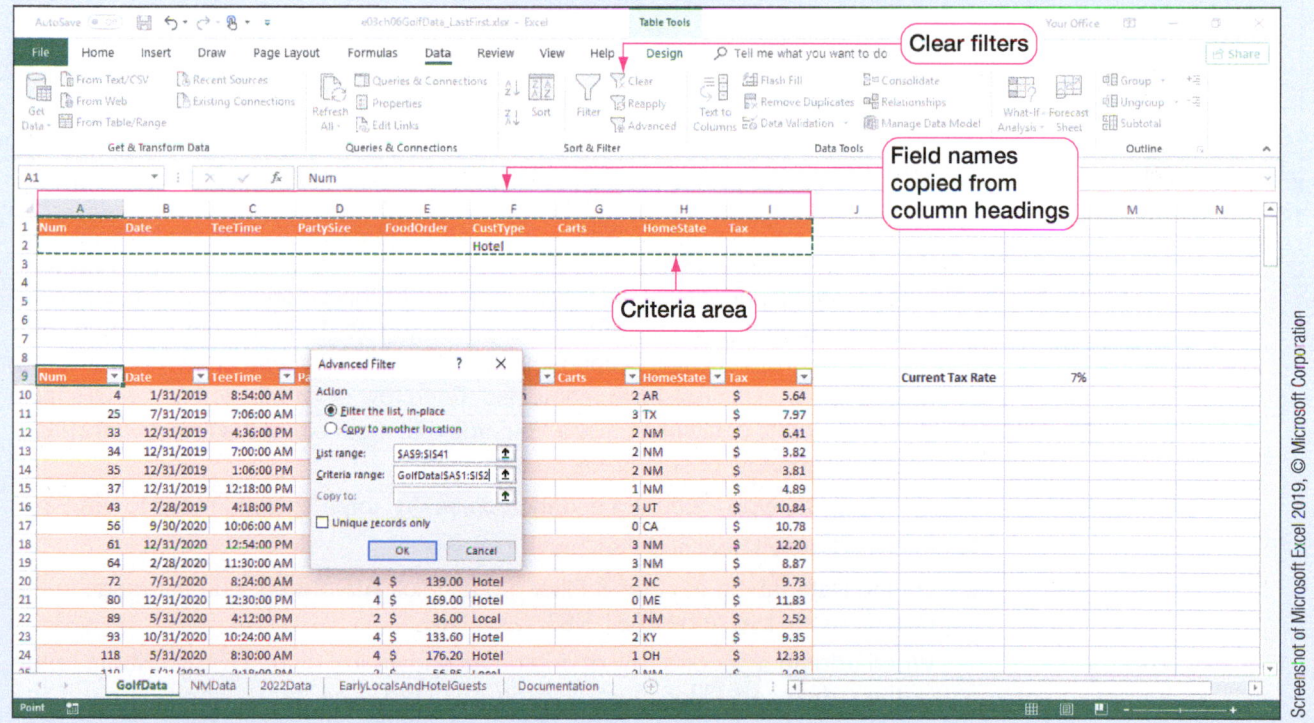

Figure 9 Advanced Filter dialog box

g. Click **OK**. The data in the table is filtered to show only the Hotel CustType transactions.

SIDE NOTE
Filter or
Advanced Filter

When an Advanced Filter
is applied, the filter arrows
disappear from the field
headings. If the Filter
button on the Data tab is
used to apply the filter to
the table again, that data
will reset, removing the
Advanced Filter results.

It is possible to add additional criteria. All criteria on the same row have to be met for the record to be shown. If only hotel customers with a party size of more than 3 are to be shown, both of those constraints must be true for the row of data to be displayed. Because all constraints are listed on one row, Excel will know to have all arguments set to true for the record to be included in the results.

h. Click cell **D2**, type **>3** and then press Ctrl + Enter.

i. On the Data tab, in the Sort & Filter group, click **Advanced**. Verify that the range in the List range box is $A$9:$I$41 and the range in the Criteria range box is $A$1:$I$2. Click **OK**.

The settings in the Advanced Filter will remain from the previous time, so the List range and Criteria range are the same as the first time the advanced filter was run. The data set should adjust to show hotel customers with party size greater than 3.

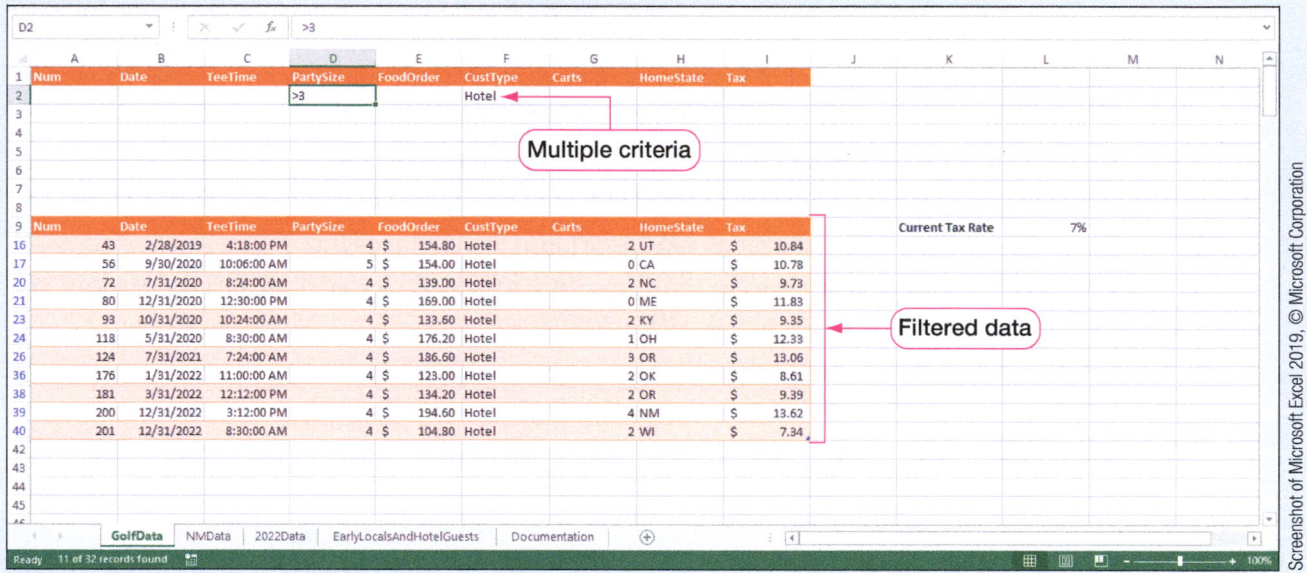

Figure 10 Advanced filter with multiple criterion

To add additional criteria, add each criterion to the criteria range. For example, to also include all records with an early morning TeeTime, before 8:00 a.m. with customer type of Local, a second row would be used. Criteria on an individual row must all be true, as has been mentioned. Each row of criteria acts as an OR, joining the two sets of filtering criteria. Records that meet either the first row of criteria or the second row of criteria will be displayed.

j. Click cell **C3**, type **<8:00 AM** and then press Tab three times to move to cell F3.

k. In cell F3, type **Local** and then press Ctrl + Enter.

l. On the Data tab, in the Sort & Filter group, click **Advanced**. Edit the range in the Criteria range box to be $A$1:$I$3. Click **OK**.

When adding a second row of criteria as shown in Figure 11, the criteria range in the Advanced Filter must also be adjusted. The same would apply if the additional row of criteria were removed from the Advanced Filter. The results will show records for hotel customers with a party size of greater than 3 or local customers with tee times earlier than 8:00 a.m. The constraints on one row will not affect the constraints on another row.

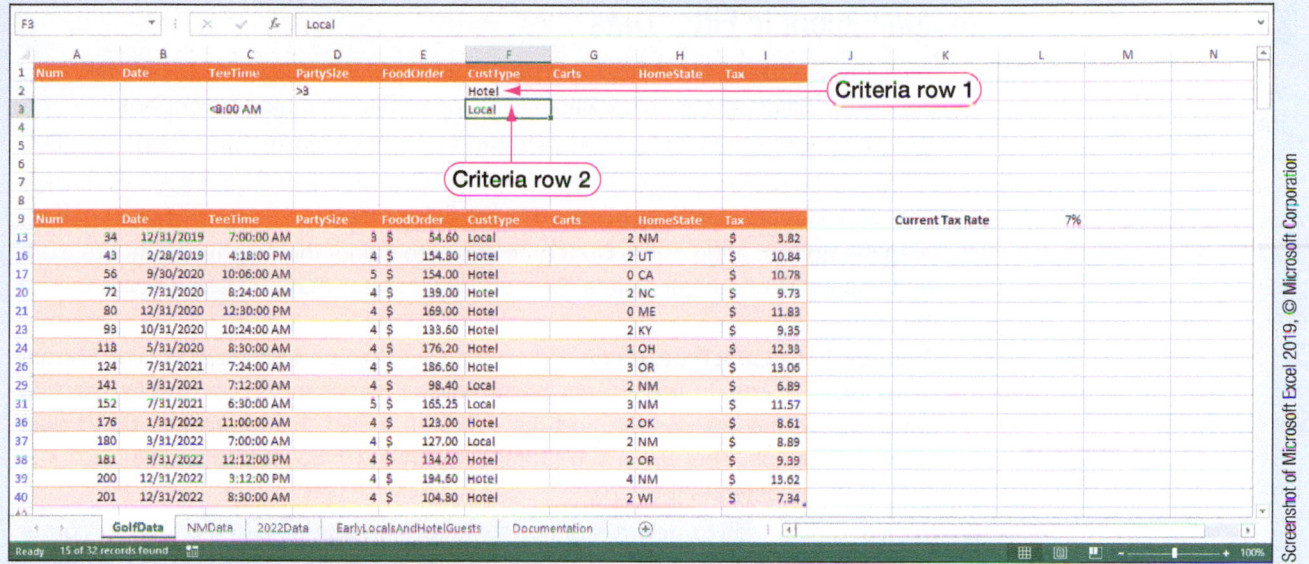

Figure 11 Advanced filter with multiple rows of criteria

m. Select the filtered range **A9:I40**, and then press Ctrl+C to copy the data.

n. Click the **EarlyLocalsAndHotelGuests** tab, click cell **A1** if necessary, and then press Ctrl+V to paste the data. Press Esc to clear the copied data from the clipboard and then adjust the column widths as necessary so that all data are visible.

o. **Save** the workbook.

CONSIDER THIS | **Extracting Table Data**

What if you want to keep the filtered data results instead of having them replaced by the next filter you run? You can do so by extracting the table data. To extract table data, do the following.

- Open the Advanced Filter dialog box.
- Select Copy to another location.
- Select the Copy to range to identify a location where you would like to extract the data. Be sure the location is blank because extracted data will replace any current data in a range of cells.
- Click OK.

Using Slicers to Filter Data

A **slicer** is a visual control that provides the user with buttons that can be used to quickly filter data in a table, PivotChart, or PivotTable. One of the benefits of using slicers is that they are easy to generate and use. Additionally, slicers indicate the current filter, so you will know exactly what data you are viewing.

In this exercise, you will create a filter for data using a slicer.

 **E06.07**

To Use Slicers to Filter Data

SIDE NOTE
Inserting Slicers
You must have a cell inside the table selected to insert a slicer.

a. Click the **GolfData** worksheet, and then click cell **A9**. Click the **Insert** tab, and then in the Filters group, click **Slicer**. The Insert Slicers dialog box opens.

b. Click to select the **CustType** and **HomeState** check boxes, and then click **OK**. Notice the filter you applied earlier is removed and the selected slicers are displayed.

c. Click and drag the **CustType slicer** so its top-left corner is in the top-left corner of **K10**.

d. Drag the bottom edge of the **CustType slicer** to adjust the height so that the extra white space is no longer visible. Do not drag it so far that you see a scroll bar on the right side.

e. Right-click the **CustType slicer**, and then select **Size and Properties**. The Format Slicer pane opens. In the Format Slicer pane, if necessary, click the **Properties** arrow to expand the section and then click to select the **Move but don't size with cells** option. This will ensure the slicer remains in cell K10 even if the column widths are adjusted in the table.

f. Click and drag the **HomeState slicer** so its top-left corner is in the top-left corner of **M10**.

g. In the Format Slicer pane, click the **Position and Layout** arrow, and then, under Layout, change the number of columns to **3** and press Enter.

h. If necessary, click the **Properties** arrow to expand the section and then click to select the **Move but don't size with cells** option.

i. **Close** ☒ the Format Slicer pane. Notice that the states are much easier to see.

SIDE NOTE
Customizing Slicers
Customizing slicers can make them more visually appealing, and more importantly, easier to use.

j. Drag the bottom edge of the **HomeState slicer** to adjust the height so that the extra white space is no longer visible. Do not drag it so far that you see a scroll bar on the right side.

k. To further customize your slicers, click the **CustType slicer**. On the Options tab, in the Slicer Styles group, click **More** ⊡. Under Dark, select **Light Orange, Slicer Style Dark 2**.

l. Click the **HomeState slicer**. On the Options tab, in the Slicer Styles group, click **More** ⊡. Under Dark, select **Light Orange, Slicer Style Dark 2**.

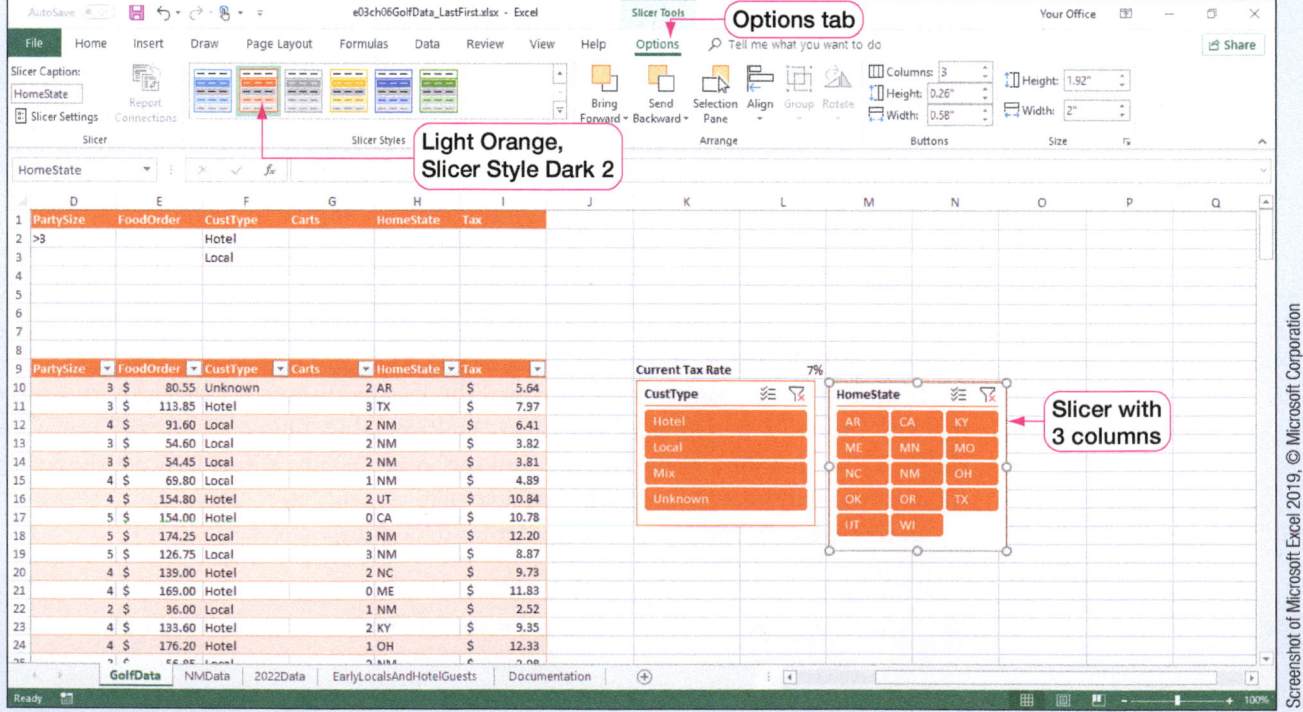

Figure 12 Customized slicers

SIDE NOTE
Selecting Multiple Criteria
Pressing Ctrl allows you to select multiple criteria on a slicer.

m. On the CustType slicer, click **Hotel** to filter the table to only display records with a hotel customer type.

n. On the HomeState slicer, click **CA**, press and hold Ctrl while clicking **KY**, **NM**, and **TX**, and then release the Ctrl key. The table now only displays records for hotel guests from the selected states.

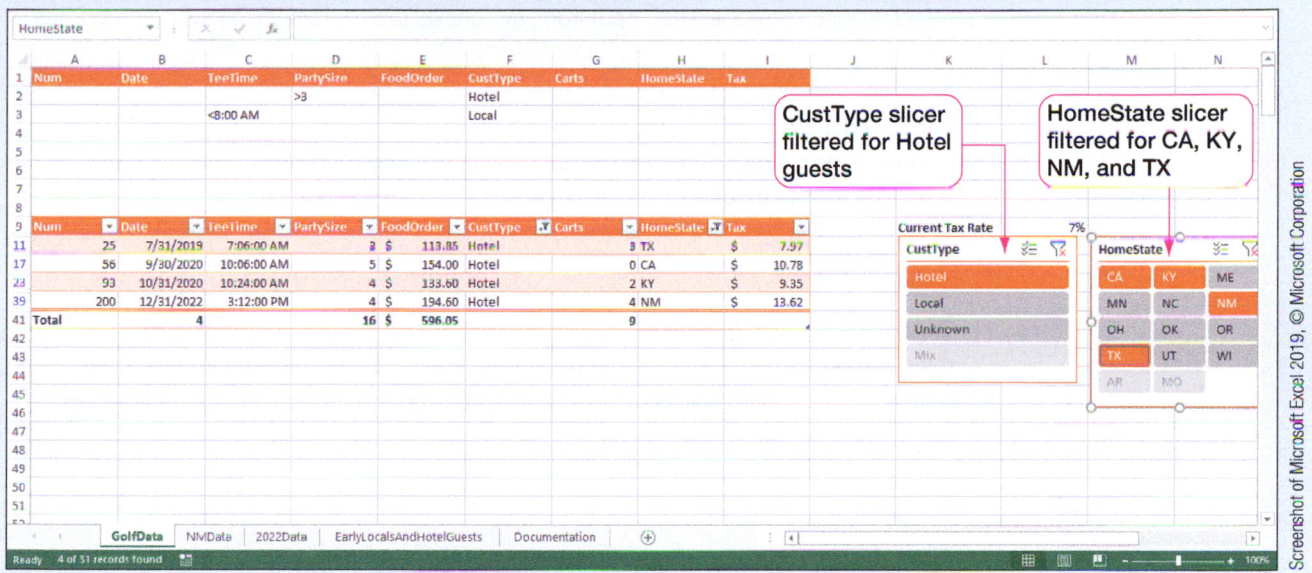

Figure 13 Filtered data using multiple slicers

o. Save  the workbook.

Summarizing a Data Set with the SUBTOTAL Function

Filters can provide answers to many questions, but they may not give you all the results you need to make sound decisions. Functions such as SUBTOTAL, AVERAGE, and COUNT functions can help to summarize the data in the data set.

In this exercise, you will summarize a data set using the SUBTOTAL function.

E06.08

To Summarize a Data Set with the SUBTOTAL Function

a. On the GolfData worksheet, click cell **A5**, type Average Food Order and then press Ctrl+Enter. Apply bold and then press Enter.

b. In cell A6, type Overall and then press Enter. In cell A7, type Filtered and then press Enter.

c. Select cells **A6:A7** and on the Home tab, in the Alignment group, click **Increase Indent**.

d. If necessary, AutoFit column **A** so that all data are visible.

e. Click cell **B6**, type =AVERAGE and then press Tab to insert the AVERAGE function.

f. Point just above the **FoodOrder** column heading in cell **E9** until the pointer changes to a black down arrow. Click to insert the GolfData[FoodOrder] structured table reference into the Average function. Press Ctrl+Enter to close the function. Apply the **Accounting** format to cell B6.

g. Click cell **B7**. Type **=SUBTOTAL** and press Tab to insert the SUBTOTAL function.

h. Press Tab to insert the 1 – AVERAGE value for the function_num argument, type a comma , and then point to just above the **FoodOrder** column heading in cell **E9** and click to insert the GolfData[FoodOrder] structured table reference as the ref1 argument.

> **Mac Troubleshooting**
> If using a Mac, press ↓ to select the 1 - Average and then press Tab to insert it as the value for the function_num argument.

> **Troubleshooting**
> If the SUBTOTAL function ScreenTip covers the 1 - Average selection, click the border of the ScreenTip and drag it to the left or to the right away from the listing.

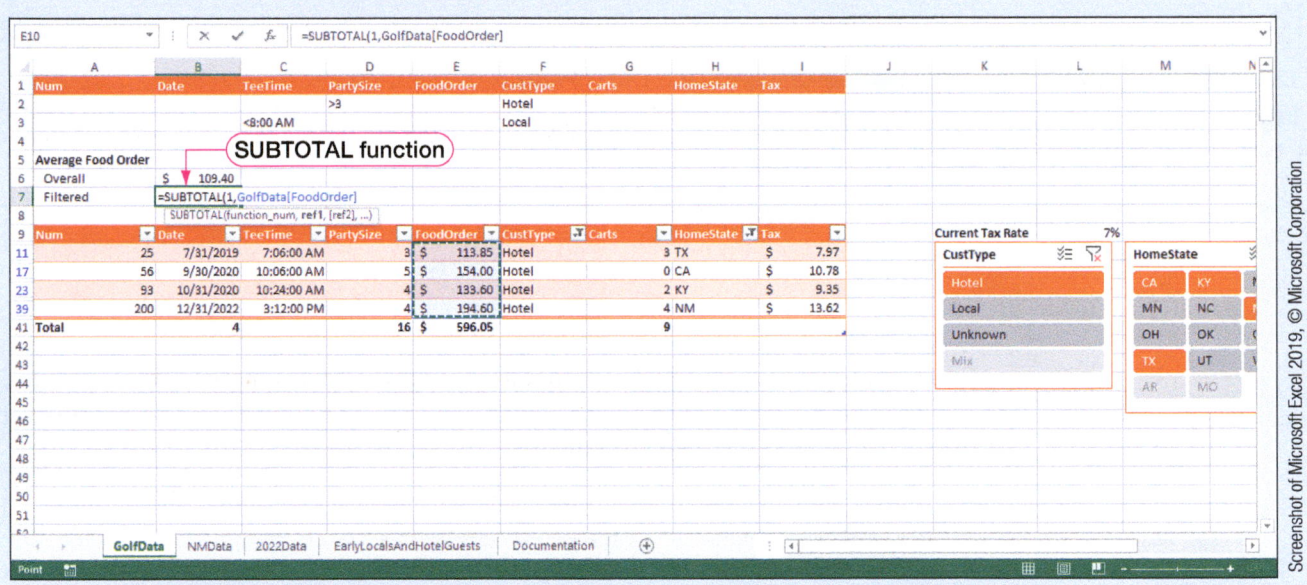

Figure 14 SUBTOTAL function

i. Press Ctrl+Enter to close the function. Apply the **Accounting** format to cell B7. The SUBTOTAL function ignores any data that is hidden because of the filter you previously applied.

j. Click cell **D5**, type Number of Records and then press Ctrl+Enter. Apply bold and then press Enter.

k. In cell D6, type Overall and then press Enter. In cell D7, type Filtered and then press Enter.

l. Select cells **D6:D7** and on the Home tab, in the Alignment group, click **Increase Indent**.

m. If necessary, AutoFit column **D** so that all data are visible.

n. Click cell **E6**, type =COUNT and then press Tab to insert the COUNT function.

o. Point and click just above the **Num** column heading in cell **A9** to insert the GolfData[Num] structured table reference into the function. Press Enter to close the function and move down to cell E7.

p. In cell **E7**. Type =SUBTOTAL and then press Tab to insert the SUBTOTAL function.

q. Press ↓ to select the 2 – COUNT function and then press Tab to insert the COUNT function into the function_num argument. Type a comma , and then point and click just above the **Num** column heading in cell **A9** to insert the GolfData[Num] structured table reference into the function. Press Ctrl+Enter to close the function.

r. Complete the **Documentation** worksheet as directed by your instructor.

s. **Save** 🖫 the workbook, **exit** Excel, and then submit the file as directed by your instructor.

> ### Grader Heads Up
> If using MyLab IT Grader, you may now submit the file as instructed. The remainder of the chapter uses a different file. Thus, it is a second project in MyLab IT Grader.

t. If you need to take a break before finishing this chapter, now is a good time.

Because you have entered several different formulas, it is now possible to see the differences within the resulting averages that have been calculated. Notice that only the SUBTOTAL function ignores hidden records and uses only visible filtered records to calculate the average. The other functions provide results based on all the records, without regard to visible and hidden records.

Organizing and Analyzing with Database Functions, PivotTables, and PivotCharts

It is possible to accomplish a great deal through the use of tables and filters—the SUB-TOTAL, logical, and retrieval functions. However, what if there is a need to really dig deep and explore a data set so you have the ability to answer all kinds of questions? What if those initial questions drive subsequent questions?

Although Excel is not a database management system (DBMS), it can store simple databases in the form of a large table of data, where each row in the table contains an individual record and each column in the table stores a particular type of data. **Database functions** are designed to easily aggregate and retrieve data from a database where specified criteria are met.

PivotTables provide a more expanded solution for exploring data. They are especially useful when you are looking at a huge table of data that can become overwhelming. A **PivotTable** is an interactive table that extracts, organizes, and summarizes source data. PivotTables are used for data analysis and looking for trends and patterns for decision-making purposes. Among other functions, a PivotTable can automatically sort, count, total, or give an average of the data stored in one table or spreadsheet. Excel then displays the results in a separate table, called a PivotTable. Here are some examples of questions PivotTables can help to answer for the pro shop.

- How many transactions does the pro shop process with cash, credit, or Apple Pay?
- How much revenue comes from members versus non-members?

- How much revenue did each employee generate last quarter?
- What was the total sales volume for the month of December?

These questions can easily be answered with a PivotTable report because PivotTables can easily group the time period to years, quarters, months, or all three. The flexibility comes from using an interface that allows the table to be built without having to create formulas and functions to do the grouping, summarizing, or calculating. And because PivotTables are interactive, they can be adjusted with a few clicks, rearranged by dragging fields, or cleared to start the process over if the layout becomes too muddled. In this section, you will develop skills for developing database functions and working with PivotTables and PivotCharts.

Construct Database Functions

Excel's worksheet structure of rows and columns allows the use of certain kinds of simple databases, and database functions are specifically designed to work with this type of data. An Excel database is a way of storing data that is made up of records (rows) and fields (columns). Different types of data can be organized in this manner, including common information such as a contact list or a list of transactions. In a database, each record is a collection of related data in a row, such as the details recorded when a product is sold, and each field is a specific piece of information, such as the ItemID being purchased. An important aspect of databases is that each record in a table contains the same fields. Thus, each transaction record may contain a transaction date field, an item code field, quantity field, and so on. Furthermore, Excel databases must include field names that are always listed as column headings in the first row.

Database functions execute common calculations such as sum, average, and count and are designed specifically for use with an Excel database. The power of database functions lies in the fact that they permit you to identify which records to include in the calculation. Consider the transactions database example. The database functions let you calculate things such as the following.

- The total revenue for transactions where more than three items were purchased
- Total number of cash transactions
- The most expensive transaction

All database functions are named by using the format DXXX(), where **XXX** is the name of the corresponding non-database Excel function. For example, in the DSUM function, the D indicates that the function is a database function, and SUM is the name of the corresponding non-database Excel function. Additionally, all database functions include the same three arguments. Using the DMAX() function as an example, the syntax is

=DMAX(database, field, criteria)

For the **DMAX** function, because the function is using data included in an Excel database, the database argument specifies the range containing the database, including the field names in the first row. The second argument—field—is the name of the database field that the calculation will use. The third argument—criteria—is the range containing the criteria that tells the function which records to use in the calculation and is a range of cells that must be at least one column wide and at least two rows high. The top row contains the field name to which the criterion applies; the cells below contains the criteria that you want to match. For example, you could use the DMAX function to find the NetRevenue that contains the highest price where more than three items were purchased.

Using Database Functions

Database functions allow for the user to specify criteria in one or more fields to explore the data with ease. When this is done, all the criteria must be evaluated to TRUE for the record to be included in the calculation. A list of database functions and their descriptions are in Table 3.

Database Function	Description
DAVERAGE	Averages the values in the field (column) of records in a list or database that match conditions you specify
DCOUNT	Counts the cells that contain numbers in a field (column) of records in the database that match the conditions you specify
DCOUNTA	Counts nonblank cells in the field (column) of records in the database that match the conditions you specify
DGET	Extracts a single value from a field (column) of a database that matches the conditions you specify
DMAX	Returns the largest number in the field (column) of records in the database that match the conditions you specify
DMIN	Returns the smallest number in the field (column) of records in the database that match the conditions you specify
DPRODUCT	Multiplies the values in the field (column) of records in the database that match the conditions you specify
DSTDEV	Estimates the standard deviation based on a sample by using numbers in a field (column) of records in a database that match conditions you specify
DSTDEVP	Calculates the standard deviation based on the entire population by using numbers in a field (column) of records in a database that match conditions you specify
DSUM	Adds the numbers in a field (column) of records in the database that match conditions you specify
DVAR	Estimates the variance based on a sample by using the numbers in a field (column) of records in a database that match conditions you specify
DVARP	Calculates the variance based on the entire population by using the numbers in a field (column) of records in a database that match conditions you specify

Table 3   Database functions

In this exercise, you will set up a criteria area on the DatabaseTotals worksheet and create database functions.

 **E06.09**

SIDE NOTE
Why Use a Table?
By converting this range of cells to a table, it can be easily expanded with additional transaction records.

To Use Database Functions

a. Start **Excel**, click **Open** in the left pane, and then double-click **This PC**. Navigate through the folder structure to the location of your student data files, and then click **e03ch06SalesAnalysis**. If a Security Warning message displays, click the **Enable Editing** button.

b. Click the **File** tab, click **Save As**, and then double-click **This PC**. In the Save As dialog box, navigate to the location where you are saving your project files, and then change the file name to e03ch06SalesAnalysis_LastFirst using your last and first name, and then click **Save**.

c. Click the **SalesData** worksheet and then click cell **A3**. Convert the range to a table by pressing Ctrl+T. In the Create Table dialog box, verify that the range $A$3:$L$24 is in the **Where is the data in your table?** box and that the **My table has headers** check box is checked, and then click **OK**.

d. On the Design tab, in the Properties group, click inside the Table Name box and type SalesData to name the table, and then press Enter. It is good practice to provide a descriptive name to any table created.

e. With the range **A3:L24** still selected, type SalesDatabase in the Name Box to create a named range for the entire table, including the column headings, and then press Enter. You will now be able to refer to the SalesDatabase named range as the database in the various database functions.

SIDE NOTE
Alternate Method for Field Name
The field name can be either the name of the column or the number of the column that you want to use in the calculations. Since NetRevenue is the 11th column, you could also type 11.

f. To set up the criteria section for use in database functions, you must have a row of column headings that match those of the database. Select the range **A3:L3**, and press Ctrl+C to copy the column headings. Click the **DatabaseTotals** worksheet, if necessary, click cell **A1**, and then press Ctrl+V to paste the column headings.

g. Click cell **B5**, type **NetRevenue** and then press Enter. This is the name of the field that will be used in the various database functions.

h. Click cell **B7**, type **=DSUM** and then press Tab to open the function.

i. Type **SalesDatabase** and then press Tab to insert the named range as the Database argument.

j. Type a comma **,** and then click cell **B5** as the field containing the values you wish to sum.

k. Type a comma **,** select the range **A1:L2** for the criteria range and then press Ctrl+Enter. Because no criteria has been specified, the result is the sum of all net revenue values from the SalesDatabase named range.

The range referenced for the criteria must be at least two rows tall, the first row contains field names from the database and the subsequent rows for specifying criteria. Database functions do support multiple rows of criteria if you need to incorporate OR criteria. However, if the range includes more than 1 criteria row and no criteria is specified in one of the rows, the database function will return values as if no criteria has been specified.

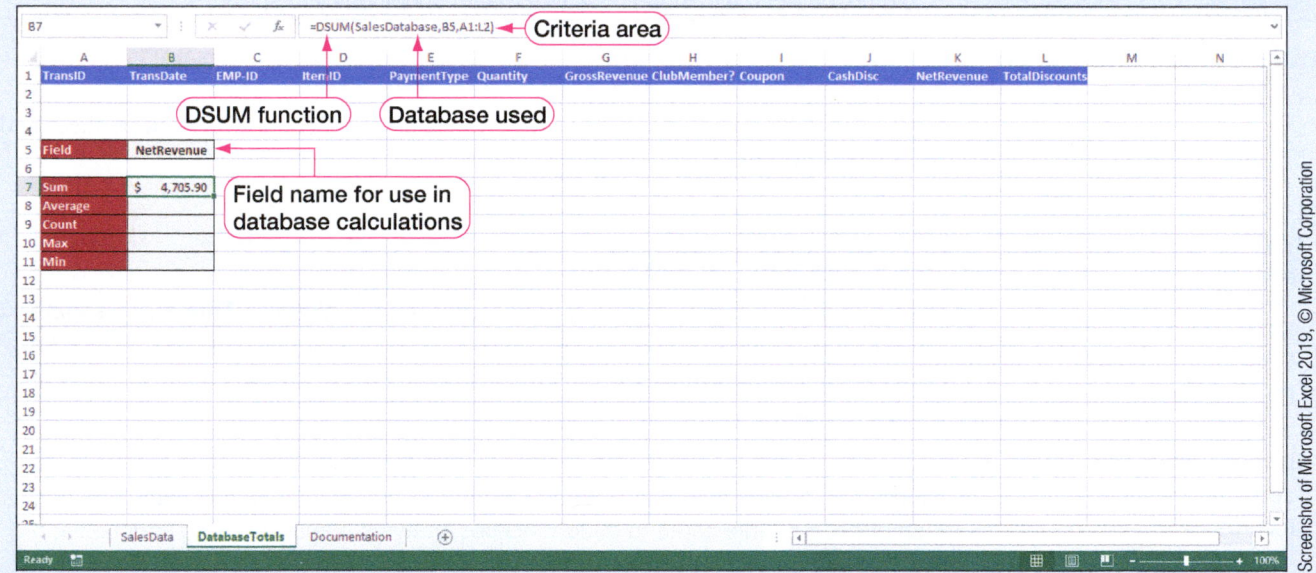

Figure 15   Database function—DSUM

l. Click cell **B8**, type **=DAVERAGE** and then press Tab to open the function.

m. Type **SalesDatabase** and then press Tab to insert the named range as the Database argument. Type a comma **,** and then click cell **B5** as the field containing the values you wish to average. Type a comma **,** select the range **A1:L2** for the criteria range, and then press Enter.

n. In cell B9, type **=DCOUNT** and then press Tab to open the function.

o. Type **SalesDatabase** and then press Tab to insert the named range as the Database argument. Type a comma **,** and then click cell **B5** as the field containing the values you wish to count. Type a comma **,** select the range **A1:L2** for the criteria range, and then press Enter.

p. In cell B10, type **=DMAX** and then press Tab to open the function.

q. Type **SalesDatabase** and then press Tab to insert the named range as the Database argument. Type a comma **,** and then click cell **B5** as the field containing the values from which you wish to return the maximum value. Type a comma **,** select the range **A1:L2** for the criteria range, and then press Enter.

r. In cell B11, type **=DMIN** and then press Tab to open the function.

s. Type **SalesDatabase** and then press Tab to insert the named range as the Database argument. Type a comma **,** and then click cell **B5** as the field containing the values from which you wish to return the minimum value. Type a comma **,** select the range **A1:L2** for the criteria range, and then press Enter.

Now that the database functions have been set up, you can easily add criteria into the second row of the criteria range and if a record in the database meets all specified criteria it will be used in the calculations.

t. Click cell **E2,** type **Apple Pay** and then press Enter to see the sum, average, count, max, and min net revenue for those records where Apple Pay was the method of payment.

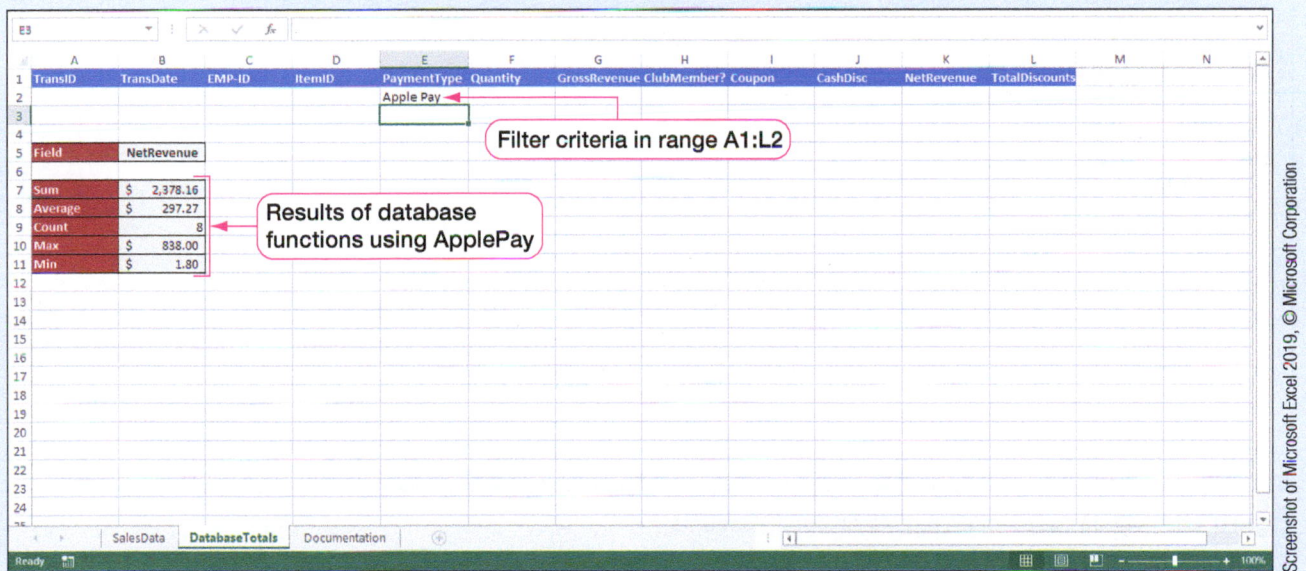

Figure 16 Database function results for Apple Pay customers

u. Click cell **B2**, type **>11/15/2022** and then press Enter. The database functions will now only calculate the values for records where the customer used Apple Pay and the transaction occurred later than 11/15/2022.

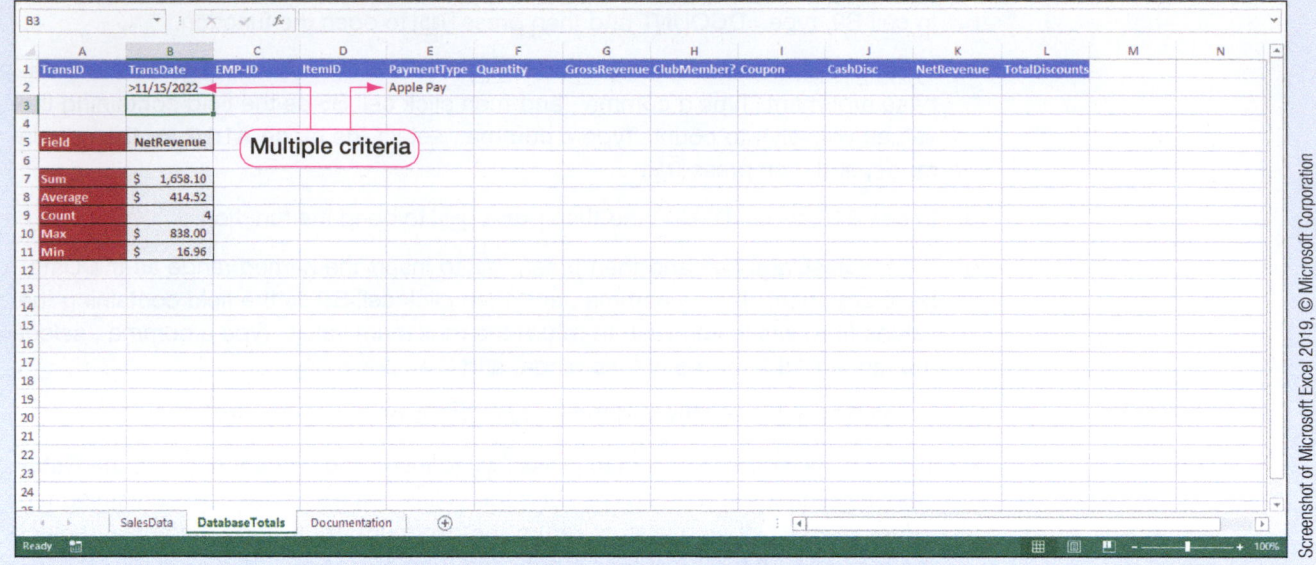

Figure 17 Database function results with multiple criteria

v. Click cell B5, type **TotalDiscounts** and then press [Enter]. The database functions are now calculated using the TotalDiscounts field in the database.

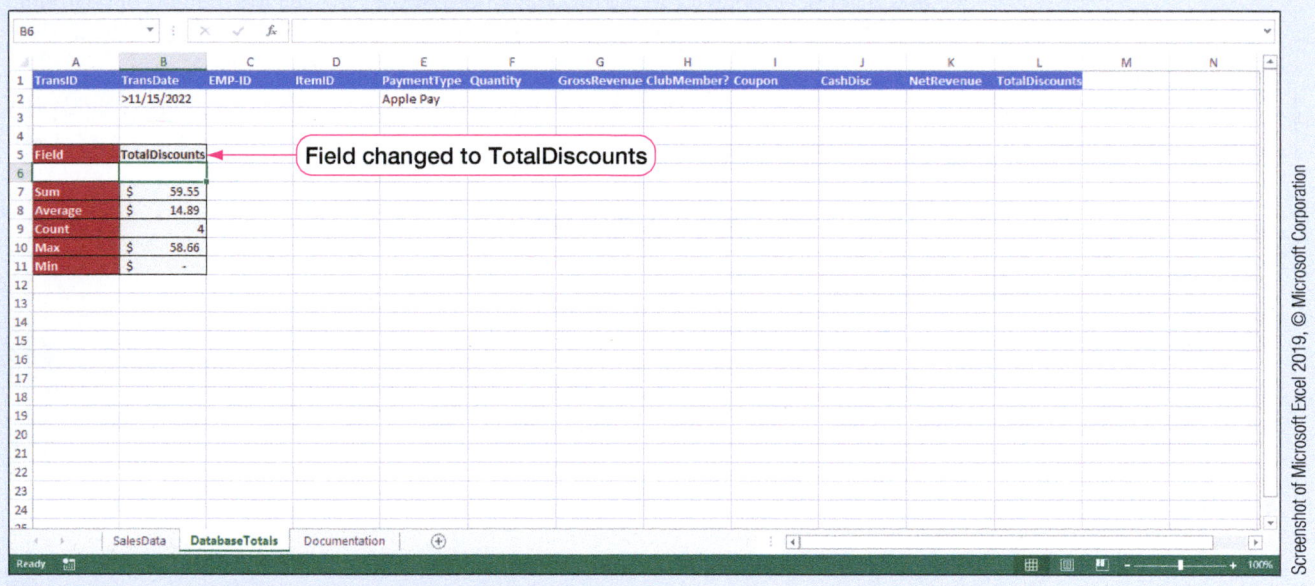

Figure 18 Database function results on TotalDiscounts

w. Save  the workbook.

S S **CONSIDER THIS** | **Changing the Field Value**

What are some possible issues with the use of these database functions? Would the formatting applied to the results when NetRevenue is the field cause confusion if Quantity was the field instead? What would the database functions return if there are no matching records? How could you modify the formula to handle possible errors?

Develop and Customize PivotTables

An understanding of the general process is helpful in working with PivotTables. First, it is important to make sure the data set is well organized and in the correct structure. A PivotTable can be created on an existing worksheet or a new worksheet. When it is created, a link or connection is established to a data source. After the data source and the location to insert the blank PivotTable have been determined, the interactive part begins. The PivotTable is blank or empty to begin with, but it can be developed by considering what data to group and what data to summarize. The final step is to explore and work with the options within the PivotTable to fine-tune the layout to fit your specific needs.

Exploring PivotTable Variations

The Recommended PivotTables feature in Excel allows you to explore your data from many different perspectives with just a few clicks. Based on the data set, Excel can recommend and create a variety of PivotTables to explore things like Total Gross Revenue for each Employee, Total Discounts by Payment Method, and so much more. The recommended PivotTables option is great if you are not exactly sure for what you are looking and just want to explore.

To Explore PivotTable Variations

a. Click the **SalesData** worksheet and then click cell **A3**.

b. Click the **Insert** tab and in the Tables group, click **Recommended PivotTables**. The Recommended PivotTables dialog box opens with several recommendations.

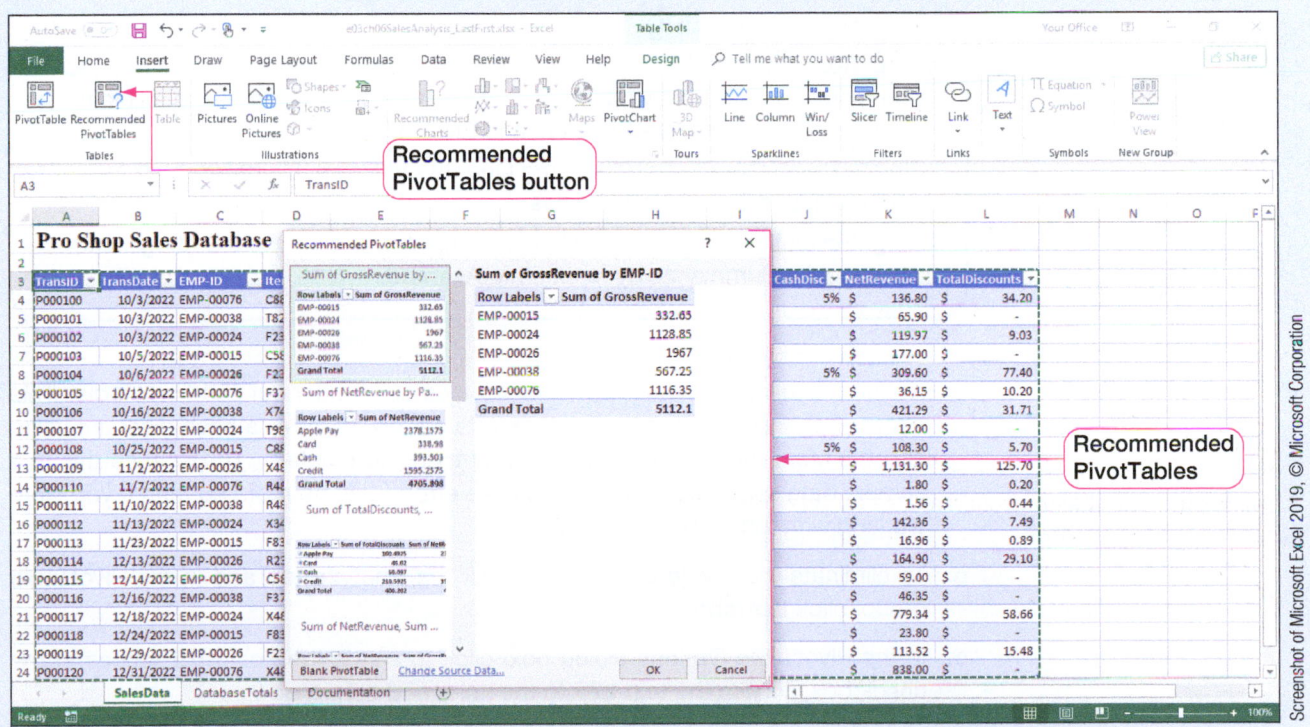

Figure 19 Recommended PivotTable options

c. Scroll through the options and select **Average of CashDisc by Quantity and ClubMember?** and then click **OK**. A new worksheet is inserted to the left of the SalesData worksheet and the recommended PivotTable is inserted. The Pivot-Table Fields pane appears on the right side of the window.

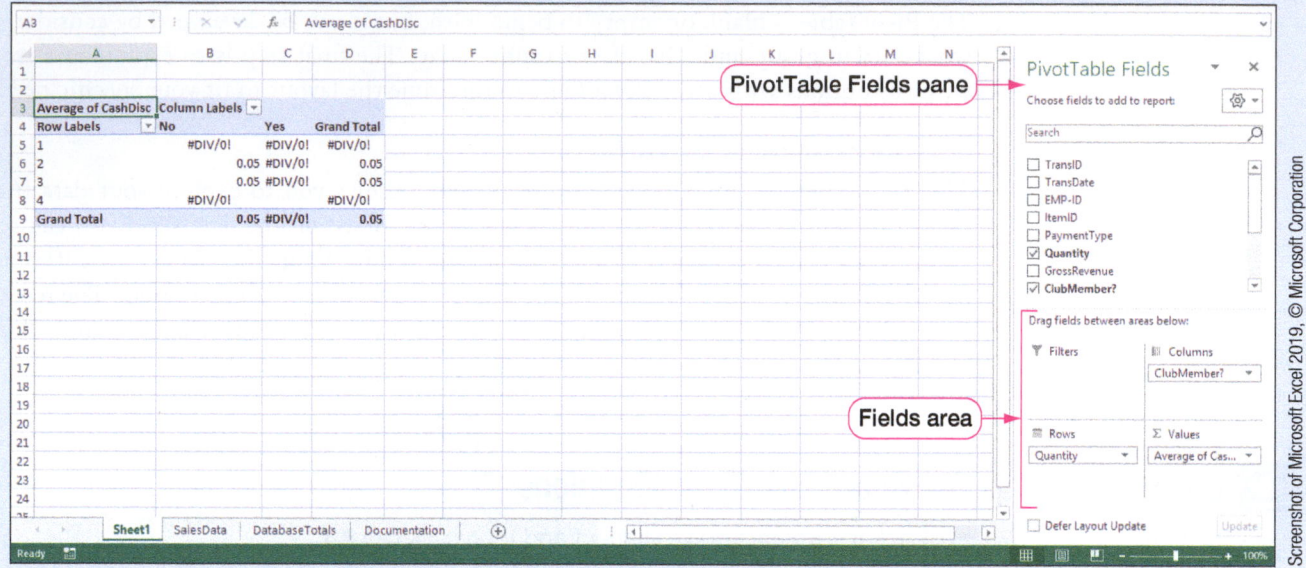

Figure 20 Average of CashDisc by Quantity and ClubMember? PivotTable

> ## Mac Troubleshooting
>
> **a.** The Recommended PivotTable automatically created on a Mac will need to be modified before moving forward. In the PivotTable Fields pane, click to deselect **TransDate**, **NetRevenue** and **EMP-ID**.
>
> **b.** In the PivotTable Fields pane, drag **Quantity** to Rows, **ClubMember?** to columns, and **CashDisc** to Values.
>
> **c.** Right-click the **CashDisc** field in the Values area, select **Field Settings**, and change the Summarize by function to **Average**.

SIDE NOTE
Contextual Tabs
You can select any cell inside the PivotTable to redisplay the PivotTable Tools contextual tabs on the ribbon.

Notice the divide by 0 errors (#DIV/0!) located throughout the PivotTable. This occurs because many records in the data set do not have a cash discount value and therefore the average calculation is trying to divide by 0. Because this is a sample data set, the prevalence of these errors may be more so than if you were working with more complete set.

d. To eliminate the divide by 0 errors, click the **Analyze** tab and in the PivotTable group, click **Options**.

e. In the PivotTable Options dialog box, click to select the **For error values show** check box, click in the **text box** to the right, and then type 0

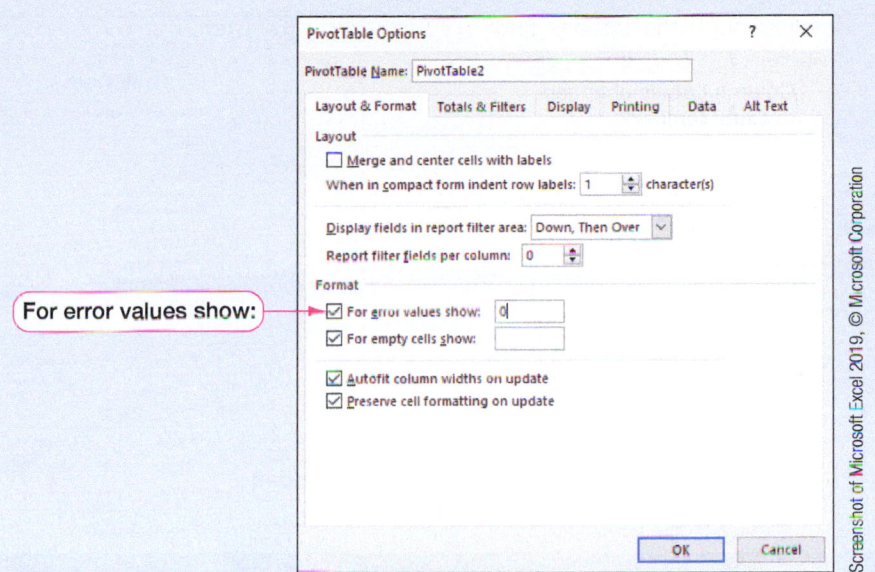

For error values show:

Figure 21 PivotTable Options dialog box

f. Click **OK** and notice that all the #DIV/0! errors are now 0. This PivotTable can be improved with just a few small changes.

g. Click cell **A4** and replace Row Labels with Quantity Sold

h. Click cell **B3** and replace Column Labels with ClubMember?

You now realize that because cash discounts are always 5% off, the average of them is not that meaningful. Once a PivotTable is created, it is very easy to change things around to explore the data from different perspectives.

i. In the PivotTable Fields pane, click to deselect the **CashDisc** check box to remove it from the PivotTable.

> ### Troubleshooting
> If you close the PivotTable Fields pane and need to display it again, first select a cell in the PivotTable. Under the PivotTable Tools contextual tab, click the Analyze tab. In the Show group, click the Show arrow if necessary, and then select Field List.

j. In the PivotTable Fields pane, click to select the **TotalDiscounts** check box to add it to the Values area. The PivotTable now displays the sum of total discounts for each quantity sold with columns that indicate whether the customer was a club member.

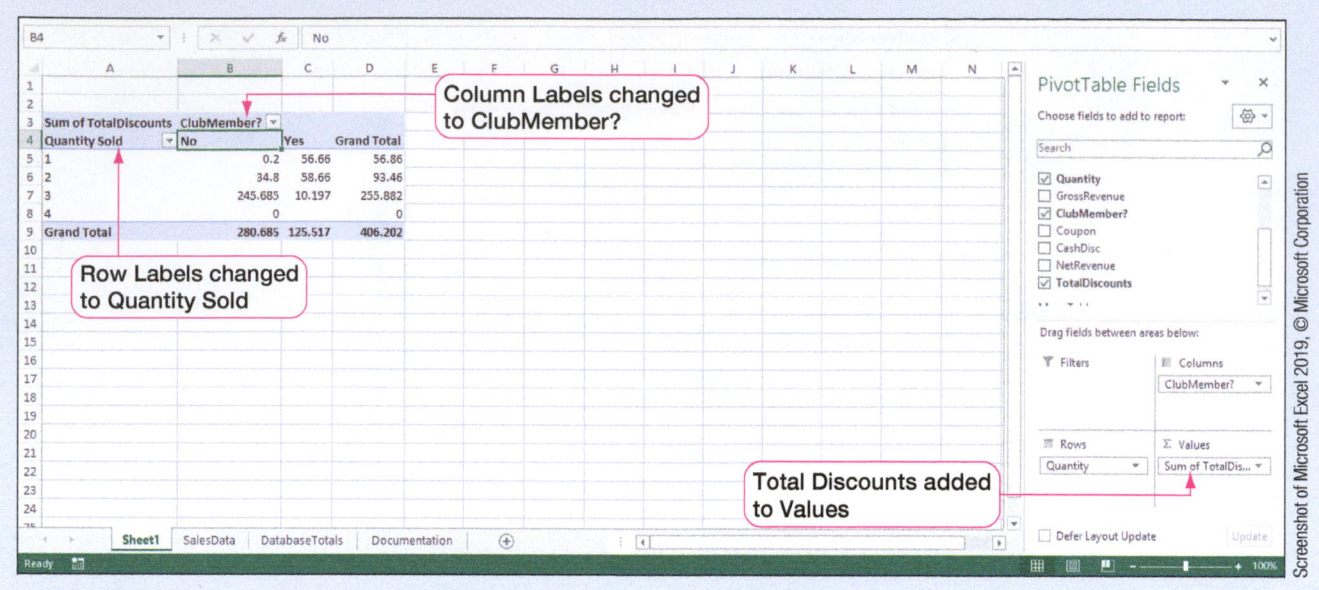

Figure 22 Sum of TotalDiscounts by Quantity PivotTable

k. Double-click the **worksheet** tab to rename it TotalDiscountsByQty and then press Enter.

l. **Save** 🖫 the workbook.

Creating a PivotTable

Creating a PivotTable manually is a two-step process: selecting the data set and location where the PivotTable will be created and working with the data fields to group and summarize the selected data. When creating a PivotTable, ensure the source data is arranged in an area with column headings representing each field and the rows representing each record, preferably with no other information or content in cells that are adjacent to the data set just like with a table. In addition, there should be clear, concise field headings in the top cell for each column of data. Excel will use these as the labels within the PivotTable. Finally, if there are automatic subtotals or other summary functions at the bottom of the data, be sure to remove these. They will cause confusion if they are incorporated into a PivotTable.

REAL WORLD ADVICE	**Consider the Fields Needed for the PivotTable**

You should consider whether you are going to add data and want to name the data set range so you can add data to the named range. Add any calculated fields to the data initially. For example, with quantity and price, there may be a need to add a new column named Revenue that is the price times the quantity. Or if there is a field that has both the city and state, you might want to separate the data into two columns so it is possible to group by city or by state. If there are potential changes, working with a table is optimal, as it makes adding fields easy, and those new fields can be incorporated into PivotTables simply by refreshing the data.

There are only two options with regard to the location of a PivotTable: A PivotTable can be created on a new worksheet or on an existing worksheet. PivotTables automatically expand and contract on a worksheet as variables are added, removed, and rearranged. Creating a PivotTable on a new worksheet will set it apart and reduce the chance that the PivotTable will interfere with or disturb other data. If a PivotTable is placed on an existing worksheet with other data, it is best to choose a location below or to the right of any existing data. This allows the PivotTable room to expand to the right or down as needed, without interfering with the existing data.

SS CONSIDER THIS | PivotTables and Hidden Data

A filter applied to the data set will not affect the PivotTable creation process. The PivotTable will ignore the filter and use all the data—including the hidden data. Why is this important when using the data for decision making?

Similar to creating an Excel table, when a PivotTable is being created from a data set, one cell within the data set should be the active cell. Excel will automatically detect the range in the process of setting up the initial PivotTable area. It is possible to adjust the data range used if Excel mistakenly includes other information that is not needed in the PivotTable data range. If the data has been established as a table, the creation of a PivotTable is based on the current range for the table.

In this exercise, you will create a PivotTable from an Excel table.

 **E06.11**

To Create a PivotTable

a. Click the **SalesData** worksheet and then click cell **A3**.

Troubleshooting

If you have a few cells selected in a data set when you begin creating a PivotTable, you may end up creating a PivotTable that has only the subset selection as the range. It is best to have only one cell selected in your data set when you create the PivotTable.

b. Click the **Design** tab, and in the Tools group, click **Summarize with PivotTable**. The Create PivotTable dialog box opens.

Troubleshooting

If the data you are using is not in a table, click the Insert tab, and then, in the Tables group, click PivotTable.

c. Verify that the SalesData table/range is selected. Verify that **New Worksheet** is selected, and then click **OK**. The PivotTable is inserted on a new sheet.

d. Double-click the **worksheet** tab, replace the Sheet name with PivotAnalysis and then press Enter. Notice the PivotTable Tools contextual tabs that appeared.

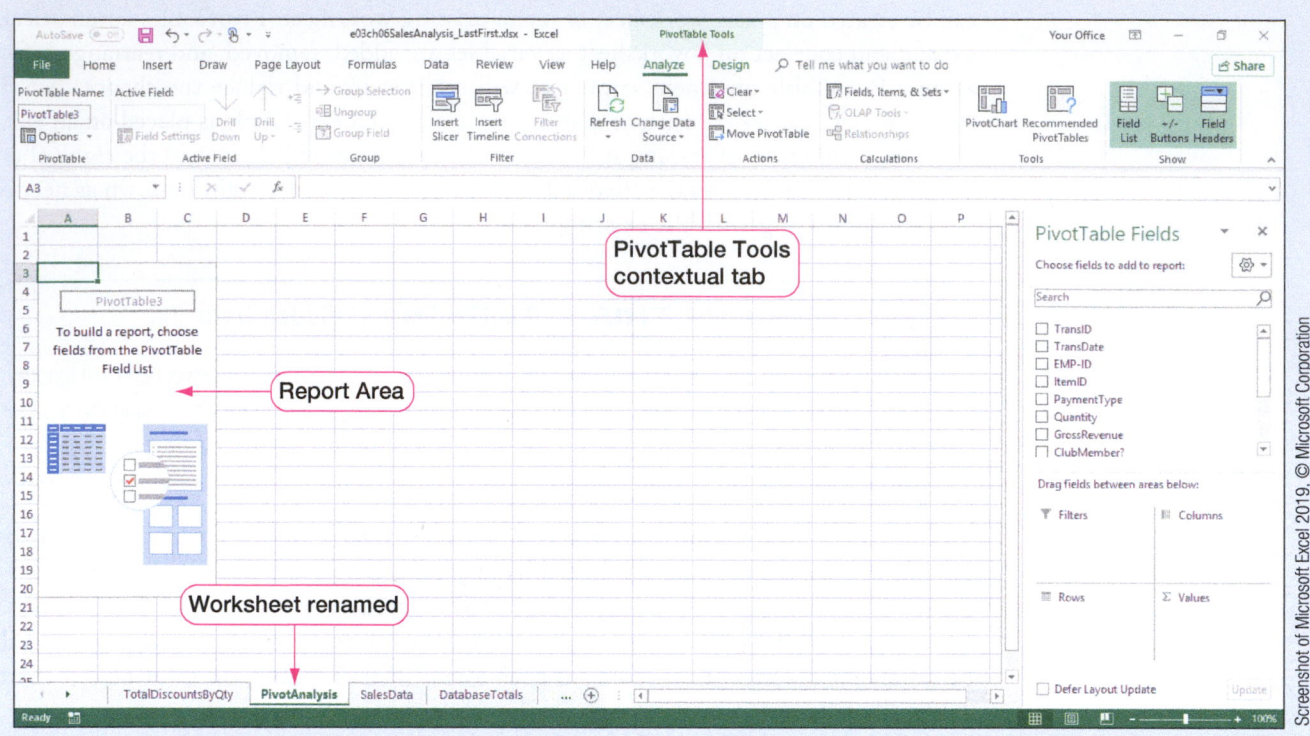

Figure 23 PivotTable contextual tabs

e. Click cell **A1**. Notice that the PivotTable Tools contextual tabs disappear and only a blank PivotTable area is showing below cell A1.

f. Click cell **A3**.

The PivotTable Fields pane will reappear on the right side of the screen. The PivotTable Tools contextual tabs are now available.

g. **Save** the workbook.

Summarizing Data with a PivotTable

Once the worksheet is set up for constructing the PivotTable, the interactive part of the process begins. The focus is to construct a table that will group and summarize subsets of the data in a useful and meaningful manner. There are a few guidelines for choosing how to arrange the fields.

It helps to distinguish fields as either grouping variables or summary variables, because these two types get placed in different areas within the PivotTable. A **grouping variable** can be thought of as any field within the data set that could be used to categorize or group for the purpose of comparison. For example, gender is a common variable used to group and analyze data. It may be necessary to compare the salaries of females with those of males. Dates are also useful for grouping data into months, quarters, and years to explore trends over time. Conversely, a **summary variable** is data that is not categorical in nature and can be aggregated by summing, counting, or averaging, such as gross revenue, quantity, or price.

Grouping variables are placed along the top or the left side of the PivotTable. The aggregation of data occurs when records in the data are grouped by selected variables. The results would be placed in the bottom-right areas of the aggregate summary. This layout is shown in Figure 24.

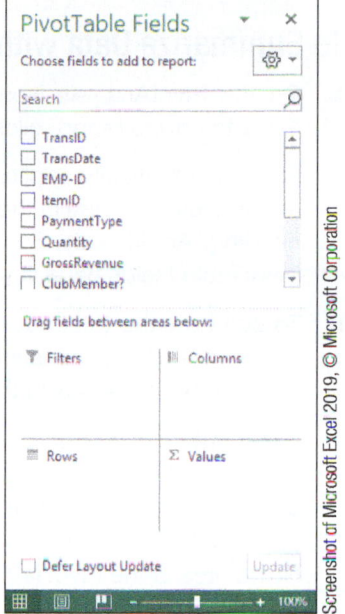

Figure 24   PivotTable layout

The grouping variables are positioned in the Columns or Rows areas at the bottom of the PivotTable Fields pane. The summary variables are positioned in the Values area. Fields are dragged from the PivotTable Fields list and dropped to any of the four quadrant areas at the bottom of the PivotTable Fields pane. Alternatively, you can click the check box beside the field names to select the field. When the check box beside a field is selected, Excel will try to guess where that field should be placed on the basis of the data values contained in the field. If it is text or dates, it will default to the Rows area. If it is numerical data, it may be considered a summary variable and placed into the Values area—the calculations area of the PivotTable. Additionally, you can place fields into the Filters area, which will allow you to filter data on the basis of the field or fields placed in that area. For example, if you choose to place a Days field into the Filters area, you could simply display data for the weekend—Saturday and Sunday. If Excel puts the field into the wrong area, it can be dragged from one area to another, or you can click the field name in the applicable area's box to access a list of options for the field, which include options to move the field's location. If a field is not needed, its check box can be unchecked to remove it from the PivotTable design. It is possible to have multiple fields in any of the PivotTable areas.

In this exercise, you will summarize data with a PivotTable to see total monthly net revenue for each payment type.

 **E06.12**

SIDE NOTE
Alternate Method for Grouping
You can also group numerical data by clicking a cell containing a value from the field and on the PivotTable Tools Analyze tab, in the Group group, click Group Field.

To Summarize Data with a PivotTable

a. On the PivotAnalysis worksheet, in the PivotTable Fields pane, under Choose fields to add to report, click to select the **NetRevenue** field check box.

Excel automatically applies the SUM aggregate function to the NetRevenue field and places the value in the PivotTable in column A under the Sum of NetRevenue heading. Additionally, Sum of NetRevenue is displayed in the Values area in the PivotTable Fields pane.

b. To see how the total net revenue breaks down by year, quarter, month, or day, you can add the transaction date field to the PivotTable. Click to select the **TransDate** check box in the PivotTable Fields pane.

Excel automatically groups the transaction dates into months and Oct, Nov, and Dec appear in the PivotTable in column A under the Row Labels heading. Next to each month is a plus sign ⊞ that can be clicked to view individual transaction dates within each month. Additionally, Months and TransDate are displayed in the Rows area in the PivotTable Fields pane.

c. Right-click cell **A4** and in the right-click menu, select **Group**. Because the sales data used in the PivotTable analysis is only a small sample, it may not seem necessary to group the dates by anything other than Months. However, when the analysis is done on multiple years of data, additional groupings will prove useful.

d. In the Grouping dialog box, click **Days** to deselect it and then click **Quarters** and **Years** so that the transaction dates will be grouped by Months, Quarters, and Years. Click **OK**. Notice that subtotals are automatically added to the year and quarter groupings.

> **Mac Troubleshooting**
> If using a Mac, press and hold ⇧Shift to select multiple grouping options.

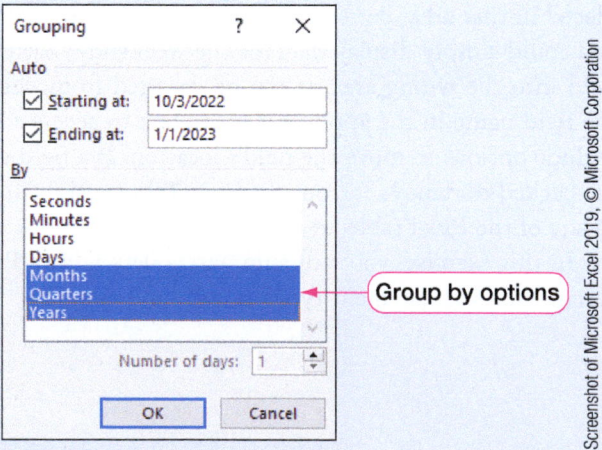

Screenshot of Microsoft Excel 2019, © Microsoft Corporation

Figure 25 Grouping dialog box

e. To further analyze the total net revenue, drag the **PaymentType** field from the PivotTable Fields list and drop it into the **Columns** area.

The PivotTable now calculates the sum of net revenue for each month and payment type. If you wanted to know about sales volume instead of net revenue, you could simply deselect NetRevenue and click the Quantity check box instead.

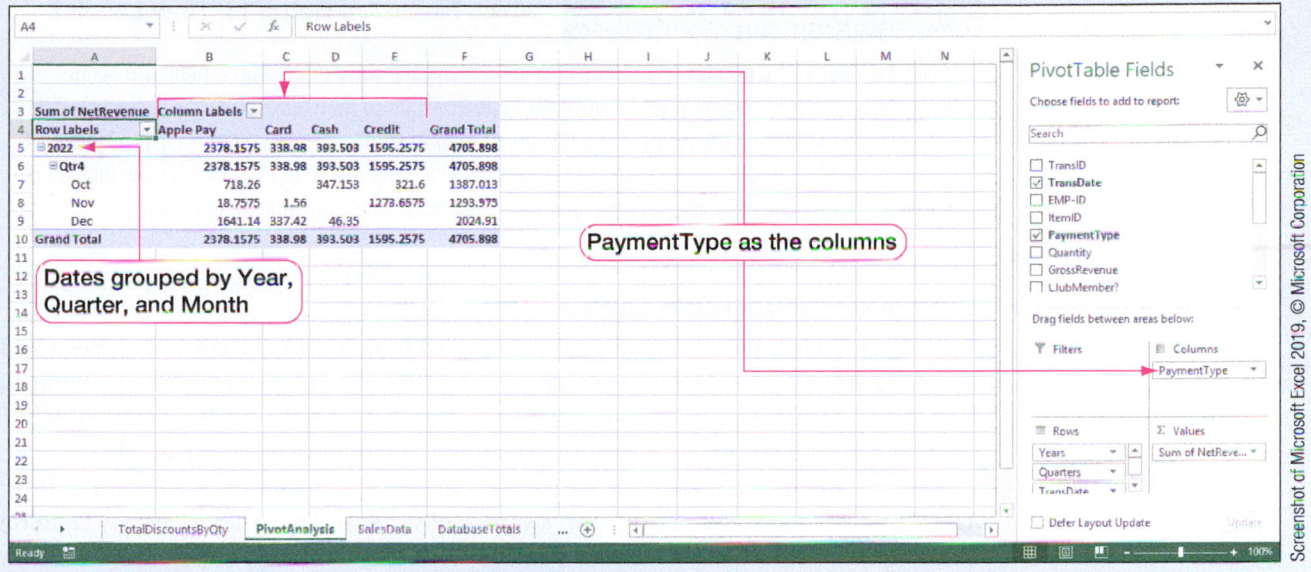

Figure 26 PivotTable—NetRevenue by date and payment type

f. Drag the **ClubMember?** field from the PivotTable Fields list and drop it into the **Filters** area so that you can easily include or exclude club members in the analysis.

g. Click the **filter arrow** ⌄ for the ClubMember? field in cell **B1** to view the filter options.

h. Select **Yes** from the filter and then click **OK** to see the net revenue for club members only.

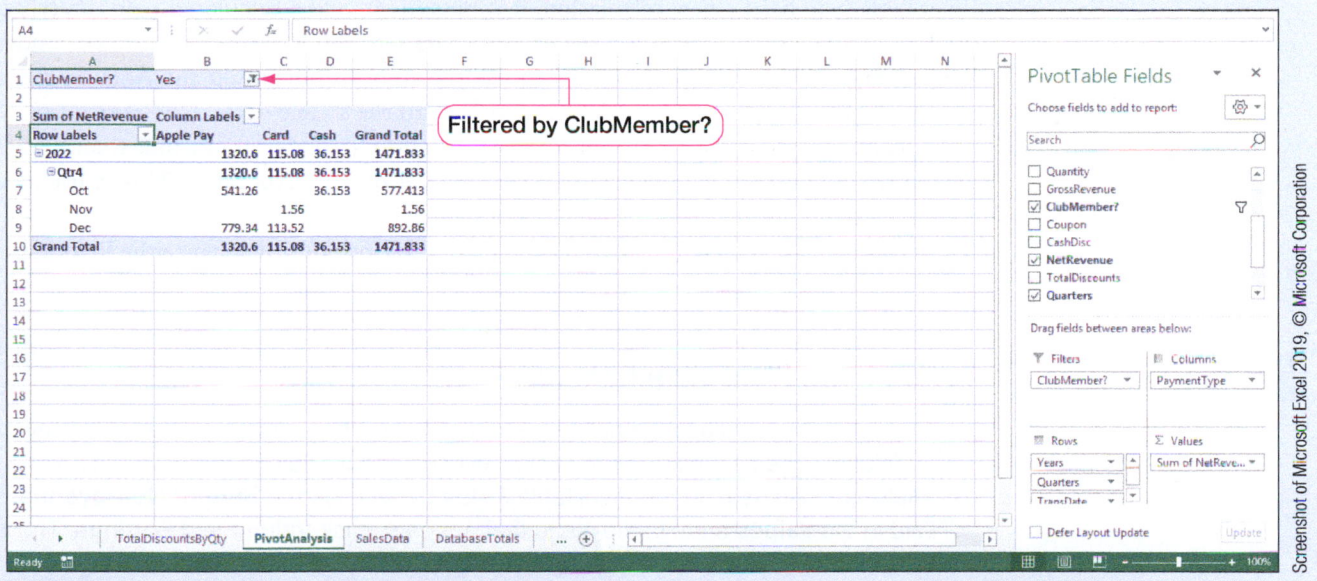

Figure 27 PivotTable—Filtered by ClubMember? field

i. **Save** 💾 the workbook.

CONSIDER THIS | **Group on Rows or Columns**

The fields for grouping could be all in the Rows area, all in the Columns area, or a mixture. What issues may arise if you have all the grouping fields as row labels or all as column labels? What would you use as a rule of thumb for the number of groups within each area?

REAL WORLD ADVICE | **Which Fields Are Better for Row Labels?**

While it is possible to choose any grouping field on either the rows or columns, there are some guidelines. Typically, you want your PivotTable to go down more than across. People are more accustomed to scrolling up or down in a document than to scrolling left or right. So if you have a lot of groups within a field, it is better to put those fields along the row side of the PivotTable instead of across the top in columns. It is better to have the user scroll up or down instead of across.

Configuring PivotTable Options

With PivotTables, two contextual tabs are available to aid in the control of PivotTable elements: Analyze and Design. The Analyze tab has all the options for fine-tuning the PivotTable. Many of these options can also be accessed by right-clicking any cell within the PivotTable. Some are very useful in creating the structure of the PivotTable.

The Design tab focuses on formatting and on the appearance of designing the Pivot-Table. Options include choosing from a variety of styles and whether to display band row and/or column colors, report layouts, and so forth. Additionally, formatting can always be done through the traditional Format Cells dialog box found by right-clicking any cell in the PivotTable. This is not recommended, though, as it will format only the selected cell. Formatting data through the Value Field Settings dialog box applies the format to all other cells within the same field. This eliminates the need to select a range of data and to be concerned with how the formatting will change as the PivotTable changes shape or is restructured.

Additionally, new fields can be added. Remember that when data is in an Excel table, it is possible to add a new field that is automatically included. If, while working with the PivotTable, you need a new calculation, it is possible to add a calculated field directly to the PivotTable without changing the original data set. You also can return to the under-lying data, add the new fields, and then use the Refresh button on the Analyze tab to update the PivotTable data for any changes made to the source data.

Finally, it is possible to change the layout, adding totals, grand totals, and labels within the PivotTable to enhance the look and feel of the PivotTable. This is useful in creating a structure that will be used in a presentation.

In this exercise, you will work with the PivotTable options to enhance the PivotTable.

 E06.13

To Configure PivotTable Options

a. The net revenue values are not formatted in a way that is appropriate for money, additionally the field name Sum of NetRevenue should be changed. On the Pivot-Analysis worksheet, in the PivotTable Fields pane, click the **Sum of NetRevenue** field in the **Values** area. In the menu that appears, click **Value Field Settings**. The Value Field Settings allow you to make changes to the field name, change the aggregate function being applied to the value, and format the numbers.

> **Mac Troubleshooting**
>
> If using a Mac, right-click the **Sum of NetRevenue** field in the **Values** area and then select **Value Field Settings**.

b. In the Value Field Settings dialog box, in the Custom Name field, replace Sum of NetRevenue with Total Net Revenue

SIDE NOTE
PivotTable Formatting
It is not recommended
to use the standard
formatting techniques
found on the Home
tab with PivotTables.
PivotTables are dynamic
and the regular format-
ting techniques will not
make use of the dynamic
attributes.

c. Click **Number Format** to open the Format Cells dialog box. Click the **Accounting** category and then click **OK**. Click **OK** again. The values are now formatted as Accounting and the custom field name, Total Net Revenue is displayed in cell A3 and in the Values area of the PivotTable Fields pane.

Appropriate formatting and labeling of your PivotTable will help to improve its readability.

d. Click cell **A4** and replace Row Labels with **Quarters by Year** If necessary, adjust the width of column A so that all data are visible.

e. Click cell **B3** and replace Column Labels with **Payment Type**

f. Right-click cell **B5**. Point to **Show Values As**, and then select **% of Grand Total**. The values change to reflect the proportion of the total. You can now easily see that in Quarter 4 of 2022, Apple Pay transactions made up 89.72% of the total revenue for that quarter.

g. Click the **Design** tab, and in the PivotTable Styles group, click **More** ⮟, and then select **White, Pivot Style Light 23**.

> **Mac Troubleshooting**
> If using a Mac, right-click cell **B5** and select **Value Field Settings**. Click the **Show data as** tab, click the arrow in the list box and select **% of Grand Total**. Click **OK**.

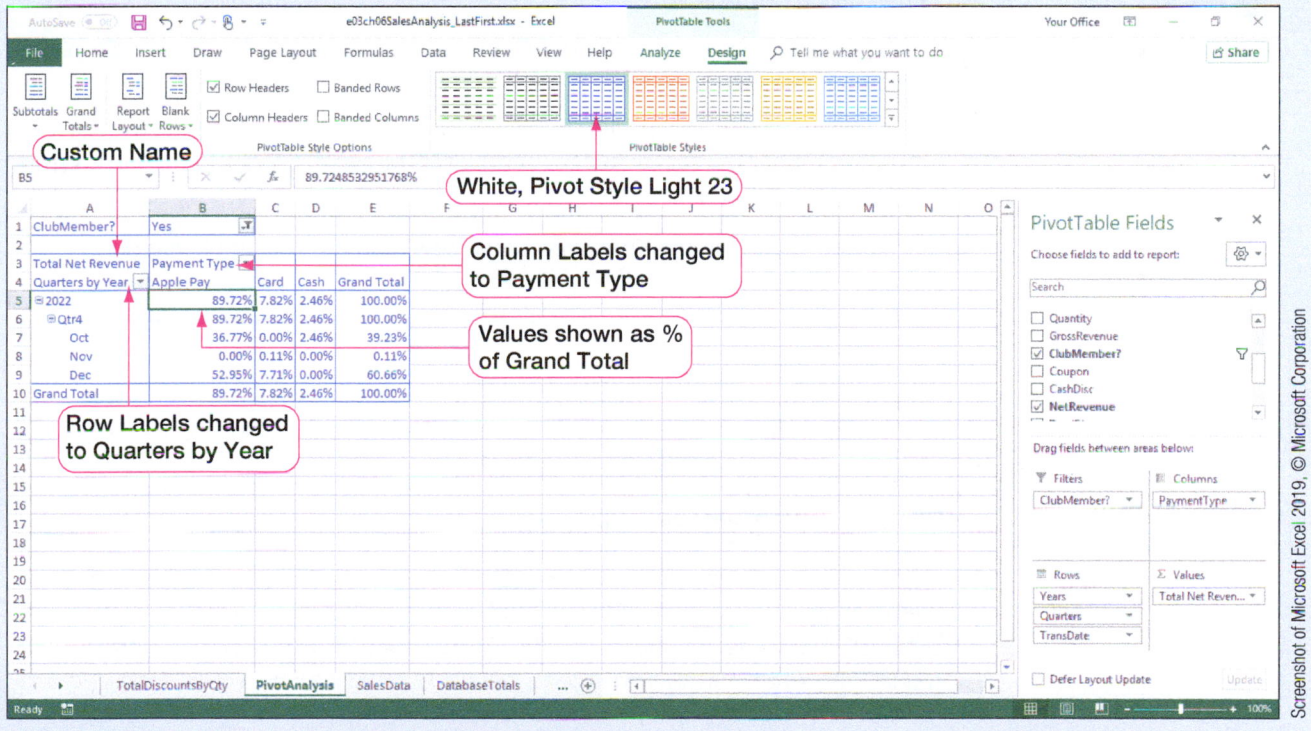

Figure 28 PivotTable—Total Net Revenue as percent of grand total

h. **Save** 🖫 the workbook.

Screenshot of Microsoft Excel 2019, © Microsoft Corporation

REAL WORLD ADVICE   **Choosing Filter Fields**

In general, the Filter field should be an overarching field that gives a big picture perspective of the data. If a Date field is used, the year should be the grouping criterion, rather than months. Fields that can be further manipulated by other fields make for good report filters. A Product field would not be as suitable a report filter as a Product Category field because a product category is a bigger picture field that can be filtered further as needed.

Adding a Slicer to the PivotTable

Finally, more options can be added by using a slicer to create yet another way to filter and explore the data. A slicer is a visual mechanism for quickly filtering data in a PivotTable. A slicer is an object that sits or floats on top of the spreadsheet that lists the data options for a field. The user can quickly select one or more of the list items to filter on the fly.

In this exercise, you will add a slicer to the PivotTable.

 **E06.14**

To Add a Slicer to the PivotTable

a. On the PivotAnalysis worksheet, click the **Analyze** tab and in the Filter group, click **Insert Slicer**. The Insert Slicers dialog box appears.

b. Click to select the **EMP-ID** check box and then click **OK** to add the employee ID slicer.

c. Move the **EMP-ID slicer** so that the top-left corner is in cell **G3** and then drag the bottom edge to adjust the height so that the extra white space is no longer visible. Do not drag it so far that you see a scroll bar on the right side.

d. Right-click the **EMP-ID slicer**, and then select **Slicer Settings**. The Slicer Settings dialog box opens.

e. Under the Header section, in the Caption box, replace EMP-ID with **Employee** and then click **OK**.

f. To further customize your slicer, click the **Employee slicer**, if necessary. Click the **Options** tab. In the Slicer Styles group, click **More**. Under Light, click **White, Slicer Style Other 2**.

g. Click **EMP-00024** in the Employee slicer view data for that employee only.

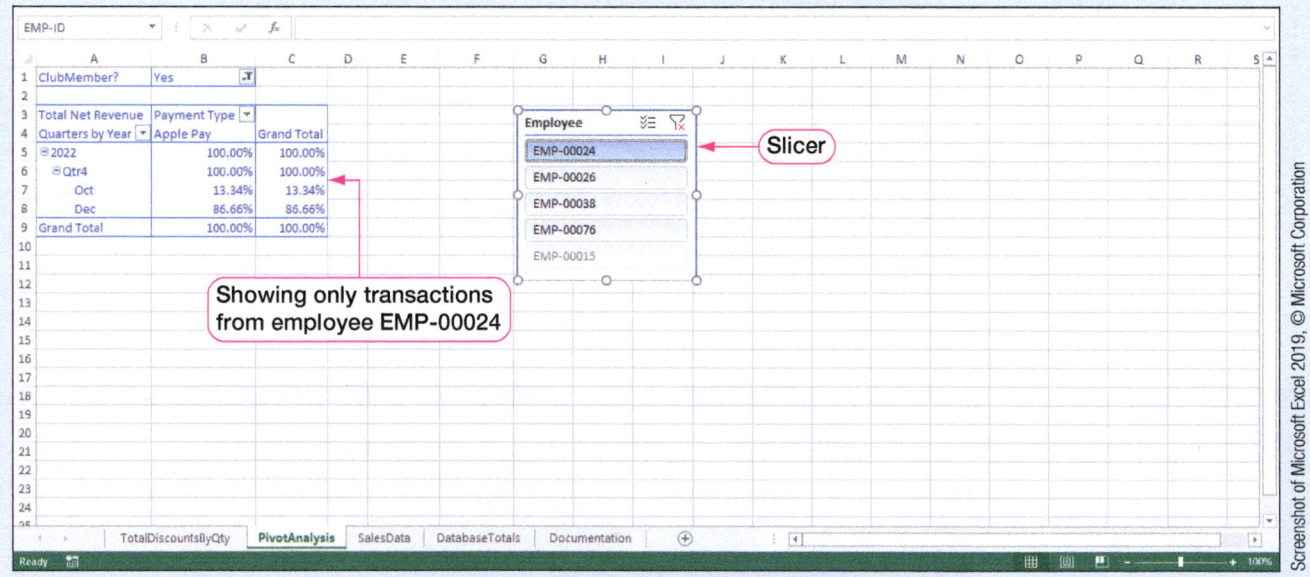

Figure 29 PivotTable and slicer with customization

h. **Save** the workbook.

REAL WORLD ADVICE	The Power of Data Modeling

Businesses can collect thousands upon thousands of rows of data every day. Some businesses can collect even more than that per hour! Think of how many transactions a large banking organization has every minute. This vast amount of data collected on a regular basis may be stored in multiple locations, making it difficult to combine in one location to perform data analysis. Basic data model functionality that is built into Excel—called PowerPivot—allows experienced Excel users to conduct more advanced data analysis and build sophisticated data models. PowerPivot allows a user to import up to one million rows of data from multiple sources, such as large corporate databases, public data feeds, spreadsheets, and text files on your computer.

Updating, Refreshing, and Drilling Down in PivotTables

There are many options for organizing and summarizing data. What happens if the data changes? What are the options for giving a subset of data to another person? These capabilities are available in PivotTables. If adding data to a PivotTable is necessary, the data source and range of data can be changed. After changes are made to the source data set, the PivotTable data should be refreshed so the changes are updated in the PivotTable as well.

With a technique called "drilling down," it is also possible to give a subset of data to people without having to provide data they do not need or should not have in the first place. **Drilling down** is a method for accessing the detailed records that were used in a PivotTable to get to the aggregated data. It allows a user to select an individual piece of data in the PivotTable and then create a copy on another worksheet of the individual records that were used to get that summary data.

REAL WORLD ADVICE	Managers Use Drilled-Down Data

The level of management position that a manager holds determines the type of data that is needed. Lower-level managers need very detailed data—that is drilled down—to make daily decisions. Senior-level managers mainly use summarized data. Think about that from a PivotTable perspective. Lower-level managers will click the plus signs to expand the fields, while senior-level managers will not. Because of these different information needs, it is important to know your audience before constructing your PivotTable.

In this exercise, you will update, refresh, and drill down data.

 **E06.15**

To Update, Refresh, and Drill Down in PivotTables

a. Click the **SalesData** worksheet. Using the following data, add a new record in row 25 of the Sales database.

Field	Data
TransID	P000121
TransDate	01/01/2023
EMP-ID	EMP-00024
ItemID	T822Z48
PaymentType	Cash
Quantity	3
GrossRevenue	98.85
ClubMember?	Yes
Coupon	
CashDisc	
NetRevenue	98.85
TotalDiscounts	0

b. Click the **PivotAnalysis** worksheet. Click cell **A3**, and then click the **Analyze** tab. In the Data group, click **Refresh**. Notice that the newly created cash transaction for EMP-00024 is added to the PivotTable analysis.

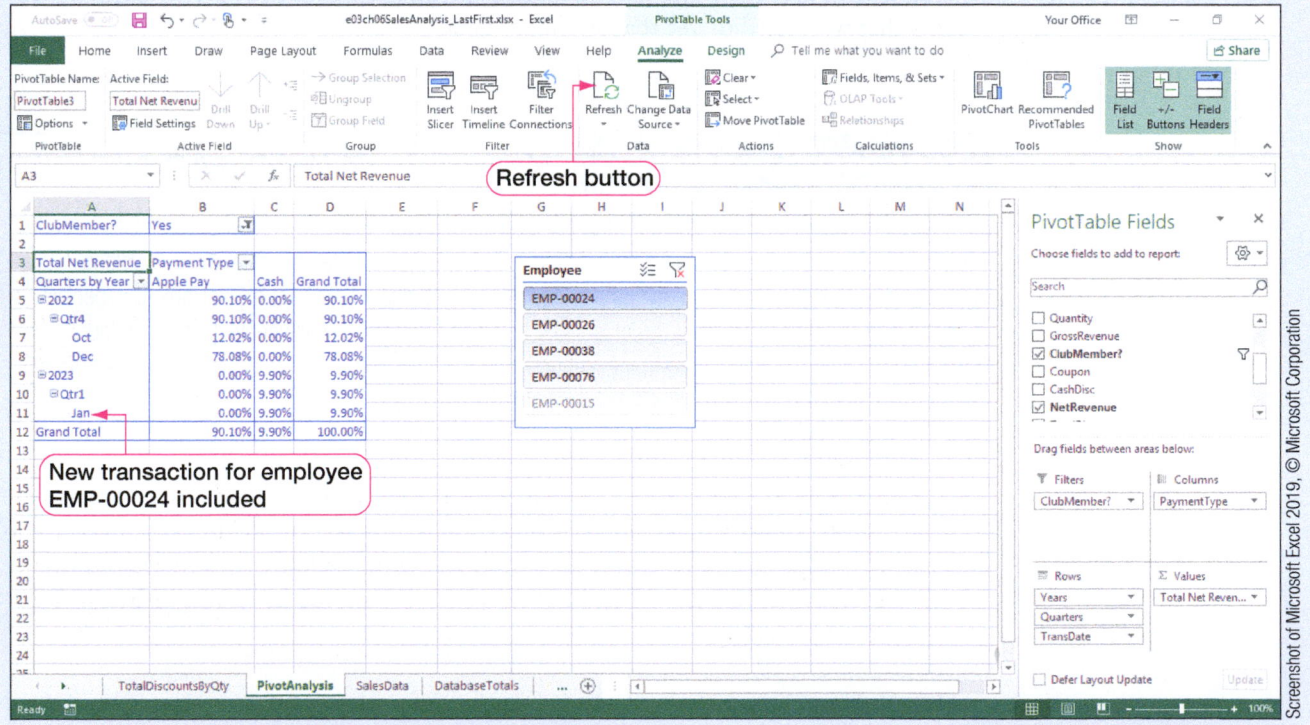

Figure 30   Refreshed PivotTable with added transaction

c. On the **Analyze** tab, in the Actions group, click the **Clear** button, and then click **Clear Filters**.

d. Click cell **B9**. This is the percentage of December 2022 net revenue from all transactions where the customer used Apple Pay.

e. Double-click cell **B9**. The action of double-clicking any cell within the PivotTable initiates the drill-down process, in which Excel will copy and paste the records that are associated with that value to another worksheet.

f. Double-click the **worksheet** tab, replace the sheet name with AplePayTransactions and then press Enter.

g. Select columns **A:L**. Click the **Home** tab, and then, in the Cells group, click **Format**. Select **AutoFit Column Width**.

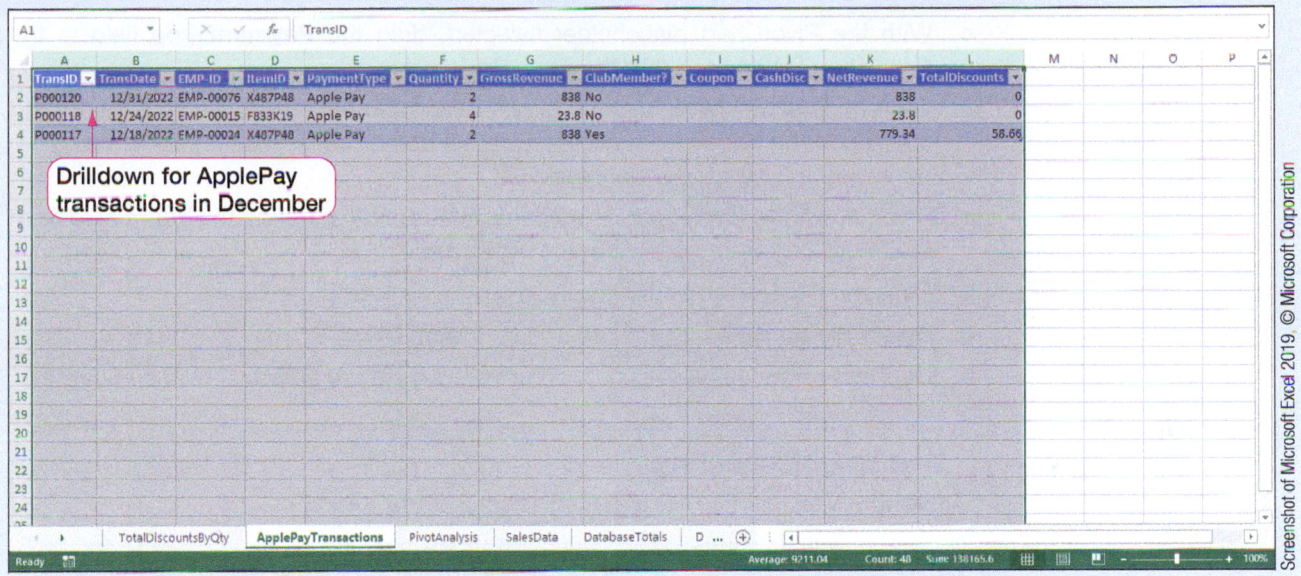

Figure 31   PivotTable drill-down Apple Pay transactions

h. **Save** 🖫 the workbook.

Develop and Customize PivotCharts

The visual representation of data through charts can be powerful. A **PivotChart** is a built-in analysis tool that allows for graphical representations of data with the added filtering capabilities of PivotTables. PivotCharts can be created directly from a PivotTable or from any other data set organized and structured appropriately for PivotTables.

PivotCharts have an added component of filtering that can be used to explore the data. Multiple PivotCharts can be associated with one PivotTable; however, because they are all tied together, best practice dictates having only one PivotChart associated with one PivotTable. Additionally, be careful when making use of a PivotChart in a presentation so that no changes occur accidentally within the PivotTable that could yield unwanted changes to the chart. Once a PivotChart has been created, all formatting elements from a regular chart are available.

Adding a PivotChart

PivotCharts provide a visual representation of the data in a PivotTable. It is easier to see a trend by looking at a "picture" of the data than by viewing the data in table format. For example, by looking at a PivotChart that displays revenue over the past 12 months, you can easily see the movement of the trends without even thinking about it. By viewing data in a PivotTable, you would need to think about whether the numbers are higher or lower than the one you previously viewed. Once you view the data in a PivotChart, it is easy to read details such as month and total revenue for each month.

In this exercise, you will add a PivotChart to a worksheet.

 **E06.16**

To Add a PivotChart

a. Click the **SalesData** worksheet, and then click cell **A3**. Click the **Insert** tab, and in the Charts group, click the top-half of the **PivotChart** button to open the Create PivotChart dialog box.

b. Verify that SalesData is in the Table/Range box and that **New Worksheet** is selected. Click **OK**. A new worksheet is inserted to the left of SalesData with placeholders for a PivotTable and PivotChart. Double-click the newly added work-sheet tab, replace the name with RevenueByPaymentType

c. With the PivotChart placeholder selected, drag the **PaymentType** field in the PivotChart Fields pane into the **Axis (Categories)** area.

d. Click to select the **NetRevenue** check box in the PivotChart Fields pane to add the field to the Values area. Excel displays a default column chart representing the net revenue for each payment type.

e. Scroll down the PivotTable Fields pane if necessary and drag the **Years** field from the PivotChart Fields pane into the Filters area.

f. Click the **Design** tab and in the Type group, click **Change Chart Type**.

g. Select **Pie** on the All Charts tab and then click **OK**.

h. On the **Design** tab, in the Location group, click **Move Chart**.

> ### Mac Troubleshooting
> If using a Mac, point to Pie and then select 2-D Pie

i. Click the **New sheet** option button and in the text box, replace the default name with RevenueByTypePivotChart Click **OK** and the chart is placed on its own worksheet.

j. Double-click the **Total chart title** and replace the text with Proportion of Revenue by Payment Type

k. Click the **Design** tab and in the Chart Styles group, apply the **Style 5** Chart Style.

l. Click the **Years filter button** to display the filter menu. Select **2022** and then click **OK** to see only 2022 transactions.

> ### Mac Troubleshooting
> If using a Mac and the Years filter button does not appear on the PivotChart, complete the following steps.
>
> a. Click the **RevenueByPaymentType** worksheet, then click the **Years filter button** in cell B1 of the PivotTable.
>
> b. Select the year **2022** and then click **OK**.
>
> c. Click the **RevenueByTypePivotChart** worksheet to return to the pivot chart.

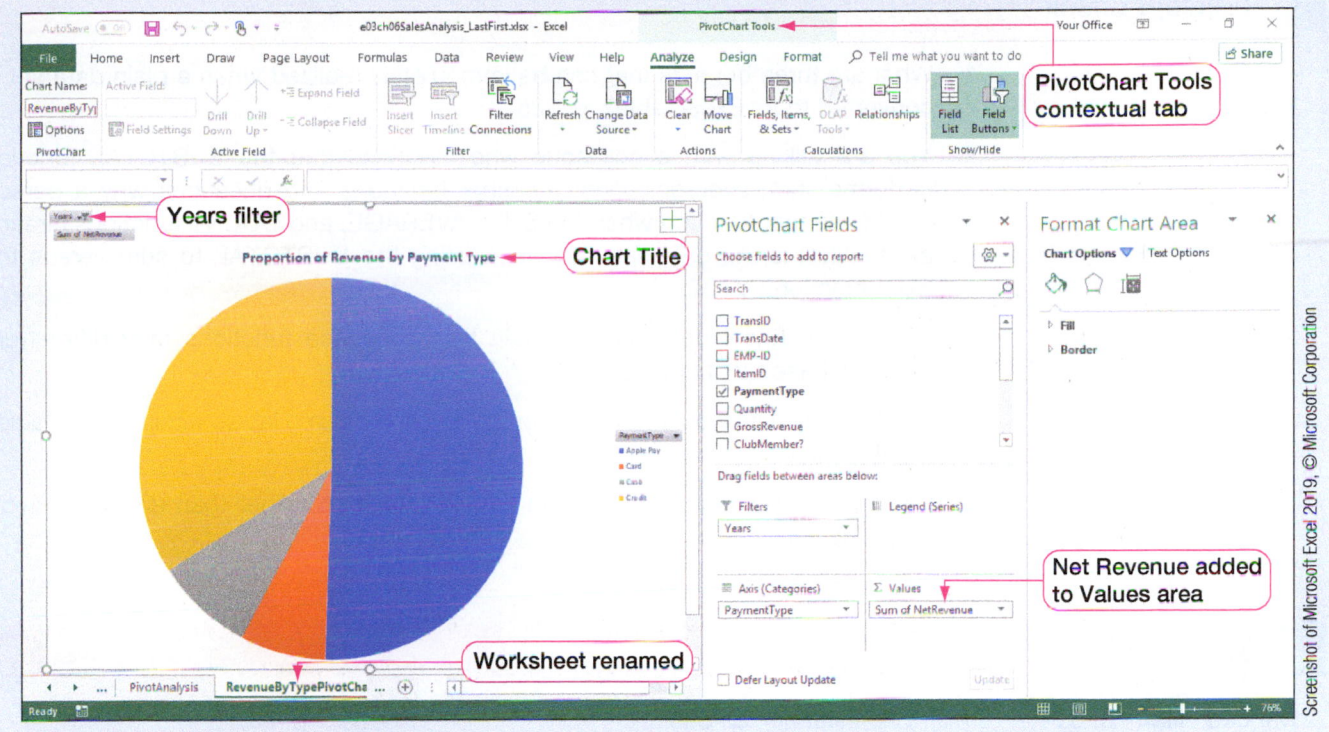

Figure 32 Customized PivotChart

m. Complete the **Documentation** worksheet as directed by your instructor.

n. **Save** 🖫 the workbook, **exit** Excel, and then submit your file as directed by your instructor.

QUICK REFERENCE   **PivotTable and PivotChart Best Practices**

When creating a PivotTable or PivotChart, remember the following.

- Once you have selected your data, ensure that the source data is arranged in an area with column headings representing each field and the rows representing each record.
- Distinguish fields as either grouping variables or summary variables.
- Format the PivotTable or PivotChart so it is easy to read and your audience understands what it is you are trying to communicate.
- Know who your audience is before you develop your PivotTable or PivotChart. It could make a difference in how much detail you display.

Concept Check

1. What are three benefits that can be immediately realized when a plain data set is converted to an Excel table? p. 325

2. You are talking with a colleague who mentions that the SUBTOTAL function performs sum, average, count, or other functions and questions why a person would use that function when the SUM, AVERAGE, and COUNT functions already exist. What is the difference between using the SUBTOTAL to sum versus the SUM function? p. 329

3. What is an Excel database? Explain how database functions may differ from non-database functions. p. 342

4. What type of data would work well for the row and column labels within a PivotTable? What are some examples? p. 352

5. Describe two benefits of using an Excel PivotChart rather than an Excel Pivot-Table. p. 361

Key Terms

Advanced Filter   p. 334
Aggregate   p. 329
Convert to Range   p. 329
Data set   p. 323
Database functions   p. 341
Drilling down   p. 359

Filtering   p. 330
Grouping variable   p. 352
Information   p. 323
PivotChart   p. 361
PivotTable   p. 341
Raw data   p. 323

Slicer   p. 337
Standard filter   p. 332
Structured reference   p. 327
SUBTOTAL function   p. 329
Summary variable   p. 352
Table   p. 324

Visual Summary

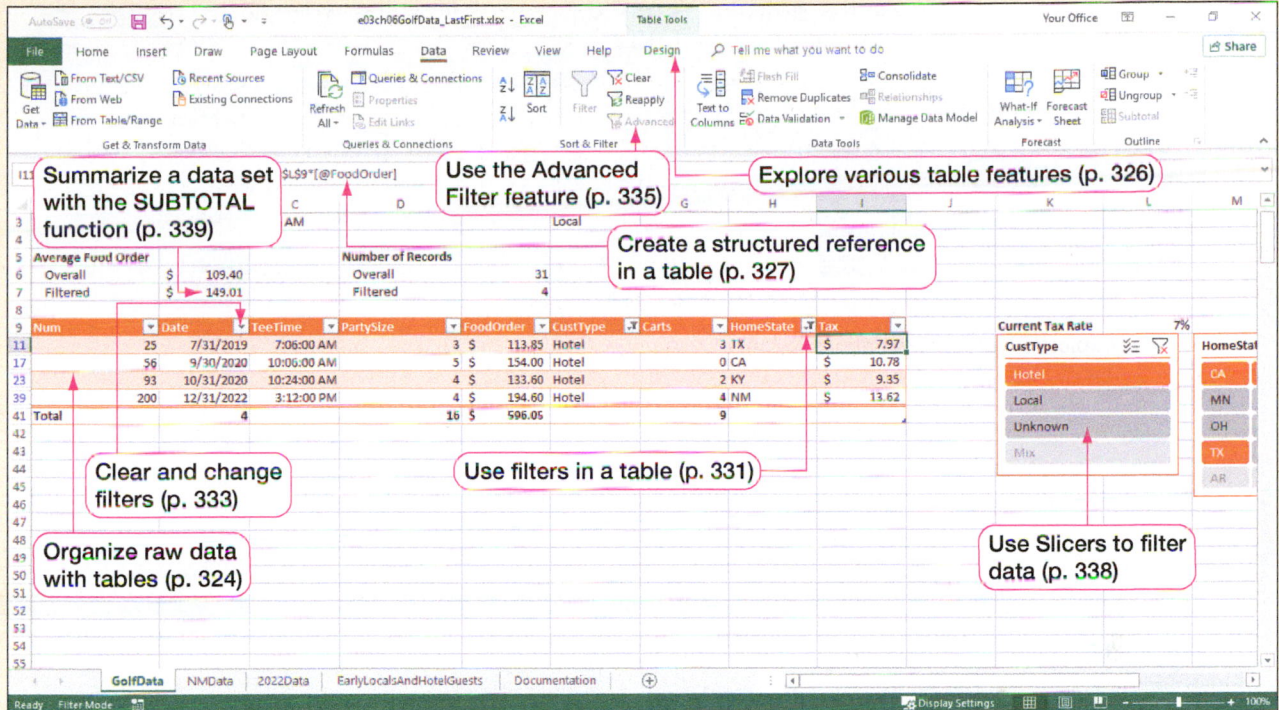

Summarize a data set with the SUBTOTAL function (p. 339)

Use the Advanced Filter feature (p. 335)

Explore various table features (p. 326)

Create a structured reference in a table (p. 327)

Clear and change filters (p. 333)

Use filters in a table (p. 331)

Organize raw data with tables (p. 324)

Use Slicers to filter data (p. 338)

Figure 33

Screenshot of Microsoft Excel 2019, © Microsoft Corporation

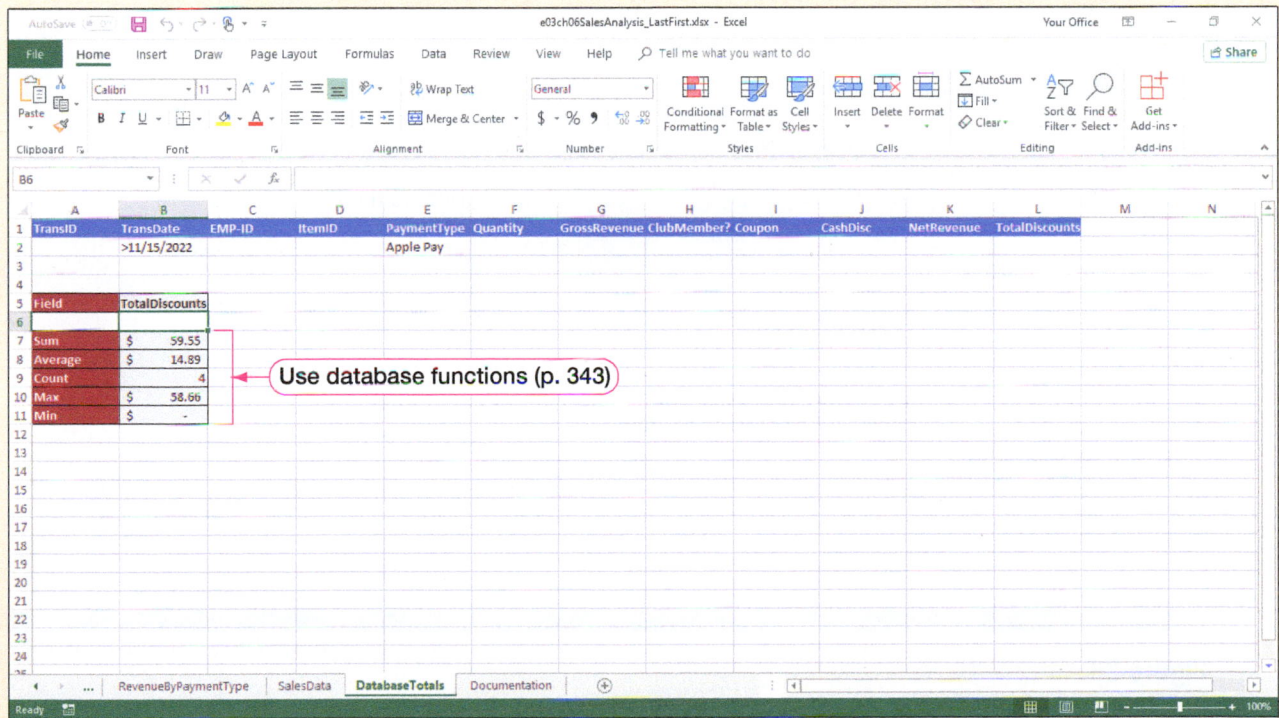

Use database functions (p. 343)

Figure 34

Screenshot of Microsoft Excel 2019, © Microsoft Corporation

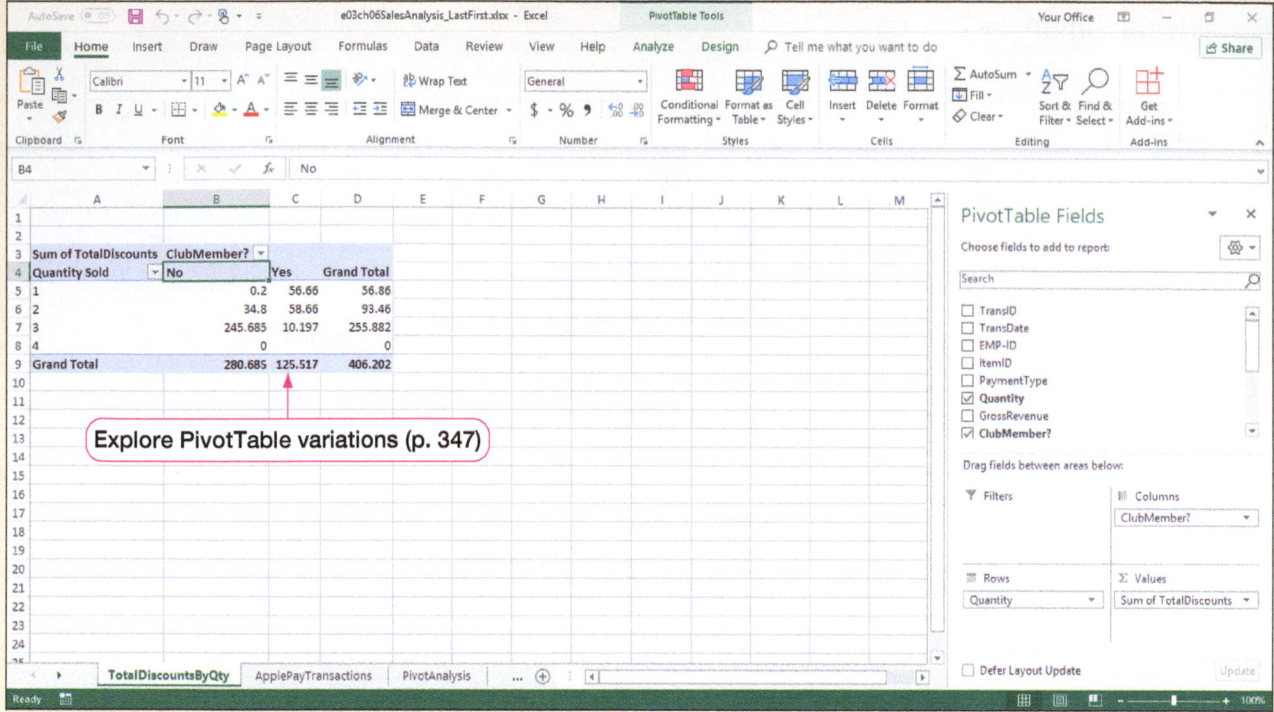

Figure 35

Screenshot of Microsoft Excel 2019, © Microsoft Corporation

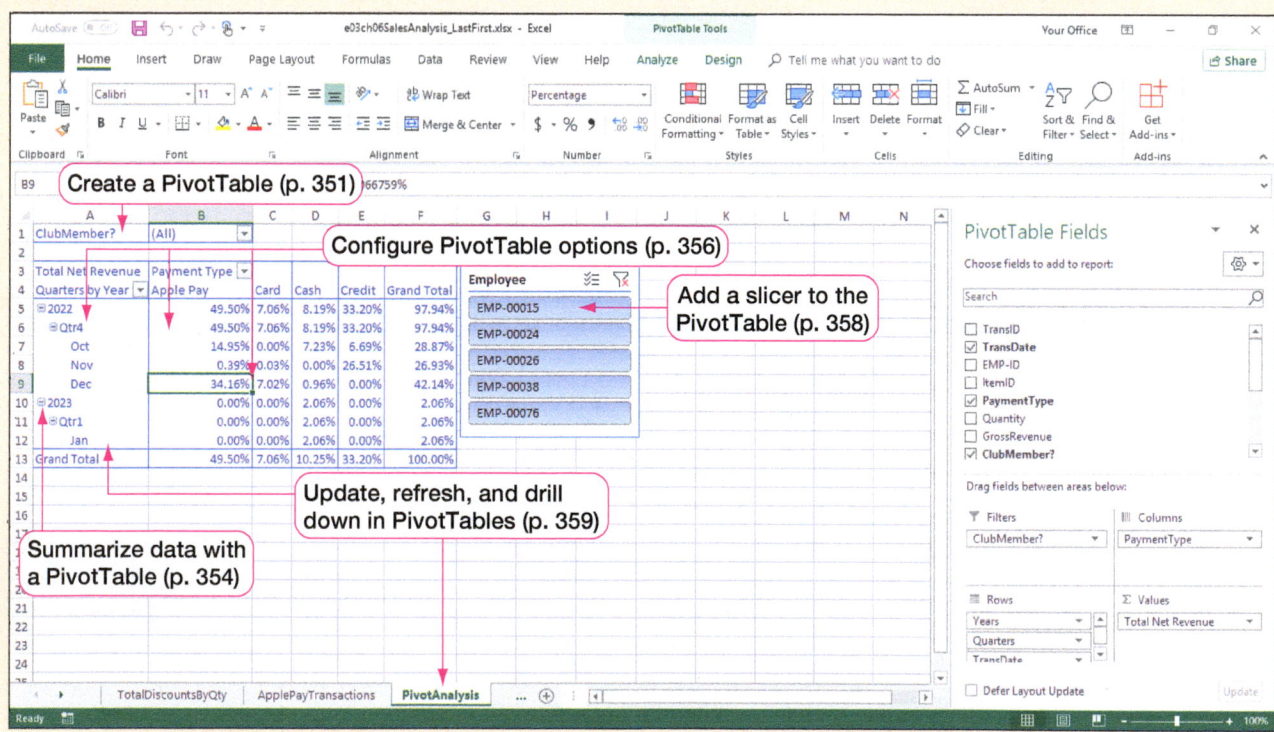

Figure 36

Screenshot of Microsoft Excel 2019, © Microsoft Corporation

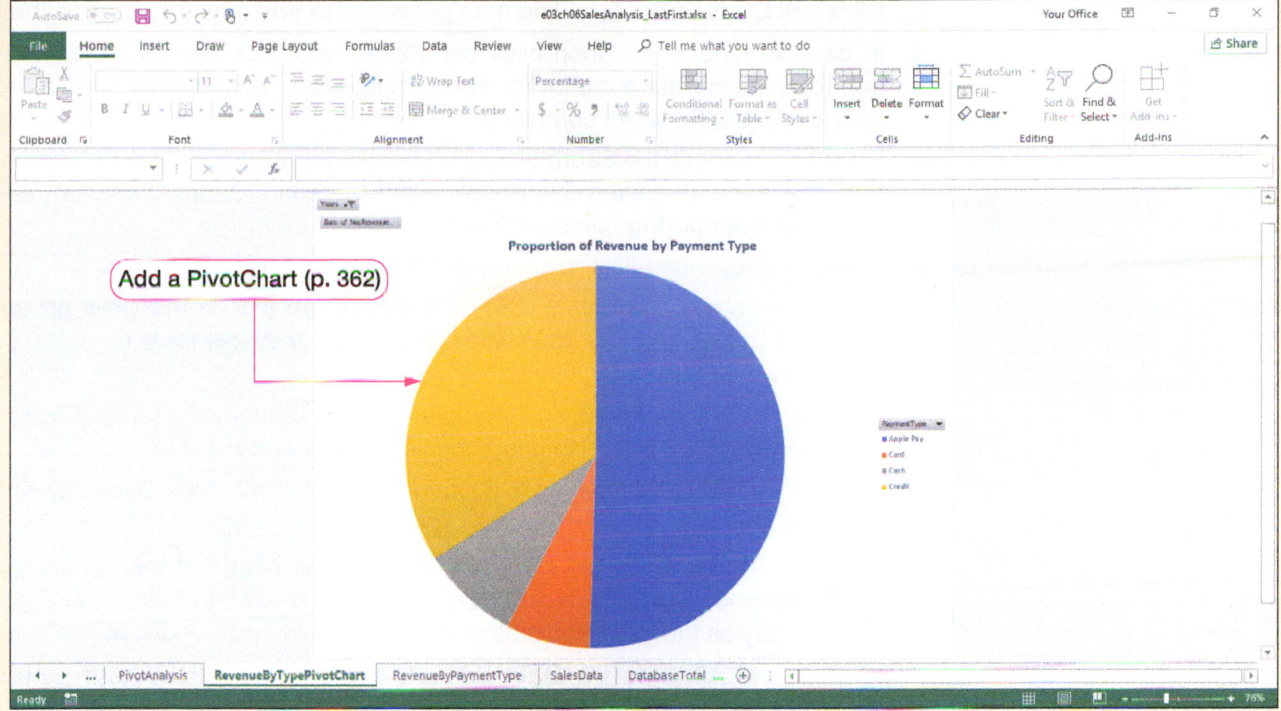

Add a PivotChart (p. 362)

Figure 37

Screenshot of Microsoft Excel 2019, © Microsoft Corporation

Practice 1

Student data file needed:

 e03ch06EmployeeSales.xlsx

You will save your file as:

 e03ch06EmployeeSales_LastFirst.xlsx

Sales & Marketing

New Employee Sales Analysis

The management team has requested data from the information systems team on new golf shop employees. The data is from the sales database and includes only sales for three employees over the period of a week. Management would like you to use that data to set up some analyses they can review.

a. Start **Excel**, click **Open** in the left pane, and then double-click **This PC**. Navigate through the folder structure to the location where you store your student data files, and then double-click **e03ch06EmployeeSales**. If a Security Warning message displays, click the **Enable Editing** button.

b. Click the **File** tab, click **Save As**, and then double-click **This PC**. In the Save As dialog box, navigate to the location where you are saving your files. In the File name box, type **e03ch06EmployeeSales_LastFirst** using your last and first name, and then click **Save**.

c. Click the **GolfShopData** worksheet. If necessary, click cell **A1**, click the **Insert** tab, and then in the Tables group, click **Table**. Verify that the table range box displays $A$1:$K$71 and the **My table has headers** check box is checked, and then click **OK**.

d. Click the **Design** tab and in the Properties group, replace Table1 with **Employee Sales** as the name of the table.

e. With the data still selected, click inside the **Name Box** and type **SalesDatabase** to create a named range for the entire table, including the column headings. This named range can be used as the Database argument in database functions.

f. Click cell **L1,** type Subtotal and then press Enter to add a new column to the table.

g. In cell **L2**, type **=** and then click cell **F2**. Type ***** click cell **G2**, and then press Enter to calculate the subtotal for each transaction. The formula should look like =[@Retail]*[@QTY] when completed.

h. Point to just above the Subtotal column heading until your mouse pointer changes to a downward black arrow, click to select the entire Subtotal column, and then apply the **Accounting** number format.

i. Create an Advanced Filter by completing the following.

- Select rows **1 through 5**. Click the **Home** tab and in the Cells group, click **Insert** to insert 5 blank rows above the EmployeeSales table to make room for an advanced filter.

- Select cell range **A6:L6**, and then press Ctrl+C to copy the range. Click cell **A1**, and then press Ctrl+V to paste the field labels in row 1.

- Click cell **C2**, and then type Clothing Click cell **K2**, type Saturday and then press Enter.

- In cell K3, type Sunday click cell **C3**, type Clothing and then press Enter. The criteria specify to only include transactions with clothing as the category and Saturday as the day OR clothing as the category and Sunday as the day.

- Click cell **A6**, click the **Data** tab, and then, in the Sort & Filter group, click **Advanced**. In the Advanced Filter dialog box, click in the **List range** box, and ensure that the range is $A$6:$L$76. Click inside the **Criteria range** box and then select **A1:L3**. Click **OK**. Four records display.

- Select cell range **A6:L73**, and then press Ctrl+C to copy the filtered data. Click the **WeekendClothingData** worksheet. If necessary, click cell **A1**, and then press Ctrl+V to paste the subset of data. Press Esc to clear the copied data from the clipboard and then adjust the column widths as necessary so that all data are visible.

j. Insert slicers to use to filter the data in the table by completing the following:

- Click the **GolfShopData** worksheet, and then click cell **C6**. Click the **Design** tab, and then in the Tools group, click **Insert Slicer**. Click to select the **Category** and **Day** check boxes, and then click **OK**. Drag the **Category slicer** so its top-left corner is in the top-left corner of **N6**. Drag the bottom edge of the **Category slicer** to adjust the height so that the extra white space is no longer visible.

- Drag the **Day slicer** so its top-left corner is in the top-left corner of **Q6**.

- To further customize your slicers, apply the **Light Blue, Slicer Style Light 5** to both slicers.

- Use the slicers to view all weekday (Monday through Friday) records for Accessories.

k. Create database functions to analyze the EmployeeSales data for clothing items where the quantity sold was >2 or shoes, of any quantity, were purchased by completing the following:

- Select cell range **A6:L6**, and then press Ctrl+C to copy the range. Click the **DatabaseTotals** worksheet. If necessary, click cell **A1**, and then press Ctrl+V to paste the field labels in row 1.

- Click cell **B5**, and then type Subtotal as the field name to use in the database functions.

- Click cell **C2**, type Clothing press Enter and in cell C3, type Shoes Click cell G2, type >2 and then press Enter. These will be used as the criteria in the database functions.

- Click cell **B7**, type =DSUM(SalesDatabase,B5,A1:L3) and then press ⏎.
- In cell B8, type =DAVERAGE(SalesDatabase,B5,A1:L3) and then press ⏎.
- In cell B9, type =DCOUNT(SalesDatabase,B5,A1:L3) and then press ⏎.
- In cell B10, type =DMAX(SalesDatabase,B5,A1:L3) and then press ⏎.
- In cell B11, type =DMIN(SalesDatabase,B5,A1:L3) and then press ⏎.

l. Create a PivotTable from the EmployeeSales table on the GolfShopData worksheet by completing the following:

- Click the **GolfShopData** worksheet, if necessary, click a cell inside the table, click the **Design** tab, and then, in the Tools group, click **Summarize with PivotTable**. Verify that the EmployeeSales table is the source and then click **OK** to insert the PivotTable onto a new sheet. Right-click the **Sheet1** worksheet tab, select **Rename**, type GolfReport and then press ⏎ to rename the worksheet.
- In the PivotTable Fields pane, in the PivotTable Fields list, click to select the **Category**, **QTY**, and **Emp_ID** check boxes.
- In the Values area, click the **Sum of Emp_ID** arrow, and then click **Move to Column Labels**.
- The Employee IDs are not informative, so they should be changed to the employee's first names.
  - Click cell **B4**, and then type Chuck
  - Click cell **C4**, and then type Jennifer
  - Click cell **D4**, and then type Allie
  - Select columns **B:D**, and then click the **Home** tab. In the Cells group, click **Format**, and then select **AutoFit Column Width** so the employee names can be seen.
- Apply **White, Pivot Style Light 27** to the PivotTable.
- Click the **Sum of QTY** field in the Values area and then select **Value Field Settings**.
- Type Sales Volume for the custom name and then click **OK**.
- Replace Row Labels in cell A4 with Category
- Replace Column Labels in cell B3 with Employee

m. Create a Clustered Column PivotChart from the PivotTable to easily compare each employee's sales volume for each category by completing the following:

- Click any cell inside the PivotTable. Click the **Analyze** tab and in the Tools group, click **PivotChart**.
- Select the **Clustered Column** chart type and then click **OK**.
- Click the **Design** tab and apply **Style 8**.
- On the PivotChart Tools Design tab, in the Chart Layouts group, click **Add Chart Element**, point to **Chart Title**, and then select **Above Chart**.
- Edit the Chart Title to read Sales Volume by Category
- On the Design tab, in the Location group, click **Move Chart**. Click the **New Sheet** button, type SalesVolumeByCategoryPivotChart for the new sheet name, and then click **OK**.

n. Click the **Documentation** worksheet. Click cell **A8**, and then type today's date Click cell **B8**, and then type your name in the Firstname Lastname format. Complete the remainder of the Documentation worksheet according to your instructor's directions.

o. Click **Save**, exit **Excel**, and then submit your file as directed by your instructor.

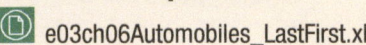

MyLab IT Grader

Student data file needed:

e03ch06Automobiles.xlsx

You will save your file as:

e03ch06Automobiles_LastFirst.xlsx

Human Resources

Sales & Marketing

Auto Sales Analysis

Community Auto Sales is considering opening a new location on the east side of town. They need to determine the types of vehicles that they would like to have on the lot for sale. They have acquired a sample data set of vehicle features and estimated manufacturer's suggested retail price (MSRP) and need your help in setting up some analysis so that they can explore their options.

a. Open the Excel file, **e03ch06Automobiles**. Save your file as e03ch06Automobiles_LastFirst using your last and first name.

b. The data on the AutoSample worksheet includes details about vehicles that the company may be interested in buying for resale. On the **AutoSample** worksheet, insert a table with headers using the data.

c. With the table selected, including the headers, create a CarDatabase named range to be used in database functions later.

d. Insert six rows above the table to make room to create an advanced filter.

e. Copy the headers in **A7:J7** and paste the headings starting in cell **A1**.

f. Using the Advanced Filter, display only the records with an Automatic transmission type, that are a Midsize vehicle size, with an MSRP of <30000

g. Copy the filtered data, including the headings, and paste a copy on the **SelectedVehicles** worksheet, starting in cell **A1**. If necessary, adjust the column widths so that all data are visible.

h. Clear the filters applied to the AutoSample data. Copy the headings and paste them onto the **DatabaseTotals** worksheet, starting in cell **A1** to begin to setup and create database functions to further analyze the data. If necessary, adjust the column widths so that all data are visible.

i. Complete the DatabaseTotals worksheet using the appropriate database functions using the **CarDatabase** named range, use the **MSRP** as the field in your calculations, and only calculate vehicles that meet all the following criteria:

- Vehicle year is newer than 2015
- Transmission type is Automatic
- highway MPG is greater than 25

j. Using the data on the **AutoSample** worksheet, create a PivotTable on a new worksheet and rename the worksheet, PivotAnalysis

- The PivotTable should use the Make field as the Rows and MSRP as the Values.
- Change the MSRP calculation so that it calculates the Average MSRP and format the field as Accounting with 2 decimal places.
- Change Row Labels in cell A3 to Vehicle Make and adjust the column width as necessary so that all data are visible.
- Create a drill-down of the Volkswagen onto a new worksheet and rename the worksheet Volkswagens Adjust the column widths so that all data are visible.
- On the PivotAnalysis worksheet, insert a **Year slicer** and position it so that its top-left corner is in cell **D2**.
- Insert a **Vehicle Style** slicer and position it so that its top-left corner is in cell **G2**.
- Use the slicers to only show convertibles and sedans with a model year of 2012, 2015, or 2016.

k. Create a Clustered Bar PivotChart from the PivotTable:

- Apply the **Style 10** chart style.
- Apply the **Monochromatic Palette 5** colors to the chart.
- Delete the Total legend from the right side of the chart.
- Edit the chart title to read Average MSRP
- Move the chart to its own worksheet with the name AverageMSRPPivotChart

l. Complete the Documentation worksheet according to your instructor's directions.

m. Save the workbook, exit Excel, and then submit your file as directed by your instructor.

Perform 1: Perform in Your Career

Student data file needed:

 e03ch06DayCare.xlsx

You will save your file as:

 e03ch06DayCare_LastFirst.xlsx

Small Business Ownership

Finance & Accounting

You run a small day care out of your home. Many of the parents, who love your interactions with their children, have begun talking to you about expanding your operations. Never having thought about opening a day care business, you have begun to research the costs involved in opening your own center. After gathering some data, you believe you can open a business. But you realize you need to analyze the data and make the data look more presentable to your investors. The workbook contains worksheets with estimated revenues and expenses over a two-year period.

a. Open the Excel file, **e03ch06DayCare**. Save your file as e03ch06DayCare_LastFirst using your last and first name.

b. On the Revenue worksheet:

- Convert the Revenue data set to a table.
- Calculate Revenue based on the # Children and Income Per columns.
- Create an Advanced Filter of your choosing to explore the data.

c. On the Expenses worksheet:

- Convert the Expenses data to a table.
- Add two slicers of your choosing to help explore the data.
- Filter the data using the slicers, copy the filtered data, and then paste a copy to a new worksheet with an appropriate sheet name.
- Insert some blank rows above the table and use SUBTOTAL functions to create three different calculations on the data that is filtered.

d. Create a PivotTable:

- Using either the Revenue or Expenses table, create a PivotTable to further explore the data.
- Create the PivotTable on a new sheet with an appropriate sheet name. Format values and cells appropriately. Add one slicer for use in filtering.

e. Create a PivotChart:

- Create a PivotChart from the PivotTable created.
- Choose an appropriate chart type and move it to its own worksheet with an appropriate sheet name.

f. Update the Documentation worksheet according to your instructor's directions.

g. Save the workbook, exit Excel, and then submit your file as directed by your instructor.

Integrating Complex Functions into Business Analysis

This business unit had two outcomes:

Learning Outcome 1:
Use Excel logical and retrieval functions to analyze data in support of decision making.

Learning Outcome 2:
Use Excel tables, database functions, PivotTables, and PivotCharts to quickly summarize and analyze large amounts of data.

In Business Unit 3 Capstone, students will demonstrate competence in these outcomes through a series of business problems at various levels from guided practice, problem solving an existing spreadsheet, and performing to create new spreadsheets.

More Practice 1

Student data file needed:

 e03Indigo5Desserts.xlsx

You will save your file as:

 e03Indigo5Desserts_LastFirst.xlsx

Indigo5 Dessert Analysis

Sales & Marketing

Robin Sanchez, the chef at Indigo5, has been discussing dessert sales with the restaurant manager, Alberto Dimas. They want to examine the production levels and the sales of their signature desserts. To do so, they have collected data from last week's sales and included it in a workbook so you can analyze the data. Once you have completed the analysis, you will present it to Chef Sanchez and Mr. Dimas so they can make marketing decisions about the restaurant's dessert menu.

a. Start **Excel**, click **Open** in the left pane, and then double-click **This PC**. Navigate through the folder structure to the location of your student data files, and then double-click **e03Indigo5Desserts**. If a Security Warning message displays, click the **Enable Editing** button.

b. Click the **File** tab click **Save As**, and then double-click **This PC**. In the Save As dialog box, navigate to the location where you are saving your project files. Change the file name to **e03Indigo5Desserts_LastFirst** using your last and first name. Click **Save**.

c. On the DessertSales worksheet, create the following named ranges to use in formulas.

- Select the cell range **O3:P9**. Click in the **Name Box**, type **EmployeeList** and then press Enter.

- Select the cell range **O13:R18**. Click in the **Name Box**, type **DessertList** and then press Enter.

d. On the DessertSales worksheet, click cell **A10**. Click the **Insert** tab, and then in the Tables group, click **Table**. Verify the range is **=$A$10:$D$210** and that the **My table has headers** check box is checked. Click **OK**.

e. To begin your analysis, create the following fields and formulas.

- Click cell **E10**. Type **Dessert** and then press Tab. In cell F10, type **Category** and then press Tab. In cell G10, type **Emp Name** and then press Tab. In cell H10, type **Revenue** and then press Enter.

- In cell E11, enter the formula **=VLOOKUP([@[Dessert ID]],DessertList,2,FALSE)** and press `Tab`. The VLOOKUP will look up the Dessert ID in the leftmost column of the DessertList named range and return the name of the dessert from the second column. FALSE indicates an exact match will be needed.

- Creme Brulee and Dutch Apple Pie are the two desserts that are prepared just before serving and are served warm. Thus, if the dessert is either of those, the category should be "Warm"; otherwise, it should be "Cool". In cell F11, enter the formula **=IF(OR([@Dessert]="Creme Brulee",[@Dessert]="Dutch Apple Pie"),"Warm","Cool")** and then press `Tab`.

- In cell G11, enter the formula **=VLOOKUP([@[Emp ID]],EmployeeList,2,FALSE)** and then press `Tab`. The VLOOKUP will look up Emp ID in the leftmost column of the EmployeeList named range and retrieve the employee's name from the second column. FALSE indicates an exact match will be needed.

- In cell H11, enter the formula **=VLOOKUP([@[Dessert ID]],DessertList,4,FALSE)*[@Qty]** and then press `Enter`. This will look up the Dessert ID in the leftmost column of the DessertList named range and retrieve the selling price from the fourth column. Then the selling price is multiplied by the quantity sold to calculate the total dessert revenue generated.

- Point to just above the **Revenue** column heading until the pointer changes to a downward black arrow, click to select the entire Revenue column, and then apply the **Accounting** number format. Select columns **E:H**. On the Home tab, in the Cells group, click **Format**, and then select **AutoFit Column Width**.

f. Create an advanced filter to explore the data in the table by completing the following.

- Select the cell range **A10:H10**, and then press `Ctrl`+`C` to copy the column headers. Click cell **A1**, and then press `Ctrl`+`V` to paste the headers.

- Click cell **D2**, and then type **>7**

- Press `Tab` two times and in cell F2, type **Warm** and then press `Enter`.

- Click cell **A10**. Click the **Data** tab, and then, in the Sort & Filter group, click **Advanced**. Confirm **$A$10:$H$210** is displayed in the List range input box. Click in the **Criteria range** input box, select cell range **A1:H2**, and then click **OK** to filter the data.

g. Calculate the following subtotals.

- Click cell **C5**, enter the formula **=SUBTOTAL(1,Table1[Revenue])** and press `Enter` to calculate the average dessert check. The "1" indicates that the formula will average the filtered records on the Revenue field for records currently displayed in the table.

- In cell C6, enter the formula **=SUBTOTAL(3,Table1[Dessert ID])** and press `Enter` to count the number of records in the table. The "3" indicates that the formula will count the nonblank cells in the Dessert ID field for records currently displayed in the table.

- In cell C7, enter the formula **=SUBTOTAL(9,Table1[Qty])** and press `Enter` to sum the number of desserts sold. The "9" indicates that the formula will sum the numbers in the Qty field for records currently displayed in the table.

h. Create slicers to further explore the data by completing the following.

- Click cell **A10**. Click the **Design** tab, and then, in the Tools group, click **Insert Slicer**. In the Insert Slicers dialog box, click the **Dessert** and **Emp Name** check boxes. Click **OK**.

- Drag the **Emp Name** slicer so its top-left corner is in the top-left corner of cell **K1**. Right-click the **Emp Name** slicer, and then select **Slicer Settings**. In the Caption box, replace Emp Name with **Employee** Click **OK**.

- Right-click the **Employee** slicer, and then select **Size and Properties**. In the Format Slicer pane, click the **Position and Layout** arrow, and then change the **Number of columns** to 2

- Close the Format Slicer pane. Drag **the bottom edge** of the slicer to adjust the height so that the extra white space is no longer visible.

- Drag the **Dessert** slicer so its top-left corner is in the top-left corner of cell **K10**. Drag the bottom-right corner of the slicer to adjust the height and width so that the extra white space is no longer visible, and all dessert names are visible.

- With the Dessert slicer still selected, press and hold [Ctrl] and then click the **Employee** slicer so that both are selected. On the **Options** tab, in the Slicer Styles group, select **White, Slicer Style Light 3**.

- In the Employee slicer, click **Alicia**, press [Ctrl], and then click **Yalonda**. In the Desserts slicer, click **Carrot Cake**, press [Ctrl], and then click **Dutch Apple Pie**.

i. Use database functions to further explore the data by completing the following.

- Clear the **Employee** and **Dessert** slicers.

- Select the range **A10:H210**. Click inside the **Name Box**, type **DessertDatabase** and then press [Enter].

- Select the range **A10:H10** to select the column headers. Press [Ctrl]+[C] to copy, click the **DatabaseTotals** worksheet, click cell **A1**, if necessary, and then press [Ctrl]+[V] to paste the column headers.

- Click cell **F2** and type **Cool** Press [Tab] and in cell **G2**, type **Wayne** and then press [Enter]. The database functions will be calculated based on records in the DessertDatabase named range that meet both criteria.

- Click cell **B5**, type **Revenue** and press [Enter]. This will be the field used in the calculations of the database functions.

- Click cell **B7**, enter the formula **=DSUM(DessertDatabase,B5,A1:H2)** and then press [Ctrl]+[Enter]. With B7 still selected, format the cell as **Accounting**.

- Click cell **B8**, enter the formula **=DAVERAGE(DessertDatabase,B5,A1:H2)** and then press [Ctrl]+[Enter]. With B8 still selected, format the cell as **Accounting**.

- Click cell **B9**, enter the formula **=DCOUNT(DessertDatabase,B5,A1:H2)** and then press [Enter].

- Click cell **B10**, enter the formula **=DMAX(DessertDatabase,B5,A1:H2)** and then press [Ctrl]+[Enter]. With B10 still selected, format the cell as **Accounting**.

- Click cell **B11**, enter the formula **=DMIN(DessertDatabase,B5,A1:H2)** and then press [Ctrl]+[Enter]. With B11 still selected, format the cell as **Accounting**.

j. Click the **Report** worksheet and create the following formulas:

- Click cell **F3**. Enter the following formula **=IF(OR(AND(E3="Day Bake",C3<$K$6), AND(E3="Fresh Bake",C3<$K$7)),"Low","Okay")** and then press [Ctrl]+[Enter] so that if the Bake Time is Day Bake and has an ending quantity lower than the Day Bake level listed in K6, the formula will return Low. The formula also returns Low if the Bake Time is Fresh Bake and the ending quantity for the Fresh Bake item is less than the Fresh Bake value listed in cell K7, otherwise Okay should be displayed.

- With F3 still selected, use the **fill handle** to copy the formula down to cell **F8**.

- Click cell **G3**. Enter the following formula **=IF(OR(D3>5,AND(F3="Low",E3= "Day Bake")),"Produce More","")** and then press [Ctrl]+[Enter] so that if the requests are greater than 5 or a Day Bake item is Low, the formula will return Produce More, otherwise a blank should be returned.

- With G3 still selected, use the **Fill handle** to copy the formula down to cell **G8**.

- Select the range **K3:Q4**, click inside the Name Box, type **DailyGoal** and then press [Enter] to create a named range that can be used in LOOKUP functions.

- Click cell **B18**, enter the formula =SUM(B11:B16)/HLOOKUP(B10,DailyGoal, 2,FALSE) and then press Ctrl + Enter. This sums the day's quantity sold and divides this value by the day's goal. The goal is found by using the HLOOKUP in the DailyGoal named range.
- With cell B18 still selected, format as **Percentage** with **0** decimal places. Use the **Fill handle** to copy the formula over to cell **H18**.
- Select the range **J12:K15**, click inside the Name Box, type GoalGrade and then press Enter to create a named range that can be used in LOOKUP functions.
- Click cell **B19**, enter the formula =VLOOKUP(B18,GoalGrade,2) and then press Ctrl + Enter. This will return the letter value based on the percent of goal met. With cell B19 still selected, use the **Fill handle** to copy the formula over to cell **G19**.

k. Create a PivotTable to analyze the dessert data by completing the following.

- Click the **DessertSales** worksheet and then click cell **A10**. Click the **Design** tab, and then, in the Tools group, click **Summarize with PivotTable**.
- In the Create PivotTable dialog box, click **OK** to create the PivotTable on a new worksheet.
- Double-click the newly inserted **sheet tab**, rename the sheet PivotTableAnalysis and then press Enter.
- In the PivotTable Fields List, check the **Qty**, **Dessert**, **Category**, and **Emp Name** check boxes.
- Drag the **Dessert** field to the Columns area.
- Click the **Design** tab, and in the PivotTable Styles group, click **More**. Under Medium, select **Light Yellow, Pivot Style Medium 5**. In the PivotTable Style Options group, click the **Banded Rows** check box.
- Click cell **A3**, type Total Quantity and then press Tab. In cell B3, type Desserts and then press Enter. In cell A4, type Dessert Type and Emp Name and then press Enter. Select columns **A:D**. Click the **Home** tab. In the Cells group, click **Format**, and then select **AutoFit Column Width**.
- In cell B3, click the **Desserts** filter button, and then click **(Select All)** to deselect all the items. Click the **Creme Brulee**, **Dutch Apple Pie**, and **New York Cheesecake** check boxes, and then click **OK**.

l. Create a PivotChart from the PivotTable by completing the following.

- Click the **Analyze** tab, and in the Tools group, click **PivotChart**.
- Click **Line**, click **Stacked Line**, the second option, and then click **OK**. Close the Fields pane.
- Click the **Design** tab, and then, in the Location group, click **Move Chart**.
- In the Move Chart dialog box, select **New sheet**. Click in the **New Sheet** box, replace Chart1 with PivotChartAnalysis and then click **OK**.
- Click the **Design** tab, and in the Chart Layouts group, click **Add Chart Element**, point to **Chart Title**, and then select **Above Chart**. Type Total Quantity Sold by Employee and Dessert Type
- In the Chart Styles group, click **Change Colors**, and then select **Colorful Palette 4**. In the Chart Styles group, click **More**, and then select **Style 13**.

m. Click the **Documentation** worksheet. Click cell **A8**, and then type in today's date. Click cell **B8**, and then type in your name in the Firstname Lastname format. Complete the remainder of the Documentation worksheet according to your instructor's directions.

n. Save the workbook, exit Excel, and then submit your file as directed by your instructor.

MyLab IT Grader

Student data file needed:
e03MovieAnalysis.xlsx

You will save your file as:
e03MovieAnalysis_LastFirst.xlsx

Sales & Marketing

Production & Operations

Dobalina Movie Analysis

Bob Dobalina runs a movie production consulting business and has worked with some of the world's most renowned directors. He has requested your help in analyzing a small sample of the movies on which he has provided consultation.

a. Open the Excel file, **e03MovieAnalysis**. Save your file as e03MovieAnalysis_LastFirst using your last and first name.

b. On the **MovieTables** worksheet, assign the MovieTitles named range to the cell range **A2:B37** and assign the MovieRatings named range to the range **D2:E37**.

c. On the **Movies** worksheet, create a table with headers using the range **A5:K32** and apply the **Light Blue, Table Style Medium 23**.

d. Use the Create from Selection named range tool to create a named range for each column, using the Top row of the table for the names.

e. In cell **J6**, enter a VLOOKUP function that will lookup the MovieID value in the leftmost column of the MovieTitles named range and return the movie name from the second column. Incorporate an IFERROR function so that if there is no MovieID, the function returns a blank. Copy the formula down through cell **J32**.

f. In cell **K6**, enter a VLOOKUP function that will lookup the MovieID value in the leftmost column of the MovieRatings named range and return the movie rating from the second column. Incorporate an IFERROR function so that if there is no MovieID, the function returns a blank. Copy the formula down through cell **K32**.

g. In cell **N5**, enter an INDEX function that will retrieve the name of the movie with the highest gross sales. Write the function using the INDIRECT function as the array argument so that the formula can be copied across to **P5**.

h. Insert **Year** and **Genre** slicers to further explore the data in the Movies table. Format the slicers as follows.

   • Position the **Year** slicer so that its top-left corner is in cell **M7**. Change the layout so that it is **2** columns and then adjust the height of the slicer so that the extra white space is no longer visible.

   • Position the **Genre** slicer so that is top-left corner is in cell **M24**. Change the layout so that it is **2** columns and then adjust the height of the slicer so that the extra white space is no longer visible and adjust the width so that all genres are visible.

   • Apply the **Light Blue, Slicer Style Dark 1** to both slicers.

i. Use the slicers to select only the movies from the **Animation**, **Adventure**, or **Action** genres that were released in **2011**, **2012**, or **2014**.

j. Copy the filtered data, including the column headers, and paste the results on the **SelectedMovies** worksheet, starting in cell **A1**.

k. On the **Movies** worksheet, in cell **B1**, enter a function that will calculate the total gross sales for records visible in the table. Format as **Accounting**.

l. In cell **B2**, enter a function that will calculate the average gross sales for records visible in the table. Format as **Accounting**.

m. In cell **B3**, enter a function that will calculate the number of movies visible in the table, using the **MovieID** field.

n. On the Directors worksheet, in cell **D2**, enter an IFS function that will determine the status of each director, based on the following conditions.

- A director is considered Elite if they have directed at least 15 movies with an average score that is greater than 6.5 or has an average score of greater than 6.8 regardless of the number of movies.
- A director is considered Premiere if they have directed at least 5 movies with an average rating of at least 6.
- All other directors should have a status of Standard
- Copy the formula down through cell **D28**.

o. Using the table on the Movies worksheet, create a PivotTable on a new worksheet and configure it according to the following.

- Name the worksheet that the PivotTable is on, PivotAnalysis
- The PivotTable should show the Average Gross Sales for each Genre (rows), with the ability to filter on Director.
- Format the Average of Gross as **Accounting** with **0** decimal places and with a custom name of Average Gross Sales
- Edit the Row Labels label to read Genres
- Apply the **Dark Blue, Pivot Style Dark 2** style to the PivotTable.

p. Use the PivotTable on the PivotAnalysis worksheet to create a 2-D Clustered Column Chart and configure the chart according to the following.

- Apply the **Style 10** Chart Style.
- Apply the **Layout 5** Quick Layout.
- Apply the **Monochromatic Palette 5** colors.
- Edit the Y axis title to read Average Gross Sales
- Edit the chart title to read Average Gross Sales by Genre
- Move the PivotChart to a new worksheet, naming the worksheet AverageGrossPivotChart
- Use the Director filter to select only the following directors: **Kevin Smith**, **Kunihiko Yuyama**, **Oliver Stone**, and **Tim Burton**.

q. Update the **Documentation** worksheet according to your instructor's directions.

r. Save the workbook, exit Excel, and then submit your file as directed by your instructor.

Critical Thinking Explain how you would modify the PivotTable to be able to see the number of movies that are in the dataset for each genre with the ability to see the data for one or more specific companies.

Problem Solve 2

 MyLab IT Grader

Student data file needed:

 e03Inventory.xlsx

You will save your file as:

e03Inventory_LastFirst.xlsx

Managing Gift Shop Inventory

Production & Operations

The gift shop staff wants to track inventory so it can reduce out-of-stock inventory items and reorder inventory more efficiently. The staff needs a template designed that will hold all the product information and then analyze daily transactions at the end of every month. You have been asked to help the gift shop employees develop a workbook that will help them manage the store's inventory. Because the staff currently does not collect this data, the gift shop manager has given you a template with a small amount of fictitious data so you can create the needed formulas and worksheets.

a. Open the Excel file, **e03Inventory**. Save your file as e03Inventory_LastFirst using your last and first name.

b. On the **Inventory** worksheet, enter a nested IF formula into cell L2 to determine the reorder status based on the following.

- A blank should be returned if the current inventory and reorder point are both blank.
- Rush should be returned if the Discontinue value is N and current inventory is less than or equal to the rush reorder point.
- Reorder should be returned if the Discontinue value is equal to N and current inventory is less than the reorder point.
- For all others, OK should be returned.
- Fill the formula down through cell L21.

c. On the **Inventory** worksheet, create an Inventory named range for the range **A2:M21**.

d. On the **InventoryAudit** worksheet, create the following named ranges.

- Range: **F3:G6** Name: Massage
- Range: **I3:J6** Name: Golf
- Range: **F10:G12** Name: Food
- Range: **I10:J12** Name: Novelty
- Range: **F16:G19** Name: Reading
- Range: **I16:J17** Name: Clothing

e. In cell **B3**, create a formula to retrieve the item within the category listed in cell B1. Enter an INDIRECT function nested in an INDEX function to return the item numbers by category. The function will reference cell B1 and return the value at the intersection of row 1, using the Category number in cell A3 and column 1. Nest the function in an IFERROR function to return a blank cell if no items exist within the category. Copy the formula down through cell B17.

This will allow you to change the value in cell B1 to another category and retrieve the desired data from the appropriate table.

f. In cell **C3**, create a formula to retrieve the projected sales for each item within the category listed in cell B1. Enter an INDIRECT function nested in an INDEX function to return the item numbers by category. The function will reference cell B1 and return the value at the intersection of row 1, using the Category number in cell A3 and column 2. Nest the function in an IFERROR function to return a blank cell if no items exist within the category. Copy the formula down through cell C17.

g. In cell **F24**, enter a formula that calculates the quantity of each item by subtracting the total out amount from the beginning inventory amount and then adding the total in amount. Copy the formula down through cell F43.

h. In cell **G24**, enter a VLOOKUP function to retrieve the CurrentInventory amount for Item A1 from the eighth column in the Inventory named range on the Inventory worksheet. Copy the formula down through cell G43.

i. In cell **J24**, enter a VLOOKUP function to retrieve the description of item A1 from the second column in the Inventory named range on the Inventory worksheet. Incorporate an IF function so that if the value retrieved is blank that a blank is displayed instead of a 0. Copy the formula down through cell J43.

j. On the **DailyTransactions** worksheet, create an advanced filter to explore the data by completing the following.

- Copy the column headers in **A10:F10** and paste them at the top of the sheet, starting in cell **A1**.
- Add the appropriate criteria so that only transactions from the Food category that were purchased on a Friday are displayed.
- Copy the filtered results, including the column headings, and paste them on the DailyTransactionsFilter worksheet, starting in cell A1.

k. On the DailyTransactions worksheet, use database functions to explore the data by completing the following.

- Clear the advanced filter.
- Create a DailyDatabase named range for the range **A10:F40**.
- In cell **B5**, type QtySold as the field to use in the calculations.
- In cell **B6**, enter a DSUM function that will calculate the total QtySold for records that meet the specified criteria.
- In cell **B7**, enter a DAVERAGE function that will calculate the average QtySold for records that meet the specified criteria.

l. Create a PivotTable to further explore the DailyTransactions data by completing the following.

- Create the PivotTable on a new worksheet with the name PivotTableAnalysis
- Place the **Category** and **Item** fields into the Rows area, the **WeekDay** field in the Columns area, and the **QtySold** field in the Values area.
- Modify the **QtySold** field so that the Sum calculation is used and use Sales Volume as the custom name.
- Change the Row Labels in cell A4 to Category/Items
- Change the Column Labels in cell B3 to Days
- Apply the **Dark Blue, Pivot Style Dark 2** PivotTable style.
- Use the Category filter to only show sales volume for the Golf, Food, and Clothing categories.

m. Update the **Documentation** worksheet according to your instructor's directions.

n. Save the workbook, exit Excel, and then submit your file as directed by your instructor.

Perform 1: Perform in Your Career

Student data file needed:

 e03TrialBalance.xlsx

You will save your file as:

e03TrialBalance_LastFirst.xlsx

Analyzing the Trial Balance

General Business

Finance & Accounting

You work for an optics manufacturing company that was recently purchased by another company. As part of the acquisition, the acquiring company changed your ledger account numbers to match their ledger account numbers. It is your responsibility to remap the trial balance for the prior years so it can be used for trending analysis.

a. Open the Excel file, **e03TrialBalance**. Save your file as e03TrialBalance_LastFirst using your last and first name.

b. On the **TrialBalance** worksheet, add a new field label in G1 named New Account and a new field label in H1 named New Dept Format both labels appropriately.

c. In cell **G2**, create a formula that will look up the account number in the Account worksheet and return the Target. Fill the formula down the column. Create named ranges, if desired, to make it easier to reference cells on other worksheets.

d. In cell **H2**, create a formula that will look up the account number in the Department worksheet and return the Target Department. Create named ranges, if desired, to make it easier to reference cells on other worksheets.

- Hint: Because the Target Department column is to the left of the SourceAcct, you cannot use a lookup function.
- If the function returns an error, it should display [None] rather than the error.
- Fill the formula down the column. Adjust the column width as necessary.

e. Convert cell range **A1:H8407** to a table and apply a style of your choice to the table.

f. Create and apply an advanced filter using the table headings and two rows of criteria.

g. Summarize the filtered data in the table by creating at least two SUBTOTAL functions. Add appropriate labels and formatting.

h. Insert at least one slicer to filter the data in the table and apply a style similar to your table. Apply a new filter to the data by selecting multiple criteria for the slicer(s). Ensure that the slicer does not cover any data.

i. Insert a new worksheet, copy the column headings of the table into row 1 of the new worksheet to use with at least two database functions to further explore the data. Create a named range to use as the Database argument. Add appropriate labels and formatting.

j. Insert a PivotTable on a new worksheet using the data in the table on the TrialBalance worksheet.
   • Ensure that the PivotTable includes values in all four areas of the PivotTable Fields pane.
   • Rename the worksheet and format the PivotTable appropriately.

k. Update the **Documentation** worksheet according to your instructor's directions.

l. Save the workbook, exit Excel, and then submit your file as directed by your instructor.

Student data file needed:

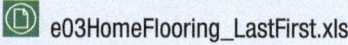 e03HomeFlooring.xlsx

You will save your file as:

e03HomeFlooring_LastFirst.xlsx

Home Flooring Options

Production & Operations

You have decided to replace the flooring in your home. However, you have a limited budget and need to review several possibilities and options. Because you are familiar with Excel, you will use an Excel workbook to help you with your decision.

a. Open the Excel file, **e03HomeFlooring**. Save your file as e03HomeFlooring_LastFirst using your last and first name.

b. The FlooringOptions worksheet contains data on various types of flooring that you are considering for several rooms in your house. Convert the dataset to a table using any table style you like.

c. The Prices worksheet contains the price per square foot for each of the options. Create a named range for the data on the Prices worksheet.

d. On the FlooringOptions worksheet add a new column to the table and retrieve the appropriate price per square foot for each item. Label and format appropriately.

e. Insert blank rows above the table to create an advanced filter using at least 1 row of criteria to select a handful of flooring options to consider.

f. From the filtered results, select three records along with the column headings and paste them into the FlooringSelection worksheet.

g. On the FlooringSelection worksheet add additional columns with data about the rooms in which you are considering new flooring. Include columns for the type of room, width and length measurements (in feet).

h. Add two additional columns to calculate the total square footage for each room as well as the price of flooring for each room.

i. Below the data, calculate the total cost of flooring.

j. All data should be labeled and formatted appropriately.

k. Create a PivotTable on a new worksheet, based on the flooring data information on the FlooringOptions worksheet, that shows the average price per square foot by type of flooring. Create a PivotChart from the PivotTable. Rename the worksheet and format both the PivotTable and PivotChart appropriately.

l. Complete the Documentation worksheet according to your instructor's directions.

m. Save the workbook, exit Excel, and then submit your file as directed by your instructor.

Perform 3: Perform in Your Team

Student data file needed:

 e03RoadHouseInventory.xlsx

You will save your file as:

 e03RoadHouseInventory_TeamName.xlsx

Managing Inventory at the Roadhouse Bar and Grill

Production & Operations

You and your team manage the Roadhouse Bar and Grill, a local restaurant that specializes in home-cooked meals for breakfast, lunch, and dinner. The owner has given you a scaled-down version of the data with one day's worth of transactions. Your team needs to manage the inventory of beverage items to ensure you have enough beverages for each day you are open for business. You decided to create a shared folder in the "cloud" so you can share the workbook with your management team.

a. Select one team member to set up the document by completing steps b–d.

b. Open your browser and navigate to https://www.onedrive.com or https://www.drive.google.com or any other instructor-assigned location. Be sure all members of the team have an account on the chosen system, such as a Microsoft or Google account.

c. Open the Excel file, **e03RoadhouseInventory**. Save your file as e03RoadhouseInventory_TeamName replacing TeamName with the name assigned to your team by your instructor.

d. Share the workbook with the other members of your team. Make sure each team member has the appropriate permission to edit the document.

e. Hold a team meeting and discuss the requirements of the remaining steps. Make an action and communication plan. Consider which steps can be done independently and which steps require completion of prior steps before being started.

f. In Excel, your team members will need to complete the following. Apply formatting such as resizing fields and use absolute cell references and relative cell references as deemed necessary.

- Create appropriate named ranges for the tables on the Tables and BeverageData worksheets.

- On the Transactions worksheet, use lookup functions to complete columns F, G, and I. Create a formula in column J to calculate the total spent on beverages based on the quantity sold and price.

- Using the data on the Transactions worksheet, insert a table and then create an appropriate named range for use in database functions. Insert rows above the table that will allow you to create and apply an advanced filter.

- Summarize the filtered data using SUBTOTAL functions and database functions.

- Create a PivotTable for the data in your table and insert it on the PivotTable-Analysis worksheet in row 10. Format the PivotTable with appropriate headings, titles, colors, and other formatting as you deem necessary. Use the PivotTable to answer the three questions at the top of the worksheet.

- Create a PivotChart on a new worksheet. Format the PivotChart with appropriate headings, titles, colors, and other formatting as you deem necessary. Name the new worksheet appropriately.

- On the BeverageData worksheet, insert a function in column G that retrieves the serving type from the Servings List on the Tables worksheet.

g. Complete the Documentation worksheet according to your instructor's directions. Minimally, include enough detail to identify which parts of the worksheets and/or workbook each team member completed.

h. In a custom header section of the Documentation worksheet, include the names of the students in your team. Spread the names evenly across each of the three header sections: left section, center section, and right section.

i. Save the workbook, exit Excel, and then submit your file as directed by your instructor.

Perform 4: How Others Perform

Student data file needed:

 e03Shipping.xlsx

You will save your file as:

 e03Shipping_LastFirst.xlsx

Shipping at ABC Distributor

Production & Operations

ABC Distributor ships to retail companies across the United States. Products are typically shipped in quantities of 20 to 500 units. The company examines shipping data to evaluate and adjust the shipments of items and reduce shipping expenses. In the spreadsheet provided, data with some analysis has been started. The company knows there are issues and would like help getting things straightened out, along with setting up and customizing additional information.

a. Open the Excel file, **e03Shipping**. Save your file as e03Shipping_LastFirst using your last and first name.

b. On the ShippingData worksheet, a table has been set up and a calculated field was added, but formulas need to be developed and possibly corrected. Create named ranges as you deem necessary or useful.

- In cell H16, the function that will retrieve the weight from the ProductWeights named range was set up, but it seems to be giving an error message in some cells. Check the formula, and make sure it will retrieve the weight correctly. Format the column appropriately.

- In cell I16, create a formula that will retrieve the Category in the second row of the Contract_Category table on the InputData worksheet, using the Weight field as the lookup value.

- In cell J16, create a formula that will find the shipping Unit_Cost by dividing ShipCost by Qty shipped.

c. On the ShippingData worksheet, create an advanced filter.

d. Set up calculations on the filtered data based on one of three data fields specified in cell B5.

- In cell B6, create a formula that will find the average of the filtered data based on the field name listed in B5. Write the formula in a way that if you were to change the value in B5 to ShipCost it would calculate the average shipping cost of the filtered data.

- In cell B7, create a formula that will find the sum of the filtered data based on the field name listed in B5. Write the formula in a way that if you were to change the value in B5 to ShipCost it would calculate the total shipping costs of the filtered data.
- Clear the criteria in row 2, and then, in cell E2, type CA as the criterion for the State. In cell C2, type >300 as the criterion for the Qty.
- In cell E6, create a formula that will average the field listed in E5 for all CA transactions.
- In cell E7, create a formula that will find the minimum of the field listed in E5 for all CA transactions.
- In cell E8, create a formula that will find the maximum of the field listed E5 for all CA transactions.
- In cell E9, create a formula that will find the sum of the field listed in E5 for all CA transactions.
- In cell J5, create a formula to find the largest ShipCost from the ShipData.
- In cell J6, knowing the largest shipping cost value in J5, create a formula to find the City location in conjunction with the row number for the largest shipping cost value in J5.
- In cell J8, create a formula to find the largest Qty shipped from the ShipData.
- In cell J9, similar to the function developed in cell J6, create a formula to find the City location for the row number that had the largest shipment quantity value in J8.

e. Based on the ShippingData worksheet, create a PivotTable on a new worksheet named PivotTableAnalysis. Insert a slicer. Format with appropriate heading, colors, and other formatting as you deem necessary.

f. Using the PivotTable, create a drill-down of your choice on a new, appropriately named worksheet.

g. Create a 3-D Clustered Column PivotChart using the data on the ShippingData worksheet. Place the PivotChart on a new worksheet. Format with appropriate headings, titles, colors, and other formatting as you deem necessary. Name the new worksheet appropriately.

h. Complete the Documentation worksheet according to your instructor's directions.

i. Save the workbook, exit Excel, and then submit your file as directed by your instructor.

Excel Business Unit 4

Build an Application with Multiple Worksheets and Workbooks

It is quite common for businesses or individuals to need to create worksheets and workbooks that are designed specially to meet their needs. Excel workbooks can also be structured to make it easier for other people to use the workbook. This business unit will explore using multiple worksheets, workbooks, and templates to tailor workbooks to meet specific needs. The business unit will also explore refining workbooks by auditing formulas, creating validation, making the workbooks user-friendly, and protecting worksheets and workbooks.

Learning Outcome 1

Use multiple worksheets, workbooks, and templates to create an Excel application.

REAL WORLD SUCCESS

"During my internship I worked in the sales department, and one of my jobs was to summarize weekly reports sent in from the various salespeople. Everyone sent their information to me in different formats, and it took a long time to pull it all together—sometimes a day or more! I finally remembered that Excel can consolidate data, so I sent a template to the salespeople and asked them to fill it in each week. Now I could open their files, consolidate the data, and in a few hours have what used to take me days to complete. The salespeople really liked how easy the template was to use, and my boss was totally impressed with my ingenuity and said she will use the method with the next intern."

– Rebecca, recent graduate

Learning Outcome 2

Perform formula auditing, use data validation, create macros, and explore worksheet and workbook protection to refine an Excel application.

REAL WORLD SUCCESS

"As an intern, one of my jobs is to do a lot of data entry each week. When I started, I was given a workbook from the last intern to use, and I had to delete the data from the previous week, then save the workbook with a different name, and then enter the new weekly data. It often took me more time to set up the workbook each week than it did to enter the data. So I created a macro to clear the data for me, and now, with the click of a button, I have the worksheet cleared and am ready to enter the new data. After that, I set up macros for all the repetitive tasks I have to do in Excel. Not only has this made my job easier, but it gives me more time to be creative, which definitely gets the attention of my boss!"

– Jarrett, intern

Microsoft Excel

Chapter 7 MULTIPLE WORKSHEETS, WORKBOOKS, AND TEMPLATES

MyLab IT Grader

Human Resources

Prepare Case

Turquoise Oasis Spa Therapist Sales and Service Analysis

The Turquoise Oasis Spa serves resort guests with a full range of services from traditional and alternative massage to aromatherapy and detoxification therapy. The spa is open seven days a week. Meda Rodate, the spa manager, would like a workbook that allows her to summarize and compare the sales of each therapist and services used for each day the spa is open.

Anna Omelchenko/Shutterstock

Student data files needed:

 e04ch07Spa.xlsx

 e04ch07SpaLink.xlsx

 e04ch07SpaLogo.jpg

 e04ch07SpaPrices.xlsx

 e04ch07SpaSales.xlsx

You will save your files as:

 e04ch07Spa_LastFirst.xlsx

 e04ch07SpaLink_LastFirst.xlsx

 e04ch07SpaPricesShared_LastFirst.xlsx

 e04ch07SpaProjects_LastFirst.xlsx

 e04ch07SpaSalesTemplate_LastFirst.xltx

 e04ch07SpaCalendar_LastFirst.xlsx

Working with Multiple Worksheets

An Excel workbook can contain many worksheets—potentially hundreds of them. A single worksheet is a two-dimensional object; the rows are one dimension, and the columns represent a second dimension. When a workbook contains more than one worksheet, the multiple worksheets can represent a third dimension as long as the worksheets share an identical layout. Data from multiple worksheets can be referenced to generate new data via formulas, functions, and consolidation. Data can be copied and pasted from one worksheet to another and can be filled from one worksheet to many worksheets. Multiple worksheets can be selected at the same time, called **grouping**, and actions such as data entry and formatting can affect all the worksheets in the group at once, greatly increasing efficiency.

Data can be accessed between worksheets by using three-dimensional (3-D) references, and even named ranges can include cells from multiple worksheets. These are called, not surprisingly, 3-D named ranges.

In this section, you will work with the Spa workbook, which contains multiple worksheets. There are three sheets—one for each therapist—that need additional information to be added as well as two additional worksheets with schedule and price information about the therapists' services. You will complete the therapists' worksheets and then add additional worksheets to come up with summary information for the three therapists.

Group Worksheets

Grouping worksheets allows you to perform certain tasks once and have those tasks affect the same cells for all worksheets in the group. There are multiple ways to group worksheets. You can click the tab of a worksheet, hold down Ctrl, and then click the worksheet tab of additional worksheets you want to include in the group. The tabs of each worksheet included in the group will be highlighted with a white—or light—background color as a visual indicator. The file name in the title bar of the window will also show [Group] to remind you that you have worksheets grouped. Alternatively, if all the worksheets you would like to group are contiguous, you can click the worksheet tab of a worksheet on one end, hold down Shift, and then click the worksheet tab on the other end of the contiguous worksheets.

Ungrouping worksheets is accomplished either by right-clicking a grouped worksheet tab and selecting Ungroup Sheets from the shortcut menu or by clicking the tab of a worksheet that is not grouped.

Opening the Starting File

Meda Rodate, the spa manager, has already started a workbook. She included data for product pricing in the PriceList worksheet and sales for December 16, 2022, in the SpaSales worksheet. She also created three additional worksheets, one for each of the spa therapists: Christy Istas, Kendra Mault, and Jason Niese. You will work with the existing worksheets to add formatting and formulas to make the workbook more useful.

In this exercise, you will open the Spa workbook.

E07.00

SIDE NOTE
Office Updates
Depending on your exact Office version, you may see Open or Open Other Workbooks.

To Open the Spa Analysis Worksheet

a. Start Excel, click **Open** in the left pane, and then double-click **This PC**. Navigate through the folder structure to the location of your student data files, and then double-click **e04ch07Spa**. If a Security Warning message displays, click **Enable Editing**.

b. Click the **File** tab, click **Save As**, and then double-click **This PC**. In the Save As dialog box, navigate to the location where you are saving your project files, and then change the file name to e04ch07Spa_LastFirst using your last and first name.

c. Click **Save**.

Grouping Worksheets

When worksheets are grouped, what you do to one worksheet happens to the other worksheets in the group. For example, you can enter data, add formatting, insert and delete rows or columns, and delete or clear cells on all the worksheets in the group. While grouping worksheets is often the most efficient way to modify a workbook, there are some Excel features that are not available for grouped worksheets. For example, conditional formatting cannot be directly applied to grouped worksheets; in that case, conditional formatting would have to be applied to each worksheet individually.

In the Spa workbook, you will group the worksheets for each of the therapists and change the tab color for all the worksheets so they are easy to identify. You will do the same for the PriceList and SpaSales worksheets. The PriceList and SpaSales worksheets contain source data; the Istas, Mault, and Niese worksheets contain the analysis. By coloring their respective worksheet tabs differently, you will create a visual differentiation between the two types of worksheets in the workbook.

In this exercise, you will group worksheets and change tab colors.

 **E07.01**

SIDE NOTE
Pin the Ribbon
If your ribbon is collapsed, pin your ribbon open. Click the Home tab. In the lower-right corner of the ribbon, click Pin the ribbon 📌.

To Group Worksheets and Change the Tab Color

a. On the **Istas** worksheet, press and hold ⎵Shift⎵, and then click the **Niese** worksheet.

   The Istas, Mault, and Niese worksheets are now grouped. Notice the Group tag next to the file name in the title bar, which indicates that you are in grouped worksheet mode.

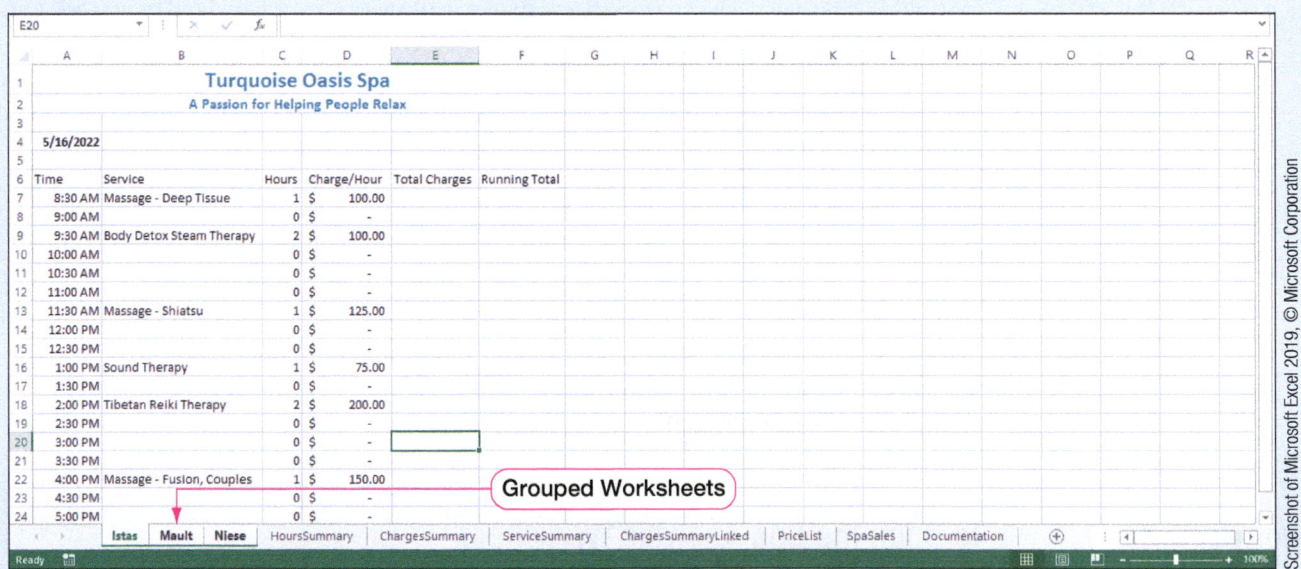

Figure 1   Worksheets grouped

b. Right-click the **Istas** worksheet, point to **Tab Color**, and then select **Blue** from the Standard Colors row.

   Notice how the tab color is added to all three worksheets.

c. Right-click the **Istas** worksheet, and then click **Ungroup Sheets**.

d. **Save** 💾 the workbook.

REAL WORLD ADVICE | Do Not Forget to Ungroup

Anyone who works with grouped worksheets occasionally forgets to ungroup them and then makes changes to several worksheets when the objective was to make changes to the visible worksheet only. If you forget to ungroup worksheets, you can quickly create more work than you saved by grouping worksheets in the first place. If you realize immediately that you still have your worksheets grouped, you can use the Undo command and then start again after you ungroup the worksheets.

Entering Data

Grouping worksheets can save a lot of data entry time. Grouped worksheets make the entry of worksheet structural elements such as titles, column headings, and row labels fast and efficient. Be careful, though. Errors made, such as misspellings or misplacement of a heading, are compounded across all grouped worksheets.

In the Spa workbook, you will group the therapists' worksheets again and enter information that will pertain to all the therapists. By grouping, the therapists' worksheets will all have the same structure, be visually consistent, and make data entry in the future much more efficient.

In this exercise, you will enter data into grouped worksheets.

 **E07.02**

To Enter Data into Grouped Worksheets

a. On the **Istas** worksheet, press and hold Shift, and then click the **Niese** worksheet.

b. Click cell **A25**, type Total and then press Ctrl+Enter.

c. Click the **Mault** worksheet. Notice that the text entered on the Istas worksheet is also in the Mault worksheet. Click the **Niese** worksheet, and you will see the same result.

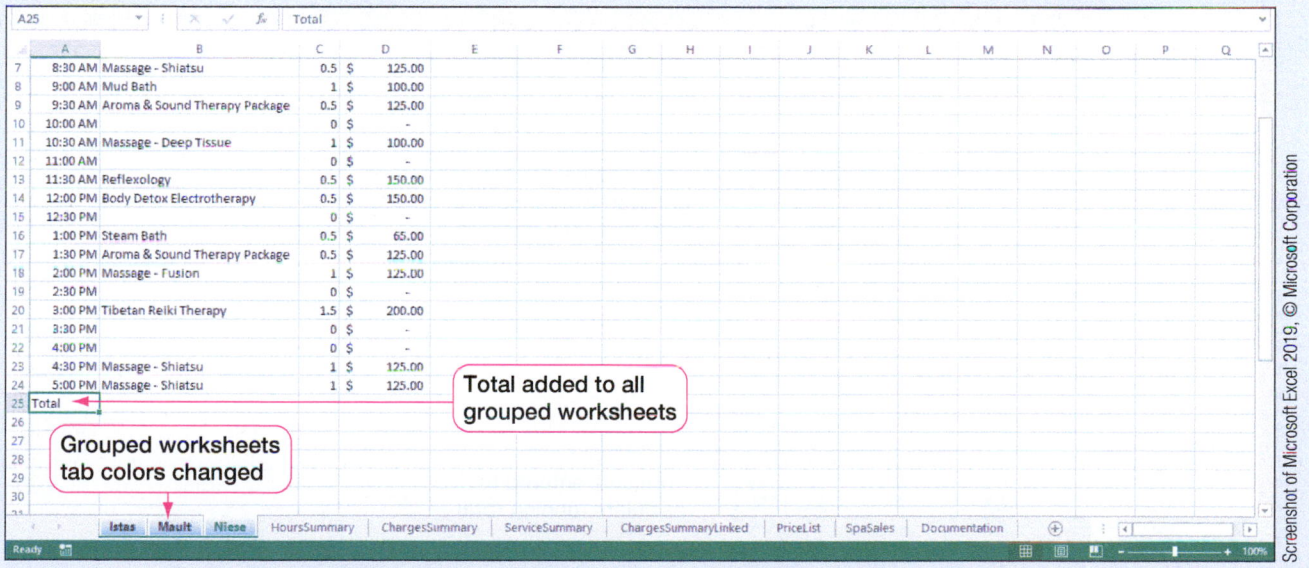

Figure 2 Data entered on Istas worksheet shows on the Niese worksheet

Leave the worksheets grouped for the next exercise.

d. **Save** the workbook.

Entering Formulas

Entering formulas into grouped worksheets is a very efficient way to simultaneously create new data in multiple worksheets and is the same as entering data in grouped worksheets. Occasionally, while a formula may appear to work on multiple grouped worksheets, the data may appear too similar on the worksheets or even incorrect. It is very important to carefully check the results of your formulas to ensure that they show the intended results.

In the Spa workbook, part of the therapists' worksheets has been added, but two columns have no data. You will add formulas to these columns to calculate both the Total Charges for each therapist and the Running Total for each therapist.

In this exercise, you will enter formulas and functions into multiple worksheets.

 **E07.03**

To Enter Formulas and Functions into Multiple Worksheets

a. Click the **Istas** worksheet. With the worksheets still grouped, click cell **E7**, type =C7*D7 and then press Ctrl+Enter. Copy the formula to cell range **E8:E24**.

This formula multiplies the Charge/Hour by the number of hours to get the total charge for each service listed. Dashes appear in place of zeroes because the Accounting number format is applied to this range of cells on the Istas worksheet.

b. Click cell **F7**, type =E7 and then press Enter. In cell **F8**, type =F7+E8 and then press Ctrl+Enter. Copy the formula in cell F8 to cell range **F9:F24**.

The Running Total should be the cumulative total for services performed. The first service will simply be the amount of that service, but all services after the first one will be the cumulative amount for the day, so each service in column E will be added to the previous service total charges in column F.

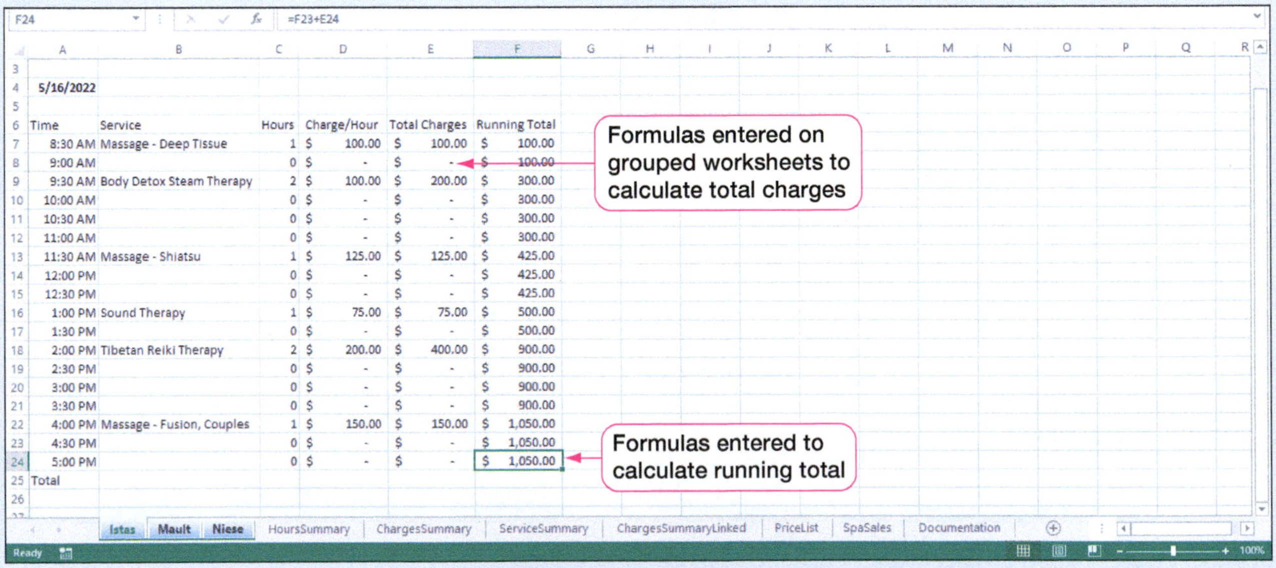

	A	B	C	D	E	F
4	5/16/2022					
6	Time	Service	Hours	Charge/Hour	Total Charges	Running Total
7	8:30 AM	Massage - Deep Tissue	1	$ 100.00	$ 100.00	$ 100.00
8	9:00 AM		0	$ -	$ -	$ 100.00
9	9:30 AM	Body Detox Steam Therapy	2	$ 100.00	$ 200.00	$ 300.00
10	10:00 AM		0	$ -	$ -	$ 300.00
11	10:30 AM		0	$ -	$ -	$ 300.00
12	11:00 AM		0	$ -	$ -	$ 300.00
13	11:30 AM	Massage - Shiatsu	1	$ 125.00	$ 125.00	$ 425.00
14	12:00 PM		0	$ -	$ -	$ 425.00
15	12:30 PM		0	$ -	$ -	$ 425.00
16	1:00 PM	Sound Therapy	1	$ 75.00	$ 75.00	$ 500.00
17	1:30 PM		0	$ -	$ -	$ 500.00
18	2:00 PM	Tibetan Reiki Therapy	2	$ 200.00	$ 400.00	$ 900.00
19	2:30 PM		0	$ -	$ -	$ 900.00
20	3:00 PM		0	$ -	$ -	$ 900.00
21	3:30 PM		0	$ -	$ -	$ 900.00
22	4:00 PM	Massage - Fusion, Couples	1	$ 150.00	$ 150.00	$ 1,050.00
23	4:30 PM		0	$ -	$ -	$ 1,050.00
24	5:00 PM		0	$ -	$ -	$ 1,050.00
25	Total					

F24 fx =F23+E24

Formulas entered on grouped worksheets to calculate total charges

Formulas entered to calculate running total

Sheet tabs: Istas Mault Niese HoursSummary ChargesSummary ServiceSummary ChargesSummaryLinked PriceList SpaSales Documentation

Screenshot of Microsoft Excel 2019, © Microsoft Corporation

Figure 3 Formulas entered to calculate Total Charges and Running Total

c. Click the **HoursSummary** worksheet to ungroup the worksheets. Click the **Mault** and then the **Niese** worksheet to view the formulas added to the worksheet.

d. **Save** 💾 the workbook.

Filling Contents Across Worksheets

Fill Across Worksheets is a command that can be used to copy cell contents, formats, or both contents and formats to worksheets in a group. The source and destination worksheets must all be included in the group. Unlike copy and paste, in which cells can be copied from one location in a worksheet to a different location in the same worksheet or a different worksheet, Fill Across Worksheets will only fill to the same location in different worksheets; for example, cell A5 in Sheet1 can only be filled to cell A5 in other worksheets.

When using Fill Across Worksheets, the decision of whether to fill All, Contents, or Formats depends on what exactly you need to copy. Choose Contents when the target worksheets are already formatted or will be formatted differently than the source worksheet.

In this exercise, you will complete the Istas worksheet and then apply the content and format to the other therapists' worksheets.

 **E07.04**

SIDE NOTE

Flash Fill Not Available
Because the worksheets are grouped, many options, including Flash Fill, are not available to use with the group.

To Fill Contents Across Worksheets

a. Click the **Istas** worksheet. Select cell range **C25:E25**, and on the Home tab, in the Editing group, click **AutoSum** ∑.

b. With the cell range C25:E25 still selected on the Istas worksheet, press and hold [Shift], and then click the **Niese** worksheet. On the Home tab, in the Editing group, click **Fill** ⬇. Select **Across Worksheets**. Click to select **Contents**.

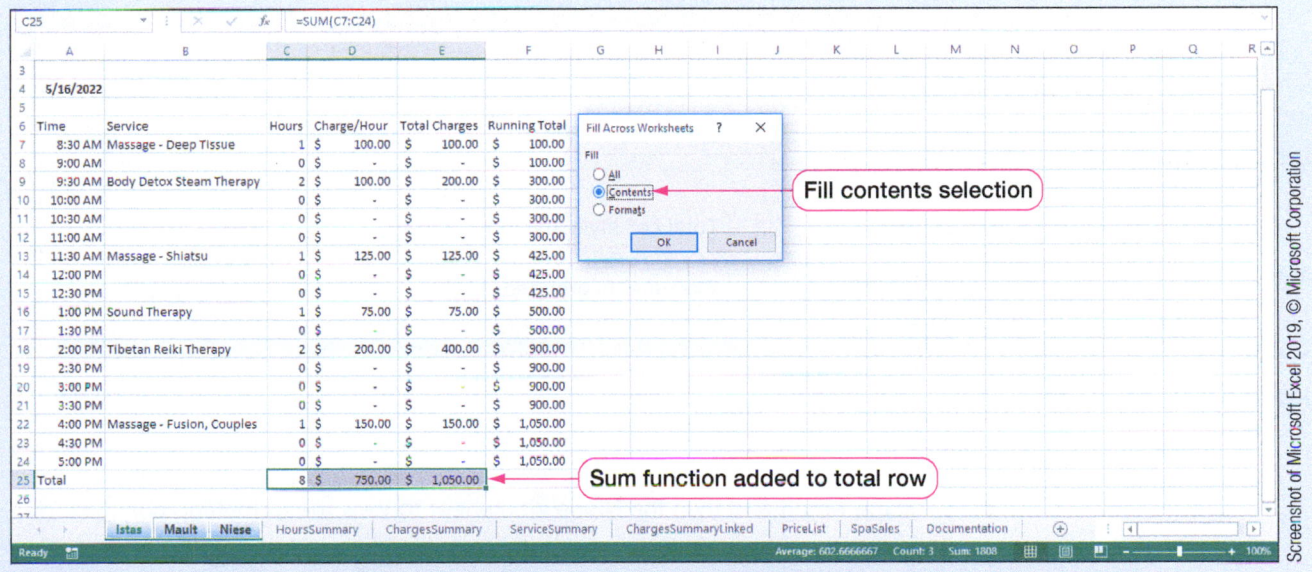

Figure 4 Fill Across Worksheets dialog box

c. Click **OK**.

Review that the SUM functions in cell range C25:E25 on the Istas worksheet were copied to both the Mault and Niese worksheets.

d. Click the **HoursSummary** worksheet to ungroup the sheets.

e. **Save** 🖫 the workbook.

Formatting Cells

By grouping worksheets, you can apply cell formatting to multiple worksheets at once. For example, any of the formatting tools in the Font, Alignment, and Number groups on the Home tab can be applied to grouped worksheets. Any ribbon tools that are not available when worksheets are grouped will be grayed out. Note that table formatting cannot be applied to grouped worksheets, nor can any modifications to cell formats—or cell contents—inside a table be applied when worksheets are grouped.

In this exercise, you will format cells on grouped worksheets.

 **E07.05**

To Format Cells on Grouped Worksheets

a. Click the **Istas** worksheet, press and hold Shift, and then click the **Niese** worksheet. Select cell range **A6:F6**. On the Home tab, in the Styles group, click **Cell Styles**, and then select **Accent5**.

b. Select cell range **C25:E25**, and in the Styles group, click **Cell Styles**, and then select **Total**. Click cell **F25** to see the formatting changes.

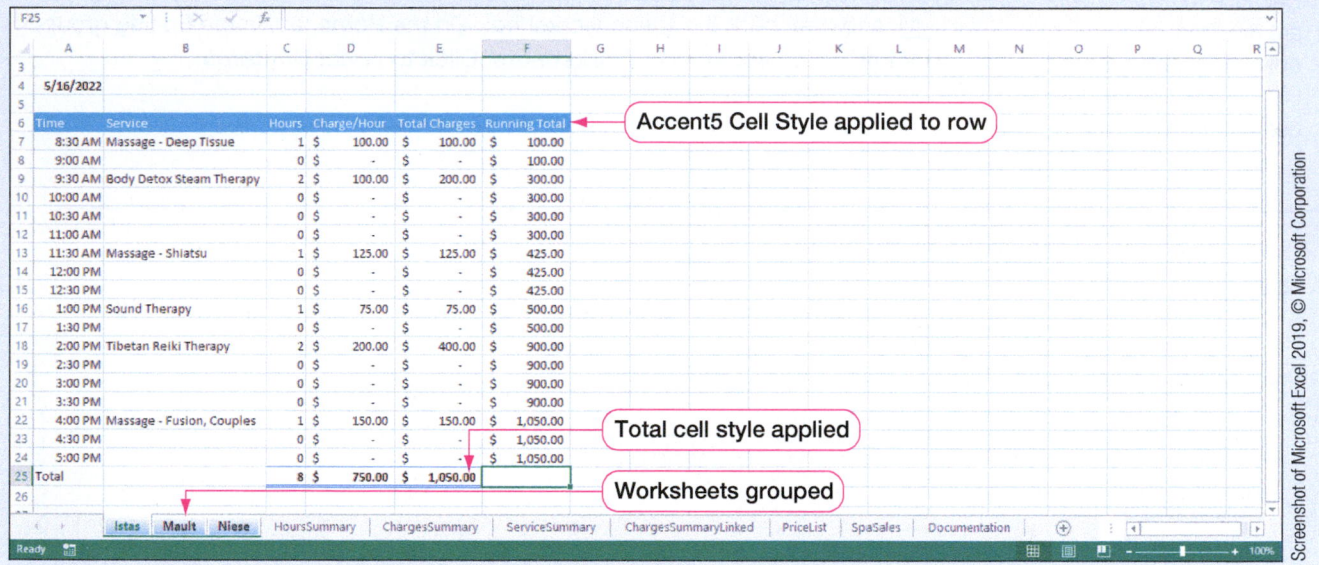

Figure 5 Cells formatted

c. Click the **Mault** and then the **Niese** worksheet to view the formatting changes.

d. Right-click the **Istas** worksheet, and then select **Ungroup Sheets**.

e. **Save** the workbook.

| REAL WORLD ADVICE | Copying and Pasting Data in Grouped Worksheets |

Data can be copied from a single worksheet into grouped worksheets. Data can be copied from one set of grouped worksheets and then pasted into the same or a different set of grouped sheets. The criteria that determines whether Clipboard data can be pasted into a new location are as follows:

- The new location must have room available such that the pasted range has exactly the same shape as the copied range.

- When multiple worksheets are grouped, the pasted range cannot overlap the copied range in any dimension; for example, copied cells from group Sheet1:Sheet2 cannot then be copied to a paste range in group Sheet2:Sheet3, but they could be pasted to Sheet1:Sheet2 as long as the rows and columns of the copied range and the paste range do not overlap.

Filling Formats Across Worksheets

Filling formats across worksheets is like filling content across worksheets, but in this case, only the formatting is applied. By using the Fill Across Worksheets command, you can copy formatting without affecting formulas and other data. You will fill the formatting from columns E and F in the Istas worksheet to the Mault and Niese worksheets. Because the content of each therapist's worksheet is unique, using Fill Across Worksheets for the formats will create identical formatting without affecting therapist-specific content.

In this exercise, you will fill formats across worksheets.

 **E07.06**

To Fill Formats Across Worksheets

a. On the **Istas** worksheet, select cell range **E7:F24**.

b. Press and hold ⌈Shift⌋, and then click the **Niese** worksheet. On the Home tab, in the Editing group, click **Fill** 🔽, and then select **Across Worksheets**. Click **Formats**, and then click **OK**.

c. Right-click the **Mault** worksheet, and then select **Ungroup Sheets**. Verify that all three worksheets have matching formatting.

d. **Save** 💾 the workbook.

| REAL WORLD ADVICE | Some Things Are Different When Worksheets Are Grouped |

- You can use worksheet grouping to reorder your worksheets but remember that the group will move as one in the reordering process. If you want to reorder the placement of worksheets within a group, the worksheets need to be ungrouped, and the reorder placement must be done manually.

- Be careful when printing. If you print when worksheets are grouped, every worksheet in the group is available to print, not just the active worksheet. The Print Preview navigation information will display the available pages for printing from the group. If you want only one worksheet to print, either specify which page or pages to print in the print options or ungroup and select the target worksheet.

- Many of Excel's commands and features are not available when worksheets are grouped—for example, the entire Data tab, table features and formatting, conditional formatting, shapes, charts, and sparklines.

Create Summary Worksheets

If your workbook contains multiple worksheets, you may want to summarize—or consolidate—the data on the multiple worksheets onto one summary worksheet. This can be useful when the worksheets represent different months' worth of data and you want to come up with a year-end summary or, in the case of the spa, you have multiple therapists and want to combine all their individual data on one summary worksheet.

One of Excel's more powerful features is the ability to reference data between worksheets. If you think of a worksheet as a two-dimensional array, then multiple worksheets in a workbook can be thought of as a three-dimensional array. Multiple worksheets represent a third dimension; therefore, references that address data across multiple worksheets are called 3-D references and 3-D named ranges. By using a 3-D formula with 3-D references, you can easily create a summary worksheet from multiple worksheets that are updated automatically as the source data is updated.

If your multiple worksheets contain either an identical structure or data with identical row and/or column labels, another option is to create a summary worksheet using the Consolidate feature. Consolidated data can be generated with or without links to the original source data. Summary data created using the Consolidate feature that is not linked is not automatically updated when the source data is changed. But if you create a summary and link the consolidated data back to the source data, then changes to source data are automatically reflected in the linked consolidation.

There are two ways in which data can be consolidated: by position and by category. **Consolidate by position** aggregates (totals) data in the same position in multiple worksheets. A summary sheet can be created but only when the source worksheets have an identical structure. **Consolidate by category** aggregates data in cells with matching row and/or column labels; the data does not need to be in the same relative position to create a summary sheet. There can be a different number of labels among the worksheets, and there can be a different mix of labels among the worksheets.

QUICK REFERENCE	When and How to Consolidate

If you want to summarize data from multiple places (worksheets or workbooks), you have several options. The option you choose will depend on where the data is located and how it is organized.

- Consolidate by position: Use this method if you want to arrange the data in all the worksheets in identical order and location.

- Consolidate by category: Use this method if you want to organize the data differently than how it is presented in the separate worksheets but use the same row and column labels so the consolidated worksheet matches the data.

- Consolidate by formula: Use this method if you want to use formulas with cell references or 3-D references to the other worksheets that you are combining because you do not have a consistent position or category of data to use.

- PivotTable report: Use this method if you want to use a PivotTable instead of a consolidation.

Creating a 3-D Reference

Three-dimensional references, or **3-D references**, allow formulas and functions to use data from cells and cell ranges across worksheets. A 3-D reference has the following structure: =worksheet name!cell reference. For example, the 3-D reference to cell C25 in worksheet Sheet3 is Sheet3!C25. Individual cells in multiple worksheets can be referenced by using a range of worksheets as well. For example, to reference cell C25 in Sheet1, Sheet2, and Sheet3—assuming that the three sheets are in that order and contiguous—the reference is specified as Sheet1:Sheet3!C25. Finally, a range of cells can be referenced across several worksheets. For example, the cell range C3:C25 in worksheets Sheet1 through Sheet3 is specified as Sheet1:Sheet3!C3:C25.

In the Spa workbook, you will delete the date entered in cell A4 of the three therapists' worksheets. Then you will change the date, so it is entered on the Istas worksheet and the other two worksheets have a 3-D reference to it.

In this exercise, you will create a 3-D reference.

 E07.07

SIDE NOTE
A Space in a Worksheet Name
In a 3-D reference, if a worksheet name includes a space, the space is replaced with an underscore.

To Create a 3-D Reference

a. On the Mault worksheet, press and hold [Shift], and then click the **Niese** worksheet. Click cell **A4**, and then press **Delete**.

b. In cell **A4**, type = and then click the **Istas** worksheet. Click cell **A4**, and then press [Ctrl]+[Enter]. This should insert a reference to cell A4 from the Istas worksheet in cell A4 on both the Mault and Niese worksheet.

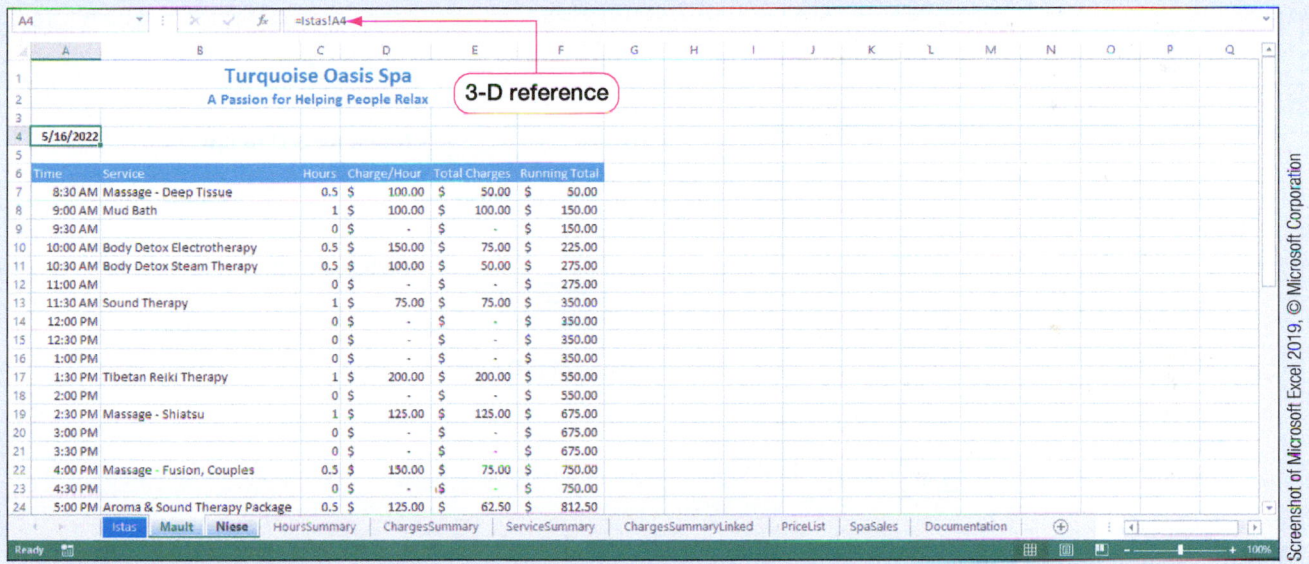

Figure 6   3-D reference

c. Click the **Istas** worksheet to ungroup the sheets.

d. **Save** 💾 the workbook.

Naming a 3-D Reference

A **3-D named range** is a named range that references the same cell or range of cells across multiple worksheets in a workbook. A 3-D named range cannot be defined in the Name box; you must use the Define Name command in the Defined Names group on the Formulas tab.

In this exercise, you will name ranges of cells so you can refer to them at a later time by the name and not the cell reference.

 **E07.08**

MAC COMPATIBILITY
Define Name
On a Mac, in the Defined Names group, click the Define Name arrow, and then select Define Name.

To Create a 3-D Name

a. On the Istas worksheet, click cell **E25**.

b. Click the **Formulas** tab, and in the Defined Names group, click **Name Manager**.

There is already one named range in the workbook: ProductTable. This name refers to cell range A2:D26 on the PriceList worksheet and is used in the VLOOKUP function in cell range D7:D24. The VLOOKUP in cell D7 is used to look up the Charge/Hour for the service entered in cell B7. The Charge/Hour is found in the table called ProductTable.

c. In the Name Manager dialog box, click **New**, and then in the Name box, type **TotalCharges3D**

d. To the right of the Refers to box, click **Collapse** 🔼. Press and hold Shift, click the **Niese** worksheet, and then click **Expand** 🔽. The Refers to box should now show ='Istas:Niese'!$E$25.

This reference is to cell E25 on the Istas worksheet, the Mault worksheet, and the Niese worksheet, in that order.

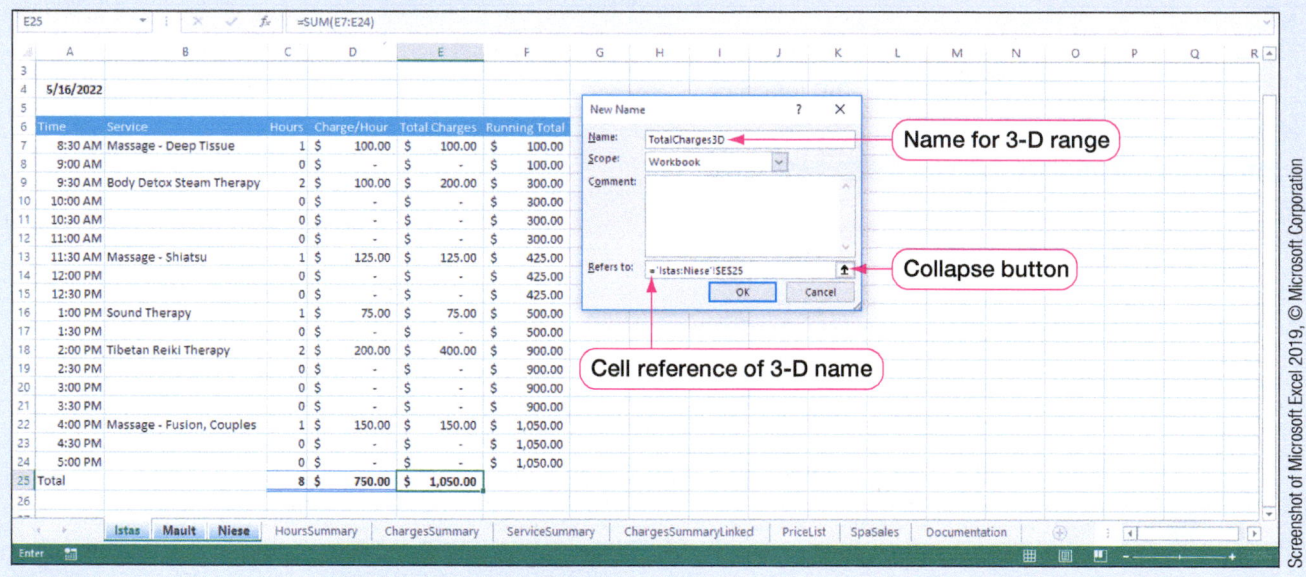

Figure 7 3-D named range added to a worksheet

e. Click **OK**, notice that TotalCharges3D is now listed in the Name Manager, and then click **Close**.

f. **Save** 🖫 the workbook.

<table>
<tr><td>**REAL WORLD ADVICE**</td><td>**Order Matters When Working with Grouped Worksheets**</td></tr>
</table>

When you assign a name to a range of cells, the first cell reference and the last cell reference are recognized, and all the cells in between are included in the range. For example, a cell range A1:C25 named "Profits" will always use the values in cell range A1:C25, no matter how you move the cells around.

Naming ranges that span multiple worksheets works the same way. The difference is that if you start with a range of worksheets, as in the case example that looks like Istas:Niese, when you rearrange the worksheets, the range will no longer be accurate. For example, if you decide to move the Mault tab to the right of the Niese worksheet, it would no longer be included in the named range Istas:Niese. You therefore must be extremely careful when you have named ranges and want to rearrange the worksheets. One option is to name a blank worksheet "Begin" to use for the first worksheet in the named range and another blank worksheet named "End" to use as the last worksheet in the range. This way, you are always reminded to keep the actual worksheets with data between the Begin and End worksheets.

Creating a 3-D Formula

When you have data on multiple worksheets and want to consolidate that data into a summary worksheet, you can use a 3-D formula. A **3-D formula** is a formula that references the same cell or range of cells across multiple worksheets in a workbook. Creating a 3-D formula is very similar to creating any other formula, but instead of typing the formula, it is generally easier to point to and click the cells. That way, you can avoid spelling errors that may make the formula incorrect.

In the Spa workbook, you will summarize the number of hours and total charges for all three therapists on a new summary worksheet. The formula for hours will be a simple 3-D formula, and the total charges will be a 3-D SUM function.

 **E07.09**

To Create a 3-D Formula

a. Click the **HoursSummary** worksheet, click cell **B7**, and then type **=** Click the **Istas** worksheet, click **C7**, and then type **+** Click the **Mault** worksheet, click **C7**, and then type **+** click the **Niese** worksheet, click **C7**, and then press Ctrl+Enter. Do not click back on the HoursSummary worksheet.

The formula you should see is =Istas!C7+Mault!C7+Niese!C7. This formula adds the values in cell C7 on all three worksheets.

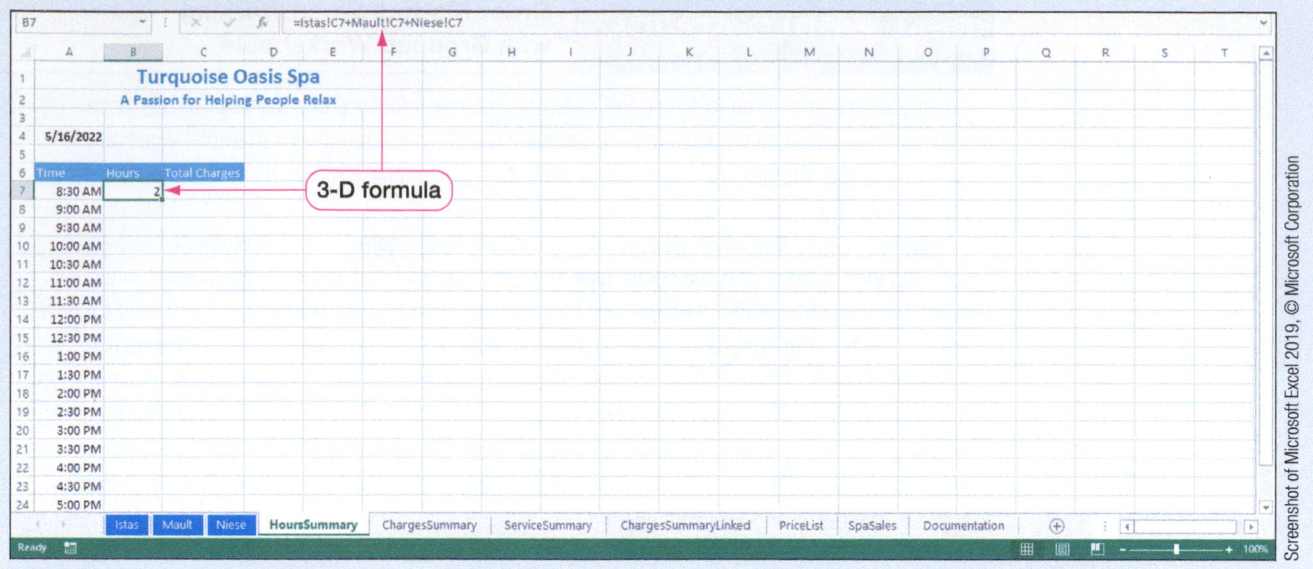

Screenshot of Microsoft Excel 2019, © Microsoft Corporation

Figure 8   3-D formula added to worksheet

Troubleshooting

If the formula appears as =Istas!C7+Mault!C7+HoursSummary!, you clicked back on the HoursSummary worksheet in error before pressing Ctrl+Enter. Click Undo and complete step a again.

b.   Copy the formula to cell range **B8:B24**.

c.   Click cell **C7**, and then type **=SUM(**

d.   Click the **Istas** worksheet, press and hold Shift, click the **Niese** worksheet, click **E7**, and then press Ctrl+Enter.

Note that Excel added the right parenthesis. The formula you should see is =SUM(Istas:Niese!E7). This formula sums the values in cell E7 on sheets Istas through Niese.

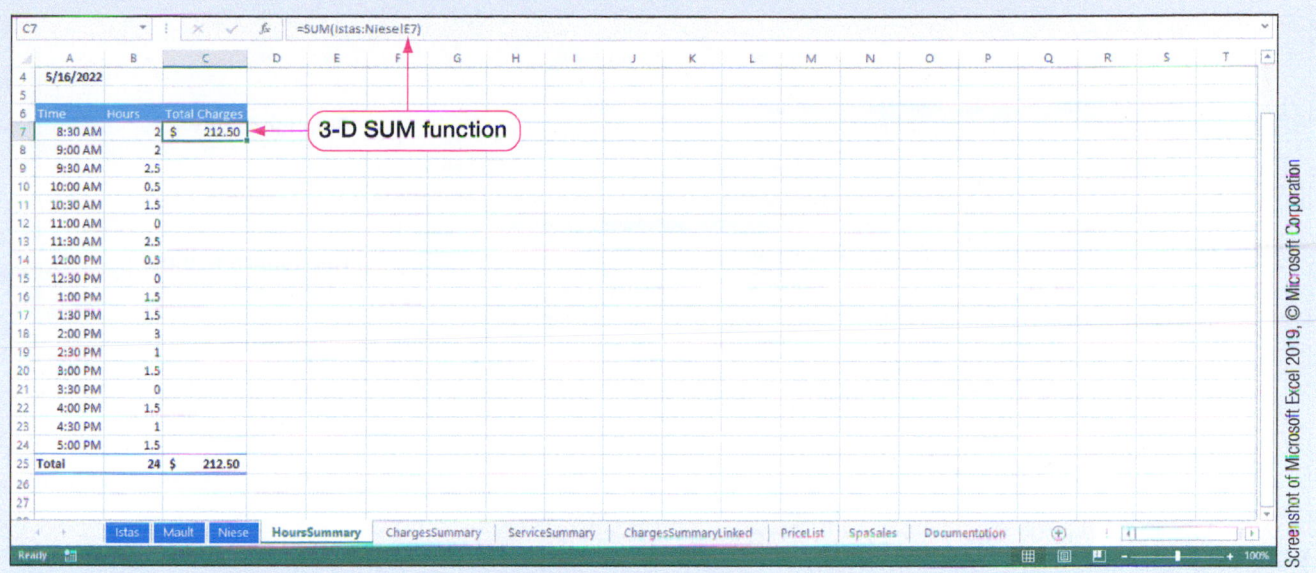

Figure 9 3-D SUM function added to worksheet

    e. Copy the formula to cell range **C8:C24**.

    f. Save  the workbook.

Consolidating Data by Position

Consolidate by position can be used to create a summary worksheet when the source worksheets all have an identical structure, such that the same location in each worksheet contains the same relative data. For example, if cell A5 contains sales discounts for bulk sales in the January worksheet, cells A5 in worksheets February through December also contain sales discounts for bulk sales. The range selected in each worksheet must include the exact same number of rows and columns in each worksheet that is part of the consolidation.

    In this exercise, you will consolidate data by position.

E07.10

To Consolidate Data by Position

    a. Click the **ChargesSummary** worksheet, and then click cell **B7**. Click the **Data** tab, and then, in the Data Tools group, click **Consolidate**. In the Consolidate dialog box, make sure **Sum** is selected in the Function box.

    b. Click the **Reference** box, click the **Istas** worksheet, and then select cell range **E7:F24**. If necessary, scroll to the left of the worksheet tabs and move the Consolidate dialog box to make the selection.

    c. Click **Add** in the Consolidate dialog box.

    d. Click the **Mault** worksheet and notice that cell range E7:F24 is still selected. Click **Add** in the Consolidate dialog box.

    e. Click the **Niese** worksheet and notice that cell range E7:F24 is still selected. Click **Add** in the Consolidate dialog box.

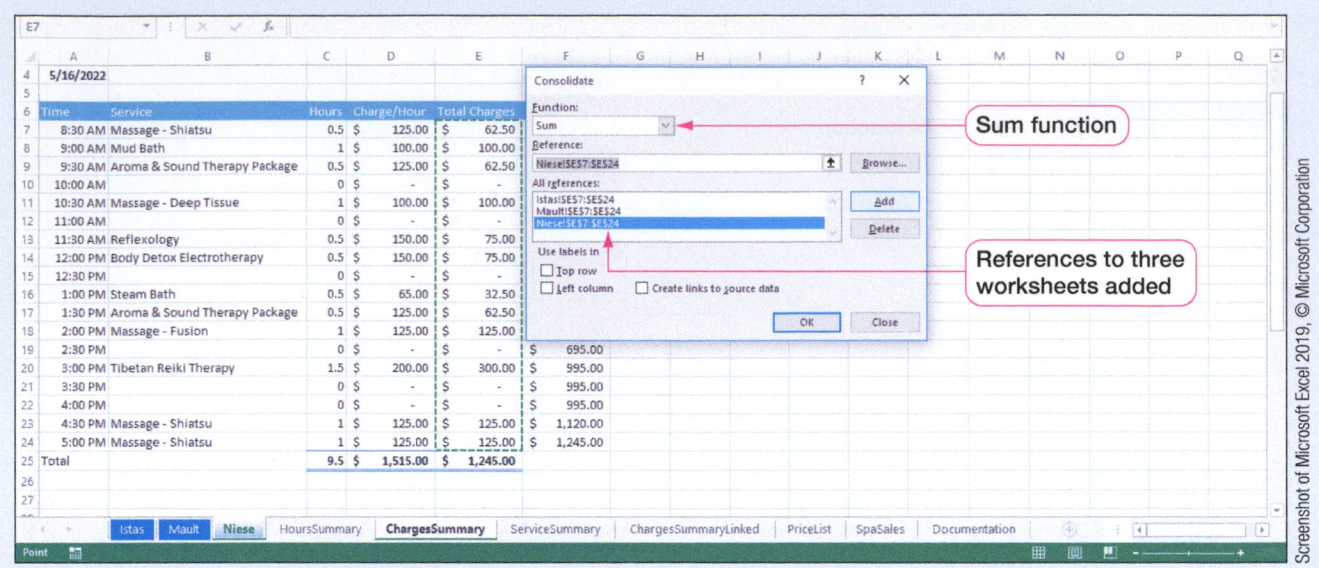

Figure 10 Ranges added to Consolidate dialog box

> f. Click **OK** in the Consolidate dialog box. Click cell **B7** and then review the formula bar. Note a value is in the cell, not a formula.
>
> g. Save  the workbook.

Consolidating Data by Category

Consolidating by category is more flexible than consolidating by position. When consolidating by category, Excel examines row and/or column headings to determine which cells should contribute to a given calculation. Data does not need to be in the same relative position between and among worksheets; it simply needs to share the same row and/or column labels. Labels can even be repeated multiple times in a single worksheet.

In the Spa workbook, you will consolidate therapists' sales by service rather than by time. Because there is no way of knowing ahead of time where specific services will be located in the source worksheets, consolidation by category is the only realistic option.

In this exercise, you will consolidate data by category.

E07.11

SIDE NOTE
Only One per Worksheet
A worksheet can store only one consolidation. If you want to create more than one consolidation, they should be placed on different worksheets.

To Consolidate Data by Category

a. Click the **ServiceSummary** worksheet, and then click cell **A6**. On the Data tab, in the Data Tools group, click **Consolidate**. In the Consolidate dialog box, make sure **Sum** is selected in the Function box, and then click the Reference box.

b. Click the **Istas** worksheet, and then select cell range **B6:E24**. Note that you do not include the Running Total because a sum of Running Total by category would be a meaningless number. Click **Add**.

c. Click the **Mault** worksheet, verify that cell range B6:E24 is selected, and then click **Add**.

d. Click the **Niese** worksheet, verify that cell range B6:E24 is selected, and then click **Add**.

e. Under the Use labels in section, select the **Top row** and the **Left column** check boxes.

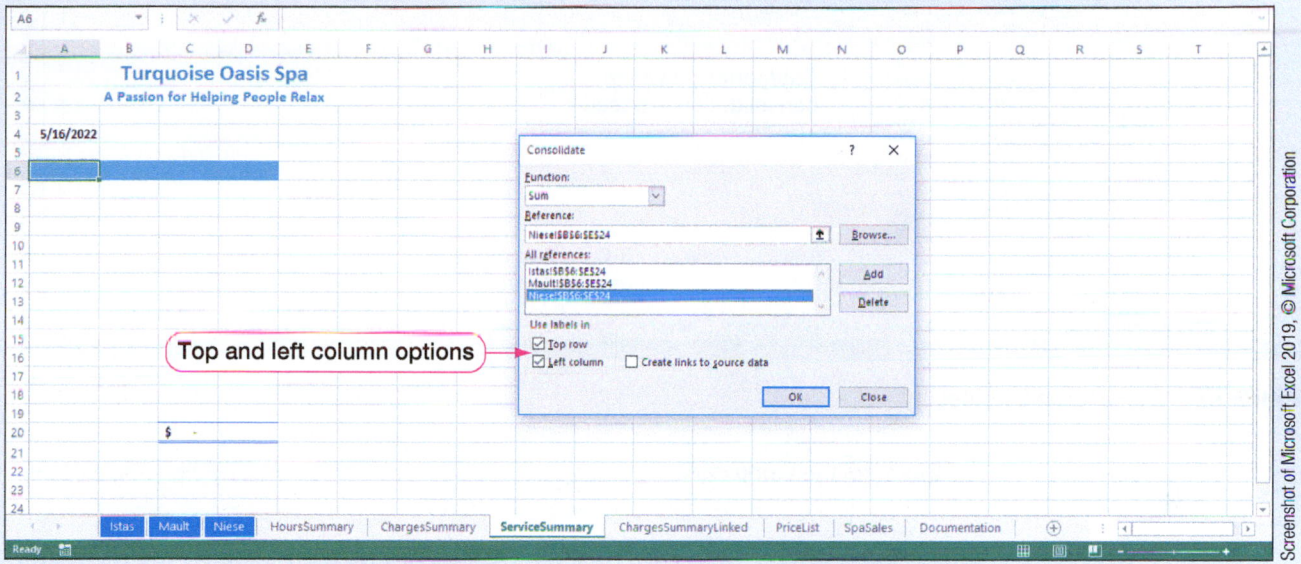

Figure 11 Consolidate dialog box options

f. Click **OK** in the Consolidate dialog box.

g. Click cell **A6**, and type Service—the Consolidate function does not copy the title of the far-left column—and then press Ctrl+Enter. Row 10 will be blank because there are rows in each worksheet for times that are blank, and this is the consolidation of those rows.

h. Select columns **A:D**. Click the **Home** tab, and in the Cells group, click **Format**, and then select **AutoFit Column Width**.

i. Click cell **D20**, type =SUM(TotalCharges3D) and then press Ctrl+Enter. This SUM function uses the 3-D named range created in an earlier exercise.

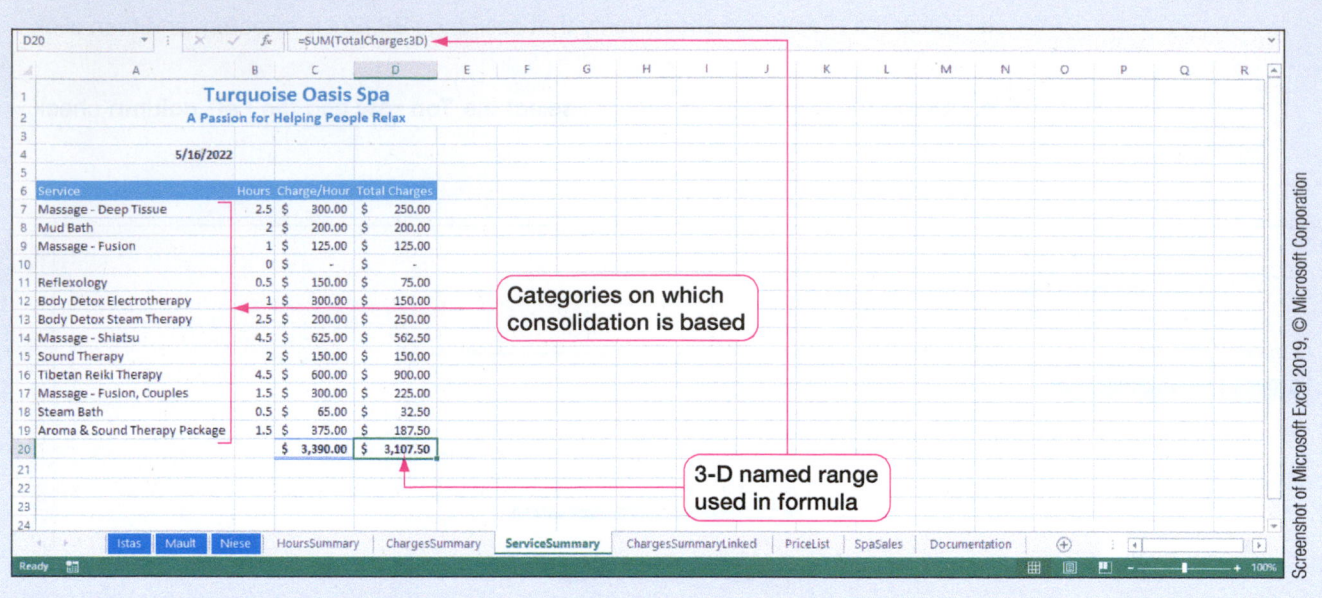

Figure 12 Consolidate by category

    j. **Save** 🖫 the workbook.

Creating Links to Source Data in a Consolidation

A data consolidation may contain links to source data that will include the cell references from other worksheets that contributed to the consolidated data result. The source cell reference details are placed into hidden rows that can be viewed if necessary.

    A consolidation that includes links to source data must be placed into a worksheet that is separate from all source data. The Consolidate feature cannot create links to the worksheet that contains the consolidation. Be aware that if you create links to source data then you will not be able to edit the data in the consolidation.

REAL WORLD ADVICE	Considerations for Including Links to Source Data

When data is consolidated and links to the source data are included, Excel will update the consolidated data when the source data changes. However, you would not be able to update the consolidated data manually. If you want to be able to update consolidated data manually, then do not create links to the source data.

In this exercise, you will create a linked consolidation of sales by appointment time.

 **E07.12**

SIDE NOTE
Alternate Method
When selecting the references to consolidate, you can also use the Collapse 🔼 and Expand 🔽 buttons in the Reference box.

To Consolidate with Links to Source Data

a. Click the **ChargesSummaryLinked** worksheet, and then click cell **A6**. Click the **Data** tab, and in the Data Tools group, click **Consolidate**. In the Consolidate dialog box, make sure **Sum** is selected in the Function box, and then, if necessary, click the **Reference** box.

b. Click the **Istas** worksheet, select cell range **A6:F24**, and then, in the Consolidate dialog box, click **Add**. Click the **Mault** worksheet, verify that cell range A6:F24 is selected, and then click **Add**. Click the **Niese** worksheet, verify that cell range A6:F24 is selected, and then click **Add**.

c. Under the Use labels in section, select the **Top row** check box, select the **Left column** check box, and then select the **Create links to source data** check box.

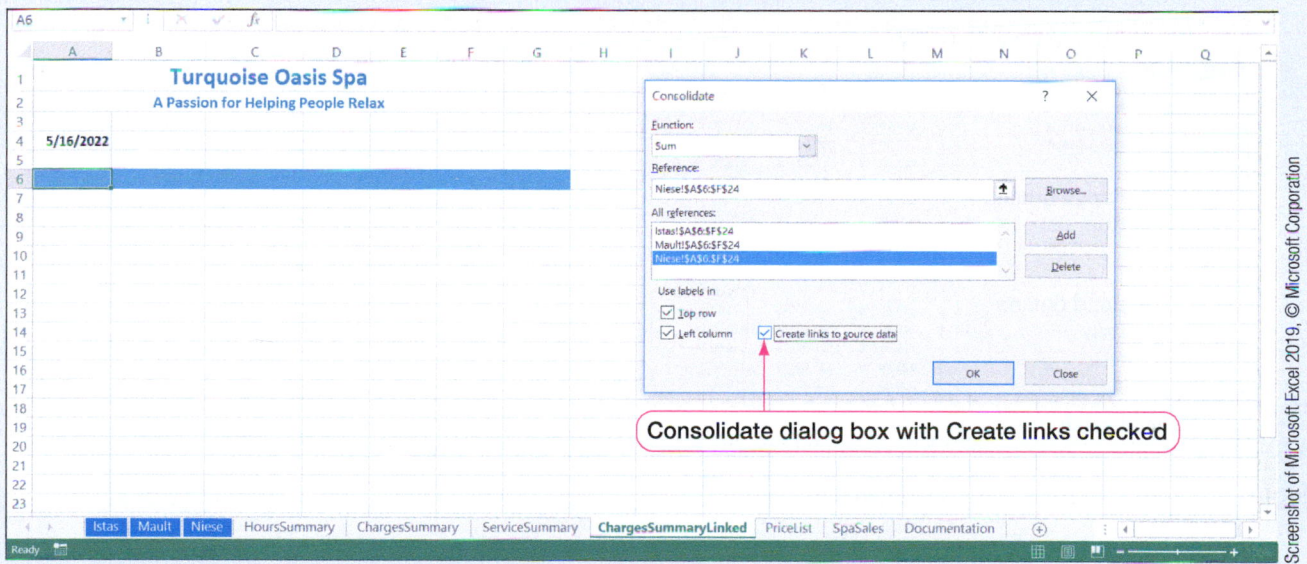

Consolidate dialog box with Create links checked

Figure 13   Consolidate dialog box with link box checked

d. Click **OK**. Select columns **A:G**. Click the **Home** tab, and in the Cells group, click **Format**, and then select **AutoFit Column Width**.

e. Select cell range **A10:A78**. The hidden rows include the links to the consolidated data. On the Home tab, in the Number group, click the **Number Format** arrow, and then select **More Number Formats**. In the Category box, click **Time**, and then in the Type box, click **1:30 PM**. Click **OK**.

f. Click the **Expand Outline** button ➕ next to row 14.

Rows 11:13, which were previously hidden, are revealed. Notice that the file name for your workbook is shown in column B. Consolidation can be used among multiple workbooks, and column B identifies the source workbook for each item of data. Because you are consolidating sheets in a single workbook, column B is irrelevant.

Notice that column C is empty. Service names are text and cannot be summated, so column C does not contain any information. Further, Charge/Hour in column E is not particularly informative. A sum of Charge/Hour is not a meaningful number—its inclusion, while necessary for consolidation, is not meaningful.

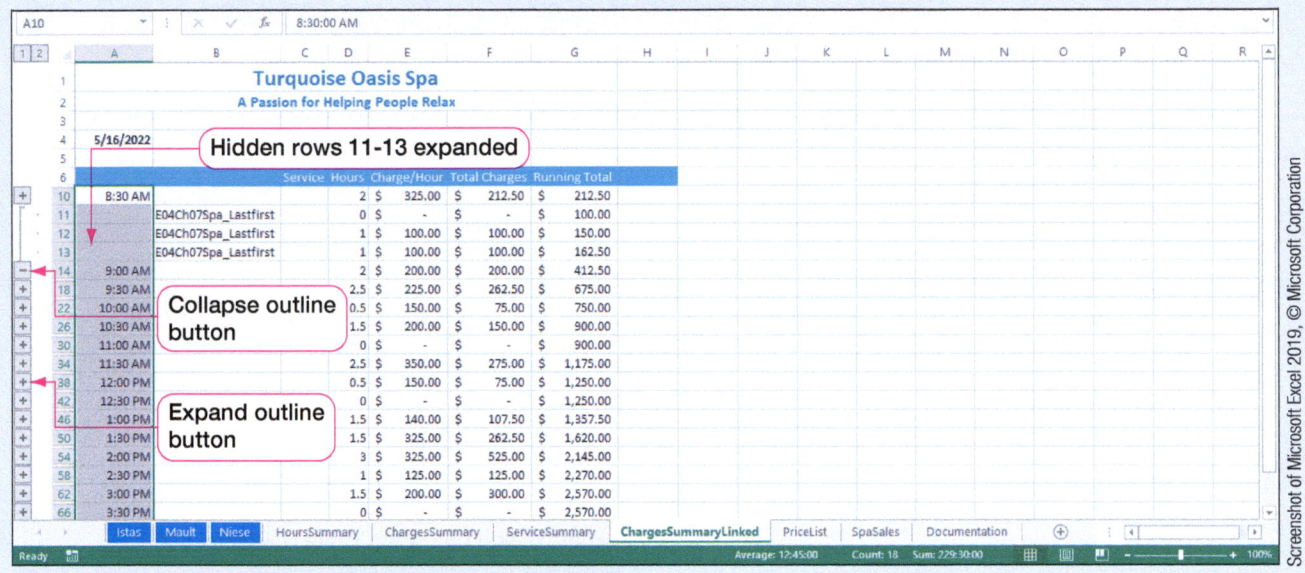

Figure 14   Hidden rows in consolidated summary

g. Click the **Level 2** outline button [2] just to the left of the Select All button ◢. The source data that contributes to each of the subtotals for a category—time in this case—is expanded.

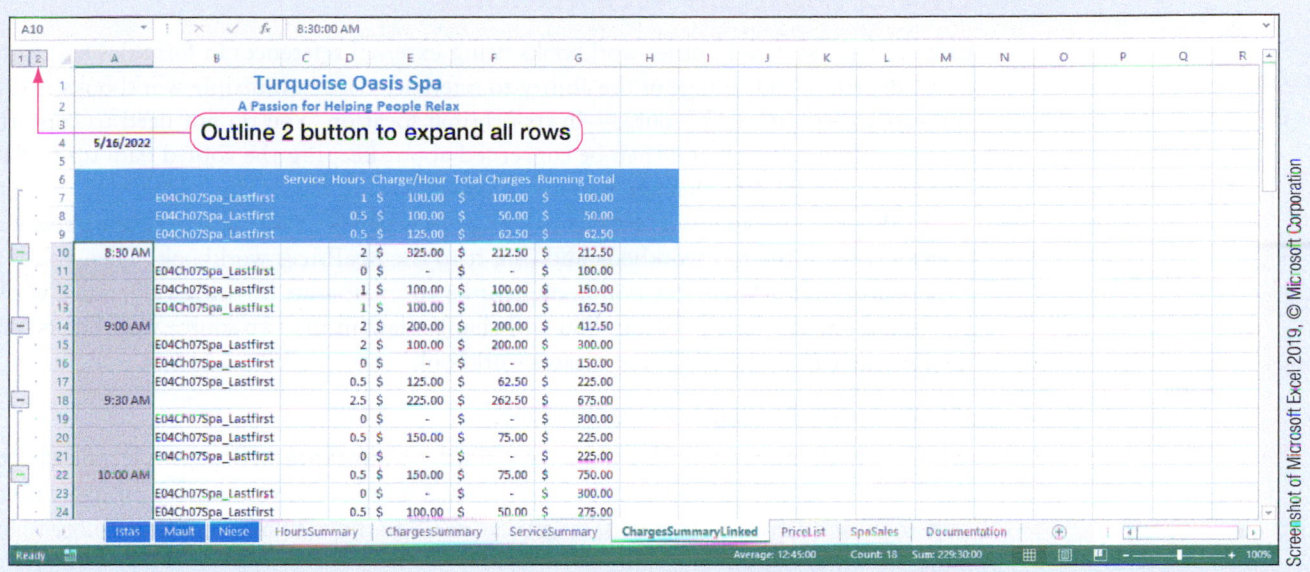

Figure 15 Level 2 outline in consolidated summary

Screenshot of Microsoft Excel 2019, © Microsoft Corporation

h. Click cell **G11**.

Notice the contents in the formula bar. The 100.00 in cell G11 came from source data in the Istas worksheet, in cell F8. Because a linked consolidation keeps track of the locations of source data, any changes to source data are automatically reflected in the consolidation.

i. Click the **Istas** worksheet, and then press Ctrl+Home.

j. **Save** 🖫 the workbook. If you need to take a break before finishing this chapter, now is a good time.

REAL WORLD ADVICE   **Consolidating between Different Workbooks**

You can consolidate not only worksheets, but also workbooks. The easiest way to do this is to have all the source workbooks open, start defining the consolidation, and then navigate to each workbook, select the source range with the mouse, and add the reference to the consolidation. This type of consolidation is useful if you have staff members using similarly structured workbooks and need to combine the data for a summary. If you know you are going to need this kind of summary information, it may be useful to provide your staff or group members with templates to work from or some other standard worksheet so that, when it comes time to collaborate, it will be quick and easy for one person to do.

Using Multiple Workbooks

Excel can access data in other workbooks using external references in formulas and functions. A primary advantage of the ability to reference data in multiple workbooks is that you can access data at its source—in its original location. You do not need to copy the data to your workbook and then be concerned about keeping the copied data up to date when the original data changes.

In this section, you will work with multiple workbooks at the same time. You will create a copy of the Spa workbook and link it to the SpaPrices workbook. Then you will create copies of the SpaPrices workbook in order to collaborate by using two source workbooks and one master workbook. You will change data in the two source workbooks, and then merge the changes into the master workbook.

Work with Multiple Workbooks

Working with multiple workbooks is very similar to working with multiple worksheets. Excel 2019 opens each workbook in an individual window, so you can use multiple monitors to view different workbooks, or you can arrange the windows on one monitor to see multiple workbooks at one time.

Data can be referenced between workbooks using 3-D ranges and formulas, so when the source workbook is updated, the changes flow through to the summary workbook. You can also choose whether to link workbooks to make the updating automatic.

Viewing Multiple Workbooks at One Time

When you want to view multiple workbooks on one screen, you can choose how they are arranged. Once you have all the workbooks open on your desktop, you can choose to arrange them in four different ways: Tiled, Horizontal, Vertical, or Cascade. How you choose to view them will be determined by how you want to work with them and your personal preference.

In this exercise, you will open another workbook along with the Spa workbook that is already open, and then you will view the two workbooks in different views.

 **E07.13**

To View Multiple Workbooks at One Time

a. If you took a break, open the **e04ch07Spa_LastFirst** workbook.

b. Click the **File** tab, and then click **Open**. Navigate to where your student data files are located, click **e04ch07SpaPrices**, and then click **Open**. Click **Enable Editing** if necessary. The two workbook windows will cascade, one in front of the other.

> #### Troubleshooting
> Do you have more than two workbooks open? All open workbooks will be included in this arrangement, so if you do not want to see a particular workbook, be sure to close it and arrange the workbooks again.

MAC COMPATIBILITY
The Tiled Feature Not Available on a Mac
Click the Window menu, click Arrange, select Tiled, and then click OK.

c. Click the **View** tab, and in the Window group, click **Arrange All**, click the **Tiled** option if necessary, and then click **OK**.

Notice that the workbooks are resized to fit on one screen. To edit a workbook, click that workbook to make it active, and then make your changes.

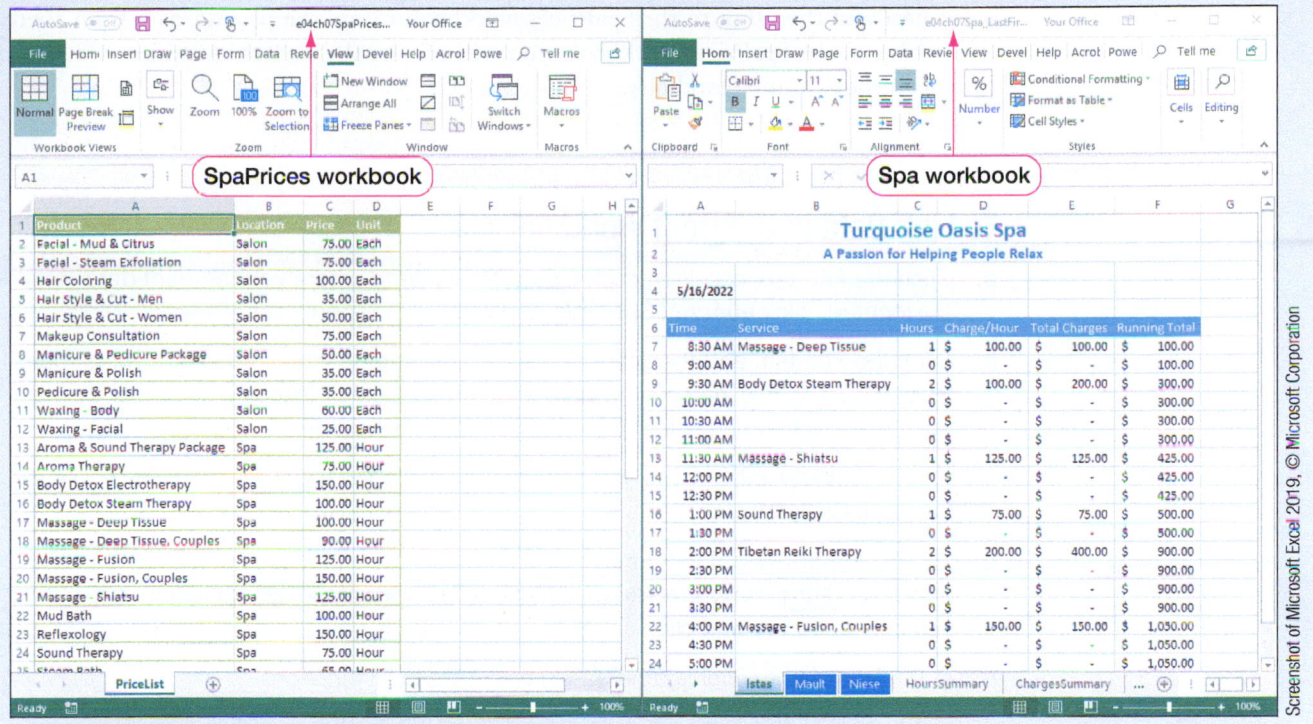

Figure 16 Workbooks arranged with the Tiled option

d. On either of the workbooks, click **Arrange All** again, click the **Horizontal** option, and then click **OK**.

Notice that the workbooks are resized to fit the width of the screen, one above the other.

e. Save and close **e04ch07Spa_LastFirst** but keep **e04ch07SpaPrices** open for use in the next exercise.

f. **Maximize** ☐ the e04ch07SpaPrices window.

Linking Workbooks

When you need data from a different workbook, the advantage to referencing that data at its source rather than copying it into your workbook is that when the source data is changed, your workbook can also be changed to reflect the most current data. Excel recognizes when a workbook is linked to another workbook or workbooks through external references, and it will prompt you when the workbook is opened and ask whether you want to update links. Which option you choose will depend on whether you want the workbook to be updated.

Linking to other workbooks does create some potential problems, however. Links to workbooks are easily broken, especially if files are moved or deleted. Excel tries to prevent this from happening by using relative addresses. In a relative link, the address of a linked workbook is defined by its location in relation to the location of the destination workbook. If either workbook is moved when the destination workbook is closed, the links will be broken. It is considered good practice to store all workbooks that are in a linked relationship together in the same folder if possible.

When you use a relative link, the reference will include the file name in brackets, the sheet name, an exclamation point, and then the following cell reference.

=[filename.xlsx] worksheet name!cell reference

In this exercise, you will use a copy of the Spa workbook that excludes the PriceList worksheet and then link to the SpaPrices workbook to use the pricing data from there. By linking to the SpaPrices workbook, you will correct the errors that appear when you first open the SpaLink workbook.

 **E07.14**

To Link Data in Different Workbooks

a. Click the **File** tab, and then click **Open**. Navigate to where your student data files are located, click **e04ch07SpaLink**, and then click **Open**.

b. Click the **File** tab, and then click **Save As**. Navigate to where you are saving your files, click the File name box, and then type e04ch07SpaLink_LastFirst using your last and first name. Click **Save**. Click **Enable Editing** if necessary.

c. Click the **View** tab, in the Window group, click **Arrange All**, and then select **Vertical**. Click **OK**.

d. On the **e04ch07SpaLink_LastFirst** workbook, click the **Istas** worksheet, press and hold Shift, click the **Niese** worksheet to group the worksheets, and then scroll if necessary and click cell **D7**.

e. In the formula bar, highlight **#REF!** in the VLOOKUP function.

Notice that all the formulas in columns D through F return a #REF! error. Because the PriceList worksheet which the formula was referring to was removed, all the formulas that referenced that worksheet have a cell reference error. You will replace that missing reference with a reference to the SpaPrices workbook.

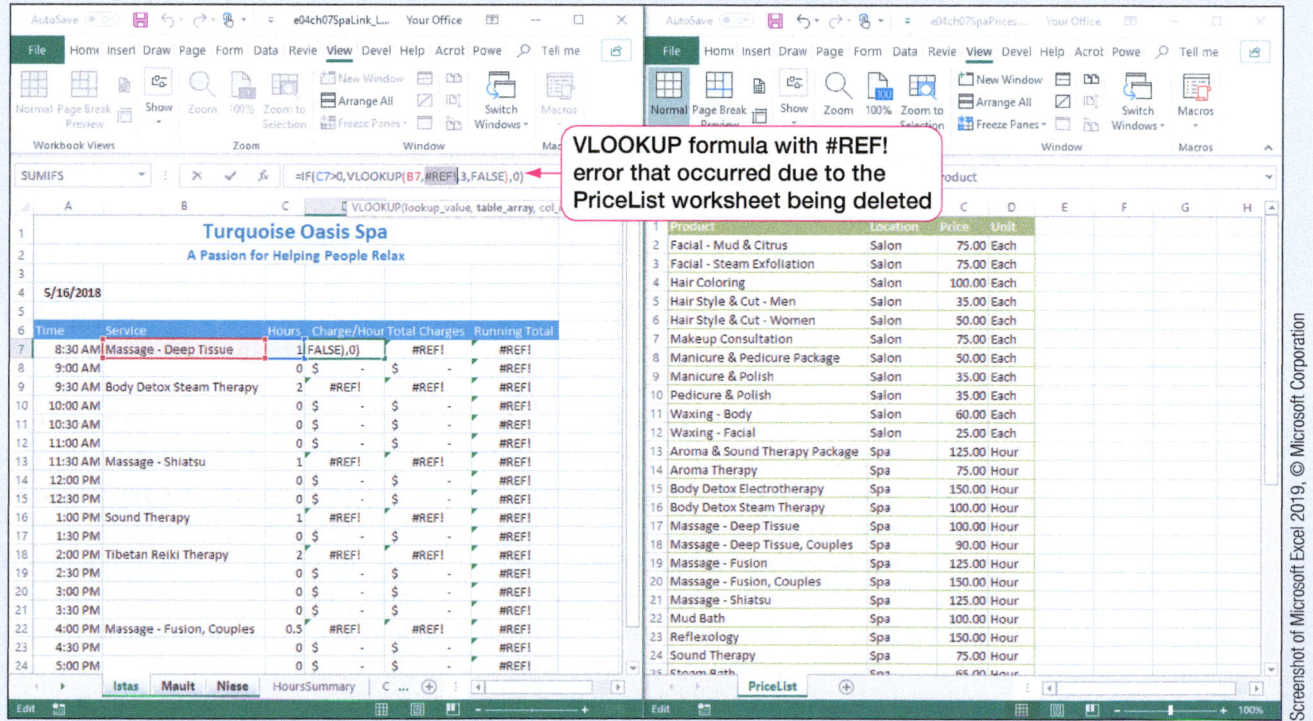

Figure 17 #REF error in the formula

f. Click the **e04ch07SpaPrices** workbook, and then select cell range **A2:D26**. This becomes the new lookup range for the VLOOKUP function.

The formula bar should show =IF(C7>0,VLOOKUP(B7,[e04ch07SpaPrices.xlsx] PriceList!$A$2:$D$26,3,FALSE),0).

> **Troubleshooting**
>
> Remember that the #REF! error in Excel ends with an exclamation point! Be sure to highlight all of #REF! in the above step, or the correction to the formula will not work. If you have difficulty using the mouse, try using the Shift + → keys to select #REF!.

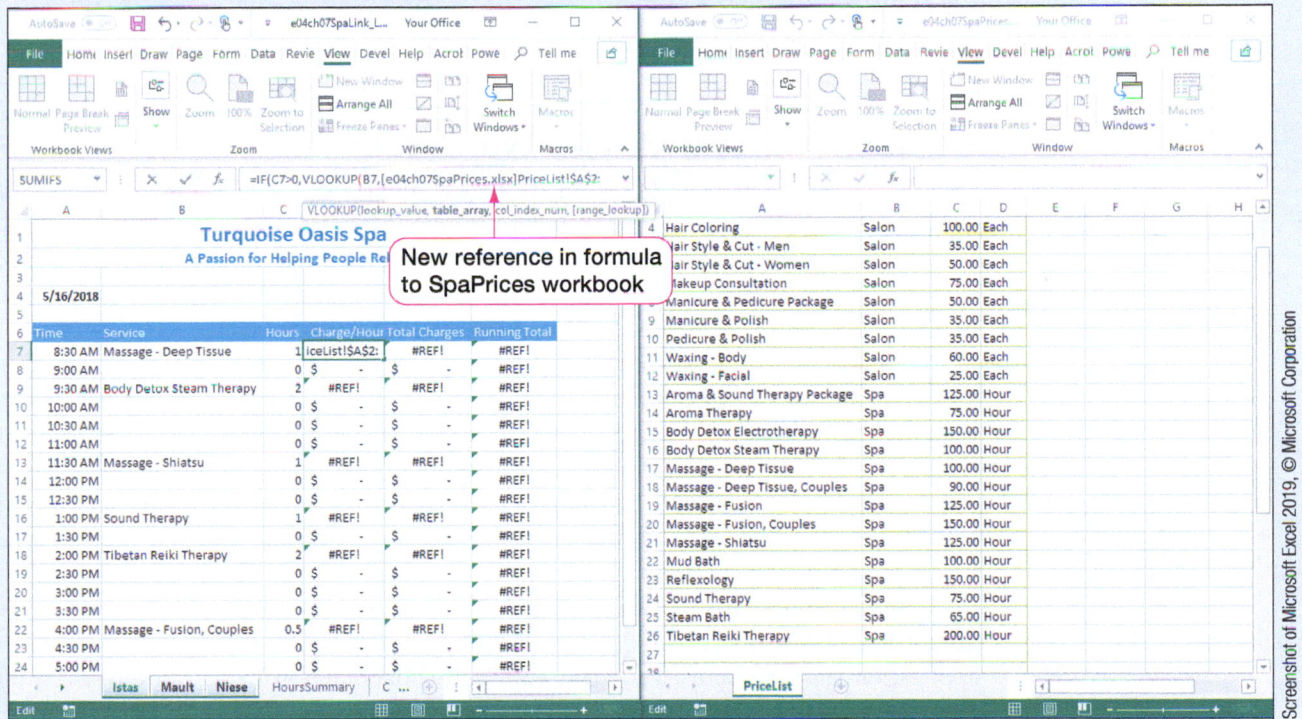

Figure 18 New reference to a workbook

g. Press Ctrl + Enter. Copy the formula in cell D7 to cell range **D8:D24**, and then press Ctrl + Home. This will eliminate all the #REF! errors on the worksheet.

h. Click the **HoursSummary** worksheet to ungroup the worksheets, **Save** 🖫 and then **Close** ✕ the workbook. Maximize the **e04ch07SpaPrices** workbook.

REAL WORLD ADVICE	Planning Linked Workbooks

- Make your links easy to track: Consider changing the formatting of a linked cell to something identifiable so you can easily identify cells with a linked formula.

- Avoid circular links: Workbooks should not have links to each other. The links should be one-way from one workbook to another. A circular link will slow down opening and updating the workbooks.

- Turn on Automatic Calculation: Source workbooks to which you link should have automatic calculation turned on to make updating quicker and error free. This is the automatic default setting, but it can be verified under Options on the File tab by opening the Options dialog box and scrolling to the Formulas section.

- Consider where you will store your files: If one file is stored on a network drive, and the other linked file is stored on your computer's hard drive, someone opening the file on the network drive will not have access to the linked file on your hard drive. This means that links will not be updated.

Collaborate Using Multiple Workbooks

Collaboration allows workbooks to be shared among different users. **Co-authoring** allows two or more users to open and work on an Excel workbook at the same time. When co-authoring, users can see each other's changes in real time—just a matter of a few seconds. Co-authoring has replaced the "Shared Workbooks" feature in the previous versions of the software due to the Shared Workbooks limitations.

To be able to use the co-authoring feature, an Office 365 subscription and the latest version of Office must be installed. Before beginning, users should be signed in with their Office subscription account. The document you wish to share will be stored in the cloud, such as the OneDrive or SharePoint Online library. Note, SharePoint sites not hosted by Microsoft will not support co-authoring. Finally, to use the co-authoring feature, files must be saved as an Excel workbook. Co-authoring does not support Strict Open XML Spreadsheet format.

Co-authoring allows individuals to work collaboratively on a workbook even if they do not have Excel installed by using Excel Online. **Excel Online** is a web-based Excel application that can be used to view, edit, and collaborate on Excel workbooks. While many of the features in Excel are available in Excel online, not all features are supported. Excel online can be used by having a OneDrive or a SharePoint account. **OneDrive** is Microsoft's online file hosting service. OneDrive allows users to store, retrieve, edit, and share files. **SharePoint** is a document management and collaboration service developed by Microsoft. It is often used as a content management system for internal purposes. SharePoint can be used to store, organize, share, and access information from any device.

To Co-Author a Workbook

Meda Rodate has requested you update the salon and spa price list. You are able to update the salon product list but will need assistance with the Spa product list in the future. Therefore, you will share the workbook with your co-workers so they will be able to update the workbook at the same time or in the future.

 **E07.15**

To Co-Author a Workbook

SIDE NOTE
Online Documents
Once you have saved a file to OneDrive or a SharePoint site, you can access it by logging into your OneDrive or Share-Point account, selecting the file, and then clicking Edit in Excel.

> **Grader Heads Up**
> The MyLab IT Grader version of this project will not complete the co-authoring workbook exercise.

NOTE: This exercise cannot be completed by yourself. Check with your instructor on how to proceed with this exercise.

a. Ensure you are logged into your **Office 365** account.

b. Click the **e04ch07SpaPrices** workbook. Click **File**, click **Save As**, and then select the online location—such as OneDrive—where you will store your data file.

c. Click **More options**, and then type **e04ch07SpaPricesShared_LastFirst** using your last and first name.

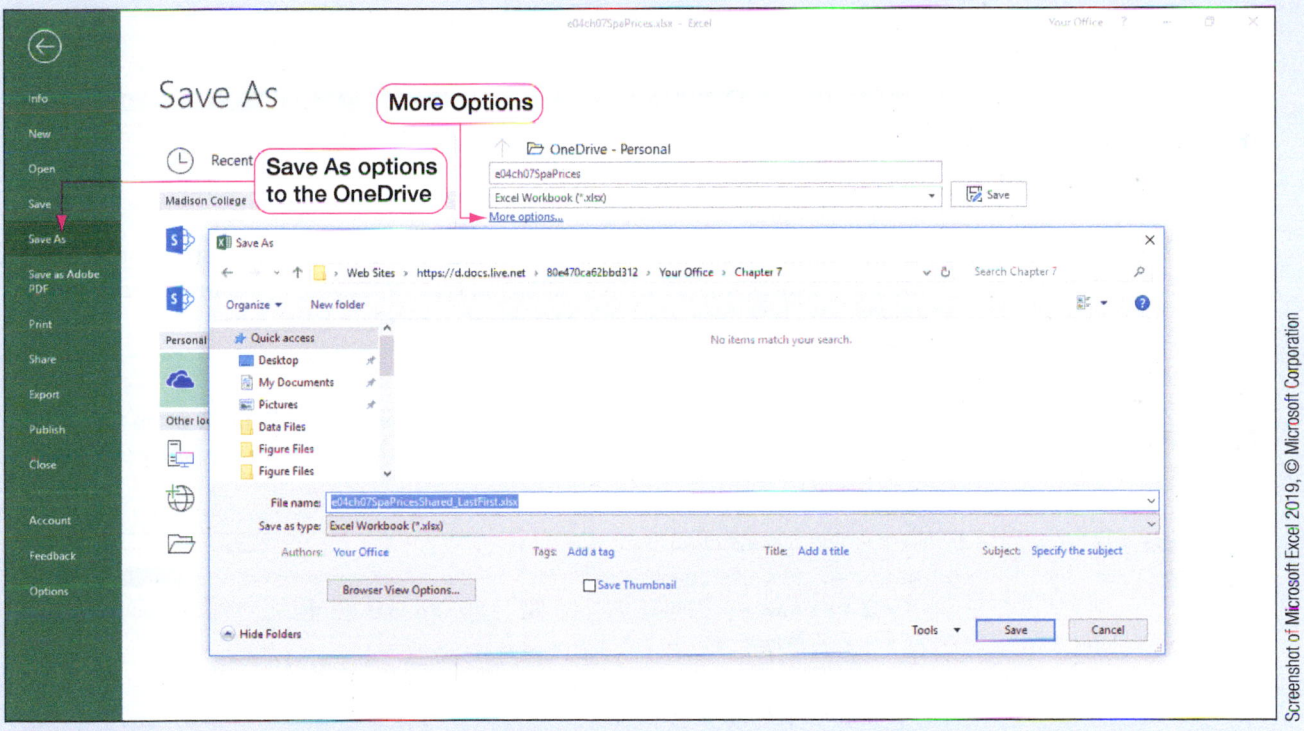

Figure 19 Saving a workbook to the OneDrive

SIDE NOTE
Alternate Method
You can also click the File tab, click Share, and then select your One-Drive account to share a workbook.

d. Click **Save**. You may see the notification stating the workbook is now being automatically saved.

Screenshot of Microsoft Excel 2019, © Microsoft Corporation

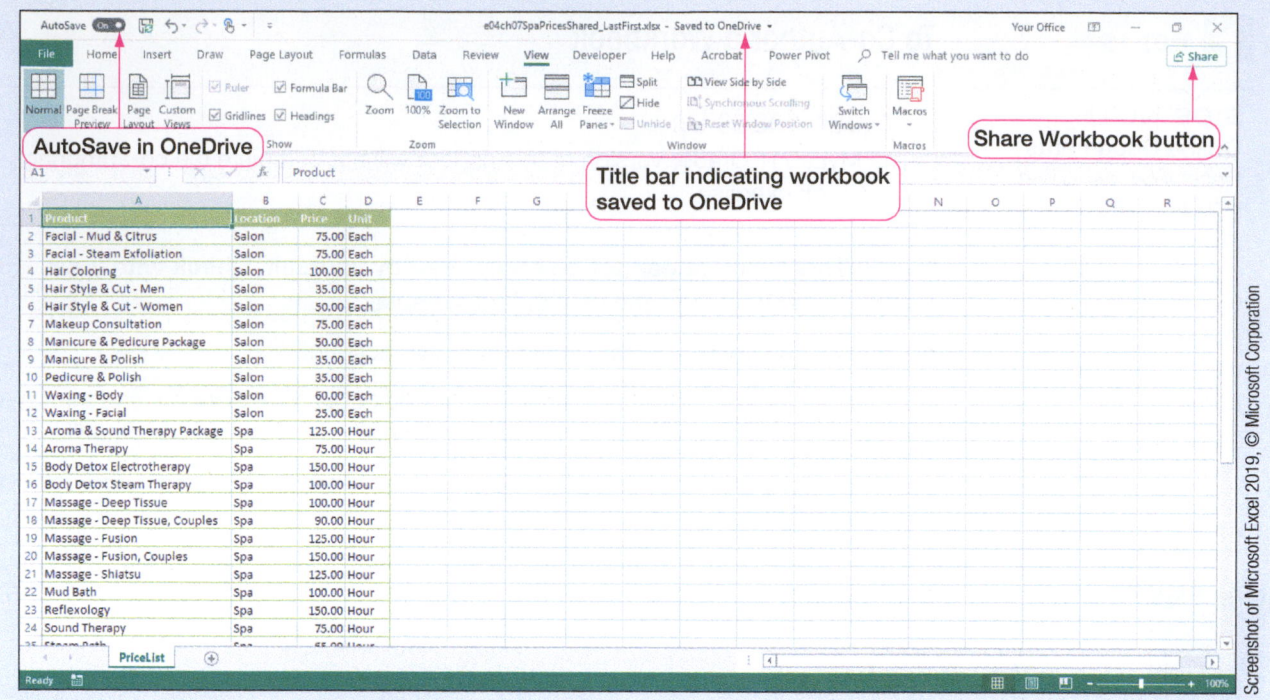

Figure 20 AutoSave in the OneDrive

Screenshot of Microsoft Excel 2019, © Microsoft Corporation

MAC COMPATIBILITY
Mac Alternate Method
There is not a Share pane on a Mac, however on the window drop down, click the File menu, click Share, and then Invite People.

e. Click **Share** in the upper-right corner of the workbook.

f. On the right-hand side of the Excel window, you will see a Share pane in which you can invite people to work on the workbook with you. In the **Invite People** box, check with your instructor on which email(s) to enter here.

g. Ensure **Can edit** is selected.

h. Type the message Please enter the new spa prices in column C once they have been updated.

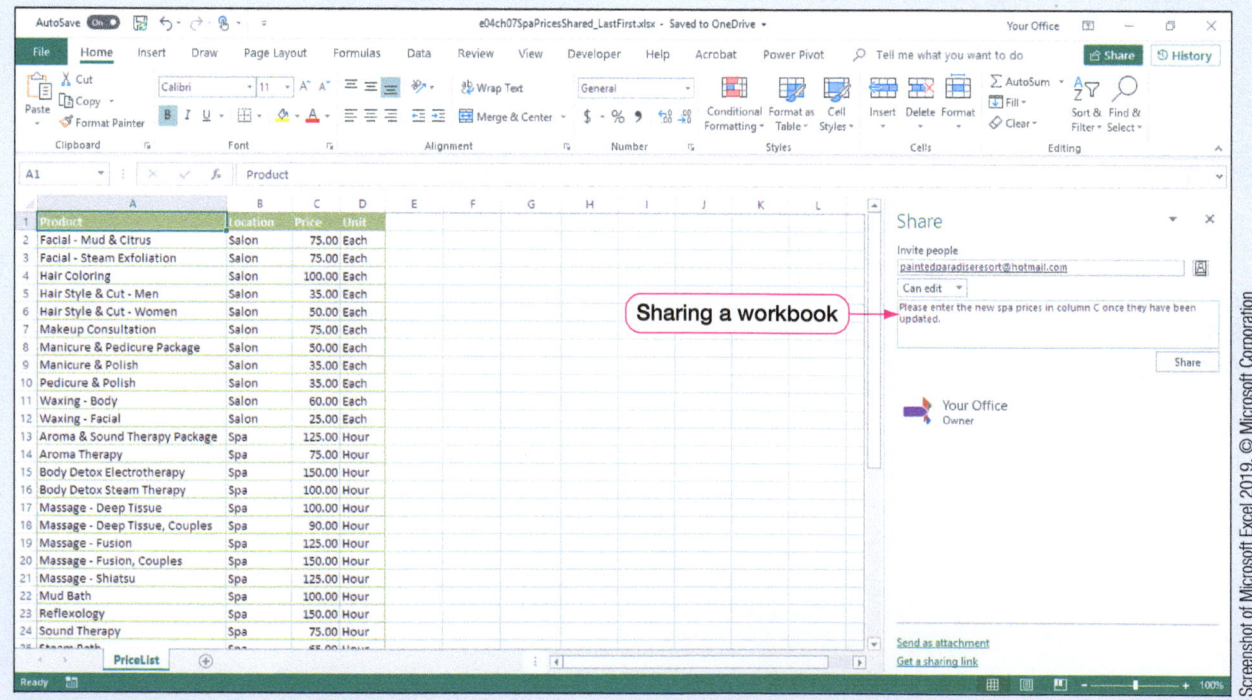

Figure 21 Sharing a workbook

Screenshot of Microsoft Excel 2019, © Microsoft Corporation

CHAPTER 7

SIDE NOTE

Excel Online

If working in Excel Online, the document owner will also be able to see other users and the changes actively being made in real time.

i. Click **Share**.

j. Enter the following data into the shared workbook.

Facial - Mud & Citrus	C2	100
Makeup Consultation	C7	100
Manicure & Pedicure Package	C8	70
Manicure & Polish	C9	45

k. Your partner or instructor should log into the email in which the workbook was shared, and then enter the following in the shared workbook.

Facial – Stream Exfoliation	C3	100
Pedicure & Polish	C10	50

l. As your partner is working, you will be able to watch their edits in real time.

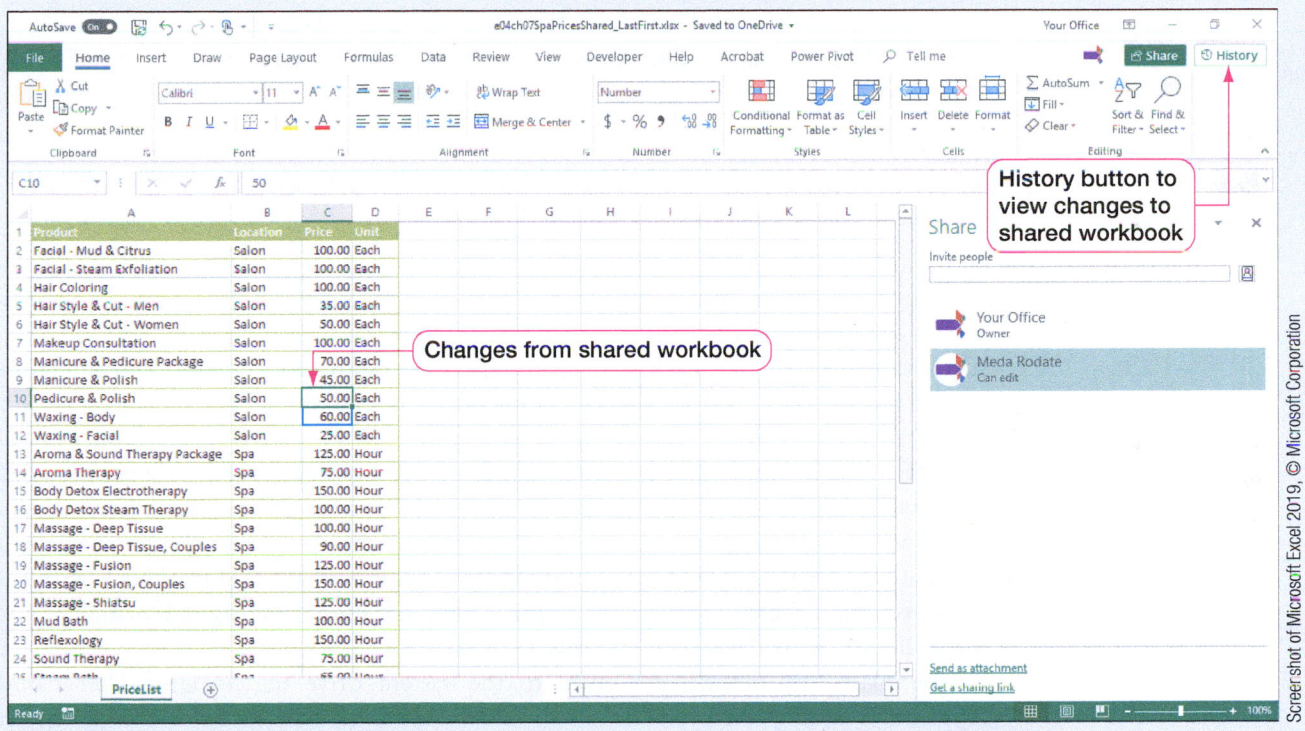

History button to view changes to shared workbook

Changes from shared workbook

Figure 22 Workbook collaboration

m. After your partner has had time to enter in the data in step k, click **Close** ⊠ to close the workbook.

n. If you are not storing your data files in OneDrive, download and save the shared workbook to the location where you are storing your files, and then exit OneDrive.

QUICK REFERENCE	Sharing a Workbook

In you are using the latest version of Excel or if you are using Office 365, you will notice the Share Workbook button is no longer available on the Review tab. Microsoft has instead moved to the co-authoring feature. If you do not have a OneDrive account, you can use the former method of sharing workbooks by following these steps:

- Click the **File** tab, click **Options**, and then select **Quick Access Toolbar**.
- Click the **Choose commands from** arrow, and then select **All Commands**.
- Scroll and select **Share Workbooks (Legacy)**, and then click **Add**.
- Scroll and select **Track Changes (Legacy)**, and then click **Add**.
- Scroll and select **Protect Sharing (Legacy)**, and then click **Add**.
- Scroll and select **Compare and Merge Workbooks**, click **Add**, and then click **OK**.
- Click the **Share Workbook** on the Quick Access Toolbar.
- On the Editing tab, click **Allow changes by more than one user** check box.
- On the Advanced tab, select the options you want to use for tracking changes, and then click **OK**.
- Click **File**, and then click **Save** to save the workbook. Shared will appear at the top of the Excel window.

Using and Creating Templates

In its simplest form, an Excel **template** is a workbook that provides a starting point for building other similar workbooks. In its intended form, a template is a worksheet framework—a worksheet that contains cell formats, structural data such as column headings and data labels, and formulas necessary to achieve the template's purpose, such as totaling invoice line items, calculating sales tax, or tracking and totaling the time spent on a project.

A template is just a workbook saved with a different file extension—the .xltx extension. If stored in the default location, templates do have one special differentiator that may make their creation advantageous: They are readily available via the File tab when a new workbook is being created. In addition, when a template is opened from the default template location, the file will be saved by default as a normal Excel workbook with the .xlsx extension, thereby leaving the original template file in its original form, ready to use again for future development needs.

Templates, by default, are saved to the system drive in the Users\User name\ AppData\Roaming\Microsoft\Templates folder. Any templates added to that folder are available from the File tab.

Any workbook can be used as a template for another workbook. Simply open a workbook and save it with the template extension and a new file name.

In this section, for the spa, you will use a local template for a to-do list. Then you will search online for a template to use for a group calendar. Finally, you will use the SpaSales workbook to create a template that the managers can use for each of the staff members.

Use Existing Templates

Microsoft Excel has several **local templates**, which are templates that are stored in the default Templates folder on your hard drive. On your hard drive, local templates are most likely stored in the Program Files\Microsoft Office\Templates\1033 folder. The number 1033 is the language ID number for English (US). This folder will change depending on which language version of Office you have installed. Templates for all the Office applications are stored in this folder.

Local templates are accessed from the File tab. You can add your own templates to the built-in templates folder by saving or moving your templates to that folder.

Using Local Templates

Local templates are the templates that are stored in the default Templates folder on your hard drive, and these are the templates you see when you click the File tab. They are commonly used, have formatting and other features already applied, and are ready for you to enter your personal data. Any data that appears in the template is there as an example, so be sure to delete that sample data before you save your workbook.

In this exercise, you will choose the Project tracker from the local templates to create a project list for the spa employees.

 E07.16

MAC COMPATIBILITY
Templates
In the search bar, type Project tracker.

To Find, Open, and Use a Local Template

a. If you took a break, open Excel. Click the **File** tab, click **New**, scroll through the list of templates, and then click **Project tracker**.

> **Troubleshooting**
>
> Microsoft frequently changes its templates, so you may not be able to find the Project tracker template as a local template. Either choose a different template that is local for this activity or search for the Project tracker template as an online template.

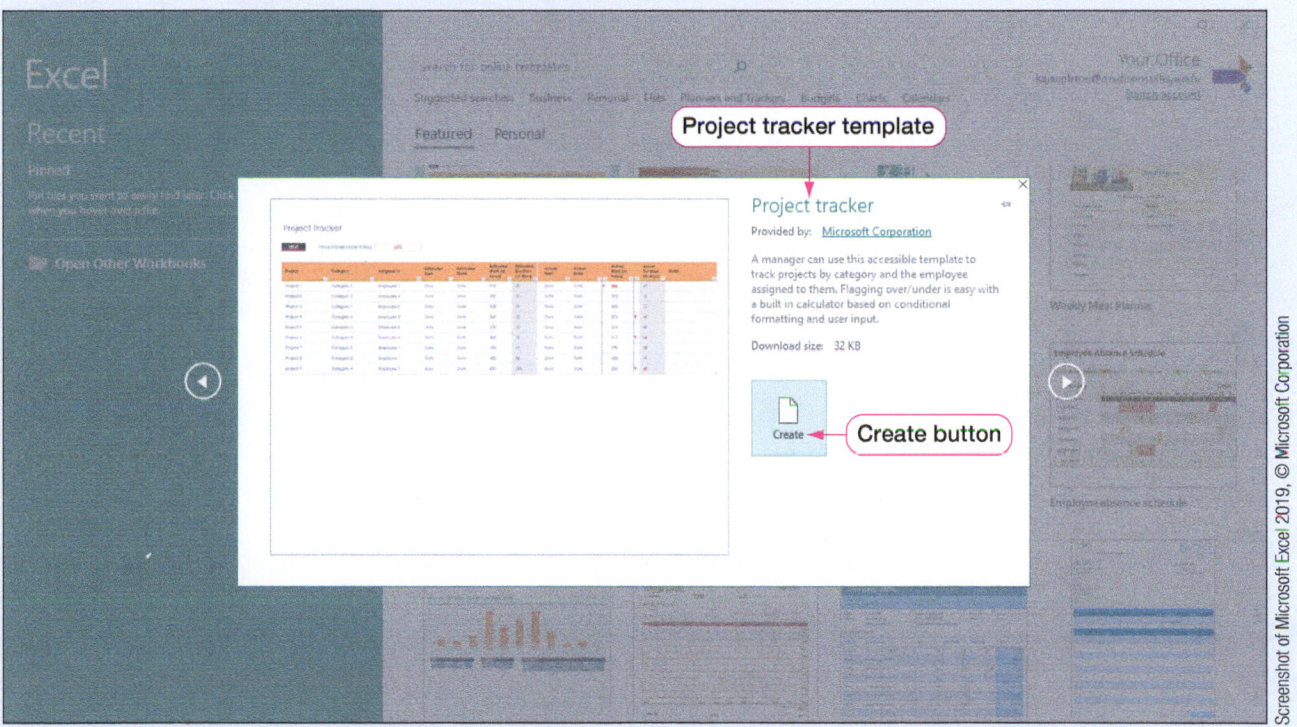

Figure 23 Creating a new template

b. Click **Create** to start using the template. Click the **File** tab, and then click **Save As**. Navigate to the folder where you are storing your files, and type e04ch07SpaProjects_LastFirst using your last and first name. Click **Save**.

c. Click the **Setup** worksheet, and then enter the following categories and employee information.

B5	Supplies	C5	Istas
B6	Inventory	C6	Niese
B7	Subscriptions	C7	Mault

d. Delete the contents of cell range **B8:B10** and then click cell **B8**.

e. Click the **Project Tracker** worksheet. Click cell **B5**, type Order supplies and then press [Tab]. In cell **C5**, click the arrow to the right of the cell. Notice the list available is the list you entered in step c. Select **Supplies**.

f. Enter the remaining data for the Spa in rows 5 and 6 as shown in the table below by replacing the sample data already there. Notice the lists available when you click certain cells. You have the option to select from the list or to type in your value.

Row	Project	Category	Assigned To	Estimated Start	Estimated Finish	Estimated Work (in hours)
5			Mault	5/7/22	5/10/22	3
6	Purge inventory	Inventory	Istas	4/3/22	4/11/22	8

g. Select cell ranges **B7:G13** and **I5:L13**, and then press [Delete] to delete the contents of the cells. This will delete only the content and none of the formatting in these cells. Click cell **B5**.

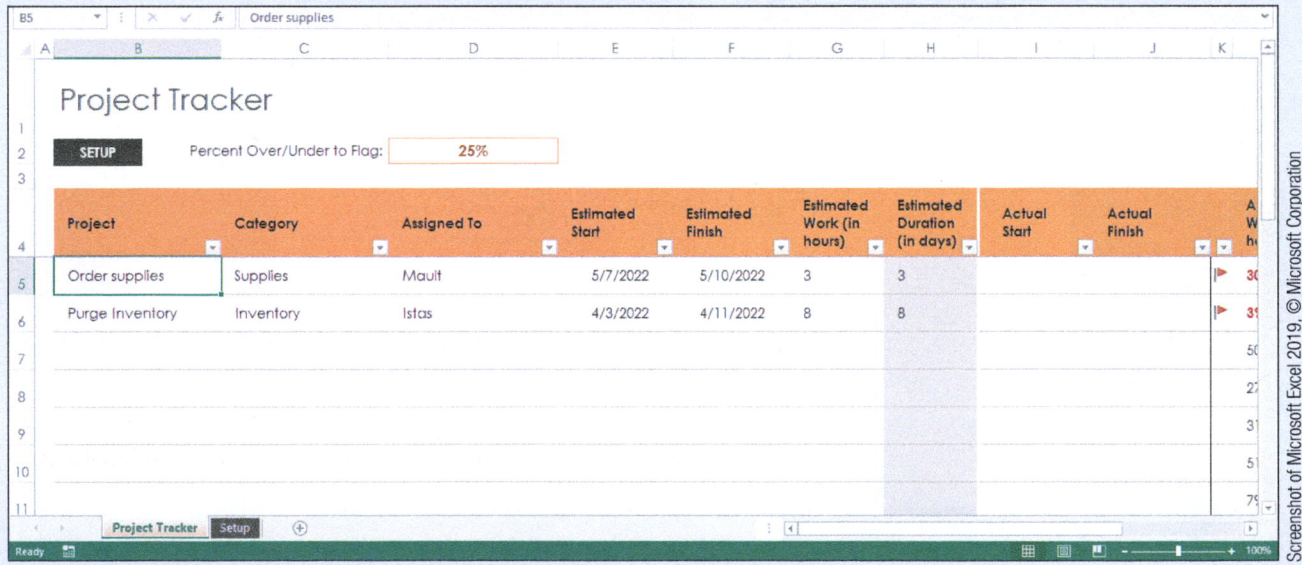

Figure 24 Workbook created from a local template

h. Save the workbook, click the **File** tab, and then click **Close**. Keep Excel open for the next exercise.

 **CONSIDER THIS** | **How Could Excel Facilitate Work as a Team?**

So far in this chapter, you have learned how to group worksheets, consolidate worksheets, merge data from individual worksheets into a master worksheet, and build and use templates. Think about a couple of group or team projects you have been involved with in your educational career, and consider how the Excel capabilities listed above might have aided your efforts with the following.

- Tracking team member contributions to a project
- Tracking project progress toward completion
- Bringing the work of team members together into one coherent final product
- Supporting a team member who is struggling with a part of the project by facilitating the involvement of other team members' assistance

How else might Excel facilitate teamwork in your education? How about in your career?

Using Online Templates

Online templates are templates stored online that can be downloaded to your hard drive. There are thousands of Excel templates available online. Microsoft, through its template site at Office.com, fosters a community of Office users who download templates posted by other users. Users can rate templates on a scale of 1 to 5 stars. User ratings are averaged, and the average is posted next to each template.

Some people are very good at generating data through formulas and functions; others are experts at presenting information graphically or at formatting tabular content attractively. Office users can post their templates to Office.com so others can benefit from their expertise.

In this exercise, you will search for an online template and then use it to create an event calendar for the spa to provide to their customers.

 **E07.17**

MAC COMPATIBILITY
Online Template
Searching for templates online is not available on a Mac.

To Find, Open, and Use an Online Template

a. Click the **File** tab, and then click **New**.

b. In the Search for online templates box at the top of the window, type business calendar Click the **Search** button 🔍.

c. Scroll down until you see **Business Calendar (any year, Sun-Sat)**. The whole title is visible when you point to the icon for the template. Click the **Business Calendar (any year, Sun-Sat)** template.

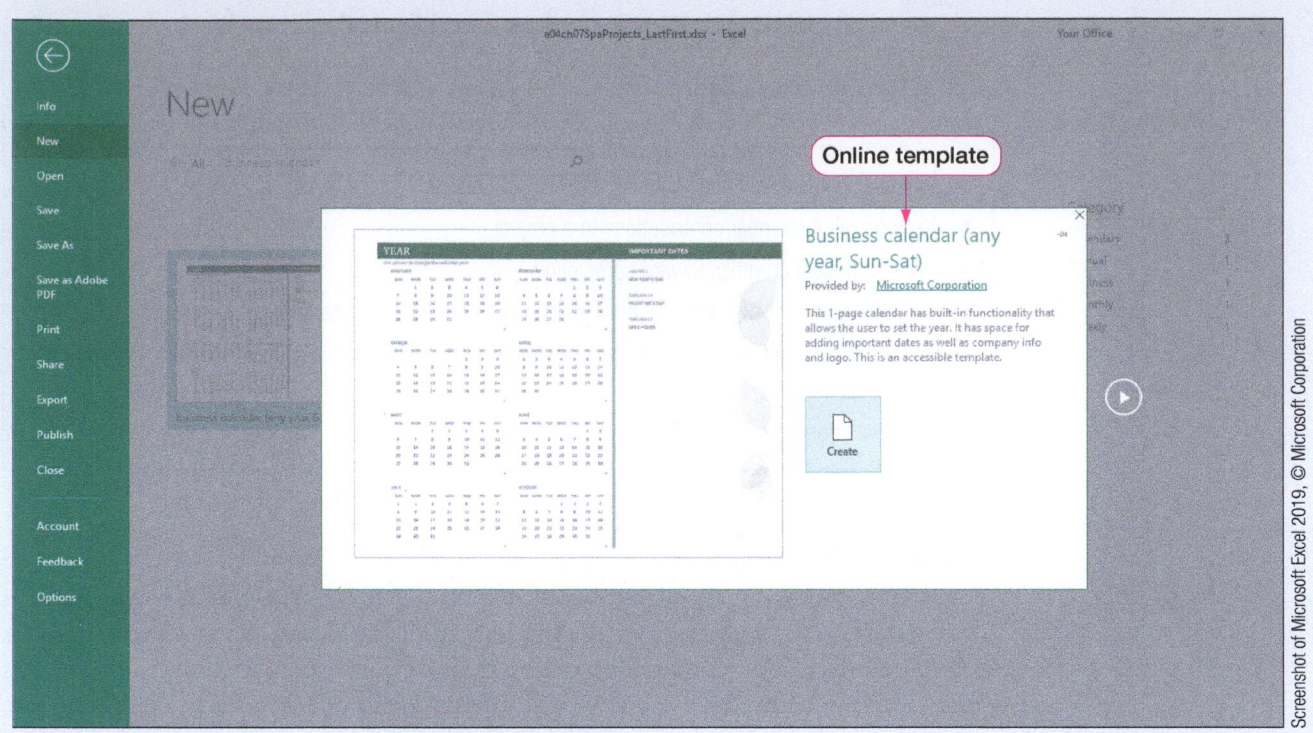

Figure 25 Small business calendar online template

d. Click **Create**. If necessary, in the Protected View bar at the top of the window, click **Enable Editing**.

e. Click the **File** tab, click **Save As**, and then navigate to where you are saving your files. In the File name box, type e04ch07SpaCalendar_LastFirst using your last and first name, and then click **Save**.

f. Review the information on the Start worksheet, and then delete the Start worksheet. On the **Yearly Calendar** worksheet, click cell **B1**, and then click the spinner next to the year. Change the year to **2022**.

g. Click cell **U44**, and then change the contents to 3356 Hemmingway Circle Change cell **U45** to Santa Fe, NM 87594 Change cell **U47** to 505.555.1564 Change cell **U48** to kmasters@paintedparadise.com Change cell **U49** to www.paintedparadiseresort.com

h. Right-click the image below the resort's website address, and then point to **Change Picture**. From the gallery, select **From File**. Navigate to your student files, select **e04ch07SpaLogo**, and then click **Insert**.

i. Click any cell to deselect the graphic, and then press $\boxed{\text{Ctrl}}$+$\boxed{\text{Home}}$. Click **Save** $\boxed{}$.

j. Click the **File** tab, and then click **Close** to close the workbook. Keep Excel open for the next exercise.

Create Templates from an Existing Workbook

Creating templates is really not different from creating workbooks. You simply remove any specific data and save the workbook as a template. You can create templates from your own workbooks, or you can create them by modifying a template to better fit your needs.

Creating a Template from a Workbook

The SpaSales workbook has the time slots and schedules for one day: December 16, 2022. This is a good format to use for other dates, especially because the Spa workbook uses this format to summarize the data. You will delete the date, service, and duration details but leave the appointment times and therapist names so each day can be updated easily. You will also change the tab name to something less specific.

 E07.18

To Create a Template from a Workbook

Grader Heads Up
The MyLab IT Grader version of this project will not complete the creation of a template.

SIDE NOTE
Alternate Method
Use the Ctrl + Shift + ↓ to select the column.

a. Click the **File** tab, click **Open**, navigate to your student files, and then click **e04ch-07SpaSales**. Click **Open**. If necessary, click **Enable Editing**.

b. Select cell range **A2:A55**, and then press Delete to delete the dates.

c. Select cell range **D2:E55**, and then press Delete to delete the service descriptions and hours.

d. Right-click the **MondaySales** worksheet, select **Rename**, type **DailySales** and press Enter. Press Ctrl + Home.

e. Click the **File** tab, click **Save As**, and then navigate to the location where you are saving your files. In the File name box, type **e04ch07SpaSalesTemplate_LastFirst** using your last and first name.

f. In the Save as type list, click **Excel Workbook**, and then select **Excel Template**. Navigate to the location where you are saving your files, and then click **Save**.

Notice the file extension of .xltx. This indicates that the file has been saved as a template.

MAC COMPATIBILITY
Mac Alternate Method
Click the File menu, select Save as Template. Type the file name in the Save As box. Select Folder in the Where arrow, and the file format "Excel Template" is already selected.

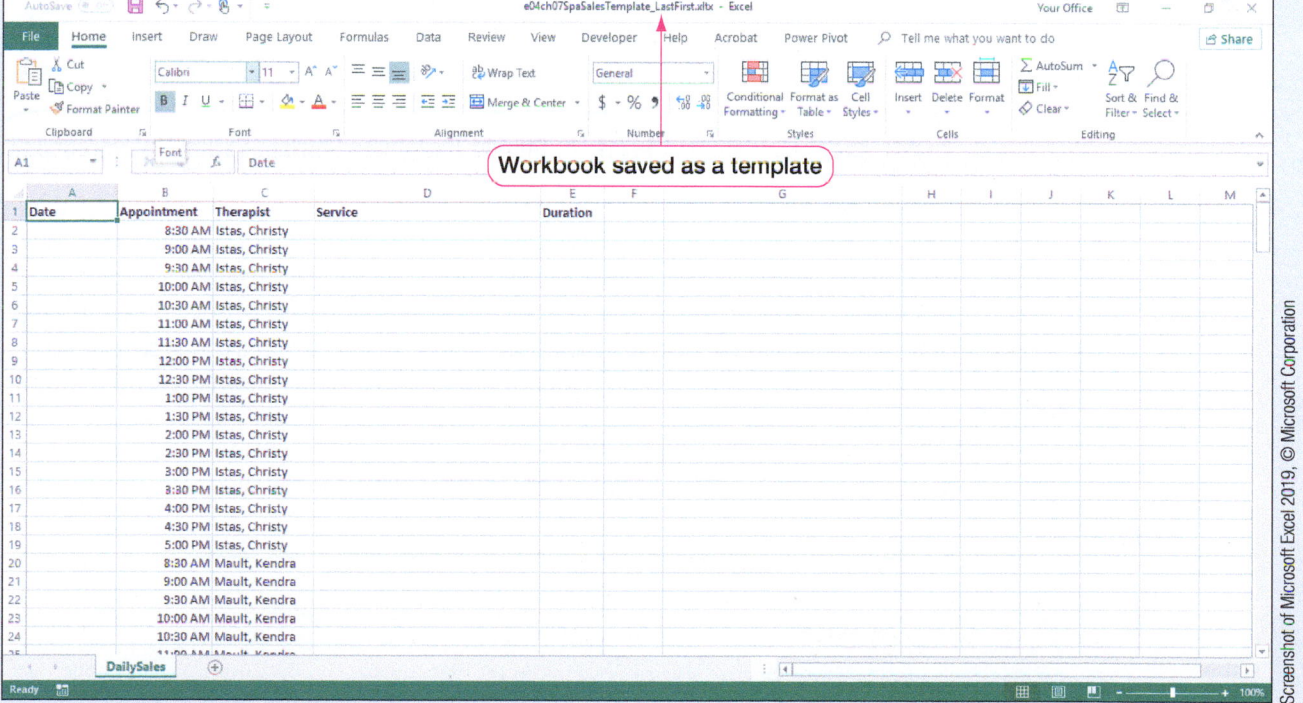

Figure 26 Excel workbook saved as a template

g. Close the template file. Navigate to the location where you are storing your files and open the file **e04ch07SpaSalesTemplate_LastFirst**. Notice the name of the workbook on the title bar includes a number 1 and is now in an Excel workbook—not template—format.

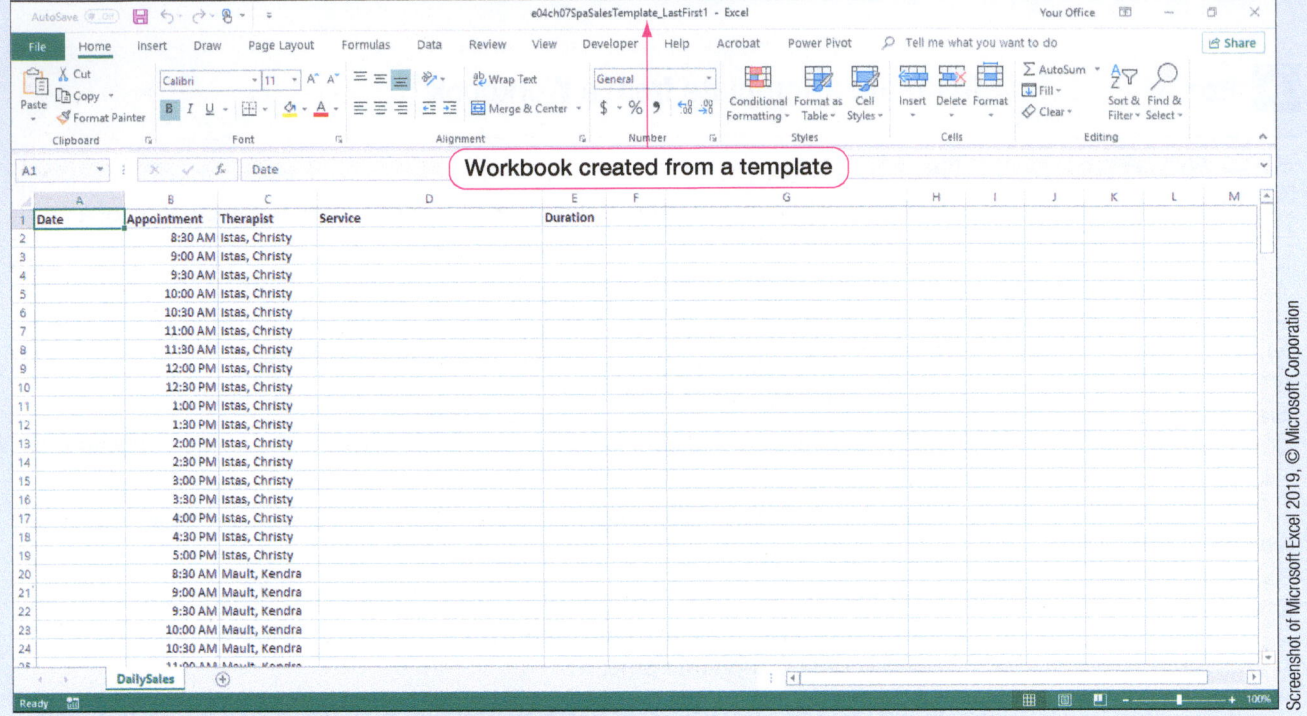

Figure 27   Excel workbook saved as a template

h. Close the workbook, exit Excel, and then submit your files as directed by your instructor.

S̲S̲   CONSIDER THIS | Should Templates Contain External References?

Templates generally are used to create worksheets or workbooks with consistent structure and format. While templates can—and often do—contain formulas, consider carefully before creating a template that includes external references to other workbooks. For such a template to be used, the linked workbook must be available in the proper location. The probability of breaking external links in a template is quite high, even if the template is well documented. It would be very easy for a user to copy the template to a new folder, open it to create a new workbook, and consequently break the external references (links).

   If you were creating a template and had to reference data in another workbook, what steps could you take to minimize the probability that the external links would get broken by someone using the template?

Concept Check

1. The ability to group worksheets creates an opportunity for you to greatly increase the efficiency of your work. List three ways in which grouping worksheets can increase your efficiency. p. 387

2. What are the three ways you can consolidate data across worksheets? When would you use each of the three ways? p. 394

3. What are the different ways you can see multiple workbooks on one screen at the same time? When might you want to do this? p. 406

4. What is the advantage of sharing a workbook? How can you keep track of all the changes made to the workbook? p. 410

5. What are local templates? With so many templates available, how do you know which ones might be better than others? p. 414

6. How do you create a custom template? Once you do, how do you make sure it shows on the File tab? p. 418

Key Terms

3-D formula   p. 397
3-D reference   p. 394
3-D named range   p. 395
Co-authoring   p. 410
Collaboration   p. 410

Consolidate by category   p. 394
Consolidate by position   p. 394
Excel Online   p. 410
Fill Across Worksheets   p. 391
Grouping   p. 387

Local templates   p. 414
OneDrive   p. 410
Online templates   p. 417
SharePoint   p. 410
Template   p. 414

Visual Summary

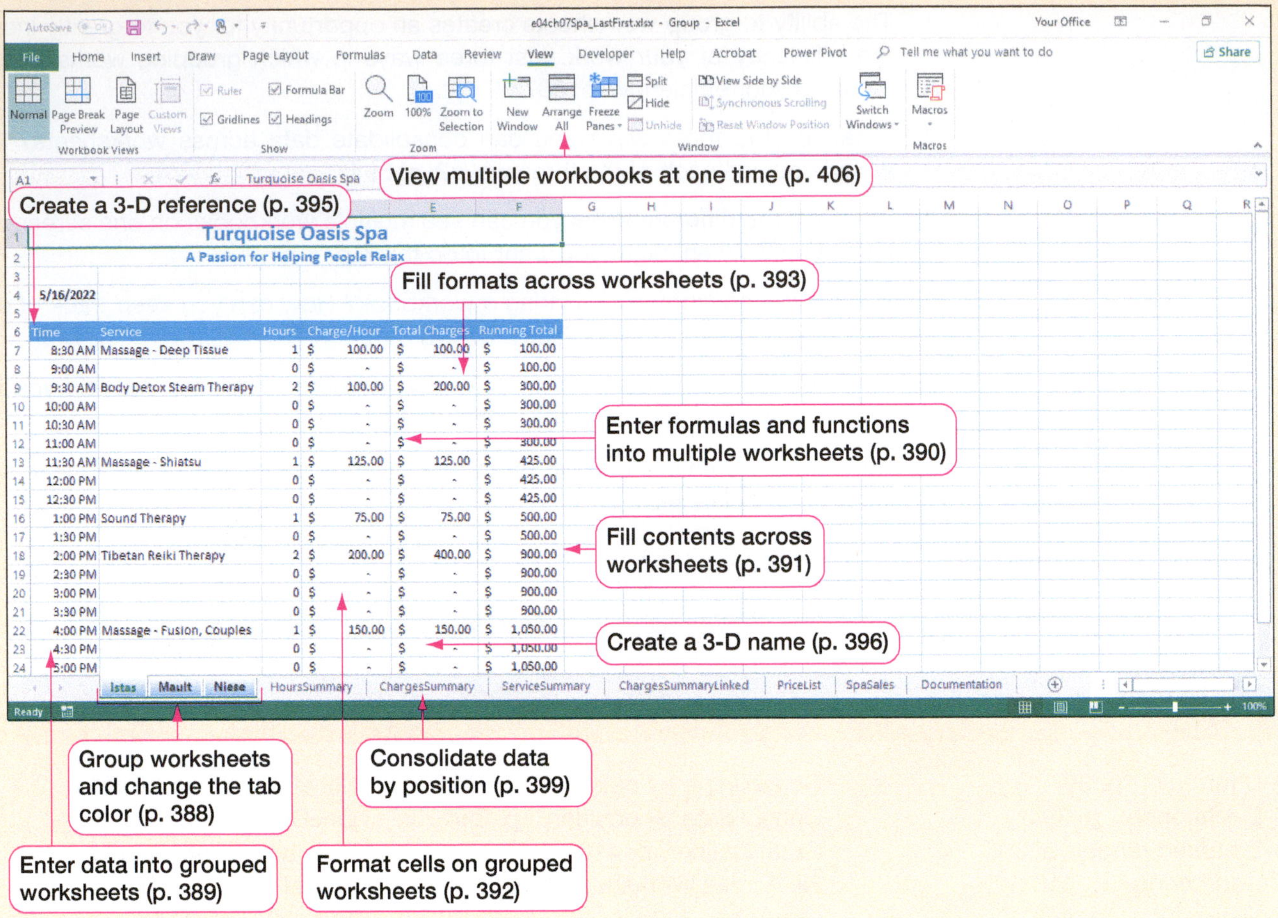

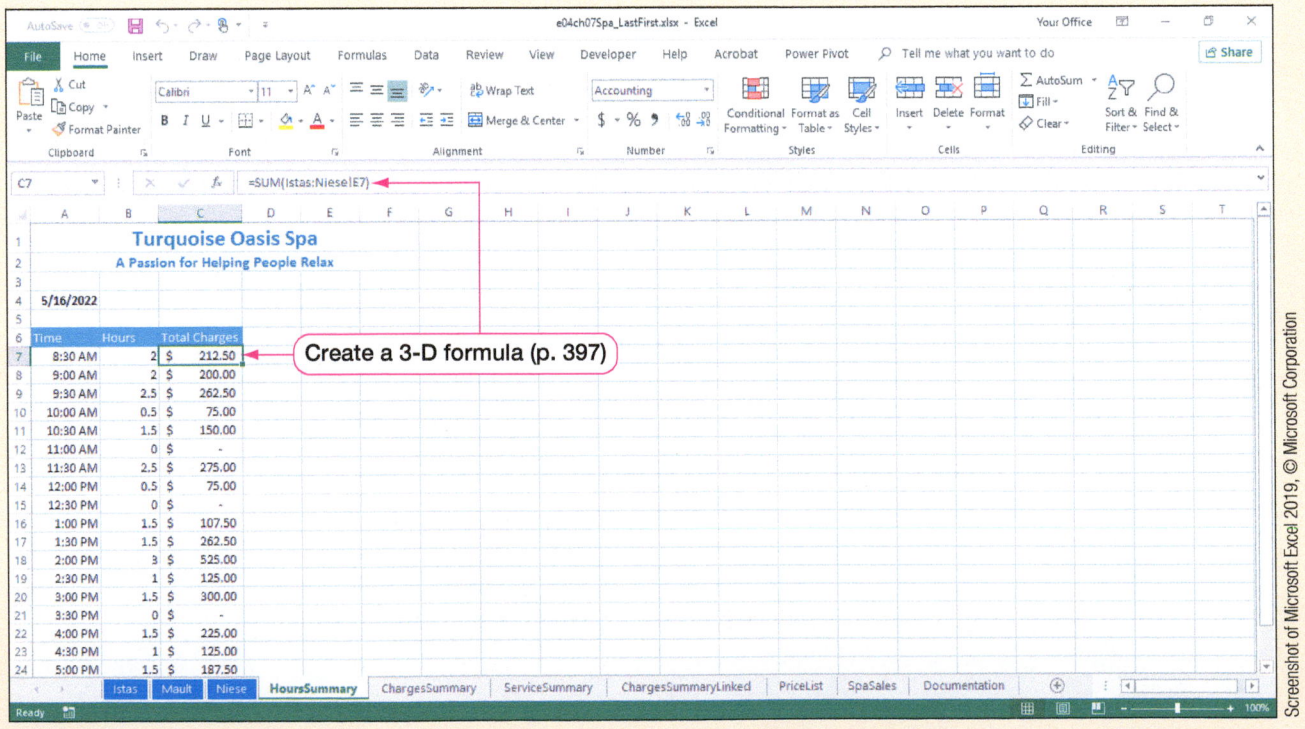

Screenshot of Microsoft Excel 2019, © Microsoft Corporation

Figure 28

Screenshot of Microsoft Excel 2019, © Microsoft Corporation

Figure 29

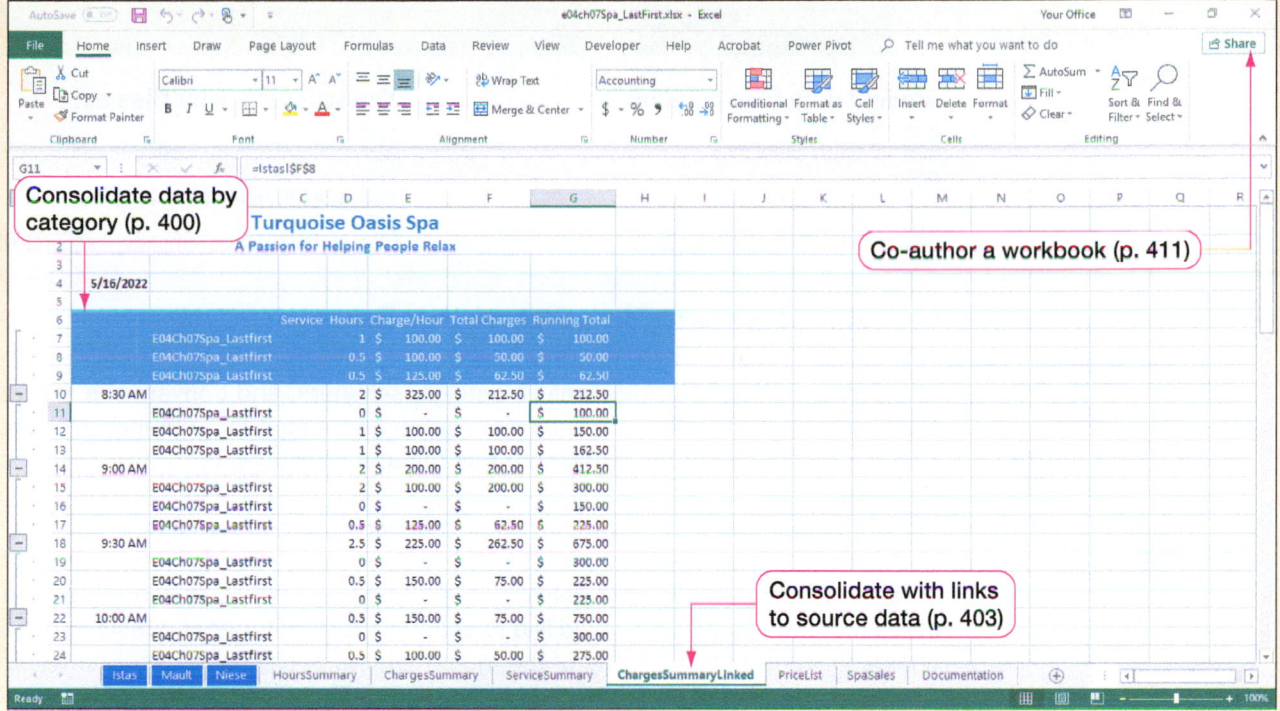

Consolidate data by category (p. 400)

Co-author a workbook (p. 411)

Consolidate with links to source data (p. 403)

Figure 30

Screenshot of Microsoft Excel 2019, © Microsoft Corporation

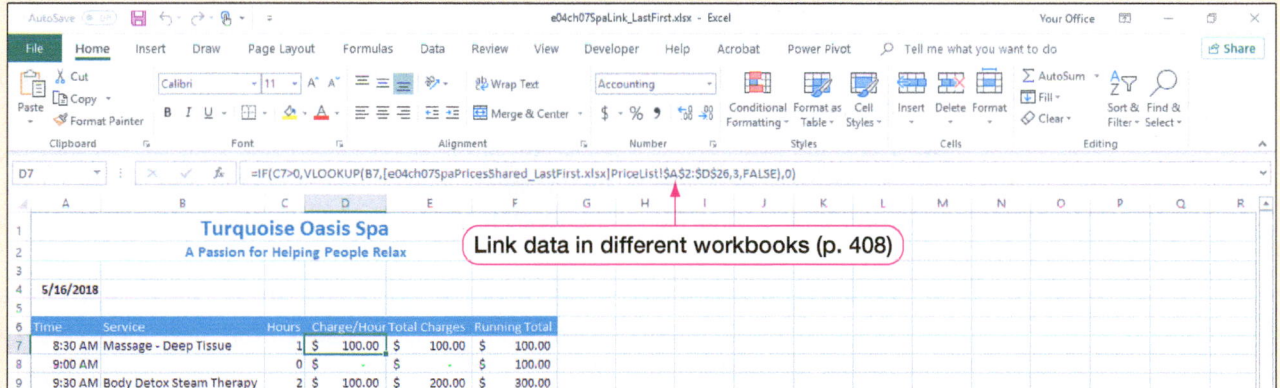

Link data in different workbooks (p. 408)

Figure 31

Screenshot of Microsoft Excel 2019, © Microsoft Corporation

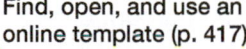

Find, open, and use an online template (p. 417)

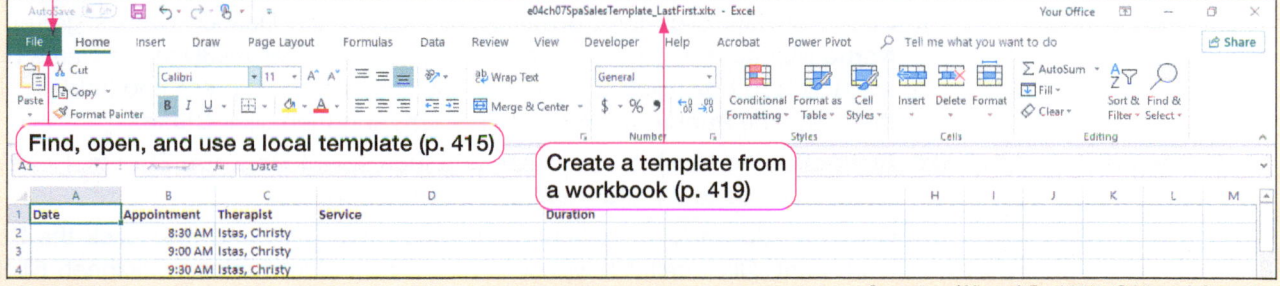

Find, open, and use a local template (p. 415)

Create a template from a workbook (p. 419)

Figure 32

Screenshot of Microsoft Excel 2019, © Microsoft Corporation

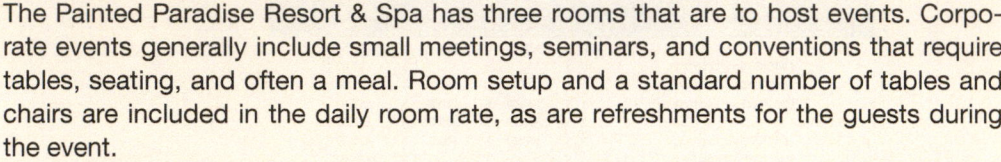

Student data files needed:

- e04ch07Event.xlsx
- e04ch07EventLink.xlsx
- e04ch07EventRooms.xlsx

You will save your files as:

- e04ch07Event_LastFirst.xlsx
- e04ch07EventLink_LastFirst.xlsx
- e04ch07EventTemplate_LastFirst.xltx

Productions &
Operations

Corporate Event Planning at the Resort

The Painted Paradise Resort & Spa has three rooms that are to host events. Corporate events generally include small meetings, seminars, and conventions that require tables, seating, and often a meal. Room setup and a standard number of tables and chairs are included in the daily room rate, as are refreshments for the guests during the event.

Patti Rochelle, the corporate event planner, has started a workbook to track each month's daily events in each of the three rooms. The first month's data was entered, but she needs help finishing the workbook and consolidating all the data into a monthly report. She would like to show the total number of guests and the total charges incurred for each day of the month and each type of event. She would also like to create a template to use every month, and she would like the daily rate to link to the external workbook that contains this information so that if the rates change, her workbook will be updated. She would also like to share her workbook with her staff so they can make changes where necessary.

a. Open Excel, click **Open** in the left pane, and then double-click **This PC**. Navigate through the folder structure to the location of your student data files, and then double-click **e04ch07Event**. If a Security Warning message displays, click the **Enable Editing** button.

b. Click the **File** tab click **Save As**, and then double-click **This PC**. In the Save As dialog box, navigate to the location where you are saving your project files, and then change the file name to e04ch07Event_LastFirst using your last and first name. Click **Save**.

c. On the Musica worksheet, press and hold Shift, and then click the **Pueblo** worksheet.

d. Right-click the **Musica** worksheet, point to **Tab Color**, and then select **Olive Green, Accent 3**.

e. Click cell **E8**, and then enter a formula to calculate the total charges. The formula should multiply the # Days and the Room Rate, using an absolute reference for the Room Rate. Enter the formula =D8*$C$5 Copy the formula to cell range E9:E38.

f. Select cell range **A7:E39**. On the Home tab, in the Editing group, click **Fill**, click **Across Worksheets**, select **Formats**, and then click **OK**.

g. Click cell **E39**, click the **Formulas** tab, and in the Defined Names group, click **Name Manager**. Click **New**, and then type TotalCharges3D in the Name box. In the Refers to box, click at the end of the cell reference, press and hold Shift, and then click the **Pueblo** worksheet. Click **OK**, and then click **Close**.

h. Right-click the **Musica** worksheet, and then select **Ungroup Sheets**. Review the changes made to the **Eldorado** and **Pueblo** worksheets.

i. Click the **Eldorado** worksheet, press and hold Shift, and then click the **Pueblo** worksheet. Click cell **A3**, type = and then click the **Musica** worksheet. Click cell **A3**, and then press Enter.

j. Click the **GuestSummary** worksheet to ungroup the worksheets.

k. On the GuestSummary worksheet, click cell **B8**, type **=** click the **Musica** worksheet, click cell **C8**, and then type **+** Click the **Eldorado** worksheet, click cell **C8**, type **+** Click the **Pueblo** worksheet, click cell **C8**, and then press Ctrl+Enter. Copy the formula to cell range **B9:B38** on the GuestSummary worksheet.

l. On the GuestSummary worksheet, click cell **C8**, and then type **=SUM(** Click the **Musica** worksheet, press and hold Shift, click the **Pueblo** worksheet, and then click cell **E8**. Press Ctrl+Enter. Copy the formula to cell range **C9:C38**.

m. Click the **RoomSummary** worksheet. Click cell **B8**, click the **Data** tab, and then, in the Data Tools group, click **Consolidate**.

n. In the Consolidate dialog box, make sure **Sum** is selected in the Function box. Click the **Reference** box, click the **Musica** worksheet, and then select cell range **C8:E38**. Click **Add**.

o. Click the **Eldorado** worksheet, verify that cell range **C8:E38** is selected, and then click **Add**.

p. Click the **Pueblo** worksheet, verify that cell range **C8:E38** is selected, and then click **Add**. Click **OK**.

q. Click cell **D39**, type **=SUM(TotalCharges3D)** and then press Enter for a result of $135,900.

r. Click the **EventsSummary** worksheet. Click cell **A7**, and then on the Data tab, in the Data Tools group, click **Consolidate**. In the Consolidate dialog box, make sure **Sum** is selected in the Function box, and then click the Reference box.

s. Click the **Musica** worksheet, and then select cell range **B7:E38**. Click **Add**.

t. Click the **Eldorado** worksheet, verify that cell range **B7:E38** is selected, and then click **Add**.

u. Click the **Pueblo** worksheet, verify that cell range **B7:E38** is selected, and then click **Add**. Click to select **Top row** and **Left column**, and then click **OK**.

v. Click cell **A7**, and then type Event

w. Click the **EventSummaryLinked** worksheet. Click cell **A7**, and then, on the Data tab, in the Data Tools group, click **Consolidate**. In the Consolidate dialog box, make sure **Sum** is selected in the Function box, and then click the **Reference** box.

x. Click the **Musica** worksheet, select cell range **A7:E38**, and then click **Add**. Click the **Eldorado** worksheet, and then click **Add**. Click the **Pueblo** worksheet, and then click **Add**. Click to select **Top row**, **Left column**, and **Create links to source data**, and then click **OK**.

y. Select cell range **A11:A131**, and then on the Home tab, in the Number group, click the **Number Format** arrow, and select **Short Date**.

z. Select columns **A:F** and then on the Home tab, in the Cells group, click **Format**, and then select **AutoFit Column Width**.

aa. Update the **Documentation** worksheet according to your instructor's directions. **Save** and **close** the workbook, but keep Excel open.

bb. Click the **File** tab, and then open **e04ch07EventLink**. If necessary, click **Enable Content**. Save the file as an Excel Workbook with the name **e04ch07EventLink_LastFirst** using your last and first name.

cc. Click the **File** tab, and then open **e04ch07EventRooms**.

dd. Click the **View** tab, and in the Window group, click **Arrange All**. Click the **Tiled** option, and then click **OK**.

ee. In the **e04ch07EventLink_LastFirst** workbook, the RoomRates worksheet has been deleted, so the reference to that worksheet shows an error. Click the **Musica** worksheet, click cell **C5**. Type **=** click the **e04ch07EventRooms** workbook, click cell **B8**, and then press Ctrl+Enter.

ff. Click the **Eldorado** worksheet, and then click cell **C5**. Type **=** click the **e04ch07EventRooms** workbook, click cell **B7**, and then press Ctrl+Enter.

gg. Click the **Pueblo** worksheet, and then click cell **C5**. Type **=** click the **e04ch07EventRooms** workbook, click cell **B6**, and then press Ctrl+Enter.

hh. Save and then **close** the **e04ch07EventLink_LastFirst** workbook.

ii. Close the **e04ch07EventRooms_LastFirst** workbook, but keep Excel open.

jj. Open the **e04ch07Event_LastFirst** workbook. Click the **Musica** worksheet, press and hold Shift, and then click the **Pueblo** worksheet.

kk. Select cell range **B8:D38**, and then press Delete to clear the contents from the cells. Right-click the **Musica** worksheet and then select **Ungroup Sheets**.

ll. Save the workbook in your student folder as a **template** named **e04ch07EventTemplate_LastFirst** using your last and first name.

mm. Save the workbook, close Excel, and then submit your files as directed by your instructor.

Problem Solve 1

MyLab IT Grader

Student data file needed:
 e04ch07Parks.xlsx

You will save your files as:
 e04ch07Parks_LastFirst.xlsx
 e04ch07ParksLink_LastFirst.xlsx
 e04ch07ParksTemplate_LastFirst.xltx

Park Management

General Business

As the newest staff member for Park Management LLC, your supervisor Andrea Ramirez has asked you to consolidate information that has been collected for each of the company's locations. Park Management LLC manages museums and parks in three states: Minnesota, Iowa, and Wisconsin. States have their own workbooks with quarterly data, and management would like to see this data consolidated into one report per state. In each workbook, there is also a sheet for Rate information, but this is not always current, so you will need to link the workbooks to the master Rate workbook that another staff member updates.

a. Open the Excel file, **e04ch07Parks**. Save your file as **e04ch07Parks_LastFirst** using your last and first name.

b. Group worksheets **Quarter1** through **Quarter4**. Create formulas in the cell range **D6:E10** to calculate the admission collected from both adult and children visitors for each location referencing the appropriate rates in the Rates worksheet. Leave the worksheet grouped.

c. In cell range **B11:E11**, calculate the total of the columns. Format cell range **B11:C11** with the Comma style and no decimals. Format cell range **D11:E11** with the Accounting Number Format.

d. With the worksheets still grouped, format cell range **B6:C10** with the Comma style no decimals. AutoFit columns **B:E**. Apply the Total cell style in cell range **B11:E11**. In cell **A11**, type **Total** Ungroup the worksheets.

e. On the **Summary** worksheet, enter a 3-D SUM function in cell range **B6:E10** to calculate the total visitors and admissions for each category and location from Quarter1 through Quarter4.

f. Use the Fill Across Worksheets feature to copy the formatting for cell range **B6:E10** from the Quarter4 worksheet to the Summary worksheet.

g. Use Fill Across Worksheets to copy the content and formatting from cell range **A11:E11** on the Quarter4 worksheet to the Summary worksheet. AutoFit columns **B:E** in the Summary worksheet only.

h. On the **LinkedSummary** worksheet, in cell **A5**, create a linked consolidation using cell range **A5:E11** from the Quarter1, Quarter2, Quarter3, and Quarter4 worksheets. Select **Top row**, **Left column**, and **Create links to source data** in the Consolidate dialog box.

i. Change the column width of column **A** to 20 hide column **B**, and use the AutoFit Column Width feature for columns **C:F**. Complete the Documentation worksheet according to your instructor's direction, and then save the workbook.

j. Save **e04ch07Parks_LastFirst** as **e04ch07ParksLink_LastFirst**

k. Delete the **Rates** worksheet, and then click the **Quarter1** worksheet. Open **e04ch07Parks_LastFirst**. Arrange the two workbooks so you can see them side by side.

l. In **e04ch07ParksLink_LastFirst**, group the Quarter1 through Quarter4 worksheets. Click cell **D6**, and then in the formula bar replace the **#REF!B6** with a reference to cell B6 on the Rates worksheet in e04ch07Parks_LastFirst. Change the cell reference **$B$6** to a relative reference—to remove the absolute reference—and then copy the formula from cell **D6** to cell range **D7:E10**. Ungroup the sheets. Save and close the e04ch07ParksLink_LastFirst workbook.

> ## Grader Heads Up
> The MyLab IT Grader version of this project does not include the creation of a template file.

m. Create a template from the **e04ch07Parks_LastFirst** to use for the other states with the same parks. Group the Quarter1 through Quarter4 worksheets, and then clear the contents from cell range **B6:C10**. Delete **Wisconsin** from cell A2 of all worksheets. Save the template as **e04ch07ParksTemplate_LastFirst**

n. **Close** the workbook, exit Excel, and then submit your files as directed by your instructor.

Critical Thinking

You used the Fill Across Worksheets to copy cell formats from the Quarter4 worksheet to the Summary worksheet. What is the benefit of using the Fill Across Worksheets feature?

Perform 1: Perform in Your Life

Student data file needed:

 e04ch07FoodPrices.xlsx

You will save your files as:

e04ch07Food_LastFirst.xlsx

e04ch07FoodPrices_LastFirst.xlsx

e04ch07FoodLink_LastFirst.xlsx

e04ch07FoodTemplate_LastFirst.xltx

e04ch07FoodTime_LastFirst.xlsx

General Business

Finance & Accounting

Softball Fundraiser

You have volunteered to help your child's softball team raise money for uniforms. As part of the fundraiser, food booths will be set up at four locations around town. You need to develop a spreadsheet that will track sales and income by product at each location. The file will need to be shared with the four booth locations, so the booth volunteers can update their sales on a regular basis. In addition, because the team will be recognizing the person with the most volunteer hours, you need to develop a time card to track the hours.

a. Open the Excel file, **e04ch07FoodPrices**. Save your file as e04ch07FoodPrices_LastFirst using your last and first name.

b. Click the Sheet1 worksheet, rename it Prices Add a heading in row 1 to identify what the workbook contains. Format each column appropriately. Save the workbook.

c. Open a new blank workbook, and save it as e04ch07Food_LastFirst using your last and first name.

d. Rename the first worksheet as Summary and add four additional worksheets. Rename the four worksheets for each food booth location. Color the tabs for the four locations to show that they contain similar data.

e. Format all five worksheets as follows:

- All columns must print on one page.

- There should be at least two rows at the top of the worksheet to hold the location of the booth and the names of the volunteers working the booth. Include a blank row between the heading above and the detail data below.

- Include columns for the item description, units sold, sales price, total sale, cost per unit, and total cost.

- Allow at least four rows for the list of products to be sold. Enter a formula that will calculate the total sale and the total cost based on the number of units sold and the sales price or cost per unit price as appropriate.

- Add a total row to the units sold, total sale, and total cost columns. Label the row, and format as appropriate.

- Format the column headings using a cell style to highlight them from the rest of the data.

- Center the Location over the columns of data, and size the font appropriately.

- Format any columns that will contain values appropriately.

f. On the Summary worksheet, in row 1, type Summary Create a 3-D formula that will add the units sold from each location worksheet. Leave the formulas in the total sale and total cost columns as previously entered. Save your changes.

g. Save the file as e04ch07FoodLink_LastFirst using your last and first name.

h. Using the **e04ch07FoodPrices_LastFirst** workbook you created earlier, link the item descriptions, sales price, and cost per unit to all five worksheets as appropriate.

i. Enter Units sold test values in all four location sheets to validate that your formulas are correct and everything is working properly. Save your changes.

j. Save the file as a template with the name e04ch07FoodTemplate_LastFirst using your last and first name. Clear any contents that are not necessary to a template. Save and close the file.

k. You have decided to use the Built-In template Time card rather than creating a file from scratch.

l. Open the **Time card** template. Save the file as e04ch07FoodTime_LastFirst using your last and first name.

m. Change Employee to Volunteer

n. Delete columns E:H.

o. Delete rows 21:22.

p. Change the Week ending date to 5/20/2022

q. Save the workbook, exit Excel, and then submit your files as directed by your instructor.

Microsoft Excel

Chapter 8 BUILDING AN APPLICATION WITH MULTIPLE WORKSHEETS AND WORKBOOKS

MyLab IT Grader

Finance & Accounting

Prepare Case

Turquoise Oasis Spa Application

Meda Rodate, manager of the Turquoise Oasis Spa, wants to improve the layout of the existing spa invoice and automate the invoice process as much as possible to ensure data accuracy and consistency. The invoice currently has formulas in the Charge/Hour and Amount columns, but they often get deleted by mistake. The therapist's name is often misspelled, the room number is often wrong, and Meda thinks the subtotal amount may not be calculating correctly. Another problem arises when the description of the service is not entered correctly, and then the charge/hour cannot be found in the lookup table.

In this chapter, you will modify an invoice application for the Turquoise Oasis Spa. Meda Rodate has started the application, but she is unable to finish it, so you will assist her. The invoice application has several requirements she cannot satisfy:

- Data validation to minimize data entry errors
- Automatically generated invoice number
- Automated data cleanup using macros
- Protection of the application to stop users from mistakenly changing application content and structure

Monika Wisniewska/Shutterstock

Student data file needed:

 e04ch08SpaInvoice.xlsx

You will save your files as:

 e04ch08SpaInvoice_LastFirst.xlsx

 e04ch08SpaInvoiceMacro_LastFirst.xlsm

Auditing Formulas

Formula auditing tools show you which cells are used in a formula and how the cells are used. Whether you are working with a worksheet you developed or one developed by someone else, being able to see all the cells that are part of a formula makes evaluating the accuracy and relevance of the formula easier. Excel's formula auditing tools include Trace Precedents, Trace Dependents, and Evaluate Formula.

Both tracing a formula and evaluating a formula are useful in understanding how a worksheet is structured. They are particularly useful if a complex formula is not producing a correct result. In this section, you will use formula auditing tools to gain a clearer understanding of how the invoice worksheet is structured and to correct an error in an invoice formula.

View Formula Precedents and Dependents

Tracing formulas draws lines from a formula to cells that supply source data (precedents) and to formulas that use the result of a formula (dependents). A **precedent cell** is a cell that supplies a value to the formula in the active cell, and a **dependent cell** is a cell whose value depends on the value in the active cell for its result. When you select to **trace precedents**, Excel automatically draws arrows from the precedent cells to the active cell. When you select to **trace dependents**, Excel automatically draws arrows from the active cell to its dependent cells. This is helpful for seeing which cells will be affected by a change to the active cell.

Opening the Starting File

Because you did not create the Spa workbook, you will audit the worksheet before you start making changes to it. This will allow you to better understand how the invoice is set up and to check for any possible errors in the formulas.

In this exercise, you will open the Spa workbook.

E08.00

SIDE NOTE
Office Updates
Depending on your exact Office version, you may see Open or Open Other Workbooks.

To Open the Spa Workbook

a. Start Excel, click **Open** in the left pane, and then double-click **This PC**. Navigate through the folder structure to the location of your student data files, and then double-click **e04ch08SpaInvoice**. If a Security Warning message displays, click **Enable Editing**.

b. Click the **File** tab, click **Save As**, and then double-click **This PC**. In the Save As dialog box, navigate to the location where you are saving your project files, and then change the file name to e04ch08SpaInvoice_LastFirst using your last and first name. Click **Save**.

Auditing Formulas with Trace Dependents and Trace Precedents

Every formula has precedents, and some formulas may also have dependents. While you can always click a cell to see the cell references included in a formula, sometimes a visual cue is helpful to see how the formula works. When you choose to trace dependents and trace precedents, Excel puts arrows on the workbook to show you how the formula in the cell is constructed. These arrows make it easier to find errors than just by looking at the cell references in the formula.

In this exercise, you will use trace precedents and trace dependents to look at the formulas to make sure they are constructed properly and work the way they are supposed to work.

 **E08.01**

SIDE NOTE
Pin the Ribbon
If your ribbon is collapsed, pin your ribbon open. Click the Home tab. In the lower-right corner of the ribbon, click Pin the ribbon.

SIDE NOTE
Office Updates
Depending on your exact Office version, your ribbon may look slightly different.

To Trace Precedents and Trace Dependents

a. On the **Invoice** worksheet, select cell **F31**.

b. Click the **Formulas** tab, and then in the Formula Auditing group, click **Trace Precedents**.

A blue arrow is displayed that begins with a blue dot in cell F16 and ends with an arrow in cell F31. The cell range F16:F30 is outlined in blue. This outlined range is a precedent to the calculation in cell F31. Notice that the precedent range F16:F30 is determining the subtotal and is missing cell F15, the first row of the invoice.

c. In the Formula Auditing group, click **Trace Dependents**.

An arrow is displayed from cell F31 to cell F33, and another arrow is displayed from cell F33 to cell F35. The formula in cell F33 is a dependent cell to the formula in cell F31, and the formula in cell F35 is a dependent cell to the formula in cell F33. This means that the value in cell F33 will depend on the value in cell F31, and the value in cell F35 will depend on the value in cell F33.

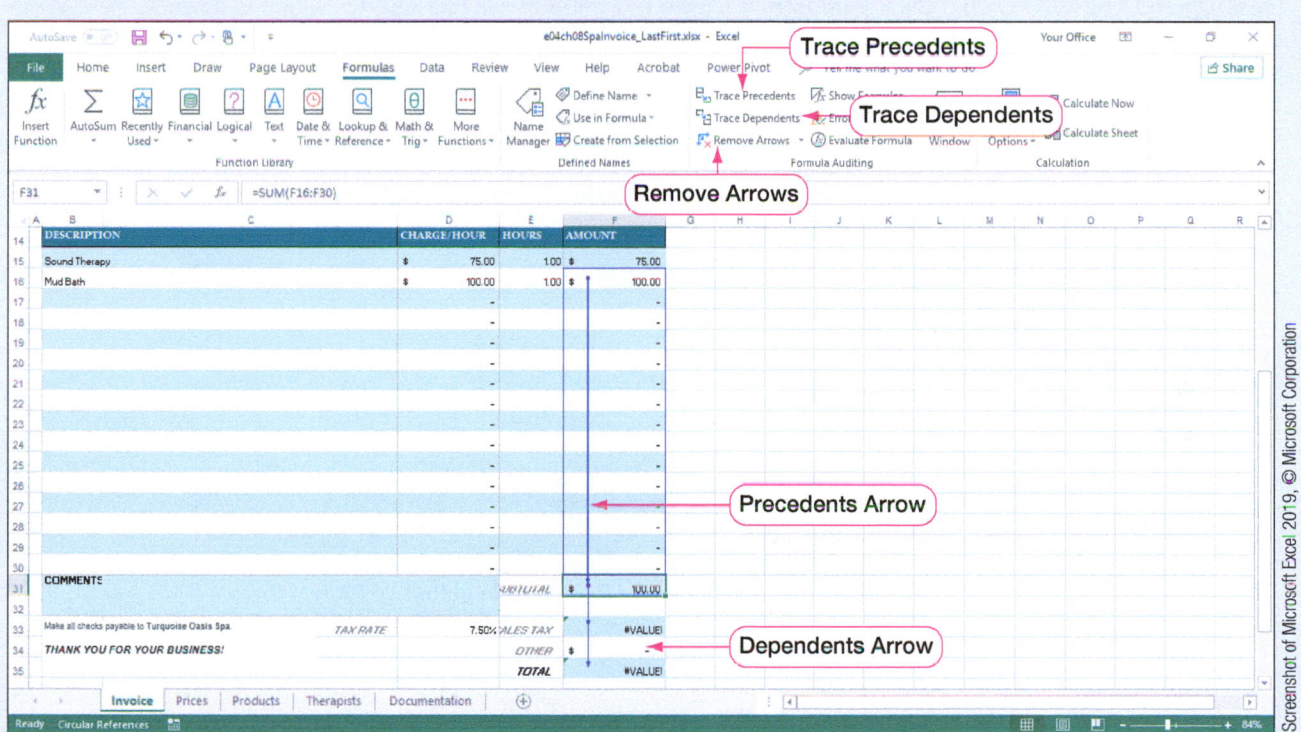

Figure 1 Trace Precedents and Trace Dependents arrows

d. In the Formula Auditing group, click **Remove Arrows**.

e. If necessary, select cell **F31**, and in the **formula bar**, change F16 to **F15** to correct the SUM function so it includes all the rows of the invoice. Press Ctrl+Enter.

f. **Save** the workbook.

Evaluate Formulas

Evaluating a formula walks you through the steps taken in calculating the result of a formula. **Evaluate Formula** is a tool that breaks down a formula into its individual pieces and evaluates each part separately so you can see how the formula works. It is similar to using trace precedents and trace dependents but without the arrows filling up the screen.

Using the Evaluate Formula Tool

In the SpaInvoice workbook, there is a problem with the calculation of the Sales Tax and the Total invoice amount because it is showing a #VALUE! error instead of a result.

In this exercise, you will use Evaluate Formula to determine what is wrong with the formula in cell F33.

 **E08.02**

SIDE NOTE
Select All Cells That Contain a Formula
Press Ctrl and type G, click Special, and then select Formulas. Notice the categories of formulas you can select. Click OK.

To Evaluate Formulas

a. On the Invoice worksheet, select cell **F33**, and then, on the Formulas tab, in the Formula Auditing group, click **Evaluate Formula**. The formula =F31*E33 is displayed in the Evaluation box.

b. Click **Evaluate**. It shows the value of cell F31 as 175, which is correct.

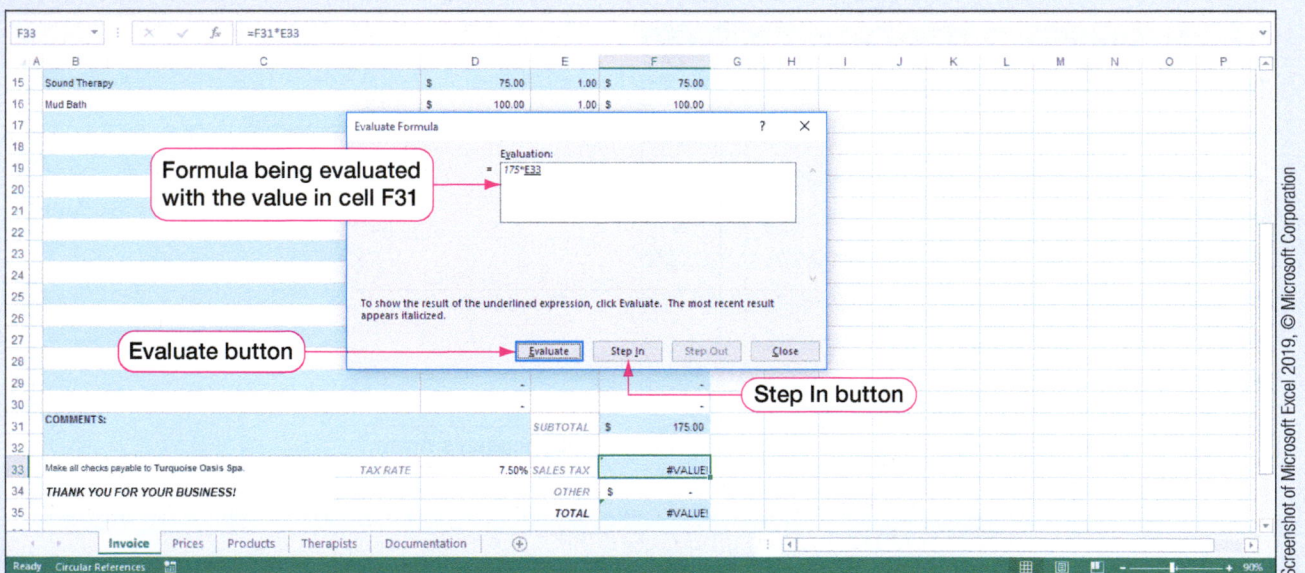

Figure 2 Evaluate Formula dialog box

MAC COMPATIBILITY
Evaluate Formulas
The Evaluate Formula command is not available on a Mac. Mac users should adjust the formulas using Edit mode.

c. Click **Step In**. This shows that the value of E33 is the text SALES TAX, which is not correct.

d. Click **Step Out** to view the cell references replaced by the values in the formula.

The value should be the sales tax rate, or 6.50%, not the text "SALES TAX." This is what is causing the #VALUE! error in the cell.

e. Click **Close**. You cannot edit a formula in evaluation mode.

f. In the formula bar, select cell **E33** and then type **D33** Press Ctrl + Enter. If necessary, click **OK** in the circular reference warning dialog box. You will correct this problem in the next exercise.

g. **Save** the workbook.

Correct Circular References

A **circular reference** is an error in a worksheet indicating a single formula that references itself or multiple formulas that reference each other. Technically, the formulas are precedents and dependents of one another. A circular reference is a problem for Excel because it means that action A requires action B to complete before it can be executed but action B requires action A to complete before it can be executed. If a workbook contains a circular reference, there will be an indication in the lower-left corner of the Excel window. While most of the time a circular reference is an error, there are advanced financial models that purposefully use circular references.

Finding and Correcting Circular References

In the SpaInvoice workbook, when you corrected the formula referencing the Sales Tax value in the preceding exercise, you saw a circular reference warning dialog box. This means there is a circular reference somewhere in the worksheet. The message in the status bar indicates that the circular reference is in cell F35.

In this exercise, you will identify and correct a circular reference.

E08.03

MAC COMPATIBILITY
No Red Arrow in Trace Precedents
Mac users will not see a red arrow when using Trace Precedents.

To Identify and Correct Circular References

a. On the Invoice worksheet, select cell **F35**, and then, on the Formulas tab, in the Formula Auditing group, click **Trace Precedents**.

The arrow is red, indicating an error. Notice that the SUM function in cell F35 includes a cell reference to cell F35, which is causing the circular reference.

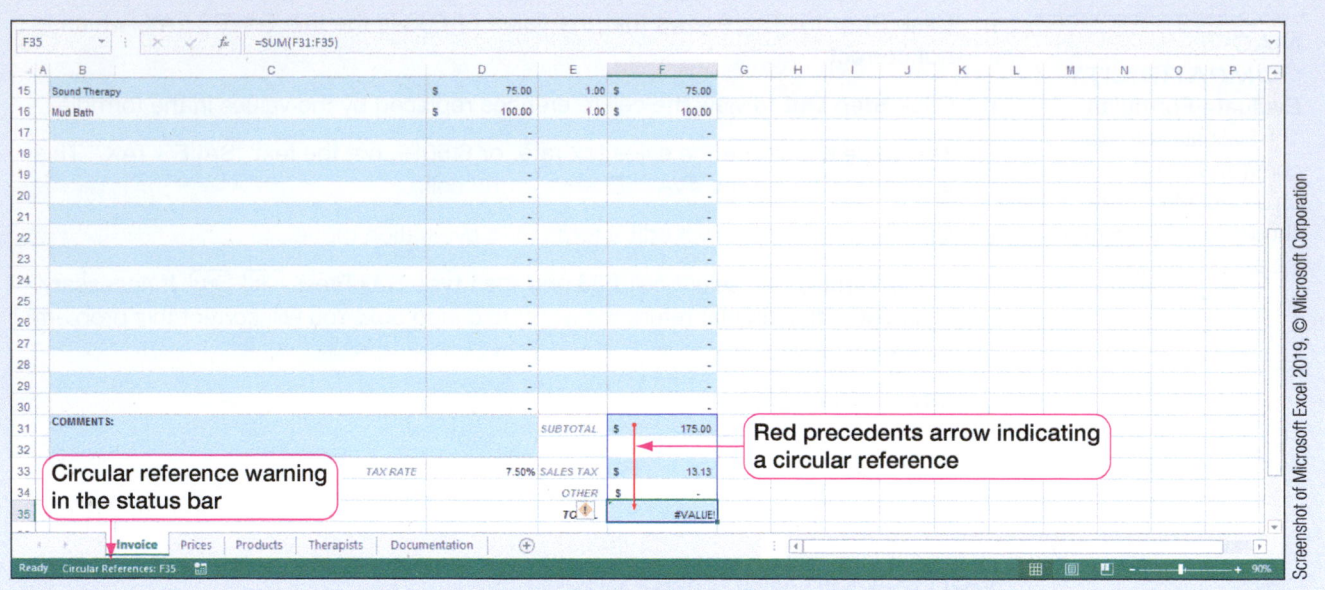

Figure 3 Circular reference as indicated by Trace Precedents

b. In the formula bar, select cell **F35** and then type **F34** Press Ctrl+Enter. This removes the trace arrow and corrects the formula.

c. **Save** 💾 the workbook.

Use the Watch Window

The **Watch Window** is an Excel feature that makes it possible to monitor cells the user considers important in a separate window. The Watch Window is particularly useful when you are making changes in one worksheet or workbook and you want to monitor the effect of your changes to values in several other worksheets or workbooks.

To include a cell in the Watch Window, the workbook that contains the cell must be open and must remain open. As soon as the workbook is closed, any cells in that workbook that are being watched are removed from the Watch Window.

Opening and Using the Watch Window

In the SpaInvoice workbook, you will set up a Watch Window to watch the subtotal, sales tax, and total cells. This way, as rows are being added to the invoice, there will be no need to scroll to the bottom to see the total.

In this exercise, you will track changes using the Watch Window.

 **E08.04**

To Track Changes Using the Watch Window

Grader Heads Up

In the MyLab IT Grader version of this project, you will not be adding a Watch Window.

MAC COMPATIBILITY

The Watch Window Doesn't Exist on a Mac

You will not be able to complete this exercise on a Mac.

a. On the Invoice worksheet, on the Formulas tab, in the Formula Auditing group, click **Watch Window** 🔲. This will open the Watch Window, which will be empty.

b. If necessary, move the Watch Window out of the way. Click cell **F31**. Press and hold Ctrl, and then select cells **F33** and **F35**. In the Watch Window, click **Add Watch**. In the Add Watch dialog box, click **Add** to confirm the cells you selected.

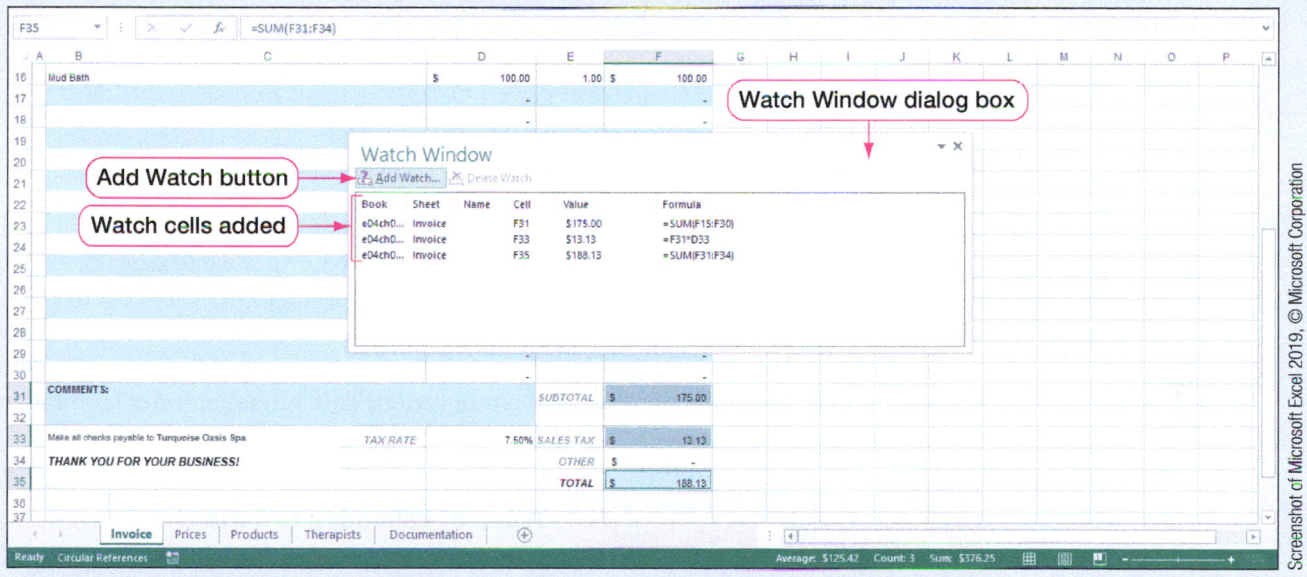

Figure 4   Watch Window

SIDE NOTE

Watch Window

To adjust the size of the docked Watch Window, click the Watch Window border and drag to desired height.

c. Drag the **title bar** of the Watch Window to the top of the worksheet window.

The Watch Window will be docked below the ribbon and stay there. You can also dock the Watch Window on the bottom, left, or right of the worksheet window. To undock the Watch Window, simply drag the title bar toward the middle of the application window.

Screenshot of Microsoft Excel 2019, © Microsoft Corporation

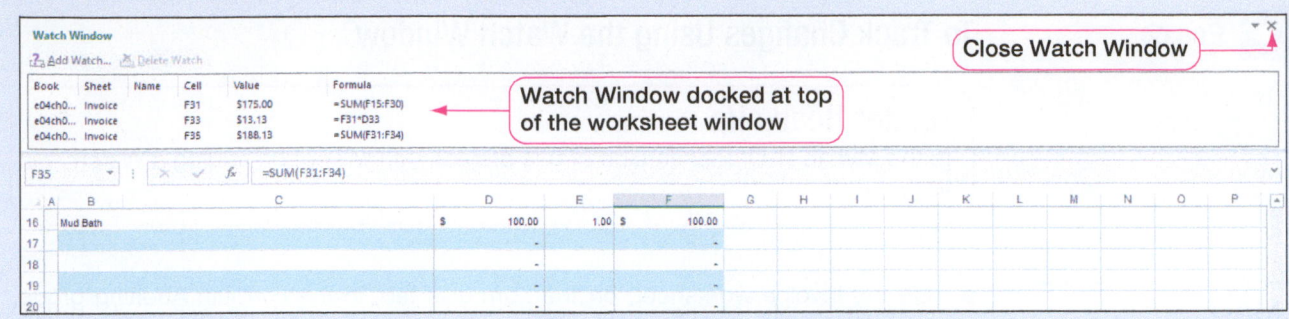

Figure 5 Watch Window docked

Screenshot of Microsoft Excel 2019, © Microsoft Corporation

SIDE NOTE
Alternate Method
You can also close the Watch Window by clicking the Close [X] button in the top-right corner of the window.

d. Select cell **E15**, type **2** and then press Ctrl+Enter. Notice that all the cells in the Watch Window changed.

e. In the Formula Auditing group, click **Watch Window** to close the Watch Window.

The Watch Window also closes when you close the workbook, so each time you open the workbook, you will have to open the Watch Window to use it; however, you will not have to add the cells again because they will be saved.

f. **Save** 💾 the workbook.

Creating Data Validation Rules

Probably the greatest single source of errors in a workbook is human error. While it is impossible to completely eliminate human error while editing a workbook, Excel provides data validation tools that can help to ensure that data entry errors are kept to a minimum. **Data validation** includes rules that determine what can and cannot be entered in specific cells. **Validation criteria** are constraints that limit what users can enter into a particular cell. In this section, you will create various data validation rules for different cells throughout the workbook.

QUICK REFERENCE	Types of Validation Criteria

- Any value: Does not validate data but does allow the use of an input message to give data entry instructions.
- Whole number: Limits the data value in a cell to a specified range of integers.
- Decimal: Limits the number of decimal places that can be used in a cell.
- List: Requires the user to select a value from a list of predefined values.
- Date: Requires that data entered into a cell represent a valid date.
- Time: Requires that data entered into a cell represent a valid time.
- Text length: Places a limit on the number of text characters that can be entered into a cell.
- Custom: Allows the user to create custom criteria by specifying a formula that data entered into a cell must satisfy to be considered valid.

Control Data Entry with Data Validation

In its simplest form, data validation restricts you to a single validation criterion per cell. For example, with a simple validation rule, you cannot specify that a cell can contain an item from a list and that it can contain a whole number. Custom validation can be used to apply multiple validation criteria to a cell, but the formulas required tend to be much more complex.

Each of the validation criteria can be specified with an Input Message and/or an Error Alert. The Input Message and Error Alert are tools to assist you in communicating data validation constraints to the user. The **Input Message** is a message that appears when a user makes a validated cell active and prompts a user before data is entered with information about data constraints. The **Error Alert** informs a user when entered data violates validation constraints.

There are three types of error alerts that can be assigned to a cell or range of cells with data validation: stop, warning, and information. A stop alert is the most restrictive of the data validation alerts. With a stop alert, if invalid data is entered, the user can only cancel or retry entering valid data. A warning alert will warn the user of an invalid data entry but allows the user to proceed or to cancel the entry. The information alert displays an error message with an information icon but allows the user to enter the invalid data.

Setting Up a List Validation

List validation is a type of data validation that presents a list of data values that the user can choose from. Data for the list must be included as part of the workbook; it cannot be in an external workbook. The SpaInvoice workbook has one validation rule created for the Description lines of the invoice. You will add more data validation rules to limit what can be entered in other cells and cell ranges.

In this exercise, you will create a list validation on the Therapist field to choose from a list of therapists that can be found on the Therapists worksheet.

 E08.05

SIDE NOTE
Hide Input Message
If you do not desire to have the input message visible when the cell is selected, remove the check from the Input Message tab in the Data Validation dialog box.

To Create and Use a List Validation

a. On the Invoice worksheet, click cell **C15**. Notice the input message which appears when the cell is selected. Data validation has already been set on cell range C15:C30. Also notice the arrow to the right of the cell.

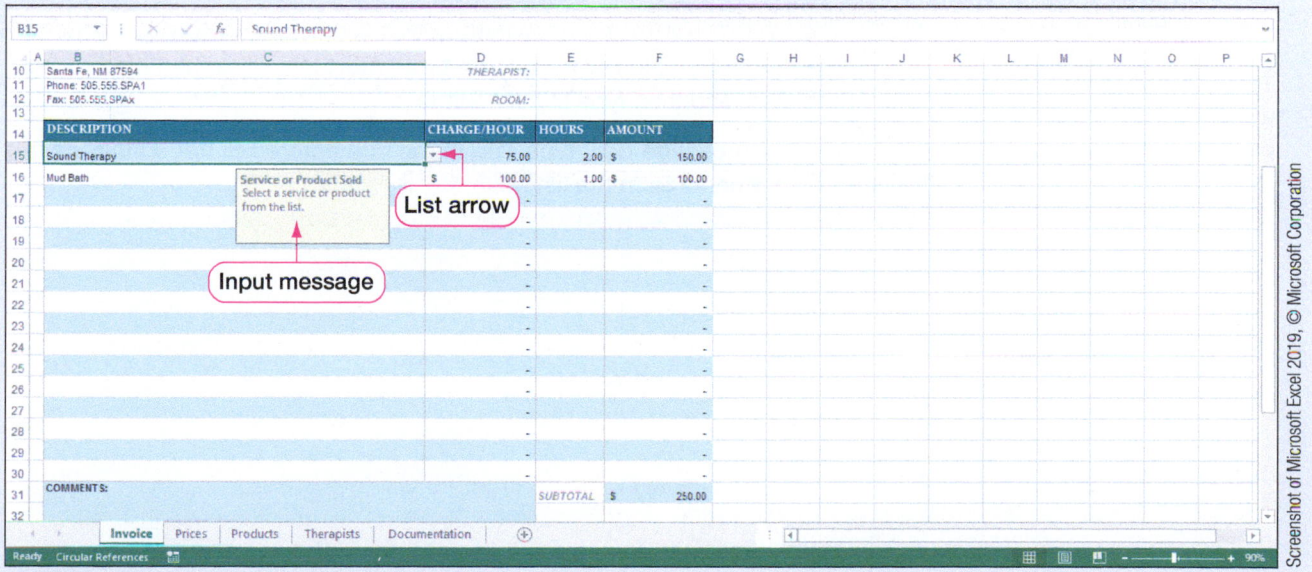

Figure 6 Validation rule present

SIDE NOTE
Why Check Ignore Blank?

If you do not check Ignore blank, Excel will return an error from the validated cell if you delete its value.

b. Click the arrow to view the data entry options. Press [Esc] to return to cell C15.

c. Click cell **E10**. Click the **Data** tab, and then in the Data Tools group, click **Data Validation**.

d. In the Data Validation dialog box, on the **Settings** tab, click the **Allow** arrow, and then select **List**. Verify that the **Ignore blank** and **In-cell dropdown** options are checked.

e. Click the **Source** box, click the **Therapists** worksheet, and then select the cell range **A2:A4**. The Source box should show =Therapists!$A$2:$A$4.

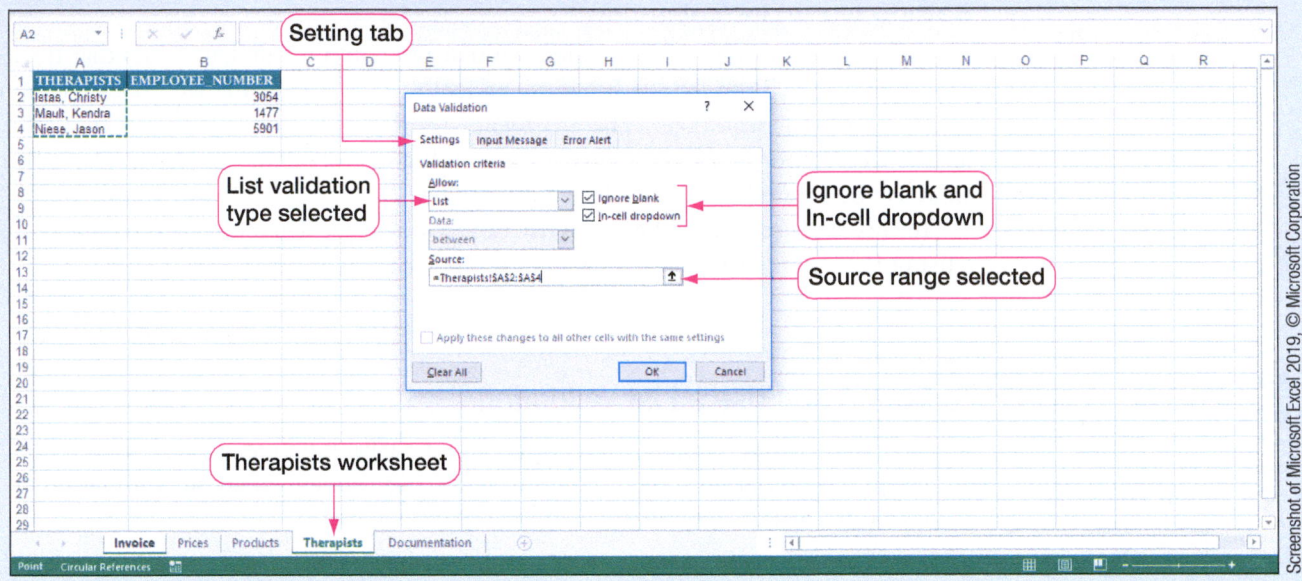

Figure 7 List data validation rule

SIDE NOTE
Named Ranges

Consider using named ranges to identify source data for list validation. They can make your worksheet easier to interpret and understand.

f. In the Data Validation dialog box, click the **Input Message** tab. Click the **Title** box, and then type Select a Therapist

g. Click the **Input message** box, and then type Select the therapist who delivered the services listed.

h. In the Data Validation dialog box, click the **Error Alert** tab. Click the **Title** box next to the Stop alert, and then type Invalid Name

i. Click the **Error message** box, type The name you entered is not a valid name. Please select a name from the list.

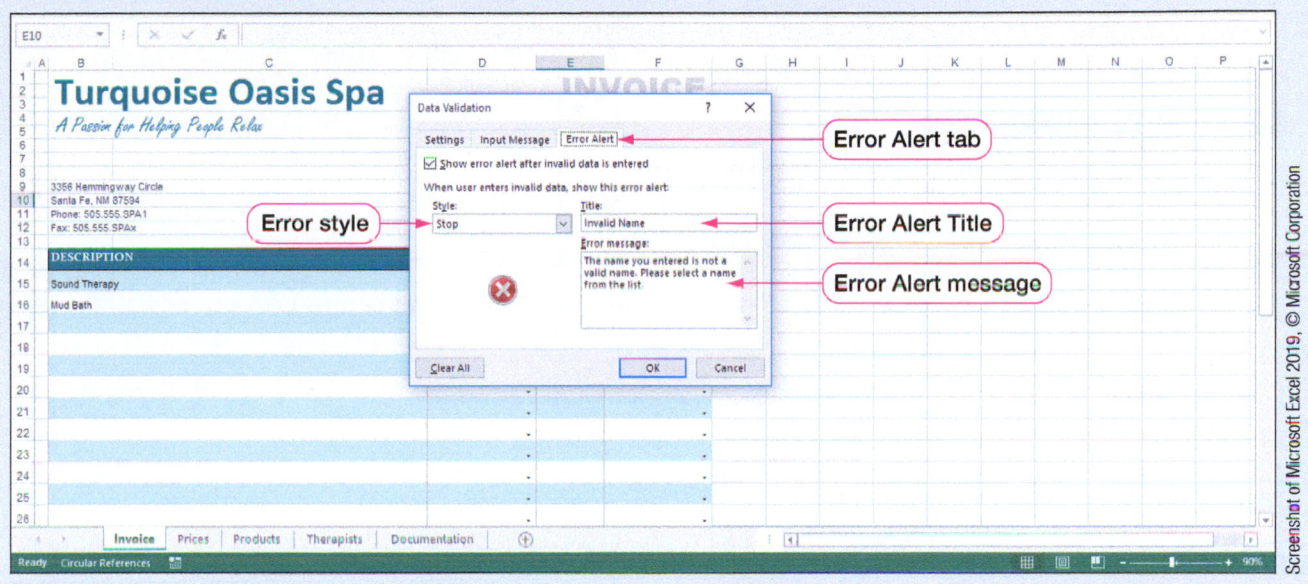

Figure 8 Error Alert tab

j. Click **OK**. Click the list arrow next to cell **E10**, and then select **Istas, Christy**.

k. **Save** the workbook.

Specifying a Decimal Validation

Decimal validation restricts users to only entering data that contains digits and allows decimal places. Validation of this type may require a minimum or maximum value depending on the criteria chosen, such as equal to, between, not equal to, not between, greater than, or less than. In the SpaInvoice workbook, the maximum number of hours for any spa service is two hours.

In this exercise, you will specify a decimal validation rule.

 **E08.06**

To Specify a Decimal Validation Rule

a. On the Invoice worksheet, select the cell range **E15:E30**. On the **Data** tab, in the Data Tools group, click **Data Validation** .

b. In the Data Validation dialog box, click the **Settings** tab, click the **Allow** arrow, and then select **Decimal**. Verify that **Ignore blank** is checked.

c. Click the **Data** box, select **less than or equal to**, and then, in the Maximum box, type **2**

d. Click the **Input Message** tab, click the **Title** box, type **Hours**

e. Click the **Input message** box, and then type **Enter the number of service hours.**

f. Click the **Error Alert** tab, and then click the **Style** arrow.

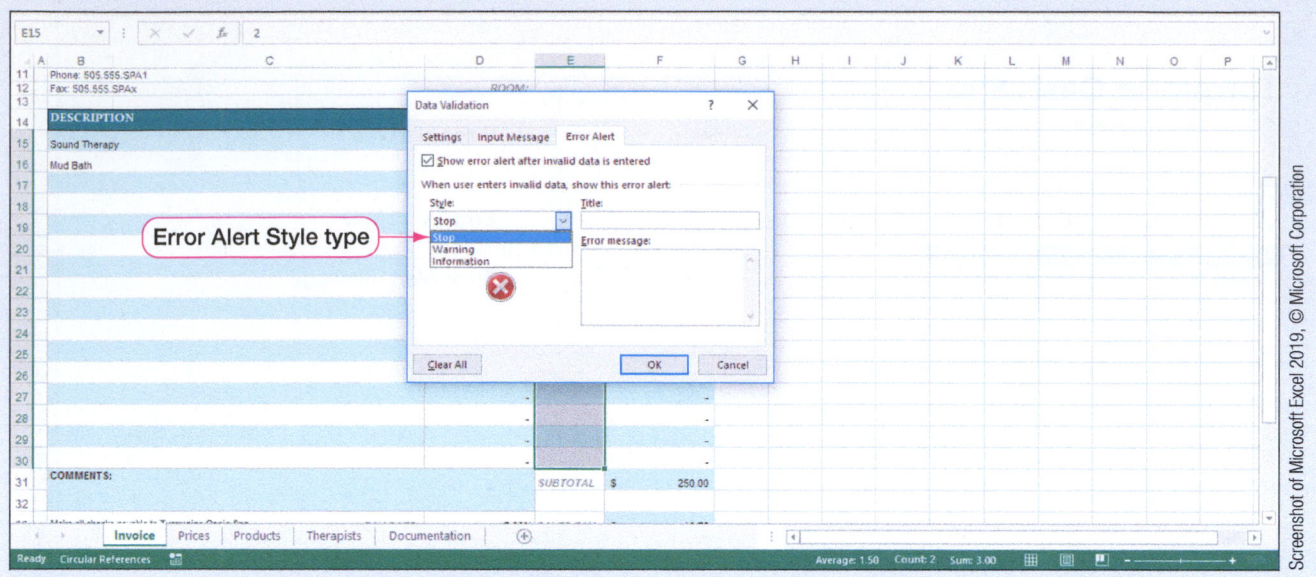

Figure 9 Data validation style

g. Select **Warning**. Click the **Title** box, and then type Invalid Value

h. Click the **Error message** box, type The hours you entered exceed the maximum recommended. and then click **OK**.

i. Click cell **E15**, and then type 3 Notice in the Invalid Value dialog box, you can click Yes to continue entering 3 hours since the cell contains a data validation Warning alert instead of a Stop alert. Press [Esc] to return the value in cell E15 to 2.

j. **Save**  the workbook.

Specifying a Date Validation

Date validation is a type of data validation that specifies that only a date can be entered into a cell. Date criteria values can be explicitly entered, referenced by a cell address, or derived from a formula.

In the SpaInvoice workbook, the date entered in cell E6 should be restricted to the current date or earlier. Thus, invoices may not be dated with a future date. The TODAY function will be used for the date criteria, so the date entered will always be compared to the current date based on the function.

In this exercise, you will limit data entry to a date.

E08.07

To Limit Data Entry to a Date

a. On the Invoice worksheet, select cell **E6**. On the Data tab, in the Data Tools group, click **Data Validation**. In the Data Validation dialog box, click the **Settings** tab, click the **Allow** arrow, and then select **Date**. Verify that **Ignore blank** is checked.

b. Click the **Data** arrow, and then select **less than or equal to**.

c. Click in the **End date** box, and then type =TODAY() This function represents the current date, which means that the invoice cannot have a date later than the current date.

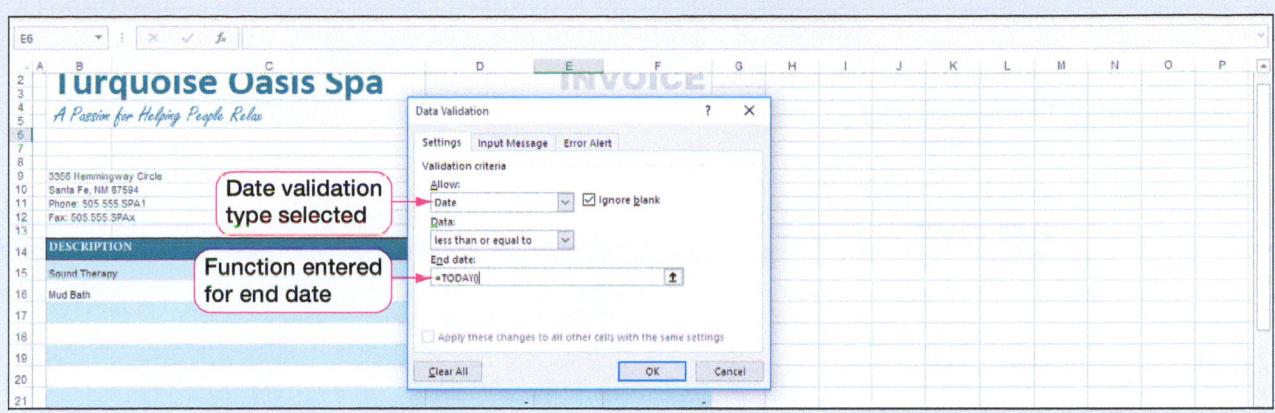

Figure 10 Date validation with formula

Screenshot of Microsoft Excel 2019, © Microsoft Corporation

d. Click the **Input Message** tab, click the **Title** box, and then type Invoice Date

e. Click the **Input message** box, and then type Enter the date in the following format: MM/DD/YYYY.

f. Click the **Error Alert** tab. If necessary, click the **Style** arrow, and then select **Stop**. Click in the **Title** box, and then type Invalid Date

g. Click the **Error message** box, type Future dates are not allowed. and then click **OK**.

h. Select cell **E6**, type =TODAY() to enter the current date, and then press Ctrl+Enter.

If you wanted to enter a date manually, that is, not using the TODAY function, as long as the date is in the correct format (MM/DD/YYYY) and is on or before the current date, it would be allowed.

i. **Save** 💾 the workbook.

Specifying a Time Validation

Time validation is a type of data validation that restricts only time values to be entered into a cell. Time validation is similar to date validation; the only difference is that in time validation, the data entered must be a time value.

In the SpaInvoice workbook, you will add validation criteria to cell E8 to ensure that only a time value between 8:30 AM and 5:00 PM—the spa hours—can be entered.

In this exercise, you will limit data entry to a time value.

 **E08.08**

To Limit Data Entry to a Time Value

a. On the Invoice worksheet, select cell **E8**. On the Data tab, in the Data Tools group, click **Data Validation** 📊. In the Data Validation dialog box, click the **Settings** tab, click the **Allow** arrow, and then select **Time**. Verify that **Ignore blank** is checked and that Data is **between**.

b. Click the **Start time** box, and then type 8:30 AM Click the **End time** box, and then type 5:00 PM

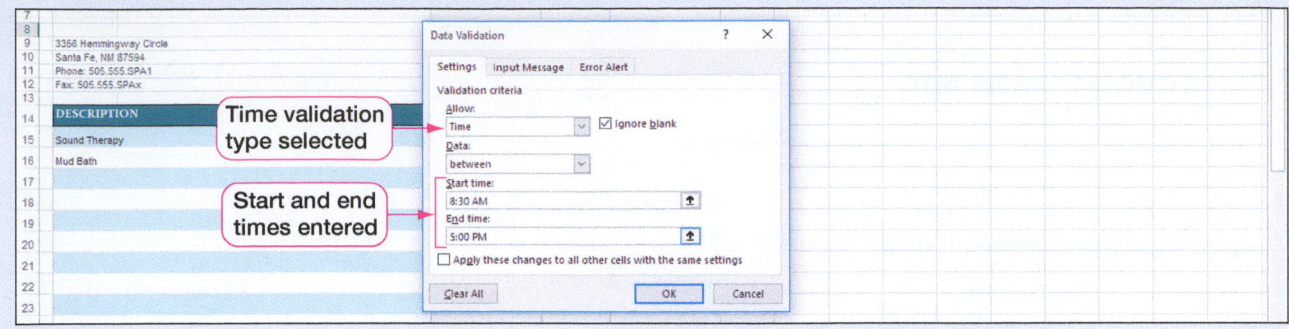

Figure 11 Time data validation

Screenshot of Microsoft Excel 2019, © Microsoft Corporation

c. Click the **Input Message** tab, click the **Title** box, and then type Appointment Time

d. Click in the **Input message** box, and then type Enter the appointment time as HH:MM AM/PM.

e. Click the **Error Alert** tab, click the **Title** box, and then type Invalid Time In the **Error message** box, type The time entered must be between 8:30 AM and 5:00 PM. and then click **OK**.

f. Select cell **E8**, type 3:00 PM and press Ctrl+Enter.

g. **Save** 🖫 the workbook.

Using Whole Number Validation

Whole number validation is a type of data validation that requires that only integers, or whole numbers, be entered in a cell. A valid range or a minimum and a maximum value may also be specified.

In the SpaInvoice workbook, you will set the range of numbers allowed in cell E12 to be between 1001 and 5140. These refer to the highest and lowest guest room numbers in the resort. You also decide to not set an input message or an error alert.

In this exercise, you will limit data entry to a whole number with a minimum and maximum value.

 **E08.09**

To Limit Data Entry to a Whole Number

> ### Grader Heads Up
> In the MyLab IT Grader version of this project, you will not be adding a Whole Number data validation.

a. On the Invoice worksheet, select cell **E12**. On the Data tab, in the Data Tools group, click **Data Validation** 🗏. In the Data Validation dialog box, click the **Settings** tab, click the **Allow** arrow, and then select **Whole number**. Verify that **Ignore blank** is checked and that Data is **between**.

b. Click the **Minimum** box, and then type 1001 Click the **Maximum** box, and then type 5140

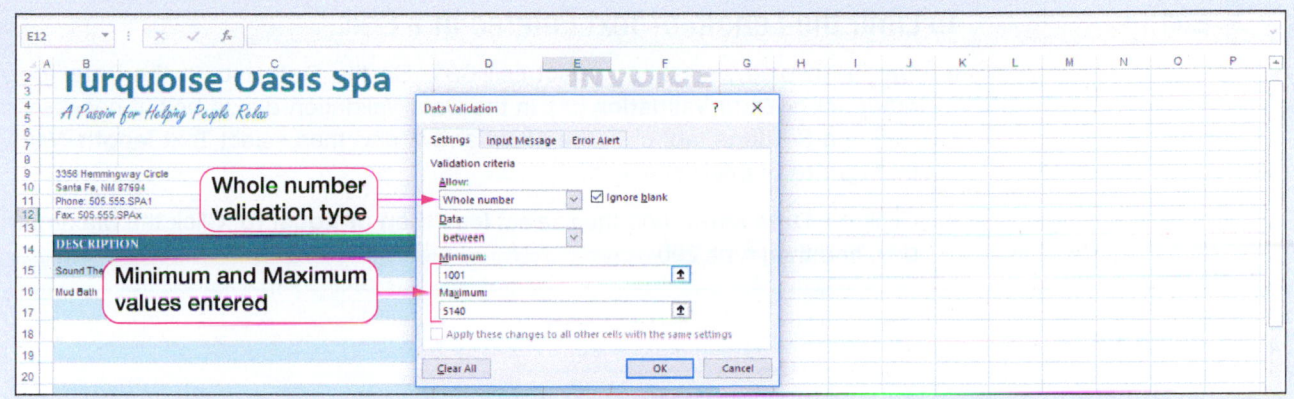

Figure 12 Whole number data validation

Screenshot of Microsoft Excel 2019, © Microsoft Corporation

    c. Click **OK** to skip entering an input message or error alert. Select cell **E12**, type **900** and then press Ctrl+Enter. You will get a Stop error alert that the value doesn't match the data validation.

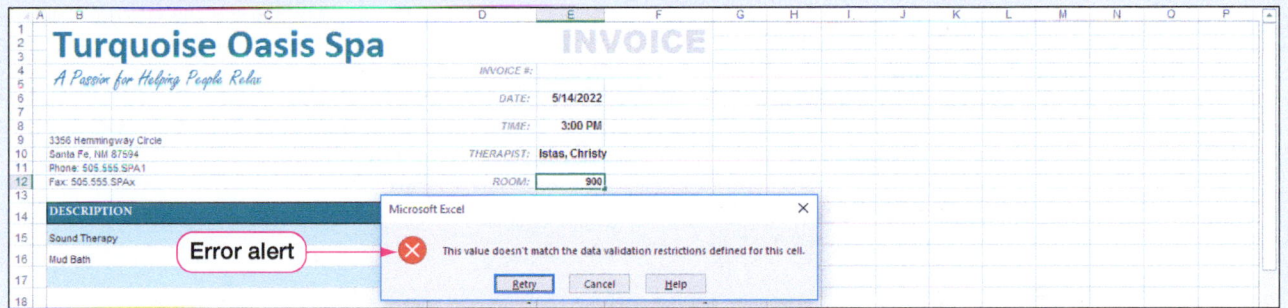

Figure 13 Error alert

Screenshot of Microsoft Excel 2019, © Microsoft Corporation

    d. Click **Cancel**. Type **1001** and then press Ctrl+Enter.

    e. **Save** 💾 the workbook.

Setting Up Text Length Validation

Text length validation is a type of data validation used to limit the number of characters that can be entered into a cell. Data from workbooks is often imported into databases that have fixed field lengths. Using text length validation on a cell that will be imported into a database can help to prevent the data from being truncated (cut off) when it is imported. Text length validation can also prevent cells from becoming too long, which may prevent a range from printing on one page, which is often a requirement for an invoice or other worksheet.

    In this exercise, you will limit data entry by the length of text entered in a cell.

 **E08.10**

To Limit the Length of Text Entered in a Cell

a. On the Invoice worksheet, select cell **C31**. On the **Data** tab, in the Data Tools group, click **Data Validation**. In the Data Validation dialog box, if necessary, click the **Settings** tab, click the **Allow** arrow, and then select **Text length**. Verify that **Ignore blank** is checked.

b. Click the **Data** arrow, and then select **less than or equal to**. Click the **Maximum** box, and then type 200

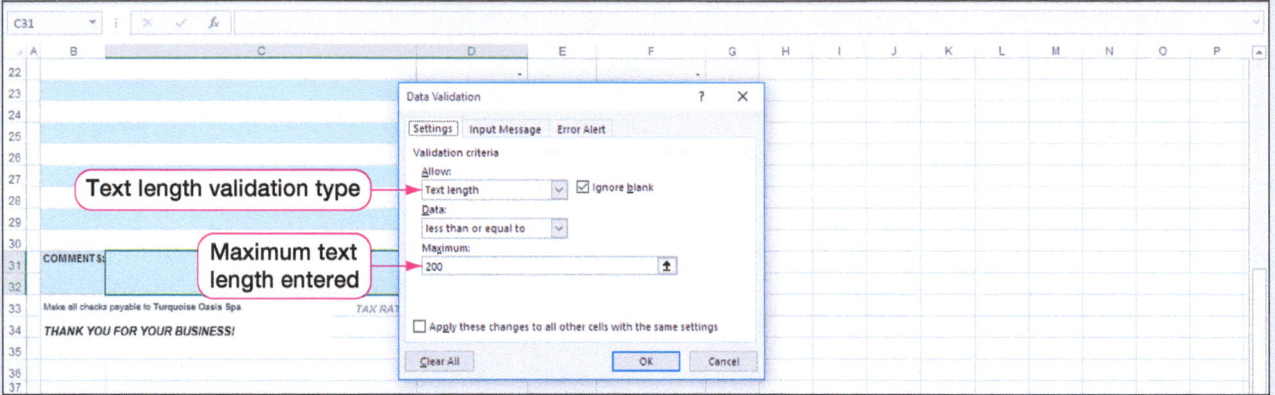

Figure 14 Text data validation

Screenshot of Microsoft Excel 2019, © Microsoft Corporation

c. Do not set an Input Message. Click the **Error Alert** tab, click the **Title** box, and then type Comments Click the **Error message** box, and then type Comments may not be more than 200 characters. Click **OK**.

d. Save the workbook.

Using Any Value Validation

Any value validation is a type of data validation that utilizes the input message to communicate rules to enter data in a cell. The moment an Any Value validated cell is made active, the Input Message is displayed as a prompt to the user. There are no criteria, data restrictions, or error messages set up with an Any Value validation.

In the SpaInvoice workbook, you will create a prompt so that when the user clicks on the Tax Rate in cell D33, a prompt appears with more information about the tax rate. There will be no value associated with the data validation and no error message, just the input message to provide information.

In this exercise, you will use data validation to display data entry prompts.

 **E08.11**

To Use Data Validation to Display Data Entry Prompts

a. On the Invoice worksheet, select cell **D33**. On the Data tab, in the Data Tools group, click **Data Validation**.

b. In the Data Validation dialog box, click the **Input Message** tab. Click the **Title** box, and then type Tax Rate

c. Click the **Input message** box, type All items and services require sales tax. and then click **OK**.

Because you are not restricting data in this cell, changes to the Settings tab and Error Alert tab should not be made.

d. Save the workbook.

Creating a Custom Data Validation

Custom validation is a more complex type of data validation that allows the user to apply multiple criteria simultaneously by using formulas. For example, you can specify a valid range of whole numbers if a number is entered and limit the length of a text value if a text value is entered.

The Painted Paradise Resort & Spa has 700 hotel rooms: 140 rooms on each of five floors. Rooms are numbered according to a codified data value. **A codified data value** is a value created by following a system of rules in which the position of information is tied to its context. Turquoise Oasis room numbers are codified values; the first digit is the floor the room is located on, and the next three digits are the room number on that floor. For example, the 79th room on floor 3 is room 3079. The lowest room number is 1001, and the highest room number is 5140.

In the previous exercise, you used whole number validation to limit the value entered for room number to a range of numbers bounded by the lowest and highest room number values in the hotel. The problem is that there are many invalid values within that range. Each floor has 140 rooms. On floor 3, room numbers range from 3001 to 3140. There are no valid room numbers from 3141 to 3999; so the majority of values allowed by whole number validation criteria used in a previous exercise are invalid.

In the SpaInvoice workbook, you will change the data validation for the room number that only specifies a minimum and maximum value and will create instead a custom validation rule that will allow only the following numbers to be entered in cell E12 for the room number: 1001–1140, 2001–2140, 3001–3140, 4001–4140, and 5001–5140.

In this exercise, you will create a custom validation rule for room numbers.

 **E08.12**

To Create a Custom Validation Rule

a. On the Invoice worksheet, select cell **E12**. Click the **Data** tab, and in the Data Tools group, click **Data Validation**.

b. In the Data Validation dialog box, click the **Settings** tab, and in the **Allow** box, select **Custom**. In the Formula box, select the existing text, and then replace it with =AND(LEFT(E12,1)<="5",LEFT(E12,1)>="1",RIGHT(E12,3)>="001",RIGHT(E12,3)<="140", LEN(E12)=4)

> **Troubleshooting**
>
> If you have trouble entering the data validation formula without making an error, type the formula into a blank cell on the Invoice worksheet. If there is no error, then copy and paste from the formula bar into the Data Validation dialog box.

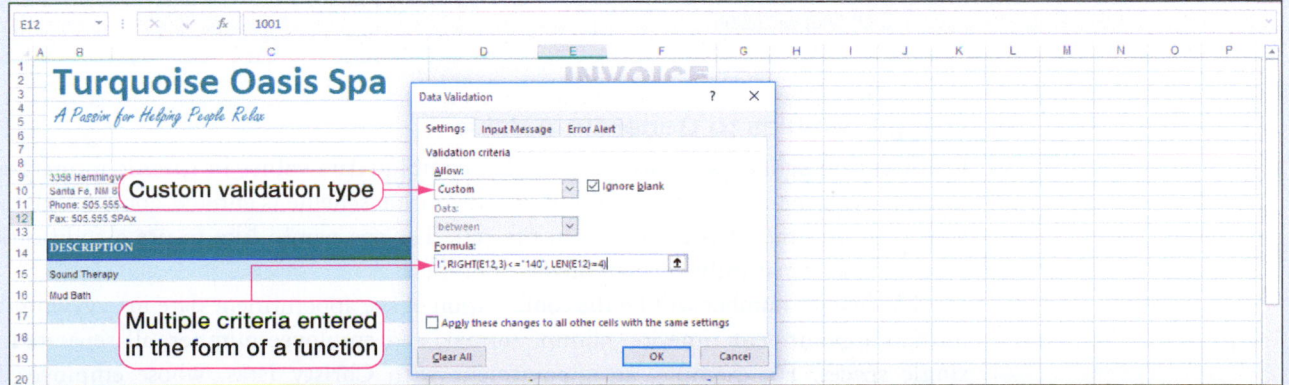

Figure 15 Custom data validation rule

Screenshot of Microsoft Excel 2019, © Microsoft Corporation

By starting with an AND function, the rule requires all the criteria in the function to be true for there not to be an error. So Excel will check the number entered in cell E12, and as long as it meets all of the following criteria, the room number will be accepted. Otherwise, the Alert Message will appear. You will learn the following text functions in chapter 9.

- The LEFT(E12,1)<="5" tests to make sure that the first digit (the digit on the left) of the room number in cell E12 is less than or equal to 5, because the resort has only five floors.

- The LEFT(E12,1)>="1" tests to make sure that the first digit of the room number is greater than or equal to 1. So together with the preceding criterion, this criterion ensures that the first digit is between 1 and 5.

- The RIGHT(E12,3)>="001" tests to make sure that the three digits to the right are greater than or equal to "001", because the room numbers on each floor start with 1.

- The RIGHT(E12,3)<="140" tests to make sure that the three digits to the right are less than or equal to 140, because the highest room number on each floor is 140.

- The LEN(E12)=4 limits the total characters entered into the cell to four.

c. Click the **Input Message** tab. Click the **Title** box, and then type Room Number

d. Click in the **Input message** box, type Enter the 4-digit room number. and click the **Error Alert** tab. Click the **Title** box, and type Error Click the **Error message** box, type Invalid room number. and then click **OK**.

e. In cell **E12**, type 3200 and then press ⟨Ctrl⟩+⟨Enter⟩. You will get an error message that the number you entered is an invalid number. Click **Retry**.

f. While still in cell **E12**, type 3120 and then press ⟨Ctrl⟩+⟨Enter⟩.

g. Save the workbook.

S̲S̲ CONSIDER THIS | **When Data Validation Might Not Be the Best Option**

Data validation is an excellent tool to use in workbooks where you want to restrict data entry to certain values or ranges of values. There may be times when a list of data is required, and data validation can require the use of that list for choosing a value.

However, there may be times when data validation rules can hinder data entry rather than enhancing it. Can you think of a time when data validation might hinder a user who is trying to enter data in a workbook? In what types of situations might that occur? Can you think of any other options available other than data validation?

Using Formulas to Generate a Value

Codification schemes consist of rules that combine data values in specific formats and locations to generate a new data value. A codification scheme is entered not through data validation but rather as a formula in the cell. The spa would like to use a codification scheme to automatically generate invoice numbers.

The invoice number will be the combination of the appointment date in "yyyymmdd" format, appointment time in "hhmm" format, and employee number, all separated by single spaces. For example, an appointment with Christy Istas, whose employee ID number is 3054, on 5/14/2022 at 2:30 PM would have an invoice number of "20220514 1430 3054."

In the SpaInvoice workbook, you will create this codification scheme in a formula that will automatically generate the invoice number based on the data entered in the invoice. You will build the formula one piece at a time until all the pieces of the codification scheme are included.

In this exercise, you will create a codification scheme for the invoice number.

 **E08.13**

SIDE NOTE
Use of Ampersand in Formulas

Use the ampersand (&) in a formula to concatenate, or join two strings together, to return one string.

To Create a Codification Scheme

a. Select cell **E4**, type **=IF(E6>0,TEXT(E6,"YYYYMMDD"),"")** and then press Ctrl + Enter. This formats the invoice number so that the date is the first part of the invoice number in the format YYYYMMDD, but it displays nothing if cell E6—the date—is empty.

b. In the formula bar, click to place the insertion point at the end of the formula. Type **&" "&IF(E8>0,TEXT(E8,"HHMM"),"")** and then press Ctrl + Enter.

There should be a space between the quotation marks that are between the ampersands so there will be a space between the time of the appointment in HHMM format and the invoice number. There should be no space between the quotation marks at the end of the IF function so that the result displays nothing for the time portion if cell E8 (the time) is empty.

c. Place the insertion point at the end of the formula. Type **&" "&IF(E10>0,VLOOKUP(E10,Therapists,2),"")** and then press Ctrl + Enter.

The formula should read: =IF(E6>0,TEXT(E6,"YYYYMMDD"),"")&" "&IF(E8>0,TEXT (E8,"HHMM"),"")&" "&IF(E10>0,VLOOKUP(E10,Therapists,2),""). There should be a space between the quotes that are between the ampersands so there will be a space between the employee number of the therapist selected and the end of the invoice number, but there should be no space between the quotation marks at the end of the IF function so it displays nothing for the therapist's employee number if cell E10 is empty. The therapist's employee number comes from the named range Therapists on the Therapists worksheet and is found by using the VLOOKUP function. The final invoice number in cell E4 should be YYYYMMDD 1500 3054, where YYYY is the four-digit year, MM is the two-digit month, and DD is the two-digit day of the current date entered in the invoice.

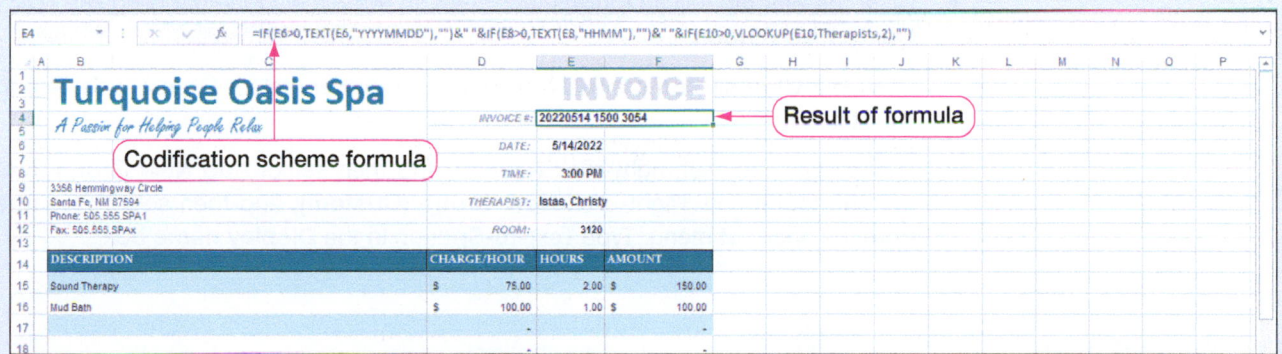

Figure 16 Codification scheme for invoice number

Screenshot of Microsoft Excel 2019, © Microsoft Corporation

d. Save the workbook.

Validating with Text-to-Speech Manually

Excel includes a **text-to-speech** feature that reads the values of text back to you. This feature requires speakers or headphones for this feature to work properly. To use the text-to-speech feature, you have to add at least one text-to-speech button to the ribbon. There are five buttons available to choose from, described in the Quick Reference.

QUICK REFERENCE	Text-to-Speech Options

There are a number of text-to-speech buttons you can add to the ribbon. The button or buttons you choose will determine how you can use the text-to-speech feature.

- Speak Cells: Click to hear the contents of the selected cell and adjacent cells.
- Speak Cells - Stop Speaking Cells: Click to stop hearing the cell contents read.
- Speak Cells by Columns: Click to hear the cell contents read in the column selected.
- Speak Cells by Rows: Click to hear the cell contents read in the row selected.
- Speak Cells on Enter: Click to hear the cell contents read when you press Enter.

This type of editing allows you to hear what you entered as well as see what you entered and can help you find mistakes you might otherwise overlook. This feature has replaced the speech recognition feature in earlier versions of Excel; however, speech recognition is still available in the different versions of Windows.

In the SpaInvoice workbook, you will add two of the Speak Cells buttons to a new group on the Review tab and use it to have the contents of a cell read to you.

In this exercise, you will use text-to-speech for data proofing.

 E08.14

To Use Text-to-Speech for Data Proofing

> **Grader Heads Up**
> In the MyLab IT Grader version of this project, you will not be adding text-to-speech to the Ribbon.

MAC COMPATIBILITY

Adding Commands on a Mac

Mac users, click the Excel menu, and then click Preferences. Under Authoring, click Ribbon & Toolbar. Select Commands Not in the Ribbon, and then select Speak Cells by Columns and Speak Cells by Rows.

a. Click the **File** tab, click **Options**, and then, in the Excel Options dialog box, click **Customize Ribbon**.

b. Click the **Choose commands from** arrow, and then select **Commands Not in the Ribbon**.

c. In the Main Tabs list, right-click **Review**, and then select **Add New Group** from the shortcut menu. Right-click **New Group (Custom)**, and then select **Rename** from the shortcut menu. Type Text-to-Speech in the **Display name** box.

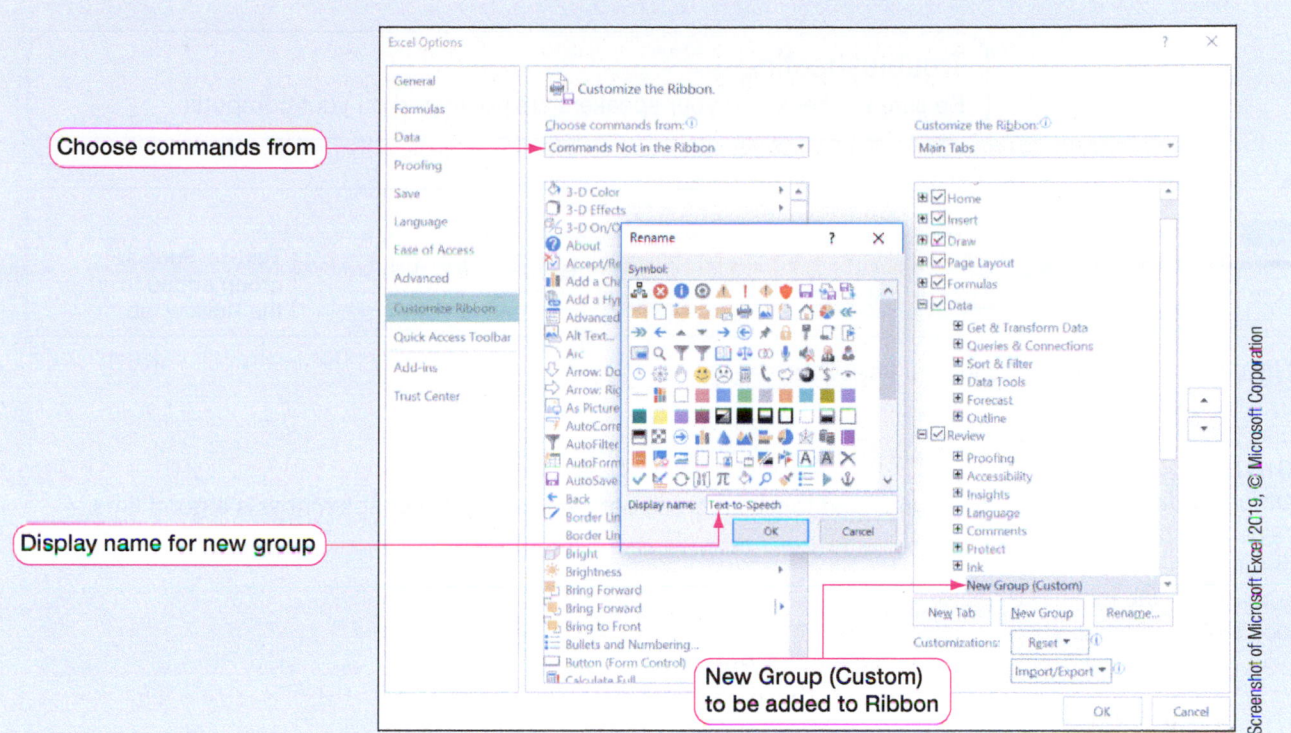

Choose commands from

Display name for new group

New Group (Custom) to be added to Ribbon

Screenshot of Microsoft Excel 2019, © Microsoft Corporation

Figure 17   New group added to Review tab

d. Click **OK**. With the new group still selected, in the Commands list, scroll down, select **Speak Cells**, and then click **Add**. Select **Speak Cells - Stop Speaking**, and then click **Add**.

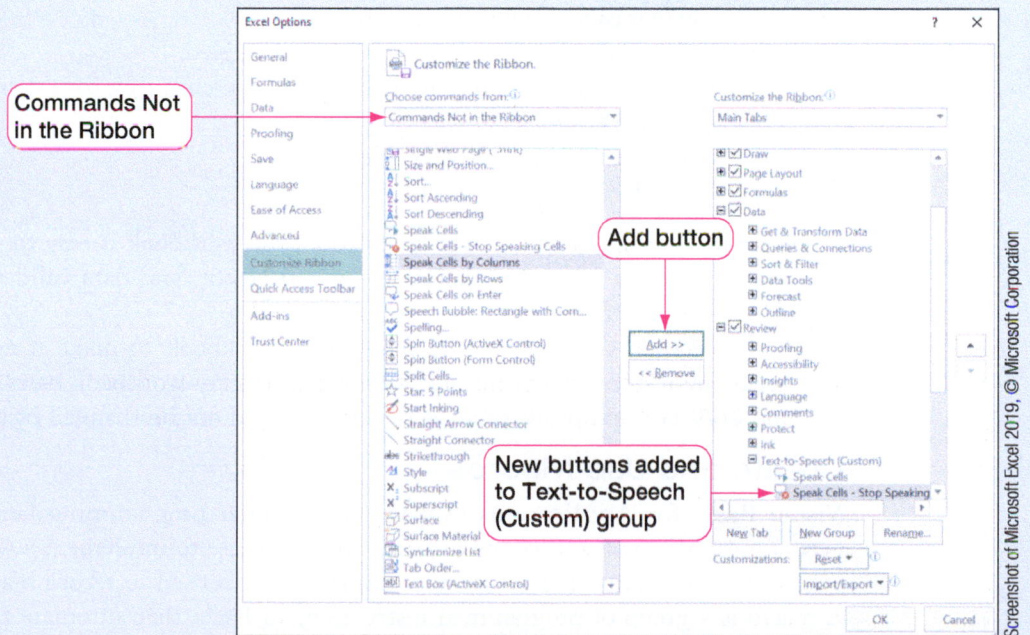

Commands Not in the Ribbon

Add button

New buttons added to Text-to-Speech (Custom) group

Screenshot of Microsoft Excel 2019, © Microsoft Corporation

Figure 18   Text-to-speech buttons to add to the ribbon

e. Click **OK**. Select cell **B15**, and then click the **Review** tab. In the Text-to-Speech group, click **Speak Cells**. When several lines have been read, click **Stop Speaking**.

> **Troubleshooting**
>
> Be sure to check that your speakers are not muted on your computer.

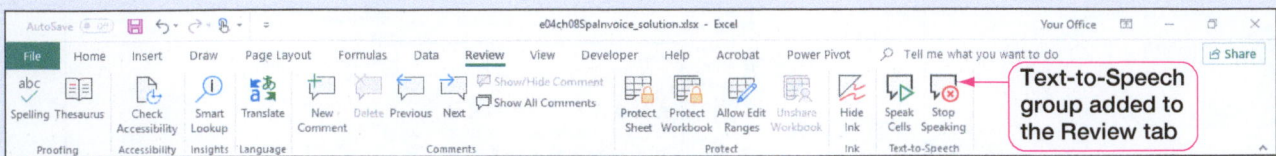

Figure 19 New buttons added to Review tab

Screenshot of Microsoft Excel 2019, © Microsoft Corporation

> **SIDE NOTE**
>
> **Office Updates**
>
> Depending on your exact Office version, your Review tab may look slightly different.

f. **Save** 💾 the workbook.

g. If you need to take a break before finishing this chapter, now is a good time.

Developing User-Friendly Excel Applications

There are many characteristics that can be listed to describe a user-friendly application, whether an Excel application or an application developed in a different technology.

- It has an easy-to-understand user interface.
- User-entered data is validated as much as is possible.
- There is easy, guided navigation.
- Unnecessary functionality is hidden or disabled.
- It offers protection from users inadvertently changing data that would break the application.
- Only essential content is visible.
- Good documentation exists.

So far, in developing the invoice application, the workbook is easy to understand—it is modeled after a standard invoice design and layout, and data validation has been applied to ensure correct data entry as much as possible.

In this section, you will modify the invoice workbook to make it an even better application by implementing macros, hiding unnecessary workbook parts such as scroll bars and gridlines, and protecting the cells that should not be changed by a user.

Create and Use Macros

Visual Basic for Applications (VBA) is a computer programming language that is part of most Microsoft Office products that users can use to implement a wide variety of enhancements to Microsoft Office applications. VBA is used to record macros in Excel. A macro is a group of programmed instructions in Excel that automate tasks and play them back when the macro is run. **A macro** is often used to automate repetitive tasks. For example, a macro may perform menu selections, data entry, data formatting, or even calculation. If a task is performed repeatedly in a worksheet, it is probably a candidate to be recorded as a macro, particularly if incorrectly performing the task could cause inaccuracy on the worksheet. The three locations where a macro can be store are described in Table 1.

Macro Option	Storage Location
This Workbook	This option stores the macro in the active workbook. The macro is available to the active workbook as well as any other open workbooks. Once the active workbook is closed, however, the macro is no longer available to other open workbooks.
New Workbook	This option saves the macro in a new workbook. The macro is available to the active workbook and any open workbooks. Once the new workbook is closed, the macro is no longer available to the active workbook or any other open workbooks.
Personal Macro Workbook	This option stores the macro in a hidden workbook that automatically opens every time you open Excel. The macro is then available to any open workbooks as well as any new workbooks that may be created.

Table 1 Locations where macros can be stored

In the SpaInvoice workbook, you will create two different macros. One macro will clear the data from the invoice, and the other will automatically apply formatting to a range of cells. Because a macro records every keystroke and mouse click, it is best practice to plan a macro before recording it to avoid recording unnecessary mouse clicks or keystrokes. If you did record any unnecessary mouse clicks or keystrokes, they can be removed from the macro; in a later exercise, you will learn how to modify a macro. Best practice is also to test your macro to make sure it works as you had planned.

First, you will set up a Trusted Location for your macro-enabled workbook so when you open it, the macros will not be blocked.

Creating a Trusted Location

When you save a workbook that contains a macro, Excel recognizes it as a potential threat, primarily because macros can contain viruses as well as legitimate commands. A **Trusted Location** is a folder that has been identified in the Microsoft Office Trust Center as a safe location for opening files that contain active code that includes macros. If a workbook in a Trusted Location is opened, macros contained in the document will be automatically enabled. If the location where the file is stored is not a Trusted Location, the Trust Center will block any macros and other items that could contain malicious code, and you will have to manually enable the content when you open it.

By default, Excel already has some Trusted Locations set up for templates and other start files. In this exercise, you will add the folder where you are saving your student files as a trusted folder.

 E08.15

MAC COMPATIBILITY
Trust Center Not Available on a Mac
The Trust Center option is not available on a Mac. On the menu bar, click Excel, click Preferences, and then click Security & Privacy. Under Macro Security, select one of the three options (Disable all macros without notification, Disable all macros with notification, or Enable all macros).

To Create a Trusted Location

> **Grader Heads Up**
> In the MyLab IT Grader version of this project, you will not be adding a Trusted Location.

a. If you took a break, open the **e04ch08SpaInvoice_LastFirst** workbook, and, if necessary, click the **Invoice** worksheet.

b. Click the **File** tab, click **Options**, click **Trust Center**, and then click **Trust Center Settings**.

c. Click **Trusted Locations**, and under Trusted Locations, click **Add new location**. In the Microsoft Office Trusted Locations dialog box, click **Browse**, navigate to the folder where you save your student files, and then select that folder.

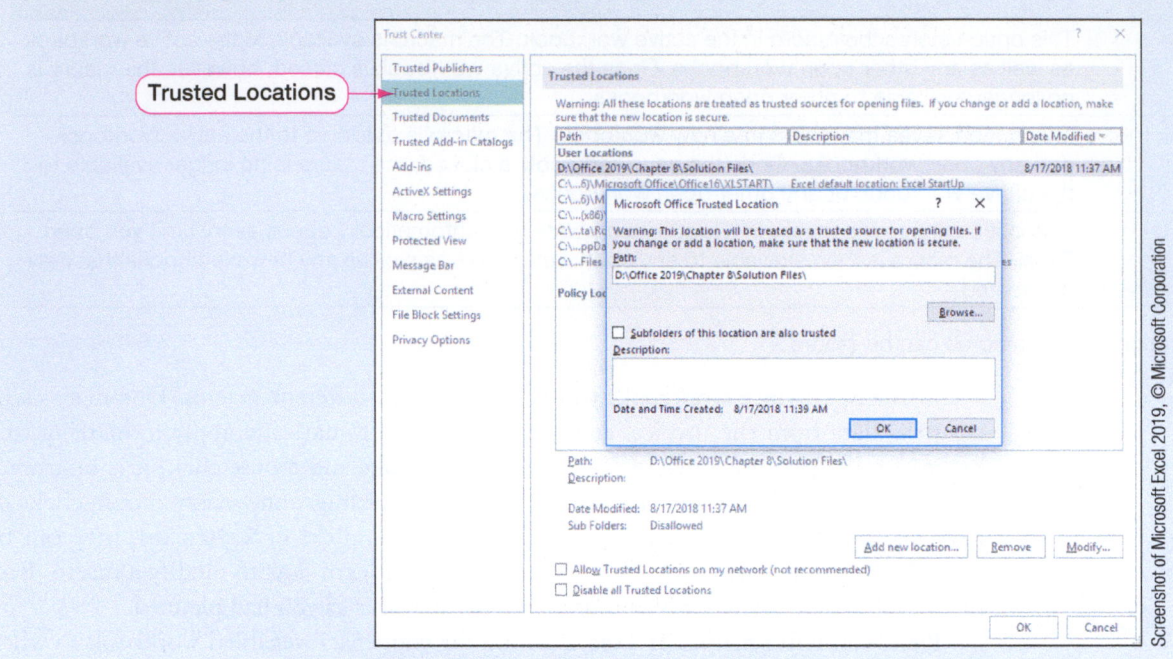

Figure 20 Trusted Center dialog box

d. Click **OK**, click **OK** again, and then verify that your folder has been added to the list of User Locations. Click **OK**, and then click **OK** again.

e. Save the workbook.

REAL WORLD ADVICE   **Trusted Locations**

Instead of setting up trusted locations, you can change Excel settings to enable all macros. However, proceed with caution. Macros can contain computer viruses and can put your computer as risk. Best practice is to disable all macros and enable them on a case-by-case basis.

Adding the Developer Tab to the Ribbon

Recording macros is generally considered an activity for worksheet developers. The Developer tab is not visible by default in Excel, so in order to record a macro, the Developer tab needs to be added to the ribbon. The **Developer tab** contains the buttons needed to create, edit, and run macros.

In this exercise, you will add the Developer tab to the ribbon so you can access the buttons necessary to create macros for the Spa workbook.

E08.16

MAC COMPATIBILITY
Trust Center Not Available on a Mac
On a Mac, on the menu bar, click Excel, click Preferences, and under Authoring, click View. Under In Ribbon, Show, select the Developer tab check box.

To Add the Developer Tab to the Ribbon

a. Click the **File** tab, click **Options**, and then click **Customize Ribbon**.

b. In the Main Tabs list on the right side of the Excel Options dialog box, click the **Developer** check box, and then click **OK**.

c. Save 🔖 the workbook.

Creating an Absolute Macro Reference

As with cell references in formulas, cell references in macros can be absolute or relative. An **absolute macro reference** affects the same cell address each time the macro is run. Absolute macro references are set when the macro is recorded. The location of the active cell when the macro is run is irrelevant. Macros are recorded with absolute references by default.

In this exercise, you will record an absolute macro to clear the current data but leave all the formulas necessary for the invoice to calculate correctly.

 E08.17

SIDE NOTE
Naming a Macro
A macro name cannot have a space. Consider using capitalization or underscores when assigning macro names.

To Record an Absolute Macro

a. On the **Invoice** worksheet, click the **Developer** tab, and in the Code group, click **Record Macro** 🔲.

b. In the Record Macro dialog box, in the **Macro name** box, type ClearCells

c. Click in the **Shortcut key** box, press and hold the [Shift] key, and then type C Ensure that Store macro in has **This Workbook** selected.

d. In the **Description** box, type To clear contents from cells.

Troubleshooting

Make sure you use an uppercase "C" when recording the macro so the shortcut keys will be [Ctrl]+[Shift]+[C]. [Shift] is added because [Ctrl]+[C] is the keyboard Copy shortcut.

Mac Troubleshooting

On a Mac, [Ctrl] is replaced by [Option]+[Command ⌘] in the Record Macro dialog box.

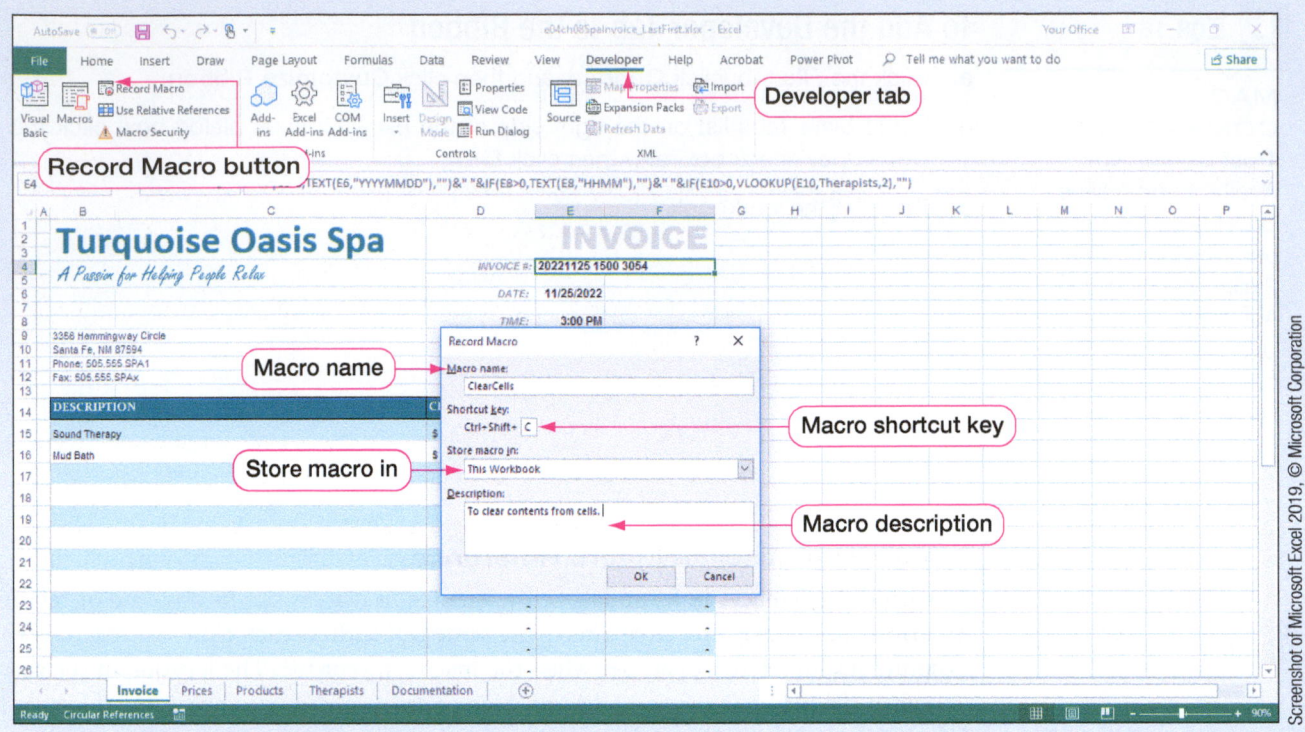

Figure 21 Macro dialog box

SIDE NOTE

Alternate Method
You can also stop recording a macro by clicking the stop recording button in the lower-left corner of the worksheet window.

SIDE NOTE

Deleting a Macro
To delete a macro, click the Developer tab, and in the Code group, click Macros, select the macro you want to delete, and then click Delete.

e. Click **OK**. Select cell **E6**, press and hold Ctrl, and then select cells **E8**, **E10**, **E12**, **B15:B30**, **C31**, and **E15:E30**.

f. Click the **Home** tab, and in the Editing group, click **Clear**, and then select **Clear Contents**. Click cell **E6**.

g. Click the **Developer** tab, and in the Code group, click **Stop Recording**.

h. Click the **File** tab, and then click **Save**. Click **No**.

To save the macro, you will have to save the workbook as a macro-enabled workbook.

i. In the Save As dialog box, in the **File name** box, type e04ch08SpaInvoiceMacro_LastFirst using your last and first name. Click the **Save as type** box, and then select **Excel Macro-Enabled Workbook**. Click **Save**.

Notice that the file extension of the macro-enabled workbook changes to .xlsm. You can add data to the invoice, then run the macro to see whether it works correctly.

j. Click in cell **E6**, enter today's date Click in cell **E8**, and enter 3:00 PM Click in cell **E10**, and select **Istas, Christy**.

k. Press Ctrl+Shift+C to test the macro.

l. **Save** the workbook.

REAL WORLD ADVICE   **A Macro Cannot Be Undone**

The effects of a macro cannot be reversed by using the Undo command. In fact, running a macro in Excel deletes the entire Undo history. If the macro is relatively simple, the easiest way to "fix" it is to delete it and start over again. The other option, discussed in the "Working with Relative Macro References" section that follows, is to modify the program in the VBA editor. This requires some knowledge of programming, so for most users, deleting the macro and starting over is generally the simplest option.

Working with Relative Macro References

Relative macro references identify cells relative to the location of the active cell when the macro was recorded. Whereas an absolute macro reference will always make changes to the same cells whenever the macro is run, a relative macro reference will make changes to the cells relative to where the active cell is located.

For example, if you want to change the formatting of the cell you are on and the cell to the right of the cell you are on, then you would record a relative macro. This way, regardless of which cell is active, the macro will affect that cell and the cell to the right of it.

When a customer is charged a special price, the spa likes to highlight that invoice item. In this exercise, you will create a relative macro to highlight a row in the invoice.

 **E08.18**

MAC COMPATIBILITY
Relative Macros Not Available on a Mac
Mac users will not be able to complete this exercise.

To Record a Relative Macro

a. On the Invoice worksheet, select cell **B15**, click the selection arrow, and choose **Facial - Mud & Citrus**. Select cell **E15**, type **1** and then press Ctrl+Enter.

b. Click cell **B15**. On the **Developer** tab, in the Code group, click **Use Relative References**. This will toggle the Use Relative References button on, which is evident by the color to which the button changes.

c. Click **Record Macro**, and in the **Macro Name** box, type HighlightItem for the macro name. Click in the **Shortcut key** box, and then type h Ensure the Store macro in box is **This Workbook**. Click in the **Description** box, type To highlight an invoice special.

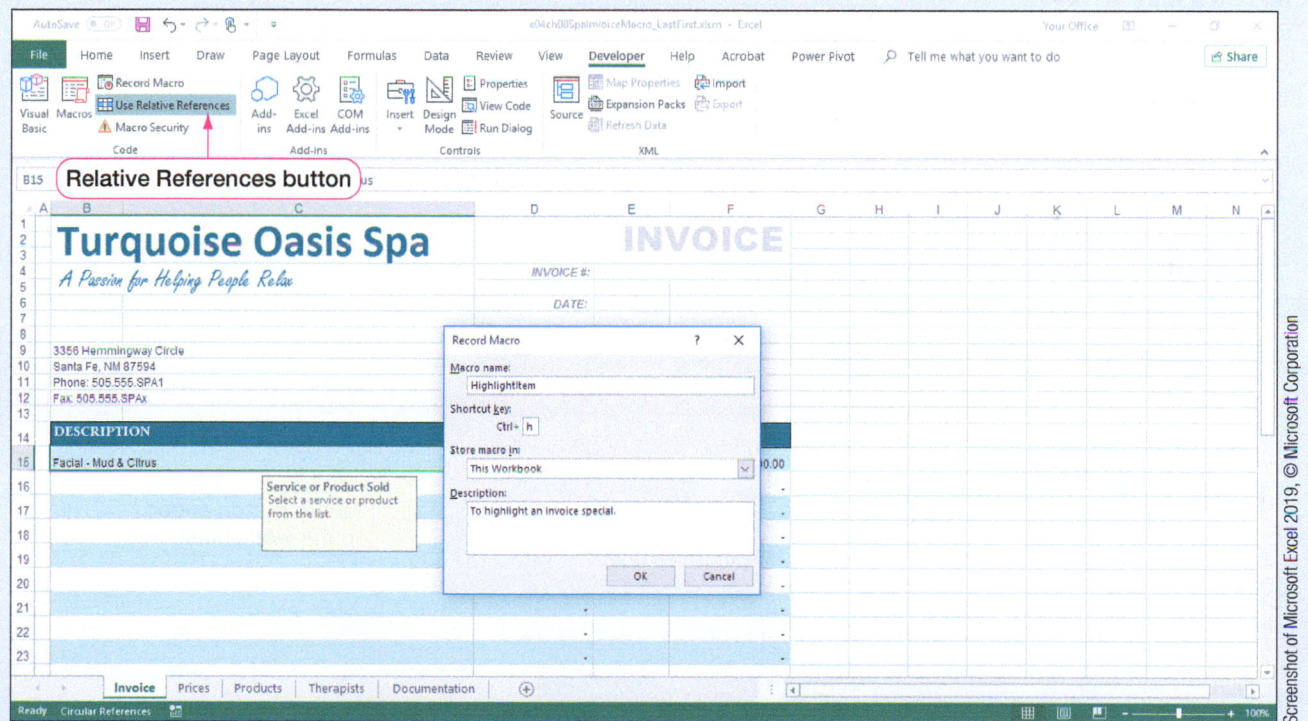

Figure 22 Relative Macro dialog box

d. Click **OK**. Select cells **B15:F15**, click the **Home** tab, and in the Font group, click **Bold**. Click the **Font Size** arrow, and then select **14**.

e. Click the **Developer** tab, and in the Code group, click **Stop Recording**.

f. Click cell **B16**, click the list arrow, and then select **Hair Coloring**. Press Ctrl+H to test the macro.

g. **Save** the workbook.

Adding a Macro to a Button

Macros can be run by using the keyboard shortcuts you apply when creating the macro, from the Developer tab, or even from a button that you can add to a worksheet. A button makes it easy for a user to run a macro with little or no knowledge of how a macro works.

In this exercise, you will create a macro button to run the ClearCells macro.

 **E08.19**

SIDE NOTE
Running a Macro from the Ribbon

To run a macro from the ribbon, click the Developer tab, and in the Code group, click Macros, select the macro name, and then click Run.

MAC COMPATIBILITY
Edit Macro Button Text on a Mac

To edit a macro button's text on a Mac, point to the button text until the cursor changes to an insertion point, and then click to edit the text.

To Create a Macro Button

a. On the Invoice worksheet, on the **Developer** tab, and in the Controls group, click **Insert**. Under Form Controls, select the **Button (Form Control)** in the top left corner. Click in the top left corner of cell **G2**, and then drag to the bottom-right corner of cell **H3** to draw the button.

b. In the Assign Macro dialog box, under Macro name, click **ClearCells**.

> **Troubleshooting**
>
> Be very careful once you have created a button to run a macro. Even when you are editing the button and its properties, if you left-click the button, the macro will run.

c. Click **OK**. Right-click the button, select **Edit Text**, delete the text, and then type Clear Invoice Right-click the button, and then select **Exit Edit Text**.

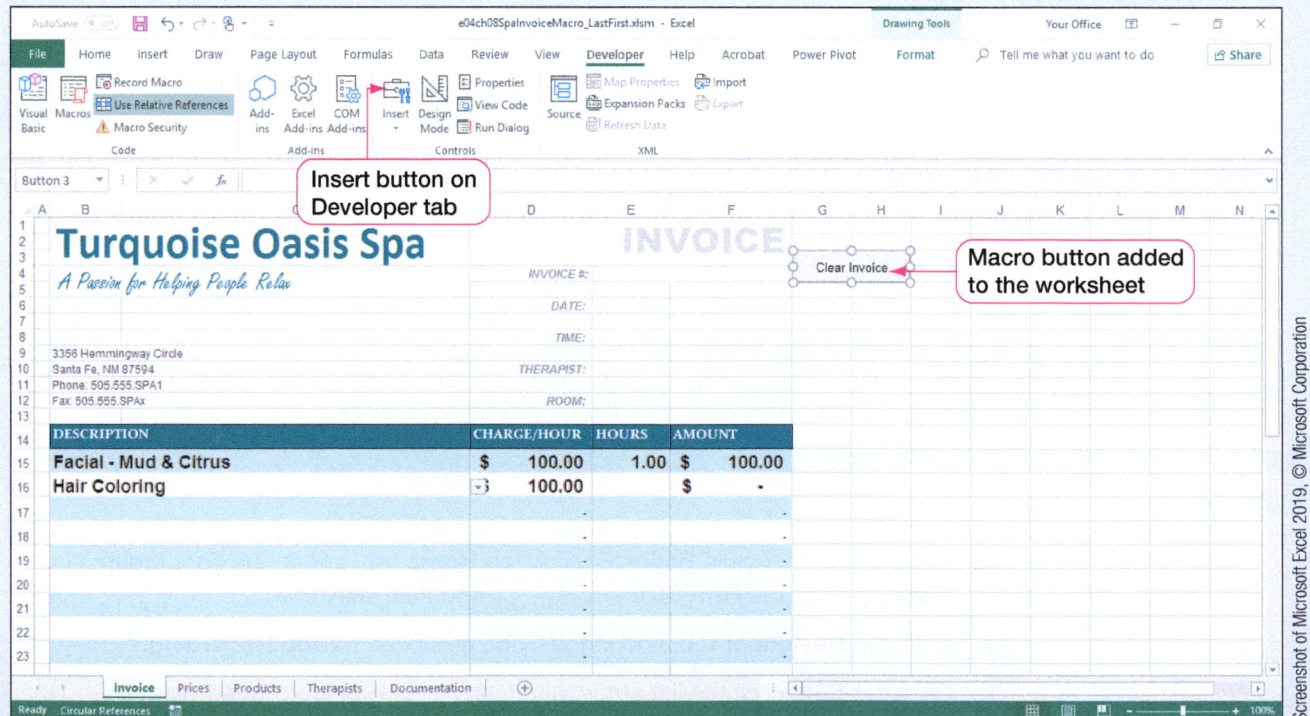

Figure 23 Macro button on the worksheet

d. Select cell **G5** to deselect the button. Click the **Clear Invoice** button to run the macro and verify that the data in the invoice is cleared.

> The ClearCells macro in this example clears the contents of the cells but does not clear the formatting, so the special formatting you applied with the HighlightItem macro is still applied to the cell range B15:F15. You will create an absolute macro to clear the formatting.

e. On the **Developer** tab, in the Code group, click **Use Relative References** to toggle it off.

f. Click **Record Macro**. In the **Macro name** box, type ClearFormatting In the **Shortcut key** box, type k Ensure that the Store macro in box is **This Workbook**. Click in the **Description** box, type To clear special highlighting from the invoice. and then click **OK**.

g. Select the cell range **B15:F30**. Click the **Home** tab, and in the Font group, click **Bold** B . In the Font group to remove the bold format, click the **Font Size** arrow 10 , and then select **9**. Click cell **B15**.

h. Click the **Developer** tab, and in the Code group, click **Stop Recording** .

i. **Save** the workbook.

Modifying a Macro

If you make a mistake when recording a macro, you can delete the macro and record a new one. Or if you know VBA, you can edit a macro and change the VBA code that Excel produced.

In the previous exercise, you recorded a ClearFormatting macro to clear any formatting applied from the HighlightItem macro. To eliminate having to run an extra macro, you will edit the ClearCells macro to include the step recorded in the ClearFormatting macro.

In this exercise, you will modify a macro using VBA.

 **E08.20**

To Modify a Macro Using VBA

a. On the Invoice worksheet, on the **Developer** tab, in the Code group, click the **Macros** button. In the Macro dialog box, in the **Macro name** list, select **ClearCells**, and then click **Edit**.

> A new Visual Basic for Applications (VBA) window opens with the actual code for the macro you recorded. All macros you have recorded will show in the window, separated from one another by a horizontal line.

Troubleshooting

The code you see in the VBA code window may not exactly match the code shown in Figure 24. Excel converts every keystroke and mouse click to VBA code when recording a macro, so any deviation from the steps in the exercise in which you created the macros—including keystrokes to correct deviations—are recorded.

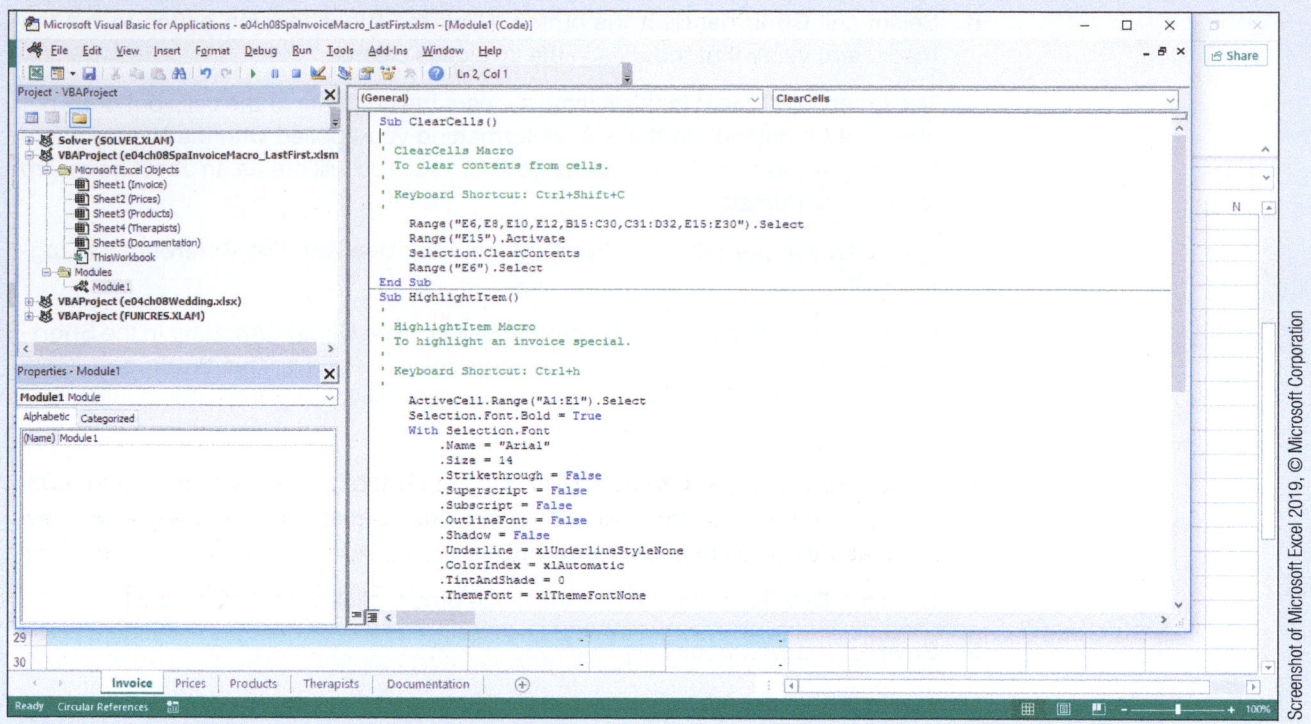

Figure 24 VBA window

b. Scroll if necessary to see the VBA code for the ClearFormatting macro.

c. Select the text that starts with **Range ("B15:F30")** and ends with **Range ("B15:C15").Select**. Press Ctrl+C.

d. Scroll to the top of the VBA window to see the ClearCells macro. Place your insertion point after the line **Range ("E6").Select**. Press Enter, and then press Ctrl+V.

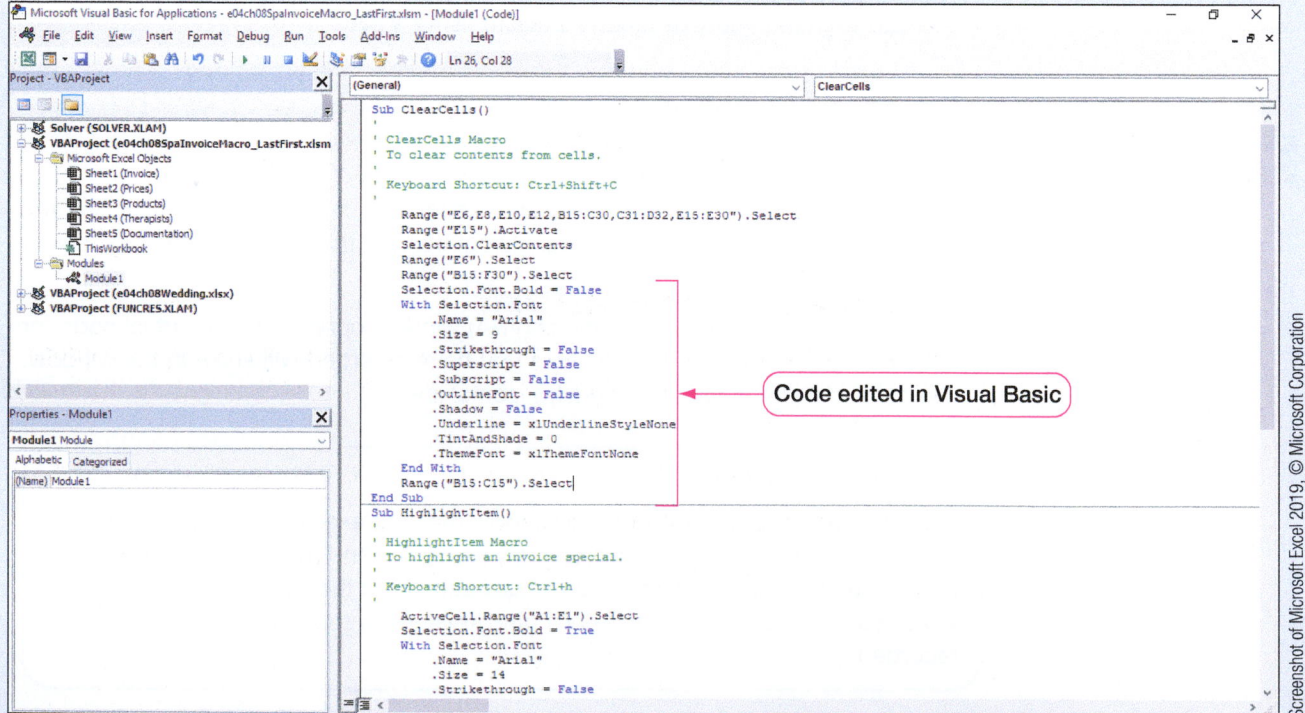

Figure 25 Edited VBA code

e. On the menu, click **File**, and then select **Close and Return to Microsoft Excel**. Your changes will be saved automatically, and the VBA window will close.

f. Click cell **B15**, and select **Facial - Mud & Citrus**. Press ⌈Ctrl⌉+⌈H⌉ to apply formatting from the HighlightItem macro.

g. Click the **Clear Invoice** button. If necessary, click the **Home** tab, and verify that the formatting in row 15 was changed back to size 9, not bold.

h. Save 💾 the workbook.

i. If you need to take a break, now is a good time.

Change How to Navigate a Workbook

Workbook navigation is defined as moving from one cell to another in a worksheet and moving between worksheets. Assisting workbook users by adding navigational aids to a workbook and by hiding worksheets and features that the user does not need makes that workbook much more usable and easier to understand, and it makes the workbook's appearance much cleaner and less intimidating.

In the SpaInvoice workbook, you will add a hyperlink to navigate to a different worksheet and then hide unnecessary worksheets, scroll bars, row and column headings, and gridlines. This will give the invoice a cleaner look and make it look less like an Excel workbook.

Navigating with Hyperlinks

A **hyperlink** is a link that opens another page or file when you click on it. In Excel, a hyperlink can open a worksheet, another workbook, a file, a picture, an e-mail address, a photo, a web page, or another program. The hyperlink can be text or a picture and makes it easy for a user to get additional information that is in another location. Screen tips can be assigned to hyperlinks to give the user more description on the purpose of the hyperlink.

In the SpaInvoice workbook, there are multiple worksheets with information about the prices, products, and therapists. Because the charge per hour is automatically filled in based on the description the user chooses, you will add a hyperlink to that heading so the user can find more information about the charge per hour.

In this exercise, you will add hyperlinks to the workbook.

 E08.21

SIDE NOTE
Editing a Hyperlink
Right-click the hyperlink, and then select Edit Hyperlink.

To Add Hyperlinks to the Workbook

a. If you took a break, open the **e04ch08SpaInvoiceMacro_LastFirst** workbook. On the Invoice worksheet, select cell **D14**, click the **Insert** tab, in the Links group, click **Link**.

b. In the **Insert Hyperlink** dialog box, in **Link to**, select **Place in This Document**.

c. In the **Type the cell reference** box, type F2

d. In the **Or select a place in this document** box, click **Prices**.

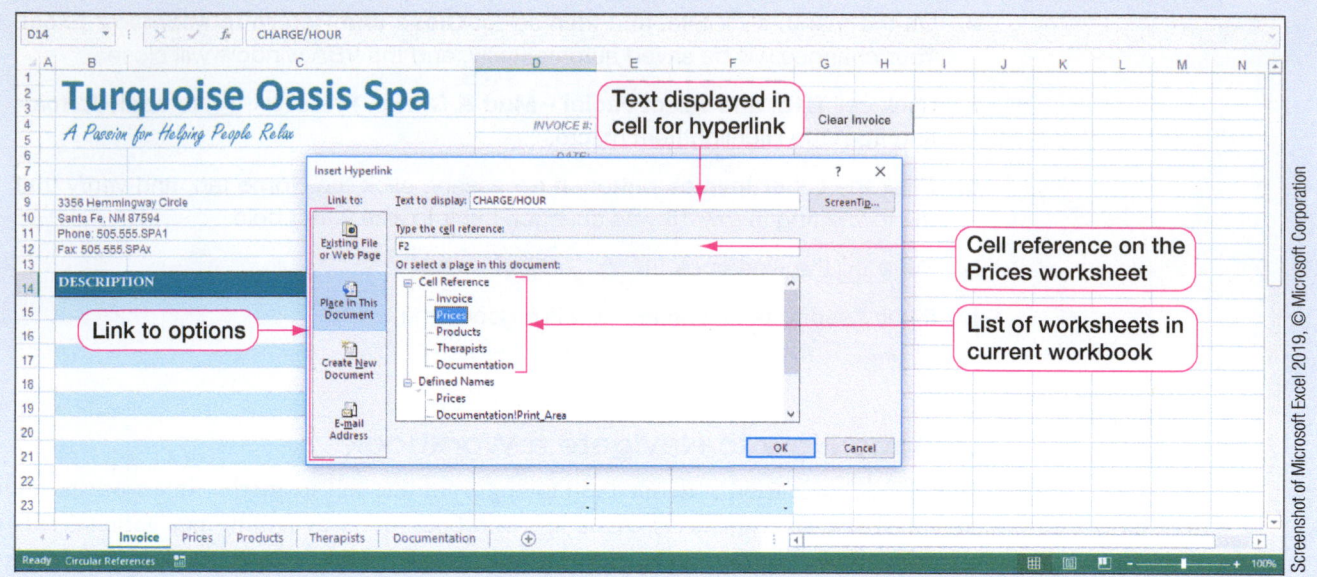

Figure 26 Inserting a hyperlink

e. Click **ScreenTip**. In the Set Hyperlink ScreenTip dialog box, type Go to Prices worksheet

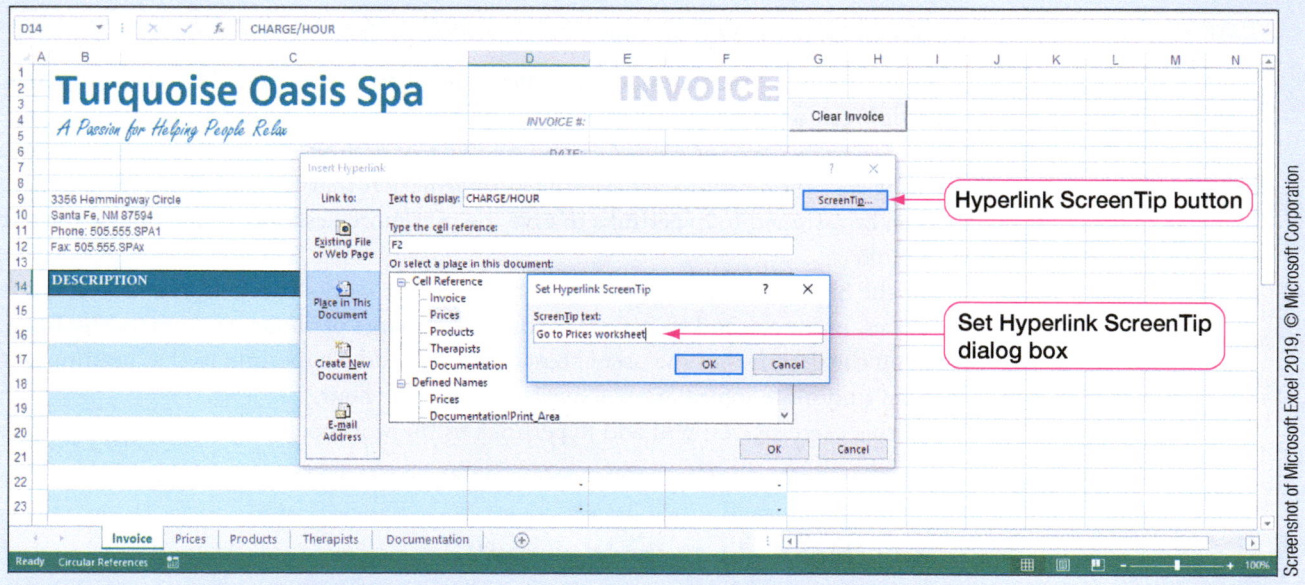

Figure 27 ScreenTip dialog box

f. Click **OK**, and then click **OK**. The font color of the text in cell D14 will change to the default font color for a hyperlink; the text will also be underlined.

g. In cell **D14**, click the hyperlink. The Prices worksheet should now be the active worksheet, and cell F2 should be the active cell.

h. On the **Insert** tab, in the Links group, click **Link**. In the **Type the cell reference** box, type **D14** In the **Or select a place in this document** box, select **Invoice**. Click **ScreenTip**. In the Set Hyperlink ScreenTip dialog box, type Return to Invoice worksheet Click **OK**, and then click **OK**.

i. Click cell **F2** to return to the Invoice worksheet.

SIDE NOTE
Link to Defined Names
You can also create links to defined names within a workbook by selecting Place in This Document and then selecting the named range.

> **Troubleshooting**
> Click and hold on a cell that contains a hyperlink until the mouse pointer changes to ⊕. The cell will be selected without accessing the hyperlink.

j. **Save** the workbook.

Hiding Worksheets

A workbook with data stored in multiple worksheets can seem cluttered and difficult to navigate. There may be times when you would prefer that users not see data or have access to background calculations and code that have been placed in another worksheet. Because this data is often required for formulas, functions, and other calculations in a workbook, the worksheets can be hidden so a user cannot easily access it.

The employee number listed on the Therapists worksheet could be considered confidential information, so you want to hide this worksheet.

In this exercise, you will hide the Therapists worksheet.

▶ **E08.22**

SIDE NOTE
Unhide a Worksheet
Right-click any worksheet tab, select Unhide, select the name of the hidden worksheet, and click OK.

To Hide a Worksheet

a. Right-click the **Therapists** worksheet, and then select **Hide** from the shortcut menu. This will hide the worksheet so it can no longer be accessed by a worksheet.

b. Click the **Invoice** worksheet.

c. **Save** 🖫 the workbook.

Hiding Worksheet Tabs

When you hide a worksheet, any hyperlinks to that worksheet will no longer work. Excel assumes that if you want the data on the worksheet hidden, then you would not want to provide access to the data through a hyperlink. However, if you do want to access the data on a worksheet through a hyperlink but not through the worksheet tab, you can hide the worksheet tabs instead. Hiding worksheet tabs will affect the whole workbook: Either all the worksheet tabs will be hidden or none of the worksheet tabs will be hidden. Once you hide the worksheet tabs, you have to show them again to continue navigating to individual worksheets, especially if you do not have hyperlinks set up to each worksheet.

In the SpaInvoice workbook, you will hide the worksheet tabs so the Charge/Hour link you created will still be functional but the tabs will not be visible. Because you created a hyperlink from the Prices worksheet to return to the Invoice worksheet, it will be okay to hide the worksheet tabs.

In this exercise, you will hide worksheet tabs.

 **E08.23**

To Hide Worksheet Tabs

Grader Heads Up
In the MyLab IT Grader version of this project, you will not be hiding worksheet tabs.

SIDE NOTE
Show Worksheet Tabs
On the File tab, click Options, click Advanced, scroll down, and check Show sheet tabs. Click OK.

a. Click the **Invoice** worksheet. Click the **File** tab, click **Options**, and then click **Advanced**. Scroll down until the **Display options for this workbook** group is visible.

Troubleshooting
If the Invoice worksheet is not the active worksheet when you hide it, you will have no way to get back to that worksheet if you do not have any hyperlinks set up. If this happens, repeat the steps to hide the worksheets, check Show sheet tabs, and click OK.

MAC COMPATIBILITY
Changing Display Options
Changing display options is done differently on a Mac. On the menu bar, click Exel, and then click Preferences. Under Authoring, click View. Under Show in Workbook, click to select the desired options.

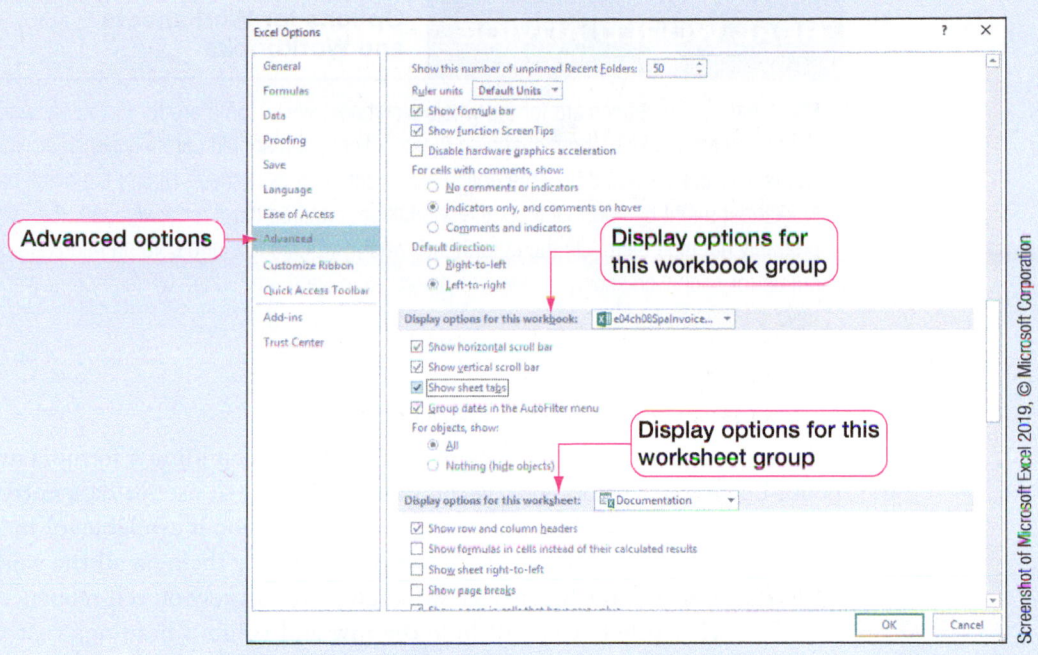

Figure 28 Display options for this workbook

b. Click **Show sheet tabs** to uncheck the option, and then click **OK**. Notice that the sheet tabs at the bottom of the window are no longer visible.

c. Save  the workbook.

Hiding Scroll Bars

Depending on the size of the worksheet and the resolution of your monitor, vertical and/or horizontal scroll bars may or may not be necessary. You can choose to hide the scroll bars, but you should do so only if all cells will be visible on one screen, regardless of the screen size. This option will affect the whole workbook, not just one worksheet.

The Spa workbook does require some scrolling, but you will hide and then unhide the scroll bars as practice. You will be able to use your mouse to scroll or the keyboard arrows to scroll if necessary, but those will be your only ways to scroll with the scroll bars hidden.

In this exercise, you will hide scroll bars.

⏵ **E08.24**

MAC COMPATIBILITY
Changing Scroll Bar Options Doesn't Exist on a Mac
If using a Mac, you will not be able to complete this exercise.

To Hide Scroll Bars

a. On the Invoice worksheet, click the **File** tab, click **Options**, and then click **Advanced**. Scroll down until the **Display options for this workbook** group is visible. Click **Show horizontal scroll bar** to uncheck the options, and then click **OK**.

Notice that the horizontal scroll bar is gone from the application window, but you can still scroll with your mouse or the arrow keys on the keyboard.

b. Click the **File** tab, click **Options**, and then click **Advanced**. Scroll down until the Display options for this workbook group is visible. Click **Show horizontal scroll bar**, and then click **OK**.

c. Save  the workbook.

REAL WORLD ADVICE

**Options for Worksheets
and Workbooks**

Some navigation options are for the whole workbook, while some are for individual worksheets. When you are thinking about changing these options, you should carefully consider what each worksheet looks like and how the option will affect each worksheet. Hiding the scroll bars for one worksheet might be fine, but if another worksheet requires them for navigation, then you should probably not hide them. On the other hand, when you hide row and column headings, this is an option for each worksheet, so one worksheet can have them hidden while another worksheet can have them showing.

Hiding Row and Column Headings

Row and column headings are helpful when you are building a formula or even a workbook, but once the workbook is complete and ready to use for data entry, the row and column headings often become unnecessary. This option is available for individual worksheets, so hiding them on one worksheet will not hide them on all the worksheets.

Data entry into the SpaInvoice workbook will not rely on cell references, because the cells are well labeled. You will hide the row and column headings that will make the workbook look more like an invoice than an Excel workbook.

In this exercise, you will hide row and column headings.

 **E08.25**

To Hide Row and Column Headings

a. On the Invoice worksheet, click the **File** tab, click **Options**, and then click **Advanced**. Scroll down until the **Display options for this worksheet** group is visible, and then click **Show row and column headers** to uncheck the option.

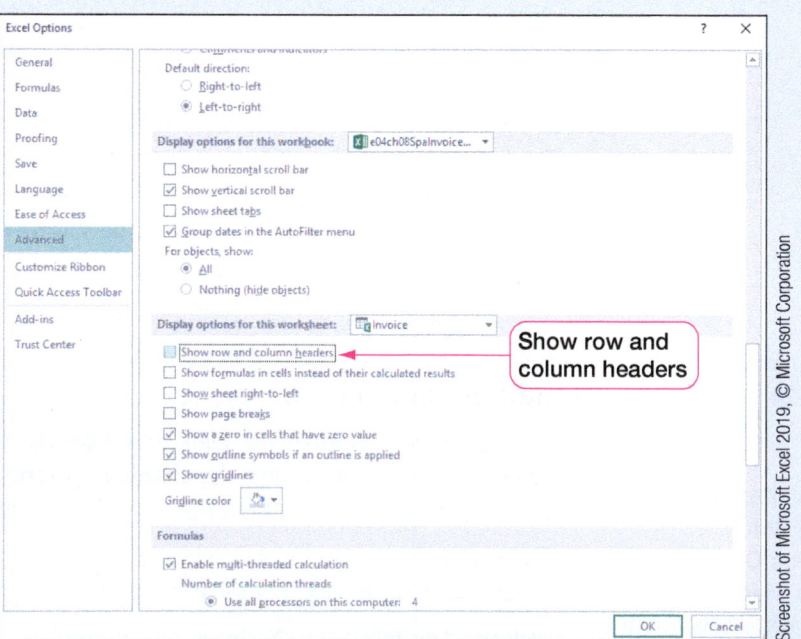

Figure 29 Display options for this worksheet

SIDE NOTE
Alternate Method
Gridlines can also be removed by clicking the File tab, Options, Advanced, and scrolling to display the options for the worksheet.

b. Click **OK**. Notice that the column headers (A, B, C) and row numbers (1, 2, 3) are no longer showing.

c. Click the **File** tab, click **Options**, and then click **Advanced**. Scroll down until the **Display options for this worksheet** group is visible, and then click **Show row and column headers** to check the option.

d. Click the **View** tab, and in the Show group, click **Gridlines** to deselect this option.

e. **Save** 💾 the workbook.

Protect Workbooks and Worksheets

Once a workbook or worksheet has been developed and tested but before you give it to other users, you may want to protect parts of the workbook that you do not want users to be able to change. If a user clicks on a cell that contains a formula and inadvertently presses [Delete], a critical part of the application could be erased. Unless the user thinks quickly enough to undo the mistake, the Excel application could be broken.

Excel allows for protection of applications in two layers: the workbook level to control who has access to the workbook and the worksheet level to protect worksheets from alteration. Ideally, only users who are authorized to use a workbook can access it, and only those who are authorized can change the contents of cells or change worksheet structures where appropriate.

At the worksheet level, there are many options available to customize the type of editing that will be allowed on the worksheet. These options are described in the following Quick Reference.

QUICK REFERENCE	Ways to Protect a Worksheet

When an option in the Protect Sheet dialog box is checked, that option will be allowed when the worksheet is protected. By default, only the first two options listed here are allowed when the worksheet is protected. The Protect Sheet dialog box lists the following options.

- Select locked cells: This is selected by default and allows the user to select cells with the Locked check box selected in the Format Cells dialog box.
- Select unlocked cells: This is also selected by default and allows the user to select cells with the Locked check box cleared in the Format Cells dialog box.
- Format cells: Enables all items in the Format cells dialog box as well as conditional formatting. However, the Protection tab and Merge Cells command remain unavailable.
- Format columns: Enables every item in the Column submenu of the Format menu.
- Format rows: Enables every item in the Row submenu of the Format menu.
- Insert columns: Allows a user to insert columns.
- Insert rows: Allows a user to insert rows.
- Insert hyperlinks: Allows a user to insert hyperlinks.
- Delete columns: Allows a user to delete any column that does not contain a locked cell.
- Delete rows: Allows a user to delete any row that does not contain a locked cell.
- Sort: Enables the Sort option on the Data tab for data in a range that does not contain a locked cell.
- Use AutoFilter: Allows a user to change filter criteria for an existing filter but not to add or delete a filter.
- Use PivotTable & PivotChart: Allows a user to make changes to an existing PivotTable or PivotChart.
- Edit objects: Removes any protection from an object except any related to the object's properties.
- Edit scenarios: Removes protection from scenarios.

Protection at the workbook level is not nearly as flexible as protection at the worksheet level. Worksheet protection allows many options for protection at the individual cell level, whereas workbook protection allows you only to require a password to open a worksheet, to lock down the structure of the workbook—prohibiting the adding, deleting, or moving of worksheets—and to mark a workbook as Final, which tells users that the worksheet they are using is the final version intended for their use.

REAL WORLD ADVICE | **Use Passwords with Caution**

Any user can turn the worksheet or workbook protection on or off. Therefore, you may want to use a password when you turn on protection. Passwords are case sensitive; can be up to 256 characters long; and can contain letters, numbers, and symbols such as #, $, !—basically any character than can be entered via the keyboard.

However, there is no way to retrieve this password if you forget what it is. This means that if you forget the password, you will not be able to turn the protection off and edit your worksheet or workbook again.

Unlocking Cells

By default, all cells in a worksheet are locked. This does not affect your worksheet until you turn on worksheet protection. Once Protect Sheet is turned on, locked cells cannot be edited. To allow editing, the cells must be unlocked before the protection is turned on.

The Spa workbook has some cells that should be locked and protected, and it has some cells into which the user will need to enter data.

In this exercise, you will unlock the cells that require data entry and then protect the worksheet but without a password. First you will show the row and column headers to make your navigation of the worksheet easier.

 E08.26

SIDE NOTE
Alternate Method
To unlock cells, you can also right-click the selection, select Format Cells, click the Protection tab, and click Locked.

To Unlock Cells and Protect a Worksheet

a. On the Invoice worksheet, select cell **E6**, press and hold Ctrl, and then select cells **E8**, **E10**, **E12**, **D14**, **C31**, and **F34** and cell ranges **B15:B30** and **E15:E30**. Click the **Home** tab, and in the Cells group, click **Format**.

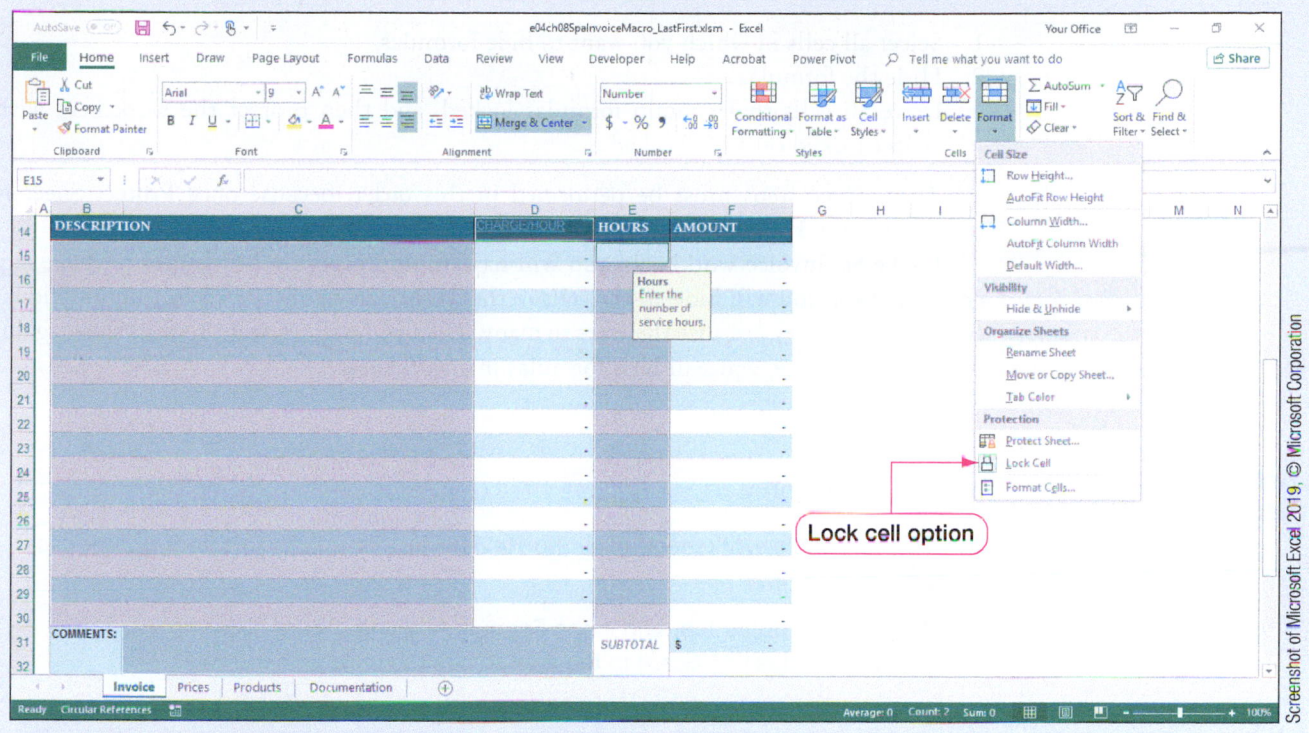

Figure 30 Lock cell option

b. Select **Lock Cell** to unlock the selected cells—for the hyperlink in cell D14 to work, the cell must be unlocked.

c. On the Home tab, in the Cells group, click **Format**, and then select **Protect Sheet**. Click **Select locked cells** to deselect the option.

SIDE NOTE
Alternate Method
To protect a worksheet, click the Review tab, and in the Protect group, click Protect Sheet.

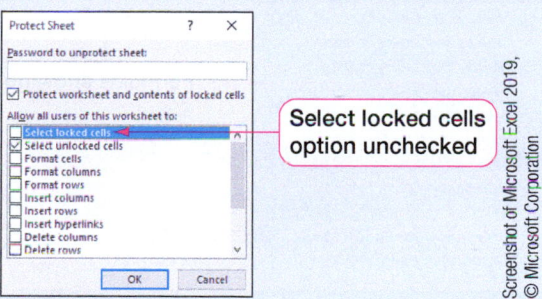

Figure 31 Protect Sheet dialog box

d. Click **OK**, click cell **B20**, and then press [Home].

Notice that the function of Home changes when the sheet is protected. Rather than moving the active cell to column A of the current row, it moves the active cell to the topmost and leftmost unlocked cell in the worksheet, which in this case is cell E6.

e. **Save** 🖫 the workbook.

Hiding Formulas

When a worksheet is protected, if cells with formulas are locked, then they cannot be selected. Therefore, if they contain a formula, that formula cannot be viewed in the formula bar. However, a user could still use the Show Formulas button on the Formulas tab to view the formula in a locked cell.

To completely hide formulas in a worksheet is a three-step process.

1. Select all cells in which you want to hide formulas.
2. Hide the formulas.
3. Leave all cells that contain formulas locked, and then protect the worksheet with Select locked cells unchecked.

These three steps must be performed in this order, because once Protect Sheet is toggled on, the Format button on the Home tab will not be available.

In the SpaInvoice workbook, you will have to unprotect the worksheet to make any changes. Then you will hide all the cells in the workbook rather than selecting individual cells with formulas, because there are so many. Then you will protect the worksheet again.

In this exercise, you will hide formulas in a worksheet.

 E08.27

To Hide Formulas

a. On the Invoice worksheet, click the **Review** tab, and in the Protect group, click **Unprotect Sheet**.

b. Click the **Formulas** tab, and in the Formula Auditing group, click **Show Formulas**. Scroll to the right to see the cells with formulas.

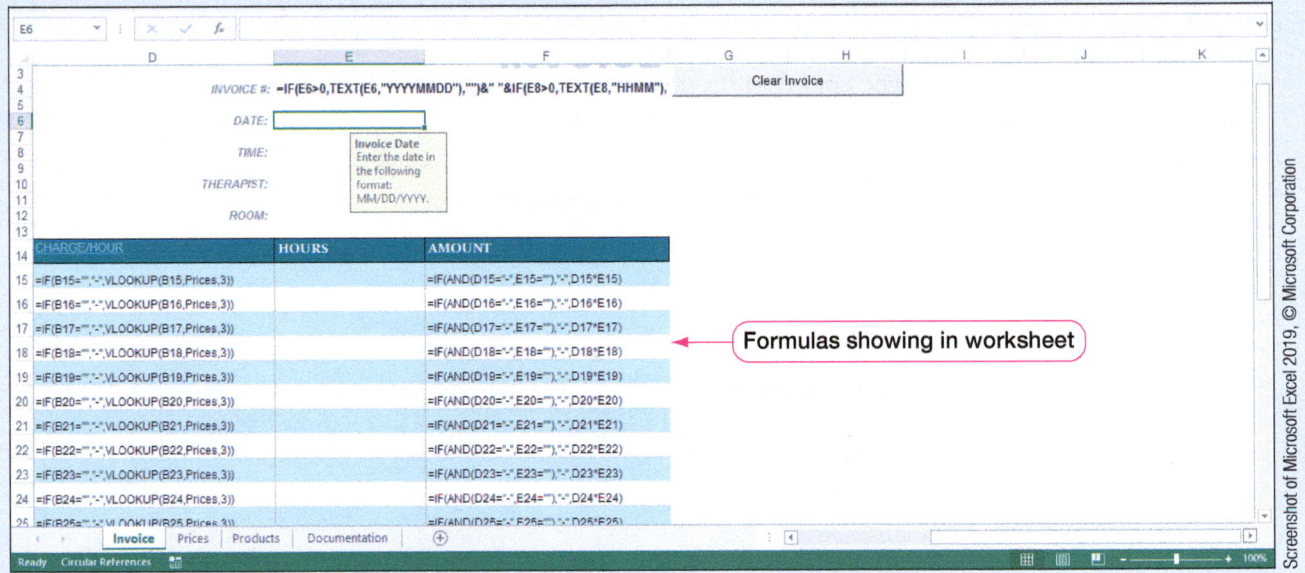

Figure 32   Worksheet in Formula View

c. Select cell **E4**, press and hold Ctrl, and select the cell ranges **D15:D30** and **F15:F30** and cells **F31**, **F33**, and **F35**. Click the **Home** tab, and in the Cells group, click **Format**, and then select **Format Cells**.

d. In the Format Cells dialog box, click the **Protection** tab, and then click the **Hidden** check box to select it.

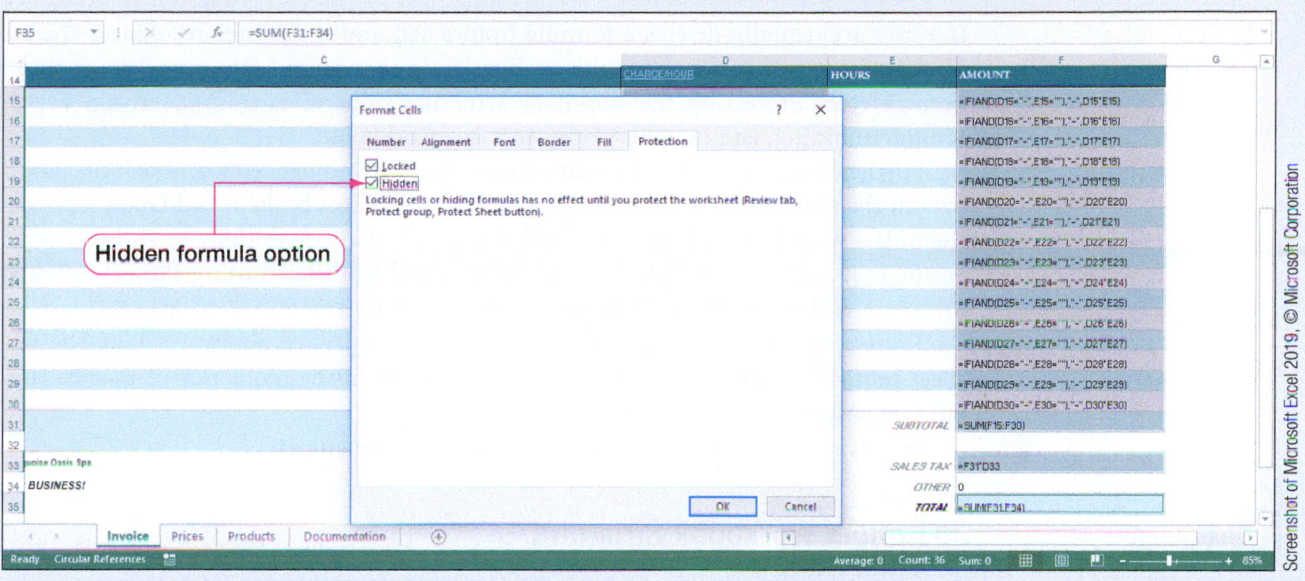

Figure 33 Hiding formulas

e. Click **OK**. On the Home tab, in the Cells group, click **Format**, click **Protect Sheet**, and then, in the Protect Sheet dialog box click **OK**.

Notice that formulas are no longer displayed. All cells that contain formulas are locked, so viewing formulas in the formula bar is not possible. The Show Formulas button will toggle on, but the formulas still will not be visible.

f. Click the **Formulas** tab, and in the Formula Auditing group, click **Show Formulas** to toggle it off. This will resize the columns to their normal width when the formulas are not showing.

g. Scroll to the left as needed to make column **A** visible.

h. Click the **File** tab, click **Options**, and then click **Advanced**. Scroll down to the Display options for this workbook, and then click the **Show horizontal scroll bar** check box to deselect it. Scroll down to Display options for this worksheet, click the **Show row and column headers** check box to deselect it, and then click **OK**.

i. **Save** 🔲 the workbook.

S CONSIDER THIS | Changing Navigation Tools and Other Features

By hiding areas of the workbook, including gridlines, row and column headings, and scroll bars as well as hiding, protecting, and locking cells, you certainly make your workbook more secure. Users who are not familiar with Excel may appreciate these enhancements because they make navigating and using the workbook simpler and often less intimidating. When you are deciding which features to hide and lock, take into consideration your end user. If your users are more advanced in Excel, can you see any frustrations they could encounter in working with a protected and locked workbook? What features might be more helpful to them, and which would be less helpful?

Protecting Workbook Structure

If a user accidentally deletes a formula from a cell and if the user recognizes the error, Undo can be used to fix the problem. But Undo cannot undelete a worksheet that has been deleted. Protecting the workbook structure stops users from inserting, deleting, hiding, unhiding, and moving worksheets in a workbook.

Further, if a user decides to rename a worksheet, any unopened workbook that accesses data in the renamed worksheet will have its 3D references broken, and Undo will not fix them. If a worksheet in your workbook is accessed by other workbooks and you want to ensure that a user cannot delete or rename a critical worksheet, using Protect Workbook Structure will secure the worksheets and their names.

Protecting the workbook structure includes an optional password. Like the worksheet protection password, if the password is lost, then the protection cannot be turned off. Use passwords with caution.

In this exercise, you will protect the workbook structure.

 **E08.28**

SIDE NOTE
Turn Off Workbook Protection
To turn off workbook protection, click the Review tab, and in the Protect group, click Protect Workbook.

To Protect Workbook Structure

a. On the Invoice worksheet, click the **Review** tab, and in the Protect group, click **Protect Workbook**.

b. In the Protect Structure and Windows dialog box, verify that **Structure** is checked.

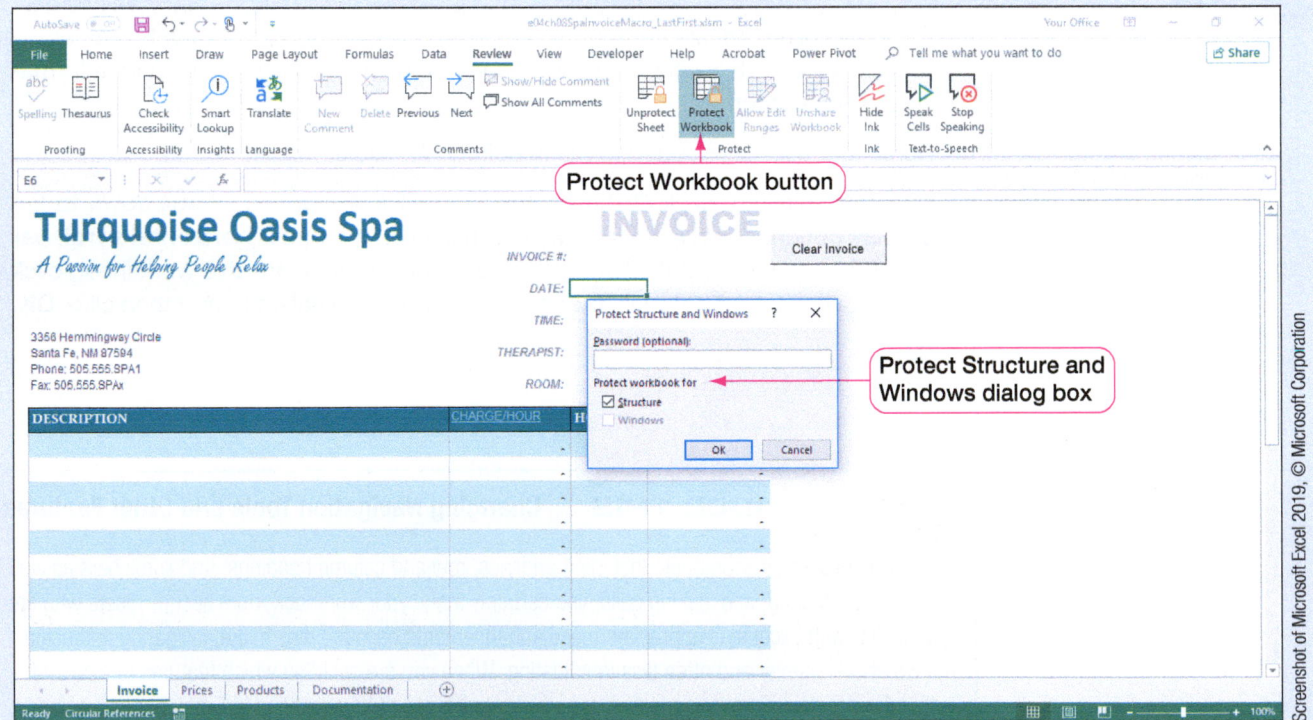

Figure 34   Protect Workbook button

c. You will not add a password in this exercise. Click **OK**.

   On the Review tab, notice that the Protect Workbook button is now toggled on—it is a different color.

d. **Save** the workbook.

REAL WORLD ADVICE

Do Not Rely Solely on Workbook Protection

Workbook protection by itself does not lend much protection to your application. Even though a user cannot delete a worksheet, the user can still delete all the content in a worksheet unless worksheet protection is enabled. Protect your workbooks with both workbook-level and worksheet-level protection.

Encrypting a Workbook

The highest level of protection is to encrypt the workbook with a password; this prevents the workbook from being opened without the password. When a password is entered into the Encrypt Document dialog box, the workbook is encrypted when it is saved. **Encryption** is a method of protecting a workbook by assigning a password that unscrambles the code once it has been opened. For the user, the net result is that after a workbook has been saved with an encryption password, the password is required to open the workbook again.

Again, use caution when assigning passwords. If the password is lost, the workbook cannot be opened. If a workbook needs to be protected because it contains sensitive content such as social security numbers, worksheet or workbook passwords are not recommended, as they can be broken with VBA coding. Instead, workbook encryption should be used.

REAL WORLD ADVICE

Back Up before You Encrypt Your Workbook

If you are going to encrypt your workbook with a password, it is a good idea to make a backup copy of the workbook without the password first. Thus, if you forget your password, you still have a copy of the workbook that you can open.

If you are concerned about security, you can always save the backup with a different name so that someone else might not be able to determine that it is the same workbook as the one with the password.

In this exercise, you will encrypt the workbook with a password.

 **E08.29**

To Encrypt a Workbook

> **Grader Heads Up**
>
> In the MyLab IT Grader version of this project, you will not encrypt the workbook with a password.

MAC COMPATIBILITY
Protecting a Workbook on a Mac
To protect a workbook on a Mac, click the Review tab, and in the Changes group, click Protect Workbook.

a. Click the **File** tab, click **Info**, click **Protect Workbook**, and then select **Encrypt with Password**.

b. In the Encrypt Document dialog box, in the **Password** box, type invoice

In Excel, passwords are case sensitive, so type very carefully.

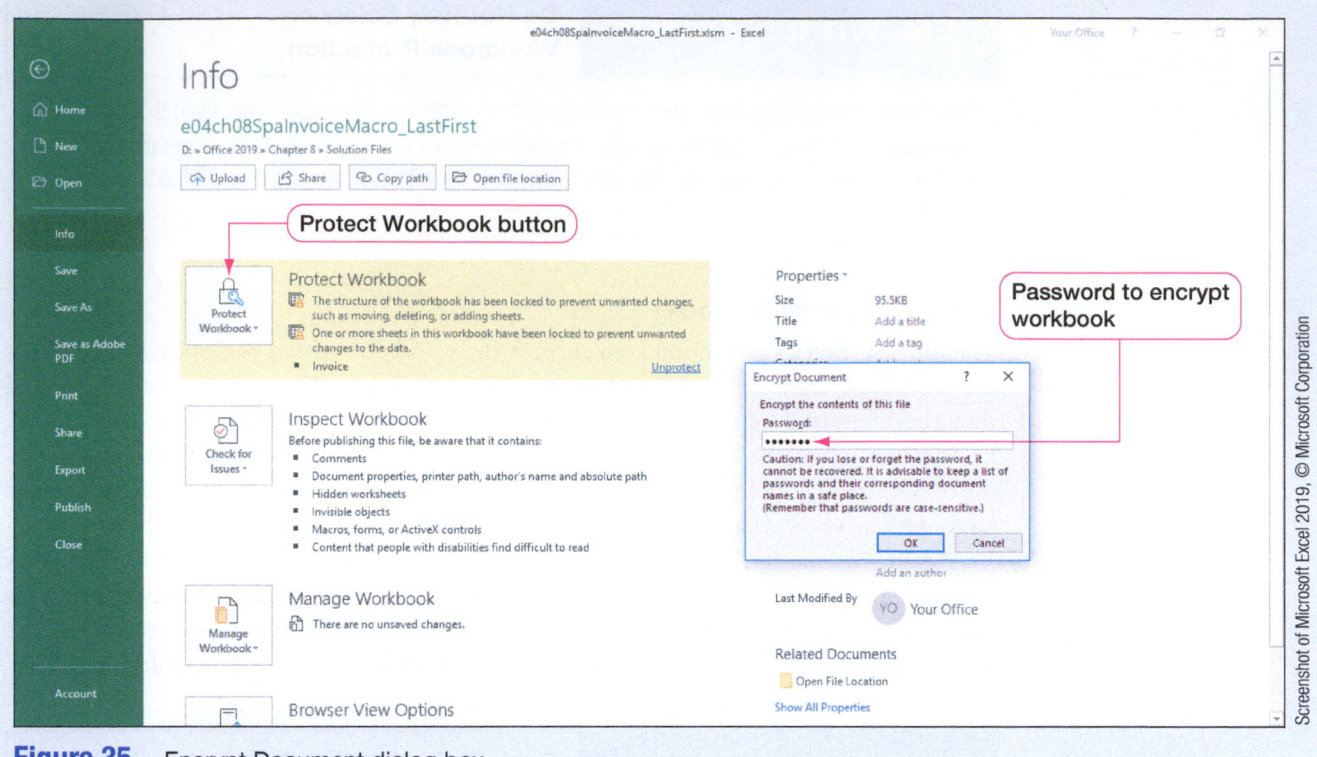

Figure 35 Encrypt Document dialog box

c. Click **OK**, and then type **invoice** again. Click **OK**. When you close and open the workbook, you will be prompted for the password.

d. Click the **Back** button ⊕. **Save** 🖫 the workbook.

Marking a Workbook as a Final Draft

When you are creating a workbook for someone else to use and have the final version complete, it is helpful to use the Mark as Final option. Mark as Final represents a means of communicating the development status of a workbook to indicate that the workbook is complete and ready for use. Mark as Final is a form of workbook protection by making a workbook read-only. However, Mark as Final is a very weak form of protection. A workbook that has been marked as final will display the Marked as Final 🖉 icon on the status bar; but even though a workbook has been marked as final, users are given the option to "Edit Anyway."

In this exercise, to indicate to Meda Rodate that the SpaInvoice workbook updates she requested are now complete, you will mark this version of the workbook as final.

MAC COMPATIBILITY
Marking a Workbook as Final Is Not Available on a Mac
If you are using a Mac, you will not be able to complete this exercise.

To Mark a Workbook as Final

a. Click the **File** tab, click **Info** if necessary, click **Protect Workbook**, and then select **Mark as Final**. Click **OK** in the alert box, and then click **OK** in the next alert box.

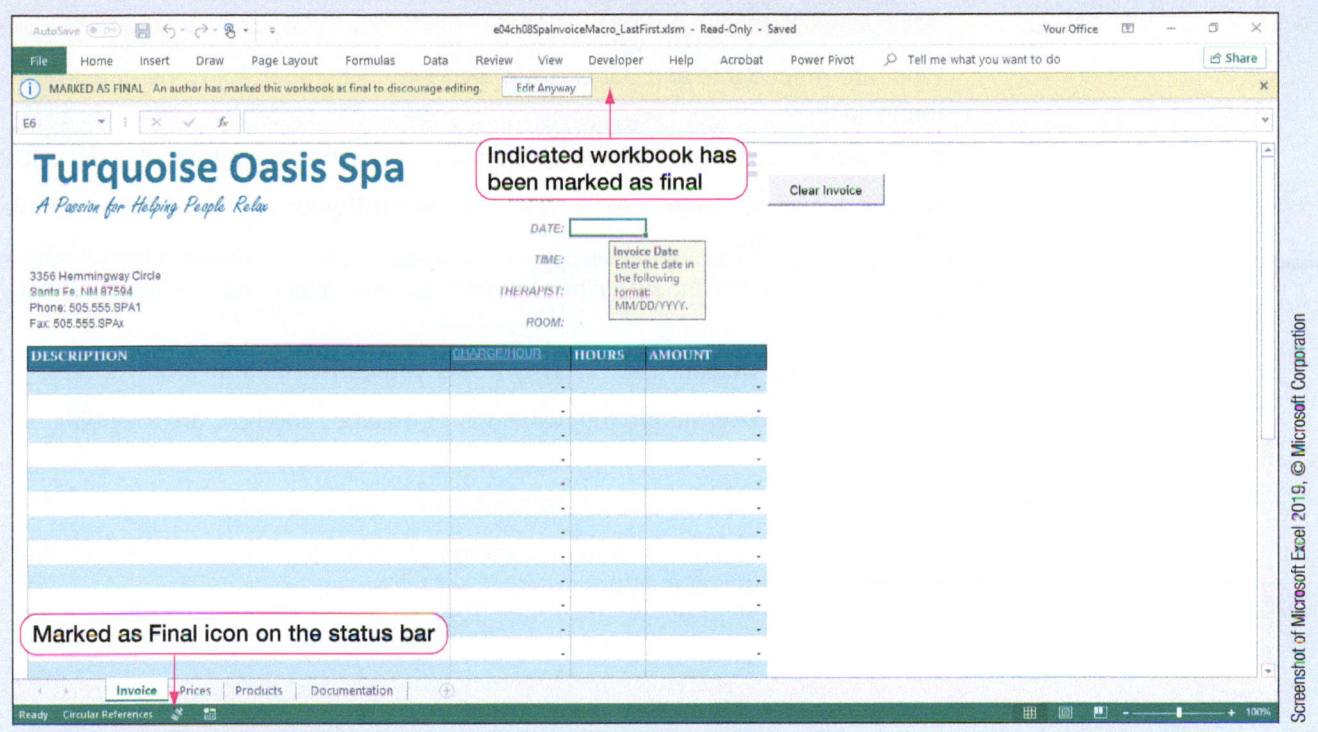

Figure 36 Indication the workbook is marked as final

b. Click the **File** tab, click **Info**, and then notice that the description under Protect Workbook says the workbook is marked as final.

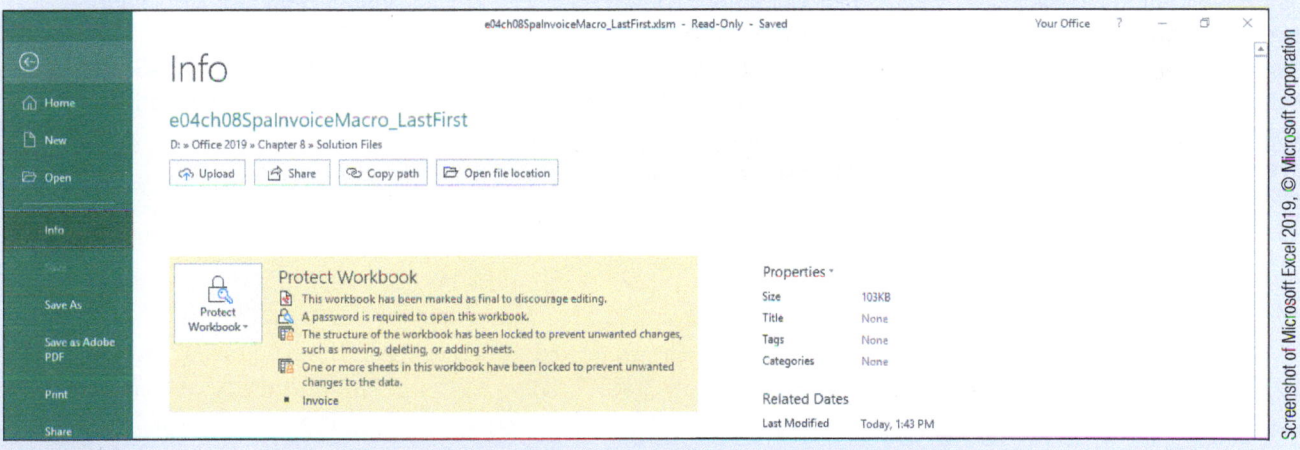

Figure 37 Workbook protection in Backstage view

c. Close the workbook, exit Excel, and then submit your file as directed by your instructor.

Concept Check

1. What are precedents and dependents, and why is it important to be able to trace them? p. 430

2. When would you use the Evaluate Formulas tool? What does the tool do? p. 432

3. What is a circular reference? How do you know if your workbook has a circular reference? p. 433

4. What is the Watch Window? When would it be beneficial to have a Watch Window open? p. 434

5. How does data validation work? Why would you use it? p. 436–437

6. What is a macro? What are the two kinds of macros, and how are they different? p. 450–455

7. Why would you want to turn off the navigational features of a workbook? p. 459

8. What is the difference between protecting a workbook structure and protecting a worksheet? p. 465–466, 470

Key Terms

Absolute macro reference   p. 453
Any value validation   p. 444
Circular reference   p. 433
Codification scheme   p. 446
Codified data value   p. 445
Custom validation   p. 445
Data validation   p. 436
Date validation   p. 440
Decimal validation   p. 439
Dependent cell   p. 430
Developer tab   p. 452

Encryption   p. 471
Error Alert   p. 437
Evaluate Formula   p. 432
Hyperlink   p. 459
Input Message   p. 437
List validation   p. 437
Macro   p. 450
Precedent cell   p. 430
Relative macro reference   p. 455
Text length validation   p. 443
Text-to-speech   p. 448

Time validation   p. 441
Trace dependents   p. 430
Trace precedents   p. 430
Trusted Location   p. 451
Validation criteria   p. 436
Visual Basic for Applications
   (VBA)   p. 450
Watch Window   p. 434
Whole number validation   p. 442

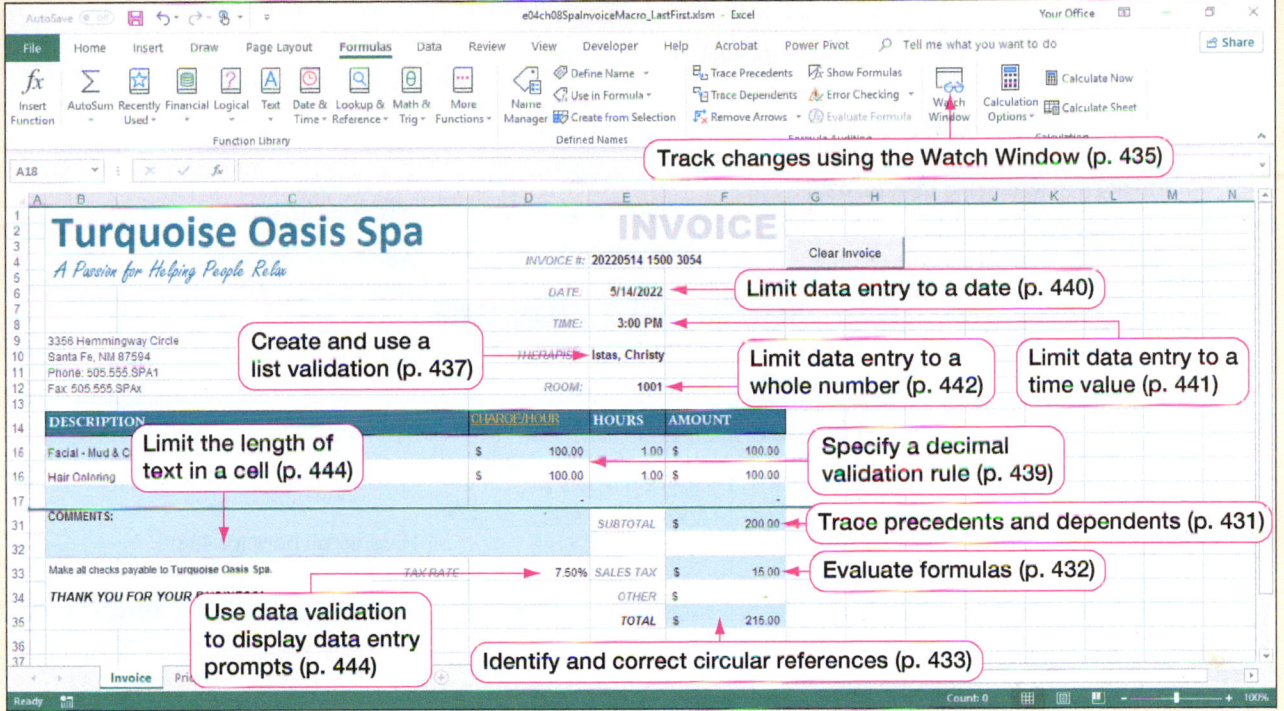

Figure 38

Screenshot of Microsoft Excel 2019, © Microsoft Corporation

Track changes using the Watch Window (p. 435)

Limit data entry to a date (p. 440)

Create and use a list validation (p. 437)

Limit data entry to a whole number (p. 442)

Limit data entry to a time value (p. 441)

Limit the length of text in a cell (p. 444)

Specify a decimal validation rule (p. 439)

Trace precedents and dependents (p. 431)

Evaluate formulas (p. 432)

Use data validation to display data entry prompts (p. 444)

Identify and correct circular references (p. 433)

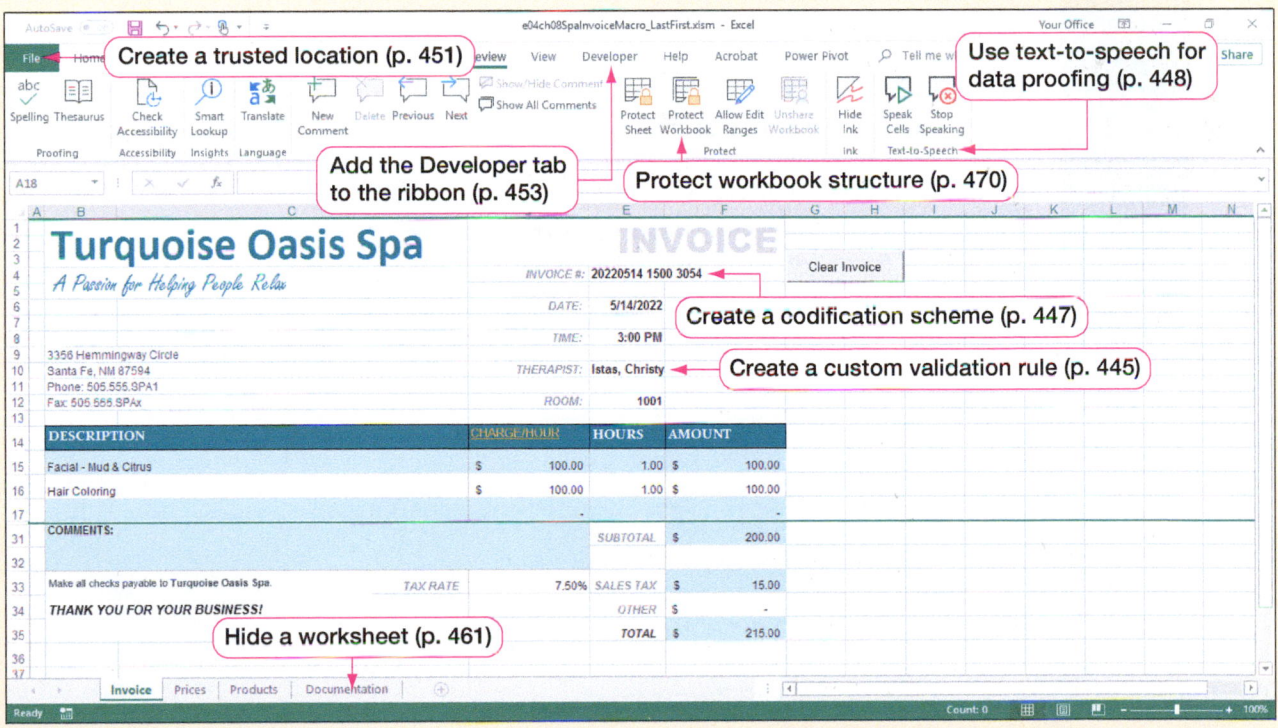

Figure 39

Screenshot of Microsoft Excel 2019, © Microsoft Corporation

Create a trusted location (p. 451)

Use text-to-speech for data proofing (p. 448)

Add the Developer tab to the ribbon (p. 453)

Protect workbook structure (p. 470)

Create a codification scheme (p. 447)

Create a custom validation rule (p. 445)

Hide a worksheet (p. 461)

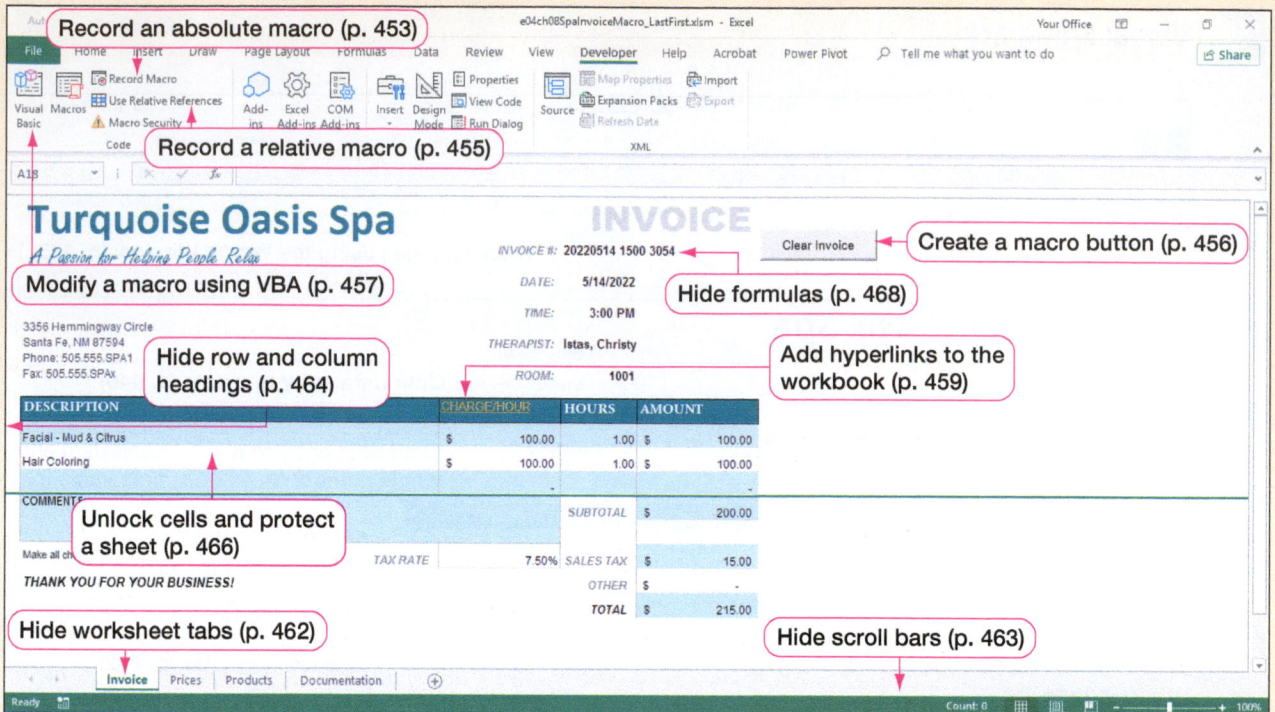

Figure 40

Screenshot of Microsoft Excel 2019, © Microsoft Corporation

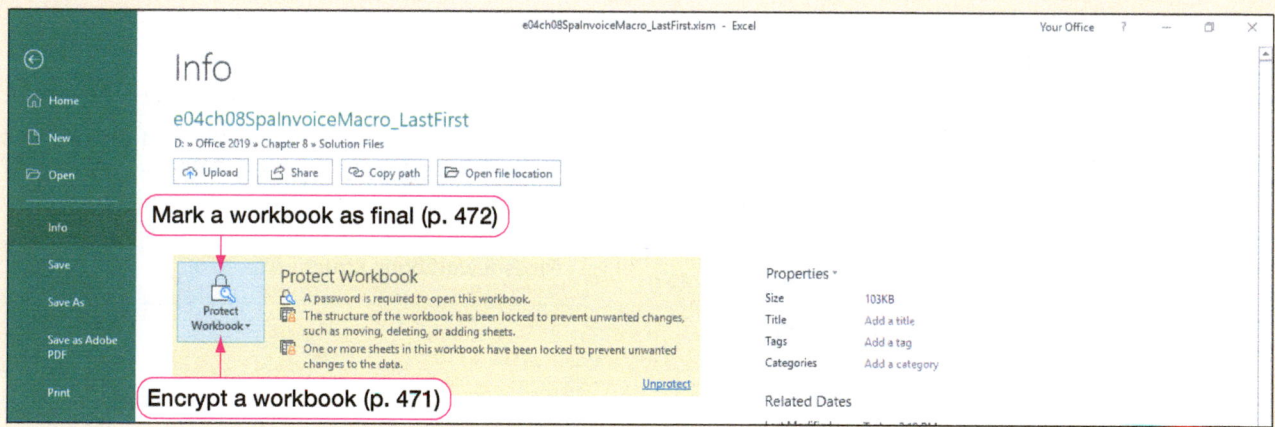

Figure 41

Screenshot of Microsoft Excel 2019, © Microsoft Corporation

Practice 1

Student data file needed:	You will save your file as:
e04ch08Wedding.xlsx	e04ch08Wedding_LastFirst.xlsm

$

Finance &
Accounting

Painted Paradise Resort Wedding Planner

Painted Paradise Resort & Spa has a wedding chapel and reception facilities capable of handling 300 people. Wedding guests stay at the hotel, dine in the restaurant, play golf, go to the spa, and shop in the gift shop, often using a wedding as an opportunity to stay at the resort for a weekend. The resort is becoming a popular wedding destination, and Patti Rochelle, the events manager, has been trying to update a workbook she uses to generate wedding cost estimates for prospective clients.

She has developed an attractive and functional design. The calculations are pretty much handled; however, her worksheet still requires a lot of manual data entry, and she would like a macro to clear data from the wedding planner after an estimate has been generated and printed.

a. Open Excel, click **Open** in the left pane, and then double-click **This PC**. Navigate through the folder structure to the location of your student data files, and then double-click **e04ch08Wedding**. If you get a warning message that there is one or more circular references in the workbook, click **OK**. If a Security Warning message displays, click **Enable Editing**.

b. Click the **File** tab, click **Save As**, and then double-click **This PC**. In the Save As dialog box, navigate to the location where you are saving your project files. Change the file name to e04ch08Wedding_LastFirst using your last and first name, and then select **Excel Macro-Enabled Workbook** in the Save as type box. Click **Save**.

c. On the **WeddingPlanner** worksheet, select the estimated cost total in cell **E34**. Click the **Formulas** tab, and then in the Formula Auditing group, click **Trace Precedents**.

   - Notice the Circular Reference warning in the status bar for cell E34. The SUM function in cell E34 includes a reference to E34 that is causing the circular reference.

   - Click in the formula bar, and then change E34 to E32

> ### Mac Troubleshooting
> If using a Mac, you will not be able to complete step d.

d. On the Formulas tab, in the Formula Auditing group, click **Watch Window**. Select cells **E16**, **E21**, **E25**, **E28**, **E32**, and **E34**, and then click **Add Watch**. In the Add Watch dialog box, click **Add**. Verify that the cells were added to the Watch Window. Dock the Watch Window to the top of the worksheet. **Close** the Watch Window.

e. Select cell **C8**. On the **Data** tab, in the Data Tools group, click **Data Validation**. You will create a rule so the number entered is between 25 and 300.

   - On the Settings tab, in the **Allow** box, select **Whole number**. In the Data box, verify that **between** is selected. In the **Minimum** box, type 50 and then, in the **Maximum** box, type 300

   - Click the **Input Message** tab, and then, in the **Title** box, type Guests In the Input message box, type Enter the estimated number of guests.

- Click the **Error Alert** tab, and then, in the **Title** box type Error In the Error message box, type The number of guests must be between 50 and 300. and then click **OK**.
- In cell **C8**, type 150

f. Select cell **C10**. On the Data tab, in the Data Tools group, click **Data Validation**. You will create a rule so the date entered must be the current date or later.

- Click the **Settings** tab. In the **Allow** box, select **Date**. In the Data box, select **greater than or equal to**. In the **Start date** box, type =TODAY()
- Click the **Input Message** tab, and then, in the **Title** box type Date In the **Input message** box, type Enter the wedding date.
- Click **the Error Alert** tab, and then, in the **Title** box, type Error In the **Error message** box, type The wedding date must be today or later. and then click **OK**.
- In cell **C10**, type =TODAY()

g. Select cell **C11**. On the Data tab, in the Data Tools group, click **Data Validation**. You will create a rule so the time entered must be between 11:00 AM and 8:00 PM.

- Click the **Settings** tab, and then, in the **Allow** box select **Time**. In the **Data** box, select **between**. In the **Start time** box, type 11:00 AM and then, in the **End time** box, type 8:00 PM
- Click the **Input Message** tab, and then, in the **Title** box, type Time In the **Input message** box, type Enter the wedding start time.
- Click the **Error Alert** tab, and then, in the **Title** box, type Error In the **Error message** box, type The start time must be between 11:00 AM and 8:00 PM. and then click **OK**.
- In cell **C11**, type 2:00 PM

h. Select the cell range **C20:C21**. On the Data tab, in the Data Tools group, click **Data Validation**. You will create a rule so the data entered must come from a list of cells on the Parameters worksheet.

- Click the **Settings** tab, and then, in the **Allow** box, select **List**. Click the **Source** box, click the **Parameters** worksheet, and then select the cell range **A9:A10**.
- Click the **Input Message** tab, and then, in the **Title** box, type Amenities In the **Input message** box, type Select an option from the list. and then click **OK**.
- In cell **C20**, click the **arrow**, and then select **Standard**.
- In cell **C21**, click the **arrow**, and then select **Deluxe**.

i. Select the cell range **C24:C25** and cell **C28**. On the Data tab, in the Data Tools group, click **Data Validation**. You will create a rule so the data entered can be selected from a list.

- Click the **Settings** tab, and then, in the **Allow** box, select **List**. Click the **Source** box, type Yes, No Click **OK**.
- In cell **C24**, click the arrow, and then select **Yes**.
- In cell **C25**, click the arrow, and then select **Yes**.
- In cell **C28**, click the arrow, and then select **No**.

j. Select cell **F10**. On the Data tab, in the Data Tools group, click **Data Validation**. You will create a custom rule so the room number entered starts with the number 1 or 2 and ends with a number less than 7; the available room numbers are 10–16 and 20–26.

- Click the **Settings** tab. In the **Allow** box, select **Custom**. Click the **Formula** box, then type =AND(LEFT(F10,1)<="2",LEFT(F10,1)>="1",RIGHT(F10,1)<"7",LEN(F10)=2)

- You will not add an Input message for this cell. Click the **Error Alert** tab. In the Title box, type Room # In the **Error message** box, type Invalid room number. Click **OK**.

- In cell **F10**, type 15

k. If necessary, add the **Developer** tab to the ribbon.

> ### Mac Troubleshooting
> The Trust Center option is not available on a Mac.

- Click the **File** tab, click **Options**, click **Customize Ribbon**, and then, under Main Tabs, click to select **Developer**. Click **OK**.

l. Assign the folder where you save your student files as a trusted location.

- Click the **File** tab, click **Options**, click **Trust Center**, click **Trust Center Settings**, and then click **Trusted Locations**.

- Click **Add new location**, browse to the folder where you save your student files, and then click **OK**. Click **OK** three times.

m. Click the **Developer** tab, and in the Code group, click **Record Macro**.

- In the Macro name box, type ClearContents In the Shortcut key box, press [Shift], and then type C Verify that the Store macro in box is **This Workbook**. In the Description, type Delete all user-entered data from the worksheet. and then click **OK**.

- Select the cell range **C5:C6**, press and hold [Ctrl], and then select the cell ranges **C8**, **C10:C11**, **C20:C21**, and **C24:C25** and cells **C28** and **F10**. Press [Delete].

- Select cell **C5**. On the Developer tab, in the Code group, click **Stop Recording**.

n. Click **Undo** to undo the changes you made recording the macro.

o. On the **Developer** tab, in the Controls group, click **Insert**, and then under Form Controls, select **Button (Form Control)**.

- Click in the top left corner of cell **E5** next to the Bride's name, and then drag to the bottom right corner of cell **F6** to size and add the button.

- Select **ClearContents**, and then click **OK**.

- Right-click the button, and then select **Edit Text**. Delete the current text, and then type Clear Information Right-click the button, and then select **Exit Edit Text**.

- Test the button.

p. Select cell **B19**. Click the **Insert** tab, and in the Links group, click **Link**.

- Select **Place in This Document**, and then under Or select a place in this document, select **Parameters**. Select the text in the **Type the cell reference** box, and then type D15 Click **ScreenTip**, and then type Click to view amenities Click **OK**, and then click **OK**.

- Click the hyperlink to go to the Parameters worksheet.

- On the **Parameters** worksheet, select cell **D15** if necessary, and then click the **Insert** tab, and in the Links group, click **Link**.

- Select **Place in This Document**, and then under Or select a place in this document, select **WeddingPlanner**. In the **Type the cell reference** box, type B19 Click **ScreenTip**, and then type Return to Wedding Planner worksheet Click **OK**, and then click **OK**.

- Click the hyperlink to return to the WeddingPlanner worksheet.

q. Click the **WeddingPlanner** worksheet, select cell **B19**, cell range **C5:C6**, cell **C8**, cell range **C10:C11**, cell **F10**, cell ranges **C20:C21** and **C24:C25**, and cell **C28**—the cells are all formatted with gray where the data is entered. Click the **Home** tab, and in the Cells group, click **Format**, and then click **Lock Cell** to unlock the selected cells.

r. Click the **File** tab, click **Options**, click **Advanced**, and do the following.

> ### Mac Troubleshooting
> If using a Mac, you will not be able to complete this step.

- Scroll down to **Display options for this workbook**, and then click **Show horizontal scroll bar** to deselect it.

- Scroll down to **Display options for this worksheet**, and then click **Show row and column headers** to deselect it. Click **OK**.

s. Click the **View** tab, and in the Show group, click to deselect the **Gridlines** check box.

t. Update the Documentation worksheet according to your instructor's directions.

u. Hide the Parameter and the Documentation worksheets.

v. Click the **Formulas** tab, and in the Formula Auditing group, click **Show Formulas**.

- Select all the cells that show a formula.

- Click the **Home** tab. In the Cells group, click **Format**, select **Format Cells**, click the **Protection** tab, and then click **Hidden**. Click **OK**.

- Click the **Formulas** tab, and in the Formula Auditing group, click **Show Formulas** again to remove the formula view.

w. Click the **Home** tab, and in the Cells group, click **Format**, and then select **Protect Sheet**. Ensure that **Select unlocked cells** is checked, and then click **OK**.

> ### Mac Troubleshooting
> If you are using a Mac, you will not be able to mark the workbook as final.

x. Click the **Review** tab, and in the Changes group, click **Protect Workbook**, verify that **Structure** is selected, and then click **OK**.

y. Click the **File** tab, click **Info** if necessary, click **Protect Workbook**, and then select **Mark as Final**. Click **OK** to save the workbook, and then click **OK** again.

z. Close the workbook, exit Excel, and then submit your file as directed by your instructor.

Problem Solve 1

MyLab IT Grader

Student data file needed:

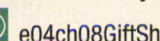 e04ch08GiftShopSales.xlsx

You will save your file as:

e04ch08GiftShopSales_LastFirst.xlsm

Finance & Accounting

General Business

Gift Shop Sales

Susan Brock, the gift shop manager, is analyzing products sold in the gift shop to determine if the current inventory should be continued or discontinued. She has given you a worksheet to track revenue on a few of the items sold in the gift shop on a trial basis for the next six months. She has asked you to help modify the workbook so employees know exactly what to enter into the revenue tracker and also set the worksheet up to avoid the possibility of deleting important formulas.

You will create a Watch Window, validation rules, and macros to make data entry as simple as possible. Then you will protect the worksheet and the workbook structure, as well as hide all the formulas, so the chance of deleting critical cells is minimized. Finally, you will mark the workbook as final so when you send it to the gift shop manager, she knows it is the version she should be using.

a. Open the Excel file, **e04ch08GiftShopSales**. Save the workbook as a **Macro-Enabled Workbook** named **e04ch08GiftShopSales_LastFirst** using your last and first name. Click **OK** at the circular error message; you will correct this in step b.

Grader Heads Up

In the MyLab IT Grader version of this project, you will not save the workbook as a macro-enabled workbook.

---

b. On the BudgetData worksheet, use **Trace Precedents** to illustrate the circular reference error in cell **E36**. Correct the formula in cell E36 by entering the correct cell range.

Grader Heads Up

In the MyLab IT Grader version of this project, you will not be adding a Watch Window.

---

c. Create a **Watch Window** to view cells **D36**, **E36**, **F36**, and **G36**.

d. Add a data validation to cell **G4** that only allows values from a list with the source data from cell range **B26:B30** on the **ListData** worksheet. The **Input Message** should have a title Reported By and the Input message Choose a name from the list. The **Error Alert** should have the Stop title Error and the Error message Please choose a name from the list.

e. Add data validation to cell **G5** that only allows today's date or earlier. Use the function =TODAY(). There will be no input message, only a stop **Error Alert** with the title Incorrect Date and the **Error message** should read Date must be today or earlier.

f. Add data validation to cell **G6** with only an **Input Message** that reads Please enter a time in the following format: HH:MM AM/PM.

g. Add data validation to cell **C37** to limit the length of the text to **200 characters**. Only include an **Error message** that reads Comments cannot exceed 200 characters.

h. Add a data validation to cell range **C9:C35** that only allow values from a list with the source data from cell range **B6:B23**, named RevenueList, on the **ListData** worksheet. The **Input Message** should have a title Choose Item and the Input message Choose an item from the list. The **Error Alert** should have the Stop title Error and the Error message Please choose an item from the list.

i. Insert a hyperlink in cell **C6** on the BudgetData worksheet that links to cell E1 on the ListData worksheet. Enter the screen tip Go to ListData

j. Insert a hyperlink in cell **E1** on the ListData worksheet that links to cell C6 on the BudgetData worksheet. Enter a screen tip Go to BudgetData Test the hyperlink to return to the BudgetData worksheet.

k. If necessary, add the **Developer** tab to the ribbon. Create an **absolute macro** that will clear the contents of all cells that data is entered into the BudgetData work-sheet by the user. Name the macro ClearContents and assign the capital letter C as the shortcut key to the current workbook only. Clear contents from the following cells: **G4:G6**, **B9:D35**, and **C37**. Select cell **G4** to make it the active cell before you stop recording.

l. Add a form control button in cell **F1** that will run the macro **ClearContents** macro. Change the text on the button to Clear Contents and then resize the button as necessary to read all the text.

m. Enter the following data in the report to test the macro:
   - In cell **G4**, using the list arrow, select **Jamie**
   - In cell **G5**, today's date
   - In cell **G6**, 2:00 PM
   - In cell **B9**, enter today's date
   - In cell **C9**, select gift shop, they sell snacks from the list arrow
   - In cell **D9**, type 3

n. Test the ClearContents macro by using the **Clear Contents** form control button.

o. On the BudgetData worksheet, unlock cells **C6**, **G4:G6**, **B9:D35**, and **C37**.

p. Hide the formulas from cell range **E9:G35**.

q. Update the Documentation worksheet according to your instructor's directions.

r. Hide the Documentation worksheet.

s. Hide the horizontal scroll bar, the row and column headers, and the sheet tabs. Hide the gridlines. Protect the worksheet. Do not allow selecting locked cells.

t. Enter the following data in the report:
   - In cell **G4**, using the list arrow, select **Jamie**
   - In cell **G5**, =TODAY()
   - In cell **G6**, 2:00 PM
   - In cell **B9**, enter today's date
   - In cell **C9**, select gift shop from the list arrow
   - In cell **D9**, type 3
   - In cell **C10**, select gift shop from the list arrow
   - In cell **D10**, type 1

u. Save the workbook. Mark the workbook as final, exit Excel, and then submit your file as directed by your instructor.

Critical Thinking

In this chapter, you learned how to protect a worksheet and a workbook. Describe a scenario when it would be important to set worksheet protection. Describe a scenario when it would be important to set workbook protection.

Student data file needed:

 e04ch08Budget.xlsx

You will save your file as:

 e04ch08Budget_LastFirst.xlsm

Watching Your Money

Finance & Accounting

You and your spouse have decided to create a 2022 budget plan to track your income and expenses. Your spouse is not very familiar with Excel, so you have decided to create a workbook that can be shared between the two of you and can easily be updated. As part of monitoring your expenses, you and your spouse have decided that any expense greater than $500 should pop up with a warning to remind you to double-check the expense.

a. Open the Excel file, **e04ch08Budget**. Save your file as a macro-enabled workbook named **e04ch08Budget_LastFirst** using your last and first name. Click OK at the circular error message; you will correct this in the next step.

b. Find and correct the circular references in the worksheet.

c. On the Budget worksheet, add a blank column between columns B and C, and enter **Type** in cell C5.

d. Enter at least three rows of data to test your validation rules. Income items should be entered as a positive number, and Expense items should be entered as a negative number. Increase column width as appropriate to accommodate your data validations.

e. Format any input cell as unlocked. All other cells should be locked, and formulas should be hidden.

f. Enter a hyperlink for the Type heading on the Budget worksheet to the Lists worksheet and include a ScreenTip. Enter a hyperlink on the Lists worksheet to switch to the Budget worksheet and include a ScreenTip. Note that on the Budget worksheet, you may need to unlock the cell which contains the hyperlink.

g. If necessary, add the Developer tab to the ribbon.

h. Add an absolute macro for use at the end of each month to copy the contents of the data entry areas of the worksheet. The macro should make a copy of the Budget worksheet to keep for future use and then clear all the data that was entered for the month. Ensure that you select the appropriate worksheet and protect and unprotect as necessary.

i. Insert a macro button on the Budget worksheet and assign the macro to the button and name the button appropriately.

j. Update the Documentation worksheet according to your instructor's directions. Hide the Lists and Documentation worksheets.

k. Hide the gridlines on the Budget worksheet. Hide the scroll bars as appropriate, and row and column headings on all worksheets.

l. Protect the workbook structure. Do not set a password.

m. Mark the workbook as final. Exit Excel, and then submit your file as directed by your instructor.

Build an Application with Multiple Worksheets and Workbooks

This business unit had two outcomes:

Learning Outcome 1:

Use multiple worksheets, workbooks, and templates to create an Excel application.

Learning Outcome 2:

Perform formula auditing, use data validation, create macros, and explore worksheet and workbook protection to refine an Excel application.

In Business Unit 4 Capstone, students will demonstrate competence in these outcomes through a series of business problems at various levels from guided practice to problem solving an existing spreadsheet and creating new spreadsheets.

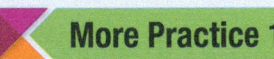
More Practice 1

Student data file needed:  e04Indigo5.xlsx

You will save your file as: e04Indigo5_LastFirst.xlsm

General Business

Indigo5 Meal and Menu Tracking

To help plan the menu at the Indigo5 restaurant, Alberto Dimas, the restaurant manager, would like to be able to see how many meals in each category are being sold each season. He has created a spreadsheet that has the meals broken down by season with the average price, average cost, and dishes sold for each category, but he is having trouble consolidating and summarizing the data. He would also like to include a form to fill out for estimates for special events. When guests plan a special event, they can pick up to four food categories. Based on the average prices of each category, Alberto would like an estimated cost for the event.

a. Open **Excel**, click **Open** in the left pane, and then double-click **This PC**. Navigate through the folder structure to the location of your student data files, and then double-click **e04Indigo5**. Click **OK** for the Circular Reference warning dialog box. If a Security Warning message displays, click **Enable Editing**.

b. Click the **File** tab, click **Save As**, and then double-click **This PC**. In the Save As dialog box, navigate to the location where you are saving your project files. Change the file name to e04Indigo5_LastFirst using your last and first name, and then select **Excel Macro-Enabled Workbook** in the Save as type box. Click **Save**.

c. On the **Winter** worksheet, press and hold Shift, and then click the **Fall** worksheet.

• Right-click the **Winter** worksheet, point to **Tab Color**, and then select the standard color **Purple**.

• On the Winter worksheet, click cell **A20**, and then type Total

• Click cell **D20**, and then type =SUM(D5:D19)

• Select the cell range **A20:D20**, and on the Home tab, in the Styles group, click **Cell Styles**, and then select **Total**.

• Right-click the **Winter** worksheet, and then select **Ungroup Sheets**.

d. Click the **YearSummary** worksheet. Click cell **D5**, and then type =SUM(Click the **Winter** worksheet, and then click cell **D5**. Press and hold Shift, click the **Fall** worksheet, type) and then press Ctrl+Enter. Use the **fill handle** to copy this formula to cell range **D6:D19**.

e. Click the **Fall** worksheet, press and hold ⌈Shift⌉, and then click the **YearSummary** worksheet. On the Fall worksheet, select cell range **D5:D19**. On the Home tab, in the Editing group, click **Fill**, and then select **Across Worksheets**. In the **Fill Across Worksheets** dialog box, click **Formats**, and then click **OK**.

f. On the Fall worksheet, select cell range **A20:D20**, and on the Home tab, in the Editing group, click **Fill**, select **Across Worksheets**, verify that **All** is selected, and then click **OK**.

g. Click the **YearSummaryLinked** worksheet.

- Click cell **A5**, and then on the **Data** tab, in the Data Tools group, click **Consolidate**. In the **Consolidate** dialog box, make sure **Sum** is selected in the Function box, and then click in the **Reference** box.

- Click the **Winter** worksheet, select cell range **A4:D19**, and then click **Add**. Click the **Spring** worksheet, and then click **Add**. Click the **Summer** worksheet, and then click **Add**. Click the **Fall** worksheet, and then click **Add**.

- Click to select the **Top row** check box, click to select the **Left column** check box, and then click to select the **Create links to source data** check box. Click **OK**.

- Use the AutoFit feature on columns A through E, select cell **A5**, and then type **Category**

- Right-click the column **B** header, and then click **Hide** to hide the column.

h. Click the **SpecialEvents** worksheet. Select cell **D15**, the estimated total. On the Formulas tab, in the Formula Auditing group, click **Trace Precedents**.

- Notice the Circular Reference warning in the status bar for cell D15. The SUM function in cell D15 includes a reference to D15, which is causing the circular reference. Click in the **formula bar**, and then change D15 to **D14**

i. Click the **Formulas** tab, and in the Formula Auditing group, click **Watch Window**. Select cells **B6**, **B8**, and **D15**, and then click **Add Watch**. Click **Add**, and then **close** the Watch Window.

> **Mac Troubleshooting**
> The Watch Window is not available on a Mac.

j. Click cell **B8**. Click the **Data** tab, and in the Data Tools group, click **Data Validation**. You will set a rule so the number entered is a whole number between 10 and 100.

- Click the **Settings** tab, and in the **Allow** box, select **Whole number**. In the **Data** box, verify that **between** is selected. In the **Minimum** box, type **10** and then, in the **Maximum** box, type **100**

- Click the **Input Message** tab. In the Title box, type **Guests** and then, in the **Input message** box, type **Enter the estimated number of guests.**

- Click the **Error Alert** tab. In the **Title** box, type **Error** and then in the **Input message** box type **The number of guests is not valid.** Click **OK**.

- In cell **B8**, type **90** and then press ⌈Enter⌉.

k. Click cell **B6**. On the Data tab, in the Data Tools group, click **Data Validation**. You will set a rule so the date entered must be after the current date.

- Click the **Settings** tab. In the **Allow** box, select **Date**. In the **Data** box, select **greater than**. In the **Start date** box, type **=TODAY()**

- Click the **Input Message** tab. In the **Title** box, type **Date** In the **Input message** box, type **Enter event date.**

- Click the **Error Alert** tab. In the **Title** box, type **Error** In the **Error message** box, type **The date must be later than today.** Click **OK**.

- In cell **B6**, type **=TODAY() +1** This will enter tomorrow's date.

l. Select cell range **B11:B14**. On the Data tab, in the Data Tools group, click **Data Validation**. You will set a rule so the data entered must come from a list of cells on the YearSummary worksheet.

- Click the **Settings** tab. In the Allow box, select **List**. Click the **Source** box, click the **YearSummary** worksheet, and then select cell range **A5:A19**.
- Click the **Input Message** tab. In the **Title** box, type Category In the **Input message** box, type Select an option from the list. Click **OK** (you will not enter an error alert).
- Select cell **B11**, click the **arrow**, and then select **Appetizer**.
- Select cell **B12**, click the **arrow**, and then select **Fish**.
- Select cell **B13**, click the **arrow**, and then select **Poultry**.
- Select cell **B14**, click the **arrow**, and then select **Desserts**.

m. **Save** your workbook.

n. If necessary, add the **Developer** tab to the ribbon. Click the **File** tab, click **Options**, click **Customize Ribbon**, and then, under Customize the Ribbon, click **Developer**. Click **OK**.

> ### Mac Troubleshooting
> Mac users, click the Excel menu, click Preferences, and then under Authoring, click View. Under In Ribbon, Show, click to select the Developer tab check box.

o. If necessary, add the location where you save your student files as a trusted location.

> ### Mac Troubleshooting
> Trusted Locations is not available on a Mac.

- Click the **File** tab, click **Options**. Click **Trust Center**, click **Trust Center Settings**, and then click **Trusted Locations**.
- Click **Add new location**, browse to the folder where you save your student files, and then click **OK**. Click **OK** again, click **OK** again, and then click **OK** again.

> ### Mac Troubleshooting
> Trust Center options are not available on a Mac. Macro options are found under Excel Preferences, Security & Privacy, and then under Macro Security, select the appropriate option.

p. Click the **Developer** tab, and in the Code group, click **Record Macro**.

- In the **Macro name** box, type ClearContents In the **Shortcut** key box, press and hold the Shift, and then type C Store the macro in **This Workbook**. In the **Description** box, type Delete all user-entered data from the worksheet. Click **OK**.
- Select cell range **B3:B4**, press and hold Ctrl, and then select cell ranges **B6:B8** and **B11:B14**. Press Delete.
- Click cell **B3**. On the Developer tab, in the Code group, click **Stop Recording**.

q. Click **Undo** to undo the changes you made in recording the macro.

r. On the Developer tab, in the Controls group, click **Insert**, and then select **Button (Form Control)**.

- Click in the top left corner of cell **G1**, and then drag to the bottom right corner of cell **H2** to size and add the button.
- Select **ClearContents**, and then click **OK**.
- Right-click the button, and then select **Edit Text**. Delete the current text, and then type Clear Form Click cell **G4** to deselect the button.

s. Click cell **A10**. Click the **Insert** tab, and in the Links group, click **Link**.

- Select **Place in This Document**, and then select **YearSummary**. Click **ScreenTip**, and enter the ScreenTip Go to YearSummary Click **OK**, and then click **OK**.

- Click the **YearSummary** worksheet. Select cell **H2**, type Special Events and then insert a hyperlink to the SpecialEvents worksheet. Enter a ScreenTip Back to SpecialEvents

t. Complete the **Documentation** worksheet according to your instructor's directions. Right-click the **Documentation** worksheet, and then select **Hide**.

u. Click the **SpecialEvents** worksheet. Select cell ranges **B3:B4**, **B6:B8**, and **B11:B14**. On the Home tab, in the Cells group, click **Format**, and then select **Lock Cell**.

v. Click the **File** tab, click **Options**, click **Advanced**, and then scroll down to the **Display options for this workbook** section.

- Click **Show horizontal scroll bar** and **Show vertical scroll bar**. This will turn off all the scroll bars for the workbook.

> ### Mac Troubleshooting
> On a Mac, click Excel Preferences, under Authoring, click View, and then select option under the Show in Workbook section.

- In the Display options for this worksheet section, click to uncheck **Show row and column headers**. This will turn off the row and column headers for the SpecialEvents worksheet. Click **OK**.

w. Click the **View** tab, and in the Show group, click to uncheck **Gridlines**. This will turn off the gridlines for the SpecialEvents worksheet.

x. Click the **Formulas** tab, and in the Formula Auditing group, click **Show Formulas**.

- Select all the cells that show a formula EXCEPT for the Event date, which is entered by the user. Also select cell **A10**, which contains the hyperlink.

- Click the **Home** tab, and in the Cells group, click **Format**, select **Format Cells**, click the **Protection** tab, and then click **Hidden**. Click **OK**.

- Click the **Formulas** tab, and in the Formula auditing group, click to uncheck **Show Formulas**.

y. Click the **Home** tab, and in the Cells group, click **Format**, and then select **Protect Sheet**. Click **Select locked** cells to uncheck the option, and then click **OK**.

z. Click the **Review** tab, in the Protect group, click **Protect Workbook**, verify that **Structure** is selected, and then click **OK**—do not set a password.

aa. Click the **File** tab, click **Info**, if necessary click **Protect Workbook**, and then select **Mark as Final**. Click **OK** to save the workbook, click **OK** again, and then close Excel. Submit your file as directed by your instructor.

> ### Mac Troubleshooting
> To protect a workbook on a Mac, click the Review tab, and then in the Changes group, click Protect Workbook. Mark as Final is not an available feature on a Mac.

Productions &
Operations

MyLab IT Grader

Student data file needed:

 e04Entertainment.xlsx

You will save your files as:

 e04Entertainment_LastFirst.xlsx

 e04EntertainmentTemplate_LastFirst.xltx

Entertainment Expenses

The Painted Paradise Resort & Spa is a favorite spot for many locals to visit on a Friday night because of the live entertainment in the Silver Moon Lounge. The lounge has quarterly contracts with 13 popular local bands; each band will play in the lounge once a quarter. Lounge manager Will Diaz would like to keep track of quarterly and yearly expenses for the entertainment. He has started a workbook but has asked you to complete it. You will begin by summarizing the quarterly worksheets and consolidating the data. You will also share a copy with the assistant manager to update any necessary items.

a. Open the Excel file, **e04Entertainment**. Save your file as e04Entertainment_LastFirst using your last and first name.

b. Group the **Q1** through **Q4** worksheets. Change the color of the **Q1, Q2, Q3**, and **Q4** worksheet tabs to **White, Background 1, Darker 50%**.

c. With the worksheets still grouped, on the **Q1** worksheet, select cell range **E4:E16**. Fill all across the worksheets (Q1:Q4).

d. On the **Q1** worksheet, select cell range **A3:F3**. Fill the format across the worksheets (Q1:Q4).

e. With the worksheets still grouped, enter a formula in cell **E17** to calculate the total of column E prices.

f. With the worksheet still grouped, enter a formula in cell **F4** that calculates the total cost based on the hours performed and the price. Copy the formula though **F16**.

g. With the worksheets still grouped, enter a formula in cell **F17** to calculate the column F total.

h. With the worksheets still grouped, format column **F** with the Accounting number format.

i. A data validation to select from the Type list from the Type worksheet has been created on the Q1 worksheet but is not on the Q2 through Q4 worksheets. On the **Q1** worksheet, add an Input message to the data validation in cell range **C4:C16**, Select entertainment type from the list. With the cell range still selected, group the **Q1:Q4** worksheets, and then fill all across the worksheets.

j. Ungroup the worksheets.

k. On the **Year** worksheet, in cell range **B4:B16**, enter a 3D formula to calculate the total amount spent on each entertainment group during **Q1:Q4**.

l. In cell **B17**, enter a formula to total the Total Cost column.

m. On the **LinkedSummary** worksheet, in cell **B4** create a linked consolidation to the cell range **F4:F16** on the **Q1:Q4** worksheets.

n. Hide the **Type** worksheet. Remove the gridlines from the **Q1:Q4** worksheets. **Save** the workbook.

Grader Heads up

In the MyLab IT Grader version of this project, you will not be creating an Excel template.

o. Save the workbook as an Excel Template named **e04EntertainmentTemplate_LastFirst** using your last and first name.

p. Group **Q1:Q4** worksheets, and then clear the data in cell range **D4:D16**. Ungroup the worksheets.

q. Save the workbook, exit Excel, and then submit your files as directed by your instructor.

Critical Thinking

In this exercise, you created a linked consolidation. What is the benefit of creating a linked consolidation versus a consolidation by position?

Problem Solve 2

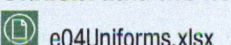 **MyLab IT Grader**

Student data file needed:

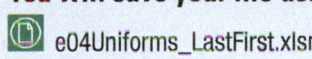 e04Uniforms.xlsx

You will save your file as:

e04Uniforms_LastFirst.xlsm

Hotel Uniform Order Tracking

Productions & Operations

The staff at Painted Paradise Resort & Spa are required to wear uniforms every day. While the hotel provides uniforms each year to staff members, occasionally employees want to order items in addition to what is provided to them. One of the recent interns at the hotel created a spreadsheet order form but never finished it. You will finish working on it so it can be distributed to the staff. You will add data validation rules, record a macro, and make the spreadsheet look less like an Excel spreadsheet and more like an online order form so it is easy to use. You will also save it as a template to make it easy for the staff members to open each time.

a. Open the Excel file, **e04Uniforms**. Click **OK** in the circular reference warning box, and then save your file as an **Excel Macro-Enabled Workbook** named **e04Uniforms_LastFirst** using your last and first name.

b. On the OrderForm worksheet, locate and correct the circular reference. The affected cell is identified on the status bar at the bottom of the window.

c. Select cell **C10** and enter a data validation rule to look up the department name from the cell range named **Departments** on the Options worksheet. Enter the Input Message title Department: Enter the input message Select a department from the list. Enter an Error Alert title Error: Enter the error message Invalid department. Select cell **C10**, and select **Front Desk**.

d. On the OrderForm worksheet, select cell range **C13:C18**, and enter a data validation rule to look up the top options from the cell range named **TopOptions** on the Options worksheet. Leave the input message and error message blank.

e. Select cell **C13**, and select **Vest**.

f. On the OrderForm worksheet, select cell range **C19:C24**, and enter a data validation rule to look up the bottom options from the cell range named **BottomOptions**. Leave the input message and error message blank.

g. On the OrderForm worksheet, select cell range **C25:C30**, and enter a data validation rule to look up the other options from the cell range named **OtherOptions**. Leave the input message and error message blank.

h. On the OrderForm worksheet, select cell range **D13:D30**, and enter a data validation rule to look up the size options from the cell range named **Sizes**. The input message and error message can be left blank. Select cell **D13**, and select **Large**. Select cell **E13**, and type 2

i. Select cell **A13** and insert a hyperlink to the defined name **Tops**. Add a screen tip Go to Top Options Select cell **A19** and insert a hyperlink to the defined name **Bottoms**. Add a screen tip Go to Bottoms Options Select cell **A25** and insert a hyperlink to the defined name **Other**. Add a screen tip Go to Other Options

j. If necessary, add the Developer tab to the ribbon. Record a macro named ClearForm with the shortcut key F in This Workbook. Add the description To clear the form for another order. Clear cell range C6:C7, cell C10, cell range C13:E30, and cell C33. Select cell C6 as the last step in your macro, and stop the recording. Undo the changes you made while recording the macro.

k. Insert a macro button in cell range F6:G7 to run the ClearForm macro. Change the button text to Clear Form Test the macro button.

l. In cell C6, enter the name Kyle Humphrey In cell C10, select **Front Desk**. In cell C13, select **Vest**. In cell D13, select **Large**. In E13, type 2

Grader Heads up

In the MyLab IT Grader version of this project, you do not add a new group to the ribbon.

---

m. If necessary, add a new group to the Review tab on the ribbon called Text-to-Speech and add the **Speak Cells** and **Stop Speaking Cells** buttons.

n. Modify the workbook for easier navigation.

- On the OrderForm worksheet, unlock the cells required for data entry (the same cells the macro clears as well as the cells containing the hyperlinks).
- Hide all formulas except the Order Date in cell C7.
- Hide the gridlines on the OrderForm worksheet.
- Hide the horizontal scroll bar on both worksheets.
- Hide row and column headings on the OrderForm worksheet.
- Protect the OrderForm worksheet to not allow the user to click in locked cells (do not use a password).
- Protect the workbook and mark the workbook as final.

o. Close Excel, and submit your files as directed by your instructor.

Perform 1: Perform in Your Career

Student data files needed:

- e04Miles.xlsx
- e04Account.xlsx
- e04Expense.xlsx

You will save your files as:

- e04Miles_LastFirst.xlsx
- e04Expense_LastFirst.xlsx
- e04ExpenseTemplate_LastFirst.xltx

Expense Report Application

Finance & Accounting

You have just started working at a new job. Your boss, Elda Rust, has asked you to recreate the current expense report, which is old and outdated. She would like users to be able to enter data only in appropriate cells and wants to ensure that invalid data is not entered. To be properly designed, your workbook should be easy to use, even for people who are unfamiliar with Excel. You have been instructed to have one worksheet for each day of the week with a consolidation worksheet.

a. Open the Excel file, **e04Miles**. Save your file as e04Miles_LastFirst using your last and first name.

b. Create a named range for cell range A2:B7.

c. Open the Excel file, **e04Expense**. Save your file e04Expense_LastFirst using your last and first name.

d. Open the Excel file, **e04Account**. Copy the data on the Lists worksheet into the e04Expense workbook on a new worksheet. Close the e04Account workbook.

e. On the ExpenseReport worksheet, in cell J10 type # of Miles

f. Select cell range B10:B26, and the delete the Table Column.

g. Clear all in cell range K4:M5.

h. In cell K4, type Date Format cell K4 the same as the SSN label in K7.

i. Insert a bottom border in cell L4.

j. Adjust the formula in cell L11. Using a VLOOKUP function, it should multiply the number of miles by the appropriate rate from e04Miles_LastFirst and sum the remainder of the items in the row.

k. Format cell range I11:I26 appropriately.

l. Change the order of cells C10 and B10. (Description will come before Account.)

m. Ensure that only a date of today or before today can be entered in cell L4.

n. Cell range B11:B25 should allow for a list of descriptions from the Lists worksheet.

o. Insert a formula in cell range C11:C25 that will look up the account number based on the description selected in the adjacent column. Adjust the formula so that errors will return a blank.

p. Hide the Lists worksheet.

q. Update the documentation worksheet according to your instructor's directions. Hide the Documentation worksheet.

r. Format the column widths appropriately across the entire table.

s. Unlock cells that would be needed for data entry. Hide all formulas. Protect the worksheet, and do not allow the selecting of locked cells.

t. Hide gridlines and row and column headings of the ExpenseReport worksheet. Protect the structure of the workbook. Save the workbook.

u. Save the workbook as a template named e04ExpenseTemplate_LastFirst using your last and first name for future use.

v. Close Excel, and then submit your files as directed by your instructor.

Perform 2: Perform in Your Life

Student data file needed:

 e04Marathons.xlsx

You will save your file as:

e04Marathons_LastFirst.xlsm

Marathons around the World

Finance & Accounting

You started running five years ago and have set a personal goal to participate in as many marathons as possible next year. However, you are not sure of all the costs that will be involved so you can budget appropriately. Fortunately, you have two upcoming marathons you can use to assist you in determining your expenses and creating your plan.

You will create a workbook that contains four worksheets. Two of the worksheets will consolidate your expenses for each marathon. You will consolidate the data from the two marathons on the third worksheet. The fourth worksheet will be used to track your expenses. At a minimum, you will need to track the following categories.

- Entrance fees
- Running club dues
- Gym memberships
- Medical
- Clothing
- Footwear
- Miscellaneous supplies
- Travel
- Lodging

a. Open the Excel file, **e04Marathons**. Save your file as an **Excel Macro-Enabled Workbook** named **e04Marathons_LastFirst** using your last and first name.

b. Rename Sheet1 Summary Rename Sheet2 Marathon1 and rename Sheet3 Marathon2 Color the tabs to visually show related tabs.

c. The Summary and the two Marathon tabs should all be set up the same, as follows.
   - Ensure that there is a Heading Row for Category and Amount.
   - List your specific categories under the heading Category.
   - Format the cells under the Amount heading appropriately. Enter appropriate amounts for the categories. Not all categories need an amount entered.
   - Ensure that there is a total row, and format it appropriately.
   - On the Summary worksheet, use a 3D reference to consolidate the data from the two marathon tabs under the Amount heading.

d. Sheet4 will contain a table that will track your expenses. Rename the sheet tab appropriately.

e. In cell A1, type Marathon1 and then, in cell B1, type Philadelphia Marathon In cell A2, type Marathon2 and then in cell B2, type Death Valley Trail Marathon

f. Leave at least one row below your headings and create the following.
   - A column for the date of the expense. Only dates in the current year and future years should be allowed.
   - A column to indicate whether the expenses belong to Marathon1 or Marathon2 listed in cell range B1:B2. You should be able to choose only from these two marathons.
   - A column for the category of expenses. These expenses should be limited to the categories on the Summary worksheet.
   - The fourth column is for a detailed description of your expense. It should be limited to no more than 30 characters.
   - The next column should contain the actual amount of your expense.
   - The last column should be a running total of your expenses.
   - Format the values in the amount and the running total as currency.
   - Fill formats from the top row of your data, down at least eight rows.
   - Create a named range for the data input area you just created, excluding the Running Total column.

g. Enter at least six rows of data to test your formulas, perform data validation, and ensure that you enter at least one line of test data for each marathon. Auto Fit all column widths as necessary.

h. Enter a formula on the Marathon1 and Marathon2 worksheets that will total the data entered on the expenses worksheet. There are two criteria that need to be met for a value to appear: The expense must be for the correct marathon, and it must match the correct category. (Hint: Use a SUMIFS formula.)

i. Create a macro that will clear the data from the expenses worksheet. (This will allow you to use the same file for your next two marathons.) Ensure that the first step of your macro is to select the Expenses worksheet.

j. Undo the actions of your macro so your data remains.

k. Add a button to the Summary worksheet that will run the macro.

l. Hide gridlines, column/row headings, and scroll bars on all worksheets in the workbook. Protect the Summary, Marathon1, and Marathon2 worksheets.

m. Update the Documentation worksheet according to your instructor's directions. Hide the Documentation worksheet.

n. Protect the structure of the workbook; do not set a password.

o. Save the workbook, exit Excel, and then submit the file as directed by your instructor.

Perform 3: Perform in Your Team

Student data file needed:

Finance & Accounting

Blank Excel workbook

You will save your file as:

e04Reimbursement_TeamName.xlsx

Team Expense Reimbursement with Summary

The organization you work for has used paper forms for years, but now that so many employees have smartphones, tablets, laptops, or other such devices, the organization would like to create electronic forms. In the past, team members have submitted their expenses individually, and it was up to the payroll manager to consolidate the information to be able to create a team summary of expenses for a project.

Your supervisor has asked you to create a workbook that can be used by teams of employees to track expenses for a project. The workbook should contain one worksheet for each team member as well as a worksheet to summarize team expenses.

a. Select one team member to set up the document by completing steps b through e.

b. Open your browser and navigate to https://www.onedrive.live.com, https://www.drive.google.com, or any other instructor-assigned location. Be sure all members of the team have an account on the chosen system, such as a Microsoft or Google account.

c. Create a new workbook, and then name it e04Reimbursement_TeamName using the team name assigned to your team by your instructor.

d. Share the spreadsheet with the other members of your team. Make sure each team member has the appropriate permission to edit the document.

e. Hold a team meeting, and discuss the requirements of the remaining steps. Make an action and communication plan. Consider which steps can be done independently and which steps require completion of prior steps before starting.

f. Team member 1 should complete the following.

- Create a worksheet to track expenses. Include the following columns: Date, Description, Hotel, Transportation, Meals, Phone, Mileage, Other, and Total. Format at least 19 rows as a table.

- Create data validation rules in the Date column to accept only dates less than or equal to today.

- Create data validation in the expense columns to restrict the values to decimals between $2.00 and $999.

- Create three more copies of the worksheet just created, one for each team member. Name each of the worksheets with the first name of one of the team members.

- Enter at least five lines of expenses on the worksheet for team member 1.

g. Team member 2 should complete the following after team member 1 has uploaded the workbook.

- On the worksheet for team member 2, enter at least five lines of expenses.

- For all four worksheets (one for each member), insert a formula in the Total column to add the columns Hotel through Other and add a total line to total expenses by each column.

h. Team member 3 should complete the following after team member 2 has uploaded the workbook.

- On the worksheet for team member 3, enter at least five lines of expenses.

- Insert a new worksheet named TeamSummary and then move it after the team member 4 worksheet.

- Add a title to the new worksheet.

- On the four member worksheets, unlock all cells that need to be opened for data entry. Hide any formulas.

i. Team member 4 should complete the following after team member 3 has uploaded the workbook.
   - On the worksheet for team member 4, enter at least five lines of expenses.
   - On the TeamSummary worksheet, consolidate all four team members' expense reports by Description. Format the results as appropriate. (Hint: Do not include the date column in the consolidation.)
   - On the TeamSummary worksheet, create hyperlinks from the TeamSummary worksheet to all four member worksheets.
   - Protect the four team members' worksheets without a password and prevent clicking on locked cells.

j. In a custom header section of the TeamSummary worksheet, include the names of the students in your team. Spread the names evenly across each of the three header sections: left section, center section, and right section.

k. On the TeamDescriptions worksheet, each team member must list his or her first and last name as well as a summary of his or her contributions.

l. Team member 1 should save the workbook and mark the workbook as final.

m. Exit Excel, and then submit the team file as directed by your instructor.

Perform 4: How Others Perform

Student data file needed:	**You will save your file as:**
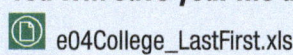 e04College.xlsm	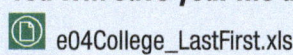 e04College_LastFirst.xlsm

Education Costs Worksheet

Finance & Accounting

A fellow student has created a workbook to track his expenses for the next two semesters of school. You like the idea of being able to do this and have asked him for the workbook so you can use it as well. You will adjust the workbook to make it work for you. You are a little confused about how the workbook works, and because he did not leave any instructions, you have to figure out on your own what he has done.

a. Open the Excel file, **e04College**. Save it as an Excel Macro-Enabled workbook named e04College_LastFirst using your last and first name. Click OK in the circular reference warning dialog box.

b. Locate and correct the circular reference.

c. On the Fall2021 and Spring2022 worksheets, create formulas in the Amount column to sum the expenses identified in column A.

d. On the TotalCosts worksheet, create a 3-D reference that sums the data from the Fall2021 and Spring2022 worksheets.

e. On the TotalCosts worksheet, if appropriate, unlock any cells for data entry, and protect the rest of the worksheet. Add hyperlinks to both the Fall2021 and Spring2022 worksheets.

f. On both the Fall2021 and Spring2022 worksheets, create a hyperlink to return to the TotalCosts worksheet.

g. Click the Fall2021 worksheet. Look at the cells with the comments (they have red triangles in the top right corner). On the Documentation worksheet, comment on what the macro does. Also comment on what kind of macro it is.

h. Save the workbook, and mark it as final. Close Excel, and submit your workbook as directed by your instructor.

Excel Business Unit 5

Manipulating Data Sets for Decision Making

Data is a big part of business, and its value and importance are increasing as collecting it from a variety of sources becomes ever easier. Learning how to collect and organize all relevant data for use in analyses is extremely important in every business. Excel is one of the most commonly used applications for data analysis in the world, and it has a variety of tools built in to facilitate sound, data-driven decision making.

Learning Outcome 1:

Understand the benefits of analyzing data sets and learn techniques to import, organize, and clean data sets from a variety of sources.

REAL WORLD SUCCESS

"I was recently asked to develop a series of reports on enrollments at the university I work for. The data on students enrolling at the university was made available to us in an Access database. By importing the data into Excel from Access, I was able to create a broad range of statistics, graphs, and reports spanning several years of data. The result was a comprehensive view of our data that provided unique insights for our university."

– Dave, alumnus

Learning Outcome 2:

Utilize various forecasting and optimization tools, such as data tables, Scenario Manager, and Solver to support decision making.

REAL WORLD SUCCESS

"I recently created a workbook detailing changes to several products our company manufactures. In the workbook, I used a data table to analyze the changes in profits resulting from different cost and demand combinations. The use of form controls and conditional formatting made the worksheet intuitive and easy to use."

– Joseph P., manager

Microsoft Excel

Chapter 9 ORGANIZE, IMPORT, EXPORT, AND CLEANSE DATA SETS

MyLab IT Grader

Sales & Marketing

Prepare Case

Red Bluff Golf Course & Pro Shop Data Integration

The Red Bluff Golf Course & Pro Shop manager, Aleeta Herriott, has asked you to create a report that analyzes costs and revenues from tournaments hosted over the past year. In the past, her staff had to reenter data manually from different sources to create this report because no one at the resort knew how to import the data. As a result, they rarely completed the report. Aleeta worries about the accuracy of the reports that were compiled because of the manual data entry. However, she did keep all the original files. Recently, a new Golf database was created to track sales and allow for easy export to Excel for analysis. Aleeta wants you to design a spreadsheet that will help her automate the process of gathering and standardizing the data from the past for analysis.

Orest Drozda/Shutterstock

Student data files needed:

 e05ch09TournamentData.xlsx

 e05ch09TournamentReport.xlsx

 e05ch09MenuOptions.xml

e05ch09MoreMenuOptions.xml

 e05ch09Customer.xml

 e05ch09Customers.csv

 e05ch09Golf.accdb

You will save your files as:

 e05ch09TournamentData_LastFirst.xlsx

 e05ch09TournamentReport_LastFirst.xlsx

Connecting to Data with Get & Transform Data

One reason for the popularity of spreadsheets is their ability to combine data and information from a wide variety of sources. Once you have advanced beyond the novice level to become a more advanced user, you will very likely need to integrate data from multiple sources. Most organizations have their data spread throughout the organization in a variety of formats on a variety of devices. Your organization may collect data on websites or network servers or in word-processing programs, databases, or even paper reports.

This data may not be immediately usable to your organization. The data may not be properly formatted or may need transforming before it is of value for analysis. For example, dates can be stored in many different formats around the world. Additionally, you may have data that needs to be transformed, such as needing to separate a customer's full name into first and last names. Excel has powerful business intelligence tools that make connecting to and transforming data simple and dynamic. The connection and any changes made to the data are saved within the query and can be repeated at any time. In this section, you will learn how to connect to external data, import it, and transform it using Get & Transform.

Understand the Importance of External Data Sets

Anything that is not stored in an Excel format (.xls or .xlsx) or not stored locally is considered to be **external data**. Spreadsheet applications such as Excel offer a wide variety of tools to help the user extract external data and integrate it into reports so that it can be actively used to make better decisions. **Get & Transform** is a business intelligence tool within Excel that enables Excel to connect to a wide variety of data sources and perform a series of recorded steps to combine and refine data for use. The process of converting data from one format to another format is called **transformation**. Transforming data can range from separating strings of text, to calculating the difference between dates, to appending sets of data from different sources together. A significant advantage to using Get & Transform is that as new records are added to external data sources, the recorded transformation steps are applied when the data connection is refreshed. This means that once the data transformation process is constructed, it can run new data whenever needed.

Common file formats that Get & Transform can connect to include comma delimited files, text files, and .accdb files from Microsoft Access. Get & Transform can connect to internet-based resources if a URL is provided and to other online systems such as Facebook, Salesforce.com, Azure, and SharePoint. Get & Transform also has built in capabilities to connect to database systems like SQL, Oracle, and SAP HANA. Microsoft continues to expand the file types and data sources that Get & Transform can connect to, along with expanding the types of transformations that can be completed.

One of the reasons that spreadsheets are such powerful tools is that they have evolved into the de facto means of consolidating diverse types of data. For example, an organization may want you to work on an analysis or report but cannot grant you access to their databases. One solution would be for them to export their data to a text format, which you can then easily import into Excel.

REAL WORLD ADVICE	Connecting to and Storing Data in Excel

After establishing a connection with Get & Transform, you can choose from several methods of storing the data in Excel. The decision on how to store data in Excel may depend on many factors, such as the size of the data set you are connecting to or the type of analysis that will be performed on the data. Later in the text, you will explore Excel's Data Model, which allows for data connects to be made without storing data in a worksheet. For particularly large or complex data sets, this may be the preferred method. Until then, all data will be imported into a worksheet for analysis.

| QUICK REFERENCE | Common Data Sources for Excel |

Source	Description
Microsoft Access (.mdb, .accdb)	Import data from relational database tables created in Access (.mdb, .accdb) formats.
HTML (.html)	Link to data stored in tabular form on websites.
Comma separated (.csv)	Convert data stored in a comma-delimited (.csv) format.
XML (.xml)	Import data stored in .xml format.
Text (.txt)	Exchange data between mainframes and other systems that use the .txt format.
SQL Server	A popular relational database server for corporate web servers.
Analysis Services	Designed to import data formatted as a data cube in SQL Server Analysis Services.
Windows Azure Marketplace	An online service in which one can subscribe to data sets, build queries, and import the queries to Excel.
Microsoft Query	A query wizard to help import data from less common or unlisted sources using ODBC (standard data conversion drivers).
Data Connection Wizard	Another query wizard for creating and maintaining connections with unlisted data sources; uses OLEDB drivers.

REAL WORLD ADVICE	Legacy Connections in Excel

Get & Transform became widely available in all versions of Excel 2016 and was previously called Power Query. In Excel 2019, it is the only method of connecting to external data on the Data tab. To enable the legacy data import wizards for connecting to Access, websites, and other sources; navigate to the Excel Options and click in the Data group.

Opening the Starting File

Data can be easily shared online between companies, within companies, and between companies and their customers. While this data can be placed into a workbook by copying from the website and pasting into a workbook, linking to a web page is a more efficient process. When the web page is linked to a workbook, the data can be updated without having to visit the web page and perform a copy-and-paste process every time the data is updated. Aleeta Herriott has asked you to import data from a web page that lists online transactions related to golf tournaments through the Painted Paradise website. In this exercise, you will begin by opening the starting file.

E09.00

SIDE NOTE
Office Updates
Depending on your exact Office version, you may see Open or Open Other Workbooks.

To Open the Starting File

a. Start **Excel**, click **Open** in the left pane, and then double-click **This PC**. Navigate through the folder structure to the location of your student data files, and then double-click **e05ch09TournamentData**. An Excel workbook will open with a variety of blank worksheets that you will use throughout this chapter.

b. Click the **File** tab, click **Save As**, and then double-click **This PC**. In the Save As dialog box, navigate to the location where you are saving your project files, and then change the file name to e05ch09TournamentData_LastFirst using your last and first name. Click **Save**.

Importing Web Data into Excel

One popular way to integrate information from web pages is to use a web query. A **query** is a question that you would ask about the data in a database such as Access. Access allows users to formulate queries in a variety of tools or languages to search for information in the database. You might think of a web query as something you could type into a search engine such as Google or Bing to search the web. However, in Excel, a **web query** is a way of importing data into a spreadsheet directly from a web page. This could be stock prices from a financial website such as http://money.msn.com, or it could be sales data from a company web server or even a table of data in a Wikipedia article.

More and more, companies are using websites to make their data available to users. Financial, governmental, and even college-related data is uploaded and refreshed daily. By linking this data to a spreadsheet via a web query, users can automatically update the data for use in their spreadsheet applications. Web queries are tied to specific URLs; if the URL changes, the web query will no longer be able to access the data. This makes it important to have the exact URL address when you are importing data.

One of Red Bluff's suppliers uses a web page to provide data on products shipped to the pro shop. This data is updated regularly. The formatting on the report is problematic and several columns need transformation steps before the data can be used for analysis. In this exercise, you will establish a web query to import data from the Red Bluff Golf Course & Pro Shop Supplier Report using Get & Transform.

 E09.01

MAC COMPATIBILITY
No Get & Transform in Office 2019 for Mac
At the time of publishing for this text, the tools discussed in this text in the Get & Transform Data group are not available in the Office 2019 for Mac versions of Microsoft Office. Instead, the previous set of tools in the group Get External Data continue to serve the purpose of importing data into Excel for the Mac versions of Office.

To Connect to and Import Web Data into Excel

a. Be sure the Suppliers worksheet is active.

b. Click the **Data** tab, and in the Get & Transform Data group, click **From Web**.

c. In the From Web dialog box, click in the **URL** box, and type the following URL: http://www.paintedparadiseresort.com/supplierreport2022.html

d. Click **OK**.

e. The Navigator window now displays the available tables to which Get & Transform can connect. Click **Supplier Report** and review the data displayed under the Table View tab. Notice that the dates appear as text entries and that the Product and Units fields are combined into a single field. You will correct this with Get & Transform.

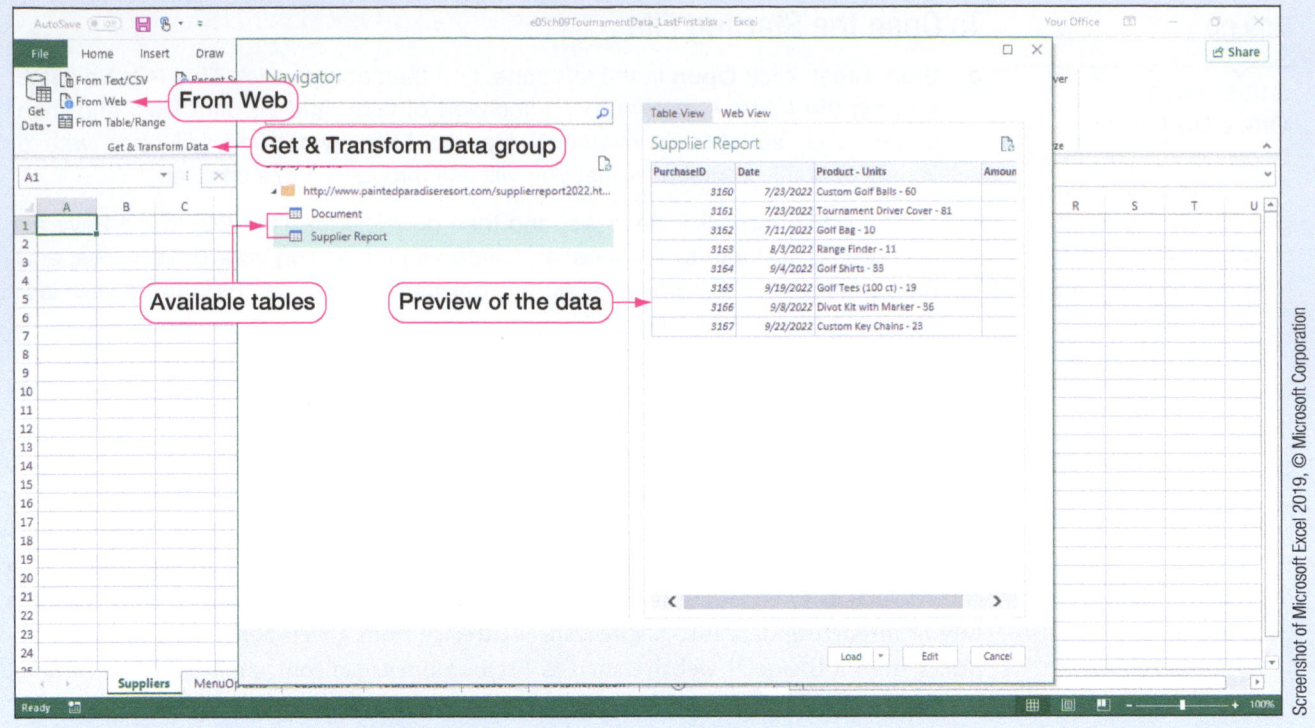

Figure 1 The Navigator window

Screenshot of Microsoft Excel 2019, © Microsoft Corporation

SIDE NOTE

Office Updates

Depending on your exact Office version, you may see the Edit button in Get & Transform be called Transform Data.

SIDE NOTE

Connection Speed

Because of the variable speed of connections and the amount of data being downloaded from a website, it may take several minutes for the data to download.

f. Click **Edit**.

g. Click the **Products-Units** heading to select the Products-Units column.

h. On the **Home** tab, in the Transform group, click **Split Column**, and then click **By Delimiter**.

i. Get & Transform should detect the hyphen character as the delimiter. If it does not, click the **Select or enter delimiter** box and then click **Custom**. Type - (a hyphen) in the next box.

j. Ensure that the option for **Each occurrence of the delimiter** is selected and then click **OK**.

Notice that there are now two columns of data, the Product names are in one and the number of units sold are in the other.

Troubleshooting

The tabs in the Editor window are highly contextual. Transformations on the Home and Transform tabs make changes to the data in their original columns. Transformations on the Add Column tab create a new column of data with the applied transformation but leave the original data in place. These columns are not connected, however, and the original data can be deleted if it is no longer needed.

k. On the Home tab and in the Close group, click the **Close & Load** arrow and then click **Close & Load To**. In the Import Data dialog box, click the option for **Existing worksheet**. Ensure cell A1 is displayed in the Existing worksheet box and then click **OK**.

New columns created

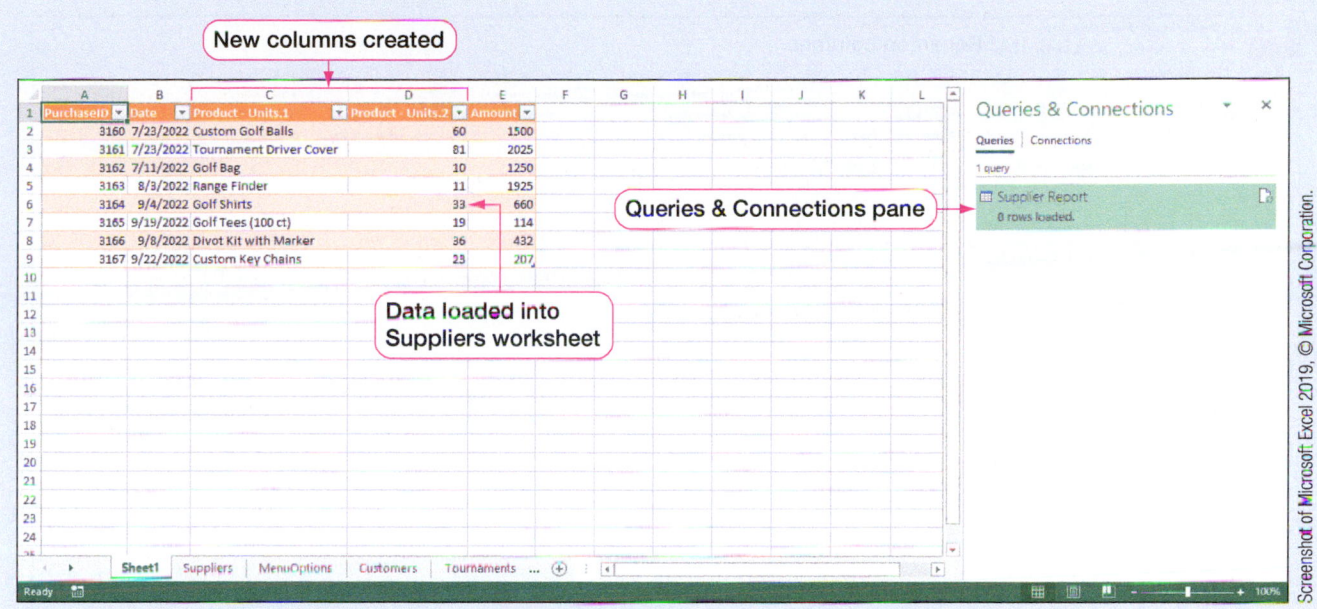

Queries & Connections pane

Data loaded into
Suppliers worksheet

Screenshot of Microsoft Excel 2019, © Microsoft Corporation.

Figure 2   The transformed data loaded to Excel

I.   **Save**  the workbook.

Modifying an Existing Get & Transform Connection

You may have noticed that the data you pulled into your spreadsheet from the web page with your original query contains column headings that were renamed during the data transformation process. For example, the heading for the new Product column was named Product-Units.1. The new column that contains the units data was renamed Product-Units.2. Get & Transform connections can be easily modified to alter existing steps or to include more steps.

Get & Transform saves all steps that have been created during the import process in the Applied Steps pane. These steps can be changed or deleted and new steps can be added in any order. In this exercise, you will modify the query by changing the column headings on the previous import.

E09.02

SIDE NOTE
Pin the Ribbon
If your ribbon is collapsed, pin your ribbon open. Click the Home tab. In the lower-right corner of the ribbon, click Pin the ribbon.

To Modify an Existing Get & Transform Connection

a.   Ensure that the Queries & Connections pane is visible. If it is not, click the Data tab, and in the Queries & Connections group, click **Queries & Connections**.

b.   In the Queries & Connections pane, double-click Supplier Report.

c.   Double-click the column heading **Products-Units.1** and type Product to rename the column.

d.   Double-click the column heading **Products-Units.2** and type Units to rename the column.

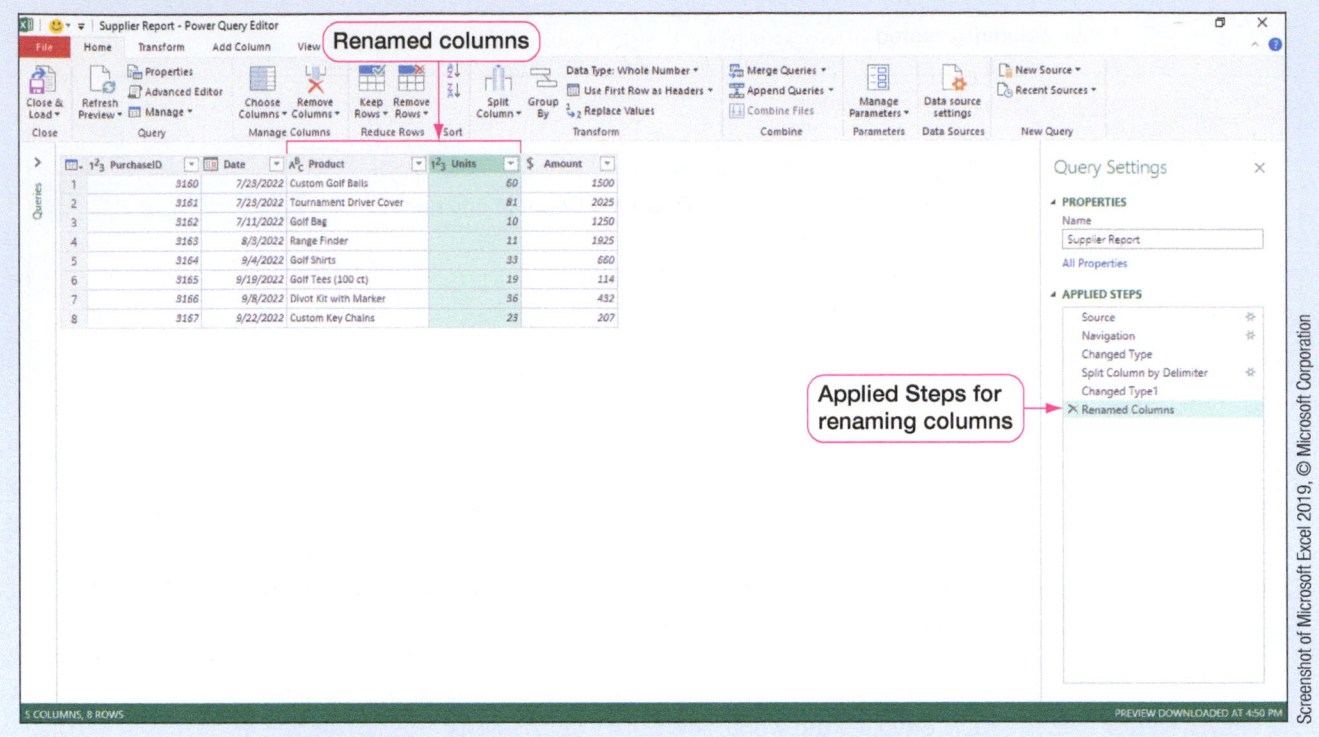

Figure 3 Modified web query

e. On the Home tab, click **Close & Load**.

f. **Save** the workbook.

SS CONSIDER THIS | **Beyond Spreadsheets**

The amount of data in the business world is growing rapidly—faster than at any time in history. Companies and governments store massive amounts of data. Facebook stores billions of photos. What kinds of data could a company like Facebook be collecting that you might not have considered? How could the information be used, both positively and negatively?

REAL WORLD ADVICE | **How Is Connecting to Web Data Different from Copying and Pasting?**

It may seem simpler just to copy the web data and paste it into your worksheet than to use a web query. In fact, you can copy and paste for the occasional import of web data. However, when you use the copy-and-paste method, you will have to spend time reformatting the data to use it in your formulas in Excel. More important, using Get & Transform to connect to web data provides a great advantage when you are creating an application that needs to be updated frequently. The Get & Transform connection will automatically update and apply any data transformations to the web data and reflect the changes in your Excel file.

Connecting to XML Data and Text Files

Two of the most common data formats for importing data into Excel are XML data and text files. In this section, you will learn how to import data in these two formats into Excel.

Understand and Import XML and Text Data

XML, or Extensible Markup Language, is an increasingly popular tool working behind the scenes in Excel. A little understanding of how it is used will take you well beyond the usual beginner's knowledge of spreadsheets. In an earlier exercise, you imported data that was stored in a table on a web page. This made it easier to import the data into Excel without reformatting it. However, in some cases, data on web pages is not stored in an organized manner. That is to say, the data may not be in a table that is easily accessible with Excel. **XML** was created to help give structure to web page data so it can be searched and processed more efficiently. XML allows users to define their own tags in order to define the content of the document.

Most web pages are coded in **HTML**, or Hypertext Markup Language. Both XML and HTML are examples of markup languages. **Markup languages** use special sequences of characters or "markups" inserted in the document to indicate how the document should look when it is displayed or printed. The markup indicators are often called "tags" and are enclosed in angle brackets (< >). These tags tell the device that will process the document what to do with it. HTML is used to format and display the web data, whereas XML was developed to help convert web data into a tabular structure so it could be easily stored and transported. Unlike HTML tags, the tags in XML actually describe the content of the data between the tags. For instance, HTML uses tags such as <H1> </H1> to help describe the formatting of the document, but XML uses tags to describe the actual content between the tags <revenue></revenue>. Because of this, XML capabilities were soon extended to databases, spreadsheets, and word processors and became the de facto standard for transmitting data between systems and different applications.

One of the most powerful aspects of XML is that you can define custom tags for content that is specific to a particular industry. In HTML, all the tags are predetermined so the browser knows how to interpret them. XML is different in that as long as you follow the rules for creating XML tags and documents, you can define the tags any way you like.

The goal of XML is to allow users to automate the storage, transmission, and processing of content. To accomplish this, XML separates the content from the format and structure of the document. To understand how to process an XML document, it is crucial to understand its structure. The structure of an XML document is described in the XML schema or data map. The **XML schema** describes the structure of an XML document in terms of what XML elements it will contain and their sequence. In Excel, the term **XML map** is synonymous with XML schema. An **XML element** includes the start and stop tags and everything in between, such as <revenue>$345,678</revenue>. The document structure is separate from the actual content of the document itself and uses a separate file with an .xsd extension. It is similar in concept to the idea of a mail merge. The content is contained in the .xml file, the formatting is described in an .xsl file, and the structure of all the data elements is laid out in the schema or .xsd file. All of these files are merged in the resulting XML document, just as a list of names and addresses is merged with a form letter in Word, as illustrated in Figure 4.

Determining the structure of any document may not be obvious. If you were to look at a book index or a table of contents, you would know just by glancing at them what these two different documents were. This is because over the years, publishers have defined what the structure of an index or table of contents should look like. It is the same way with schemas. You can define the structure of a sales order document to contain the customer number, name, date, product ID, cost, and total cost. All of these would be represented as elements within the XML schema. So, when processing an XML file, Excel looks for an existing XML schema to check whether it has received a valid XML document. Thus, it can automate the processing of XML files because it knows what to expect because the parts of the document are defined by the schema.

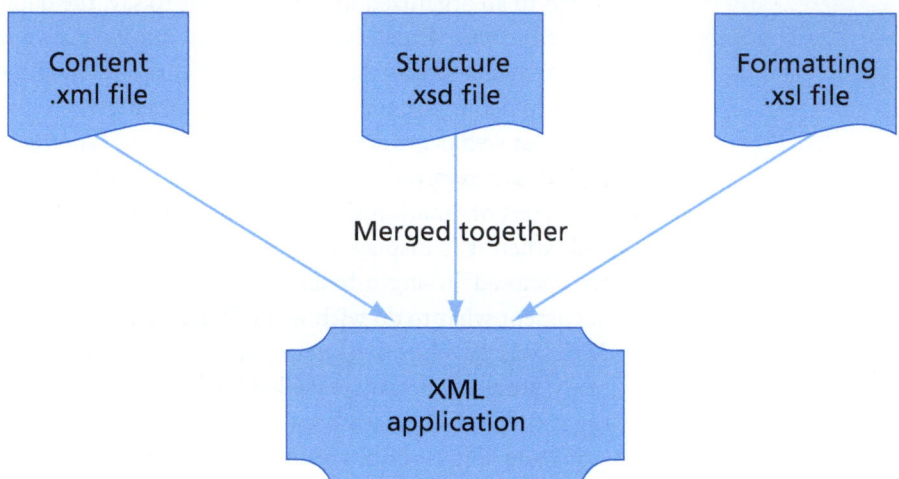

Figure 4   XML document files

Importing XML Data

The Red Bluff Golf Course & Pro Shop uses the Indigo5 restaurant to cater food and drinks for many of its hosted tournaments. A list of current menu options and pricing has been sent to you as an XML file. By being saved in this XML document, the data can be electronically transmitted, queried, and stored. Get & Transform can connect to XML files in a similar manner as it connects to websites. Queries created by Get & Transform can be refreshed by clicking the Refresh button in the Data tab, or by right-clicking a query in the Query & Connections pane and selecting Refresh. So whenever you refresh a Get & Transform connection to an XML source, it automatically connects to the source to import the changes and update the data on your worksheet.

In this exercise, you will import an XML document of menu options and pricing into the MenuOptions worksheet.

 E09.03

To Import XML Data

a. Click the **MenuOptions** worksheet.

b. On the Data tab, in the Get & Transform Data group, click **Get Data**, point to **From File**, and then click **From XML**.

c. In the Import Data dialog box, navigate through the folder structure to the location of your student data files, and then double-click **e05ch09MenuOptions**.

d. In the displayed dialog box, click **Edit**. You will notice that initially only two columns and one row has been imported. Click the first cell that reads **Table** to see a preview of the data in the XML file.

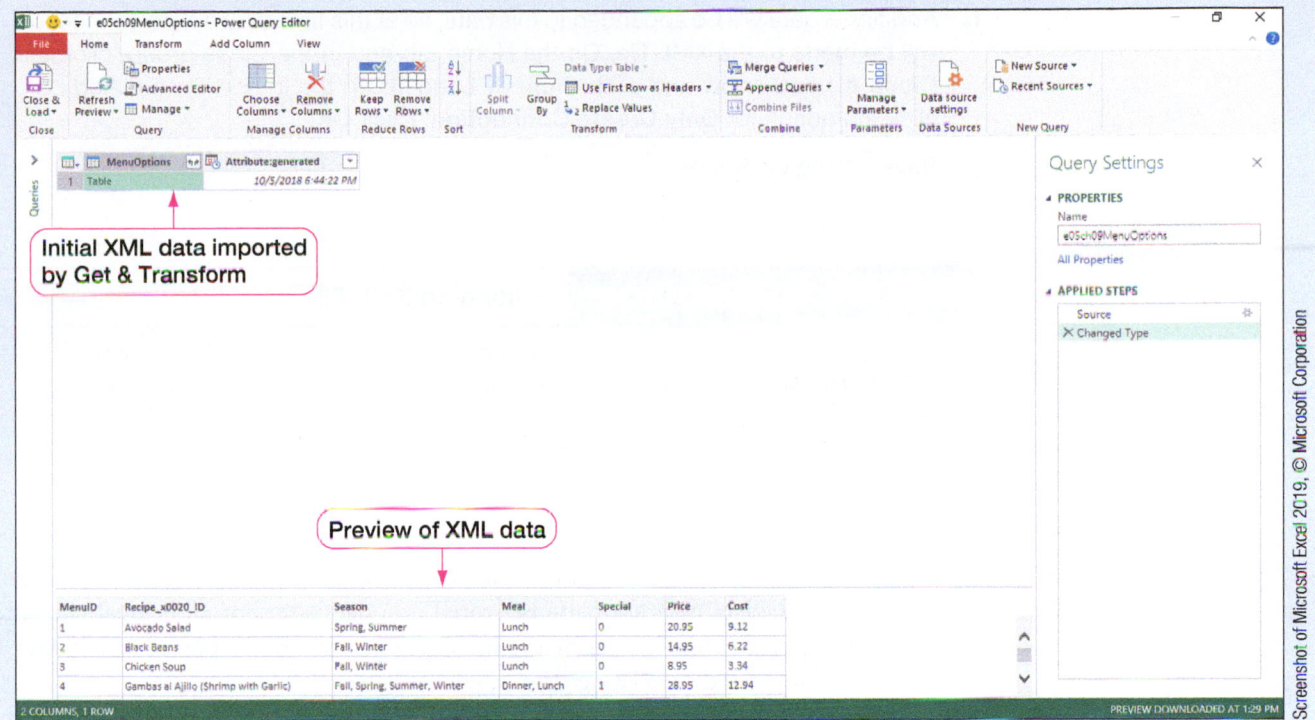

Figure 5 XML document connection in Get & Transform

e. Click the Expand button 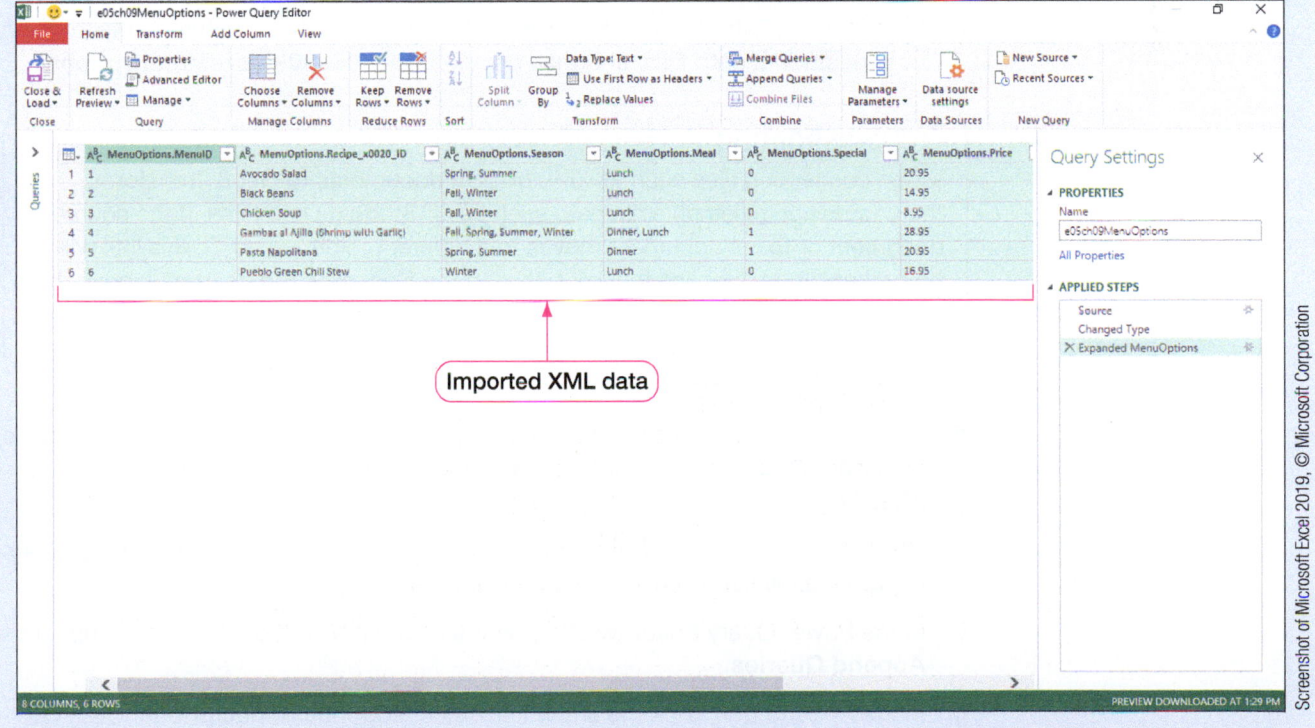 to view a list of possible fields to include in the query. Ensure that all fields are selected and click **OK**. The data from the XML file now appears in the Query Editor window.

Figure 6 XML document imported into Get & Transform

f. Additional data will be appended to this data, so at this time only a data connection will be made to the XML file. On the Home tab and in the Close group, click the **Close & Load** arrow and click **Close & Load To**. In the Import Data dialog box, click the option for **Only Create Connection**. Click **OK**.

g. Save  the workbook.

REAL WORLD ADVICE	Editing an XML File

Data in an XML file may not always be formatted exactly the way you will need it. If you need to modify an XML file, you can use a simple text editor such as Notepad or WordPad to open and save changes to an XML file.

Appending Multiple Queries

Often, data from multiple data sources can be combined into a single data set. For example, customer data may normally be stored in a database, but additional customer data may be received from a special event. This data can be imported using Get & Transform and appended to existing data.

In this exercise, you will import an XML document containing additional menu options and pricing and merge it with the prior query.

E09.04

To Append Data

a. Click the MenuOptions worksheet.

b. On the Data tab, in the Get & Transform Data group, click **Get Data**, point to **From File**, and then click **From XML**.

c. In the Import Data dialog box, navigate through the folder structure to the location of your student data files, and then double-click **e05ch09MoreMenuOptions**.

> ### Troubleshooting
> When connecting files such as XML or CSV documents to Get & Transform, the connection relies on a file path such as C:\Student Data Files. If the source document or Excel document moves to a different folder on a PC, this link will be broken. To reestablish the link between the files, click the gearbox icon in the Source step in the list of Applied Steps in Get & Transform and click the browse button to locate the source file.

d. Click **Edit**. You will notice that initially only two columns and one row appear to be imported. Click the first cell that reads **Table** to see a preview of the data in the XML file.

e. Click the Expand button to view a list of possible fields to include in the query. Ensure that all fields are selected and click **OK**.

f. In the Power Query Editor window, on the Home tab, in the Combine group, click **Append Queries**.

g. In the Append box, click the arrow and select **e05ch09MenuOptions**. Click **OK**.

h. Notice that all of the fields imported are formatted as text. Click the heading for the **MenuOptions.Price** column. On the Home tab, in the Transform group, click **Data Type** and then click **Currency**. Data types can also be changed from within the column headings.

i. Click the heading for the **MenuOptions.Cost** column. Click **ABC** $\begin{smallmatrix}A^B_C\end{smallmatrix}$ and click **Currency**.

j. The first column of data is confusing as the MenuIDs are repeated. Click the heading for the **MenuOptions.MenuID** column and press Delete to remove the column from the query.

k. Click the **Add Column** tab, and in the General group, click the **Index Column** arrow, and then click **From 1**.

l. Click the **Index** column heading and drag it to the far left of the query.

m. Double-click the **Index** heading and, type **MenuID** and press Enter.

n. Scroll to the right to view the last column of data in the query. Click the heading for the **Attribute:generated** column and press Delete to remove the column from the query.

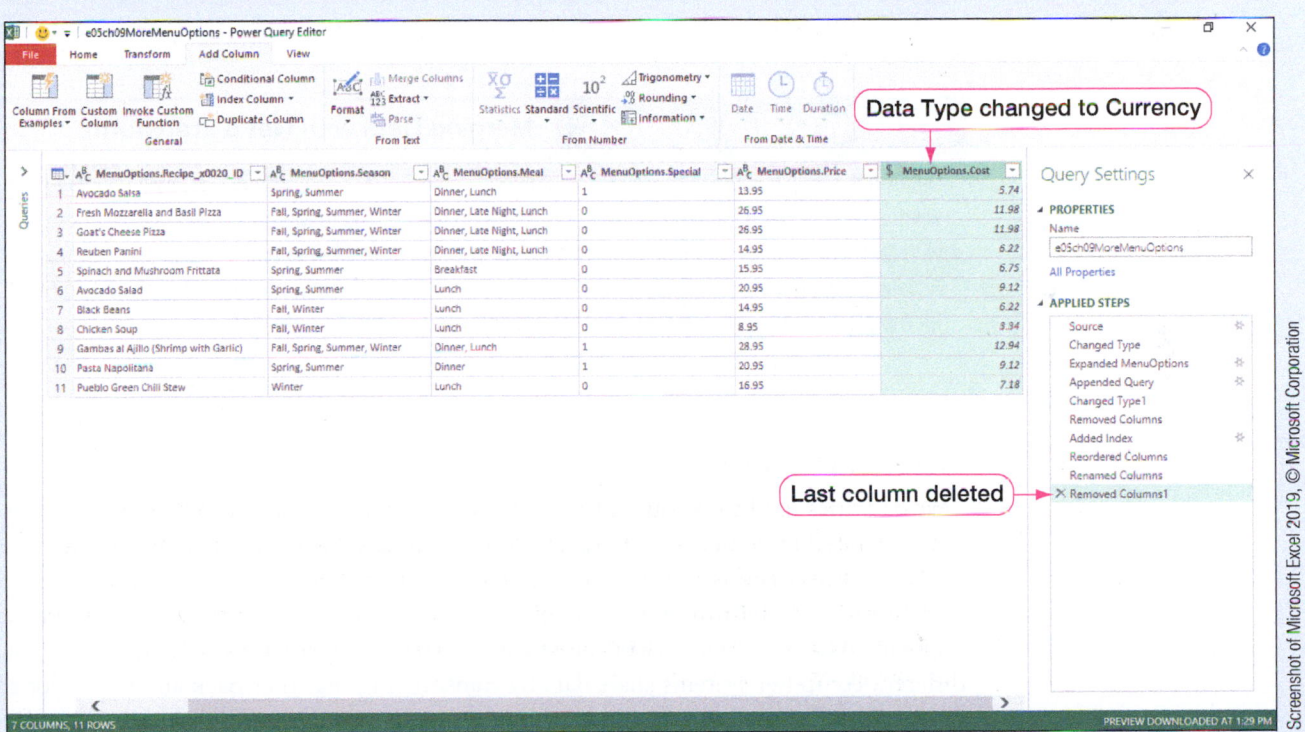

Figure 7 Appended XML data in Get & Transform

o. On the Home tab, in the Close group, click the **Close & Load** arrow and click **Close & Load To**. In the Import Data dialog box, click the option for **Existing worksheet**. Click ⬆ and click cell **A1** on the **MenuOptions** worksheet.

p. Click ⬇ and click **OK**.

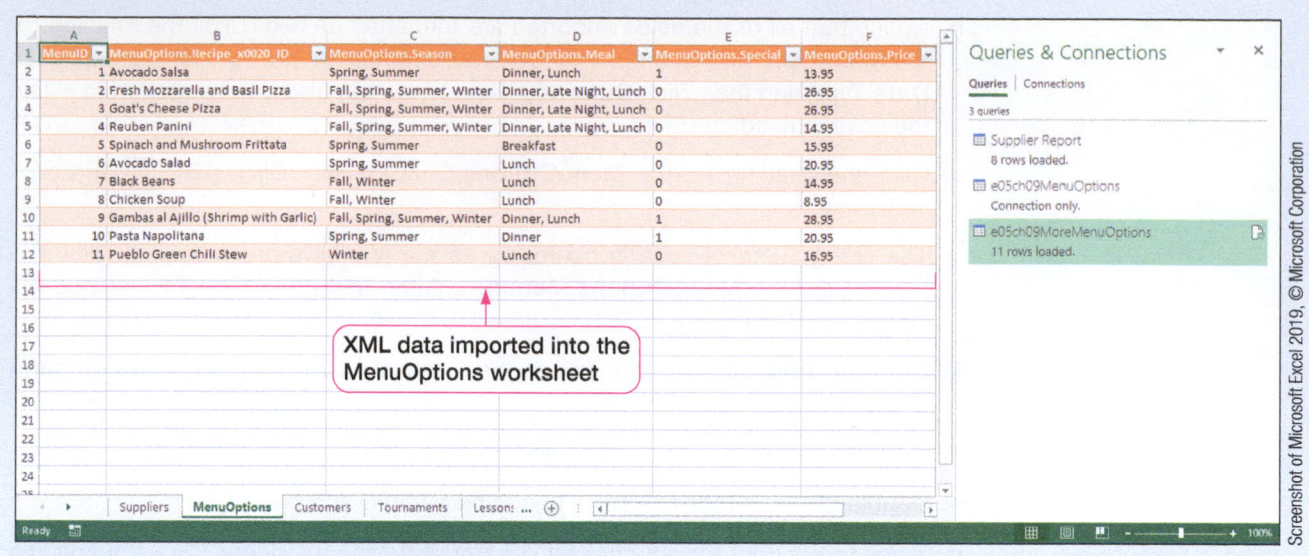

Figure 8 XML document imported into Excel

q. **Save** 💾 the workbook.

Screenshot of Microsoft Excel 2019, © Microsoft Corporation

REAL WORLD ADVICE **Merging Data with Get & Transform**

Data from multiple sources can also be combined using Get & Transform. In the Power Query Editor window, on the Home tab and in the Combine group are options to Merge and Append queries with that have already been created. This works in a similar fashion to building queries in Microsoft Access or using a VLOOKUP function in Excel to create a new column of data. The only requirement for merging queries is a common field that can be used to join the data sets.

Importing Text Files

Text data files used to be called flat files because they were structured as simple lines of data separated by delimiters. **Text data** consists of any grouping of characters, numbers, or dates. A **text file** is just a simple container of text data that is structured by the use of delimiters. A **delimiter** is a way of indicating the beginning and end of a text data segment. As a container of data, a text file can transmit virtually any kind of data. Many different computer systems share data by transmitting text files back and forth. For that reason, text files are one of the most commonly used computer file formats. Text files—also called ASCII files—have no metadata associated with them, so they are not used for transmitting graphics, formulas, or any special formatting. In this context, **metadata** is simply data about data. For digital graphics, metadata could include when the image was created, source information, keywords, format instructions, and captions.

Like XML and HTML files, text files can be imported in two different ways: either one file at a time by opening the file in Excel or by creating a connection that is maintained between the file source and the target workbook. If you are going to use the application often and the external data will change frequently, you will want to maintain a live connection. Otherwise, you can just import the text files as needed. The two methods are similar and easy to accomplish in Excel.

Text files are known as plain text because they contain just text, without any formatting. No special fonts, images, or hyperlinks are allowed. What makes the text understandable is the use of delimiters to separate the data. The use of a delimiter tells the receiving computer when the next data value begins. The most common file types that use delimiters are .csv, .txt, and .prn, as shown in Table 1.

File Type	Sample			
.csv — comma separated	PNum,PName,Shipped,Quantity			
	59313,XL Golf Shirts,3/15/19,35			
	72316,Men's Shoe,2/5/19,10			
	47423,Head covers,3/6/19,20			
.txt — tab delimited	PNum	PName	Shipped	Quantity
	59313	XL Golf Shirts	3/15/19	35
	72316	Men's Shoe	2/5/19	10
	47423	Head covers	3/6/19	20
.prn — space delimited	PNum PName Shipped Quantity			
	59313 XL_Golf_Shirts 3_15_19 35			
	72316 Mens_Shoe 2_5_19 10			
	47423 Head_covers 3_6_19 20			

Table 1 Common delimited text file formats

You can import a text file by simply clicking the File tab to open Backstage view, clicking Open, navigating to the file, and then clicking Open. This is a quick way to view the data, and it often works well enough for your immediate needs. However, if you want to take advantage of all the text import features and any transformations that need to be made, you can use the From Text/CSV function of Get & Transform.

Red Bluff's web developer has exported some customer data from the new Red Bluff website and saved it as a text file. The customers in this list have indicated that they are interested in attending future golf tournaments. In this exercise, you will connect to the data from the text file and transform several fields before importing the data into the Customers worksheet.

 E09.05

To Connect to Text Files

a. Click the **Customers** worksheet. Click the **Data** tab, and in the Get & Transform Data group, click **From Text/CSV**.

b. In the Import Data dialog box, navigate through the folder structure to the location of your student data files, and then double-click **e05ch09Customers**.

c. Examine the data in the Navigator window and click **Edit**.

d. In the Query Editor window, click the **Customer Full Name** column. Click the **Add Column** tab, and in the General group, click the **Column From Examples** arrow, and then click **From Selection**.

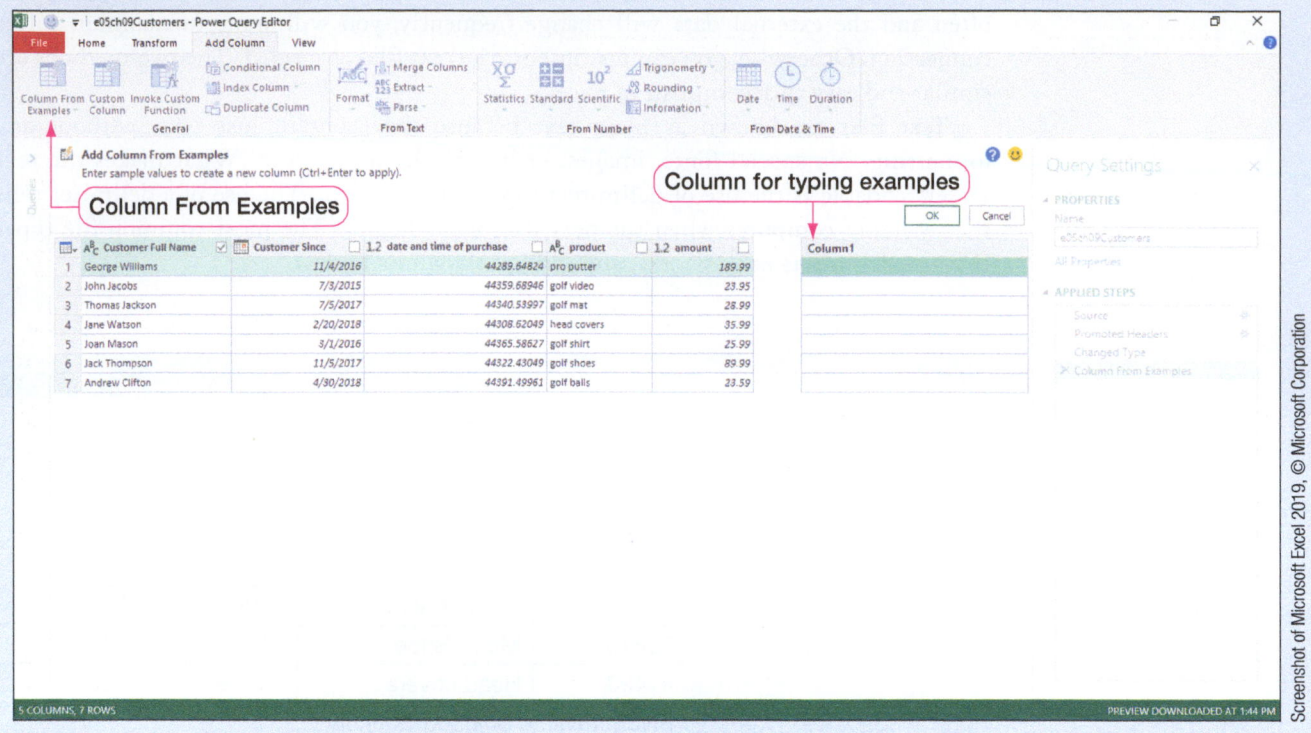

Figure 9 Add Column from Examples

e. Double-click the first cell of Column1, type George and press Enter.

Notice that Get & Transform correctly guesses your example, and fills a list of first names into the column. Click **OK**.

f. Double-click the **Text Before Delimiter** heading, type Customer First Name and press Enter.

g. Click the **Customer Full Name** heading.

h. On the Add Column tab, in the General group, click the **Column From Examples** arrow, and then click **From Selection**.

i. Double-click the first cell of Column1, type Williams and press Enter. Notice that Get & Transform correctly guesses your example, and fills a list of last names into the column. Click **OK**.

> **Troubleshooting**
>
> Be sure to examine the column of examples that Get & Transform displays. At times the data may be complex enough that Get & Transform needs more examples to get the correct data extracted from the original column. In those instances, simply click on the cell that is incorrect and type the correct value. Excel will adjust and learn the new pattern.

j. Double-click the **Text After Delimiter** heading, type Customer Last Name and press Enter.

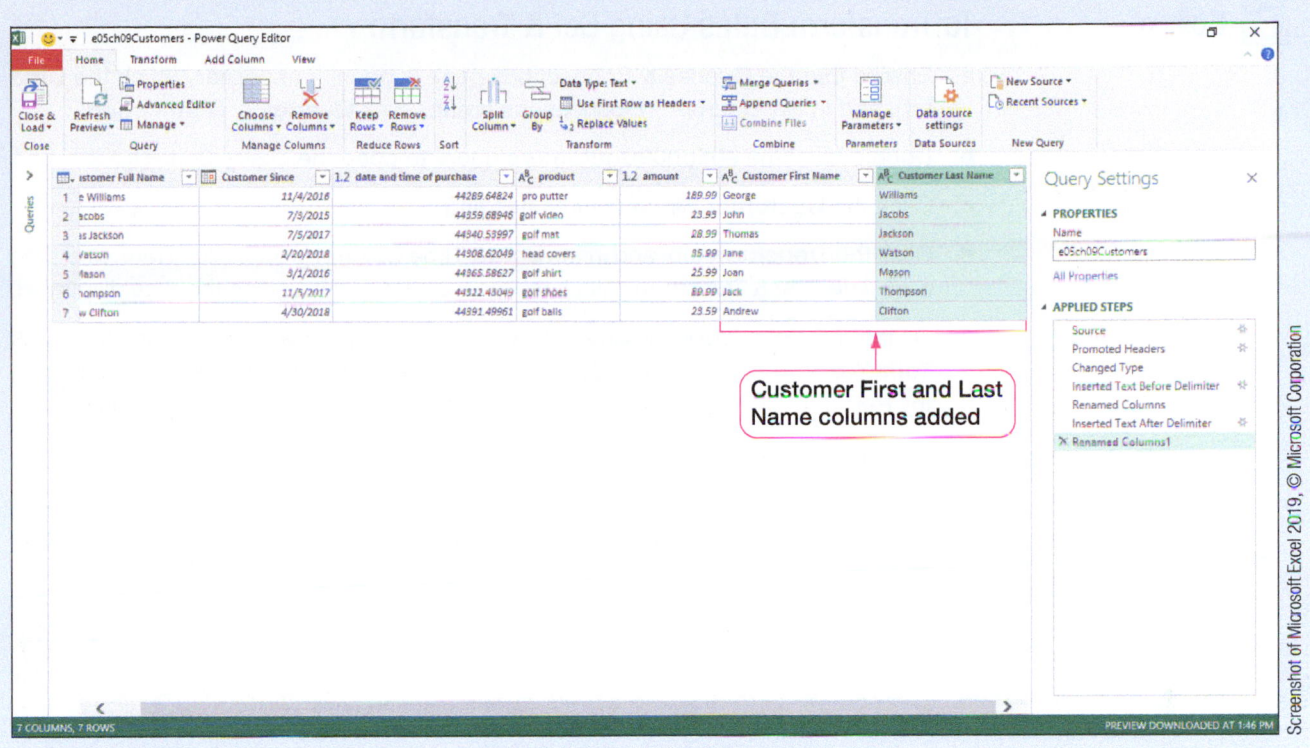

Customer First and Last
Name columns added

Screenshot of Microsoft Excel 2019, © Microsoft Corporation

Figure 10 Customer First Name and Customer Last Name columns

k. Click the **Customer Full Name** heading and press Delete.

l. Click the **product** heading.

m. Click the **Transform** tab, and in the Text Column group, click the **Format** arrow and then click **Trim** to remove leading spaces in some product names.

n. On the Home tab, in the Close group, click the **Close & Load** arrow and click **Close & Load To**. In the Import Data dialog box, click the option for **Existing worksheet**. Click and then click cell **A1** on the **Customers** worksheet. Click and then click **OK**.

o. Save the workbook.

Working with Dates in Get & Transform

Dates can often be difficult to work with in data sets. Often you may be given a date that needs to be displayed as an age, or perhaps the date field contains a time stamp that is not needed for analysis. Excel contains a number of useful functions for working with dates. Get & Transform also contains several features that make working with dates in external data sets easy.

The customer data you have been given contains two issues. The Customer Since field contains a date. Aleeta Herriot has asked that this data be transformed to display the number of years the customer has been with the Red Bluff Golf Course & Pro Shop. Also, the time portion of the date and time stamp in the date and time of purchase field needs the time removed. In this exercise, you will use Get & Transform to transform the dates as requested.

 **E09.06**

To Transform Dates Using Get & Transform

a. Ensure that the Queries & Connections pane is open. If necessary, click the **Data** tab, and in the Queries & Connections group, click **Queries & Connections**.

b. Double-click the **e05ch09Customers** query to open the Query Editor.

c. Click the **Customer Since** column heading.

d. Click the **Transform** tab, and in the Date & Time Column group, click **Date**, and then click **Age**. Get & Transform calculates the number of days since the date displayed.

e. On the Transform tab, in the Date & Time Column group, click **Duration**, and then click **Total Years**. The column now displays the years each person has been a customer of the Red Bluff Golf Course & Pro Shop; however, the data also shows fractions.

f. On the Transform tab, in the Number Column group, click **Rounding**, and then click **Round Down**.

g. Double-click the **Customer Since** heading, type Years as a Customer and press Enter.

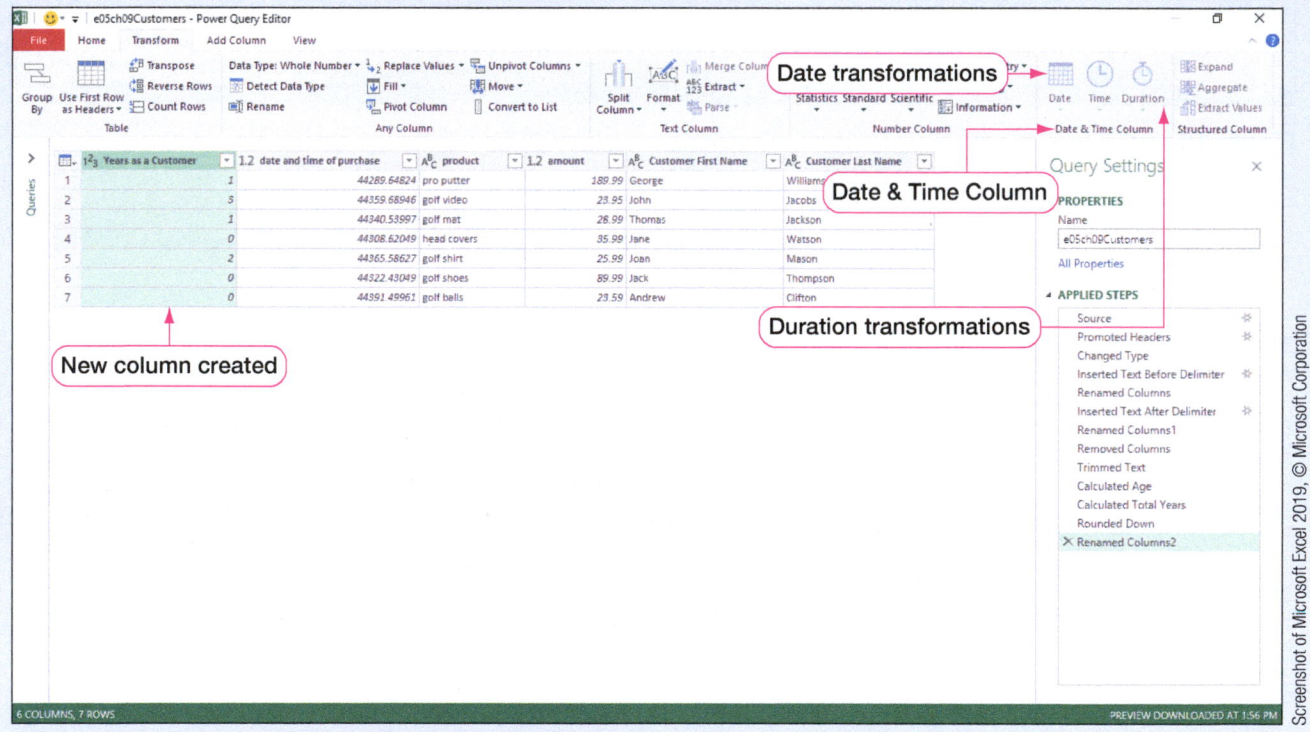

Figure 11 Customer Since column transformed to years

h. Click the **date and time of purchase** column heading.

i. Click the **Home** tab, and in the Transform group, click **Data Type**, and then click **Date/Time**. This option displays the entire date and time for the purchase.

j. In the Transform group, click **Data Type**, and then click **Date**. A message box is displayed that clarifies whether you want to replace the current step or add a new step. Click **Replace current**. The time stamp has now been removed from the column of data.

k. Double-click the **date and time of purchase** heading, type Date of Purchase and press Enter.

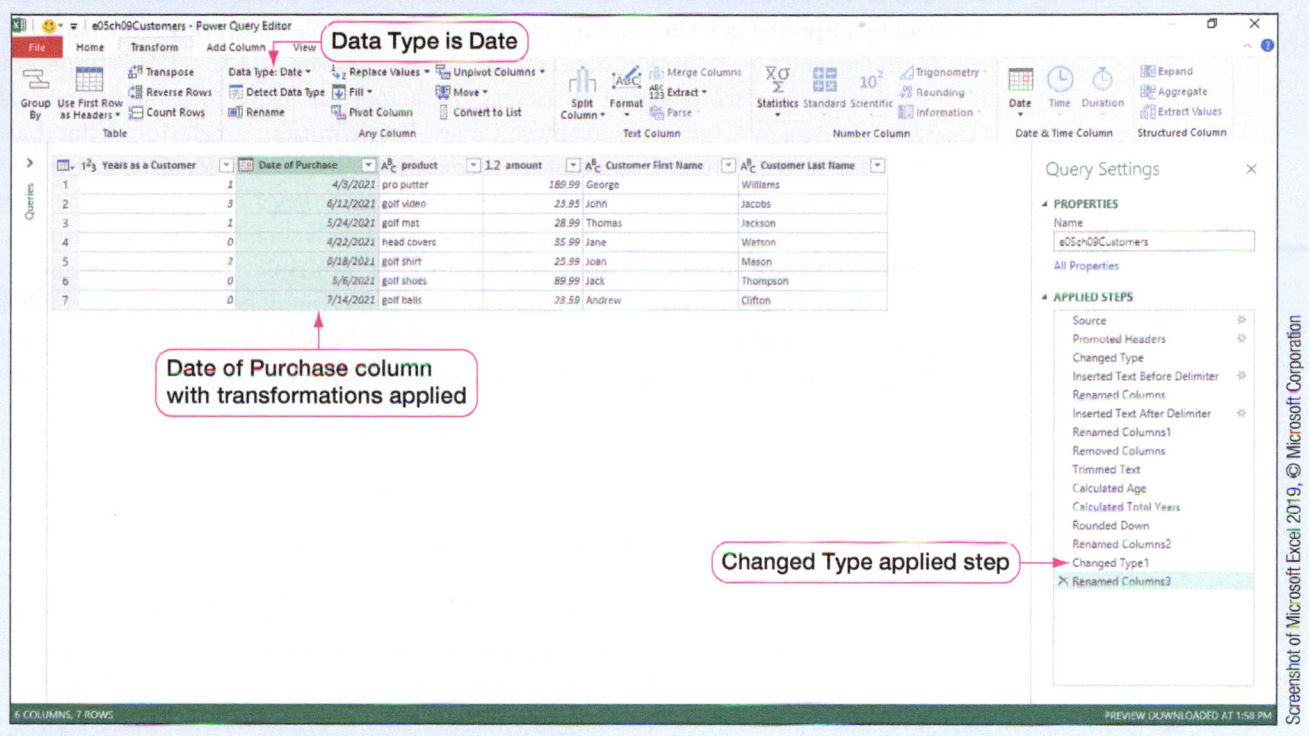

Figure 12   Date of Purchase column in the Query Editor

l. On the Home tab, in the Close group, click **Close & Load**.

m. **Save** 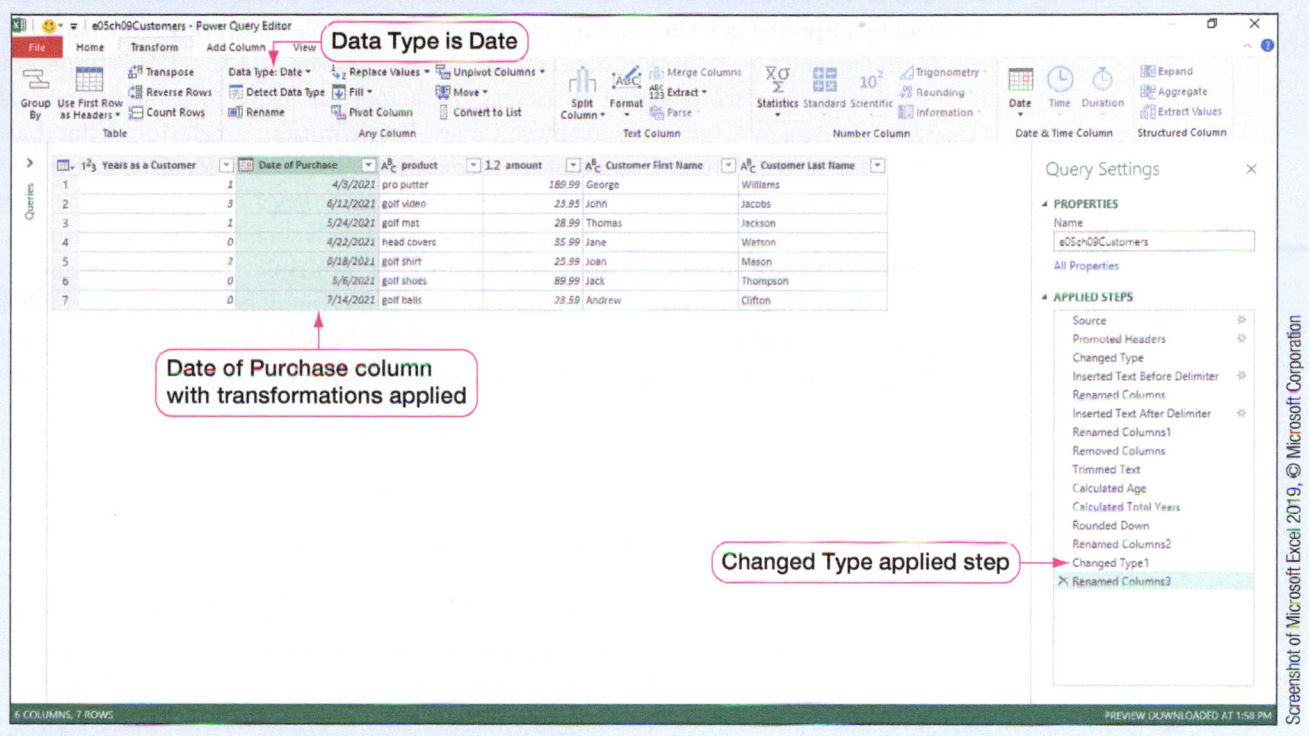 the workbook.

REAL WORLD ADVICE | **Private Data in Spreadsheets**

Data privacy is a very important topic. One of the primary means of breaching customer data is through gaining access to a file that contains private data. An available option in the Properties of any query or connection is to Remove data from the external data range before saving the workbook. If checked, this option will remove any data stored from the data query when the workbook is closed. Removing this data is one means of securing your workbook. These options can be accessed by opening the Queries & Connections pane and right-clicking on the desired query.

Connect to an Access Database

Data may be collected and stored in a database such as Access and then imported into Excel. This process leverages Excel's powerful charting and analysis features. It also protects the data in the Access database, as Excel will import only a copy of the data, leaving the original data safely in the Access database. Over the years, Excel has evolved, making it easier to move data back and forth between Access and Excel. In this section, you will learn how to connect your Excel spreadsheet to the data in an Access database.

Connecting to an Access Database

At the most basic level, you can copy and paste data from an Access table into a blank Excel worksheet. Within Access, users also have the option of exporting tabular data into an Excel format. For longer-term projects, you can create a permanent connection between an Access database and the Excel application using Get & Transform. This live data can be imported as a simple table or even as a PivotTable report or PivotChart.

To understand how to import data from an Access database into Excel, it is important to review how the data is stored in Access. As a tool for using relational databases, Access stores data as a set of one or more tables. By definition, a **relational database** is a collection of tables linked together by shared fields. Each table consists of rows and columns, each row being uniquely identified by a primary key field. The **primary key** functions as a unique identifier for each row or record. Fields such as Customer_Number or Part_Number are commonly used as primary keys. Multiple tables are designed to be linked by joining a common field. In such cases, the primary key field of one table is connected to a common field of another table in which the field for the other table is not a primary key. This field is then known as a **foreign key** field when linked to a primary key field in another table.

With a little background, you can quickly understand the basics of relational databases such as Access. Figure 13 shows the tblPayments table from the Red Bluff Golf Course & Pro Shop database that tracks payments for upcoming tournaments. Across the top, you can see all the field labels, and each row represents a single payment record. The PaymentID field is the unique identifier for each payment. This field functions as the primary key field. The primary key is automatically generated by Access. Important data for the golf course and the pro shop is kept in other tables for employees, members, and member lessons. Information in each of these different tables is linked through the primary key in one table being shared as the foreign key in another table.

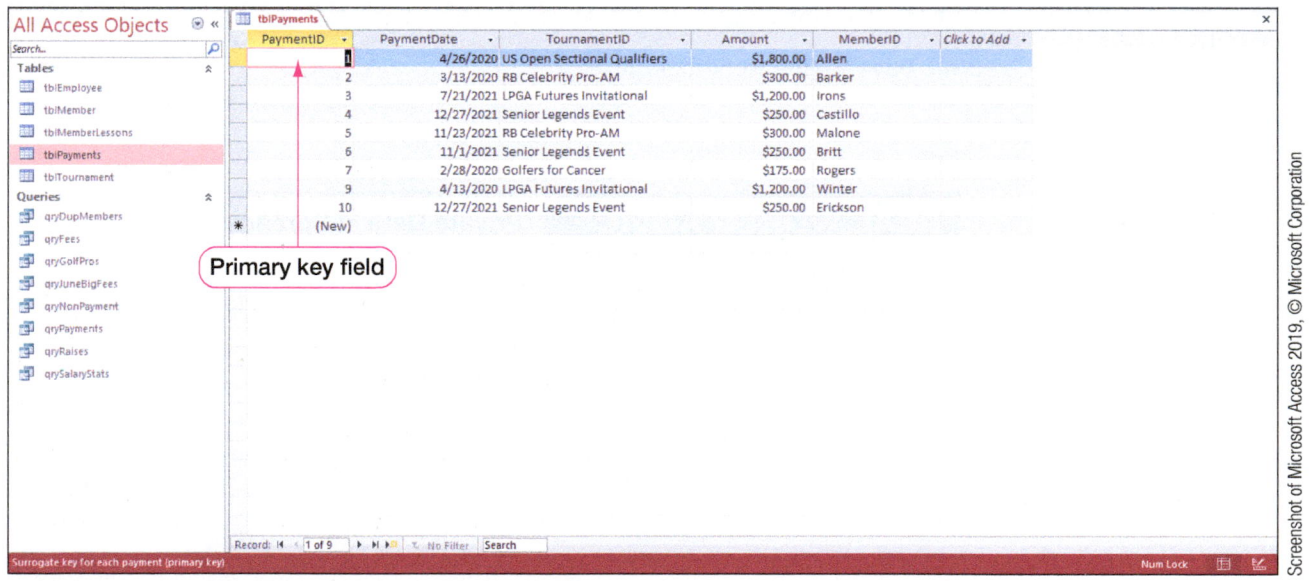

Figure 13   Payment table in Access for the Red Bluff Golf Course & Pro Shop

In this exercise, you will import the qryPayments query results from the Golf database into the Tournaments worksheet. This query organizes various data from the database concerning the tournaments that Red Bluff members have paid entry fees to attend. After the data has been imported into Excel, it can be analyzed further.

 **E09.07**

To Connect to an Access Database Using Get & Transform

a. Click the **Tournaments** worksheet.

b. Click the **Data** tab, in the Get & Transform Data group, click **Get Data,** point to **From Database,** and then click **From Microsoft Access Database**.

c. In the Import Data dialog box, navigate through the folder structure to the location of your student data files, and then double-click **e05ch09Golf**.

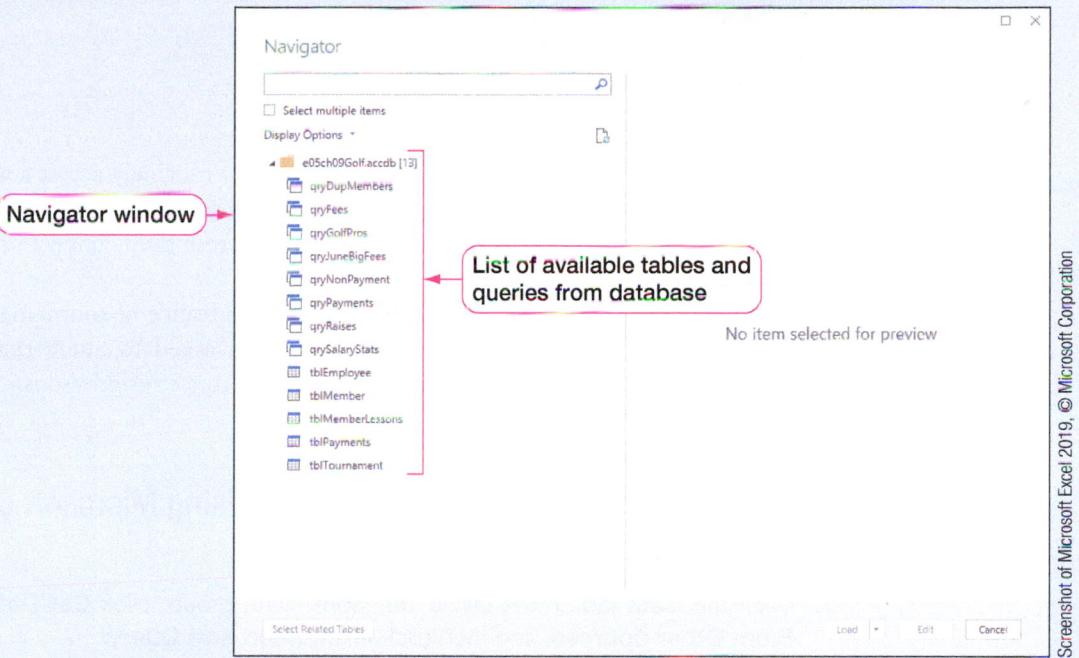

Figure 14   Connecting to an Access database

Screenshot of Microsoft Excel 2019, © Microsoft Corporation

SIDE NOTE
Drag Access Data into Excel
You can import tables and queries from Access by dragging the object from the Navigation Pane and dropping it into the desired starting cell.

d. In the Navigator window, click **qryPayments** and then click **Edit**.

e. Click the **PaymentDate** column heading.

f. On the Home tab, and in the Transform group, click **Data Type**, and then click **Date**.

g. Click the **StartDate** column heading.

h. On the Home tab, and in the Transform group, click **Data Type**, and then click **Date**.

i. On the Home tab and in the Close group, click the **Close & Load** arrow and click **Close & Load To**. In the Import Data dialog box, click the option for **Existing worksheet**. Click ⬆ and click cell **A1** on the **Tournaments** worksheet. Press Enter and then click **OK**.

j. **Save** 🖫 the workbook.

Importing Data from an Access Database Using Microsoft Query

Sometimes, instead of importing a complete table into an Excel worksheet from Access, users prefer to pick and choose specific fields. Perhaps you want to create a PivotTable report showing sales by region and country. **Microsoft Query** is a special tool to help users import individual data fields into their Excel applications. Excel has a query wizard built into its Microsoft Query function that can be a very powerful aid for linking a worksheet to an Access database.

QUICK REFERENCE | Microsoft Query

Microsoft Query has built-in drivers that make it easy to retrieve data from these common databases:

- Access
- SQL Server
- Paradox
- Oracle
- dBASE
- Text files

It is very common for business users to use Excel to routinely access a wide variety of data sources in the course of their work. By using Microsoft Query to access external data, users do not have to redo the query; they can simply refresh their connection to the source data so the Excel application reflects any changes.

Red Bluff members often sign up for lessons in advance of tournaments they have signed up to attend. In this exercise, you have been asked to query the golf course's database to better understand this consumer behavior concerning lessons.

 E09.08

To Import Data from an Access Database Using Microsoft Query

a. Click the **Lessons** worksheet.

b. Click the **Data** tab, in the Get & Transform Data group, click **Get Data,** point to **From Other Sources,** and then click **From Microsoft Query**.

c. In the Choose Data Source dialog box, select **MS Access Database**, ensure that **Use the Query Wizard to create/edit queries** is checked, and then click **OK.**

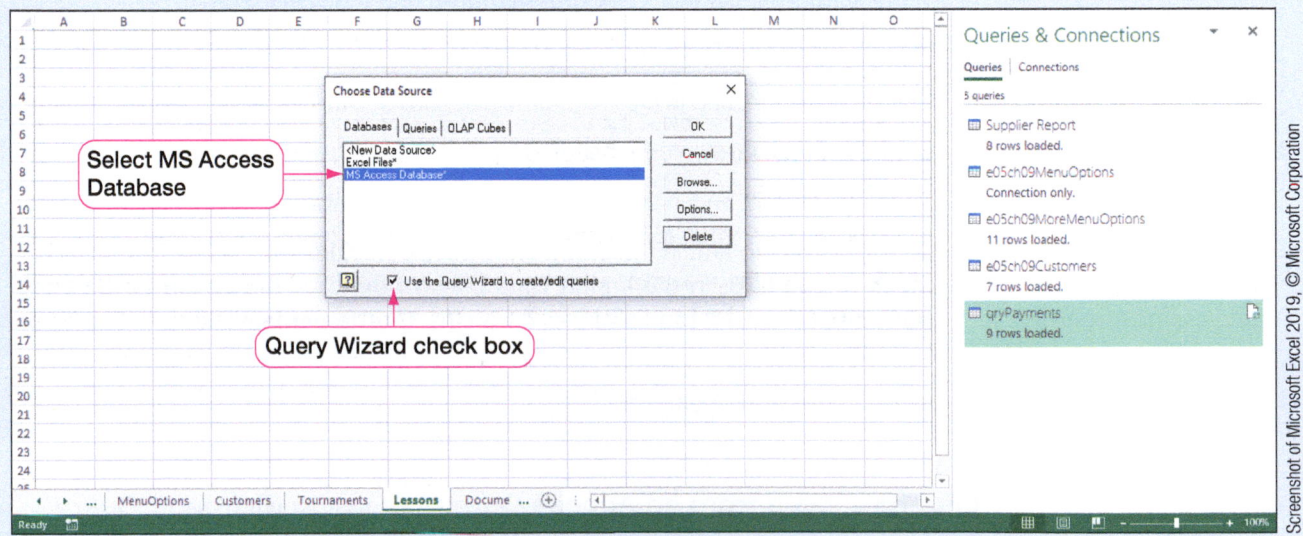

Figure 15 Connecting to an Access database with Microsoft Query

d. In the Select Database dialog box, under Directories, double-click the **folder** where your student data files are stored, and then, under Database Name, select **e05ch09Golf**. Click **OK**.

e. In the Query Wizard - Choose Columns dialog box, scroll through the list of tables and columns until you see the qryFees query, and then click the **Expand Outline** button ⊞, to the left of qryFees, to see the available fields.

f. Double-click to select and move **LastName** to the Columns in your query box. Using the same technique, double-click the **FirstName**, **ScheduledDate**, and **Fee** fields to move them into the Columns in your query list.

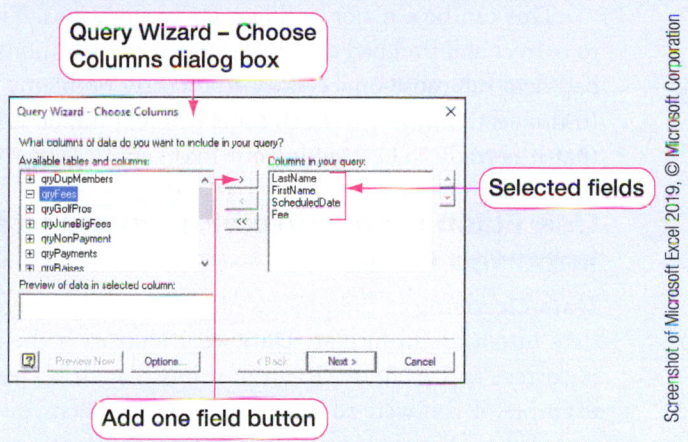

Figure 16 Selecting fields for Microsoft Query

g. Click **Next**, click to select the **ScheduledDate** field, click the first **Filter** arrow, and then click **is greater than or equal to**. In the input box to the right, type 6/1/2022

h. Ensure that the **And** operator is selected, click the next **Filter** arrow, and then click **is less than or equal to**. In the input box to the right, type 6/30/2022

i. Click **Fee**, click the first **Filter** arrow, and then click **is greater than or equal to**. In the input box to the right, type 150

j. Click **Next**. Click the **Sort by** arrow, select **LastName**, and then accept the default Ascending order. Click the **Then by** arrow, select **FirstName**, and then keep the Ascending option.

k. Click **Next**, verify that Return Data to Microsoft Excel is selected, and then click **Finish**.

l. Verify that **Existing worksheet** is selected and that the input box displays =$A$1, and then click **OK**. The Access data is imported and displayed, starting in cell A1.

m. Save 💾 the workbook. Click the **File** tab, click **Close** to close the workbook, and then submit your file as directed by your instructor. If you need to take a break before finishing this chapter, now is a good time.

Grader Heads Up

If you are using MyLab IT Grader, this is the end of the first MyLab IT Grader project, Part A. This project continues in Part B, which is a separate MyLab IT Grader project.

Making Data Useful

If data has been provided to your company as a website, database connection, or one of the file types previously mentioned; Get & Transform is a terrific tool to use in Excel to import and transform the data. But Get & Transform may not always be the most efficient tool to use. You may already have data within an Excel workbook or the data may be in such a poor state that Get & Transform cannot clean the data.

The data in Excel might still require some manipulation to fit the data to your needs, such as formatting it differently and cleansing the data before it can be used for decision-making purposes. Sometimes this is straightforward and entails simply using the spelling checker or using the Find and Replace feature. Other times, it may require extensive reformatting or reorganization of multiple columns.

This can be a major problem for corporations. The cost to businesses in labor-hours to correct and find bad data is estimated to be billions of dollars each year. The impact of bad data can cause unnecessary a nd costly problems in bad decisions based on the data. In this section, you will learn some efficient methods to save time when cleansing data so that it is ready to be used in your Excel applications.

Use Flash Fill and Text Functions to Cleanse Imported Data

Data cleansing is the process of fixing obvious errors in the data and converting the data into a useful format. **Data verification** is the process of validating that the data is correct and accurate. Keep in mind that data cleansing is not data verification. For example, if you were to cleanse phone numbers, you would fix or mark as questionable a record with a four-digit phone number. If you were to verify a phone number, you would call the phone number and verify that it reached the person it purported to call. Data verification is very costly in both time and money. Therefore, for the majority of data, most companies will conduct only data cleansing and not necessarily data verification.

Using Flash Fill to Cleanse Text Data

Excel has a feature called Flash Fill that can make data cleansing easier and faster than using traditional text functions. Like the Column From Examples feature in the Get & Transform Query Editor, **Flash Fill** recognizes simple patterns in data as you type and automatically fills in values for text and numeric data. Because Flash Fill involves less typing than traditional text functions, it can be easier to use on touch-enabled devices. Before you use the Flash Fill feature, there are a couple of key points to keep in mind. For Flash Fill to work, you must type in a column or row that adjoins your existing data. There cannot be a blank column or row between the data and where you are typing. Also, Flash Fill works only on relatively simplistic data sets and is not updated automatically if data is changed or added.

Flash Fill works by examining the pattern of data in the cell next to where you are typing. If a pattern can be detected, a suggested fill will be displayed in the column in which you are typing. On the RegistrationData worksheet, the first names and middle initials of the customers from the tournament golf club giveaway are still in a single column. In this exercise, you will use Flash Fill to separate the First Name into a separate column so that letters can be prepared to send to the entrants.

 **E09.09**

To Use Flash Fill to Cleanse Text Data

Grader Heads Up

If you are using MyLab IT Grader for this project, note that Part B begins here as a separate MyLab IT Grader project.

a. Open the Excel file, **e05ch09TournamentReport**. Save your file as e05ch09TournamentReport_LastFirst using your last and first name.

b. On the RegistrationData worksheet, click cell **B2**.

c. Type Carter, and then press Enter to move to cell B3.

d. Type J

Notice that as you type, Flash Fill recognizes the pattern of the data you are trying to enter. A list of all of the first names from column A will appear as suggestions in column B.

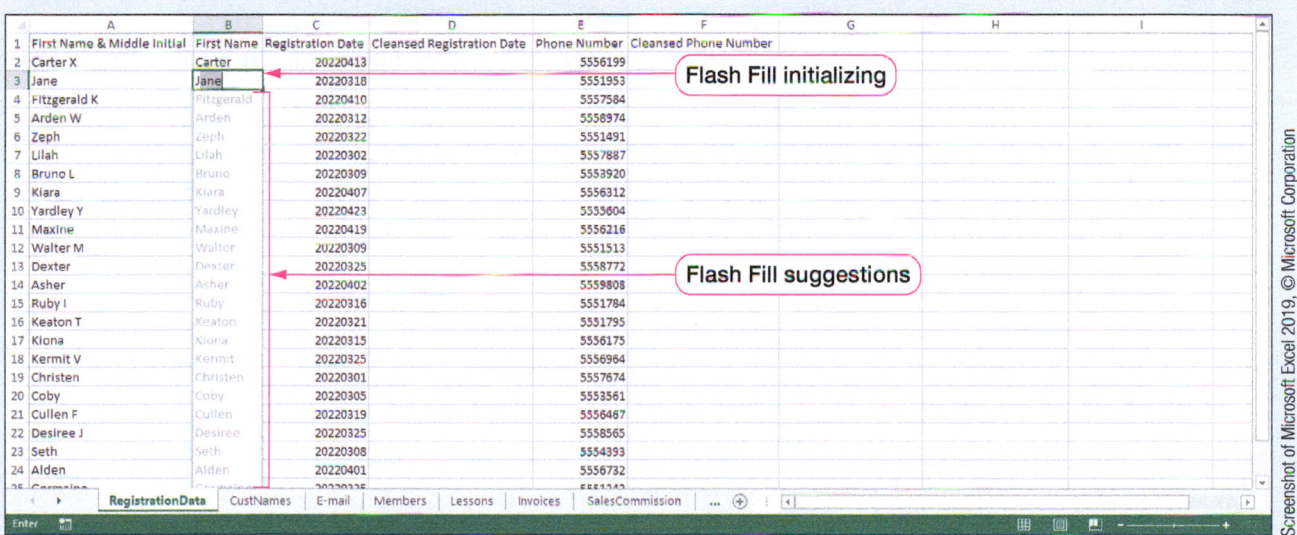

Figure 17 Using Flash Fill to cleanse text data

e. Press Enter to accept the changes suggested by Flash Fill.

Troubleshooting

Flash Fill relies on consecutive actions in order to offer a suggestion. If you click on another cell or press a button on the keyboard between typing "Carter", pressing Enter, and typing "J", Flash Fill will not offer a suggestion.

f. **Save** the workbook.

REAL WORLD ADVICE	**When to Use Get & Transform versus Flash Fill**

Both Get & Transform and Flash Fill are quick and powerful data transformation tools. While they share some similarities, Get & Transform should be the preferred tool when your data is located outside of Excel or requires periodic updates. Flash Fill is a great tool for a one time use on a data set.

Using Flash Fill to Cleanse Numeric Data

Flash Fill is disabled by default on numeric data. When using the Flash Fill feature on numeric data, you may need to provide an additional example of how the data should be arranged. The Flash Fill feature then can be used through the Data tab in the ribbon.

The registration dates that were provided are in numeric format but not in a format that Excel recognizes as a date. The dates provided are in YYYYMMDD format; for cell C2, the date appears as 20220413. Flash Fill can be used in this situation to reorganize the date into the MM/DD/YYYY format, or 4/13/2022 for cell C2. Additionally, the phone number in cell E2 was provided as 5556199 and needs to be displayed as 555-6199.

In this exercise, the registration date and entrant phone numbers will be properly formatted by using Flash Fill.

 E09.10

SIDE NOTE
Alternative Method
Pressing Ctrl + E is the equivalent of clicking Flash Fill on the Data tab.

To Use Flash Fill to Cleanse Numeric Data

a. Click cell **D2**, type **4/13/2022** and then press Enter.

b. In cell **D3**, type **3/18/2022** and then press Enter.

   Notice that no suggestions from Flash Fill appear.

c. On the Data tab, in the Data Tools group, click **Flash Fill**. Flash Fill will complete the list of dates through cell D26.

d. Click cell **F2**, type **555-6199** and then press Enter.

e. In cell **F3**, type **5** and then notice the suggestions that appear from Flash Fill. Because you are mixing text in with the phone numbers, Flash Fill will make suggestions.

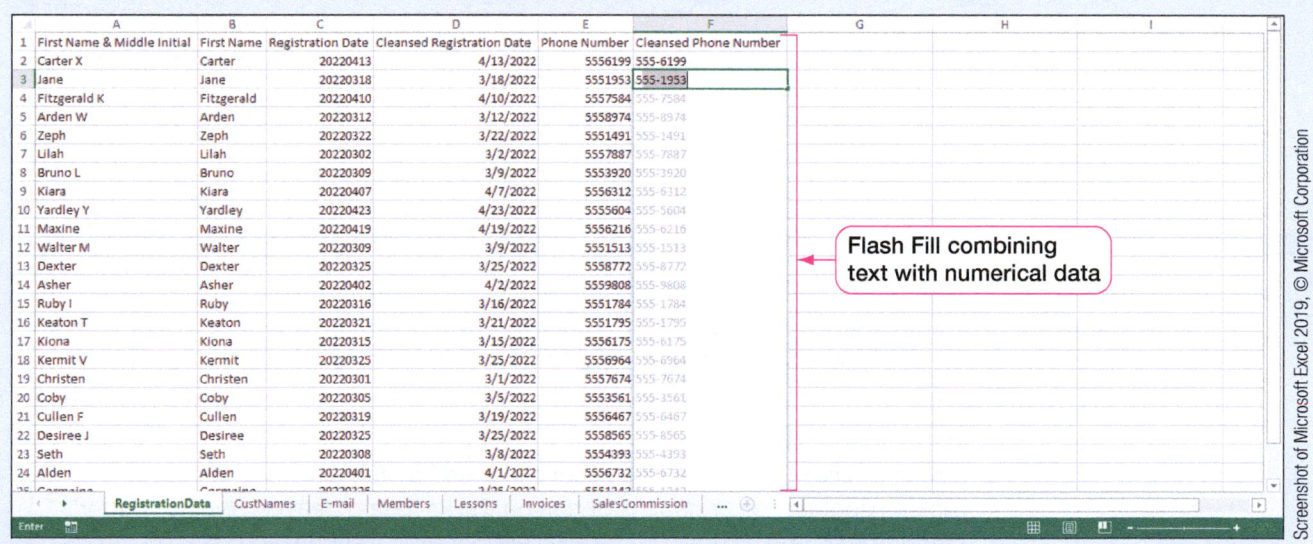

Figure 18 Using Flash Fill to cleanse numeric data

f. Press Enter to accept the suggestions.

g. **Save** 💾 the workbook.

Using Text Functions to Cleanse Data

Previously, you imported text data into Excel with Get & Transform. Recall that text data involves strings of characters. Do not be confused by this term because it can include special characters, spaces, and numbers as well as letters. Text is a very generic data type. Often, data from external sources can easily be cleaned up with proper formatting, for example, formatting number values into currency values. Excel offers a range of **text functions** that help to manage text data. Excel text functions help to manipulate and standardize data and can offer additional tools to automate the process.

QUICK REFERENCE	Common Text Functions	
Function Name	**Description**	**Example**
CLEAN(text)	Removes any nonprinting characters from a text string. The CLEAN function removes the first 32 nonprinting character codes, but it does not remove nonprinting character codes for higher values.	If cell A2 contains =CHAR(6)&"text", =CLEAN(A2) will leave only "text".
LOWER(text)	Converts a text string to all lowercase characters.	=LOWER(Apt. 4B) will result in "apt. 4b".
PROPER(text)	Capitalizes only the first letter in each word of a text string; the remaining characters are in lowercase.	If cell A2 contains the string "this is a TITLE", =PROPER(A2) returns "This Is A Title".
TRIM(text)	Removes all spaces from text except for single spaces between words; this includes extra spaces at the beginning or the end of the string.	If cell A2 contains the string " profit margin", =TRIM(A2) would remove the extra spaces to yield "profit margin".
UPPER(text)	Converts all the characters in a text string to uppercase.	=UPPER("total") will result in the word "TOTAL".

S **CONSIDER THIS** | **Why Should You Care about Bad Data?**

Have you ever received mail in which your name or address was misspelled? This is one example of how bad data is propagated. At some point, your name was entered into a database incorrectly, and then that list of names was sold to others. Studies indicate that the total cost to businesses from bad data is well into the billions of dollars. How else does bad data get into the system? What are some basic steps you could take to prevent or minimize the problem?

Text functions help users to extract and standardize their data in ways that make life easier; a little knowledge of these functions can reap big rewards. One of the golf club manufacturers is sponsoring a hole-in-one prize for an upcoming tournament. If one of the tournament participants gets a hole in one on hole 9, he or she will receive a free set of golf clubs. To be eligible for the prize, customers filled out entry cards, and the information was entered into a database.

The formulas you use in other spreadsheet applications will malfunction when they encounter the irregular spacing found in the Name column of the spreadsheet you have been given (see Figure 19). Consider the contents of cell A2. The text is typed in all capital letters, and there are additional spaces and nonprinting characters. Only the first letter of each string of text should be capitalized. There is also an extra space between the "THOMAS" and the "M" that needs to be removed.

Three helpful functions can change the case of characters in a string of text. The **LOWER** function can be used to change uppercase characters to lowercase, and the **UPPER** function can be used to change all characters in a cell to uppercase. The **PROPER** function will capitalize only the first letter of each word in the text string while changing the other characters to lowercase. The **TRIM** function will remove extra spaces from a string of text.

REAL WORLD ADVICE | **Cleansing Nonprintable Characters**

Cleansing extra spaces is only half the problem. Many times, there are nonprinting characters that are not easily visible—such as a hard return or other unseen characters that are often transferred from Internet data. This can be quite frustrating when you are performing a logical test on that data or using one of the LOOKUP functions. If you do not have clean data with all the extra spaces or unprintable characters removed, you will get an error message.

The **CLEAN** function removes nonprintable characters, such as line breaks, but will leave other characters.

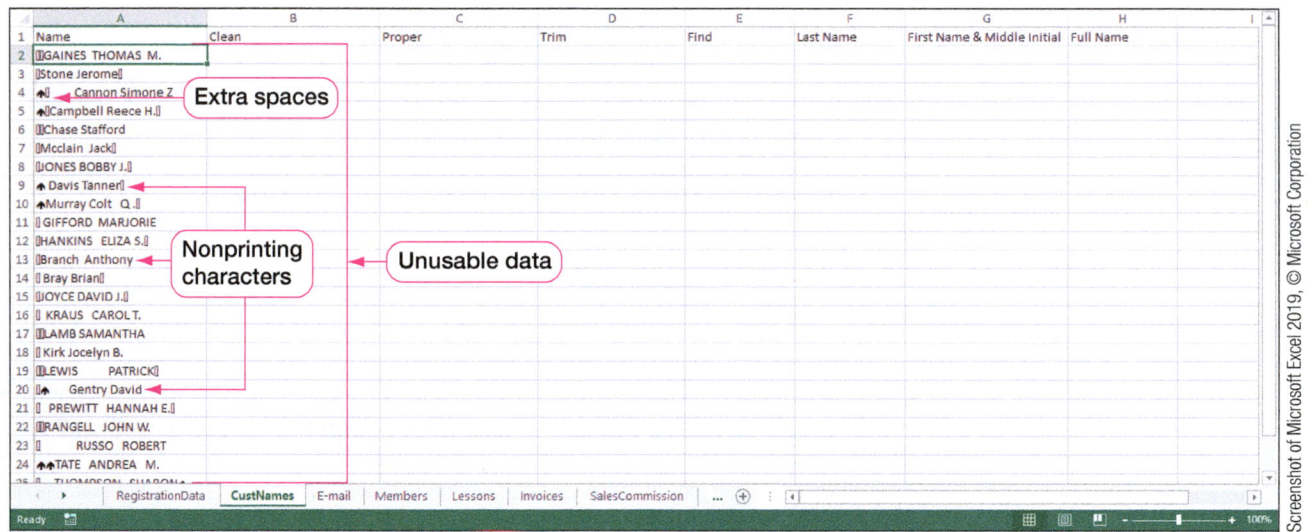

Figure 19 Unusable data needing to be cleansed

In this exercise, you will use text functions to cleanse the data in the spreadsheet.

 **E09.11**

To Use Text Functions to Cleanse Data

a. Click the **CustNames** worksheet, click cell **B2**, type **=CLEAN** and then press [Tab] to insert the function. Click cell **A2**, and then press [Enter] to complete the function. Notice that the function has removed the nonprinting characters that were found on the left side of the name.

b. Click cell **B2**, and then double-click the **fill handle** to copy the function down to B26. Resize the column as needed to fit the contents.

c. Click cell **C2**, type **=PROPER** and then press [Tab] to insert the function. Click cell **B2**, and then press [Enter] to complete the function. Notice that the function capitalized only the first letter of each name; the rest of the characters were left in lowercase.

d. Click cell **C2**, and then double-click the **fill handle** to copy the function down to C26. Resize the column as needed to fit the contents.

e. Click cell **D2**, type **=TRIM(** and then press [Tab]. Click cell **C2**, and then press [Ctrl]+[Enter]. The TRIM function will remove any extra spaces before or after the names as well as extra spaces between names.

f. Double-click the **fill handle** to copy the function down to D26. Resize the column as needed to fit the contents.

> **SIDE NOTE**
> **Alternate Method**
> Text functions can be nested together to achieve more efficiency. =CLEAN(PROPER (TRIM(B2))) will provide the same result.

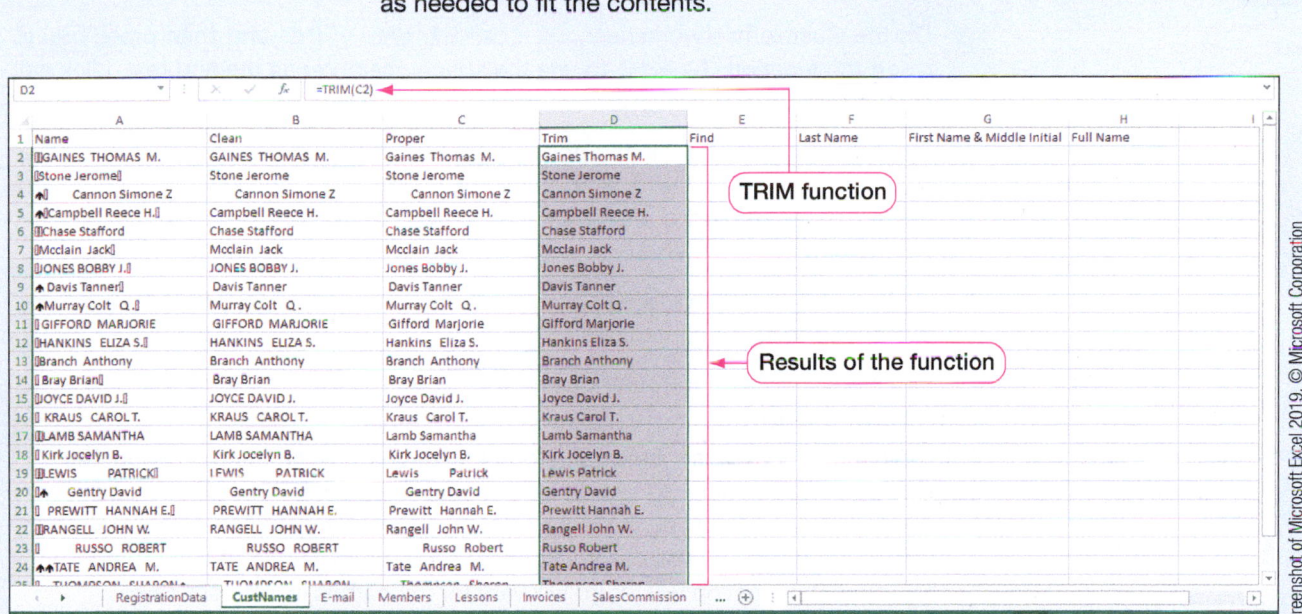

Figure 20 CLEAN, PROPER, and TRIM functions applied

g. **Save** 💾 the workbook.

Manipulate Data Using Text Functions

Imported data can often contain strings of text that need to be manipulated in addition to being cleansed to be useful in a spreadsheet analysis. The text functions in Excel can be used to separate or reorganize strings of text so they can be better used.

Using the LEFT and FIND Functions to Separate Data

Consider the contents of cell D2 on the CustNames worksheet. For tasks such as mail merges, breaking the name into first, middle, and last columns would be useful. This can be accomplished in many ways. One method would be to find the space character between the last name and first name in the string of text. Once it has been located, everything in front of that space could be removed, leaving only the first name and the middle initial.

The **FIND** function is useful for finding where a specific string of text is located within a larger string. The FIND function returns a number that represents the position, from the left, where a specific string of text begins. The **LEFT** function can be used to extract a specific number of characters from a string of text beginning at the left side of the string.

In this exercise, you will use the LEFT and FIND function to separate the Last Name from the full name in column D.

 **E09.12**

To Use Text Functions to Separate Data

a. On the CustNames worksheet, click cell **E2**, type **=FIND** and then press ⎡Tab⎦ to insert the function. Type **" "**, to use the space character as the find text, click cell **D2**, and then press ⎡Ctrl⎦+⎡Enter⎦.

   The FIND function returns the position number of the first space character in cell D2. The position of this space character is important because throughout the entire column of names, the space character is always located just after the last name.

b. Double-click the **fill handle** to copy the formula down to E26. Resize the column as needed to fit the contents.

> #### Troubleshooting
>
> In step a of this exercise, be careful to put a space between the double quotes to indicate the character to search for is a space character. This function will return a number telling you the location of the character specified as the first function argument—in this case, a space. As can be expected, the number of characters the function will return will vary for the names in different cells.

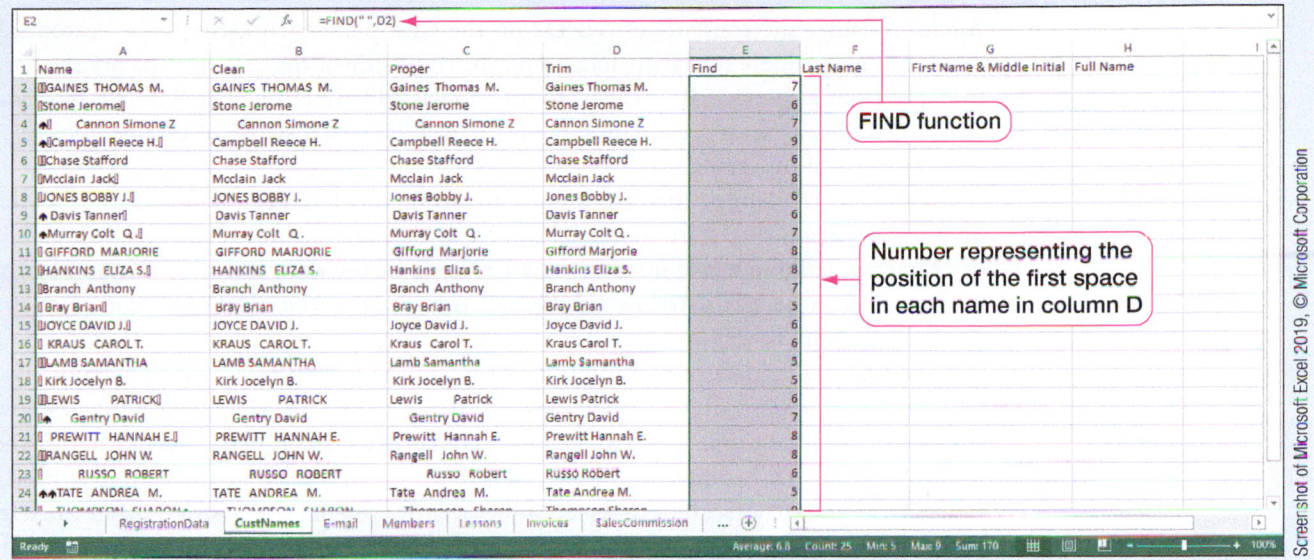

Figure 21 Using the FIND function

Screenshot of Microsoft Excel 2019, © Microsoft Corporation

SIDE NOTE
Using TRIM

Instead of removing extra spaces from a text function by subtracting position numbers, you could use the TRIM function.

c. Click cell **F2**, type **=LEFT** and then press [Tab] to insert the function. Click cell **D2**, type **,** and click cell **E2**, type **-1** and then press [Ctrl]+[Enter].

d. Double-click the **fill handle** to copy the formula down to F26. Resize the column as needed to fit the contents.

The LEFT function examines the text in cell D2. The second argument tells the LEFT function how many characters to return from the left. Consider the last name in cell D2: "Gaines". This name is six characters long. Because the space found in D2 occurs at the seventh position, you can subtract one from E2 to return the first six characters.

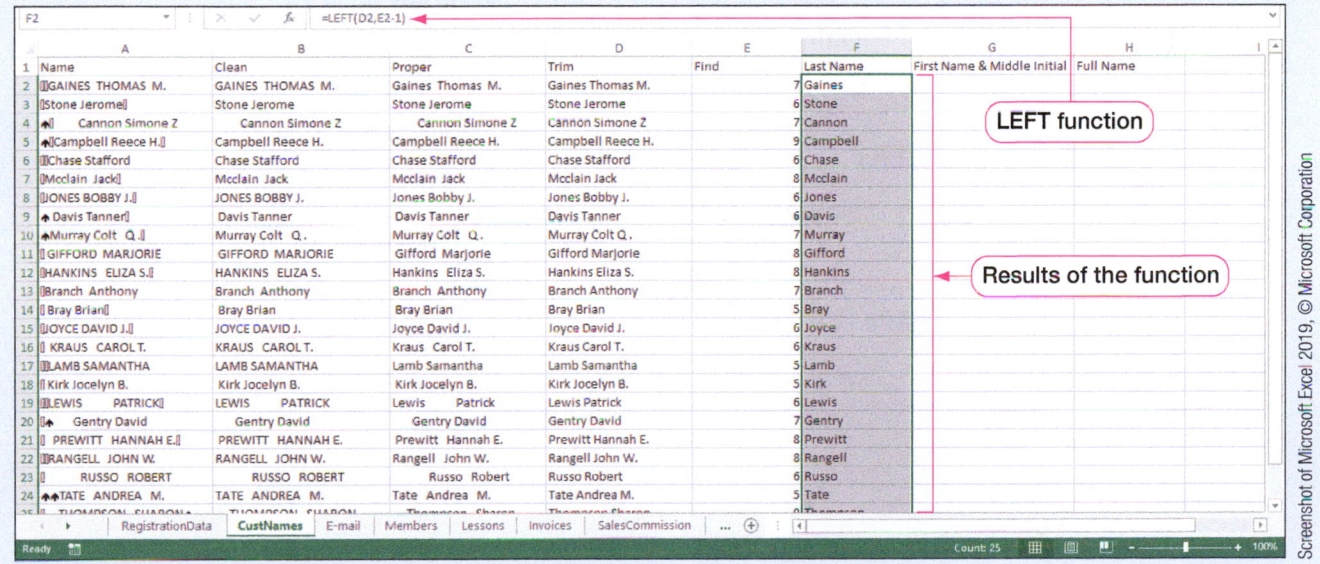

Figure 22 Using the LEFT function

Screenshot of Microsoft Excel 2019, © Microsoft Corporation

e. **Save** the workbook.

Using Text Functions to Separate Data from the Right Side of a Cell

Again, consider the contents of cell D2 on the CustNames worksheet. The customer's first name and middle initial are located on the right side of the cell. To separate the data from the right side of a cell, it is best to use the RIGHT function. The **RIGHT** function can be used to extract a specific number of characters from a string of text beginning at the right side of the string.

There are challenges that are unique to using the RIGHT function, as it is the only text function that starts from the right side of a text string. If the desired number of characters is not a static number for all records in the data set, then the number of characters must be calculated by subtracting the result of the FIND function from the result of the LEN function.

The **LEN** function is a useful way to calculate the length of a specified string. The basic syntax contains only one argument: the string of text of which you want to know the length. So if you typed =LEN("Gaines Thomas M."), the function would return the result of 16, which includes the space characters and the period at the end. The FIND function, as you may recall, returns a number that represents the position, from the left, where a specific string of text begins.

Examine all of the names in column D, and you will see that the space character (" ") is what consistently appears directly to the left of the text to be extracted. So if you typed =FIND(" ", "Gaines Thomas M."), the function would return the result of 7, the location of the first space in the string. Subtracting the first 7 characters from the 16 total characters, results in 9, which is the number of desired characters from the right to extract "Thomas M." See Figure 23 for an illustration of how these functions work together.

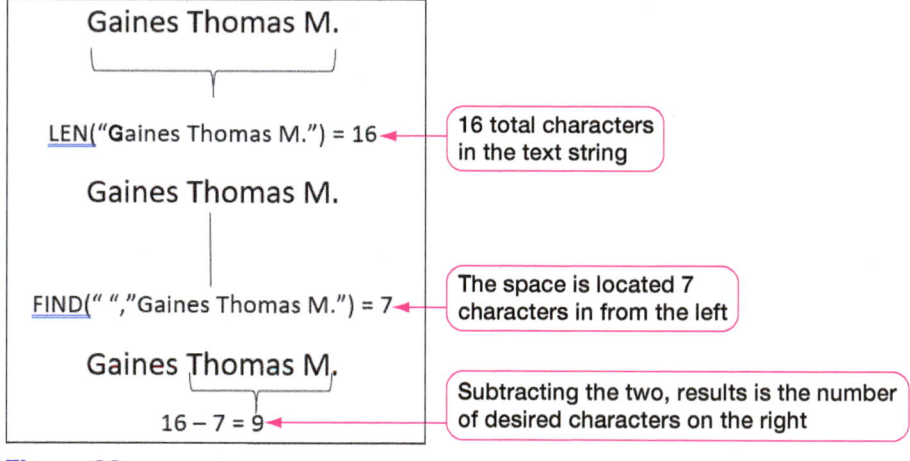

Figure 23   LEN – FIND

In this exercise, you will use text functions to separate the first name and initial from the name in column D.

 **E09.13**

To Use Text Functions to Separate Data from the Right Side of a Cell

a. Click cell **G2**, type **=RIGHT** and then press [Tab] to insert the function. Click cell **D2**, type **,LEN** and then press [Tab] to insert the function. Click cell **D2**, type **)-** and then click cell **E2**. Type **)** and then press [Ctrl]+[Enter].

b. Double-click the **fill handle** to copy the formula down to G26. Resize the column as needed to fit the contents.

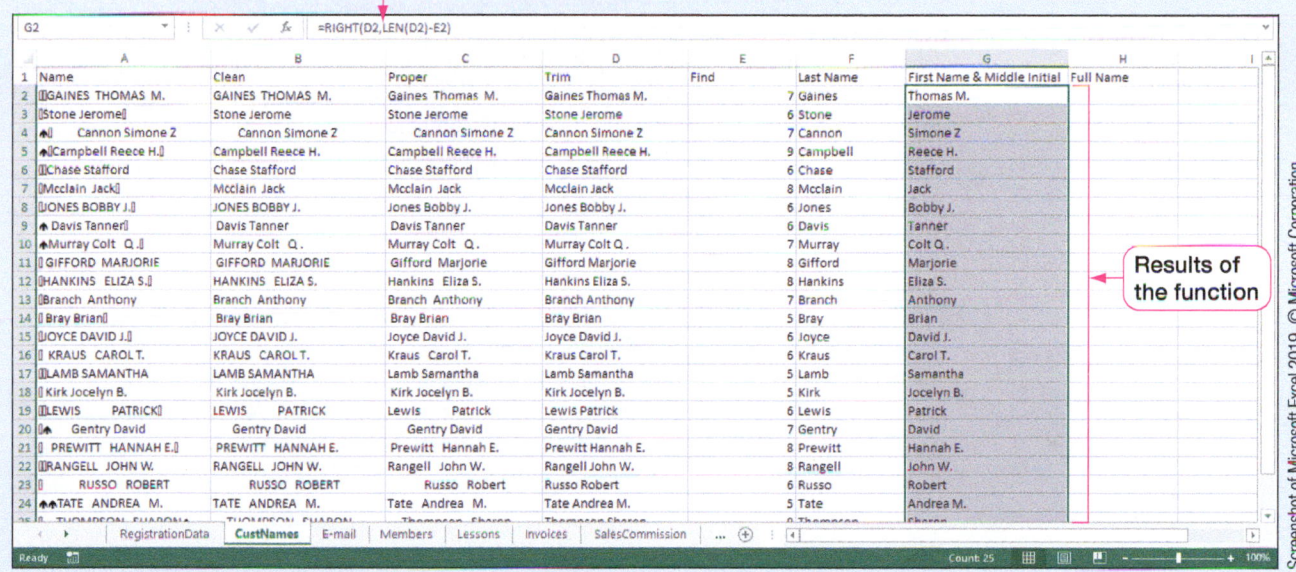

RIGHT function, using LEN – FIND to determine number of characters from the right to display

Results of the function

Figure 24 Text string separated from the right

c. **Save** 🖫 the workbook.

Screenshot of Microsoft Excel 2019, © © Microsoft Corporation

Here are some additional text functions to consider along with a description of what each one does.

Function Name	Description	Example
FIND(find_text, within_text, [start_num])	Locates a particular string of data within a second text string and returns the number of the starting position of the first text string from the starting position of the second text string. The "start_num" is an optional parameter giving a position within the string where the search will start. If the "start_num" is omitted, the position is assumed to be 1.	=FIND(" ","ABC corp.") will return the value of 4, because the space is the fourth character.
LEFT(text,[num_chars])	This function returns the characters in a text string based on the number of characters you specify, starting with the far-left character in the string. The text argument is a string of text or a cell reference to text data, and the num_chars argument specifies the characters to extract.	If cell A2 contains the text string "sale price", then =LEFT(A2,4) will return the word "sale".
LEN(text)	This function returns the number of characters, including spaces, in a text string.	If cell A2 contains the string "Excel 2019", then =LEN(A2) will return the number "10".
MID(text,start_num,num_chars)	This function returns a specific number of characters from a text string, starting at the position you specify and based on the number of characters you specify.	If cell A2 contains the string "purchase price", then =MID(A2,10,10) yields "price". It takes ten characters starting at the tenth position. If num_chars exceed the remaining string length, MID returns to the end of the string.
REPLACE(old_text, start_num, num_chars, new_text)	Replaces part of a text string, based on the number of characters you specify, with a different text string. Old_text is the original string, start_num is the position to start replacing text, num_chars is the number of characters to replace, and new_text is the new string to place in that position.	If cell A2 contains "2019", then =REPLACE(A2,3,2,"22") results in "2022" by starting at the third position and replacing two characters with "22".
RIGHT(text, [num_chars])	Returns the characters in a text string based on the number of characters you specify, starting from the far-right character position.	If cell A2 contains the string "item price", then =RIGHT(A2,5) will result in "price".

(Continued)

QUICK REFERENCE	Additional Text Functions (Continued)	
Function Name	**Description**	**Example**
SEARCH(find_text, within_text, [start_num])	Locates one text string within a second text string and returns the number of the starting position of the first text string from the starting character of the second text string. This function is not case sensitive.	If cell A2 contains the string "revenue", =SEARCH("e",A2,6) returns "7" as the position of the next "e" after the starting position of six characters. If the start_num argument value of 6 is omitted, the formula would return 2.
SUBSTITUTE(text, old_text, new_text, [Instance_num]).	Similar to REPLACE. This function substitutes new_text for old_text in a text string. "Text" is the text string or the cell reference to text data.	If cell A2 contains "sales data", then =SUBSTITUTE (A2,"sales","cost") results in "cost data".

Concatenating Strings of Text

Concatenating data refers to combining or joining multiple strings of data to form a single string. In the current worksheet data example, the goal is to change the name order from the original version of last name, first name, and middle initial to a result of first name and middle initial followed by last name. It would be useful to show it all together in a single field. The previous exercise separated the name data; all that is needed is to string it together in the desired order. There are a variety of ways to accomplish this in Excel. You can manually string together data using the ampersand (&), for instance, or you can use the CONCAT function to string together data to join into one cell.

CONCAT is a text function used to join strings of text together using up to 254 individual arguments. Each argument in the function can be a string or text, a cell reference, or a range of cells. One of the advantages of using this function is that it allows the user to do some formatting of the data at the same time if needed, such as nesting the function in combination with the PROPER function to have the first character in each word capitalized.

In the data provided, the first name plus middle initial appears in column G, and the last name is stored in column F. In this exercise, you will join the data in columns G and F, using the ampersand, as it accomplishes the same thing as the CONCAT function with less typing.

 **E09.14**

SIDE NOTE
The CONCATENATE Function
The CONCAT function replaces CONCATENATE that was previously used in Excel. CONCATENATE is still available for backward compatibility.

To Concatenate Strings of Text

a. Click cell **H2**, then type **=**. Click cell **G2**, type **&" "&** click cell **F2**, and then press Ctrl + Enter.

b. Double-click the **fill handle** to copy the formula down to H26. Resize the column as needed to fit the contents. Cell H2 now displays "Thomas M. Gaines", combining the results of G2 and F2 with a space character between them.

Troubleshooting

Are spaces missing between the names in the final result? Check to see whether a space was typed between the double quotes in the formula. Recall that in addition to text from a cell reference, quotes can be used to string together additional characters—in this case, a space between the words.

Ampersands used to join cells and text string

Results of joining cells and text string

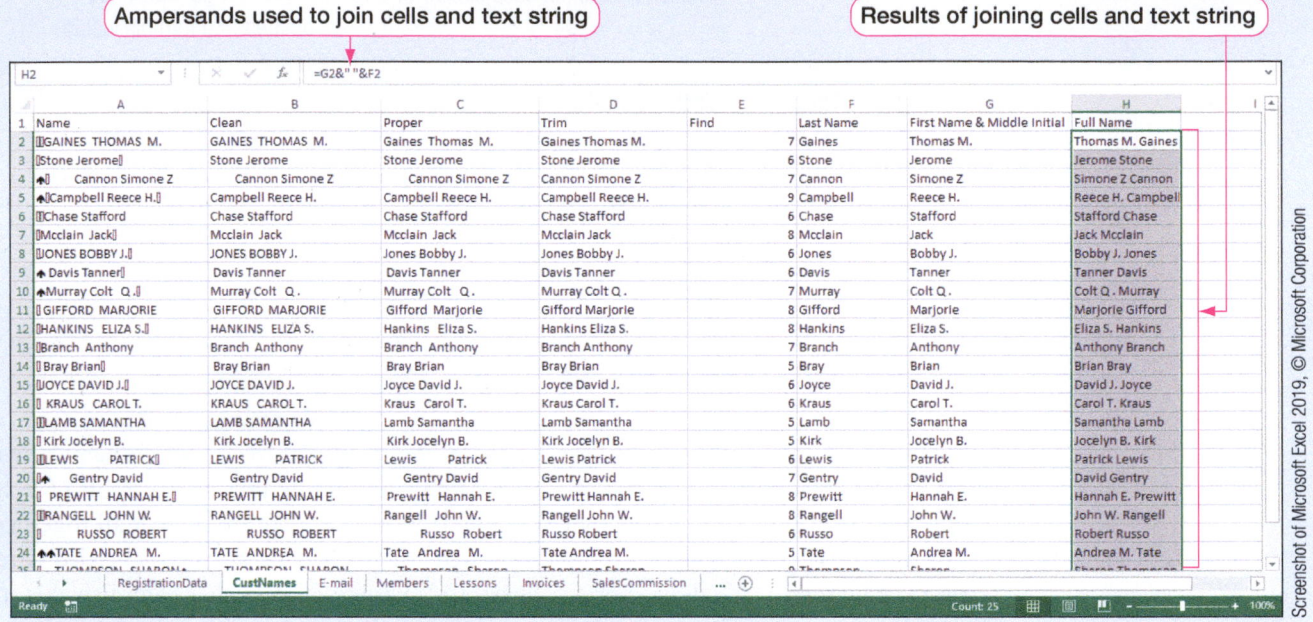

Figure 25 Using the ampersand to concatenate strings of text

c. **Save** the workbook.

REAL WORLD ADVICE | **Recognizing Data Patterns Is Important**

The secret to understanding how to cleanse your data is realizing that there are character patterns in the data. Delimiters such as commas and spaces in between words can become crucial signposts that the resourceful Excel user can exploit with text functions. When you see a character pattern in your data, you can use the FIND function to find just about anything, especially commas and spaces. Once you start looking for character patterns, you will be amazed at how many there are.

CONSIDER THIS | **Variations in Data Entry**

Given the sample name data in the CustNames worksheet exercises, what formula or formulas could be used to extract the middle initial data? What if some of the data contained a full middle name? What formula(s) could be used to take into account this variation in data?

Using Text Functions to Separate Data from the Middle of a Cell

On the E-mail worksheet, you have been provided with a list of e-mail addresses for members who have registered for an upcoming tournament. However, the addresses were copied and pasted into a single column from an e-mail application, and the results contain the member's full name and additional unnecessary characters. In order to easily access the e-mail address for future use, the e-mail address portion of the text string must be separated into a new column. A function similar to CONCAT, called TEXTJOIN, will allow the creation of a quick e-mail list for the tournament. **TEXTJOIN** is a new function in Excel that concatenates text and can include a delimiter between each string of text.

Examine the e-mail address in cell B2. Notice that there are three parts to the address: The member's name is located on the left side of the cell, the text "mailto:" is located in the middle of the cell, and the e-mail address is located on the right side of the cell inside of bracket characters. To accomplish the task of isolating the address into a new column, you will need to use the FIND, MID, and LEN functions.

The **MID** function works in a similar fashion to the LEFT function in that it returns characters from a cell from left to right. The difference is that the second argument of the function allows you to direct MID to begin returning characters from the middle of a cell. Because the starting position of where the e-mail address begins is different for each string of text, you will use the FIND function to locate the colon (":") in the string, as the e-mail address always begins three characters after the colon.

In this exercise, you will use various text functions to isolate the e-mail addresses in column B and combine them into a single cell to create an e-mail list.

 **E09.15**

To Use Text Functions to Separate Data from the Middle of a Cell

a. Click the **E-mail** worksheet, and then click cell **C2**.

b. Type **=FIND** and then press Tab to insert the function. Type **":"** to use the colon character as the find text, type , and click cell **B2**, and then press Ctrl+Enter. The colon is the 22nd character from the left of cell B2.

The colon appears in the cell as part of the text that is copied and pasted from e-mail applications such as Outlook. It can be used to identify where the actual e-mail address begins. Therefore, determining where the colon is in each of the e-mail addresses will prove to be very useful.

c. Double-click the **fill handle** to copy the formula down to C21.

d. Click cell **D2**, type **=LEN** and then press Tab to insert the function. Click cell **B2**, and then press Ctrl+Enter.

Determining the total length of the address will be useful in calculating how many characters to extract to isolate the e-mail address.

e. Double-click the **fill handle** to copy the formula down to D21.

f. Click cell **E2**, type **=MID** and then press Tab to insert the function. Click cell **B2**, type , click cell **C2**, and then type **+3** to complete the argument for the start number of the MID function.

By adding three characters from where the colon is positioned, the first character retrieved by the MID function will be the 25th character from the left, the "j".

g. Click cell **D2**, type - click cell **C2**, type **-3** and then press Ctrl+Enter.

The length of the text needed for each e-mail address will vary. By starting with the length of each cell and then subtracting the location of the colon and another three positions, the mid function will retrieve 20 characters, or 45-22-3=20.

h. Double-click the **fill handle** to copy the formula down to E21.

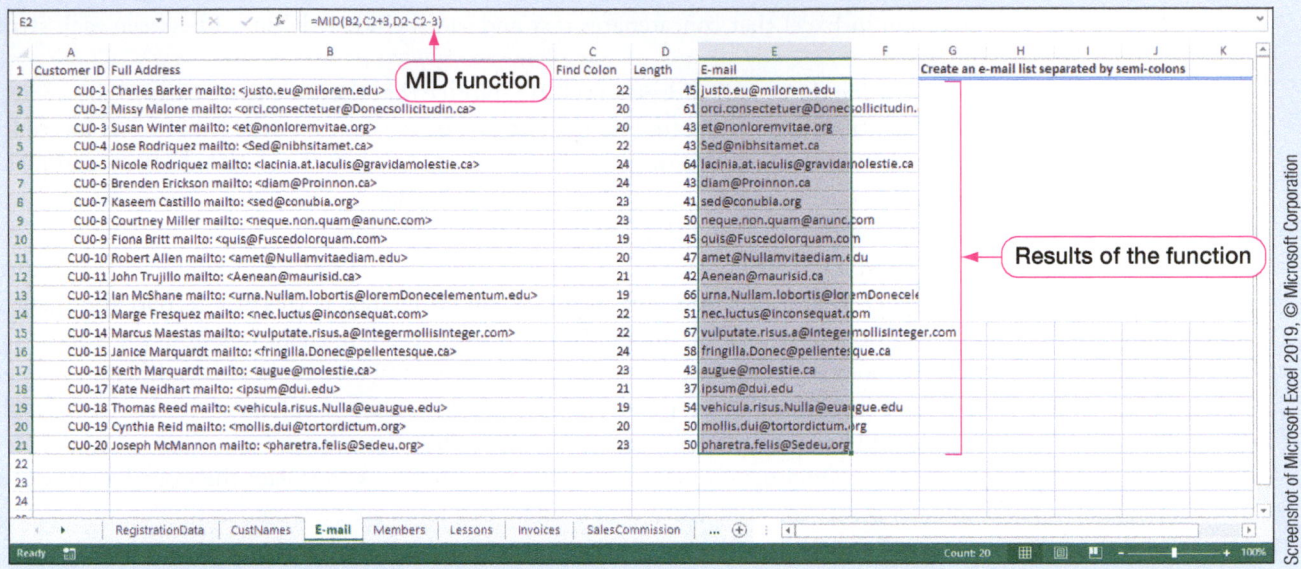

Figure 26 Using the MID function to retrieve e-mail addresses

i. Click cell **G2**, type **=TEXTJOIN** and then press Tab to insert the function. Type "**; ",** and then press Tab to choose TRUE for the ignore empty argument.

> **Troubleshooting**
> Be sure to type a semicolon and a space for the delimiter argument in the TEXTJOIN function. This inserts an extra space between the e-mail addresses, making them easier to read.

j. Type **,** and then click to select the range from **E2 to E21**. Press Ctrl+Enter to complete the function.

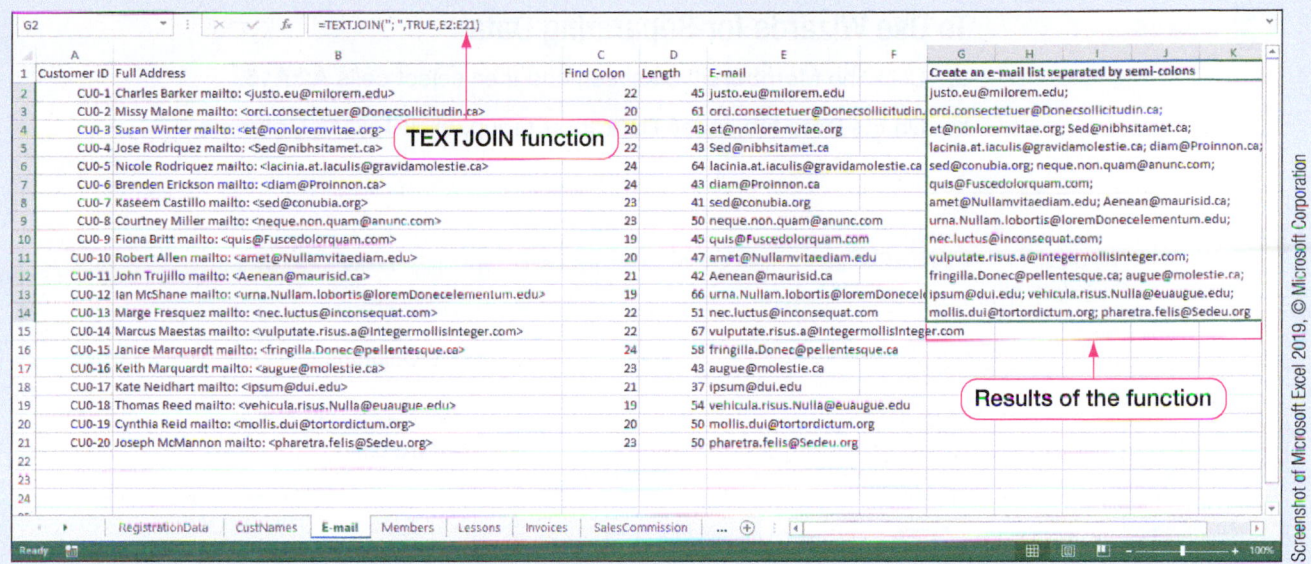

Figure 27 Results of the TEXTJOIN function

k. Save 💾 the workbook.

Screenshot of Microsoft Excel 2019. © Microsoft Corporation

QUICK REFERENCE	Which Function to Use?

How do you know when to use the LEFT, RIGHT, and MID functions if they all work in a similar manner?

1. If the desired text starts on the left side of the cell, use the LEFT function.
2. If the desired text starts from the right side of the cell and is consistently located relative to the right side of the cell, use the RIGHT function.
3. If the desired text is in the middle of a text string, use the MID function.

Separate Data Using Wizards

You have already separated data using the LEN and FIND functions. Excel provides a special wizard called the **Convert Text to Columns Wizard** for separating simple data cell content. This wizard can often provide another option to consider whenever it can be applicable. This is a very handy Excel feature because it walks you through the whole process of separating your data and gives you control over a variety of formatting options.

Using Wizards for Separating Data

Aleeta Herriott has provided you with a list of names of golf course members who have registered for tournaments but who have not yet purchased anything at the pro shop. The pro shop would like to target them in a new promotion to offer them a 10% discount. In this exercise, you will separate the name data into two separate fields, using the Convert Text to Columns Wizard.

 **E09.16**

To Use Wizards for Separating Data

a. Click the **Members** worksheet, and then select cells **A2:A15**.

b. On the **Data** tab, in the Data Tools group, click **Text to Columns**.

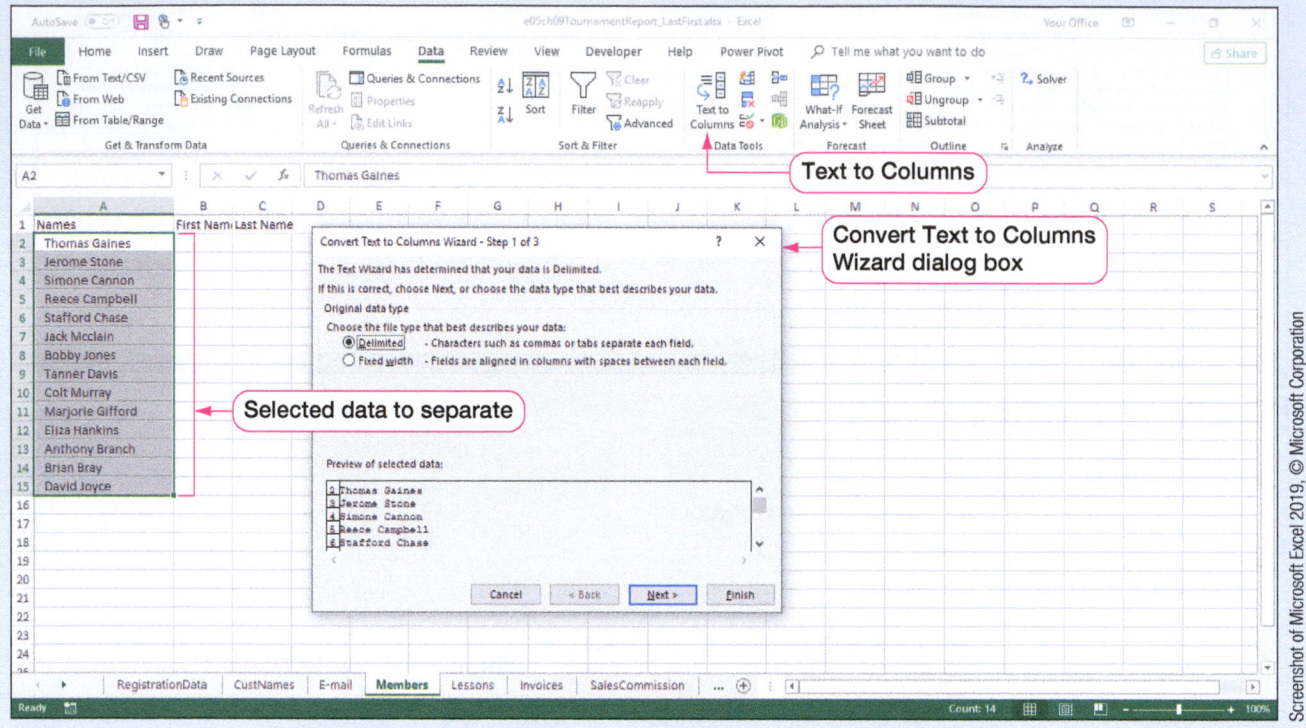

Figure 28 Convert Text to Columns Wizard

c. In the Convert Text to Columns Wizard, under Choose the file type that best describes your data, make sure **Delimited** is selected, and then click **Next**.

d. Under Delimiters, select the check box next to **Space**, click to uncheck the check box next to **Tab**, and then click **Next**.

e. Click in the **Destination** box, change the destination cell reference to **$B$2**, and then click **Finish**.

> **Troubleshooting**
>
> By default, the Convert Text to Columns Wizard will begin the output of the data in the first cell you selected. The result will be to paste the separated data over the original data. It is best practice to change the destination cell to begin to the right of your original data if possible.

f. Resize columns **B** and **C** as needed to fit the contents.

g. **Save** the workbook.

REAL WORLD ADVICE **Wizard versus Text Functions versus Flash Fill**

There are many tools in Excel to cleanse and reorganize data. The main goal is always to reach for the tool that fulfills the goal at hand in the most efficient manner. Now that you have seen how to transform data with Get & Transform, text functions, Flash Fill, and the Convert Text to Columns Wizard, how do you know which one to choose over the others?

- Get & Transform is designed for data that is being imported into Excel. It is particularly powerful when the data also requires transformation and can automate both the import and transformation process.

- The Convert Text to Columns Wizard is designed for simple cell content, so if you are separating text data rarely and the data fits the requirements of the wizard, the Convert Text to Columns Wizard will be the easiest and most efficient to use.

- If you will be converting or cleaning data repetitively and the data is already stored in Excel, text functions are the best option.

- Flash Fill works well with consistently organized data and is optimized for working on touch-enabled devices.

Removing Duplicates

It is easy to enter a customer contact more than once or to have multiple customer entries when merging customer data from multiple sources. This is one of the most common data entry errors. Even when steps are taken to minimize redundant data, there is a chance that duplicate entries will still result.

Excel provides an easy tool for removing duplicate entries: the **Remove Duplicates** button found on the Data tab in the Data Tools group. In the Remove Duplicates dialog box, you specify which columns you want the wizard to check. Excel searches whichever columns you have selected and prompts you to remove any duplicates that it finds. However, use this tool with caution because it will not show what Excel is about to delete.

You have been asked to examine data that was manually entered concerning golf lessons attended by members of the golf club before a tournament in the past year. Because each member can attend only one lesson per day, any duplicate values should be removed. The record contains the member's last name, date of the lesson, and fee. In this exercise, you will use the Remove Duplicates tool to remove any duplicate entries on the Lessons worksheet.

 **E09.17**

To Remove Duplicates

a. Click the **Lessons** worksheet, and then select the data in cells **A1:C18**.

b. On the Data tab, in the Data Tools group, click **Remove Duplicates**.

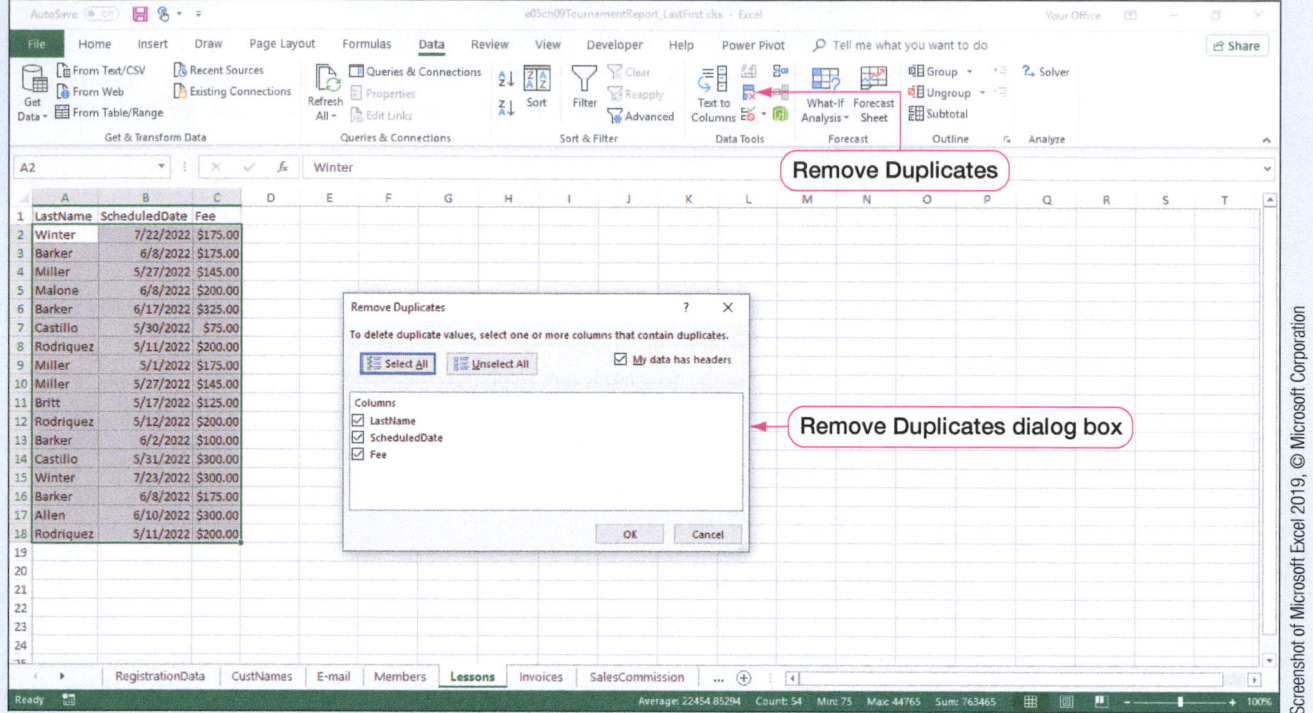

Figure 29   Remove Duplicates dialog box

c. Ensure that all three columns are selected to check for duplicates, and then click **OK**.

d. Excel returns a message saying 3 duplicate values found and removed; 14 unique values remain. Click **OK**.

e. Save 💾 the workbook.

REAL WORLD ADVICE   **Identifying Duplicate Data**

Identifying duplicate data can be a time-consuming and challenging task. While the best practice is to use a unique identifier or primary key for each record, duplicate data can still be created. Before removing data from a data set, be sure to thoroughly investigate the records to ensure that they are true duplicates.

Using Conditional Formatting to Identify Duplicates

In the previously discussed methods for removing duplicates, Excel automatically deletes the records once it finds them and you click OK without specifying which records were deleted. If it is necessary to examine the records first, you can identify duplicates by using conditional formatting. Before Excel 2007, you had to write a complex logical test formula with conditional formatting to achieve the same result. Recent versions of Excel have made this task much easier to perform. With the Conditional Formatting feature, Excel has a special predefined rule for identifying duplicate values.

The accounts manager at the Red Bluff Golf Course & Pro Shop has asked you to go through a list of invoices for items related to several past tournaments to identify whether there are any duplicates among them. In this exercise, you will not be deleting any of the data; rather, you will simply highlight duplicate records for further investigation. In viewing the long list of numbers, it is apparent that the most efficient and simplest method would be to create a conditional formatting rule in Excel to highlight any duplicate invoices.

 **E09.18**

To Use Conditional Formatting to Identify Duplicates

a. Click the **Invoices** worksheet, click cell **A2**, and then press `Ctrl`+`Shift`+`↓` to select cells A2:A277.

b. Click the **Home** tab, and in the Styles group, click **Conditional Formatting**.

c. In the gallery that appears, point to **Highlight Cells Rules**, and then select **Duplicate Values**.

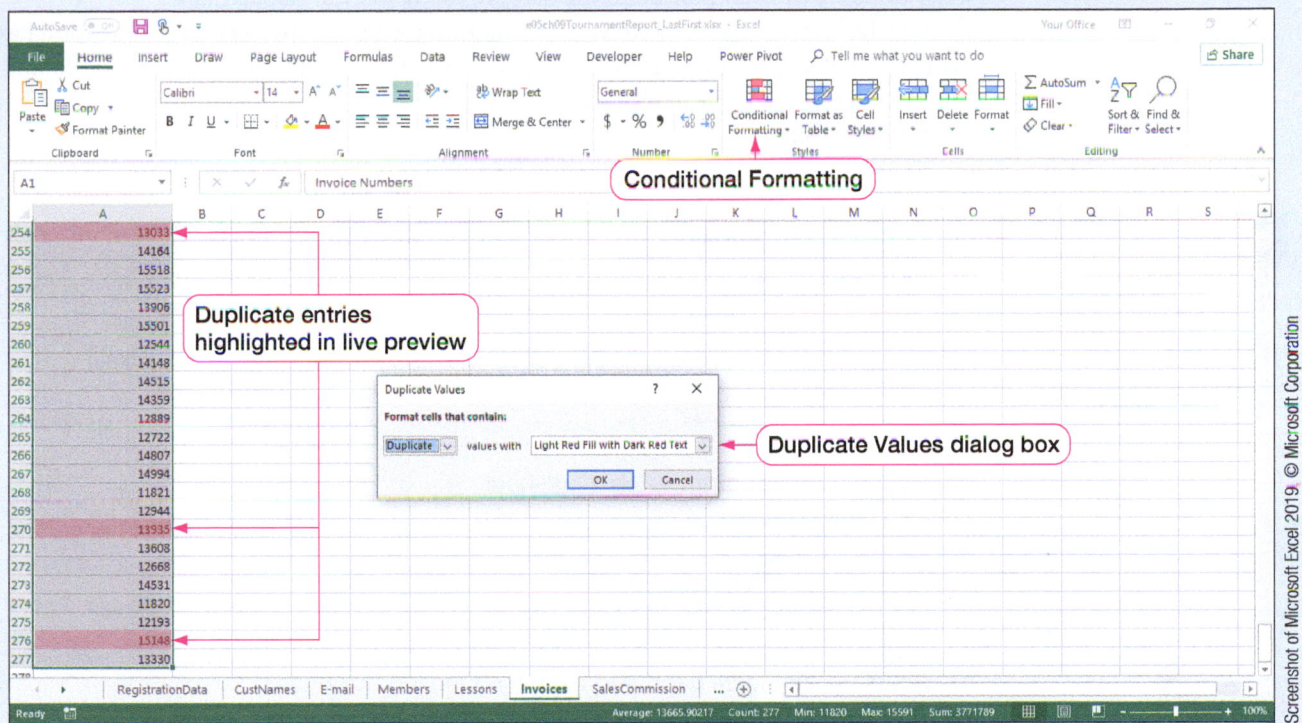

Figure 30   Using Conditional Formatting to identify duplicates

d. Accept the default entries in the Duplicate Values dialog box, and click **OK**. The duplicate values are now highlighted.

e. Press `Ctrl`+`Home` to return to cell A1. In the Editing group, click **Sort & Filter**, and then click **Filter**.

f. In cell A1, click the **filter** arrow ⏷, and point to **Sort by Color**, and then click the **light red rectangle**. This will allow for easier viewing of the duplicate records.

g. **Save** 💾 the workbook.

> **Grader Heads Up**
>
> If you are using MyLab IT Grader, this is the end of the first MyLab IT Grader project, Part B. This project continues in Part C, which is a separate MyLab IT Grader project.

Cleanse Date-Related Data

One of the biggest problems in combining data from a variety of sources is coming up with a standard date format. Some users include a full, four-digit year; others use two digits. Some include a zero with single-digit months; others do not. Furthermore, different countries order the date components completely differently.

Another problem with dates is that sometimes when you import web data into Excel or you paste it in as text from an external source, the default format for the dates is a text format. These text dates are usually left-aligned instead of right-aligned, and they may be marked with an error indicator icon (if error checking is turned on). This creates problems when the date field is used in other calculations, such as when you create a PivotTable and want to group the data by date.

Cleansing Dates with the DATEVALUE Function

The **DATEVALUE** function converts a date in a text format into a serial date value. In Excel, a date is a number in which the value is calculated as the number of days since December 31, 1899. So January 1, 1900, is equivalent to a value of 1 in this system. Converting dates into serial values is what allows you to use dates in mathematical calculations.

You have been asked to convert the dates on a list of invoices related to purchases made for the next Seniors Golf tournament at the Red Bluff Golf Course & Pro Shop. In this exercise, you will cleanse these dates, which then can be used in PivotTables or other means of analysis.

 E09.19

To Cleanse Dates with the DATEVALUE Function

> ### Grader Heads Up
> If you are using MyLab IT Grader for this project, note that Part C begins here as a separate MyLab IT Grader project.

a. Click the **SalesCommission** worksheet.

b. Click cell **D2**, type **=DATEVALUE** and then press Tab to insert the function. Click cell **B2**, and then press Ctrl+Enter.

c. In the Number group, click the **Number Format** arrow, and then select **Short Date** as the format for the cell.

d. Double-click the **fill handle** to copy the function down to D11.

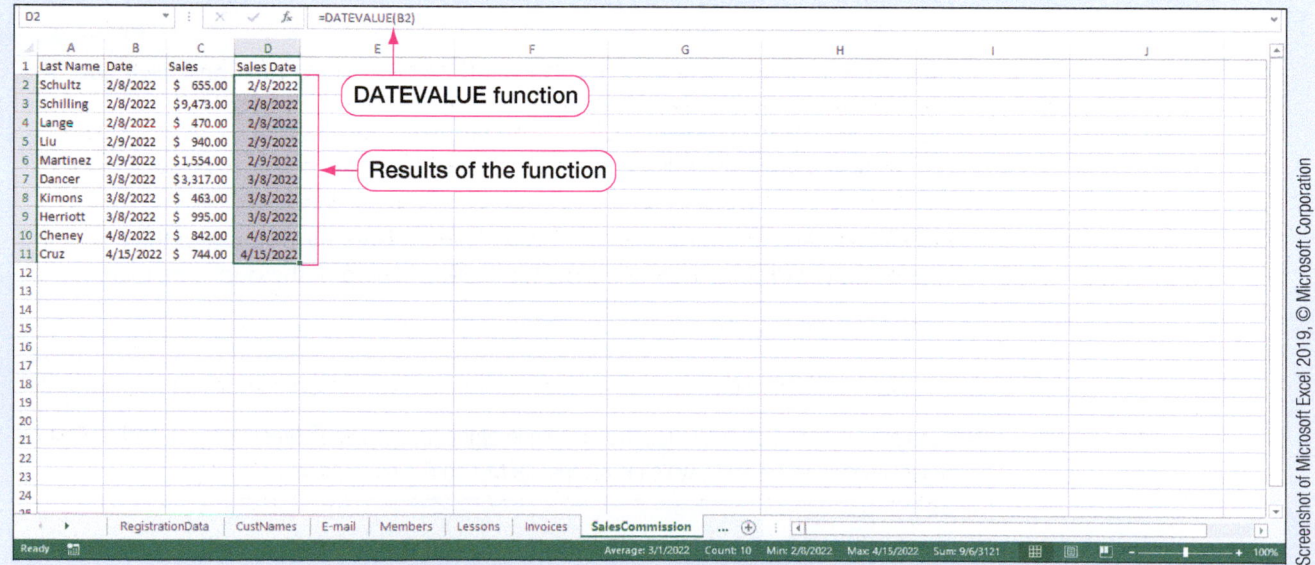

Figure 31 Using the DATEVALUE function

e. **Save** the workbook.

| REAL WORLD ADVICE | How to Tell if Dates Work |

In the prior exercise, the dates seen in B2 and D2 look the same. Highlight the range B2:B11, and the status bar of Excel will display a count of the cells, 10. This indicates that Excel sees the data in the cells as text and will not be able to perform calculations on the data. Select the range D2:D11, and the status bar displays an average and a sum in addition to the count. This means Excel can work with the dates as numeric values.

Reconstructing Dates Using Text to Columns

Because there are many different date formats, working with dates can be very tricky. For example, the standard European format for dates is DD/MM/YY, whereas in the United States, the standard is MM/DD/YY. Excel contains several date functions that make working with dates and converting dates much easier.

The date data from the Red Bluff Celebrity Pro-Am Tournament concerning purchases made at the pro shop before the 2022 tournament is in the European DD/MM/YYYY format. In this exercise, you will use the Convert Text to Columns Wizard to change the date format on a list of purchases.

 E09.20

To Reconstruct Dates Using Text to Columns

a. Click the **Purchases** worksheet, and then select cells **B2:B11**.

b. Click the **Data** tab, and in the Data Tools group, click **Text to Columns**.

c. In the Convert Text to Columns Wizard, under Choose the file type that best describes your data, select **Fixed width**, and then click **Next**.

> ### Troubleshooting
>
> Before attempting to rearrange dates by using the LEFT, RIGHT, and MID text functions, keep in mind that Excel stores dates as a serial number, and it is the cell formatting that displays this serial number in a date format. The LEFT function extracts a specified number of characters from a text string starting from the far-left character. The RIGHT function does the same starting from the far-right character. And the MID function extracts characters starting in the middle of the text string. So applying the LEFT function to a date will return only the specified numbers beginning on the left of the serial number for that date. You can extract the day, month, and year from a date field by using Convert Text to Columns or applying the DAY, MONTH, YEAR functions.

d. There are no column breaks to add, remove, or move, so click **Next**.

e. Under Column data format, click **Date**, click the **Date** arrow, and then click **DMY**. Click the Destination box, and then adjust the cell reference by typing $C$2 Click **Finish**. Resize the columns if necessary to show all the dates.

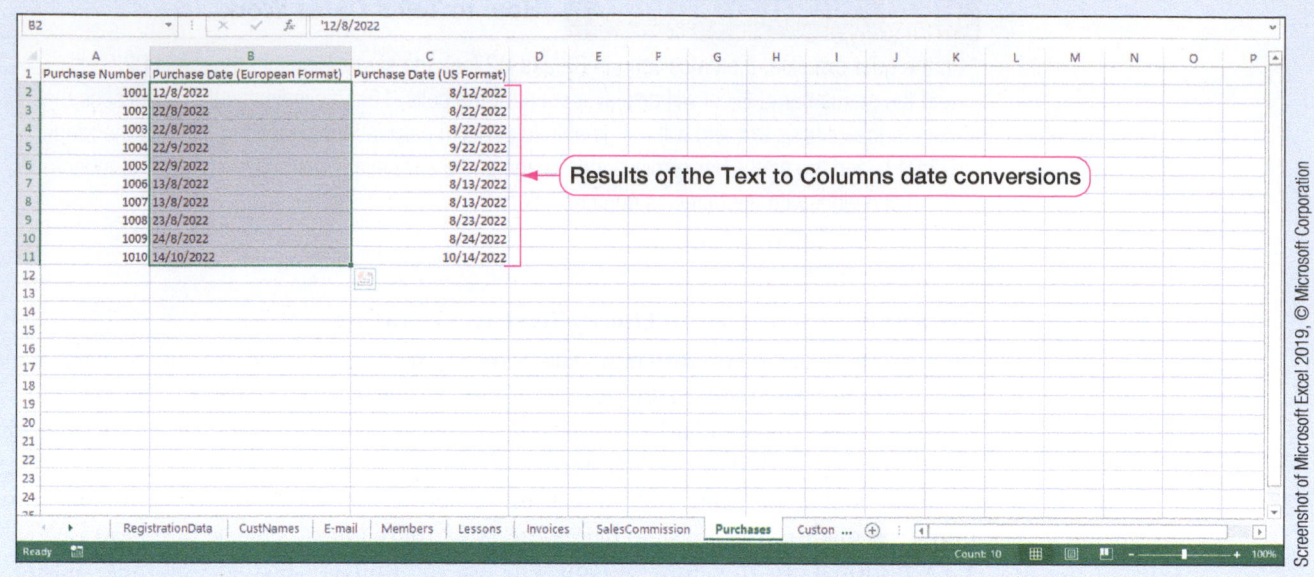

Figure 32 Dates in European format converted to U.S. format using Text to Columns

    f. Save 🖫 the workbook.

Creating Dates with Date Functions

Excel has many features that can help you to process date-related data. It might seem that working with dates in Excel is a confusing process. But any businessperson can tell you that doing calculations with dates and manipulating them is something that you are sure to encounter. Knowing how to apply some of the more sophisticated functions of Excel will increase your value to almost any company.

Aleeta Herriott has been so impressed with your work that she has asked for your help in sorting out some data from customer transactions that occurred just after the Red Bluff Celebrity Pro-Am tournament. The data has already been imported from the .csv file for a summary sales report and converted into an Excel format. But it still has some strange-looking date fields that are preventing Aleeta from running her own Excel formulas. When the raw data was first imported, it looked as if the source system put the name of the day (such as Tuesday) in front of the standard date format for the Ord_Date field. In addition, the standard date format of the data was imported into Excel as three separate fields with the headings Ord_Year, Ord_Day, and Ord_Month. Technically, there is nothing wrong with the data itself, but with several hundred thousand transactions in the report, it makes doing any date-related calculations challenging.

The **DATE** function returns the sequential serial number that represents a particular date. Making use of the DATE function allows a quick conversion of the data in the three separate fields because you can find the serial date with the arguments =DATE(year, month, day).

QUICK REFERENCE	Common Date Functions in Excel
Function Name	**Description**
DATE(year, month, day)	Returns the sequential serial number that represents a particular date.
DATEVALUE(date_text)	Returns the serial number of the date represented by date_text. Use DATEVALUE to convert a date represented by text to a serial number.
DAY(serial_number)	Returns the day of the month from a date entry. The serial_number argument has to be a serial date or cell reference to a date format-ted cell. The DATE function can be used to determine the serial number if needed.
MONTH(serial_number)	Returns the month (i.e., 1–12) of the date entry.
NETWORKDAYS(start_date, end_date, [holidays])	Returns the number of whole working days between two given dates.
WEEKDAY(serial_number, [return_type])	Returns the day of the week corresponding to a date (1–7). The optional return_type argument allows you to change how days are counted.
WORKDAY(start_date, days, [holidays])	Returns the corresponding date that is the number of days from the start_date, minus weekends and holidays. The start_date must be in serial or date format.
YEAR(serial_number)	Returns the year corresponding to a date. This works for years from 1900 to 9999.

In this exercise, you will use the DATE function to combine the separate date fields into one complete date.

 **E09.21**

To Create Dates with Date Functions

a. Click the **CustomerTransactions** worksheet, and then right-click the **column heading** for column E.

b. Click **Insert**. Click cell **E1**, type Complete_Date and then press Enter. Resize column E to fit if necessary.

c. In cell E2, type =DATE, and then press Tab to insert the function. Click cell **B2** and type , click cell **D2**, type , click cell **C2**, and then press Ctrl+Enter.

d. Click the **Home** tab, and in the Number group, click the **Number Format** arrow, and then select **Short Date** to format the value as a date. Double-click the **fill handle** to copy the function down to E15.

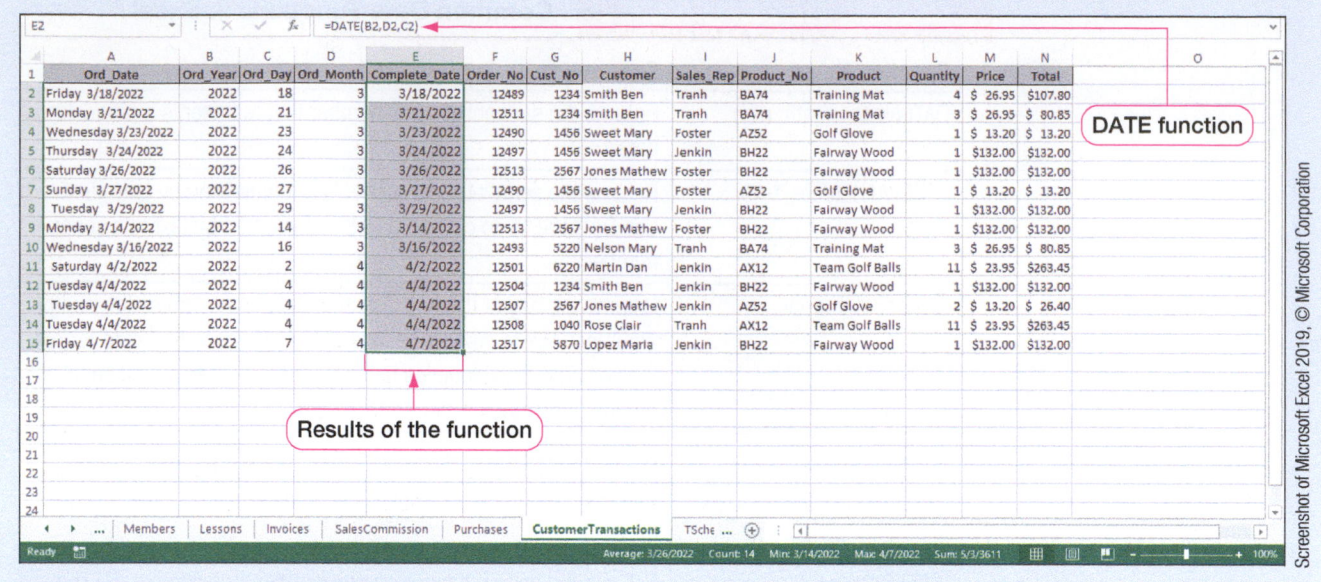

Figure 33 Using the DATE function

e. **Save** the workbook.

Using the NETWORKDAYS and TEXT Functions

Because the Red Bluff Golf Course is famous for its competitive layout and challenging greens, it is often asked to host golf tournaments. It currently hosts several major and minor tournaments each year. The most popular event is the Senior Legends tournament, which occurs in December. Golf tournaments must be scheduled years in advance, and members have to be alerted about them so that they know to expect times when the course will be unavailable to them. It is also important for the maintenance staff to schedule enough workdays to keep everything looking nice and for the inventory in the pro shop to be restocked in time for each event.

With this in mind, Barry Cheney, the Red Bluff Golf Course manager, has asked you to help him build a long-term tournament schedule report. In talking with him, you learned that he would really like to keep track of the number of working days he has between events so he can give members and staff plenty of notice before an event. With a little research, you discovered a function called **NETWORKDAYS**, which can be used to calculate the number of available workdays between two given dates. Its syntax looks like this: =NETWORKDAYS(start_date, end_date, {holidays}).

The optional holidays argument at the end allows users to factor in how specific holidays might reduce the number of available work days. Additional research shows that the TEXT function can be used to display the name of the day by using the dddd format as one of the arguments. The **TEXT** function allows you to display numeric data as text in addition to using special formatting strings to display the text.

In this exercise, you will use the NETWORKDAYS and TEXT functions to help build the long-term tournament schedule report.

E09.22

To Use the NETWORKDAYS and TEXT Functions

a. Click the **TSchedule** worksheet. Click cell **G5**.

b. Type **=NETWORKDAYS** and then press Tab to insert the function.

c. Click cell **F5**, type **,** and then click cell **E6** to calculate the number of workdays between the end of one tournament and the beginning of the next, and then type **,**

d. Click and drag cell **I5** down to cell **I12**, to select the range of holidays in 2022. Press the F4 key to create an absolute cell reference to the range, and then press Ctrl+Enter.

e. Double-click the **fill handle** to copy the function down to G9.

   Notice that cell G9 shows a negative number. This is because the formula in G9 does not refer to the correct start date for the next golf tournament.

f. To correct the error, click cell **G9**, and then click the **formula bar** to edit the **E10** cell reference. Select the text **E10**, type **E13** and then press Enter. The negative number should change to a positive 60.

g. Do the same for the 2023 Season tournament schedule. Click cell **G13**. Type **=NETWORKDAYS** and then press Tab to insert the function.

h. Click cell **F13**, type **,** click cell **E14**, and then type **,**

i. Click and drag cell **J5** down to cell **J12**. Press the F4 key to create an absolute cell reference to the range, and then press Ctrl+Enter.

j. Click cell **G13**, and click and drag the **fill handle** down to cell G16.

   Notice that you do not need to copy down to G17. For the 2023 season, the start date for the first 2024 event is unavailable. Therefore, you cannot calculate the available workdays between the 2023 Senior Legends event and the next event, because the schedule for 2024 is unknown at this time.

k. Click cell **H5**, type **=TEXT** and then press Tab to insert the function. Click cell **E5**, type **,"dddd"** and then press Ctrl+Enter.

l. Click and drag the **fill handle** down to cell H9. This allows you to determine the day of the week each event will start.

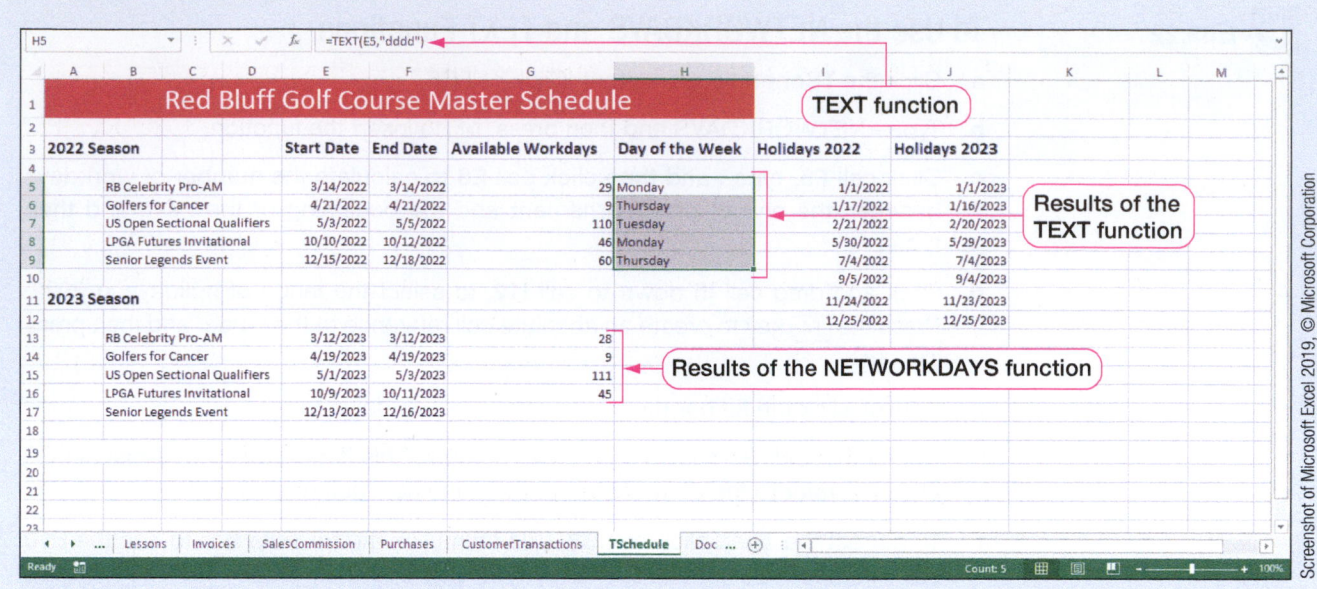

Figure 34 Results of the NETWORKDAYS and TEXT functions

m. Click cell **H5**, and then press Ctrl+C to copy the formula in H5. Select the range **H13:H16**, and then press Ctrl+V to paste the formula into the range.

n. Save 💾 the workbook, exit Excel, and then submit your file as directed by your instructor.

Concept Check

1. What is a web query? How is it used to import data into Excel? p. 497

2. What is a markup language? Give two examples, and describe how they are useful. p. 503

3. What are the benefits of importing data from an Access database into Excel? p. 513

4. How are character patterns in data used to help cleanse and manipulate data within a cell? p. 518

5. What does the Flash Fill feature do in Excel? How does Flash Fill handle text and numeric data differently? p. 524

6. What are text functions? How are they used for cleansing data? p. 533

7. Why is it important to cleanse date-related data? p. 537

Key Terms

CLEAN   p. 522
CONCAT   p. 529
Convert Text to Columns
  Wizard   p. 533
Data cleansing   p. 518
Data verification   p. 518
DATE   p. 540
DATEVALUE   p. 538
Delimiter   p. 508
External data   p. 497
FIND   p. 524
Flash Fill   p. 518
Foreign key   p. 514
Get & Transform   p. 497

HTML   p. 503
LEFT   p. 524
LEN   p. 526
LOWER   p. 522
Markup language   p. 503
Metadata   p. 508
Microsoft Query   p. 515
MID   p. 531
NETWORKDAYS   p. 542
Primary key   p. 514
PROPER   p. 522
Query   p. 499
Relational database   p. 514
Remove Duplicates   p. 535

RIGHT   p. 526
TEXT   p. 542
Text data   p. 508
Text file   p. 508
Text functions   p. 521
TEXTJOIN   p. 531
Transformation   p. 497
TRIM   p. 522
UPPER   p. 522
Web query   p. 499
XML   p. 503
XML element   p. 503
XML map   p. 503
XML schema   p. 503

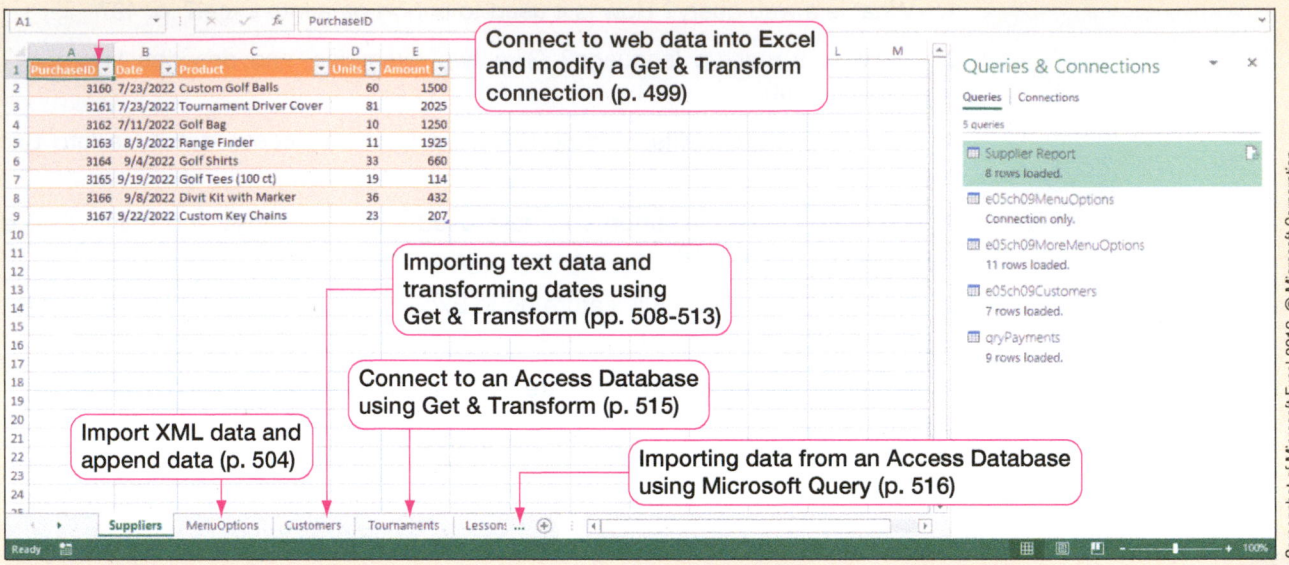

Figure 35

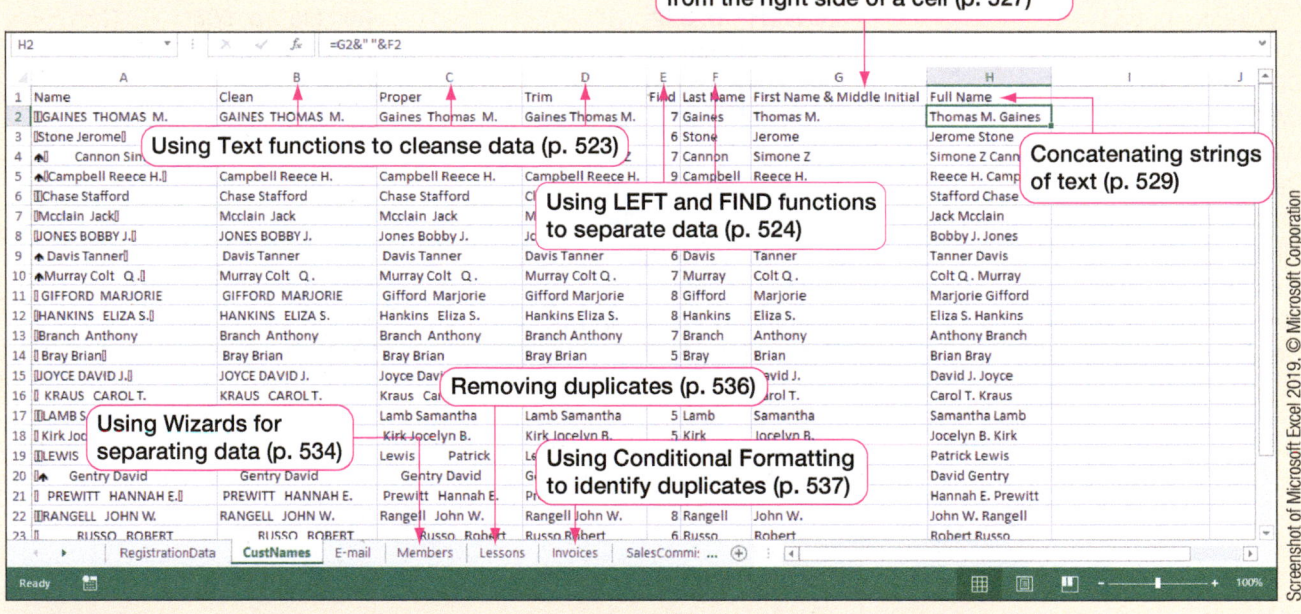

Figure 36

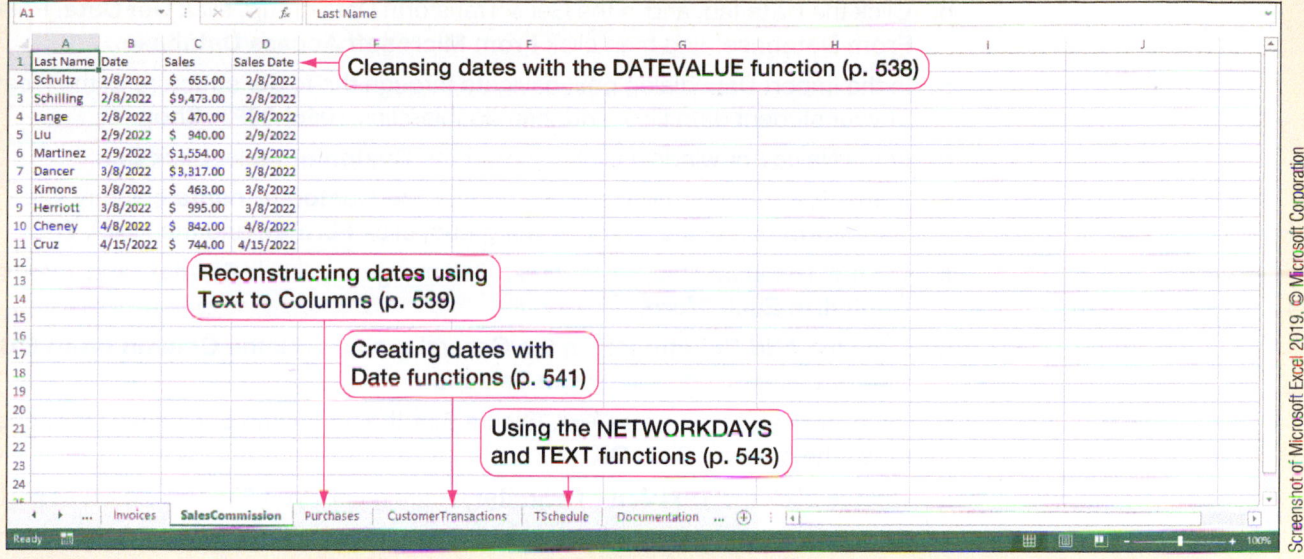

Figure 37

Practice 1

Student data files needed:

e05ch09Newsletter.xlsx

e05ch09ProShop.accdb

You will save your file as:

e05ch09Newsletter_LastFirst.xlsx

Red Bluff Golf Course & Pro Shop Special Promotions Spreadsheets

Sales & Marketing

The Red Bluff Golf Course & Pro Shop regularly runs special promotions to sell golf equipment and clothing. When customers visit the Pro Shop website, they can opt to receive electronic copies of the Pro Shop newsletter via e-mail. The website administrator then updates an Access database containing the customer information at the end of every week. Recently, customers who visited the pro shop opted to receive the newsletter by writing their name and e-mail address on a sign-up sheet. At the end of the day, these names were entered into an Excel workbook. You have been asked to take the data contained in the workbook and integrate it with the customer data from the Access database. All that combined data then needs to be cleansed so it can be used to send out e-mail versions of the pro shop newsletter.

a. Open the Excel file, **e05ch09Newsletter**. Save it as e05ch09Newsletter_LastFirst using your last and first name. If necessary, enable content.

> **Mac Troubleshooting**
>
> At the time of publishing for this text, the tools discussed in this text in the Get & Transform Data group are not available in the Office 2019 for Mac versions of Microsoft Office. Instead, the previous set of tools in the group Get External Data continue to serve the purpose of importing data into Excel for the Mac versions of Office.

b. Click the **Data** tab, and in the Get & Transform Data group, click **Get Data**. Point to **From Database**, and then click **From Microsoft Access Database**.

c. In the Import Data dialog box, navigate through the folder structure to the location of your student data files, and then double-click **e05ch09ProShop**.

d. In the Navigator window click to select the **Customer** table. Click **Edit**.

e. In the Query Editor, click the heading for the **Customer name** column. Click the **Transform** tab, in the Text Column group, click **Format**, and then click **Trim**.

f. On the Transform tab, in the Text Column group, click **Format**, and then click **Capitalize Each Word**.

g. Click the **Add Column** tab, in the General group, click the **Column From Examples** arrow, and then click **From Selection**.

h. Type Bree and then press Enter. Ensure that the first name of all customers copied down the column. Click **OK**.

i. Double-click the **Text After Delimiter** heading and type First Name Press Enter

j. Click the heading for the **Customer name** column. On the Add Column tab, in the General group, click the **Column From Examples** arrow, and then click **From Selection**.

k. Type Workman and then press Enter. Ensure that the last name of all customers copied down the column. Click **OK**.

l. Double-click the **Text Before Delimiter** heading and type Last Name and press Enter

m. Click the heading for the **Customer name** column and then press Delete.

n. Click and drag the **Customer email address** column to the right of the Last Name column.

o. Click the **Home** tab and in the Close group, click the **Close & Load** arrow and click **Close & Load To**. In the Import Data dialog box click the option for **Existing worksheet**. Ensure cell A1 is displayed in the Existing worksheet box and then click **OK**.

p. Click the **InStoreNewsletter** worksheet tab.

q. Click cell **C2**, type =TRIM and then press Tab to insert the function. Click cell **A2**, and then press Ctrl+Enter. Double-click the **fill handle** to copy the formula down to cell C15. Resize the column as needed to fit the contents.

r. Click cell **D2**, type =PROPER and then press Tab to insert the function. Click cell **C2**, and then press Ctrl+Enter. Double-click the **fill handle** to copy the formula down to cell D15. Resize the column as needed to fit the contents.

s. Click cell **E2**, type =FIND and then press Tab to insert the function. Type ",", click cell **D2**, and then press Ctrl+Enter. Double-click the **fill handle** to copy the formula down to cell E15. Resize the column as needed to fit the contents.

t. Click cell **F2**, type =LEFT and then press Tab to insert the function. Click cell **D2**, type ,E2-1 and then press Ctrl+Enter. Double-click the **fill handle** to copy the formula down to cell F15. Resize the column as needed to fit the contents.

u. Click cell **G2**. Type =RIGHT and then press Tab to insert the function. Click cell **D2**, type ,LEN and then press Tab to insert the function. Click cell **D2**, type)-E2-1) and then press Ctrl+Enter. Double-click the **fill handle** to copy the formula down to cell G15. Resize the column as needed to fit the contents.

v. Click **Save**, exit Excel, and then submit your file as directed by your instructor.

Problem Solve 1

MyLab IT Grader

Student data files needed:

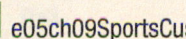 e05ch09SportsCustomers.xlsx

e05ch09SportsCustomers.accdb

You will save your file as:

e05ch09SportsCustomers_LastFirst.xlsx

Sales & Marketing

Sports Store Customers

Joe Nelson has a small sports equipment store that has a growing list of customers. The different supervisors have been saving customer information in different formats. Joe would like to have all the data in an Excel spreadsheet. He has asked you to take on the task of getting the data together and putting them in the formats he would like for his planned marketing effort.

a. Open the Excel file, **e05ch09SportsCustomers**. Save it as e05ch09SportsCustomers_LastFirst using your last and first name. If necessary, enable content.

> ### Mac Troubleshooting
>
> At the time of publishing for this text, the tools discussed in this text in the Get & Transform Data group are not available in the Office 2019 for Mac versions of Microsoft Office. Instead, the previous set of tools in the group Get External Data continue to serve the purpose of importing data into Excel for the Mac versions of Office.

b. Import the data from the query **qryCustomer** in the **e05ch09SportsCustomers .accdb** database using Get & Transform. Edit the data to perform the following transformations.

c. Use the Clean and Trim transformations on the Transform tab in the Query Editor to remove extra spaces and nonprintable characters from the Customer name column.

d. Use the Capitalize Each Word transformation to proper case the names in the Customer name column.

e. Separate the names in the Customer name column into new columns named First Name and Last Name For example, Customer name Dunlap, Jeremy should have a First Name of Jeremy and a Last Name of Dunlap.

f. Use the Trim transformation to remove any extra spaces in the First Name and Last Name columns that may have been created during the prior step.

g. Delete the **Customer name** column.

h. On the Add Column tab, in the General group, use the Column From Examples transformation to separate the Address column in three new columns named Street Address City and State For example, 6813 Ligula Av., Santa Fe NM should have a Street Address of 6813 Ligula Av., a City of Santa Fe, and State of NM.

i. Delete the Address column and arrange the remaining columns in the following order: First Name, Last Name, Street Address, City, State.

j. Load the **CustomerDatabase** worksheet in cell **A2**.

k. **Save** the workbook, exit Excel, and then submit your file as directed by your instructor.

Student data file needed:

 e05ch09HOA.xlsx

You will save your file as:

e05ch09HOA_LastFirst.xlsx

Finance & Accounting

Sales & Marketing

Investing in Homes

You volunteer for your homeowner association (HOA). The HOA has decided to invest in several stocks. To fund the investment, they are asking for donations from local businesses as a way to invest in the local community. The HOA officers have obtained a list of the businesses in the neighborhood and have asked you to create a spreadsheet with the list of names so they can send out a mailing. In addition, they have asked you to show them recent populations in the United States listed by each state.

a. Open the Excel file, **e05ch09HOA**. Save it as e05ch09HOA_LastFirst using your last and first name. If necessary, enable content.

b. Insert the **file name** in the left section of the footer on the **Businesses** worksheet.

c. On the **Businesses** worksheet, use **Flash Fill** to cleanse the data in additional columns using the following guidelines.

- The names of the Customers should be arranged with the first name, a space, and then the last name.

- The phone number should be displayed in standard phone number format: (xxx) xxx-xxxx.

- The ZIP Code should be displayed with a hyphen between the first five digits and the last four digits.

d. Resize the columns as needed to fit the contents.

e. Delete any duplicate records, using the Remove Duplicates tool. A duplicate record is one in which all columns contain the same data.

Mac Troubleshooting

If you are doing this Perform case on a Mac, step f cannot be completed on a Mac.

---

f. The HOA would like to see a listing of all U.S. States and their respective populations. This data is best imported into Excel with Get & Transform. You may include additional information in this data import such as U.S. Territories and the District of Columbia if that information is available. You may use the website or data source of your choice, although you might find that https://en.wikipedia.org works well for web connections in Excel.

g. Resize the columns as needed to fit the contents on each worksheet.

h. Save the workbook, exit Excel, and then submit your file as directed by your instructor.

Microsoft Excel

OBJECTIVES

1. Perform break-even analysis   p. 552
2. Analyze variables in formulas through the use of data tables   p. 559
3. Use Goal Seek to determine values needed to achieve an objective   p. 565
4. Use the Scenario Manager to create scenarios   p. 568
5. Create scenario reports   p. 571
6. Understand the use of the Solver add-in   p. 573
7. Solve complex problems using Solver   p. 574
8. Generate and interpret Solver answer reports   p. 580

Chapter 10 DATA TABLES, SCENARIO MANAGER, AND SOLVER

MyLab IT Grader

Production & Operations

Prepare Case

The Red Bluff Golf Course & Pro Shop Business Planning Analysis

Barry Cheney, the golf course manager at the Red Bluff Golf Course & Pro Shop, has been considering expanding the clubhouse to accommodate a steady increase in business. This expansion could include more space for the pro shop and more guest accommodations. Barry will need to provide a detailed analysis of past sales along with sales forecasts to assure William Mattingly, the resort's CEO, that the money spent on the improvements and expansion will have positive financial benefits for Red Bluff. To increase management's understanding of the current capacities, Barry has collected data about traffic, sales, and product mix. He has asked you to analyze this data using Excel's What-If Analysis tools.

Justasc/Shutterstock

Student data file needed:

 e05ch10ExpansionAnalysis.xlsx

You will save your file as:

 e05ch10ExpansionAnalysis_LastFirst.xlsx

Examining Cost-Volume-Profit Relationships

Managers need to analyze business data to help them plan and monitor the organization's day-to-day operations. **Cost-volume-profit (CVP) analysis** is the study of how cost and sales volume are related and the effect their relationship has on profit. Management relies on the accounting department to provide the data needed to perform CVP analysis. This data allows management not only to perform CVP analysis but also to examine operational risks as a suitable cost structure is chosen.

Consider the Red Bluff Golf Course & Pro Shop. Organizations such as this do not simply decide to renovate or expand operations based on an impulse. Nor do they decide to acquire an existing business or open a new location that way. Managers spend a great deal of time analyzing past sales data along with projected future sales data to determine whether every strategy from beginning to end has the desired results in mind: increased profit or greater market share.

For example, if Red Bluff does expand or renovate its business, in what ways will it expand or renovate? Will the expansion include more space for the pro shop, an indoor golf simulator, or areas for guests to relax? Will it be for storing more of the retail products sold in the pro shop? Or will Red Bluff simply upgrade existing facilities? Management needs to know what the most popular services are before making any decisions about the types of areas to add. What about revenue? If a loan is taken out and Red Bluff's costs rise because of the interest on the loan, what sales volume or revenue does Red Bluff need to generate to cover the increased costs? CVP analysis is a way of evaluating the relationships among the fixed and variable costs, the sales volume—in terms of either units or dollars—and the profits. In this section, you will create a break-even analysis, work with conditional and custom formatting, use Goal Seek, and create data tables to analyze data.

Perform Break-Even Analysis

CVP analysis is used to help understand how changing volumes of sales or revenue affect profits. One of the main CVP analysis tools is **break-even analysis**, which can help managers understand the relationships among cost, volume, and profit. Managers can use break-even analysis to calculate the break-even point in sales volume or dollars, estimate profit or loss at any level of sales volume, and help in setting prices. The **break-even point** is the sales level at which revenue equals total costs; in other words, there is neither a profit nor a loss. Understanding how profit on an item or service is affected by other variables requires an analysis of the costs. This analysis helps to identify the items or services for which the profit changes as sales volume changes and those for which it does not.

When calculating the break-even point, you need to consider the fixed, variable, and mixed costs. **Fixed costs** are expenses that never change regardless of how much product is sold or how many services are rendered. For example, when the golf course is open for business, it must pay management salaries, insurance, depreciation of building and equipment, and some other costs, regardless of how many customers they have during the day. **Variable costs**, by contrast, do change according to how many products are sold or services are rendered. For example, with every new golf course membership, Red Bluff provides three personalized golf balls to the new member. The cost of ordering the customized golf balls depends on how many memberships are sold. Thus, the cost of the supplies used varies depending on the services rendered. **Mixed costs** are costs that contain a variable component and a fixed component. Consider utilities, such as electricity and water. Utility companies charge a specific amount; electric companies charge per kilowatt-hour used, and water companies charge a base fee and then an additional amount per gallon used, but the bill will vary depending on the usage per billing cycle.

To determine the break-even point, the golf course needs to consider all costs before it can determine its profit. For example, consider the Red Bluff Golf Course & Pro Shop golf polo shirts. The manufacturer charges $22.79—a variable cost—to produce one shirt. The total variable cost would be the variable cost per polo shirt multiplied by the number of polo shirts ordered. The manufacturer charges $15,000 per production run—a fixed cost—regardless of how many shirts are manufactured. This fee covers the costs that the manufacturer incurs to set up the production line. Red Bluff sells the golf polo shirts for $49.99 and would need to sell approximately 552 to break even. A graph displaying this analysis is shown in Figure 1.

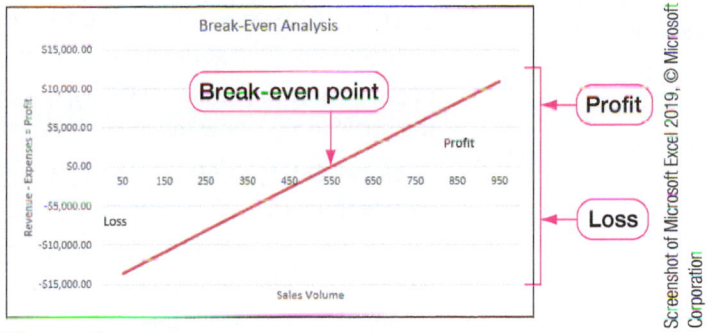

Figure 1   Break-even analysis chart

Opening the Starting File

Barry Cheney is considering raising the price of golf lessons. He has given you a workbook that includes information for some of the business activities, such as costs, prices, revenues, and profits, as provided by the accounting department. In this exercise, you will begin by opening the file.

E10.00

SIDE NOTE
Office Updates
Depending on your exact Office version, you may see Open or Open Other Workbooks.

To Open the Starting File

a. Start **Excel**, click **Open** in the left pane, and then double-click **This PC**. Navigate through the folder structure to the location of your student data files, and then double-click **e05ch10ExpansionAnalysis**. An Excel workbook opens that contains several worksheets containing information for a variety of business activities.

b. Click the **File** tab, click **Save As**, and then double-click **This PC**. In the Save As dialog box, navigate to the location where you are saving your project files, and then change the file name to e05ch10ExpansionAnalysis_LastFirst using your last and first name. Click **Save**.

Performing a Break-Even Analysis

The Red Bluff Golf Course & Prop Shop offers golf lessons to its clients for a fee of $140.00 per lesson. The cost for each golf lesson is composed of both fixed and variable costs. In this exercise, by conducting a break-even analysis, you will determine the minimum number of clients Red Bluffs needs to have signed up for golf lessons to offset the costs.

▶ E10.01

SIDE NOTE
Pin the Ribbon
If your ribbon is collapsed, pin your ribbon open. Click the **Home** tab. In the lower-right corner of the ribbon, click Pin the ribbon .

To Perform a Break-Even Analysis

a. If necessary, click the **Break-Even Analysis** worksheet. Click cell **D6**, type = click cell **D4**, type * and then click cell **D5**. Press Enter to calculate the gross revenue from golf lessons.

b. Click cell **D13**, type =SUM and then press Tab to insert the function. Select cells **D9** through **D12**, and then press Enter to calculate the total fixed costs of providing golf lessons.

c. Click cell **D15**, type = click cell **D6**, type * and then click cell **C15**. Press Enter to calculate the total commission the golf instructors will earn.

SIDE NOTE
**No Value Displays
in Cell D6**
Once you enter a value
in cell D4, all zeros will
be replaced with values.

d. In cell D16, type = click cell **C16**, type * and then click cell **D4**. Press Enter to calculate the total cost of supplies.

e. In cell D17, type = click cell **D15**, type + and then click cell **D16**. Press Enter to calculate the total variable costs.

f. In cell D18, type = click cell **D13**, type + and then click cell **D17**. Press Enter to calculate the total expenses.

g. In cell D19, type = click cell **D6**, type — and then click cell **D18**. Press Enter to calculate the net income—how much profit the golf course will generate from golf lessons.

h. Click cell **D4**, type 50 and then press Ctrl+Enter to try to find the break-even point. Notice that your net income is still negative (–$1,648.10).

i. In cell D4, type 60 and then press Ctrl+Enter to try to find the break-even point. Notice that your net income is still negative (–$537.60). However, you are getting closer to finding the break-even point.

j. In cell D4, type 65 and then press Ctrl+Enter. Notice that your net income finally has become positive: $17.65. Thus, Red Bluff would need 65 clients to sign up for golf lessons before it would make a profit. If more than 65 clients sign up for golf lessons, more profit will be generated.

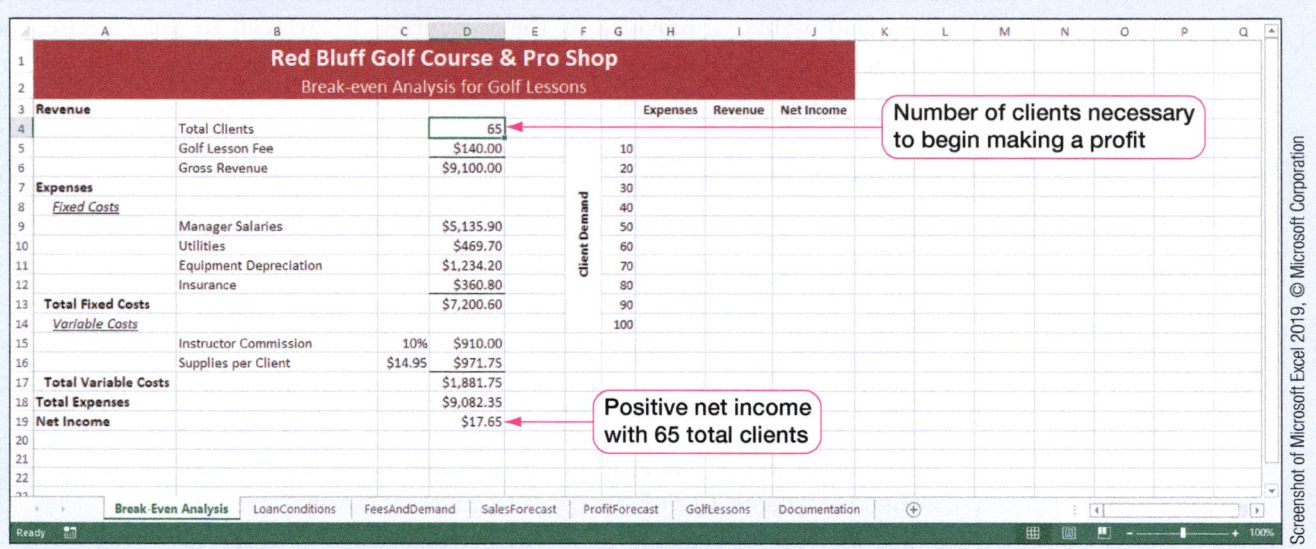

Figure 2 Working with a break-even analysis

k. **Save** the workbook.

S_S **CONSIDER THIS** | **What Are Your Costs?**

Have you ever thought about what type of costs you experience on a daily basis? Consider costs such as paying tuition, buying lunch, making a car payment, or paying student organization dues? Can you determine which of these would be fixed, variable, or mixed costs?

Using the Scroll Bar to Perform a Break-Even Analysis

Managers use break-even analysis to determine the minimum volume the business needs to make and sell if it is a manufacturer—or buy and sell if it is a retail business—to be sustainable. Once you know a variable cost per unit and total fixed costs, you can calculate the break-even point. By knowing the break-even point, you can set sales goals, prices, and employee hours. When you entered various numbers in the previous exercise, you were performing what-if analysis. **What-if analysis** is the use of several different values in one or more formulas to explore all the various results. These different values are called variables. A **variable** is a value that you can change to see how the change affects other values. Throughout your career, your day will consist of what-if questions. For example, "What if you sell more golf lessons at a lower price? Would you generate more net revenue than if you sold fewer at a higher price?"

REAL WORLD ADVICE | **The Operative Word Is "Tool"**

The operative word in what-if analysis tools is "tool." It is important to understand that these tools help managers analyze data so the manager can make the best decision based on the information he or she has. Analyzing data is only one component of decision making. Managers make decisions through exploring different options as well as reviewing documents, personal knowledge, or business models to identify and solve problems and make decisions. These tools support organizational decision-making activities and are a method of analyzing and interpreting data.

Another way to determine the break-even point in Excel is by using a scroll bar. The **scroll bar** is a form control that allows you to change a number in a target cell location in single-unit increments. The scroll bar is a type of **scenario tool** because of the ability to calculate numerous outputs in other cells by referencing the target cell in formulas and functions. When you use scenario tools to aid in decision making, you are performing what-if analysis. For example, Red Bluff managers can use the scroll bar to change the number of clients and price of each golf lesson to determine when the business will meet and exceed its profit goal. This can be a challenge to determine whether you were to perform this analysis manually—by entering random numbers into cells—because it is extremely time consuming and you do not want users to make physical changes to your spreadsheet model. Additionally, in many cases, when the price increases, the total number of items that can be sold will decrease. In this example, the higher the price of a golf lesson, the fewer clients Red Bluff will have booking the service.

REAL WORLD ADVICE | **The Scroll Bar Can Be Used with the VLOOKUP Function**

If you are given a table of data, such as quantity and price information, you can use a VLOOKUP function to help connect values. For example, when the lesson fee is changed in cell D5, the VLOOKUP function will display a new value—Total Clients—in cell D4. When the values in cells D4 and D5 change, the results in Gross Revenue, Instructor Commission, Supplies per Client, Total Variable Costs, Total Expenses, and Net Income also change.

QUICK REFERENCE | **Adding the Developer Tab**

Before you can add a scroll bar, you first need to add the Developer tab. Click the File tab, click Options, and then click Customize Ribbon. On the right side of the window, under Customize the Ribbon, click to select the check box next to Developer under the Main Tabs list. Click OK.

In this exercise, you will incorporate the scroll bar form control into the break-even analysis to make it easier to determine the number of clients necessary for Red Bluff to break even.

 **E10.02**

To Use the Scroll Bar to Perform a Break-Even Analysis

a. Click the **Developer** tab, and then, in the Controls group, click **Insert**.

b. Click **Scroll Bar (Form Control)** ▤, and then draw the scroll bar in the area of cells **E4** through **E17**. Be careful to avoid selecting the ActiveX Scroll Bar from the Insert menu.

MAC SIDE NOTE
Displaying the Developer Tab
On a Mac, point above the ribbon to display the Excel menu bar. Click Excel, and then click Preferences. In the Excel Preferences window, under Authoring, select Ribbon & Toolbar. In the right pane, under Customize the Ribbon, click to select the Developer check box and click Save.

> ### Mac Troubleshooting
> Add the scrollbar control horizontally and then change the height and width on the Shape Format tab so that it appears vertical. The Height should be about 3" and the Width 0.5".

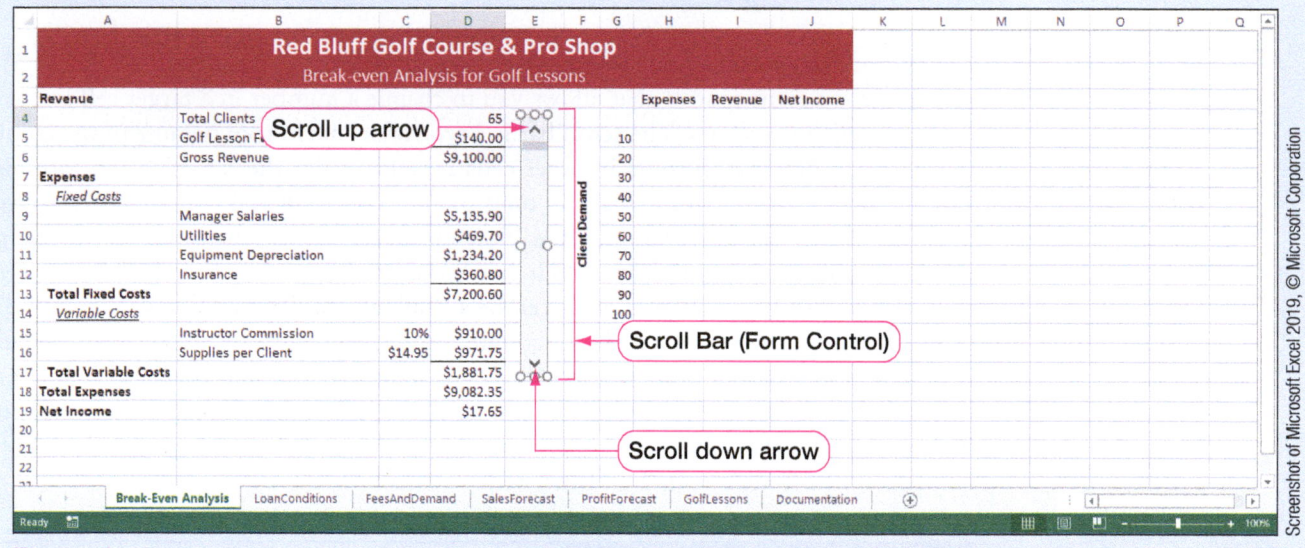

Figure 3 Break-even analysis using the scroll bar

SIDE NOTE
Alternative Method
You can also right-click the scroll bar and then click Format Control to enter the scroll bar properties.

c. On the Developer tab, in the Controls group, click **Properties**. In the Format Control dialog box, click the **Control** tab, if necessary. Because you want to analyze the net income from 60 to 120 clients, you need to type the following criteria in the Format Control dialog box.

- Current value: type **65**

- Minimum value: type **60**

- Maximum value: type **120**

- Incremental change: leave at the default value of 1

- Page change: leave at the default value of 10

- Cell link: click cell **D4**, moving the dialog box if necessary

SIDE NOTE
Circles Around the Edge
The circles around the edge mean the control is active. To deactivate the control, click a blank area away from it.

> ### Mac Troubleshooting
> On a Mac, right-click the Scroll Bar control and select Format Object to access the properties.

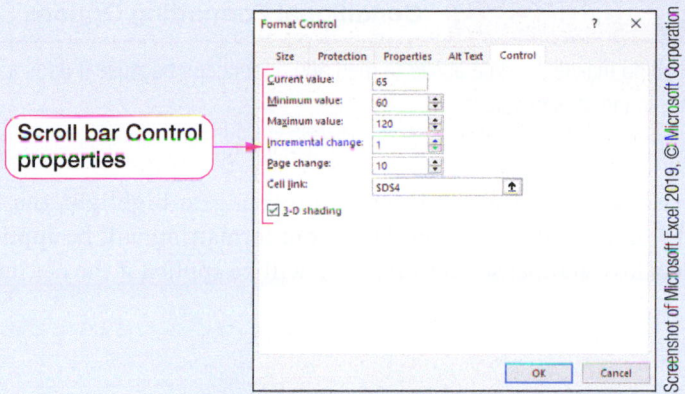

Scroll bar Control properties

Figure 4 Format Control dialog box

Screenshot of Microsoft Excel 2019, © Microsoft Corporation

SIDE NOTE
Select an Existing Control
To select an existing control object, press Ctrl, and then click the control.

d. Click **OK**, click a cell away from the scroll bar to deactivate the scroll bar, and then click the **up** arrow on the scroll bar.

You will notice that the value in cell D4 decreases. Analyze the net income for 50 to 120 clients.

e. Scroll down to the maximum value of 120 by clicking the **down** arrow on the scroll bar.

Notice that with 120 clients, the golf course would make a profit of $6,125.40.

f. Scroll up until you have a net income that is at the break-even point. Notice that the golf course would have to service 65 clients to make a profit.

g. Save the workbook.

CONSIDER THIS | **How Would You Use the Scroll Bar?**

Using the scroll bar can be a quick and easy method to find the break-even point once the spreadsheet has been formulated. How could you find the break-even point if you wanted higher pricing? Would it be easier to type values into the fee and clients cells? Would you rather change the data on the worksheet with a scroll bar? Which would be more efficient?

Using Conditional Formatting

When you format fonts, borders, alignment, fill colors, and so on, you are making the spreadsheet easier for you to use and read. The same is true of conditional formatting. **Conditional formatting** applies custom formatting to highlight or emphasize values that meet specific criteria, as seen in Table 1. This kind of formatting is called conditional because the formatting occurs when a particular condition is met. For example, a manager may want to highlight cells for employees who exceeded monthly sales quotas or products that are selling below cost.

Conditional Formatting	Description
Highlight Cells Rules	Highlights cells with a fill color, font color, or border if values are greater than a value, less than a value, between two values, equal to a value, or duplicate values
Top/Bottom Rules	Formats cells with values in the top 10 items, bottom 10 items, top 10%, bottom 10%, above average, below average, or other customizable values
Data Bars	Applies a color gradient or solid fill bar; the width of a solid fill bar symbolizes the current cell's value as compared to other cells' values
Color Scales	Formats different cells with different colors; one color is assigned to the lowest group of values, another color is assigned to the highest group of values, and gradient colors are assigned to other values
Icon Sets	Inserts an icon from the icon palette in each cell to point out values as compared to each other

Table 1 Conditional Formatting

QUICK REFERENCE | Conditional Formatting Options

Conditional formatting makes the data easier to read and understand because it adds a visual or graphical element to the cells or values.

In this exercise, you will use conditional formatting to highlight the Net Income value, in cell D19, in two different ways. One set of formatting will be applied if the net income results in a loss; another set of formatting will be applied if the net income results in a profit.

 **E10.03**

To Use Conditional Formatting

a. Click cell **D19**. Click the **Home** tab, and then in the Styles group, click **Conditional Formatting**. Point to Highlight Cells Rules, and then click **Less Than** to open the Less Than dialog box.

b. In the Format cells that are LESS THAN box, type **0** On the right side of the dialog box, click the **with arrow**, click to select the **Red Text** option, and then click **OK**.

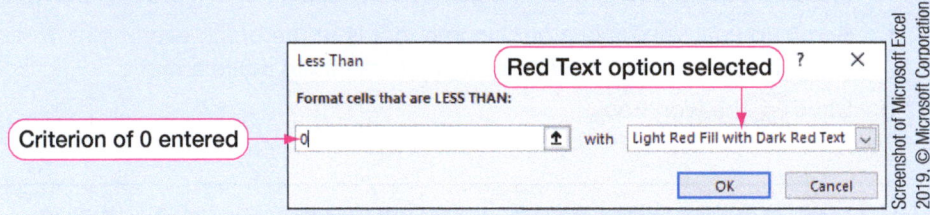

Figure 5 Less Than dialog box

c. In the Styles group, click **Conditional Formatting**, and then point to Highlight Cells Rules, and then click **Greater Than** to open the Greater Than dialog box.

d. In the Format cells that are GREATER THAN box, type **0** Click the **with arrow** on the right side of the dialog box, click to select the **Green Fill with Dark Green Text** option, and then click **OK**.

e. Click the **up** arrow on the scroll bar.

Notice that when the net income becomes a negative number, the font changes to red. This makes it easier for users to identify when the golf course has not reached the break-even point.

f. **Save** 💾 the workbook.

QUICK REFERENCE | Custom Formatting Can Be Created

Not only can you apply preset conditional formatting within Excel but you can also create your own formatting properties for fill colors, font colors, border colors, and so on. There are three ways to create custom formatting in Excel. Begin each option by clicking the Conditional Formatting button.

1. Point to Highlight Cells Rules, and after selecting a rule, click the arrow to choose a color, and click Custom Format.

2. Click New Rule.

3. Click Manage Rules to open the Conditional Formatting Rules Manager dialog box. The color can be changed for an existing rule by choosing Edit Rule.

| REAL WORLD ADVICE | How Much Is Too Much? |

Have you ever seen a document or web page that is so busy with colors and graphics that it is too difficult to read? Where do you draw the line when using conditional formatting or custom formatting? Not only can too much formatting make worksheets difficult for your audience to read, but it can make the worksheets difficult for you to maintain. Although formatting gives you more control over styles and icons, improved data bars, and the ability to highlight specific items and display data bars for negative values to more accurately illustrate your data visuals, consider what the repercussions can be if you format too much. Think about someone who is visually impaired or color-blind. What is appealing to you may not be easy for someone else to read.

Analyze Variables in Formulas Through the Use of Data Tables

Excel contains three types of what-if analysis tools: Goal Seek, Data Tables, and Scenario Manager. A **data table** takes sets of input values, determines possible results, and displays all the results in one table on one worksheet. Because data tables focus on only one or two variables, the results are easy to read and share in tabular form. Although it is limited to only one or two variables, a data table can include as many different variable values as needed.

Using One-Variable Data Tables

A **one-variable data table** has input values that are listed either down a column, referred to as column-oriented, or across a row, referred to as row oriented. A one-variable data table can help you analyze how different values of one variable in one or more formulas will change the results of those formulas. The formulas that are used in a one-variable data table must refer to only one input cell. For example, you can use a one-variable data table to see how different interest rates affect a monthly car payment by using the PMT function. In this case, the interest rate cell would be the input cell of the one-variable data table. The results display all possible interest rates provided in a data table after

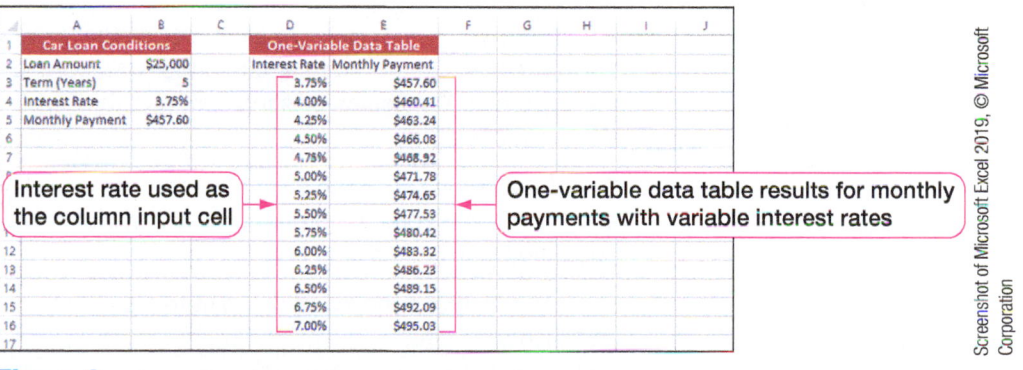

Figure 6 Analyzing data with a one-variable data table

Excel performs a what-if analysis on these variables, as shown in Figure 6.

In this exercise, you will help to create two one-variable data tables: one determines how much the monthly payment on a loan would be based on varying interest rates; the other determines how the changes in client demand for golf lessons will affect the expenses, revenue, and net income. You will also apply some conditional formatting to add emphasis and increase the readability of the worksheets. Finally, you will build a traditional cost-volume-profit chart based on the one-variable data table that will further analyze the break-even point for golf lesson pricing.

 **E10.04**

To Use One-Variable Data Tables

a. Click the **LoanConditions** worksheet, click cell **D3**, type **5**, and then press Enter. In cell D4, type **6** and then press Enter. Select the cell range **D3:D4**, and then drag to fill down to cell **D9**. Click cell **E2**, type **=** click cell **B6**, and then press Enter.

b. Right-click cell **E2**, and then select **Format Cells**. In the Format Cells dialog box, if necessary, click the **Number** tab. Under Category, click **Custom**, and then click the **Type** box. Delete any existing text, and then type "Monthly Payment" (including the quotation marks) to hide the results of the formula and display the typed text as a column heading. Click **OK**, and then select the range **D2:E9** to select the data for your data table.

c. Click the **Data** tab, and then in the Forecast group, click **What-If Analysis**, and click **Data Table** to open the Data Table dialog box.

d. Click in the **Column input** cell box, click cell **B4**, and then click **OK**. Notice that Excel calculated the monthly payment for each interest rate.

e. Select the range **E3:E9**. Click the **Home** tab, and then in the Styles group, click **Conditional Formatting**. Point to Data Bars, and then, under Gradient Fill, select **Green Data Bar**.

SIDE NOTE
Using Cell B4 as the Column Input Cell
The interest rates used are listed in a column. This is why you entered the interest rate location—cell B4—into the column input cell box.

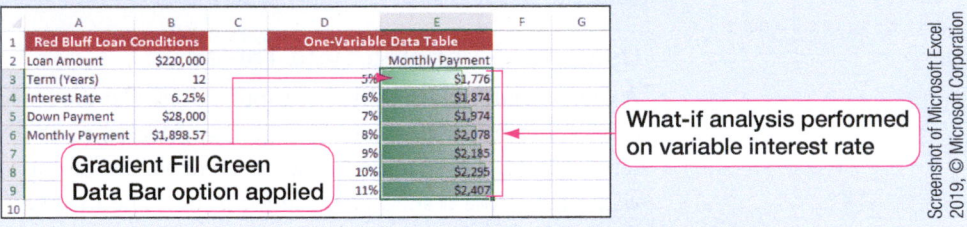

Figure 7 One-variable data table with conditional formatting

f. Click the **Break-Even Analysis** worksheet, and then click cell **H4**. Type **=** click cell **D18**, and then press Tab. In cell I4, type **=** then click cell **D6**, and press Tab. In cell J4, type **=** click cell **D19**, and then press Enter.

g. Select the range **H4:J4**, right-click any of the **selected cells**, and then select **Format Cells**. On the Number tab, under Category, click **Custom**, and then click the **Type** box. Delete any existing text, and then type **;;;** to hide the results of the formulas. Click **OK**.

h. Select the range **G4:J14** to select the data for your data table. Click the **Data** tab, and then in the Forecast group, click **What-If Analysis**, and click **Data Table** to open the Data Table dialog box.

i. Press Tab to move the insertion point to the Column input cell box, click cell **D4**, and then click **OK**.

Notice that Excel calculated the expenses, revenue, and profit based on client demand.

SIDE NOTE
Hiding Formulas in Data Tables
Excel requires at least one formula to be referenced for a data table. Having them visible does not add any value, so custom formatting is often used to hide them.

j. Select the range **J5:J14**. Click the **Home** tab, and then, in the Styles group, click **Conditional Formatting**. Point to **Highlight Cells Rules**, and then click **Less Than** to open the Less Than dialog box. In the Format cells that are LESS THAN box, type **0** click the **with** arrow in the box to the right, and then, if necessary, click the **Light Red Fill with Dark Red Text** option. Click **OK**.

k. Click **Conditional Formatting** again, point to Highlight Cells Rules, and then click **Greater Than** to open the Greater Than dialog box. In the Format cells that are GREATER THAN, type **2000** click the **with** arrow in the box to the right, and then click the **Green Fill with Dark Green Text** option. Click **OK**.

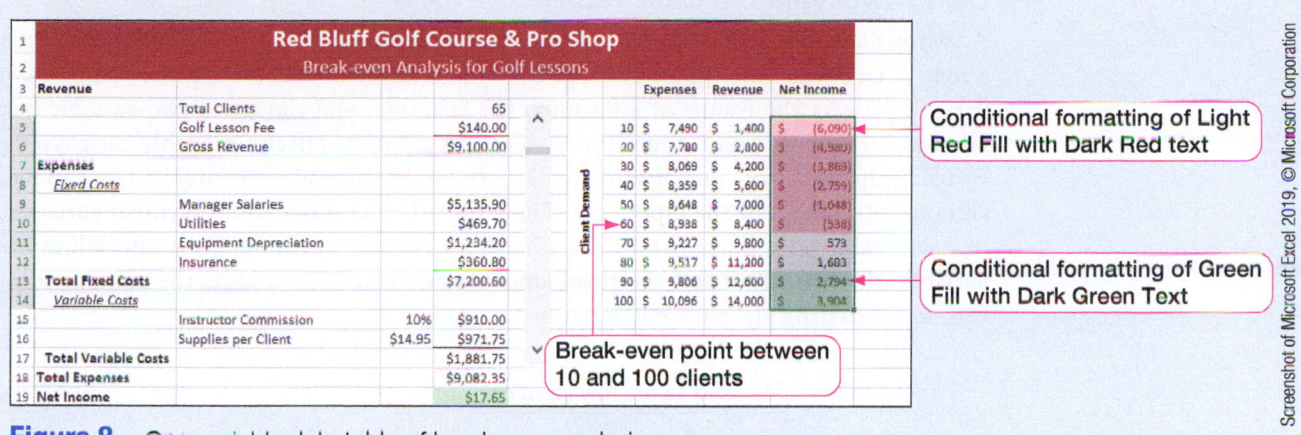

Figure 8 One-variable data table of break-even analysis

Screenshot of Microsoft Excel 2019, © Microsoft Corporation

SIDE NOTE
Data Tables Automatically Updated
If you change the formula used as a row or column input, the data table will be updated automatically.

l. Select the range **G3:I3**, hold down Ctrl, and then select the range **G5:I14**. Click the **Insert** tab, and then in the Charts group, click **Line** , and then select **Line** in the 2-D Line category. Click the **border edge** of the Line chart, and then drag to move it until the top-left corner is in cell **F16**.

m. Click **Chart Elements** ⊞, click the **arrow** to the right of Axis Titles, and then click the check box for **Primary Horizontal.**

n. Click the **horizontal axis title** text box, and type Client Demand

o. Click the **Chart Title** text box, and type Cost-Volume-Profit

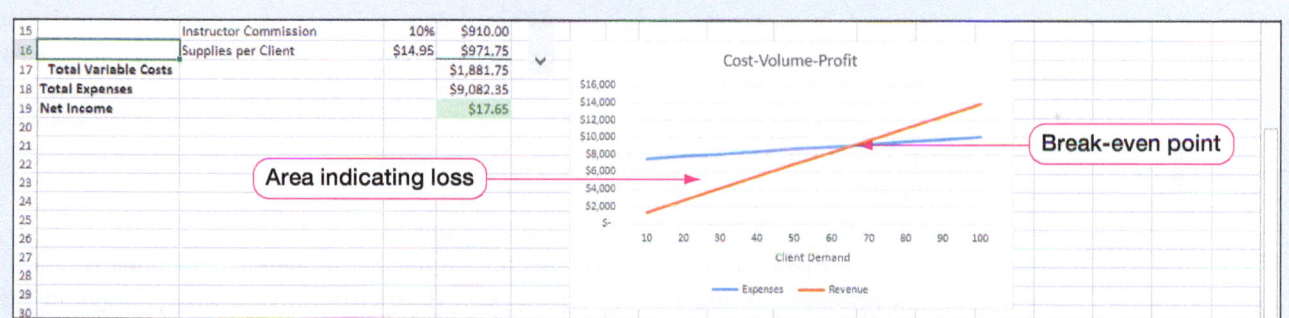

Figure 9 Traditional cost-volume-profit chart

Screenshot of Microsoft Excel 2019, © Microsoft Corporation

p. Click any cell outside the chart to deselect it. Press Ctrl+Home to select cell A1.

q. **Save** 🖫 the workbook.

S̲S̲ CONSIDER THIS | **What Does the Chart Tell You?**

Have you ever heard that a picture is worth a thousand words? Look at the chart you just created. Can you tell where the break-even point is? Is it easier to look at the chart and tell instantly, or is it easier to look at the data table?

Using Two-Variable Data Tables

A two-variable data table has input values that are listed both down a column and across a row. A **two-variable data table** can help you analyze how changing the value of two variables affects the results of a formula. For example, you can use a two-variable data table to see how different interest rates and loan amounts affect a monthly car payment by using the PMT function as shown in Figure 10. In this case, the interest rate and loan amount cells would be the input cells. The results display all possible payment variations in a data table after Excel performs a what-if analysis using the interest rate cell as one variable, the row input cell, and loan amounts as the other variable, the column input cell, in calculating the payment variations.

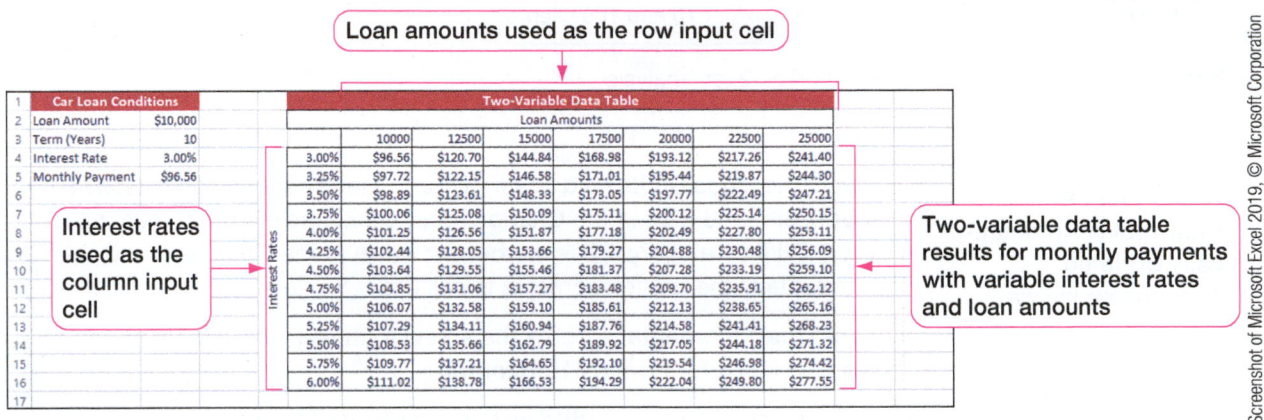

Figure 10   Two-variable data table for a car loan

A two-variable data table can be useful when you want to analyze the relationships among cost, sales volume, and profit. When doing so, you need to consider how demand affects the price of a product or service. The analyses you have performed thus far have assisted in determining the break-even point for products and services. Additionally, you have considered the quantity of products that may be sold or the number of clients that may be serviced. The bottom line is that these analyses have clearly indicated how this relationship between the price and revenue affects demand.

A product or service is **elastic**—or responsive to change—if a small change in price is accompanied by a large change in the quantity demanded. The opposite is also true. A product is **inelastic**—or not responsive to change—if a large change in price is accompanied by a small amount of change in demand. This effect is known as the price elasticity of demand and can be calculated by dividing the change in quantity demanded by the change in price. When you are calculating the elasticity as shown in Figure 11, some assumptions do need to be made about your business and how any changes in price will affect demand. The quotient is conveyed as an absolute value because it is assumed that demand will never increase when prices increase.

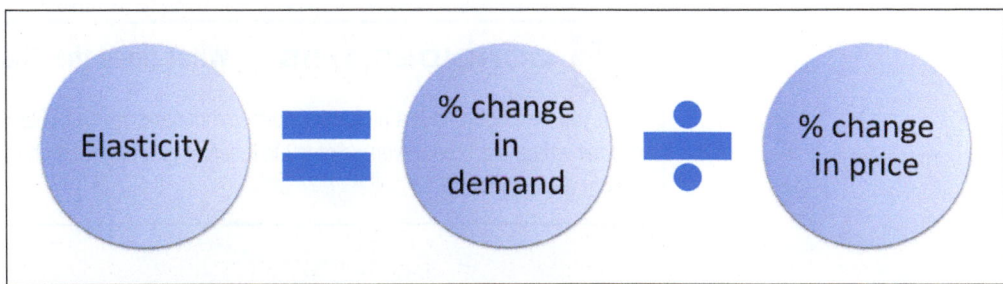

Figure 11   Elasticity formula

For example, the Red Bluff manager may assume that if he increases the price of golf lessons by 15%, demand will decrease by 20%. When calculating the elasticity, you are calculating the price elasticity of demand. Thus, if Barry wanted to calculate the elasticity of demand, the equation would be as shown in Figure 12.

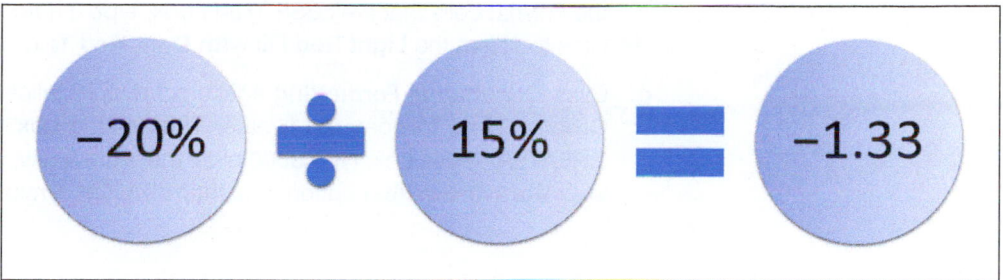

Figure 12   Elasticity calculation of price increase for golf lessons

In this formula, a decrease in demand of 20% divided by a 15% increase in price equals −1.33. Elasticity calculations can be evaluated as absolute values. Here, the elasticity value is 1.33. However, instead of having to calculate and interpret elasticity, you can use a two-way data table to view how the price of a product or service responds to change.

REAL WORLD ADVICE	A Two-Variable Data Table Is Not Calculating Elasticity

The two-variable data table you are creating does not actually tell you about the elasticity of price versus demand. It calculates the outcomes of varying prices of golf lessons and client demand. In determining selling prices or financing a project, the risk is that the yield will not generate enough revenue to cover operating costs and to repay debt obligations. A two-variable data table gives you another way of assessing the risk associated with pricing a product or service at a certain level or anticipating a specific level of demand.

In this exercise, you will create a two-variable data table to determine how much net income would be generated for golf lessons based on varying prices and varying client demand.

 **E10.05**

To Use Two-Variable Data Tables

a. Click the **FeesAndDemand** worksheet, click cell **E3**, type = click cell **B7** to reference the Net Income formula that Excel will use to calculate your data table, and then press Enter.

b. Right-click cell **E3**, and then click **Format Cells**. On the Number tab, under Category, click **Custom**, click the **Type** box, delete any text, and then type ;;; to use custom formatting to hide the formula results. Click **OK**.

c. Select the range **E3:L16** to select the data for your data table. Click the **Data** tab, then, in the Forecast group, click **What-If Analysis**, and then click **Data Table** to open the Data Table dialog box.

d. With the insertion point in the Row input cell box, click cell **B3**, and then press Tab to move to the Column input cell box. Click cell **B2**, and then click **OK**.

Notice that Excel calculated the net income for the combination of client demand and golf lesson fees.

e. Select the range **F4:L16**, and then click the **Home** tab. In the Number group, click the **Number Format** arrow [General], and then click **Currency**.

f. On the Home tab, in the Styles group, click **Conditional Formatting**, point to Highlight Cells Rules, and then click **Less Than** to open the Less Than dialog box. In the Format cells that are LESS THAN box, type 0 If necessary, click the **with** arrow, click to select the **Light Red Fill with Dark Red Text** option, and then click **OK**.

g. Click **Conditional Formatting** again, point to Highlight Cells Rules, and then click **Greater Than** to open the Greater Than dialog box. In the Format cells that are GREATER THAN box, type 3500 click the **with** arrow, click to select the **Green Fill with Dark Green Text** option, and then click **OK**. Press Ctrl+Home to select cell A1.

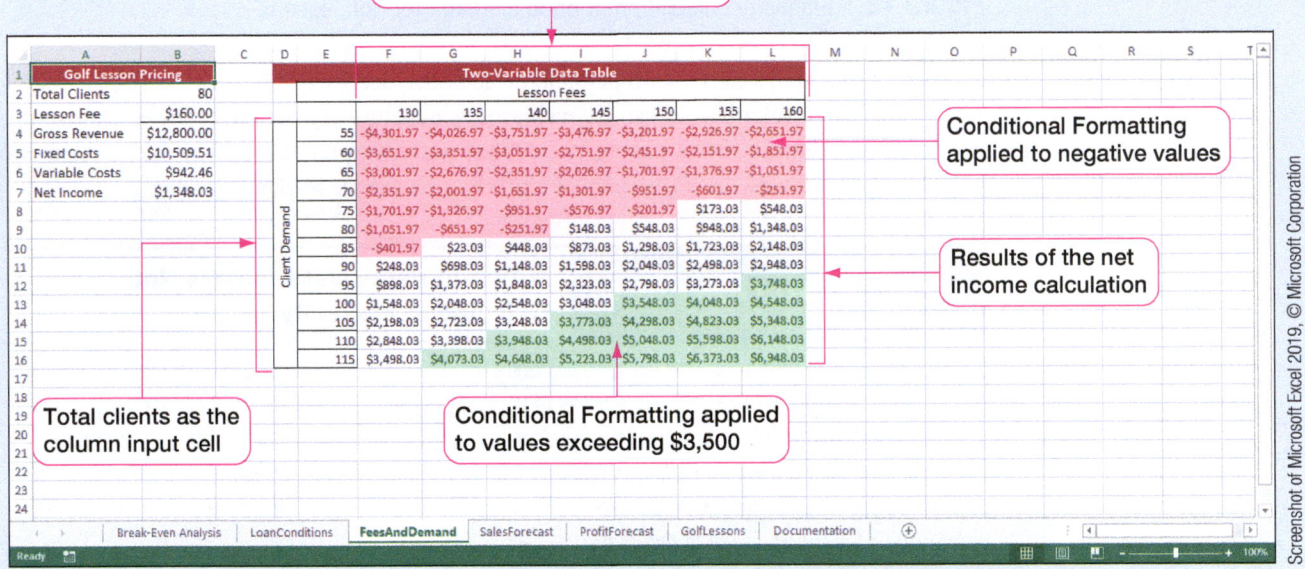

Figure 13 Two-variable data table of lesson fees and client demand

h. Save 💾 the workbook.

QUICK REFERENCE | **Interpreting Elasticity**

Products and services are often evaluated by their elasticity. When interpreting elasticity, consider the following.

- Relatively elastic: If the elasticity is greater than 1, demand is very responsive to changes in price.

- Relatively inelastic: If the elasticity is less than 1, large changes in price will cause small changes in demand.

- Perfectly elastic: For high elasticity values, any change in price causes a vast change in demand.

- Perfectly inelastic: For elasticity values of zero, a change in price has no influence on demand.

- Unit elastic: For elasticity values of 1, any change in price results in an equal and opposite change in demand.

Use Goal Seek to Determine Values Needed to Achieve an Objective

Goal Seek is another scenario tool that maximizes Excel's cell-referencing capabilities and enables you to find the input values needed to achieve a goal or objective. To use Goal Seek, you select the cell—variable cell—containing the formula that will return the result you are seeking. Once you have selected the cell, indicate the target value you want the formula to return. Then, finally, select the location of the input value that Excel can change to reach the target. In simpler terms, when you perform Goal Seek, Excel is manipulating the data much as you would in an algebraic equation that requires you to solve for x.

Through a process called **iteration**, Goal Seek repeatedly enters new values in the variable cell to find a solution to the problem. Iteration continues until Excel has run the problem 100 times or has found an answer that is within .001 of the target value you specified. Because Goal Seek calculates so quickly, you save significant time and effort. Without Goal Seek, you would have to manually type one number after another in the formula or a related cell to attempt to find the solution.

Using Goal Seek

In this exercise, you will use Goal Seek to determine the number of boxes of golf balls and high-performance golf polo shirts Red Bluff needs to sell to meet its sales goals as well as the selling price of golf shorts and golf umbrellas required to meet its sales goals.

To Use Goal Seek

a. Click the **SalesForecast** worksheet, and then click cell **E5**.

b. Click the **Data** tab, and then in the Forecast group, click **What-If Analysis**, and then click **Goal Seek** to open the Goal Seek dialog box. Excel automatically selects the active cell as the Set cell value—in this case, cell E5.

> Red Bluff wants to set a sales goal of $27,500 for stock golf balls. Because you know the selling price and target goal, you can calculate the quantity of boxes needed to sell to meet the sales goal.

c. Click the **To value** box, type 27500 press [Tab] to move to the By changing cell box, and then click cell **C5**.

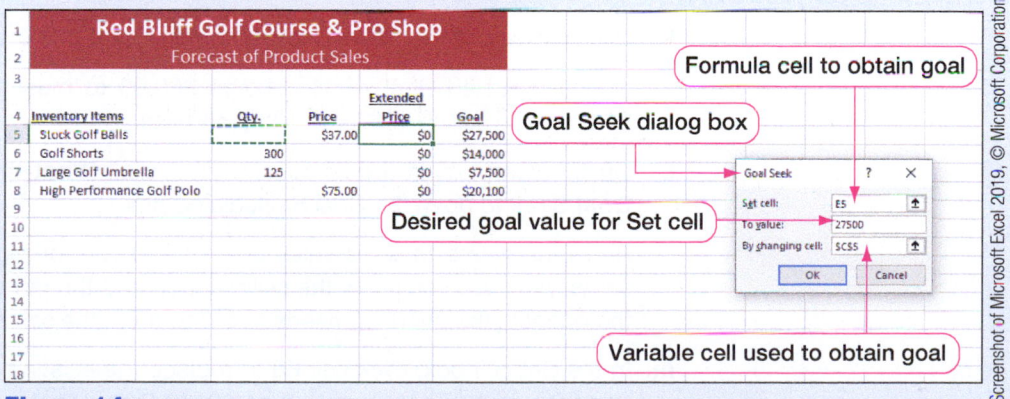

Figure 14   What-if analysis using Goal Seek

d. Click **OK** twice to run Goal Seek, and then **close** the Goal Seek Status dialog box.

> Notice that to reach its $27,500 sales goal for stock golf balls, Red Bluff would need to sell 743.24 packages of golf balls.

e. Click cell **C5**. Click the **Home** tab, then, in the Number group, click the **Number Format** arrow `General`, click **Number**, and then click the **Decrease Decimal** button twice to format with no decimal places because the pro shop cannot sell part of a package of golf balls.

> ## Troubleshooting
>
> If Excel displays in the Goal Seek Status dialog box that it could not find a viable solution, click Cancel, and then ensure that you have entered the correct values in the Goal Seek dialog box. Some rules to keep in mind: Verify that the Set cell box contains a formula, the To value box contains the result desired for the formula, and the By changing cell box contains a reference to the cell that can be adjusted to achieve the goal.

f. Click the **Data** tab, and then in the Forecast group, click **What-If Analysis**. Click Goal then click Goal Seek to open the **Goal Seek** dialog box.

Red Bluff wants to set a sales goal of $14,000 for golf shorts. Because you know the quantity and target goal, you can calculate the price that must be charged to meet the sales goal.

g. In the Set cell box, replace the existing cell reference by clicking cell **E6**, press Tab, and then, in the To value box, type **14000** Press Tab to move to the By changing cell box, and then click cell **D6**.

h. Click **OK** twice to run Goal Seek, and then **close** the Goal Seek Status dialog box.

Notice that Red Bluff should charge $46.67 to meet its sales revenue goal of $14,000 from selling 300 pairs of golf shorts.

i. On the Data tab, in the Forecast group, click **What-If Analysis**, and then click **Goal Seek** to open the Goal Seek dialog box.

Red Bluff wants to set a sales goal of $7,500 for large golf umbrellas. Because you know the quantity and target goal, you can calculate the price that must be charged to meet the sales goal.

j. In the Set cell box, click cell **E7** to replace the existing cell reference, press Tab, and then, in the To value box, type **7500** Press Tab to go to the By changing cell box, and then click cell **D7**.

k. Click **OK** twice to run Goal Seek, and then **close** the Goal Seek Status dialog box.

Notice that Red Bluff should charge $60.00 to meet its sales revenue goal of $7,500 from selling 125 large golf umbrellas.

l. On the Data tab, in the Forecast group, click **What-If Analysis**, and then click **Goal Seek** to open the Goal Seek dialog box.

Red Bluff wants to set a sales goal of $20,100 for high-performance golf polo shirts. Because you know the selling price and the target goal, you can calculate the quantity the pro shop needs to sell to meet the sales goal.

m. In the Set cell box, click cell **E8** to replace the existing cell reference, press Tab, and then, in the To value box, type **20100** Press Tab to go to the By changing cell box, and then click cell **C8**.

n. Click **OK** twice to run **Goal Seek**, and then **close** the Goal Seek Status dialog box.

Notice that if 268 high-performance golf polo shirts are sold, the sales revenue goal of $20,100 will be met.

o. Click cell **C5**. Click the **Home** tab, and then in the Clipboard group, click **Format Painter**, and select the cell range **C6:C8** to copy the Number format settings to these cells. Press Ctrl+Home to select cell A1.

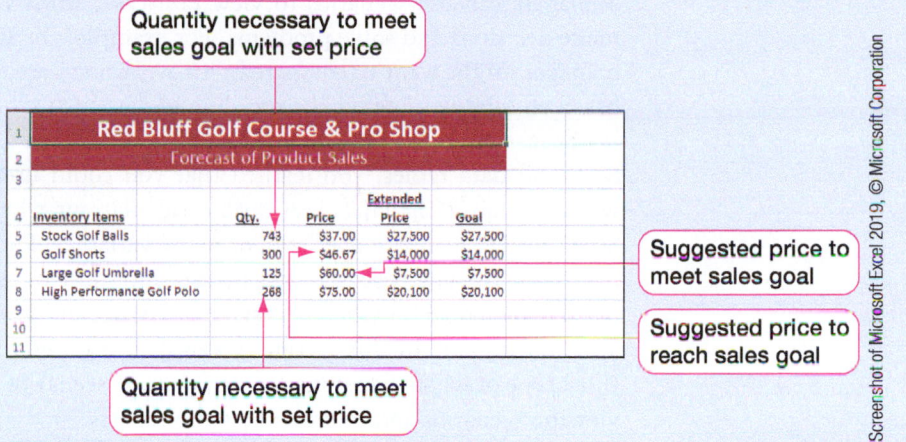

Figure 15 Results of Goal Seek analysis

p. **Save** 🖫 the workbook.

If you need to take a break before finishing this chapter, now is a good time.

REAL WORLD ADVICE | **Goal Seek Can Be Used for Basic Forecasting**

When managers forecast, they are estimating or predicting future occurrences of sales, manufacturing needs, inventory, and so on, by looking at past data, such as the past three years of sales trends. Goal Seek determines the unknown value that produces a desired result, such as the number of $32 boxes of stock golf balls the pro shop must sell to reach its goal of $25,000. Goal Seek is simple because it is streamlined, can calculate only one unknown value, and can be helpful in a variety of forecasting efforts.

QUICK REFERENCE | **Changing Excel's Iteration Settings**

Excel's default iteration settings can be changed by completing the following steps.

1. Start Excel, and then click the File tab.
2. Click Options.
3. Click Formulas in the left pane.
4. Under Calculation options, click Enable iterative calculation.
5. Select the Maximum Iterations and Maximum Change you would like Excel to perform.
6. Click OK.

Using the Scenario Manager

A **scenario** allows you to build a what-if analysis model that includes variable cells linked by one or more formulas or functions. By running the scenarios, you can compare multiple variables and their combined effects on the various calculated outcomes. Managers can use scenarios to view best-case, worst-case, and most likely scenarios to make decisions and solve problems. For example, the Red Bluff Golf Course & Pro Shop manager might want to compare best-case, worst-case, and most likely scenarios for sales based on sales volumes at the pro shop in a week.

Scenarios can be most beneficial because they can use multiple variables. Using Goal Seek and data tables, you learned that you could use what-if analysis tools when you want to analyze the effects on various calculations when inputting one or two variables. Scenarios can evaluate one, two, or many variables. For example, the Red Bluff manager may want to view best-case, worst-case, and most likely scenarios of the pro shop's total net income based on variable costs, fixed costs, and gross revenue of both retail products and golf lessons. In this section, you will learn how to use the **Scenario Manager**, the third type of what-if analysis tool, to manage scenarios by adding, deleting, editing, and viewing scenarios and to create scenario reports.

Use the Scenario Manager to Create Scenarios

You can use scenarios to predict the outcome of different situations in your spreadsheet. Before creating a scenario, you need to design your worksheet to contain at least one formula or function. This formula or function will rely on other cells and can have different values inserted into it. The significant step in creating the various scenarios is identifying the various data cells whose values can differ in each scenario. You can then select these cells—known as **changing cells**—in the worksheet before you open the Scenario Manager dialog box. Once the Scenario Manager dialog box is open, you can enter and define the different scenarios. Each scenario includes a scenario name, input or changing cells, and the values for each input cell.

Designing a Scenario

Barry Cheney would like you to determine how much net income—profit—the Red Bluff Golf Course & Pro Shop is forecasted to generate based on varying retail sales, revenue from services rendered, and variable costs.

In this exercise, you will enter the formulas that will help to calculate each scenario.

 **E10.07**

To Design a Scenario

a. If you took a break, open the **e05ch10ExpansionAnalysis_LastFirst** workbook.

b. Click the **ProfitForecast** worksheet.

c. Click cell **D6**, type **=SUM** and then press Tab to insert the function. Select cells **D4:D5** to calculate the forecasted total or gross revenue, and then press Enter.

d. Click cell **D13**, type **=SUM** and then press Tab to insert the function. Select cells **D9:D12** to calculate the total forecasted fixed costs, and then press Enter.

e. Click cell **D15**, type **=** click cell **D6**, type * and then click cell **C15** to calculate the forecasted employee commissions. Press Enter.

f. In cell D16, type **=** click cell **D13**, type + and then click cell **D15** to calculate the forecasted total expenses. Press Enter.

g. In cell D17, type **=** click cell **D6**, type − and then click cell **D16** to calculate the forecasted net income. Press Enter.

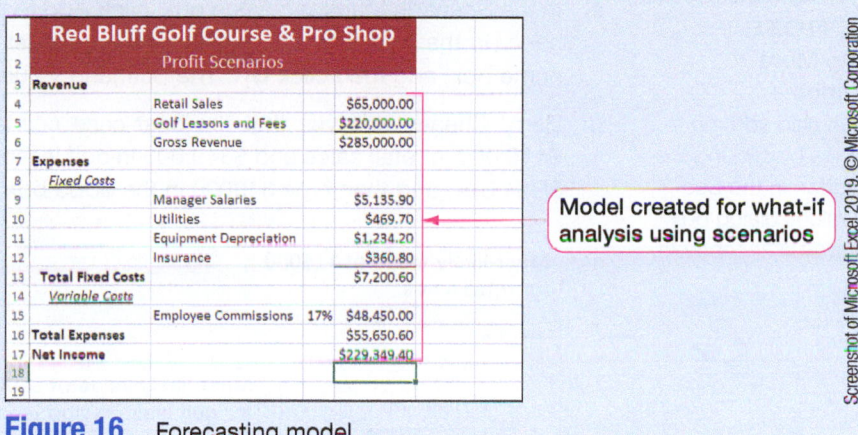

Figure 16 Forecasting model

h. **Save** 🖫 the workbook.

Adding, Deleting, and Editing Scenarios

Once you have identified the changing cells—which can be anywhere on your worksheet—you can then select these cells in the worksheet before you open the Scenario Manager dialog box, or you can enter the target cells directly into the Scenario Manager dialog box as well as entering and defining the different scenarios. Each scenario represents different what-if conditions to evaluate the spreadsheet model. Once scenarios have been added, they are stored under the name you assigned to them. The number of scenarios you can create is limitless.

In this exercise, you will use the Scenario Manager to create various profit scenarios for the Red Bluff Golf Course & Pro Shop.

 **E10.08**

To Add, Delete, and Edit Scenarios

a. On the **ProfitForecast** worksheet, select the range **D4:D5**. These will be your changing cells.

b. Click the **Data** tab, and then, in the Forecast group, click **What-If Analysis**, and select **Scenario Manager** to open the Scenario Manager dialog box.

c. In the Scenario Manager dialog box, click **Add** to begin creating your first scenario. In the Add Scenario dialog box, type Most Likely Scenario in the Scenario name box.

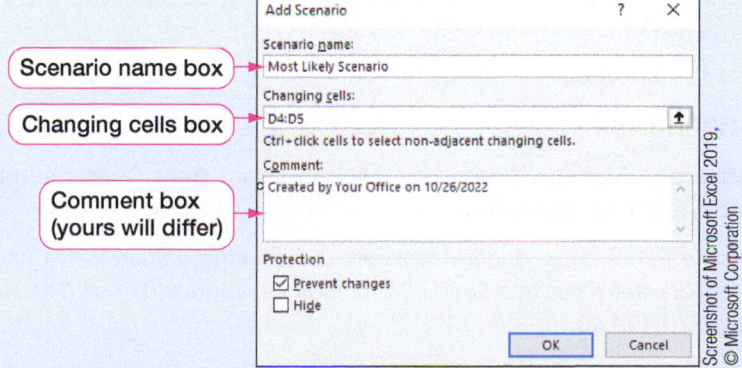

Figure 17 Add Scenario dialog box

d. Click **OK**. The values that are entered in cells D4 and D5 are the most likely scenario values. Click **OK**.

SIDE NOTE
Adding More Scenarios
You can also add more scenarios by clicking the Add button in the Scenario Values dialog box. Either way is acceptable.

e. In the Scenario Manager dialog box, click **Add** to begin creating your second scenario. In the Add Scenario dialog box, type Best Case Scenario in the Scenario name box, and then click **OK**. The Scenario Values dialog box will open.

f. Barry Cheney believes that the best-case scenario would result in revenue of $115,000 in retail sales and $340,000 in golf lessons and fees. Type 115000 in the $D$4 box, and then type 340000 in the $D$5 box.

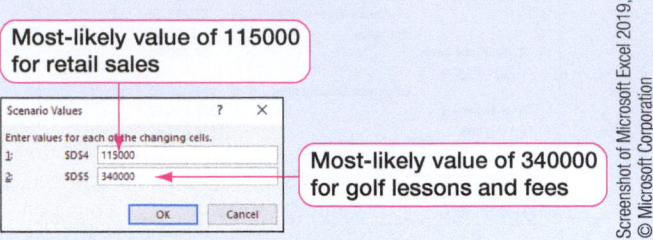

Figure 18   Scenario Values dialog box

g. Click **OK**, and then in the Scenario Manager dialog box, click **Add**.

h. In the Add Scenario dialog box, type Worst Case Scenario in the Scenario name box, and then click **OK**. The Scenario Values dialog box will open.

i. Barry Cheney believes that the worst-case scenario would result in revenue of $40,000 in retail sales and $90,000 in golf lessons and fees. Type 40000 in the $D$4 box, type 90000 in the $D$5 box, and then click **OK**.

j. Because Barry has already created a forecast with the most likely scenario values entered, he decided that he does not need this scenario and e-mails you to let you know. In the Scenario Manager dialog box, under Scenarios, click to select **Most Likely Scenario**, and then click **Delete** to delete the most likely scenario.

SIDE NOTE
Use Caution When Deleting Scenarios
Excel does not give a delete confirmation before deleting scenarios.

k. Barry also informed you that the worst-case scenario would have retail sales forecasted at $35,000. In the Scenario Manager dialog box, under Scenarios, click to select **Worst Case Scenario**, click **Edit**, and in the Edit Scenario dialog box, click **OK**.

l. In the $D$4 box of the Scenario Values dialog box, change 40000 to 35000, and then click **OK**.

Viewing Scenarios

After you create the scenarios, you can view the results by using the Show button at the bottom of the Scenario Manager dialog box. This is helpful to double-check whether the values entered in each scenario are accurate. Excel will replace the existing values in your spreadsheet with those entered into each scenario. In this exercise, you will view the various scenarios created.

 **E10.09**

To View Scenarios

a. In the Scenario Manager dialog box, click to select **Best Case Scenario** under Scenarios, and then click **Show**.

Notice how Excel automatically replaces the existing values in D4 and D5 with $115,000 for retail sales and $340,000 for Golf Lessons and Fees. The Net Income result is $370,499.40.

b. Under Scenarios, click to select the **Worst Case Scenario**, and then click **Show**.

Notice how Excel automatically replaces the existing values in D4 and D5 with $35,000 for retail sales and $90,000 for Golf Lessons and Fees. The Net Income result is $96,549.40.

Create Scenario Reports

Although you can view your scenarios while the Scenario Manager dialog box is open, you will probably want to view them side by side to compare the results. Additionally, it is not possible to print and distribute the scenarios very easily this way. You can create a Scenario Summary report automatically by clicking the Summary button in the Scenario Manager dialog box. A **Scenario Summary report** lists the results of scenarios side by side, allowing the outcomes to be easily compared. The Summary button opens the Scenario Summary dialog box where you can choose the type of report you would like to create.

Generating a Scenario Summary Report

By selecting the Scenario Summary option, you can create a worksheet that includes subtotals and the results of the scenarios.

In this exercise, you will create a Scenario Summary report so that Barry Cheney can view the current scenario modeled in the worksheet along with the best-case and worst-case scenarios.

 **E10.10**

To Generate a Scenario Summary Report

a. In the Scenario Manager dialog box, click **Summary** to open the Scenario Summary dialog box.

b. Leave the Report type at the default selection of Scenario summary, verify the Result cell is **D17**, and then click **OK**.

   Notice that Excel adds a new worksheet named Scenario Summary to your workbook.

c. Format the Scenario Summary report so it is easier to read. Select cells **B6:C6**, click the **Home** tab, and then in the Alignment group, click **Merge & Center**, and replace the $D$4 text by typing Retail Sales Press Enter.

d. Select cells **B7:C7**, click **Merge & Center**, and replace the $D$5 text by typing Lessons and Fees Press Enter. Adjust the width of column C so that the text can be read.

e. Select cells **B9:C9**. Click **Merge & Center**, and then replace the $D$17 text by typing Net Income Press Enter.

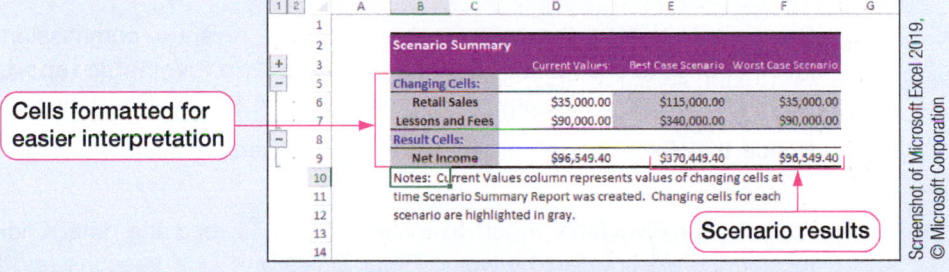

Figure 19 Scenario Summary report

f. **Save** the workbook.

Generating a Scenario PivotTable Report

A scenario PivotTable report can also be created automatically by clicking the Summary button in the Scenario Manager dialog box. The Summary button opens the Scenario Summary dialog box, where you can choose the Scenario PivotTable report option. A **Scenario PivotTable report** summarizes the results of various scenarios side by side in a

PivotTable format. In this exercise, you will create a Scenario PivotTable report that will allow management even more manipulation of data because of the two-dimensional view the report provides.

 **E10.11**

To Generate a Scenario PivotTable Report

a. Click the **ProfitForecast** worksheet.

b. Click the **Data** tab, and then in the Forecast group, click **What-If Analysis**. Click **Scenario Manager** to open the Scenario Manager dialog box.

c. In the Scenario Manager dialog box, click to select the **Best Case Scenario**, and then click **Edit**.

d. Barry Cheney wants to determine whether the Red Bluff Golf Course & Pro Shop can still be profitable if the employees earn different commissions based on sales. In the Edit Scenario dialog box, click the **Changing cells** box to place the insertion point after the range D4:D5, and then type **,C15** Click **OK**.

e. In the Scenario Values dialog box, in the $C$15 box, verify that the value displays 0.17 to reflect the commission of 17%, and then click **OK**.

f. In the Scenario Manager dialog box, click to select **Worst Case Scenario**, and then click **Edit**.

g. In the Edit Scenario dialog box, click the **Changing cells** box to place the insertion point after the range D4:D5, and then type **,C15** Click **OK**.

h. In the Scenario Values dialog box, click the **$C$15** box, delete the 0.17 value, type **0.095** to change the commission to 9.5%, and then click **OK**.

i. Barry also wants you to re-create the most likely scenario. In the Scenario Manager dialog box, click **Add**, type **Most Likely Scenario** in the Scenario name box, and then click **OK**. Your D4:D5, C15 changing cells will automatically be entered into the Changing cells box.

j. Type the following values for each changing cell in each box of the Scenario Values dialog box. Type **40000** in box 1, type **177500** in box 2, and type **0.12** in box 3.

k. Click **OK**, and then, in the Scenario Manager dialog box, click **Summary** to open the Scenario Summary dialog box.

l. Barry wants to view the ending values for gross revenue, commission, and net income. Click to change the Report type to **Scenario PivotTable report**, click the **Result cells** box, delete any existing text, type **D6,C15,D17** and then click **OK**.

Notice that Excel added a new worksheet named Scenario PivotTable to your workbook.

m. Format your PivotTable report to make it easier to read the data. Click cell **A1**, replace the existing text by typing **Retail Sales and Golf Lessons and Fees** and then press Enter. Click the **Home** tab and then in the Cells group, click **Format**. Click **Column Width**. In the Column width box, set the width of column A to **34** Click **OK**.

n. In cell **A2**, type **Scenario PivotTable Report** press Enter, select the range **A2:D2**, and then click **Merge & Center**. Click the **Bold** button ⓑ, click the **Font Size** arrow ⌷, and then click **16**.

o. Click cell **A3**, type **Scenarios** and then press Tab.

p. Add headings to your data. In cell **B3**, type **Gross Revenue** and then press Tab. In cell **C3**, type **Commission** and then press Tab. In cell **D3**, type **Net Income** and then press Enter.

q. Select the range **B3:D3**, and then in the Alignment group, click **Center**.

r. In the Cells group, click **Format**, and then click **Column Width**. In the Column width box type **14** and click **OK**.

s. Select the range **B4:B6**, hold down Ctrl, select the range **D4:D6**, then click the **Number Format** arrow, and then click **Currency**. Click the **Decrease Decimal** button two times to format with no decimal places.

t. Select the range **C4:C6**, click the **Number Format** arrow General, and then click **Percentage**. Click the **Increase Decimal** button once to format with one decimal place, and then press Ctrl+Home to return to cell A1.

Scenario results in PivotTable format

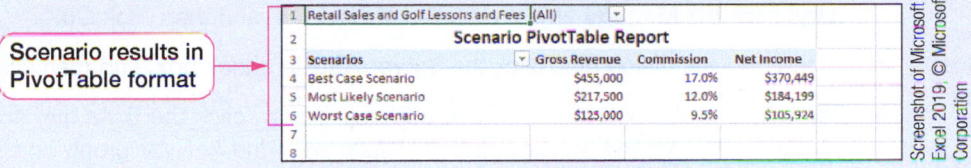

Figure 20 Scenario PivotTable report

u. **Save** the workbook.

If you need to take a break before finishing this chapter, now is a good time.

Using Solver

An important item to note is that there is no true or right answer on whether, or by how much, to raise prices. The answer depends in part on the businessperson's notion of how much demand he or she believes there is likely to be at the various prices and what that relationship is for that particular business. It may be risky to raise the price very high because a higher price will have lower demand, which means that fewer units are likely to be sold at the higher price. However, if the demand stays the same or is higher than expected, the profit potential is also higher. In this situation, a tool such as Solver can help to give a businessperson enough information to make an educated decision.

Excel's **Solver** is an add-in that helps to optimize a problem by manipulating the values for several variables with constraints that you determine. A **constraint** is a rule you establish when formulating your Solver model. You can use Solver to find the highest, lowest, or exact value for a specific outcome by adjusting values for selected variables. Business managers can use Solver to minimize or maximize the output based on the constraints. For example, the golf course manager could use Solver to determine a sales strategy that will help the golf course maximize its profit, given a specific mix of services provided to clients. In this section, you will learn how to load the Solver add-in; find optimal solutions by setting objectives, changing variable cells, and defining constraints. You will then generate a Solver answer report; and save and restore a Solver model.

Understand the Use of the Solver Add-In

Solver is one of many add-ins installed by default with Excel. However, it is not displayed on the ribbon by default. An **add-in** is an application with specific functionality geared toward accomplishing a specific goal. Because companies other than Microsoft develop the add-ins, they are not automatically activated when Excel is installed.

Loading the Solver Add-In

To use Solver, you need to activate the add-in. This is a one-time setup task; once you have activated the Solver add-in, it will appear on the Data tab on the ribbon each time you launch Excel. In this exercise, you will load the Solver add-in.

 E10.12

MAC SIDE NOTE
Loading the Solver Add-In
Point above the ribbon to display the menu bar and click Tools. At the bottom of the menu, click Excel Add-ins. In the Add-ins dialog box, click to select the Solver Add-in check box and click OK.

To Load the Solver Add-In

a. If you took a break, open the **e05ch10ExpansionAnalysis_LastFirst** workbook.

b. Click the **File** tab, click **Options**, and then click **Add-ins**.

c. At the bottom of the View and manage Microsoft Office Add-ins pane, if necessary, click the **Manage** arrow, click **Excel Add-ins**, and then click **Go**.

d. In the Add-Ins dialog box, click the **Solver Add-in** check box, and then click **OK**.

e. To verify that the Solver add-in was added properly, click the **Data** tab, and then check to see that the Solver button is displayed in the Analyze group on the right side of the ribbon.

Solve Complex Problems Using Solver

The purpose of using Solver is to perform what-if analysis to solve more complex problems and to optimize the outcome. When you **optimize**, you are finding the best way to do something. For example, Barry Cheney may want to find the best product mix of the pro shop's retail products to maximize profitability. He could use Solver to find the values of certain cells in a spreadsheet that optimize—maximize or minimize—a certain objective. Thus, Solver helps to answer this type of optimization problem.

Before configuring the Solver constraints, you need to ensure that you create a spreadsheet model that can be used to manipulate the values for your variables. This involves creating a target cell, which defines the goal of your problem. For example, Barry may create a formula that calculates total revenue. Additionally, you need to select one or more variable cells that Solver can change to reach the goal. You should evaluate your spreadsheet as you define your goal, identify one or more variables that can change in attaining the chosen goal, and then determine the limitations of the spreadsheet model. These variable cells are used to formulate the three Solver parameters: objective cell, changing cells, and constraints.

Your worksheet can also contain other values, formulas, and functions that use the target cell and the variable cells to reach the goal. For Solver to work properly, the formula in the target cell must reference and depend on the variable cells for part of its calculation. If you do not construct your Solver model in this format, you will get an error message that states, "The Set Target Cell values do not converge."

REAL WORLD ADVICE	Solver Can Be Used for Many Analyses

The Excel Solver add-in can be a powerful tool for analyzing data. In many financial planning problems, an amount such as the unpaid balance on a loan or the amount saved in a retirement fund changes over time. Consider a situation in which a business borrows money. Because only the principal of the monthly payment reduces the unpaid loan balance, the business may want to determine how it can minimize the total interest paid on the loan if it pays more than the minimum payment each month.

Setting the Objective Cell and Variable Cells

The **objective cell** contains the formula that creates a value that you want to optimize—maximize, minimize, or set to a specific value. For example, the golf course manager may want to maximize the gross revenue of golf lessons by analyzing the number of customers per day in relation to the total number of instructors employed. The golf course manager would have to consider many factors; however, deciding the actual goal of using Solver is the first step in creating a Solver analysis.

Solver works with a group of cells, called variable cells, which take part in calculating the formulas in the objective and constraint cells. Solver adjusts the values in the variable cells to satisfy the limits on constraint cells and return the result you want for the objective cell.

The golf course manager wants you to find the total number of clients, the number of hours of lessons per day, and the number of instructors on duty needed to maximize net income. The worksheet you were given was previously set up with functions to calculate the net income.

 **E10.13**

To Set the Objective Cell and Variable Cells

a. Click the **GolfLessons** worksheet.

b. On the Data tab, in the Analyze group, click **Solver**.

c. Because Barry Cheney wants to maximize the net income, the cell that holds the net income will become the objective cell. In the Solver Parameters dialog box, click in the Set Objective box, and then click cell **D20**, moving the Solver Parameters dialog box if necessary.

d. Because you need to maximize the net income, set the objective to **Max**, which is Excel's default value.

e. Two variables that will have an effect on the net income are the total number of clients and the number of instructors on duty. Click in the By Changing Variable Cells box, and then select cells **D4:D5**.

> ### Troubleshooting
> Pressing ⎆Enter or otherwise running Solver at this point will generate an error if the steps in the next exercise are not completed.

Defining Constraints

Constraints are the rules or restrictions that your variable cells must follow when the Solver performs its analysis. For example, if Barry Cheney wants to maximize the net income on the basis of how many golf lessons are given per day, he would have to consider how many hours per day the course is open, how many instructors work per day, and how long it takes to give a lesson. In addition, the cost of supplies can vary depending on how many clients the instructors have. In this exercise, you will use the Solver Parameters dialog box to identify the various constraints in the model.

 **E10.14**

To Define Constraints

a. In the Solver Parameters dialog box, click **Add** to enter the first constraint. The Add Constraint dialog box will open.

b. The golf course can have no more than four instructors scheduled at any given time. On the **GolfLessons** worksheet, in the Add Constraint dialog box, in the Cell Reference box, click cell **D5**. If necessary, click the arrow, to select **<=** in the mathematical operators box, and then, in the Constraint box, type **4**

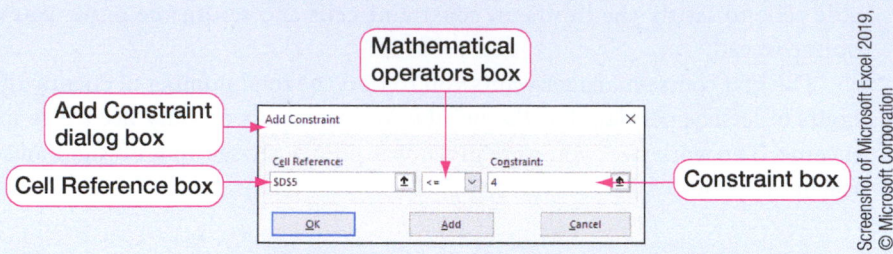

Figure 21 Add Constraint dialog box

c. Click **Add** to save the first constraint and add another constraint.

d. Lessons can last from 45 minutes to 90 minutes each, and the golf course is open for 11 hours per day. This means that instructors can give anywhere from 7 to 14 lessons per day. Communicating this requires you to enter two constraints. In the Add Constraint dialog box, in the Cell Reference box, reference cell **D4**. Click the **arrow**, select **>=** in the mathematical operands box, and then, in the Constraint box, type **7**

e. Click **Add**, and then, in the Add Constraint dialog box, in the Cell Reference box, reference cell **D4**. Click the **arrow**; select **<=** in the mathematical operands box if necessary; and then, in the Constraint box, type **14**

f. In the Add Constraint dialog box, click **Add**. Because the instructors cannot service part of a client, you have to add a constraint to ensure that the value returned for cell D4 is a whole number. In the Add Constraint dialog box, in the Cell Reference box, reference cell **D4**. Click the **arrow** and select **int** in the mathematical operands box. Excel will enter the word "integer" in the Constraint box. Click **Add**.

g. Because Red Bluff cannot have part of an instructor working, you have to add a constraint to ensure that the value returned for cell D5 is a whole number. In the Add Constraint dialog box, in the Cell Reference box, reference cell **D5**. Click the **arrow** and select **int** in the mathematical operands box.

h. Click **OK**. Notice that the five constraints you entered appear under the Subject to the Constraints list of the Solver Parameters dialog box. Leave the Solver Parameters dialog box open for the next step.

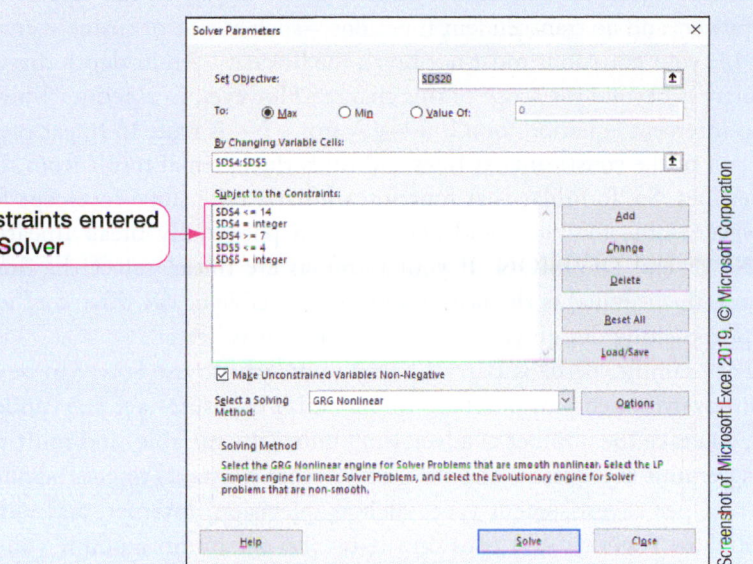

Constraints entered into Solver

Screenshot of Microsoft Excel 2019, © Microsoft Corporation

Figure 22 Solver Parameters dialog box

QUICK REFERENCE	Constraints That Can Be Overlooked

The integer constraint—int—mandates that the values in the variable cells remain whole numbers. For example, the manufacturers of Red Bluff's retail products—such as golf balls and golf gloves—will not produce partial products. Thus, to guarantee that the variable cell values remain whole numbers, you need to create integer constraints for them.

The greater than or equal to zero constraint requires the variable cell values remain greater than or equal to zero when you run Solver. For example, the manufacturers of Red Bluff's retail products will not produce negative amounts of product. However, a negative value in a changing variable cell could possibly produce higher results in the objective cell. By default, the Make Unconstrained Variables Non-Negative check box is selected to guarantee that the variable cells remain greater than or equal to zero. If you want to let a variable cell be negative, you can uncheck the Make Unconstrained Variables Non-Negative check box and create a constraint that allows this to occur, such as D7>=−50.

One item to note: If Solver takes too long to solve, you can press `Esc` to break Solver and stop running the analysis.

Selecting a Solving Method

Three solving methods are available within the Solver Parameters dialog box: Simplex LP, Evolutionary, and Generalized Reduced Gradient (GRG) Nonlinear. These solving methods relate to **linear programming** (LP), which is a mathematical method for determining how to attain the best outcome, such as the maximum profit or the lowest cost, in a given mathematical model, such as your spreadsheet, for a list of requirements—constraints—represented as linear relationships. Thus, linear programming is a specific case of mathematical programming. When you run Solver, this mathematical programming is occurring behind the scenes.

The **Simplex LP method** is a linear model in which the variables are not raised to any powers and no transcendent functions—such as sine or cosine—are used. To use Simplex LP, your equations must not break the linearity. An in-depth discussion of algebraic linearity is beyond the scope of this chapter. However, in algebra, "linear" means that the slope-intercept equation for a line—y = mx + b—is true. In linear programming, Excel plots all of the constraints as lines and finds the optimal result from the intersections of those lines. So, formulas that function similar to the slope-intercept formula are linear. However, some functions and operators can potentially break linearity, such as MIN, MAX, IF, and DIVISION. If your formulas are linear, select the Simplex LP method because this method is the fastest and most reliable of the three methods. In fact, if you can purposefully design your models as linear, it is better.

For example, perhaps Barry Cheney wants you to use Solver to be able to determine what advertisements to purchase to maximize exposures yet stay under budget. In this case, you take the number of advertising units (the variable) and multiply it by the exposures per unit (a constant) and the cost (another constant) to get the number of exposures and cost per advertisement type, such as television, internet, and radio. Then you add all of those together and constrain it by the maximum amount you can spend, along with any other constraints. Then you optimize for maximum exposures. Notice that you multiplied the variable cells by a constant and then added them together, similar to the slope-intercept formula. Thus, if the constraints were plotted on a chart, the lines would be linear, as illustrated in Figure 23.

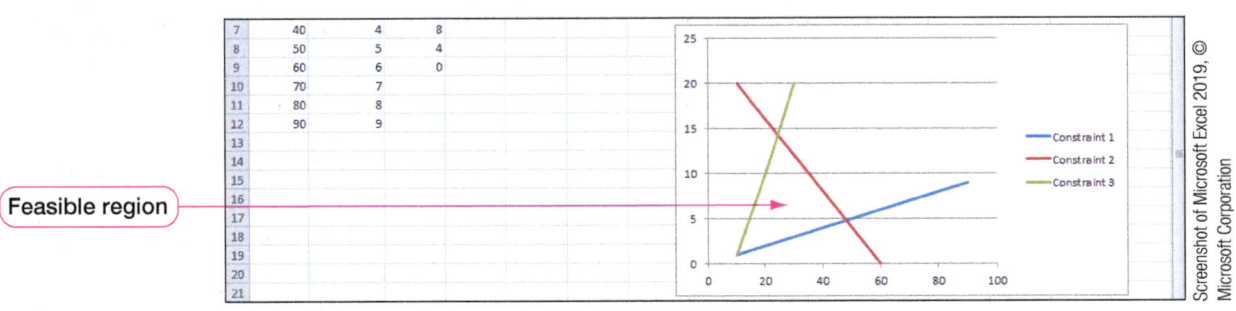

Figure 23   Linear chart with three linear constraints

The **GRG Nonlinear method** is used for more complex models that are nonlinear and smooth. It is also the default method that Excel's Solver uses. Smooth means that when the constraints are graphed, a curve of some kind exists: concave, convex, a wave, and so on. Generally, the model is smooth when it uses trigonometric functions or exponentials, multiplies the variables together, and so on. A nonlinear model is one in which just one of the constraint lines breaks the linearity of the model. You may have several constraints that are linear but one constraint line that breaks the linearity of the model, as shown in Figure 24.

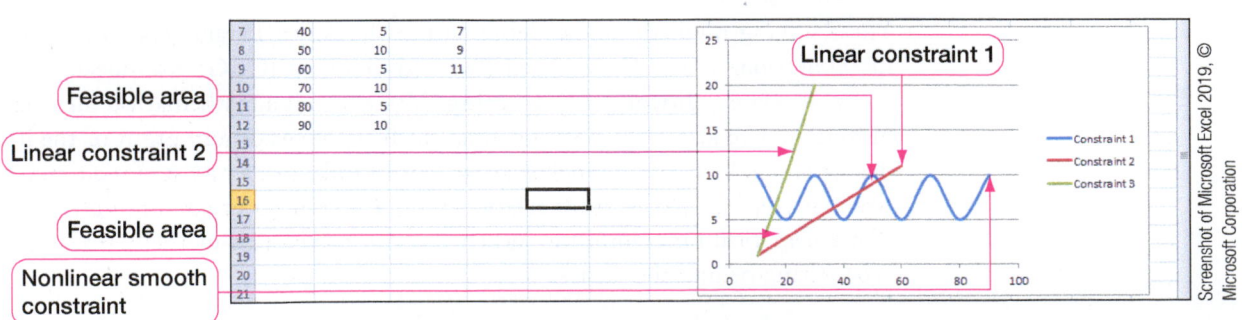

Figure 24   Nonlinear chart with two feasible areas

In the GRG Nonlinear method, Excel uses an iterative process and starting point. You tell Excel where to start, and it starts moving along the constraint lines—linear and nonlinear. The starting point is typically zero unless specific individualized business knowledge would indicate otherwise. As it moves along the graph lines, Excel is looking for peaks when maximizing and valleys when minimizing. When it finds a significant enough peak or valley, Excel finds an optimal answer. If you give Excel a different starting point, Excel may find a different locally optimal answer, particularly if a higher peak or a lower valley exists far away from the starting point that you used the first time. Thus, the GRG Nonlinear method is less reliable than the Simplex LP method. However, the Simplex LP method is limited in what can be modeled because linearity must be maintained.

There is a setting in GRG Nonlinear to help resolve this potential issue. You can take advantage of the Multistart method. This allows Excel to have multiple start points to compare all of the locally optimal answers. By way of this comparison, Excel can potentially find a probabilistically global optimal answer.

Finally, integer constraints break the linearity of a model even if you set it to use Simplex LP. Thus, integer constraints force GRG Nonlinear and a special branching method that takes longer. Also, if the model is actually linear, setting the method to GRG Nonlinear will force a linear model to be solved with GRG Nonlinear.

The **Evolutionary method** is used when a worksheet model is nonlinear and nonsmooth; thus, it is the most complex model. "Nonsmooth" means that the line takes sharp bends or has no slope at all. Typically, these are models that use functions—such as VLOOKUP, PMT, IF, and SUMIF—to derive values based on or derived from the variable cells or changing cells. The Evolutionary method does not make any assumptions about the underlying functions and formulas relationship. Thus, the Evolutionary method uses randomness to pick a population of candidates. Then it uses the variables (changing cells) and evaluates the result (target cell) for each candidate. It holds the population of candidate answers to help pick the next set of variables to test. The Evolutionary method's name is inspired by nature itself. As the method picks random variables, it will use natural selection to reuse certain variables from the population that seem to yield better results. It will also use a crossover effect to combine variables from two known good answers in the population. Further, it will also randomly "mutate" to create new candidates for the population that may or may not be better than the other candidates.

This means that the Evolutionary method cannot guarantee the most optimal result but only the best result it found. Thus, every time you run the Evolutionary method, you might get a different answer. The Evolutionary method takes more processing power and time than the other methods. The only way the Evolutionary method knows when to stop is based on the user-defined setting for length of time, number of iterations, or number of candidates. Therefore, the Evolutionary method is best only in situations that cannot be adequately modeled with an optimal answer method—that is, Simplex LP or GRG Nonlinear. Using the Evolutionary method is beyond the scope of this chapter.

With all three methods, scalability can be an issue. If there is a wide scale for the object or constraint values, it can cause issues in Solver. If you are dealing with numbers that differ by several magnitudes, consider revising the model to express the values differently. For example, instead of listing the number to purchase as 2,000,000, express the number as 2,000 in units of thousands. Although there is an automatic scaling setting, best practice is to uncheck this setting.

Start with Simplex LP. If your model is nonlinear, Solver will notify you. At that point, you can try the GRG Nonlinear model. Try the Evolutionary model in cases when Solver still cannot seem to converge on—gather or develop—a solution. One of these three models will eventually give you an optimal or good solution.

Generate and Interpret Solver Answer Reports

When you run Solver, an answer report is created in a new worksheet and named "Answer Report." Other items to be considered in producing a Solver Answer Report include the type of report you want to generate—Answer, Sensitivity, Limits, or Population—as well as deciding how you want your worksheet to look after you run the Solver. When the Evolutionary Solving method is used, the Population report is also available. In cases when Solver finds an optimal solution and there are no integer constraints, two additional reports are available: the sensitivity report and the limits report.

Generating a Solver Answer Report

After you define the objective, variable cells, constraints, and solving method, you are ready to generate a Solver answer report. After you run Solver, you have several options before the report is generated. Once Solver displays a message that states it found a solution, you can choose the type of report that you want: Answer, Sensitivity, Limits, or Population. The **Solver Answer Report** lists the objective cell and the changing cells with their corresponding original and final values for the problem, input variables, and constraints. In addition, the formulas, binding status, and slacks are given for each constraint. The **Solver Sensitivity Report** provides information about how sensitive the solution is to small changes in the formula for the target cell. This report displays the shadow prices for the constraint—the amount the objective function value changes per unit change in the constraint. Because constraints are often determined by resources, a comparison of the shadow prices of each constraint provides valuable information about the most effective place to apply additional resources to achieve the best improvement. This report can be created only if your Excel model does not contain integer or Boolean—the values 0 and 1—constraints. The **Solver Limits Report** displays the achieved optimal value and all the input variables of the model with the optimal values. Additionally, the report displays the upper and lower bounds for the optimal value. A variable cell could vary without changing the optimal solution. Finally, the **Solver Population Report** displays various statistical characteristics about the given model, such as how many variables and rows it contains.

You can also choose how you want your Excel model to behave, either restoring it to the original values or keeping the Solver solution. If you restore the original values, the original values that were entered into the variable cells before running Solver are restored. This can be helpful in case you have to run Solver again, because it keeps you from having to manually change the values back to what they were when you began. If you choose to keep the Solver solution, you will be able to see the final outcome on both the Answer Report and the Excel model. Regardless of which option you choose, you will still be able to run Solver over and over again as needed. In this exercise, you will generate a Solver Answer Report using the GRG Nonlinear method.

To Generate a Solver Answer Report

a. In the Solver Parameters dialog box, if necessary, click the **Select a Solving Method** arrow, and then click to select **GRG Nonlinear** solving method because the changing cells are being multiplied together.

b. Click **Options**, click the **All Methods** tab if necessary, and verify that the **Use Automatic Scaling** check box is unchecked.

c. Click the **GRG Nonlinear** tab. If necessary, click to select the **Use Multistart** check box, and then click to uncheck the **Require Bounds on Variables** check box. Click **OK**.

d. Click **Solve** at the bottom of the Solver Parameters dialog box.

e. In the Solver Results dialog box, verify that the **Keep Solver Solution** option is selected. This will display your optimal results on the spreadsheet as well as your report.

f. Under Reports, on the right side of the Solver Results dialog box, click to select **Answer**.

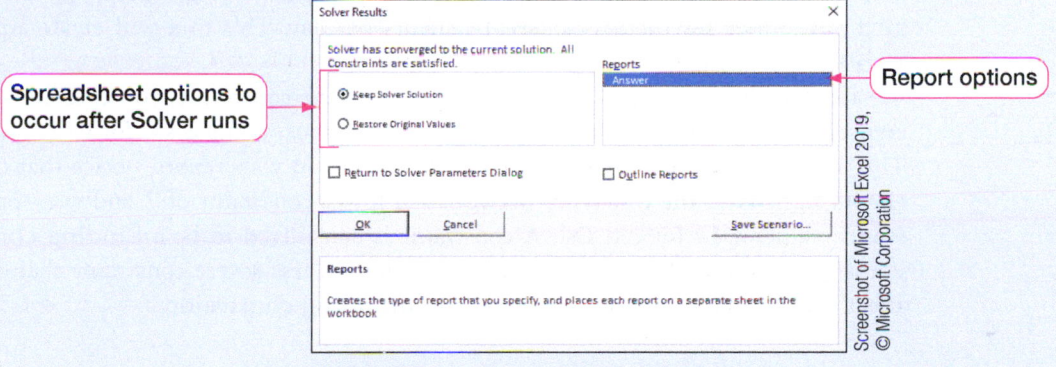

Figure 25 Solver Results dialog box

g. Click **OK**. Notice that a worksheet tab named Answer Report 1 now exists in the workbook.

h. Click the **Answer Report 1** worksheet, and then **Save** 💾 the workbook.

Interpreting a Solver Answer Report

The Solver answer report is divided into four sections: report details, objective cell information, variable cell information, and constraints information. The first three sections of the Answer Report you just created are shown in Figure 26. The report details section displays information about the Solver report: report type, filename, worksheet that contains the Excel model, the date and time the report was created; Solver Engine details; and Solver Options that you set at the time you created the report.

The second section reports information about the objective cells: cell references; cell names; whether you searched for the minimum, maximum, or a specific value; and the original and final objective cell values. For example, in this model, you were trying to maximize the net income. Before Solver was run, the net income value was –$1,908.65; however, once Solver ran, the net income was maximized. The result indicated that the golf course could make $7,302.00 in profit.

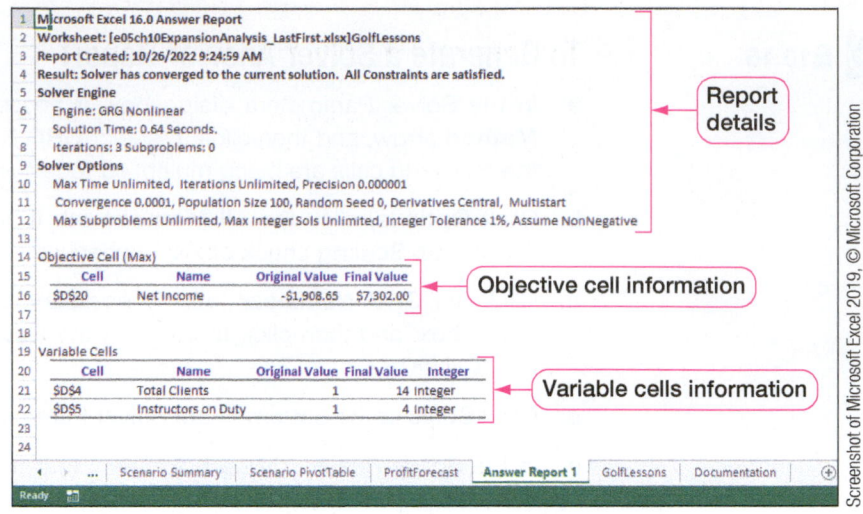

Figure 26   Solver Answer report

The third section displays information about the variable cells: cell references, variable cell names, original cell values, and final cell values. In your report, you can see that each of the four instructors can see 14 clients per day. This mix will create a profit of $7,302.00 per day.

The fourth section displays information about the constraints you entered—cell references, descriptions, new cell values, formulas, status, and slack—for each constraint. This section of the report can be seen in Figure 27. In your report, notice that the total clients slack is 7, the difference between the lower constraint of 7 and the upper constraint value of 14 for cell D4. A constraint is considered to be a **binding constraint** if changing it also changes the optimal solution. A less severe constraint that does not affect the optimal solution is known as a **nonbinding constraint**.

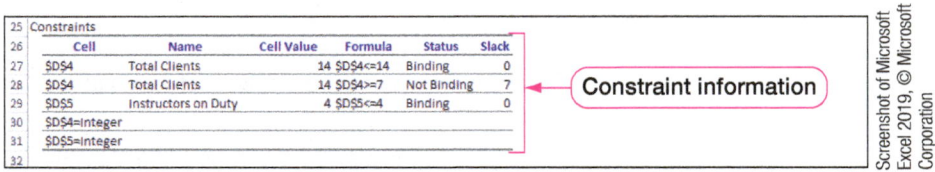

Figure 27   Constraints in the Solver Answer report

One point to note is that if you change your Excel model or Solver parameters, you must run Solver again to create an updated report. The names of new reports will be "Answer Report" followed by consecutive numbering: 1, 2, 3, and so on. Simply delete the reports you no longer need.

 **CONSIDER THIS** | **Why Is It Important to Know How to Read Solver Reports?**

You have spent a considerable amount of time creating your Solver answer report. Why do you think it is so important to be able to understand what the output data for the answer report is telling you? How would analyzing the data and interpreting the output affect management decisions? What factors would you consider when setting the variable constraints for any adjustments to the Solver model?

Saving and Restoring a Solver Model

When you save your workbook, the most recent Solver settings are automatically saved, even if you have multiple worksheets in which you created Solver parameters. For example, if you have made changes to your Solver constraints, the previous ones will not be saved. You can save your Solver settings as you work; that way, you can apply previous settings again in the future. By saving the Solver model, you save the objective cells, variable cells, and constraints, and Excel places this information in a few cells on the worksheet. Solver models can be easily saved and reloaded by clicking the Load/Save button in the Solver Parameters dialog box.

 CONSIDER THIS | **How Could You Use Solver?**

Have you ever wondered what you need to get on your outstanding assignments and exams to earn a specific grade in a course? Or have you wondered how much of a salary increase you would need to budget for a specific purchase or how to meet certain goals for retirement? How could you configure Solver to determine the optimal solution? Which Solver model would you use to solve your problem? Which type of report would you choose?

 **E10.16**

To Save and Restore a Solver Model

a. Click the **GolfLessons** worksheet. You will restore the original values in this worksheet. Click cell **D4**, type **1** and then press Enter. In cell D5, type **1** and then press Enter. On the Data tab, in the Analyze in Excel group, click **Solver**.

b. In the Solver Parameters dialog box, click **Load/Save** to open the Load/Save Model dialog box.

c. Excel guides you through the process. Because you are saving this model, Excel prompts you to select a specific number of cells. In this case, Excel needs nine cells to write the objective cell, variable cell, and constraint data. However, you need to specify only the starting cell. Click inside the box in the Load/Save Model dialog box, click cell **A23**, and then click **Save**.

Once the Solver model was saved, the Solver Parameters dialog box reopened. Notice how Solver placed data in nine cells beginning with A23.

d. Barry Cheney is thinking about opening the golf course for more hours during the day—possibly being open for up to 16 hours per day. In the Solver Parameters dialog box, under Subject to the Constraints, click to select **$D$4 <= 14** from the list of constraints, and then click **Change**.

e. In the Change Constraint dialog box, in the Constraint box, change the value of 14 to **25**. By adding additional hours and 15-minute lessons, additional clients can be served. Click **OK**.

f. If Barry extends the golf course operating hours, he will need to schedule more instructors each day. He knows that a minimum of four instructors will need to work; however, there could be up to seven scheduled in a given day. In the Solver Parameters dialog box, under Subject to the Constraints, click to select **$D$5 <= 4** from the list of constraints, and then click **Change**.

g. In the Change Constraint dialog box, click the **arrow**, and then click to select **>=** in the mathematical operands box. Click **OK**.

h. Click **Add** to add a new constraint that will limit the maximum number of instructors on duty to 7. In the Add Constraint dialog box, in the Cell Reference box, reference cell **D5**. If necessary, click the **arrow** and select **<=** in the mathematical operands box, and then, in the Constraint box, type **7** Click **OK**.

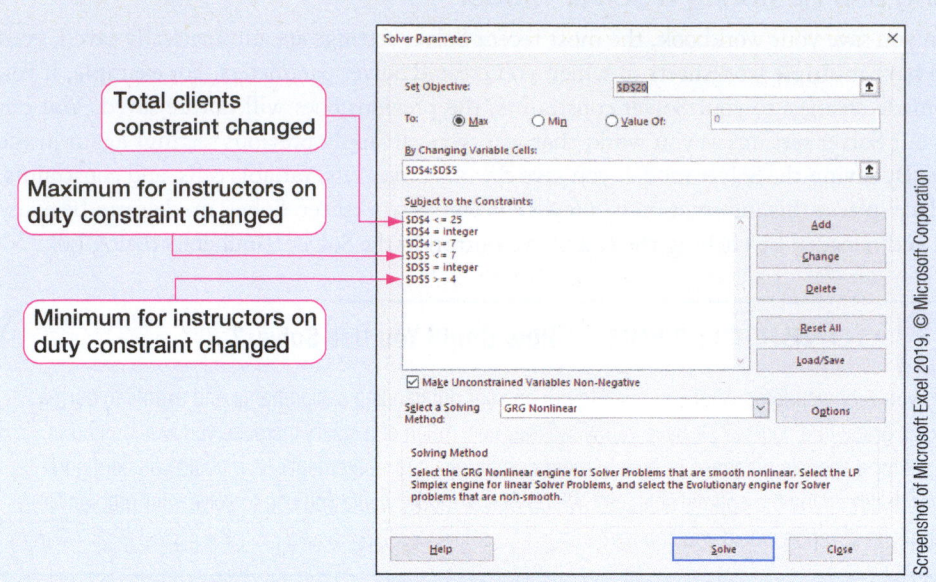

Total clients constraint changed

Maximum for instructors on duty constraint changed

Minimum for instructors on duty constraint changed

Figure 28 New model constraints loaded into the Solver Parameters dialog box

i. Click **Load/Save** to open the Load/Save Model dialog box, reference cell **B23** in the box, and then click **Save**.

j. In the Solver Parameters dialog box, click **Solve** to run Solver and open the Solver Results dialog box.

k. Click to select the **Restore Original Values** option, and then on the right side of the Solver Results dialog box under Reports, click to select **Answer**. Click **OK**.

Notice that a worksheet named Answer Report 2 now exists and that on the Golf-Lessons worksheet, the values in cells D4 and D5 were reset to 1.

l. Click the **Answer Report 2** worksheet.

Notice that Red Bluff can maximize the instructors' schedule and realize a net income of $27,486.55 per day.

m. Save the workbook, exit Excel, and then submit your file as directed by your instructor.

S S CONSIDER THIS | **What Does Answer Report 2 Tell You?**

Does it benefit the golf course management to stay open additional hours? How much more—if any—net income can the golf course generate on a daily basis? How many instructors will need to work each day? What else does the Solver Answer report tell you?

QUICK REFERENCE | **Saving Solver Parameters**

You can save the last selections in the Solver Parameters dialog box with a worksheet by saving the workbook. Each worksheet in a workbook may have its own Solver selections, and all of them are saved. You can also define more than one problem for a worksheet by clicking Load/Save to save problems individually.

When you save a model, enter the reference for the first cell of a vertical range of empty cells in which you want to place the problem model. When you load a model, enter the reference for the entire range of cells that contains the problem model.

Concept Check

1. Why do managers use CVP analysis, and what does it help them learn about their business? p. 552

2. Discuss the difference between using a two-variable data table and calculating elasticity in analyzing costs. p. 559

3. Give three examples of how you could use Goal Seek. Describe how Goal Seek uses iteration to find the solution. p. 565

4. What are scenarios used for, and how can analyzing scenarios assist managers in decision making? p. 568

5. What are the two different types of Scenario Summary reports, and what are some ways in which they are useful? p. 571

6. What is Solver? What can Solver help managers determine? p. 573

7. What are the three main parameters needed to use Solver? Briefly define all three. p. 574

8. What does a Solver Answer report outline? Why is the option to Restore Original Values helpful? p. 580

Key Terms

Add-in   p. 573
Binding constraint   p. 582
Break-even analysis   p. 552
Break-even point   p. 552
Changing cell   p. 568
Conditional formatting   p. 557
Constraint   p. 573
Cost-volume-profit (CVP)
   analysis   p. 552
Data table   p. 559
Elastic   p. 562
Evolutionary method   p. 579
Fixed cost   p. 552

Goal Seek   p. 565
GRG Nonlinear method   p. 578
Inelastic   p. 562
Iteration   p. 565
Linear programming   p. 577
Mixed cost   p. 552
Nonbinding constraint   p. 582
Objective cell   p. 575
One-variable data table   p. 559
Optimize   p. 574
Scenario   p. 568
Scenario Manager   p. 568
Scenario PivotTable report   p. 571

Scenario Summary report   p. 571
Scenario tool   p. 555
Scroll bar   p. 555
Simplex LP method   p. 578
Solver   p. 573
Solver Answer Report   p. 580
Solver Limits Report   p. 580
Solver Population Report   p. 580
Solver Sensitivity Report   p. 580
Two-variable data table   p. 562
Variable   p. 555
Variable cost   p. 552
What-if analysis   p. 555

Performing break-even analysis (p. 553)

Using the scroll bar to perform a break-even analysis (p. 556)

Using conditional formatting (p. 558)

Using Goal seek (p. 565)

Using two-variable data tables (p. 562)

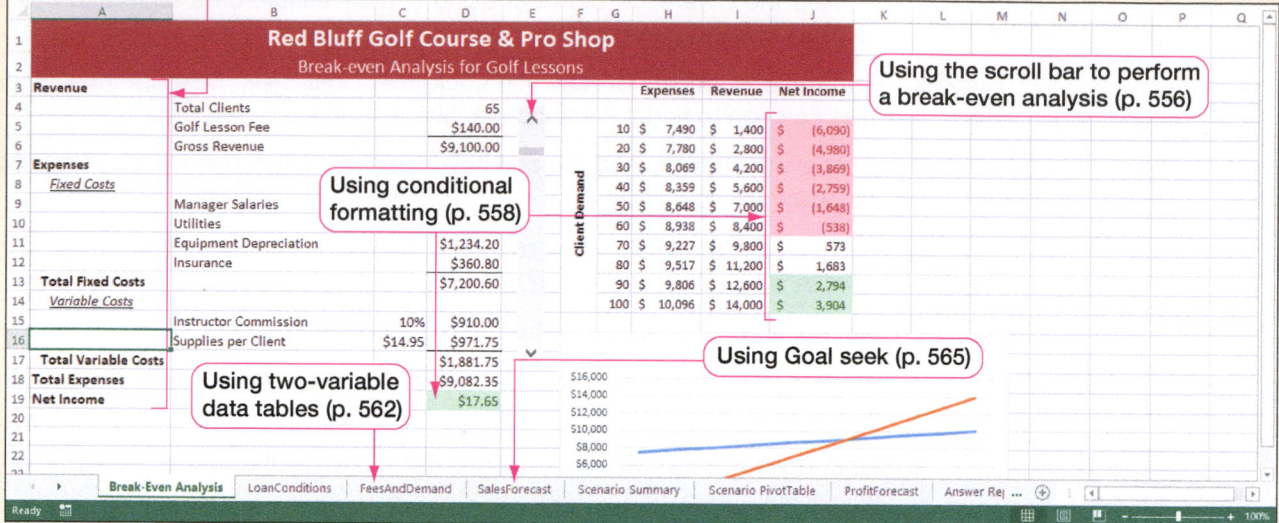

Figure 29

Screenshot of Microsoft Excel 2019, © Microsoft Corporation

Adding, deleting, and editing scenarios (p. 569)

Designing a scenario (p. 568)

Viewing scenarios (p. 570)

Generating a scenario summary report (p. 571)

Generating a scenario PivotTable report (p. 572)

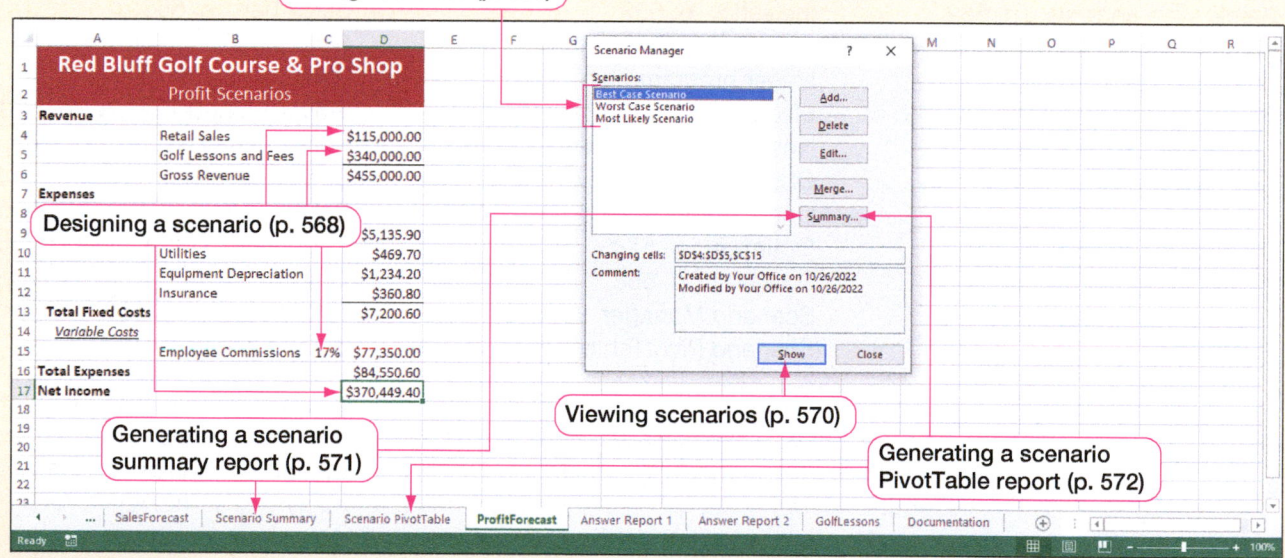

Figure 30

Screenshot of Microsoft Excel 2019, © Microsoft Corporation

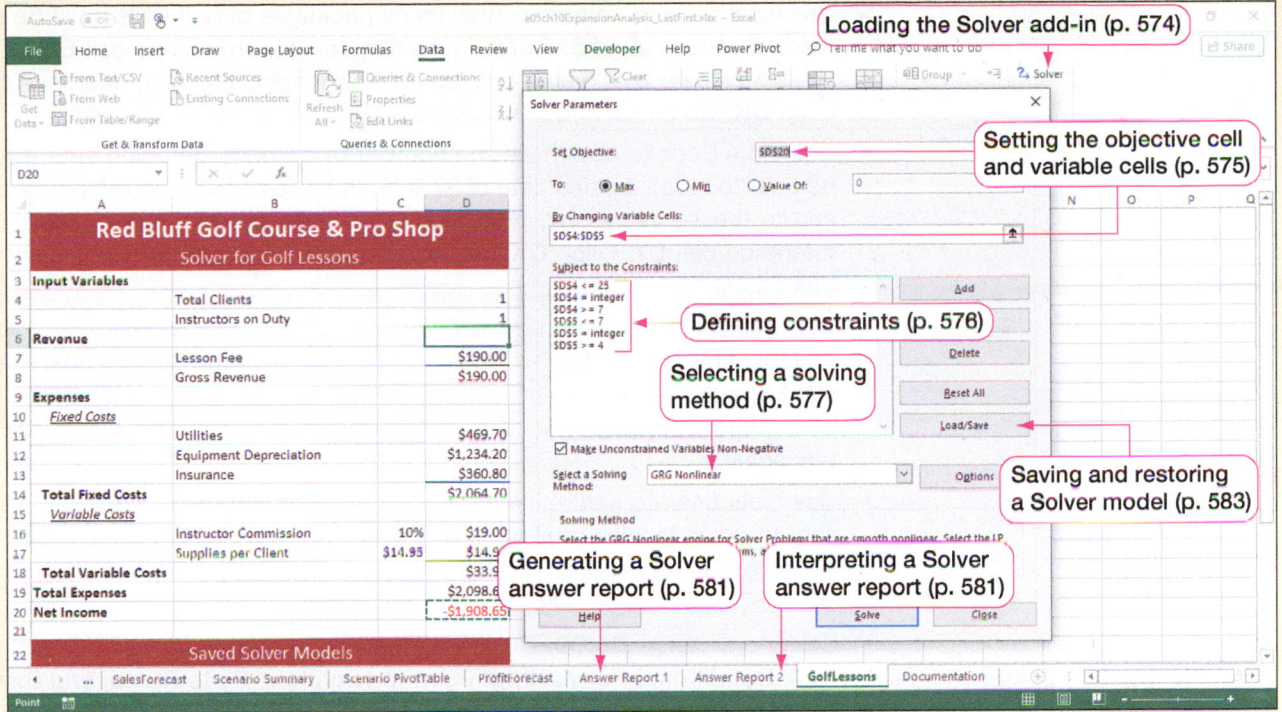

Figure 31

Screenshot of Microsoft Excel 2019, © Microsoft Corporation

Practice 1

Student data file needed:

 e05ch10Forecast.xlsx

You will save your file as:

 e05ch10Forecast_LastFirst.xlsx

Forecasting at the Red Bluff Golf Course & Pro Shop

Sales & Marketing

The Red Bluff Golf Course & Pro Shop needs to analyze current sales trends and forecast prices for the upcoming year to ensure that it is maximizing profit. Barry Cheney, the manager, is not certain whether the prices he is currently charging are going to help him reach his sales goals. Additionally, he needs some guidance about how many hours a day the golf course should be open for business as well as how many employees he should schedule during operating hours to maximize net income. Barry has asked you to perform what-if analyses using a break-even analysis, data tables, Goal Seek, scenarios, and Solver. He has given you templates and data to use to create your analysis. Upon completion, you will need to present your findings to him.

a. Open the Excel file **e05ch10Forecast**. Save your file as **e05ch10Forecast_LastFirst** using your last and first name. If necessary, enable content.

b. Complete the following tasks to forecast prices and sales quantities of specific products, using Goal Seek.

• If necessary, click the **ProductsAndSales** worksheet, and then click cell **E5**. Click the **Data** tab, and then in the Forecast group, click **What-If Analysis**, and select **Goal Seek** to open the Goal Seek dialog box.

• Use Goal Seek to determine the selling price of golf umbrellas necessary to reach a sales goal of $9,450 if 265 are sold. In the To value box, type **9450** and then, in the By changing cell box, reference cell **D5**. Click **OK** two times, and then open the Goal Seek dialog box again.

- Use Goal Seek to determine how many packages of golf balls must be sold to reach a sales goal of $28,875. In the Set cell box, reference cell **E6**. In the To value box, type 28875 and then, in the By changing cell box, reference cell **C6**. Click **OK** two times, and then open the Goal Seek dialog box again.

- Use Goal Seek to determine the number of graphite golf club sets that must be sold to reach a sales goal of $7,875. In the Set cell box, reference cell **E7**, and in the To value box, type 7875 and then, in the By changing cell box, reference cell **C7**. Click **OK** two times, and then open the Goal Seek dialog box again.

- Use Goal Seek to determine the number of platinum ladies' complete golf sets that must be sold to reach a sales goal of $9,730. In the Set cell box, reference cell **E8**, and in the To value box, type 9730 and then, in the By changing cell box, reference cell **C8**. Click **OK** two times, and then open the Goal Seek dialog box again.

- Use Goal Seek to determine the selling price of golf club cleaning kits necessary to reach a sales goal of $2,620 if 125 are sold. In the Set cell box, reference cell **E9**, and in the To value box, type 2620 and then, in the By changing cell box, reference cell **D9**. Click **OK** two times.

- Select cell range **D5:D9**. Click the **Home** tab, and then in the Styles group, click **Conditional Formatting**. Point to **Highlight Cells Rules**, and then click **Greater Than**. In the Format cells that are GREATER THAN box, type 200 Click the **with** arrow, and then click **Custom Format**. Under Font style, click **Bold**, and then click **OK** two times to apply bold to the product prices when the price is greater than $200. Press Ctrl + Home to select cell A1.

c. Complete the following tasks to forecast the best-case, worst-case, and most likely scenarios using Scenario Manager.

- Click the **MonthlyForecasting** worksheet. Click the **Data** tab, and then in the Forecast group, click **What-If Analysis**. Click **Scenario Manager** to open the Scenario Manager dialog box.

- Use Scenario Manager to configure the most likely scenario for this monthly forecast. Click **Add**, and then in the Scenario name box, type Most Likely Scenario and press Tab. In the Changing cells box, reference cells **D4:D5**, press and hold Ctrl, and then reference cell **C15**. The values that are currently on the spreadsheet are the values for the most likely scenario. Click **OK** two times.

- Use Scenario Manager to configure the worst-case scenario for this monthly forecast. Click **Add** to begin creating your second scenario, and in the Scenario name box, type Worst-case Scenario and then click **OK**. In row 1, type 86000 in row 2, type 140000 in row 3, type 0.08 and then click **OK**.

- Use Scenario Manager to configure the best-case scenario. Click **Add** to begin creating your third scenario. In the Scenario name box, type Best-case Scenario and then click **OK**. In row 1, type 230000 in row 2, type 403000 in row 3, type 0.055 and then click **OK**.

- In the Scenario Manager dialog box, view each of your scenarios by clicking each scenario's name in the listing box, and then click **Show**. Click Summary to create a **Scenario Summary** report, if necessary, and in the Result cells box, reference cell **D18**. Then click **OK**.

- Click the **Scenario Summary** worksheet if necessary. To add headings to your data, delete the cell reference headings in cells **C6**, **C7**, **C8**, and **C10**. Click cell **B6**, type Retail sales and then press Enter. In cell B7, type Equipment sales and then press Enter. In cell B8, type Commission and then press Enter. Click cell **B10**, type Net income and then press Enter. If necessary, format the font as bold.

- Click the **MonthlyForecasting** worksheet. On the Data tab, in the Forecast group, click **What-If Analysis**, click **Scenario Manager** to open the Scenario Manager dialog box, and then click **Summary**. Select the **Scenario PivotTable** report option. If necessary, in the Result cells box, reference cell **D18**, and then click **OK**.

- If necessary, click the **Scenario PivotTable** worksheet to format the report to make it easier to read. In cell **A1**, type Monthly Forecasting Solution press [Enter], and then set the width of column A to 27 In cell **A2**, type Scenario PivotTable Report and press [Enter]. Merge and center the range **A2:B2**; change the font size to **16** point; then apply **Bold**. In cell **A3**, type Scenarios and then press [Tab]. In cell B3, type Net Income and then press [Enter]. In the PivotTable Fields pane, in the Σ VALUES area, click **Net Income**, and then click **Value Field Settings**. Click **Number Format**, and in the Format Cells dialog box, click **Currency**. Then click **OK** twice. Resize the width of column B as needed.

d. Complete the following tasks to create a Solver Answer report that determines the maximum net income that can be generated.

- Click the **NetIncomeForecast** worksheet, click the **Data** tab, and then in the Analysis group, click **Solver**.

- In the Solver Parameters dialog box, in the Set Objective box, reference cell **D23**, and then, in the By Changing Variable Cells box, reference cells **D4:D5**. Click **Add** to begin entering your constraints.

- The pro shop can be open from 11 to 17 hours per day, depending on what Barry Cheney decides. In the Solver Parameters dialog box, click **Add** to add a constraint. In the Add Constraint dialog box, in the Cell Reference box, reference cell **D4**. Click the **arrow**, and select **>=** in the mathematical operands box. Then, in the Constraint box, type 11 Click **Add**, and then create a second constraint when the value in cell **D4** is <=17

- Click **Add**. The pro shop can have two to six employees working per day, depending on the day and time of year. Using the techniques you have practiced, create a constraint when the value in cell **D5** is >=2 Click **Add**, and then create another constraint when the value in cell **D5** is <=6

- Click **Add**. The hours and employees must be integers. Using the techniques you have practiced, create a new constraint when the value in cell **D4** is an integer. Click **Add**, and then create another constraint when the value in cell **D5** is an integer. Click **OK**.

- To save your Solver model with the six constraints, click **Load/Save**. In the Load/Save Model dialog box, reference cell **A25**, click **Save**, and then click **Solve** to run Solver. Click **Restore Original Values**, click **Answer** under Reports, and then click **OK** to create a Solver answer report.

e. Complete the following tasks to create a two-variable data table with conditional formatting that will help to analyze the break-even point.

- Click the **GolfPricing** worksheet. The net income in cell D19 is the output cell that will be used in the data table to help determine the break-even point when the golf fee and total number of golfers vary. Click cell **G5**, and then type = reference cell D19, and press [Ctrl]+[Enter]. To format cell G5 to hide the results of the function, right-click cell **G5**, and then click **Format Cells**.

- On the Number tab, click to select the **Custom** category, and then click inside the **Type** box. Delete any existing text, and then type ;;;

- Click **OK**. Select the range **G5:R21** to select the data for your data table.

- On the Data tab, in the Forecast group, click **What-If Analysis**, and then click **Data Table** to open the Data Table dialog box. Reference cell **D5** in the Row input cell box, reference cell **D4** in the Column input cell box, and then click **OK**.

- Select the range **H6:R21**, and then format the cells as **Currency**. To view all the data, widen the columns if necessary.

- On the Home tab, in the Styles group, click **Conditional Formatting**. Point to **Highlight Cells Rules**, and then click **Less Than** to open the Less Than dialog box. In the Format cells that are LESS THAN box, type **0** If necessary, click to select the **Light Red Fill with Dark Red Text** option, and then click **OK**.

- Click **Conditional Formatting** again. Then point to **Highlight Cells Rules**, and click **Greater Than** to open the Greater Than dialog box. In the Format cells that are GREATER THAN box, type **3500** and then click to select the **Green Fill with Dark Green Text** option, and click **OK**. Press Ctrl + Enter.

f. Save the workbook, exit Excel, and then submit your file as directed by your instructor.

Problem Solve 1

MyLab IT Grader

Student data file needed:

 e05ch10Schedule.xlsx

You will save your file as:

 e05ch10Schedule_LastFirst.xlsx

Production & Operations

Scheduling Employees

The Painted Paradise Resort & Spa is working on getting a handle on its expenditures on part-time labor. The management feels that there is some opportunity to improve scheduling to reduce costs in some areas. One area has the requirements that the schedules be five days a week with two days in a row off. With these constraints, they would like to build an optimal schedule (from a cost perspective). Management is also considering the impact of raises and potential benefits increases due to new regulations.

a. Open the Excel file **e05ch10Schedule**. Save your file as e05ch10Schedule_LastFirst using your last and first name. If necessary, enable content.

b. The Schedule worksheet has the possible schedules each employee can work (rows 5–11). The 1s represent the days worked, and the 0s represent the days off (so each schedule has two days in a row off). The range D5:D11 contains the number of employees assigned to the schedule in the corresponding row. This range will need to be changed to fulfill the scheduling needs.

c. In cell **F13**, enter a formula that will calculate the total number of employees scheduled to work Sunday for all schedules A-G. Begin by multiplying the number of employees for schedule A, in cell D5, by the value representing whether or not employees are working that day in cell F5. Be sure to make the reference to cell D5 an absolute cell reference so that, when finished, the formula can be copied across the row. So far the result of the formula is 0 because schedule A has people scheduled off on Sunday. Next, add to the product, the number of employees scheduled to work Sunday for schedule B. Continue with the formula by adding a similar calculation for schedules C–G, making an absolute cell reference for each cell in column D.

d. Copy the formula over to **L13**.

e. In cell **D18**, calculate the total number of shifts scheduled, using the range F13:L13.

f. In cell **D20**, enter a formula that calculates the payroll for the week, which is the product of shifts scheduled and cost per employee per day.

g. Using Solver, minimize the Payroll/Week for the resort by determining the optimal number of employees to have assigned to each schedule. Remember these points as you complete the Solver Parameters dialog box.

   • The number of people in the range F13:L13 must be greater than or equal to the demand (range F15:L15) so there are enough people working for that day's needs.

   • The number of employees scheduled in D5:D11 must be greater than zero.

   • Solve this model, using the Simplex LP method.

   • Keep the Solver solution in the model.

   • Create an Answer report.

h. On the **Part-Time Expenses** sheet, in cell **E8**, insert a formula to calculate the total annual part-time wage expense. The Benefit % is an estimate in the form of a percentage of total wages. It needs to be added to the cost of wages based on the average part-time hours and the average hourly rate.

i. Create nine scenarios based on the Part-Time Expenses. These scenarios are based on the possibilities management sees for next year.

   • The first three scenarios are based only on a variation in hours. The number given is the expected hours needed for next year. The actual hours may go as low as 85% of the 225,000 hours expected and as high as 120% of the 225,000 hours expected. Create three scenarios that show the effect of average, minimum, and maximum usage of hours on the Total PT Wage Expense. Use the 225,000 expected hours for the Avg scenario. Name the scenarios Avg Hours and Min Hours and Max Hours

   • The next three scenarios are for the same three levels of hour usage but with a 3.5% increase in the wage rate. Name these three scenarios Avg Hours w/Raises and Min Hours w/Raises and Max Hours w/Raises

   • The last three scenarios are with the same three hours levels but with a 3% increase in wage rate and a Benefit % estimate of 35%. Name these three scenarios Avg Hours w/Raises&Benefits and Min Hours w/Raises&Benefits and Max Hours w/Raises&Benefits

j. Display the results of the nine scenarios created in the prior step by creating a scenario summary. Delete the row labels in **column C**. Replace the row labels by typing the following in the appropriate cell in **column B**: Part Time Hours and Part Time Wage and Part Time Benefits and PT Wage Expense Adjust the width of column B so that all labels are visible. The nine scenarios will display the data in a column for each scenario.

k. Save the workbook, exit Excel, and then submit your file as directed by your instructor.

Critical Thinking   Explain why you were able to use the Simplex LP method in the optimization model that you created. Briefly interpret each of the four sections in the Solver Answer report generated from the model.

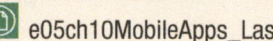
Student data file needed:

e05ch10MobileApps.xlsx

You will save your file as:

e05ch10MobileApps_LastFirst.xlsx

Finance &
Accounting

Mobile Applications

You are investigating the possibility of developing applications (apps) for smartphones. After some research on the development process for mobile apps, you have determined that you can sell your app for $1.29 per download. You must pay a developer fee of $125 to sell your mobile app. When you sell your mobile app, the online store you are working with will charge you 25% per download, so your revenue on each download will be 75% of the selling price of the app. As part of this project, you will need to purchase a new laptop computer. A new laptop will cost $1150. You will create a break-even model to investigate how many apps you will need to sell to make a profit on your new app. In addition to your new app, the company you work for has just finished developing three new apps that will be released in the coming weeks. They would like your help in forecasting sales given the selling price and sales goal of each new app.

a. Open the Excel file, **e05ch10MobileApps**. Save your file as e05ch10MobileApps_LastFirst using your last and first name. If necessary, enable content.

b. On the Break-EvenAnalysis worksheet, complete the following tasks to create your break-even analysis, using a scroll bar, and build a traditional cost-volume-profit chart from a one-variable data table that will help to analyze the break-even point.

   • In cell D7, calculate the gross revenue made from the number of apps sold in D4, the unit price in D5, and the percent per download in D6.

   • In cell D12, calculate the total fixed costs.

   • In cell D14, calculate the net income.

c. Insert a scroll bar in the area of cells E4 through E14. Format the scroll bar with the following criteria.

   • Current value: 1275

   • Minimum value: 1275

   • Maximum value: 1375

   • Incremental change: 10

   • Page change: Leave the default value of 10

   • Cell link: D4

d. In cells G4:I4, create references to the Total Fixed Costs, Revenue, and Net Income from column D. Format the cells using semicolons (;) so that the results of the calculation are not visible in the worksheet.

e. Fill in the Total Fixed Costs, Revenue, and Net Income columns (range G5:I14), using a data table. Format the range as appropriate for the data.

f. Use conditional formatting to apply Gradient Fill Green Data Bars to the Net Income column of the data table.

g. Using the data table columns for Apps Sold, Total Fixed Costs, and Revenue, insert a line chart that displays the Total Fixed Costs and Revenue as series data and the Apps Sold as the Horizontal (Category) Axis. Delete the chart title if necessary. Move the chart so that the top-left corner of the chart is aligned with the top-left corner of F17.

h. On the **ForecastedSales** worksheet in cells D5:D7, calculate the extended price of the three new apps your company is going to release.

i. Using the extended price and the sales goal in cells E5:E7, use Goal Seek to find the quantity to sell in column B.

j. Save the workbook, exit Excel, and then submit your file as directed by your instructor.

Manipulating Data Sets for Decision Making

This business unit had two outcomes:

Learning Outcome 1:
Understand the benefits of analyzing data sets and learn techniques to import, organize, and clean data sets from a variety of sources.

Learning Outcome 2:
Utilize various forecasting and optimization tools, such as data tables, Scenario Manager, and Solver to support decision making.

In Business Unit 5 Capstone, students will demonstrate competence in these outcomes through a series of business problems at various levels, from guided practice to problem solving an existing workbook and performing to create new workbooks.

More Practice 1

Student data file needed:

 e05Indigo5.xlsx

You will save your file as:

 e05Indigo5_LastFirst.xlsx

Indigo5 Restaurant

Finance & Accounting

Production & Operations

Management at Indigo5, a five-star restaurant that caters to local patrons in addition to clients of the Painted Paradise Resort & Spa, has outsourced its data collection processes to a new firm in town. The data already collected, which is stored in the e05Indigo5 workbook, is not compatible in its current form with the database that Indigo5 now uses to store this data. You will need to use your knowledge of Excel functions to cleanse the data so it can be imported into the database.

Additionally, Indigo5's executive chef, Robin Sanchez, is regularly updating data in her database to make certain she has all the ingredients and recipes the kitchen needs to offer the high-quality food for which the restaurant is known. You have been asked to build a spreadsheet model that will assist managers in answering what-if questions about product pricing when Chef Sanchez wants to add a new menu item.

a. Open the Excel file, **e05Indigo5**. Save it as e05Indigo5_LastFirst using your last and first name. If necessary, enable content.

b. On the FoodCategories worksheet, separate the category number from the value in cell **A2** using Flash Fill. In cell **B2**, type CAT01 and then press Enter. In cell **B3**, type CAT02 and then press Enter.

c. Click the **Data** tab, and in the Data Tools group, click **Flash Fill** to complete the list of categories in column B.

d. Click cell **C2**. Separate the description of the category from the value in cell **A2** using Flash Fill. In cell **C2**, type Appetizer and then press Enter. In cell **C3**, type Sea and notice the suggestion Flash Fill provides. Press Enter to accept the suggestion, and complete the list of descriptions in column C.

e. Click the **Reviews** worksheet. You will need to convert the text in cell A2 to proper case. Click cell **E2**, type =PROPER and then press Tab to insert the function. Click cell **A2**, and then press Ctrl+Enter to complete the formula. Double-click the **fill** handle in cell **E2** to copy the formula down the column. If necessary, apply AutoFit to the column so that all contents are displayed.

f. You will need to convert the numbers in cell **B2** into an acceptable date format. Click cell **F2**, and complete the following.

- Type **=DATE** and then press ⎵Tab to insert the function.

- Type **LEFT** and then press ⎵Tab to insert the LEFT function.

  The LEFT function will be used to extract the four characters from the left side of cell B2 that represent the year.

- Click cell **B2**, type **,4),** type **MID** and then press ⎵Tab to insert the MID function.

  The MID function will be used to extract the two characters in the middle of cell B2 that represent the month.

- Click cell **B2**, type **,5,2),RIGHT** and then press ⎵Tab to insert the RIGHT function.

  The RIGHT function will be used to extract the two characters from the right of cell B2 that represent the day.

- Click cell **B2**, type **,2))** and then press Ctrl+Enter to end the nested function.

  The final formula should be =DATE(LEFT(B2,4),MID(B2,5,2),RIGHT(B2,2))

- Double-click the **fill** handle in cell F2 to copy the formula down the column. If necessary, apply AutoFit to the column so that all contents are displayed.

g. Complete the following tasks to perform a break-even analysis for a new menu item. Fixed expenses have been spread evenly among all menu items.

- Click the **Break-even Analysis** worksheet. Click cell **D6**, type **=** click cell **D4**, type ***** click cell **D5**, and then press Enter to calculate the gross revenue, that is, the amount of money generated from selling the new menu item.

- Click cell **D13**, type **=SUM** and press ⎵Tab to insert the function. Select the cell range **D9:D12**, and then press Enter to calculate the total fixed costs. Click cell **D15**, type **=** click cell **D4**, type ***** click cell **C15**, and then press Enter to calculate the total food cost based on how many items were sold.

- In cell **D16**, type **=** click cell **D13**, type **+** click cell **D15**, and then press Enter to calculate the total expenses. In cell **D17**, type **=** click cell **D6**, type **-** click cell **D16**, and then press Enter to calculate the net income, that is, how much profit the restaurant will generate from the new menu item.

- Apply conditional formatting to cell **D17** with the Custom Format option so numbers that are less than zero are displayed in red text and numbers that are greater than zero are displayed in green text, and then enter quantities in cell **D4** until you find the break-even point.

- Click cell **G4**, type **=** click cell **D16**, and then press ⎵Tab. In cell **H4**, type **=** click cell **D6**, and then press ⎵Tab. In cell **I4**, type **=** click cell **D17**, and then press Enter. Select cell range **G4:I4** to format with the formula results hidden. Right-click any of the cells in the selected cell range, and then click **Format Cells**. On the Number tab, select the **Custom** category, click in the **Type box**, remove any existing text, and then type **;;;** Click **OK**.

- Select the cell range **F4:I18** for your data table. Click the **Data** tab, and in the Forecast group, click **What-If Analysis**. Click **Data Table** to open the Data Table dialog box. Press ⎵Tab to move to the Column input cell box, reference cell **D4**, and then click **OK**.

- Select the cell range **I5:I18**, click the **Home** tab, and in the Styles group, click **Conditional Formatting**. Point to Color Scales, and then select **Green - White - Red Color Scale**.

- Select the cell range **G3:H3**, press and hold Ctrl, and then select the cell range **G5:H18**. Click the **Insert** tab, and in the Charts group, click **Insert Line or Area Chart**, and then, in the 2-D Line category, click **Line**. Click the border edge of the chart, and then drag to reposition the top-left corner into cell F20.

- Click the **Chart Tools Design** tab, and in the Data group, click **Select Data**, and then, under Horizontal (Category) Axis Labels, click **Edit**. With the insertion point in the Axis label range box, select the cell range **F5:F18**. Click **OK** two times.
- Click **Chart Elements**, click the **Axis Titles** arrow, and then select **Primary Horizontal**. Type Total Ordered and then press Enter. Click the **Chart Title** box, type Break-Even Analysis and then press Enter.
- Click an empty cell to deselect the chart.

h. Save the workbook, exit Excel, and then submit your file as directed by your instructor.

Problem Solve 1

MyLab IT Grader

Student data files needed:

 e05HotelFinancials.xlsx

e05HotelSales.accdb

You will save your file as:

e05HotelFinancials_LastFirst.xlsx

Finance &
Accounting

Production &
Operations

Financial Analysis for the Painted Paradise Resort & Spa

The hotel manager has asked for your help in conducting an analysis of sales for several of the room types offered at the Painted Paradise Resort & Spa. First, you have been asked to conduct a sales forecast of three popular rooms. This information has been stored in an Access database and will need to be imported before any analysis can be completed. A list of potential customers from a new marketing campaign has also been included in the workbook you have been given. The data needs to be cleansed before it can be used. Finally, you have been asked to create three different sales scenarios for the hotel.

a. Open the Excel file **e05HotelFinancials**. Save your file as e05HotelFinancials_ LastFirst using your last and first name.

b. Establish a connection to the data in the table **tblRoomTypes** in the e05Hotel-Sales database using Get & Transform. Edit the data before importing it to Excel.

c. On the Transform tab, and in the Text Column group, use Split Column to separate the RoomType column. Split the columns using the left parentheses character.

d. On the Transform tab, and in the Any Column group, use Replace Values to remove the right parentheses character from the RoomType.2 column.

e. Trim both columns to remove any extra spaces. Rename RoomType.1 to RoomType and RoomType.2 to NumberOfBeds Close and Load the data to cell **A3** on the **SalesForecast** worksheet.

f. In cell **E3**, type Quantity and enter 1 as the quantity for each record that was imported.

g. In cell **F3,** type Extended Price and in the cell range **F4:F6**, calculate the extended price for each room type by multiplying the room rate by the quantity.

h. In cell **G3**, type Goal and in cells **G4** and **G5**, type 3500 In cell **G6**, type 8500

i. Use Goal Seek to find the appropriate quantities of each room type in order for the extended price to meet the goals you typed in cell range G4:G6.

j. Format the cell range **E4:E6** as **General** with 0 decimal places.

k. Format the cell ranges **D4:D6** and **F4:G6** as **Currency** with 0 decimal places.

l. Adjust the column widths so that all data is visible.

m. On the **NewCustomers** worksheet, complete the following steps to cleanse the data in columns A through D.

- In cell **E2**, use the appropriate function to cleanse the nonprinting characters from cell **B2**. Copy the function down through cell **E11**.

- In cell **F2**, use the appropriate function to display the street address from **C2** in proper case. Copy the function down through cell **F11**.

- The data in the cell range **D2:D11** contains the customer's home city and state. The last two characters in each cell contain the state abbreviation. In cell **G2**, use the appropriate functions to display only the city from **D2**. Be certain to remove extra spaces from the city name. Copy the function down through cell **G11**.

- In cell **H2**, use the appropriate function to display only the state abbreviation from cell **D2**. Copy the function down through cell **H11**.

n. On the **Scenarios** worksheet, complete the following tasks to create a Scenario PivotTable Report.

- Use the Scenario Manager to add a Most-likely scenario Use the cell range **D5:D7** as the Changing cells. The current values on the worksheet will be your Most-likely scenario values.

- Add a new scenario named Best-case scenario In the Scenario Values dialog box, type 40 in **row 1**, type 65 in **row 2**, and type 80 in **row 3**.

- Add a new scenario named Worst-case scenario In the Scenario Values dialog box, type 12 in **row 1**, type 24 in **row 2**, and type 50 in **row 3**.

- Create a Scenario PivotTable Report using cells **E8**, **C20**, and **C22** as your Result cells.

o. Complete the following tasks to format the report with appropriate headings and formatting.

- In cell **A1**, type Room Reservations

- In cell **B3**, type Gross Revenue

- In cell **C3**, type Total Expenses

- In cell **D3**, type Net Income

- Format the gross revenue, total expenses, and net income data as **Currency**, and **AutoFit** the widths of the columns as needed.

p. Save the workbook, exit Excel, and then submit your file as directed by your instructor.

Problem Solve 2

MyLab IT Grader

Student data files needed:

 e05ProductMix.xlsx

 e05SampleCustomers.txt

You will save your file as:

 e05ProductMix_LastFirst.xlsx

Product Mix Optimization

Production & Operations

3-D CustomAble Designs is a medical device company that utilizes 3-D printing technology to manufacture wheelchairs. It offers a standard model for the majority of its customer base but has recently started implementing a design-your-own-chair service in which the chairs can be customized with some unique features and designs. You have been asked to use your knowledge of Excel to help the company clean up some of its customer names that were corrupted when exported from its CRM system.

You have also been asked to help with a Solver model that will help to determine the optimal mix of standard and custom wheelchairs necessary to maximize profit, given several labor and material constraints.

a. Open the Excel file **e05ProductMix**. Save your file as e05ProductMix_LastFirst using your last and first name.

b. Establish a connection to the tab-delimited text file **e05SampleCustomers** using Get & Transform. Edit the query.

c. On the Home tab, in the Transform group, use **Split Column** to split the columns by a delimiter. If the Tab character is not autodetected, select it from the list.

d. Use the first row as headers and change the MostRecentPurchase field to a data type of **Date**.

e. Clear any nonprinting characters and extra spaces from the text in the **Customer-Name** column.

f. Display the names in proper case.

g. All of the names are arranged by last name, a space character, and the first name of the customer. Split the names into two columns titled, LastName and FirstName and remove any extra spaces.

h. Close and Load the customer names into cell **A1** of the **RecentCustomers** worksheet.

i. On the MaximizeProfits worksheet, complete the following so that a linear Solver model can be created.

   • In cell **B18**, calculate the revenue of custom-designed wheelchairs, using the selling price in cell **F8** and the number of units produced in cell **B11**. Copy the formula over to cell **C18** to calculate the revenue from standard wheelchairs.

   • In cell **B21**, calculate the costs of labor for custom-designed wheelchairs by multiplying the hourly rate in cell **B5** by the number of hours necessary to create a custom wheelchair in cell **F5** by the number of custom wheelchairs produced in cell **B11**. Use appropriate cell referencing so that the formula can be copied down to cell **B23** to calculate the costs of primary and additional materials for custom wheelchairs and can be copied over to calculate all costs for standard wheelchairs.

   • In cell **B25**, calculate the profit of custom wheelchairs by subtracting the total costs from the revenue. Copy the formula over to cell **C25** to calculate the profit from standard wheelchairs.

   • In cell **D18**, calculate the total revenue by adding the revenue from custom and standard wheelchairs. Copy and paste the formula into the cell range **D21:D23** and cell **D25**.

j. Create a Solver model using the GRG Nonlinear method by completing the following steps.

   • Set the objective to maximize the total profit in cell **D25**.

   • Set the changing cells to be the number of units to produce in the cell range **B11:C11**.

   • Create a constraint that will ensure that the number of units to produce will be whole numbers.

   • Create a constraint that will ensure that the number of units produced will not exceed the maximum expected demand in the cell range **B13:C13**.

   • Create a constraint that will ensure that the used resources in the cell range **F12:F14** will not exceed the available resources in the cell range **H12:H14**.

k. Save the Solver model for use later, starting in cell **A28**.

l. Run Solver and create a Solver Answer Report.

m. Save the workbook, exit Excel, and then submit your file as directed by your instructor.

Critical Thinking Discuss some reasons why the optimal product mix to maximize profits did not involve producing as many custom wheelchairs as the estimated maximum demand. Also, which constraint forced this model to use the GRG Nonlinear method instead of the Simplex LP method?

Perform 1: Perform in Your Life

Student data file needed:

e05ReceptionBudget.xlsx

You will save your file as:

e05ReceptionBudget_LastFirst.xlsx

Reception Budget What-If Analysis

Production & Operations

You are planning a wedding. Your fiancé has asked you to create an Excel workbook to ensure that the two of you do not go over budget. Your goal with this workbook is to determine what happens to your budget when the number of guests changes, when the cost of the meal goes up, and so on.

a. Open the Excel file **e05ReceptionBudget**. Save the file as e05ReceptionBudget_LastFirst using your last and first name.

b. Add a scroll bar to the Budget worksheet within the cell range E5:E25 that will allow you to determine what happens when the number of guests varies, using the following properties.

   • Current and minimum value of **120**

   • Maximum value of **320**

   • Incremental and page change of **10**

   • Link the scroll bar to the appropriate cell

c. Given the current estimates on the worksheet, use the scroll bar to determine the maximum number of guests you can have at the reception without exceeding the amount available.

d. Create a two-variable data table that determines what happens to your budget if you add more people or the cost of the meal changes. You haven't decided on a caterer yet, but your current estimates are between $45 per person and $105 per person.

   • Format the various budget remaining amounts in the data table appropriately.

   • Add appropriate conditional formatting to the data table so that budgets with a positive value are highlighted in one way, those with negative values are highlighted in another way, and the break-even point is highlighted in a third way.

e. There is one break-even point, where the number of guests is above 200 and the cost of the meal result in your budget having $0 remaining. Enter this information next to your two-variable data table in cells C29 and C30.

f. Use the Scenario Manager to create two different scenarios, named appropriately, that will calculate the remaining budget with two different guest counts and cost per meal amounts.

g. Create a Scenario Summary Report to show your remaining budget with the two different scenarios created. Provide descriptive labels for the summary report.

h. Make the following modifications on the **Bands** worksheet.

   • Using the Address column, create three new columns that will store the street address, city, and state from the Address column. Use text functions to separate everything before the comma for the street address. Then separate the remaining data into columns using the appropriate delimiter or character location.

- Create a new column and use Flash Fill formulas to concatenate the appropriate phone number formatting symbols to each phone number, for example, (520) 345-3536.
- Create another new column and use Flash Fill to insert a hyphen between the first five characters of the Zip Code and the four-character extension.
- Adjust the column widths so that all data are visible.
- Use the Remove Duplicates tool to delete any duplicate data.

i. Save the workbook, exit Excel, and submit your file as directed by your instructor.

Perform 2: Perform in Your Career

Student data files needed:

Blank Excel Workbook

e05IncomeProjections.txt

You will save your file as:

e05IncomeProjections_LastFirst.xlsx

Income Projections

Finance & Accounting

Production & Operations

An analyst recently helped your company to project its net income for the next several years on the basis of prior-year data. Unfortunately, the data was provided in a text file rather than an Excel workbook. This has made it very hard for your company to analyze the data. Your supervisor has asked you to convert the data into Excel and perform basic analysis on the data to present to the Planning Committee.

a. Start **Excel** and create a new blank workbook. Save the workbook as e05IncomeProjections_LastFirst using your last and first name.

b. Establish a connection to the e05IncomeProjections text file using Get & Transform.

c. Use the first row as the heading row, and replace all of the periods in the first column with space characters.

d. Close and Load the data onto a blank workbook in cell A1 of the first worksheet. Change the tab name to Data

e. Format the workbook as follows.
- Create a new worksheet and change the tab name to BreakEven
- Create a title for the worksheet. Copy the imported data (including the column headings) and paste only the values to the BreakEven worksheet.
- Add any rows as desired to make the data more visually appealing.
- Format as desired.

f. Add formulas where appropriate to complete the analysis.

g. Add a scroll bar to the worksheet. This will allow you to determine your operating profit as more units are sold. The scroll bar should be connected to the year 4 Units data. Your maximum plant capacity is 30,000 units. Use 500-unit increments.

h. Determine the break-even point for year 4, and enter the data in an appropriate location on the worksheet.

i. For the year 4 data, create a one-variable data table based on number of units to review the Revenue, Expenses, and Operating Profit. Use conditional formatting to highlight positive numbers and negative numbers in different ways. Apply appropriate formatting as desired.

j. Create a Cost Volume Profit Chart on a Chart Sheet. Ensure that all data and the sheet tab are labeled appropriately, and apply an appropriate chart style.

k. Insert a new worksheet and change the name to Solver. Copy the data for the year 4 projection from the BreakEven worksheet to the Solver worksheet.

l. Use Solver to create an Answer Report that shows the maximum operating profit possible by changing the number of units, the materials, labor, and variable overhead unit costs, as well as meeting the following constraints.

- You cannot produce more than 30,000 units with your current equipment, and you can produce only whole units.
- The unit cost of materials can range from $15.20 to $17.60.
- The unit cost of labor can range from $23.75 to $27.50.
- The unit cost of variable overhead can range from $5.70 to $6.60.

m. Solve the model with the GRG Nonlinear method and create an Answer Report.

n. Save your Solver model on the Solver worksheet for future use.

o. Save the workbook, exit Excel, and submit your file as directed by your instructor.

Perform 3: Perform in Your Team

Student data file needed:

 e05InventoryAnalysis.xlsx

You will save your file as:

 e05InventoryAnalysis_TeamName.xlsx

The Other Bar and Grill Inventory Management

Production & Operations

You are the bar manager at the Other Bar and Grill, a local restaurant that specializes in fresh-cooked meals for breakfast, lunch, and dinner. The general manager has given you an Excel workbook that contains data about the beverages offered and sold. You need to manage the inventory of beverage items to ensure that you have enough beverages for each day you are open for business and to determine pricing for special drink items. Additionally, the database used for keeping track of inventory has been corrupted, causing some issues with the inventory data. You will need to use your knowledge of Excel to clean the inventory data.

a. Select one team member to set up the document by completing steps b–e.

b. Open your browser and navigate to https://www.onedrive.live.com https://www.drive.google.com or any other instructor-assigned location. Be sure all members of the team have an account on the chosen system.

c. Open the Excel file **e05InventoryAnalysis**. Save your file as e05InventoryAnalysis_TeamName using the name assigned to your team.

d. Create a new worksheet at the beginning of the workbook, and then rename Sheet1 as Contributors List the names of the team members on the worksheet, then add a heading above the name to read Team Members Include any additional information on this worksheet required by your instructor.

e. Share the workbook with the other members of your team. Make sure each team member has the appropriate permission to edit the document.

f. On the DrinkForecast worksheet, complete the following tasks to forecast prices for drink specials.

- In the cell range **D5:D9**, enter a formula that increases this year's quantity sold by 20%. Format the results appropriately.
- In the cell range **F5:F9**, enter a formula that calculates the extended price for next year's forecast.
- The current prices are located in the cell range **E5:E9**. Use Goal Seek to determine new prices in the cell range E5:E9 based on the revenue goals for next year, located in the cell range **G5:G9**.
- Adjust the column widths so that all data are visible.

g. On the DrinkScenarios worksheet, complete the following tasks to create a Scenario summary report.

- In the cell range **E4:E8**, enter a formula that calculates the extended price for next year's forecast. In cell **E9**, enter a formula that calculates the gross revenue.

- In cell **E18**, enter a formula that calculates the variable cost for all drinks sold.

- Open the Scenario Manager. Add a Worst-case scenario and then use the Qty cells as the changing cells. The current values on the worksheet will be your Worst-case scenario values.

- Add a new scenario named Best-case scenario Use the following values as your Scenario values.

  Mojito: 185

  Fuzzy Navel: 65

  Strawberry Daiquiri: 50

  Pina Colada: 35

  The Other Special: 220

h. Add a new scenario named Most-likely scenario Use the following values as your Scenario values.

Mojito: 175

Fuzzy Navel: 50

Strawberry Daiquiri: 35

Pina Colada: 25

The Other Special: 165

i. Create a Scenario Summary Report using the net income cell as your result cell. Format your report with the appropriate row headings and then resize columns if necessary.

j. On the Inventory worksheet, complete the following steps to cleanse the data provided.

- Remove any duplicates that exist in the Inventory worksheet. Duplicate records occur where two or more rows are identical.

- The stock code should consist of all uppercase letters. Create a new column with the appropriate function to display the stock code correctly.

- Create a new column labeled ItemCode. Construct the item code by combining first the corrected stock code and then the item number.

- The data in the Category/Brand column has been corrupted the most. There are several spaces before and after the data that need to be removed. There are also symbols that need to be removed from the data. Additionally, the category and brand should be in two separate columns. Display the corrected values in their own columns labeled Category and Brand. The category data should be in proper case. Use as many columns to the right of the Inventory data as you need to accomplish these tasks.

- Use functions or Flash Fill to separate the units and measurement into two separate columns.

k. Save the workbook, exit Excel, and then submit your file as directed by your instructor.

Perform 4: How Others Perform

Student data files needed:

 e05OnlineOrderAnalysis.xlsx

 e05OnlineOrders.accdb

You will save your file as:

 e05OnlineOrderAnalysis_LastFirst.xlsx

Troubleshooting Online Orders

Finance & Accounting

The company you work for uses an online system to sell and ship its products to customers. It would like to begin analyzing this data, and management has compiled a subset of the data in an Access database. The company had a previous intern attempt an analysis, but he was not able to work well with the data in its current format. You have been asked to import the data into Excel and cleanse it for further analysis. Additionally, you have been asked to check the what-if analysis that was begun for the Exfoliator product the company sells. The intern attempted to build the what-if analysis, but your manager believes that some mistakes were made in the file.

a. Open the Excel file **e05OnlineOrderAnalysis**. Save your file as e05OnlineOrderAnalysis_LastFirst using your last and first name.

b. Establish a connection to the qryTransactionDetails query from the e05Online-Orders.accdb Access database using Get & Transform. Complete the following steps.

   • The data in the TransactionDate field represents the transaction date but is stored as text. The data in the ShippingDate field represents the shipping date for the product but is also stored as text. Both columns are in the YYYYMMDD format. Convert both columns to Date format.

   • Close and Load the data to cell **A1** of the **Transactions** worksheet.

c. Using the two date columns created in the prior step, calculate the number of workdays between the date of the transaction and the shipping date. Your calculation should exclude weekends and any holidays. A listing of 2022 and 2023 holidays can be found in the Holidays worksheet.

d. Establish a connection to the tblCustomers table from the e05OnlineOrders.accdb database file using Get & Transform. Complete the following steps to cleanse the data.

   • Delete the tblTransactionDetails column.

   • Separate the FullName field into two new fields. Do not delete the FullName field and rename the new fields appropriately.

   • Close and Load the data to cell **A1** of the **Customers** worksheet.

e. Complete the following tasks on the **ExfoliatorAnalysis** worksheet to correct the mistakes.

   • Apply appropriate formatting to all numeric values.

   • Check the series data for the chart to ensure that they are correct, and then correct them as needed.

   • Check all existing formulas to ensure that they are correct, and then correct them as needed.

   • In column I, ensure that the conditional formatting identifies values less than zero with a light red fill and dark red text while values greater than zero have a light green fill and dark green text.

   • Ensure that the data table is set up correctly, including hiding any references to formulas using custom formatting.

f. Save the workbook, exit Excel, and then submit your file as directed by your instructor.

Excel Business Unit 6

Building Financial and Statistical Models

Businesses are generating and consuming vast amounts of data. This data can be utilized to make informed business decisions. To accomplish this, the data can be analyzed by using a wide variety of tools in Excel. Functions in Excel can be used to calculate regular payments, interest rates, and the total interest and principal paid on a loan. Creating an amortization schedule will facilitate tracking of the interest and principal paid on a loan for each periodic payment. Bond and investments can also be analyzed by using Excel functions along with calculating the depreciation of assets. A statistical analysis can be completed in Excel by using functions or the Data Analysis add-in. These tools can also be used to predict business outcomes, find relationships between data, and predict future values using a regression analysis.

Learning Outcome 1

Using Excel financial functions, construct a loan analysis, calculate cumulative interest and principal, create an amortization schedule, analyze bonds and investments, and calculate depreciation of assets.

REAL WORLD SUCCESS

"As an intern in the accounting department of an electric engineering company, I was asked to transfer some accounting documents to an Excel workbook. During the process, I was able to identify an error in how the company calculated the depreciation of one of their assets."

– Emily, recent graduate

Learning Outcome 2

Understand statistical language, understand the basic types of data, conduct a statistical analysis using Excel functions and the Data Analysis add-in, predict outcomes using probability distributions, use correlations and covariance to find relationships in data, and use regression analysis to predict future values.

REAL WORLD SUCCESS

"After graduation, I got a job at a small e-marketing firm. The managers were looking over some numbers to decide whether or not they should acquire a smaller company. They had decided to go with the acquisition until someone used statistics to analyze the distribution of the data. It turned out that a few outliers were skewing the numbers and it would have been a very bad decision to acquire the company. I never thought statistics had a place in business until I witnessed firsthand how just a few simple statistical methods can prevent bad decisions."

– James, recent graduate

Microsoft Excel

Chapter 11 LOAN AMORTIZATION, INVESTMENT ANALYSIS, AND ASSET DEPRECIATION

MyLab IT Grader

Finance & Accounting

Prepare Case

The Turquoise Oasis Spa Financial Analysis

Painted Paradise Golf Resort & Spa CEO William Mattingly recently announced that Genisys Corporation, a large technology company, will soon break ground on its new corporate headquarters about three miles from the resort. In addition, Genisys has proposed a partnership with the resort to provide lodging, recreation conferences, and other services to Genisys Corporation staff, executives, and VIP guests. Turquoise Oasis managers Irene Kai and Meda Rodate believe that the new relationship with Genisys Corporation has the potential to double the spa's revenue. To handle the increased business, they plan several upgrades and improvements. The spa will have to handle more simultaneous clients while maintaining high-quality service. The managers would like you to prepare an analysis of several options to finance these improvements and eventual expansion.

Pixel-Shot/Shutterstock

Student data file needed:

 e06ch11Finance.xlsx

You will save your file as:

 e06ch11Finance_LastFirst.xlsx

Constructing a Loan Analysis

Businesses need to have a positive cash flow to survive. **Cash flow** is the movement of cash into and out of a business. The measurement of cash flow can be used to determine a company's value and financial situation. The statement of cash flow is particularly helpful in assessing a company's short-term viability, which includes its abilities to collect cash from customers and to pay bills. The longer a company stays profitable and the better it manages its cash flow, the better its viability. Once a company's value and financial situation have been determined, banks can use that information to determine the company's eligibility for business loans.

From a personal perspective, individuals deal with managing money on a regular basis. People need to understand not only how to successfully invest their money, but also how loans work—such as a car loan, a student loan, or a home loan, known as a mortgage. Personal finance is similar to managing an organization's cash flow except that it relates to the individual's or family's monetary choices. It addresses the ways in which individuals or families obtain, budget, save, and spend money—taking into account various economic risks and future life events, such as getting married or having a family.

An **economic risk** occurs when a chosen act or activity might not generate enough revenue to cover operating costs and repay debt obligations. This notion suggests that a choice has an effect on the outcome. Potential losses themselves may also be called risks. Almost any human endeavor, whether personal or professional, carries some type of risk, but some are riskier than others. For example, the Turquoise Oasis Spa may decide to obtain a bank loan to fund an expansion. Before the bank agrees to finance the loan, it will need to consider many factors, including the spa's cash flow and short-term viability. This will help the bank to determine the level of risk—whether the spa is likely to be able to repay the loan on time and in full.

Excel includes financial functions to use for business and personal analysis, and financial management. It is important to understand the purpose and features of each function so you can apply them to a specific task or problem. These financial functions are designed to calculate the monthly payment and other components of a loan, determine the future value of an investment, compare and contrast different investment opportunities, and calculate the depreciation of assets over time. In the following section, you will conduct a loan analysis using the PMT, RATE, and NPER functions.

Construct a Loan Analysis with PMT, RATE, and NPER

Many businesses and individuals need to borrow money—it is a fact of life. If you need to apply for a loan, you will want to know the monthly payment, which depends on such factors as the loan terms: the principal amount, the interest rate, and the length of the loan. The type of loan that the Turquoise Oasis Spa is considering is an amortized loan. An amortized loan is a loan with scheduled periodic payments consisting of both principal and interest. This is different from other types of loans that have interest-only payment features and balloon payments.

Opening the Starting File

In this exercise, you will open an Excel workbook and begin conducting a loan analysis on four different loan options to fund the Turquoise Oasis Spa expansion.

To Open the e06ch11Finance Workbook

a. Start Excel, click **Open** in the left pane, and then double click **This PC**. Navigate through the folder structure to the location of your student data files, and then double-click **e06ch11Finance**.

> ### Grader Heads Up
> If you are using MyLab IT Grader, this is the beginning of the first MyLab IT Grader project Part A.

b. Click the **File** tab, click **Save As**, and then double-click **This PC**. In the Save As dialog box, navigate to the location where you are saving your project files, and then change the file name to **e06ch11Finance_LastFirst** using your last and first name. Click **Save** 🖫.

Using the PMT Function

The payment function, or **PMT function**, can be used to calculate a payment amount on the basis of constant payments and a constant interest rate. Payments on business loans, mortgages, car loans, or student loans can be calculated. For example, if the managers of the Turquoise Oasis Spa have determined that they need to borrow $250,000 to help fund the spa's expansion and the bank is charging 6.25% interest over a ten-year period, the managers can use the PMT function to determine what the monthly payment would be.

REAL WORLD ADVICE	Additional Costs of a Loan

The payment amount returned by the PMT function includes principal and interest but no taxes, reserve payments, private mortgage insurance, or fees that may be associated with the loan. Be sure to include other fees and charges when calculating your actual expenses associated with a loan. Additional costs can be quite substantial. If you fail to consider them, you may obtain a loan that you cannot afford.

To use the PMT function for the Turquoise Oasis Spa's loan, you have to understand the structure of the function and what each function argument is determining. The PMT function calculates payments for a loan for a fixed amount with a fixed interest rate and for a fixed period of time. The PMT function syntax uses five arguments. The first three are required, and the last two are optional: (1) interest rate per period (rate), (2) number of periods (nper), (3) present value (pv), (4) future value (fv), and (5) type (type). Notice that the optional arguments are represented by square brackets.

=PMT(rate, nper, pv, [fv], [type])

The **rate** argument is the periodic interest rate—the interest rate of the loan. For example, if the annual percentage rate (APR) is 12% and you make monthly payments, the periodic rate—the rate charged per period and in this case, per month—is 1%. This is calculated by dividing the APR by 12, the number of months in a year.

> ### CONSIDER THIS | Determining the Per Period Rate of Interest
> The key to determining the rate of interest per period is in the total number of payments and/or how frequently the payments are made each year. If they are monthly payments, then you need to divide the rate argument by 12. By what would you divide the rate if the payments were made quarterly? What if they were made yearly?

The **nper** argument is the total number of payments that will be made to pay the loan in full. The term of the loan is generally specified in years; however, payments are made several times a year. If the loan is for five years and you make 12 monthly payments, you would calculate the nper by multiplying the number of years by the number of payments in one year. Thus, five years times 12 monthly payments equals 60, which is the number to use in the formula.

The **pv** argument is the present value of the loan, also known as the principal when used in the PMT function. Usually, the loan amount is used as the present value. The PMT function in Excel returns a negative number if all arguments are positive. This is due to the nature of cash flow. Whether the perspective is from the borrower or the lender determines whether the present value is entered as a positive or negative argument.

When viewed from the borrower's perspective, incoming cash flows are "positive," whereas outgoing flows are "negative." In calculating the loan from the borrower's perspective, the pv argument is positive because the borrower receives the cash—a cash inflow. Thus, the PMT function returns a negative amount because the borrower will pay that amount every period—a cash outflow.

In calculating a loan from the bank, or lender's, perspective, the pv argument is negative because the bank pays the money to the borrower—a cash outflow. Thus, the PMT function returns a positive amount because the bank will receive that payment every period—a cash inflow.

Best practice in calculating a loan payment or amortization is to do the calculations from the bank's perspective. Thus, to avoid receiving a negative answer, you can type a negative sign in front of the present value, ensuring a positive payment value. When you are working with financial functions, to avoid getting a wildly incorrect answer, it is important to keep in mind from whose perspective the problem is being calculated.

QUICK REFERENCE | **Cash Flows**

Cash Inflow: A lender or bank is receiving cash in a loan agreement.

Cash Outflow: A lender or bank is paying cash in a loan agreement.

The **fv** argument—future value of the loan—is the balance you want to reach after the last payment has been made. Consider any type of loan that you may have. The ultimate goal is to pay off the loan, meaning that the future value would be zero. If fv is omitted—because it is an optional argument—Excel assumes that the future value is zero.

 CONSIDER THIS | **Using the fv Argument**

A business may lease office equipment and then make regular payments throughout the term of the lease. At the end of the lease, the business may have the option to purchase the equipment for a specific price, which is determined at the lease signing. The amount would be entered in the fv argument of the PMT function. What are some other uses of the fv argument?

The **type** argument indicates when the payments are due—at either the beginning (1) or the end (0) of a period, such as the end of a month, quarter, or year. If type is omitted (because it is an optional argument), Excel assumes that the value is 0, indicating an end of the period payment.

The Turquoise Oasis Spa can use the PMT function to calculate the monthly payment on Loan Option 1 for $250,000 at 6.25% annual interest rate over a ten-year period. Thus, the PMT function arguments would be as follows.

- Rate: 6.25% divided by 12 months = 0.5208%

- Nper: 10 years * 12 months = 120 months

- Pv: –$250,000—Recall that this argument is negative because it represents an out-flow of money.

Because the future value and type arguments are not given, you would end the PMT function after entering the present value and calculate the monthly payment as $2,807.00. If you do not have a future value and the payment is made at the end of the period, you can stop at principal—the pv argument—and just type your ending parenthesis.

=PMT(.0625/12,10*12,–250000)

The amount of the payment can change depending on when the payment needs to be made—at either the beginning or the end of a period—because of how interest is calculated. If the payments are made at the beginning of a period, the total interest that will be paid on the loan is lower because the principal is being paid down faster. The **principal** is the unpaid balance amount of the loan. Because the future value is not given and you want to enter 1 in the type argument, you would type two commas after the present value argument to indicate that you want to skip the future value argument. The PMT function calculates the monthly payment as $2,792.46 and would be entered as follows.

=PMT(.0625/12,10*12,–250000,,1)

 CONSIDER THIS | **What-If Analysis for a Loan**

How could referencing cells with the loan terms allow you to perform what-if analysis? In **what-if analysis**, several different values are used in one or more formulas to explore all the various results. What if you decided that you could not afford the loan payments? How could you modify the interest rate, loan amount, and terms to find a payment that you can afford?

In this exercise, you will calculate a loan payment using the PMT function. For determining cash flows, the calculations will be from the bank's perspective.

 E11.01

SIDE NOTE
Pin the Ribbon
If your ribbon is collapsed, pin your ribbon open. Click the **Home** tab. In the lower-right corner of the ribbon, click Pin the ribbon ⊡.

To Calculate Loan Payments Using the PMT Function

a. This workbook includes information for some of the financing options collected by the managers. On the **LoanAnalysis1–3** worksheet, click cell **B10**, and then examine the formula in the cell.

The pv argument of the PMT function is negative. This indicates that the calculation is from the bank's perspective. The bank will have to pay that amount at the beginning of the loan—a cash outflow.

b. Click cell **B11**, and then type **=PMT(** to begin the PMT function. Click cell **B7**, type **/** and then click **B9** to calculate the rate argument. Because your payments will be monthly, you divide cell B7 by cell B9 to convert the annual interest rate into a monthly interest rate.

c. Type **,** to move to the nper argument.

d. Click cell **B8**, type * and then click cell **B9** to calculate the number of periods in the loan. Because the loan is for 10 years and each year will have 12 payments, there will be 10 × 12, or 120, payments.

e. Type , to move to the pv argument.

f. Type – to indicate that the present value is negative, since this calculation is from the bank's perspective—a cash outflow. Click cell **B6** to select the beginning loan amount. Type ,,1) to omit the fv argument and indicate that payments are due at the beginning of the period.

g. Press Ctrl+Enter. The completed function in cell B11 should appear as =PMT(B7/ B9,B8*B9,–B6,,1). Notice that the difference between the periodic payment amounts in cells B10 and B11 depends on when the payment is made.

h. **Save** 💾 the workbook.

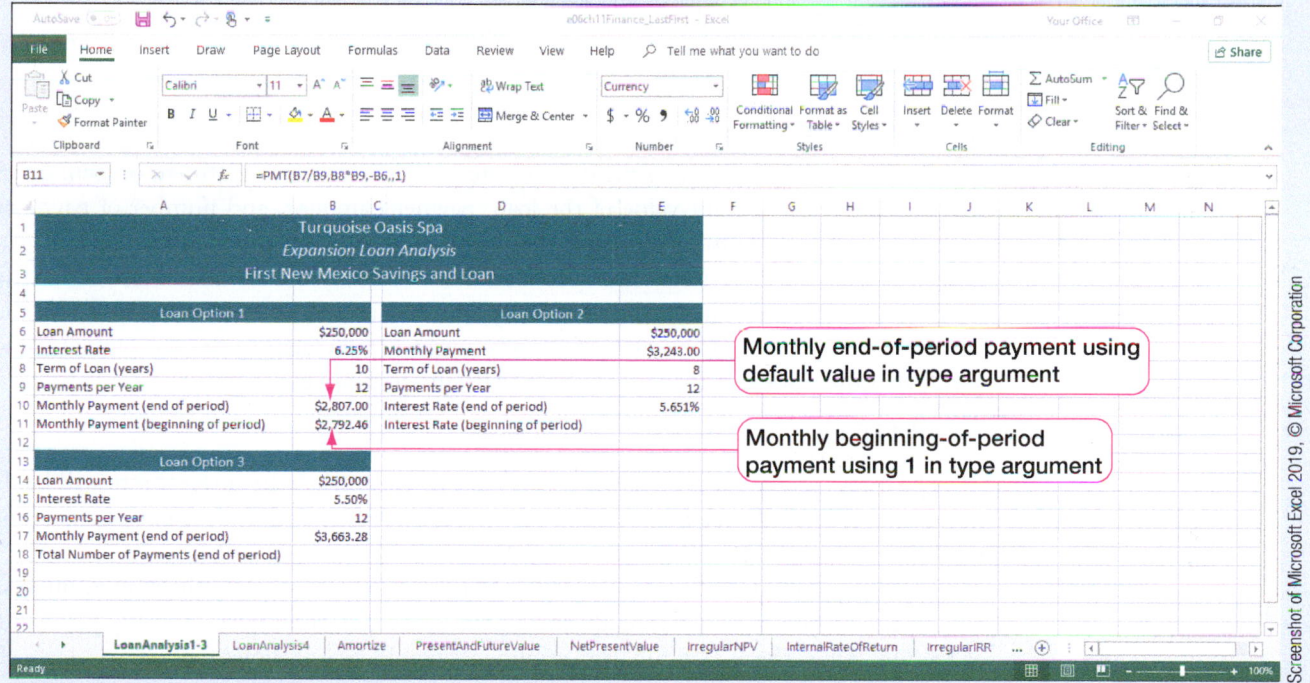

Figure 1 Loan analysis using the PMT function

Screenshot of Microsoft Excel 2019, © Microsoft Corporation

QUICK REFERENCE | **Understanding the PMT Function Syntax**

The PMT function syntax has the following arguments.

Argument	Description
rate	The interest rate per period for the loan. Required.
nper	The total number of periods (payments) for the loan. Required.
pv	The present value, or the total amount that a series of future payments is worth now; also known as the loan amount. Required.
fv	The future value, or a cash balance you want to attain after the last payment has been made. If fv is omitted, it is assumed to be 0 (zero); that is, the future value of a loan is 0. Optional.
type	The number 0 (zero) or 1; indicates when payments are due. Optional. Set type equal to 0—or omit—if payments are due at the end of the period. Set type equal to 1 if payments are due at the beginning of the period.

Using the RATE Function

The **RATE function** calculates the interest rate per period for an investment or loan, given that you know the present value of the loan, payment amount, and number of payment periods. This can be useful if you do not have all the information you need to calculate loan payments with the PMT function or you would like to verify the actual interest rate of the loan. The RATE function syntax uses six arguments. The first three are required, and the last three are optional: (1) number of periods (nper), (2) payment (pmt), (3) present value (pv), (4) future value (fv), (5) type (type), and (6) interest rate guess (guess).

=RATE(nper, pmt, pv, [fv], [type], [guess])

The **guess** argument is used when you want to guess what the interest rate will be. If nothing is entered, Excel assumes that the guess is 10%. If RATE does not calculate, or results in a #NUM! error, you can enter a guess value between 0 and 1.

The Turquoise Oasis Spa can use the RATE function to calculate the annual interest rate on Loan Option 2 for $250,000 to be paid over eight years with monthly payments of $3,243. Thus, the RATE function arguments would be as follows.

- Nper: 8 years * 12 months = 96 months
- Pmt: $3,243
- Pv: $250,000

=RATE(8*12,3243,−250000)

Because the future value, type, and guess arguments are optional, you would end the RATE function after entering the present value and calculate the interest rate as 0.565%. It is important to note that the result in this case is the monthly interest rate because you used 12 times the number of loan years. If you were making payments quarterly and used 4 times the number of loan years or annually, the number of loan years only, Excel would calculate the rate as quarterly or annually. If you wanted to calculate the annual interest rate from the monthly result, you could simply multiply the rate by 12. As a result, the bank would be charging the Turquoise Oasis Spa 5.651% annually.

=RATE(8*12,3243,−250000)*12

In this exercise, you will use the RATE function to calculate the interest rate for a loan for which the payment is due at the beginning of the period. For determining cash flows, the calculations will be from the bank's perspective.

 **E11.02**

To Calculate the Interest Rate of a Loan Using the RATE Function

a. Click cell **E10**, and notice that the RATE function has already been entered for the end of period Interest Rate. The RATE function returns 5.651%.

b. Click cell **E11**, and then type =RATE(to begin the RATE function.

c. Click cell **E8**, type * and then click cell **E9** to calculate the nper argument.

d. Type , to move to the pmt argument. Click cell **E7** to supply the monthly payment amount for the RATE function. Type , to move to the pv argument.

e. Type – and then click cell **E6**. This will calculate the present value of the loan as negative for the RATE function, indicating that it is being calculated from the bank's perspective. The bank will have to pay that amount at the beginning of the loan—a cash outflow.

f. Type ,,1)* and then click cell **E9** to calculate the annual interest rate for a loan where the payment is made at the beginning of the period. Press Ctrl + Enter.

g. The completed function in cell E11 should appear as =RATE(E8*E9,E7,–E6,,1)*E9. Notice that the annual interest rate is 5.780% when the payment is made at the beginning of the period.

> ### Troubleshooting
> If the RATE function returns #NUM! instead of the expected interest rate, then check to make sure there is a negative sign before the pv argument. For the RATE function to work, either the pmt argument or the pv argument must be negative.

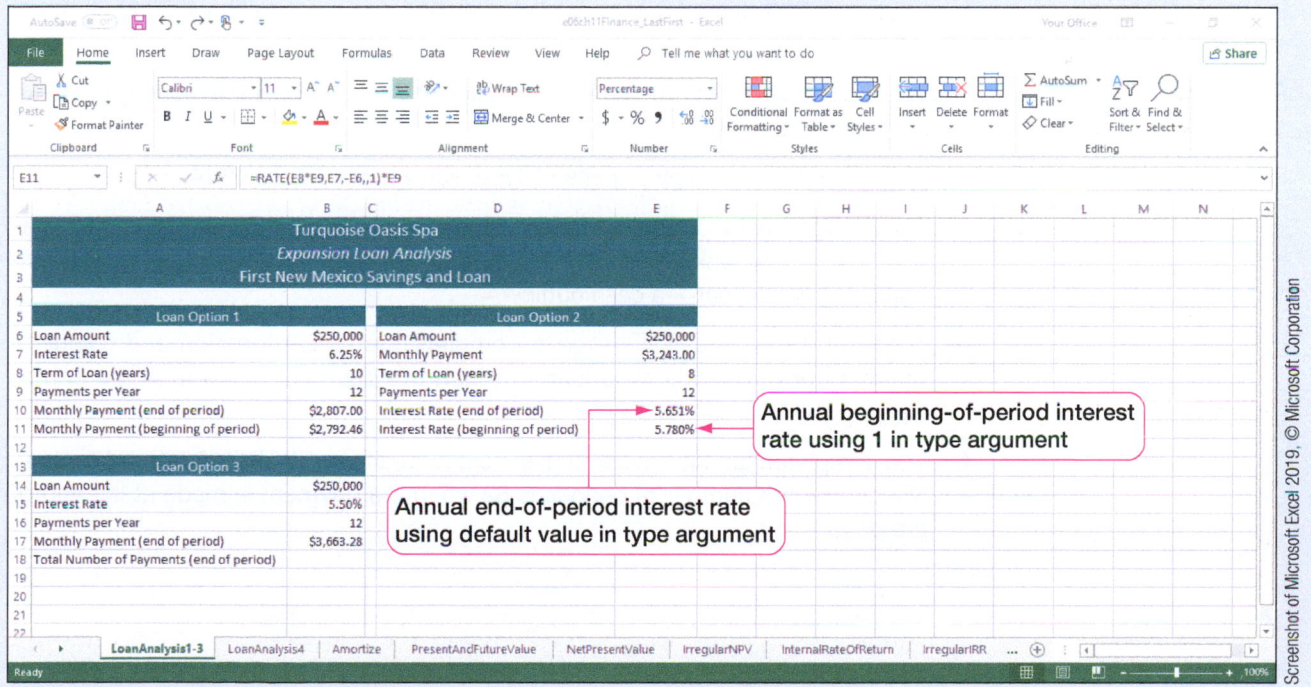

Figure 2 Loan analysis using the RATE function

h. Save the workbook.

Using the NPER Function

The number of periods function, or **NPER function**, calculates the number of payment periods for an investment or loan if you know the loan amount, interest rate, and payment amount. The NPER function syntax uses five arguments. The first three are required, and the last two are optional: (1) rate (rate), (2) payment (pmt), (3) present value (pv), (4) future value (fv), and (5) type (type).

=NPER(rate, pmt, pv, [fv], [type])

The Turquoise Oasis Spa can use the NPER function to calculate the number of periods on Loan Option 3 for a $250,000 loan with an annual rate of 5.50% if the monthly payment is $3,663.28, paid at the end of the period. Thus, the NPER function arguments would be as follows.

- Rate: 5.50%
- Pmt: $3,663.28
- Pv: $250,000

=NPER(.055/12, 3663.28, −250000)

In this exercise, because the future value and type arguments are optional, you will end the NPER function after entering the present value and calculate the number of periods as 82. For determining cash flows, the calculations will be from the bank's perspective.

 **E11.03**

To Calculate the Total Number of Periods Using the NPER Function

a. Click cell **B18**, and then type **=NPER(** to begin the NPER function.

b. Click cell **B15**, type **/** and then click cell **B16** to calculate the monthly interest rate.

c. Type **,** to move to the pmt argument. Click cell **B17** to supply the monthly payment for the NPER function.

d. Type **,** to move to the pv argument. Type **−** and then click cell **B14**.

   The pv argument of the NPER function is negative. This indicates that the calculation is from the bank's perspective. The bank will have to pay that amount at the beginning of the loan—a cash outflow.

e. Type **)** and then press ⌈Ctrl⌉+⌈Enter⌉ to complete the NPER function and calculate the number of periods for a loan in which the payment is made at the end of the period.

f. The completed function in cell **B18** should appear as =NPER(B15/B16,B17,−B14). Notice that the number of periods is 82 when the payment is made at the end of the period.

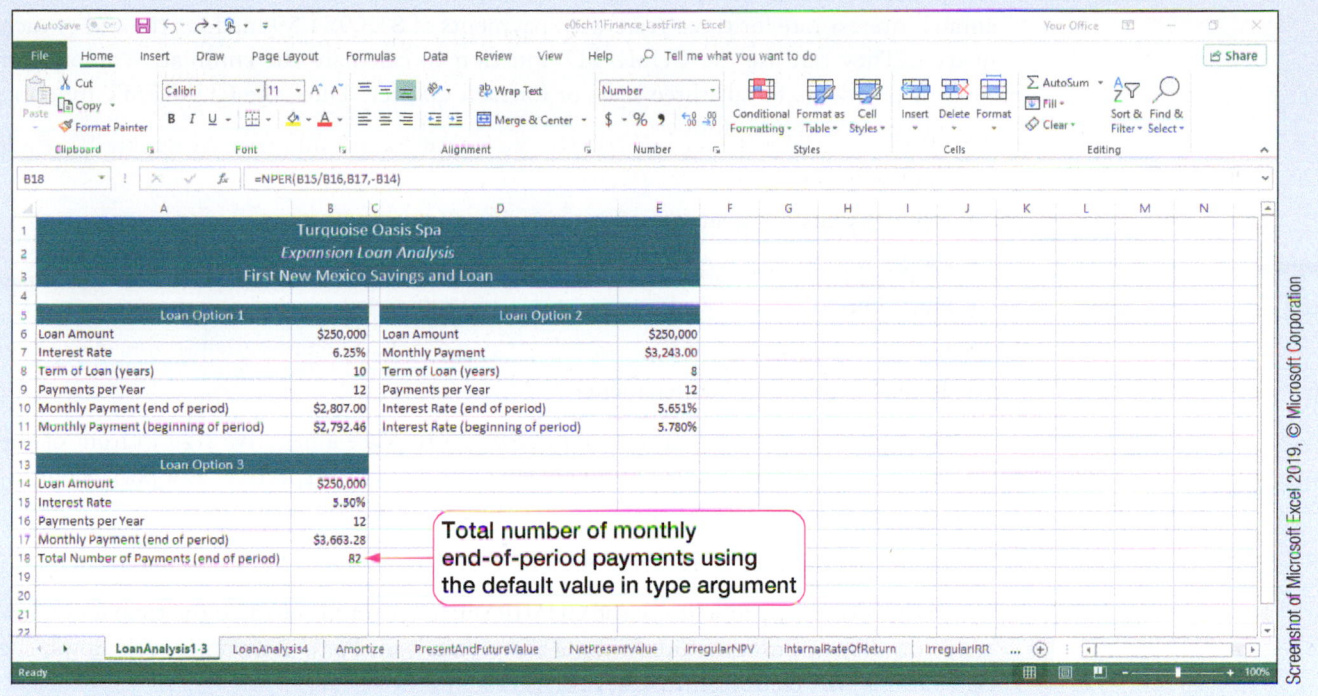

Figure 3 Loan analysis using the NPER function

    g. Save 🖫 the workbook.

Calculate Cumulative Interest and Principal Using CUMIPMT and CUMPRINC

Each loan payment in an amortized loan is made up of a principal amount and an interest amount. There are times when you will want to know the total interest or principal amount being paid over a particular time period. Consider a mortgage. If someone is paying on a mortgage, they can use the amount of interest paid throughout the year as a deduction on their federal income taxes. Thus, knowing the amount of cumulative interest paid can make it easier to complete this section on a tax return.

Using the CUMIPMT Function

The cumulative interest payment function, or **CUMIPMT function**, can be used to calculate the amount of interest paid over a specific number of periods, such as quarterly, annually, or for the whole term of the loan. Thus, if you do not want to calculate a running total of the interest paid, you can total the payments between two payment periods. The CUMIPMT function syntax uses six arguments, all of which are required: (1) rate (rate), (2) number of periods (nper), (3) present value (pv), (4) start period (start_period), (5) end period (end_period), and (6) type (type).

    =CUMIPMT(rate, nper, pv, start_period, end_period, type)

    The two new arguments are start_period and end_period; they indicate the period numbers during the life of the loan. Start_period defines the start payment period for the interval you want to sum. The end_period defines the end payment period.

The Turquoise Oasis Spa is also considering Loan Option 4 for $250,000 at an 8.65% annual interest rate for three years with payments of $18,984.59 made at the end of each quarter. They can use the CUMIPMT function to calculate the cumulative amount of interest payments for all three years or for each quarter. Thus, the CUMIPMT function arguments would be as follows.

- Rate: 8.65%
- Nper: 3 years * 4 quarters = 12 quarterly payments
- Pv: $250,000
- Start_period: 1
- End_period: 12
- Type: 0—end of period payments

With this function, Excel does not allow you to place a negative sign in front of the pv argument. Thus, to display numbers from the bank's perspective, as a positive number, you can simply place a negative sign before the function name.

=–CUMIPMT(.0865/4, 3*4, 250000, 1, 12, 0)

In this exercise, you will use the CUMIPMT function to calculate the total and quarterly cumulative interest paid during a three-year loan. For determining cash flows, the calculations will be from the bank's perspective.

 **E11.04**

To Calculate Cumulative Interest Payments Using the CUMIPMT Function

a. Click the **LoanAnalysis4** worksheet. Click cell **B13**, and type =–CUMIPMT(to begin the CUMIPMT function. The negative sign indicates that the CUMIPMT function is from the bank's perspective. The bank will receive the interest payments on the loan—a cash inflow.

b. Click cell **B7**, type / and then click cell **B9** to calculate the interest rate for the CUMIPMT function.

c. Type , to move to the nper argument. Click cell **B8**, type * and then click cell **B9** to calculate the number of periods.

d. Type , to move to the pv argument. Click cell **B6**, which contains the present value of the loan.

e. Type ,1 to move to the start_period argument and begin calculating interest in the first period.

f. Type ,12 to move to the end_period argument and stop calculating interest in the twelfth period. Type ,0) to calculate the total cumulative interest payments for the life of the loan based on payments being made at the end of the period. Press Ctrl+Enter.

The completed function in cell B13 should appear as =–CUMIPMT(B7/B9,B8*B9,B6,1,12,0). Notice that the cumulative interest is $36,517.43 when the payment is made at the end of the period.

g. Click cell **B17**, and type =–CUMIPMT(to begin the CUMIPMT function that will calculate the interest paid in the first quarterly payment. The negative sign indicates the CUMIPMT function is from the bank's perspective. The bank will receive the quarterly interest payment on the loan—a cash inflow.

h. Click cell **B7**, and press F4 to lock the cell reference. Type **/** and click cell **B9**. Press F4 to lock the cell reference. This calculates the rate for the CUMIPMT function and locks the cell references so that the formula can be copied down the column later.

i. Type **,** to move to the nper argument. Click cell **B8**, and press F4 to lock the cell reference. Type ***** and click cell **B9**. Press F4 to lock the cell reference. This calculates the number of periods for the CUMIPMT function and locks the cell references so that the formula can be copied down the column later.

j. Type **,** to move to the pv argument. Click cell **B6**, which contains the present value of the loan, and then press F4 to lock the cell reference.

k. Type **,** to move to the start_period argument. Click cell **A17**, which contains a 1, indicating the first quarterly payment. This cell reference will need to stay relative to the current cell when copied down the column.

l. Type **,** to move to the end_period argument. Click cell **A17**, which contains a 1, indicating the first quarterly payment. As the function is copied down the column, the CUMIPMT function will calculate the interest paid in each period.

m. Type **,0)** to move to the type argument and calculate the periodic interest for the first quarterly payment. Press Ctrl+Enter. The completed function in cell B17 should appear as =–CUMIPMT($B$7/$B$9,$B$8*$B$9,$B$6,A17,A17,0).

n. Double-click the **fill handle** to copy the formula down to cell **B28**. Notice that the amount of the cumulative interest payments decreases with each quarterly payment because the amount of principal is less after each quarterly payment.

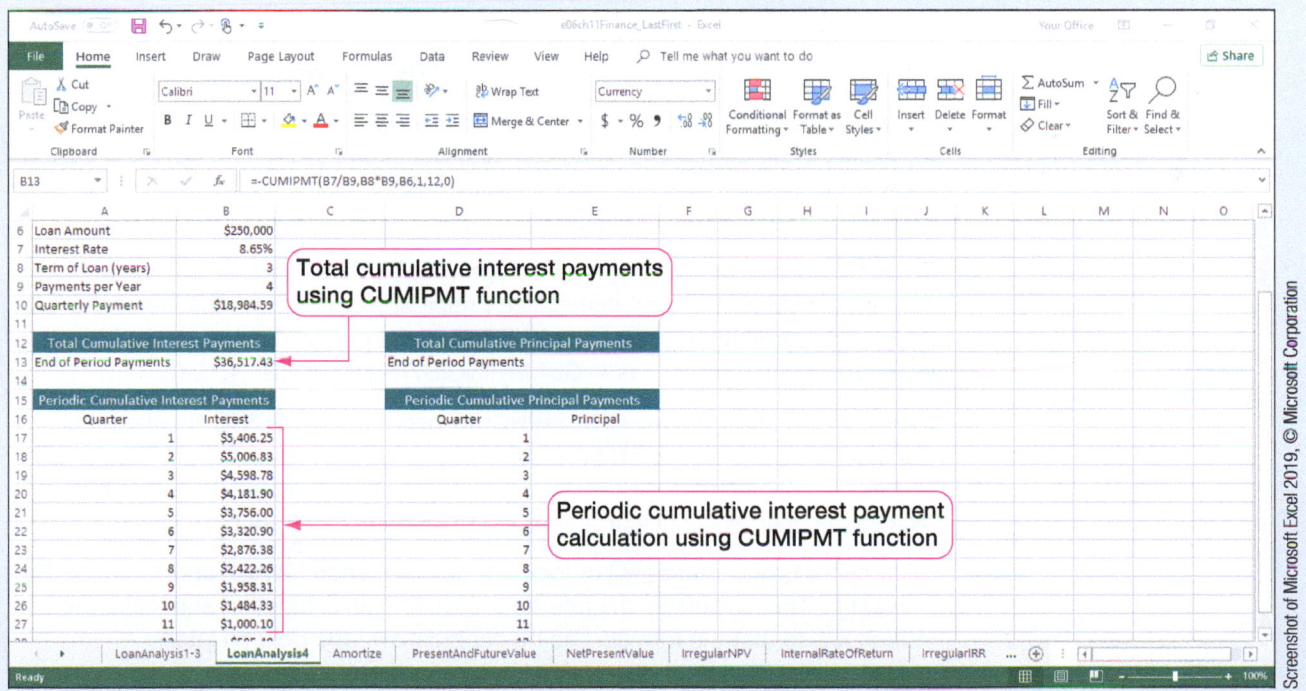

Figure 4 Loan analysis using the CUMIPMT function

o. **Save** 💾 the workbook.

Using the CUMPRINC Function

Similar to the CUMIPMT function, the cumulative principal function, or **CUMPRINC function**, can be used to calculate the amount of principal paid over a specific number of periods, such as quarterly or annually. Thus, if you do not want to calculate a running total of the principal paid, you can total the payments between two payment periods. The CUMPRINC function syntax uses the same six arguments that the CUMIPMT uses, all of which are required. As in using the CUMIPMT function, you cannot place a negative sign in front of the pv argument. To display numbers as a positive result, you can simply place a negative sign before the function name.

=–CUMPRINC(rate, nper, pv, start_period, end_period, type)

In this exercise, you will use the CUMPRINC function to find the total cumulative principal paid per year for the loan. For determining cash flows, the calculations will be from the bank's perspective.

 **E11.05**

To Calculate Cumulative Principal Payments Using the CUMPRINC Function

a. Click cell **E13**, and type =–CUMPRINC(to begin the CUMPRINC function. The negative sign indicates that the CUMPRINC function is from the bank's perspective. The bank will receive the principal interest payment on the loan—a cash inflow.

b. Click cell **B7**, type / and then click cell **B9** to calculate the quarterly interest rate.

c. Type , to move to the nper argument. Click cell **B8**, type * and then click cell **B9** to calculate the total number of payments.

d. Type , to move to the pv argument. Click cell **B6** to reference the loan amount.

e. Type , to move to the start_period argument. Type 1 to indicate that you want to calculate the cumulative principal paid, beginning in the first payment period. Type ,12 to move to the end_period argument and indicate that you want to stop calculating the cumulative principal paid in the twelfth payment period.

f. Type , to move to the type argument. Type 0) and press `Ctrl`+`Enter` to finish the function and calculate the total cumulative principal payments for the life of the loan based on payments being made at the end of the period. The completed function in cell E13 should appear as =–CUMPRINC(B7/B9,B8*B9,B6,1,12,0).

g. Click cell **E17**, and type =–CUMPRINC(to begin a CUMPRINC function that will calculate the cumulative principal paid each quarter of the loan period. The negative sign indicates the CUMPRINC function is from the bank's perspective. The bank will receive the quarterly principal interest payment on the loan—a cash inflow.

h. Click cell **B7**, and press `F4` to lock the cell reference. Type / and click cell **B9**. Press `F4`. This calculates the rate for the CUMPRINC function and locks the cell references so that the formula can be copied down the column later.

i. Type , to move to the nper argument. Click cell **B8**, and then press `F4`. Type * and click cell **B9**. Press `F4` to lock the cell references.

j. Type , to move to the pv argument. Click cell **B6** to reference the current loan amount and then press `F4`.

k. Type , to move to the start_period argument. Click cell **D17** to reference the first quarter as the starting period.

l. Type **,** to move to the end_period argument. Click cell **D17** to reference the first quarter as the ending period.

m. Type **,0)** and press Ctrl+Enter to calculate the cumulative principal paid in the first quarterly payment. The completed function in cell E17 should appear as =–CUMPRINC($B$7/$B$9,$B$8*$B$9,$B$6,D17,D17,0).

n. Double-click the **fill handle** to copy the formula down to cell **E28**. Notice that the value of the cumulative principal payments increases with each quarterly payment. This is because with each payment, the principal gets smaller and therefore less interest is accruing per period on the amount and more of the payment goes toward paying off the principal.

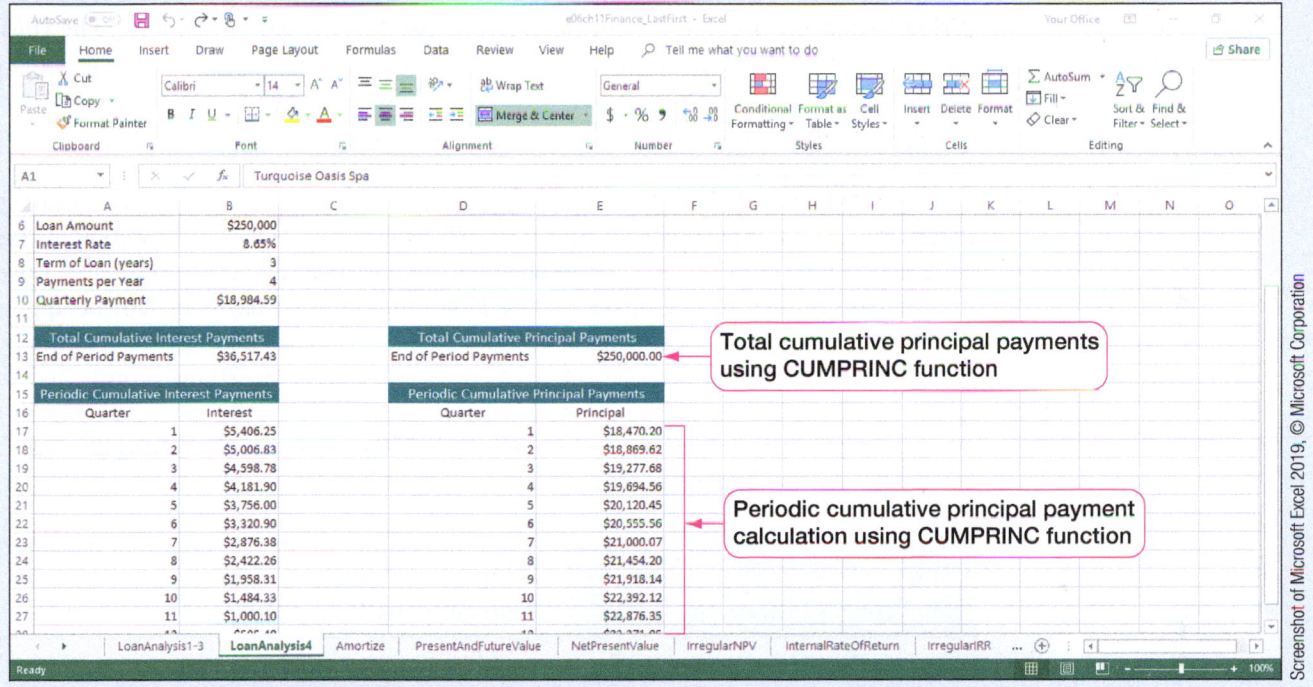

Figure 5 Loan analysis using the CUMPRINC function

o. Save the workbook.

Create an Amortization Schedule Using PPMT and IPMT

With the financial functions you have learned so far, you have some effective tools to help you make an informed decision about which loan option is best to finance the expansion project. Another tool that can help with the decision is an amortization table.

The term **amortize**, with respect to loan balances, refers to repaying the balance of a loan over a period of time in multiple installments—or payments. An **amortization schedule** is a table that calculates the interest and principal payments along with the remaining balance of the loan for each period. Similar to the CUMIPMT and CUM-PRINC functions, which calculate the cumulative amount of interest and principal paid over a specified period of time, the IPMT and PPMT functions calculate the interest and principal portions that make up each periodic payment.

Using the PPMT and IPMT Functions

The principal payment function, or **PPMT function**, calculates how much of a specific periodic payment is going toward the principal amount of a loan. The PPMT function syntax uses six arguments. The first four are required, and the last two are optional: (1) interest rate per period (rate), (2) period (per), (3) number of periods (nper), (4) present value (pv), (5) future value (fv), and (6) type (type).

The syntax of the PPMT function is very similar to that of the PMT function, with the addition of the period (per) argument. The **per** argument is a number that must be between 1 and nper and is the specific period for which a loan payment is being applied. As you make payments on an amortized loan, the amount you pay each period is the same, but how much of that payment is being applied toward the principal increases over time. The per argument is needed to keep track of each payment.

The interest payment function, or **IPMT function**, calculates how much of a specific periodic payment is going toward the interest that has accrued on the loan. The IPMT function syntax is the same as that of the PPMT function. When you begin making payments on an amortized loan, in the beginning, the majority of the amount being paid goes toward interest that has accrued on the remaining balance; this amount decreases over time as the principal is paid down.

Turquoise Oasis Spa could use an amortization table to analyze the loan options for additional improvements. For example, Irene Kai would like to borrow $30,000 for new equipment and to pay this loan off in one year. By creating an amortization table showing the date of each payment, she can see how much of each payment will be applied to the interest and to the principal as well as the balance of the loan. After creating the amortization table, she finds that the payment would be $2,588.20 per month, and the salon would end up paying $1,058.43 in interest over the life of the loan. In this section, you will create an amortization table to help Irene Kai analyze the repayment schedule to determine whether the payments are within the spa's budget.

REAL WORLD ADVICE	Things to Check in an Amortization Table

There are four things that you can check to ensure that you have accurately constructed your amortization table.

- The final remaining balance value in your table should be zero.

- A given periodic payment (PMT) will equal the sum of the interest payment (IPMT) and the principal payment (PPMT).

- The sum of the principal payments (PPMT) will always equal the loan amount. If you add interest, it will be the total amount paid over the course of the loan term in both interest and principal.

- All interest and principal paid should equal the sum of all the payments made.

  You can check your calculations in one easy step. Highlight a range of cells, such as the IPMT and PPMT calculations for the first period, and Excel displays the Average, Count, and Sum for the selection in the status bar located at the bottom of the Excel window.

Creating an Amortization Schedule

When you create an amortization table, start with the simplest configuration. Initially, you should calculate the payment number, the payment amount, the interest and principal portions, and an ending balance for each payment. You can always add more details and complexity later. In this exercise, you will create an amortization table for the new equipment loan. The total number of payments is already calculated in cell G5 of the Amortize worksheet. For determining cash flows, the calculations will be from the bank's perspective.

SIDE NOTE

Interest Payments

Notice how the interest portion of each payment decreases as the loan is paid off—from $161.25 to $13.84 at the end.

SIDE NOTE

Remaining Balance

Interest payments are the costs associated with the loan and are never deducted from the beginning balance.

To Create an Amortization Schedule

a. Click the **Amortize** worksheet. Click cell **G6**, and then type **=PMT(** to begin the PMT function.

b. Click cell **C6** to reference the annual interest rate. Type **/** and then click cell **C8** to reference the number of payments per year. This calculates the monthly interest for the PMT function.

c. Type **,** to move to the nper argument. Click cell **G5** to reference the number of payments.

d. Type **,–** to move to the pv argument. The calculations are from the bank's perspective. The bank will have to pay that amount at the beginning of the loan—a cash outflow.

e. Click cell **C5**, type **)** and then press Ctrl+Enter to reference the loan amount and calculate the payments that will be made at the end of the period. The completed function in cell G6 should appear as =PMT(C6/C8,G5,–C5). Notice that the monthly payment will be $2,588.20.

f. Click cell **G7**, and then type **=**. Click cell **G5**, type * and then click cell **G6** to calculate the total amount that will be paid. Press Enter, and notice that the total amount that will be paid on the loan is $31,058.43.

g. In cell G8 type **=** Click cell **G7**, type **–** and then click cell **C5** to calculate the total interest that will be paid on the loan. Press Ctrl+Enter and notice that the total interest that will be paid on the loan is $1,058.43.

h. Click cell **C12**, type **=** and then click cell **C5** to reference the beginning balance of the loan and begin creating your amortization schedule.

i. Press Tab, and type **=** Click cell **G6**, press F4, and then press Ctrl+Enter to enter your payment. Double-click the **fill handle** to copy the formula down to cell **D23**. The total in D24 should equal your results in cell G7.

j. Click cell **E12**, and then type **=IPMT(** to begin the IPMT function.

k. Click cell **C6** to reference the annual interest rate and then press F4. Type **/** and click cell **C8**. Press F4 to reference the number of payments per year and calculate the monthly interest.

l. Type **,** to move to the per argument. Click cell **A12**, as this will be the first period of interest.

m. Type **,** to move to the nper argument. Click cell **G5**, and press F4 to reference the total number of payments.

n. Type **,** to move to the pv argument. Type **–** and click cell **C5**. Press F4 to reference the loan amount. The pv argument of the IPMT function is negative. This indicates that the calculation is from the bank's perspective. The bank will have to pay that amount at the beginning of the loan—a cash outflow.

o. Type **)** and press Ctrl+Enter to complete the function and calculate how much of the monthly payment is being applied to the interest portion of the loan. The completed function in cell E12 should appear as =IPMT($C$6/$C$8,A12,$G$5,–$C$5). Double-click the **fill handle** to copy the formula down to cell **E23**. The total in E24 should equal your results in cell G8.

p. Click cell **F12**, and then type **=PPMT(** to begin the PPMT function.

q. Click cell **C6**, and press F4 to reference the annual interest. Type **/** and click cell **C8**. Press F4 to reference the payments per year and calculate the monthly interest.

r. Type **,** to move to the per argument. Click cell **A12**, as this will be the first period of principal payments.

s. Type **,** to move to the nper argument. Click cell **G5**, and press F4 to reference the total number of payments.

t. Type **,** to move to the pv argument. Type **–** and click cell **C5**. Press F4 to reference the loan amount. The pv argument of the PPMT function is negative. This indicates that the calculation is from the bank's perspective. The bank will have to pay that amount at the beginning of the loan—a cash outflow.

u. Type **)** and press Ctrl+Enter to calculate how much of the monthly payment is being applied to the principal portion of the loan. The completed function in cell F12 should appear as =PPMT($C$6/$C$8,A12,$G$5,–$C$5). Double-click the **Auto-Fill** handle to copy the formula down to cell **F23**. Notice how the principal portion of the payment increases as the loan is paid off, with $2,426.95 total principal being paid in the first payment and $2,574.36 total principal being paid in the last payment. The total principal in F24 should equal the loan amount in C5.

v. Click cell **G12**, and then type **=**. Click cell **C12**, type **–** and click cell **F12** to calculate the remaining balance after each payment by subtracting the principal payment from the beginning balance. Press Ctrl+Enter, and double-click the **fill handle** to copy the formula down to cell **G23**. Note that the calculations will be negative until you fill in the beginning balance.

w. Your beginning balance for the next payment will be the same as the ending balance after the previous payment. Click cell **C13**, type **=** and then click cell **G12** to calculate the beginning balance for the second period. Press Ctrl+Enter, and double-click the **fill handle** to copy the formula down to cell **C23** to supply the beginning balance for the remaining periods.

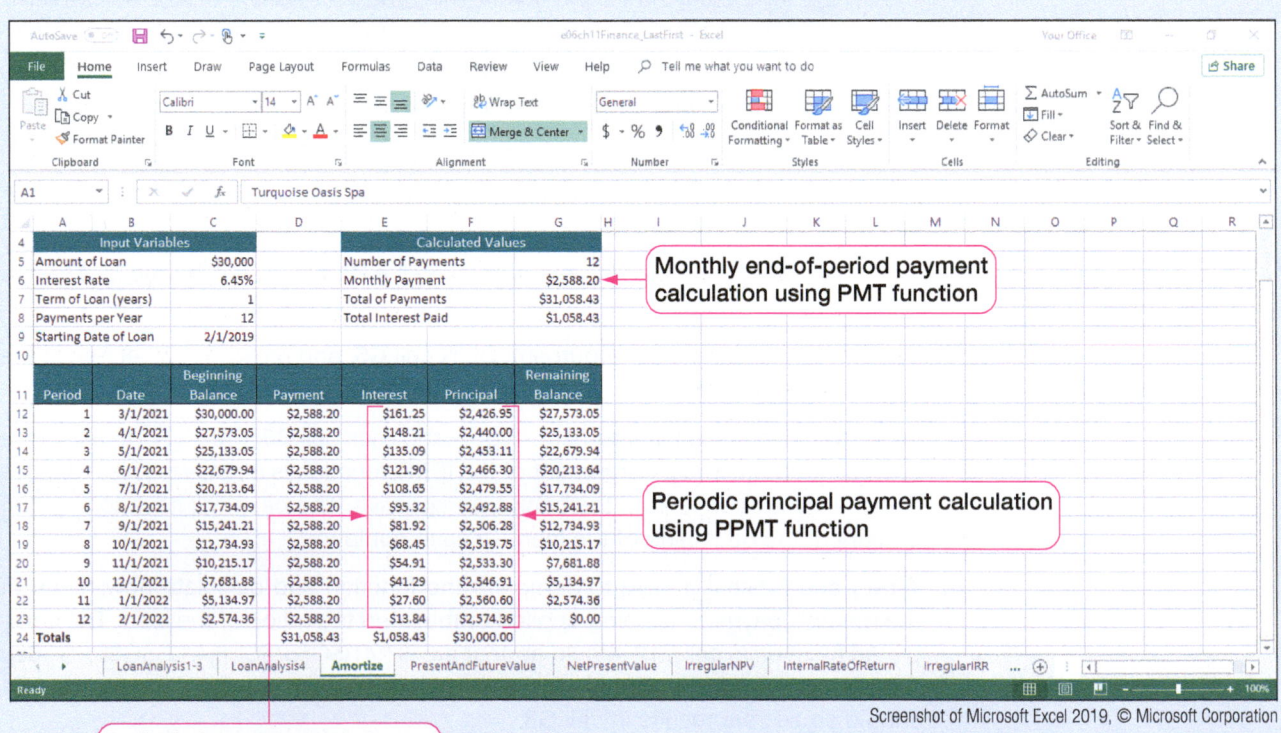

Periodic interest payment calculation using IPMT function

Figure 6 Amortization schedule

x. Save 🖫 the workbook. If you need to take a break before finishing this chapter, now is a good time.

Grader Heads Up

If you are using MyLab IT Grader, this is the end of the first MyLab IT Grader project Part A. This project continues in Part B which is a separate MyLab IT Grader project.

REAL WORLD ADVICE	Selecting the Right Loan

In deciding among several different loan options with various terms, rates, and payment frequencies, it is important to get the big picture. Time plays an important role in the total cost of a loan. If you can afford larger payments, you could save a lot of money by selecting a 15-year loan over a 30-year loan as you will likely pay less interest. Be sure to use all the tools available to you to thoroughly analyze your options so that you can make the most informed decision possible.

Constructing a Financial Analysis of Investments

In addition to analyzing possible expansion finance options from a bank, managers at the Turquoise Oasis Spa would like to analyze some possible investment opportunities to help finance the expansion and generate revenue in the long term. Whether it is a business or an individual investing money, analyzing how the investments are performing is a critical part of the investment process. There are many methods by which money can be invested. Stocks and bonds are two examples of a category of investment called securities.

A **security** is a legal document that can be bought and sold and holds some financial value. Stocks are categorized as equity securities because the company gives partial ownership of its equity, defined as total assets minus total liabilities, by selling stock in the company. Bonds are categorized as debt securities because the company is indebted to the people who loan the company money through the purchase of bonds.

In terms of economic risk, a bond is typically considered less risky, in part because if a company fails, the debt owed to the bondholders is top priority and shareholders would lose any money invested in the company. A lower-risk investment can also mean a lower return on that investment. A **return on investment (ROI)** is the ratio of the amount of money gained or lost from an investment relative to the initial amount invested. A stockholder takes on more risk than a bondholder and therefore has the potential for a higher ROI if the company is successful. In this section, you will learn how to analyze various investment options from bonds to individual retirement accounts.

Analyze Bonds Using PV and FV

Generally speaking, the way bonds work is that an investor loans a company money for a specified period of time by purchasing a bond certificate. Typically, bonds have a fixed interest rate, and the bondholder receives annuity payments either annually or semiannually throughout the life of the bond. An **annuity** is a recurring amount paid or received at specified intervals. Once the specified time period of the bond has been reached, the bondholder is issued the value of the bond.

There are four basic concepts integral to understanding bonds. The first is par value. The **par value**—or face value—is how much the bondholder will receive at maturity. **Maturity** is the second concept and refers to the length of time before par value is returned to the bondholder. Most bond maturities range from 1 to 30 years, but they can have a range anywhere from 1 day to 100 years or more. The third concept is coupon. **Coupon** is the interest rate the bond pays. Typically, the coupon payments are made to the bondholder annually or semiannually until the bond reaches maturity. For most bonds, the coupon rate does not vary for the life of the bond. The fourth concept is **yield**.

In its most basic terms, yield is the amount of annual interest, expressed as a percentage of the par value, and determines how much investors will receive on their investment.

There are several different types of yield in referring to bonds. **Nominal yield** is the same as the coupon or interest rate. It is information provided when the bond is purchased and is considered the least helpful when it comes to analyzing the true value of a bond. **Current yield** considers the current market price of the bond, which may differ from the par value, and gives you a different yield rate on that basis. For example, consider the following: You purchase a bond with the following values on the open market for $800.

> Par Value: $1,000
> Coupon: 6% annually
> Maturity: 1 year

If the bond's purchase price was the same as the par value, the nominal yield would be the same as the coupon of 6%, and you would have $1,060 ($1,000 * .06 = $60) at the end of the year when the bond reaches maturity. However, since the bond was purchased for $800, a more accurate yield calculation would be the current yield of 7.5% ($60/$800 = 7.5%). **Yield to maturity**, or YTM, is another yield calculation that takes into account the current market price and the time to maturity and assumes that coupon payments are reinvested at the bond's coupon rate. YTM is the most useful calculation in determining the value of a bond investment and the most difficult to calculate.

Using the PV Function

Regardless of how you decide to invest your money—whether you are saving for a home, college, or retirement—if you understand the basics of analyzing your investment portfolio, you will be able to assess its performance. One of the functions that can help you analyze an investment is the present value function, or PV function. The **PV function** is used to calculate the present or current value of a series of future payments on an investment. In other words, it calculates what the investment would be worth in today's dollars. It uses the same five arguments seen in other financial functions: (1) rate (rate), (2) number of periods (nper), (3) payment (pmt), (4) future value (fv), and (5) type (type). If you do not know the payment, you must enter the future value.

> =PV(rate, nper, pmt, [fv], [type])

For example, if you were given the option of receiving $250,000 today or $300,000 seven years from now, which would you choose? Excel's PV function can help to determine the smarter choice. Assume that if you took the $250,000 today, you could invest that in a guaranteed risk-free bond at 3% yield rate for seven years. Using the PV function to calculate the present value of $300,000 with a discount rate of 3% for seven years, you see that the $300,000 seven years from now results in a lower present value— $243,927.45—than $250,000 today.

> =–PV(0.03,7,0,300000)

Turquoise Oasis Spa managers are considering a different option for financing part of the expansion: investing in a company bond with the following values.

> Par value: $75,000
> Maturity: 5 years
> Coupon: 5.50%
> YTM: 7.75%

The first step in determining whether or not this is a worthy investment is to calculate the present value of the investment. In this exercise, you will use the PV function to calculate the present value of the investment. For determining cash flows, the calculations will be from the bank's perspective.

E11.07

SIDE NOTE
Coupon Rate
The coupon rate is used to calculate the amount of the annuity payment paid to the bondholder.

SIDE NOTE
Yield to Maturity
If it is known, using the YTM rate in the PV function gives a much more accurate prediction of the present value of the bond.

To Calculate the Present Value of a Bond

a. If you took a break, open the **e06ch11Finance_LastFirst** workbook.

> **Grader Heads Up**
> If you are using MyLab IT Grader, this is the beginning of the second MyLab IT Grader project Part B.

b. Click the **PresentAndFutureValue** worksheet. Click cell **B8**, type **=** and then click cell **B6** to reference the Coupon Rate.

c. Type ***** and click cell **B5**. Press Ctrl+Enter to reference the Par Value and calculate the coupon payment that will be paid to the bondholder one time a year for five years.

d. Click cell **B10**, and then type **=–PV(** to begin the PV function. The negative sign indicates that the PV function is from the bank's perspective. The bank will receive the bond amount—a cash inflow.

e. Click cell **B9** to reference the yield to maturity rate.

f. Type **,** to move to the nper argument. Click cell **B7** to reference the maturity in years.

g. Type **,** to move to the pmt argument. Click cell **B8** to reference the annual coupon payment.

h. Type **,** to move to the fv argument. Click cell **B5**, type **)** and press Ctrl+Enter to calculate the present value of the investment as a positive number. Notice that the present value of this particular bond is worth only $68,217.67, which is less than $75,000 and therefore not a good investment.

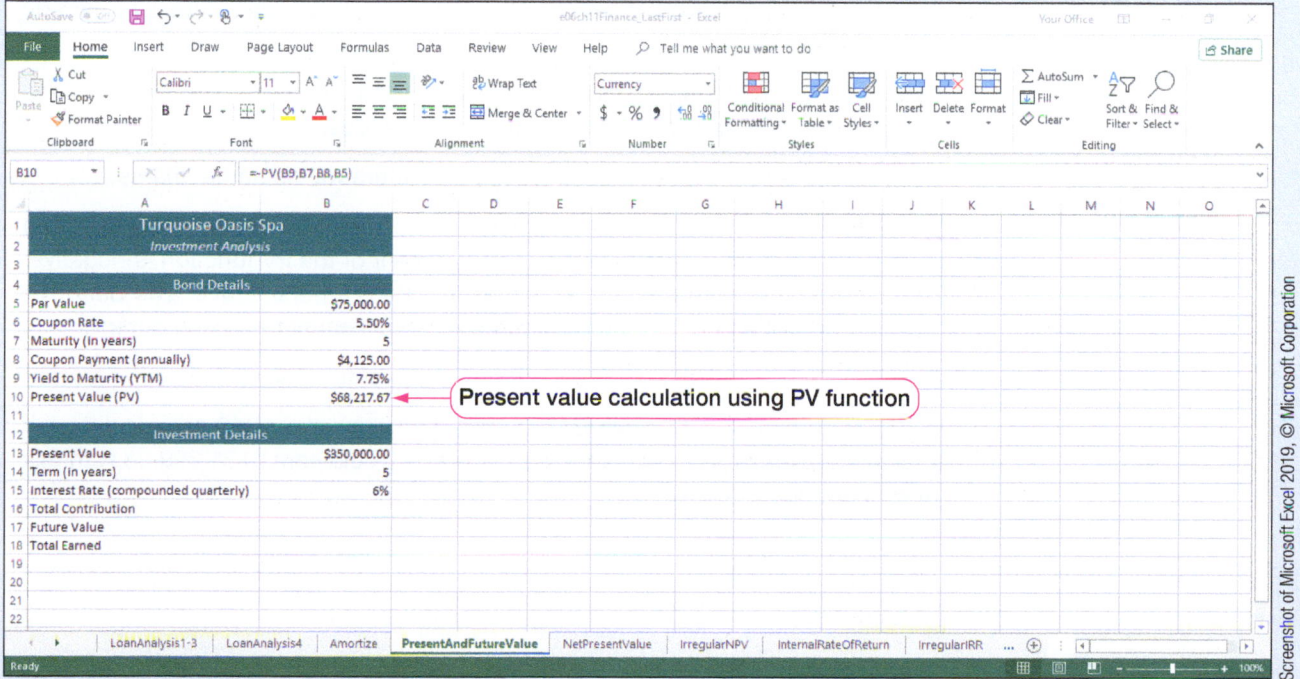

Figure 7 Calculating the present value of a bond

i. **Save** 💾 the workbook.

Using the FV Function

The future value function, or **FV function**, is used to calculate the value of an investment with a fixed interest rate and term, as well as to calculate periodic payments over a specific period of time. The FV function syntax uses five arguments. The first three are required, and the last two are optional: (1) rate (rate), (2) number of periods (nper), (3) payment (pmt), (4) present value (pv), and (5) type (type). If you do not know the payment, you must enter the present value.

=FV(rate, nper, pmt, [pv], [type])

For example, you might decide to start saving for retirement and want to use the FV function to calculate how much money you would have by the age of 65. By using the FV function, you can determine how much your Individual Retirement Account (IRA) would be worth when you retire. If you contributed $2,500 per year to your IRA for 40 years—a total of $100,000—with an interest rate of 8% annually, you would have nearly $650,000.

=FV(.08,40, −2500)

Turquoise Oasis Spa managers are considering investing money that would be provided by private investors. This would require them to wait for five years to allow the investment to grow. Payments and interest will be calculated quarterly. In this exercise, you will use the FV function to help the managers make their decision. For determining cash flows, the calculations will be from the bank's perspective.

 E11.08

Compound Interest
The interest rate must be divided by 4 and the term multiplied by 4 to account for the quarterly compounded interest.

To Calculate the Future Value of an Investment

a. Click cell **B16**. Type **=** and click cell **B13**. Press Enter to reference the present value, as the total investment will be a one-time, lump-sum investment.

b. In cell B17, type **=FV(** to begin the FV function.

c. Click cell **B15**, and type **/4** to reference the interest rate and calculate the quarterly interest rate.

d. Type **,** to move to the nper argument. Click cell **B14**, and type ***4** to reference the length of the term and calculate the number of periods.

e. Type **,** to move to the pmt argument. Type **0** as there will be no payments.

f. Type **,** to move to the pv argument. Type **−** and then click **B13** to reference the present value of the investment. The PV argument of the FV function is negative. This indicates that the calculation is from the bank's perspective. The bank will have to pay that amount at the beginning of the investment—a cash outflow.

g. Type **)** and press Enter to calculate the future value of this investment.

h. In cell **B18**, type **=**. Click cell **B17**, type **−** and then click **B16** to calculate the total earned. Press Ctrl+Enter. Notice that the spa would earn $121,399.25 with this investment option.

626   CHAPTER 11 | Microsoft Excel

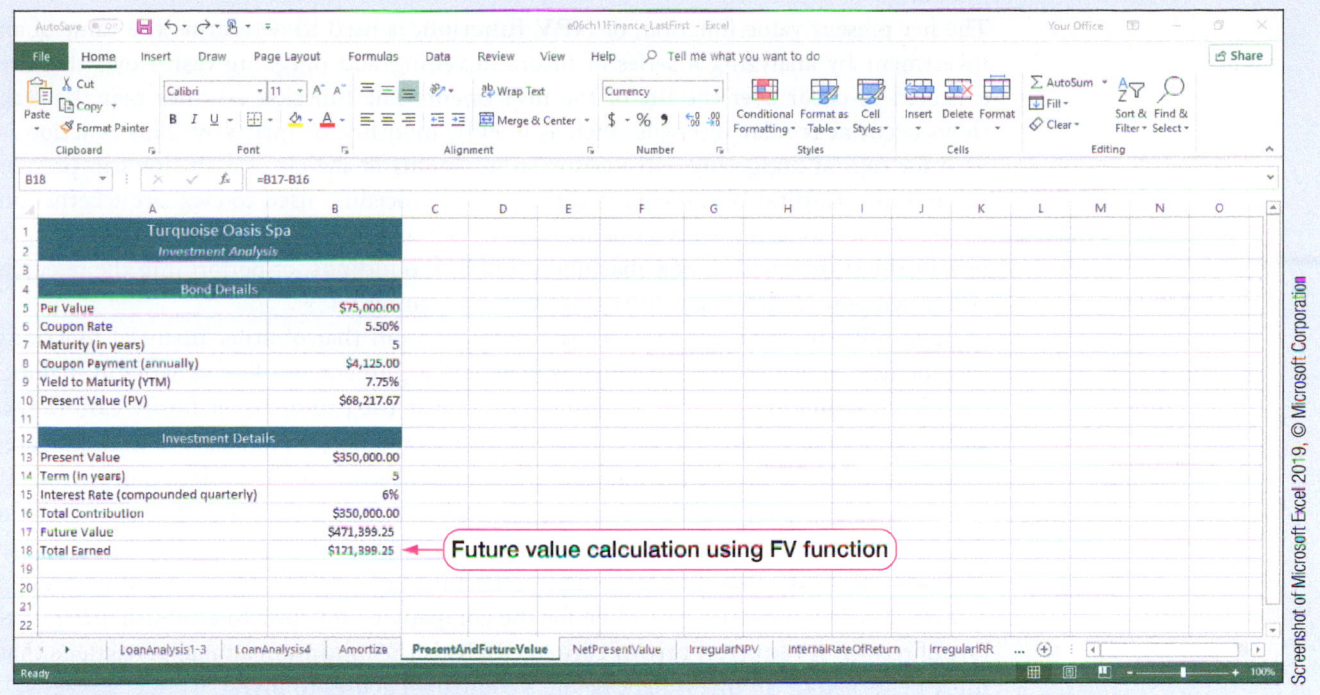

Figure 8 Calculating the future value of an investment

i. **Save**  the workbook.

SS CONSIDER THIS | **Should Turquoise Oasis Spa Wait Until It Makes Money?**

Turquoise Oasis Spa could earn more than enough money to complete the upgrades and expansion if it accepted the money from the private investors and invested the money. Would this be a wise decision if it requires waiting five years to let the investment grow? What repercussions could the managers face if they do wait? Could it affect the amount of revenue that the spa will generate?

REAL WORLD ADVICE | **Making Assumptions with PV and FV**

The PV and FV functions do not take all factors into consideration. For example, inflation is not accounted for in the calculation. Further, the PV and FV functions rely on a guaranteed, constant rate. Many investments, such as investing in stocks, are not a simple or guaranteed rate. These functions will help you make better-informed decisions. However, these functions do not take into account all variables.

Analyze Investments Using NPV, XNPV, IRR, and XIRR

Bond investments should be a part of any well-rounded investment portfolio. However, investors must also take into consideration other investment opportunities that may be higher risk but also offer a higher return. One method of analyzing various investment opportunities is to compare the projected future cash flow generated from the investment to that of a risk-free investment, such as a bond.

Using the NPV Function

The net present value function, or **NPV function**, is used to determine the value of an investment by analyzing a series of future incoming and outgoing cash flows that are expected to occur over the life of the investment. The function assumes that the cash flows occur at regular intervals, such as weekly, monthly, or quarterly. This function is used for capital budgeting and measures the surplus or deficit of cash flows in present value terms. **Capital budgeting** is the planning procedure used to evaluate whether an organization's long-term investment plans—such as acquiring a business or starting a new business, purchasing new machinery and new buildings, or performing the research and development of new products—are worth pursuing.

The NPV function syntax is a little different from that of other financial functions and includes rate and value arguments. The rate argument is a key variable in making the NPV calculation as accurate as possible, as it is used to discount future cash flows. There are several different approaches a company may take to calculate a discount rate. One approach is to decide the rate that the capital needed for the project could return if it were to be invested in a risk-free bond or other low-risk investment. For example, if a risk-free government bond could return 5%, then 5% would be used as the discount rate on the future cash flows to analyze the profitability of the investment based on today's dollars. Another approach would be for the company or investor to establish a required rate of return. A **required rate of return (RRR)** is the minimum annual percentage that must be earned by an investment before a company chooses to invest.

=NPV(rate, value1, [value2],...) + −initial investment

The value1 argument is required; subsequent value arguments are optional. The ellipsis dots indicate that additional arguments can be entered; Excel allows for 1 to 254 values to be entered. The NPV function uses the order of the value arguments to interpret the order of cash flows. Be sure to enter your values in the correct sequence, in which the value1 argument is the amount of estimated cash inflow for period 1 and not the initial amount of the investment in year 0. The initial investment amount must be subtracted outside of the NPV function to calculate the true net present value. Note that many times, the initial investment amount is recorded as a negative number. In that case, the initial investment would be added outside of the NPV function.

The managers at Turquoise Oasis Spa can use the NPV function to see whether it benefits them financially to invest in new equipment for the spa. Given an estimate of cash flows that would be generated with the new equipment and a discount rate based on a risk-free bond option, they can calculate whether the purchase of new equipment produces positive financial benefits. Suppose the spa invests $137,500 with a discount rate of 8% and the estimated cash inflows over the next three years were as follows.

Year 1: $58,450.00
Year 2: $46,612.00
Year 3: $34,003.00

The net present value would result in a loss of −$16,424.67. Therefore, this would not be a good investment for Turquoise Oasis Spa, which could earn more money by investing in a risk-free bond. If the NPV results in a negative value, then the investment should be rejected. However, if the NPV results in a value greater than 0, then the investment should be considered.

=NPV(.08,58450,46612,34003) + −137500

Turquoise Oasis Spa managers are considering the equipment—such as massage tables, salon chairs, and sinks—that they want to purchase to complete the improvements and expansion. In this exercise, you will use estimated cash inflows as a result of the new equipment for use in your net present value analysis. The initial investment will be $100,000 with a discount rate of 4.57%. For determining cash flows, the calculations will be from the bank's perspective.

 **E11.09**

SIDE NOTE
Net Present Value
Any investment that yields a positive NPV should be considered. If the NPV is negative, it is not a good option.

To Calculate the Net Present Value of an Investment

a. Click the **NetPresentValue** worksheet. Click cell **B10**, type = and then click cell **B6** to reference the initial investment amount, which will be the cash outflow for year 0. Press Ctrl+Enter.

b. Click cell **B15**, and then type **=NPV(** to begin the NPV function.

c. Click cell **B5** to reference the discount rate.

d. Type , to move to the value1 argument. Click cell **B11**, and drag to cell **B13** to select cells B11:B13, the cash flows for three years.

e. Type)+ and then click cell **B10** to end the NPV function and add the value of the initial investment. Press Ctrl+Enter to calculate the net present value of the investment. The complete function in B15 should appear as =NPV(B5,B11:B13)+B10. Notice that although the estimated cash inflows of the investment had not changed from the example above and what is contained in the worksheet, the result of the NPV function yields a positive value of $28,259.36 versus –$16,424.67. This is due to the lower discount rate being a key factor in the calculation.

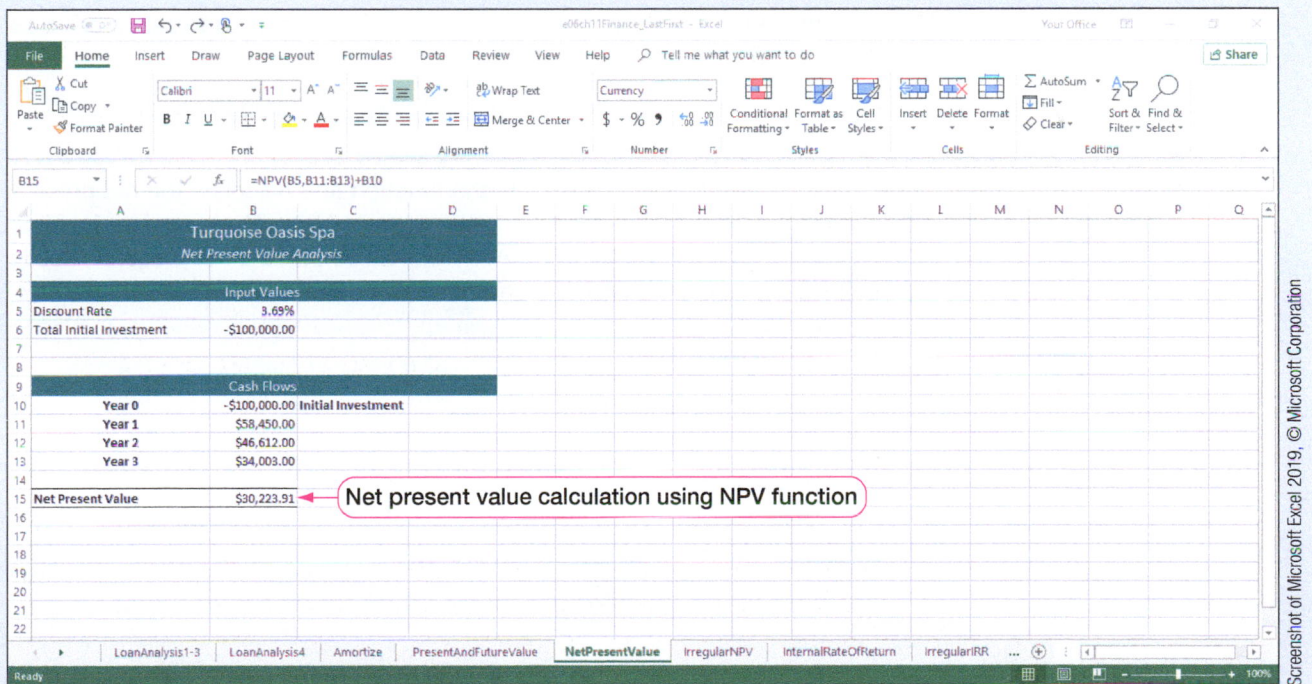

Figure 9 Net present value of an investment

f. **Save** 💾 the workbook.

Using the XNPV Function

Similar to NPV, the irregular net present value function, or **XNPV function**, determines the value of an investment or business by analyzing an irregular time series of incoming and outgoing cash flows. The XNPV function syntax is a little different from that of the NPV function and includes rate, values, and dates arguments, all of which are required. The values argument corresponds to payments, and one of these values must be a negative value, which will most likely represent the initial loan disbursement. The dates argument corresponds with when the payments were made, including the date of the initial investment. All subsequent dates must be after the initial investment date, but they may be listed in any order.

=XNPV(rate, values, dates)

Turquoise Oasis Spa managers are considering another investment option that will require an initial investment amount of $90,000 with estimated cash inflows occurring irregularly over the next two years. In this exercise, you will use the XNPV function to calculate the net present value of the investment with a required return rate of 10%. For determining cash flows, the calculations will be from the bank's perspective.

 **E11.10**

To Calculate an Irregular Net Present Value of an Investment

a. Click the **IrregularNPV** worksheet. Click cell **B20**, and then type **=XNPV(** to begin the XNPV function.

b. Click cell **B4** to reference the required rate of return.

c. Type **,** to move to the values argument. Click cell **B7**, and drag to select cell **B18** to reference the cash flows from 4/1/2019 to 9/1/2021.

d. Type **,** to move to the dates argument. Click cell **A7**, and drag to select cell **A18** to reference the dates of the cash flows.

e. Type **)** and press Ctrl+Enter to complete the function and calculate the net present value of the investment based on the irregular cash flows. The complete function should appear as =XNPV(B4,B7:B18,A7:A18). Notice that the net present value is –$1,962.91; therefore, it does not meet the required rate of return of 10%.

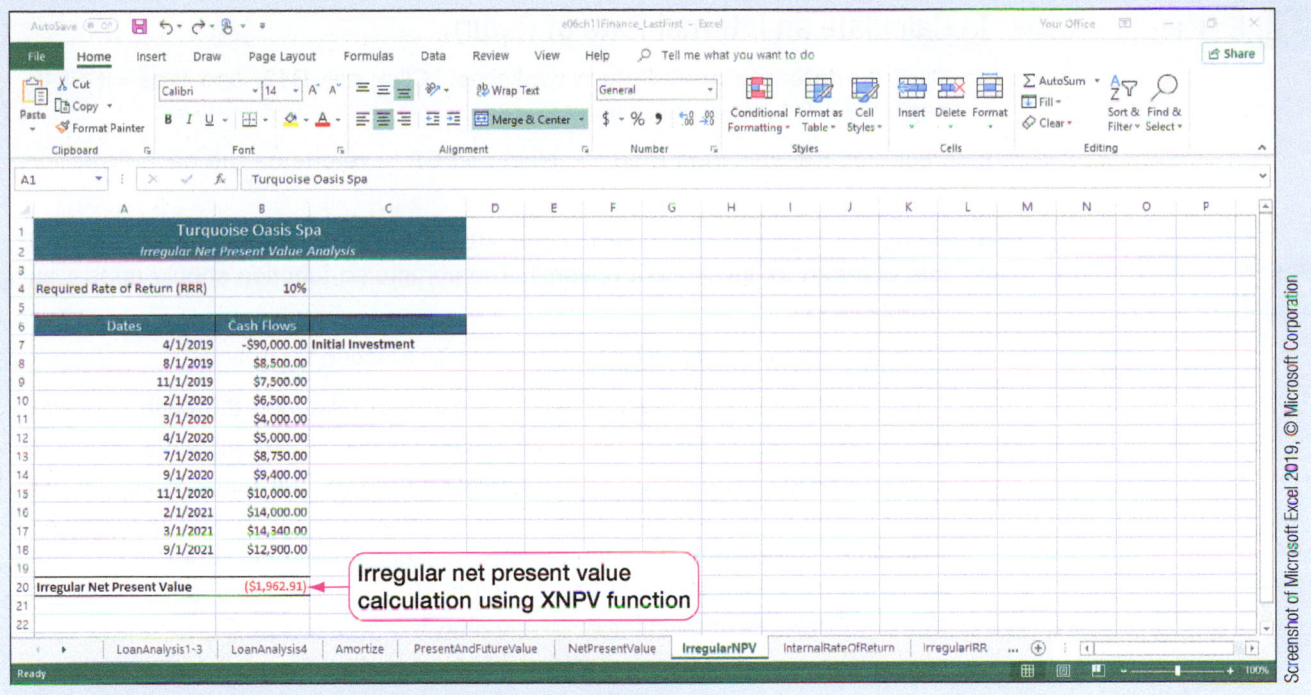

Figure 10 Irregular net present value of an investment

f. **Save** 🖫 the workbook.

Using the IRR Function

The internal rate of return function, or **IRR function**, indicates the profitability of an investment and is commonly used in business to assist in choosing between investments. This function is generally used in capital budgeting to measure and compare how profitable a potential investment is. The IRR of an investment is the rate that makes the net present value of both positive and negative cash flows equal to zero. In other words, the IRR function determines the discount rate at which you would break even on an investment. If an investment's IRR is higher than an interest rate generated by a risk-free investment, such as a government bond, then the investment should be chosen. If you are comparing multiple investment options, the investment with the highest IRR would be considered the best and should be chosen first, assuming that all investments have the same amount of initial investment. The IRR function has two arguments, which you have seen in previous financial functions—values and guess—and returns a percentage.

=IRR (values, [guess])

Turquoise Oasis Spa can use the IRR function to see which investment would be the best option. For example, suppose option 1 requires an initial investment of $125,000 with yearly cash flows of $40,000 totaling $160,000 over a four-year period, while option 2 requires the same initial investment of $125,000 with yearly cash flows also totaling $160,000 but over a six-year period and with a majority of the investment's return occurring in the first two years. In this exercise, you will analyze the internal rate of return on each of these investments. Knowing that the current rate of a risk-free investment is 10.50%, management can make a more informed decision about which option is in the best financial interest of the company. For determining cash flows, the calculations will be from the bank's perspective.

 **E11.11**

To Calculate an Internal Rate of Return

a. Click the **InternalRateOfReturn** worksheet. Click cell **B13**, and type **=IRR(** to begin the IRR function for option 1.

b. Click cell **B5**, and then drag to select cell **B9** to reference the cash flows for option 1.

c. Type **)** and then press ⌈Ctrl⌉+⌈Enter⌉ to complete the function and calculate the internal rate of return for investment option 1. The completed function should appear as =IRR(B5:B9).

d. Click cell **E13**, and type **=IRR(** to begin the IRR function for option 2.

e. Click cell **E5**, and then drag to select cell **E11** to reference the cash flows for option 2.

f. Type **)** and then press ⌈Ctrl⌉+⌈Enter⌉ to complete the function and calculate the internal rate of return for investment option 2. The completed function should appear as =IRR(E5:E11). Notice that both investment options have a higher internal rate of return than the risk-free investment option of 10.50%. However, option 2 has the higher IRR and should be chosen over option 1.

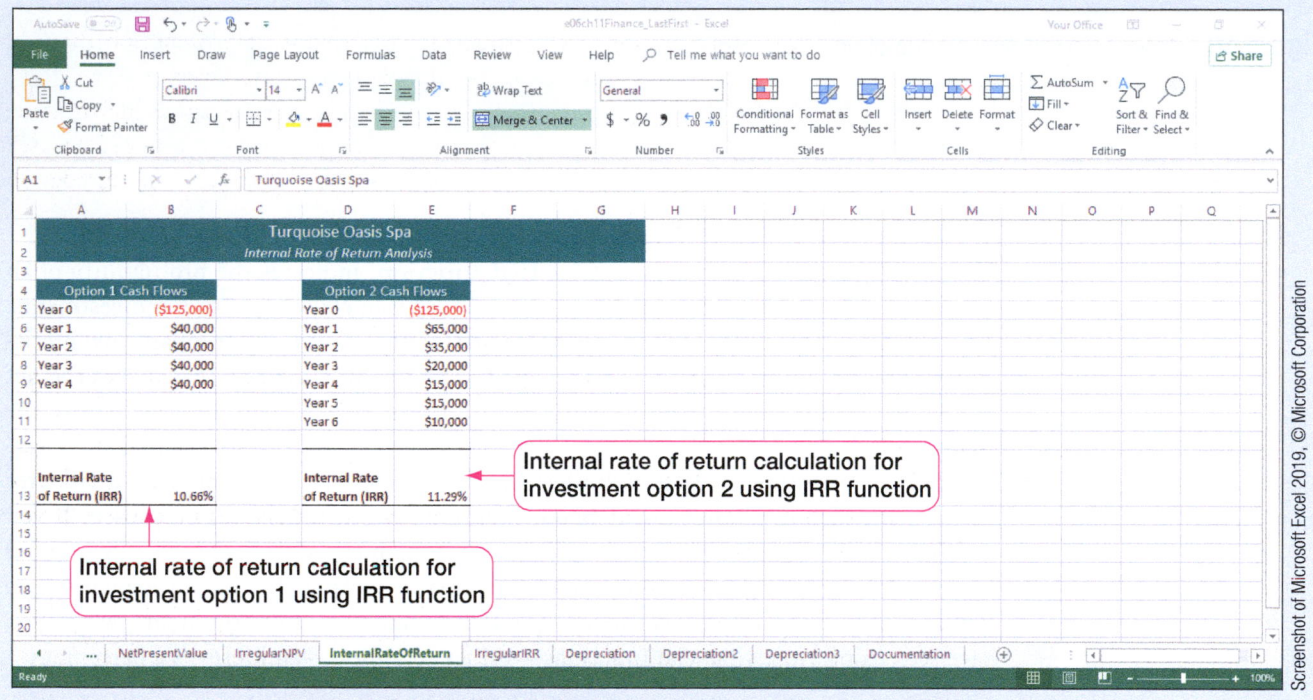

Figure 11 Comparing investments with the internal rate of return

g. **Save** 💾 the workbook.

S S **CONSIDER THIS** | **Making an Investment Decision**

At first glance, investment option 1 above may have seemed like the better choice, since the total return of $160,000 was realized in four years instead of six. However, the IRR function returns a higher rate of return for option 2. What do you think was the primary cause for the higher rate? Why?

Using the XIRR Function

Another way to analyze the rate of return is to use the irregular internal rate of return function, or XIRR function. The difference between the IRR function and the XIRR function is that the IRR function assumes that the cash flows are periodic, whereas the **XIRR function** analyzes a series of cash flows that are irregular or not periodic. The syntax of the XIRR function is similar to that of the IRR function with the addition of the dates argument. Additionally, as in the XNPV function, the series of values must contain at least one positive value and one negative value. The dates argument corresponds with when the payments were made, including the date of the initial investment. The first payment date indicates the beginning of the schedule of payments. All subsequent dates must be after the initial investment date, but they may be listed in any order.

=XIRR(values, dates, [guess])

Turquoise Oasis Spa managers are considering another investment option that will require an initial investment amount of $130,000 with estimated cash inflows occurring irregularly over the next two years. In this exercise, you will use the XIRR function to calculate the internal rate of return of the investment to determine whether or not it meets the 9.75% required rate of return. For determining cash flows, the calculations will be from the bank's perspective.

 **E11.12**

To Calculate an Irregular Internal Rate of Return

a. Click the **IrregularIRR** worksheet. Click cell **B17**, and type **=XIRR(** to begin the XIRR function.

b. Click cell **B7**, and drag to select cell **B15** to reference the cash flows.

c. Type **,** to move to the dates argument. Click cell **A7**, and drag to select cell **A15** to reference the dates.

d. Type **)** and then press Ctrl+Enter to complete the function and calculate the irregular internal rate of return. The completed function should appear as =XIRR(B7:B15,A7:A15). Notice that this investment has an internal rate of return of 5.61% and does not meet the required rate of return of 9.75%.

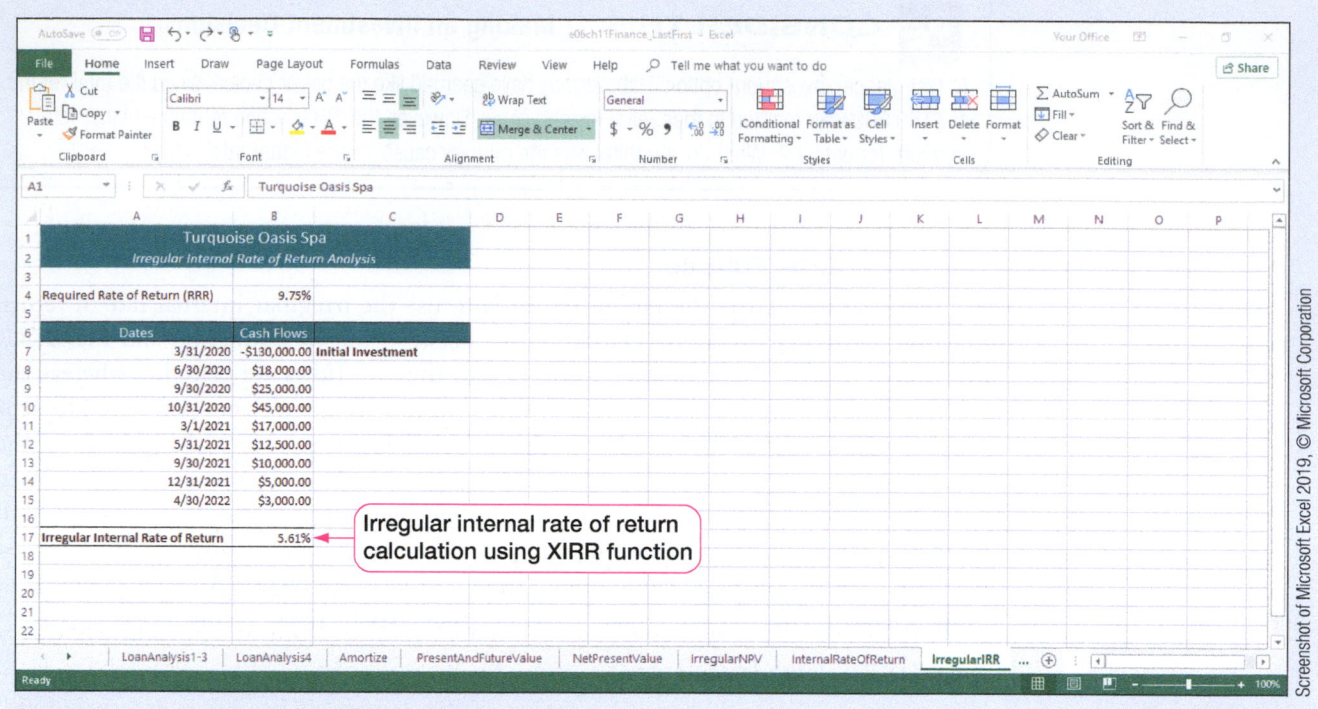

Figure 12 Irregular internal rate of return analysis

    e. Save 🖫 the workbook.

Calculating the Depreciating Value of Business Assets

Businesses are required, for tax and reporting purposes, to show that the original value of the property they purchase—such as buildings, vehicles, and equipment—is reduced—or depreciated—over time as the business "uses up" these assets. In this section, you will learn how to calculate the depreciation of assets, using three different approved methods.

QUICK REFERENCE   **Methods of Depreciation**

There are several accounting methods to depreciate an asset, and the IRS allows a business to choose whichever method is most advantageous as long as the same method is used throughout the life of the asset.

1. Straight-line depreciation (SLN)—The simplest and most commonly used method. Assumes that the value of the asset loses the same amount of value each year of its life.

2. Declining balance depreciation (DB)—Assumes that the value of an asset depreciates more in the first year than in the second year.

3. Double declining balance depreciation (DDB)—Requires that the straight-line depreciation method be used first to calculate the total percentage of the asset that is depreciated in the first year and doubles it. Each subsequent year of the asset's life, that same percentage is multiplied by the remaining balance to be depreciated.

Calculate the Depreciation of Assets Using the SLN, DB, and DDB Functions

As you learned, an amortization table can be used to analyze loan balances and repayments. A company can also use amortization tables to show the appropriate accounting or net book value of its tangible assets—such as machinery, equipment, buildings, vehicles, or property—for tax or reporting purposes. The **net book value** is equal to the original cost of the asset minus depreciation and amortization. To create an amortization table for asset depreciation, you would use functions that allow you to calculate the present value, future value, and depreciation of the asset over its useful life. When you depreciate the original cost of tangible assets, you first need to know the rules for depreciating the particular assets, because there are different rules for different types of assets. Depreciation represents a reduction in the amount of the original cost of a fixed asset that is used to reduce income as an expense for accounting and tax purposes. The idea is that because the item generates income over time, you should be able to deduct from that income the amount of the resource—or asset—used.

To calculate the depreciated value, you need to know the original cost of the asset, the asset's useful life, the asset's **salvage value,** and the rate at which the asset depreciates over time. The salvage value is what the asset is estimated to be worth at the end of its useful life. It is assumed that over time, these assets decline in value because of deterioration and obsolescence and therefore should be depreciated. Depreciation functions provide a method that matches the decline in value with the income that results from using the assets. In addition, you have to know what depreciation method the IRS expects you to apply to particular types of assets. The IRS, Generally Accepted Accounting Principles, and International Financial Reporting Standards all have specific requirements for depreciating assets and reporting depreciation based on the type of asset being depreciated.

To report the net book value of tangible assets, a depreciation schedule must be maintained. A **depreciation schedule** records the date when the asset was placed into service, a calculation for each year's depreciation, and the accumulated depreciation. An asset remains on the depreciation schedule until the asset becomes fully depreciated or is taken out of service—sold or discarded. Finally, the depreciation schedule should be evaluated annually to ensure accuracy. With a growing business and increased inventory, the Turquoise Oasis Spa must prepare a depreciation schedule for its tangible assets.

REAL WORLD ADVICE	Have You Thought about Depreciating Your Assets?

Have you ever run your own business? Maybe you owned a lawn mowing service. Suppose you purchased your own riding lawn mower. Come tax time, one method to reduce your taxes is by using depreciation. Rather than taking the full cost out in one year, you can take out a portion over several years. This is particularly useful for high-priced items.

Using the SLN Function

One way that you can calculate depreciation is using the straight-line depreciation function, or SLN function. The **SLN function** calculates the depreciation of an asset for a specified period using the fixed declining balance method. This means that the amount of money that is depreciated is the same for each year of the life of the asset. This is the easiest type of depreciation to calculate and is the depreciation method used by the majority of small businesses. The SLN function syntax uses three arguments, all of which are required: (1) initial cost of asset (cost), (2) salvage value (salvage), and (3) useful life (life) in numbers of years. The salvage value can be set to zero if that is what the expected salvage value is.

=SLN(cost, salvage, life)

Turquoise Oasis Spa managers need to track the tangible assets—such as massage tables, salon chairs, and sinks—that they previously purchased. In this exercise, you will create a straight-line depreciation table given the cost of the asset, salvage value, and useful life of the assets.

 **E11.13**

To Create a Straight-Line Depreciation Schedule

a. Click the **Depreciation** worksheet. Click cell **B8**, and type **=SLN(** to begin the SLN function.

> **Troubleshooting**
>
> If you cannot see the Depreciation worksheet, you may need to click ⋯ to the right of the tabs to see additional worksheets.

b. Click cell **B3**, and press **F4** to lock the cell reference and reference the cost of the assets so that the formula can be copied down the column later.

c. Type **,** to move to the salvage argument. Click cell **B4**, and press **F4** to reference the salvage value of the assets.

d. Type **,** to move to the life argument. Click cell **B5**, and press **F4** to reference the useful life of the assets.

e. Type **)** and press **Ctrl+Enter**. Double-click the **fill handle** to copy the function down to **B12**. The complete function should appear as =SLN($B$3,$B$4,$B$5).

f. Click cell **C8**, type **=** and then click cell **B8** to reference the accumulated depreciation for the first year. Press **Enter**.

g. In cell C9, type **=** and then click cell **C8** to reference the accumulated depreciation for the first year.

h. Type **+** and click cell **B9**. Press ⌐Ctrl⌐+⌐Enter⌐ to reference the accumulated depreciation for year 2. The completed formula should appear as =C8+B9. Double-click the **fill handle** handle to copy the formula down to **C12**.

i. Click cell **D8** and type **=**. Click cell **B3**, and then press ⌐F4⌐ to reference the cost of the assets and lock the cell reference so that the formula can be copied down the column later.

j. Type **−** and click cell **C8**. Press ⌐Ctrl⌐+⌐Enter⌐ to calculate the book value at the end of the first year. Double-click the **fill handle** to copy the function down to **D12**. Notice that the book value at the end of year five is $3,871—the same as the estimated salvage value.

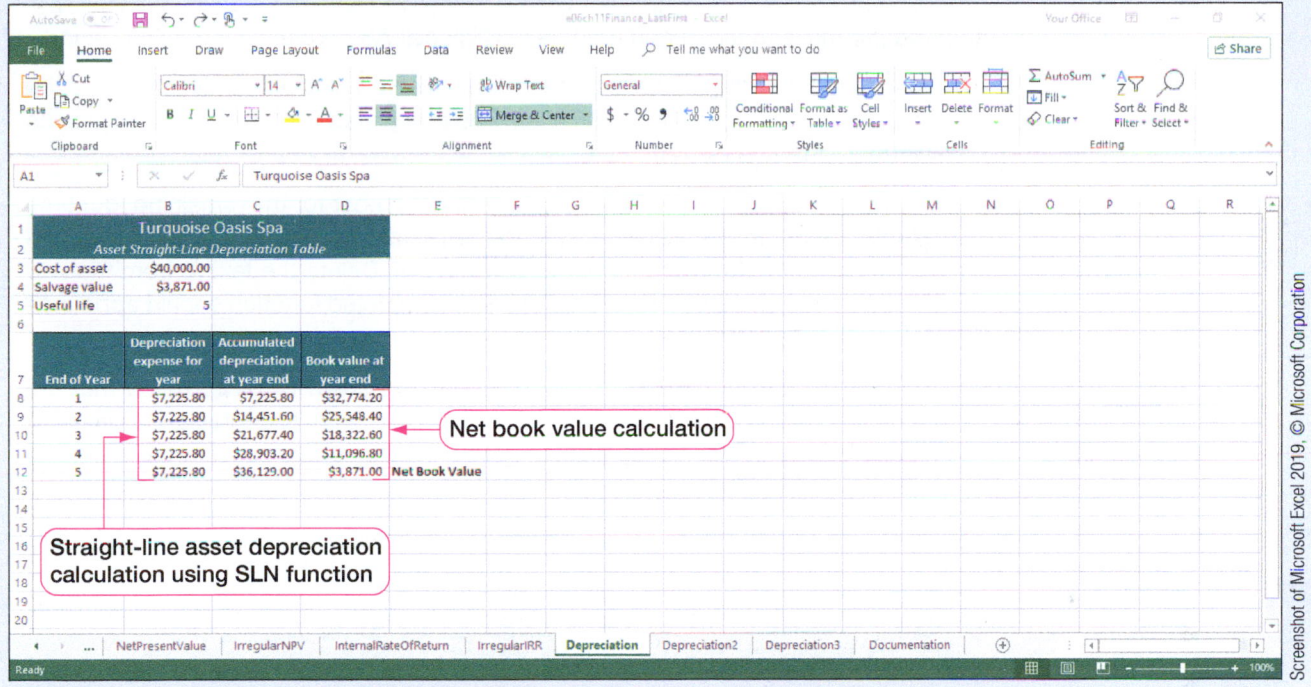

Figure 13 Straight-line asset depreciation table

k. **Save** 💾 the workbook.

Using the DB Function

Another way in which you can calculate depreciation is by using the declining balance function, or DB function. The **DB function** calculates the depreciation of an asset for a specified period using the fixed declining balance method. The difference between the DB function and the SLN function is that when you use the DB function, you can specify the period and month when the asset was placed into service. Thus, instead of spreading the cost of the asset evenly over its life, as you did with the SLN function, the DB function calculates the depreciation of the asset at an accelerated rate, which results in higher depreciation in earlier periods and progressively declining depreciation in each succeeding period. Because the month argument is optional, Excel assumes that the value is 12 if a value is omitted.

=DB(cost, salvage, life, period, [month])

In this exercise, you will calculate depreciation using the DB function.

 **E11.14**

To Create a Declining Balance Depreciation Schedule

a. Click the **Depreciation2** worksheet. The equipment was placed into service at the beginning of May of the first year. Therefore, the period for the first year will be eight—May through December is eight months. Click cell **B8**, and then type **=DB(** to begin calculating the declining balance depreciation of the asset.

b. Click cell **B3**, and press F4 to reference the cost of the assets.

c. Type **,** to move to the salvage argument. Click cell **B4**, and press F4 to reference the salvage value of the assets.

d. Type **,** to move to the life argument. Click cell **B5**, and press F4 to reference the useful life of the assets.

e. Type **,** to move to the period argument. Click cell **A8** to reference the first period.

f. Type **,** to move to the month argument. Type **8)** and press Ctrl+Enter to calculate the depreciation over an eight-month span. The completed function should appear as =DB($B$3,$B$4,$B$5,A8).

g. The equipment will be used from January to December for the remaining four time periods. Click the **Home** tab, and in the Clipboard group, click **Copy**. Click cell **B9**, and click **Paste**. Double-click to edit the cell. Delete the text **,8** from the end of the function and then press Ctrl+Enter. The completed function should appear as =DB($B$3,$B$4,$B$5,A9).

h. Double-click the **fill handle** to copy the function down to **B12**. Notice that the depreciation is declining as the periods increase with a depreciation value of $1,413.72 in year five. Notice that the net book value of the asset at the end of its useful life is $5,788.00.

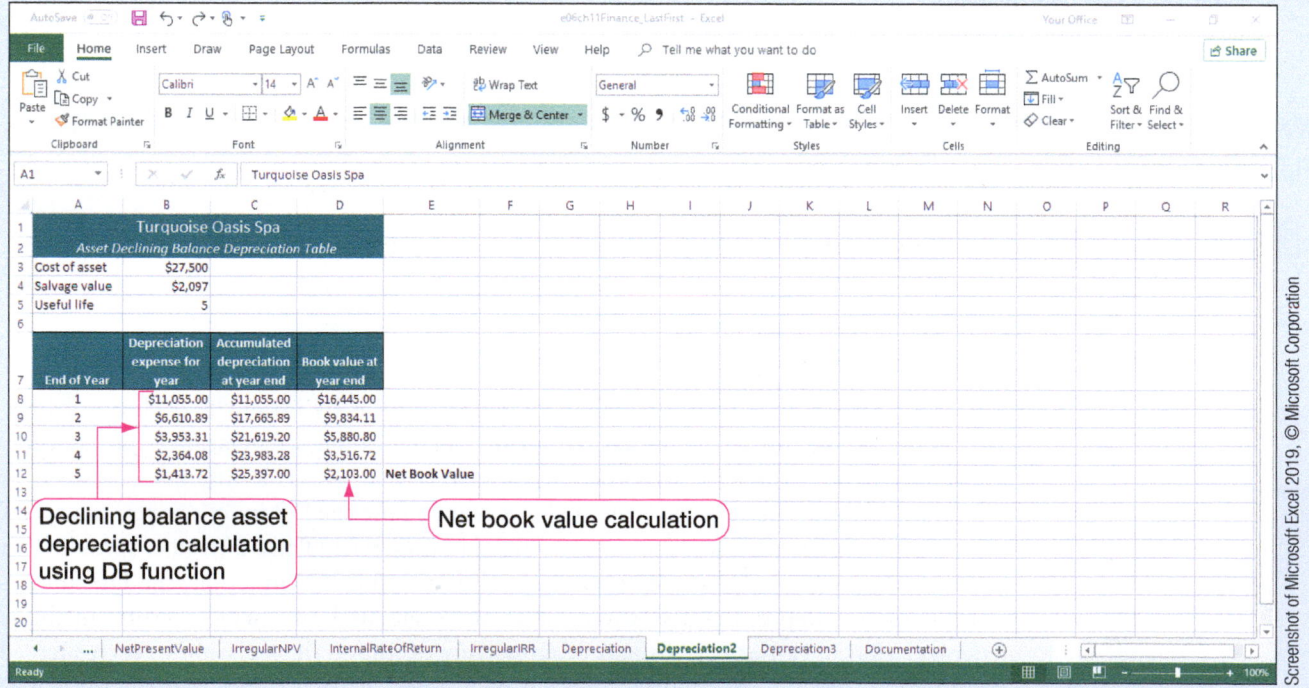

Figure 14 Declining balance asset depreciation table

i. **Save** 🖫 the workbook.

REAL WORLD ADVICE	The Salvage and Net Book Values Do Not Match

The declining balance method assumes that depreciation is more rapid earlier in the asset's life. Notice that the book value at year end in year five is greater than the salvage value. Remember that instead of spreading the cost of the asset evenly over its life, as you did with the SLN function, the DB function calculates the depreciation of the asset at an accelerated rate, which results in decreasing depreciation charges each succeeding period.

Using the DDB Function

Still another way in which you can calculate depreciation is by using the double declining balance function, or DDB function. The **DDB function** calculates the depreciation of an asset for a specified period using the double declining balance method. With the straight-line depreciation method, the useful life of the asset is divided into the total cost to arrive at an equal amount per year. The DDB function permits twice the straight-line annual percentage rate to be applied each year. For example, if you have a straight-line depreciation that is depreciating assets over a five-year period, the annual depreciation amount would be 20%. If the initial cost is $1,000, the depreciation would be 20% × $1,000 = $200 each year until the asset reaches a net book value of zero. With the double declining balance method, the depreciation amount would be 40% each year; 40% × $1,000 = $400 in the first year, 40% × $600 = $240 in the second year, and so on.

The DDB function syntax uses five arguments, four of which are required: (1) initial cost of asset (cost), (2) salvage value (salvage), (3) useful life (life), (4) period for which you want to calculate the depreciation (period), and (5) rate at which the balance declines (factor). The **factor** argument is optional; it is the rate at which the balance declines. If factor is omitted, Excel assumes the value to be 2 (the double declining balance method). The salvage value can be set to zero if that is what the expected salvage value is.

=DDB(cost, salvage, life, period, [factor])

In this exercise, you will calculate depreciation using the DDB function.

 E11.15

To Create a Double Declining Balance Depreciation Schedule

a. Click the **Depreciation3** worksheet. Click cell **B8**, and type **=DDB(** to begin the DDB function.

b. Click cell **B3**, press F4 to reference the cost of the assets, and then lock the cell reference so that the formula can be copied down the column later.

c. Type , to move to the salvage argument. Click cell **B4**, and press F4 to reference the salvage value of the assets.

d. Type , to move to the life argument. Click cell **B5**, and press F4 to reference the useful life of the assets.

e. Type , to move to the period argument. Click cell **A8** to reference the first period.

f. Type) and press Ctrl+Enter to calculate the double declining balance depreciation of the asset, and then double-click the **fill handle** to copy the function down to **B12**. Notice that you would be able to deduct higher depreciation on your taxes. However, your net book value at the end of the five years would be less than it would be if you used the DB function.

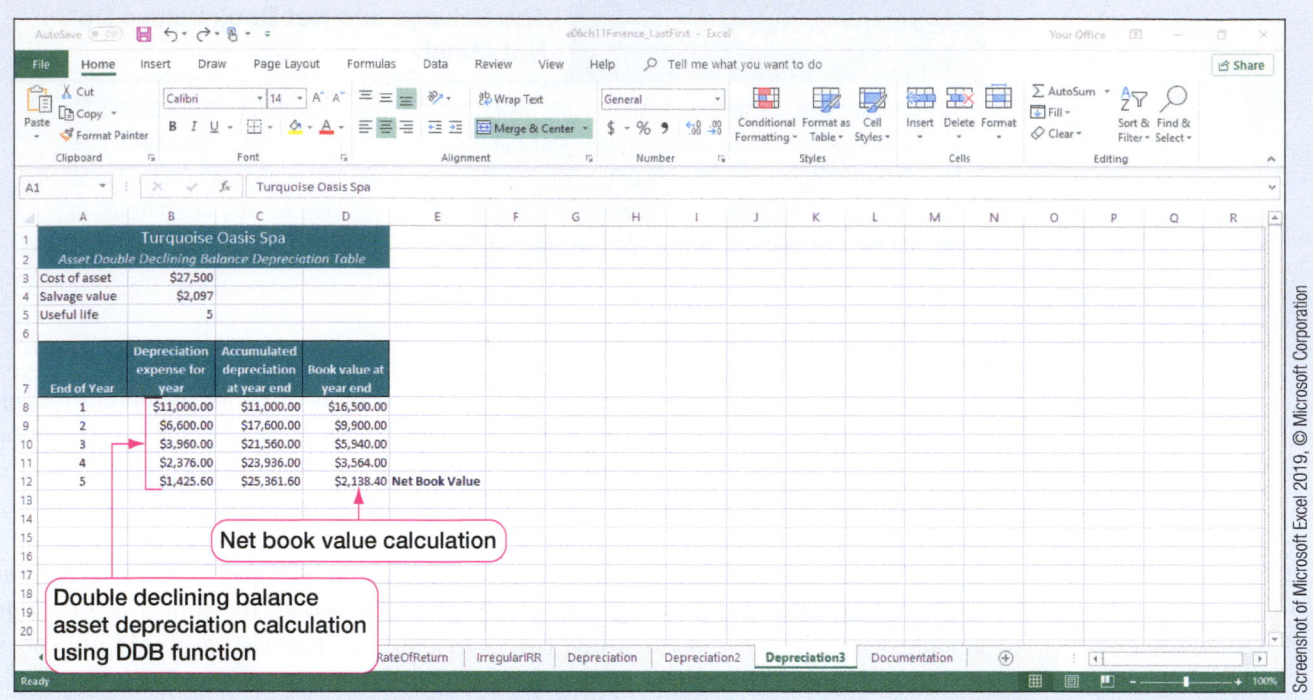

Figure 15 Double declining balance asset depreciation table

g. Insert the **file name** in the left custom footer section of the Header/Footer tab in the Page Setup dialog box on all worksheets in the workbook.

h. Complete the Documentation worksheet according to your instructor's directions.

i. **Save** 💾 the workbook, exit Excel, and then submit your file as directed by your instructor.

Grader Heads Up

If you are using MyLab IT Grader, this is the end of the second MyLab IT Grader project Part B.

REAL WORLD ADVICE | **Choosing a Depreciation Method**

Accountants use depreciation as a method to approximate the value that assets lose over time. As property ages and wears out or becomes obsolete, you can calculate the depreciation and use it as a potential tax write-off. You learned three different methods to calculate depreciation of assets. All of the depreciation methods are allowed, according to the IRS. You should consult with an accountant before making a final decision about how you depreciate an asset.

Concept Check

1. What does the PMT function calculate? Describe the required arguments of the PMT function. p. 607

2. Explain the CUMIPMT function and its arguments. Why would it be beneficial to know the cumulative interest paid in a particular time period? p. 615

3. What is an amortization schedule and what is its purpose? p. 619

4. How does estimating the present value of an investment lead to better financial decisions? p. 623

5. Discuss how the IRR and NPV functions can help in making informed financial decisions. p. 627

6. What are the differences between the three functions used to calculate asset depreciation discussed in this chapter? p. 635

Key Terms

Visual Summary

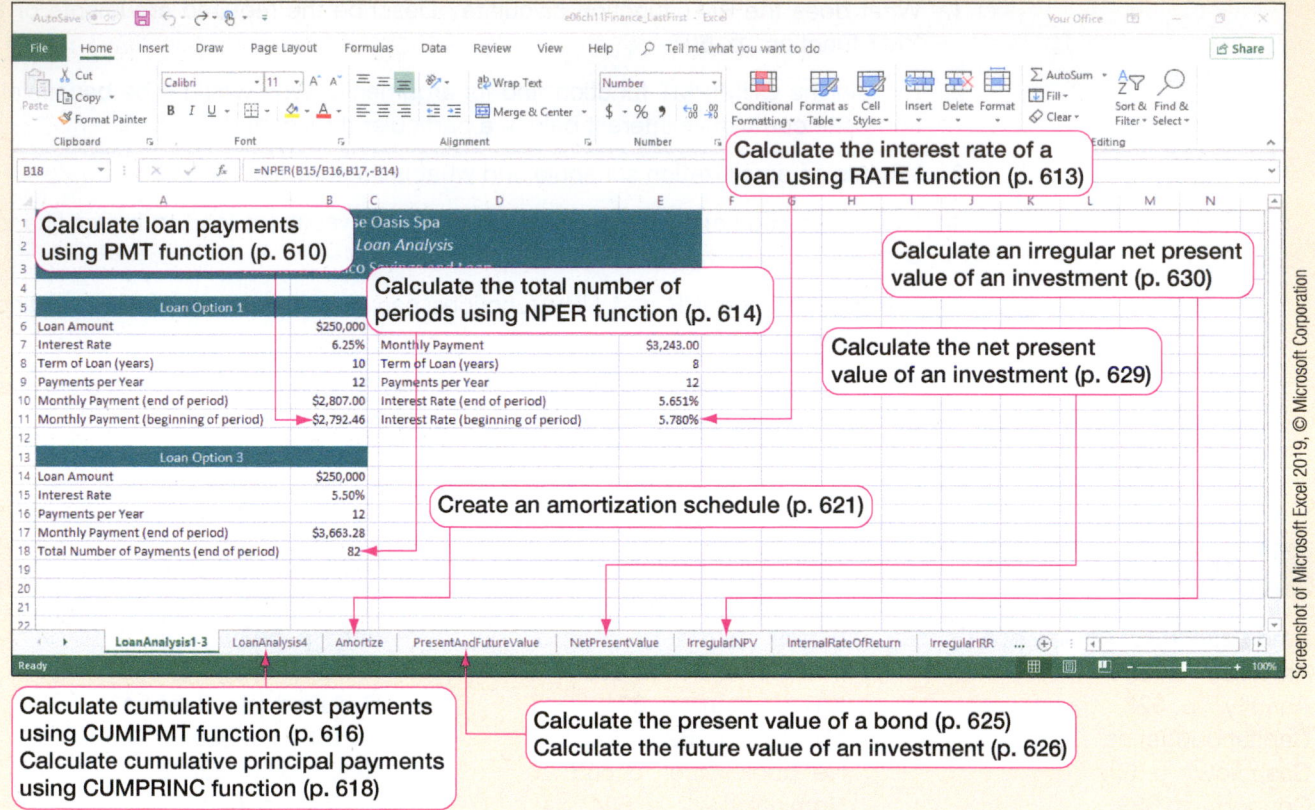

Figure 16

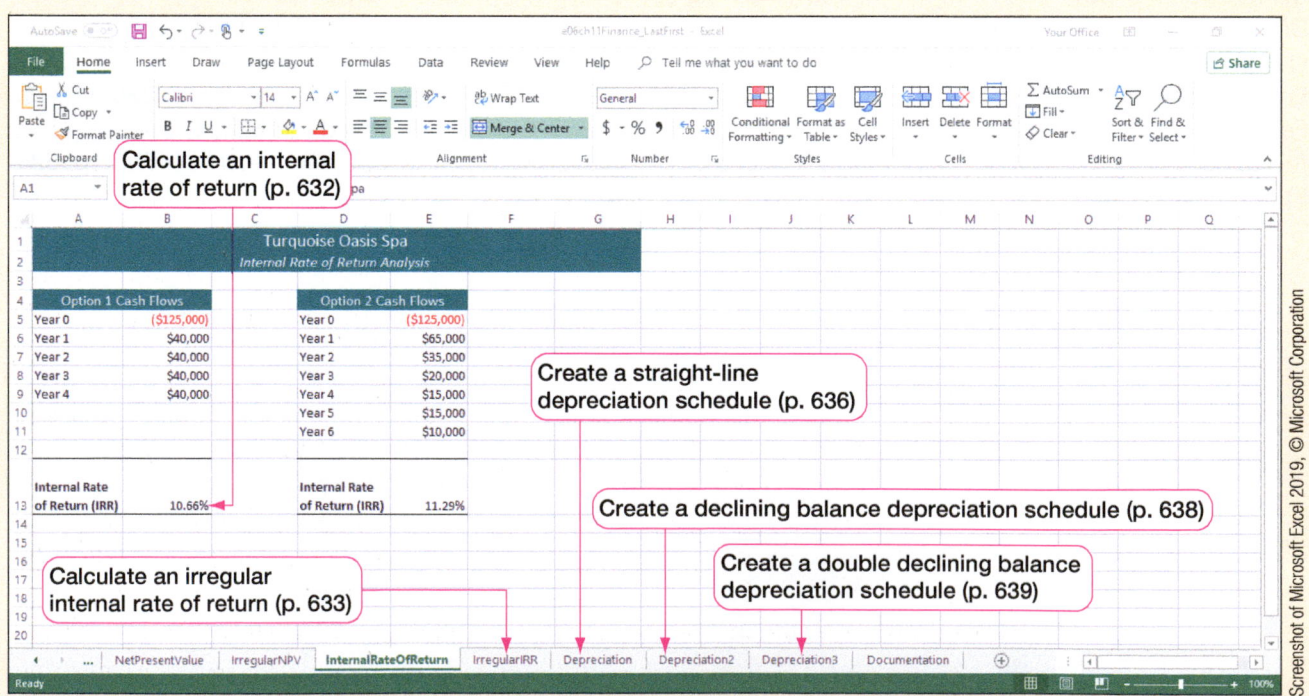

Figure 17

Student data file needed:

 e06ch11Equipment.xlsx

You will save your file as:

 e06ch11Equipment_LastFirst.xlsx

Loan Analysis and Depreciating Equipment at the Red Bluff Golf Course & Pro Shop

Finance & Accounting

The Red Bluff Golf Course & Pro Shop obtained a loan two years ago to purchase new golf carts for its members to use. Unfortunately, the manager, Barry Cheney, has not kept very good records for the loan or for the depreciation of the golf carts. You have been asked to create a loan analysis and depreciation schedule. The Red Bluff Golf Course & Pro Shop has been making monthly payments, due at the end of the period, but it has not kept track of the actual loan—such as interest and principal. Additionally, depreciation has not been written off on yearly taxes. Mr. Cheney wants to begin writing off a portion of the cost of the golf carts this year, but he is not sure whether he should use a straight-line depreciation or declining balance method. You need to calculate both schedules and report your findings to him so he can get them approved by his accountant. Barry has given you a template to use to create your analysis. For determining cash flows, the calculations will be from the bank's perspective.

a. Open the Excel file, **e06ch11Equipment**. Save your file as e06ch11Equipment_ LastFirst using your last and first name.

b. On the Analysis worksheet, click cell **A10**, and then type =PMT(A6/D6,B6*D6,−C6) to calculate the monthly payment of the loan. Press Tab. The pv argument of the PMT function is negative. This indicates that the calculation is from the bank's perspective. The bank will have to pay that amount at the beginning of the loan—a cash outflow.

c. In cell B10, type =IPMT(A6/D6,1,B6*D6,−C6) to calculate the interest portion of the monthly payment. Press Tab. The pv argument of the IPMT function is negative. This indicates that the calculation is from the bank's perspective. The bank will have to pay that amount at the beginning of the loan—a cash outflow.

d. In cell C10, type =PPMT(A6/D6,1,B6*D6,−C6) to calculate the principal portion of the monthly payment. Press Tab. The pv argument of the PPMT function is negative. This indicates that the calculation is from the bank's perspective. The bank will have to pay that amount at the beginning of the loan—a cash outflow.

e. In cell D10, type =−CUMIPMT(A6/D6,B6*D6,C6,1,12,0) to calculate how much interest was paid during the first year of the loan. Press Tab. The negative sign indicates that the CUMIPMT function is from the bank's perspective. The bank will receive the principal interest payment on the loan—a cash inflow.

f. In cell E10, type =−CUMPRINC(A6/D6,B6*D6,C6,1,12,0) to calculate how much principal was paid during the first year of the loan, and then format the cell as Currency if necessary. Press Ctrl+Enter. The negative sign indicates that the CUMPRINC function is from the bank's perspective. The bank will receive the principal interest payment on the loan—a cash inflow.

g. Click cell **B16**, and then type =IRR(B14:E14) to calculate the internal rate of return of the investment based on the expected cash flows in years 2020–2022. Press Ctrl+Enter.

h. Create a straight-line depreciation schedule by completing the following tasks.

- Click cell **H10**, type =SLN($G$6,$H$6,$I$6) and then press Ctrl+Enter. Double-click the **fill handle** to copy the function down to **H14**.

- Click cell **I10**, and then type =H10 to calculate the accumulated depreciation for the first year. Press Enter.

- In cell I11, type =I10+H11 to calculate the accumulated depreciation for year 2, press Ctrl+Enter, and then double-click the **fill handle** to copy the function down to **I14**.
- Click cell **J10**, type =$G$6–I10 to calculate the book value at the end of year 1 by subtracting the accumulated depreciation at the end of year one from the initial cost. Press Ctrl+Enter, and then double-click the **fill handle** to copy the function down to **J14**.

i. Create a declining balance depreciation schedule by completing the following tasks.

- Click cell **H17**, type =DB($G$6,$H$6,$I$6,G17) and then press Ctrl+Enter. Double-click the **fill handle** to copy the function down to **H21**.
- Click cell **I17**, type =H17 and then press Enter to calculate the accumulated depreciation for the first year.
- In cell I18, type =I17+H18 and then Ctrl+Enter to calculate the accumulated depreciation for year 2. Double-click the **fill handle** to copy the function down to **I21**.
- Click cell **J17**, type =$G$6–I17 and then press Ctrl+Enter to calculate the book value at the end of year 1 by subtracting the accumulated depreciation at the end of year 1 from the initial cost. Double-click the **fill handle** to copy the function down to **J21**.

j. Create a double declining balance depreciation schedule by completing the following tasks.

- Click cell **H24**, type =DDB($G$6,$H$6,$I$6,G24) and then press Ctrl+Enter. Double-click the **fill handle** to copy the function down to **H28**.
- Click cell **I24**, type =H24 and then press Enter to calculate the accumulated depreciation for the first year.
- In cell I25, type =I24+H25 and then press Ctrl+Enter to calculate the accumulated depreciation for year 1. Double-click the **fill handle** to copy the formula to **I28**.
- Click cell **J24**, type =$G$6–I24 and then press Ctrl+Enter to calculate the book value at the end of year 1 by subtracting the accumulated depreciation at the end of year 1 from the initial cost. Double-click the **fill handle** handle to copy the function down to **J28**.

k. Click the **Documentation** worksheet. Complete the Documentation worksheet according to your instructor's direction.

l. Save the workbook, exit Excel, and then submit your file as directed by your instructor.

Finance &
Accounting

MyLab IT Grader

Student data file needed:

 e06ch11Building.xlsx

You will save your file as:

 e06ch11Building_LastFirst.xlsx

New Investment Analysis

Flanky's, a small manufacturer of custom clothing for dogs and cats, is considering the purchase of a new building as part of its long-term strategic plan. You have been asked to conduct an analysis on the loan as well as an investment analysis using the NPV function based on an estimated series of cash flows generated by the new building and a required rate of return of 22%. For determining cash flows, the calculations will be from the bank's perspective.

a. Open the Excel file, **e06ch11Building**. Save your file as e06ch11Building_LastFirst using your last and first name.

b. On the **BuildingAnalysis** worksheet, and in cell C5, calculate the amount to finance by subtracting the starting capital from the purchase price of the building.

c. In cell C10, calculate the end of period quarterly payment amount using the PMT function. Be sure the result is displayed as a positive number.

d. In cell C11, calculate the total cumulative interest that will be paid on the loan for all 28 end-of-the-period quarterly payments. Format as Currency. Be sure the result is displayed as a positive number.

e. In cell C13, calculate the total cost of the loan by adding the amount financed to the total cumulative interest.

f. In cell F13, calculate the net present value of the investment using the NPV function. If necessary, format cell F13 as Currency with two decimal places. You have just calculated the net present value.

g. In cell I7, calculate the straight-line depreciation value of the building for year 1, and copy the formula down through year 7.

h. In cells J7:J13, calculate the accumulated depreciation amount for each year.

i. In cells K7:K13, calculate the book value of the asset at the end of each year of its useful life.

j. In cell I17, calculate the declining balance depreciation value of the building for year 1, and copy the formula down through year 7.

k. In cells J17:J23, calculate the accumulated depreciation amount for each year.

l. In cells K17:K23, calculate the book value of the asset at the end of each year of its useful life.

m. Select cells **I23:K23**, and in the Font group, click the **Border arrow**, and then click **Thick Bottom Border**.

n. Complete the Documentation worksheet according to your instructor's directions.

o. Save the workbook, exit Excel, and then submit your file as directed by your instructor.

Student data file needed:

 e06ch11Home.xlsx

You will save your file as:

e06ch11Home_LastFirst.xlsx

Purchasing a Home

Finance &
Accounting

You want to purchase a home in the future. You have decided to begin setting money aside each month that can be used toward your down payment. Your goal is to have 20% down when you are ready to purchase your home. To help determine how much you should save and how long it will take, you have decided to create an Excel workbook to track your progress and help you visualize your success.

a. Open the Excel file, **e06ch11Home**. Save your file as e06ch11Home_LastFirst using your last and first name.

b. Create a blank worksheet, and then rename the worksheet Home

c. Enter the following data, and label appropriately.

- Enter the amount you are planning to be able to pay for the home you want to purchase, $280,000

- Enter a formula to calculate the amount of down payment you will need, 20% of home purchase value.

- Enter the amount of interest you will earn, 0.0125%

- Enter the amount of money you are setting aside, $1,250/month.

d. Enter formulas to answer the questions below, labeled appropriately.

- How long would you need to save money to arrive at your 20% down payment?

- You want to buy a home within two years. In a blank cell, using the information above, calculate the amount you would need to set aside each month to accomplish this goal.

- You do not earn enough money to set $1,250 aside each month. Using the original information, what rate of interest would you need to earn to keep the monthly payments at $1,000?

- If you could set aside $1,600 at 2.65% interest, how much money would you have saved after two years?

e. Based on your analysis, you will not be able to buy a home after two years unless you invest in low-risk bonds. You were able to find a short-term bond in which to invest. The par value is $15,000, the coupon rate is 4.75% annually, the maturity is two years, and the yield to maturity is 7.5%.

- Enter the data above in separate cells labeled appropriately.

- Create a formula to calculate the coupon payment and label.

- Determine the present value of the bond, and label appropriately.

f. You are not sure it will benefit you to save the money. You decide to see what difference saving the money will mean as you make your future loan payments. Click the **Amortization** worksheet. Complete the two amortization schedules for the first year of each loan using IPMT and PPMT functions.

g. To the right of your amortization schedules, calculate the total amount of savings due to the down payment.

- Calculate the difference in the total cumulative payments made over the life of the loan for the two schedules.

- From the result, subtract the original $50,000 deposit you made.

- Confirm the result of your calculation by calculating the total cumulative interest payments made for the life of the loan for each loan. Subtract the two calculated cumulative interest payments. These calculations show the amount you have saved by having a down payment on your loan as well as borrowing less money.

h. Format both worksheets to provide a professional appearance.

i. Save the workbook, exit Excel, and then submit your file as directed by your instructor.

Microsoft Excel

Chapter 12 BUSINESS STATISTICS AND REGRESSION ANALYSIS

MyLab IT Grader

Sales & Marketing

Prepare Case

The Turquoise Oasis Spa: Using Statistics in Decision Making

Like managers of other businesses, the managers at the Turquoise Oasis Spa face a lot of uncertainty in making decisions about the strategic direction of the company. Their current decision to fund an expansion of the spa comes with considerable uncertainty about how it will affect their future. Various statistical methods can be applied to business data to help make more informed decisions with more certainty about expected outcomes. Business statistics can be applied to many areas of a business, such as financial analysis, production, operations, and marketing. Thus, the uncertainty can be managed to some extent.

The managers of the Turquoise Oasis Spa would like you to use various statistical methods to analyze their business data to help them understand the data better so that they may make better-informed decisions.

Kudla/Shutterstock

Student data file needed:

 e06ch12Statistics.xlsx

You will save your file as:

 e06ch12Statistics_LastFirst.xlsx

Applying Basic Statistical Methods to Business

Businesses today collect large amounts of data about the everyday operations of the company, from prices of raw materials to the number of links clicked on the company website. With so much data so easily available, it is becoming increasingly important that people in business understand how to use that data to make good strategic decisions. Statistical methods can be used to analyze business data to support good decision making.

Statistics is the practice of collecting, analyzing, and interpreting data. There are two major branches of statistics: descriptive statistics and inferential statistics. **Descriptive statistics** is the process of deriving meaningful information from raw data. An example of the use of descriptive statistics would be to calculate the total revenue that a spa package generates over the course of a year.

Inferential statistics is the process of taking data from a sample of the population and making predictions about the entire population. An example of the use of inferential statistics would be to survey 100 random customers about their opinions on a new service being offered at the spa. Managers at the spa can use the results of that random sample to make assumptions about whether the new spa service would go over well. Inferential statistics relies heavily on laws of probability.

Probability is the likelihood that some event will occur based on what is already known. Statistics typically describe what has already happened, and probability describes what is likely to happen in the future. In this section, you learn some of the foundational terminology used in statistics and conduct basic statistical analyses using Excel to gain a better understanding of business data.

Understand the Language of Statistics

Businesses can use various statistical methods in many areas to get a better understanding of the organization. Statistics can be used to determine the effectiveness of advertising campaigns, to understand what factors contribute to the demand for your products, to spot seasonal trends in the sales of certain products, and much more.

Before you get too far into various statistical methods and how businesses can use them, you must understand some common statistical terms. Discussions of statistics constantly refer to data. **Data** are the values that describe an attribute of an object or an event. Almost anything can be considered data, from an employee's salary to the number of spa packages sold to the cost of the latest marketing campaign. A **data set** is a collection of related data consisting of observational units and variables. An **observational unit** is a person, object, or event about which data are collected. For example, in a data set consisting of gender, salary, and name of employees, the employees are the observational unit, and the variables are the gender, salary, and names.

Discussions of statistics often refer to populations and samples. In statistics, a **population** is defined as an entire collection of people, animals, plants, or whatever on which you may collect data. For the spa, a population could be the entire population of all guests who ever received spa services. However, by the time you collect the data for the entire population, the spa has likely had more customers, so you would have to collect more data, during which time there may be still more customers. Very rarely are statistics based on populations, as collecting all the data would be too costly and too time consuming. Instead, statistics focuses on samples. A **sample population** is a subset of a population. In particular, work with statistics relies heavily on random samples. A **random sample** is a subset of a population that has been selected by using methods in which each element of the population has an equal chance of being selected. The more random the sample, the more accurate the statistical analysis will be, in part because randomness eliminates bias.

Business professionals who use statistical analysis to support their decision making rely heavily on probability distributions. A **probability distribution** describes all the possible values and likelihoods that a given variable can be within a specific range. The probability distribution can be in the form of a graph, table, or formula. There are two general classifications of probability distributions: discrete probability distributions and continuous probability distributions. The classifications are determined on the basis of whether the probabilities are associated with discrete variables or continuous variables.

A **discrete variable** is a variable that can have only a finite number of values and all possible values are known. Examples of discrete variables in business are performance classifications of employees, the number of bars of soap in a box, and the number of different services a spa offers its customers. A **continuous variable** can contain an infinite number of different values within a range. Examples of continuous variables in business are the time between sales transactions, the weight of a package for shipping, and the amount of money a customer spends in any given visit.

Opening the Starting File

You will be using various statistical methods and analysis to better understand the products, revenue, sales volume, and customers of Turquoise Oasis Spa. You will also use various statistical functions to calculate the probability of meeting or exceeding various business goals and to discover relationships between variables that may be useful in making predictions. In this exercise, you will open the workbook containing the data you have been asked to analyze.

E12.00

SIDE NOTE
Office Updates
Depending on your exact Office version, you may see Open or Open Other Workbooks.

To Get Started

a. Start **Excel**, click **Open** in the left pane, and then double-click **This PC**. Navigate through the folder structure to the location of your student data files, and then double-click **e06ch12Statistics**.

Grader Heads Up
If you are using MyLab IT Grader, this is the beginning of the first MyLab IT Grader project Part A.

b. Click the **File** tab, click **Save As**, and then double-click **This PC**. In the Save As dialog box, navigate to the location where you are saving your project files, and then change the file name to **e06ch12Statistics_LastFirst** using your last and first name. Click **Save**.

Understand the Basic Types of Data

Figure 1 illustrates the four basic levels of data used in statistics: nominal data, ordinal data, interval data, and ratio data. Each level adds to the next; thus, ordinal data is also nominal data, and so on. Having a strong understanding of these levels will help you to understand how to use various statistical functions and methods and how to interpret the results correctly.

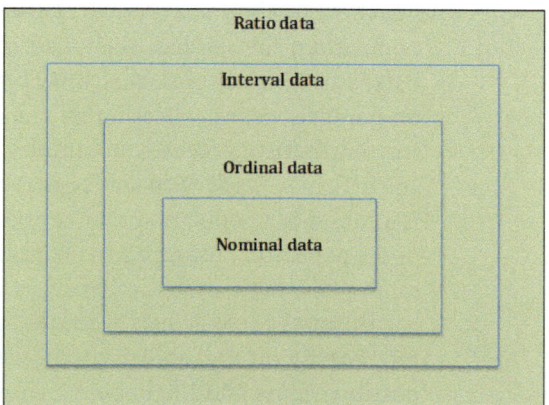

Figure 1   Four levels of data

Nominal data uses numbers for categorical or classification purposes only. Nominal variables are often used to categorize responses in a survey. For example, where respondents answer "Yes" or "No" to a specific question, nominal variables could be used to categorize the responses, such as 1 = Yes and 2 = No. It is also common to use nominal variables to categorize gender, such as 1 = Female and 2 = Male. It is important to note that some statistical functions, such as Average and Sum, would be meaningless to apply to nominal data.

Ordinal data uses numbers to rank data as first, second, third, and so on based on some scale. Ordinal data is useful in situations in which it is difficult to obtain accurate measurements. Some statistical analysis can be applied to ordinal data to derive additional meaning. For example, if a product is tested 100 times and the rate at which it fails is recorded on a scale of 1 to 10, then the average of all the product's failure rates on the scale could be useful. Ordinal data is more useful than nominal data in terms of what information can be derived, but having the actual time measurements of failure would be better.

Interval data measures the size of the difference between values. For example, with interval data, you know not only that one product test succeeded and one product test failed (nominal data) or that one product failed faster than another product (ordinal data), but also the difference in time intervals between when a product test failed and when a product test was successful.

Ratio data is similar to interval data except that the differences between the data can be quantified and proportions can be specified. For example, interval data may indicate that product 1 failed after 15 tests and product 2 failed after only five tests. Ratio data could state that product 1 passed three times as many tests as product 2 did.

Conduct Basic Statistical Analyses in Excel

Excel has many built-in functions that can be used to conduct basic statistical analysis on data. Knowledge of how to use even the most basic statistical functions can increase your understanding of the data and enable better decision making. In this section, you will assist the managers of the Turquoise Oasis Spa to better understand their data using basic statistical analysis.

Using the RAND Function to Generate a Random Sample

Randomness in selecting a sample from a population is crucial in conducting effective and accurate statistical analyses. The RAND function in Excel is one method that can help in creating a random sample. The function generates a random number between 0 and 1. The RAND function does not have any arguments.

RAND()

RAND is considered a volatile function because it generates a new number each time the worksheet is calculated. This means that every time any cell is edited or a new formula is created, the value generated by the RAND function will change. It is common practice to use Excel's Copy and Paste Values feature to prevent the values from changing once they have been generated. It is important to note that the values generated by this function are not truly random. Because an algorithm is used to generate the values, it is possible to predict what the next number generated will be; however, it is random enough to work in most situations.

Managers at the Turquoise Oasis Spa would like to select 10 random customers who visited the spa on a given day to take part in a survey about new services that the spa is considering. They plan to use the results of the survey to make decisions about which services to offer. You have been provided with the customer IDs of 34 customers who visited the spa on May 11, 2019. In this exercise, you will use the RAND function to generate 34 random values. You will then use the random values to sort the customer IDs in a random order for selection.

 **E12.01**

To Create a Random Sample Using RAND()

SIDE NOTE
Pin the Ribbon
If your ribbon is collapsed, pin your ribbon open. Click the Home tab. In the lower-right corner of the ribbon, click Pin the ribbon ⊟.

a. On the **RandomSample** worksheet, click cell **B3**, type **=RAND()** and then press Ctrl+Enter to generate a random value between 0 and 1.

b. Use the **fill handle** to copy the function down to cell **B36**.

c. Press Ctrl+C to copy the random values. On the Home tab, in the Clipboard group, click the Paste arrow 📋, and then, in the Paste Values group, click **Values** 📋 to replace the formula with its values.

SIDE NOTE
Random Sample
Because of the volatility of the RAND function, your results will be different from the image in Figure 2.

d. Select the cell range **A2:B36**. Click the **Data** tab, and in the Sort & Filter group, click **Sort**. Click **My data has headers** if necessary. Click the **Sort by** arrow, and then select **RAND** as the column to use for the sort. Click **OK**.

e. Select the cell range **A3:A12**.

f. Press Ctrl+C to copy.

g. Click cell **E3**, and then press Ctrl+V to paste the 10 randomly selected customer IDs.

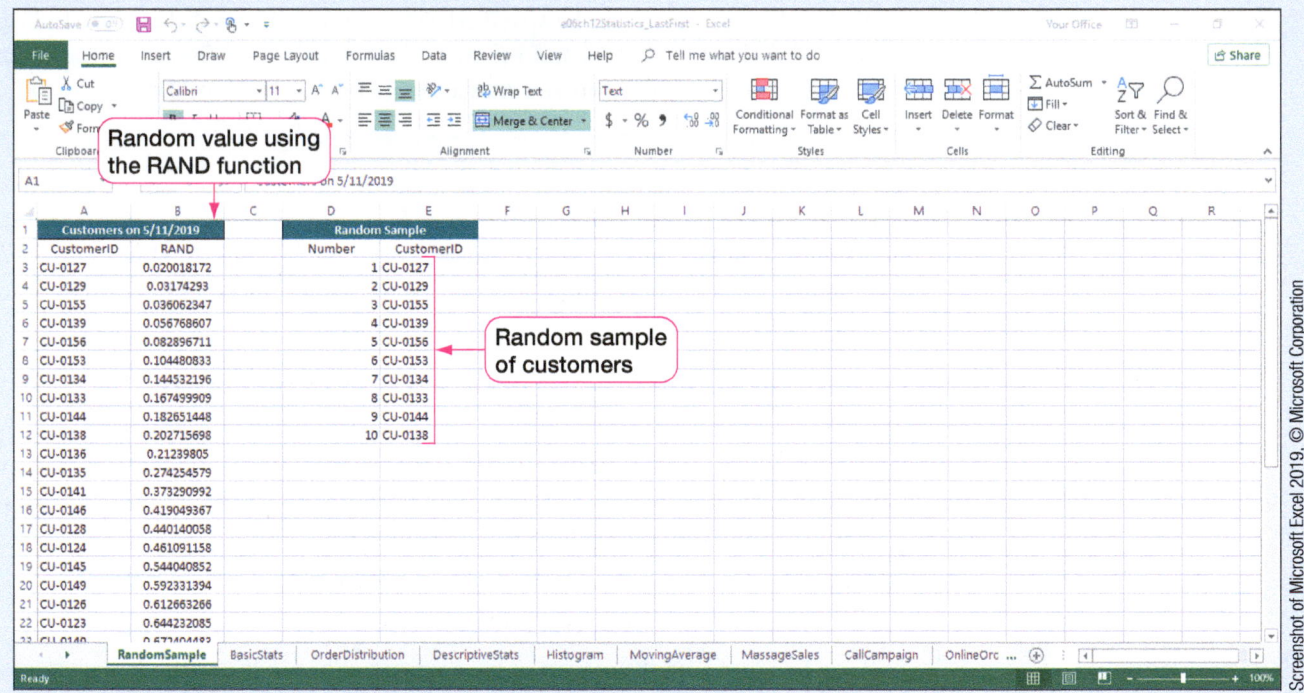

Figure 2 Creating a random sample with the RAND function

h. **Save** 💾 the workbook.

Calculating the Mean, Median, and Mode of a Data Set

Three of the most basic descriptive statistics used are mean, median, and mode. Each of these calculations attempts to define the central tendency of a data set. The **central tendency** refers to the way in which data tends to cluster around some value. The **mean** is the average of all the variables in a sample, often referred to as the arithmetic mean. The **median** describes which value falls in the middle when all the values of the sample are sorted in ascending order. For example if there are seven variables, the median value is the fourth variable in the list, where there are three variables above and three variables below. If the total number of variables is even, then the median value is the mean of the two middle variables. The **mode** is the value that appears most often in a sample. Modes are useful only with discrete data that is sorted in either ascending or descending order. If there are multiple values in a data set that appear the same number of times, then the mode will be reported in Excel as the value that appears first: the lowest value if the values are sorted in ascending order or the highest value if the values are sorted in descending order.

QUICK REFERENCE	Calculating the Central Tendency of a Data Set

Mean, Median, and Mode

- Mean: The sum of all values in a data set divided by the total number of values
- Median: The middle value that separates the higher and lower halves of a data set
- Mode: The value that appears most often in a data set with discrete variables

To calculate the mean in Excel, the AVERAGE function is used. The only arguments inside the AVERAGE function are the values from which an average is to be calculated.

=AVERAGE(number1, [number2],…)

To calculate the median of a data set in Excel, the MEDIAN function is used. Again, the only arguments needed are the values from which the median value is to be calculated.

=MEDIAN(number1, [number2],…)

To calculate the mode of a data set in Excel, one of two functions is used: MODE. SNGL or MODE.MULT. MODE.SNGL returns the value that appears most often in a data set. If more than one variable occurs most frequently, this function returns only the first one. The only arguments used by this function are the values from which a mode is to be calculated.

=MODE.SNGL(number1, [number2],…)

MODE.MULT is an array function that returns a vertical array of the values that occur most often in a data set. If more than one value occurs most frequently, this function returns all of them. The only arguments used by this function are the values from which modes are to be calculated.

=MODE.MULT(number1, [number2],…)

The Turquoise Oasis Spa often sells its house brand of essential oils to independent massage therapists who practice in the area. Management would like to find out whether a random sample of orders placed over the past year has a central tendency. In this exercise, you will use the data provided to calculate the mean, median, and mode.

 **E12.02**

To Calculate the Mean, Median, and Mode of a Data Set

a. Click the **BasicStats** worksheet. On this worksheet, a random sample of 34 orders with the quantity of items sold in each order is provided.

b. Click cell **G2**, and then type **=AVERAGE(** to begin the AVERAGE function.

c. Click cell **C2**, and drag to select cell **C35**. Type **)** and press Enter to calculate the mean of the number of units sold in the sample data set.

d. In cell **G3**, type **=MEDIAN(** to begin the MEDIAN function.

e. Click cell **C2**, and drag to select cell **C35**. Type **)** and press Enter to calculate the median sales quantity value in the sample data set.

Notice that because the number of values is an even number, the MEDIAN function returns the two middle values, which are 13.

f. In cell **G4**, type **=MODE.SNGL(** to being the MODE function.

g. Click cell **C2**, and drag to select cell **C35**. Type **)** and press Enter to calculate the most frequently occurring value in the sample data set.

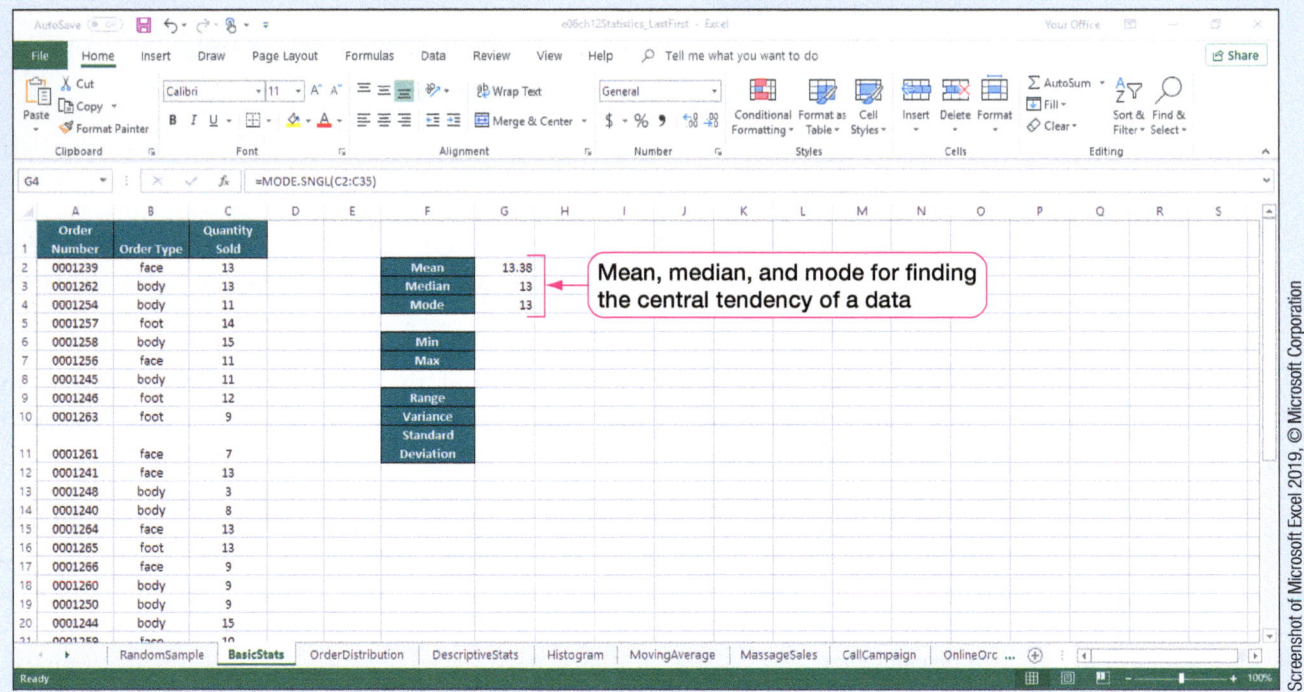

Figure 3 Calculating the mean, median, and mode of a data set

h. **Save** 💾 the workbook.

Calculating the Range, Variance, and Standard Deviation

Calculating the range, variance, and standard deviation of a data set is used to determine the dispersion of a data set. Knowing how a data set is dispersed can provide a better understanding of the data than the mean, median, and mode alone. For example, if a company lists its mean salary as $245,000, one might conclude that all salaries at the company are reasonably close to the mean. However, learning more about the dispersion of the salaries by calculating the range, variance, and standard deviation could reveal a much different picture of the salary distribution.

The **range** is the difference between the highest and lowest value in the data set. A range is the simplest method to calculate the dispersion of a data set and can provide a rough idea of how the data set is dispersed. However, a range can be misleading as a measure of spread if the data set consists of one excessively low value and/or one excessively high value. To calculate the range of a data set, the MIN and MAX functions are used. Subtracting the minimum value from the maximum value provides the range in a data set.

Variance is a calculation used in statistics to determine how far the data set varies from the mean. The higher the variance calculation, the more dispersed the data set. The smaller the variance, the more closely the data centers on the mean. Variance provides a more accurate picture of the dispersion of a data set than a range, but because of the way it is calculated, the value is not in the same units as the mean.

To calculate the variance of a data set in Excel, one of two functions is used: VAR.S or VAR.P. VAR.S is used to calculate the variance of a sample data set, and VAR.P is used to calculate the variance of a data set consisting of an entire population. Since most statistical analyses are based on random samples, VAR.S is used more often. The only arguments required are the values from which the variance is to be calculated.

=VAR.S(number1, [number2],…)

The **standard deviation** is the most commonly used method for determining the average spread of a data set from the mean. Mathematically, the standard deviation is calculated by taking the square root of the variance. It is most useful because its value is in the same unit as the median and therefore is easiest to interpret.

To calculate the standard deviation of a data set in Excel, one of two functions is used: STDEV.S or STDEV.P. STDEV.S is used to calculate the standard deviation of a sample set of data, and STDEV.P is used to calculate the standard deviation of a data set consisting of an entire population. Again, since most statistical analyses are based on random samples, STDEV.S is used most often. The only arguments required are the values from which the standard deviation is to be calculated.

=STDEV.S(number1, [number2],…)

Often, just calculating the central tendency of a data set is not enough. In fact, just finding the central tendency may lead to incorrect assumptions about the data due to possible outliers. **Outliers** are values that are abnormally different from the other values in a random sample. In this exercise, you will calculate the range, variance, and standard deviation of the random sample data set in order to understand how the data is distributed.

 **E12.03**

To Calculate the Dispersion of a Data Set

a. Click cell **G6**, and then type **=MIN(** to begin the MIN function.

b. Click cell **C2**, and drag to select cell **C35**. Type **)** and press Enter to calculate the minimum value in the sample.

c. In cell **G7**, type **=MAX(** to begin the MAX function.

d. Click cell **C2**, and drag to select cell **C35**. Type **)** and press Enter to calculate the maximum value in the sample.

e. Click cell **G9**. Type **=** click cell **G7**, and then type **-** Click cell **G6**, and press Enter to calculate to calculate the range of values in the sample.

f. In cell **G10**, type **=VAR.S(** to begin the VAR.S function.

g. Click cell **C2**, and drag to select cell **C35**. Type **)** and press Enter to calculate the variance of the sample.

h. In cell **G11**, type **=STDEV.S(** to begin the STDEV.S function.

i. Click cell **C2**, and drag to select cell **C35**. Type **)** and press Ctrl+Enter to calculate the standard deviation of the sample.

Notice that the standard deviation is quite small, at only 4.24, indicating that the sales values stay somewhat close to the mean.

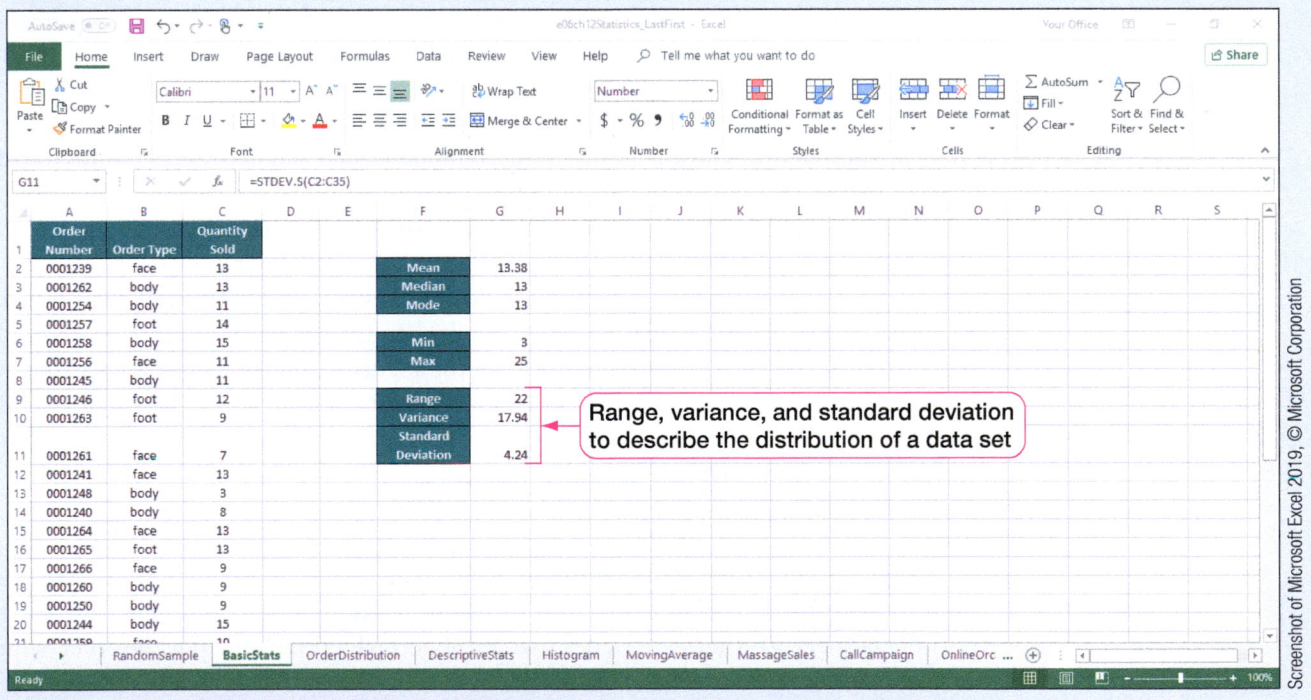

Figure 4 Calculating the dispersion of a data set

j. **Save** the workbook.

Visualize Outliers with a Box and Whisker Chart

As was previously mentioned, outliers are data that are abnormally different from other values in the data set. Defining outliers can be accomplished in many ways. The key to understanding outliers in your data is to determine where outliers are in relation to the rest of your data. A box and whisker chart, a new chart type available in Excel 2019, provides an efficient method of visualizing the distribution of your data and highlights outliers as part of the chart. Box and whisker charts visually represent several key statistical measures. First, they show the median and the mean of the data in relation to the distribution of the data. Next, they graphically represent the first and third quartiles of the data.

A **quartile** is a descriptive statistic that divides data into four equal groups, or quartiles. Each quartile consists of 25% of the data. The first quartile splits the lower quarter of the data from the upper three-quarters of the data. The second quartile is equal to the median of the data and splits the data into equal halves. The third quartile splits the lower three-quarters of the data from the upper quarter of the data. Figure 5 shows a graphical representation of quartile data.

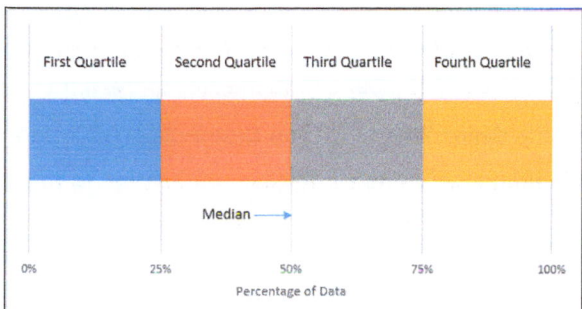

Figure 5 Distribution of data represented with quartiles

Box and whisker charts display outliers in the data. Figure 6 shows a box and whisker chart.

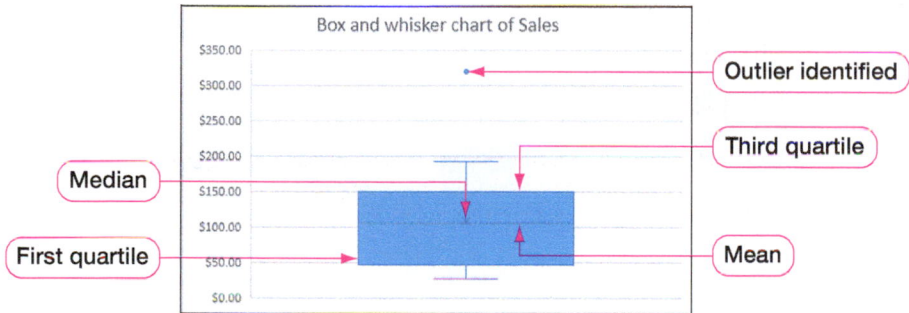

Figure 6 Box and whisker chart

The box portion of the chart shows the middle 50% of the data. The lower border of the box is the first quartile, and the upper border of the box is the third quartile. The length of the box is called the interquartile range, or IQR. The **interquartile range** is the difference between the third and first quartiles of data. The line across the box is the median of the data, the second quartile. The ☒ on the chart represents the mean of the data. The lines emanating from the box are the whiskers. The lower line represents the lower quartile of data, and the upper line represents the upper quartile of data.

Outliers in the data appear as a small circle outside of the whiskers. For box and whisker charts, outliers are calculated by measuring the distance from the edge of the box on the chart. If a data point is 1.5 times the interquartile range above the third quartile, it is considered an outlier. Likewise, if a data point is 1.5 times the interquartile range below the first quartile, it is considered an outlier.

In this exercise, you will visualize the distribution of the quantities sold in the random sample of data for which you previously calculated statistics.

 **E12.04**

To Create a Box and Whisker Chart

a. Select the cell range **B1:C35**, click the **Insert** tab, and in the Charts group, click **Insert Statistic Chart** ⬛.

> **Mac Troubleshooting**
> On a Mac, the ScreenTip says Statistical.

b. Select **Box and Whisker**.

   A box and whisker chart is inserted into the worksheet. Notice the outliers for the face box and whisker, indicating that the orders consisting of 8 and 25 products are abnormal in comparison to the rest of the data.

c. Click the **Chart Title**, and type Distribution of Orders

d. Move the chart so that it covers the cell range **I2:P15**, and click outside of the chart to deselect it.

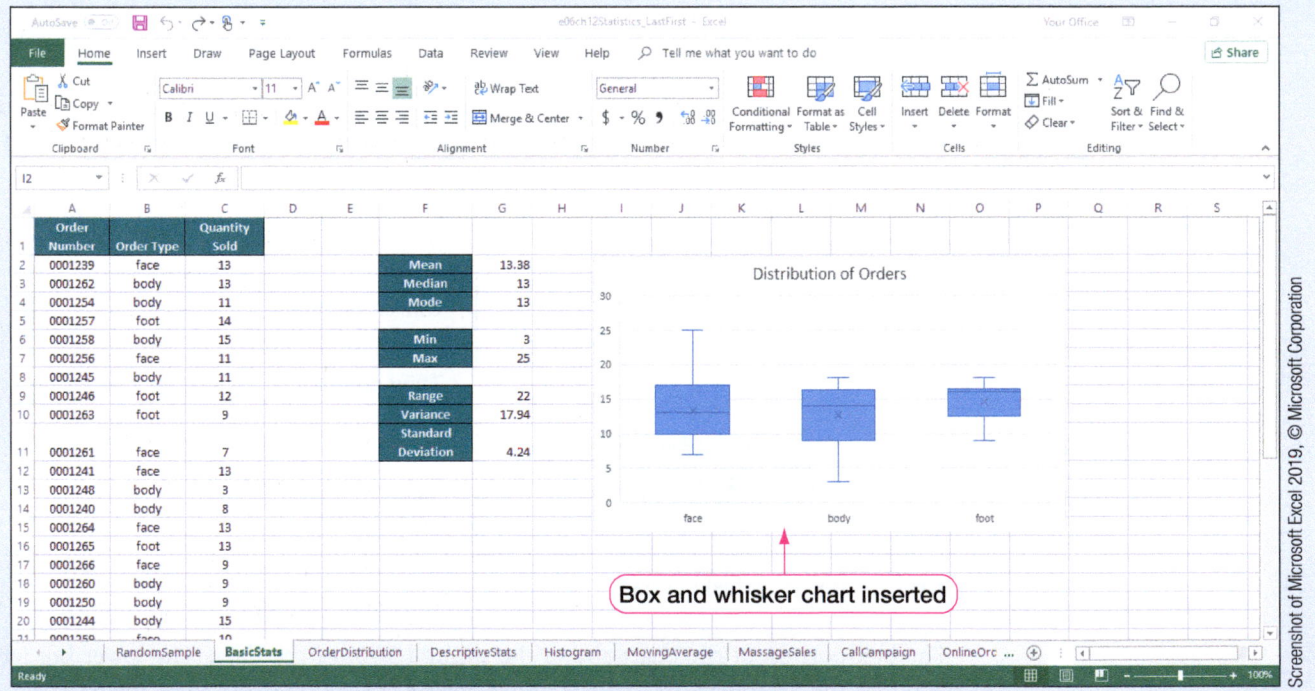

Figure 7   Box and whisker chart of quantities ordered

e. **Save** 💾 the workbook.

Creating a Frequency Distribution Using the FREQUENCY Function

Businesses often have to work with data sets that contain thousands of records or more. In working with large data sets, it can be useful to group the data into bins. **Bins** are the intervals into which you want to group your data. For example, the Turquoise Oasis Spa places orders for cases of bath salts through a wholesaler. To summarize several orders worth of data, it may prove beneficial to determine how many orders of bath salts were for 1 to 10 cases, for 11 and 20 cases, for 21 to 30 cases, for 31 to 40 cases, and for more than 40 cases.

The FREQUENCY function in Excel is an array function that creates a frequency distribution that calculates how often values occur within a bin. An **array function** is a function that can perform multiple calculations on one or more items in an array. Array functions look different from other functions because curly brackets { } are required for the function to calculate correctly.

The FREQUENCY function uses two arguments: (1) Data_array; and (2) Bins_array.

{=FREQUENCY(Data_array, Bins_array)}

The Data_array argument is an array of or a reference to a set of values from which you want to count the number of times a particular range of values occurs. Blank cells and cells that contain text are ignored in this argument.

The Bins_array argument is an array or reference to the upper values of the intervals you want to group the values in the Data_array argument into.

The FREQUENCY function always returns one additional value than there are bins referenced in the Bins_array argument. For example, if there are four bins consisting of 10, 20, 30, and 40, the function will return five values, including a count of values in the Data_array argument that are equal to more than 40, that is, counts of $1 \leq 10$, $11 \leq 20$, $21 \leq 30$, $31 \leq 40$, and > 40.

Since the FREQUENCY function is an array function, once it has been typed into a cell, you must press Ctrl + Shift + Enter instead of just Enter for it to calculate properly. Array functions are often referred to as "CSE" functions because of the keys pressed to create the function.

You have been given a random sample of 29 orders. In this exercise, you will use the FREQUENCY array function to group the number of cases ordered into the bins provided in column D.

 **E12.05**

To Summarize Data into Bins Using the FREQUENCY Function

a. Click the **OrderDistribution** worksheet. Select the cell range **E2:E6**, and type **=FREQUENCY(** to begin the FREQUENCY function.

b. Click cell **B2**, and drag to select cell **B30**. Type **,** and then click cell **D2**. Drag to select cell **D5**, type **)** and then press Ctrl + Shift + Enter to make the function an array function.

When creating a frequency table using the FREQUENCY function, you must select a range of cells that is one more than the number of cells containing the bin values. Notice that the frequency table provides a count of orders that were for 1 to 10 cases, between 11 and 20 cases, between 21 and 30 cases, between 31 and 40 cases, and more than 40 cases.

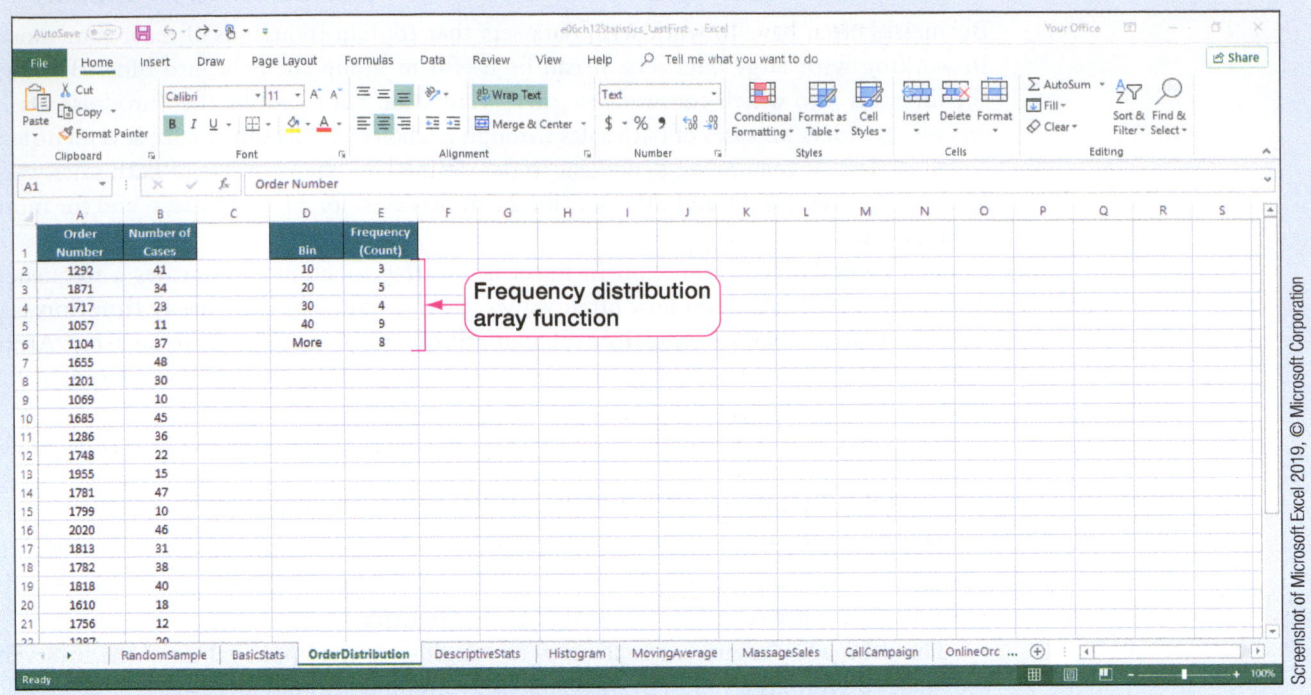

Figure 8 Summarizing data into bins with the FREQUENCY function

c. Click cell **D6**, and then type More as the label for the number of orders with more than 40 items.

> **Troubleshooting**
>
> If the FREQUENCY function is not returning expected results, be sure there are curly brackets surrounding the function. This indicates that it is an array function. {=FREQUENCY(B2:B30, D2:D5)}. If there are no curly brackets, then you must delete the functions and start over with step b.

d. Save the workbook.

Generate Descriptive Statistics and Other Analyses Using the Data Analysis Add-In

The Data Analysis add-in allows you to conduct a variety of statistical analyses with ease. For example, instead of typing out individual functions to calculate the mean, median, mode, variance, and standard deviation, you can generate all of those and more using the Data Analysis add-in.

Adding the Data Analysis Add-In

Depending on the options that were selected when Excel was installed, the Data Analysis add-in may or may not be available by default in Excel. In this exercise, you will manually install the Data Analysis add-in.

 **E12.06**

SIDE NOTE

Hover to See Icon Information

When you are presented with a set of icons such as the chart types, you can point to an icon, and a ScreenTip appears to offer descriptive information.

To Add the Data Analysis Add-In

a. Click the **File** tab, click **Options**, and then click **Add–ins**.

> ### Mac Troubleshooting
> On a Mac, click the Tools menu, click Excel Add-ins, click the Analysis ToolPak checkbox, and then click OK.

b. At the bottom of the Excel Options dialog box, ensure that **Excel Add-ins** is selected in the Manage box, and then click **Go**.

c. In the Add-Ins dialog box, click to select the **Data Analysis** check box, and then click **OK**.

d. Click the **Data** tab, and in the Analyze group, verify that the Data Analysis add-in is now available.

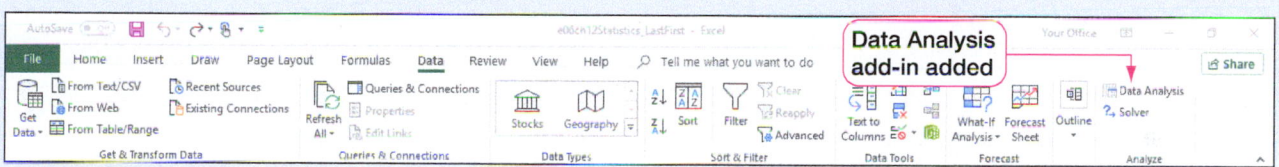

Figure 9   Data Analysis button added to the Data tab

Screenshot of Microsoft Excel 2019, © Microsoft Corporation

e. **Save** 💾 the workbook.

Generating Descriptive Statistics

Many of the statistical analyses that you have employed with Excel functions and more can be automatically generated by using the Data Analysis Descriptive Statistics tool.

The managers of the Turquoise Oasis Spa have provided you with a sample set of data containing monthly revenue amounts for the last year. In this exercise, you will generate descriptive statistics on the sample data set to gain a better understanding of the data.

 **E12.07**

To Generate Descriptive Statistics Using the Data Analysis Add-In

a. Click the **DescriptiveStats** worksheet.

b. On the **Data** tab, in the Analysis group, click **Data Analysis**.

c. Select **Descriptive Statistics** from the Data Analysis dialog box, and then click **OK**.

d. In the Descriptive Statistics dialog box, click the **Input Range** box, and then select the cell range **B1:B13**.

e. Next to Grouped By, be sure that **Columns** is selected.

f. Click to select the **Labels in First Row** check box, indicating that the first row contains the Sales Revenue label.

g. Under Output options, click to select **Output Range**, click the **Output Range** box, and then click cell **E1**.

h. Click the **Summary statistics** check box, and then click **OK**.

Notice that many of the basic statistical calculations are generated automatically, including mean, median, mode, range, variance, and standard deviation. Notice that the value for the mode of the data is #N/A because there is no value in the data that occurs more than once.

i. Resize columns **E** and **F** to fit the contents by double-clicking the line between column E and column F and the line between column F and column G in the heading.

The results of the descriptive statistics output show that the spa's monthly revenues were relatively steady throughout the year with a standard deviation of approximately 2,697.

j. Save 🖫 the workbook.

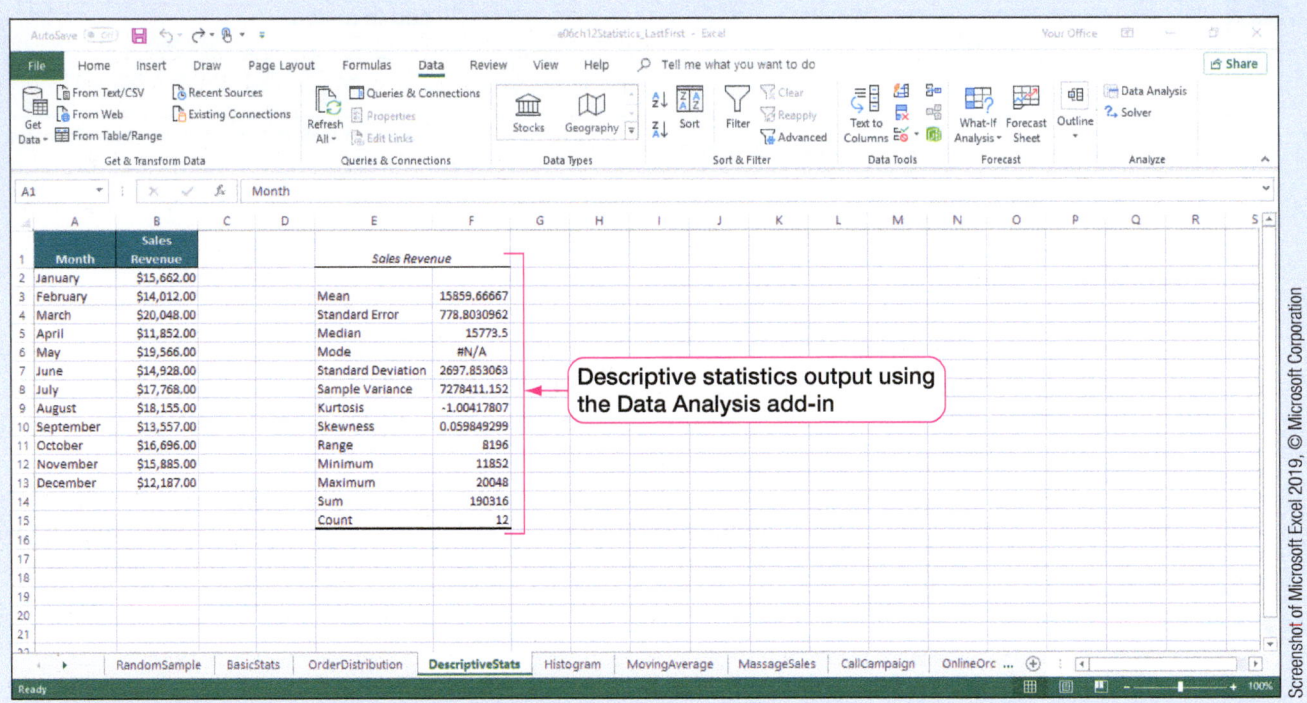

Figure 10   Descriptive statistics output

QUICK REFERENCE **Descriptive Statistics**

Below is a list of statistical functions and descriptions that are generated by the Descriptive Statistics tool in the Data Analysis add-in.

Statistical Function	Description
Mean	The average of the variables in the sample
Standard error	Used to determine how accurate the sample mean predicts the population mean by dividing the standard deviation by the square root of the sample size
Median	The middle value(s) when all the values of the sample are sorted in ascending order
Mode	The value that appears most often in a sample. If there is no Mode, then #N/A will appear
Standard deviation	The most commonly used method for determining the average spread of a data set from the mean
Sample variance	A measure of how far the data in the sample are spread from the mean
Kurtosis	Characterizes the peakedness or flatness of a distribution compared to the normal distribution
Skewness	Characterizes the degree of asymmetry of a distribution around its mean
Range	The difference between the largest and smallest values in the sample
Minimum	The smallest value in the sample
Maximum	The largest value in the sample
Sum	The sum of all values in the sample
Count	The count of all values in the sample

Using a Histogram to Visualize Data in Bins

Earlier, you created a frequency distribution using the FREQUENCY array function in Excel. Frequency distributions can be visualized by using a histogram. A **histogram** is a statistical graph that summarizes the distribution of data and how the data fits into defined bins. In prior versions of Excel, histograms were created with the Data Analysis add-in or by using carefully crafted column charts. Excel 2019 has introduced histograms as a default chart type. On the Histogram worksheet tab, sample data from 30 customers is provided, along with the number of items each of these customers has purchased over the course of one year. In this exercise, you will create a histogram to visualize the distribution of data.

 **E12.08**

To Create a Histogram

a. Click the **Histogram** worksheet.

b. Select the cell range **A1:B31**, click the **Insert** tab, and in the Charts group, click **Insert Statistic Chart** .

> **Mac Troubleshooting**
> On a Mac, the ScreenTip says Statistical.

c. Select **Histogram**. A histogram is placed into the chart. By default, a histogram may not be formatted in a way that is descriptive of the data.

d. Double-click the **horizontal axis** to open the Format Axis pane. Click the **Bin width** option button, and in the text box clear the default text, type **10** and then press [Enter]. This will divide the data into six bins. Each bin contains data points over a 10-point interval. For example, the first bin contains data points from 23 to 33.

e. Click the **Chart Title** box and then type Histogram of Items Purchased and then click outside of the chart to deselect it.

f. **Close** ⊠ the Format Axis pane and move the histogram chart so that it is within the range **E4:K18**.

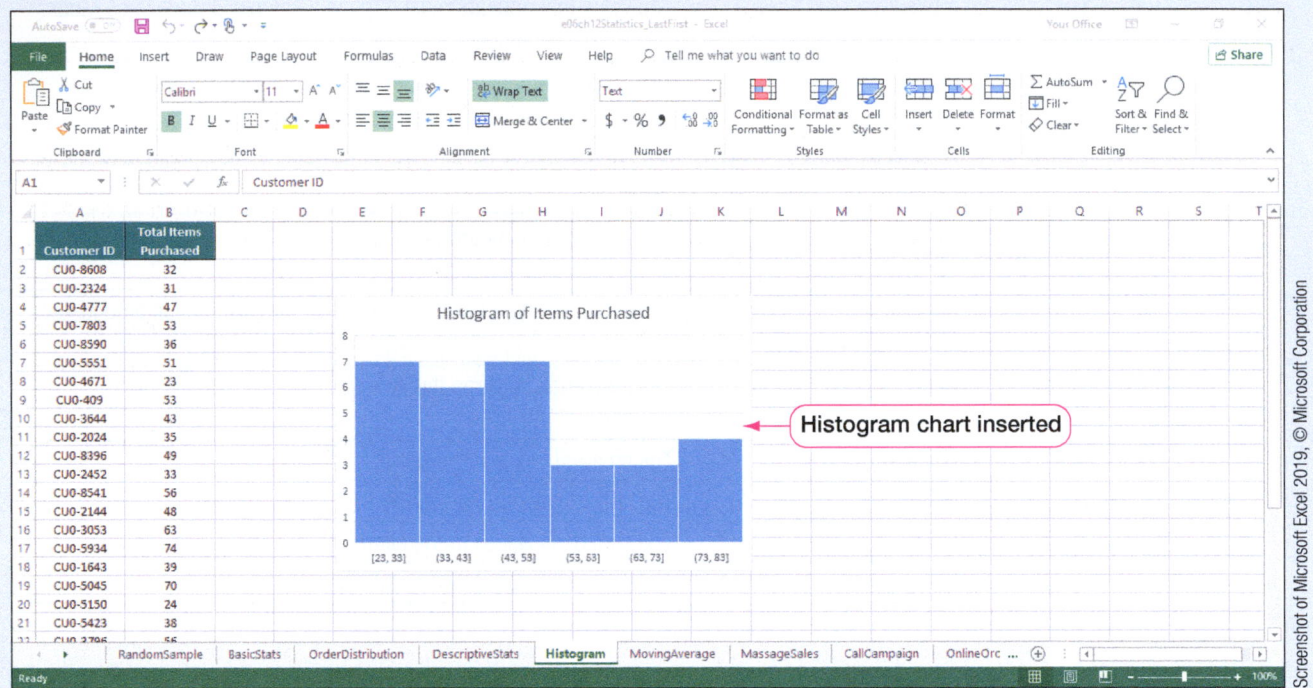

Figure 11 Histogram of items purchased

g. **Save** 🖫 the workbook.

Screenshot of Microsoft Excel 2019, © Microsoft Corporation

REAL WORLD ADVICE | **Creating Bin Values**

Although Excel automatically generates bin values, you may want to define your own bin ranges depending on the amount of data you have sampled. There are several common methods of calculating the number and width of bins in data. You can also use the Underflow and Overflow bin options for extreme data points in your sample.

Calculating a Moving Average

A useful calculation for businesses that want to track sales over time, for example, is called a moving average. A **moving average** calculates the average of values over time on the basis of specified intervals. For example, a business may wish to see the average sales for every three months in a given year. Moving averages can be useful in spotting trends over a period of time by smoothing out any fluctuations that may occur during each consecutive interval. Moving average data can be used to create charts that show whether the value is trending upward or downward.

You have been provided with monthly sales data for the past year. In this exercise, you will calculate a moving average for every three months to determine whether there is an upward or downward trend over the course of the year.

 **E12.09**

SIDE NOTE
Expecting #N/A Values
The moving average for the first two months returns #N/A. This is due to the intervals being set to 3.

To Calculate a Moving Average Using the Data Analysis Add-In

a. Click the **MovingAverage** worksheet.

b. Click the **Data** tab, in the Analysis group, click **Data Analysis**.

c. In the list of Analysis Tools, select **Moving Average**, and then click **OK**.

d. In the Moving Average dialog box, click the **Input Range** box, and then select the cell range **B2:B13**.

e. Click the **Interval** box, and type **3** to set the interval for every three months.

f. Click the **Output Range** box, and then click cell **C2**.

g. Click to select the **Chart Output** check box to include a chart, and then click **OK**.

h. Edit the chart title to read Moving Sales Average edit the horizontal axis label to read Months and then edit the vertical axis label to read Sales Click outside the chart to deselect it.

Notice the difference between the Actual and Forecast lines included in the chart. This indicates that despite the fluctuations in monthly sales, the overall trend is fairly flat with neither an upward nor a downward trend.

i. **Close** ☒ the Format Axis pane if necessary and move the moving average chart so that it is within the range **E2:L13**.

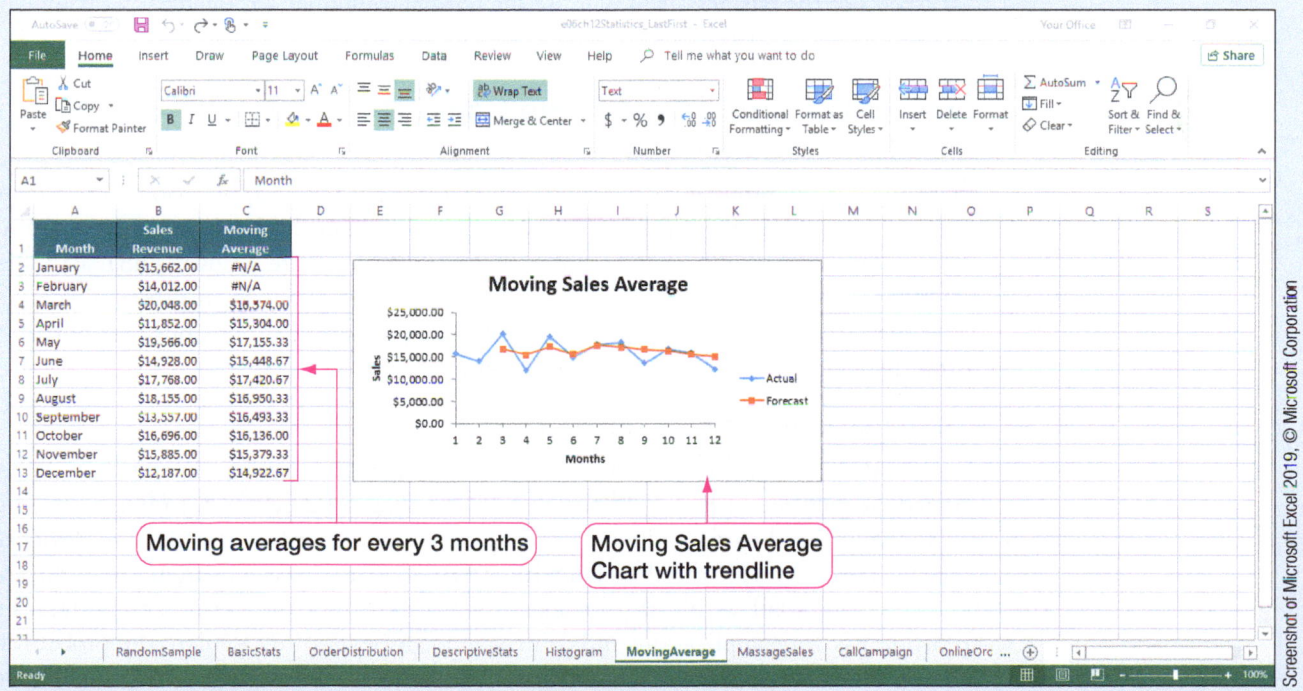

Figure 12   Calculating a three-month moving average

j. Save 🖫 the workbook. If you need to take a break before finishing this chapter, now is a good time.

Grader Heads Up

If you are using MyLab IT Grader, this is the end of the first MyLab IT Grader project Part A. This project continues in Part B which is a separate MyLab IT Grader project.

CONSIDER THIS | **Selecting Appropriate Intervals**

In calculating a moving average, it is important that the interval chosen is appropriate for the data. What interval would be appropriate for a call center that makes thousands of calls in a day? For a small business that makes an average of 10 outside sales a day?

Applying Probability Distributions to Business

All businesses operate on a large amount of uncertainty. Small businesses such as the Turquoise Oasis Spa tend to experience more volatility than large organizations and can therefore benefit greatly from using probability distributions to estimate future outcomes and events. Probability distributions are useful in predicting demand for products and services, successful marketing campaigns, effectiveness of advertising, and much more.

In this section, you will use several different probability distributions to predict various aspects of the business. You will use the normal, binomial, exponential, Poisson, and hypergeometric distributions.

Predict Business Outcomes Using Probability Distribution Functions

Excel offers many probability distribution functions with wide applications across many different industries of business, science, engineering, and mathematics. The probability distribution functions most commonly used in business are NORM.DIST, BINOM. DIST, EXPON.DIST, POISSON.DIST, and HYPGEOM.DIST. In this section, you will assist the managers at the Turquoise Oasis Spa in predicting various business outcomes using these probability distribution functions.

Using the NORM.DIST Function

A **normal distribution** is one of the most important distributions in statistics. When charted, as pictured in Figure 13, it takes on the shape of a bell and is often referred to as the "bell-shaped curve," where 68% of all values occur within one standard deviation from the mean, 95.45% of values fall within two standard deviations from the mean, and 99.8% of values fall within three standard deviations from the mean. The normal distribution has wide applications in business and can be used to calculate the probability of sales, the number of customers to expect in a given week, employee performance, and operations, to name a few.

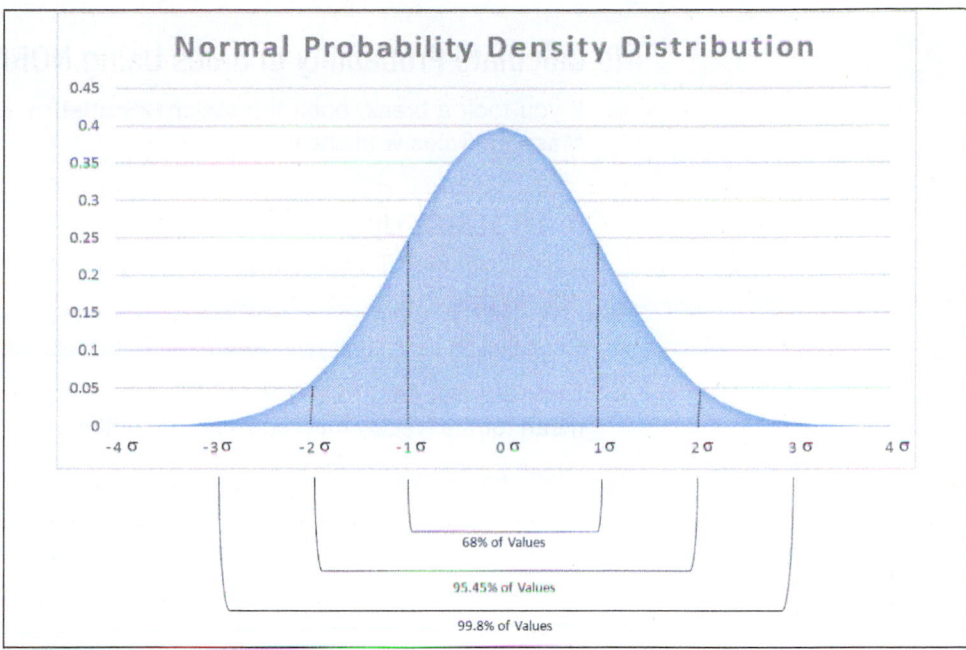

Figure 13 Normal probability density distribution

QUICK REFERENCE	Normal Distribution

- Many economic, social, and natural events follow the normal distribution.
- 68% of values will fall within one standard deviation from the mean.
- 95.45% of values will fall within two standard deviations from the mean.
- 99.8% of values will fall within three standard deviations from the mean.

The **NORM.DIST** function can be used to calculate the probability of an event occurring by using the mean and standard deviation of a continuous variable data set, assuming that the data follows a normal distribution. The NORM.DIST function uses four arguments: (1) x, (2) mean, (3) standard_dev, and (4) cumulative.

=NORM.DIST(x, mean, standard_dev, cumulative)

- The x argument is the value for which you want to calculate the probability of occurrence.
- The mean argument is the average value in the data set.
- The standard_dev argument is the standard deviation of the data set.
- The cumulative argument accepts either a TRUE or a FALSE value. If TRUE, the result will be the probability of a value being less than or equal to the value of the x argument, known as the **cumulative distribution function**. If FALSE, the result will be the probability of a value being equal to the value of the x argument, known as the **probability density function**.

Statistically, the probability of a specific x value for continuous data is 0, but the FALSE argument can be used to create a probability distribution of the data set.

Managers at the spa want to know how likely it is that they will exceed their goal of selling 30 massages over the course of the next week. You have been given data of weekly massage sales for the past seven weeks to use in your calculation. In this exercise, you will use the NORM.DIST function to calculate the probability of various sales levels in the data.

 **E12.10**

To Calculate Probability of Sales Using NORM.DIST

a. If you took a break, open the **e06ch12Statistics_LastFirst** workbook. Click the **MassageSales** worksheet.

> **Grader Heads Up**
>
> If you are using MyLab IT Grader, this is the beginning of the second MyLab IT Grader project Part B.

b. Click cell **E1**, and then type **=AVERAGE(** to begin the AVERAGE function.

c. Click cell **B3**, drag to select cell **B9**, type **)** and then press Enter to calculate the mean for the weekly massage sales quantities.

d. In cell **E2**, type **=STDEV.S(** to begin the STDEV.S function.

e. Click cell **B3**, drag to select cell **B9**, type **)** and then press Ctrl+Enter to calculate the standard deviation of the sample of weekly massage sales volume.

f. Click cell **E4**, type **30** and then press Enter as the desired minimum sales goal in week 8.

g. In cell **E5**, type **=1-NORM.DIST(** to begin the NORM.DIST function. By default, the NORM.DIST function returns the probability of a value being less than or equal to the x value. Therefore, if the desired probability is for a value greater than the x value, you have to subtract the result from 1.

h. Click cell **E4**, and then type **,** to move to the mean argument.

i. Click cell **E1**, and then type **,** to move to the standard_dev argument.

j. Click cell **E2**, and then type **,** to move to the cumulative argument.

k. Type **TRUE)** and press Ctrl+Enter to calculate the probability of selling more than 30 massages in week 8.

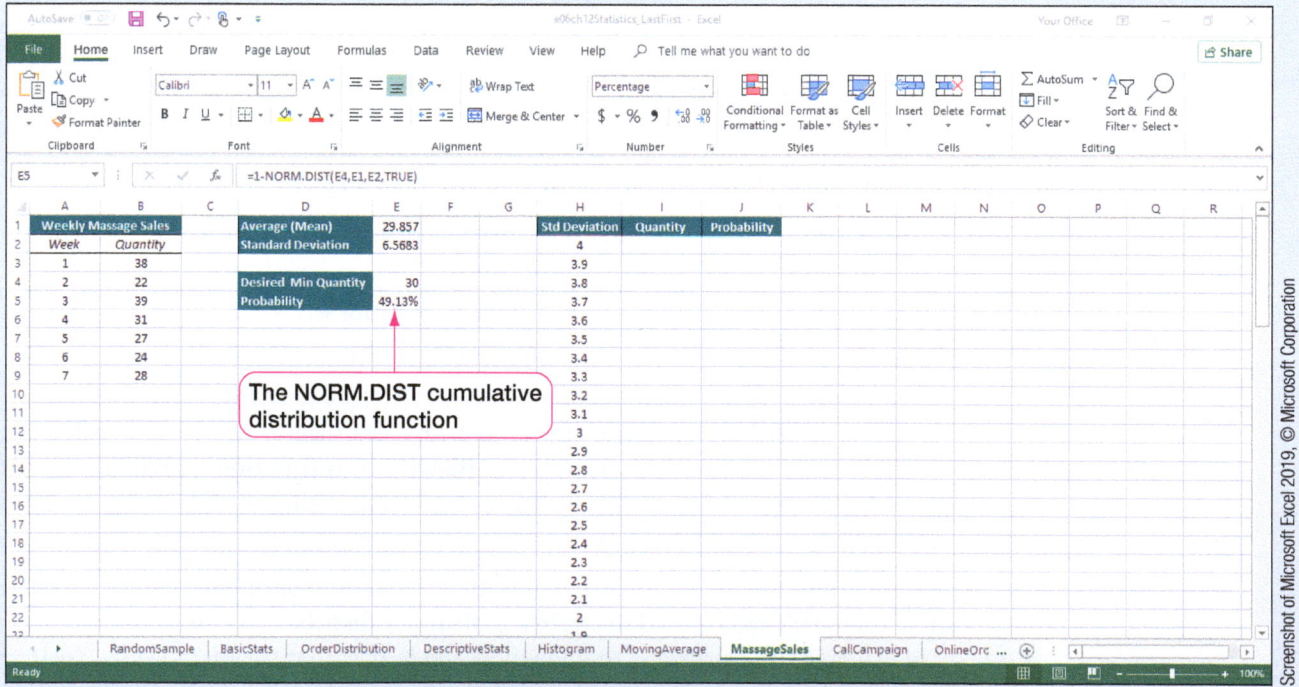

Figure 14 Probability of breaking a sales goal using the NORM.DIST function

l. Save 🖫 the workbook.

Charting a Normal Distribution

Visualizing the normal distribution of the weekly massage sales can help the managers of the spa to understand what the expectations should be for future weeks. In this exercise, you will create a chart that visualizes the normal distribution by first calculating the probability of values occurring within four standard deviations of the mean, both positive and negative.

 **E12.11**

To Visualize a Normal Distribution with a Scatter Chart

a. On the MassageSales worksheet, click cell **I2**.

b. Type **=** and click cell **H2**. Type ***** click cell **E2**, and then press ⌐F4⌐ to lock the reference so that the formula can be copied down the column.

c. Type **+** click cell **E1**, and then press ⌐F4⌐. Press ⌐Ctrl⌐+⌐Enter⌐ to calculate the number of massages sold if the unit quantity were equal to four standard deviations above the mean.

d. Use the **fill handle** to copy the formula down to **I82** (four standard deviations below the mean).

e. Click cell **J2**, and then type **=NORM.DIST(** to begin the NORM.DIST function.

f. Click cell **I2**, and then type **,** to move to the mean argument.

g. Click cell **E1**, press ⌐F4⌐, and then type **,** to move to the standard_dev argument.

h. Click cell **E2**, press ⌐F4⌐, and then type **,** to move to the cumulative argument.

i. Type **FALSE)** and then press ⌐Ctrl⌐+⌐Enter⌐ to calculate the probability that the spa will sell a number of massages that are exactly four standard deviations above the mean in a given week.

j. Use the **fill handle** to copy the formula down to **J82**.

k. Select the cell range **I2:J82**, and then click the **Insert** tab. In the Charts group, click the **Insert Scatter (X, Y) or Bubble Chart** button, and then select the **Scatter with Smooth Lines** chart.

l. Move the chart to within the cell range **A11:F23**.

m. Click the **Chart Title** text box, and then type **Weekly Sales Distribution**

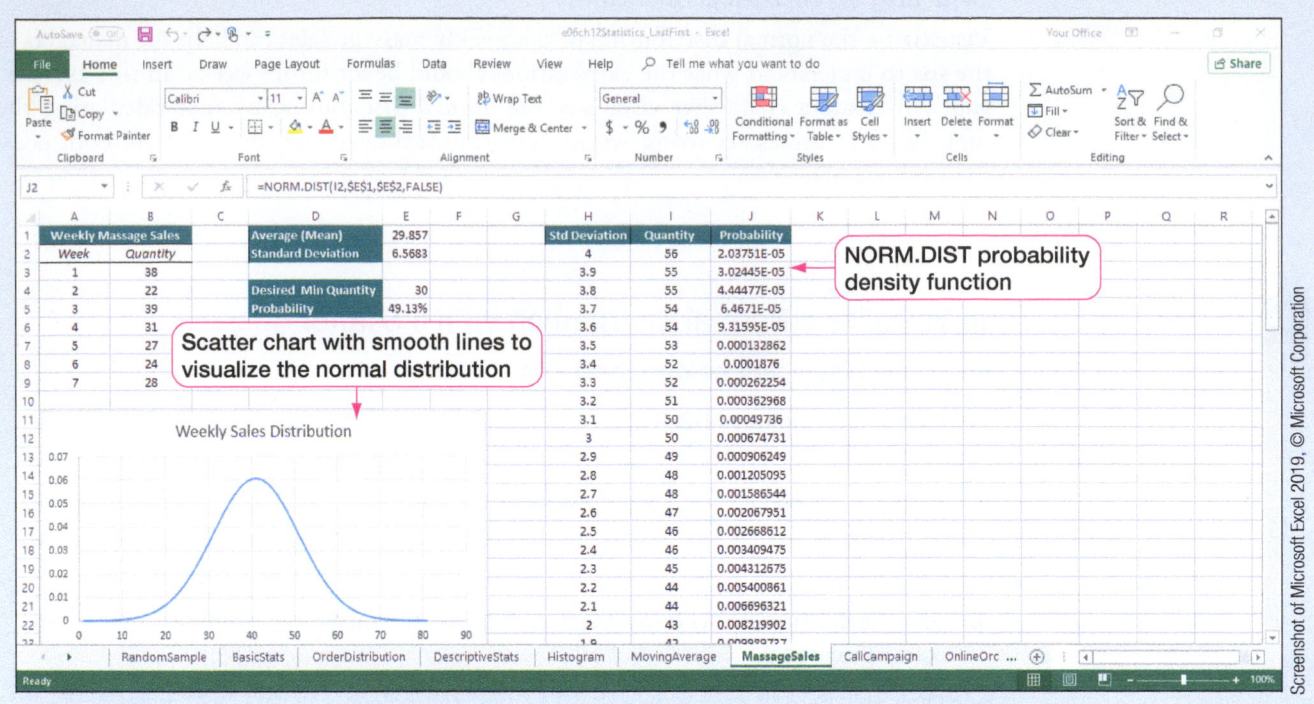

Figure 15 Visualizing the normal distribution with a scatter chart

n. **Save** 💾 the workbook.

Using the BINOM.DIST Function

The spa initiated a phone campaign to get current and former customers to subscribe to its health and beauty magazine. After 30 phone calls, there was a 35% success rate of converting a prospective customer, or lead, to a paid subscriber. Statistical analysis could be applied to this data to calculate the probability of successfully converting 0 leads, 1 lead, 2 leads, and so on. The binomial distribution can do just that. The binomial distribution is a very common probability distribution that has many applications in business. The **binomial distribution** is a discrete probability distribution that is used to model the number of successful trials based on the total number of trials and the rate of success.

The BINOM.DIST function uses four arguments: (1) number_s, (2) trials, (3) probability_s, and (4) cumulative.

=BINOM.DIST(number_s, trials, probability_s, cumulative)

- The number_s argument is the number of successes for which you want to calculate the probability of occurrence.

- The trials argument is the number of independent trials that have taken place. For the spa, it is the number of subscription phone calls placed.

- The probability_s argument is the probability of success for each trial. This is based on the data previously collected, in which 35% of the phone calls placed resulted in the person signing up for the mailing list.

- The cumulative argument accepts either a TRUE or a FALSE value. If TRUE, the result will be the probability of a value being less than or equal to the value of the x argument, known as the cumulative distribution function. If FALSE, the result will be the probability of a value being equal to the value of the x argument, known as the probability density function.

Figure 16 shows how a binomial probability density distribution may look when charted.

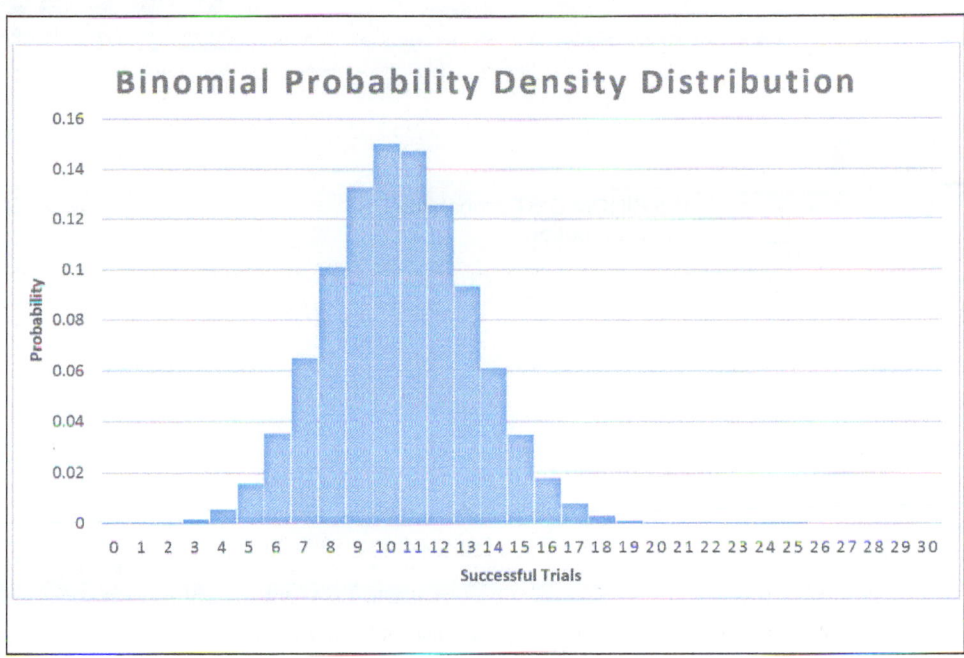

Binomial Probability Density Distribution

Figure 16 Binomial probability density distribution

In this exercise, you will use the BINOMIAL.DIST function to calculate the probability of success during a phone campaign, given a sample size of 30 and a 35% success rate.

 **E12.12**

To Calculate the Probability of Success Using BINOM.DIST

a. Click the **CallCampaign** worksheet.

b. Click cell **B5**, and type =BINOM.DIST(to begin the BINOM.DIST function.

c. Click cell **A5**, and then type , to move to the trials argument.

d. Click cell **B1**, press F4, and then type , to move to the probability_s argument.

e. Click cell **B2**, press F4, and then type , to move to the cumulative argument.

f. Type FALSE) and press Ctrl+Enter to calculate the probability that exactly 0 out of 30 calls will result in a successful sign-up.

g. Use the **fill handle** to copy the formula down to **B35**.

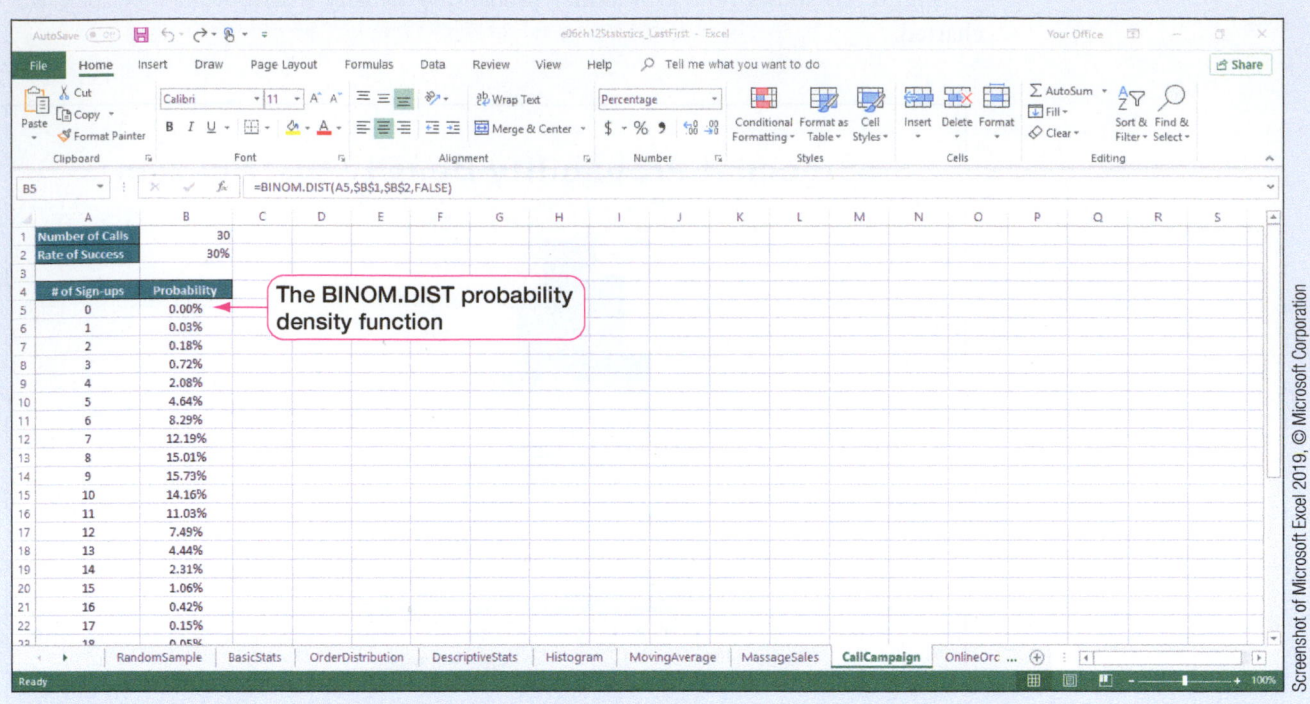

Figure 17 Probability of success using the BINOM.DIST function

h. **Save** 🖫 the workbook.

Notice that the most likely number of successful sign-ups is nine out of every 30 phone calls, at 15.73%. Managers at the spa can use this information as a way to set expectations for each phone representative. If a representative is able to consistently outperform the most likely number of sign-ups, then perhaps a best practice can be established to increase the overall rate of success.

Using the EXPON.DIST Function

Managers at the Turquoise Oasis Spa have been tracking how frequently online sales of their spa products have been occurring. They would like to estimate when the next 10 online orders will occur. The exponential distribution can do just that. The **exponential distribution** is a continuous probability function that models the times between events. The EXPON.DIST function uses three arguments: (1) x, (2) lambda, and (3) cumulative.

=EXPON.DIST(x, lambda, cumulative)

- The x argument is the value representing the number of events for which you want to calculate the probability of occurrence.

- The lambda argument is the inverse of the mean and is calculated by dividing 1 by the mean value.

- The cumulative argument accepts either a TRUE or a FALSE value. If TRUE, the result will be the probability of a value being less than or equal to the value of the x argument, known as the cumulative distribution function. If FALSE, the result will be the probability of a value being equal to the value of the x argument, known as the probability density function.

Figure 18 shows how an exponential cumulative distribution may look when charted.

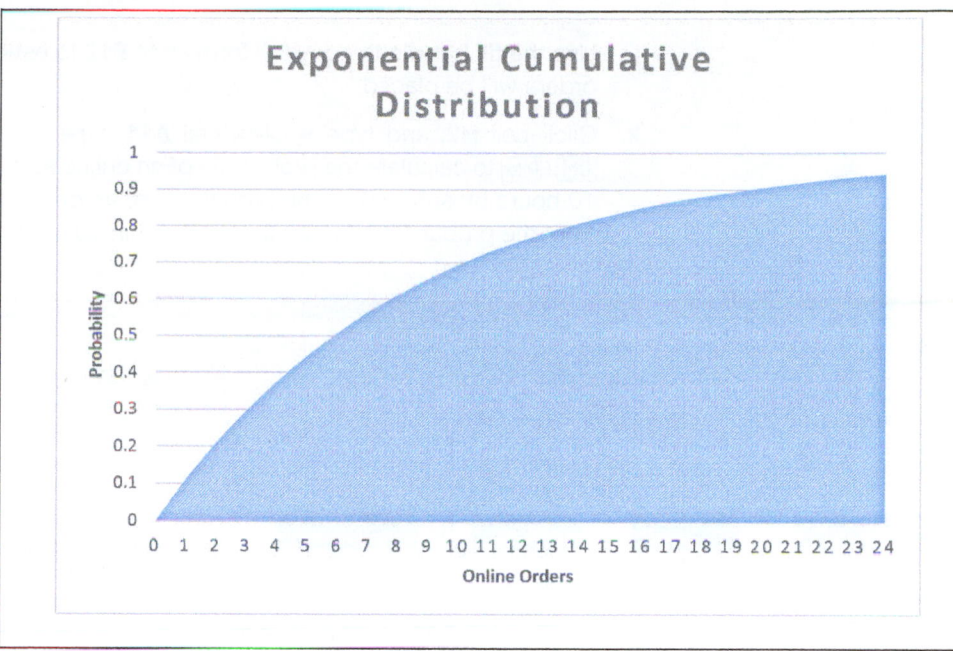

Figure 18 Exponential cumulative distribution

In this exercise, you will use the EXPON.DIST function to calculate the probability of a sale.

 **E12.13**

To Calculate the Probability of When a Sale Will Occur Using EXPON.DIST

a. Click the **OnlineOrder** worksheet.

b. Click cell **A2**, and then type **=EXPON.DIST(** to begin the EXPON.DIST function.

c. Type **B2,** to move to the lambda argument.

d. Type **1/** click cell **D2**, and then press F4. Type **,** to move to the cumulative argument.

e. Type **TRUE)** and press Ctrl+Enter to calculate the probability of an online sale taking place in 1 hour or less. The final function should appear as =EXPON.DIST(B2,1/$D$2,TRUE).

f. Use the **fill handle** to copy the function to **A25**.

Notice the various probabilities for sales taking place within the next 1 to 24 hours. Since TRUE was used for the cumulative argument, each of the probabilities is for a value less than or equal to the x value.

g. Click cell **F3**, and then type **=IFERROR(VLOOKUP(RAND(),**

h. Click cell **A2**, drag to select cell **B25**, and press F4. Type **,** to move to the col_index_num argument.

i. Type **2,TRUE),1)** to complete the formula. The final formula should appear as =IFERROR(VLOOKUP(RAND(),$A$2:$B$25,2,TRUE),1). This formula uses the VLOOKUP function to look up a random probability value generated by the RAND function. Where an approximate match is found, it returns the number of hour(s) when a sale will occur from column B. The IFERROR function is necessary because if the random variable generated is less than the probability of a sale occurring in 1 hour or less, the result would be an error and should be 1.

SIDE NOTE
Random Probabilities
Because of the volatility of the RAND function, your results will be different from the image in Figure 19.

j. Use the **fill handle** to copy the formula to **F12** to estimate when the next 10 online orders will be placed.

k. Click cell **H2**, and type **=** Click cell **A11**, type **-**, and then click cell **A6**. Press Ctrl+Enter to calculate the probability of an online sale occurring within the next 5 to 10 hours by subtracting the probability of an online sale occurring within 5 hours from the probability of one occurring within 10 hours or less.

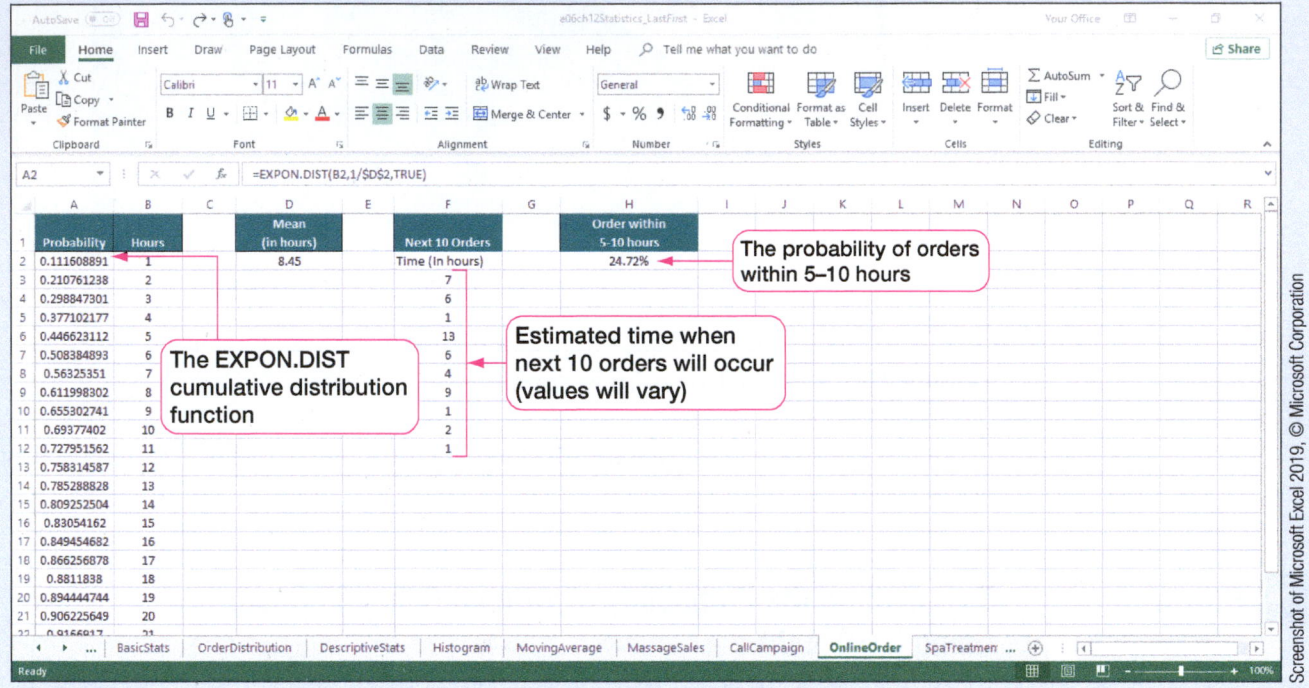

Figure 19   Predicting the time of online sales using EXPON.DIST

l. Save 🖫 the workbook.

Managers could use this statistical model to ensure that the technology used to support online sales can support the number of online sales expected to occur throughout the day.

REAL WORLD ADVICE   **Continually Monitoring Statistics**

These important statistics should be tracked continually and consistently. As the company grows, you may find that the average time between orders will decrease and additional employees and/or web and database servers may be required to process the orders.

Using the POISSON.DIST Function

Managers at the Turquoise Oasis Spa have provided three weeks of spa services sales data and are interested in predicting the number of spa services that will be sold over the next seven days. The Poisson distribution can do just that. The **Poisson distribution** is a discrete probability function that has wide business applications. It is used most often to predict demand for a product or service.

The Poisson distribution calculates the probability that a specified number of events will occur based on the mean of the data set. The POISSON.DIST function uses three arguments: (1) x, (2) mean, and (3) cumulative.

=POISSON.DIST(x, mean, cumulative)

- The x argument is the value representing the number of events for which you want to calculate the probability of occurrence.

- The mean argument is the value representing the mean of the data set.

- The cumulative argument accepts either a TRUE or a FALSE value. If TRUE, the result will be the probability of a value being less than or equal to the value of the x argument, known as the cumulative distribution function. If FALSE, the result will be the probability of a value being equal to the value of the x argument, known as the probability density function.

Figure 20 shows how a Poisson cumulative distribution may look when charted.

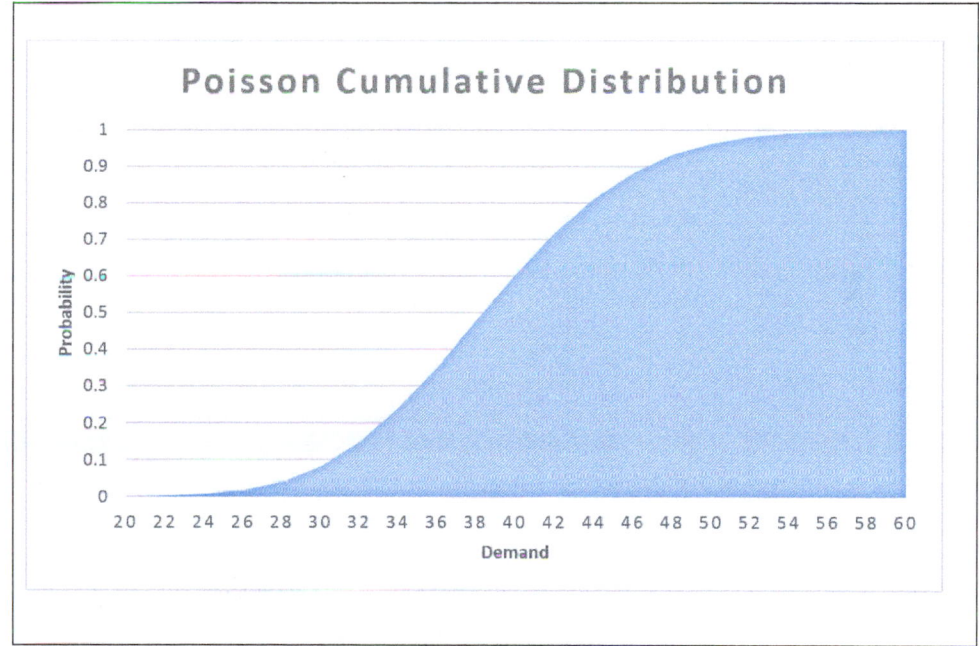

Figure 20   Poisson cumulative distribution

In this exercise, you will use the POISSON.DIST function to predict the number of orders that will be placed in the next week.

 **E12.14**

To Predict the Number of Orders Placed in the Next Week Using POISSON.DIST

a. Click the **SpaTreatments** worksheet.

b. Click cell **D2**, and then type **=POISSON.DIST(** to begin the POISSON.DIST function.

c. Click cell **E2**, and then type **,** to move to the mean argument.

d. Click cell **B25**, press ⌨F4⌨, and then type **,** to move to the cumulative argument.

e. Type **TRUE)** and then press ⌨Ctrl⌨+⌨Enter⌨ to calculate the probability of selling 20 or fewer spa treatments. The completed function should appear as =POISSON.DIST(E2,$B$25,TRUE).

f. Use the **fill handle** to copy the function down to **D22** (60 or fewer).

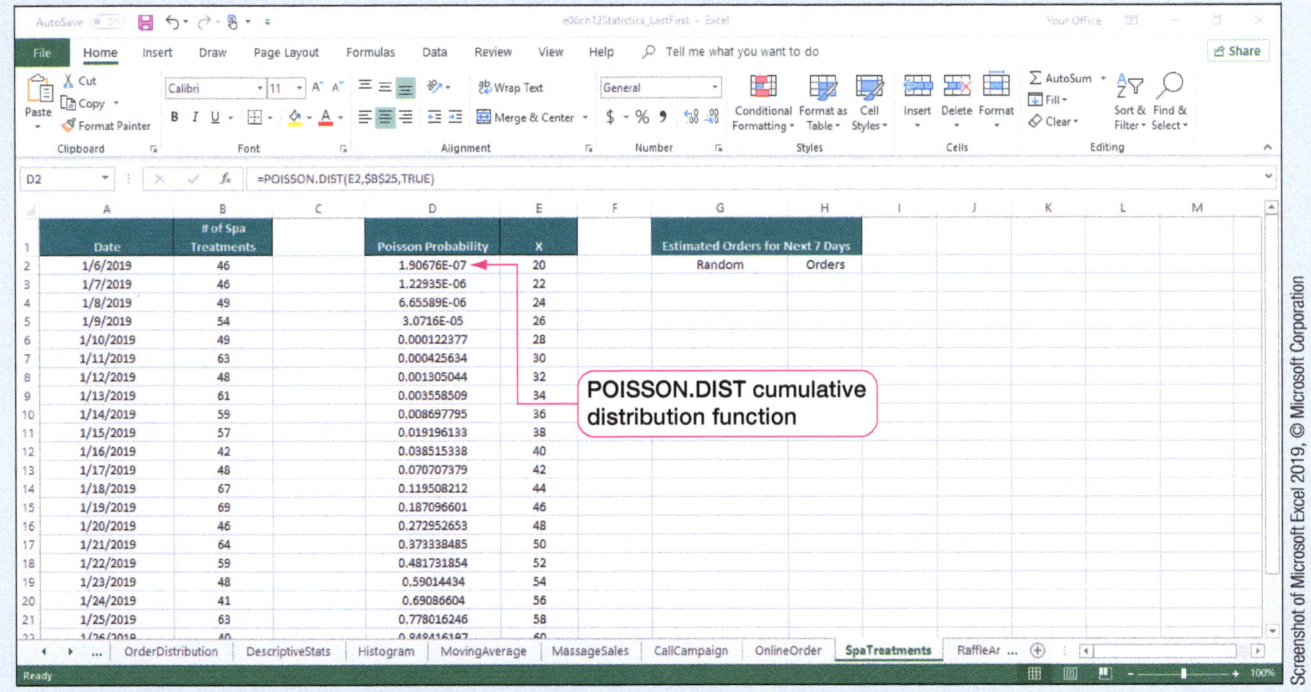

Figure 21 Using the POISSON.DIST function

Screenshot of Microsoft Excel 2019, © Microsoft Corporation

SIDE NOTE
Random Probabilities
Because of the volatility of the RAND function, your results will be different from the image in Figure 21.

g. Click cell **G3**, type **=RAND()** and then press ⌨Ctrl⌨+⌨Enter⌨ to generate a random decimal between 0 and 1. This will serve as a random probability to aid in estimating the orders for the next week.

h. Use the **fill handle** to copy the function down to **G9**.

i. With the cell range **G3:G9** selected, on the Home tab, in the Clipboard group, click **Copy**. Click the **Paste** button arrow, and then, under the **Paste Values** heading, click **Values** to replace the volatile RAND function with the values it generated.

j. Click cell **H3**. Type **=VLOOKUP(** click cell **G3**, and type **,** to move to the table array argument.

k. Click cell **D2**, drag to select cell **E22**, and then press ⌨F4⌨.

l. Type **,2,TRUE)** and then press ⌨Ctrl⌨+⌨Enter⌨ to complete the function.

m. Use the **fill handle** to copy the function down to **H9**.

Notice that the VLOOKUP function uses the randomly generated probability value as the lookup value in the function. It then looks for an approximate match in the Poisson Probability column and returns the corresponding number of spa treatment orders in the same row. Managers at the Turquoise Oasis Spa now have an estimated number of spa treatments for the next seven days.

n. Save 🖫 the workbook.

Managers at the spa can use this statistical model to assist in scheduling massage therapists for the week to be sure they have enough therapists available to meet the likely demand.

Using the HYPGEOM.DIST Function

Managers at the Turquoise Oasis Spa are planning to have a grand reopening once the expansion is complete. To help generate buzz about the event, they will be giving away raffle tickets to customers who use the spa services throughout the month of June. The winner will be allowed to draw 10 envelopes from a barrel of 100 envelopes consisting of 80 spa certificates worth $50 each and 20 complete spa packages worth $500 each. The managers would like to know the probability that the winner will draw one of the $500 prizes, two of the $500 prizes, three of the $500 prizes, and so on. The hypergeometric distribution can do just that. The **hypergeometric distribution** is a discrete population distribution that calculates the probability of drawing a specific number of target items from a collection without replacement.

The HYPGEOM.DIST function uses five arguments: (1) sample_s, (2) number_sample, (3) population_s, (4) number_pop, and (5) cumulative.

=HYPGEOM.DIST(sample_s, number_sample, population_s, number_pop, cumulative)

- The sample_s is the value representing the number of target items for which you want to calculate the probability of occurrence.
- The number_sample argument is the specific number of items that are to be drawn.
- The population_s argument is the specific number of target items in the collection.
- The number_pop argument is the total number of items in the collection.
- The cumulative argument accepts either a TRUE or a FALSE value. If TRUE, the result will be the probability of a value being less than or equal to the value of the x argument, known as the cumulative distribution function. If FALSE, the result will be the probability of a value being equal to the value of the x argument, known as the probability density function.

Figure 22 shows how a hypergeometric probability density distribution may look when charted.

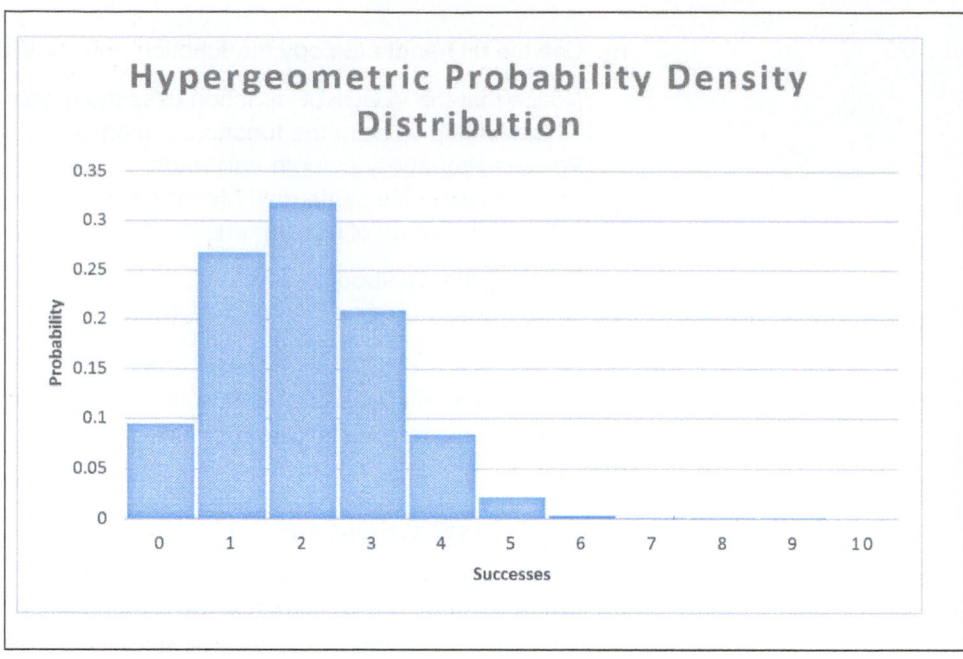

Figure 22 Hypergeometric probability density distribution

In this exercise, you will use the HYPGEOM.DIST function to calculate the probability of someone winning the spa's contest.

 **E12.15**

To Calculate the Probability of Drawing the Top Prize Using HYPGEOM.DIST

a. Click the **RaffleAnalysis** worksheet.

b. Click cell **E2**, and then type **=HYPGEOM.DIST(** to begin the HYPGEOM.DIST function.

c. Click cell **A2**, and then type **,** to move to the number_sample argument.

d. Click cell **B2**, and then type **,** to move to the population_s argument.

e. Click cell **C2**, and then type **,** to move to the number_pop argument.

f. Click cell **D2**, and then type **,** to move to the cumulative argument.

g. Type **FALSE)** and then press ⌃Ctrl+⏎Enter to calculate the probability of the winner drawing exactly 0 top prize envelopes. The completed function should appear as =HYPGEOM.DIST(A2,B2,C2,D2,FALSE). Use the **fill handle** to copy the formula down to **E12** (exactly 10 top prize envelopes).

h. Click cell **F2**. Type **=(** click cell **A2**, and type ***500)** to calculate the cost of a customer drawing the top prize.

i. Type **+(** click cell **B2**, type **-** and click cell **A2**, to calculate the number of envelopes left to draw.

j. Type **)*50** and press ⌃Ctrl+⏎Enter to calculate the total cash value of envelopes drawn if 0 are top prizes. The completed formula should appear as =(A2*500)+(B2-A2)*50. Use the **fill handle** to copy the formula down to **F12**.

k. Click cell **G2**, and then type = Click cell **E2**, type * click cell **F2**, and then press Ctrl+Enter to calculate the expected value of the drawing based on the probability of drawing 0 top prize envelopes and the total cash value of 10 $50 envelopes. Use the **fill handle** to copy the formula to **G12**.

The total expected value of the 10 envelopes drawn by the winner should equal $1,400.00.

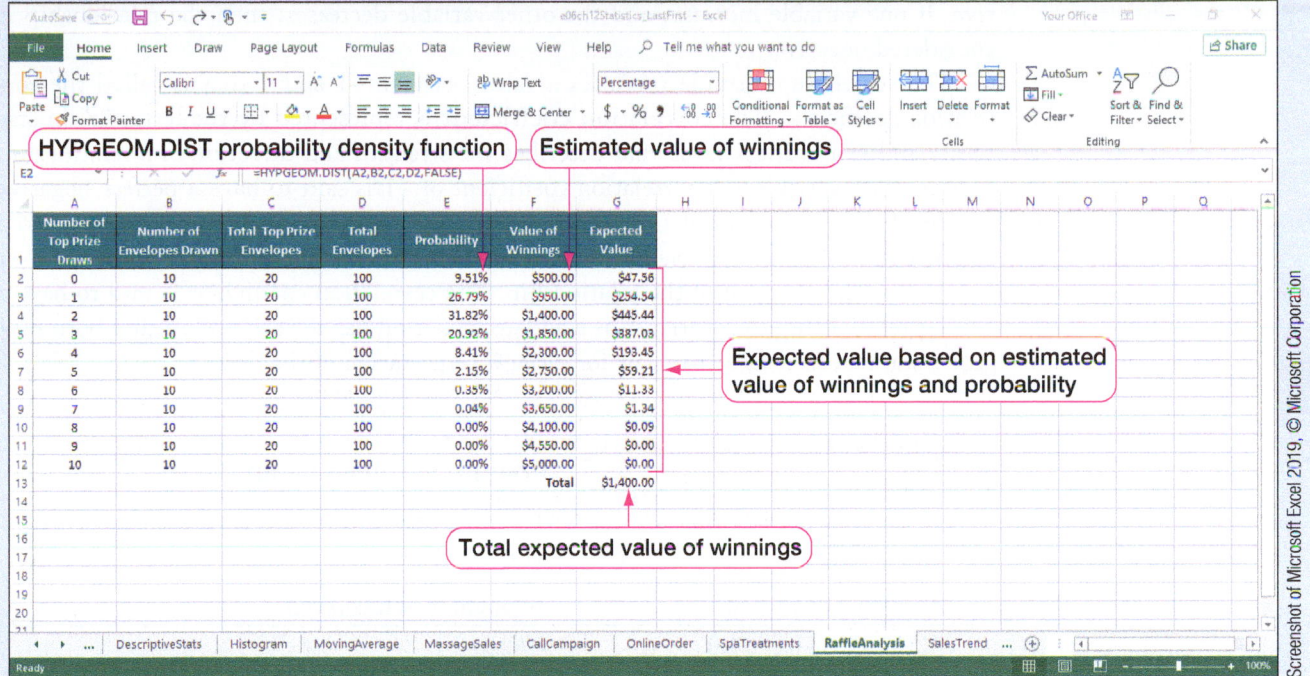

Figure 23 Calculating the probability of drawing the top prize using the HYPGEOM.DIST function

l. **Save** 💾 the workbook.

Raffles and contests like this can raise awareness of a company's existence and services offered, increasing customer traffic. It is important for management to be able to estimate the total costs of the contest winnings in case the winner is extremely lucky and beats the odds.

Finding Relationships in Data

So far, you have learned the benefits of basic statistical analysis in gaining a better understanding of data as well as the benefits of probability distributions in predicting the likelihood that certain events will occur. Identifying relationships in data can help you to answer these questions: Did the most recent marketing campaign increase sales? Do the age and gender of your customers have anything to do with how much money they spend? To understand how to answer these and similar questions and then move to predicting outcomes, you need to understand the concepts of correlation and regression.

In this section, you will learn to identify relationships in your data using covariance and correlation functions as well as regression analysis to identify trends, relationships between variables, and make predictions.

Find Relationships in Data Using COVARIANCE.S and CORREL

Managers at the Turquoise Oasis Spa are interested in knowing whether there is a relationship between the age of their clients and the amount of money the clients spend. The covariance and correlation formulas are used to describe linear relationships between data. **Covariance** is a formula that can calculate the relationship between two variables, such as age and dollars spent, as well as the direction of the relationship. If one variable increases and the other variable also increases, then the relationship is considered positive. If one variable increases and the other variable decreases, then the relationship is considered negative.

The correlation formula produces a value between −1 and 1 that is called the correlation coefficient. The **correlation coefficient** is represented by the letter "r" in statistics and is a unitless value that describes the strength and direction of a relationship between two variables. A correlation coefficient of −1 is said to have a perfect negative relationship, a coefficient of 1 is considered to have a perfect positive relationship, and a coefficient of 0 is said to have no linear relationship. The closeness of the value to −1 or 1 describes the strength of the relationship. The correlation coefficient is said to have a similar relationship to covariance as standard deviation has to variance, in that both provide a standardized value to allow for easier interpretation of the data.

QUICK REFERENCE | Strength of Relationship

Generally speaking, the following values can be used to determine whether the relationship between the two variables is strong, moderate, weak, or very weak.

Correlation Coefficient	Strength of Relationship
−1.0 to −0.5 or 0.5 to 1.0	Strong
−0.5 to −0.3 or 0.3 to 0.05	Moderate
−0.3 to −0.1 or 0.1 to 0.3	Weak
−0.1 to 0.1	Very weak or none

REAL WORLD ADVICE | Correlation Does Not Equal Causation

A correlation coefficient of 0.889 tells you only that there is a strong positive relationship between the two variables. It does not mean that an increase in one variable actually causes the other variable to increase. Be sure to keep in mind that correlation does not imply causation.

Using the COVARIANCE.S Function

To calculate the covariance in Excel, one of two functions is used: COVARIANCE.S or COVARIANCE.P. COVARIANCE.S is used to determine a relationship between two variables in a sample; COVARIANCE.P is used to determine a relationship between two variables in an entire population. You will use COVARIANCE.S, since you are dealing with sample sets of data. The only arguments are the arrays of cells that contain the two variables.

=COVARIANCE.S(array1, array2)

The value that the COVARIANCE.S function returns can be difficult to interpret at times because it is not standardized. A covariance of 7, for example, can be interpreted as a positive relationship, but the strength of that positive relationship can only be said to be weaker than it would be if the number had been 10.

Managers at the spa assume that, to a certain extent, the age of a client may be related to how much money the client spends at the spa. For example, someone who is 40 years old could spend more money than someone who is 20 years old. In this exercise, you have been given a random sample of sales data along with the ages of the customers to use Excel to determine whether there is a relationship between age and revenue and the strength of that relationship.

 **E12.16**

To Determine the Relationship between Two Variables Using COVARIANCE.S

a. Click the **SalesTrend** worksheet.

b. Click cell **D2**, and then type **=COVARIANCE.S(** to begin the COVARIANCE.S function.

c. Click cell **A2**, drag to select cell **A37**, and then type **,** to move to the array2 argument.

d. Click cell **B2**, and drag to select cell **B37**. Type **)** and then press Ctrl+Enter to calculate the covariance between age and sales at the Turquoise Oasis Spa.

Notice that the COVARIANCE.S function returns 605.0268, indicating a relationship between age and sales amount. The relationship is positive in that as the age of the customer increases, so does the amount of money they spend at the spa.

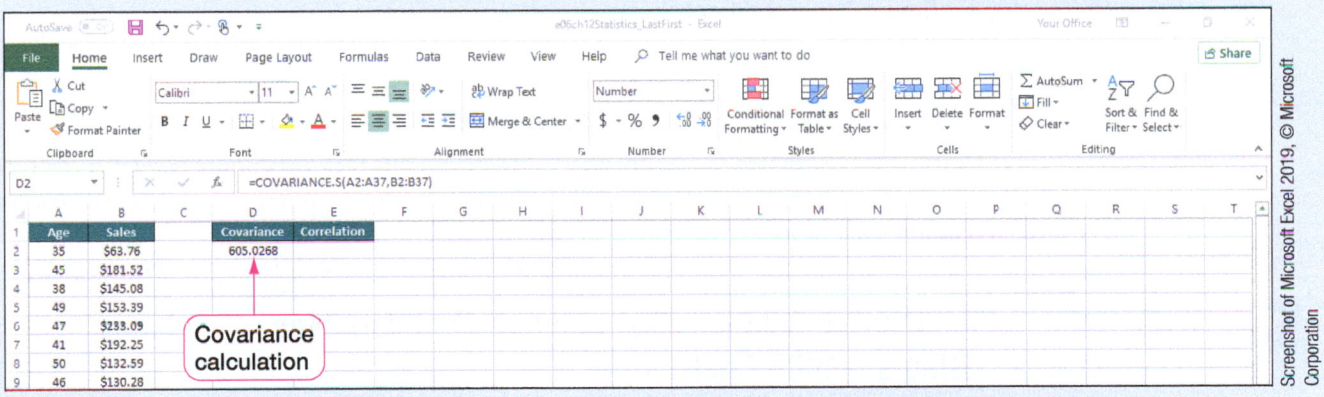

Figure 24 Determining the relationships between two variables using the COVARIANCE.S function

e. Save ▣ the workbook.

Using the CORREL Function

To calculate the correlation coefficient between two variables in Excel, the CORREL function is used. The only arguments are the arrays of cells that contain the two variables.

=CORREL(array1, array2)

In this exercise, you will use the CORREL function to calculate the correlation coefficient of the age of customers and the amount they have spent at the spa.

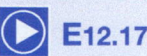 **E12.17**

To Calculate a Correlation Coefficient Using CORREL

a. On the SalesTrend worksheet, click cell **E2**.

b. Type **=CORREL(** to begin the CORREL function.

c. Click cell **A2**, drag to select cell **A37**, and then type **,** to move to the array2 argument.

d. Click cell **B2**, drag to select cell **B37**, and then type **)**. Press Ctrl+Enter to calculate the correlation coefficient between age and sales.

Notice that the correlation coefficient is approximately 0.65, indicating a strong positive correlation between age and sales.

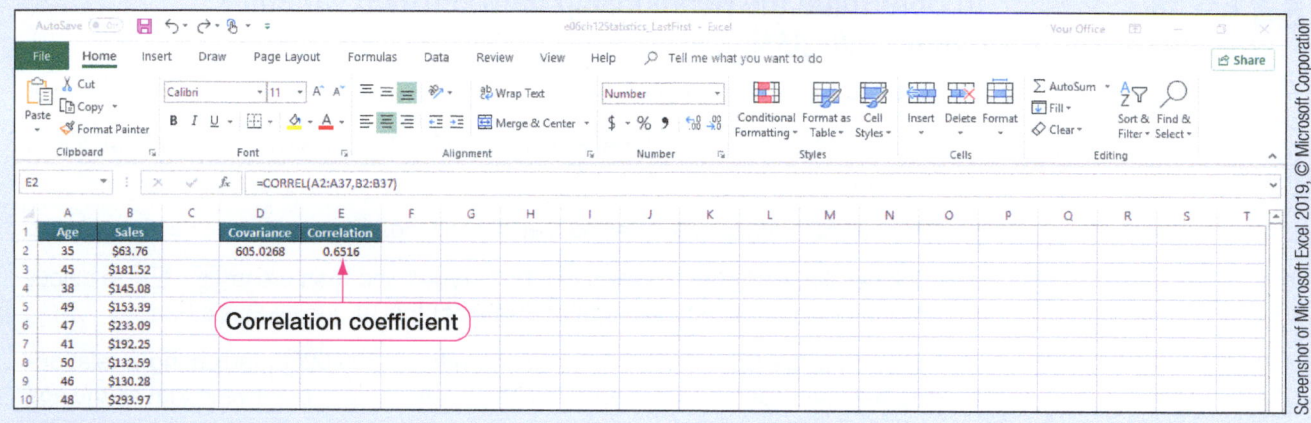

Figure 25   Calculating a correlation coefficient using the CORREL function

e. **Save** 💾 the workbook.

Visualizing Relationships with a Scatter Chart

Correlation coefficient values are easy to interpret, but it is often more powerful to create a chart that illustrates that relationship visually. In this exercise, you will visualize a correlation using a scatter chart.

 **E12.18**

MAC COMPATIBILITY

Quick Analysis Tool

There is no Quick Analysis tool on a Mac. On a Mac, click the Insert tab, and in the Charts group, click X Y Scatter and then click Scatter. The ScreenTip on the chart says X Y Scatter.

To Visualize Relationships between Two Variables Using a Scatter Chart

a. On the SalesTrend worksheet, select the cell range **A1:B37**.

b. Click the **Quick Analysis** tool 📊 at the bottom of the range selection, click **Charts**, and then click **Scatter**.

c. Click the **Chart Elements** button ⊞ next to the chart, and then click to select the **Axis Titles** and **Trendline** check boxes.

> ### Troubleshooting
>
> There is no Chart Elements button on a Mac. To do this on a Mac, on the Chart Design tab, in the Chart Layouts group, click Add Chart Element, point to Axis Titles, and then click Primary Vertical. Click Add Chart Element, point to Axis Titles, and then click Primary Horizontal. Click Add Chart Element, point to Trendline, and then click Linear.

d. Click the **Vertical Axis** Title text box, and then type Sales Revenue

e. Click the **Horizontal Axis** Title text box, and then type Age

f. Edit the chart title to read Sales-Age Correlation

g. Move the scatter chart into the cell range **D4:J17**.

Notice that the trendline with its upward slope also indicates a strong positive relationship between the age of the clients of the spa and the amount of money spent.

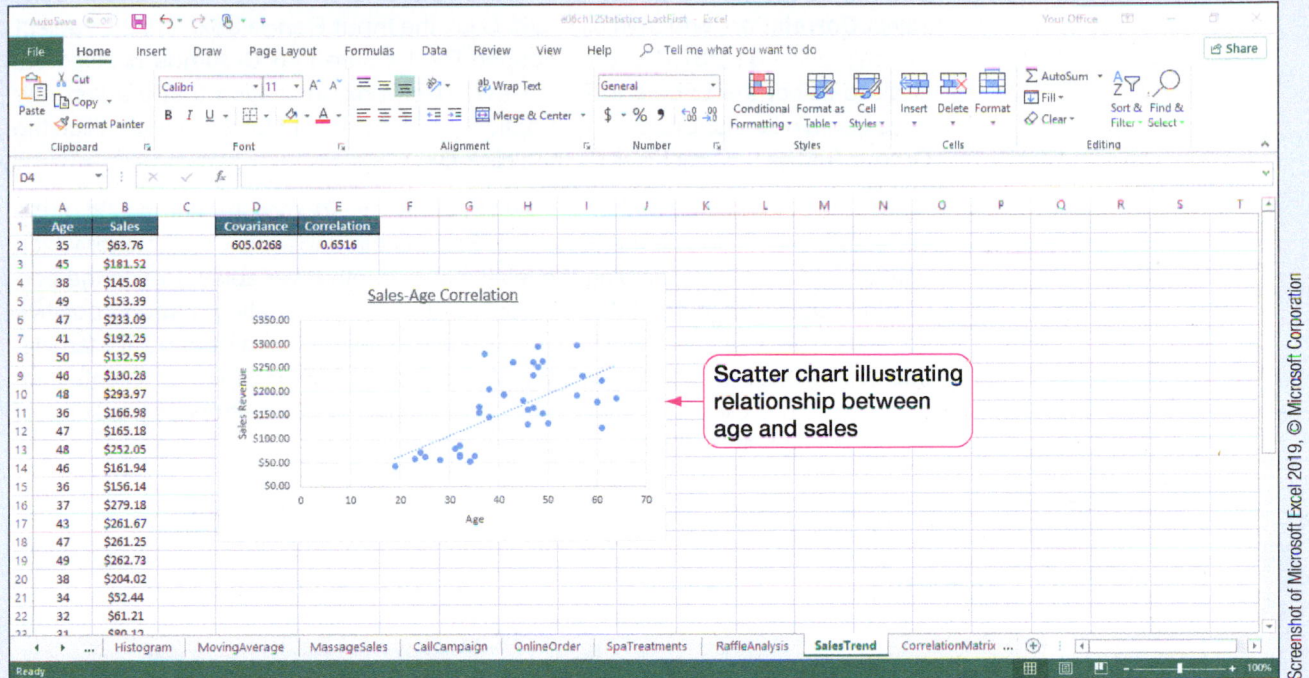

Screenshot of Microsoft Excel 2019, © Microsoft Corporation

Figure 26   Scatter chart with a trendline

h. **Save** 🖫 the workbook.

Determine Relationships between Multiple Variables Using a Correlation Matrix

Calculating the correlation coefficient using the CORREL function is useful to determine the type and strength of a relationship between two variables. However, in business, there may be several independent variables that affect a dependent variable. For example, age of customers may not be the only variable that has a relationship with revenue; gender and income could also be factors.

Using the Data Analysis Add-in to Create a Correlation Matrix

To calculate the correlation coefficients of several different variables, the Data Analysis add-in offer a method to create a correlation matrix. In this exercise, you create a correlation matrix of three different variables. You have been given a random sample of customer data with age and gender along with the amount of money spent on a given visit to the spa. Because gender is listed as either male or female in the data set provided, you must first convert it to numerical nominal data using an IF function.

 **E12.19**

To Create a Correlation Matrix Using the Data Analysis Add-In

a. Click the **CorrelationMatrix** worksheet.

b. Click cell **B2**, and then type **=IF(** to begin an IF function.

c. Click cell **A2**, type **="Male",1,2)** and then press Ctrl+Enter to create nominal data that can be used in the correlation calculation for gender, where Male = 1 and Female = 2.

d. Use the **fill handle** to copy the formula to **B37**.

e. Click the **Data** tab, and then click **Data Analysis**. In the list of Analysis tools, select **Correlation**, and then click **OK**. Click the **Input Range** box, and then select the cell range **B1:D37**. Next to Grouped By, be sure that **Columns** is selected. Click to select the **Labels in First Row** check box, indicating that the first row does contain labels. Under Output options, click to select **Output Range**, click the **Output Range** box, click cell **F1**, and click **OK**.

f. Adjust the columns to be able to view the contents. To interpret the results of the correlation matrix, locate the Sales row. Sales is the dependent variable for which you are interested in observing the relationship to other variables. Notice the correlation coefficient in cell G4 is approximately 0.746, indicating a strong positive correlation between gender and sales. Since you used 1 for male and 2 for female, this means that the spa can expect higher revenues from their female clients than from their male clients. In fact, it appears that gender is a stronger predictor of sales than age, at 0.652.

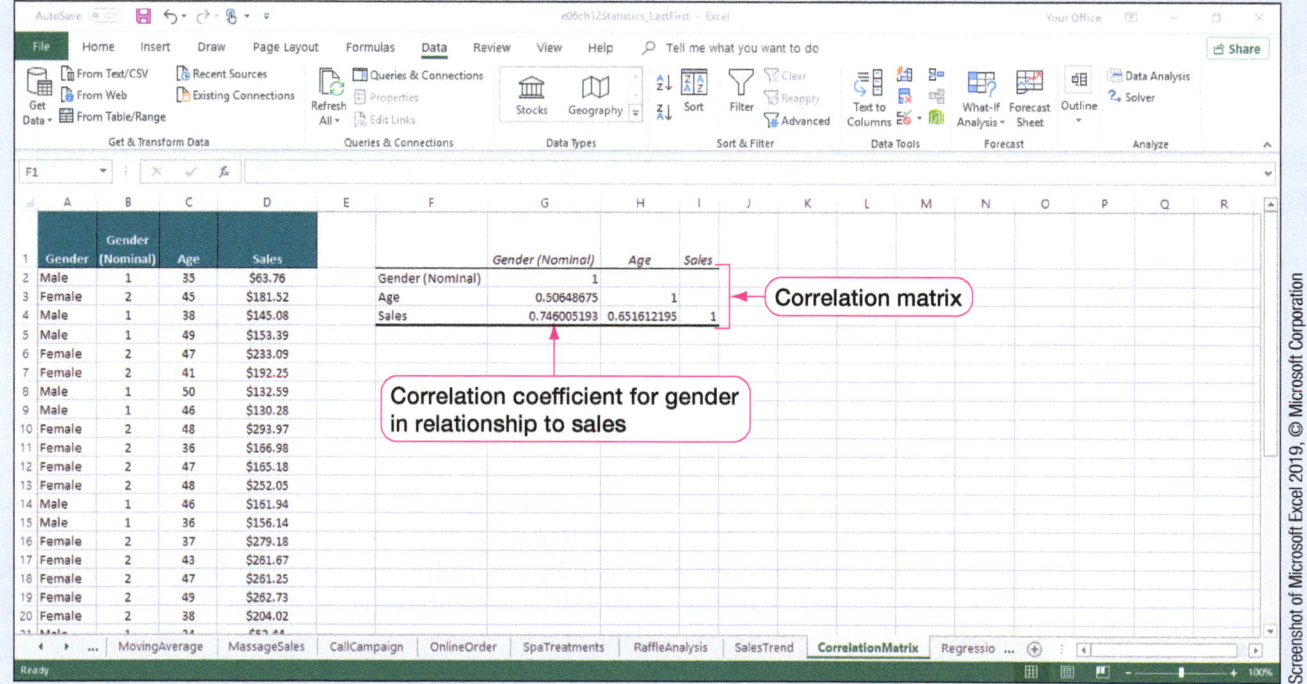

Figure 27 Correlation matrix showing the relationship between multiple variables

g. **Save** the workbook.

CHAPTER 12

> **SS CONSIDER THIS** | **Direction of Relationship**
>
> In the example above, you attributed the value of 1 for male and 2 for female. The result of the correlation matrix indicated a strong positive relationship between gender and sales. What would happen to the direction of the relationship between gender and sales if you attributed the value of 1 to female and 2 for male?

Use Regression Analysis to Predict Future Values

The next step in statistical analysis is to put your assumptions to the test and determine whether the relationships between the data are strong enough to make predictions about future events. **Regression analysis** is a method used to predict future values by analyzing the relationships between two or more variables. You will examine the relationship between age and gender of your clients and sales a bit further to determine whether the combination of age and gender is a good predictor of revenue.

Creating a Regression Analysis Using the Data Analysis Add-In

Excel's Data Analysis add-in provides an easy way to conduct a regression analysis on two or more variables. One distinction between the variables that must be made up front is which variable is the dependent variable and which is the independent variable. In this scenario, the sales are the dependent variable because sales are what you want to be able to predict. Age and gender become the independent variables, and you want to be able to measure the effectiveness of them as a predictor of sales. In this exercise, you will use the Data Analysis add-in to create a regression analysis.

 E12.20

To Conduct a Regression Analysis Using the Data Analysis Add-In

a. Click the **Regression** worksheet.

b. On the **Data** tab in the Analyze group, click **Data Analysis**.

c. In the list of Analysis Tools, select **Regression**, and then click **OK**.

d. Click the **Input Y Range** box, and then select the cell range **C1:C37** as the dependent variable of sales.

e. Click the **Input X Range** box, and then select the cell range **A1:B37** as the independent variables of age and gender. Note that in Excel the independent variables must be in adjacent columns.

f. Click the **Labels** check box to indicate that the label fields were included in the selection.

g. Under Output options, click to select **Output Range**. Click the **Output Range** box, click cell **E10**, and then click **OK**.

h. Adjust the columns as necessary so that all values are visible in the SUMMARY OUTPUT.

i. **Save** the workbook.

The summary output produced by the Regression tool includes a lot of information. However, the key to its interpretation is in three values.

- R-squared
- Intercept coefficient
- Age coefficient

The **R-squared** value, in cell F14 of the SUMMARY OUTPUT, was calculated by squaring the correlation coefficient, labeled as Multiple R in the output. This provides a more conservative estimate of the independent variables' ability to predict the value of the dependent variable.

As you can see, the R-squared value is approximately 0.657, or 65.7%. This can be interpreted as age and gender accounting for 65.7% of the sales revenue generated by a customer.

The **intercept coefficient** value, in cell F26 of the SUMMARY OUTPUT, is the value at which a regression line will cross the y-axis and is used in the slope intercept formula to predict values.

The intercept coefficient value is approximately –46.7.

The regression equation includes the intercept coefficient value (approximately –72.3), along with the age coefficient and gender coefficient to predict the value of the dependent variable. The age coefficient in cell F27 is approximately 2.46, and the gender coefficient in cell F28 is approximately 87.08.

The resulting regression equation in the context of age, gender, and sales is as follows:

Sales (Y) = (age * 2.46) + (gender * 87.08) + –72.3

In this exercise, you will create regression equations for several combinations of age and genders.

 E12.21

To Use the Regression Equation to Predict Values

a. Click cell **G3**, and type =(to begin constructing the regression equation.

b. Click cell **E3**, type * click cell **F27**, and press ⌷F4⌷.

c. Type)+(click cell **F3**, and type *. Click cell **F28**, press ⌷F4⌷, and type)+

d. Click cell **F26**, press ⌷F4⌷, and then press ⌷Ctrl⌷+⌷Enter⌷ to complete the regression equation to predict the sales revenue generated by a client who is 45 years of age and female.

e. Use the **fill handle** to copy the formula to **G6**.

   Notice that the sales revenue estimate based on age is closer to some of the actual values near the same age and gender but farther away on others. This is because, as the R-squared value indicates, age and gender account for only 65.7% of the revenue. Other variables also have an effect on revenue, such as income levels, time of visit, and perhaps even weather.

f. **Save** 🖫 the workbook.

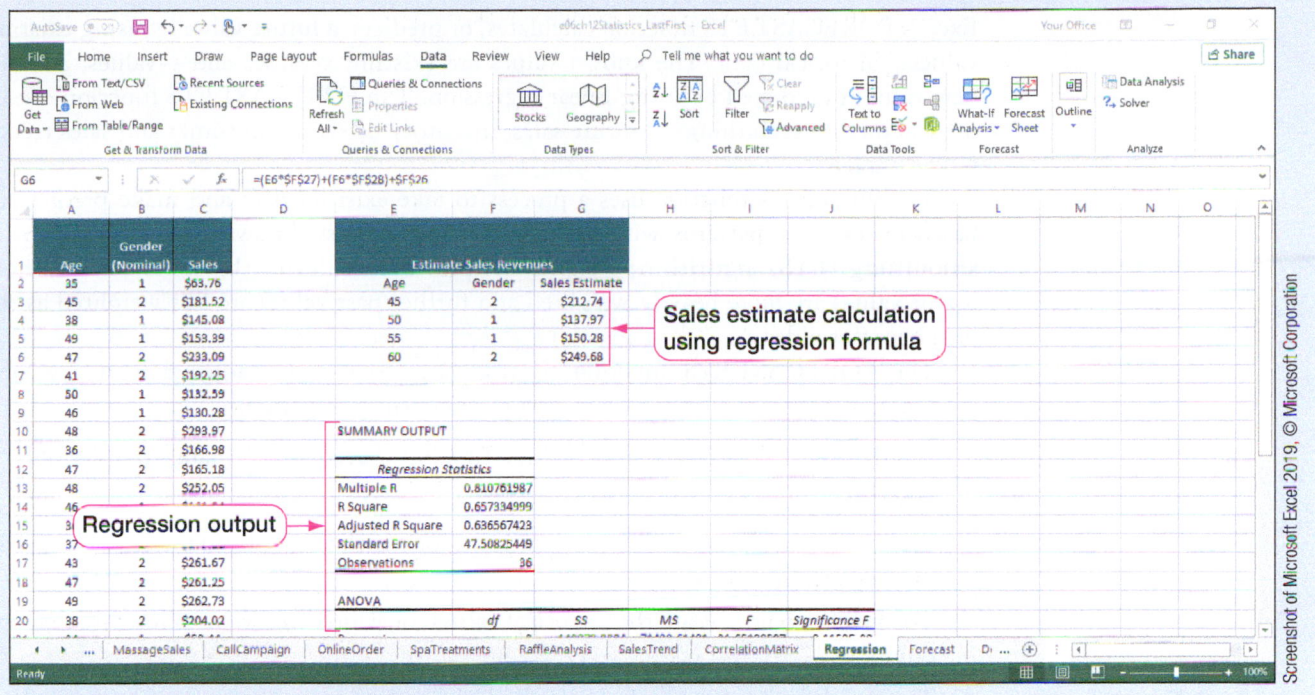

Figure 28 Regression analysis and predicted sales values

REAL WORLD ADVICE | **Residuals**

The Regression tool can automatically produce Sales estimates using the regression equation by checking the Residuals check box in the Regression dialog box. These estimates can then be compared to the corresponding actual Sales data.

You could improve the accuracy of this statistical model by collecting additional customer data and running the regression analysis with other independent variables. Additional or alternative independent variables could increase the R-squared value, possibly indicating a more accurate predictor(s) of sales revenue.

Generally, the overall model is considered statistically significant in predicting the dependent variable if the Significance F value (in cell J21) is less than 0.05. Each independent variable is considered statistically significant if its p-value (cells I27 and I28) is less than 0.05.

Predict Future Values Based on Historical Data

Historical data can provide a tremendous insight to an organization's ability to predict the future. The **FORECAST.ETS function** returns a prediction of a future value based on historical data. You will examine the relationship between age of your clients and sales to determine whether age is a good predictor of sales revenue.

Using the FORECAST.ETS Function

Excel's FORECAST.ETS function calculates, or predicts, a future value by using existing values—historical data. The known values are existing x-values and y-values, and the new value is predicted by using linear regression. The FORECAST.ETS function can be used to predict such things as future sales, inventory needs, or consumer and sales trends to name a few.

The forecast.ets function uses a process to take existing data and make predictions based on existing patterns within the data. This process, known as the **exponential smoothing (ETS) algorithm**, weights the previous values in the series so that more recent values are more heavily weighted and further past values are less weighted as the data becomes older.

The FORECAST.ETS function uses six arguments: (1) target_date, (2) values, (3) timeline, (4) seasonality, (5) data_completion, (6) aggregation.

=FORECAST.ETS(target_date, values, timeline, [seasonality], [data_completion], [aggregation])

- The target_date argument is the data point for which you want to predict a value and can be date/time or numeric.

- The values argument are the historical values for which you want to forecast the next points.

- The timeline argument references the independent array or range of numeric data. The dates in the timeline must have a consistent step between them and cannot be zero; however, the dates do not need to be sorted as the FORECAST.ETS function will sort the values automatically.

- The seasonality argument determines the length of the seasonal pattern. The default value of 1 means Excel detects seasonality automatically and uses positive, whole numbers for the length of the seasonal pattern. 0 indicates no seasonality, meaning the prediction will be linear. Positive whole numbers will indicate to the algorithm to use patterns of this length as the seasonality. For any other value, FORECAST.ETS will return the #NUM! error. The maximum supported seasonality is 8,760—number of hours in a year. Any seasonality above that number will return the #NUM! error.

- The data_completion argument accounts for up to 30% missing data. 0 will indicate the algorithm to account for missing points as zeros. The default value of 1 will account for missing points by completing them to be an average of the adjacent points.

- The aggregation argument will aggregate multiple points that have the same time stamp. The argument is a numeric value indicating which method will be used to aggregate several values with the same time stamp. The default value of 0 will use AVERAGE. Other options are SUM, COUNT, COUNTA, MIN, MAX, MEDIAN.

In this exercise, you will use the FORECAST.ETS function to calculate how much revenue the spa will generate based on past revenue.

 **E12.22**

To Predict Values Using the FORECAST.ETS Function

a. Click the **Forecast** worksheet, click cell **C16**, and then type **=B16** Press `Enter`.

b. In cell C17, type **=FORECAST.ETS(** to begin the FORECAST.ETS function.

c. Click cell **A17** and type **,**

d. Click cell **B5**, drag to select cell **B16**, press `F4`, and then type **,** to move to the timeline argument.

e. Click cell **A5**, drag to select cell **A16**, press `F4`, and then type **,** to move to the seasonality argument.

f. Type **1** and then type **,** to move to the date_completion argument.

g. Type **1)** and then press `Ctrl`+`Enter`.

h. Use the **fill handle** to copy the formula to **C40**. Format the range C17:C40 as **Currency**.

Notice that the sales revenue forecast based on past sales data is higher in the first part of 2020 but declines as time progresses. This is because the historical data is not yet available for 2020. As the forecast is created, the function can currently only use data from the 2019 performance year.

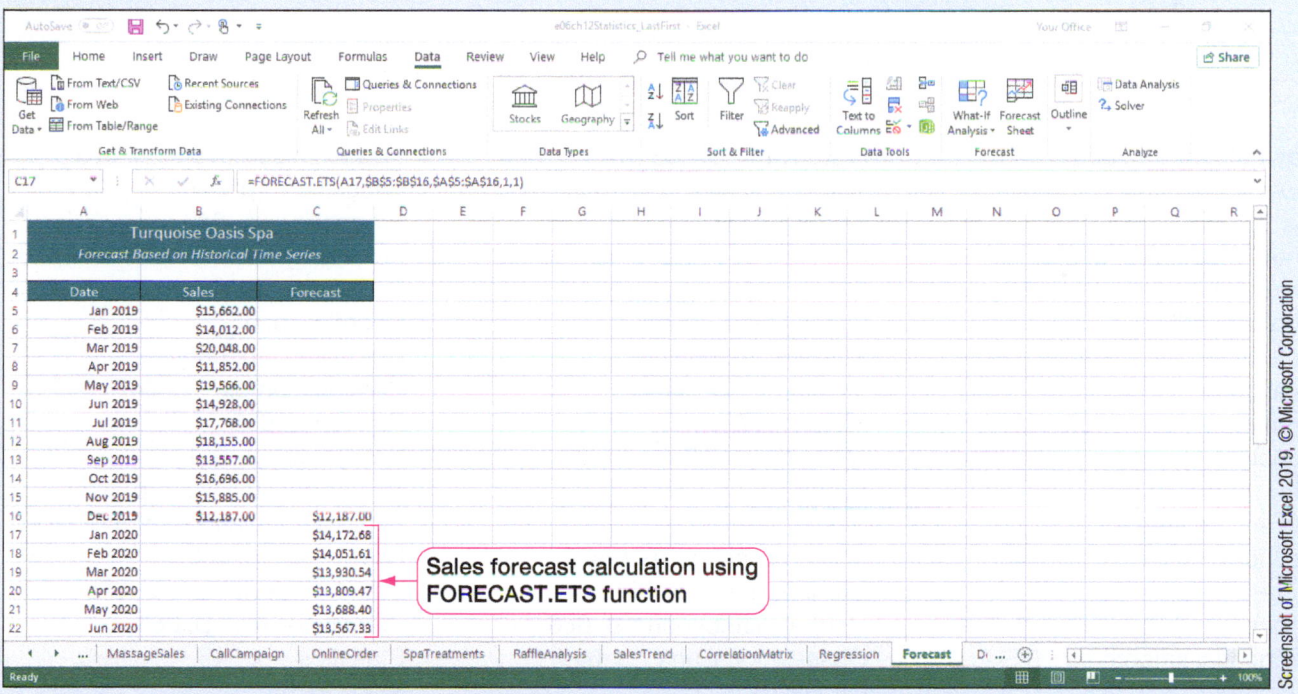

Figure 29 Creating a forecast using the FORECAST.ETS function

i. Complete the Documentation worksheet according to your instructor's directions.

j. **Save** the workbook, exit Excel, and then submit your file as directed by your instructor.

Grader Heads Up

If you are using MyLab IT Grader, this is the end of the second MyLab IT Grader project Part B.

Screenshot of Microsoft Excel 2019, © Microsoft Corporation

Concept Check

1. Discuss the difference between population and sample data. Which one is used more often in statistics? Why? p. 649

2. Describe the four types of data used in statistics. What is an example of each type? pp. 650–651

3. Discuss how calculating the range, variance, and standard deviation of a data set can help to spot differences in two data sets with the same mean. p. 655

4. What is a histogram, and how is it beneficial for understanding data? p. 657

5. What are two probability distributions used in business? What is one practical application for each? p. 666

6. What are covariance and correlation, and what can they tell you about data? p. 680

7. What can be learned from a correlation matrix? p. 683

8. What is the R-squared value, and how is it related to the correlation coefficient? p. 686

9. What can be learned from using historical data to forecast? p. 687

Key Terms

Array function   p. 659
Binomial distribution   p. 670
Bins   p. 659
Central tendency   p. 653
Continuous variable   p. 650
Count   p. 663
Correlation coefficient   p. 680
Covariance   p. 680
Cumulative distribution
   function   p. 667
Data   p. 649
Data set   p. 649
Descriptive statistics   p. 649
Discrete variable   p. 650
Exponential distribution   p. 672
Exponential smoothing (ETS)
   algorithm   p. 688
FORECAST.ETS function   p. 687

Histogram   p. 663
Hypergeometric distribution   p. 677
Inferential statistics   p. 649
Intercept coefficient   p. 686
Interquartile range   p. 657
Interval data   p. 651
Kurtosis   p. 663
Maximum   p. 663
Mean   p. 653
Median   p. 653
Minimum   p. 663
Mode   p. 653
Moving average   p. 664
Nominal data   p. 651
Normal distribution   p. 666
Observational unit   p. 649
Ordinal data   p. 651
Outliers   p. 655

Poisson distribution   p. 675
Population   p. 649
Probability   p. 649
Probability density function   p. 667
Probability distribution   p. 649
Quartile   p. 657
R-squared   p. 686
Random sample   p. 649
Range   p. 655
Ratio data   p. 651
Regression analysis   p. 685
Sample population   p. 649
Skewness   p. 663
Standard deviation   p. 655
Standard error   p. 663
Statistics   p. 649
Sum   p. 663
Variance   p. 655

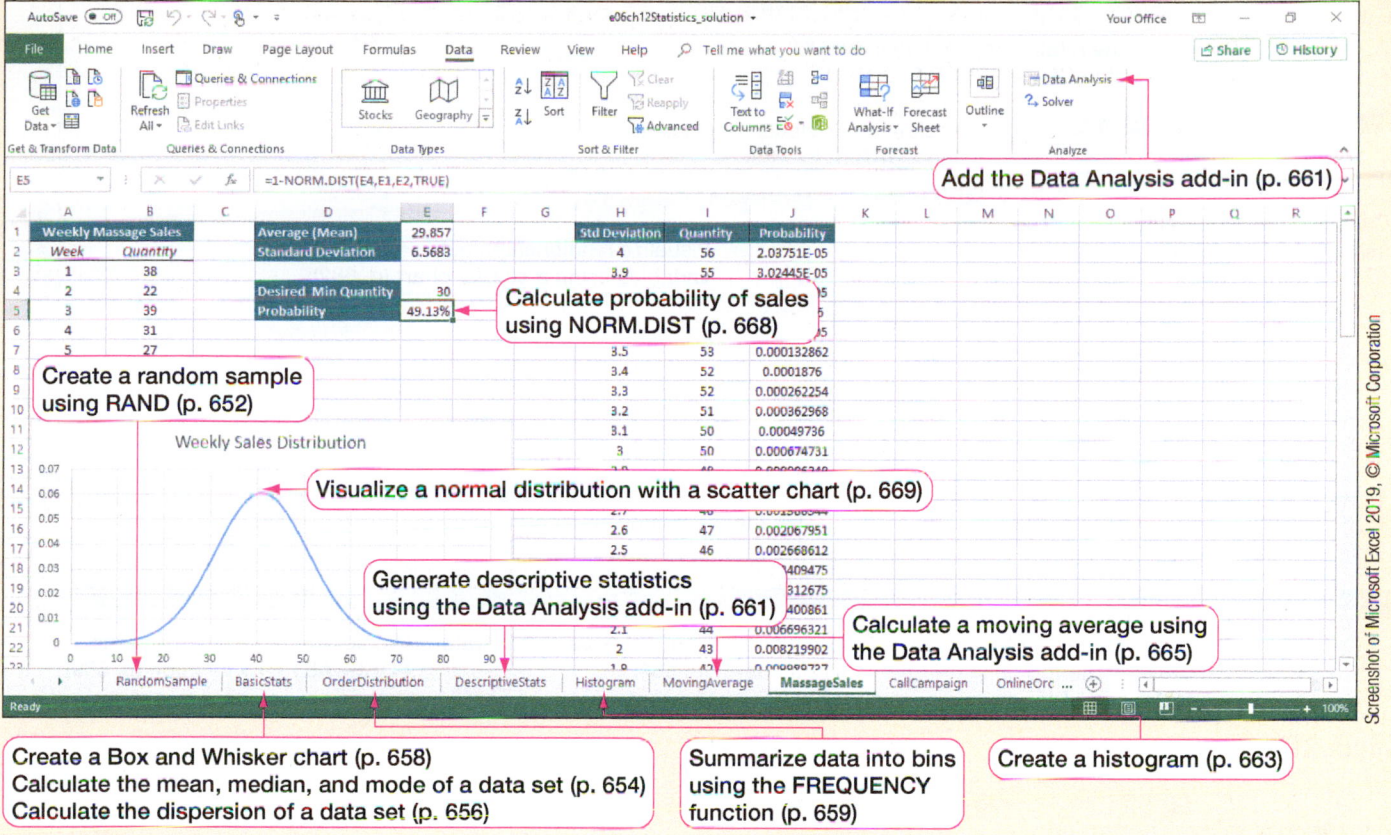

Add the Data Analysis add-in (p. 661)

Calculate probability of sales using NORM.DIST (p. 668)

Create a random sample using RAND (p. 652)

Visualize a normal distribution with a scatter chart (p. 669)

Generate descriptive statistics using the Data Analysis add-in (p. 661)

Calculate a moving average using the Data Analysis add-in (p. 665)

Create a Box and Whisker chart (p. 658)
Calculate the mean, median, and mode of a data set (p. 654)
Calculate the dispersion of a data set (p. 656)

Summarize data into bins using the FREQUENCY function (p. 659)

Create a histogram (p. 663)

Figure 30

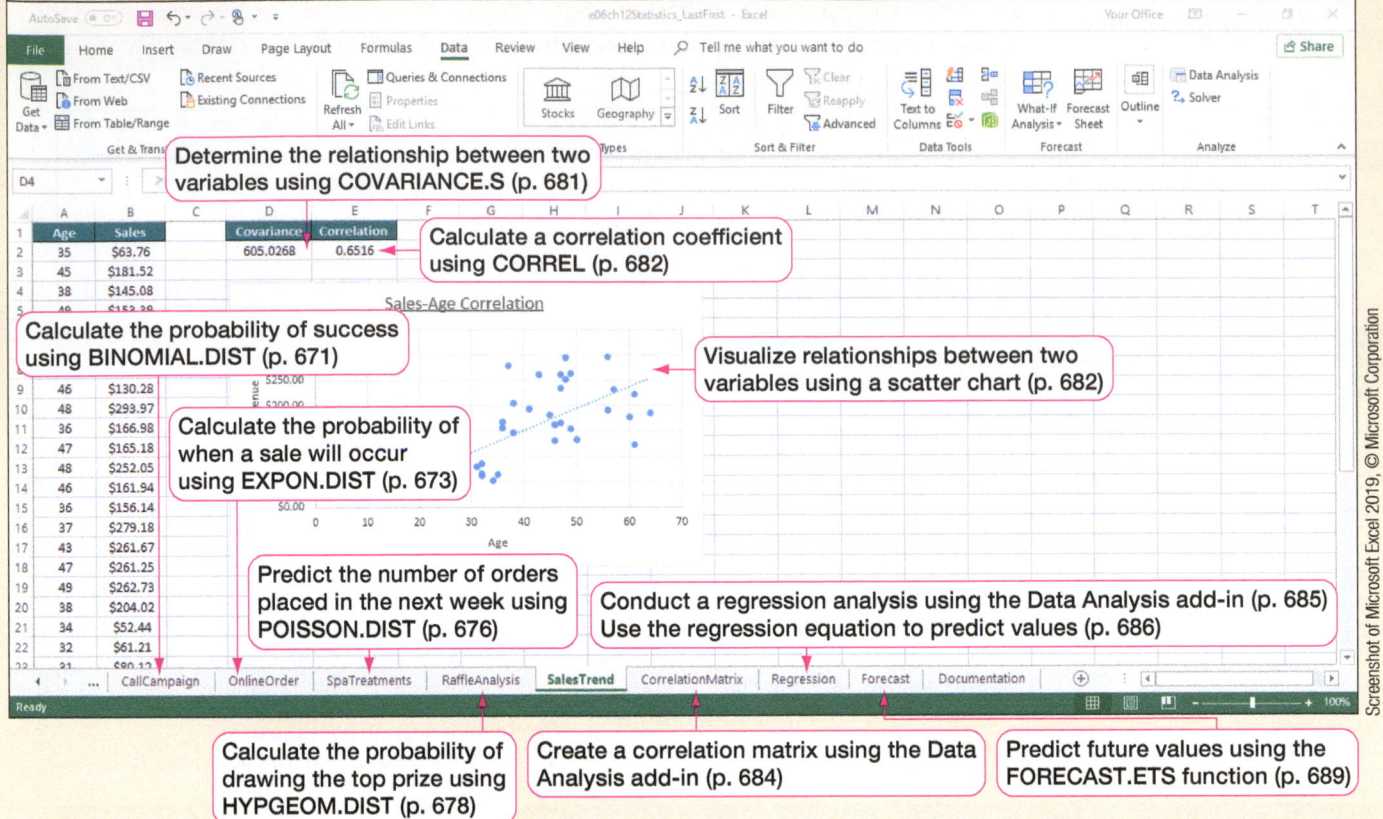

Determine the relationship between two variables using COVARIANCE.S (p. 681)

Calculate a correlation coefficient using CORREL (p. 682)

Calculate the probability of success using BINOMIAL.DIST (p. 671)

Visualize relationships between two variables using a scatter chart (p. 682)

Calculate the probability of when a sale will occur using EXPON.DIST (p. 673)

Predict the number of orders placed in the next week using POISSON.DIST (p. 676)

Conduct a regression analysis using the Data Analysis add-in (p. 685)
Use the regression equation to predict values (p. 686)

Calculate the probability of drawing the top prize using HYPGEOM.DIST (p. 678)

Create a correlation matrix using the Data Analysis add-in (p. 684)

Predict future values using the FORECAST.ETS function (p. 689)

Figure 31

Practice 1

Student data file needed:

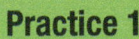 e06ch12Sales.xlsx

You will save your file as:

e06ch12Sales_LastFirst.xlsx

Statistical Analysis of Sales Data

Sales & Marketing

Angela is the president of PetInk, a company that specializes in memorializing pets in charcoal drawings. Her company has been extremely successful in selling charcoal sketches along with pet supplies and grooming services. She has collected data for four regions within the United States over the past year and has realized the need for analyzing her sales data. You will create a workbook that includes statistical analyses so she can better understand her business, such as predicting sales and the probability of reaching the forecasted sales figures.

a. Open the Excel file, **e06ch12Sales**. Save your file as e06ch12Sales_LastFirst using your last and first name.

b. Click the **Sales Data** worksheet if necessary, click cell **K2**, and then type =AVERAGE(E3:E962) to calculate the mean sales revenue. Press Enter.

c. In cell K3, and then type =STDEV.S(E3:E962) to calculate the standard deviation. Press Enter.

d. In cell K4, and then type =COVARIANCE.S(E3:E962,F3:F962) to calculate the covariance between the monthly sales and the number of items sold. Press Enter.

e. In cell K5, type **=CORREL(E3:E962,F3:F962)** to calculate the correlation coefficient that describes the type and strength of the relationships between the two variables. Press Enter.

f. Create a box and whisker chart that displays the sales revenue. Select the cell range **E3:E962**. Click the **Insert** tab, and in the Charts group, click **Insert Statistic Chart**, and then click **Box and Whisker**.

g. Reposition the chart to fit within the cell range **J7:M20**. Change the Chart Title to **Revenue**

h. Create a histogram that displays the sales volume. Select the cell range **F3:F962**. Click the **Insert** tab, in the Charts group, click **Insert Statistic Chart**, and then click **Histogram**.

i. Reposition the chart to fit within the cell range **J22:N36**. Change the Chart Title to **Sales Volume**

j. Click outside the chart area, click the **Data** tab, and then in the Analysis group, click **Data Analysis**. In the Data Analysis dialog box, select **Regression**, and then click **OK**.

k. Click the **Input Y Range** box, and then select the cell range **F2:F962**. Click **the Input X Range** box, and then select the cell range **E2:E962**. Click the **Labels** check box. Click to select **Output Range**, click the **Output Range** box, click cell **N2**, and then click **OK**. Adjust the columns as necessary so all the data from the Summary Output can be viewed.

Notice that in the box and whisker chart, there are several data points with large revenue values. The correlation indicates a moderate correlation. The model would not be considered statistically significant, as the Significance F value is greater than 0.05.

l. Click the **Store Successes** worksheet. In cell **B1**, type 80 as the number of company stores. Press Enter. In cell **B2**, type .22 as the success rate of total stores meeting the sales forecast. Press Enter.

m. Click cell **B5**, type **=BINOM.DIST(A5,$B$1,$B$2,FALSE)** to calculate the probability of there being exactly 0 successes using the binomial distribution function. Press Ctrl+Enter. Use the **fill handle** to copy the function to **B45**.

n. Complete the **Documentation** worksheet according to your instructor's direction.

o. Save the workbook, exit Excel, and then submit the file as directed by your instructor.

Problem Solve 1

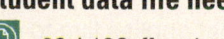

Student data file needed:	You will save your file as:
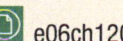 e06ch12Coffee.xlsx	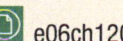 e06ch12Coffee_LastFirst.xlsx

Sales & Marketing

Sales Volume Analysis

Coffee House Blues is a local coffee shop that offers tasty coffee beverages and live blues and blues-inspired music. You have been asked to conduct some statistical analysis on the shop's sales volume data. Coffee House Blues is also in the middle of promoting an upcoming blues festival and would like you to calculate the probabilities of selling specific numbers of tickets.

a. Open the Excel file **e06ch12Coffee**. Save your file as **e06ch12Coffee_LastFirst** using your last and first name.

b. Click the **SalesVolume** worksheet tab if necessary. In cell **G1**, calculate the mean of the sales volume. In cell **G2**, calculate the sample standard deviation.

c. In cell **B2**, calculate the probability of selling the exact number of products calculated in cell **A2**, using the normal distribution function and the mean and sample standard deviation calculated in the prior step. Use the **fill handle** to copy the formula to **B82**.

d. Create a **Scatter with Smooth Lines** chart to graph the distribution of sales volume and probabilities.

e. Change the chart title to Sales Volume Distribution

f. Reposition the chart within the cell range **E4:K18**.

g. Click the **Tickets** worksheet. In cell **B1**, type 50 as the number of people contacted in the trial.

h. In cell **B2**, type .25 as the success rate of selling tickets to the festival. Format the cell as **Percentage**.

i. In cell **B5**, calculate the probability of there being exactly 0 successes using the binomial distribution function. Format the cell as **Percentage** with **3** decimal places.

j. Use the **fill handle** to copy the function to **B55**.

k. Click the **Forecast** worksheet. In cell **C15**, reference the sales for the last available month in the series.

l. In cell **C16**, use the forecast function to determine what the sales revenue will be for January 2020.

m. Use the **fill handle** to copy the formula to **C27**.

n. Complete the **Documentation** worksheet according to your instructor's directions.

o. Save the workbook, exit Excel, and then submit the file as directed by your instructor.

Critical Thinking   You created a sales forecast based upon historical sales data. How could the upcoming blues festival affect the sales forecast?

Perform 1: Perform in Your Career

Student data file needed:

 e06ch12Thick.xlsx

You will save your file as:

 e06ch12Thick_LastFirst.xlsx

Errors, Errors, and More Errors

Production & Operations

You work for a coating company that applies film to glass. The film applied to the glass has a specific thickness it must achieve. In the past, your company has experienced quality issues that have resulted in higher costs, lower revenue, and dissatisfied customers. As a result, your company is considering the purchase of a new machine to improve the quality. The vendor of the machine has graciously allowed your company a trial use of the machine to ensure that you can obtain the necessary quality. Twenty-five units have been run through the machine, and the thickness of the film has been measured. Your boss has asked you to perform a statistical analysis on the data to determine whether the company should purchase the machine. The results have been input into a workbook.

a. Open the Excel file **e06ch12Thick**. Save it as e06ch12Thick_LastFirst

b. On the Thickness worksheet, the cell range B4:B28 contains the results of the 25 tests in micrometers. Use the Data Analysis add-in to insert the Descriptive Statistics.

c. Enter the desired thickness of 542 micrometers, and calculate the probability of obtaining a film that is exactly that thickness.

d. Create 11 Bins between 452.5 and 453.5 in increments of 0.1 to use in the CSE formula FREQUENCY.

e. Create a Histogram chart. Accept the default number of bins, and label the chart appropriately.

f. Create a Moving Average Chart, available in the Data Analysis add-in. The interval should be 2.

g. Create a box and whisker chart to visualize any outliers in the data. Label the chart appropriately, and remove the primary horizontal axes.

h. Create a Binomial Distribution using 15 trials and the probability of success of 75%.

i. Given that the film must be 542 +/– 0.2 micrometers thick, should your company purchase the machine? Enter your decision in cell B2 (Yes or No).

j. Format the worksheet appropriately.

k. Complete the Documentation worksheet according to your instructor's directions.

l. Save the workbook, exit Excel, and then submit the file as directed by your instructor.

Building Financial and Statistical Models

This business unit had two outcomes:

Learning Outcome 1:
Using Excel financial functions, construct a loan analysis, calculate cumulative interest and principal, create an amortization schedule, analyze bonds and investments, and calculate depreciation of assets.

Learning Outcome 2:
Understand statistical language, understand the basic types of data, conduct a statistical analysis using Excel functions and the Data Analysis add-in, predict outcomes using probability distributions, use correlations and covariance to find relationships in data, and use regression analysis to predict future values.

In Business Unit 6 Capstone, students will demonstrate competence in these outcomes through a series of business problems at various levels, from guided practice to problem solving an existing spreadsheet and performing to create new spreadsheets.

More Practice 1

Student data file needed:

e06Barbeque.xlsx

You will save your file as:

e06Barbeque_LastFirst.xlsx

Borrowing Money for a New Business

Finance &
Accounting

You have been complimented many times on your cooking ability, and people love your barbeque. In the past, you have catered events out of your home. You would like to purchase a food truck and begin to sell your barbeque and other specialties to local customers. To apply for a business loan, you need to set up a model that will help you analyze the loan you need to move forward with your plan. You will develop a spreadsheet model to help determine how much of a loan you can afford. You also want to analyze last year's sales data using statistical functions and calculate the depreciation of assets.

a. Start **Excel**, click **Open** in the left pane, and then double-click **This PC**. Navigate through the folder structure to the location of your student data files, and then double-click **e06Barbeque**. A workbook opens displaying investment options for the business.

b. Click the **File** tab, click **Save As**, and then double-click **This PC**. In the **Save As** dialog box, navigate to the location where you are saving your project files, and then change the filename to e06Barbeque_LastFirst using your last and first name. Click **Save**.

c. On the **Loan Amortize** worksheet, complete the following tasks to calculate the number of loan payments, the end of the period payments, the total to be paid, and the total interest to be paid.

- Click cell **G5**, type =C7*C8 and then press Enter.
- In cell **G6**, type =PMT(C6/C8,G5,-C5) and then press Enter.
- In cell **G7**, type =G6*G5 and then press Enter.
- In cell **G8**, type =G7-C5 and then press Enter.

d. Complete the following tasks to construct an amortization schedule in the cell range C12:G35.

- Click cell **C12**, type =C5 and then press Tab.
- In cell **D12**, type =$G$6 and then press Tab.

- In cell **E12**, type =IPMT($C$6/$C$8,A12,$G$5,-$C$5) and then press Tab.
- In cell **F12**, type =PPMT($C$6/$C$8,A12,$G$5,-$C$5) and then press Tab.
- In cell **G12**, type =C12-F12 and then press Enter.
- Click cell **C13**, type =G12 and then press Ctrl + Enter. Use the fill handle to copy the formula down to cell **C35**.
- Select range **D12:G12**. Use the fill handle to copy the formula down to range **D13:G35**.

e. Create formulas to calculate the cumulative interest and cumulative principal.

- Click cell **I12**, type =-CUMIPMT($C$6/$C$8,$G$5,$C$5,$A$12,A12,0) and then press Ctrl + Enter. Use the fill handle to copy the formula down to cell **I35**.
- Click cell **J12**, type =-CUMPRINC($C$6/$C$8,$G$5,$C$5,$A$12,A12,0) and then press Ctrl + Enter. Use the fill handle to copy the formula down to cell **J35**.

f. Click the **Depreciation** worksheet. Click cell **B16**, type =IRR(B14:E14) and then press Enter to calculate the internal rate of return.

g. Complete the following tasks to calculate the straight-line depreciation schedule of the equipment.

- Click cell **H10**, type =SLN($G$6,$H$6,$I$6) and then press Ctrl + Enter. Use the fill handle to copy the formula down to cell **H14**.
- Click cell **I10**, type =H10 and then press Enter. In cell **I11**, type =I10+H11 and then press Ctrl + Enter. Use the fill handle to copy the formula down to cell **I14**.
- Click cell **J10**, type =$G$6-I10 and then press Ctrl + Enter. Use the fill handle to copy the formula down to cell **J14**.

h. Complete the following tasks to calculate the declining balance depreciation schedule.

- Click cell **H17**, type =DB($G$6,$H$6,$I$6,G17) and then press Ctrl + Enter. Use the fill handle to copy the formula down to cell **H21**.
- Click cell **I17**, type =H17 and then press Enter. In cell **I18**, type =I17+H18 and then press Ctrl + Enter. Use the fill handle to copy the formula down to cell **I21**.
- Click cell **J17**, type =$G$6-I17 and then press Ctrl + Enter. Use the fill handle to copy the formula down to cell **J21**.

i. Complete the following tasks to calculate the double declining balance depreciation schedule.

- Click cell **H24**, type =DDB($G$6,$H$6,$I$6,G24) and then press Ctrl + Enter. Use the fill handle to copy the formula down to cell **H28**.
- Click cell **I24**, type =H24 and then press Enter. In cell **I25**, type =I24+H25 and then press Ctrl + Enter. Use the fill handle to copy the formula down to cell **I28**.
- Click cell **J24**, type =$G$6-I24 and then press Ctrl + Enter. Use the fill handle to copy the formula down to cell **J28**.

j. Click the **Statistical Analysis** worksheet. Complete the following tasks to create descriptive statistics from the 2019 sales data.

- Click the **Data** tab, and then, in the Analyze group, click **Data Analysis**. In the Data Analysis dialog box, select **Descriptive Statistics**, and then click **OK**.
- In the **Input Range** box, type $B$3:$B$15 verify that **Columns** is selected as the Grouped By option, and then check the **Labels in first row** check box.
- Click **Output Range**, and in the **Output Range** box, type $D$4 and then check the **Summary statistics** check box. Click **OK**.

k. Click cell **H13**, and then type =1-NORM.DIST(H12,E6,E10,TRUE) and then press Ctrl + Enter to calculate the probability of selling 300 racks of ribs in week eight.

l. Click cell **K4**, type =J4*$E$10+$E$6 to calculate what the sales revenue would be if it were equal to four standard deviations above the mean, and then press

$\boxed{\text{Ctrl}}$ + $\boxed{\text{Enter}}$. Use the fill handle to copy the formula down to **K84** (four standard deviations below the mean).

m. Click cell **L4**, type **=NORM.DIST(K4,$E$6,$E$10,FALSE)** to calculate the probability that the sales revenue will be exactly four standard deviations above the mean in a given week, and then press $\boxed{\text{Ctrl}}$ + $\boxed{\text{Enter}}$. Use the fill handle to copy the formula down to **L84** (four standard deviations below the mean).

n. Select cells **K4:L84**, and then click the **Insert** tab. In the Charts group, click **Insert Scatter (X, Y) or Bubble Chart**, and then select the **Scatter with Smooth Lines** chart. Move the chart so the top-left corner is in the top-left corner of cell **A22**. Resize the chart so the bottom-right corner is in the bottom-right corner of cell **H39**. Click the **Chart Title** text box, and then replace Chart Title with Weekly Sales Revenue

o. Complete the **Documentation** worksheet according to your instructor's direction.

p. Click **Save**, exit Excel, and then submit your file as directed by your instructor.

 Problem Solve 1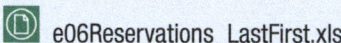

MyLab IT Grader

Student data file needed:

📄 e06Reservations.xlsx

You will save your file as:

📄 e06Reservations_LastFirst.xlsx

Hotel Reservations Analysis and Predictions

Sales & Marketing

The majority of reservations for the hotel at the Painted Paradise Resort & Spa are made online. On average, an online reservation is placed every 26.8 minutes. You have been asked to use the exponential probability distribution function to estimate when the next online reservations will take place. You will also calculate a moving average of weekly revenues and use the Poisson probability distribution to estimate the number of reservations over the next five days.

a. Open the Excel file **e06Reservations**. Save your file as e06Reservations_LastFirst using your last and first name.

b. On the **OnlineReservations** worksheet, create a statistical model that will estimate when the next 10 online reservations will occur, as well as the probability of an online reservation occurring within 12–20 minutes.

- In cell **A5**, use the Exponential probability distribution function to calculate the probability that the next online reservation will be made within two minutes. Use the fill handle to copy the function down to cell **A34**.

- In cell **D3**, create a formula that will estimate when the next 10 online reservations will take place, using a random variable. Use the fill handle to copy the function down to cell **D12**. If the formula results in an error, the value **2** should be displayed.

- In cell **F2**, create a formula that will calculate the probability of the next online reservation occurring within 12–20 minutes.

c. On the **ReservationRevenue** worksheet, create a moving average and a statistical model that will estimate the number of room reservations each day for the next five days.

- In cells **C2:C13**, use the Data Analysis add-in to create a Moving Average for every three weeks. Include a chart with the output. Position the chart so that the upper left corner begins in cell **A15**.

- In cell **F25**, calculate the mean number of reservations.

- Create a statistical model using the Poisson distribution function. In cell **H2**, use the Poisson probability distribution function to calculate the probability of 50 or fewer reservations. Use the fill handle to copy the function down to **H22**.
- In cells **K3:K7**, use the RAND function to create random variables. Copy and Paste Values so that the random variables do not change every time the worksheet recalculates.
- In cells **L3:L7**, create a formula that will estimate the number of reservations that will take place over the next five days. If the formula results in an error, the value **50** should be displayed.

d. Complete the **Documentation** worksheet according to your instructor's direction.

e. Save the workbook, exit Excel, and then submit the file as directed by your instructor.

Problem Solve 2

MyLab IT Grader

Student data file needed:

 e06Investments.xlsx

You will save your file as:

 e06Investments_LastFirst.xlsx

Investment Analysis

Production & Operations

You have been asked to analyze some investments for the company for whom you work. The first is a bond analysis in which you are given the par value, coupon rate, maturity, and yield to maturity for two different bonds to consider. For each bond, you will calculate the present value to determine which investment is better. Next you will analyze the historical performance of two stocks to compare for investing.

a. Open the Excel file **e06Investments**. Save your file as e06Investments_LastFirst using your last and first name.

b. On the **Bond Analysis** worksheet, use the values provided to calculate the coupon payment for each bond in cells B5 and C5.

c. In cell **B7**, calculate the present value of the first bond, using the data provided and the coupon payment.

d. In cell **C7**, calculate the present value of the second bond, using the data provided and the coupon payment.

e. Add formatting to the worksheet to provide a professional appearance.

f. The **Historical Performance** worksheet contains closing stock prices for two stocks in the cell ranges **B2:B37** and **C2:C37**. Calculate the mean, median, sample standard deviation, min, max, and range for each of the closing stock prices. Place the calculations for Stock #1 in the cell range F2:F7 and the calculations for Stock #2 in the cell range G2:G7. Format the calculations appropriately.

g. Create two histograms to further explore the distribution of the closing prices for each stock. Place the first histogram approximately in the cell range **E9:K22**. Place the second histogram in the cell range **M9:S22**.

h. Change the title of the first histogram to Stock #1 Closing Prices and then change the title of the second histogram to Stock #2 Closing Prices

i. Complete the **Documentation** worksheet according to your instructor's direction.

j. Save the workbook, exit Excel, and then submit the file as directed by your instructor.

Critical Thinking

Considering the present values you calculated for each of the bonds on the Bond Analysis worksheet, which bond would you choose? Examining the stock data further, what differences exist in the stock performances? What other types of charts would be appropriate for examining the data provided?

Student data file needed:

 Blank Excel workbook

You will save your file as:

e06Portfolio_LastFirst.xlsx

Personal Investment Analysis

Finance & Accounting

Financial decisions are a part of our lives, and knowing how to properly analyze investment options is crucial to making good investment decisions. In this exercise, you will analyze two different investment options.

a. Start **Excel**, and then create a new workbook. Save the file as e06Portfolio_LastFirst using your last and first name.

b. Rename the Sheet1 worksheet to Option1

c. Set up the worksheet to calculate the irregular net present value of an investment by using the following information.

- Initial investment amount: $10,000.00
- Discount rate of 3.75% and then format as **Decimal** with 2 decimal places.
- Expected incoming cash flows are to occur on the following dates:

Dates	Cash Flows
1/1/2022	–$10,000.00
2/15/2022	$2,750.00
4/15/2022	$2,500.00
8/20/2022	$2,350.00
10/20/2022	$1,900.00
12/20/2022	$850.00

- Format all cash flow values as **Currency**.

d. Add a new worksheet to the right of Option1, and then name it Option2

e. Set up the worksheet to calculate the present value of an investment bond using the following information.

- Par Value: $10,000.00
- Coupon Rate: 7%
- Maturity: 3 years
- YTM: 5.2%

f. Calculate the annual coupon payment.

g. Calculate the present value of the bond. Be sure the function returns a positive value.

h. Format all cells with appropriate formatting.

i. Add a new worksheet to the right of Option2, and name it Option3

j. Set up the worksheet to calculate the internal rate of return of an investment, using the following expected future cash flows.

Year	Cash Flow
0	–$10,000.00
1	$4,950.00
2	$2,450.00
3	$1,750.00

k. Calculate the internal rate of return based on the series of expected cash flows.

l. Add formatting to each worksheet to give the file a professional appearance.

m. Insert the **filename** in the left custom footer section of the Header/Footer tab in the Page Setup dialog box on all worksheets in the workbook.

n. Save the workbook, exit Excel, and then submit the file as directed by your instructor.

Perform 2: Perform in Your Career

Student data file needed:	**You will save your file as:**
e06Buy.xlsx	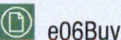 e06Buy_LastFirst.xlsx

Do We Need to Buy?

Production & Operations

You work for a motherboard manufacturing company in the Quality Assurance department. In your job, you are responsible for testing the motherboards to ensure that the proper voltage is getting to all components. On the basis of recent test results, you believe your company may need to consider purchasing a new solder wave board. Because these machines usually cost millions of dollars, you want to ensure that you have all your data validated and verified before you bring your findings to management. A failure rate greater than 2% is considered abnormal. Your immediate supervisor has begun a workbook with the most recent findings, which you will use to complete your analysis.

a. Open the Excel file **e06Buy**. Save the file as **e06Buy_LastFirst** using your last and first name.

b. On the **Volts** worksheet, use the Data Analysis add-in to generate Descriptive Statistics concerning the Volts data in column B. Place the output in cell **D4**. Autofit the contents of the columns to see all of the data.

c. Insert the CSE formula **FREQUENCY**, using the Bin array in the cell range **G6:G16**.

d. Create a box and whisker chart of the Volts data, and place the chart so that the upper left corner starts in cell **J5**. Delete the horizontal axis label, and provide an appropriate chart title.

e. Create a Moving Average Chart, available in the Data Analysis add-in. The interval should be **2**.

f. Move or adjust the chart(s) and data to improve the appearance of your worksheet.

g. The box and whisker chart identifies an outlier in your data. In which batch did the outlier appear? Place your answer in cell **B2**.

h. On the **Analysis** worksheet, calculate the monthly payments on the two loans on the worksheet. The first loan is for the repair of the machine; the second loan is for the purchase of a new one.

i. Complete the two partial amortization schedules, using IPMT and PPMT functions.

j. At the top of each amortization schedule, calculate the total interest and principal paid.

k. Complete the **Documentation** worksheet according to your instructor's direction.

l. Save the workbook, exit Excel, and then submit the file as directed by your instructor.

Student data file needed:

 Blank Excel workbook

You will save your file as:

 e06NewProduct_TeamName.xlsx

New Product Investment

Finance & Accounting

You and a team of three to five other students have been presented with an investment opportunity. You need to conduct some statistical analysis on this new product investment opportunity. You will use the normal probability distribution to analyze the possible rates of return. You will also use the binomial probability distribution to analyze the number of successful trials one can expect from the product.

a. Select one team member to set up the database by completing steps b–d.

b. Open your browser, and navigate to https://www.onedrive.live.com, https://www.drive.google.com, or any other instructor-assigned location. Be sure all members of the team have an account on the chosen system, such as a Microsoft or Google account.

c. Create a new blank workbook and name it e06NewProduct_TeamName using the name assigned to your team.

d. Rename Sheet1 as Contributors List the names of the team members on the worksheet, and then add a heading above the names to read Team Members Include any additional information on this worksheet as required by your instructor.

e. Share the spreadsheet with the other members of your team. Make sure each team member has the appropriate permission to edit the document.

f. Create a new worksheet entitled ProductInvestment Set up the worksheet to create a normal probability distribution table, using the following information.

- Mean rate of return is 13.4%
- Standard deviation of the rate of return is 4.15%
- Create column headings for Standard Deviations ROR and Probability
- Under the **Standard Deviations** heading, create a column of values ranging from 4 to –4 in increments of .01.
- Under the **ROR** heading, calculate the value of ROR as four standard deviations from the mean, and then use the fill handle to copy the formula down the column.
- Under the **Probability** heading, calculate the probability that the ROR is exactly four standard deviations from the mean, and then use the fill handle to copy the function down the column.

g. Create a scatter chart with Smooth Lines to visualize the normal distribution.

- Give the chart a title of ROR Probability Distribution
- Adjust the horizontal axis to have a minimum value of –10% and a maximum value of 30%
- Change the Label Position of the vertical axis to Low
- Position the chart near the top of your probability distribution table.

h. Create a new worksheet entitled ProductTesting. The manufacturers of the new product claim that the product's battery will last for 12 hours 90% of the time. Set up the worksheet to calculate the probability of successful trials based on the following information.

- Number of Trials: 150
- Success Rate: 80%

- Calculate the probability of exactly 110 successful trials.
- Calculate the probability of no more than 125 successful trials.
- Calculate the probability of more than 125 successful trials.

i. Insert the **filename** in the left custom footer section of the Header/Footer tab in the Page Setup dialog box on all worksheets in the workbook. In a custom header section, include the **names** of the students in your team. Spread the names evenly across each of the three header sections: left section, center section, and right section.

j. Save the workbook, exit Excel, and then submit the file as directed by your instructor.

Perform 4: How Others Perform

Student data file needed:
    e06Decisions.xlsx

You will save your file as:
    e06Decisions_LastFirst.xlsx

Sales & Marketing

Finance & Accounting

Analysis to Support Decision Making

Robert Smith, owner of a small but growing clothing store, is looking for ways to fund an expansion. He had an intern attempt to conduct some analysis on a possible loan and other investments, but Robert suspects that the analysis is not accurate, and he does not want to make any decisions until he is sure he can trust the analysis. The intern also attempted to conduct some statistical analysis on the business. Examine the worksheet, and correct any mistakes in the formulas and functions.

a. Open the file **e06Decisions**. Save your file as **e06Decisions_LastFirst** using your last and first name.

b. On the **LoanAnalysis** worksheet, you will find a number of visible errors in the loan analysis conducted by an intern.

- Examine the function in cell **B6**. The RATE function is returning a #NUM! error message instead of the APR. Correct the formula, and then make sure it returns the correct APR according to the loan information in the cells above. Each loan payment is to be made at the beginning of the period.

- Examine the principal and interest payment formulas in the cell range **C11:D11**. The sum of those two calculations does not equal the monthly payment in cell B2. Correct both formulas so they equal the monthly payment, and then use the fill handle to copy the formulas down to the end of the amortization schedule.

c. Click the **Investments** worksheet tab. On this worksheet, you will find errors in various formulas and functions that cause the investment analysis to lead to bad decisions.

- Examine the formula in cell **B5** that is calculating the coupon payment. Make the necessary correction so the coupon payment is calculated correctly.

- Examine the PV function in cell **B7** for errors. The function is missing a cell reference for one of the arguments. Make the necessary corrections.

- Examine the NPV function in cell **E13** for errors. Make the necessary corrections to ensure that the Net Present Value is being calculated correctly.

d. Click the **Stats** worksheet. On this worksheet, you will find errors in various statistical functions.

- Examine the function in cell **B7**. This function should calculate the probability of earning no more than $13,000 in sales revenue. Examine the function, and then make the appropriate changes.

- Examine the function in cell **B8**. This function should calculate the probability of earning more than $12,500 in sales revenue. Examine the function, and then make the appropriate changes.

- Examine the function in cell **D6**. This function should calculate the probability of the next customer entering the store within the next five minutes. Examine the function, and then make the appropriate changes. Use the fill handle to copy the function down to cell **D17**.

- Examine the function in cell **L3**. The function in the cell range L3:L9 should calculate the frequency of values based on the data in the cell range I3:I17 and the bins in the cell range K3:K8. The function is an array function but has been created incorrectly. Examine the function, and then make the appropriate changes.

e. Complete the **Documentation** worksheet according to your instructor's direction.

f. Save the workbook, exit Excel, and then submit the file as directed by your instructor.

Excel Business Unit 7

Enabling Decisions with Data Visualization and VBA

Businesses must make decisions quickly and accurately to maintain a competitive advantage in the global market. They can use digital dashboards to make sense of the vast amounts of data they are collecting. Features in Excel such as Power Pivot, Power View, form controls, and Visual Basic for Applications can create powerful dashboards that can be used to quickly gain information and knowledge from data. Power Pivot can connect data from various sources and visualize the data with PivotTables and PivotCharts. Power View can create sophisticated interactive visualizations. Form controls can enhance the usability and control data input on a worksheet. Finally, Visual Basic for Applications can provide powerful enhancements for dashboards. When combined, these tools can create powerful decision making applications.

Learning Outcome 1

Use Excel to develop dashboards and gain business insight using the Power Pivot, PivotTables, and PivotCharts.

REAL WORLD SUCCESS

"Over the summer, I worked as a consultant for a small clothing store in the Midwest. The management there was just starting to realize the benefits of making data-driven decisions. They used Excel for various accounting tasks but never really thought of using it to analyze large amounts of data. I was able to use the Power Pivot feature in Excel to build a data model that allowed for easy analysis of millions of records from multiple sources and create a simple dashboard to track various metrics. As a result, that company is making progress toward its goal of expanding its store locations."

– Lupe, recent graduate

Learning Outcome 2

Enhance spreadsheets with form controls and VBA. Utilize VBA to create custom functions, looping procedures, events based actions, and to secure a workbook.

REAL WORLD SUCCESS

"I interned for an auto parts manufacturing plant last summer and was asked to assist with a data cleansing project. The person working on the project had spent hours cleaning the data and was not getting very far. I was able to use a little bit of VBA to loop through thousands of rows in a matter of minutes."

– Francis, recent graduate

Microsoft Excel

Chapter 13 THE EXCEL DATA MODEL AND BUSINESS INTELLIGENCE

MyLab IT Grader

Sales & Marketing

Prepare Case

The Red Bluff Golf Course & Pro Shop Dashboards, KPIs, and Data Visualizations

Management at the Red Bluff Golf Course & Pro Shop has been collecting data on the business for the past three years. The managers are looking for ways to create visualizations of their data to help make important strategic decisions about the future of the company and to solicit private investments in Red Bluff. You have been given access to a sample set of sales data from 2019 to 2021 and have been asked to conduct further analysis, create some useful visualizations of the data, and put together a dashboard of charts and tools for management to easily see the business from multiple perspectives. You will use the business intelligence features in Excel that are scalable for use with millions of records.

Mooinblack/Shutterstock

Student data files needed:

 e07ch13Sales.accdb

 e07ch13Analytics.xlsx

You will save your file as:

 e07ch13Analytics_LastFirst.xlsx

Exploring the Importance of Business Intelligence

Business intelligence is not just a buzzword. **Business intelligence (BI)** refers to a variety of software applications that are used to analyze an organization's data to provide management with the tools necessary to improve decision making, cut costs, and identify new opportunities. The role of BI has increased over the last decade because the amount of data being collected by businesses continues to grow at a rapid rate.

This increasing dependence on BI has manifested itself in many forms in the business community over the past few years. The most recent trend, which shows no signs of slowing, is the desire for digital dashboards. **Digital dashboards** are mechanisms that deliver BI in graphical form. Dashboards provide management with a big picture view of the business, usually from multiple perspectives using various charts and other graphical representations. The abundance of data, the need for access to real time data, and the ability to use that data to make better business decisions drive companies to utilize digital dashboards. In this section, you will learn about the dashboard design concepts, explore the Excel data model, conduct some analysis, and build a dashboard.

 CONSIDER THIS | **Decisions, Decisions, Decisions . . .**

A typical manager engages in a multitude of different tasks and decisions each day. These often involve interacting with many different people, using a variety of different channels and technologies. The number of channels and technologies a manager must master is growing. Do you think technology increases, decreases, or holds steady the volume and speed of decision making today?

Understand the Basics of Dashboard Design

Dashboards are becoming more and more important today as a tool for helping managers run their businesses. Dashboards are no longer just for executives, and are being integrated at all levels of the business and in many different industries. You will likely encounter them in other classes as you discuss management techniques such as Balanced Scorecards and Six Sigma. Both of these management initiatives involve generating key performance indicators and dashboard reports for all levels of the organization. Using dashboards, everyone from the CEO to the delivery truck driver can have a personalized view of information to see quickly and easily how well they are performing.

The design of a dashboard has just as much of an impact on its effectiveness as does the data displayed. Think of the dashboard in a car. The gauges and layout of the dashboard are designed to help the driver make better decisions and interpret important things such as relative speed, gas consumption, and critical malfunctions in a very immediate and effective way. The driver must monitor the situation constantly and make crucial decisions about what to do with the car. An effective dashboard supports effective decision making.

This analogy holds true for the "driver" of a company. A manager must be able to quickly review and monitor the current health of the company and make decisions in a timely manner to correct problems. A dashboard can be a huge help to a manager because it is specifically organized to provide relevant alerts and monitor the business as a whole. Typically, dashboards are oriented around specific business activities, such as sales analysis, cash flow, employee productivity, and customer service. Some typical features of a dashboard might include the following:

- A visually oriented single-screen user interface that is intuitive and easy to navigate
- Interactive controls that allow the user to customize the data display

- Integration of multiple types of data from a variety of sources
- Data that is updated frequently so it reflects the current situation
- Information oriented toward a specific problem or decision
- A layout that does not require a lot of training to use effectively

In Excel, dashboard components typically consist of tables, PivotTables, PivotCharts, conditional formatting, and other features. There are also some basic design concepts that you need to take into consideration when creating a dashboard.

Keeping It Simple

Adding more and more data and charts to a dashboard can be tempting. However, you must always keep in mind the basic principle: When it comes to a dashboard, less is more. If users cannot easily interpret your dashboard, then you may have made it too complicated. An overly complicated dashboard is not usable as a management tool. Remember that one of the primary goals is to help the user navigate and interpret a large quantity of data at a glance.

Making Sure It Is Well Defined

Stay focused on a specific business problem. A company can track product sales, employee productivity, customer complaints, revenue, portfolio value, machine defects, and so on. However, doing all of these in the same dashboard is ill advised. As a rule, the more defined you can make your theme, the more useful your users will find the dashboard.

Knowing Your Users

Not all users are alike. They can have different decision-making styles. You can increase the success of your dashboard by taking personal preferences into account whenever possible. You should interview the main users of the dashboard to see what they would find most useful. The earlier you can let them see your dashboard design, the fewer headaches you will have later in the project. Changes are easier to make early in development than they will be when you are almost done.

Defining Crucial KPIs

A **key performance indicator (KPI)** is a quantifiable measure that helps managers to define progress toward both short-term and long-term goals. Some KPIs are year-to-date (YTD) sales growth, customer satisfaction, call resolution rates, and percent of market share, as shown in the Quick Reference table. In fact, every functional area of business has its own set of commonly used KPIs. Often, many firms in the same industry will all focus on similar KPIs because they are so critical to the nature of their business — for example, profit margin.

QUICK REFERENCE · Commonly Used Business KPIs

Business Area	KPI
Accounting	• Gross profit
	• Operating margin
	• Cumulative annual growth rate
	• ROI (Return on Investment)
	• Cost of goods sold
Finance/Accounting	• Gross yield
	• Price-to-earnings ratio (P/E)
	• Earnings before interest, taxes, depreciation, and amortization (EBITDA)
	• Earnings per share (EPS)
	• Budget ratio
Marketing/Sales	• Market share by segment
	• Customer churn rate (rate of growth or decline of customers)
	• Customer lifetime value
	• Cost per lead
	• Productivity by channel
Personnel	• Productivity ratios
	• Turnover rates
	• % overtime
	• Employee satisfaction rates
	• % absenteeism
Operations	• Out of stock %
	• Defect rate
	• Production cycle time
	• On-time delivery
	• % downtime
Customer Service	• Customer satisfaction
	• First call resolution rate
	• Average wait time
	• % of dropped calls
	• Time per call
IT	• Access speed
	• Site click-through
	• System availability
	• Service satisfaction levels
	• Project success rates

Using Strategic Placement

A good dashboard should help to summarize complex data so users can interpret the information at a glance. The dashboard needs to make it as easy as possible for users to read and understand the data. The layout of the dashboard can have a big impact on its usability. Figure 1 illustrates the regions of a screen to which a user's eyes tend to pay attention, according to research conducted by the Poynter Institute.

1	1	2	3
1	1	2	2
2	2	2	3
3	3	3	3

Figure 1   Design layout priority zones

Designing with White Space

Empty space on the screen that gives the eyes a place to rest is called **white space**. White space helps to keep a design simple, accessible, and visually pleasing to users. It is not necessarily white, just devoid of content. There is no rule for how much white space to include in your design. You should include more white space than you initially think is necessary. However, including too much white space may mean that you are wasting valuable screen space. Including the right amount of white space can give an elegant feel to your dashboard and make it easier for the user to read.

Opening the Starting File

You will use various tools to create data visualizations using Map Charts, create and modify a data model in Excel using Power Pivot, conduct some analysis, and create a dashboard using Excel's Power View. In this exercise, you will open the starting file.

E13.00

SIDE NOTE
Office Updates
Depending on your exact Office version, you may see Open or Open Other Workbooks.

To Open a Workbook

a. Start **Excel**, click **Open Other Workbooks** in the left pane, and then double-click **This PC**. Navigate through the folder structure to the location of your student data files, and then double-click **e07ch13Analytics**. A workbook opens to which you will add dashboards.

b. Click the **File** tab, click **Save As**, and then double-click **This PC**. In the **Save As** dialog box, navigate to the location where you are saving your project files, and then save the file as e07ch13Analytics_LastFirst using your last and first name. Click **Save**.

The following commercially available products exist to make it easy to create complex dashboards:

- Tableau
- Cognos
- Hyperion
- Dundas
- Corda
- SQL Server Analysis Services
- Oracle Business Intelligence

While these programs may be powerful and effective, they all suffer from two significant drawbacks. First, they require a software purchase; although some tools are nominally "free," the free or trial versions may have limited functionality and/or may not be legal to use for your company. Second, off-the-shelf software nearly always requires that its users have that software installed on their computers.

There are many benefits to using Microsoft Excel to create digital dashboards:

- Minimal costs: Not every business is a multibillion-dollar business that can afford to purchase top-of-the-line BI software, but most businesses use Microsoft Office. Leveraging the capabilities of Microsoft Excel is a very cost-effective solution without compromising too much on usability and functionality.
- Broad familiarity: From the entry-level sales representative to the CEO, familiarity with Excel is widespread. People who have some experience with Excel will spend less time learning how to use the dashboard and more time getting value from what is displayed than would be necessary with the other products.
- Flexibility: With the appropriate know-how, Excel can be much more flexible in the variety of analytics it can provide in a dashboard than many off-the-shelf solutions. Such features as PivotTables, AutoFilters, Form controls, and Power View allow you to create mechanisms that allow the audience multiple perspectives of the data.
- Rapid development: Having the capability to create your own reporting mechanisms in Excel can reduce your reliance on the IT department's resources. With Excel, not only can you develop reporting mechanisms faster, but you can also have the flexibility to adapt more quickly to changing requirements.
- Compatibility with Microsoft Power BI Desktop Suite: Dashboard created in Excel can be imported into Microsoft's Power BI Desktop Suite. Dashboards created in the Power BI Desktop Suite can be shared via the internet and via apps on mobile platforms.

REAL WORLD ADVICE | **Dashboard Design and the Systems Development Life Cycle**

Creating dashboards requires far more preparation than a standard Excel model does. It requires closer communication with business leaders, stricter data modeling techniques, and following certain best practices. The systems development life cycle (SDLC) provides a structure for managing complex IT projects. One of the SDLC models is broken into six stages: analyze, design, develop, implement, test, and maintain. Following this SDLC model can provide the necessary guidance for creating an effective dashboard.

Explore the Data Model

You can create many different types of models using Excel. For example, a financial model can be useful in evaluating loans or investments, a statistical model can be useful in predicting demand for a particular product, and a Solver model can be used to determine the optimal number of workers to hire to maximize profits. Excel 2019 provides the ability to create a data model. A **data model** is a collection of tables and their relationships that reflect the real-world relationships between business functions and processes—for example, how products relate to inventory and sales or how customers relate to revenues and sales volume. This feature allows your analysis to integrate data from multiple tables, effectively creating a relational data source inside Excel.

Relational data is a topic traditionally reserved for databases such as Microsoft Access; however, with this functionality in Excel, you need to have a basic understanding of relational data. **Relational data** is data about a person, place, or event that is stored in multiple tables. For example, the data about employees is stored in an employee table, and data about the products that the company sells is stored in a products table. These two tables may be related through the transactions that take place when the employees sell the products. Most organizations store their data in a relational database to ensure that their data is secure, accurate, and consistent. Before Excel 2013, it was very complicated and time-consuming to integrate relational data into an analysis.

Data can be added to the data model from a variety of sources. Data from two or more tables imported from an external data source such as an Access database or SQL Server are automatically added to the data model. Data in a text file, in a range of cells, organized into tables, or in a SharePoint list can also be added to the data model. These connections can be created using the Get & Transform tools found on the Data tab in Excel.

Importing Data with Get & Transform

Get & Transform is a powerful business intelligence tool that is used to discover data, connect it to your workbook, and transform the data into a more useful state. The tool is discussed in more depth in Chapter 9. Previously available as a separate download, called Power Query, Get & Transform is now the default method for connecting to external data with Excel. Several types of external data connections are supported such as Internet connections via URLs, from a variety of standalone files, from a wide array of database connections, from SharePoint lists, and from Microsoft's Azure service.

The benefit of using a tool such as Get & Transform is that it not only imports your data but also can clean and transform the data before the data is imported into a worksheet. An added benefit is that the steps used to clean and transform the data can be stored as part of the data query and are then applied when a data connection is refreshed.

The database you have been given contains a list of employees in the table tblEmployees. The last names of the employees have been typed in as all lowercase text. Additionally, the hire date field contains a date-time stamp. For the purposes of this analysis, the time portion of the field needs to be removed. In this exercise, you will import the data with Get & Transform and transform the last name and hire date fields.

 **E**13.01

To Import Data into Excel Using Get & Transform

> **Mac Troubleshooting**
>
> At the time of publishing for this text, the tools discussed in this text including the Get & Transform Data group and the Excel Data Model are not available in the Office 2019 for Mac versions of Microsoft Office. Instead, the previous set of tools in the group Get External Data continue to serve the purpose of importing data into Excel for the Mac versions of Office. PivotTables, Pivot-Charts, and other Excel functions can be used to create the charts and tables from this chapter.

a. On the SalesDashboard sheet, click the **Data** tab, and then in the Get & Transform Data group, click **Get Data**.

b. Point to **From Database**, and then select **From Microsoft Access Database**.

c. Browse to your student data files, select **e07ch13Sales**, and then click **Import**. The Navigator window will now show a list of all tables in the database.

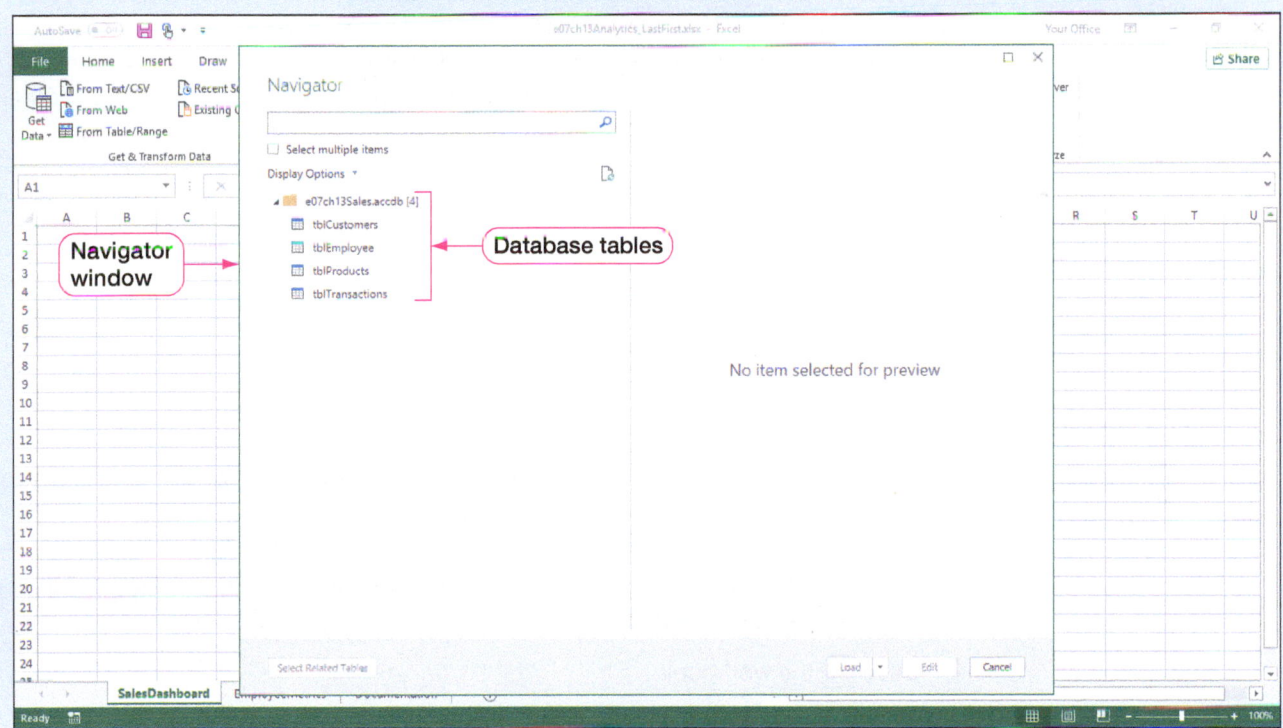

Figure 2   The Navigator window

Screenshot of Microsoft Excel 2019, © Microsoft Corporation

SIDE NOTE

Pin the Ribbon

If your ribbon is collapsed, pin your ribbon open. Click the Home tab. In the lower-right corner of the ribbon, click Pin the ribbon 📌.

d. Click the **tblEmployee** table, and then click **Edit**. This will open the Power Query Editor.

e. Click the **LastName** column. Click the **Transform** tab, and in the Text Column group, click **Format**, and then click **Capitalize Each Word**.

Notice that the column now contains last names in the proper case, with the first letter of each work capitalized.

SIDE NOTE
Applied Steps

Each step in the import process is listed in the Applied Steps portion of the Query Settings and will be executed on the data when the connection is refreshed.

f.   Click the **HireDate** column. On the Transform tab, in the Date & Time Column group, click **Date**, and then click **Date Only**.

Notice that the time portion of the column has been removed. The data can now be loaded into Excel.

g.   Click the **Home** tab, and then, in the Close group, click **Close & Load**. The table is now loaded into a new worksheet with the changes to the LastName and HireDate columns.

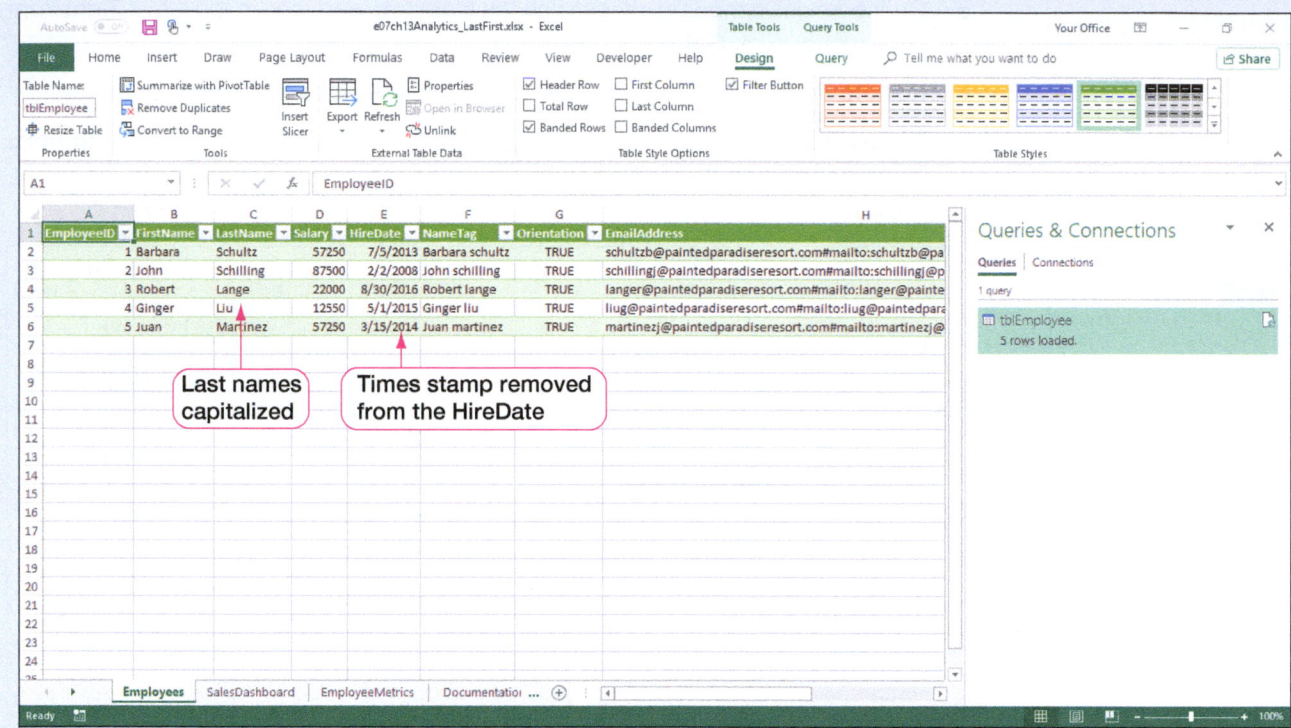

Figure 3   tblEmployee table loaded into Excel

Screenshot of Microsoft Excel 2019, © Microsoft Corporation

h.   Click any **blank cell** to deselect the table. Rename the worksheet **Employees** and **Close** ☒ the Queries & Connections pane.

i.   **Save** 🖫 the workbook.

Building a Data Model Using an Access Database

Many organizations store data inside a relational database such as MySQL or Oracle or in a database management system such as Microsoft Access. Earlier versions of Excel have allowed for data connections from external sources, but Excel now can maintain the relationships between multiple tables. The e07ch13Sales database contains some sample sales data from Red Bluff Golf Course & Pro Shop that will form the foundation of your analysis. In this exercise, you will connect to the database and import all the tables into your workbook.

 **E13.02**

To Create a Data Connection to an Access Database

a.   Click the **Data** tab and then, in the Get & Transform Data group, click **Get Data**.

b.   Point to **From Database**, and then select **From Microsoft Access Database**.

c. Browse to your student data files, select **e07ch13Sales**, and then click **Import**.

d. In the Navigator window, click to select the **Select multiple items** checkbox.

e. Click the check boxes to select the **tblCustomers**, **tblProducts**, and **tblTransactions** tables in the database.

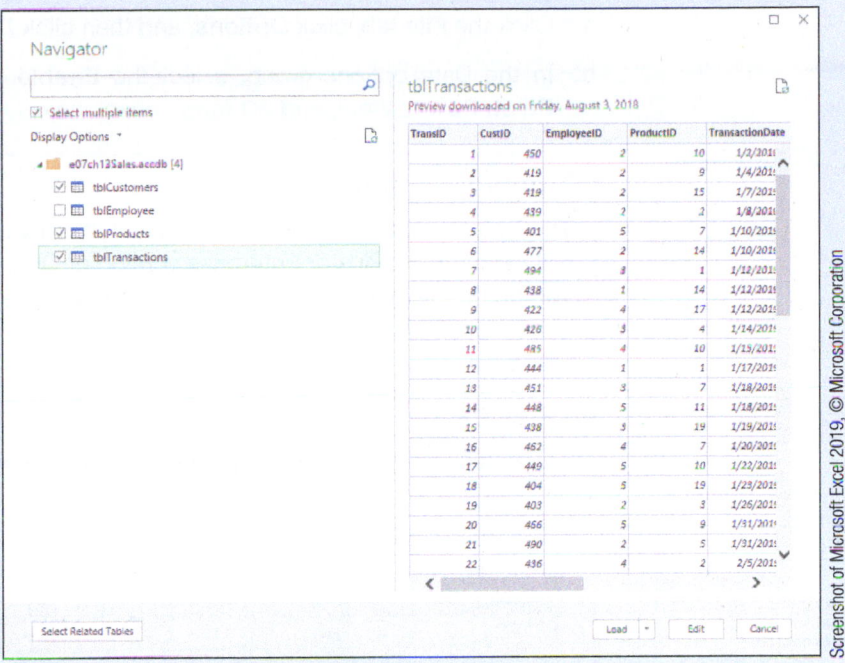

Figure 4   The Navigator window

f. Click the **Load arrow** and click **Load To**. In the Import Data dialog box, if necessary, click to select **Only Create Connection**.

Notice that the Add this data to the Data Model check box is selected by default.

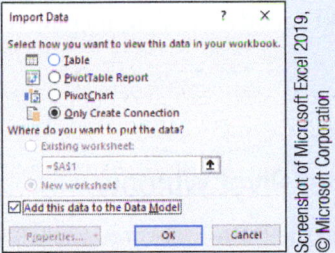

Figure 5   Import Data dialog box

g. Click **OK**.

h. Save 🖫 the workbook.

Exploring the Power Pivot Window

Now that you have imported relational data into the Excel workbook, a data model exists. As was stated previously, this makes it easy to integrate data from multiple tables in your analysis. To view and edit the data model, you must enable the Data Analysis add-ins. These include Power Pivot, Power View, and 3D Maps. In this exercise, you will enable the Data Analysis add-ins to view the data model that you created in the previous exercise. The Data Analysis add-ins are available in most versions of Office 365; however, Power View is only available in the ProPlus and Enterprise subscriptions.

 **E13.03**

To Enable the Data Analysis Add-Ins

a. Click the **File** tab, click **Options**, and then click **Data**.

b. In the Data options group, select the **Enable Data Analysis add-ins: Power Pivot, Power View, and 3D Maps** check box.

> ### Troubleshooting
> The Data Analysis add-ins are available in most versions of Office 365. You will need the ProPlus or Enterprise version of Office 365 to use Power View. If you do not have an option to Enable Data Analysis add-ins check your Office subscription type.

c. Click **OK**.

Notice that the Power Pivot tab that has been added to the ribbon.

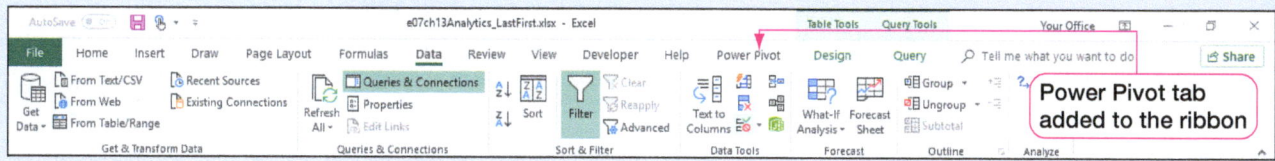

Figure 6   Power Pivot tab displayed

Screenshot of Microsoft Excel 2019, © Microsoft Corporation

d. Save  the workbook.

The Power Pivot add-in is now installed. Power Pivot is the tool in Excel that allows you to interact with and modify the data model. In this exercise, you will explore the Power Pivot window.

 **E13.04**

To Explore the Power Pivot Window

a. Click the **Data** tab, in the Data Tools group, click **Go to the Power Pivot Window**. If necessary, maximize the Power Pivot window.

Notice that a Power Pivot window opens separately from the workbook. The default view of the data model resembles a traditional Excel workbook, with each table appearing on a separate worksheet. The Excel workbook remains open in the background and can be easily viewed by closing the Power Pivot window.

The Home tab allows you to perform a variety of tasks, including adding new data from a variety of data sources; refreshing your data model to sync with changes made in the source data; creating PivotTables and PivotCharts; formatting, sorting, and filtering data; creating simple calculations and KPIs; and changing views.

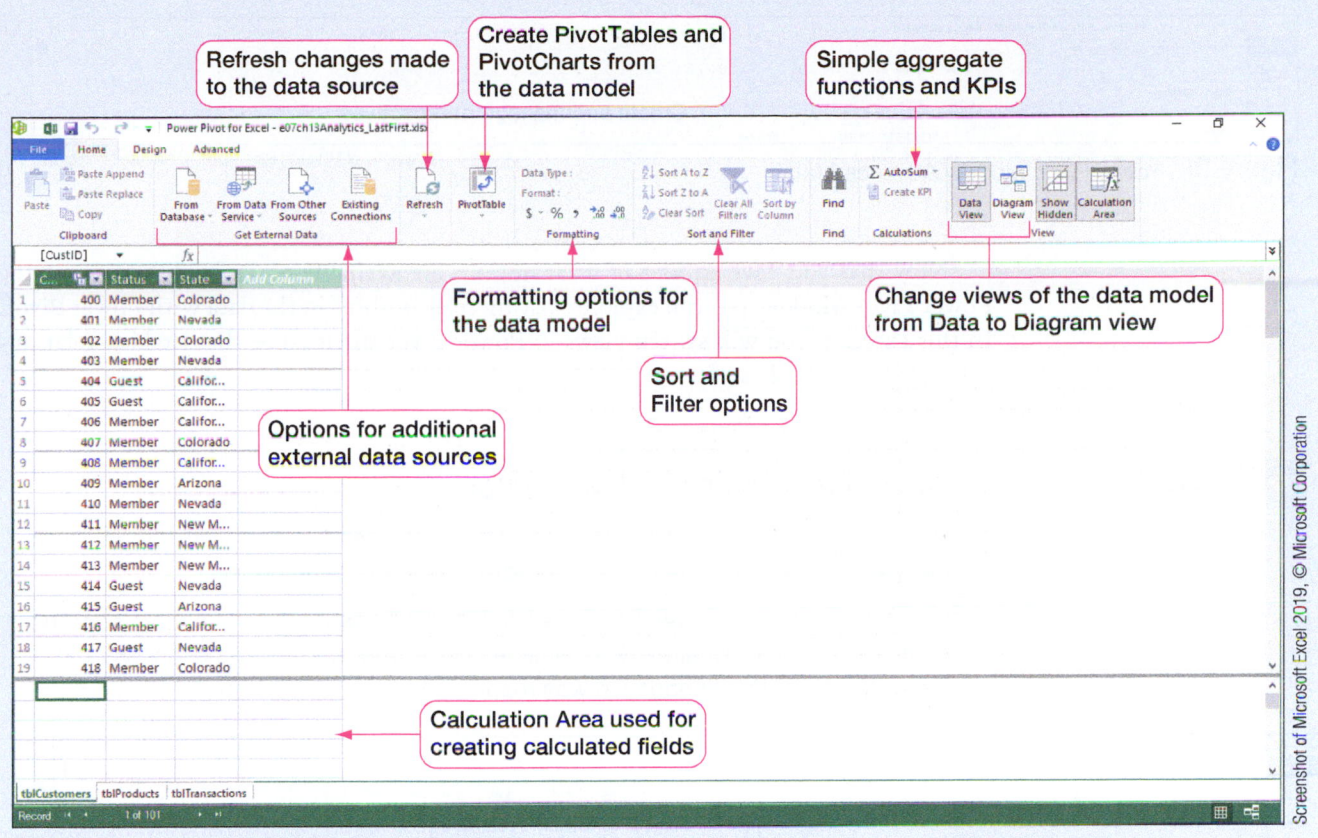

Refresh changes made to the data source

Create PivotTables and PivotCharts from the data model

Simple aggregate functions and KPIs

Formatting options for the data model

Change views of the data model from Data to Diagram view

Options for additional external data sources

Sort and Filter options

Calculation Area used for creating calculated fields

Screenshot of Microsoft Excel 2019, © Microsoft Corporation

Figure 7 Power Pivot window Home tab

b. Click the **Design** tab.

The Design tab gives you the ability to modify table properties, create more complex calculated fields, create and edit relationships between worksheets, and more.

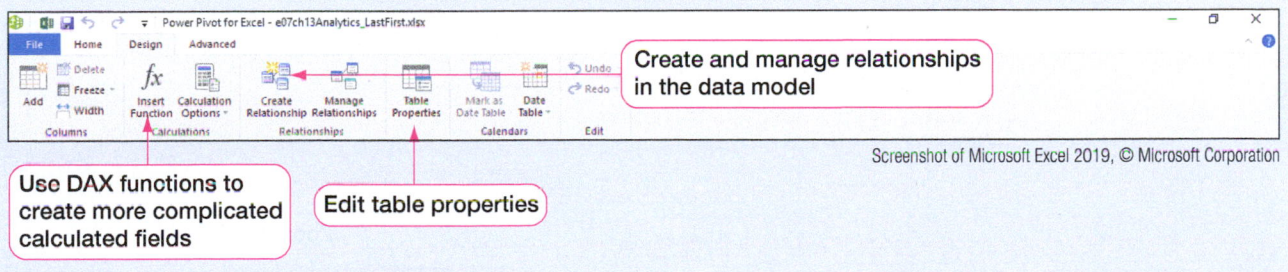

Create and manage relationships in the data model

Use DAX functions to create more complicated calculated fields

Edit table properties

Screenshot of Microsoft Excel 2019, © Microsoft Corporation

Figure 8 Power Pivot window Design tab

c. Click the **Advanced** tab.

The Advanced tab includes options that go beyond the scope of this book but include changing and managing different data perspectives for a particular user group or business scenario and allowing for easier navigation of very large data sets.

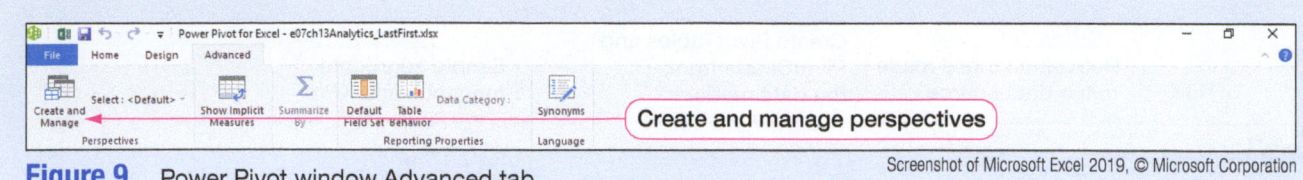

Screenshot of Microsoft Excel 2019, © Microsoft Corporation

Figure 9   Power Pivot window Advanced tab

Now that you have an idea of what options are available on each of the tabs in the Power Pivot window, you can explore existing relationships in the data with Power Pivot. In this exercise, you will switch views in Power Pivot to visualize the database relationships from the database file.

 **E13.05**

To View Relationships in Power Pivot

a. In the Power Pivot window, click the **Home** tab, and in the View group, click **Diagram View** to see the current relationships in the data model.

b. If necessary, to view all relationships, click **Fit to Screen** on the zoom bar. The relationships that are already established were imported from the Access database when the data connection was made.

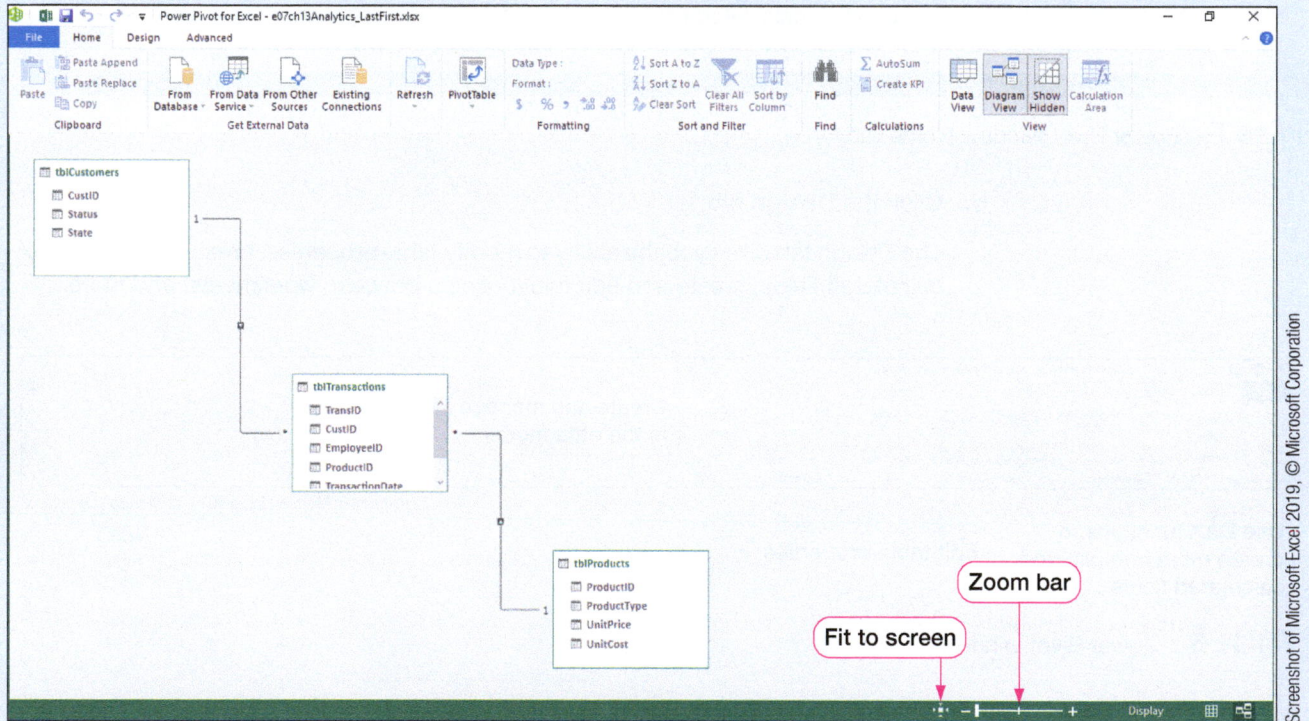

Screenshot of Microsoft Excel 2019, © Microsoft Corporation

Figure 10   Power Pivot window Diagram View

c. In the View group, click **Data View** to switch back to viewing all the data in the data model.

d. **Save** the workbook.

Adding a Table to the Data Model

Comprehensive data analysis often requires data from different sources. A human resources database might keep track of employees who have attended a required training session, and a separate sales database might keep track of online sales and in-person sales. Often, additional data may need to be incorporated into the data model to make it easier to conduct certain analyses. For example, in a previous exercise, you imported the tblEmployee table into the Employees worksheet. This data needs to be related to the rest of the Access tables for the data model to be complete. In this exercise, you will add this table to the data model.

 **E13.06**

To Add an Excel Table to the Data Model

a. Minimize ▬ the Power Pivot Window to view the Excel workbook.

b. Click the **Employees** worksheet if necessary, and then click anywhere in the Excel table.

c. Click the **Power Pivot** tab, and then, in the Tables group, click **Add to Data Model**.

The Power Pivot window opens, and you see the data from the tblEmployee table added to a worksheet labeled tblEmployee.

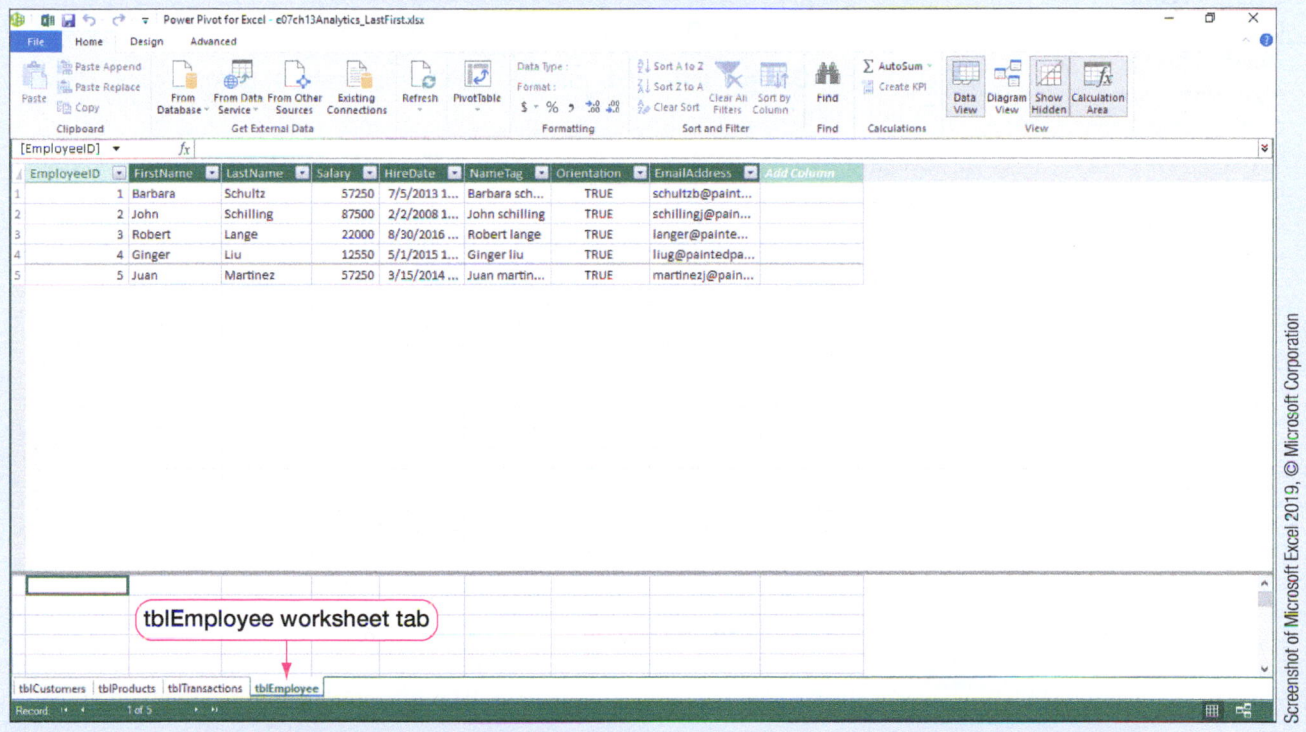

Figure 11 tblEmployee added to the data model

d. **Save** 🖫 the workbook.

Create Advanced Data Models Using Power Pivot

Power Pivot and Excel not only give you the ability to conduct analyses on data from multiple sources but also allow you to do more advanced data modeling in Power Pivot. Power Pivot allows you to create calculated columns and calculated fields and to establish KPIs all within Excel; these can then be used in PivotTables, PivotCharts, and other analysis tools. The data provided in the e07ch13Sales database did not include all the data needed for the various analyses. The managers of the Red Bluff Golf Course & Pro Shop would like you to create additional columns that calculate the revenue, costs, and profit earned from each transaction as well as calculated fields that calculate the total profit earned. You will then use those calculations to create KPIs that will measure each employee's effectiveness in terms of meeting monthly and yearly profit goals.

Creating Relationships in the Data Model

When data is imported from a relational database, only the data that has predefined relationships in the database is imported into the data model. In a business, data can come from multiple sources. For example, a company may keep important information about employee training programs in a separate human resources database. If that data were needed for analysis, it could be imported into the data model, and a relationship could be established to the tblEmployee table.

You added data from the tblEmployee table to the data model, and as of now, this data has no relationship with any of the other tables in the data model. In this exercise, you will create a relationship between the tblEmployee table and the tblTransactions table.

 **E13.07**

SIDE NOTE
Creating Relationships
Alternatively, you can create relationships between objects in Diagram view by dragging fields from one object to another.

To Create Relationships in the Data Model

a. In the Power Pivot window, click the **tblTransactions** worksheet.

b. Click the **EmployeeID** column heading to select the column.

c. Click the **Design** tab, and then, in the Relationships group, click **Create Relationship**.

d. Confirm that tblTransactions is selected in the first box and select **EmployeeID** from the list of columns.

e. Select **tblEmployee** from the second box, and then select **EmployeeID** from the list of columns.

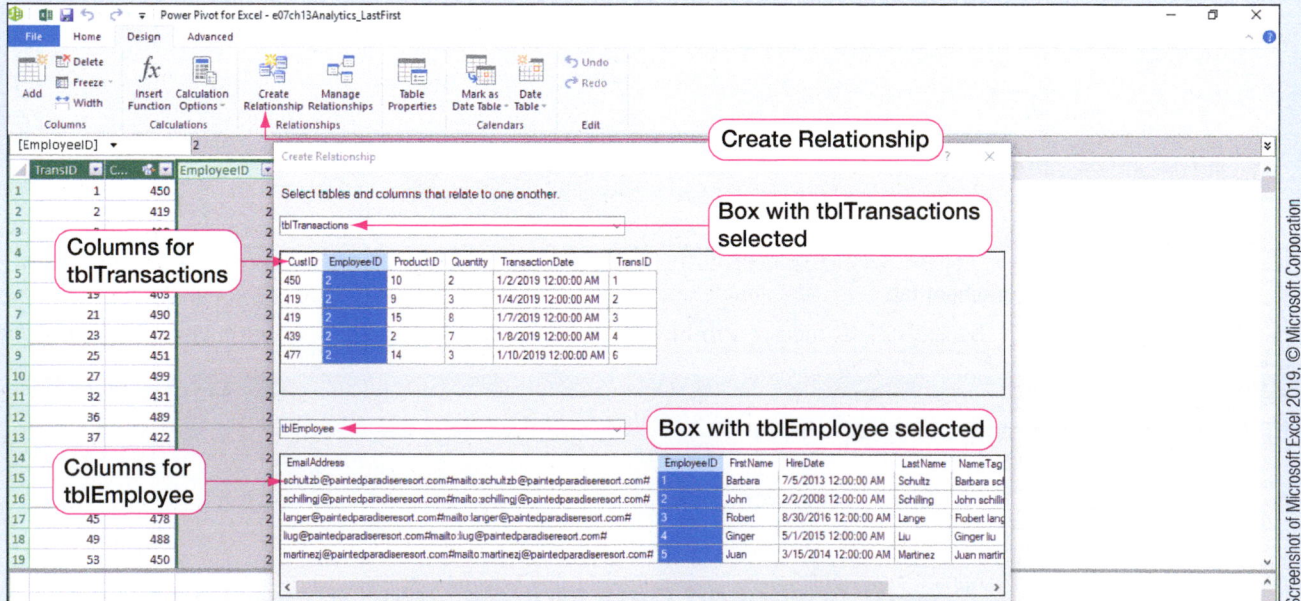

Figure 12 Create Relationship dialog box

f. Click **OK**.

g. Click the **Home** tab, and then, in the View group, click **Diagram View** to see the new relationship.

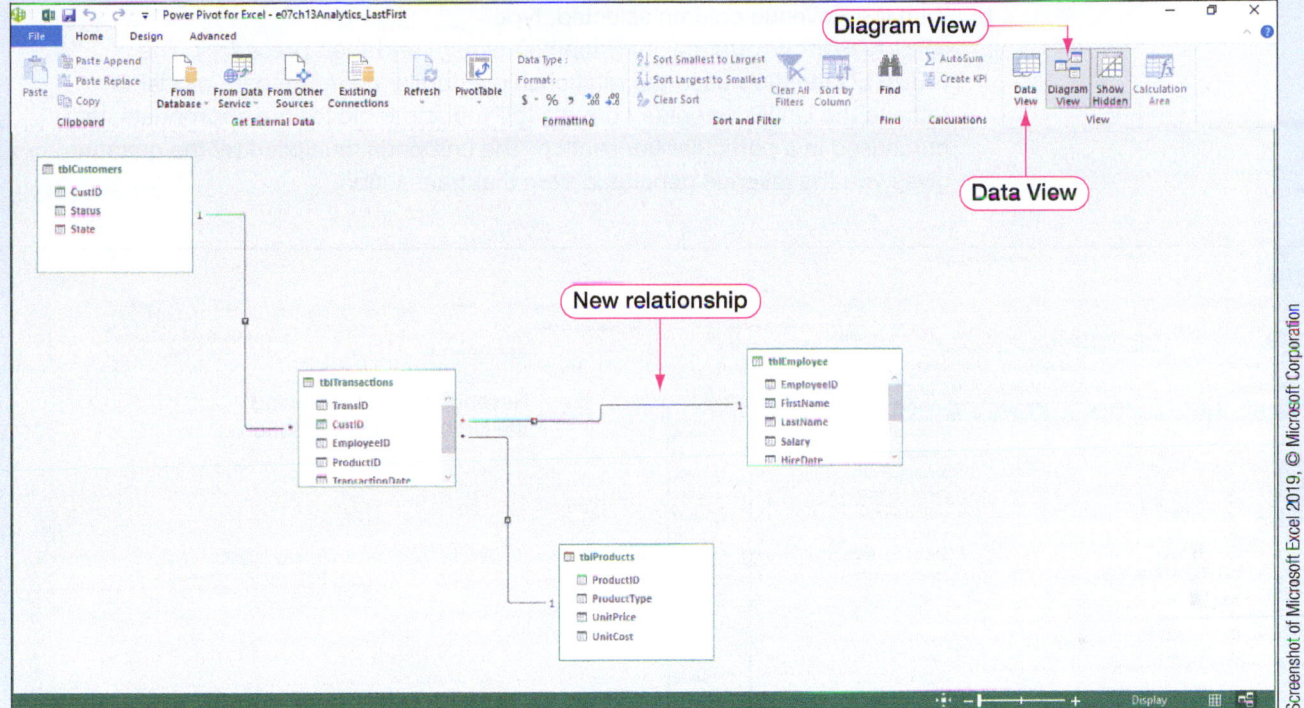

Figure 13   Diagram view with new relationship

h. On the Home tab, and then, in the View group, click **Data View** to return to the Data view of the Power Pivot window.

i. **Save** the workbook.

Adding Calculated Columns in Power Pivot

A calculated column is created inside the Power Pivot window and is based on data that is already a part of the data model. The data imported from the Access database included the quantity of items sold in each transaction along with the cost of the product and the selling price. However, these values exist in different tables. The managers at the Red Bluff Golf Course & Pro Shop would like you to include revenue, costs, and profit in future analyses.

In this exercise, you will create calculated columns for revenue, costs, and profit in the tblTransactions table. To accomplish this, you will use a category of functions called Data Analysis eXpressions (DAX). A DAX function called RELATED is used exclusively inside the Power Pivot window and belongs to, and essentially works the same as, a LOOKUP function. It uses the relationships established in the data model to retrieve a value from a related table to be used in a calculation in another table.

 **E13.08**

To Create a Calculated Column

a. On the tblTransactions worksheet, double-click the **Add Column** column heading, type Revenue as the new column heading, and then press Enter.

b. With the Revenue column selected, type **=RELATED(tblProducts[UnitPrice])*[Quantity]** and then press Enter. The RELATED function uses the relationship established in the data model to retrieve the UnitPrice value from the tblProducts table for the appropriate item purchased in a particular transaction. The unit price multiplied by the quantity gives you the revenue generated from that transaction.

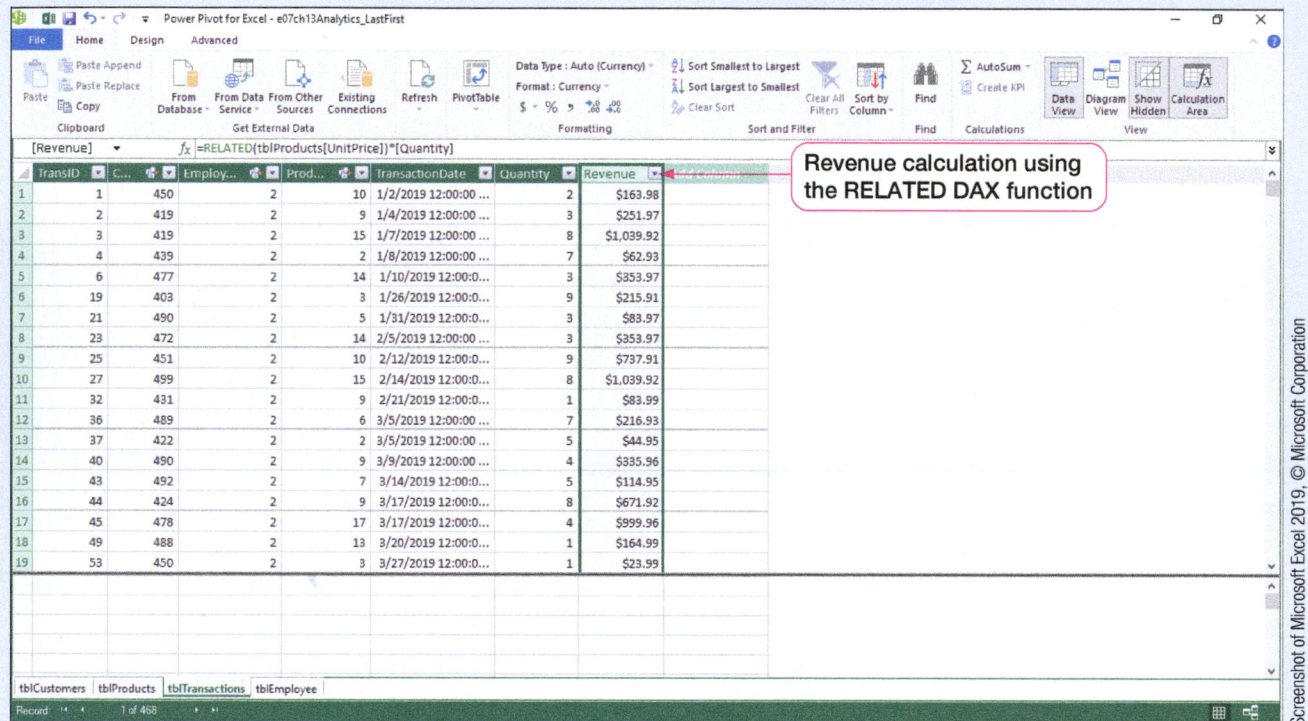

Figure 14 Calculated column of revenue

c. Double-click the next **Add Column** column heading, type Costs as the name for a second calculated column, and then press Enter.

d. With the Costs column selected, type =RELATED(tblProducts[UnitCost])*[Quantity] and then press Enter to calculate the costs associated with each transaction.

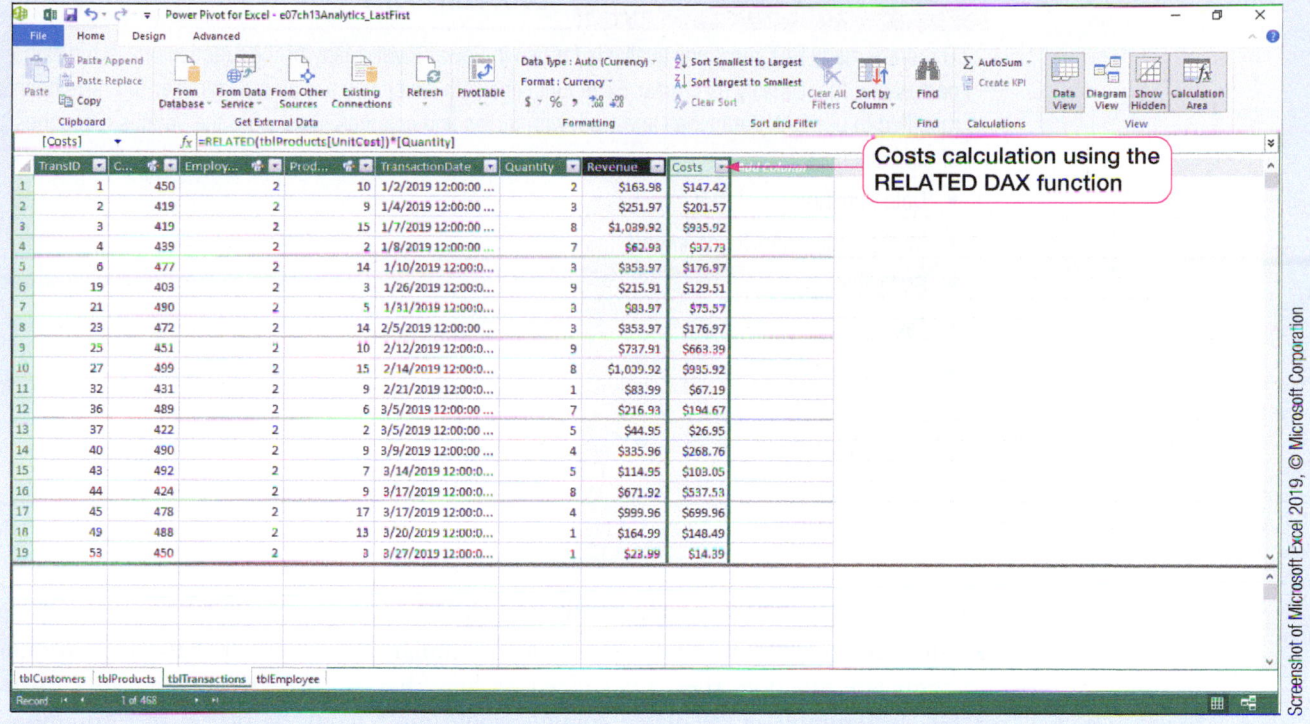

Figure 15 Calculated column of costs

e. Double-click the next **Add Column** column heading, type **Profit** as the name for a third calculated column, and then press [Enter].

f. With the Profit column selected, type **=[Revenue]-[Costs]** to calculate the profit generated from each transaction, and then press [Enter].

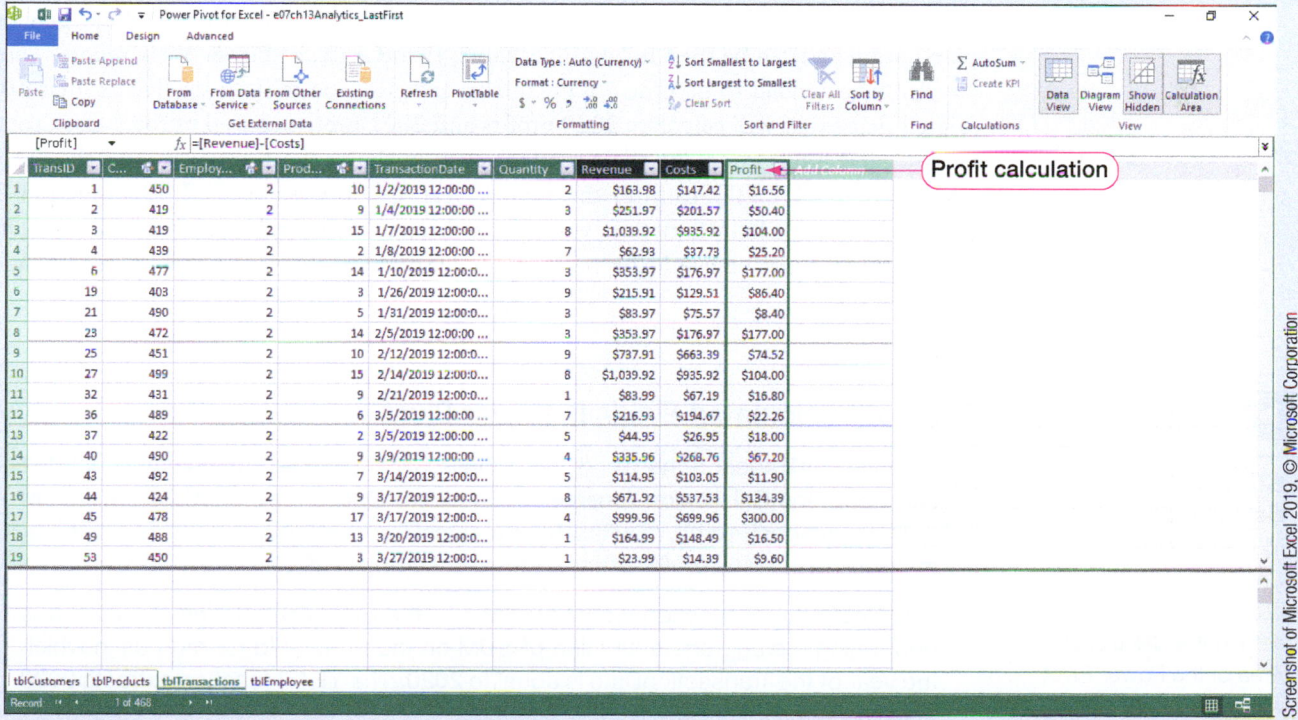

Figure 16 Calculated column for profit

g. **Save** 🔲 the workbook.

QUICK REFERENCE | **DAX Functions**

There are many DAX functions available for use in Power Pivot. Many of the functions have the same names and functionality as regular Excel functions with which you are already familiar but have been modified to use DAX data types and work with tables and columns. Below are the various categories of DAX functions.

- Date and Time
- Mathematical and Trigonometric
- Statistical
- Text
- Logical
- Filter
- Information
- Parent/Child

Adding Calculated Fields in Power Pivot

A calculated column and a calculated field are similar in that both are based on a formula or aggregate function; they differ based on how they are used in analysis. In a Pivot-Table, for example, a calculated column would most likely be placed in a column or row, whereas a calculated field would be placed in the Values area. There are two types of calculated fields, referred to as measures in earlier versions of Power Pivot: implicit and explicit. An **implicit calculated field** is created when you drag a field such as Sales or Quantity Sold into the Values area of a PivotTable. The calculation takes place, but a new calculated field is not being created. Implicit calculated fields can use only standard aggregate functions such as AVERAGE, SUM, COUNT, and MAX. An **explicit calculated field** is created when a formula is typed in the Calculation Area of the Power Pivot window. Explicit calculated fields can use a wide variety of functions beyond general aggregation and can be used in any PivotTable, PivotChart, or Power View report. They can also be extended to become a KPI. In this exercise, you will create five explicit calculated fields that will calculate 2020 profits and 2021 profits as well as total costs, total revenue, and total profits for all individual years in the data set. You will use the DAX function, CALCULATE, to filter the data by year. Using the CALCULATE function in conjunction with a SUM function, you can conditionally sum values in Power Pivot. The CALCULATE function can incorporate multiple filters, such as year, month, region, and employee ID.

 **E13.09**

SIDE NOTE
Calculated Fields in Power Pivot
Calculated fields can be created in any of the cells in the Calculation Area of the Power Pivot window.

To Create Calculated Fields in Power Pivot

a. Click the **tblTransactions** worksheet if necessary, scroll left as needed, click the first cell in the Calculation Area below EmployeeID, and type **=CALCULATE(SUM (tblTransactions[Profit]),YEAR(tblTransactions[TransactionDate])=2020)** Press Enter to calculate the total profit for transactions occurring in 2020.

The CALCULATE function works similarly to the SUMIFS function in Excel. It is performing the aggregate function of SUM on the Profit field for records in which the year of the TransactionDate is equal to 2020. The YEAR function extracts 2020 from the TransactionDate field for filtering.

SIDE NOTE

AutoComplete in Power Pivot

To avoid errors in your Power Pivot functions, use the AutoComplete feature as you type.

Troubleshooting

If the Calculation Area is not visible in the Power Pivot window, on the Home tab, in the View group, click Calculation Area.

b. Change the default name of **Measure 1** to **2020 Profit**

c. On the Home tab, in the Formatting group, click the **Format** arrow, and then select **Currency**.

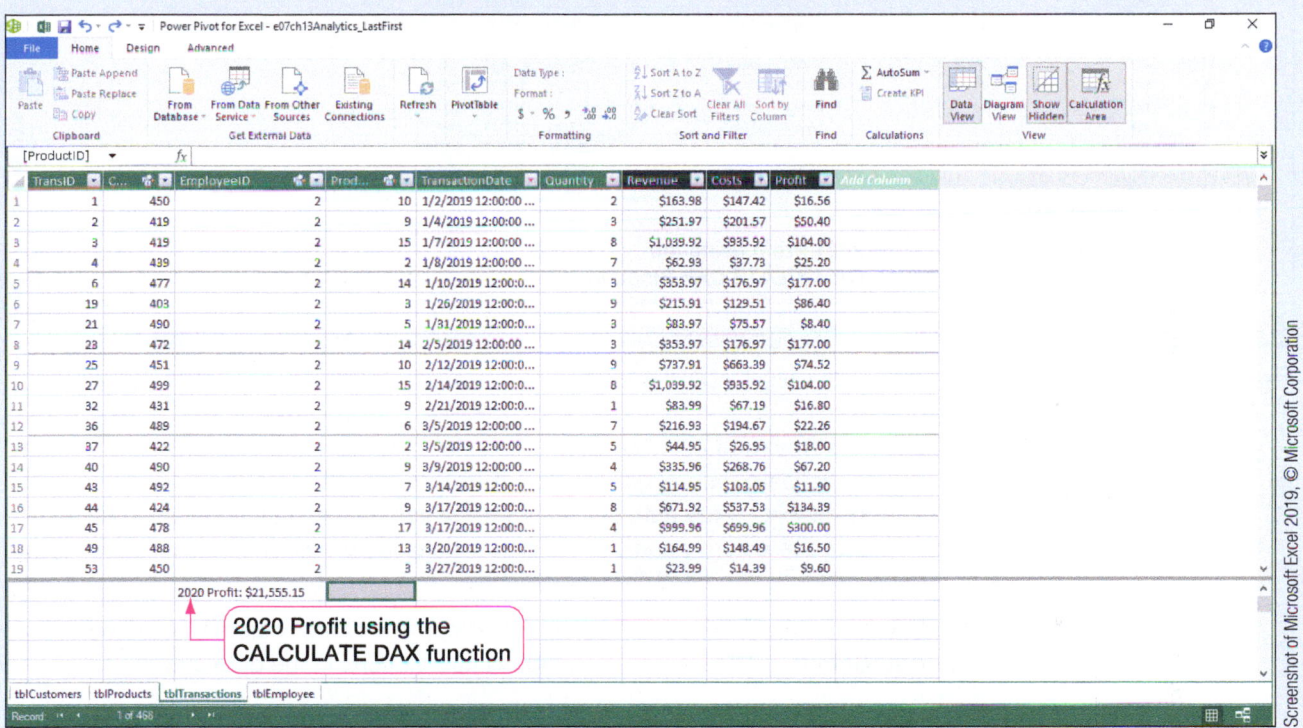

2020 Profit using the CALCULATE DAX function

Figure 17 Calculated field for 2020 profit using CALCULATE

SIDE NOTE

Viewing the Results of the Calculated Field

The results of the calculated field can be viewed by expanding the width of the cell or by pointing to the calculation.

d. Click the cell to the right in the Calculation Area under the ProductID column to create a second calculated field, type **=CALCULATE(SUM(tblTransactions[Profit]), YEAR(tblTransactions[TransactionDate])=2021)** and then press Enter. This will calculate the total profit for transactions occurring in 2021.

e. Change the default name of **Measure 1** to **2021 Profit**

f. On the Home tab, in the Formatting group, click the **Format** arrow, and then select **Currency**.

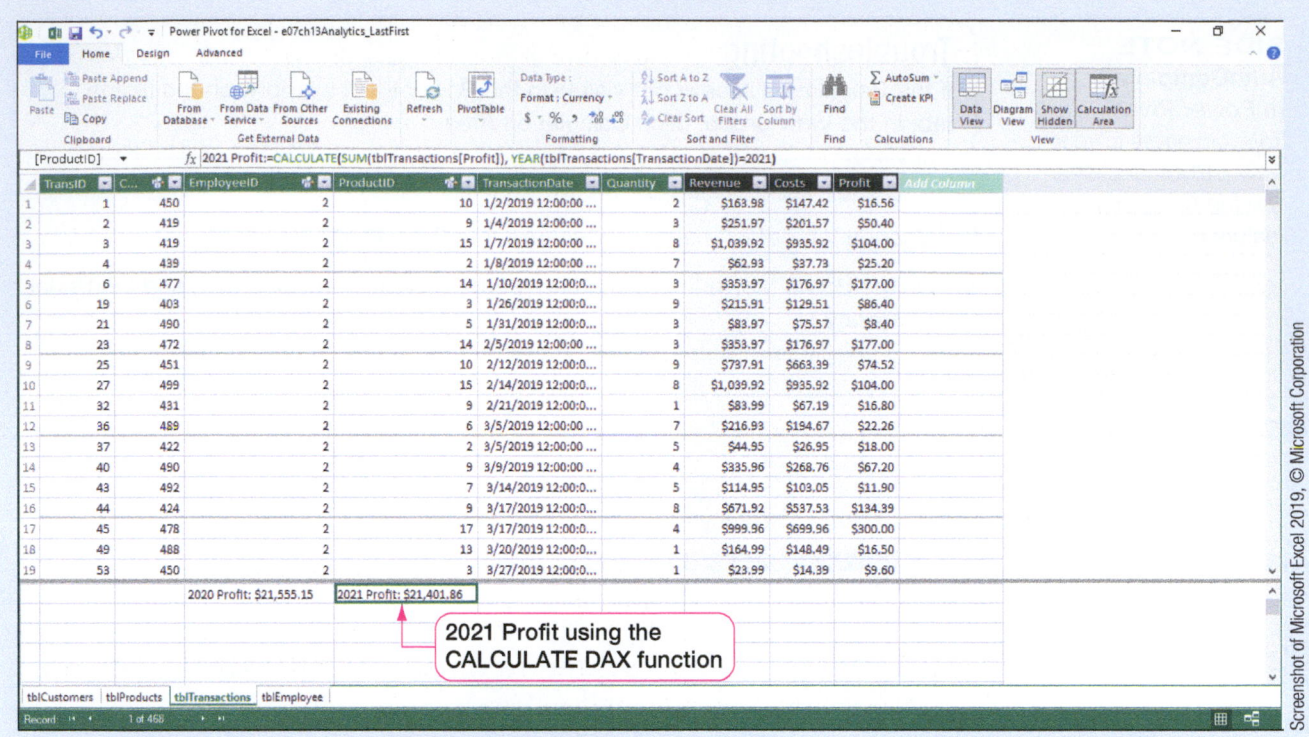

Figure 18 Calculated field for 2021 profit using CALCULATE

g. Click the **Revenue** column heading to select the Revenue column. On the Home tab, in the Calculations group, click **AutoSum** to calculate the total revenue for all transactions in the data set. AutoSum uses the Sum function to add up all the values in the column and places a new calculated field in the Calculation Area below the column, titled Sum of Revenue.

h. Click the **Costs** column heading to select the Costs column, and then click **AutoSum** to calculate total costs for all transactions in the data set.

i. Click the **Profit** column heading to select the Profit column, and then click **AutoSum** to calculate the total profits for all transactions in the data set.

j. **Save** 💾 the workbook.

QUICK REFERENCE	Naming Calculated Fields

There are a few things to consider in naming your calculated fields.

- Choose names that easily identify the calculations they will perform, as they will be visible in all PivotTable and PivotChart field lists.
- Each calculated field should be given a unique name within a table.
- Avoid names that have already been given to calculated columns within the same workbook.

Defining a Key Performance Indicator

Calculated fields can be extended to become KPIs. The managers of the Red Bluff Golf Course & Pro Shop would like you to create some KPIs that will measure employee performance. A KPI in Power Pivot includes the following: base value, target value, and status thresholds. A **base value** is a calculated field that resolves to a value. A base value, for example, can be the calculated field created as an aggregate of 2021 Profit. A **target value** can be either another calculated field that resolves to a value or an absolute value. A target value, for example, can be the aggregate of 2020 Profit or a monthly sales goal that every employee should meet. Finally, a **status threshold** is defined by the range between a high value and low value. In Excel, the status threshold is displayed with a graphic providing a visual indicator of the status of the base value compared to the target value.

KPIs can be positive, negative, or bidirectional. A **positive KPI** is defined when the greater the value, the better the KPI, such as a company's profit. A **negative KPI** is defined when the greater the value, the worse the KPI, such as the number of sick days in a specific time period. A **bidirectional KPI** is defined when the value becomes worse the farther it deviates from the target value in either direction. For example, the temperature for storing a particular product may be a bidirectional KPI; damage could occur if the temperature gets too cold or too hot.

In this exercise, you will define a KPI to help management measure employee performance. The KPI will measure each employee's monthly profit earnings against an absolute target value of $4,000.

REAL WORLD ADVICE	KPIs without Power Pivot

KPIs were a part of business long before Power Pivot became available. If your company is using a previous version of Excel without Power Pivot, you can use Conditional Formatting Icon Sets instead to indicate proximity to various KPI goals.

E13.10

SIDE NOTE

Define Status Thresholds

The low and high threshold values can also be typed directly into the boxes attached to the sliders.

To Create a KPI with an Absolute Target Value

a. On the **tblTransactions** worksheet, in the Calculation Area, click the **Sum of Profit** calculated field.

b. Click the **Home** tab, and then, in the Calculations group, click **Create KPI**.

c. In the Key Performance Indicator (KPI) dialog box, confirm that **Sum of Profit** is selected as the KPI base field (value).

d. Under Define target value, click to select the **Absolute value** button, click in the **Absolute value** box, and then type 4000

e. Under Define status thresholds, click and slide the low value threshold—on the left side of the box—to **2800**. Click and slide the high value—on the right side of the box—to **3800**.

f. Under Select icon style, click to select the second icon style.

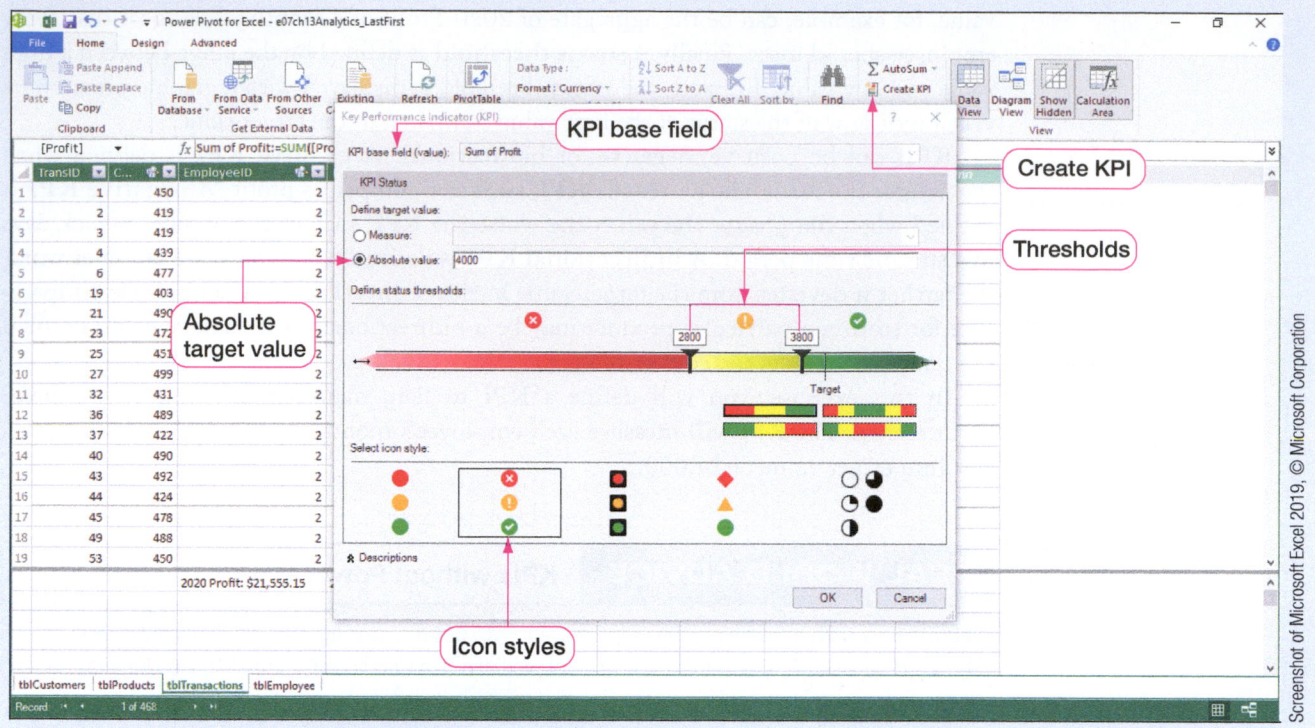

Figure 19 KPI dialog box: Absolute target value

g. Click **OK**. Notice that the **KPI indicator** ▦ is now to the right of the calculated field.

h. **Save** 🖫 the workbook.

Create a KPI Using a Calculated Target Value

The KPI for profit was created by using an absolute value. This value will not change until the KPI itself is edited. To create a more dynamic measure, KPIs can be created by using calculations in the data model. In this exercise, you will create a KPI with a calculated field as the target value. The KPI will measure each employee's 2021 profit earnings against his or her 2020 profit earnings.

 **E13.11**

To Create a KPI with a Calculated Target Value

a. On the **tblTransactions** worksheet, in the Calculation Area, click the **2021 Profit** calculated field.

b. On the **Home** tab, and then, in the Calculations group, click **Create KPI**.

c. In the Key Performance Indicator (KPI) dialog box, confirm that **2021 Profit** is selected as the KPI base field (value).

d. Under Define target value, click the **Measure** arrow, and then select **2020 Profit**.

e. Under Define status thresholds, click and slide the right threshold value to **105%** and the left value to **80%**.

f. Under Select icon style, ensure that the second icon style is selected.

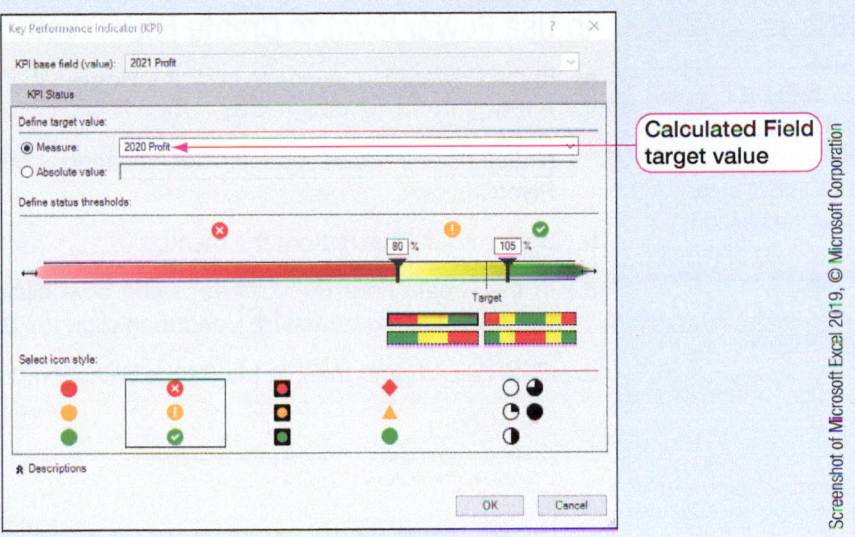

Figure 20 KPI dialog box: calculated target value

g. Click **OK**.

h. **Save** 🖫 the workbook.

Create PivotTables and PivotCharts with Power Pivot

PivotTables and PivotCharts are a major component in any dashboard, and with Excel 2019, they can be created with data from multiple sources without any additional software or add-ins as long as the data is relational data. Having Power Pivot enabled gives you more options than a traditional PivotTable offers. Not only can you create a single Pivot-Table or PivotChart on a worksheet with Power Pivot, but you can also create a PivotTable and PivotChart on the same worksheet as well as two PivotCharts arranged vertically or horizontally or four PivotCharts on the same worksheet. The managers of the Red Bluff Golf Course & Pro Shop want to get a better understanding of the sales data over the past three years. You have been asked to create a simple dashboard consisting of four Pivot-Charts and slicers to be able to easily view different aspects of the sales data. **Slicers** are visual controls that allow you to quickly and easily filter your data in an interactive way. They can be used to replace the filter icons in PivotCharts. Slicers are not compatible with versions of Excel before 2010.

Creating a Simple Sales Dashboard with PivotCharts

The Power Pivot window has options to create multiple PivotCharts on the same work-sheet using data from all connected data sources. This can be an easy way to create a simple dashboard for management to get a better picture of how things in a particular business area are going. In this exercise, you will create dashboard consisting of four PivotCharts.

 **E13.12**

To Use Power Pivot to Create Four PivotCharts

SIDE NOTE
AXIS (CATEGORIES)
Fields placed in the AXIS (CATEGORIES) area make up the horizontal axis (x-axis) of the PivotChart.

a. In the Power Pivot window, click the **Home** tab if necessary. Click the **PivotTable** arrow.

Notice the various options for creating combinations of PivotTables and PivotCharts.

b. Select **Four Charts** from the menu.

c. In the Create Four PivotCharts dialog box, click **Existing Worksheet**, click the **Collapse Dialog** button ⬆, and then click the **SalesDashboard** worksheet.

d. Click cell **A1**, and then, in the Range Selection dialog box, click **OK**.

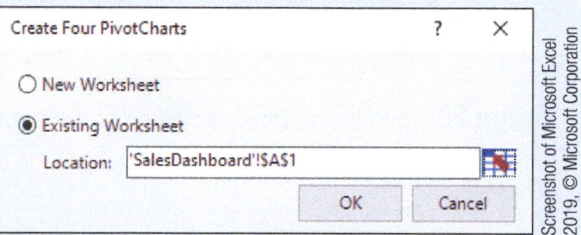

Figure 21   Create Four PivotCharts dialog box

SIDE NOTE
Search for a Field
You can also add fields from the PivotChart Fields pane by typing the name of the field in the Search Bar.

e. Click **OK** again to create the layout for four PivotCharts.

f. Complete the following tasks to create a PivotChart comparing the 2019 costs and the 2019 revenue by month.

- If necessary, click **Chart 1**. In the PivotChart Fields pane, click **tblTransactions** to view the available fields, and then drag the **TransactionDate** field to the **Axis (Categories)** area at the bottom of the PivotChart Fields pane.

  Notice that the TransactionDate field is automatically grouped into Year, Quarter, and Month in addition to showing the individual dates.

- Drag the grouping for **TransactionDate (Year)** to the **Filters** area.

- Remove the grouping for **TransactionDate (Quarter)** by dragging the field out of the Axis (Categories) area and into the worksheet.

- Remove the **TransactionDate** field by dragging the field out of the Axis (Categories) area and into the worksheet.

- If necessary, expand **tblTransactions**. Select the **Revenue** field to add it to the **Values** area.

- If necessary, expand **tblTransactions**. Select the **Costs** field to add it to the **Values** area.

- On the chart, click the **TransactionDate (Year)** filter, expand the options, and then select **2019**. Click **OK**.

- Right-click the **chart**, and then select **Change Chart Type**. In the Change Chart Type dialog box, click **Combo**. In the Choose the chart type and axis for your data series area, for the Sum of Revenue series, click the **Chart Type** arrow, and select **Line**.

- Click **OK**. This combo chart allows you to easily compare the costs and revenue from each month.

- Click the **Analyze** tab, and then, in the PivotChart group, in the Chart Name box, type Sales-Costs-2019 and press Enter to name the chart.

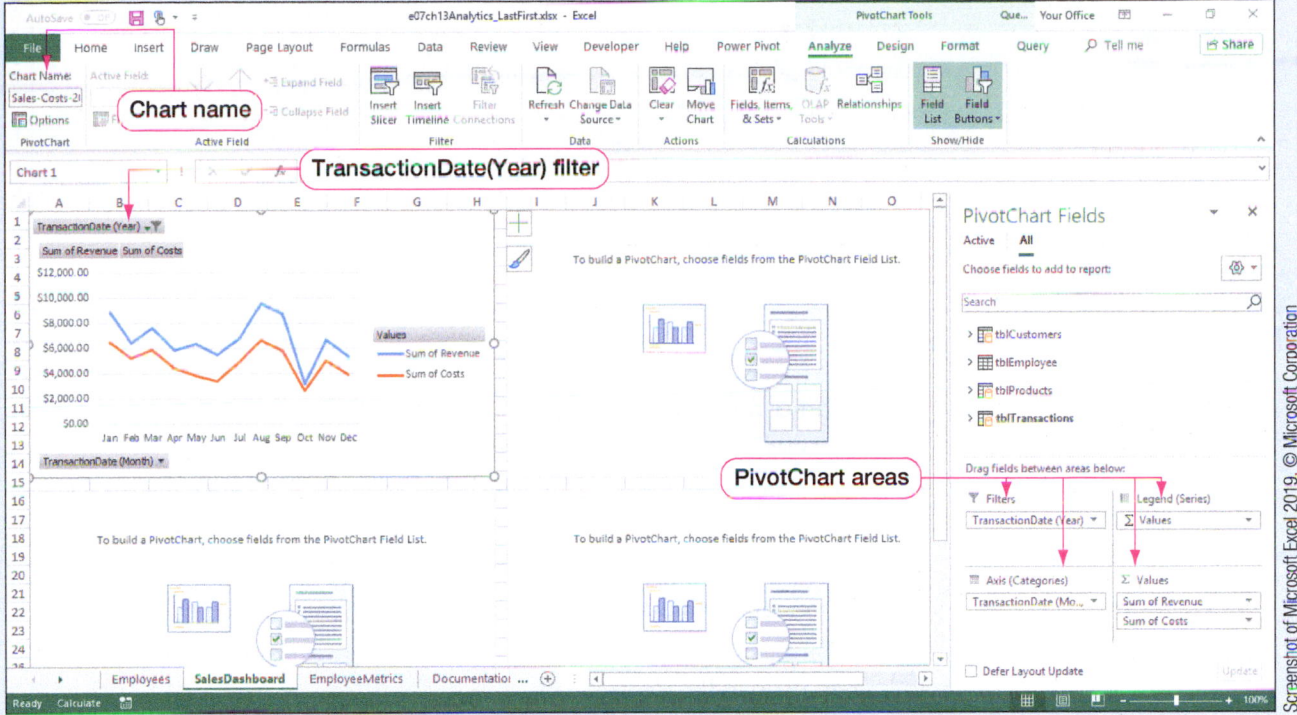

Figure 22   Combo chart for Sales-Costs-2019

g. Click **Chart 2**, the chart below Chart 1, and then complete the following tasks to create a PivotChart comparing the 2020 costs and the 2020 revenue by month.

- If necessary, in the PivotChart Fields pane, click **All** under the PivotChart Fields heading to view all available tables in the data model. Click **tblTransactions** to view the available fields, and then drag the **TransactionDate (Month)** field to the **Axis (Categories)** area.

- Drag the **TransactionDate (Year)** field into the **Filters** area.

- Click to select the **Revenue** check box, and then click to select the **Costs** check box to add the fields to the **Values** area.

- On the chart, click the **TransactionDate (Year)** filter, expand the options, and then select **2020**. Click **OK**.

- Right-click the **chart**, and then select **Change Chart Type**.

- In the Change Chart Type dialog box, click **Combo**, and change the Chart Type of the Sum of Revenue to **Line**. Click **OK**.

- On the Analyze tab, in the PivotChart group, click the **Chart Name** box, and then type Sales-Costs-2020 to name the chart.

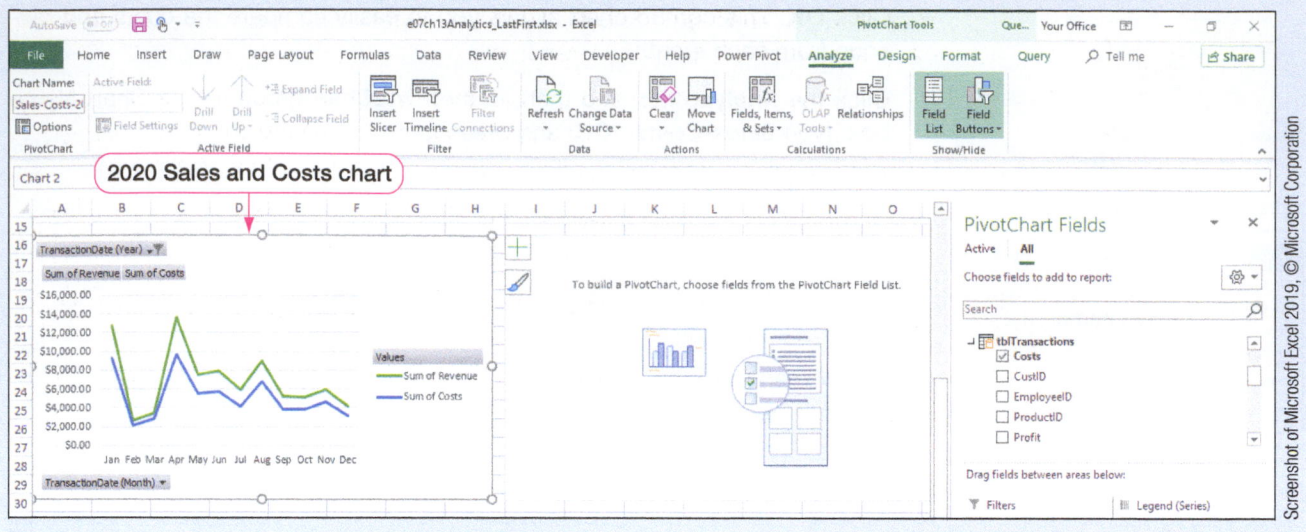

Figure 23 Combo chart for Sales-Costs-2020

h. Click **Chart 3**, and then complete the following tasks to create a PivotChart comparing the 2021 costs and the 2021 revenue by month.

- If necessary, in the PivotChart Fields pane, click **All** under the PivotChart Fields heading to view all available tables in the data model. Click **tblTransactions**, and then drag the **TransactionDate (Month)** field to the **Axis (Categories)** area.

- Drag the **TransactionDate (Year)** field into the **Filters** area.

- Click to select the **Revenue** check box, and then select the **Costs** check box to add them to the **Values** area.

- On the chart click the **TransactionDate (Year)** filter, expand the options, and then select **2021**. Click **OK**.

- Right-click the **chart**, and then select **Change Chart Type**.

- In the Change Chart Type dialog box, click **Combo**, and change the Chart Type of the Sum of Revenue to **Line**. Click **OK**.

- On the Analyze tab, in the PivotChart group, click the **Chart Name** box, and then type Sales-Costs-2021 to name the chart.

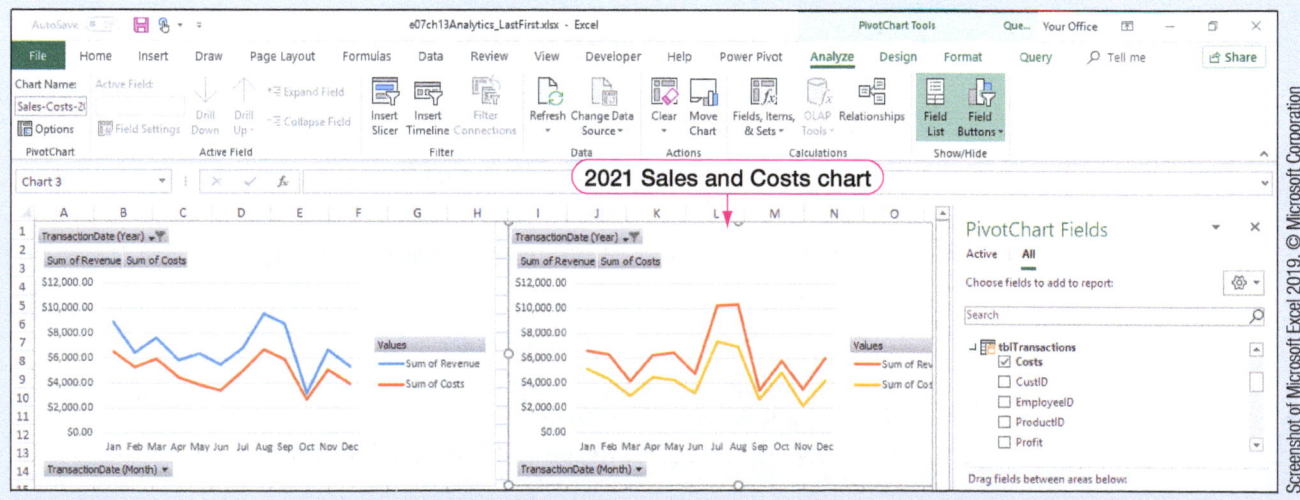

Figure 24 Combo chart for Sales-Costs-2021

i. Click **Chart 4**, and then complete the following tasks to create a PivotChart based on all sales from 2019-2021 by employee.

- In the PivotChart Fields pane, click **All** under the PivotChart Fields heading to view all available tables in the data model. Click **tblEmployee** to view the available fields, and then drag the **LastName** field to the **Axis (Categories)** area.

- Scroll down, click **tblTransactions** to view the available fields, and then select the **Revenue** check box to add it to the **Values** area.

- Right-click the **chart**, select **Change Chart Type**, and then, in the Change Chart Type dialog box, click **Bar**. Click **OK**.

- On the Analyze tab, in the PivotChart group, click the **Chart Name** box, and then type Employee-Sales-2019-2021 to name the chart.

> **Troubleshooting**
>
> Some of the axis values on the charts may be out of place or overlapping. You will improve the formatting of the charts in the next exercise.

j. **Save**  the workbook.

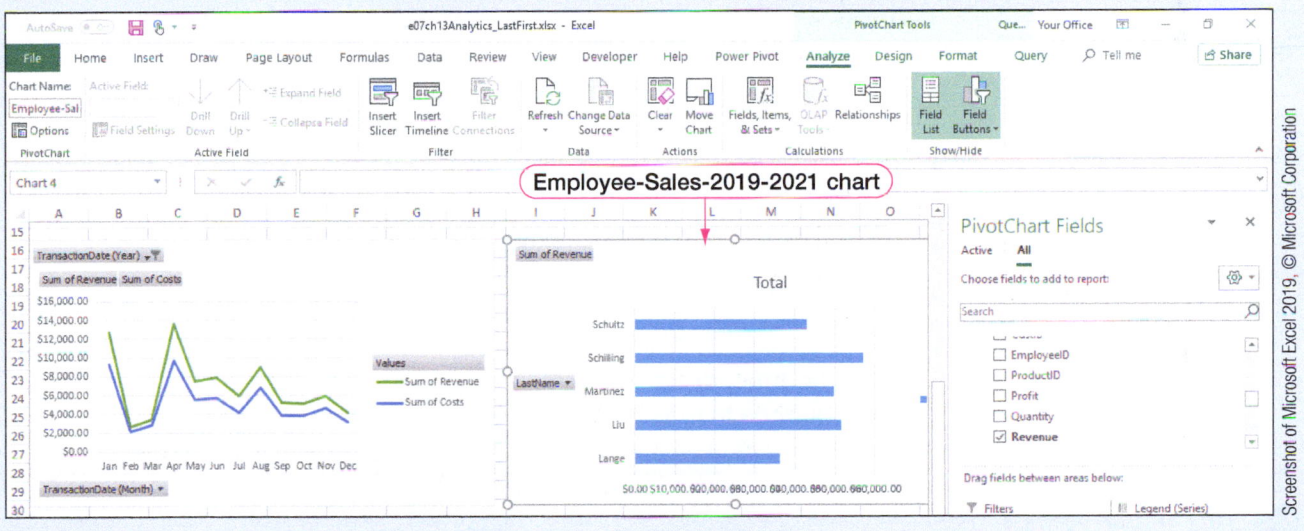

Figure 25 Bar chart for Employee-Sales-2019-2021

Improving Design with Chart Elements and Styles

Dashboards should be visually appealing without being distracting. Some simple and modest modifications to the charts can increase their readability and create a better user experience. In this exercise, you will improve the design of the dashboard by changing the chart titles and modifying other chart elements.

E13.13

To Improve Dashboard Design

a. Click the **Sales-Costs-2019** chart, and then complete the following tasks.

- Click **Chart Elements** ⊞ next to the chart, and then click to select **Chart Title** to add a chart title above the chart.

- Edit **Chart Title** to read 2019 Sales and Costs

- Click **Chart Styles** 🖊 next to the chart, and then select **Style 3** from the Style list. Click **Chart Styles** 🖊 to close the Chart Styles gallery.

- Click the **Analyze** tab if necessary, and then in the Show/Hide group, click **Field Buttons** to hide the filters on the PivotChart.

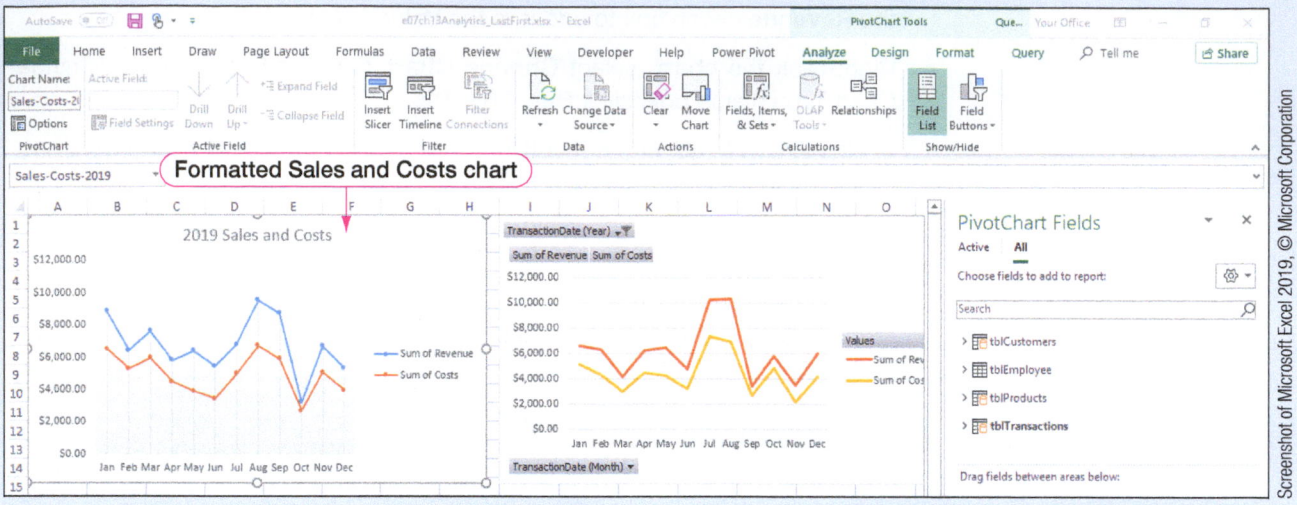

Figure 26 2019 Sales and Costs combo chart formatted

b. Click the **Sales-Costs-2020** chart, and then complete the following tasks.

- Click **Chart Elements** ➕, and then click **Chart Title** to add a chart title above the chart.

- Edit **Chart Title** to read 2020 Sales and Costs

- Click **Chart Styles** 🖊, and then select **Style 3** from the Style list. Click **Chart Styles** 🖊 to close the Chart Styles gallery.

- Click the **Analyze** tab if necessary, and then, in the Show/Hide group, click **Field Buttons** to hide the filters on the PivotChart.

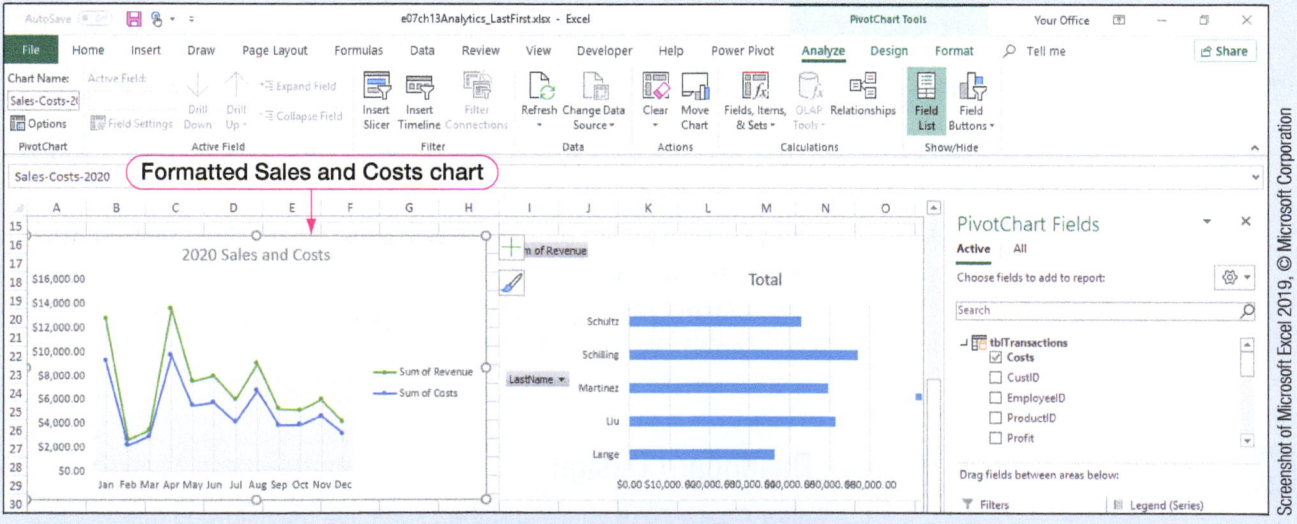

Figure 27 2020 Sales and Costs combo chart formatted

c. Click the **Sales-Costs-2021** chart, and complete the following tasks.

- Click **Chart Elements** ⊞, and then click **Chart Title** to add a chart title above the chart.

- Edit **Chart Title** to read 2021 Sales and Costs

- Click **Chart Styles** 🖌, and then select **Style 3** from the Style list. Click **Chart Styles** 🖌 to close the Chart Styles gallery.

- Click the **Analyze** tab, if necessary, and then, in the Show/Hide group, click **Field Buttons** to hide the filters on the PivotChart.

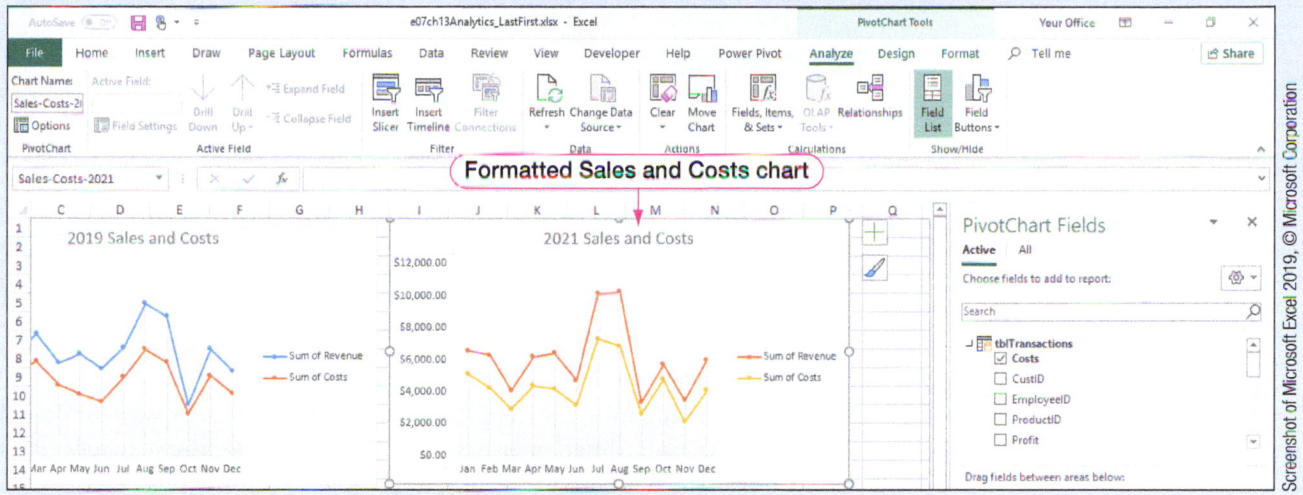

Figure 28   2021 Sales and Costs combo chart formatted

d. Click the **Employee-Sales-2019-2021** chart, and then complete the following tasks.

- Edit **Chart Title** to read 2019-2021 Sales by Employee

- Click the **Format** tab, and then, in the Current Selection group, select **Horizontal (Value) Axis** from the Chart Elements menu. Click **Format Selection**.

- In the Format Axis pane, expand the **Number** section, select **Currency** from the Category list, change the **Decimal places** to 0, and **Close** ⊠ the Format Axis pane.

- Click **Chart Styles** 🖌, and then select **Style 3** from the Style list. Click **Chart Styles** 🖌 to close the Chart Styles gallery.

- Click the **Analyze** tab, and then, in the Show/Hide group, click **Field Buttons** to hide the filters on the PivotChart.

- Click the **chart legend** to select it, and then press Delete .

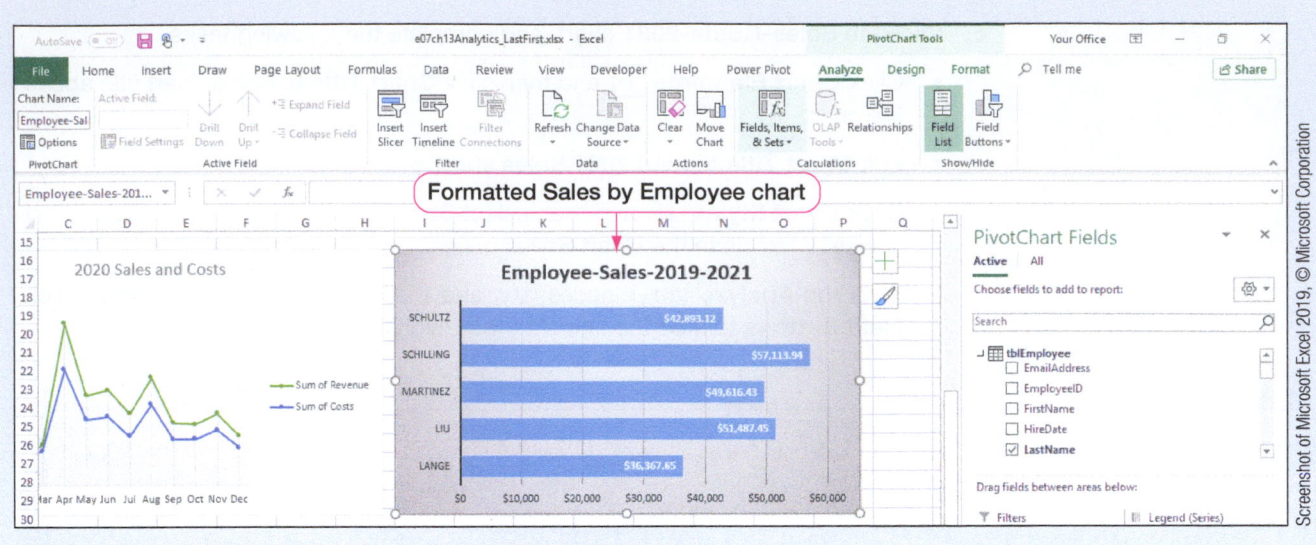

Figure 29 2019–2021 Sales by Employee bar chart formatted

 e. **Save**  the workbook.

Enhancing a Dashboard with Slicers

The current dashboard with four pivot charts lacks an easy and efficient way to filter the sales data to see the data from different perspectives. For example, the managers at the Red Bluff Golf Course & Pro Shop would like to be able to see the sales and costs for particular product categories or type of guest or even by employee. In this exercise, you will be adding slicers to the dashboard.

▶ E13.14   To Add Slicers

 a. Click the **SalesDashboard** worksheet if necessary, and then click the **2019 Sales and Costs** chart.

 b. Click the Analyze tab if necessary, and then, in the Filter group, click **Insert Slicer**.

 c. In the Insert Slicers dialog box, click the **All** tab.

 d. Scroll to the **tblCustomers** table, and if necessary, expand to view the table fields. Click to select the **Status** check box.

 e. Scroll to the **tblEmployee** table, and if necessary, expand to view the table fields. Click to select the **LastName** check box.

 f. Scroll to the **tblProducts** table, and if necessary, expand to view the table fields. Click to select the **ProductType** check box.

 g. Click **OK** to create a slicer for each of the checked boxes.

 h. If necessary, click the **ProductType** slicer to select it. On the Options tab, in the Slicer group, click **Report Connections**.

 i. In the Report Connections dialog box, confirm that **Sales-Costs-2019** is checked, and then click **Sales-Costs-2020**, **Sales-Costs-2021**, and **Employee-Sales-2019-2021** to connect the ProductType slicer to all the charts.

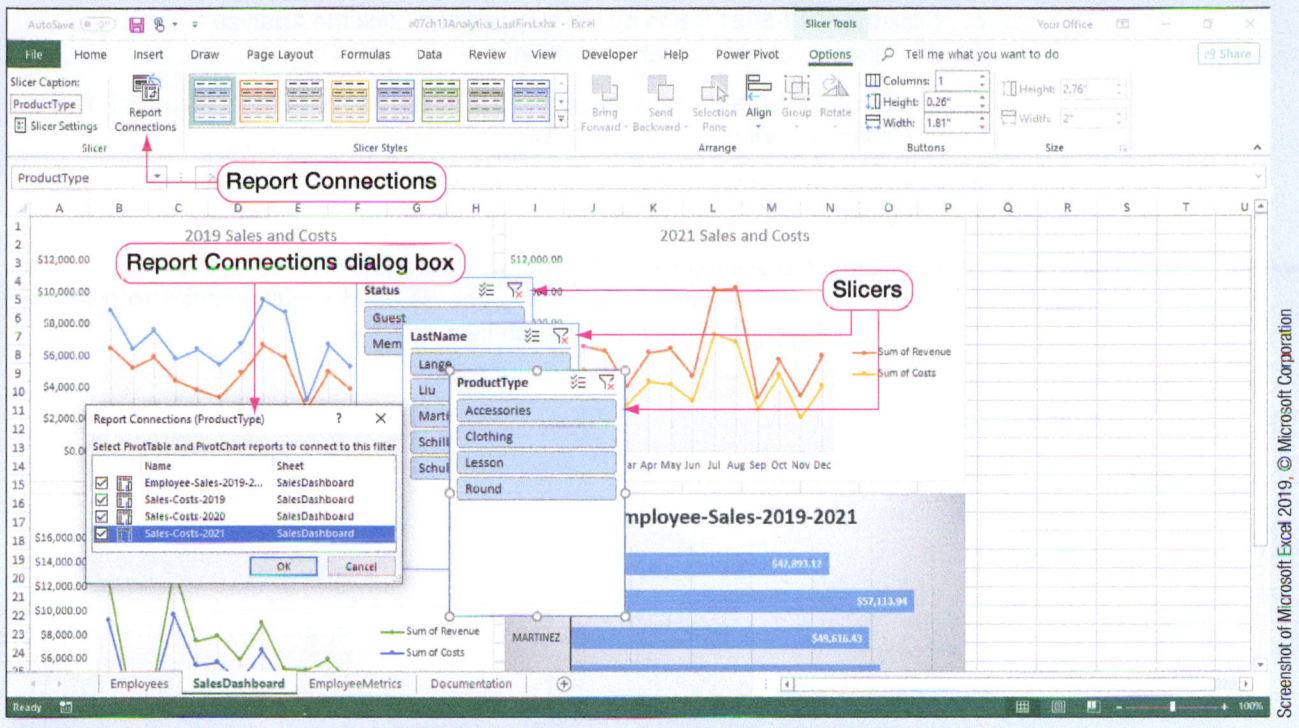

Figure 30 Report Connections (ProductType) dialog box

j. Click **OK**.

k. Repeat steps h–j for the LastName and Status slicers.

l. Reposition the right side of the **2021 Sales and Costs** and **2019-2021 Sales by Employee** charts at the right edge of column **S** to make room for the slicers.

m. Reposition and resize the **slicers** to fit between the charts within columns I through K.

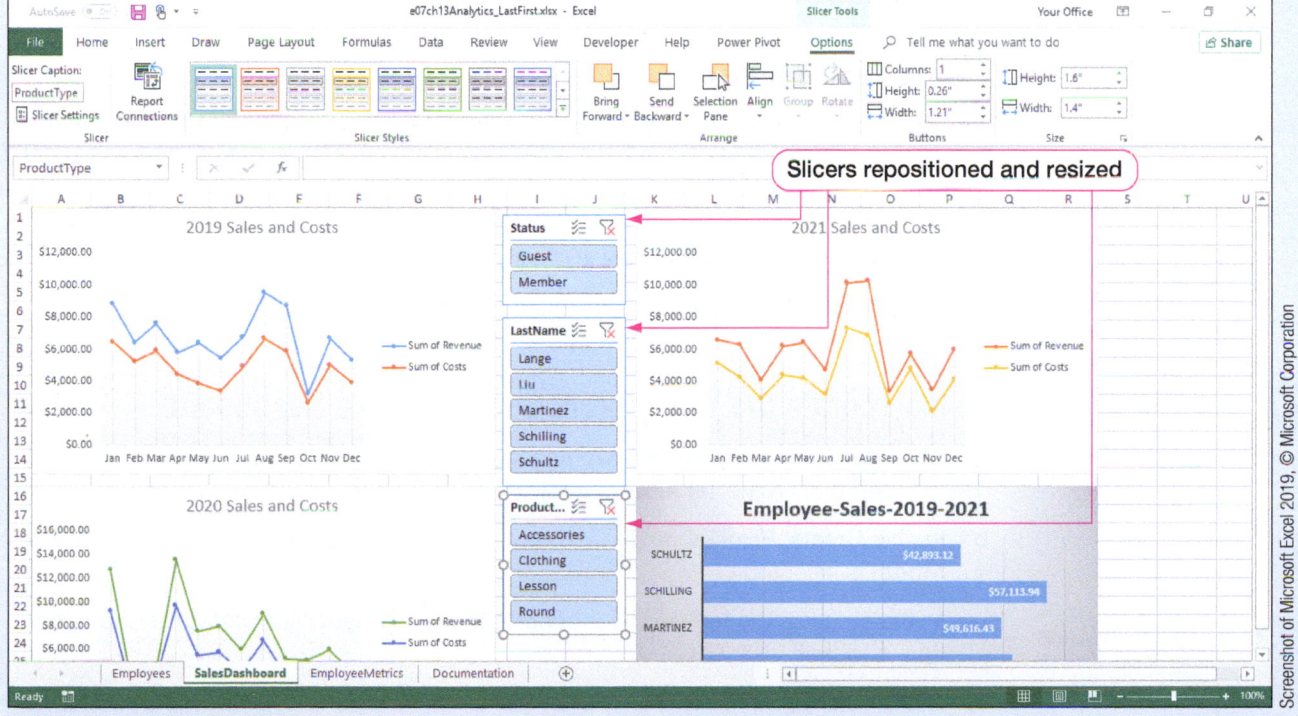

Figure 31 SalesDashboard with Status, LastName, and ProductType slicers

n.   Click the **2019-2021 Sales by Employee** chart, click the **Analyze** tab, and then, in the Filter group, click **Insert Timeline**.

o.   Click to select the tblTransactions field **TransactionDate**, and then click **OK** to add a timeline slicer to the dashboard.

p.   Resize and reposition the **slicer** to the right of the 2019-2021 Sales by Employee bar chart.

Notice that the Sales Dashboard now has easy and effective ways to filter the data displayed in the charts. Multiple fields can be used simultaneously to filter the data by holding Ctrl while clicking each field.

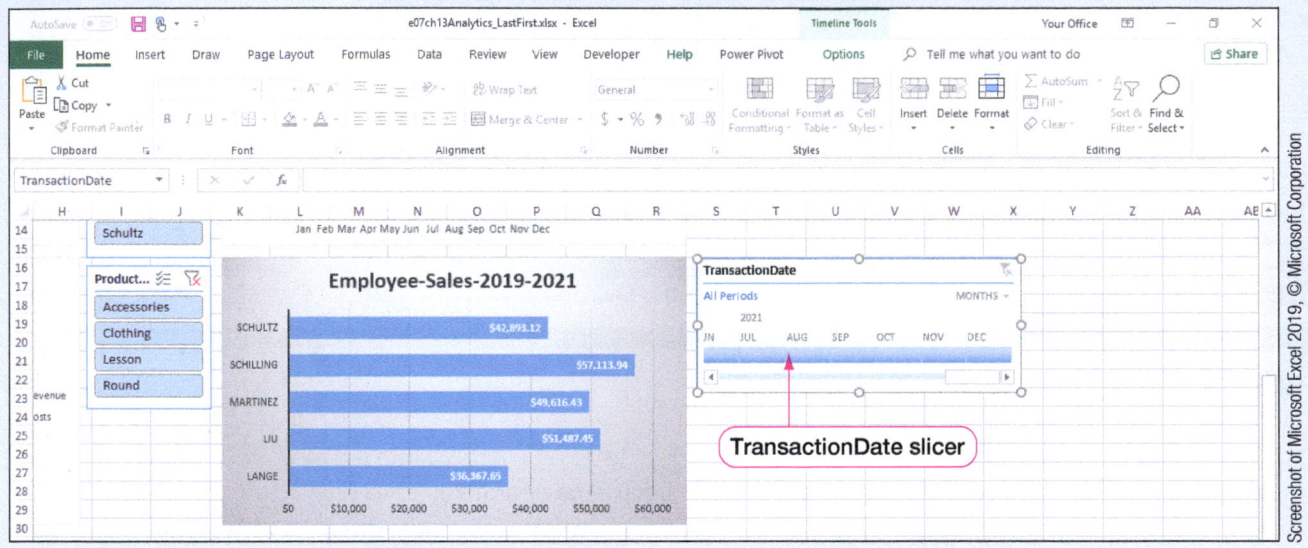

Figure 32   SalesDashboard with timeline slicer

q.   **Save**  the workbook.

Incorporating KPIs into a Dashboard

In earlier exercises, you created two KPIs. One KPI measures profit earnings to an absolute target value of $4,000, and the other compares 2021 profit earnings against 2020 profit earnings. These KPIs can be incorporated into PivotTables with additional values and/or filters.

In this exercise, you will create another dashboard displaying the profit goal KPI and additional analysis.

E13.15

To Incorporate the Yearly Profit Goal KPI into a Dashboard

a.   Click the **EmployeeMetrics** worksheet, and then click cell **A1**. Click the **Insert** tab, and then in the Tables group, click **PivotTable** to create a PivotTable.

b.   In the Create PivotTable dialog box, ensure that **Use this workbook's Data Model** is selected.

c.   In the Existing Worksheet field, confirm that **EmployeeMetrics! A1** is the Location, and then click **OK**.

d.   In the PivotTable Fields pane, click **All**. Click to expand the **tblEmployee** table, and then drag the **LastName** field to the Rows area.

e. Scroll down to **tblTransactions**, and then drag the **TransactionDate (Year)** field to the Rows area, below LastName.

f. Click to select **Profit** and add the field to the Values area. If necessary, click to expand the **tblTransactions** table. Click the **Sum of Profit KPI** to expand it, and then select **Status** to add the KPI status threshold symbols to the PivotTable.

Notice that both Lange and Schilling fell below the bottom threshold value of $2,800 in one of the years.

g. Make the following changes to the PivotTable.

- Click cell **A1**, and then edit Row Labels to read Employee by Year

- Click cell **A1** again if necessary. Click the **Home** tab, and then, in the Alignment group, click **Wrap Text** to wrap the new label in cell A1.

- Click cell **B1**, and then edit **Sum of Profit** to read Yearly Profit

- Click cell **C1**, and then edit **Sum of Profit Status** to read $4,000 Goal Status

- Adjust the width of columns **A**, **B**, and **C** to automatically fit to their contents.

- Click the **Analyze** tab, and then, in the PivotTable group, change the PivotTable Name to Profits-2019-2021

h. Close the **PivotTable Fields** pane.

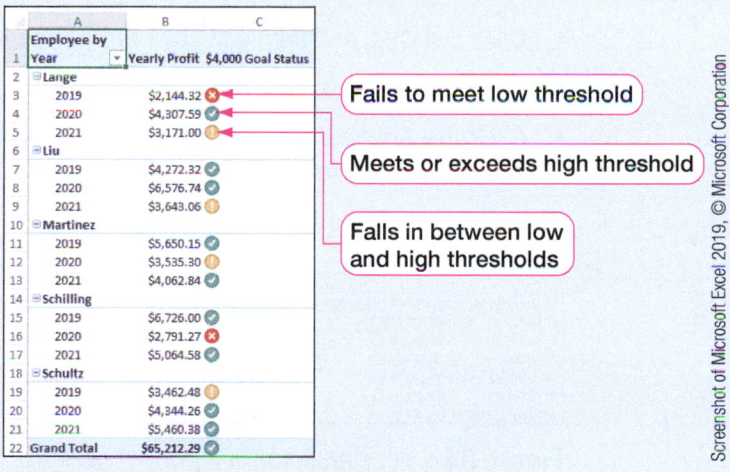

Figure 33 Yearly Profit KPI in a PivotTable

i. **Save** the workbook.

Incorporating KPI Values and Status Fields into a PivotTable

The status field of a KPI from the data model displays icons in the PivotTable. The value calculated by the KPI can also be displayed in a PivotTable, using the status field of the KPI. You have been asked to create a PivotTable that uses the 2021 profit KPI to measure employee performance. In this exercise, you will incorporate the KPI in a PivotTable that displays employees' 2021 profits.

 **E13.16**

To Incorporate the 2021 Profit KPI into a Dashboard

a. On the EmployeeMetrics worksheet, click cell **A24**.

b. Click the **Insert** tab, and then, in the Tables group, click **PivotTable**.

c. In the Create PivotTable dialog box, ensure that **Use this workbook's Data Model** is selected.

d. In the Existing Worksheet field, confirm that **EmployeeMetrics! A24** is the Location, and then click **OK**.

e. In the PivotTable Fields pane, click **All**. Click to expand **tblEmployee**, and then drag the **LastName** field to the Rows area.

f. Scroll down and click to expand **tblTransactions**, expand the **2021 Profit KPI**, and then click **Value (2021 Profit)** to add the calculated field to the Values area.

g. Click **Status** to add the KPI status threshold symbols to the PivotTable.

Notice that employees Lang and Liu fell below the lowest threshold of 80% of 2020 profits and the remaining three employees met or exceeded the highest threshold value of 105% of 2021 profits. The total profits for 2021 fell within 80% and 105% of the 2020 profits.

h. Make the following changes to the PivotTable.

- Click cell **A24**, and then edit Row Labels to read Employees

- Click cell **C24**, and then edit 2021 Profit Status to read % of 2020 Goal

- Adjust the width of columns **A**, **B**, and **C** to automatically fit to their contents.

- Click the **Analyze** tab, and then, in the PivotTable group, change the PivotTable Name to Profits-2021

i. Close the **PivotTable Fields** pane.

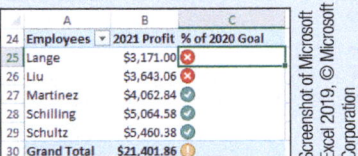

Figure 34   2021 Profit KPI in a PivotTable

j. **Save** 🖫 the workbook.

Incorporating KPIs into PivotCharts

In previous exercises, you added KPIs into PivotTables for analysis on a dashboard. KPIs can also be incorporated into PivotCharts created from the data model. In this exercise, you will incorporate the Sum of Profit KPI into a chart to add a visualization that shows how each employee's yearly profits compare to the goal.

 **E13.17**

To Incorporate the KPI Goal into a Combo Chart

a. Click on the **EmployeeMetrics** worksheet, and then click cell **D1**. Click the **Insert** tab, and then, in the Charts group, click **PivotChart**.

b. In the Create PivotChart dialog box, ensure that **Use this workbook's Data Model** is selected.

c. In the Existing Worksheet field, confirm that **EmployeeMetrics! D1** is the Location, and then click **OK**.

d. In the PivotChart Fields pane, click **All**. Click to expand **tblEmployee**, and then drag the **LastName** field to the Axis (Categories) area.

e. Scroll down, click **tblTransactions**, and then drag the **TransactionDate (Year)** field to the Axis (Categories) area below LastName.

f. Click **Profit** to add the calculated field to the Values area.

g. Click the **Sum of Profit KPI** to expand it, and then click **Goal** to add the KPI target value to the Values area.

h. Right-click the **chart object**, and then select **Change Chart Type**.

i. In the Change Chart Type dialog box, click **Combo**.

Notice the line chart in which the yearly profit goal of $4,000 appears as a line across the chart.

j. Click **OK**.

k. Make the following changes to the chart:

- Click **Chart Elements** ⊞, and then click **Chart Title** to add a chart title above the chart.

- Edit **Chart Title** to read 2019-2021 Profit Goals

- Click the **Format** tab, and then, in the Current Selection group, select **Series "Sum of Profit"** from the Chart Elements list.

- In the Current Selection group, click **Format Selection**. In the Format Data Series pane, adjust the Gap Width to 100%. **Close** ⊠ the Format Data Series pane.

- Click the **Chart Styles** ✎ next to the chart, and then select **Style 8** from the Style list. Click **Chart Styles** ✎ to close the gallery.

- Click the **Analyze** tab, and then, in the PivotChart group, edit **Chart Name** to read Profit-2019-2021

- On the Analyze tab, in the Show/Hide group, click **Field Buttons** to hide all filters.

- Reposition the chart to fit within the cell range **D4:K18**.

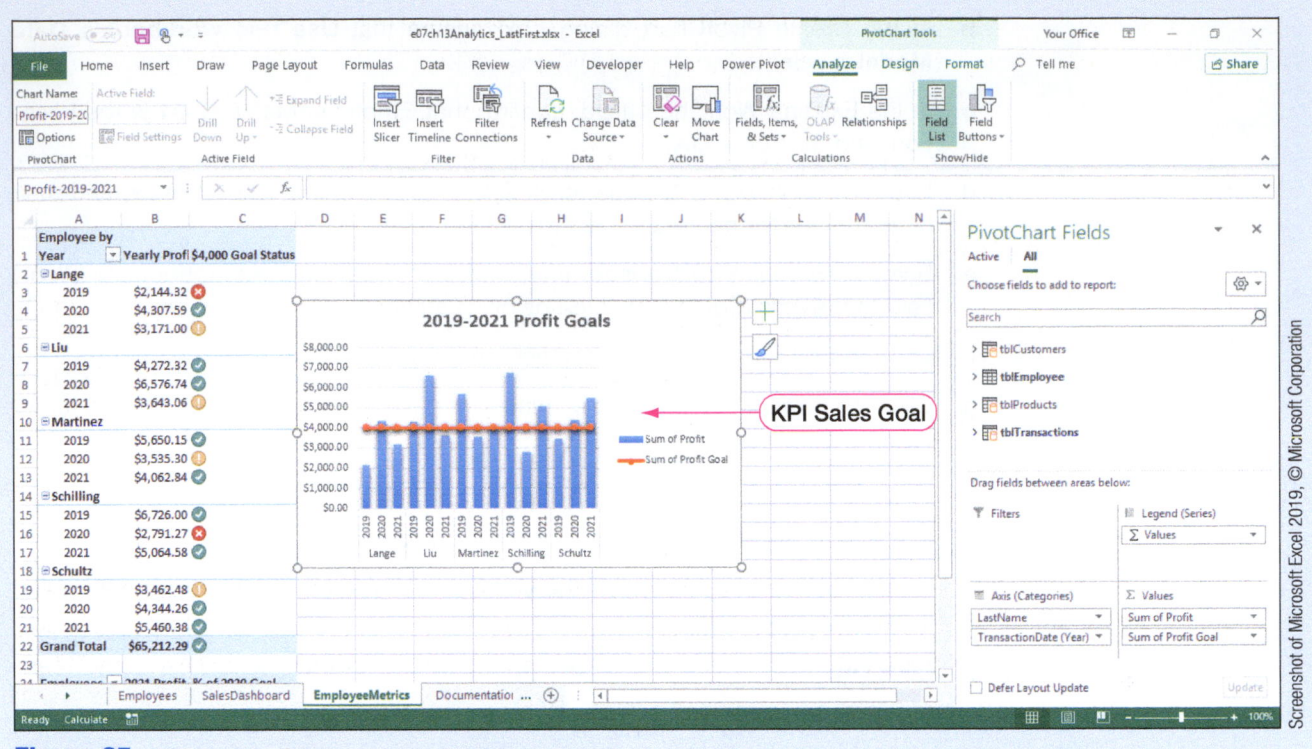

Figure 35 KPI goal added to combo chart

    l. **Save** 🖫 the workbook.

Creating PivotTables with Sparklines

Another common method of representing data graphically for dashboards created in Excel is to use sparklines. **Sparklines** are miniature charts that provide a way to graphically summarize a row or column of data in a single cell. There are three different types of sparklines: line, column, and win/loss. The managers of the Red Bluff Golf Course & Pro Shop feel that they would benefit from comparing trends in sales revenue from each sales representative. In this exercise, you will create a PivotTable and add sparklines that illustrate the trend over each month of 2021 for each sales representative.

 **E13.18**

To Add Sparklines to a PivotTable

    a. Click the **EmployeeMetrics** worksheet, and then click cell **A34**. Click the **Insert** tab, and then, in the Tables group, click **PivotTable** to insert another PivotTable into the Dashboard.

    b. In the Create PivotTable dialog box, ensure that **Use this workbook's Data Model** is selected.

    c. In the Existing Worksheet field, confirm that **EmployeeMetrics! A34** is the Location, and then click **OK**.

    d. In the PivotTable Fields pane, click **All**. Click to expand **tblEmployee**, and then drag the **LastName** field to the Rows area.

    e. Scroll down, click **tblTransactions**, drag **TransactionDate (Year)** to the Filters area, and then drag the **TransactionDate (Month)** field to the Columns area.

f. Click to select **Revenue** and add the calculated field to the Values area.

g. Make the following changes to the PivotTable.

- Click the **TransactionDate (Year)** report filter, and select **2021**. Click OK.

- Click cell **A34**, and then edit Sum of Revenue to read 2021 Monthly Revenue

- Click cell **B34**, and then edit Column Labels to read Months

- Click cell **A35**, and then edit Row Labels to read Employees

- Click the **Design** tab, and then, in the Layout group, click **Grand Totals**. Select **On for Columns Only**.

- Adjust the width of columns A through M to automatically fit to the contents.

- Click the **Analyze** tab, in the PivotTable group, edit **PivotTable Name** to Revenues-2021Trends

h. Click cell **N35**, type 2021 Trends as a column heading for the sparklines, and then press Enter.

i. Click cell **N36**. Click the **Insert** tab, and then, in the Sparklines group, click **Line**.

j. In the Create Sparklines dialog box, in the Data Range box, select the cell range **B36:M40**. In the Location Range box, select the cell range **N36:N40**, and then click **OK**.

k. Click the **Design** tab, and then, in the Show group, select the check boxes for **High Point** and **Low Point** to highlight the lowest and highest monthly profits for each employee.

l. Select the cell range **M34:M35**. Click the **Home** tab, and then, in the Clipboard group, click **Format Painter** to copy the formatting of the selected cells. Select the cell range **N34:N35** to paste the formatting to the selected cells.

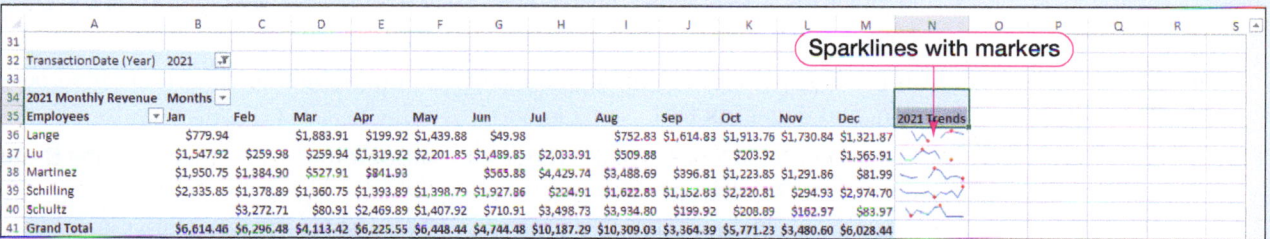

Figure 36   EmployeeMetrics dashboard with PivotTable and Sparklines

Screenshot of Microsoft Excel 2019, © Microsoft Corporation

m. **Save** the workbook.

Use Map Charts for Data Visualizations

Updates to Excel through Office 365 have included a variety of new chart types. One of these new chart types is the Map Chart. Previously map charts were only available in Excel through Add-ins from the Office Store or other third-party providers. The Office Store has many useful add-ins available, including a category of Map visualizations. Many of the add-ins are free to try but can be purchased for additional functionality.

The ability to visualize data based on geographical data is a powerful analysis tool. Being able to visualize your customer base, store locations, or shipping routes through a map visual can lead to many useful insights. The easiest method of organizing data for a Map Chart is to use a PivotTable. However, certain types of charts in Excel are not compatible with PivotTables, including Map Charts. Table 1 illustrates which chart types can be created with PivotCharts. Fortunately, there is an easy method for overcoming this that converts a PivotTable to formulas.

The advantage to this is that the layout of the cells containing the resulting functions is more flexible than it is with PivotTables. The functions can also continue to retrieve updates from the data model and can be connected to multiple slicers. The functions are also compatible with all Excel chart types, if the data is correctly organized. The disadvantage is that the cells no longer contain the interactivity that PivotTables offer in terms of sorting, filtering, expanding, or collapsing data.

Chart Creation	Chart Type
Chart types that can be created from PivotTable data	Line, Pie, Bar, Area, Surface, Radar, Combo
Chart types that cannot be created from PivotTable data	Scatter, Map, Stock, Treemap, Sunburst, Histogram, Box & Whisker, Waterfall, and Funnel.

Table 1   Chart Types That Can Be Created with PivotCharts

Incorporating Bing Maps Visualization

Red Bluff Golf Course & Pro Shop tracks some demographic information about its customers, including their home states. In this exercise, you will incorporate state and revenue data from the data model and chart it by using the Map Chart type.

To Use the Map Chart

a. Click the **EmployeeMetrics** worksheet, and then click cell **L8**. Click the **Insert** tab, and then, in the Tables group, click **PivotTable** to insert another PivotTable into the dashboard.

b. In the Create PivotTable dialog box, ensure that **Use this workbook's Data Model** is selected.

c. In the Existing Worksheet field, confirm that **EmployeeMetrics! L8** is the Location, and then click **OK**.

d. In the PivotTable Fields list, scroll down to **tblCustomers**, and then drag the **State** field to the Rows area.

e. Scroll down to **tblTransactions** and then select **Revenue** to add it to the Values area.

f. Make the following changes to the PivotTable.

- Click cell **L8**, and then edit **Row Labels** to read State

- Click the **Design** tab, and then, in the Layout group, click **Grand Totals**. Select **Off for Rows and Columns**.

- Click the **Analyze** tab, in the Filter group, click **Insert Timeline**. Click **TransactionDate** and click **OK**. Click **Months** and select **Years**.

- Move the timeline so that the upper left corner is located in cell **L1** and adjust the size of the timeline as need to fit it between the top of the worksheet and the PivotTable.

g. Click cell **L8**. Click the **Analyze** tab, and in the Calculations group, click **OLAP Tools**, and then click **Convert to Formulas**. The PivotTable has been converted to formulas which are still linked to the timeline slicer.

h. Click the **Insert** tab, and then, in the Charts group, click **Maps** 🌐 and select **Filled Map** . If necessary, click **Accept** to the message asking to send data to Bing.

SIDE NOTE
More Add-Ins
Clicking the Store icon will open a window that will allow you to explore additional add-ins for Excel.

i. Position the upper left corner of the chart to begin in cell **L8**.

j. Edit **Chart Title** to read Annual Revenue by State

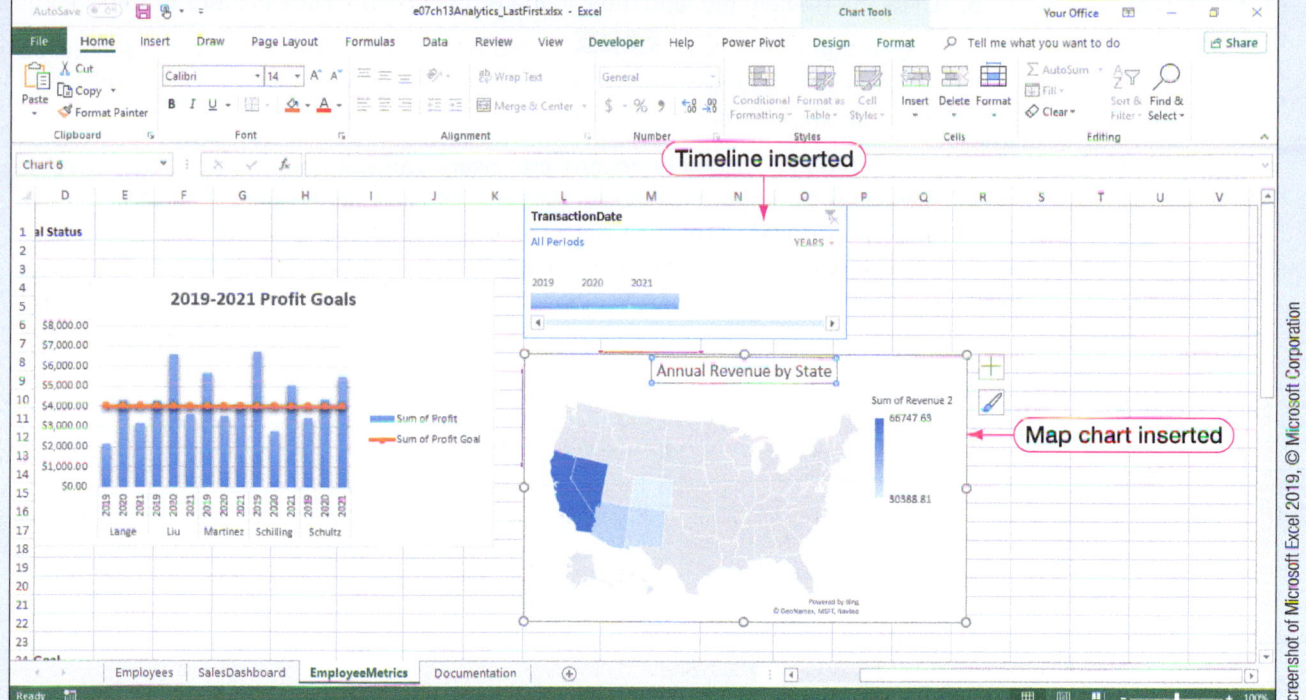

Figure 37 Map chart inserted

k. **Save** 🖫 the workbook.

REAL WORLD ADVICE | **Using PivotTable to Chart Data**

Organizing data for a Treemap or Box & Whisker chart can be time-consuming and difficult without using a PivotTable. But the same process used in the prior exercise can work for these chart types as well. Construct the data with a PivotTable as needed and then convert the PivotTable to OLAP formulas and any chart can be created.

Prepare a Dashboard for Production

Once a dashboard has been designed to meet the business requirements, there are several steps you need to take to get it ready for use. This process may include protecting various worksheets and cells from accidental mistakes, hiding various elements from the user that are not necessary for the dashboard, and making some simple design modifications to enhance the user experience.

Protecting Excel Worksheets

Because dashboards are designed for the specific needs of end users, it is important to ensure that once the dashboard contains all the required data, certain protections are in place to avoid accidental deletion of various objects or incorrect modifications. The managers at the Red Bluff Golf Course & Pro Shop who will be benefiting from these dashboards are not as comfortable with Excel as you are, and they do not want to accidentally delete data or otherwise compromise the data. In this exercise, you will protect the important elements of the workbook.

 **E13.20**

SIDE NOTE
Protect Sheet and Edit Objects
To be able to manipulate slicers, you must allow users to Edit Objects, which allows changes to the PivotCharts.

To Protect a Worksheet

a. Click the **SalesDashboard** worksheet.

b. Click the **Review** tab, and then, in the Protect group, click **Protect Sheet**.

Notice that in the Protect Sheet dialog box, there is an option to set a required password to unprotect the worksheet. This may be necessary to prevent intentional attempts to destroy the data.

c. Scroll through options of actions that users can still perform if the worksheet is protected, and then click **Select locked cells** and **Select unlocked cells** to clear the check boxes. Click **Use PivotTable & PivotChart** and **Edit objects** to allow the PivotCharts and slicers to be used.

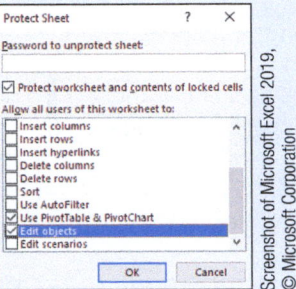

Figure 38 Protect Sheet dialog box

d. Click **OK**. With the sheet protected, no cells can be selected, no additional data can be added to the worksheet, and no columns or rows be inserted or deleted.

e. Click the **EmployeeMetrics** worksheet.

Before protecting the worksheet, make sure that all columns have been adjusted to automatically fit to their contents.

f. Click the **Review** tab, and then, in the Protect group, click **Protect Sheet**.

g. Scroll through the options of actions that users can still perform if the worksheet is protected, and then click **Select locked cells** and **Select unlocked cells** to clear the check boxes. Click **Use PivotTable & PivotChart** and **Edit objects** to allow for the PivotTable filters to be used.

h. Click **OK**.

i. Save the workbook.

SS CONSIDER THIS | Using Excel Web Add-Ins

Excel Web Add-ins encourage and facilitate sharing and collaboration. However, the Excel Web App does not support all the features available in the full desktop version of Excel, such as Protect Sheets. What other things should you take into consideration, depending on how you expect users to access your Excel workbook?

Hiding Unnecessary Screen Elements

Many of the interactive elements of Microsoft Excel can be hidden from users. Normally, controls such as the ribbon and scroll bars are useful and necessary parts of working with Excel. However, when a dashboard is presented to a user, it is preferable to hide any unnecessary objects that may distract the user from the dashboard's content. In this exercise, you will hide screen elements from the dashboard.

 **E13.21**

SIDE NOTE

Toggle the Ribbon
You can expand and collapse the ribbon by pressing Ctrl + F1.

To Hide Screen Elements

a. Click the **View** tab.

b. In the Show group, click the **Gridlines** and **Headings** check boxes to deselect them.

c. Right-click the **Employees** worksheet, and then select **Hide** to hide the worksheet from view.

d. Press Ctrl + F1 to minimize the ribbon and maximize dashboard space. If necessary, click the **EmployeeMetrics** worksheet.

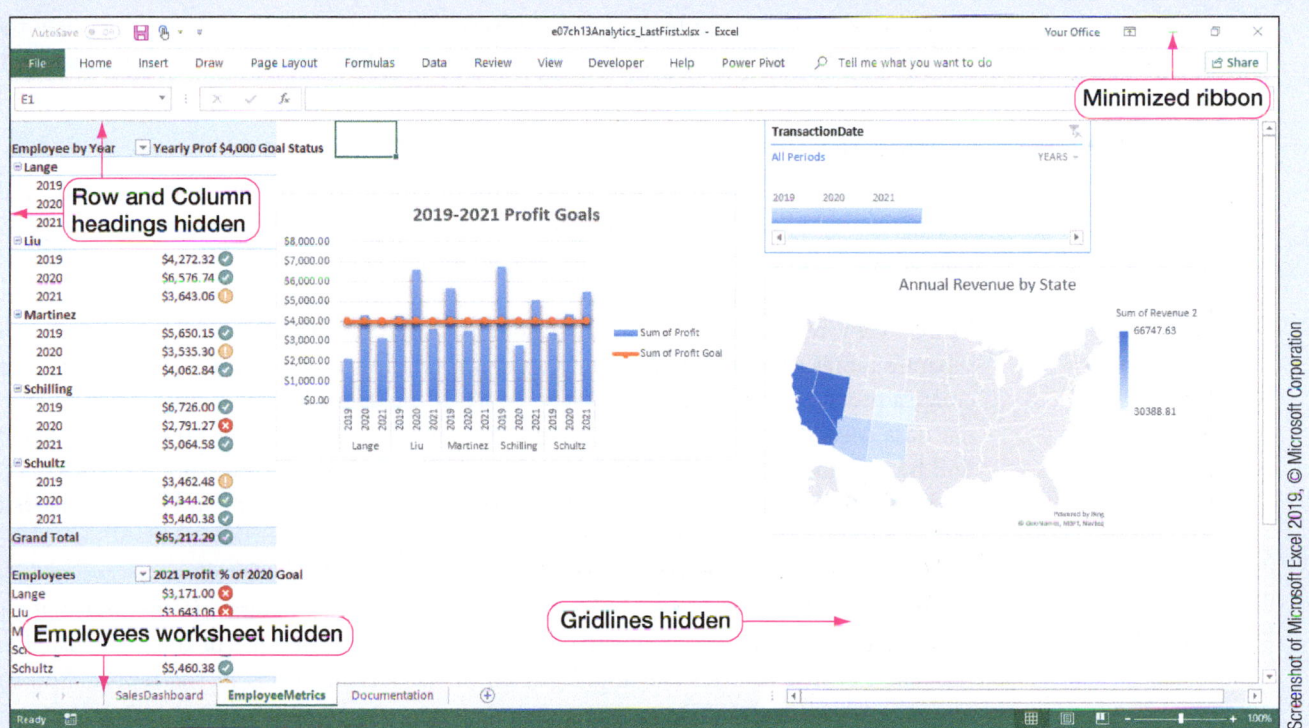

Figure 39 EmployeeMetrics dashboard with elements hidden

e. **Save** 💾 the workbook. If you need to take a break before finishing this chapter, now is a good time.

| REAL WORLD ADVICE | Hiding Screen Elements |

You may be tempted to hide the Vertical and Horizontal scroll bars under Display options for this workbook if all of the elements fit on your screen. However, consider the various screen sizes that may be used to view the data. Smaller screens and those with lower resolutions may not be able to view all the data if those screen elements are hidden.

Exploring the Benefits of Personalized Business Intelligence

Dashboards are great for people who know exactly what questions they have and what answers they want to derive from the data. However, it is often necessary to view data from multiple perspectives first, to gain a better understanding of the data, before those questions can be known. Microsoft knows that being able to quickly analyze large amounts of data is extremely important for business intelligence. This is why Power Pivot was integrated in Excel, beginning with Excel 2013. Microsoft also understands the benefits of being able to quickly analyze that data visually, which is where Power View comes in.

Power View, combined with Power Pivot in Excel, provides all the BI tools necessary to lead to better decision making. In this section, you will explore the Power View tool and create a report for the managers of the Red Bluff Golf Course & Pro Shop that demonstrates some of the key features.

Generate Visual Reports with Power View

Power View in Excel offers powerful data visualization tools that were once available only in third-party BI applications. **Power View** is an interactive data visualization, exploration, and presentation experience that encourages the creation of ad hoc reports.

Power View reports are created from data that has been added to the data model. A Power View report can be created without the use of Power Pivot by using data from separate tables or ranges. However, by creating relationships using Power Pivot, you can create a much more robust Power View report. If the data model is connected to an external data source and that source contains updated information, any Power View reports will be refreshed to accommodate the updated data. In Power View, you can quickly create a variety of data visualizations, from tables to pie, bar, column, and bubble charts to maps and more.

Beyond quick and easy visualizations, Power View allows for several ways to filter the data. Power View uses metadata in the data model to determine the relationships between the different tables and fields used in the report. Because of this, one visualization can be used to filter and highlight all of the visualizations in the report. You can also take advantage of a filter area to filter data on a single visualization or to all of them.

Slicers can also be added to a Power View report. Slicers allow you to easily filter the data in multiple visualizations, similar to how slicers work in Excel. In addition to slicers, Power View allows for easy sorting of data and switching to full-screen mode for some visualizations.

Installing the Silverlight Plug-In

Excel's Power View requires that Microsoft's Silverlight be installed. **Silverlight** is a powerful tool for creating interactive user experiences. It is a free plug-in powered by the .NET framework and is compatible with multiple browsers, devices, applications, and operating systems.

 **E13.22**

To Install Microsoft Silverlight

a. If you took a break, open the **e07ch13Analytics** workbook, and, if needed, click the **EmployeeMetrics** worksheet.

b. Open your browser, and navigate to www.microsoft.com/silverlight/

> **Troubleshooting**
>
> If you receive a message from the Microsoft website that your browser is not fully compatible, try using another browser such as Microsoft Edge.

c. Click **DOWNLOAD NOW** to begin the download and installation process of the latest version of Silverlight.

d. Follow the prompts to download and install Silverlight, and then close your browser.

Inserting a Power View Report Sheet

The Power View report sheet has a fixed size, unlike other worksheets in Excel. There are no scroll bars, and the report sheet may remind you of a PowerPoint slide. When you first insert a Power View report sheet, three panes are visible: The Design pane, the Filters pane, and the Power View Fields pane. Before any data is added to the Power View report, the options available on the Power View tab on the ribbon are limited to a few, such as Undo and Redo, setting a theme, adding a picture or image, refreshing the data, and creating and editing relationships in the data model. Additional contextual tabs will become available once you begin creating the report. In this exercise, you will insert a new Power View report sheet into the workbook and explore the layout.

 **E13.23**

To Insert a Power View Report Sheet

a. Press `Ctrl`+`F1` to expand the ribbon if necessary. Click the **File** tab, and then click **Options**.

b. Click **Customize Ribbon**, and then click the **Choose commands from** arrow, and select **Commands Not in the Ribbon**.

c. Scroll until you see **Insert a Power View Report**, and click to select it.

d. Under the Main Tabs list, click to select **Insert**, and then click **New Group**. Click **Rename**, and type Reports Click **OK**.

e. Click **Add**.

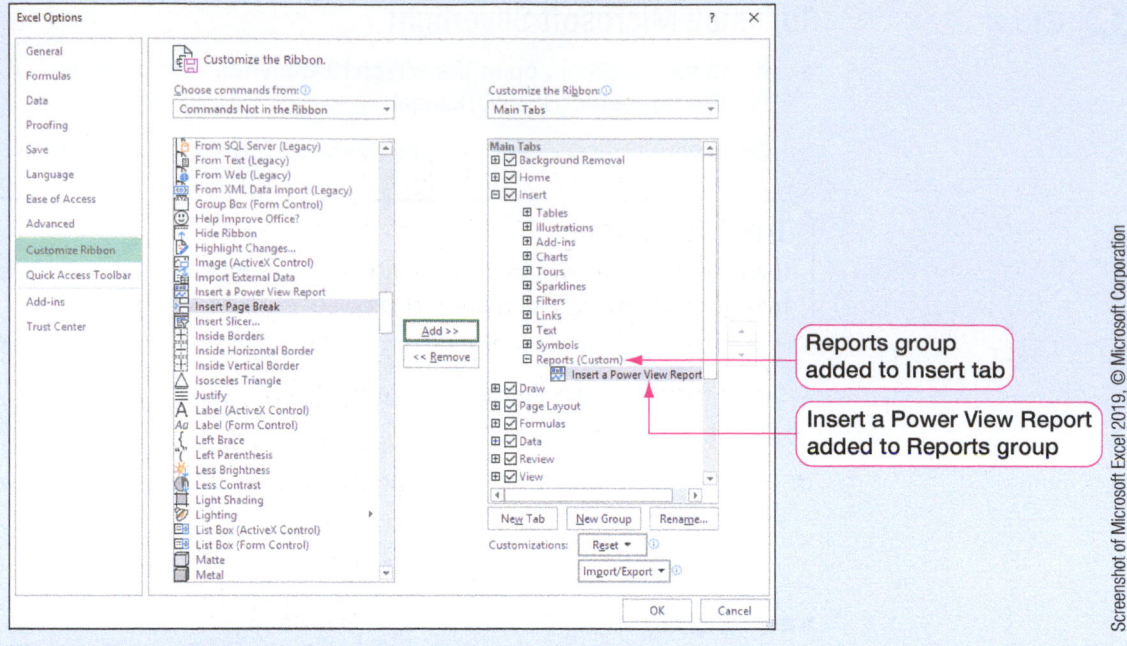

Screenshot of Microsoft Excel 2019, © Microsoft Corporation

Reports group added to Insert tab

Insert a Power View Report added to Reports group

Figure 40   Customizing the ribbon to add Power View

f.   Click **OK**.

A new group will now appear in the Insert tab on the far right of the screen containing the Power View icon.

> **Troubleshooting**
>
> If you do not have Silverlight installed, you will be prompted to install it before you can continue. If necessary, click Install Silverlight, and follow the prompts. Once it has been installed, click Reload.

g.   Click the **Insert** tab, and in the Reports group, click **Power View**.

> **Troubleshooting**
>
> If you receive an error on the prior step, Silverlight may be blocked on your PC. Follow the steps at this Microsoft Support page to enable Silverlight.
> https://support.office.com/en-us/article/flash-silverlight-and-shockwave-controls-blocked-in-microsoft-office-55738f12-a01d-420e-a533-7cef1ff6aeb1?ui=en-US&rs=en-US&ad=US

h.   Examine the various components that make up the Power View report builder.

i.   Click the **Click here** to add a title text, and type Red Bluff Golf Course & Pro Shop Sales Report

j.   Click the **Power View** tab, and then, in the Themes group, click **Themes**. Select **Hardcover** in the seventh row of the fourth column to add a theme to the Power View Report.

k.   In the Themes group, click **Background**, and then select **Dark1 Vertical Gradient**.

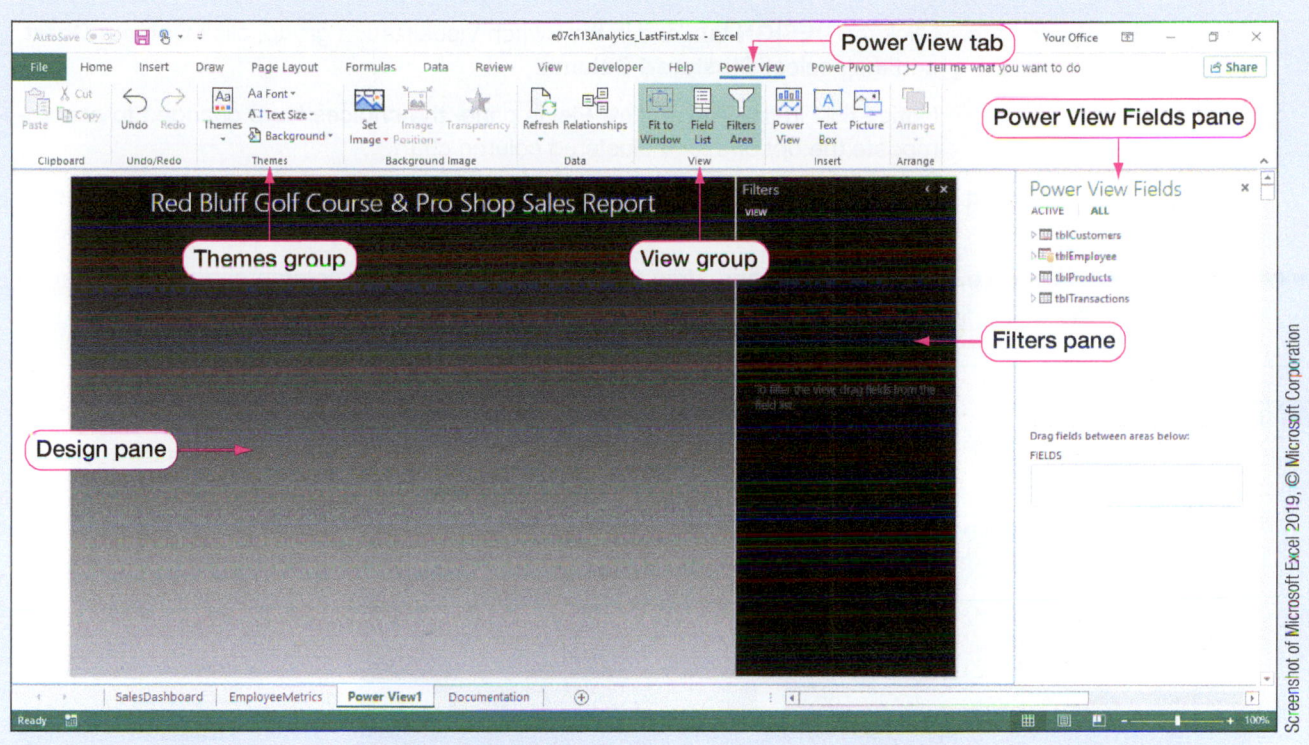

Figure 41 Power View report builder

l. **Save**  the workbook.

Creating a Visualization with Multiples

Power View allows you to create visualizations called multiples. **Multiples** are series of identical charts that have the same x- and y-axes but contain different values. These repeating charts make it easier to compare many different values at the same time. When you create multiples, Power View creates a container with one chart for each of the values. For example, if you have a column chart of monthly sales, you could add a year field to the multiples field and have one column chart for each year. There are two different types of multiples: vertical multiples and horizontal multiples. **Vertical multiples** will expand across the width of the container and wrap down the container in the available space. If all multiples do not fit in the available space, a vertical scroll bar is also added. **Horizontal multiples** expand across the available space in the container; if additional space is needed, a horizontal scroll bar is added.

In this exercise, you will create a clustered column chart with horizontal multiples to display the monthly sales from year to year.

E13.24

To Create Multiples

a. On the **InteractiveDashboard** worksheet, scroll through the Power View Fields pane, and then expand **tblTransactions** to view available fields.

b. Select **TransactionDate (Month)** and **Σ Revenue**.

Notice that once data has been added to the Design pane, the DESIGN tab appears on the ribbon.

c. Click the **DESIGN** tab, and in the Switch Visualization group, click **Column Chart**, and then select **Clustered Column**.

Notice that in the Power View Fields pane, the choices have changed to accommodate the options for a clustered column chart.

d. In the Power View Fields pane, click the **TransactionDate (Year)** arrow, and select **Add as Horizontal Multiples**.

e. In the Design pane, drag the edge of the clustered column chart to the right so that all three charts are visible.

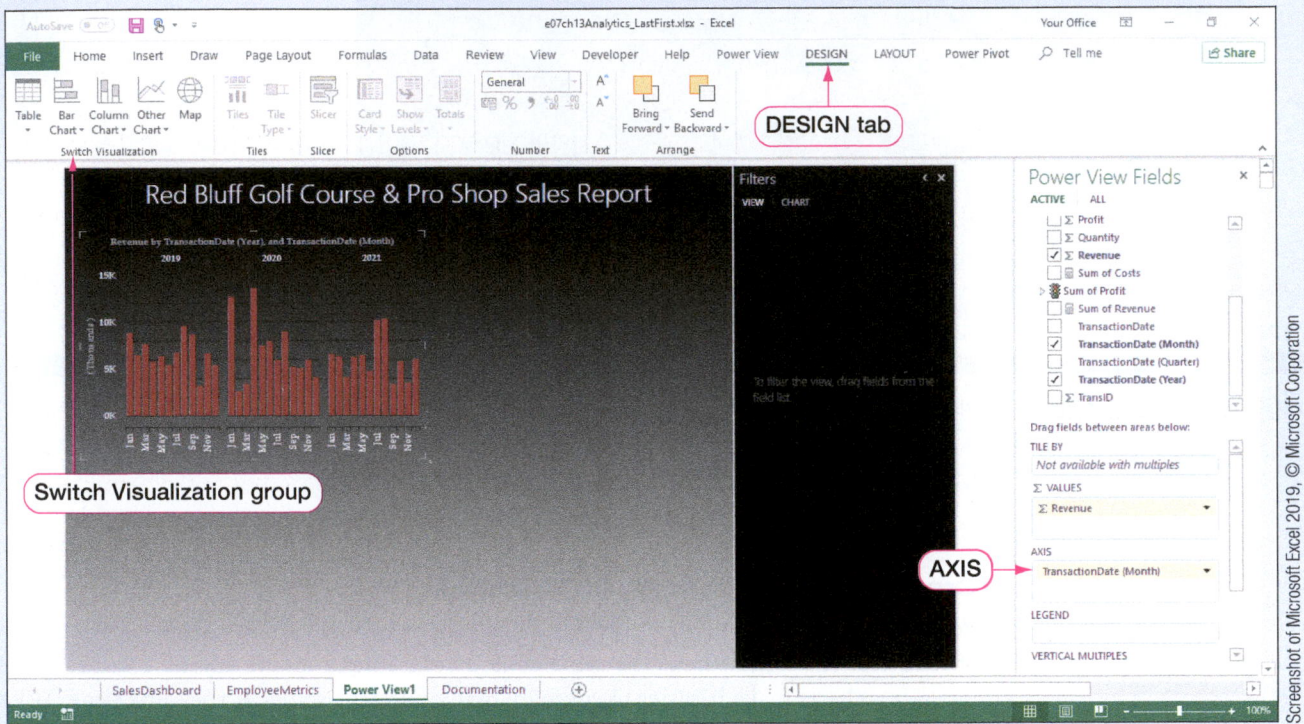

Figure 42   Horizontal Multiples visualization

f. Point to the chart, and click the **Pop out** icon in the top right corner of the chart to see the chart in full-screen view.

g. Click the **Pop in** icon to return the chart to its previous size.

h. **Save** the workbook.

Creating a Visualization with Tiles

Multiples are a great way to see all the charts at one time. However, that may not always be the most effective way to analyze data. Power View offers a visualization feature called tiles. **Tiles** provide a dynamic navigation strip that allows you to navigate through a series of charts based on a particular value, such as a chart that visualizes sales by employee with tiles for each product category. This allows the user to quickly see data from a specific product category with the click of a tile.

In this exercise, you will create a bar chart visualization that will compare total sales for each employee with tiles based on product type.

 **E13.25**

To Create a Bar Chart with Tiles

a. Click the **Power View** tab, and then, in the View group, click **Field List**, if necessary, to display the Power View Fields pane. Click an empty area of the Design pane to deselect the chart.

b. In the Power View Fields pane, expand **tblEmployee**, and then select **LastName**. Notice that a new table is being created to the right of the chart.

c. In the Power View Fields pane, scroll down to **tblTransactions**, and then select **Σ Revenue**.

d. On the DESIGN tab, in the Switch Visualization group, click **Bar Chart**. Select **Clustered Bar**.

e. In the Design pane, expand the size of the clustered bar chart so all values are visible.

f. In the Power View Fields pane, scroll up and expand **tblProducts**, and then drag **ProductType** to the **TILE BY** area. This will change the dimensions of the chart.

g. Drag to expand both the tile container and the clustered bar chart to be the same height as the clustered column chart.

Notice that with a tile container, there is no longer an option to Pop out 🔲 on the chart.

h. Close the Filters pane and the Power View Fields pane.

i. Click on the various tiles to see how the employee sales compare for other product types.

j. Explore the ability to filter all visualizations by clicking the bar for the last name **Lange** on the Revenue by LastName bar chart.

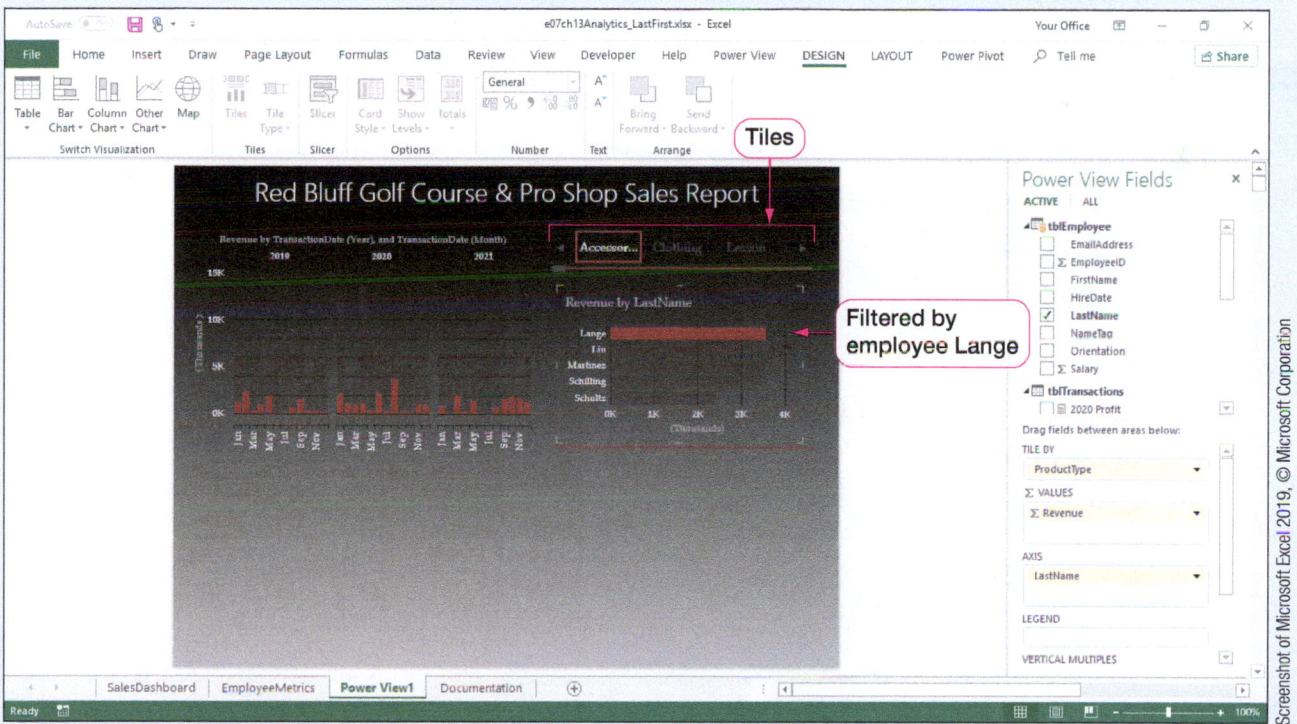

Figure 43 Power View report filtered by employee Lange

k. Click anywhere inside the chart container, but not on a bar, to remove the filter.

l. **Save** 🔲 the workbook.

Creating a Map Visualization in Power View

The Bing Maps app is one way to create data visualizations that illustrate data with a geographic element. However, the Bing Maps app has limited interactive capabilities. Beyond zooming and panning around, there is no interaction. Excel's Power View report includes a map visualization that can be used with filters or slicers or even to filter other charts in the report. In this exercise, you will create a map visualization to add to the Power View report.

 **E13.26**

To Create a Map Visualization in Power View

a. Click an empty area below the **clustered column chart**.

b. Click the **Power View** tab, and then, in the View group, click **Field List** to display the Power View Fields pane. In the Power View Fields pane, expand **tblCustomers** if necessary, and then click to select **State**. Expand **tblTransactions** if necessary, select **TransactionDate (Year)**, and then select **Σ Revenue**.

c. On the **DESIGN** tab, in the Switch Visualization group, click **Map**. If necessary, click **Enable Content** in the Privacy Warning bar.

d. If necessary, drag the Map under the clustered column chart. Drag the **right-middle sizing handle** to the right to expand the width of the Map visualization. Click **Zoom Out** 🔲 so that the following states are visible: California, Nevada, Arizona, Colorado, and New Mexico.

e. On the Map visualization, on the legend, click **2019** to filter all other visualizations to show only 2019 revenue.

f. **Close** the Power View Fields pane.

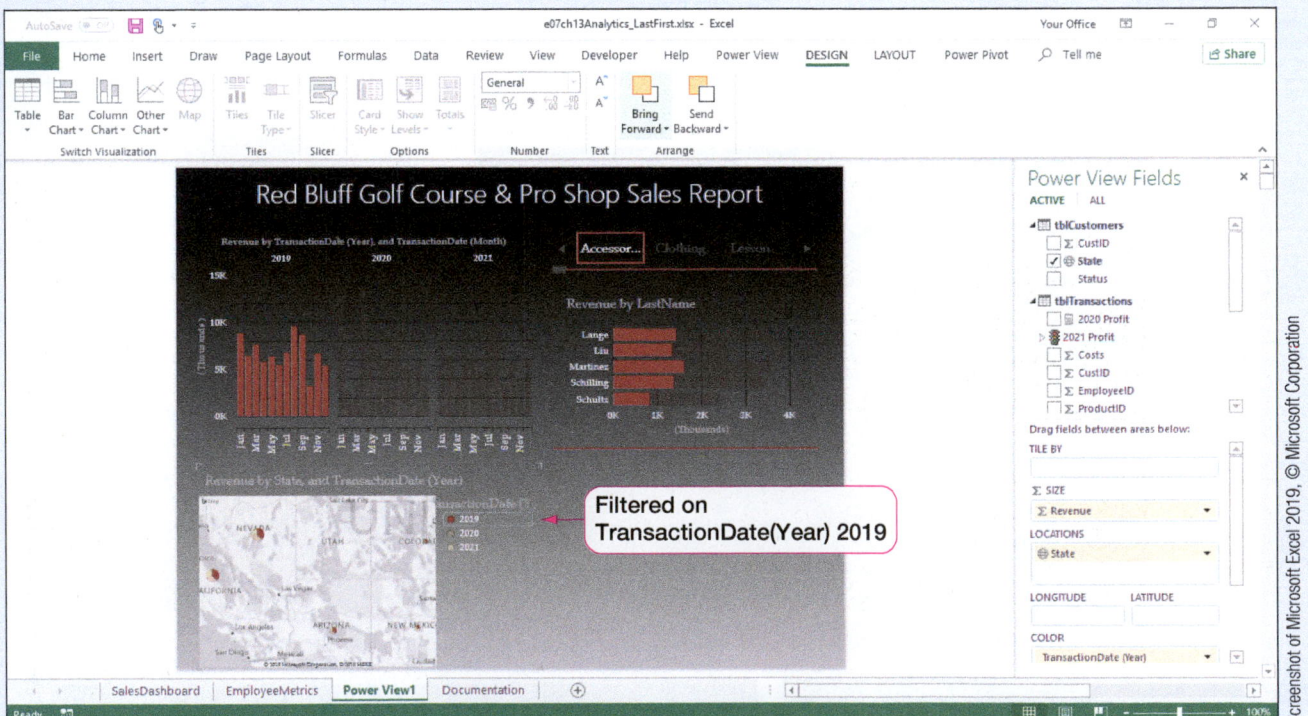

Figure 44 Power View report filtered to TransactionDate (Year) 2019

g. Click just below the **TransactionDate (Year)** legend to clear the 2019 filter.

h. **Save** 🔲 the workbook.

Adding Slicers to a Power View Report

Slicers in a Power View report work just as they do in an Excel worksheet, allowing an easy way to filter data and charts with the click of the button. As you have already seen, the Power View report makes it easy to filter data from other data visualizations. However, it is often useful to add slicers for data that is not necessarily a part of any of the visualizations. In this exercise, you will add Status and ProductType slicers to the report that will allow the managers of the Red Bluff Golf Course & Pro Shop to see the revenue for members and guests as well as any particular product type.

 **E13.27**

To Add Slicers to a Power View Report

a. Click the **Power View** tab, and in the View group, click **Field List** to view the Power View Fields pane. Click an empty area of the Design pane to the right of the map.

b. Expand **tblCustomers** if necessary, and then click to select **Status**.

c. On the **DESIGN** tab, in the Slicer group, click **Slicer** to create a slicer from the Status field.

d. Adjust the height of the Status slicer by dragging the bottom middle sizing handle up to just below Member.

e. Click an empty area below the **Status** slicer. In the Power View Fields pane, if necessary click **ALL**, then expand **tblProducts** if necessary, and then click **ProductType**.

f. On the DESIGN tab, in the Slicer group, click **Slicer** to create a slicer from the ProductType field.

g. Drag the **ProductType** slicer below the Status slicer. Adjust the size appropriately.

h. Use the slicers to filter the report to show only revenue from **Member** and **Clothing**.

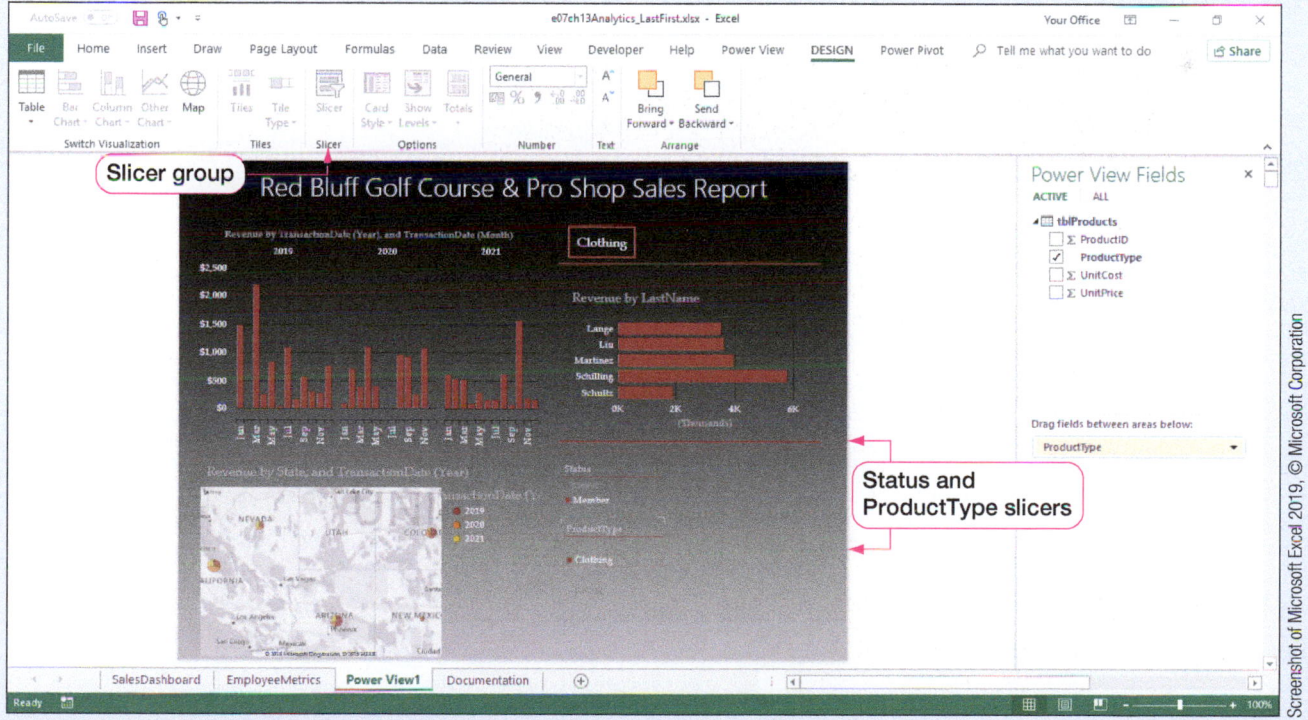

Figure 45 Slicers added to Power View report

i. Close the Power View Fields pane.

j. Click **Clear Filter** ⊞ on the Status and ProductType slicers.

k. Complete the **Documentation** worksheet according to your instructor's directions.

l. **Save** 🖫 the workbook, exit Excel, and then submit your file as directed by your instructor.

The data business intelligence tools included in Excel: Get & Transform, Power Pivot, and Power View, can all be used to create dynamic dashboards to give businesses enhanced decision making abilities. While these tools are available within the familiar Excel environment, a version of them also exists outside of Excel as a separate piece of software called the Power BI Desktop Suite. The **Power BI Desktop** is a free tool for analysts to develop powerful visualizations, models, reports, and analytics made for content developers. The Power BI Desktop Suite combines enhanced versions of the three tools into a single suite of software designed to connect to a multitude of data sources and visualize this data. The appendix to this text contains more in-depth coverage of the Power BI Desktop Suite.

Concept Check

1. What are some basic design concepts to consider when you are creating a digital dashboard? p. 707

2. Describe the data model, and explain how it can improve data analysis. p. 712

3. Discuss some of the advanced data modeling techniques made possible by Power Pivot. p. 719

4. Describe how Power Pivot can be used to create a simple dashboard, and discuss a few simple ways to enhance the value of a dashboard. p. 729

5. When creating a PivotTable for use with a map chart, why must the PivotTable be converted to formulas before the map chart can be created? What are two other chart types that require this same process? p. 743–744

6. What are some changes recommended to prepare a dashboard for production, and why are they recommended? p. 745

7. What are the benefits of a Power View report, and how is it different from a dashboard? p. 748

Key Terms

Base value   726
Bidirectional KPI   727
Business intelligence (BI)   707
Data model   712
Digital dashboard   707
Explicit calculated field   724
Get & Transform   712
Horizontal multiples   751
Implicit calculated field   724

Key performance indicator
  (KPI)   708
Multiples   751
Negative KPI   727
Positive KPI   727
Power BI Desktop   756
Power View   748
Relational data   712
Silverlight   748

Slicer   729
Sparkline   742
Status threshold   727
Target value   726
Tiles   752
Vertical multiples   751
White space   710

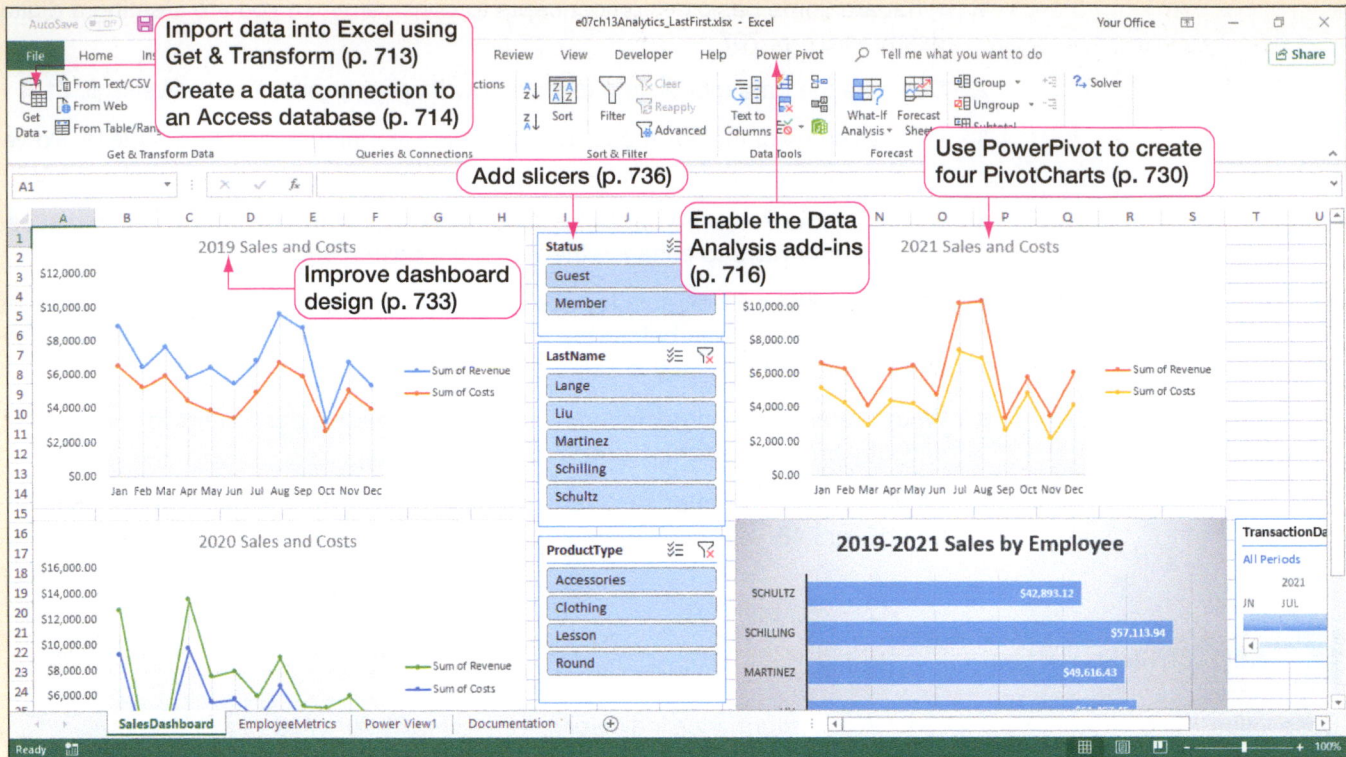

Figure 46

Screenshot of Microsoft Excel 2019, © Microsoft Corporation

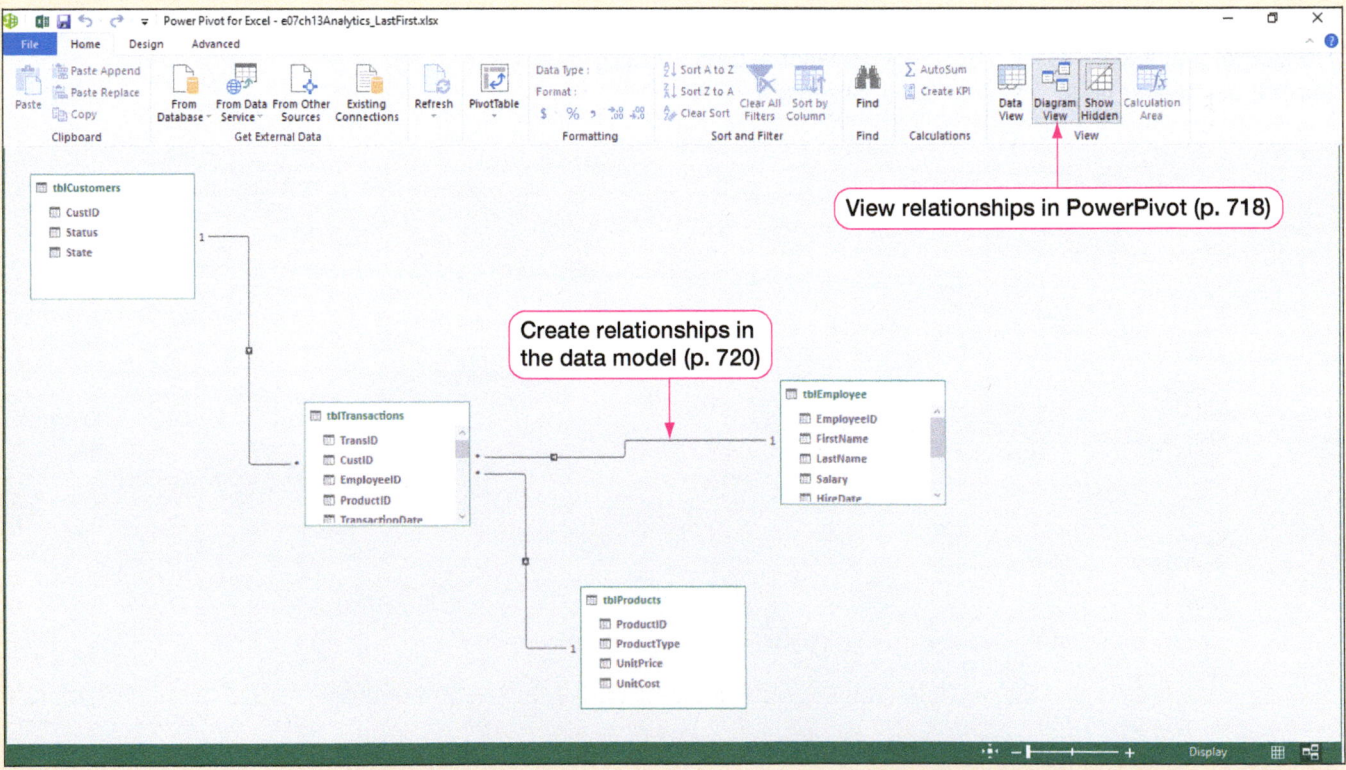

Figure 47

Screenshot of Microsoft Excel 2019, © Microsoft Corporation

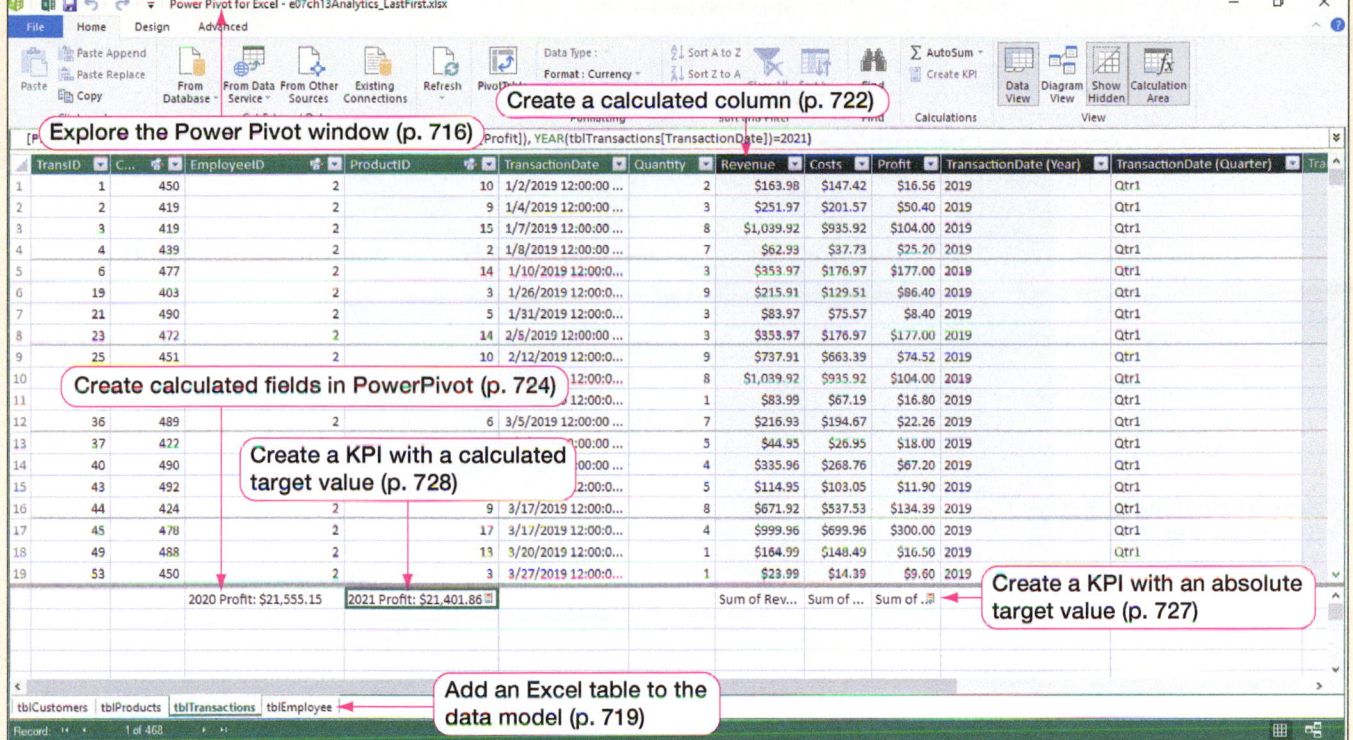

Figure 48

Screenshot of Microsoft Excel 2019, © Microsoft Corporation

The following callouts appear in Figure 48:

- Explore the Power Pivot window (p. 716)
- Create a calculated column (p. 722)
- Create calculated fields in PowerPivot (p. 724)
- Create a KPI with a calculated target value (p. 728)
- Create a KPI with an absolute target value (p. 727)
- Add an Excel table to the data model (p. 719)

Figure 49

Screenshot of Microsoft Excel 2019, © Microsoft Corporation

The following callouts appear in Figure 49:

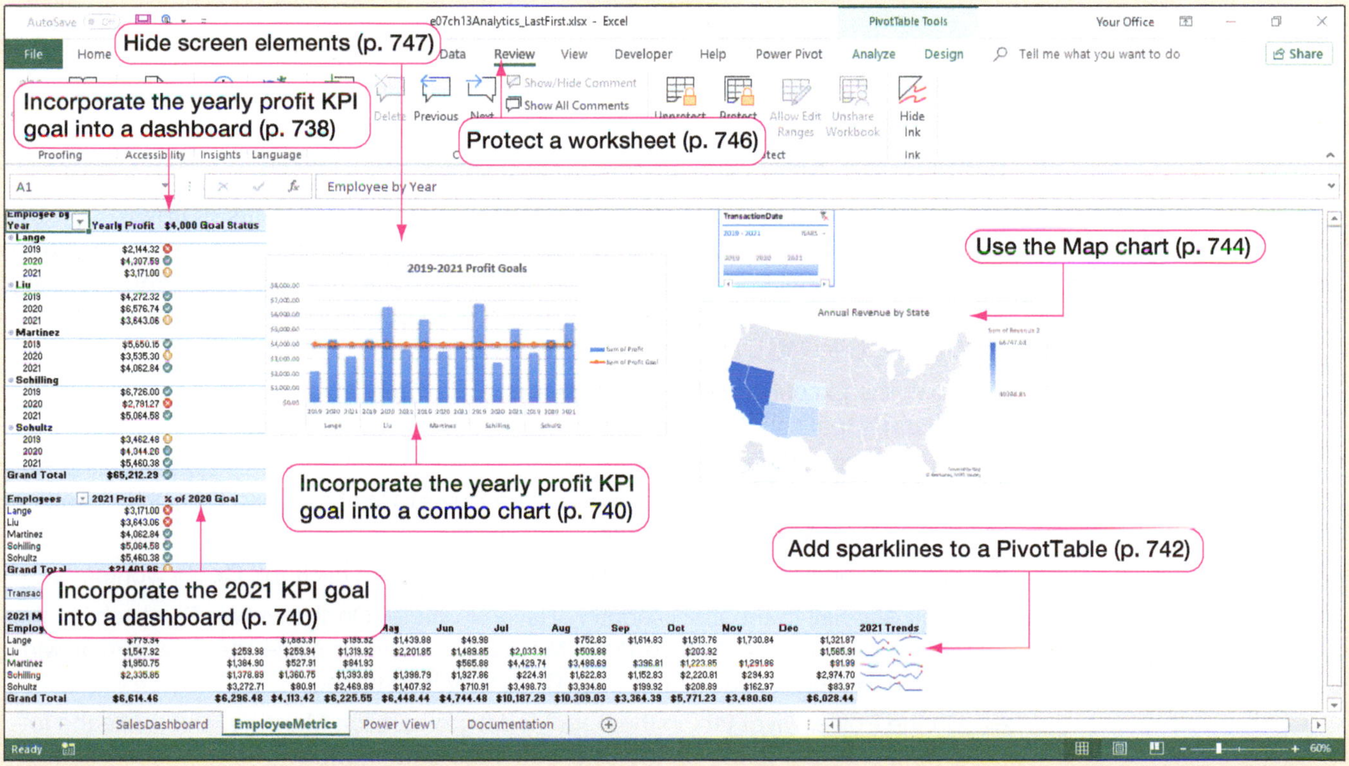

- Hide screen elements (p. 747)
- Incorporate the yearly profit KPI goal into a dashboard (p. 738)
- Protect a worksheet (p. 746)
- Use the Map chart (p. 744)
- Incorporate the yearly profit KPI goal into a combo chart (p. 740)
- Add sparklines to a PivotTable (p. 742)
- Incorporate the 2021 KPI goal into a dashboard (p. 740)

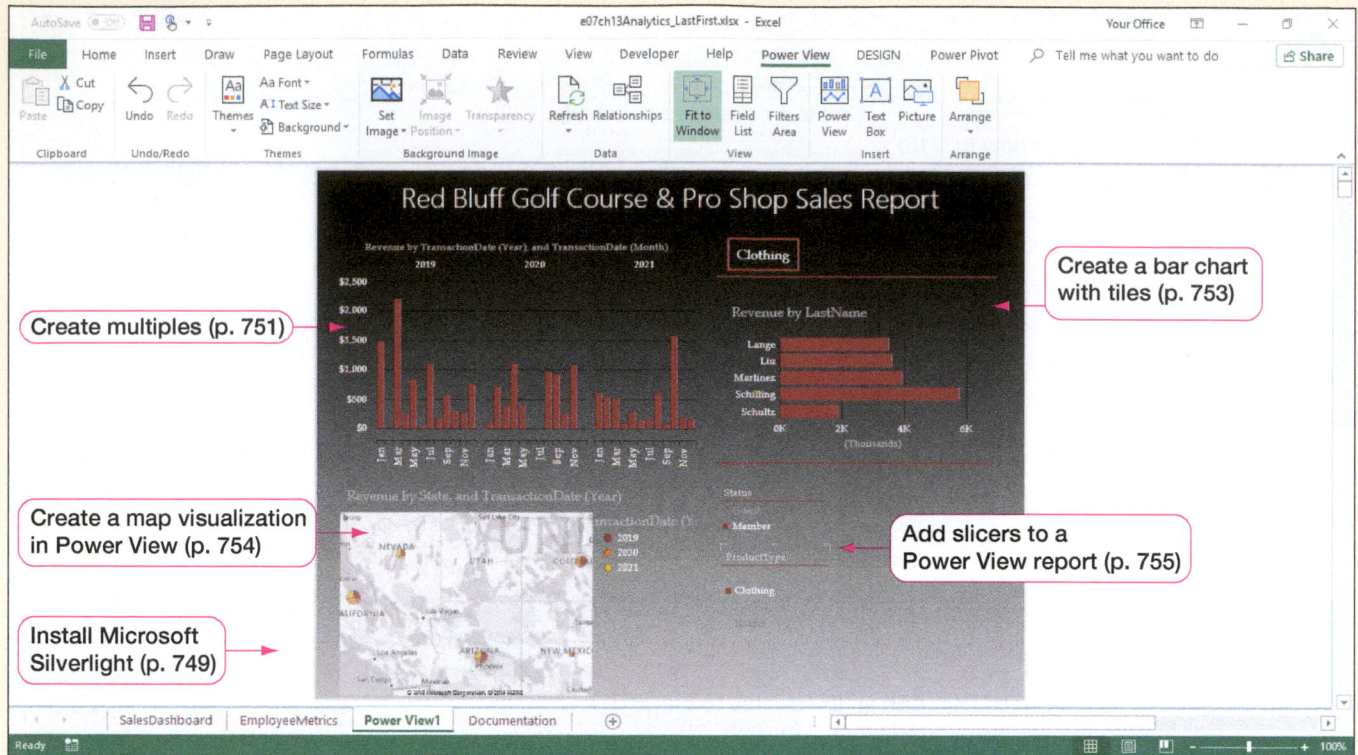

Create multiples (p. 751)

Create a bar chart with tiles (p. 753)

Create a map visualization in Power View (p. 754)

Add slicers to a Power View report (p. 755)

Install Microsoft Silverlight (p. 749)

Figure 50

Screenshot of Microsoft Excel 2019, © Microsoft Corporation

Practice 1

Student data file needed:	You will save your file as:
e07ch13SpaRevenue.xlsx	e07ch13SpaRevenue_LastFirst.xlsx

Sales & Marketing

Advanced Analysis at the Turquoise Oasis Spa

Managers at the Turquoise Oasis Spa have read about the benefits of Power View for exploring their data. They have provided you with some sample data and need you to create a data model that they can use to build their Power Pivot report. In this exercise, you will create a data model with the data provided, and then you will create calculated fields, calculated columns, KPIs, and relationships.

a. Open the Excel file **e07ch13SpaRevenue**. Save your file as **e07ch13SpaRevenue_LastFirst** using your last and first name.

b. Click the **SalesData** worksheet, and then click any cell in the Turquoise Oasis Spa Sample Sales 2019-2021 table. Click the **Power Pivot** tab, and then, in the Tables group, click **Add to Data Model**.

c. Minimize or close the Power Pivot window, and then click the **Goals** worksheet.

d. Click any cell in the 2021 Monthly Revenue table. On the Power Pivot tab, in the Tables group, click **Add to Data Model**. Minimize or close the PowerPivot window, and then repeat for the Total Orders by Rep table.

e. On the Power Pivot tab, in the Data Model group, click **Manage**, and make the following changes to the SpaSales sheet in the data model.

  • Double-click the **Add Column** column heading, type Revenue and then press Enter. Type =[UnitPrice]*[QuantitySold] and then press Enter. Click the **Home** tab, and then, in the Formatting group, click the **Format** arrow, and then select **Currency**.

- Double-click the **Add Column** column heading, type Costs and then press Enter. Type =[UnitCost]*[QuantitySold] and then press Enter. On the Home tab, in the Formatting group, click the **Format** arrow, and then select **Currency**.

- Double-click the **Add Column** column heading, type Profit and then press Enter. Type =[Revenue]-[Costs] and then press Enter. On the Home tab, in the Formatting group, click the **Format** arrow, and then select **Currency**.

f. Click the **RevGoals2021** worksheet, and then make the following changes to the RevGoals2021 worksheet in the data model.

- Select the **MonthlySalesActual** column. On the Home tab, in the Formatting group, click **Format** arrow, and then select **Currency**.

- Select the **MonthlySalesGoal** column. On the Home tab, in the Formatting group, click **Format** arrow, and then select **Currency**.

- Select both the **MonthlySalesActual** and **MonthlySalesGoal** columns, and then, in the Calculations group, click **AutoSum** to create two calculated fields in the Calculation Area: Sum of MonthlySalesActual and Sum of MonthlySalesGoal.

- In the Calculation Area, click the **Sum of MonthlySalesActual** calculated field, and then, in the Calculations group, click **Create KPI**.

- Under Define target value, in the Measure box, select **Sum of MonthlySalesGoal**.

- Under **Define status thresholds**, click and slide the low value threshold to **75%** and the high value threshold to **100%**.

- Under **Select icon style**, select the second option from the left.

- Click **OK**.

g. Create a relationship in the data model between the SpaSales table and the OrdersByRep table by completing the following tasks.

- Click the **OrdersByRep** worksheet in the Power Pivot window, and then select the **SalesRep** column.

- Click the **Design** tab, and then, in the Relationships group, click **Create Relationship**.

- In the second box, select **SpaSales**.

- Select the **SalesRep** from the list of columns, and then click **OK**.

h. Create a PivotTable to visualize the monthly revenue goal.

- On the Home tab, click **PivotTable**, and then click **PivotTable**.

- Click **Existing Worksheet**, click the **Collapse Dialog** button, and then click the **Dashboard** worksheet.

- Click cell **A1**, and then, in the Range Selection dialog box, click **OK** and then click **OK**.

- In the PivotTable Fields pane, click to expand the **RevGoals2021** table. Drag **Month-Year** to the Rows area. A new field named Month-Year (Month) will be created. Remove **Month-Year** from the Rows area.

- Click to expand the **Sum of MonthlySalesActual** KPI field. Drag the **Value (Sum of MonthlySalesActual)** and **Status** fields to the Values area.

i. Click the **Documentation** worksheet. Click cell **A8**, and then type in today's date. Click cell **B8**, and then type in your first and last name. Complete the remainder of the **Documentation** worksheet according to your instructor's direction.

j. Save the workbook, exit Excel, and then submit the file as directed by your instructor.

Problem Solve 1

MyLab IT Grader

Student data file needed:

 e07ch13Metrics.xlsx

You will save your file as:

 e07ch13Metrics_LastFirst.xlsx

Milligan's Boutiques

Sales & Marketing

Tammy Milligan owns a chain of small boutique stores in Ohio, Michigan, Illinois, and Indiana. She is a big believer in the benefits of BI for measuring progress and making strategic decisions. She has provided you with some sample sales data and would like you to create a dashboard that will give her an overview of how her business is doing. In this exercise, you will build a data model based on the sample data and create a dashboard, complete with KPIs and a map that shows which states are generating the most orders.

a. Open the Excel file **e07ch13Metrics**. Save your file as e07ch13Metrics_LastFirst using your last and first name.

b. On the **SalesData** worksheet, add each of the three tables to the data model.

c. Edit the data model by completing the following tasks on the SalesData2021 worksheet.

- Format the PurchaseDate field as ***3/14/2001**.
- Format the Price field as **Currency**.
- Create a calculated column named Revenue and type =[Price]*[Quantity] to calculate the revenue generated from each sale.
- Format Revenue as **Currency**.
- Create a calculated field for the sum of revenue.
- Create a KPI that measures the Sum of Revenue value against the absolute value of $500.00. Maintain the default thresholds of 200 and 400, and select the fourth set of icon styles.
- Create a relationship between SalesData2021 and VolumeByEmp, using the EmployeeID field.

d. Refer to Figure 51 and the following steps to create a dashboard for Milligan's Boutique. In the Power Pivot window, create a **Chart and Table (Horizontal)** combination on the **MetricsDashboard** worksheet in cell B2.

e. Format the PivotChart by completing the following.

- Drag the **Category** field from SalesData2021 to the Axis (Categories) area.
- Drag the **Quantity** field from SalesData2021 to the Values area to calculate the sum of quantity sold.
- Change the chart type to a **Pie** chart.
- Apply **Style 9** to the PivotChart.
- Add a Chart Title that reads Volume Sales by Category
- Hide all field buttons.
- Add a Timeline slicer connected to the PivotChart and position below the chart. Apply the Timeline Style **Light Green**, **Timeline Style Light 6** to the slicer.

f. Format the PivotTable by completing the following.

- Drag the **LastName** field from VolumeByEmp to the Rows area.
- Drag the **Sum of Revenue Value** field from SalesData2021 to the Values area.
- Drag the **Sum of Revenue KPI** Status field to the Values area.
- Name the PivotTable EmployeeRevGoals
- Rename the **Row Labels** heading in J2 as Employees

- Rename the **Sum of Revenue** heading in K2 as 2021 Revenue
- Rename the **Sum of Revenue** Status heading in L2 as $500 Goal Status If necessary, resize the column to fit the text.
- Apply the PivotTable Style **Light Green, Pivot Style Medium 14** to the PivotTable.

g. In the Power Pivot window, create a PivotTable on the MetricsDashboard worksheet in cell **B25**, and complete the following.

- Drag the **State** field from OrdersByState to the Rows area and the Orders field to the Values area.
- Convert the PivotTable to formulas.

h. Insert a Filled Map chart on the MetricsDashboard worksheet, and complete the following.

- Change the chart title to Number of Orders by State
- Position the map within the cell range **B25:H39**.

i. Prepare the dashboard for production by completing the following.

- Hide the SalesData worksheet.
- Hide the column and row headings as well as the gridlines on the MetricsDashboard worksheet.
- Protect the worksheet, allowing only **Use PivotTable & PivotChart** and **Edit objects**.
- Minimize the ribbon.

j. Complete the Documentation worksheet according to your instructor's directions.

k. Save the workbook, exit Excel, and then submit the file as directed by your instructor.

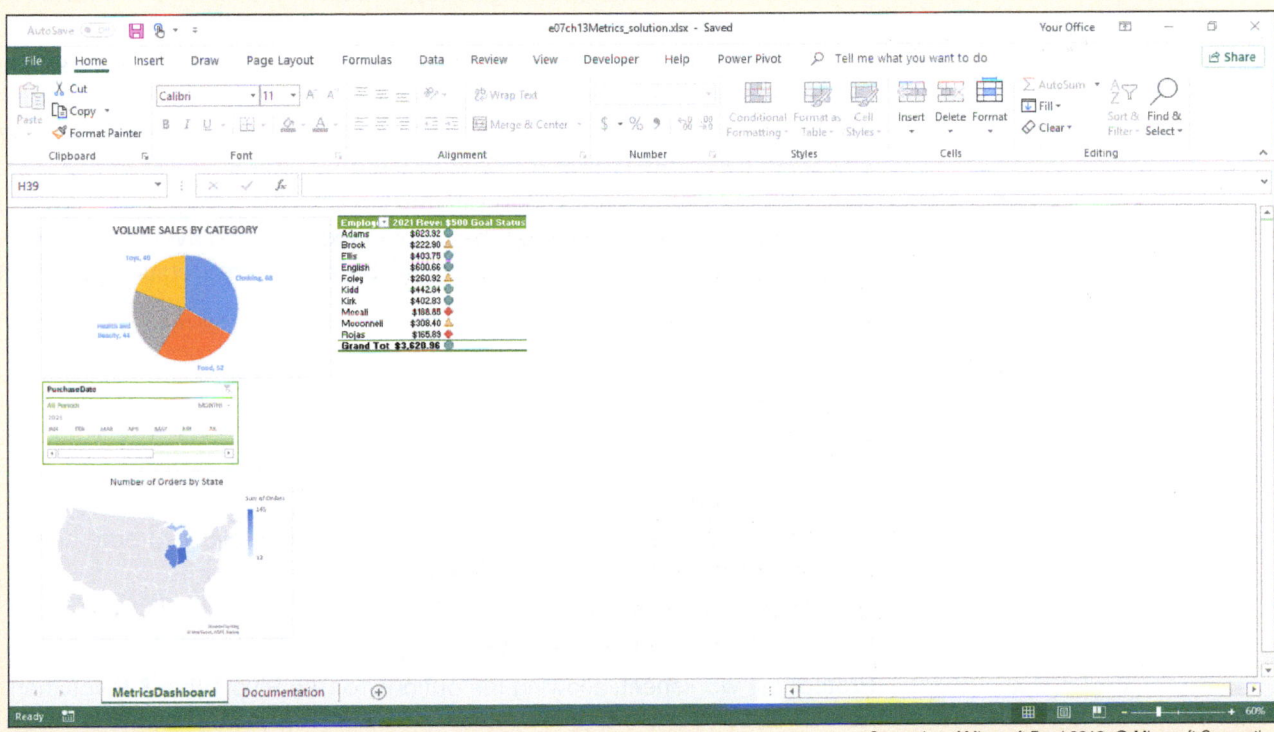

Figure 51   Metrics dashboard

Screenshot of Microsoft Excel 2019, © Microsoft Corporation

Student data files needed:

 Blank Excel Workbook

 e07ch13Dashboard_data.txt

You will save your file as:

e07ch13Dashboard_LastFirst.xlsx

Visualizing Customers

Information Technology

Your boss has asked you to create a dashboard to review the sales for October 2021. He would like to see the sales by week and the average sales by week in dollars and quantity. He would like to see whether there is any correlation between the amount and the quantity sold in a week.

a. Start Excel, and then create a new blank workbook. Save the workbook as e07ch13Dashboard_LastFirst using your last and first name.

b. Rename Sheet1 as Dashboard

c. Import the data from the tab-delimited text file **e07ch13Dashboard_data.txt** using Get & Transform.

- Add this data to the data model, and create only a connection to the data file.

d. Make the following changes to the data in the Power Pivot window.

- Format the **Date** field as ***3/14/2001**.

- Format the **Unit Price** as **Currency**.

- Add a calculated column named Revenue that multiplies the Qty and Unit Price. Format the column as **Currency**.

- Add a calculated column named Week to determine the week number. Use the **WEEKNUM** formula with the Date field as the argument.

- Add an AutoSum to the Qty column and the Revenue column.

e. Use the Power Pivot window to generate a dashboard with **Two Charts (Vertical)** on the **Dashboard** sheet.

f. Chart 1 should be a combo chart with the week as the category; the values should contain the revenue on the primary axis and the quantity on the secondary axis. Revenue should be a clustered column chart, and the quantity should be a line chart with a secondary axis.

g. Chart 2 should be a combo chart with the week as the category; the values should contain the average revenue on the primary axis and the average quantity on the secondary axis. Average revenue should be a clustered column chart, and the quantity should be a line chart.

h. Make the following changes to both charts.

- Apply **Quick Layout 3**.

- Add primary horizontal and vertical axis titles.

- Provide appropriate text for the chart title and both axis titles.

- Hide field buttons.

i. Add a slicer for the customer name, and connect the slicer to both charts. Move the slicer so it does not cover any data.

j. Hide gridlines and headings.

k. Format the workbook to print on one page.

l. Protect the worksheet, allowing the options to Use PivotTable & PivotChart and to Edit objects.

m. Save the workbook, close Excel, and then submit the file as directed by your instructor.

Microsoft Excel

Chapter 14 VISUAL BASIC FOR APPLICATIONS—VBA

MyLab IT Grader

Sales & Marketing

Prepare Case

The Red Bluff Golf Course & Pro Shop Spreadsheet Enhancement with Form Controls and VBA

Managers at the Red Bluff Golf Course & Pro Shop have been using dashboards to keep track of sales from golf lessons, clothing, accessories, and so on. You have been given access to a workbook with a sample dashboard and Power View report based on the sales from 2017 to 2019. You have been asked to use some of the developer tools—including form controls and VBA—to enhance the dashboard and Power View report, provide more security, and add new functionality.

Samot/Shutterstock

Student data file needed:

 e07ch14Dashboards.xlsx

You will save your files as:

 e07ch14Dashboards_LastFirst.xlsm

 e07ch14Dashboards_LastFirst.xlsx

Enhancing the Readability and Interactivity of Dashboards

A **digital dashboard** is a tool that delivers business intelligence in graphical form. Dashboards provide management with a big picture view of the business, usually from multiple perspectives using various charts and other graphical representations. Simple dashboards may consist of a few charts that represent sales data over a particular period of time or from various perspectives, such as product category or department. Dashboards are typically designed to encourage interaction with the user. **Slicers** are one way to encourage interaction. Slicers are visual controls that allow you to quickly and easily filter your data in an interactive way. If you are interested in knowing how to create dashboards in Excel, please refer to Chapter 13 of this book. In this section, you will use form controls to encourage more interaction with dashboards and create dynamic labels to increase the readability of a dashboard.

Enhance Spreadsheets with Form Controls

Form controls have many uses in Excel. A **form control** is an object that can be placed into an Excel worksheet, providing the functionality to interact with your models. Form controls can be used to help users select data by providing menus, lists, spinners, and scroll bars. In the context of dashboards, form controls can provide a simple way to interact with your analysis in a way that is backward compatible with earlier versions of Excel.

Opening the Starting File

You have been given access to a workbook that is connected to the Red Bluff Golf Course & Pro Shop sales database with an existing dashboard and Power View report. You will use a variety of developer tools to enhance the functionality of the dashboard and Power View report. Some of the changes you will make to the workbook require it to be saved as a macro-enabled workbook. In this exercise, you will open the starting file and save it as a macro-enabled workbook.

E14.00

To Open a Workbook and Save It As a Macro-Enabled Workbook

> ### Grader Heads Up
> The MyLab IT Grader version of this project uses only xlsx versions of the Excel workbook. You will create the MyLab IT Grader version of this file in the following exercises along with an xlsm copy of the workbook.

SIDE NOTE
Office Updates
Depending on your exact Office version, you may see Open or Open Other Workbooks.

a. Start **Excel**, click **Open Other Workbooks** in the left pane, and then double-click **This PC**. Navigate through the folder structure to the location of your student data files, and then double-click **e07ch14Dashboards**.

b. Click the **File** tab, and click **Save As**. Click **Browse**, click the **Save as type** arrow, and then select **Excel Macro-Enabled Workbook (*.xlsm)**. Navigate to the location where you are saving your project files, and then change the filename to e07ch14Dashboards_LastFirst using your last and first name. Click **Save**.

> ### Troubleshooting
> The files for this chapter must be opened with macros enabled. You may have opened the file from a trusted location as seen in Chapter 8. If you are not using a trusted location, you can enable macros by clicking the File tab, Options, Trust Center, Trust Center Settings, Macros Settings, and Enable All Macros.

Adding the Developer Tab

Form controls in Excel are located on the Developer tab of the ribbon. In this exercise, you will add the Developer tab to the ribbon.

 E14.01

SIDE NOTE
Pin the Ribbon
If your ribbon is collapsed, pin your ribbon open. Click the Home tab. In the lower-right corner of the ribbon, click Pin the ribbon.

SIDE NOTE
Developer Tab
If you already have the Developer tab added to your ribbon, you can skip this exercise.

To Add the Developer Tab

a. Click the **File** tab, and then click **Options**.

b. In the Excel Options dialog box, in the left pane, click **Customize Ribbon**.

c. In the Main Tabs list, click the **Developer** check box.

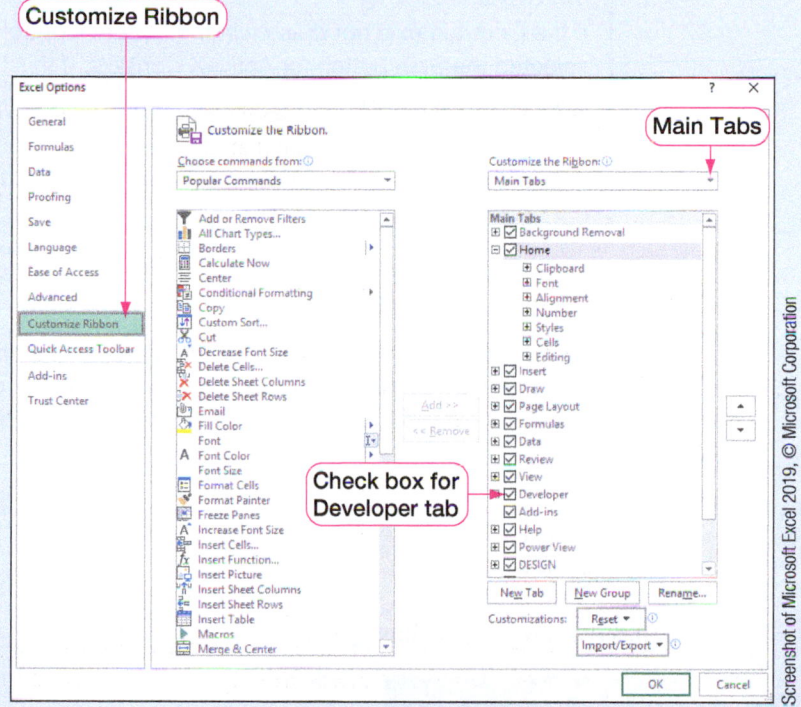

Figure 1   Excel Options dialog box

d. Click **OK**.

Adding a Spin Button

Spin buttons and scroll bars can enhance a user's experience with a dashboard. A **spin button**, also referred to as a spinner, is a form control that is linked to a specific cell. As the up and down arrows on the button are clicked, the value in the linked cell increases and decreases accordingly. In this exercise, you will create a simple spin button to provide the user with an easy way of increasing and decreasing the year of the sales data.

 **E14.02**

To Add a Spin Button

a. Click the **RevenueDashboard** worksheet. This worksheet consists of a simple dashboard with charts, tables, slicers, and sparklines.

b. Click cell **A19**. Click the **Developer** tab, and then, in the Controls group, click the **Insert** arrow.

c. Under Form Controls, click **Spin Button (Form Control)** 🔼.

d. To insert the Spin Button, drag a **vertical rectangle** in cell **A19** to the right of the year value.

e. Right-click the **spin** button, and then select **Format Control**.

f. In the Format Control dialog box, on the Control tab, select the value in the **Current value** box, and then type 2017

> ### Troubleshooting
>
> If the Control tab is not present in the Format Control dialog box, you may have selected the Spin button for ActiveX Controls. If this happened, delete the control, and repeat steps b–f.

g. Select the value in the **Minimum value** box, and then type 2017

h. Select the value in the **Maximum value** box, and then type 2019

i. Confirm that the Incremental change box contains **1**. Click the **Cell link** box, click **A19**, and then click **OK**.

j. Click cell **A19** to deselect the spin button, and then test the added functionality by clicking the up and down arrows to increase and decrease the year, and observe the changes in the table below and the chart to the right.

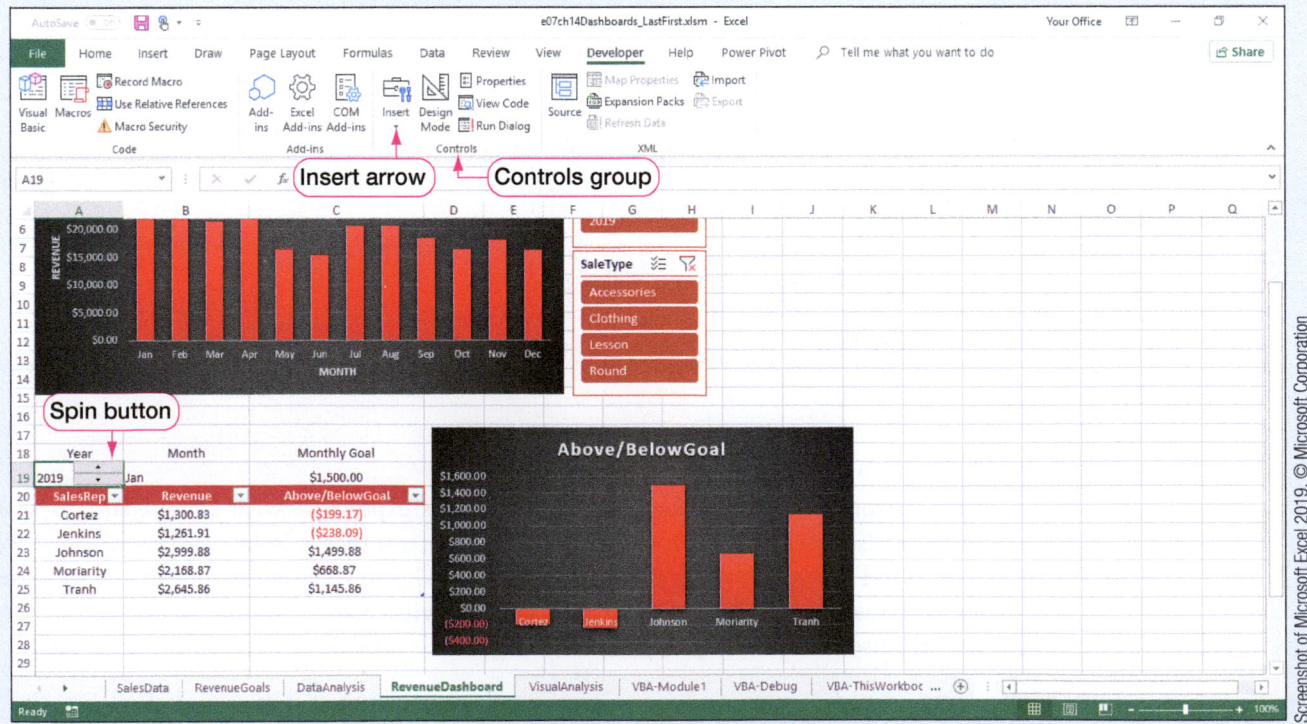

Figure 2 Spin button added

k. **Save** 💾 the workbook.

Creating a Lookup Table to Use with Form Controls

Some form controls, such as the scroll bar, require some additional work to create the values that will be used by the object. Creating a lookup table and using the VLOOKUP function is a common approach to linking values to various form controls. In this exercise, you will create a lookup table for months to use with a scroll bar control.

 **E14.03**

To Create a Lookup Table

a. Click the **DataAnalysis** worksheet.

b. Click cell **E1**, type 1 and then press Tab. Type Jan and press Enter.

c. In cell **E2**, type 2 and then press Tab. Type Feb and press Ctrl+Enter.

d. Select the cell range **E1:F2**. Click the **fill** handle, and drag to the cell range E12:F12 to create a listing of months from Jan to Dec.

e. Select the cell range **E1:F12**. Click in the **Name** box, type Month_Range and then press Enter to create a named range for the lookup table.

f. Click the **RevenueDashboard** worksheet, click cell **B17**, and then type 1 This value will be used as the lookup value in the VLOOKUP function to retrieve the appropriate month from the Month_Range named range.

g. Click cell **B19**, select **the text**, and then type the following function: =VLOOKUP(B17, Month_Range, 2, False)

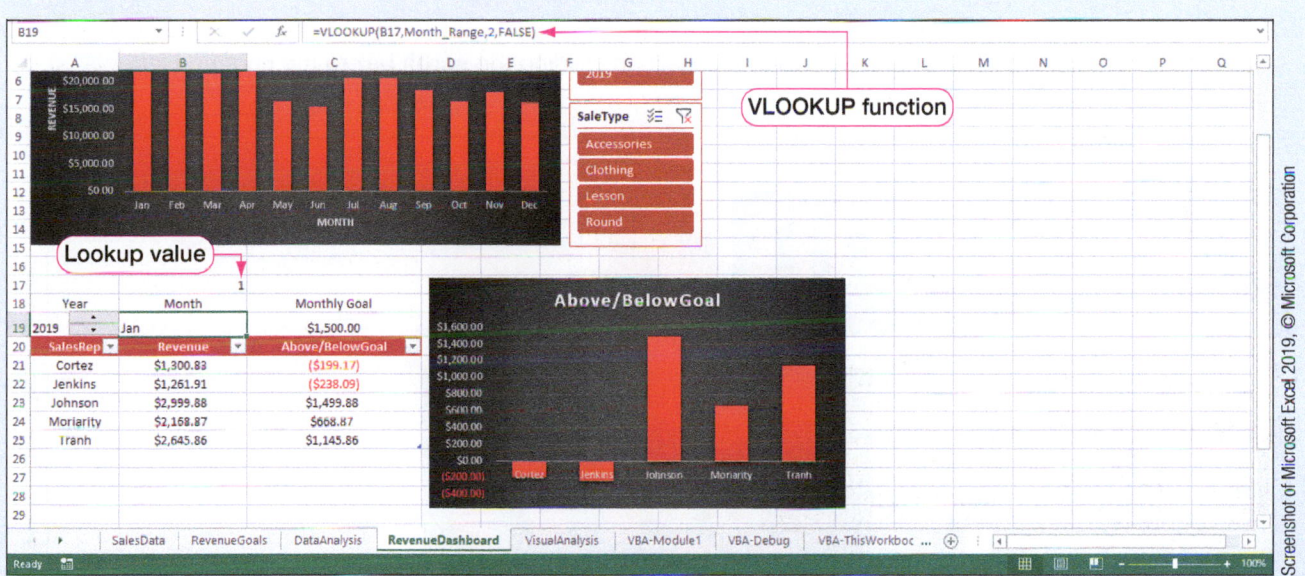

Figure 3 VLOOKUP function added

h. Press Ctrl+Enter and then **Save** 💾 the workbook.

Adding a Scroll Bar

Now that you have created a lookup table with the appropriate values and have added the VLOOKUP function to cell B19, you will add the scroll bar form control. A **scroll bar** has a function very similar to that of the spin button. However, with a scroll bar, the value of the linked cell is increased or decreased by sliding the scroll bar to the left or right. In this exercise, you will create a scroll bar so that the user can easily scroll through different months.

 **E14.04**

To Add a Scroll Bar

a. If necessary, click the **Developer** tab, and then, in the Controls group, click the **Insert** arrow. Under Form Controls, select **Scroll Bar (Form Control)** ▦.

b. Drag a **horizontal rectangle** in cell **B19** to the right of the value.

c. Right-click the **scroll bar**, and then select **Format Control**.

d. In the Format Control dialog box, on the Control tab, select the value in the **Current value** box, and then type **1**

e. Select the value in the **Minimum value** box, and then type **1**

f. Select the value in the **Maximum value** box, and then type **12** Leave the existing values in the Incremental change and Page change boxes.

g. Click the **Cell link** box, click cell **B17**, and then click **OK**.

h. Click cell **B17**, and then change the font color to white so that it is not visible in the model.

i. Test the added functionality by sliding the **scroll bar** to the right and left.

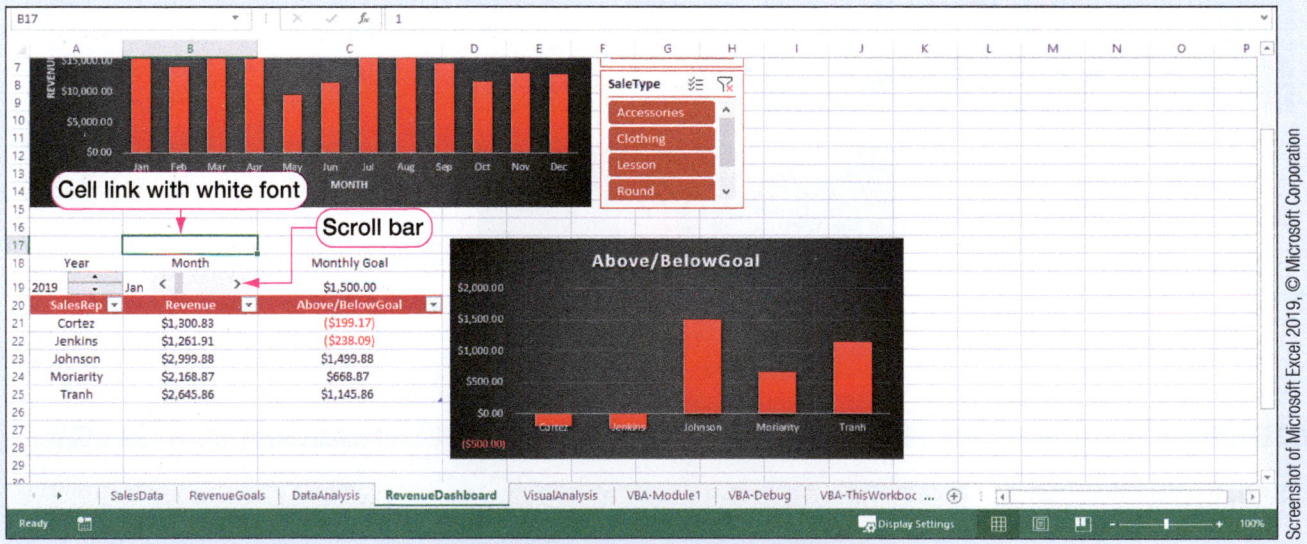

Figure 4 Scroll bar added

j. **Save** 🖫 the workbook.

Creating Dynamic Labels

Labels are critical to dashboard design and can add clarity to the graphics being displayed. Dynamic labels offer additional clarity in PivotCharts by displaying the year and/or month that is being displayed when filtered. In this exercise, you will create dynamic labels on the Sales Revenue chart.

 **E14.05**

To Create Dynamic Labels

a. Click the **Insert** tab, and then, in the Text group, click **Text Box**.

b. Drag to create a box in the top left corner of the **Sales Revenue column chart**.

c. Click the **formula bar**. Type = click the **DataAnalysis** worksheet, and then click cell **B1**. Press Enter.

> **Troubleshooting**
>
> If you did not click the formula bar before typing =, then the cell reference will not work. Just delete the typed =, click the formula bar, and type = again.

d. On the **Home** tab, in the Font group, increase the font size to 14 Click the **Fill Color** arrow, and then select **No Fill** to remove the default white fill.

e. Click the **Font Color** arrow, and then select **White, Background 1**.

f. Click the **Format** tab, and then, in the Shape Styles group, click the **Shape Outline** arrow. Select **No Outline**.

g. Test the functionality of the dynamic label by clicking on different years in the Year slicer. If necessary, adjust the size of the text box to accommodate the value.

    You will now add another dynamic label for the SaleType.

h. Click the **Insert** tab, and then, in the Text group, click **Text Box**.

i. Drag to create a box in the top right corner of the **Sales Revenue column chart**.

j. Click the **formula bar**. Type = click the **DataAnalysis** worksheet, and then click cell **B2**. Press Enter.

k. On the Home tab, in the Font group, increase the font size to 14 Click the **Fill Color** arrow, and then select **No Fill** to remove the default white fill.

l. Click the **Font Color** arrow, and then select **White, Background 1**.

m. Click the **Format** tab, and then, in the Shape Styles group, click the **Shape Outline** arrow. Select **No Outline**.

n. Click **Accessories** in the SaleType slicer, and then adjust the size of the box to accommodate the value.

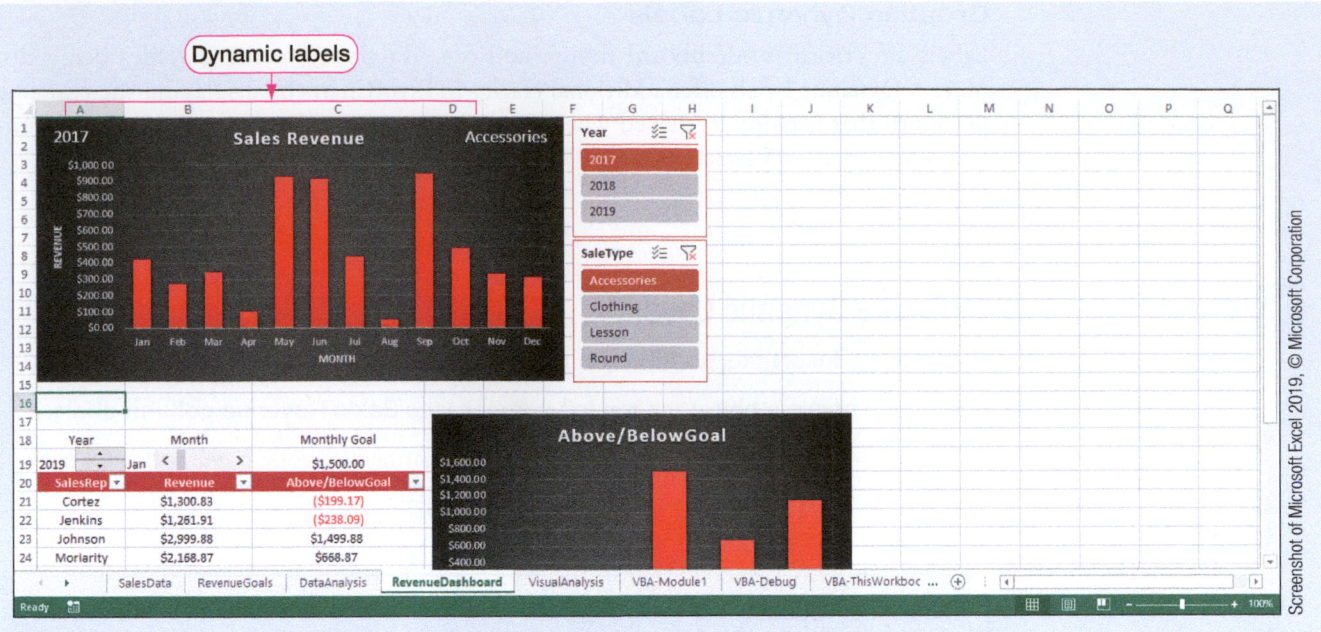

Figure 5 Dynamic labels added

o. **Save** 💾 the workbook. If you need to take a break before finishing this chapter, now is a good time.

Leveraging the Power of Visual Basic for Applications (VBA)

Visual Basic for Applications (VBA) is a powerful programming language that is part of most Microsoft Office applications: Word, Access, Excel, and PowerPoint. VBA allows a user to implement a wide variety of enhancements to any of these applications. VBA is particularly valuable in automating repetitive tasks; in that way, it is similar to macros, but it provides additional tools that can enhance the functionality and usability of an Excel application. VBA is considered a very basic form of object-oriented programming. **Object-oriented programming (OOP)** uses a hierarchy of objects—also called classes—as the focus of the programming. VBA manipulates objects by using the methods and properties associated with them. In this section, you will explore the various components of VBA and create simple procedures that will enhance an Excel workbook and provide additional security to protect the data.

Understand the Components of VBA

The key to using VBA effectively to enhance your dashboard or any other Excel application is to understand Excel's object model. An **object model** is a hierarchical collection of objects, consisting of properties, methods, and events that can be manipulated by using VBA. Excel is made up of several dozen objects. Objects are combinations of data and code that are treated as a single unit including workbooks, worksheets, charts, and PivotTables—and even Excel itself is an object. **Objects** can also serve as containers for other objects. For example, Excel is an object called an application. This application object contains workbook objects, workbook objects contain worksheet objects, and worksheet objects contain cell range objects. Figure 6 shows a partial object model for Excel.

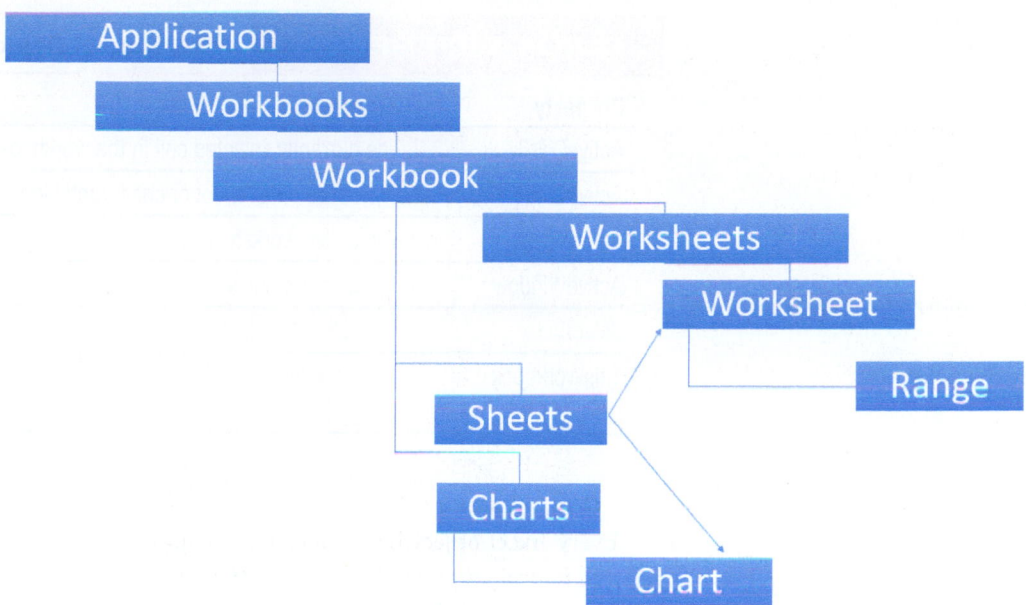

Figure 6   Partial hierarchical object model

Objects are often grouped together into what are called **object collections**. For example, a worksheet is an object in a workbook, and all worksheets in a workbook collectively are also an object. A particular object can be referenced inside a collection by referring to the object collection and then the name or number that represents that specific member of that collection. For example Sheets("Sheet2") is a reference to a worksheet with the name Sheet2 that is a member of the Sheets object collection.

QUICK REFERENCE	Object Collections
Object Collection	**Description**
Workbooks("Book1")	Refers to a workbook named Book1
Sheets("Sheet1")	Refers to a worksheet named Sheet1
Range("A2:C23")	Refers to the range of cells A2:C23
Charts(2)	Refers to the second chart in a workbook
ChartObjects(3)	Refers to the third embedded chart in a worksheet
Windows(3)	Refers to the third open Excel workbook window

When you refer to a particular object using VBA, the objects need to be referred to in their hierarchical structure. For example, to refer to cell A1 in a specific worksheet, you would need the following code.

Application.Workbook(workbookname.xlsx).Sheets("Sheet1").Range("A1")

The periods between each object are referred to as separators. **Separators** indicate the distinction between the object container and the member of that container.

Having to type the entire hierarchy each time a particular object is used can be tedious. Therefore, VBA provides special object names that can be used to refer to specific objects. For example, ActiveCell refers to the specific cell that is currently selected in the workbook.

QUICK REFERENCE | VBA Special Object Names

Property	Description
ActiveCell	The currently selected cell in the workbook
ActiveChart	The active chart sheet or chart contained in a ChartObject on a worksheet
ActiveSheet	The active worksheet
ActiveWindow	The active window
Selection	The selected object. It could refer to a range object, shape, chart, and so on
ThisWorkbook	The workbook object that contains the VBA procedure being executed. This object may or may not be the same as the ActiveWorkbook object.

Every Excel object has properties. **Properties** are attributes of an object that can be referred to or manipulated by using VBA. For example, the cell range object has properties such as value and address.

QUICK REFERENCE | Properties of Common Objects

Object	Property	Description
Workbooks	Name	The name of the workbook
	Path	The directory in which the workbook resides
	Saved	Whether or not the workbook has been saved
	HasPassword	Whether or not the workbook has a password
Worksheets	Name	The name of the worksheet
	Visible	Whether or not the worksheet is visible
Range	Address	The cell reference of the range
	Comment	A comment attached to the cell
	Formula	The formula entered in the cell
	Value	The value entered in the cell
Chart	ChartTitle	The text of the chart's title
	ChartType	The type of chart: bar, column, line
	HasLegend	Whether or not the chart has a legend

An object's properties can be easily modified with a simple expression: Object.Property = expression. For example, to rename a worksheet that is currently selected, using VBA, you would type the following expression: ActiveSheet.Name = "NewSheetName".

Excel objects also have methods. A **method** is an action that an object is able to perform. For example, one of the methods for a Range object is ClearContents. When this method is called, values would be cleared from the range. The basic syntax required to call an object's method is as follows.

ObjectName.Method

For example, to clear the values in the cell range A1:A5, you would type the following.

Range("A1:A5").ClearContents

QUICK REFERENCE — Common Methods and Descriptions

Object	Method	Description
Workbooks	Close	Closes the workbook
	Protect	Protects the workbook
	SaveAs	Saves the workbook with a specified file name
Worksheets (SheetName)	Delete	Deletes the worksheet
	Select	Selects and displays the worksheet
Range	Clear	Clears all content in the range
	Copy	Copies the values in the range to the Clipboard
	Merge	Merges the cells in the range
Chart (ChartName)	Copy	Copies the chart to the Clipboard
	Select	Selects the chart
	Delete	Deletes the chart
Worksheets	Select	Selects all the worksheets in the workbook
Charts	Select	Selects all chart sheets in the workbook

Methods often have parameters that must be included to use the method on the object. A **parameter** is a variable used to refer to data provided to a method. For example, the Workbook object has a SaveAs method that requires the file name as a parameter. Most methods contain required and optional parameters. The basic syntax for providing parameters in a method is as follows:

object.method parameter1: = value, parameter2:= value2

For example,

ActiveWorkbook.SaveAs Filename:="NewWorkbookName", FileFormat:=52

saves the active workbook as NewWorkbookName.xlsm.

QUICK REFERENCE — Common FileFormat Values

FileFormat Value	File Extension
51	.xlsx
52	.xlsm
6	.csv
−4158	.txt

Exploring the Visual Basic Editor

The **Visual Basic Editor (VBE)** is the tool built into Microsoft Office that is used for creating and editing VBA. At the top of the VBE screen is the title of the workbook that is currently open and being edited. Directly under the application title are the File menu and Standard toolbars, which are visible by default. On the left side of the Visual Basic Editor is the Project Explorer. The **Project Explorer window** contains a hierarchical list of all the objects in open workbooks, including macros, modules, and worksheets. VBA in an Excel workbook can be contained either in a specific worksheet, in the specific workbook, or within a module. Below the Project Explorer window is the Properties window. The **Properties window** contains a list of all the properties of a selected object such as name, size, and color. Depending on your system settings, the Properties window may not be displayed by default when the VBE is opened. The larger window on the right of the Visual Basic Editor is the Code window. The **Code window** is where all the VBA code is typed and where VBA generated by a recorded macro can be viewed and edited. The VBA code is stored in modules. A **module** is simply a container for code. In this exercise, you will explore the VBE and insert a new module.

 **E14.06**

SIDE NOTE
Displaying the VBE
You can press Alt + F11 to access the VBE and toggle back and forth between the VBE and the Excel workbook.

To Explore the VBE

a. If you took a break, open the **e07ch14Dashboards_LastFirst** workbook and, if needed, click the **RevenueDashboard** worksheet. Click the **Developer** tab, and in the Code group, click **Visual Basic**. If necessary, **Maximize** the window.

b. If the Analysis ToolPak Add-in is installed in Excel, you will see an open Code window with FUNCRES.XLAM in the title bar. **Close** this window if necessary.

c. Click **Insert**, and then select **Module**.

Notice the Project Explorer window, Properties window, and Code window.

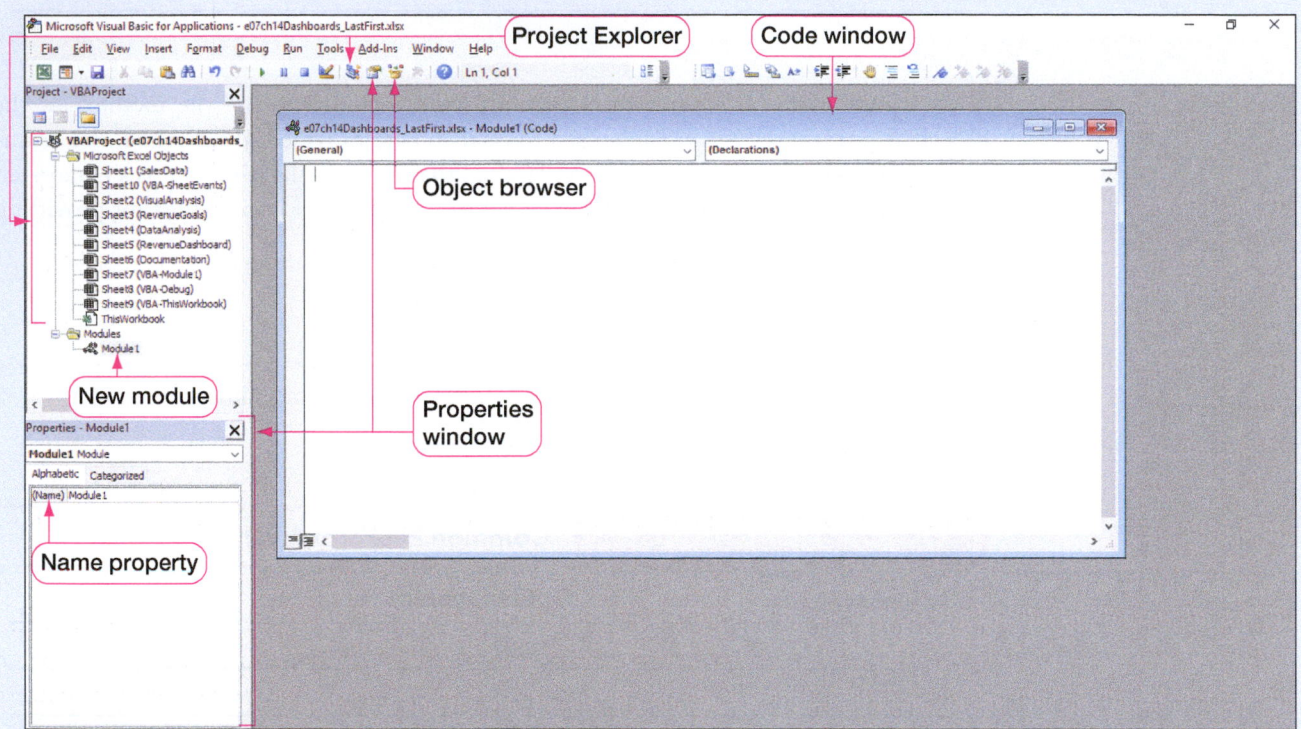

Microsoft Visual Basic 2019, © Microsoft Corporation

Figure 7 The Visual Basic Editor

SIDE NOTE
Displaying the Windows
If you close the Project Explorer, you can press Ctrl and type R to display it. Pressing F4 will display the Properties window if it is closed.

d. In the Properties window, click inside the Name box. Replace the **Module1** text with **e07ch14Module1_LastFirst** using your last and first name.

The two primary types of procedures that are supported by VBA are Sub procedures and function procedures. **A Sub procedure** performs an action on your project or workbook, such as renaming a worksheet or clearing filtered values from PivotTables. **A function procedure** is a group of VBA statements that perform a calculation and return a single value. Function procedures are often used to create custom functions that can be entered in worksheet cells. You can have zero or hundreds of Sub procedures and functions written within a single module. Modules are most often used to store any public procedures that are not driven by events such as the opening of a workbook. If a Sub procedure is to run when a workbook opens or a worksheet becomes active, then it is typically stored in the workbook or worksheet object to take advantage of the Procedure menu at the top of the Code window.

REAL WORLD ADVICE | **Organizing VBA Code by Type**

If you have several Sub procedures within a workbook, it can easily become challenging to keep track of where a specific Sub procedure is within a module. It is best to group your Sub procedures together by what they do into separate modules, renaming the module appropriately to describe the kind of procedures it contains. For example, Sub procedures that format a workbook can all be grouped into one module, and Sub procedures that are used to manipulate data can be stored in another.

CONSIDER THIS | **Public versus Private Sub Procedures**

There are public and private Sub procedures. By default, Excel makes all Sub procedures public, which means that they can be accessed or called by any module in the workbook and are available to be accessed in the Macro window. If a Sub procedure is private, it can only be called from within the module it is defined within, and the code is viewable only inside the VBE. What are some advantages and disadvantages of creating public and private Sub procedures?

Create Custom Functions with VBA

Function procedures can provide custom calculations that are used frequently in a business and are not part of the extensive functions available in Excel. These custom functions do not have to be complicated, but they can be created to ensure consistency in calculations.

To create a function procedure, you must first declare that it is a function and then provide the function with a name and an opening parenthesis. After the opening parenthesis, you must provide a name for the value or values that the function needs to perform its calculation and declare the data type(s) that Excel should expect from the value(s). A closing parenthesis is required to end the function.

Function Commission (salesTotal As Currency)

The next line of code is where the calculation of the function is defined. Simply type the FunctionName, declared in the first line, an equal sign, followed by the ValueName, defined in the first line, and then the calculation you would like the function to perform.

Commission = salesTotal * .15

In this example, the function Commission would be calculated by multiplying the value supplied by the user by .15. The value supplied by the user could be a number typed into the function or a cell reference.

Creating a Function Procedure

In this exercise, you will create a custom function that will take the total sales value and multiply it by 15% to calculate the total commission paid.

 **E14.07**

SIDE NOTE

Capitalization

Capitalization is important in programming. Once a procedure has been named or a variable has been declared, the VBE will autocorrect for capitalization.

To Create a Function Procedure

a. Click inside the **Code window**, declare a function procedure by typing Function COMMISSION(salesTotal As Currency) and then press Enter.

The Function key word is what tells Excel that you are creating a function procedure. COMMISSION is the name given to the function. The value that the function will use in its calculation is named salesTotal and will be a Currency data type.

b. Type the comment 'This function will multiply the total sales amount by 15% and then press Enter.

c. Type COMMISSION = salesTotal * 0.15 and then press Enter.

Note that COMMISSION is the name of the function and must be assigned a value for the function procedure to return a value to the worksheet.

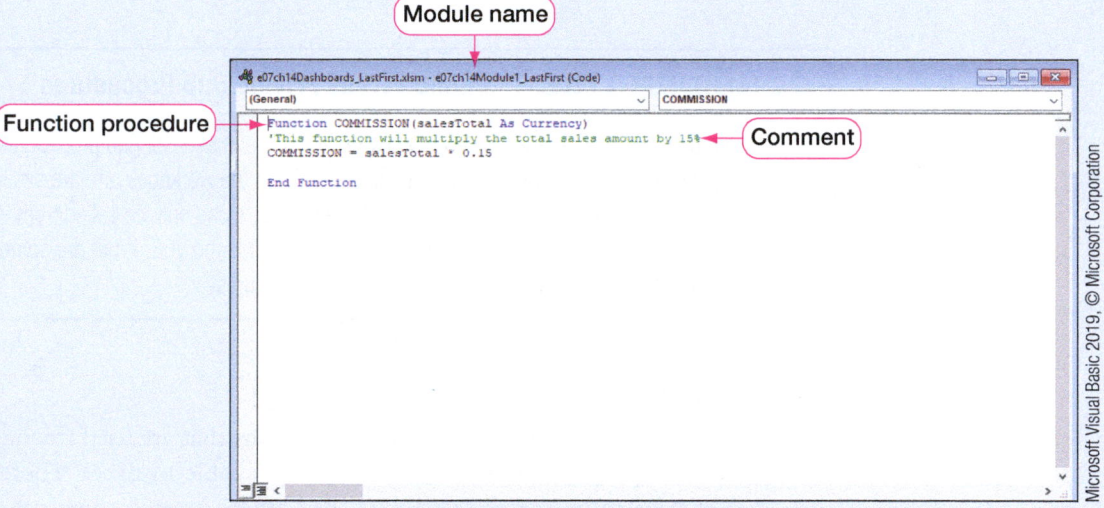

Figure 8 COMMISSION function procedure

d. **Save** the workbook.

Using a Custom Function

Now that you have created a new function in the VBE, it can be used in any worksheet in the workbook. In this exercise, you will use the newly created function in the RevenueDashboard worksheet.

 **E14.08**

To Use a Custom Function

a. Press Alt + F11 to switch to the workbook.

b. On the RevenueDashboard worksheet, click cell **A27**, type Total Sales and then press Tab.

c. In cell **B27**, type =SUM(RevenueGoals[Revenue]) to sum the values of the Revenue column in the RevenueGoals table. Press Ctrl + Enter.

d. Format cell B27 as **Currency**.

e. Click cell **A28**, type Commission and then press Tab.

f. In cell **B28**, type =COMMISSION(B27) to use the COMMISSION function. Press Ctrl + Enter.

   The COMMISSION function multiplies the value in cell B27 by 0.15 to calculate the commission.

g. Format cell B28 as **Currency**.

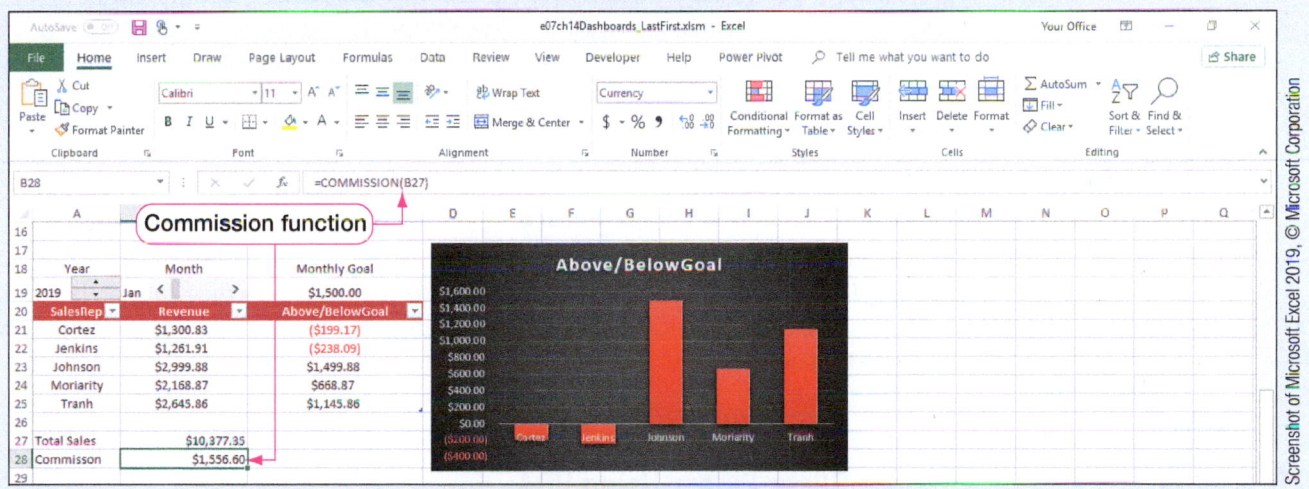

Figure 9 COMMISSION function used

h. **Save** 💾 the workbook.

Improve Readability of VBA with Formatting and Structure

An important aspect of writing VBA is making sure the code is easy to read so that you and others can interpret what is happening. This means frequently using indentation, comments, and line breaks. This is especially true in working with more complex code.

   You need to take extra steps to keep the code legible and to document what steps you are taking and why. This will make it easier on you and others who may need to edit, analyze, or troubleshoot the code. One of these extra steps will be using the Tab key to create indentations in the code.

Commenting code in VBA is an excellent way of explaining the purpose and intention of a procedure. This way, you can add straightforward documentation about what the procedure is doing and what steps to take next. If you are developing more complicated procedures, you might want to leave yourself notes about what still needs to be completed or what statements are not working as expected. Adding comments in the Code window is as simple as typing an apostrophe at the beginning of the line of code. The (') symbol tells the VBE to ignore any text following the apostrophe on a line of the code.

Also, the VBE interprets code on a line-by-line basis, which means that if you type part of a statement on a line and press Enter before the end of the statement, it will create a syntax error. So lengthy statements may become difficult to read, because without pressing Enter, the lines of code will extend continuously to the right. However, placing a space followed by an underscore character at the end of the first line of code and pressing Enter will break the code to a second line. This tells the VBE that the two lines of code should be treated as one.

REAL WORLD ADVICE | **Using the Macro Recorder to Learn VBA**

An easy way to gain a better understanding of how VBA works is to use the Macro Recorder to generate VBA code for actions you want to complete. See Chapter 8 for information about recording macros. The code that is generated can be useful in identifying the key elements of the language and how the objects, properties, methods, and events work together to accomplish specific tasks.

Using VBA to Clear Slicer Filters

The RevenueDashboard worksheet contains two slicers used for filtering on Year and SaleType. In this exercise, you will write VBA code that will clear the filters on both slicers. You will be calling the ClearManualFilter method for the SlicerCaches collection that is part of the ThisWorkbook object.

 E14.09

SIDE NOTE
Naming Sub Procedures

Names for Sub procedures must begin with a letter and cannot contain any spaces.

SIDE NOTE
View the Object Browser

Press F2 in the VBE to display the Object Browser, which shows properties, methods, and events for an object.

To Clear Slicer Filters Using VBA

a. Press Alt + F11 to switch back to the VBE. Click inside the Code window just below the End Function statement, type Sub clearSlicers() and then press Enter to create a new Sub procedure.

b. To add a comment to the Sub procedure, type 'This code clears all slicer filters specified and press Enter. The (') symbol at the beginning of the line indicates that it is a comment and not a line of code that Excel needs to execute.

c. Type ThisWorkbook.SlicerCaches("Slicer_Year").ClearManualFilter and then press Enter.

d. Type ThisWorkbook.SlicerCaches("Slicer_SaleType").ClearManualFilter and then press Enter.

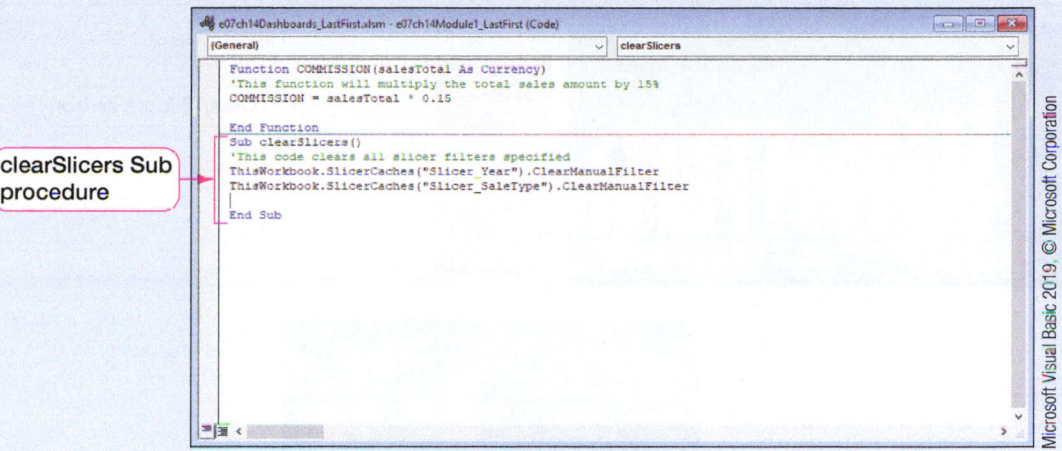

clearSlicers Sub procedure

Figure 10   clearSlicers Sub procedure

e. Click **Save** .

f. To test the VBA code, press [Alt]+[F11] to toggle back to the workbook. Click **2017** on the Year slicer, and click **Accessories** on the SaleType slicer.

g. Press [Alt]+[F11] again to toggle back to the editor. Press [F5] to run the clearSlicers Sub procedure.

h. Press [Alt]+[F11] again to toggle back to the workbook, and observe all the slicer filters have now been cleared.

i. **Save** the workbook.

Assigning VBA Code to a Button Control

The clearSlicers Sub procedure is not very useful without giving the user a way of running the code from the dashboard. Sub procedures can be added to command buttons for easy access. In this exercise, you will add a command button to the RevenueDashboard that runs the clearSlicers Sub procedure.

E14.10

To Assign a Sub Procedure to a Button Control

a. Click the **Developer** tab, and then, in the Controls group, click the **Insert** arrow. Under Form Controls, select **Button (Form Control)** ▭.

b. Drag to create a **rectangular button** to the right of the **Year** slicer, within the cell range **L1:M2**.

c. In the Assign Macro dialog box, select **clearSlicers**, and then click **OK**.

d. Right-click the **button** form control, and then select **Edit Text**. Delete the existing button text, type Clear Slicers and then click outside the button to confirm the change.

e. To test the functionality of the new button, apply some filters using the slicers, and then click the **Clear Slicers** button to clear them.

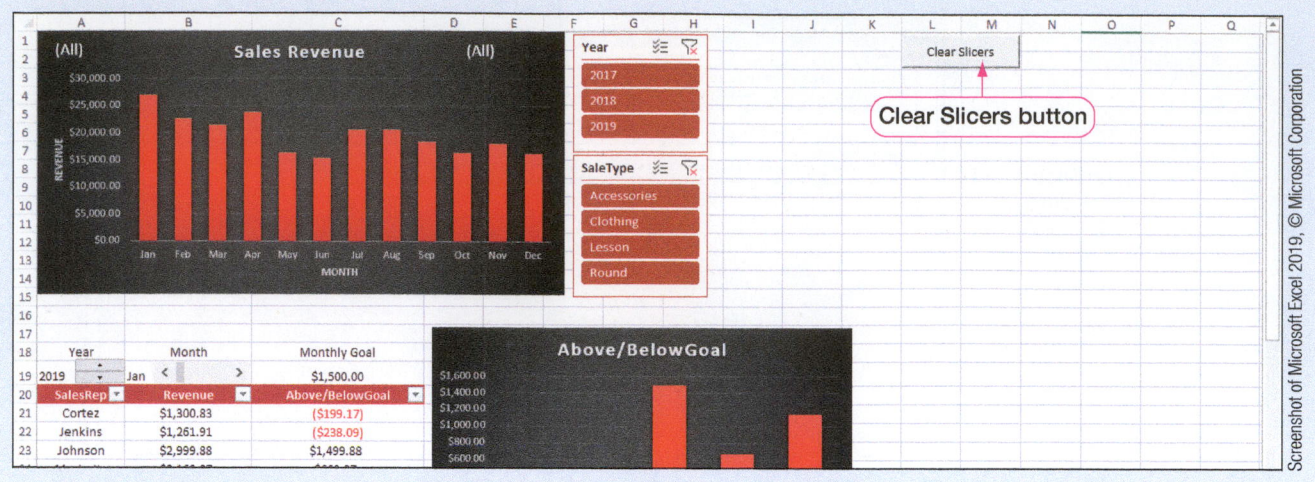

Figure 11 Clear Slicers button

f. **Save** 💾 the workbook.

Troubleshoot VBA

You may have encountered some errors when you attempted to write VBA code. Some of the errors may have been caused by pressing Enter to break up a line of code without inserting a space and an underscore or by some other syntax error. With those types of errors, the VBA code cannot be executed until the problem is corrected. The other common VBA error is called a run-time error. A **run-time error** occurs when code containing improper logic is executed. A message will then be displayed containing a description of the error. The VBE includes a tool called the debugger to help troubleshoot run-time errors. When the debugger is used, the code is executed one line at a time to make it easy to identify the exact point where the run-time error occurs.

Debug VBA

In this exercise, you will create a new module and enter a simple Sub procedure. The Sub procedure will contain an obvious error to help you learn how to use the VBE debugger.

 E14.11

SIDE NOTE
Debug Mode
You can also enter debugging mode by clicking the Debug menu and then selecting Step Into.

To Debug VBA

a. Press **Alt**+**F11** to switch to the VBE. Click **Insert**, and then select **Module**.

b. In the Properties window, select the text in the **Name** property, type **e07ch14DebugVBA_LastFirst** using your last and first name, and then press **Enter**. Click in the **Code Window**.

c. Any spelling errors in this code are intentional for the purposes of this exercise. Please type this code exactly as follows.

- Type **Private Sub troubleShoot ()** and then press **Enter**.

- Type **Sheets("RevenuDashboard").Range("A16"). Valu = "Red Bluff Monthly Revenue"** and then press **Enter**.

d. Press **F8** to enter debug mode. Notice that the first line of code is highlighted in yellow.

Mac Troubleshooting

Mac Troubleshooting

F8 can not be used to do this on a Mac. Instead, click Debug/Step Into on the File menu OR Shift/Cmd/I to highlight the first line of code. Repeat the command to highlight the second line and an error dialog box displays. Click Debug. Fix the error and press ⎇Shift⎇ ⎇Command ⌘⎇ one more time. Repeat until the errors are corrected.

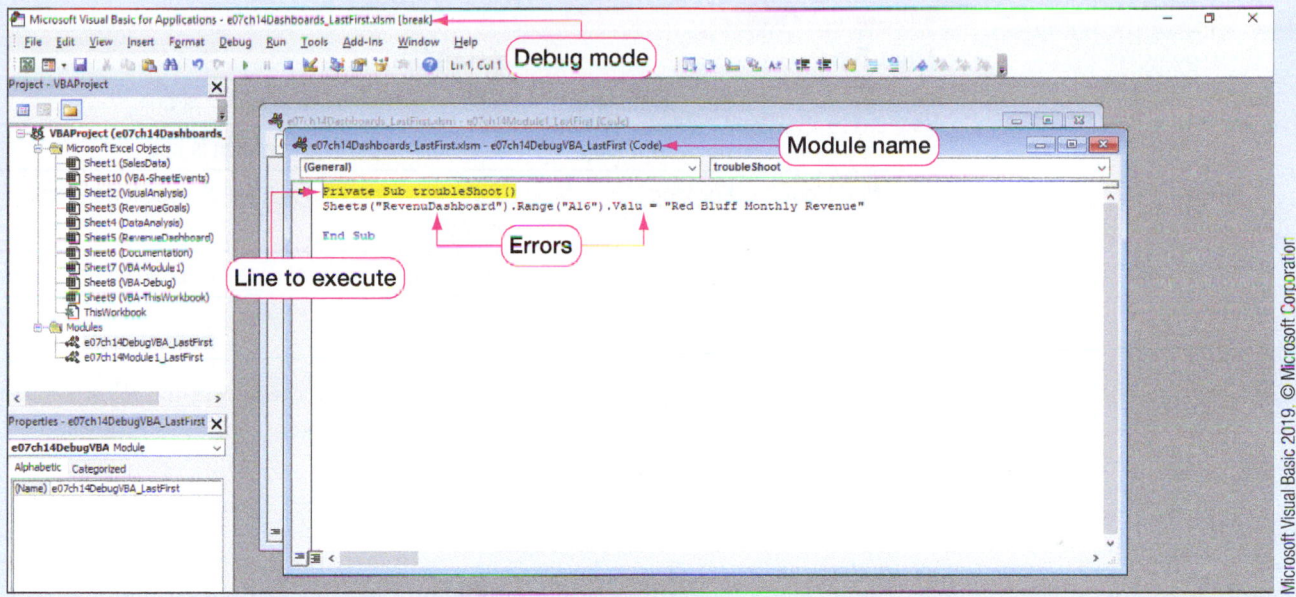

Figure 12   VBA debug mode

e. Press F8 again to execute that line of code. No warnings or errors are displayed, and the next line of code is now highlighted.

f. Press F8 again to execute the second line of code. A run-time error is displayed, stating Subscript out of range.

This error can occur for a variety of reasons, but a very common one is when the code refers to an object that does not exist in the workbook. In this case, the name of the sheet is misspelled.

g. Click **Debug**. Correct the spelling of the sheet name to RevenueDashboard and then press F8 to execute the second line again.

h. Another error message is displayed, indicating that the object does not support this property or method. Click **Debug**, and then notice that the Value property is misspelled as **Valu**. Correct the spelling of the Valu property to Value and then press F8 to execute the second line again.

i. The second line of code executes without any additional errors, and the first line of code in e07ch14Module1_LastFirst is highlighted. Press F8 to exit debugging mode.

j. Press Alt + F11 to switch back to the workbook. Notice that the text has been added to cell A16.

k. **Save** 🖫 the workbook.

Create and Use Loops in VBA

The clearSlicers Sub procedure created earlier to automatically clear the filters from the Years and SaleType slicers was effective, but if more slicers are added to the dashboard, the procedure has to be modified to include the additional slicers. A more effective use of the VBA code would be to use what is called a loop. A **loop** is used to execute a series of statements multiple times. The number of times the code is executed can be determined by a specified number until a condition is true or false, or the code can continue to execute however many objects there are in a collection. There are essentially two categories of loops: Do loops and For...Next loops.

QUICK REFERENCE		Types of Loops in VBA
Loop Type		**Description**
Do Loop	**Do...While loop**	Loops while a specified condition is true
	Do...Until loop	Loops until a specified condition is true
For...Next loop	**For loop**	Loops until a specified number of loops have been completed
	For...Each loop	Loops through an object collection or an array

The appropriate loop type needed to be able to clear the filters for all slicers in a workbook is the For...Next loop. The syntax of the For...Next loop is as follows.

For Each element In group

code to execute

Next element

In the context of using the For...Each loop to loop through a collection of objects, the element is the object, and the group is the collection of those objects. In the syntax of the For...Each loop, the data type of the element and group must be the same. This often requires that in the VBA code, before the loop begins, variables be declared with a data type specified.

Declaring a Variable

A **variable** is space in a computer's memory that is given a name and is used to store a value of a specified data type. To create a variable, the space needs to be allocated in the computer's memory. This is known as dimensioning or declaring a variable. VBA abbreviates this as Dim, and it is a required keyword before a variable can be created.

The syntax for declaring a variable and assigning a data type to it is as follows.

Sub procedureName ()

Dim variableName As DataType

End Sub

QUICK REFERENCE	Restrictions to Naming Variables

As in naming procedures, there are specific requirements that must be taken into consideration in naming variables.

1. Variable names must start with a letter and not a number.

2. Variable names cannot have more than 250 characters.

3. Variable names cannot be the same as any one of Excel's key words. For example, a variable cannot be named "Sheet" or "Workbook".

4. Spaces are not allowed in variable names. You can separate words either by capitalizing the first letter of each word or by using the underscore character.

You can also declare multiple variables and assign them all a data type at one time by using the following syntax.

Sub procedureName ()

Dim variable1 As DataType1, variable2 As DataType2, variable3 As DataType3

End Sub

There are several data types in VBA; the most common ones are Currency, String, Single, Double, Boolean, and Variant.

QUICK REFERENCE	Common VBA Data Types	
Name	**Description**	**Example**
Boolean	Used in true or false variables	True or False
Integer	Numeric data type for whole numbers	125
Long	Numeric data type for large integer numbers	9,000,000,000
Currency	Numeric data type that allows for four digits to the right of the decimal and 15 to the left	1234.67
Single	Numeric data type used for numbers that can contain fractions	125.25
Double	Numeric data type used for large numbers that can contain fractions	9,000,000,000.25
Date	Stores date and time data	7/1/2018 8:35:56 AM
String	A variable length of text characters	"A message to the user"
Variant	The default data type if none is specified; can store numeric, string, date/time, empty, or null data	125, "Hello," 7/1/2018, etc.

In this exercise, you will begin working toward creating a For…Each loop that will clear the filters on any number of slicers that may be added to the RevenueDashboard worksheet. First, you will need to declare a variable to use within the For…Each loop.

 **E14.12**

To Declare a Variable

a. Press [Alt]+[F11] to switch to the VBE.

b. Click the **e07ch14Module1_LastFirst** Code window, click just below the End Sub statement of the clearSlicers procedure, and then press [Enter].

c. Create a new Sub procedure by typing **Sub slicerLoop()** and then press [Enter].

d. Type the following comment: **'This code will loop through all slicers in the workbook and clear all filters** and then press [Enter].

e. Declare a variable of the SlicerCache type by typing **Dim slicers As SlicerCache** and then press [Enter] twice to make the code easier to read. Now that you have created a variable of the type SlicerCache, you are now ready to begin the For … Each loop.

Creating a For...Each Loop

In order to clear slicer filters for any slicer object in the book, a different property of the SlicerCache object must be used. By using the ClearAllFilters property instead of ClearManualFilters, the code will now apply to text and timeline slicers in the workbook. In this exercise, you will create the VBA code to loop through all of the SlicerCache objects in the collection of SlicerCaches in the ThisWorkbook object.

 **E14.13**

To Create a For...Each Loop

a. Begin the loop by typing For Each slicers In ThisWorkbook.SlicerCaches and then press Enter twice.

This line of code is what begins the loop. Excel will go through each of the SlicerCache objects in the collection of SlicerCaches and perform the next line of code.

b. Create the code to execute by typing slicers.ClearAllFilters and then press Enter twice.

c. End the loop by typing Next slicers and then press Enter.

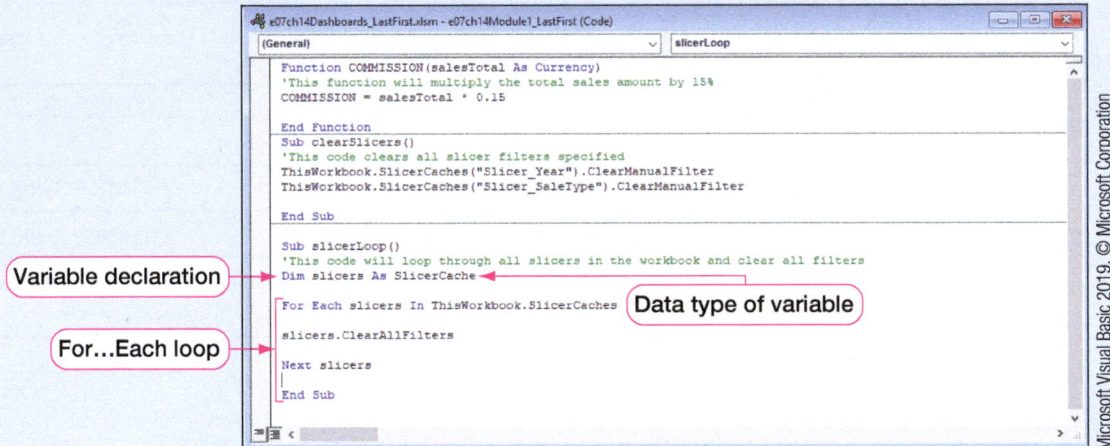

Figure 13 slicerLoop Sub procedure

d. **Save** 💾 the workbook.

Adding Slicers to Test Loop Effectiveness

Now that you have created a For...Each loop to accommodate the addition of more slicers on the RevenueDashboard worksheet, you can add new slicers and keep the functionality of the Clear Slicers button. In this exercise, you will add two additional slicers, filter the chart using all four slicers, and run the loop by clicking the Clear Slicers button.

 **E14.14**

To Test Effectiveness of the For...Each Loop

a. Press Alt + F11 to switch to the RevenueDashboard worksheet, and then click the **Sales Revenue** column chart.

b. Click the **Analyze** tab, and then in the Filter group, click **Insert Slicer**.

c. Check the boxes for **SalesRep** and **Status**, and then click **OK**.

d. If necessary, click the **Status** slicer, and then resize it to 1" in height and 1.5" in width. Click the **Options** tab, and then, in the Slicer Styles group, select **Rose, Slicer Style Dark 3** in the Dark category.

e. Click the **SalesRep** slicer, and then resize it to 2" in height and 1.5" in width. Click the **Options** tab, and then, in the Slicer Styles group, select **Rose, Slicer Style Dark 3** in the Dark category.

f. Reposition the **Status** and **SalesRep** slicers to the right of the Year and SaleType slicers. Position the SalesRep slicer above the Status slicer. If necessary, right-click the **Clear Slicers** button, and then drag to the right to make room for the slicers.

g. Select the **Year** and **SaleType** slicers. On the Options tab, in the Slicer Styles group, select **Rose, Slicer Style Dark 3** from the Dark category.

h. Use each of the four slicers to filter the Sales Revenue column chart, and then click the **Clear Slicers** button.

   Notice that because the Clear Slicers button is still assigned to the clearSlicers procedure, the additional slicers are not affected by the code.

i. Right-click the **Clear Slicers** form control button, and then select **Assign Macro**.

j. Select **slicerLoop** to change the macro assigned to the button, and then click **OK**.

k. Click **any cell** to deselect the Clear Slicers button.

l. Click the **Clear Slicers** button to confirm that the code now affects all slicers and that there are no errors.

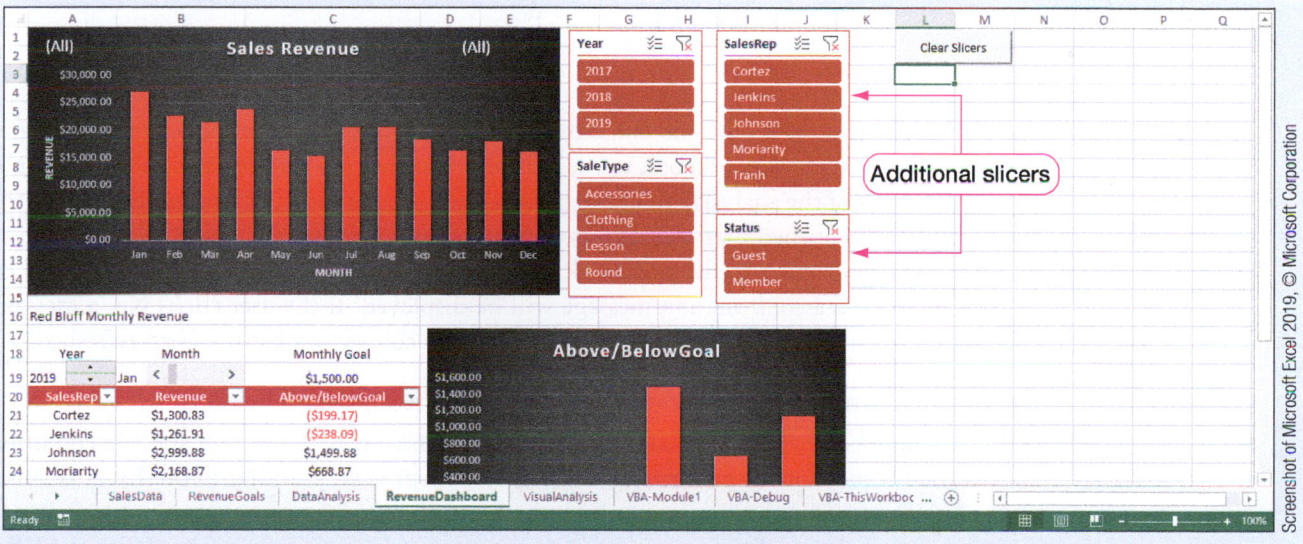

Figure 14   Additional slicers added

m. **Save** 💾 the workbook.

Assign VBA Procedures to Events

VBA code can be executed by a variety of methods, most commonly by assigning the code to a button or by setting up the code to execute when an event occurs. An **event** is an action initiated either by a user or by VBA code. An example of an event at the application level would be when a user creates a new workbook; an event at the workbook level would be when a user opens or closes a workbook.

QUICK REFERENCE		Common Events
Object	**Event**	**Description**
Application	SheetCalculate	Detects when formulas in any worksheet have been recalculated
	NewWorkbook	Detects when a user creates a new workbook
	WorkbookBeforeClose	Occurs after a user closes a workbook but before Excel actually closes it
Workbook	Open	Detects when a workbook is opened
	BeforeClose	Runs specified code before a workbook closes
	BeforeSave	Occurs after a user has clicked Save but before Excel actually saves the file
Worksheet	Activate	Detects when a specified worksheet is activated
	Deactivate	Detects when a specified worksheet is no longer the active sheet
	Change	Detects when any cell in a specified worksheet is changed

If the managers like the enhancements you make to the workbook, they will connect the data in the workbook to their database so that the most recent data available is always part of the analysis. You have been asked to create code that will execute when the workbook is opened that will display a message asking whether the user wants to refresh the data connection in the workbook. If the user clicks Yes, the data connection will be refreshed and a confirmation message will be displayed. If the user clicks No, a message will be displayed informing the user that the data connection has not been refreshed.

Incorporating Conditional Statements into VBA

The most basic method of running VBA commands in response to a specific condition is the If conditional statement. A VBA IF statement is very similar to the Excel IF function. The main difference is that with the Excel IF function, you are limited to only one outcome if the condition is true and one outcome if the condition is false. With the VBA If-Then-Else control structure, there is virtually no limit to the number of commands and logic that can be applied. The basic syntax of the If-Then-Else structure is as follows.

If Condition Then

Commands if condition is true

Else

Commands if condition is false

End If

The condition portion of the structure is an expression that is resolved to either true or false. If it is true, then the first set of commands is run; otherwise, the second set of commands is run. In this next exercise, you will create an If-Then-Else statement in which the condition is to check how the user responds to a message box asking whether or not to refresh the data connection. The commands will make use of message boxes. A **message box** is a dialog box object that is created by using the MsgBox command. The message box is used to display an informative message to the user and includes buttons the user can interact with. The MsgBox syntax is as follows:

MsgBox("Message Text", Buttons, "Message Title")

The only required argument in the MsgBox is the Message text or Prompt argument.

In this exercise, you will incorporate an If statement into a Sub procedure. This exercise requires a more complicated procedure; therefore, you will be including comments and adding extra white space to make the code easier to read and understand.

 **E14.15**

To Incorporate Conditional Statements

a. Press Alt + F11 to switch to the VBE.

b. Click the **Code window**, click just below the End Sub statement of the slicerLoop procedure, and then press Enter.

c. Create a new procedure by typing Sub refreshData() and then press Enter.

d. Type the following comment: 'This line of code will display a message box to the user and then press Enter twice.

e. To create a message box, type dataConnection = MsgBox("Would you like to refresh the data connection?", vbQuestion + vbYesNo, "Data Connection") and then press Enter twice.

   The message box will display a question mark and Yes/No buttons because you typed vbQuestion + vbYesNo for the buttons argument of the message box.

   This line of code creates a message box with the message text, a question style with Yes and No buttons, and a title of Data Connection. The user's response of Yes or No will be stored in the dataConnection variable.

f. Type the following comment block.

   'This If statement will refresh the data connection and display a confirmation message

   'if the user clicks Yes to the message box. If the user clicks no, another message box

   'will be displayed informing the user that the data connection was not refreshed

g. Press Enter twice, and then begin the If statement by typing If dataConnection = vbYes Then and then press Enter twice. This line of code will check the value of the message box, and if the user clicks the Yes button, it will execute the next block of code.

h. Type ThisWorkbook.Connections("ThisWorkbookDataModel").Refresh and then press Enter twice. This line of code, when executed, will refresh the dashboard with any changes made to the data model. This will be useful once the dashboard is connected to the sales database.

i. To create a confirmation message box, type MsgBox ("The data connection has been refreshed.") and then press Enter twice. Type Else to begin the Else statement, and then press Enter twice.

j. To create a message box if the user clicks No, type **MsgBox ("The data connection has not been refreshed.")** and then press Enter twice.

k. To end the If statement, type **End If** and then press Enter.

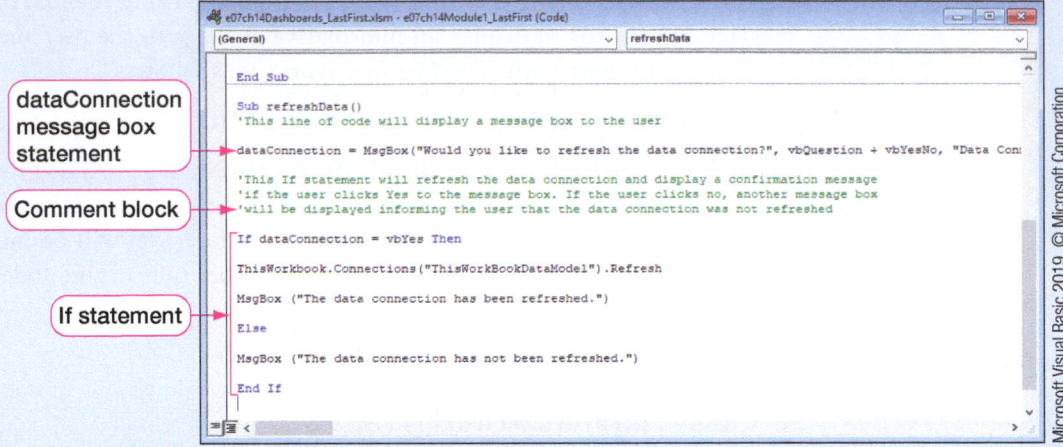

dataConnection message box statement

Comment block

If statement

Figure 15 refreshData Sub procedure

l. **Save** 💾 the workbook.

Microsoft Visual Basic 2019, © Microsoft Corporation

REAL WORLD ADVICE **Refreshing a Data Connection When a Workbook Opens**

In the previous exercise, you prompted the user to refresh a data connection when the workbook opens. Using VBA to automate this further, the sub routine could simply refresh without prompting the user. Additionally, if the data was stored in an external source, such as an Access Database, the VBA code to refresh the data connection would work equally as well. In this scenario, if the user of the workbook was frequently offline, or if the data connection to the database was unavailable, giving the user the option to not refresh would avoid VBA errors or additional coding to avoid producing the errors.

Assigning a VBA Procedure to the Open Event

The refreshData Sub procedure is not complete. It should run every time the workbook is opened. By using the Call statement, a Sub procedure can be run from within another Sub procedure. In this exercise, you will call the procedure to execute when the workbook opens, using the Open event in the ThisWorkbook object.

 **E14.16**

SIDE NOTE
Using the Object and Procedure Lists
Alternatively, you can select Workbook from the Object list at the top of the Code window and select Open from the Procedure list.

To Assign a VBA Procedure to the Open Event

a. If necessary, press Alt + F11 to switch to the VBE. If necessary, click to expand Microsoft Excel Objects in the Project Explorer window. Double-click the **ThisWorkbook** object to open the Code window for ThisWorkbook.

b. To create a new private Sub procedure for the Open event, type **Private Sub Workbook_Open()** and then press Enter.

c. To call the refreshData procedure, type **Call refreshData** and then press Enter.

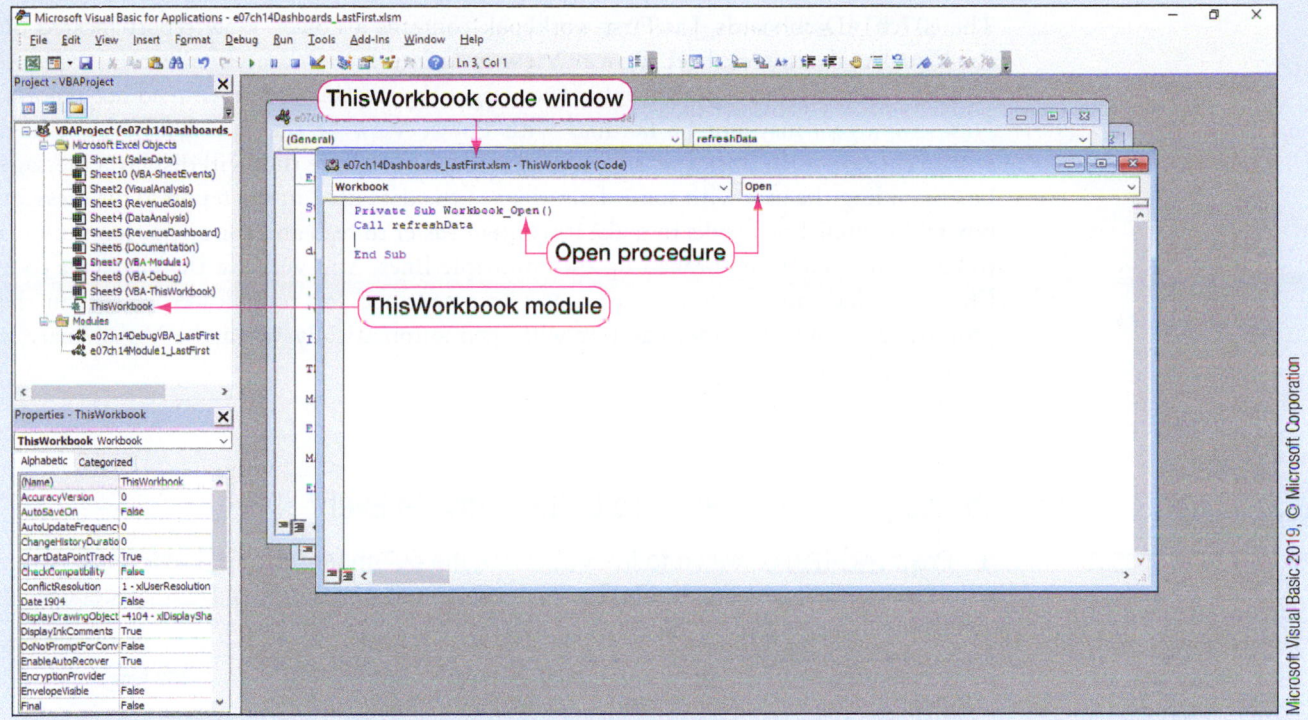

Figure 16 Call procedure from Open event

    d. Click **Save** 🖫.

    e. Close the VBE and the workbook. If prompted to save the workbook, click **Save**.

    f. Test the **procedure** by opening the workbook again. Notice the Data Connection message box.

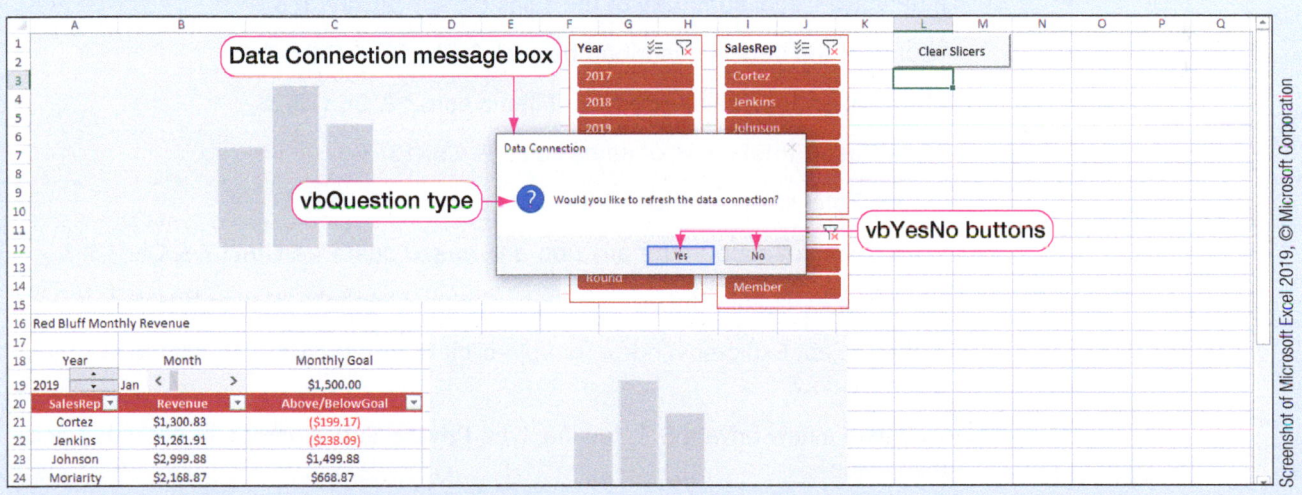

Figure 17 Data Connection message box

    g. Click **Yes**, and then click **OK**.

Assigning a VBA Procedure to the Activate Event

The e07ch14Dashboards_LastFirst workbook contains a Power View report located on the VisualAnalysis worksheet. **Power View** is an interactive data visualization, exploration, and presentation experience that encourages the creation of beautiful ad hoc reports. New employees may not be familiar with Power View or the information contained within the report. In this exercise, you will create a procedure that will display a message box providing the user with some definitions of the data used in the report. This message box will include line breaks to make its content easier to read and concatenation symbols to allow the code to be broken up into multiple lines. You will use the character code Chr(13) to indicate a carriage return and an ampersand (&) to concatenate text in the prompt argument. The message box will open automatically when the VisualAnalysis worksheet is activated.

 E14.17

MAC COMPATIBILITY
Power View Availability
Power View is not available in Office 365 for Mac.

To Assign a VBA Procedure to the Activate Event

a. Press [Alt]+[F11] to switch to the VBE. Click the **e07ch14Module1_LastFirst** code window, click just below the End Sub statement of the refreshData procedure, and then press [Enter].

b. To create a new Sub procedure, type Sub powerView() and then press [Enter].

c. Type the following comment block:

'This procedure displays a message box providing definitions for data used in the report.

'It will be assigned to the Activate event of the VisualAnalysis worksheet.

d. Press [Enter] twice.

e. In this step, press [Enter] after each underscore character. To create the message box, type Description = MsgBox("This report is designed to provide you with an interactive visual summary of the sales data. " & Chr(13) & _

"Some of the data is described below." & Chr(13) & Chr(13) & _

"TotalSales: Total sales revenue of items sold." & Chr(13) & _

"TotalCosts: Total costs of items sold." & Chr(13) & _

"Profit: Total sales revenue - total unit costs." & Chr(13) & _

"This does not account for any non-unit based costs." & Chr(13) & Chr(13) & _

"Feel free to explore the visualizations.", vbInformation, "Power View")

f. In the Project Explorer window, double-click **Sheet2(VisualAnalysis)** to view the Code window.

g. To create a new private Sub routine, type Private Sub Worksheet_Activate() and then press [Enter].

h. To call the powerView routine, type Call powerView and then press [Enter].

i. Click **Save** 🖫.

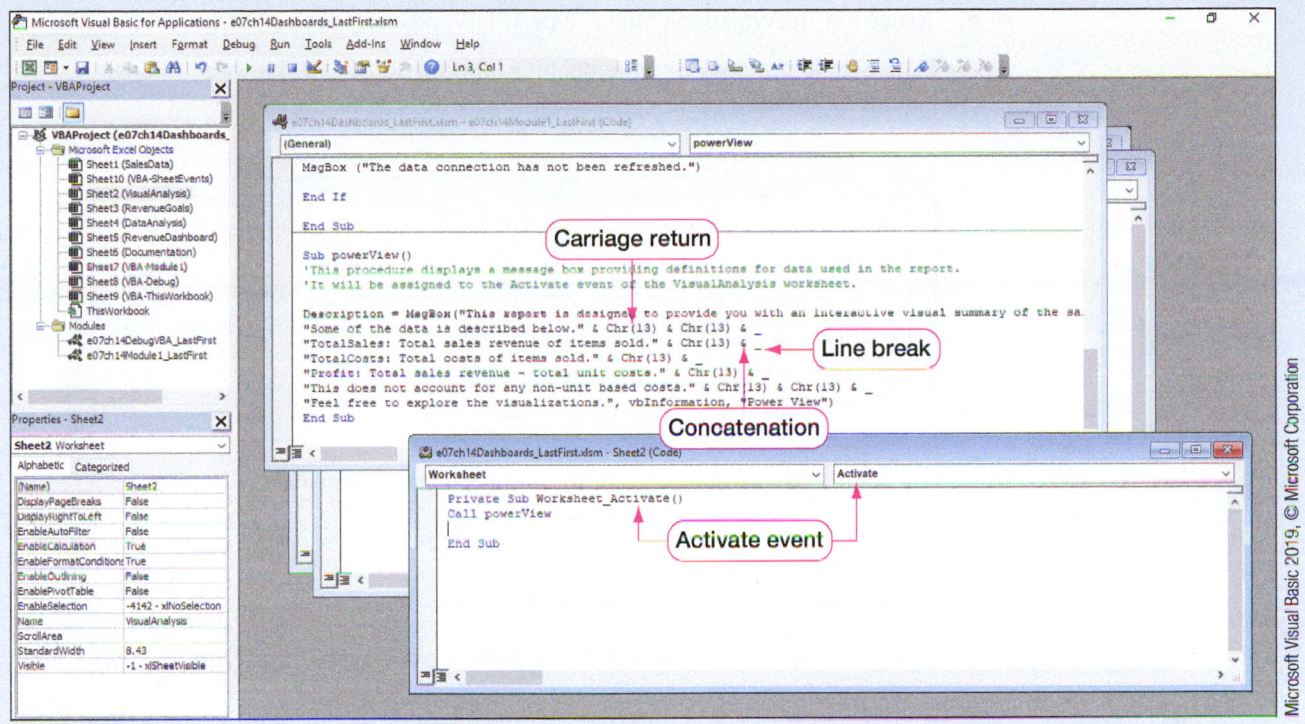

Figure 18 powerView Sub procedure on Active event

j. Press `Alt` + `F11` to switch back to the workbook, and then click the **VisualAnalysis** worksheet to see the message. Click **OK** to close the message box. The visualization is then generated.

Enhance a Workbook

VBA can enhance a workbook in a variety of ways. As previously demonstrated, VBA can automate routine or repetitive tasks. It can change the interface of Excel, either temporarily or permanently. For example, VBA can be used to hide the ribbon or add and remove gridlines, headings, and the formula bar. It can make a common task, like closing and saving a workbook, easier to execute.

Closing a Workbook with VBA

In this exercise, you will use the Close property of the ThisWorkbook object to close and save the workbook.

 **E14.18**

To Close a Workbook with VBA

a. Click the **RevenueDashboard** worksheet. Press `Alt` + `F11` to switch to the VBE.

b. Click the **e07ch14Module1_LastFirst** code window, click just below the End Sub statement of the powerView procedure, and then press `Enter`.

c. To create a Sub procedure, type Sub saveAndClose() and then press `Enter`.

d. To add the following comment, type 'This procedure will save and then close the workbook and then press `Enter` twice.

e. To use the ThisWorkbook object, type **ThisWorkbook.Close** and then press SpaceBar .

Notice that optional arguments now appear for SaveChanges, Filename, and RouteWorkbook.

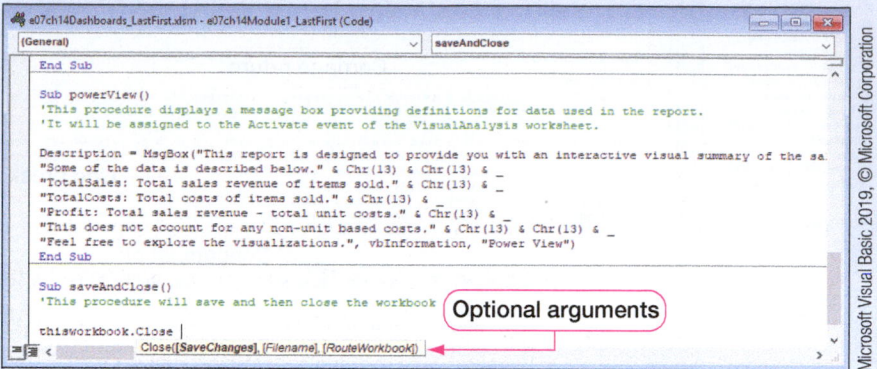

Figure 19 ThisWorkbook.Close arguments

f. To save changes to the workbook before closing the file, type **True** and then press Enter .

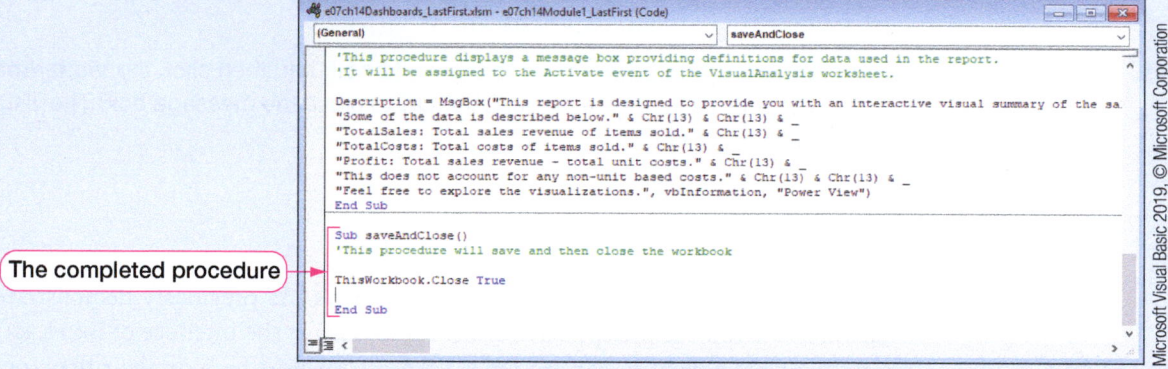

Figure 20 The completed saveAndClose procedure

g. Press Alt + F11 to switch to the RevenueDashboard worksheet.

h. Click the **Developer** tab, and then, in the Controls group, click the **Insert** arrow. Under Form Controls, select **Button (Form Control)** ⬜.

i. Drag to create a **rectangular button** below the **Clear Slicers** button, within the cell range **L11:M13**.

j. In the Assign Macro dialog box, select **saveAndClose**, and then click **OK**.

k. Right-click the **button** form control, and then select **Edit Text**. Delete the existing button text, type Save and Close and then click outside the button to confirm the change.

l. To test the functionality of the new button, click the **Save and Close** button. Reopen the **e07ch14Dashboards_LastFirst** workbook, and notice that all changes have been saved.

m. Save 💾 the workbook.

Altering the User Interface with VBA

Hiding the gridlines and headings of a worksheet provides a more professional appearance to a dashboard. It also provides more space on the screen for view data and visualizations. Additional space can be gained by hiding the formula bar. While gridlines and headings are settings that apply only to a specific worksheet, the formula bar is an Excel application–level setting. Removing it with a VBA command will remove it permanently from Excel until it is added back either via the ribbon or an additional VBA command. In this exercise, you will use the Activate and Deactivate worksheet events to selectively remove gridlines, headings, and the formula bar from the RevenueDashboard worksheet.

 **E14.19**

To Alter the User Interface with VBA

a. Switch to the VBE. Click the **Sheet5 (RevenueDashboard)** module.

b. To create a new private Sub procedure for the Activate event, type Private Sub Worksheet_Activate() and then press Enter.

c. To add the following comment, type 'This procedure will hide gridlines, headings, and the formula bar and then press Enter twice.

d. To hide gridlines, type ActiveWindow.DisplayGridlines = False and then press Enter.

e. To hide headings, type ActiveWindow.DisplayHeadings = False and then press Enter.

f. To hide the formula bar, type Application.DisplayFormulaBar = False and then press Enter.

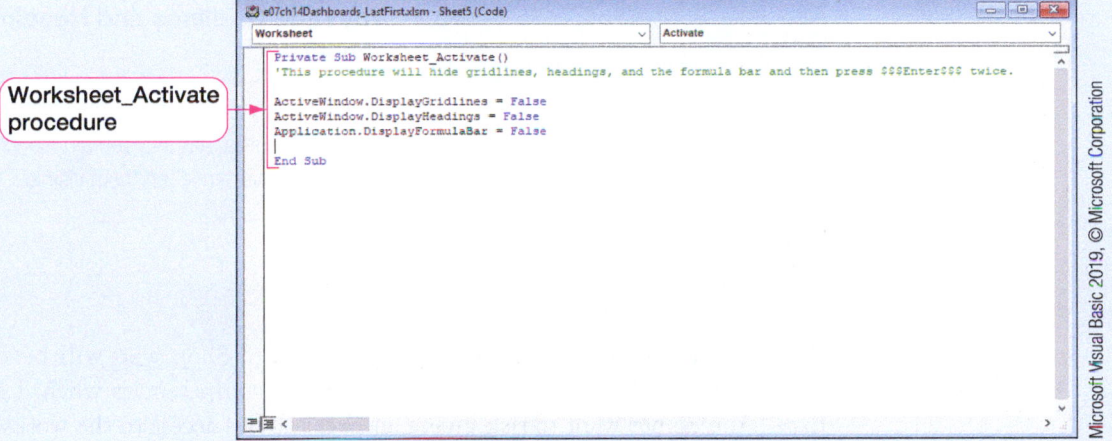

Worksheet_Activate procedure

Figure 21 The Worksheet_Activate procedure

g. To create a new private Sub procedure for the Deactivate event, click after the **End Sub** line and press Enter. Type Private Sub Worksheet_Deactivate() and then press Enter.

h. To add the following comment, type 'This procedure displays the formula bar and then press Enter twice.

i. To show the formula bar, type Application.DisplayFormulaBar = True and then press Enter.

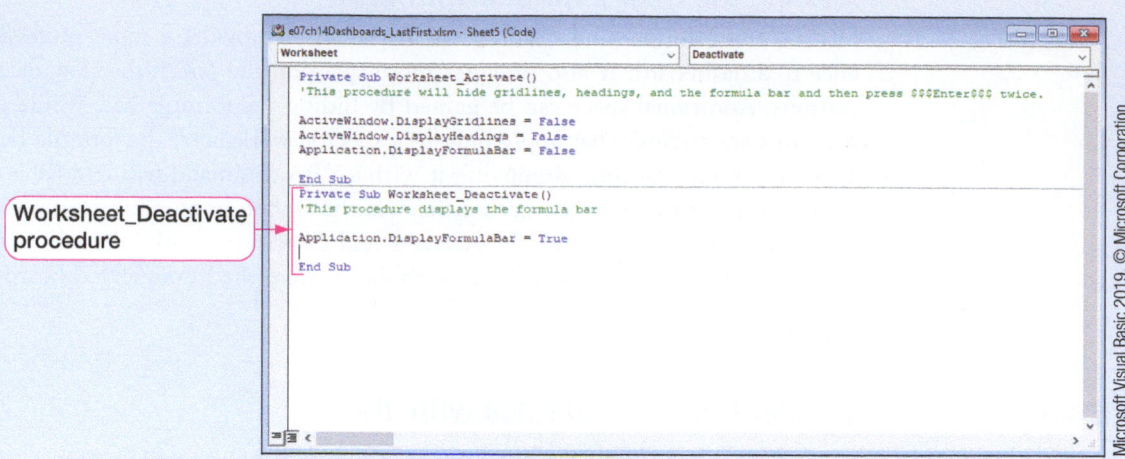

Worksheet_Deactivate procedure

Figure 22 The Worksheet_Deactivate procedure

j. Test the new event procedures by selecting a different worksheet and then clicking back to the RevenueDashboard. Notice that the worksheet gridlines and headings on the RevenueDashboard are no longer visible. Also notice that the formula bar is not visible while the RevenueDashboard is selected but reappears when the SalesData worksheet is selected.

k. Click **Save** 🖫.

REAL WORLD ADVICE | **Why Hide Gridlines and Headings with VBA?**

Once gridlines and headings are turned off on the View tab on the ribbon, they remain hidden until the options are checked again. Hiding them with VBA ensures that they remain hidden in the event that someone making modifications to the worksheet inadvertently left them visible.

Protect and Secure a Workbook

The managers at the Red Bluff Golf Course & Pro Shop who will benefit from Excel dashboards and Power View reports have varying competencies when it comes to using Excel. You do not want to risk giving an Excel novice access to the worksheets that contain the raw data where he or she could potentially damage or delete the data.

Protecting worksheets from intentional or unintentional modification can be done by simply hiding the worksheets in the Excel workbook. However, those worksheets can easily be made visible with a right-click or through the Options menu under the File tab. VBA provides a more secure method of hiding worksheets by using the xlVeryHidden property.

Using the xlVeryHidden Property

In this exercise, you will use xlVeryHidden and assign it to the Visible property of the Sheet object to hide specific worksheets in the workbook. The sheets that are hidden by assigning this to the Visible property cannot be made visible without altering the VBA code.

 **E14.20**

To Make Sheets Very Hidden

a. Click the **SalesData** worksheet. Press [Alt]+[F11] to switch to the VBE.

b. Click the **e07ch14Module1_LastFirst** code window, click just below the End Sub statement of the powerView procedure, and then press [Enter].

c. To create a Sub procedure, type Sub hideSheets() and then press [Enter].

d. To add the following comment, type 'This procedure will make the SalesData, RevenueGoals, and DataAnalysis worksheets hidden and then press [Enter] twice.

e. To hide the SalesData worksheet, type Sheets("SalesData").Visible = xlVeryHidden and then press [Enter].

f. To hide the RevenueGoals worksheet, type Sheets("RevenueGoals").Visible = xlVeryHidden and then press [Enter].

g. To hide the DataAnalysis worksheet, type Sheets("DataAnalysis").Visible = xlVeryHidden and then press [Enter].

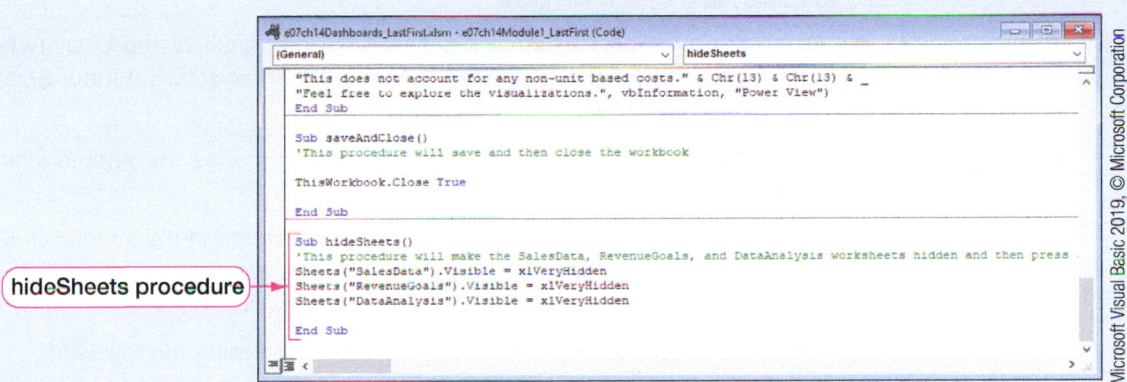

Figure 23 hideSheets Sub procedure

h. Click **Save** 💾.

i. Press [F5] to run the procedure. Press [Alt]+[F11] to switch back to the workbook, and then observe that the three worksheets are no longer visible.

Providing Access to Hidden Worksheets

Some managers may need to access the raw data in a workbook and should not be required to know VBA to be able to unhide those worksheets. In this exercise, you will create a procedure that, upon execution, will prompt the user for a password to make the hidden sheets visible. This will require the use of an input box. An **input box** is an effective way of using VBA code to increase the interactivity of a dashboard by prompting the user for information and storing that information in a variable to be used later.

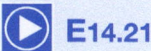 **E14.21**

To Provide Access to Hidden Sheets

a. Press [Alt]+[F11] to switch back to the VBE.

b. Click the **e07ch14Module1_LastFirst** code window just below the End Sub statement of the hideSheets procedure, and then press [Enter].

c. To create a new Sub procedure, type **Sub showSheets ()** and then press [Enter].

d. Type the following comment block.

'This procedure will prompt the user for a password if they wish to view

'the hidden worksheets. If the password is correct, the sheets will

'be made visible

e. Press [Enter] twice.

f. To declare a new variable to store the password, type **Dim password as String** and then press [Enter].

g. To provide the password variable with the password, type **password = "Show Sheets"** and then press [Enter].

h. To create a variable to store the password response of the user, type **access = InputBox("Enter the password to view hidden sheets:", "Show Sheets")** and then press [Enter] twice.

i. Type the following comment: **'The If statement makes the sheets visible if the password is correct** and then press [Enter].

j. To begin the If statement to compare the value stored in the access variable from the Input Box to the password variable, type **If access = password Then** and then press [Enter].

k. Make the sheets visible if the condition is true by typing the following.

Sheets("SalesData").Visible = True and then press [Enter].

Sheets("RevenueGoals").Visible = True and then press [Enter].

Sheets("DataAnalysis").Visible = True and then press [Enter].

l. Type **Else** to begin the code if the condition is false, and then press [Enter].

m. To create a message box that informs the user of an invalid password, type **invalid = MsgBox("The password is invalid", vbCritical, "Invalid Password")** and then press [Enter].

n. End the If statement by typing **End If** and then press [Enter].

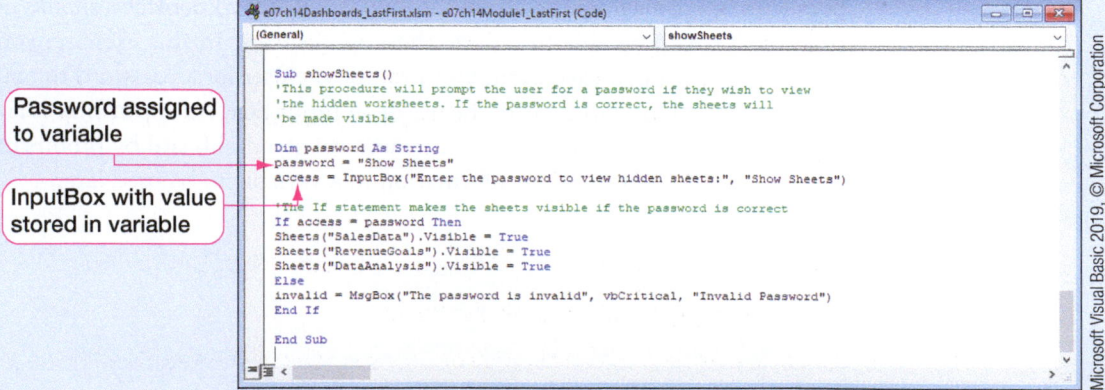

Figure 24 showSheets Sub procedure

o. Click **Save** 💾. Press Alt + F11 to switch back to the workbook.

p. Click the **RevenueDashboard** worksheet tab if necessary. Assign the show-Sheets macro to a button on the RevenueDashboard worksheet by completing the following tasks.

- Click the **Developer** tab, and then, in the Controls group, click the Insert arrow. Under Form Controls, select **Button (Form Control)** 🔲.

- Drag a **rectangular button** within the range **L6:M8**, as shown in Figure 25.

- In the Assign Macro dialog box, select **showSheets**, and then click **OK**.

- Select the **button text**, type View Hidden Sheets and then click any cell to deselect the button.

- Click the **View Hidden Sheets** button, type Show Sheets as the password, and then click **OK**. Confirm that the three sheets are now visible.

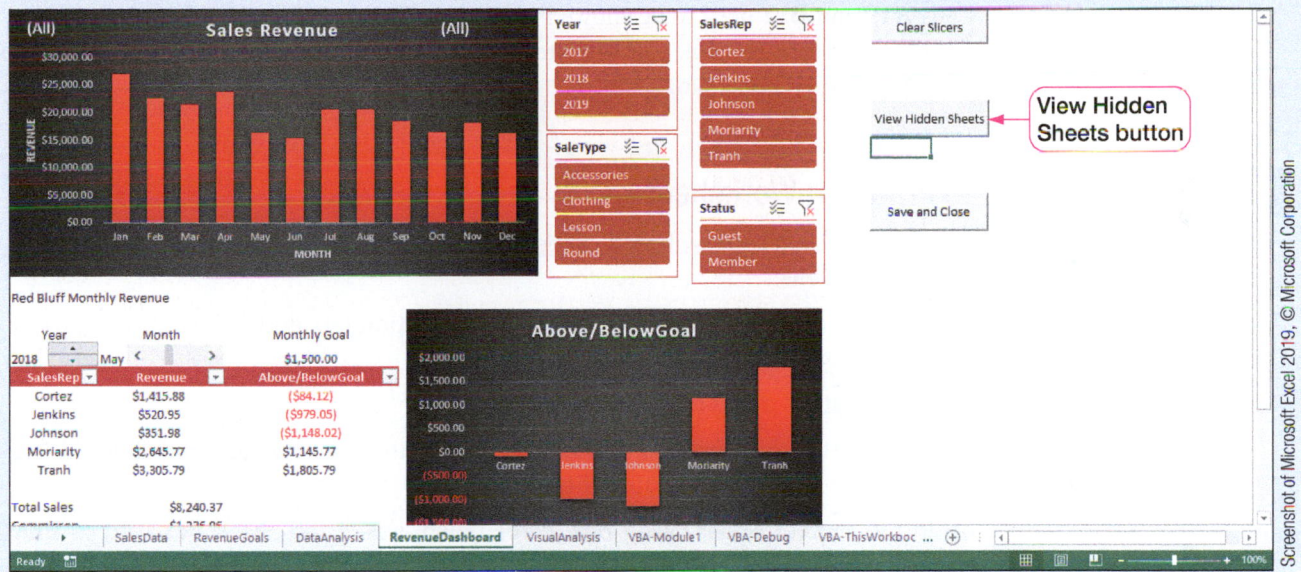

Figure 25 View Hidden Sheets button

q. Click **Save** 💾.

Assigning a Procedure to the BeforeClose Event

Now that the hidden sheets are visible, you will need to run the hideSheets procedure again so that no unauthorized person can access the sheets. In this exercise, you will call the hideSheets procedure to execute when the BeforeClose event occurs.

 **E14.22**

To Call a Procedure on the BeforeClose Event

a. Press Alt + F11 to switch to the VBE.

b. In the Project Explorer window, double-click **ThisWorkbook** to open the Code window.

c. Click the **Procedures** arrow, scroll up, and then select **BeforeClose**. A new Private Sub procedure is created for the BeforeClose event that will execute after the user has clicked Close but before Excel closes the workbook.

d. To call the hideSheets procedure, type Call hideSheets and then press Enter.

e. Click **Save** 💾. **Close** ☒ the VBE, and then **Close** ☒ the workbook.

f. Open the **e07ch14Dashboards_LastFirst** workbook, and, if necessary, click Enable Content. Click **No** when prompted to refresh the data connection, click **OK**, and then verify that the three worksheets are now hidden.

Protecting a Worksheet

The RevenueDashboard worksheet is now in its final state and needs to be protected to prevent unintentional changes. Before the worksheet is protected, you need to ensure that the cells that must be allowed to be changed to use the dashboard are not locked. Cells A19 and B17 need to be allowed to change. They are linked to the spin button and the slider. In this exercise, you will protect the RevenueDashboard worksheet and allow cells A19 and B17 to change.

 **E14.23**

To Protect a Worksheet

a. On the RevenueDashboard worksheet, right-click cell **A19**, and then select **Format Cells**.

b. In the Format Cells dialog box, click the **Protection** tab, and then click the Locked check box to deselect **Locked**. Click **OK**.

c. Repeat steps a and b for cell **B17**.

d. On the RevenueDashboard worksheet, click the **Review** tab, and then, in the Changes group, click **Protect Sheet**.

e. In the Protect Sheet dialog box, scroll down, select the check box next to **Edit objects**, and then click **OK**. The worksheet is now protected but still fully functional.

f. Click **Save** 💾.

Protecting the VBA Code with a Password

Protecting the VBA code with a password ensures that no unauthorized person will access the code. It is considered best practice to export any VBA modules as text files before protecting them with a password. Thus, if the password is lost or the workbook becomes corrupt, you will have a copy of the VBA code. In this exercise, you will export the VBA modules and then protect the VBA with a password.

 **E14.24**

To Protect the VBA Code with a Password

a. Press Alt + F11 to switch to the VBE.

b. Double-click to open the **e07ch14Module1_LastFirst** module. Press Ctrl + A to select all the text and press Ctrl + C to copy the text.

c. Press Alt + F11 to switch to the Excel workbook. Click the **VBA-Module1** worksheet and if necessary, click cell **A1**. Press Ctrl + V to paste the VBA code into the worksheet.

d. Press **Alt**+**F11** to switch to the VBE.

e. Double-click to open the **e07ch14DebugVBA_LastFirst** module. Press **Ctrl**+**A** to select all the text and press **Ctrl**+**C** to copy the text.

f. Press **Alt**+**F11** to switch to the Excel workbook. Click the **VBA-Debug** worksheet and if necessary, click cell **A1**. Press **Ctrl**+**V** to paste the VBA code into the worksheet.

g. Press **Alt**+**F11** to switch to the VBE.

h. Double-click to open the **ThisWorkbook** module. Press **Ctrl**+**A** to select all the text and press **Ctrl**+**C** to copy the text.

i. Press **Alt**+**F11** to switch to the Excel workbook. Click the **VBA-ThisWorkbook** worksheet and if necessary, click cell **A1**. Press **Ctrl**+**V** to paste the VBA code into the worksheet.

j. Press **Alt**+**F11** to switch to the VBE.

k. Double-click to open the **Sheet2(VisualAnalysis)** module. Press **Ctrl**+**A** to select all the text and press **Ctrl**+**C** to copy the text.

l. Press **Alt**+**F11** to switch to the Excel workbook. Click the **VBA-SheetEvents** worksheet and if necessary, click cell **A1**. Press **Ctrl**+**V** to paste the VBA code into the worksheet.

m. Press **Alt**+**F11** to switch to the VBE.

n. Double-click to open the **Sheet5(RevenueDashboard)** module. Press **Ctrl**+**A** to select all the text and press **Ctrl**+**C** to copy the text.

o. Press **Alt**+**F11** to switch to the Excel workbook. Click the **VBA-SheetEvents** worksheet and click cell **G1**. Press **Ctrl**+**V** to paste the VBA code into the worksheet.

p. Press **Alt**+**F11** to switch to the VBE. On the menu click **Tools**, and then select **VBAProject Properties**.

q. Click the **Protection** tab, and then, in the Lock project area, select the **Lock project for viewing** check box.

r. Click the **Password** field, and then type P49%rwn

s. Click the **Confirm password** field, and then type P49%rwn again.

t. Click **OK**.

u. **Close** ☒ the VBE, and then click **Save** 🔲. The password will not take effect until the workbook is closed. Close the workbook.

v. Open the **e07ch14Dashboards_LastFirst** workbook. Click **No** to the Data Connection prompt, and then click **OK**. Press **Alt**+**F11** to switch to the VBE.

w. If necessary, click **View**, and then click **Project Explorer** to view the Project Explorer window. Double-click **VBA Project (e07ch14Dashboards_LastFirst .xlsm)**. Type P49%rwn in the VBAProject Password dialog box, and then click **OK**. If necessary, click to expand VBAProject (e07ch14Dashboards_LastFirst.xlsm) to view the modules.

x. Click **Save** 🔲. Press **Alt**+**F11** to switch to the workbook. Complete the Documentation worksheet.

y. Click **File**, **Save a Copy**, and then, in the File Type box, click the **arrow**. Click **Excel Workbook (*.xlsx)** and then click **Save**. Click **Yes** to the warning box that VBA features will be removed.

z. Save your workbook, exit Excel, and submit your file as directed by your instructor.

Concept Check

1. What are form controls, and how can they be used to enhance interactivity with a dashboard? p. 766

2. Describe the object model in Excel. p. 772

3. What are function procedures, and how can organizations use them? p. 777

4. What are some common practices that can help to improve the readability and understanding of VBA code? p. 779

5. Describe the purpose of debug mode in the VBE and why it is useful. p. 778

6. List the categories of loops used in VBA, and describe each type of loop. p. 783–784

7. Describe three scenarios in which assigning a VBA procedure to an event would enhance the workbook. p. 788

8. What can be done to ensure that unauthorized changes are not made to a workbook? p. 796

Key Terms

Code window   p. 776
Digital dashboard   p. 766
Do…Until loop   p. 784
Do…While loop   p. 784
Event   p. 788
For loop   p. 784
For…Each loop   p. 784
Form control   p. 766
Function procedure   p. 777
Input box   p. 797
Loop   p. 783
Message box   p. 789

Method   p. 774
Module   p. 776
Object   p. 772
Object collection   p. 773
Object model   p. 772
Object-oriented programming
   (OOP)   p. 772
Parameter   p. 775
Power View   p. 792
Project Explorer window   p. 775
Property   p. 774
Properties window   p. 776

Run-time error   p. 782
Scroll bar   p. 770
Separator   p. 773
Slicer   p. 766
Spin button   p. 767
Sub procedure   p. 777
Variable   p. 784
Visual Basic for Applications
   (VBA)   p. 772
Visual Basic Editor (VBE)   p. 775

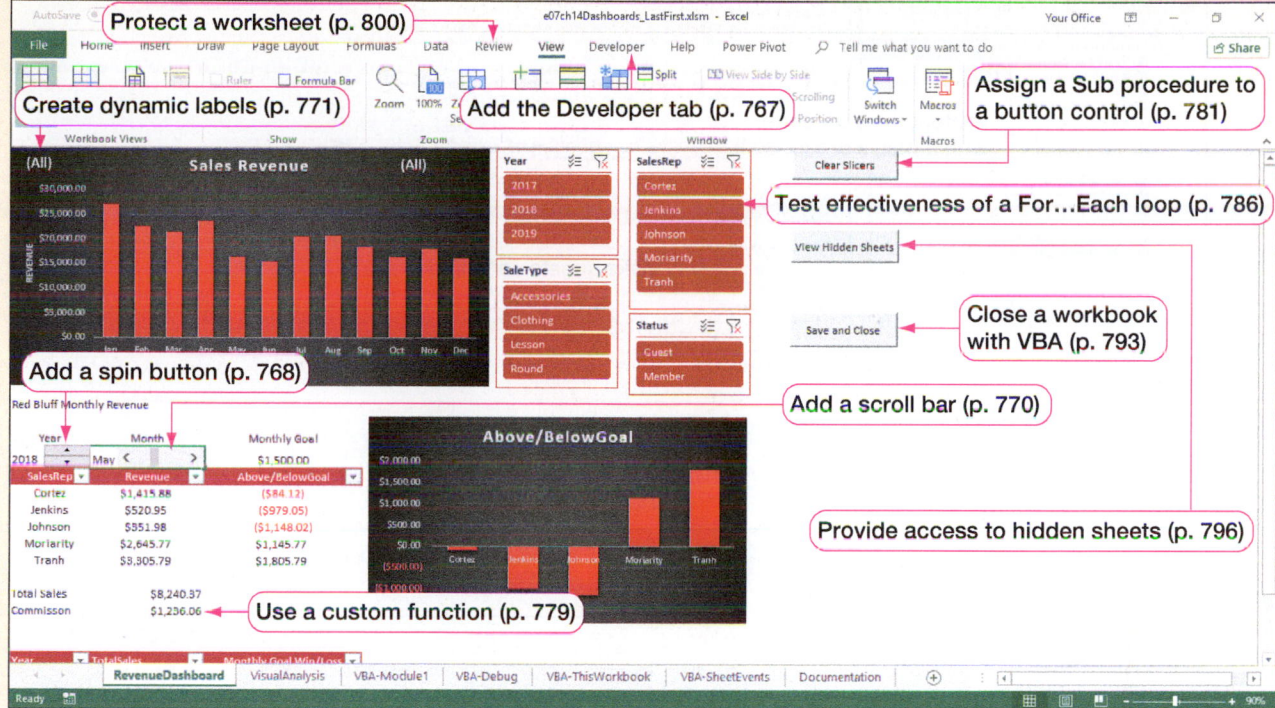

Figure 26

Screenshot of Microsoft Excel 2019, © Microsoft Corporation

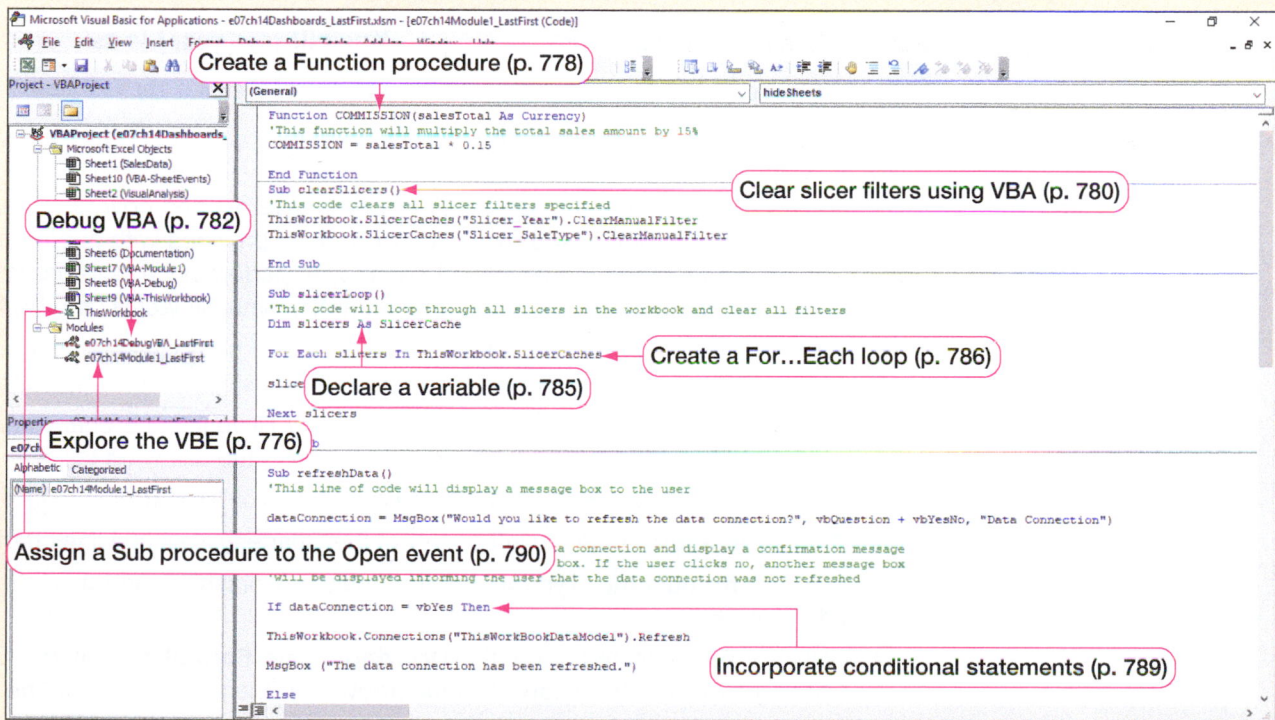

Figure 27

Microsoft Visual Basic 2019, © Microsoft Corporation

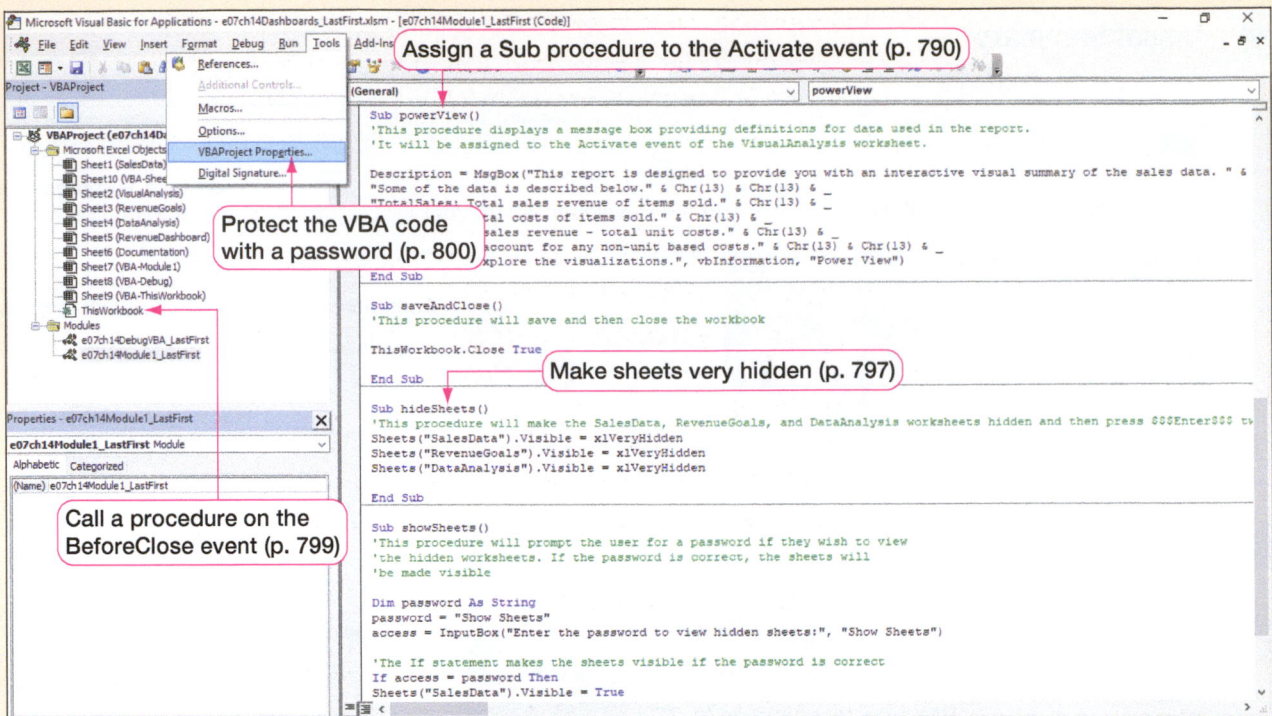

Assign a Sub procedure to the Activate event (p. 790)

Protect the VBA code with a password (p. 800)

Make sheets very hidden (p. 797)

Call a procedure on the BeforeClose event (p. 799)

Figure 28

Microsoft Visual Basic 2019, © Microsoft Corporation

Sales & Marketing

Practice 1

Student data file needed:

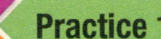 e07ch14Reviews.xlsx

You will save your file as:

 e07ch14Reviews_LastFirst.xlsm

Enhancing the Performance Review Dashboard

Managers at the Red Bluff Golf Course & Pro Shop have realized how form controls and VBA can enhance their dashboards. You have been provided with another dashboard that can be used to aid managers in employee performance reviews. You will enhance the dashboard by adding some form controls, dynamic labels, and VBA.

a. Start **Excel**, and then open the **e07ch14Reviews** workbook. Save it as a Macro-Enabled Workbook named e07ch14Reviews_LastFirst using your last and first name.

b. Click the **Dashboard** worksheet. On the Quarterly Revenue line chart, create a dynamic label based on the **Year** slicer by completing the following tasks.

  • Click the **Insert** tab, and then, in the Text group, click **Text Box**.

  • Drag a **rectangle** in the top left corner of the Quarterly Revenue line chart.

  • Click the **formula bar**. Type = click the Analysis worksheet, and then click cell **B1**. Press [Enter].

  • With the box selected, click the **Drawing Tools Format** tab. In the Shape Styles group, click the **Shape Outline** arrow, and then select **No Outline**.

  • Click the **Home** tab, and then, in the Font group, increase the font size to 16

  • Adjust the size of the box as necessary to accommodate the font size.

c. Repeat step b to add a dynamic label in the top left corner of the Revenue and Costs combo column chart and the Total Revenue pie chart. Use cell **B14** from the **Analysis** worksheet for this step.

d. Add a spin button form control to cell I23 by completing the following tasks.

- Click the **Developer** tab, and then, in the Controls group, click the **Insert** arrow. Select **Spin Button (Form Control)**.
- Drag the small square **Spin** button in the cell range I22:I23 to the right of the year label and year value.
- Right-click the **Spin** button, and then click **Format Control**.
- Type 2017 in the Current and Minimum value fields.
- Type 2019 in the Maximum value field.
- Click the **Cell link** field, click cell I23, and then click **OK**.

e. Create a lookup table to be used with a scroll bar form control by completing the following tasks.

- Click the **Analysis** worksheet. Click cell I1, type Value and then, in the cell range I2:I5, type the values 1 2 3 and 4
- Click cell J1, type Quarter and then, in the cell range J2:J5, type the values Q1 Q2 Q3 and Q4
- Select I1:J5, click the **Name** box, and then type Quarters to give the range of cells a name.

f. On the Dashboard worksheet, add a scroll bar to the right of Q1 in cell J23 by completing the following tasks.

- Click the **Dashboard** worksheet, click cell J21, and then type the number 1 to be used as the lookup value.
- Click cell J23, and then type =VLOOKUP(J21,Quarters,2,FALSE)
- On the Developer tab, in the Controls group, click the Insert arrow, and then select the **Scroll Bar (Form Control)**.
- Drag a **horizontal rectangle** in cell J23 to the right of the Q1 text.
- Right-click the **Scroll Bar**, and then select **Format Control**.
- Type 1 in the Current value and Minimum value fields.
- Type 4 in the Maximum value field.
- Click the **Cell link** field, click cell J21, and then click **OK**.
- Click cell J21, click the **Home** tab, and then in the Font group, change the font color to **White, Background 1**.

g. Create a VBA Sub procedure that will clear filters in all slicers in the workbook, even if more slicers are added, by completing the following tasks.

- Press Alt + F11 to switch to the VBE, click **Insert**, and then select **Module**.
- In the Properties window, click the **Name** field, and then type ReviewModule _LastFirst using your last and first name.
- Click the **Code window**, type Sub clearSlicers () and then press Enter.
- Type the following comment: 'This code will loop through all the slicers in the workbook and clear all filters and then press Enter twice.
- Type Dim allSlicers As SlicerCache to declare a variable with a data type of SlicerCache, and then press Enter twice.
- Type For Each allSlicers In ThisWorkbook.SlicerCaches and then press Enter twice.
- Type allSlicers.ClearManualFilter and then press Enter twice.
- Type Next allSlicers and then press Enter.

h. On the Dashboard worksheet, assign the Sub procedure to a Button form control by competing the following tasks.

- Press [Alt]+[F11] to switch to the workbook.
- On the Developer tab, in the Controls group, click the **Insert** arrow, and then select **Button (Form Control)**.
- Drag a **button** within the cell range **J1:K3**. In the Assign Macro dialog box, select **clearSlicers**, and then click **OK**.
- Edit the button text to Clear Slicers and then, if necessary, adjust the size of the button so that all text is visible.

i. Add the **SalesRep** slicer to the dashboard by completing the following tasks.

- Click the **Quarterly Revenue** line chart.
- Click the **Analyze** tab, and then, in the Filter group, click **Insert Slicer**.
- Click the **SalesRep** check box, and then click **OK**.
- Resize the **SalesRep** slicer to 1.5" in width and 2" in height.
- Reposition the **SalesRep** slicer to fit within the cell range **J5:K14**, in between the Year and SaleType slicers and the pie chart.
- Click the **Options** tab, and then, in the Slicer Styles group, select **Light Green, Slicer Style Dark 6**.
- On the **Options** tab, click **Report Connections**, click the **PivotTable2** check box, and then click **OK**.

j. Click the **Documentation** worksheet. Click cell A8, and then type in today's date. Click cell **B8**, and then type your first and last name. Complete the remainder of the **Documentation** worksheet according to your instructor's direction.

k. Save your workbook, exit Excel, and submit your file as directed by your instructor.

Problem Solve 1

 MyLab IT Grader

Student data file needed:

 e07ch14Goals.xlsm

You will save your file as:

 e07ch14Goals_LastFirst.xlsm

Goals and Results

Sales & Marketing

You recently started a new job. Your predecessor began a file to track the company sales by year, by quarter, and by sales representative. The dashboard is supposed to calculate the commission payout based on a changing percentage for a month/year. You have been asked to complete this dashboard.

a. Open the **Excel** workbook **e07ch14Goals**. Save your file as a Macro-Enabled Workbook named e07ch14Goals_LastFirst using your last and first name.

b. On the **Lookups** worksheet, create a list of month numbers and month names.

c. On the **Dashboard** worksheet, above the Goals table in cell **B22**, create a lookup formula that will return the month name based on the month number entered in cell E22.

d. Add a spin button to cell **A22** to change the year. It should allow the years to change between 2021, 2022, and 2023.

e. Add a scroll bar across cells B22 and C22 that changes the month name. It should be linked to the month number in cell **E22**. As the user changes the month, the name displayed should be updated accordingly. Change the appropriate properties of the control so that months 1 through 12 can be selected.

f. Create a Clustered Column chart based on the data in the Goals table that shows sales representatives who are above/below goal. Position the chart so that it covers the highlighted month number cell.

g. Use **Chart Style 4** for the chart so it is consistent with the other chart on the worksheet.

h. Add slicers to the Sales by Quarter chart for **Year** and **Rep**. Format and size appropriately in the white space next to the Chart.

i. Create two dynamic labels for the Sales by Quarter chart. Add two text boxes to the chart; one text box should be linked to the PivotTable field **Year**, and the other should be linked to the PivotTable field **Rep**. The PivotTable for both fields is located on the Analysis worksheet.

j. Create a Sub procedure to clear the two slicers. Use a For…Each loop to account for additional slicers being added to the workbook.

k. Review the Commission macro. There is an error in the macro, and it will not run. Correct the macro.

l. Add comments to the Commission macro so future users will know what each step of the macro does.

m. Run the macro with a commission rate of 20%.

n. Insert a button on the Dashboard worksheet that will run the macro to clear the slicers. Place the button to the right of the Sales by Quarter chart. Edit the text of the Button to Clear Slicers

o. Create a Sub procedure that will hide gridlines, row and column headers, and the formula bar when the Dashboard sheet is activated.

p. Create a Sub procedure that displays the formula bar when the Dashboard sheet is deactivated.

q. Complete the Documentation worksheet according to your instructor's direction.

r. Save your workbook, exit Excel, and submit your file as directed by your instructor.

Critical Thinking A common step in creating a dashboard is to use the Protect Worksheet feature found on the Review tab. Given the dashboard built in this exercise, what problems might be associated with protecting the Dashboard worksheet? How could these issues be corrected to provide full functionality of the Dashboard and still protect the worksheet?

Perform 1: Perform in Your Life

Student data file needed:
 Blank Excel workbook

You will save your file as:
 e07ch14Expenses_LastFirst.xlsm

Personal Expenses Dashboard

Finance & Accounting

Keeping track of personal expenses is the first step to becoming financially independent. If you can keep track of what you spend your money on, then you may be able to find areas where you can save money to afford a car payment or start paying back any student loans. In this exercise, you will create a few simple charts on a dashboard based on data that you will provide. You will then enhance the dashboard by adding form controls and VBA.

a. Start **Excel**, create a new blank workbook, and then save it as a Macro-Enabled Workbook with the name e07ch14Expenses_LastFirst using your last and first name.

b. Rename Sheet1 to ExpenseData and use this worksheet to make a table of expenses. Be sure to make a note of the date, a description of the expense, the amount of the expense, and the category to which the expense belongs. Some examples of categories may be Food, School, Entertainment, Rent, ATM withdrawal, and the like. If you have a bank account, you may be able to export a file of expenses from the bank's website.

c. Create two additional worksheets in the workbook, then rename one Analysis and the other Dashboard

d. You will use the Analysis worksheet to create any lookup tables necessary for use with form controls such as scroll bars, spin buttons, or PivotTables.

e. Create two charts and one table on the Dashboard worksheet based on the data on the ExpenseData and/or Analysis worksheets. One of the charts should be created from the data in the Excel table.

f. Add two slicers to the Dashboard worksheet that will allow you to filter the data in the chart.

g. Create a table on the Dashboard worksheet showing expense data from different days or months by category. Add one form control, either a spin button or scroll bar, to change the day or months.

h. Create a VBA module named ExpenseModule_LastFirst using your last and first name.

i. Create a VBA Sub procedure that will loop through all slicers and clear the filters, and then assign that Sub procedure to a form control button on the Dashboard worksheet.

j. Create a VBA Sub procedure that will close the file and save any changes made to the file. Assign the Sub procedure to a form control button on the Dashboard worksheet.

k. Save your workbook, exit Excel, and submit your file as directed by your instructor.

Enabling Decisions with Data Visualization and VBA

This business unit had two outcomes:

Learning Outcome 1:

Use Excel to develop dashboards and gain business insight using the Power Pivot, PivotTables, and PivotCharts.

Learning Outcome 2:

Enhance spreadsheets with form controls and VBA. Utilize VBA to create custom functions, looping procedures, events based actions, and to secure a workbook.

In Business Unit 7 Capstone, students will demonstrate competence in these outcomes through a series of business problems at various levels from guided practice to problem solving an existing workbook and performing to create new workbooks.

More Practice 1

Student data files needed:

 e07Indigo5.accdb

 e07Metrics.xlsx

You will save your file as:

 e07Metrics_LastFirst.xlsm

Restaurant Metrics

Sales & Marketing

Robin Sanchez, owner and chef of the Indigo5 restaurant, would like to start paying closer attention to the sales data in order to make strategic decisions about the future of the restaurant. Robin has provided you with a small sample of sales data from 2020-2021 in an Access database. You have been asked to import the data into the Excel data model, conduct some analysis, create a simple dashboard, and then enhance it with some simple VBA.

a. Start **Excel**, click **Open Other Workbooks** in the left pane, and then double-click **This PC**. Navigate through the folder structure to the location of your student data files, and then double-click **e07Metrics**. A workbook opens displaying a blank worksheet.

b. Click the **File** tab, click **Save As**, and then double-click **This PC**. In the Save As dialog box, navigate to the location where you are saving your project files, and then, in the Save as type box, select **Excel Macro-Enabled Workbook**. Change the filename to **e07Metrics_LastFirst** using your last and first name. Click **Save**.

c. Import the Employees table to the workbook, and transform the FirstName and HireDate fields.

- Click the **Data** tab. In the Get & Transform Data group, click **Get Data**, point to **From Database**, and then click **From Microsoft Access Database**.

- Browse to your student data files, select **e07Indigo5**, and then click **Import**.

- In the Navigator window, Click the **Employees** table, and then click **Edit**.

- In the Power Query Editor window, click the **FirstName** column. Click the **Transform** tab, and in the Text Column group, click **Format**, and then select **Capitalize Each Word**.

- Click the **HireDate** column. On the Transform tab, in the Date & Time Column group, click **Date**, and then select **Date Only**.
- Click the **Home** tab, and in the Close group, click **Close & Load**.
- Rename the worksheet Employees

d. On the **SalesDashboard** worksheet, import the data from the e07Indigo5 database into the Excel data model by completing the following.
- Click the **Data** tab. In the Get & Transform Data group, click **Get Data**, point to **From Database**, and then click **From Microsoft Access Database**.
- Browse to your student data files, select **e07Indigo5**, and then click **Import**.
- In the Navigator window, select **Select multiple items**.
- Click the **ProductCategories** and **Transactions** check boxes to select the tables in the database, and then click the **Load** arrow.
- Click **Load To** and in the Import Data dialog box, ensure that the **Only Create Connection** option and **Add this data to the Data Model** options are checked.
- Click **OK**.
- Close the **Queries & Connections** pane.

e. On the **Employees** worksheet, click anywhere in the table. Click the **Power Pivot** tab; and then, in the Tables group, click **Add to Data Model**. If the Power Pivot tab is not visible, you will need to install the Add-in as explained in Chapter 13.

f. Enhance the data model by completing the following.
- In the Power Pivot window, click the **Design** tab, and then, in the Relationships group, click **Create Relationship**.
- In the Create Relationship dialog box, **Employees** should be selected in the first drop down list. Click **ServerID** in the list of columns. Select **Transactions** in the second drop down list and select **ServerID** in the list of columns. Click **OK**.
- Click the **Transactions** worksheet, and then click the **TransDate** column heading. Click the **Home** tab, and then, in the Formatting group, click the **Format** arrow. Select ***3/14/2001**.
- Double-click the next **Add Column** column heading, and then type EstimatedRevenue Press [Enter], and then type =RELATED(ProductCategories [AvgPrice])*[Qty] and then press [Enter].

g. To create a calculated field just below the ServerID column, click in the Calculation Area, and then type 2020Revenue:=CALCULATE(sum(Transactions[Estimated Revenue]),YEAR(Transactions[TransDate])=2020)

h. On the Home tab, in the Formatting group, click the **Format** arrow, and then select **Currency**.

i. To create another calculated field just below the CategoryCode column, click in the Calculation Area, and then type 2021Revenue:=CALCULATE(sum(Transactions [EstimatedRevenue]), YEAR(Transactions[TransDate])=2021)

j. On the Home tab, in the Formatting group, click the **Format** arrow, and then select **Currency**.

k. Create a new KPI for Sales Revenue by completing the following.
- Click the **2021Revenue** calculation. Click the **Home** tab, and then, in the Calculations group, click **Create KPI**.
- In the Create KPI dialog box, under Define target value, in the Measure box, select **2020Revenue** from the calculated field list.
- Adjust the status thresholds to be a low of 90% and a high of 105%
- Click **OK**.

l. Create a simple dashboard by completing the following.

- On the **Home** tab, click the **PivotTable** arrow, and then select **Chart and Table (Horizontal)**.

- In the Create PivotChart and PivotTable (Horizontal) dialog box, click **Existing Worksheet**, click the **Range Selection** button, and then click the **SalesDashboard** worksheet. Click cell **A1**.

- Click **OK**, and then click **OK** again.

m. Create a PivotChart by completing the following.

- In the PivotChart Fields pane, expand **Transactions**, and then drag **Estimated Revenue** into the Values.

- Expand **ProductCategories**, and then drag **CategoryDescr** into the Axis (Categories) area.

n. Improve the design of the PivotChart by completing the following.

- Click the **Design** tab, and in the Chart Styles group, click **More**, and then select **Style 6**.

- Edit the Chart Title text to be Indigo5 Revenue

- Click the chart **legend**, and press $\boxed{\text{Delete}}$.

- Click the **Analyze** tab, and then, in the Show/Hide group, click the **Field Buttons** icon to remove the filter buttons from the PivotChart.

o. Create a PivotTable by completing the following.

- Click the **PivotTable1** placeholder, and then, in the PivotTable Fields pane, expand **Employees**. Drag **FirstName** into the Rows area.

- Expand **Transactions**, expand **2021Revenue**, and then drag **Value (2021Revenue)** into the Values area. Drag **Status** into the Values area.

p. Add slicers to the PivotChart by completing the following.

- Click the **Indigo5 Revenue** chart. On the **Analyze** tab, in the Filter group, click **Insert Slicer**.

- In the Insert Slicers dialog box, click the **All** tab, and then click the check box for **CategoryDescr**. Click **OK**.

- With the CategoryDescr slicer still selected, on the **Options** tab, in the Slicer group, click **Report Connections**.

- If necessary, click the check box for **PivotTable1**, and then click **OK**.

- Click the **Indigo5 Revenue** chart, and on the Analyze tab, in the Filter group, click **Insert Timeline**. Click to select the check box for **TransDate**, and then click **OK**.

q. Modify the slicers by completing the following.

- Select the **CategoryDescr** slicer. On the **Options** tab, in the Slicer Styles group, select **White, Slicer Style Other 2**.

- On the Options tab, in the Buttons group, click in the **Columns** box, and change the value to 2

- On the Options tab, in the Size group, click the **Width** box, and change the value to 1.1

- Reposition the slicer so that the top left corner of the slicer is positioned in cell **J9**.

- Click the **TransDate** timeline slicer. On the Options tab, in the Timeline Styles group, select **Light Blue, Timeline Style Light 5**.

- In the timeline slicer, click the **MONTHS** arrow, and select **YEARS**. On the Options tab, in the Size group, click the **Width** box, and change the value to 1.5
- Reposition the slicer to fit within the range **B16:D22**.

r. Create a VBA Sub procedure using a For...Each loop to clear all slicers by completing the following.
- Press Alt + F11 to switch to the VBE.
- Click **Insert**, and then select **Module**.
- In the Properties Window, select the text in the **Name** property, and then type Indigo5VBA_LastFirst using your last and first name.
- Click the **Code Window**, type Sub clearSlicers () and then press Enter.
- To add a comment to the procedure, type 'Procedure clears all slicers in workbook using a For Each loop. and press Enter twice.
- To declare a variable with a data type of SlicerCache, type Dim slicers as SlicerCache and then press Enter.
- To create a For...Each loop, type For Each slicers in ThisWorkbook.SlicerCaches and then press Enter. Type slicers.ClearAllFilters and then press Enter. Type Next slicers and then press Enter twice.
- Press Alt + F11 to switch to the workbook.

s. Add a button to the dashboard to clear all slicers. Click the **Developer** tab, and then, in the Controls group, click the **Insert** arrow. Click **Button (Form Control)**, and drag to create a rectangular button within the cell range **F16:G17**. In the Assign Macro dialog box, click **clearSlicers** and click **OK**.

t. Right-click the **button** form control, and then click **Edit Text**. Delete the existing button text, and then type Clear Slicers Click outside the button to confirm the change.

u. Click the **Documentation** worksheet. Click cell **A6**, and then type in today's date Click cell **B6**, and then type in your first and last name Complete the remainder of the Documentation worksheet according to your instructor's directions.

v. Save the workbook, exit Excel, and then submit your file as directed by your instructor.

Problem Solve 1

MyLab IT Grader

Student data files needed:

e07DataModel.xlsx

e07HotelData.accdb

You will save your file as:

e07DataModel_LastFirst.xlsm

Advanced Data Modeling and Power View Report for the Hotel

Sales & Marketing

Managers at the Painted Paradise Resort & Spa hotel keep track of reservations in a database and would like to be able to view the data differently. You have been asked to create a data model in Excel based on the data in the database file provided. You will then create a Power View report so that the managers can view the reservation data with charts and visualizations.

a. Open the Excel file **e07DataModel**. Save your file as a Macro-Enabled Workbook with the name e07DataModel_LastFirst using your last and first name.

b. Create a connection to the **e07HotelData** database located with your student files using Get & Transform Data on the Data tab.

- Click any cell outside of the existing tables on the **HumanResources** worksheet.
- Select all tables in the database.
- Create only a connection to the data and add the data to the Data Model.

c. Add the tables on the **HumanResources** worksheet to the data model.

- Create a relationship between the HumanResources3 data and the JobCodes data using the JobID fields.

d. On the **Reservations** worksheet, in the Power Pivot window, format the **CheckInDate** and **CheckOutDate** fields as ***3/14/2001**.

e. Create a new calculated column on the Reservations worksheet to the right of the DiscountID column.

- Name the calculated column AmountDue
- Calculate the amount due after the discount has been applied to the SubTotal, for example, SubTotal * (1- Discount). Use the RELATED DAX function to retrieve the appropriate Discount amount from the DiscountTypes data.

f. Create a new calculated field on the Reservations worksheet just below the ID column.

- Name the calculated field 2021Revenue
- Use the CALCULATE function to sum the AmountDue column for reservations that took place in 2021.
- Format as **Currency**.

g. Create a new calculated field on the Reservations worksheet just below the 2021Revenue calculated field.

- Name the calculated field 2022Revenue
- Use the CALCULATE function to sum the AmountDue column for reservations that took place in 2022.
- Format as **Currency**.

h. Create a KPI based on the following information.

- Use the 2022Revenue calculated field as the base field (value).
- Use the 2021Revenue calculated field as the Measure.
- Set the minimum status threshold to 95%
- Set the maximum status threshold to 110%
- Select the second set of icons.

i. Close the Power Pivot window, and click in a blank cell on the HumanResources worksheet. Insert a Power View worksheet to the right of the HumanResources worksheet.

- Rename the Power View1 worksheet HotelReport
- Apply the **Flow** theme (located in the seventh row of the first column).
- Apply the **Dark2 Solid** Background.
- Add a title of 2021-2022 Reservations Report

j. Create a map visualization that illustrates the number of reservations made from each state.

- Use the GuestState field from the Guests data and the ID field from the Reservations data.
- Summarize the ID field by using Count (Distinct).

- Use the ResYear field from the Reservations Data as the HORIZONTAL MULTIPLES.
- Use the RoomType as the COLOR.
- Adjust the size of the map visualization to fill the top half of the Design pane, below the title.

k. Create a table that illustrates the monthly revenue generated in 2022 along with the KPI icon status icon.
   - Use the ResMonth field from the Reservations data.
   - Use the 2022Revenue Value and Status from the Reservations KPI data.
   - Place the table under the map visualization in the bottom left portion of the Design Pane.

l. Create a clustered bar chart that illustrates the Amount Due for each discount type.
   - Use the Description field from the DiscountType data.
   - Use the AmountDue field from the Reservations data.
   - Create a tile by using the ResYear field from the Reservations data.
   - On the Layout tab, in the Synchronize group, click the **Axes** arrow, and select **Horizontal Axis the Same Across All Tiles**.
   - Place the clustered bar chart under the map visualization in the bottom right portion of the Design pane.
   - Close the Power View Fields pane and the Filters Area.

m. Click the **HumanResources** worksheet. Open the VBE and insert a new module. Create a Sub procedure that will display a message box that will be displayed when the HotelReport Power View sheet is activated. Provide the user with the following information:
   - Describe the worksheet as an interactive visual summary.
   - Define the AmountDue calculation.
   - Define the 2022Revenue calculation.
   - Define the 2022Revenue Status settings.
   - Use line breaks to make its content easier to read and concatenation symbols to allow the code to be broken up into multiple lines.
   - Call the Sub routine whenever the HotelReport worksheet is activated.

n. Create another Sub procedure that closes and saves the file. Add a Button Form Control to the worksheet, assign the Sub procedure to the button, and change the Button text to Save and Close

o. Complete the **Documentation** worksheet according to your instructor's directions.

p. Save the workbook, exit Excel, and submit your file as directed by your instructor.

Critical Thinking

Revisit the Power View report constructed in this exercise. What changes could be made to the report to increase its analysis capabilities? Consider the table containing the revenue generated by month that contains the KPI status. If this were converted into a chart, what would be the best choice of chart types, and how would the KPI be best visualized?

Problem Solve 2

MyLab IT Grader

Student data file needed:

 e07Dashboard.xlsx

You will save your files as:

 e07Dashboard_LastFirst.xlsm

e07HotelVBA_LastFirst.txt

Production & Operations

Enhancing the Hotel Dashboard with VBA

The managers at the Painted Paradise Resort & Spa hotel use a dashboard to keep track of their top guests at the hotel and to track revenues by room type. You have been asked to enhance the dashboard and make it more secure by adding dynamic labels to the charts and using VBA.

a. Open the Excel file **e07Dashboard**. Save your file as a **Macro-Enabled Workbook** with the name e07Dashboard_LastFirst using your last and first name.

b. Click the **Dashboard** worksheet, and create dynamic labels for Year and Quarter on the Top Guests by Nights Stayed clustered column chart.

- Use cell B1 on the Analysis worksheet as the value for the Year dynamic label. Place it in the top left corner of the chart, and increase the font size to 16.

- Use cell B2 on the Analysis worksheet as the value for the Quarter dynamic label. Place it in the top right corner of the chart, and increase the font size to 16.

c. Create a Quarter dynamic label on the 2022 Revenue & Goal combo chart.

- Use cell B2 on the Analysis worksheet as the value for the Quarter dynamic label. Place it in the top right corner of the chart, increase the font size to 16, and remove the outline.

d. Insert a new VBA module in the VBE with the name e07HotelVBA_LastFirst using your last and first name.

e. Create a new Sub procedure that will loop through all the slicers on the Dashboard worksheet and clear the filters.

- Name the Sub procedure clearSlicers

- Use the name slicers as your variable of the data type **SlicerCache**.

- Create a For . . . Each loop to loop through each of the slicers in the ThisWorkbook.SlicerCaches collection.

- Create an extra space in between lines of code to make it easier to read.

f. Add a Button (Form Control) onto the Dashboard worksheet within the cell range G2:G3. Assign the clearSlicers Sub procedure to the button, and edit the button text to be Clear Slicers

g. Create a new Sub procedure in the e07HotelVBA_LastFirst module that will use the xlVeryHidden method to hide the Data and Analysis worksheets. Name the Sub procedure hideSheets

h. Assign the hideSheets Sub procedure to the BeforeClose event in the ThisWorkbook Code window.

i. Create a new Sub procedure in the e07HotelVBA_LastFirst module that will display an input box requesting a password to unhide the Data and Analysis worksheets.

- Name the Sub procedure showSheets

- Name the variable to store the password psw, and set the data type to String.

- Assign the value Password1234 to the psw variable.

- Create an input box. You will store the response of the input box in a variable named access Type Enter the password to view the worksheets as the prompt. Type Show All Sheets as the title.

- Insert an If statement that checks whether the value stored in the **psw** variable is equal to the value stored in the **access** variable.
- If the two values are equal, change the visible property of the Data and Analysis worksheets to True.
- If the two values are not equal, display a message box with the Invalid Password as the prompt.

j. Add a Button (Form Control) onto the Dashboard worksheet within the cell range G7:G8. Assign the showSheets Sub procedure to the button, and edit the button text to be Show Sheets

k. Export the e07HotelVBA_LastFirst module as a .txt file with the same name.

l. Complete the **Documentation** worksheet according to your instructor's directions.

m. Save the workbook, exit Excel, and submit your files as directed by your instructor.

Perform 1: Perform in Your Life

Student data files needed:

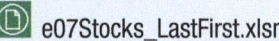 Blank Excel workbook

e07Stock.txt

You will save your file as:

e07Stocks_LastFirst.xlsm

Master Trader

Finance & Accounting

You have invested in several stocks and want to review how well your investments have done. You believe this will be easier to review if you can visually represent the data, so you have decided to create a dashboard to showcase your results.

a. Start **Excel**, and then create a new workbook. Save your file as a **Macro-Enabled Workbook** with the name e07Stocks_LastFirst using your last and first name.

b. Rename Sheet1 as Dashboard

c. Use Get & Transform to connect to the data from the tab-delimited text file named **e07Stock.txt**. No transformations should be necessary.
- Add this data to the data model, and create only a connection to the data file.

d. Make the following changes to the data in the PowerPivot window.
- Format the **Date** field as *3/14/2001.
- Format the **Open**, **High**, **Low,** and **Closing** fields as **Currency**.
- Add a calculated column called Change that subtracts the Open value from the Closing value, and format the column as **Currency**.

e. Use the Power Pivot window to generate a dashboard with **Two Charts (Horizontal)** on the Dashboard worksheet.

f. Chart 1 should be a Clustered Bar chart with the Date as the Category; the Values should contain the Average Open and Closing amounts. Display only Months in Categories area of the chart.

g. Make the following changes to chart 1.
- Add a chart title.
- Move the legend to the bottom of the chart.
- Apply Style 2.
- Remove the field buttons from the chart.

h. Chart 2 should be a Combo chart with the Date as the Category; Values should contain the Average High on the Primary Axis and the Average Change on the Secondary Axis. Both variables should be Line charts. Display only Months in Categories area of the chart.

i. Make the following changes to chart 2.
   - Add a chart title.
   - Apply Style 4.
   - Apply Quick Layout 3.
   - Move the legend to the bottom of the chart.
   - Remove the field buttons from the chart.

j. Add a slicer for the Stock and connect the slicer to both charts.

k. Add a timeline for the Date and connect the timeline to both charts. Change the Periods to Quarters.

l. Create a Sub procedure that will clear all slicers in the workbook.

m. Add a button to the Dashboard worksheet to run the macro.

n. Hide gridlines and headings.

o. Protect the worksheet allowing the options to Use PivotTable & PivotChart and to Edit objects.

p. Save the workbook, exit Excel, and submit your file as directed by your instructor.

Perform 2: Perform in Your Career

Student data file needed:	You will save your file as:
e07Online.xlsx	e07Online_LastFirst.xlsm

Managing Online Goals

Production & Operations

You are in charge of managing five employees at a computer recycling company. Your company has created an online portal your customers can use to contact you when it is time for a pickup, rather than calling a customer service agent directly. The system has been designed to randomly select the next employee in a grouping. Because there are goals your employees need to meet, you want to analyze the data from the last year to ensure that workloads are being distributed as evenly as possible.

a. Open the Excel file **e07Online**. Save your file as a **Macro-Enabled Workbook** with the name e07Online_LastFirst using your last and first name.

b. Add each of the four tables on the Data worksheet to the Data Model in Power Pivot.

c. Add the following relationships in Power Pivot.
   - Between the SalesData table, Customer field and the Customers table, ID field.
   - Between the SalesData table, Employee field and the Employees table, Code field.
   - Between the SalesData table, Month field and the Months table, Month Number field.

d. Create a new column on the Months tab named MonthSort. Construct the field to display the month number, a hyphen, and the month name. January should display as "01-January".

e. In Power Pivot, on the SalesData worksheet, format the Amount column as **Currency**.

f. Add a calculated field that calculates the sum of the Amount column.

g. Create a KPI with the sum of the Amount column as the base field and an absolute value of 100000 as the target value. Adjust the thresholds to be 90000 and 100000 Use the fourth icon style option.

h. Create a simple dashboard on a new worksheet, using **Chart and Table (Horizontal)**.

i. Rename the new worksheet **Dashboard**

j. Add another PivotChart from Power Pivot to the Dashboard worksheet below the existing PivotChart.

k. Create and format the two charts and PivotTable using the following steps.

- The first chart should show the Sales by Employee for October, November, and December. Use the MonthSort field to properly sort the months. Place the legend at the bottom of the chart.

- The second chart should show Sales by Month. Use the MonthSort field to properly sort the months. Remove the chart legend.

- For each chart, hide the field buttons and add a chart title.

- Your PivotTable should show the Employee Name, the value of the employee's KPI, and the Status.

l. Add a slicer for the Customer name that is connected to both PivotCharts. Place the slicer in the cell range J11:K19.

m. Create a Sub procedure that will clear the slicer.

n. Add a button to the Dashboard worksheet to run the macro. Place the button under the slicer.

o. Protect the worksheet, allowing the options to Use PivotTable & PivotChart and to Edit objects.

p. Hide gridlines and headings on the **Dashboard** worksheet.

q. Complete the **Documentation** worksheet according to your instructor's direction.

r. Save the workbook, exit Excel, and submit your file as directed by your instructor.

Perform 3: Perform in Your Team

Student data file needed:	**You will save your file as:**
e07Analysis.xlsx	e07Analysis_TeamName.xlsx

Team Analysis

Sales & Marketing

A local department store would like to reap the benefits of using data analysis to make strategic decisions about the future of the business. You will collaborate with a team of three to five other students to develop a data model in Excel and use it to create a simple dashboard.

a. Select one team member to set up the database by completing steps b—e.

b. Start Excel, and then open the **e07Analysis** workbook located with your student files.

c. Save the workbook as e07Analysis_TeamName using the team name assigned to your team by your instructor.

d. Open your browser and navigate to https://www.onedrive.live.com, https://www.drive.google.com, or any other instructor-assigned location. Be sure all members of the team have an account on the chosen site, such as a Microsoft or Google account.

e. Upload the **e07Analysis_TeamName** workbook to your account, and then share it with your team members, ensuring that each member has permission to edit the document.

f. Examine the steps below, and meet with your team members to discuss who should take on which tasks. Some steps will need to be done before others can be completed.

g. Add each of the **tables** on the Data worksheet to the data model.

h. Establish the appropriate **relationships** between the tables based on common fields.

i. Format the **fields** in the Power Pivot window appropriately.

j. On the **Transactions** worksheet, create a calculated column for Revenue using the Transactions and Products data, and then format it as **Currency**.

k. On the **Transactions** worksheet, create a calculated field for 2019 Total Revenue, using the appropriate DAX function, and then format it as **Currency**.

l. On the **Transactions** worksheet, create a calculated field for 2020 Total Revenue, using the appropriate DAX function, and then format it as **Currency**.

m. Create one more **calculated field** of your choosing, and then format it appropriately.

n. Create two KPIs of your choosing, one with an absolute value as the target value and one with a calculated field as the target value.

o. Create a dashboard on the Dashboard worksheet, using data from the data model. At a minimum, the dashboard must include the following items.

- Add two **PivotCharts**, one of which displays the KPI goal in a combo chart.
- Add one **PivotTable** that displays the other KPI status value.
- Add two **slicers** that are connected to either both PivotCharts or one PivotChart and the PivotTable.
- Format all of the items to create a professional-looking dashboard.

p. Complete the **Documentation** worksheet according to your instructor's direction. At a minimum, include enough detail to identify which parts of the worksheets or workbook each team member completed.

q. In a custom header section for all worksheets, include the **names** of the students in your team. Spread the names evenly across each of the three header sections: left section, center section, and right section.

r. Save the workbook, exit Excel, and submit your file as directed by your instructor.

Perform 4: How Others Perform

Student data file needed:

 e07Retail.xlsm

You will save your file as:

 e07Retail_LastFirst.xlsm

Dashboard Errors

Sales & Marketing

Peter Shaw, a manager at Goods & Stuff, a small retail store in the Midwest, attempted to create a dashboard to keep track of sales. The dashboard is not working as expected, and he is getting error messages when he tries to run some VBA code. In this exercise, you will examine the dashboard and then make the necessary changes.

a. Start Excel, and then open **e07Retail**. Save your file as e07Retail_LastFirst using your last and first name.

b. Explore the elements on the Dashboard worksheet. Notice that the slicer is not working. When you use the spin button and scroll bar, an error message appears.

c. Unprotect the worksheet, and then unlock the cells linked to the form controls.

d. Use the **Month** slicer, and notice that the label on the Revenue by Category pie chart does not change.

e. Modify the value in the box on the pie chart to be a dynamic label for Month, using the appropriate field on the Analysis worksheet.

f. Protect the worksheet, ensuring that the slicer object can still be used.

g. Click the **Show All Sheets** button, and then use Debug mode to locate and fix the error in the showSheets Sub procedure.

h. Save and close the workbook, and you will notice another VBA error message. Enter Debug mode, and then locate and fix the method causing the error.

i. Save and close the workbook.

j. Open the workbook again, click the **Show All Sheets** button, and then type Pwd1234 as the password to show all sheets.

k. Save the workbook, exit Excel, and submit your file as directed by your instructor.

Microsoft Excel

LEVERAGING MICROSOFT'S POWER BUSINESS INTELLIGENCE ("BI") DESKTOP SUITE

Prepare Case

Finance & Accounting

Sales & Marketing

Painted Paradise Red Bluff Golf Course & Pro Shop Sales Visualization

Management at the Red Bluff Golf Course & Pro Shop has been collecting data on sales transactions for the past three years. The managers are looking for ways to better visualize their data to help make important strategic decisions about the future of the company. You have been given access to a sample set of sales data from 2019–2021 and have been asked to harness the capabilities of the Microsoft Power Business Intelligence ("BI") Desktop Suite to go beyond what Excel alone can do.

OBJECTIVES

1. Install and connect the Power BI Desktop   p. 822

2. Understand the Power BI Desktop, relationships, and filled maps   p. 828

3. Work with calculations, treemaps, and drill downs   p. 832

4. Understand calendar tables and date measures   p. 836

5. Visualize trends with gauges, forecasting, and slicers   p. 842

Jannoon028/Shutterstock

Student data files needed:

e00AppendixSales.accdb

e00AppendixProShopAnalytics.pbix

You will save your file as:

e00AppendixProShopAnalytics_LastFirst.pbix

Working with Microsoft's Power Business Intelligence ("BI") Desktop Program

For many years, businesses have collected data—the equivalent of metaphorical oceans full of data. At the same time, businesses have struggled with leveraging that data. Imagine a self-driving car. The amount of data being measured every millisecond by the car is vast—including speed, trajectory, location, and sensors. Every millisecond, a sensor monitors how close the front-right tire is to the closest object or whether the windshield wipers should come on from rain detection. That data is important for the self-driving car to navigate the streets. However, making sense of every individual data point quickly becomes overwhelming. Various systems have been developed to leverage all of this data and convert it into business intelligence and business analytics.

Microsoft has developed many capabilities in Microsoft Excel to connect to data, model data, and visualize data. Chapter 13 of this book covers the capabilities native to Microsoft Excel. However, Microsoft has further developed a separate suite called Power Business Intelligence suite or the "Power BI" for short. This suite allows businesses to easily leverage both analytics and intelligence into day-to-day operations. This Power BI suite competes with other expensive software packages such as Tableau and JMP from SAS. The Power BI suite has two distinct advantages—content creation is free and the interface is comfortable for Excel users. This Appendix will show you the Power BI suite and how it can go above and beyond the capabilities of Excel.

Install and Connect the Power BI Desktop

The Power BI suite is composed of two pieces—the Power BI Desktop and the Power BI service. The **Power BI Desktop** is a free tool for analysts to develop powerful visualizations, models, reports and analytics—made for content developers. The **Power BI service** is an online, paid service that allows the analyst to share these reports in an interactive form—made for content consumers. In other words, an analyst can develop reports for free and with a subscription share it with any employee at their business—and the employee can interact with those reports on a phone, a Mac, or a PC. Sharing the files created in the Power BI Desktop only requires the paid subscription and a push of a button. Thus, this Appendix will focus on the analyst's role in creating business intelligent content in the Power BI Desktop—and will not cover the Power BI Service.

Downloading and Installing the Power BI Desktop

Before you can begin to look at the data from the Red Bluff Golf Course & Pro Shop, you need to install the Power BI Desktop. Microsoft Office 365 updates automatically according to your version or selected update cycle. For most users, this cycle is a rolling update every six months. At the time this book was written, the Power BI Desktop was on a monthly rolling update cycle. Importantly, updates to the Power BI Desktop are *not* automatically installed. In order to get updates, you have to uninstall, redownload, and install the new version. As you work through this Appendix, keep in mind that your interface could look different depending on the future Microsoft updates. In this next section, you will download and install the Power BI Desktop.

 **E00.01**

To Download and Install the Power BI Desktop Suite

a. Open Edge or other browser and navigate to https://powerbi.microsoft.com/en-us/downloads/ If necessary, scroll down. Under Microsoft Power BI Desktop, click **Advanced download options**.

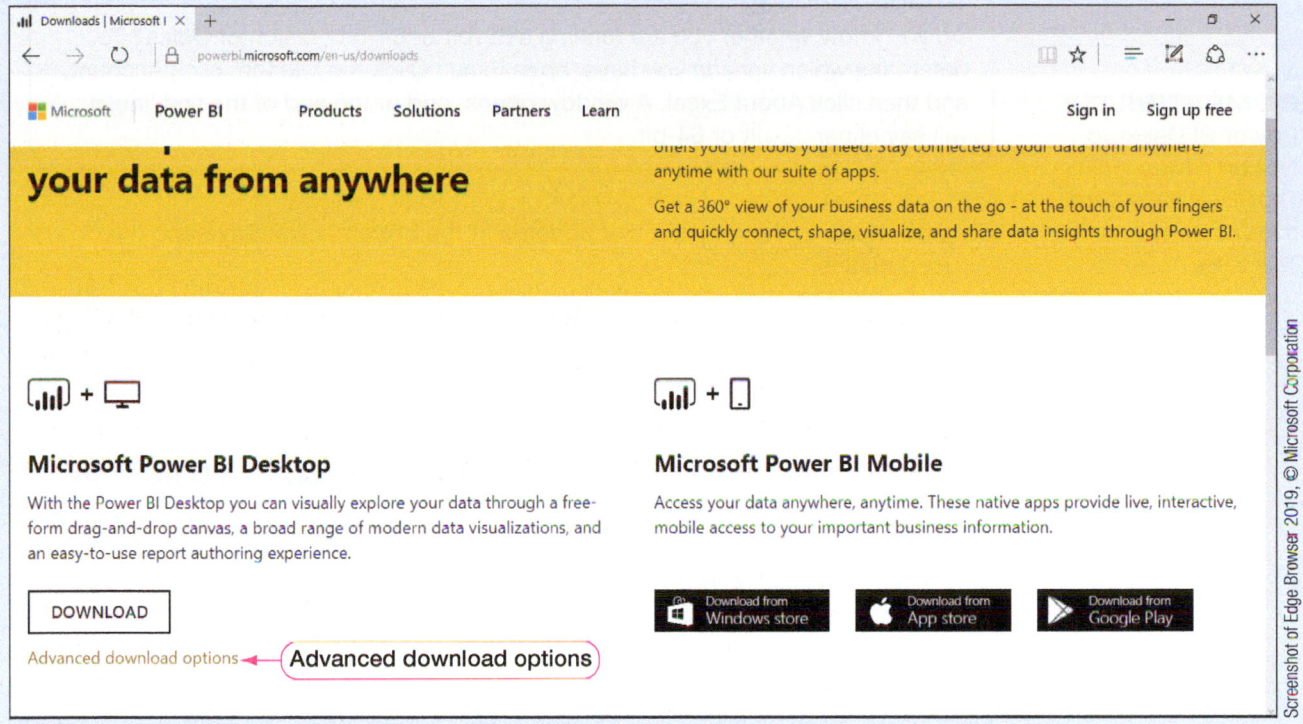

Figure 1 Advanced download options

b. If necessary, scroll down. Click the **Select Language** arrow, click **your preferred language**, and then click **Download**.

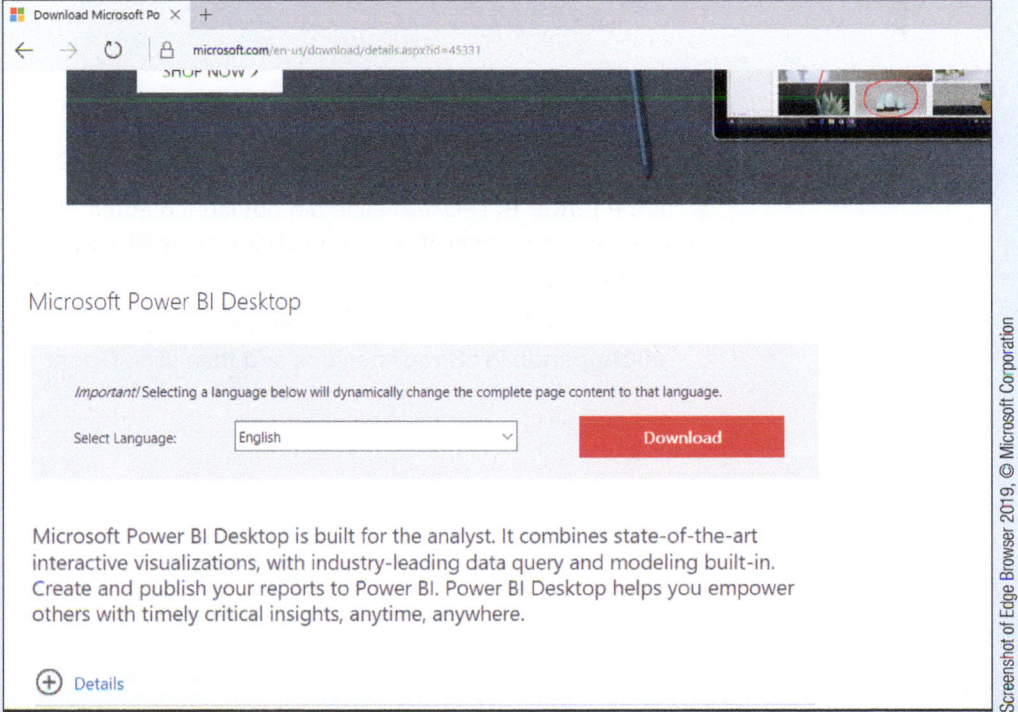

Figure 2 Select Language

c. Check the box next to the **PBIDesktop.msi** or **PBIDesktop_x64.msi** version (32 or 64 bit). **Importantly, this must match your version of MS Office to utilize connections with Access and Excel.**

MAC COMPATIBILITY
Power BI Desktop Not on a Mac
The Power BI Desktop does not exist on a Mac. This entire Appendix must be completed on a PC.

> ### Troubleshooting
> Do you know whether you are running a 32-bit or 64-bit version of Office? To determine which version you have, open Excel. Click the File tab, click Account, and then click About Excel. A window opens, and at the end of the first line, it will say either 32-bit or 64-bit.

d. Click **Next**. In the gray bar that appears at the bottom, click **Save** and the download begins.

e. After the download completes, click **Run**. Follow the prompts to install the Power BI Desktop suite.

Launching and Connecting the Power BI Desktop to a Database

After you launch the Power BI Desktop, you must first connect to your data. The data is not stored in the Power BI Desktop file. You can connect to local sources such as text files, Excel files, and Access databases. Local connections are an absolute connection. If you connect to an Access database and later move the database file, the connection in the Power BI file will break. In business, cloud technologies can store the data to allow all employees easy access, for example, connecting to Google Analytics, Azure, and Salesforce. With cloud connections, the connection is seamless to the content consumers—they will automatically connect no matter where they are or what device they access the Power BI suites from. Because not all readers of this book have access to the same cloud sources, this Appendix will use a local Access database. You can connect to more than one kind of data. In this next section, you will open the Power BI Desktop and connect to an Access Database.

 **E00.02**

To Launch and Connect the Power BI Desktop to a Database

a. If the Power BI Desktop suite did not launch automatically after installation, click ⊞ and type Power BI Find and click **Power BI Desktop**. If necessary, create an account.

b. On the Start screen, click **Open other reports**. Browse to select **e00AppendixProShopAnalytics** and then click **Open**.

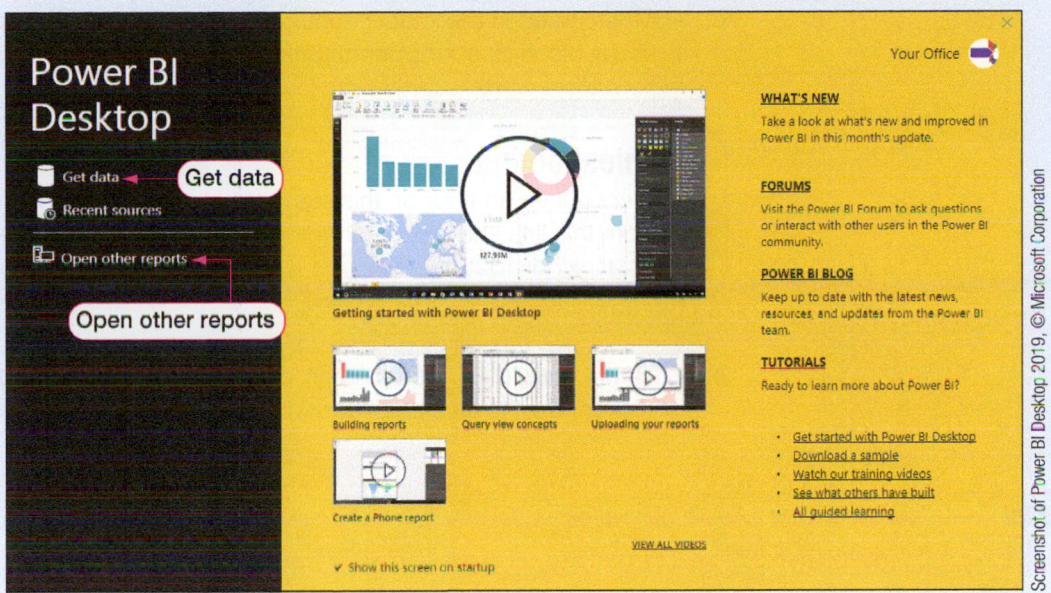

Figure 3 Power BI Desktop start screen

c. On the Home tab, in the External data group, click **Get Data** and then click **More**. In the Get Data dialog box, click **Database**, and then click **Access database**. Click **Connect**. Get Data in the Power BI Suite is very similar to Get & Transform in Excel.

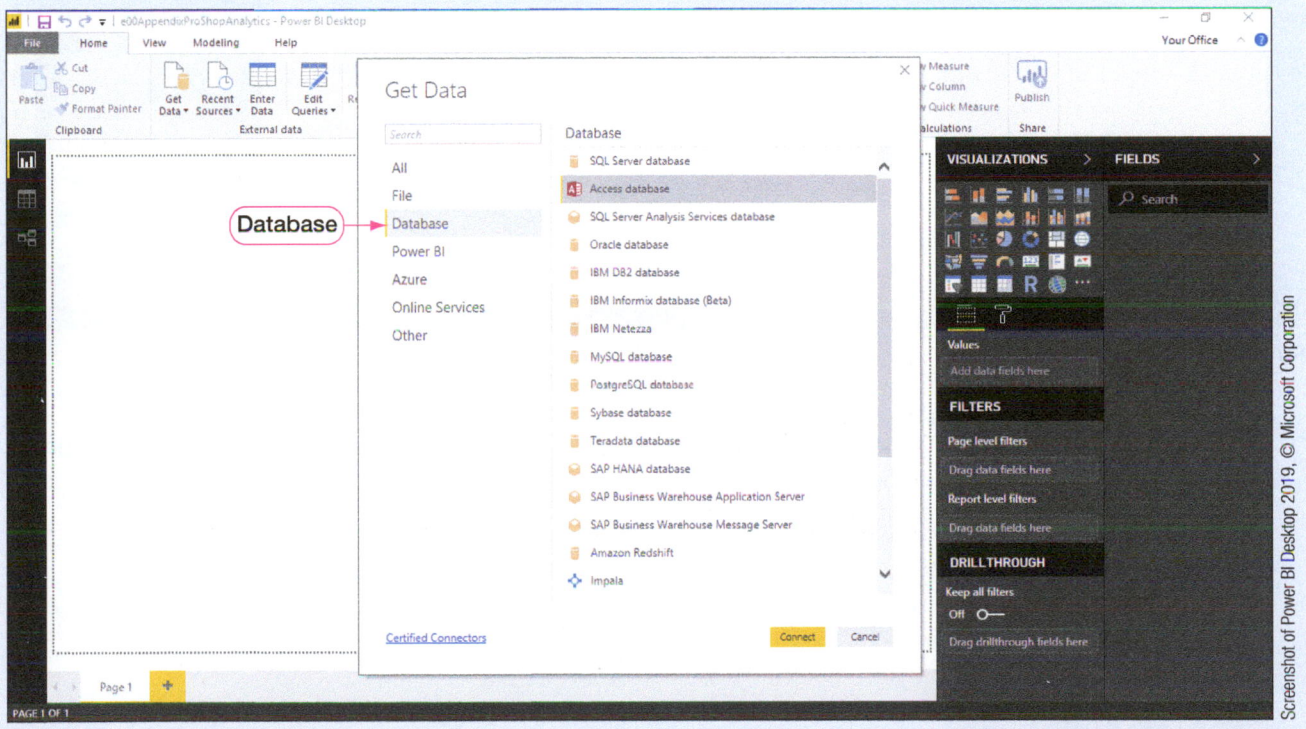

Figure 4 Get data screen

d. Navigate through the folder structure to the location of your student data files, and then double-click **e00AppendixSales.accdb**. If necessary, click **Open**.

> **Troubleshooting**
>
> If you encounter an error on this step, download the Access Connector application from this link and install it: https://www.microsoft.com/en-us/download/details.aspx?id=13255.

e. Click the **check box** next to each of the four tables in the database. As each one is clicked, the Power BI Desktop will show a sample of the data in the table.

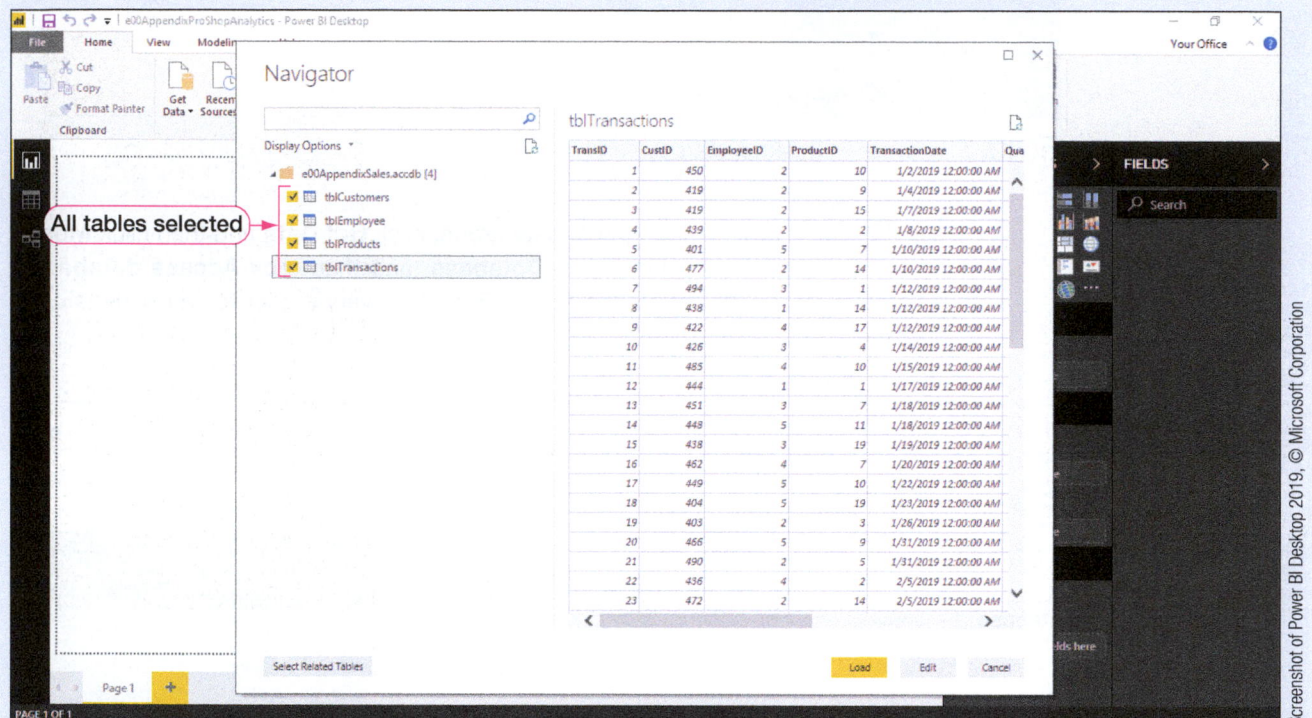

Figure 5   Navigator window

f. Click **Edit**. This opens the Power Query Editor. Chapters 9 and 13 covered parts of the Power Query Editor that exists in Excel. While not covered in this Appendix, all of the capabilities covered earlier in Excel work here as well.

Troubleshooting

If you do not see the Power Query window, it may have opened behind the Power BI Desktop window. On the taskbar, point to the Power BI Desktop and click on the preview of the Power Query window.

g. On the Home tab, in the Close group, click **Close & Apply**. You return to the Power BI Desktop, and the tables from the database are connected.

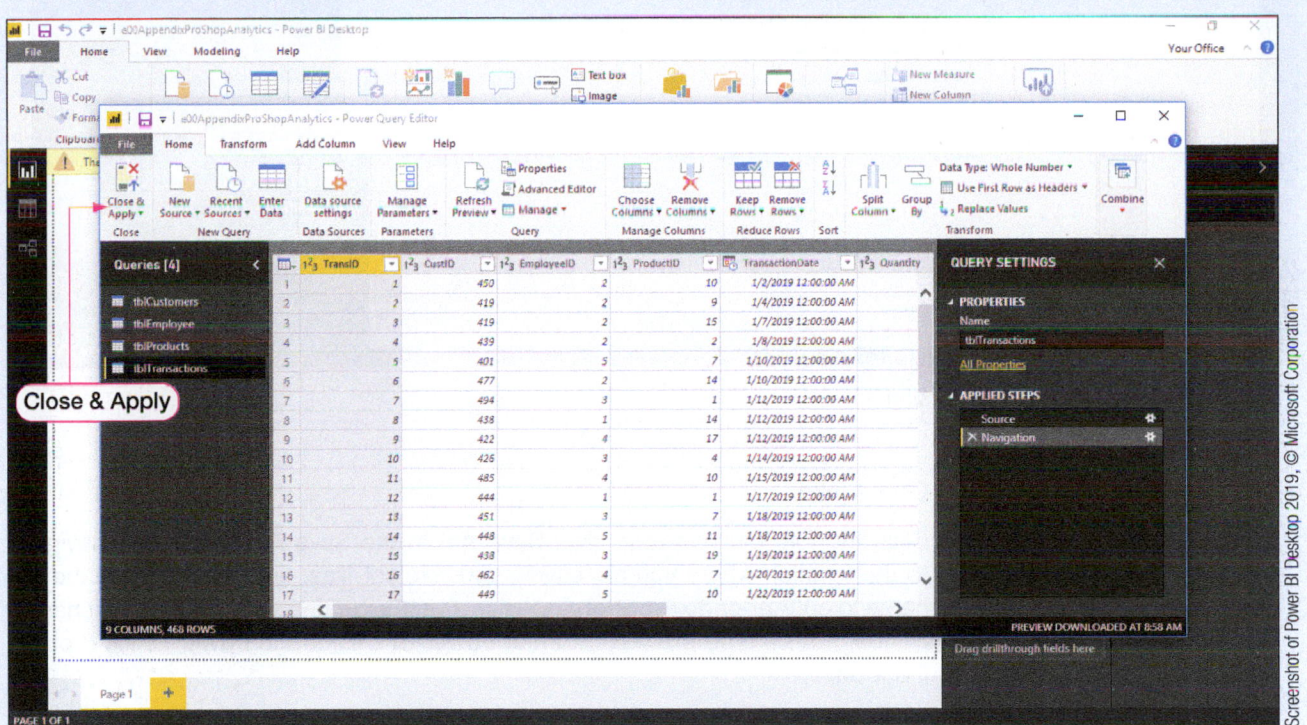

Close & Apply

Figure 6 Power Query Editor

h. On the Help tab, in the Help group, click **About**. This will show you the version you have installed. The Power BI Desktop is updated regularly and could cause your version to look differently than the instructions in this text. Version 2.63.3272.40461 32-bit (October 2018) was used to write this text. Remember that to get updates in the Power BI Desktop, you have to uninstall, redownload, and reinstall the program.

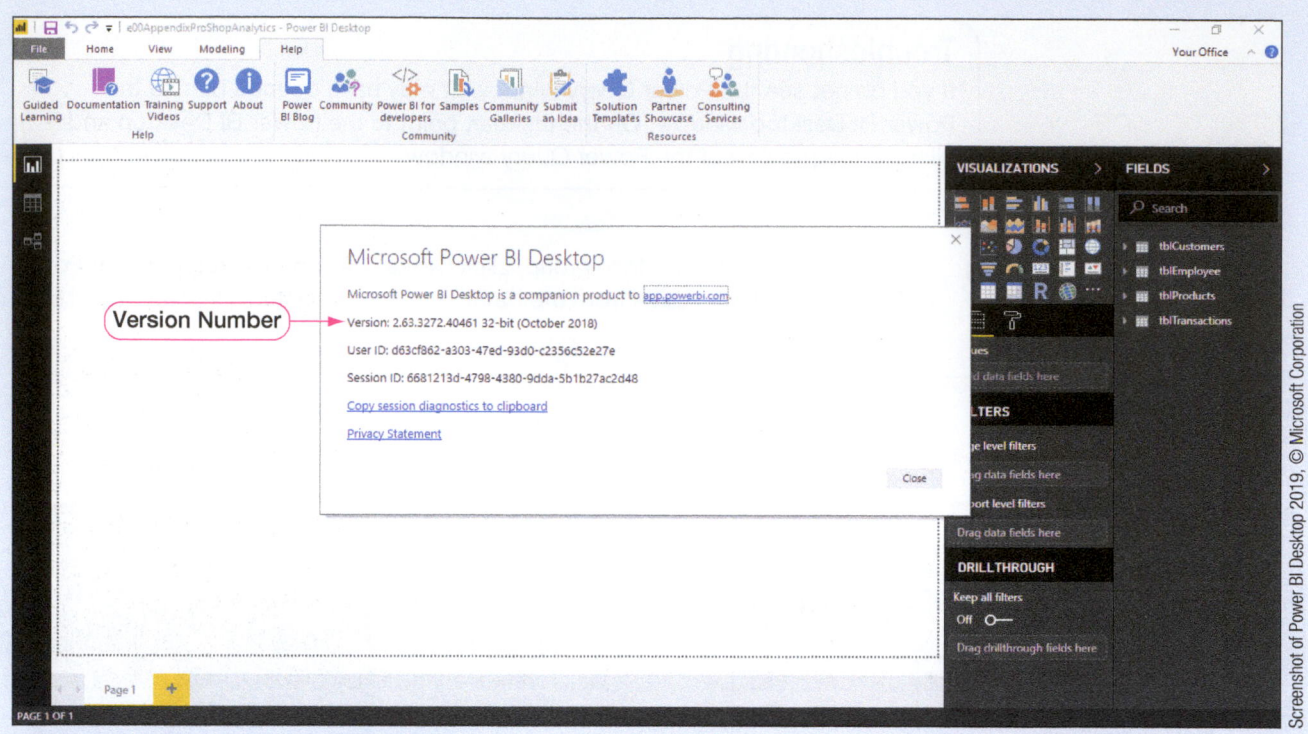

Figure 7 Power BI Desktop version

i. Click **Close**.

j. Click the **File** tab and then click **Save As**. In the Save As dialog box, navigate to the location where you are saving your project files, and then change the file name to e00AppendixProShopAnalytics_LastFirst using your last and first name. Notice, the file type extension for the Power BI Desktop is Power BI file (*.pbix). Click **Save**.

Understand the Power BI Desktop, Relationships, and Filled Maps

The Power BI interface-shown in Figure 8—has three different views: Report ![icon], Data ![icon], and Relationships ![icon]. By default, you open in the **Report view** where you build visualizations and which is very similar to Power View in Excel. **Visualizations** can be many different kinds of connected visual content, for example a table, map, line, column, waterfall, and many more. In the **Data view**, you can create additional calculations and see the data and is very similar to Excel's Power Pivot. In the **Relationships view**, you can see all of the tables and how they are related to one another and is very similar to Data Model in Excel and Relationships window in Access.

In Report view, you can create multiple reports on different page tabs similar to Excel worksheets. The white pane is where your report and visualizations are created. On the right, you have two important panes. You have the **VISUALIZATIONS pane** where you create, configure, and format the visualizations—such as a map. You also have the **FIELDS pane** where you can access and see all of the tables and fields available for use.

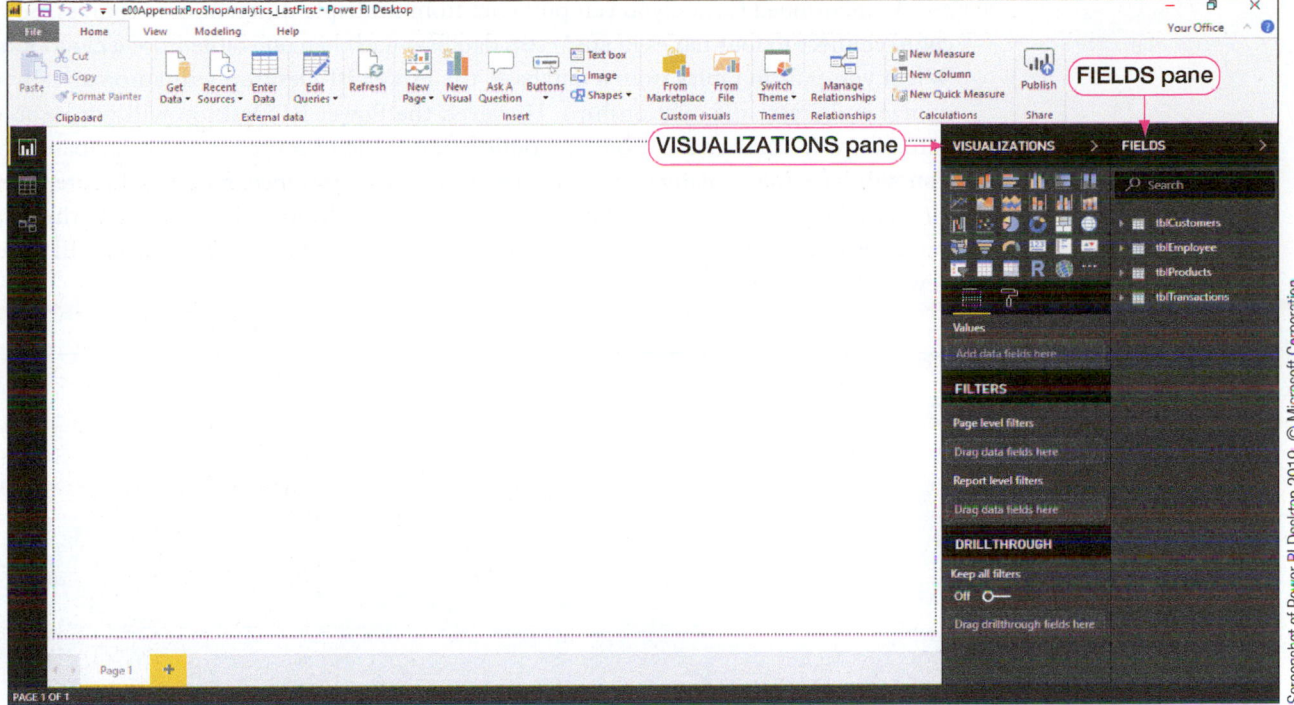

Figure 8 Power BI Desktop interface

Understanding Relationships

Many data sets come from a relational database. Other sources can be a flat data set or a Web API. A full discussion of relational databases, keys, relationships, and normalization are outside the scope of this Appendix. A flat data set has only one table—and that table has everything you need. However, flat databases tend to have a lot of redundancy. Web APIs tend to be connections that are not fully flat or fully relational. Knowledge of these concepts are very helpful in connecting different data sources properly. This Appendix will briefly discuss relationships. For full coverage of relational databases, please see the *Microsoft Office 365® Access™ 2019 Comprehensive* book.

A **relationship** is how the data in one data set connects to another data set through common fields known as keys. A **primary key** field is a field that uniquely identifies the record and can only occur once. A **foreign key** is a field in a data set that stores a value that is the primary key in *another* data set. It is called foreign because it does not identify a record in this data set; it identifies a record in another—foreign—data set. A foreign key can appear in the same data set many times.

Illustratively, you could have one data set called customer. In that data set, you have a field called Customer ID. The Customer ID is a primary key because each customer has their own unique number—two customers cannot share the same number. Also, you have another data set called transactions. The transactions data set lists out all of the transactions and should have its own primary key that uniquely represents each transaction—such as Transaction ID. Also in the transaction data set, you have a Customer ID. The Customer ID in the transactions data set is a foreign key. It represents the customer who made the transaction and you hope the Customer ID is in the data set many times—because this means the customer has made many different transactions (or purchases) from you. When you create a relationship, you tell the Power BI Desktop that the Customer ID in the customer table is the same as the Customer ID in transactions. Thus, even though the transactions data set only has the Customer ID—and not the customer's name or other information—the Power BI Desktop will be able to use the relationship to pull that additional data such as customer name from the customer data set.

As mentioned earlier, you can pull data from multiple different data sources. So, you could connect to four tables in an Access database and then one table from a cloud source. When you pull in tables from a database, the Power BI Desktop will automatically recognize and create the relationships. However, the Power BI Desktop will not be able to automatically connect the table you pulled from a cloud source to your database tables. You will have to manually create a relationship in that instance. Examine Figure 9 below for the relationships that the Power BI Desktop has already imported from the Access database and incorporated into the data model. Later in the Appendix, you will create a new table and learn how to manually create relationships.

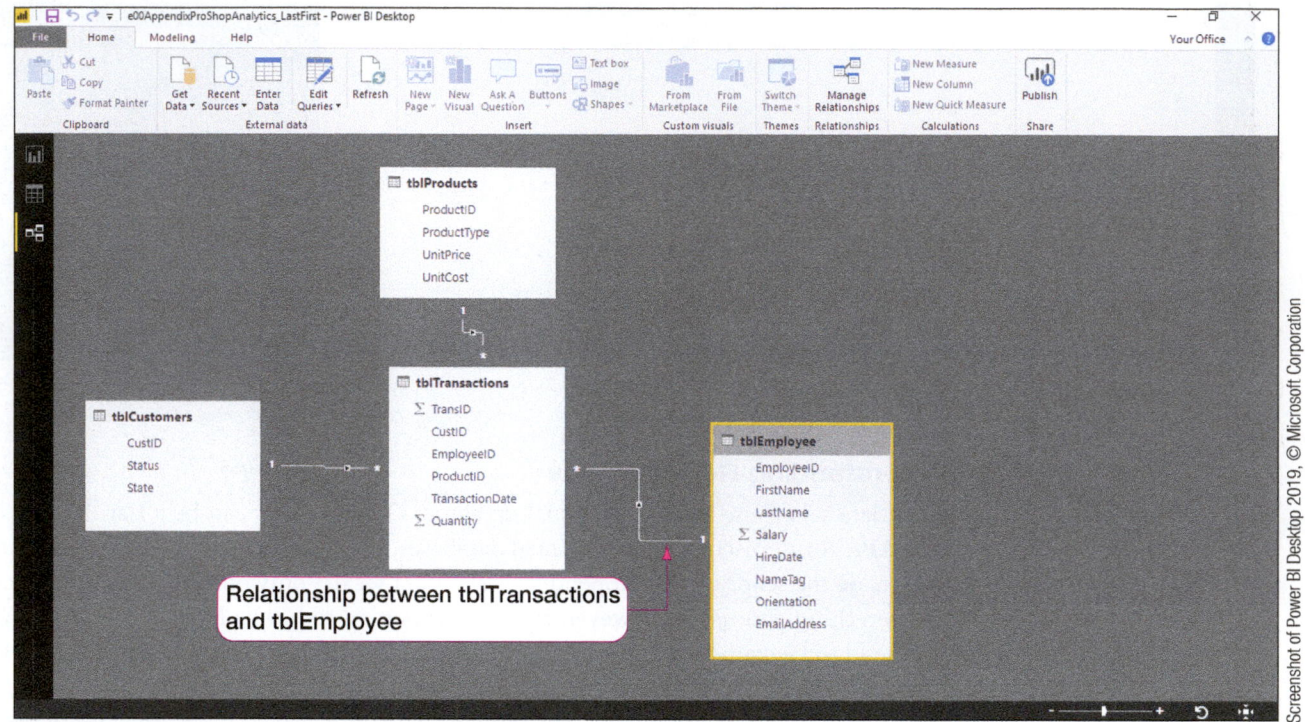

Figure 9 Relationships imported from the database

Creating a Filled Map Visualization

Map visualizations can be very powerful. Map charts can be created in Excel, and Power View can create detailed maps. However, the Power BI Desktop has several different map types and has rich features not found in Excel. **A Map visualization** allows you to represent locational data such as country, state, zip code, or geological coordinates on a map. In this next exercise, you will represent the total quantity sold in the entire database by state.

 E00.03

To Create a Filled Map of Sales

a. In the VISUALIZATIONS pane, click **Filled map** ▦.

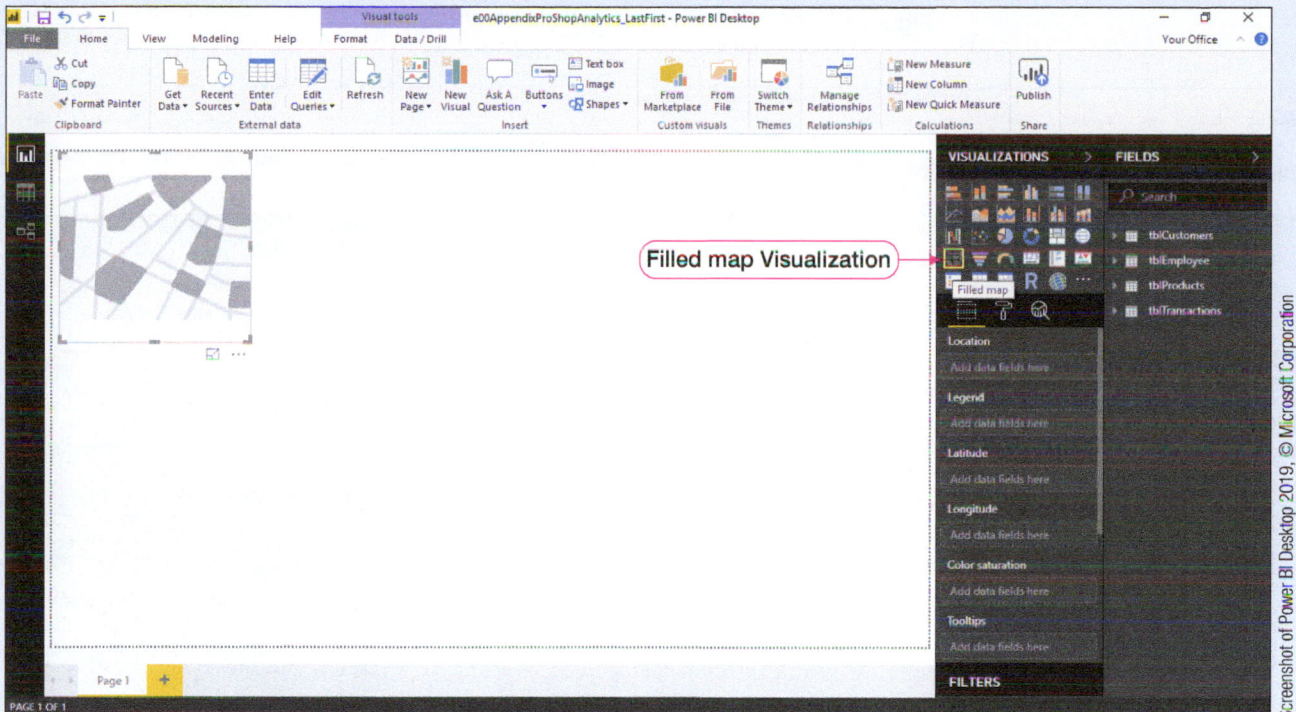

Figure 10 Filled map visualization

b. In the FIELDS pane, click the **arrow** next to tblCustomers to see the fields available in the tblCustomers table.

c. Click and drag the **State** field from the FIELDS pane to the VISUALIZATIONS pane under Location where it says **Add data fields here**.

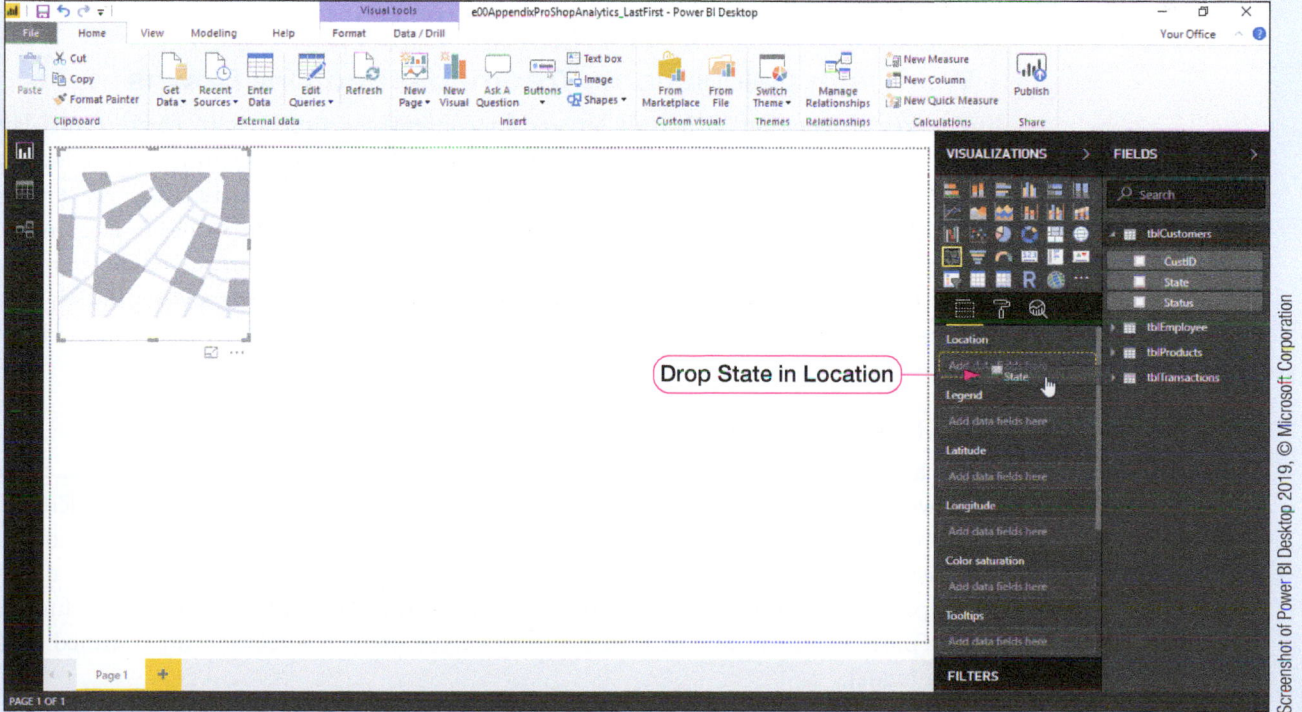

Figure 11 Drop in the State field for location

d. From the tblTransactions table, add **Quantity** to the Color saturation.

e. In the VISUALIZATIONS pane, click **Format**. Click **Title** and increase the Text size to **16**. Using the sizing handles, resize the map to approximately the size in Figure 12.

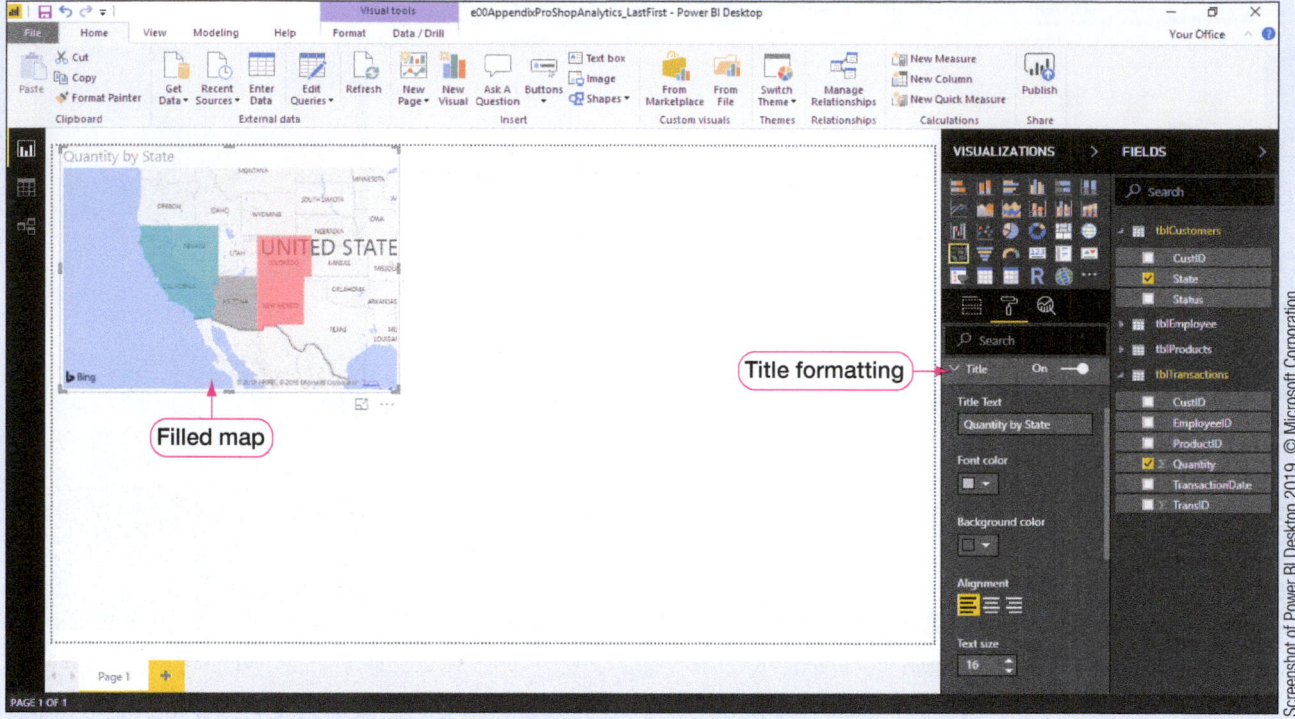

Figure 12 Fill map for Quantity by State

f. **Save** the document.

Work with Calculations, Treemaps, and Drill Downs

The key to creating insightful reports for content consumers is to create multi-layer reports that are interactive, allowing the person using the report to peel back layers of the data. To do this, sometimes you will need to add new calculations that do not exist in the data set—but whose components do exist to calculate the value. In fact, in good relational database design, calculations should never be stored in the data sets but are calculated instead. The Power BI Desktop also allows you to create a visualization called a Treemap—which you can also create in Excel—but the Power BI Desktop provides the ability to drill down into the data to unfold layers or different data perspectives.

Understanding and Creating Calculations

In the golf data, no field exists that calculates revenue in any of the database tables. However, there are fields called Quantity and UnitPrice. Thus, you can add a calculation to create a field called Revenue. To accomplish this, you will use a category of functions called Data Analysis eXpressions (DAX). These are the same kinds of functions used in Chapter 13 in Excel. In particular, you will use the **RELATED function**—a function that pulls a value from a field in a different table using the relationships defined in the data model.

The RELATED function takes the syntax below. Where the syntax says Column, you give the calculation a name. The RELATED function only has one argument, Column-Name. This is a reference to the field in another table.

RELATED function syntax:
Column = RELATED(ColumnName)

Example revenue calculation:
Revenue = tblTransactions[Quantity] * RELATED(tblProducts[UnitPrice])

 E00.04

To Create a Calculation and Use the RELATED Function

a. Click **Data** ⊞ in the left pane. This takes you to Data view.

b. In the FIELDS pane, click the **tblTransactions** table.

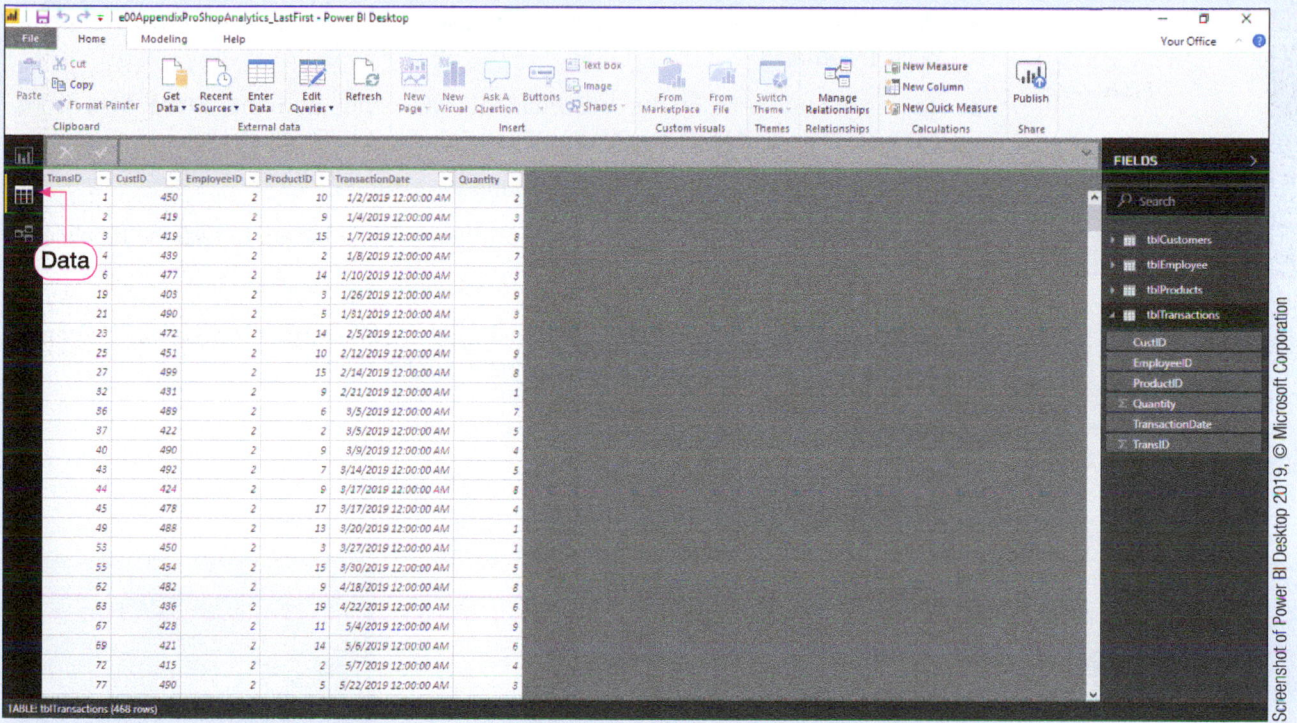

Figure 13   tblTransactions open in Data view

c. On the Home tab, in the Calculations group, click **New Column**.

d. In the formula bar, delete **Column =** and then type Revenue = tblTransactions [Quantity] * RELATED(tblProducts[UnitPrice])

SIDE NOTE
Alternate Method
Instead of typing everything, you can also use the arrow keys and tab to select when the appropriate options appear.

e. Press Enter and the column is added.

f. Click **Report** 📊 to switch back to Report View.

g. Click anywhere in the white space to deselect the filled map.

h. **Save** 💾 the document.

Creating a Treemap and Drill Down

While Treemaps can be created in Excel, you must know how to precisely set up the data. The Power BI Desktop makes Treemaps easy and drillable. A **Treemap visualization** represents hierarchical data in the form of a rectangle with smaller rectangles inside where the size of the rectangles represents the value. The size of the overall rectangle represents the total of all data, whereas the size of the smaller inside rectangles represents the value of a subcategory. For example, you could have a Treemap representing all revenue where the inside smaller, nested rectangles size represents the amount of revenue from a particular state. Further, you can add another layer of grouping such as product type. So, if the user drills into a particular state, such as Nevada, the Treemap evolves to show the overall size of the rectangle represents all the revenue in Nevada, and the smaller inside rectangles sizes represents the revenue of each product type in Nevada. In this next exercise, you will create a Treemap of revenue by State and then ProductType.

 **E00.05**

To Create a Treemap and Drill Down

a. Without any of the other visualizations selected, in the VISUALIZATIONS pane click **Treemap** .

b. To the Group area in the VISUALIZATIONS pane, add the **State** field from tblCustomers and then the **ProductType** field from tblProducts.

c. Add **Revenue** from tblTransactions to the Values area.

d. Click **Format** . Click the On\Off toggle next to **Data labels** to turn the labels on.

e. Click **Title** and increase the Text size to **16**.

Notice, even though ProductType was added under Group, the Treemap does not show it. To see the ProductType, you need to drill down.

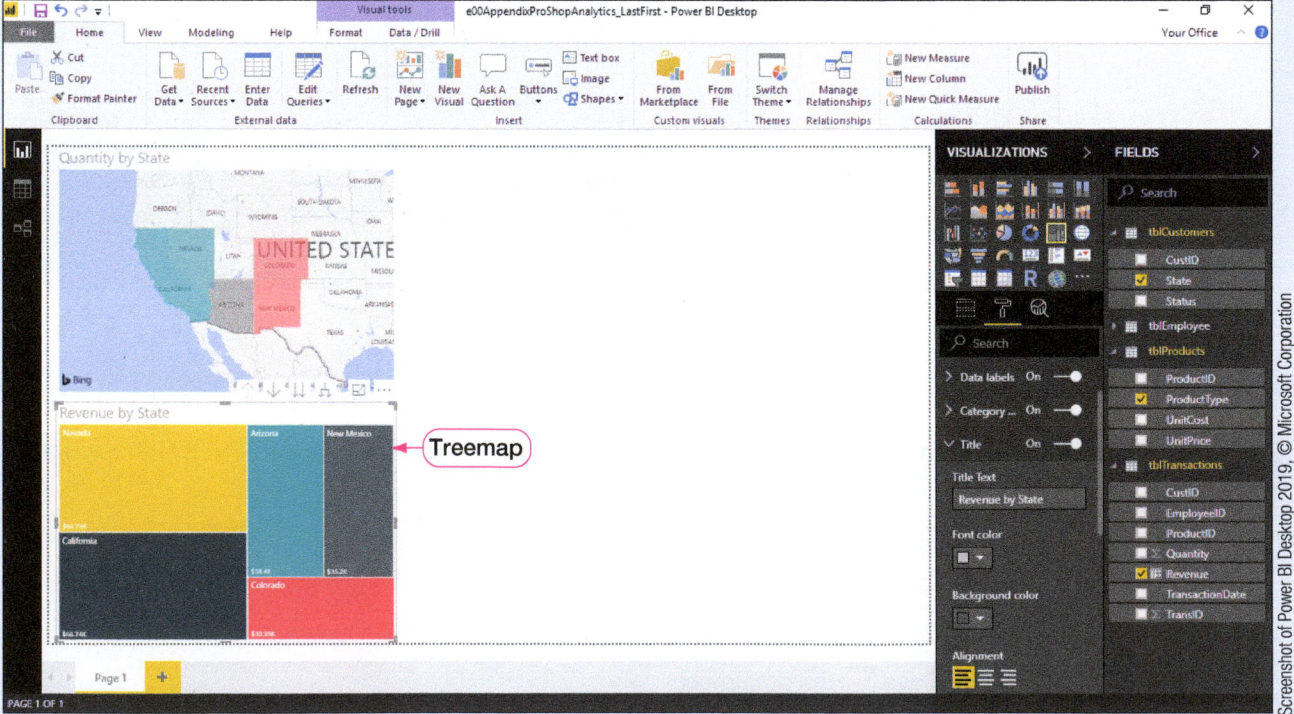

Figure 14   Treemap

f. On the Data / Drill tab, in the Data actions group, click **Drill down**. Now, when a state on the Treemap is clicked, it will drill down into the Product Types for that state.

g. In the Treemap, click on the **Nevada** tile. The Treemap then drills down into ProductType.

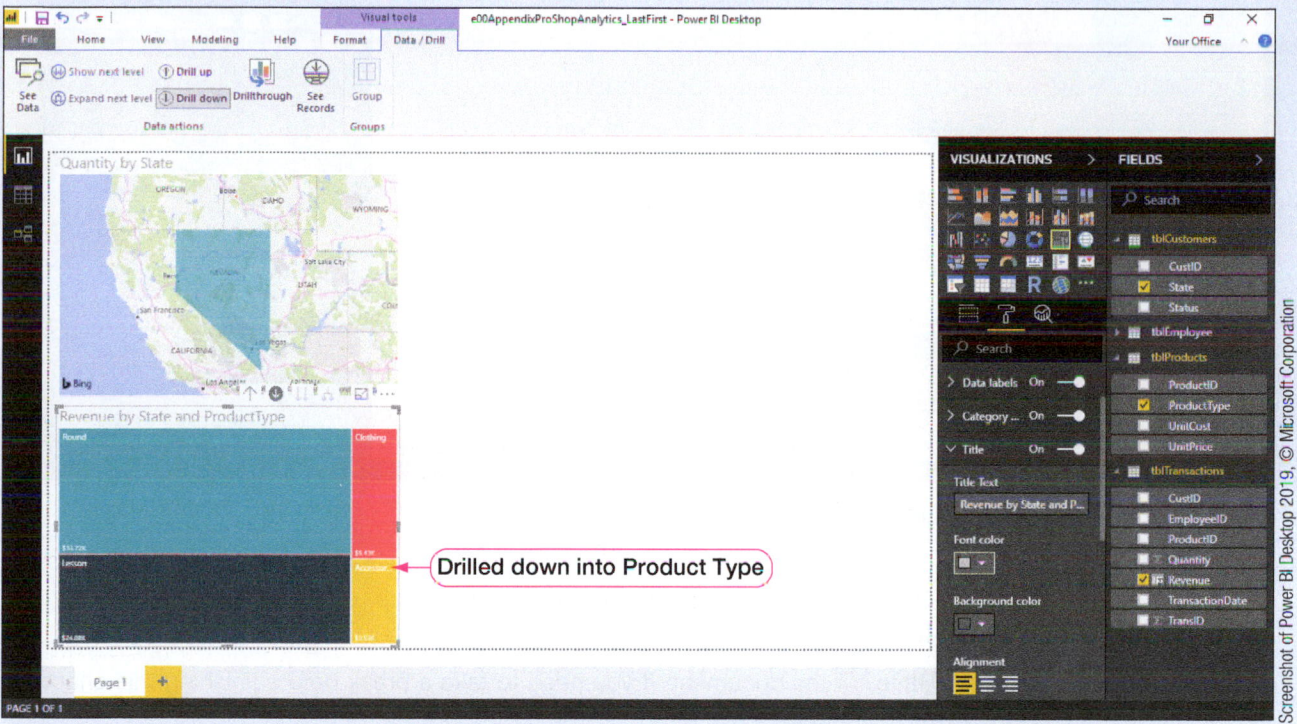

Figure 15   Treemap drilled down into Product Type

h. On the Data / Drill tab, in the Data actions group, click **Drill up**. This returns the Treemap to the highest level.

i. On the Data / Drill tab, in the Data actions group, click **Expand next level**. This combines both levels and shows each product type per state as a different tile in the Treemap.

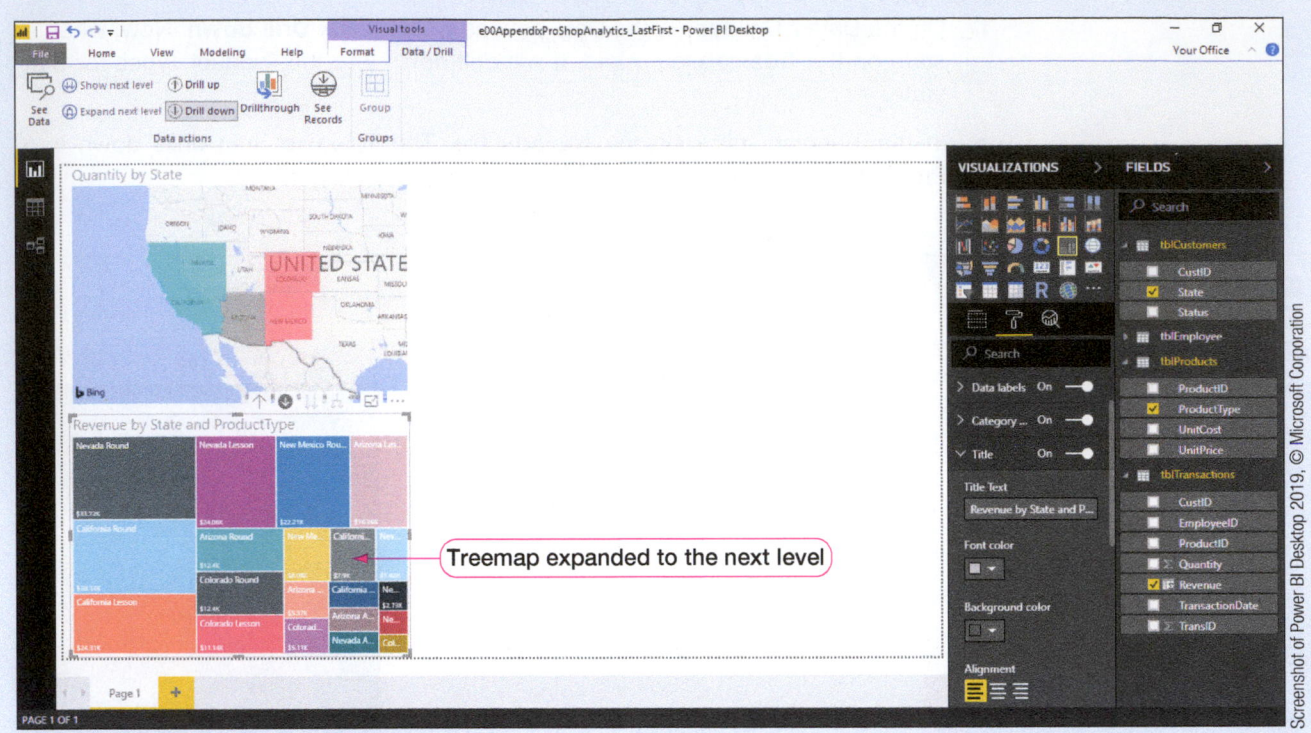

Figure 16 Treemap expanded to the next level

> **j.** On the Data / Drill tab, in the Data actions group, click **Drill up**. This returns the Treemap to the highest level.
>
> **k.** **Save** 🖫 the document. If you need to take a break before finishing this chapter, now is a good time.

Working with Analytics and Time Intelligence in Visualizations

The Power BI Desktop contains a rich feature set of analytical tools that can further enhance visualizations. Adding trend lines, forecasting, or customized Measures to visualizations takes only a few clicks of a mouse and adds insight to your analysis. The Power BI Desktop also has **Time Intelligence** calculations that allow you to easily compare time hierarchy in years, quarters, months, and days. For example, you can compare this quarter's earnings to the same quarter last year. This system of functions can be extremely useful in creating key performance indicators and other metrics for measuring progress in business.

Understand Calendar Tables and Date Measures

Time Intelligence functions in the Power BI Desktop require the presence of a table that can serve as a calendar for reference in calculations. Fortunately, the Power BI Desktop contains functions that automate the creation of calendar tables to facilitate the use of Time Intelligence functions. Once a calendar table has been added to the Power BI Desktop file, Time Intelligence functions can be used as Measures. These Measures can be located in any of the tables in the Power BI Desktop file.

Creating a Calendar Table and Relating It to Other Tables

As previously discussed, you need a table or data set with dates in it to use Time Intelligence functions. Since this table will be new, it will need to have a relationship to other data in the model. When creating the table, it is important to know what date range you are working within. For example, you would not want to start the calendar table at a date past when your company data ends. The Power BI Desktop allows you to define the start and end dates for the table. These values can be modified at any time.

The **CALENDAR function** creates a new table with one field named Date and populates the field with dates automatically based on a given start and end date. This function creates a **Calculated Table**—a table created from a function that automatically populates the data in the new table. The CALENDAR function takes the following syntax. In the syntax where it says Table, you give the new table a name. The CALENDAR function has two arguments, StartDate and EndDate.

The CALENDAR function syntax:
Table = CALENDAR(StartDate,EndDate)

Example creating a table called tblCalendar:
tblCalendar = CALENDAR("1/1/2019","12/31/2021")

In the next exercise, you will create the calendar table and establish a relationship.

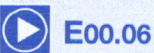 **E00.06**

To Create a Calendar Table

a. If you took a break, open the e00AppendixProShopAnalytics_LastFirst document.

b. Click **Data** .

c. Click the Modeling tab, and in the Calculations group, click **New Table**.

d. In the formula bar, delete **Table =** and type
tblCalendar = CALENDAR("1/1/2019","12/31/2021")

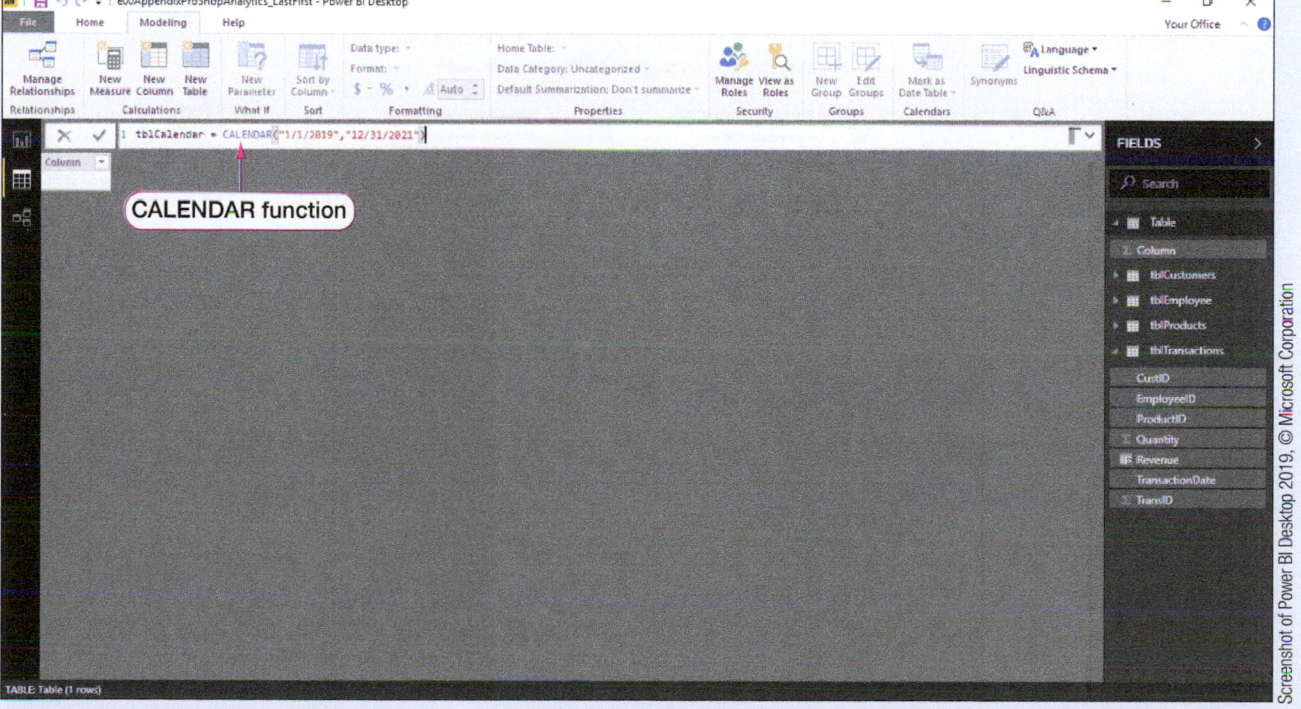

Figure 17   Calendar formula

e. Press **Enter**. The Power BI Suite creates the table and populates the data.

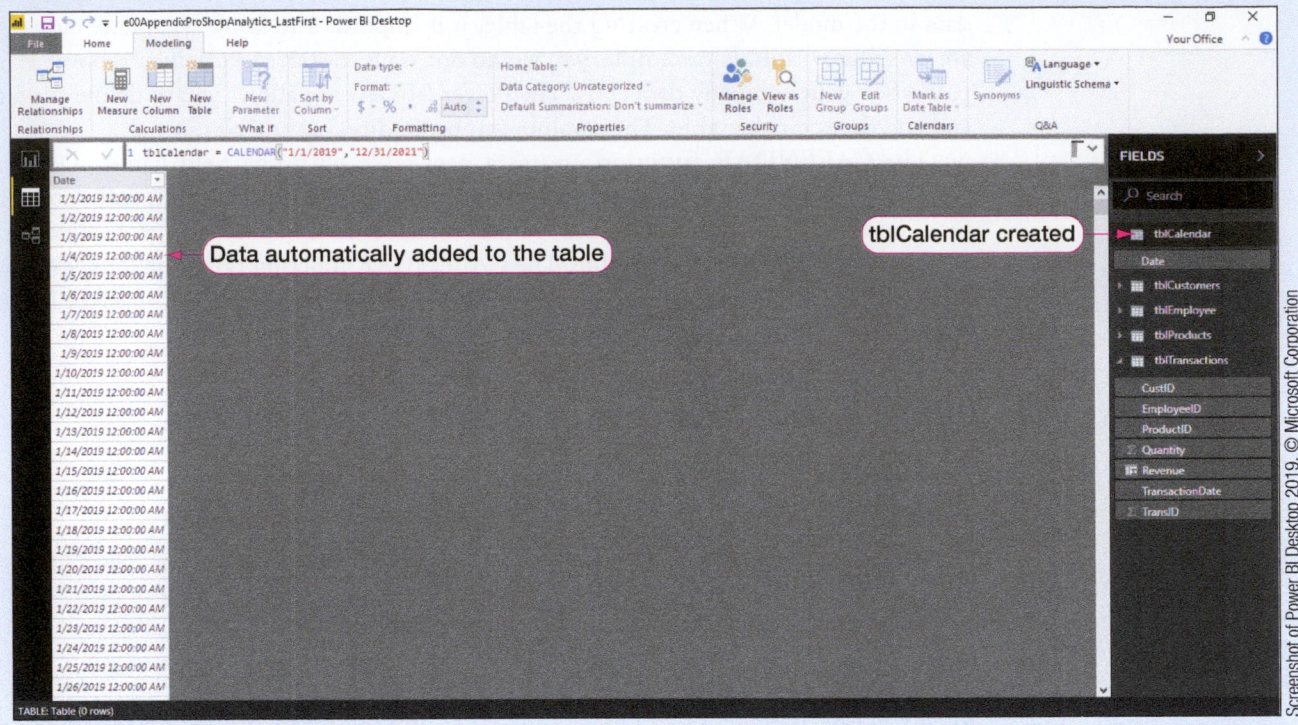

Figure 18　Calendar table created

f. Before you can use the dates from the tblCalendar table, you must create a relationship to one of your existing tables. On the Modeling tab, in the Relationships group, click **Manage Relationships**.

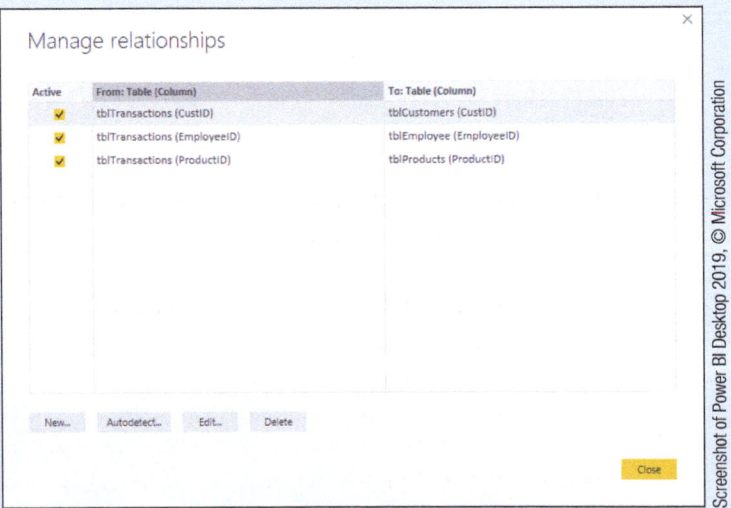

Figure 19　Manage Relationships window

g. In the Manage relationships window, click **New**.

h. In the first drop-down, select **tblCalendar** and then click to select the **Date** field.

i. In the second drop-down, select **tblTransactions**, and then click to select the **TransactionDate** field.

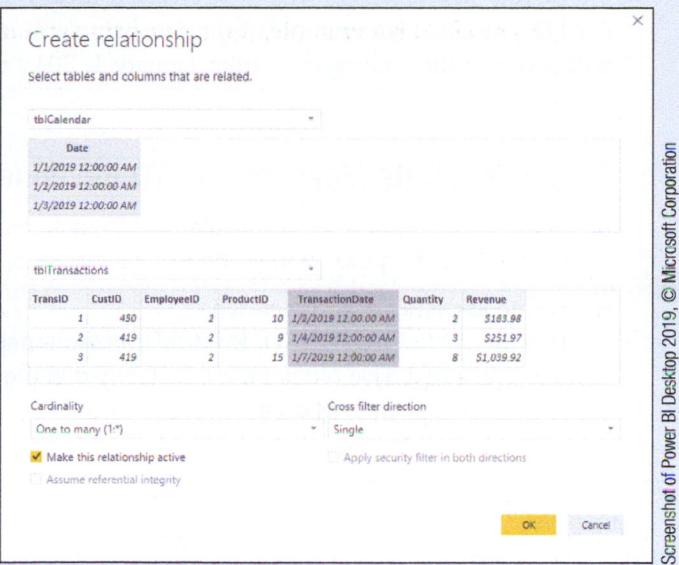

Screenshot of Power BI Desktop 2019, © Microsoft Corporation

Figure 20   New relationship between tblCalendar and tblTransactions

j. Make sure that **Make this relationship active** was automatically checked and then click **OK** to close the Create relationship window.

k. Click **Close** to close the Manage relationships window.

Now that you have a calendar table that is related to another existing table, you can add it to any visual to automatically create a date hierarchy of Year, Quarter, Month, Day.

l. Save 🔲 the document.

Creating a Year to Date Measure

A measure in the Power BI Desktop calculates a result from an expression and is then available in the FIELDS pane to use in visualizations. The measure is always calculated according to the interactions on a report. This allows for dynamic data exploration. Measures are created in Report or Data view and are available in the Field List while building visualizations. Measures can be simple SUM functions to more complex DAX or Time Intelligence functions. There are many different time intelligence functions that are available.

The **TOTALYTD function** calculates an expression from the first day of the year to the specified date. The TOTALYTD function takes the syntax below. Where Measure is in the syntax, you give the measure a name. The TOTALYTD function has two required arguments and two optional arguments. The Expression argument is the desired calculation between the first day of the year to the date specified in the second argument. The Dates argument should reference the Date field in your calendar table. The Filter and YearEndDate arguments are optional and will not be used in this text. However, they allow you to add a filter to the calculation and change the end date of a year. By default, the Power BI Desktop uses a normal calendar year.

The TOTALYTD syntax:
Measure = TOTALYTD(Expression, Dates, [Filter], [YearEndDate])

An example TOTALYTD function:
RevenueYTD = TOTALYTD(SUM(tblTransactions[Revenue]),tblCalendar[Date])

In this next exercise, you will create a measure that calculates the Year to Date ("YTD") revenue. For example, if the date being evaluated is June 10, 2019, this measure will give you the total revenue from January 1, 2019 to June 10, 2019.

 **E00.07**

To Create a Date Measure for YTD Revenue

a. In the FIELDS pane, click **tblCalendar** to make sure that tblCalendar is selected. On the Modeling tab, in the Calculations group, click **New Measure**.

b. Delete **Measure =** and then type
RevenueYTD = TOTALYTD(SUM(tblTransactions[Revenue]),tblCalendar[Date])
and press Enter. This Measure will be located in the Calendar table but will not appear as a column of data.

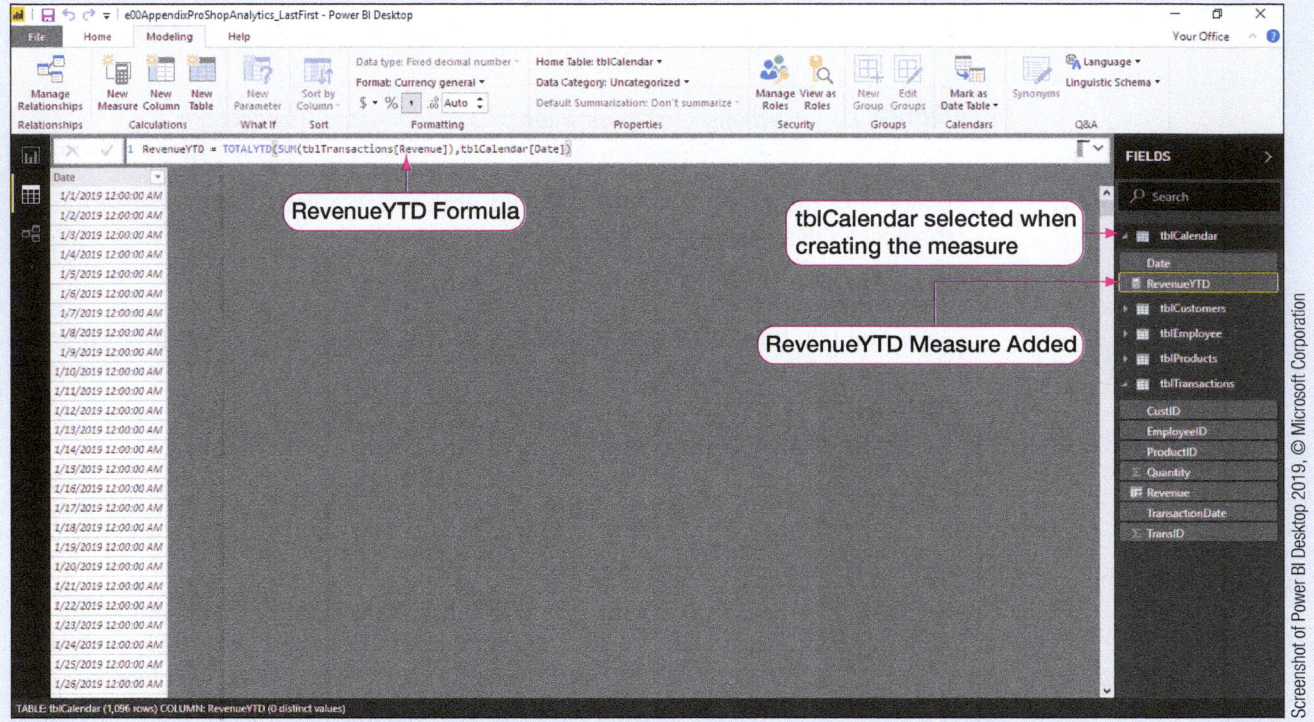

Figure 21   Year to Date Revenue Measure

The PowerBI Suite has many different functions available to do date calculations. The TOTALYTD will sum the revenue from January first of the given year to that date in time.

c. **Save** the document.

Creating a Table and Line Chart Showing Year-to-Date Trends

You can create a table to show values and a line chart to visually represent a trend over time. Line visualizations are useful to show trends over time and compare to Measure—such as year to date revenue or revenue at that point in time last year. In the next exercise, you will create a table and line chart to show how the revenue and year to date revenue compare.

 **E00.08**

To Create a Table Analyzing Monthly Revenue for 2019 along with YTD Revenue

a. Click **Report** ▥.

b. With no other visualizations selected in the workspace, in the VISUALIZATIONS pane, click **Table** ▥.

c. To the Values area in the VISUALIZATIONS pane, drag **Date** from the tblCalendar table, **Revenue** from the tblTransactions table, and then the **RevenueYTD** field from tblCalendar—in that order.

> **Troubleshooting**
>
> If you add these three fields in a different order, you can click and drag them into the proper order with Date on top, then Revenue, and then RevenueYTD.

d. In the VISUALIZATIONS pane, in the Values area, click the arrow next to the Date field and select **Date**.

A table is created that shows the revenue for each day and the year to date sum of revenue from that particular year.

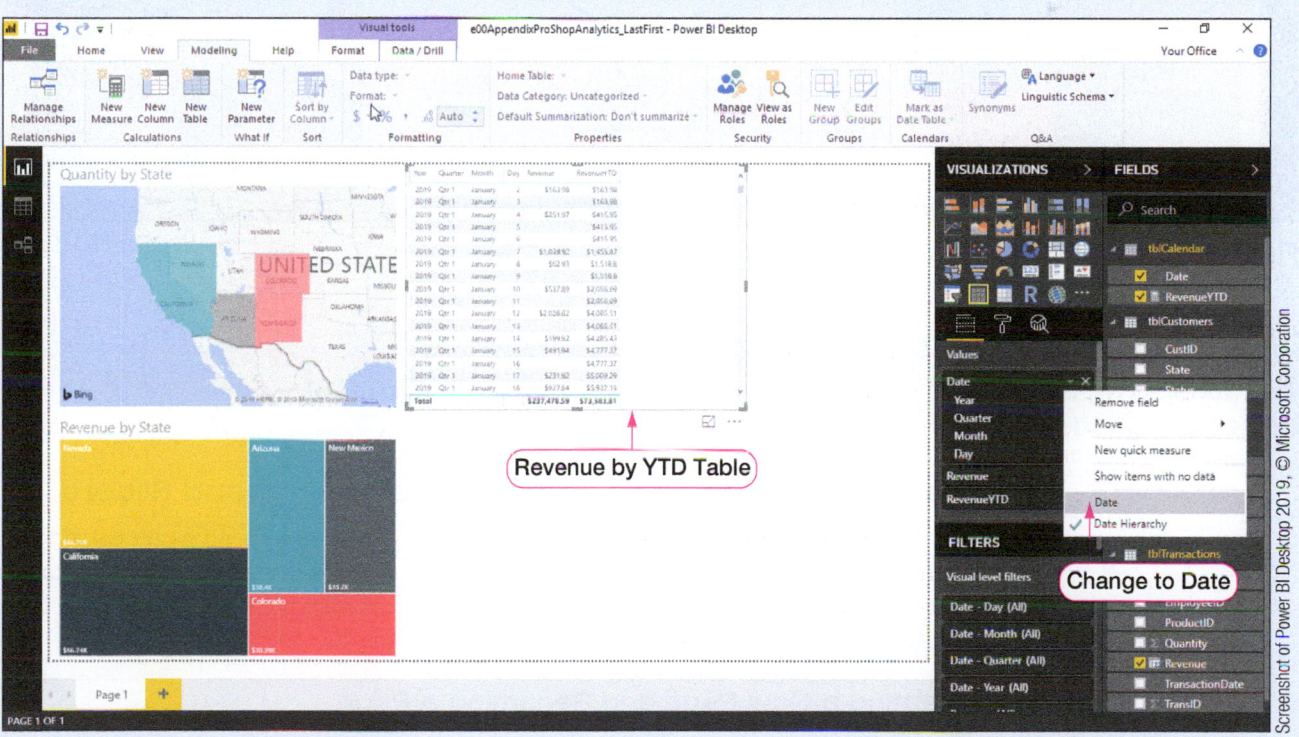

Figure 22 Table with RevenueYTD

e. With the table selected, press `Ctrl`+`C` and then `Ctrl`+`V` to create a second copy of the table. Click and drag the new table below the first table.

f. With the second table selected, in the VISUALIZATIONS pane, click **Line chart** . This creates a line chart based off the settings from the table.

This visualization shows seasonality of the revenue and the year to date revenue for that point in time.

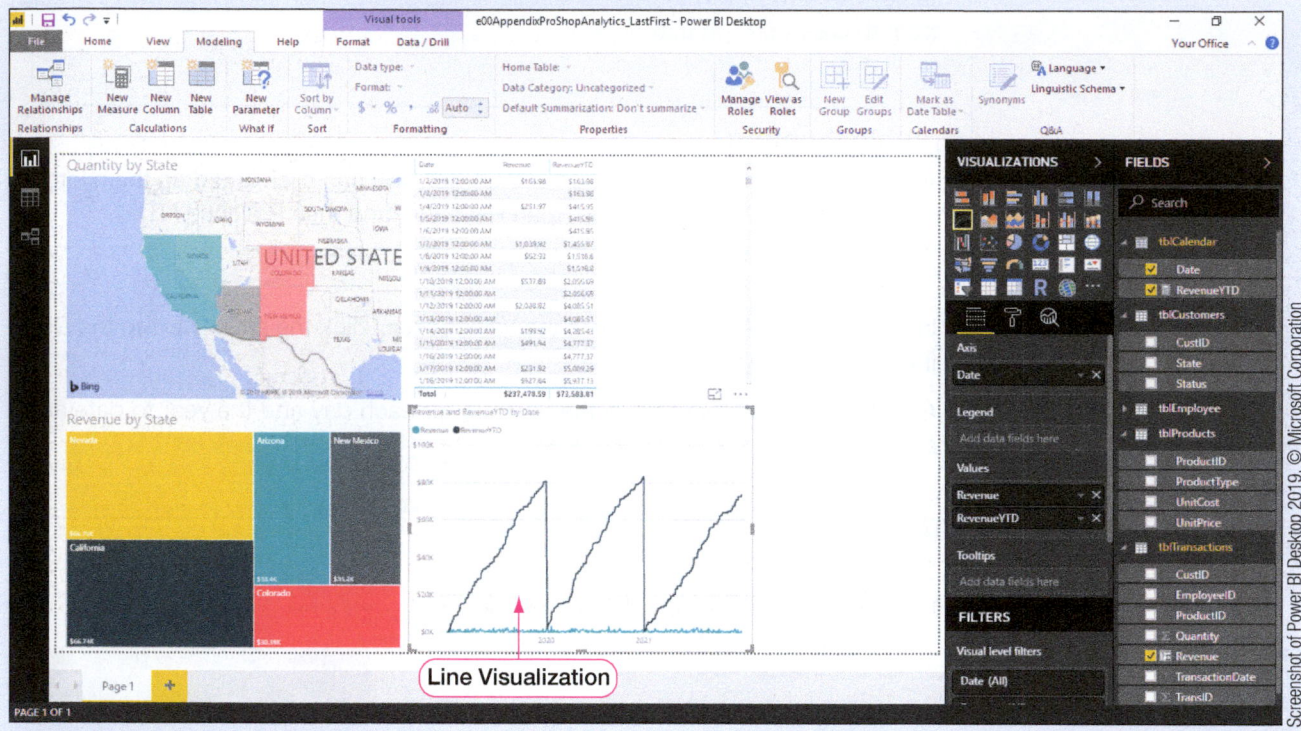

Figure 23 Line visualization

g. **Save** the document.

Visualize Trends with Gauges, Forecasting, and Slicers

Once you know how to create Measures, you can create various different visualizations with those Measures, such as the Gauge visualization. You can also add trends, forecasting, and slicers. To finish off a report, you can also control which interactions affect other visualizations.

Creating a New Page and Renaming a Page

The current page does not have room for additional visualizations. In this next exercise, you will rename the current page and add a new page to add more visualizations.

 **E00.09**

To Create a New Page and Rename a Page

a. In the bottom-left corner of the window, right-click the Page 1 tab, and select **Rename Page**.

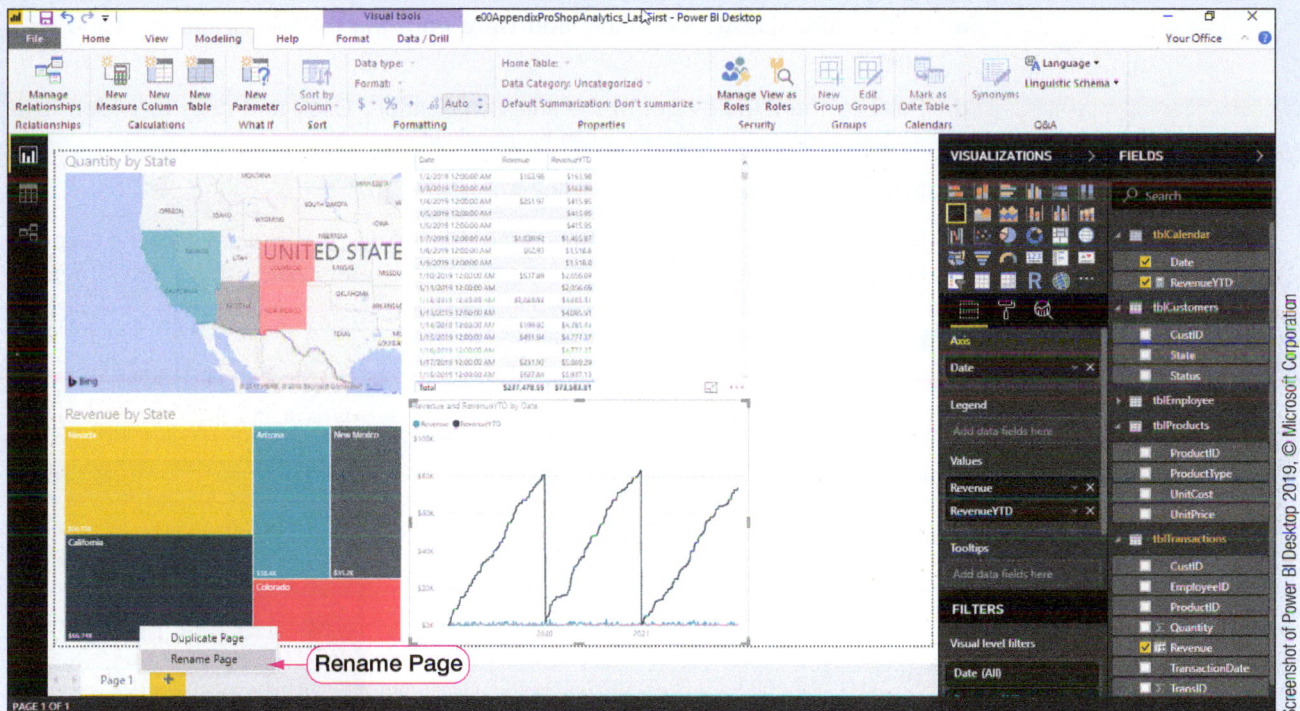

Figure 24 Renaming a page

b. Type Revenue and press Enter.

c. Click **New page** ⊞.

d. Right-click the new Page 1 and select **Rename Page**. Type Trends and press Enter.

e. Save 🖫 the document.

Creating a Line Chart with Trends and Forecasting

The Power BI Desktop can quickly and easily add both trends and forecasting. When you add a trend, the Power BI Desktop adds a linear trend line. If you add a forecast line to predict into the future, the Power BI Desktop forecasts using a method known as exponential smoothing. You can also add constant lines like average sales. In the next exercise, you will create a line chart with an average, trend, and forecasting line.

Screenshot of Power BI Desktop 2019; © Microsoft Corporation

 **E00.10**

To Create a Line Chart with Trends and Forecasting

a. On the Trends page, in the VISUALIZATIONS pane, click **Line chart** ⬈.

b. In the VISUALIZATIONS pane, add the **Revenue** field from the tblTransactions table to the Values area.

c. In the VISUALIZATIONS pane, add **Date** from the tblCalendar table to the Axis area.

d. Point to the middle-right of the line visualization. Click and drag to **widen** it to visualization to be approximately **twice** as wide.

e. In the VISUALIZATIONS pane, click **Analytics** ⬚.

f. Click the **arrow** to the left of Trend Line. Click **Add**. You can see that the revenue has been trending down.

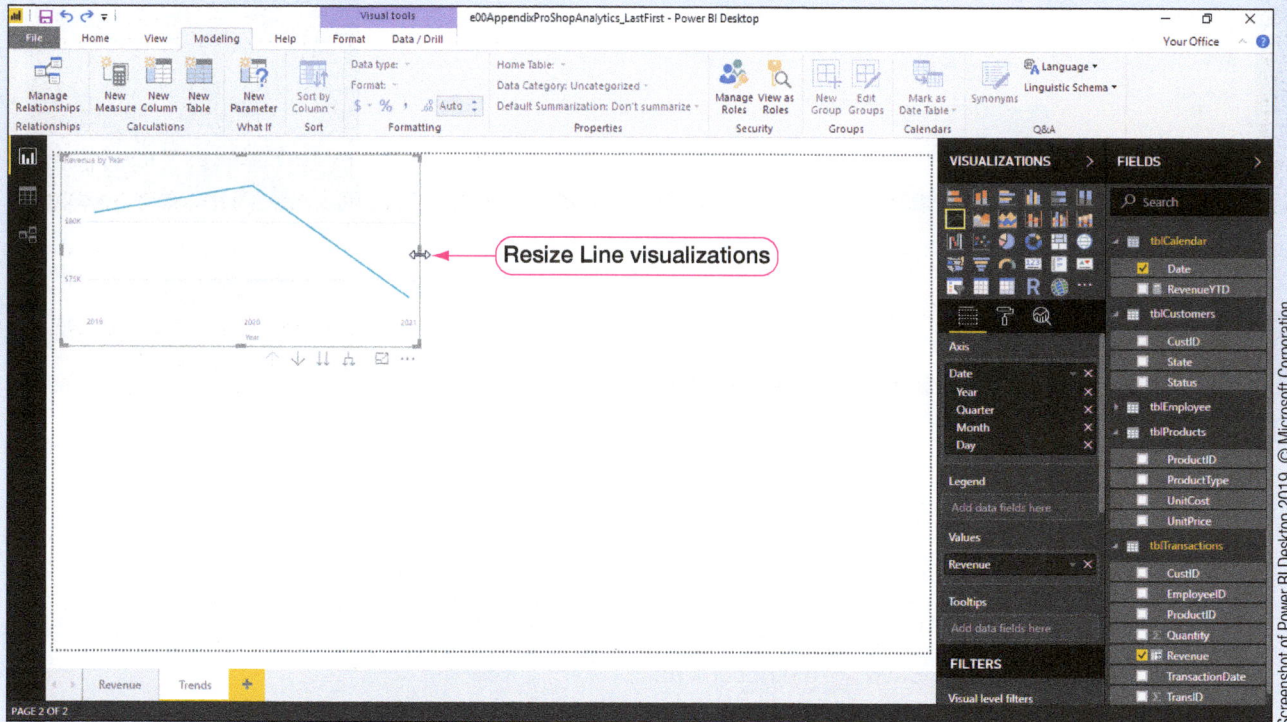

Figure 25 Resize Line visualization

g. Click the **arrow** to the left of Trend Line to collapse the Trend Line options.

h. Click the **arrow** to the left of **Average Line**. Click **Add**. You can see a line representing the average. The revenue for 2021 is much lower than the three-year average.

i. Click the **arrow** to the left of **Average Line** to collapse the **Average Line** options.

j. Click the **arrow** to the left of **Forecast**. Click **Add**.

k. In the Forecast options change the **Forecast Length** to **1** and then click **Apply**.

This analysis only includes three years of data. By default, the forecast tried to project 10 points—or years with this data—into the future using a method called exponential smoothing. Three years of data is not really enough to project more than one year into the future.

l. Point to the year **2022** in the forecast. A card will appear showing you the bounds of the forecast.

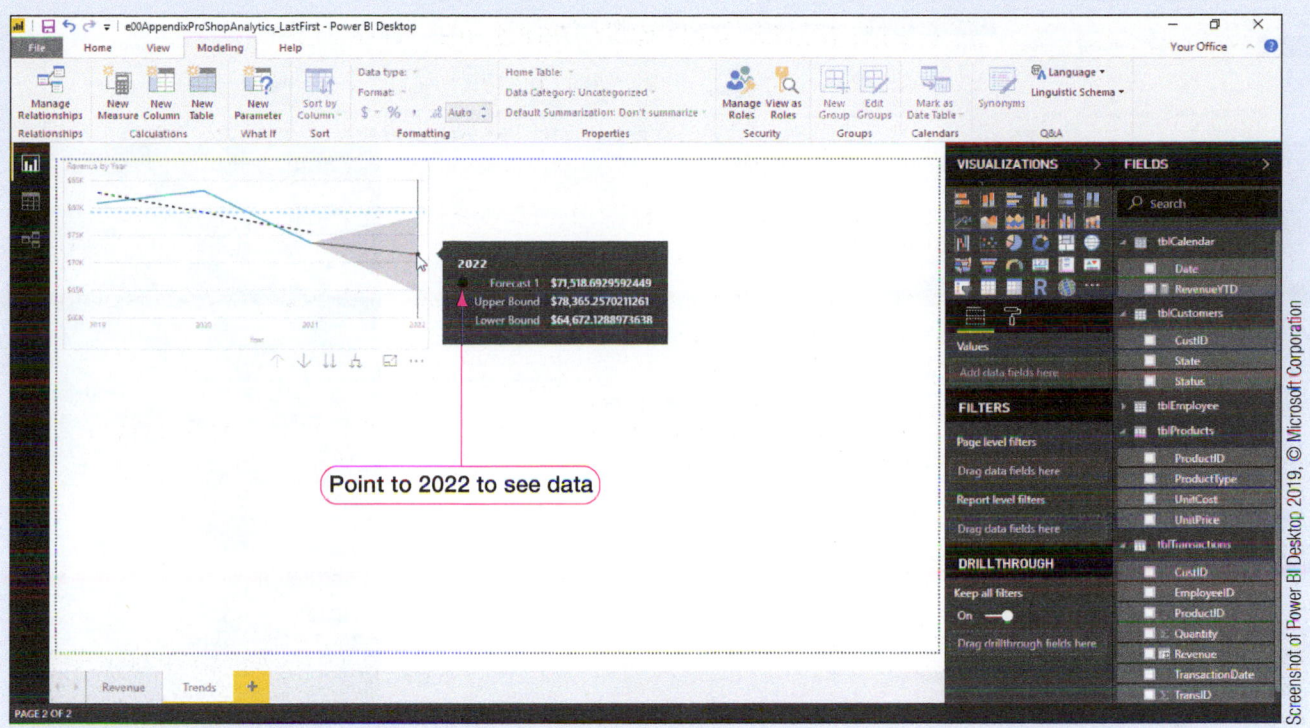

Figure 26 Trend, Average, and Forecasting

m. Click anywhere in the **white space** on the page to deselect the line visualization.

n. **Save**  the document.

Creating a Slicer

In the previous exercise, you saw that revenue is trending and forecasting down. Slicers provide a way for users to filter the data to a smaller subset. In the next exercise, you will add a slicer for product type. You will then look at the different product types to see if all of them are trending and forecasting downward.

E00.11   To Create Slicers

a. In the VISUALIZATIONS pane, click **Slicer** .

b. In the FIELDS pane, click to select the check box for the **ProductType** field in the tblProducts table and add it to the Field area.

c. Point to the **Double-line** in the slicer and click and drag the slicer to the right of the line visualization that shows trend, average, and forecast.

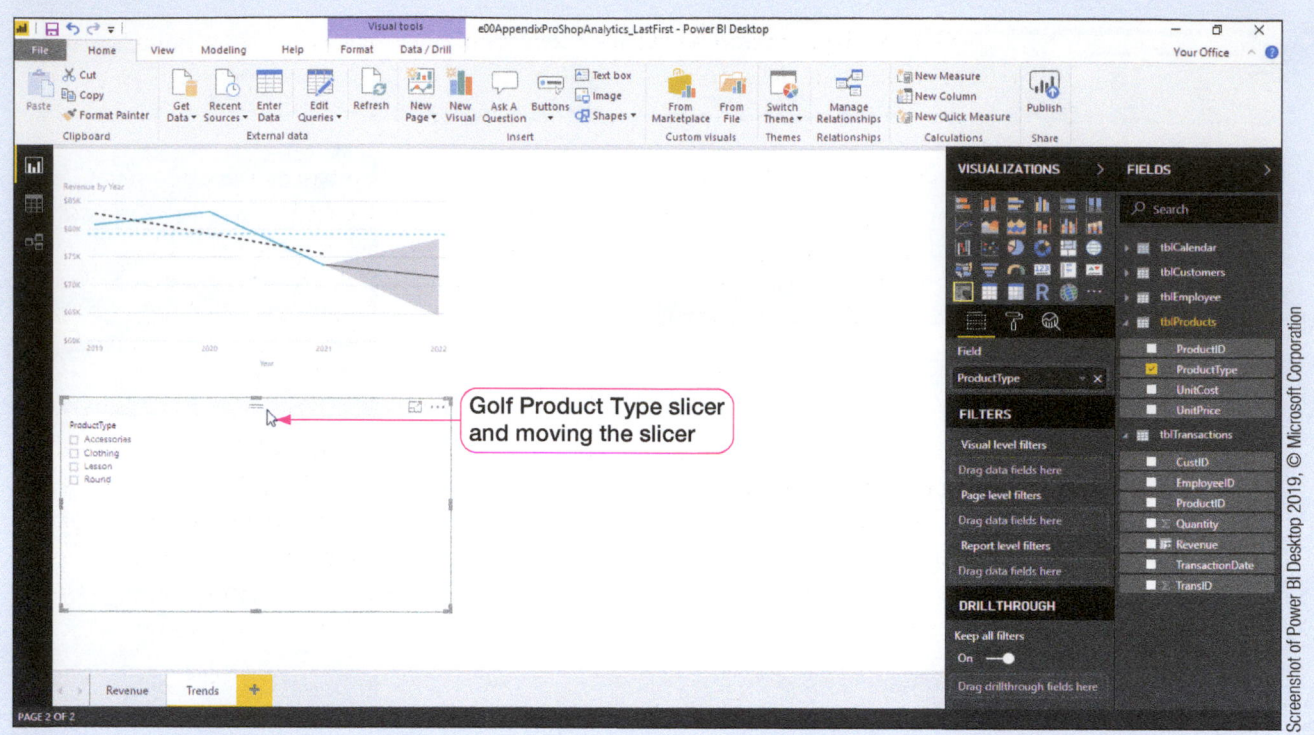

Figure 27 Moving a slicer

    d. In the slicer, click **Round**. The line visualization is updated to show only the product type of golf Round. You can see that while overall revenue has trended downward, golf rounds are trending upward.

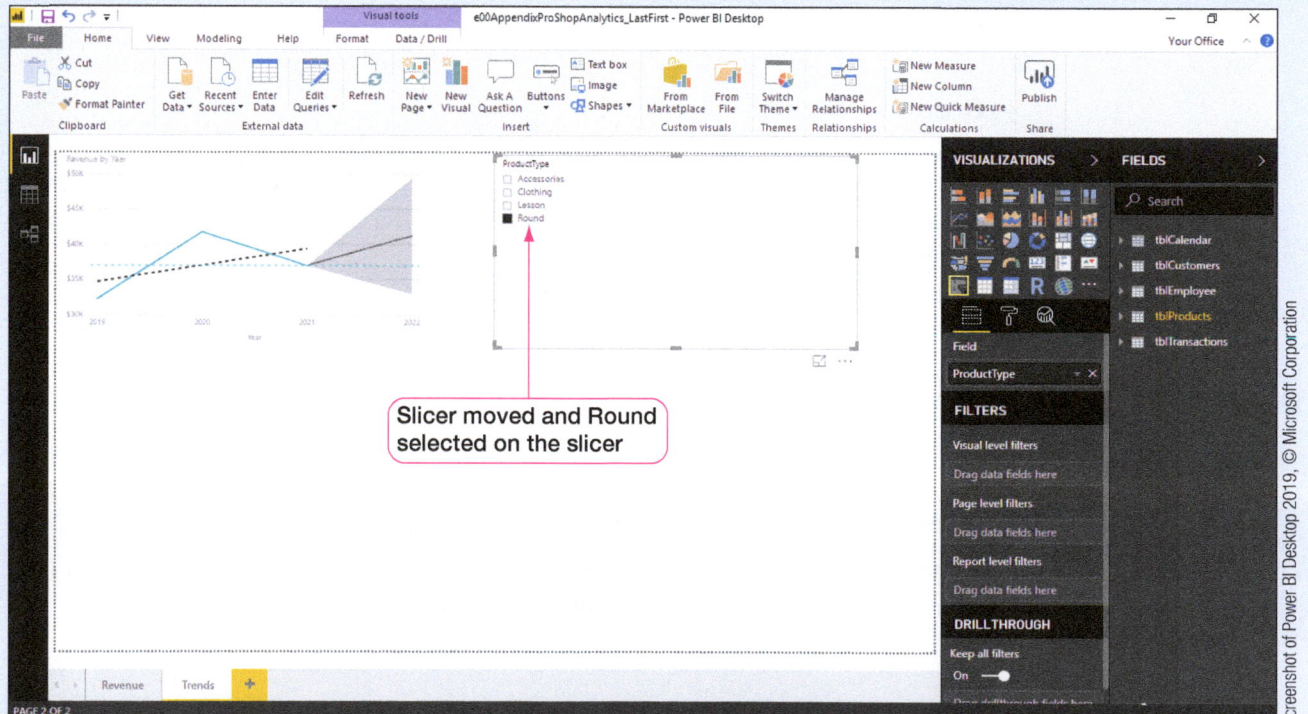

Figure 28 Visualization filtered to golf rounds

    e. Click **Round** again to clear the slicer and show all revenue again.

    f. **Save** the document.

Creating Additional Date Measures

A **Gauge visualization** shows how a current value relates to a minimum, target, and maximum value. Measures will calculate the values for the minimum, target, and maximum. To make those calculations, you will use the CALCULATE and PREVIOUSYEAR functions.

The **CALCULATE function** evaluates an expression based on the specified filters—similar to a COUNTIFS or SUMIFS in Excel. The CALCULATE function syntax is below. The CALCULATE function has two arguments—Expression and Filter. The Expression is the desired calculation—such as sum or count. The Filter argument specifies what subset of data the calculation should be performed on.

The CALCULATE syntax:
Measure = CALCULATE(Expression, {Filter1}, ...)

The **PREVIOUSYEAR function** returns the date of the previous year from the current data being evaluated and takes the following syntax. The PREVIOUSYEAR function has two arguments—Dates and YearEndDate. The Dates argument should reference the Date field in the calendar table. The YearEndDate argument is optional and allows you to change the end of year date. By default, the Power BI Desktop uses a normal calendar year.

The PREVIOUSYEAR syntax:
Measure = PREVIOUSYEAR(Dates, {YearEndDate})

An example of CALCULATE and PREVIOUSYEAR functions:
MinRevenue = CALCULATE(SUM(tblTransactions[Revenue]),PREVIOUSYEAR (tblCalendar[Date]))*.05

The example above will calculate the sum of all revenues that occurred in the prior year, and will then multiply the result by .5. This Measure represents 50% of the revenue from the prior year.

In the next exercise, you will create a gauge that will set a target, a minimum and maximum. The gauge will tell the golf shop how the revenue is currently doing. The data is dynamic; if the year is only in Quarter 1, the gauge may show low. However, when the data is refreshed in the next quarter, you will see the gauge move up. To create a gauge, you will need some additional Measures as well. In particular, you will set the minimum for the gauge to 50% of the revenue from the prior year. You will set the target of revenue to be 110% of the revenue from the prior year. Lastly, you will set the maximum value of revenue to 150% of the prior year.

 **E00.12**

To Create Additional Date Measures

a. Click the **Modeling** tab, and in the Calculations group, click **New Measure**.

b. In the formula bar, delete **Measure =** and then type
MinRev = CALCULATE(SUM(tblTransactions[Revenue]),
PREVIOUSYEAR(tblCalendar[Date])) * .5

This will set the minimum bounds for the next visualization to 50% of the prior year's revenue.

c. Press Enter.

d. On the **Modeling** tab, in the Calculations group, click **New Measure**.

e. In the formula bar, delete **Measure =** and then type
MaxRev = CALCULATE(SUM(tblTransactions[Revenue]),
PREVIOUSYEAR(tblCalendar[Date])) * 1.5

This will set the maximum bounds for the next visualization to 150% of the prior year's revenue.

f. Press Enter.

g. On the **Modeling** tab, in the Calculations Group, click **New Measure**.

h. In the formula bar, delete **Measure =** and then type
TargetRev = CALCULATE(SUM(tblTransactions[Revenue]),
PREVIOUSYEAR(tblCalendar[Date])) * 1.1

This will set the target value for the next visualization to 110% of the prior year's revenue.

i. Press Enter.

j. **Save**  the document.

Creating a Gauge

In the prior exercise, you created measures that management determined were appropriate for the golf shop—a Minimum of 50% Revenue from prior year, a Target of 110% Revenue from prior year, and a Maximum of 150% Revenue from prior year. In the next section, you will create a gauge to show how revenue is holding up to the Measures you created.

▶ **E00.13**

To Create a Gauge

a. Click anywhere in the white space so that none of the visualizations or slicers are selected.

b. On the Trends page, in the VISUALIZATIONS pane, click **Gauge**.

c. In the VISUALIZATIONS pane, add **Revenue** from the tblTransactions table to the Value area.

d. In the VISUALIZATIONS pane, add the **MinRev** Measure from the tblCalendar table to the Minimum value area.

e. In the VISUALIZATIONS pane, add the **MaxRev** Measure from the tblCalendar table to the Maximum value area.

f. In the VISUALIZATIONS pane, add the **TargetRev** Measure from the tblCalendar table to the Target value area.

Notice that the gauge does not show anything yet. Currently, the gauge is applying to all data. A slicer is needed to pick which year to put on the gauge.

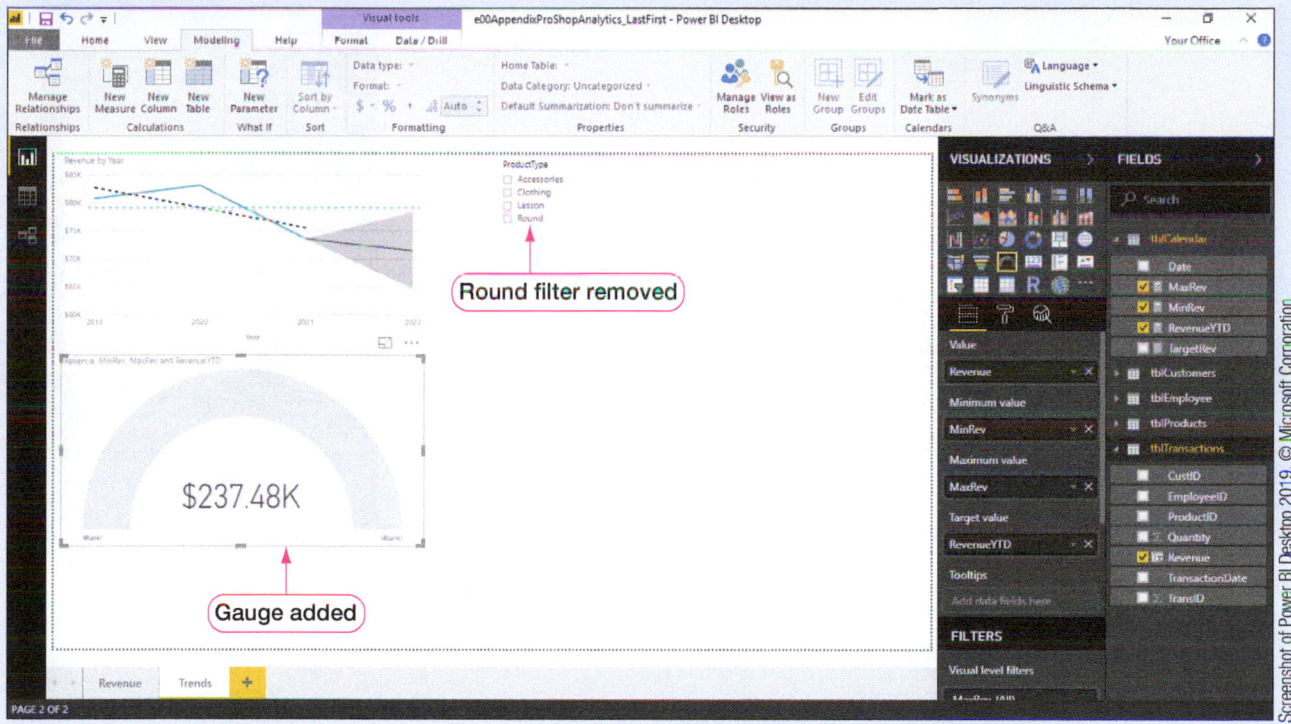

Figure 29   Gauge setup

g. Click in the **white space** so the gauge is no longer selected.

h. In the VISUALIZATIONS pane, click **Slicer**. If needed, move the slicer to the right of the gauge.

i. In the FIELDS pane, navigate to the **Date** field in tblCalendar and check the **box**.

j. In the VISUALIZATIONS pane under Field, click the **arrow** to the right of Date and then select **Date Hierarchy**.

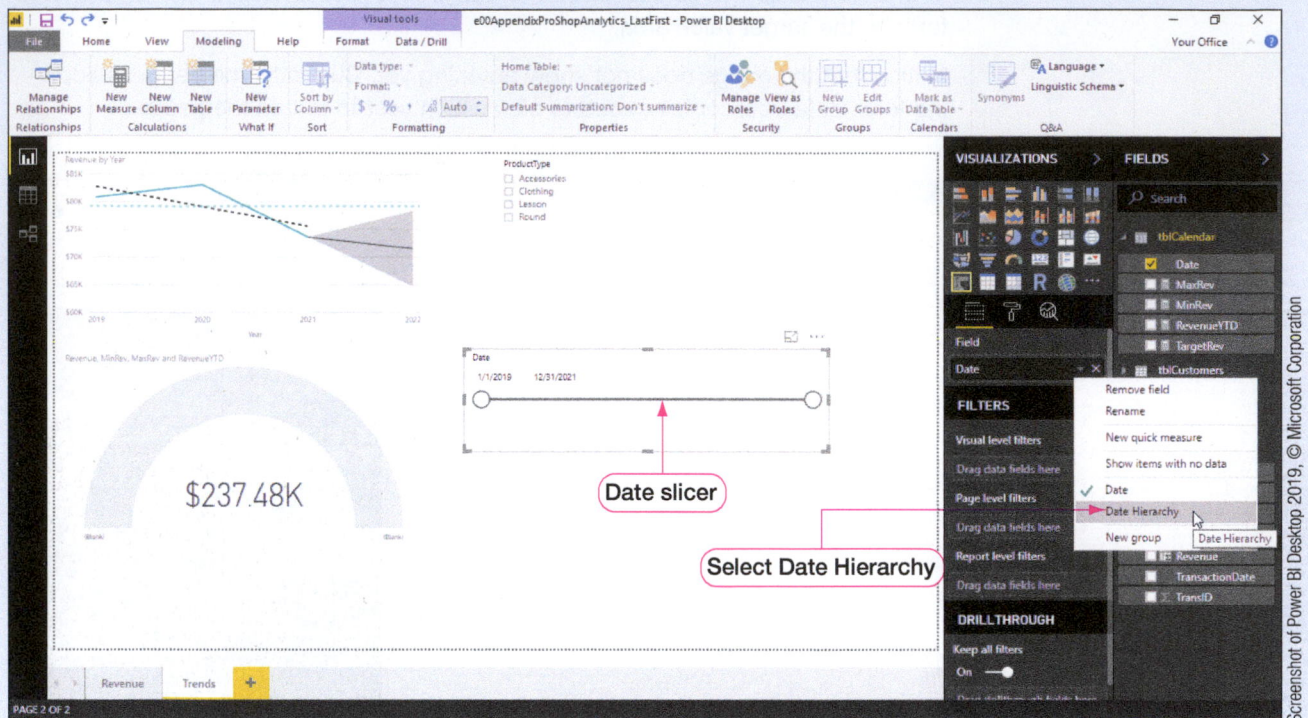

Figure 30   Date slicer

k. With the slicer selected, click **Select the type of slicer** 🖑 and then select **List**.

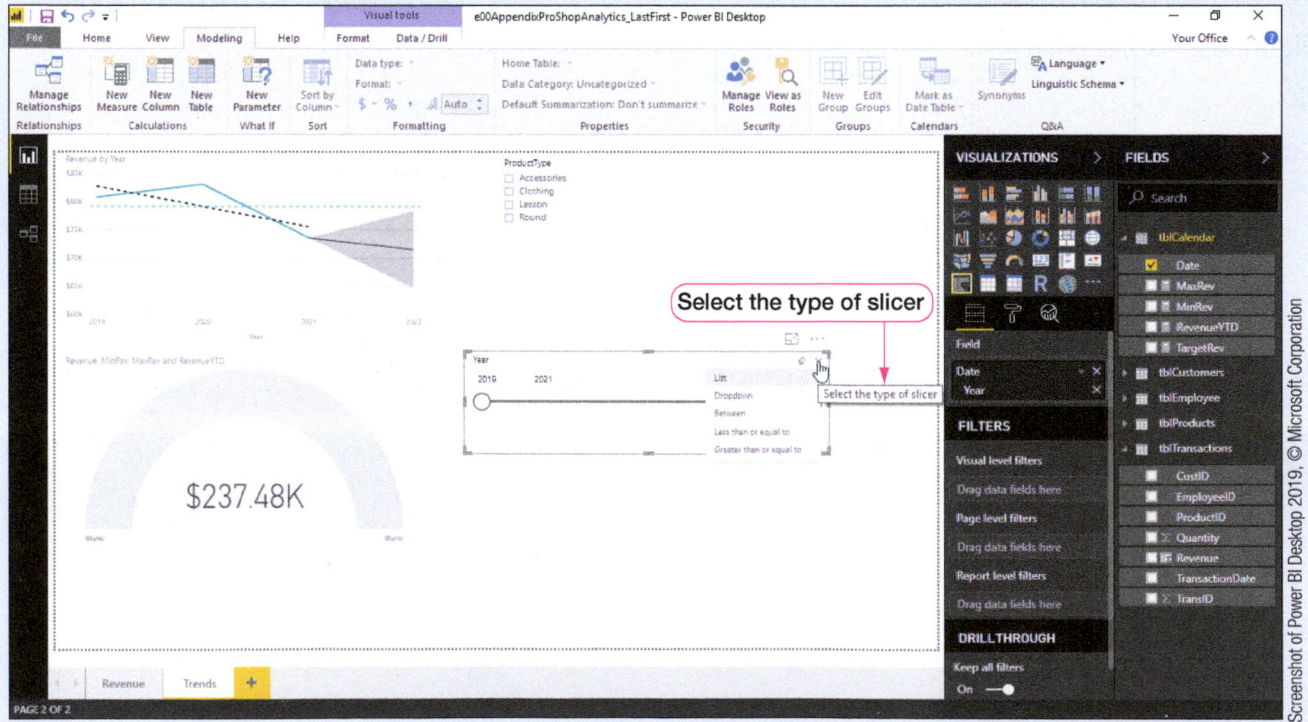

Figure 31   Date slicer as List type

l. Click **2021** in the slicer. Now, the gauge is working properly showing that year 2021 has not reached a 110% of the prior year—2020. However, it also narrowed the forecasting line visualization to only 2021—which is not desired. You will fix this in the next exercise.

m. Click the **Gauge Visualization** to select it. The title for the gauge is not very descriptive and should be updated so it can be more easily understood.

n. In the VISUALIZATIONS pane, click Format 🔧. Then click on the **arrow** to the left of Title. In the Title Text box, delete **Revenue, MinRev, MaxRev and TargetRev**. Then type Yearly 110% of Prior Year Target Gauge and then press Enter.

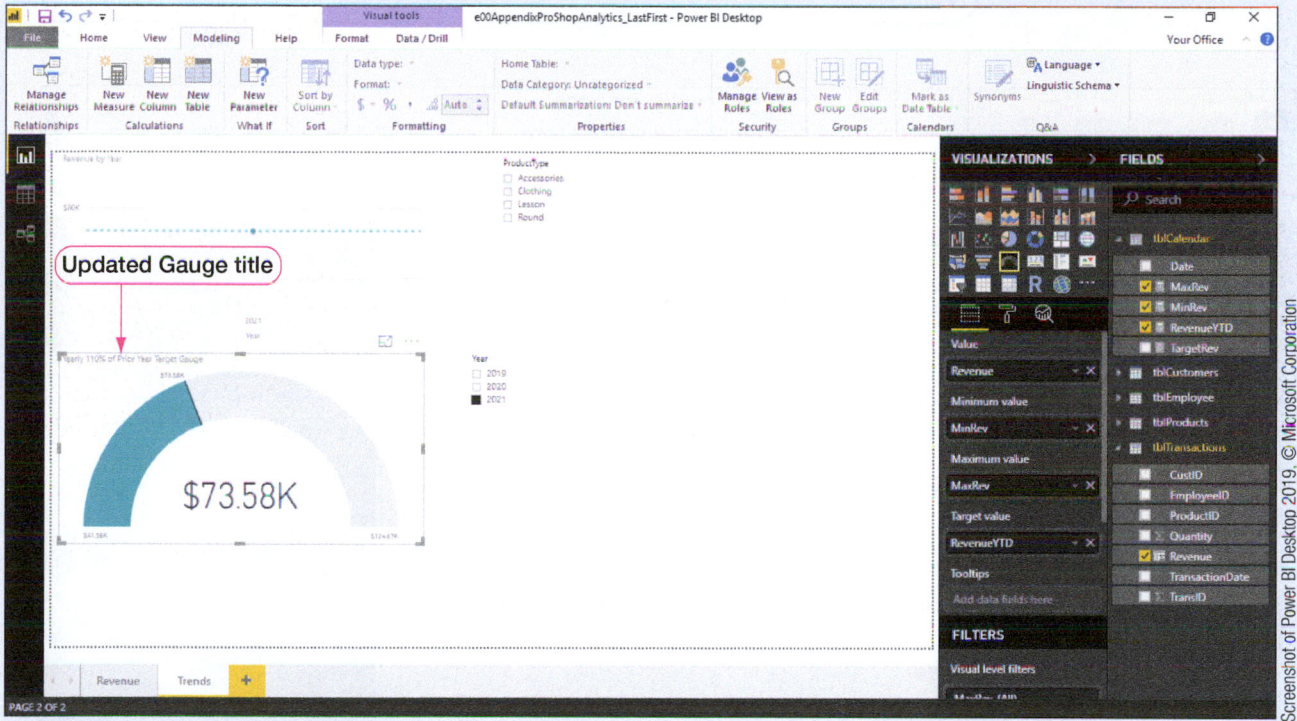

Figure 32   Gauge with updated title

o. **Save** 💾 the document.

Controlling Interactions

As you saw in the prior exercise, all of the visualizations, filters, and slicers on a page are by default connected to one another. However, that may not always be desirable. In the next exercise, you will manage the interactions to prevent unwanted connections.

 **E00.14**

To Control and Edit Interactions

a. Click on the **Year slicer** to select it.

b. Click the Format tab and then in the Interactions group, click **Edit interactions**. Additional options are displayed on the other visualizations.

> **Troubleshooting**
>
> Make sure there is room between the top visualizations and bottom visualization. Feel free to move your visualizations if needed to give more room. Otherwise, you have trouble seeing and selecting the None.

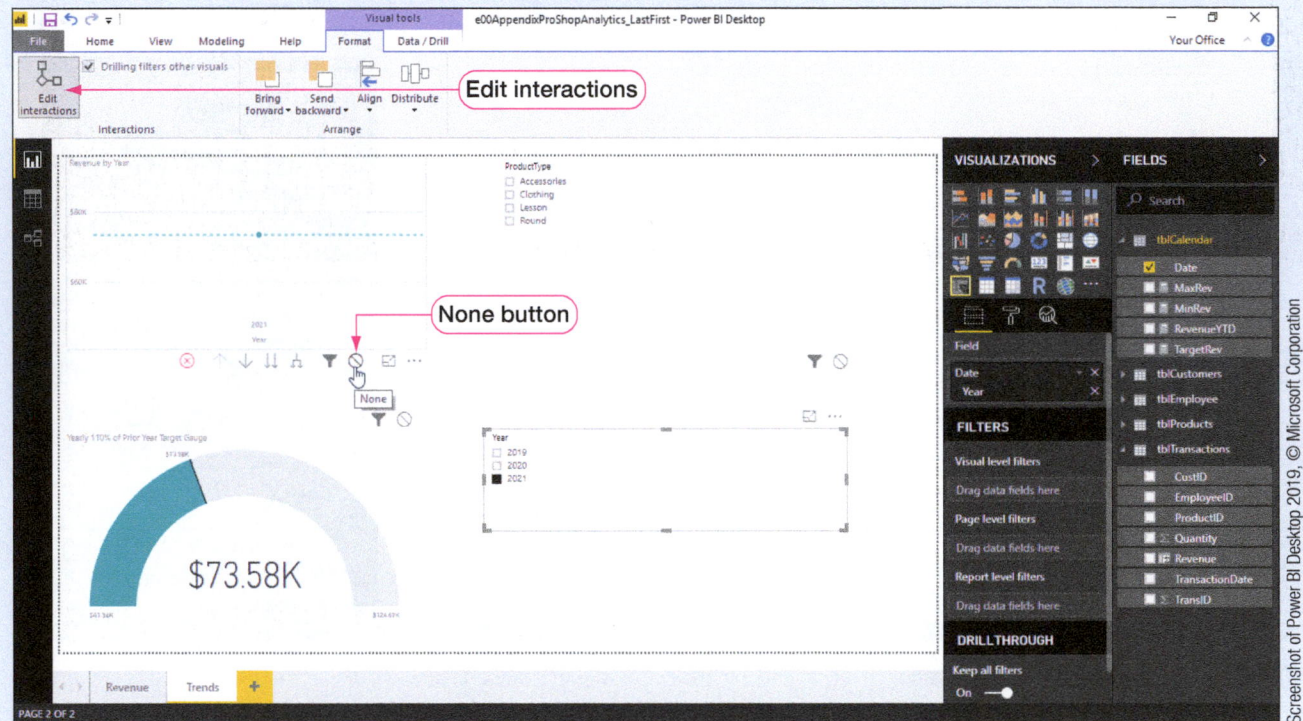

Figure 33 Edit Interactions

c. Click **None** for both the Line Visualization in the upper-left corner and the ProductType slicer in the upper-right corner. This turns off updating those when the year slicer is changed. Now, only the gauge will change based on the year selected. Because you have not edited the interactions for the Product Type slicer, the Product Type slicer will still change both the gauge and line visualization.

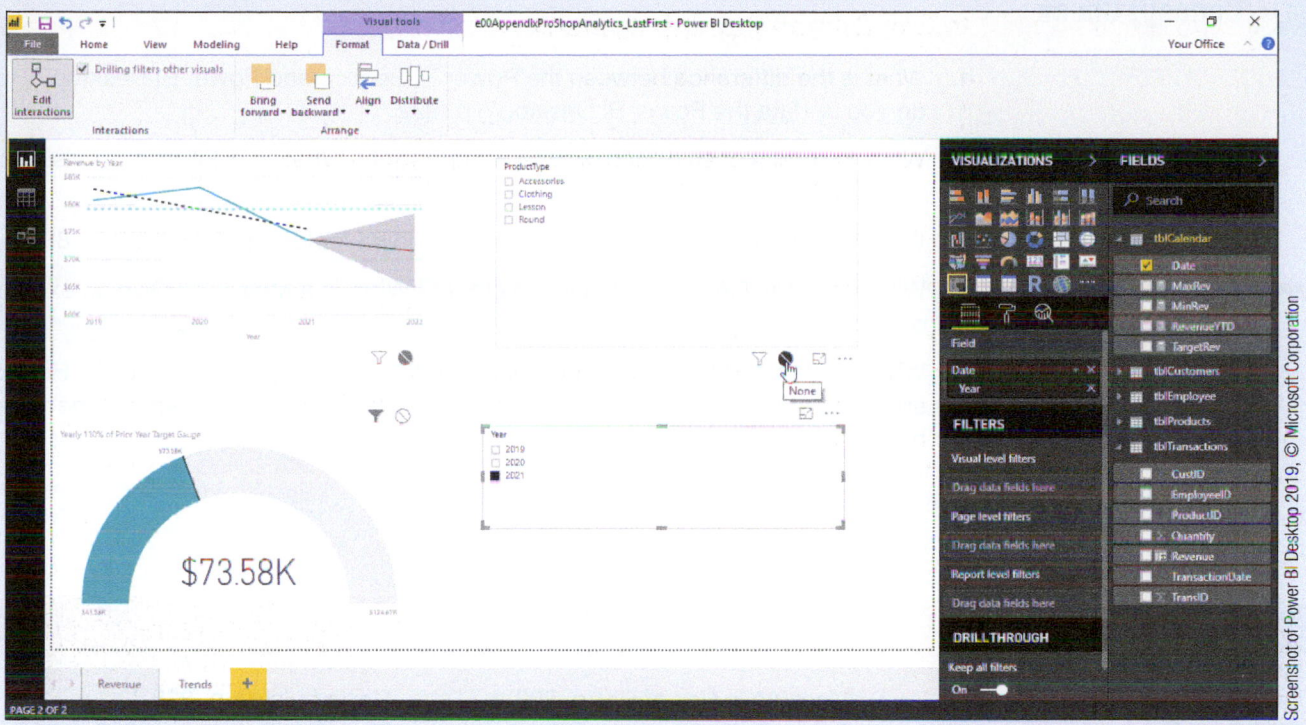

Figure 34 Final Trends page

Screenshot of Power BI Desktop 2019, © Microsoft Corporation

d. **Save** 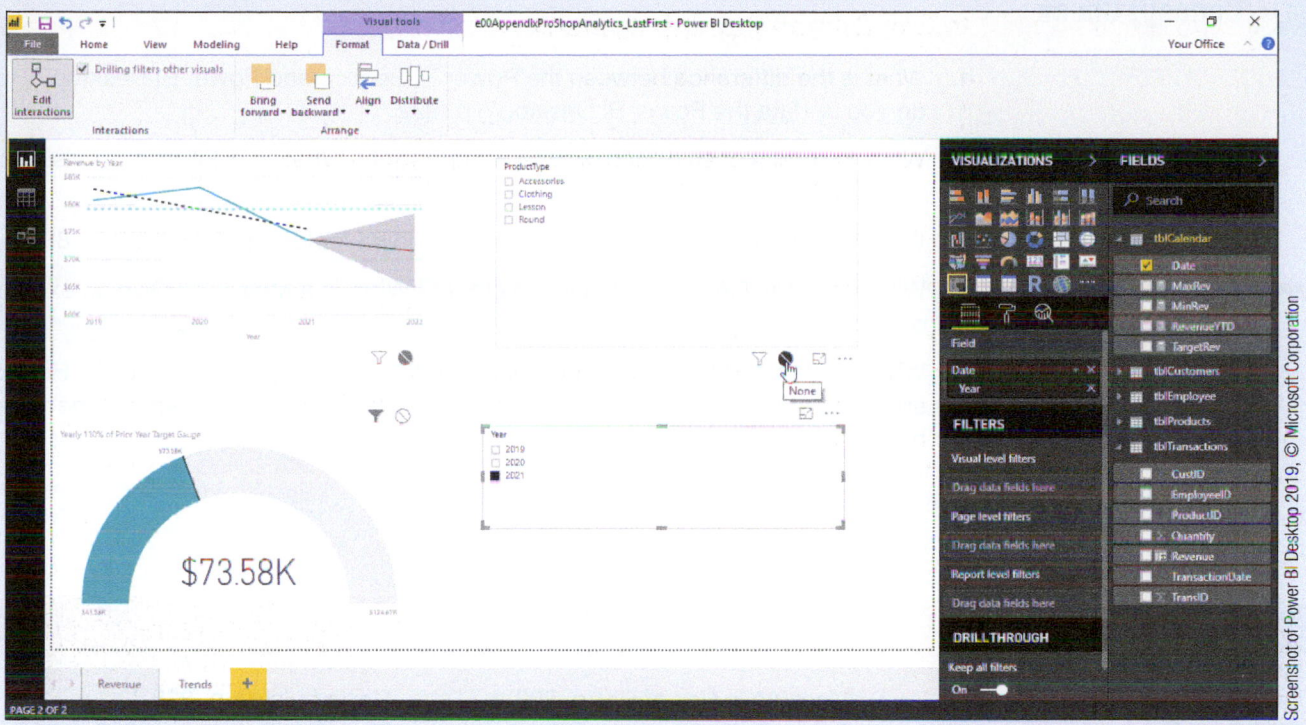 the document.

REAL WORLD ADVICE | **Free Data**

Do you want to test your skills? You can get free data sets online from many different locations. You can download something on a topic that interests you and see what insights you can find! Try some of these sites.

- https://www.census.gov/
- https://www.cdc.gov/datastatistics/
- http://data.gov
- http://data.europa.eu/euodp/en/data/
- https://registry.opendata.aws/
- https://www.cia.gov/library/publications/the-world-factbook/
- https://www.healthdata.gov/
- https://registry.opendata.aws/
- http://www.google.com/publicdata/directory
- https://www.gapminder.org/data/

Concept Check

1. What is the difference between the Power BI Service and Power BI Desktop? How do you update the Power BI Desktop? p. 822

2. What is a relationship, and why is it important? What is a Filled map visualization? p. 828

3. What is a Treemap, and what does the drill down feature accomplish? p. 832

4. What does the CALENDAR function create? What is a Measure? Give an example of one. p. 836

5. What kinds of trends and forecasting can be added to a visualization? How do slicers interact with the visualizations? What is a Gauge and what three things must be specified to create a Gauge? p. 842

Key Terms

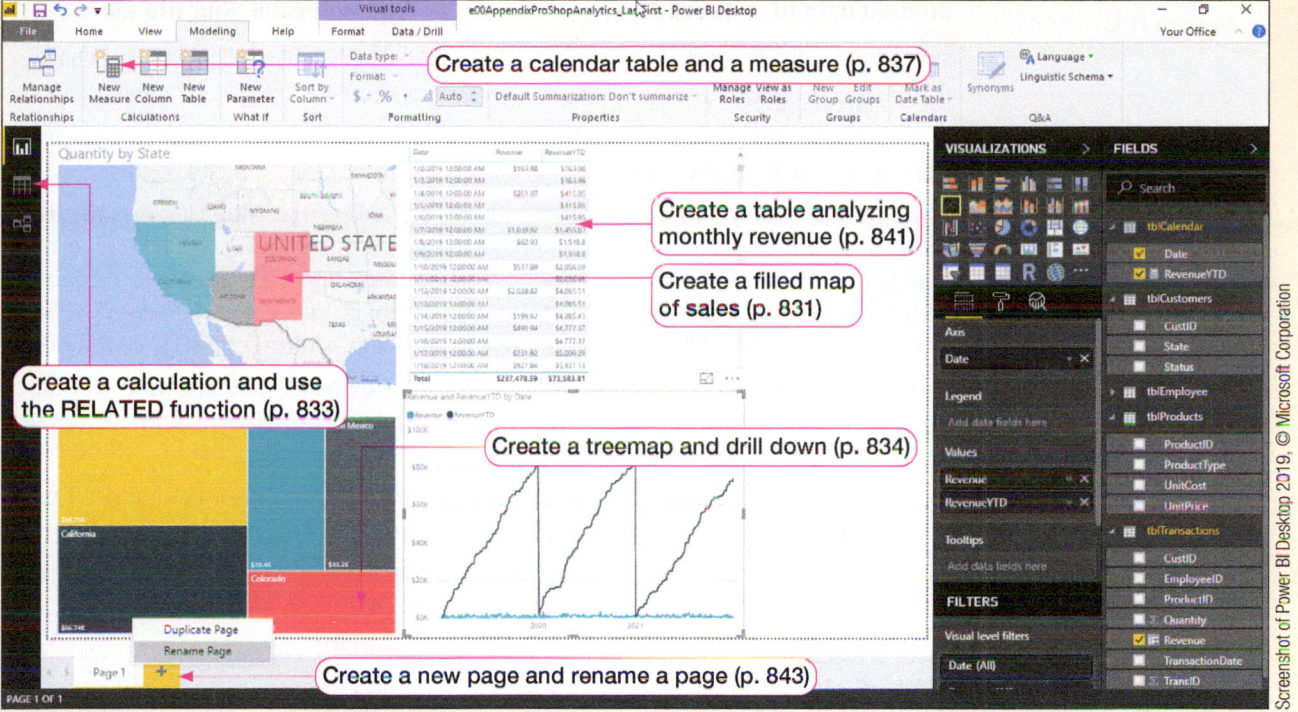

Figure 35

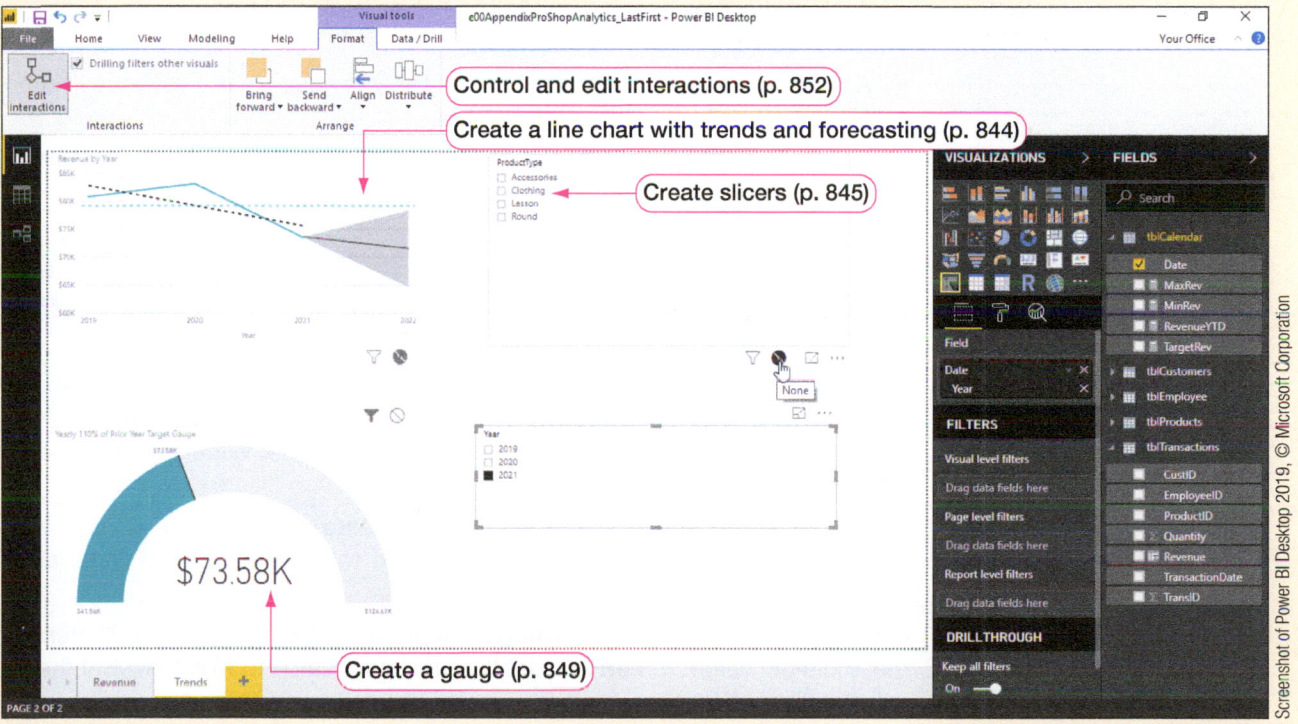

Figure 36

Screenshot of Power BI Desktop 2019, © Microsoft Corporation

MyLab IT Grader

Student data files needed:

 e00AppendixSpa.accdb

e00AppendixSpa.pbix

You will save your file as:

e00AppendixSpa_LastFirst.pbix

Finance &
Accounting

Turquoise Oasis Spa

The spa has three years of spa product sales data. The spa manager has asked you to build an analytics dashboard to evaluate the sales of the spa products. The manager specifically asked for a way to see how sales from one year measured against prior years. In the spa, management set this year's goals to be a minimum of 40% of the prior year, a target of 105% of the prior year, and a maximum of 140% of the prior year.

a. Open the file e00AppendixSpa.pbix in the Power BI Desktop and get all of the tables from **e00AppendixSpa.accdb**. Save your file as e00AppendixSpa_LastFirst using your last and first name.

b. Create a new field in tblPurchase called Revenue The new field should calculate revenue based on the Quantity sold in tblPurchase and the Price in tblProduct.

c. Using the CALENDAR function, create a table called tblProdCalendar that has a start date of 1/1/2019 and an end date of 12/31/2022

d. Create the following Measures in tblProdCalendar.

- A Measure that calculates revenue summed according to the revenue earned that year to that date. Name the Measure YTDRev

- A Measure that calculates 40% of the previous year's revenue. Name the Measure MinRev

- A Measure that calculates 105% of the previous year's revenue. Name the Measure TargetRev

- A Measure that calculates 140% of the previous year's revenue. Name the Measure MaxRev

e. Establish a relationship between **tblProdCalendar Date** field and **tblPurchase PurchaseDate** field.

f. Rename **Page 1** to Revenue

g. On the Revenue page, add a **Treemap** visualization. The Values should be **Revenue**. The Group should be first **PurchaseType** and then **Category**. Set the title for the Treemap to Revenue by PurchaseType and Category

h. On the Revenue page, add a **Filled map** visualization. The Location should be **CustState**. The Color saturation should be **Revenue**. Resize the map to take up approximately a fourth of the page in the lower-left side. Widen the Treemap to be the same width.

i. On the Revenue page, add a **Line chart** with **Date** as the Axis. For the values use the fields **Revenue** and **YTDRev**. Make sure to set the Date to Date (not Date Hierarchy).

j. On the Revenue page, add a **Gauge** visualization. Set the Value to **Revenue**. Set the Minimum value to **MinRev**. Set the Maximum value to **MaxRev**. Set the Target value to **TargetRev**.

k. Add a **Slicer** and move it to the right of the Gauge. Set the Slicer type to **List** and set the date to **Date Hierarchy**. Select the year **2022**.

l. Notice, the line chart changes based on the slicer. Change the **interactions** so the slicer does not change the line chart.

m. Add a new page and name it **Trends**.

n. Add a **Line** visualization and resize to fit the entire page. Set Axis to **Date** and Values to **Revenue**.

o. For the Line visualization, under Format, set the **Y-Axis** Start to 10000 To the Line Visualization, add a **Trend** line and a **Forecast**. Set the Forecast to a **Forecast length** of 2 points.

p. **Save** the document, and click **Close** to exit the Power BI Desktop. Submit your files as directed by your instructor.

Critical Thinking The manager asked you to answer a few specific questions. What state has the highest sales revenue over all the years? What is the spa's best year? Of the online sales, what is the highest product category? Make sure you pay attention to the slicer. Under trends, are sales trending upward or downward? Submit your answer as directed by your instructor.

Perform 1: Perform in Your Career

Student data file needed:

 e00AppendixRentals.accdb

You will save your file as:

 e00AppendixRentals_LastFirst.pbix

Exploring Car Rental Data

General Business

You are an intern at a regional car dealership. You are interested in creating a demo of what Power BI can do for your manager at work. You are hoping to persuade your boss that the Power BI Desktop will be useful and hoping he will be willing to also subscribe to the Power BI Service. Your manager provided you with some data from the past couple of years to use in your demonstration. If you use a previous year gauge, your boss would like the minimum to be 60% of the prior year, a target of 108% of the prior year, and a maximum of 125% of the prior year. The best demo will show visualizations that provide insight and interactivity.

a. Open the Power BI Desktop and get all of the tables from e00AppendixRentals.accdb. Save your file as e00AppendixRentals_LastFirst using your last and first name.

b. Include a calendar table that is related to a date field.

c. Include at least one calculated column.

d. Include at least three Measures.

e. Include at least four of the following:

- Line Chart
- Trend and/or Forecasting Line
- Treemap
- Filled Map
- Slicer
- Gauge

f. Where appropriate, control or limit interactions.

g. Save the document, and close Power BI Desktop. Submit your file as directed by your instructor.

Microsoft Excel

Appendix B KEYBOARD SHORTCUTS AND MAC COMPATIBILITY

Shortcut Keys and Commands

Basic Tasks	Windows	Mac
Open a new workbook	Ctrl+N	Command ⌘+N
Print a workbook	Ctrl+P	Command ⌘+P
Save a workbook	Ctrl+S	Command ⌘+S
Save As	F12	Command ⌘+Shift+S
Close open workbook	Ctrl+F4	Command ⌘+W
Close open workbook(s) and exit Excel	Alt+F4	Command ⌘+Q

Editing and Formatting Text	Windows	Mac
Apply bold	Ctrl+B	Command ⌘+B
Apply italic	Ctrl+I	Command ⌘+I
Apply underline	Ctrl+U	Command ⌘+U
Center selection	Ctrl+E	Command ⌘+E
Copy selected text	Ctrl+C	Command ⌘+C
Cut selected text	Ctrl+X	Command ⌘+X
Delete character to left of insertion point	Backspace	Delete
Delete character to right of insertion point	Delete	fn+Delete
Edit active cell	F2	Ctrl+U
Find and Replace	Ctrl+F	Ctrl+F
Insert line break in a cell	Alt+Enter	Option+return
Paste copied or cut text	Ctrl+V	Command ⌘+V
Select all	Ctrl+A	Command ⌘+A
Toggle absolute or relative cell reference	F4	Command ⌘+T
Undo last action	Ctrl+Z	Command ⌘+Z

Navigation and Selection	Windows	Mac
Extend selection (in direction of arrow)	`Ctrl`+`Shift`+arrow	`Command ⌘`+`Shift`+arrow
Move to cell A1 of worksheet	`Ctrl`+Home	`Command ⌘`+`Home` `fn`+`Command ⌘`+Left arrow (Macbook)
Move to end of worksheet	`Ctrl`+End	`Command ⌘`+`End` `fn`+`Command ⌘`+Right arrow (Macbook)
Select adjacent cells	`Shift` (click to select)	`Shift` (click to select)
Select nonadjacent cells	`Ctrl` (click to select)	`Command ⌘` (click to select)

Some Windows features display a contextual tab with other related tabs below it. The Mac ribbon does not display contextual tabs.

Windows Contextual Tab/Tab	Corresponding Mac Tab
Chart Tools/Design	Chart Design
Chart Tools/Format	Chart Format
Drawing Tools/Format	Shape Format
Picture Tools/Format	Picture Format
PivotTable Tools/Analyze	PivotTable Analyze
PivotTable Tools/Design	Design
Sparkline Tools/	Sparkline Design
Slicer Tools/Options	Slicer
Table Tools/Table	Table

Basic Tasks

Open a Workbook

1. Point above the Excel ribbon to display the File menu and click **Open**.
2. Click **On my Mac** and navigate to the folder where your document is stored.
3. Select the file and click **Open**.

Save a Workbook

1. Point above the Excel ribbon to display the File menu and click **Open**.
2. In the **Save As** box, enter the file name.
3. In the **Where** box, select the location to which you are saving the file.
4. If necessary, click the **File Format arrow** and choose **Excel Workbook(.xlsx)**
5. Click **Save**.

Collapse and Expand the Ribbon

1. To collapse the ribbon, click the tab that is currently active.
2. To expand the ribbon, click the active tab again.

Print a Workbook

1. Display the File menu and click **Print**.
2. In the dialog box, choose the options for the printer and number of copies.
3. To view more options, click **Show Details**. Select orientation, what to print, margins or other options as needed.
4. To set the scaling for the worksheets, select the **Scale to fit** check box and specify the number of pages wide by number of pages tall.

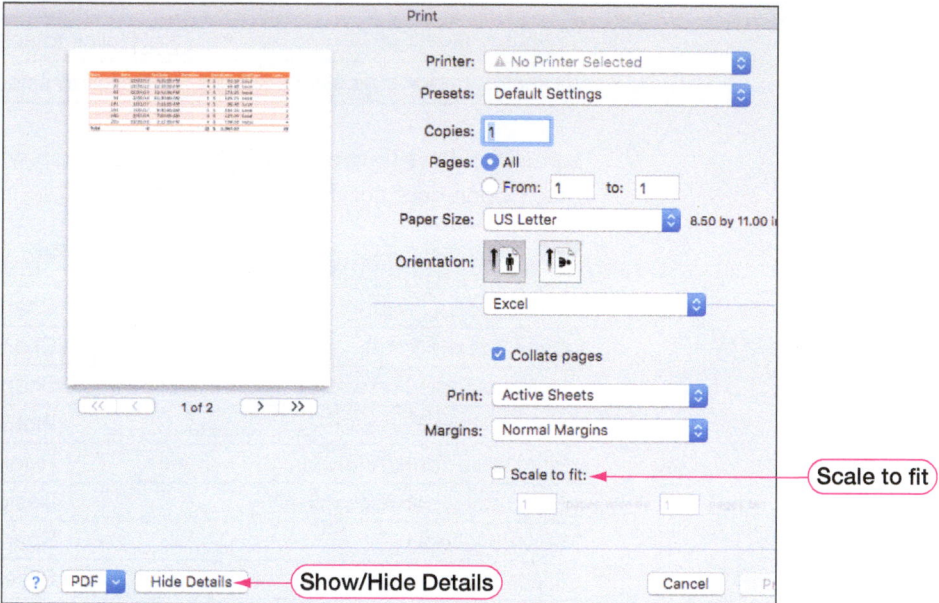

Courtesy of Apple Inc., © Microsoft Corporation

Editing and Formatting Data

Use Find and Select/Replace

1. Point above the ribbon to display the menu bar and click **Edit**. Point to **Find**, and then click **Find**. You can choose options to search in the workbook or the current sheet, search by rows or columns, match the case, or find entire cells.
2. In the Find dialog box, click **Replace**. In the Find what box, enter the text to find, and in the Replace with box, enter the replacement text. You can also click Replace directly on the Edit/Find menu.
3. Click **Replace** to replace just the next occurrence of the search text or **Replace All** to replace all occurrences of the text.

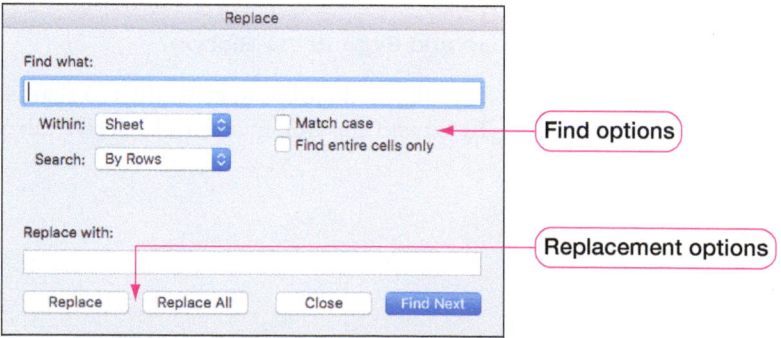

Courtesy of Apple Inc., © Microsoft Corporation

Use Paste Options

1. Select the range of cells to be copied, click where you want to paste the copied cells, and right-click to display a shortcut menu.
2. Select **Paste Special** to open the Paste Special dialog box. In this dialog box, you can select the same options available on the Paste Options menu in Windows.

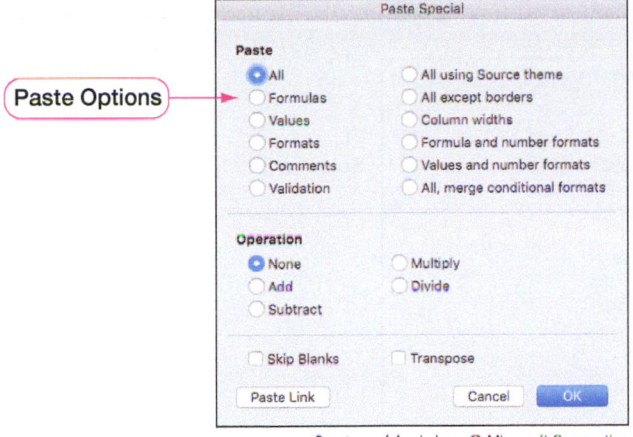

Courtesy of Apple Inc., © Microsoft Corporation

Apply Conditional Formatting

On the Mac, the conditional formatting dialog box is different from the Windows dialog box.

1. To apply conditional formatting, select the range to be formatted, and on the Home tab, click **Conditional Formatting**. If desired, point to a rule selection such as Top/Bottom Rules and select an option like Top 10 Items. The New Formatting Rule dialog box is displayed with the options set to the selected rule.
2. Edit the rule as desired; for example, change 10 to 1 to display the top value in the selected range. You can change the value in the Format with as well.
3. To create a custom format, click the **Format with** arrow and select Custom Format to open the Format Cells dialog box. Click OK.
4. When you are done, click OK to close the New Formatting Rule dialog box.

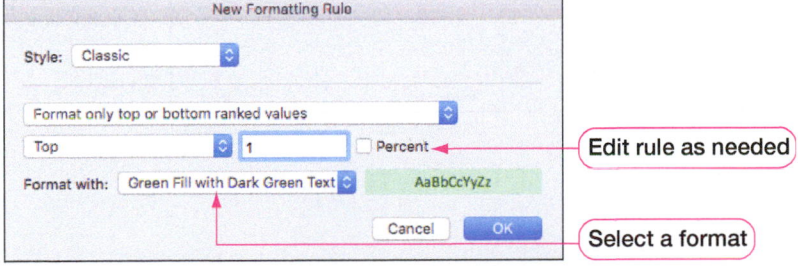

Courtesy of Apple Inc., © Microsoft Corporation

Working with Formulas and Functions

Use the Formula Builder

On a Mac, the Insert Function button next to the formula bar opens the Formula Builder pane rather than the Insert Function dialog box as in Windows.

1. Click the **Insert Function** button next to the formula bar or on the Formulas tab, in the Function Library group, select a function. The Formula Builder pane will open on the right.

2. Select the desired function from the list and click the **Insert Function** button.

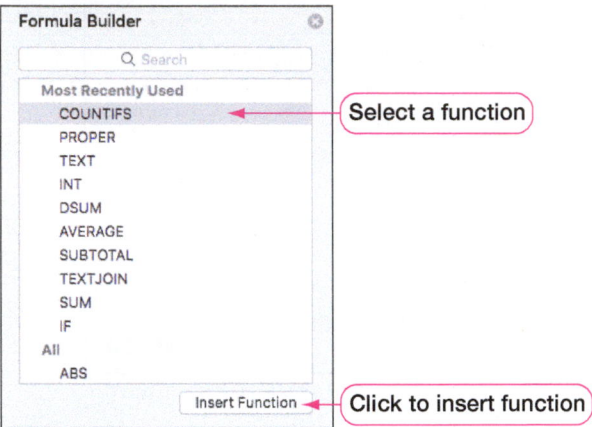

Courtesy of Apple Inc., © Microsoft Corporation

3. In the Formula Builder pane, select the range or ranges for the function arguments. If the function allows multiple criteria ranges, select the cells for Criteria_range1, click the ⊞ **button** and select additional ranges as needed. Click **Done**.

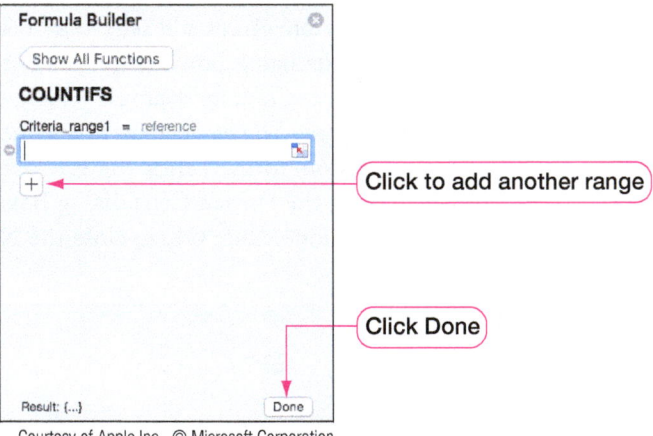

Courtesy of Apple Inc., © Microsoft Corporation

4. Close the Formula Builder pane.

Add or Edit a Named Range

On a Mac, there is no Name Manager feature. Named ranges are added, edited, or removed in the Define Name dialog box.

1. On the **Formulas** tab, in the **Defined Names** group, click **Define Name** to open the Define Name dialog box.
2. To add a named range, enter the range name in the **Enter a name for the data range** box, click the Collapse Dialog button and select the range. Click the ⊞ **button** to add another name and keep the dialog box open or click OK to close the dialog box.
3. To edit a named range, select the name in the **Names in workbook** list and edit the range in the **Select the range of cells** box.
4. To remove a name, select the name in the Names in workbook list and click the ⊟ **button**.

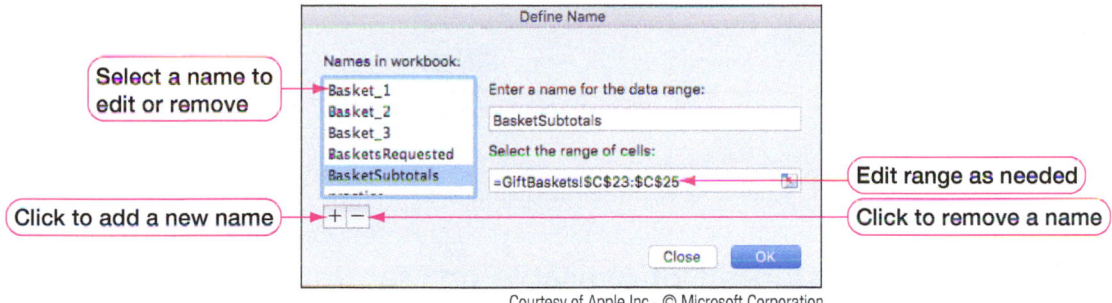

Courtesy of Apple Inc., © Microsoft Corporation

5. Click OK when done.

Change Field Settings in a PivotTable

1. To change field settings in a PivotTable, in the **Values** area, right-click the field to display a shortcut menu, and then click **Field Settings**.

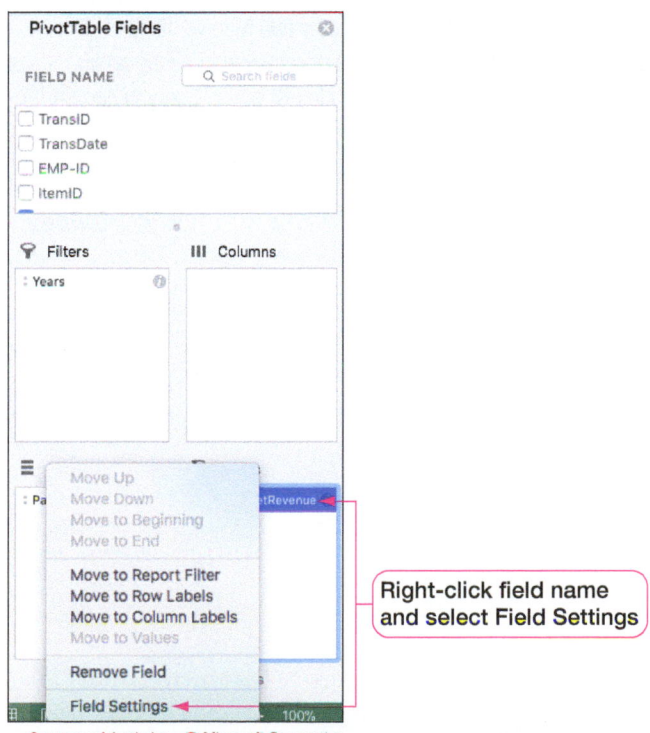

Courtesy of Apple Inc., © Microsoft Corporation

2. The PivotTable Field dialog box is displayed. You can change the field name, or change the aggregate function applied.
3. To change the format of the numbers, click the **Number button** to open the Format Cells dialog box and select a number format as desired.

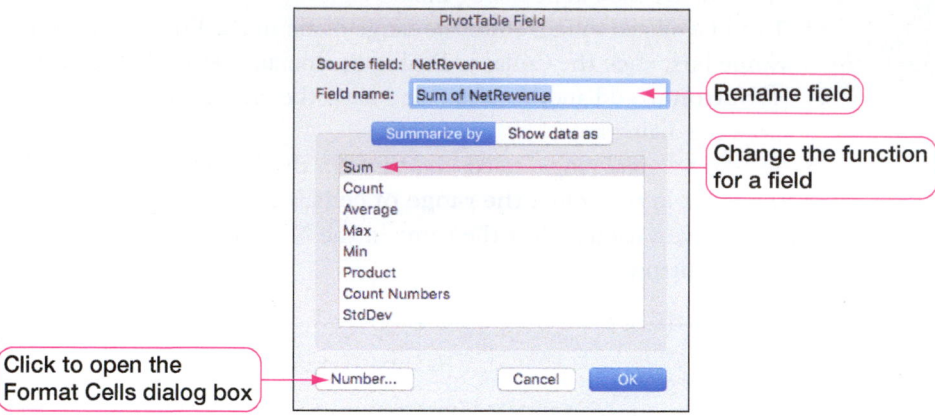

Courtesy of Apple Inc., © Microsoft Corporation

4. Click **OK** to close the dialog box.

Features Not Available on Mac (at Time of Publication)

- Get & Transform Data Tools
- Power Query
- Power Pivot
- Power View

REAL WORLD ADVICE **Microsoft Updates**

There may be some differences in fonts, themes, colors, and screen tips as well as available features between the Window and Mac versions of Office 2019. Updates happen frequently, and new features may be added or removed in either version. If you don't see the exact option specified in an exercise, select the closest option that you can find.

Microsoft Excel

Appendix C EXCEL MICROSOFT CERTIFICATION REFERENCE

MOS Excel 2019			
MOS Obj #	MOS Objective	Your Office Chapter	Your Office Section Heading
1.	**Manage Worksheets and Workbooks**		
1.1	**Import data into workbooks**		
1.1.1	Import data from .txt files	Chapter 9	Importing Text Files
1.1.2	Import data from .csv files	Chapter 9	Importing Text Files
1.2	**Navigate within workbooks**		
1.2.1	Search for data within a workbook	Common Features	Finding Text, and Replacing Text
1.2.2	Navigate to named cells, ranges, or workbook elements	Chapter 1	Navigating Within Worksheets (Ch1)
		Chapter 3	Modifying Named Ranges (Ch3)
1.2.3	Insert and remove hyperlinks	Chapter 8	Navigating with Hyperlinks
1.3	**Format worksheets and workbooks**		
1.3.1	Modify page setup	Chapter 1	Changing Page Orientation and Print Range
1.3.2	Adjust row height and column width	Chapter 1	Adjusting Column Width and Row Height
1.3.3	Customize headers and footers	Common Features	Using the Help Pane and ScreenTips (Common Features)
		Chapter 1	Adding Headers and Footers (Ch1)
1.4	**Customize options and views**		
1.4.1	Customize the Quick Access toolbar	Online	Customizing the Quick Access Toolbar
1.4.2	Display and modify workbook content in different views	Chapter 1	Using Worksheet Views
1.4.3	Freeze worksheet rows and columns	Online	Freezing Worksheet Rows and Columns
1.4.4	Change window views	Chapter 7	Work with Multiple Workbooks
1.4.5	Modify basic workbook properties	Online	Modifying Document Properties
1.4.6	Display formulas	Chapter 2	Showing Functions and Formulas

MOS Excel 2019

MOS Obj #	MOS Objective	Your Office Chapter	Your Office Section Heading
1.5	**Configure content for collaboration**		
1.5.1	Set a print area		
1.5.2	Save workbooks in alternative file formats	Chapter 1	Exporting a Workbook to PDF (Ch1)
		Chapter 8	Creating an Absolute Macro (Ch1)
1.5.3	Configure print settings	Chapter 1	Changing Page Margins and Scaling
			Changing Page Orientation and Print Range
1.5.4	Inspect workbooks for issues	Online	Inspecting a Workbook for Issues
2.	**Manage Data Cells and Ranges**		
2.1	**Manipulate data in worksheets**		
2.1.1	Paste data by using special paste options	Chapter 2	Using Paste Options/Paste Special
2.1.2	Fill cells by using Auto Fill	Chapter 1	Using Series (Auto Fill)
2.1.3	Insert and delete multiple columns or rows	Chapter 1	Inserting and Deleting Columns or Rows
2.1.4	Insert and delete cells	Chapter 1	Inserting and Deleting Cells, Clearing Cells, and Cell Ranges
2.2	**Format cells and ranges**		
2.2.1	Merge and unmerge cells	Chapter 1	Merging and Centering versus Center Across Selection
2.2.2	Modify cell alignment, orientation, and indentation	Chapter 2	Aligning Cell Content
2.2.3	Format cells by using Format Painter	Common Features	Opening Shortcut Menus and Format Painter
		Chapter 2	
2.2.4	Wrap text within cells	Chapter 1	Wrapping Text and Line Breaks
2.2.5	Apply number formats	Chapter 2	Opening an Excel Dialog Box
2.2.6	Apply cell formats from the Format Cells dialog box	Chapter 2	Using the Font Group and the Font Dialog Box
2.2.7	Apply cell styles	Common Features	Using the Style Gallery with Live Preview
		Chapter 2	Using Built-in Cell Styles (Ch2)
2.2.8	Clear cell formatting	Chapter 1	Inserting and Deleting Cells, Clearing Cells, and Cell Ranges
2.3	**Define and reference named ranges**		
2.3.1	Define a named range	Chapter 3	Creating Named Ranges Using the Name Box
			Creating Named Ranges from Selections
2.3.2	Name a table	Online	Naming a Table
2.4	**Summarize data visually**		
2.4.1	Insert Sparklines	Chapter 4	Exploring Sparklines
2.4.2	Apply built-in conditional formatting	Chapter 2	Highlight Values in a Range with Conditional Formatting
			Applying Conditional Formatting to Assess Benchmarks using Icon Sets
2.4.3	Remove conditional formatting	Chapter 2	Removing Conditional Formatting

MOS Excel 2019			
MOS Obj #	MOS Objective	Your Office Chapter	Your Office Section Heading
3.	**Manage Tables and Table Data**		
3.1	**Create and format tables**		
3.1.1	Create Excel tables from cell ranges	Chapter 6	Organizing Raw Data with Tables
3.1.2	Apply table styles	Chapter 6	Exploring Various Table Features
3.1.3	Convert tables to cell ranges	Online	Converting a Table to a Cell Range
3.2	**Modify tables**		
3.2.1	Add or remove table rows and columns	Chapter 6	Creating a Structured Reference in a Table
3.2.2	Configure table style options	Chapter 6	Exploring Various Table Features
3.2.3	Insert and configure total rows	Chapter 6	Exploring Various Table Features
3.3	**Filter and sort table data**		
3.3.1	Filter records	Chapter 6	Using Filters in a Table
3.3.2	Sort data by multiple columns	Online	Sorting Data on Multiple Columns
4.	**Perform Operations by Using Formulas and Functions**		
4.1	**Insert references**		
4.1.1	Insert relative, absolute, and mixed references	Chapter 3	Using Relative Referencing
			Using Absolute Referencing
			Using Mixed Referencing
4.1.2	Reference named ranges and named tables in formulas	Chapter 5	Using the VLOOKUP Function
		Chapter 6	Creating a Structured Reference in a Table
4.2	**Calculate and transform data**		
4.2.1	Perform calculations by using the AVERAGE(), MAX(), MIN(), and SUM() functions	Chapter 2	Using the SUM, COUNT, AVERAGE, MIN, and MAX Functions
4.2.2	Count cells by using the COUNT(), Counta(), and COUNTBLANK() functions	Chapter 2	Using the SUM, COUNT, AVERAGE, MIN, and MAX Functions
		Chapter 3	Using Statistial Functions
4.2.3	Perform conditional operations by using the IF() funciton	Chapter 3	Using Logical Functions
		Chapter 5	Constructing an IF Function
4.3	**Format and modify text**		
4.3.1	Format text by using RIGHT(), LEFT(), and MID() functions	Chapter 9	Using the LEFT and FIND Functions to Separate Data
4.3.2	Format text by using UPPER(), LOWER(), and LEN() functions	Chapter 9	Using Text Functions to Cleanse Data
4.3.3	Format text by using the CONCAT() and TEXTJOIN() functions	Chapter 9	Concatenating Strings of Text/Using Text Functions to Separate Data from the Middle of a Cell

MOS Excel 2019			
MOS Obj #	MOS Objective	Your Office Chapter	Your Office Section Heading
5.	Manage Charts		
5.1	Create charts		
5.1.1	Create charts	Chapter 4	Creating Column Charts
			Creating Pie Charts
			Creating Line Charts
			Creating Bar Charts
			Creating Scatter Charts
			Creating Area Charts
			Creating Combination Charts
			Creating Sunburst Charts
5.1.2	Create chart sheets	Chapter 4	Placing Charts on a Chart Sheet
5.2	Modify charts		
5.2.1	Add data series to charts	Online	Add a Data Series to a Chart
5.2.2	Switch between rows and columns in source data	Chapter 4	Changing the Data and Appearance of a Chart
5.2.3	Add and modify chart elements	Chapter 4	Changing the Data and Appearance of a Chart
			Analyzing with Trendlines
5.3	Format charts		
5.3.1	Apply chart layouts	Chapter 4	Changing the Data and Appearance of a Chart
5.3.2	Apply chart styles	Chapter 4	Modifying an Existing Chart
5.3.3	Add alternative text to charts for accessibilty	Online	Adding Alternative Text to Objects for Accessibility

Microsoft Excel

Appendix D EXCEL EXPERT MICROSOFT CERTIFICATION REFERENCE

MOS Excel 2019 Expert			
MOS Obj #	MOS Objective	Your Office Chapter	Your Office Section Heading
1.	Manage Workbook Options and Settings		
1.1	Manage workbooks		
1.1.1	Copy macros between workbooks	Online	Copying Macros between Workbooks
1.1.2	Reference data in other workbooks	Chapter 7	Linking Workbooks
1.1.3	Enable macros in a workbook	Chapter 14	Opening the Starting File
1.1.4	Manage workbook versions	Online	Managing Workbook Versions
1.2	Prepare workbooks for collaboration		
1.2.1	Restrict editing	Chapter 14	Protect and Secure a Workbook
1.2.2	Protect worksheets and cell ranges	Chapter 8	Unlocking Cells (Ch8)
		Chapter 14	Hiding Formulas (Ch8)
			Protect and Secure a Workbook
1.2.3	Protect workbook structure	Chapter 8	Protecting Workbook Structure
1.2.4	Configure formula calculation options		
1.2.5	Manage comments	Online	Managing Notes and Comments
1.3	Use and configure language options		
1.3.1	Configure editing and display languages	Online	Configure Editing and Display Languages
1.3.2	Use language-specific features	Online	Use Language-Specific Features
2.	Manage and Format Data		
2.1	Fill cells based on existing data		
2.1.1	Fill cells by using Flash Fill	Chapter 9	Use Flash Fill and Text Functions to Cleanse Imported Data
2.1.2	Fill cells by using advanced Fill Series options	Online	Populating Cells by Using Advanced Fill Series Options

MOS Excel 2019 Expert

MOS Obj #	MOS Objective	Your Office Chapter	Your Office Section Heading
2.2	**Format and validate data**		
2.2.1	Create custom number formats	Online	Creating Custom Number Formats
2.2.2	Configure data validation	Chapter 8	Setting Up a List Validation (and throughout the chapter)
2.2.3	Group and ungroup data	Chapter 6	Summarizing Data with a PivotTable
2.2.4	Calculate data by inserting subtotals and totals	Chapter 6	Summarizing a Data Set with the SUBTOTAL Function
2.2.5	Remove duplicate records	Chapter 9	Removing Duplicates
2.3	**Apply advanced conditional formatting and filtering**		
2.3.1	Create custom conditional formatting rules	Chapter 10	Using One-Variable Data Tables (and throughout the chapter)
2.3.2	Create conditional formatting rules that use formulas	Chapter 2	Using Conditional Formatting to Assess Benchmarks Using Font Formatting
2.3.3	Manage conditional formatting rules	Chapter 2	Using Conditional Formatting to Assess Benchmarks Using Icon Sets
3.	**Create Advanced Formulas and Macros**		
3.1	**Perform logical operations in formulas**		
3.1.1	Perform logical operations by using nest functions including the IF(), IFS(), SWITCH(), SUMIF(), AVERAGEIF(), COUNTIF(), SUMIFS(), AVERAGEIFS(), COUNTIFS(), MAXIFS(), MINIFS(), AND(), OR(), and NOT() functions	Chapter 3 / Chapter 5	Using Logical Functions (and throughout the chapter) / Constructing an IF Function (and throughout the chapter)
3.2	**Look up data by using functions**		
3.2.1	Look up data by using the VLOOKUP(), HLOOKUP(), MATCH(), and INDEX() functions	Chapter 5	Using the VLOOKUP Function (and throughout the chapter)
3.3	**Use advanced date and time functions**		
3.3.1	Reference date and time by using the NOW() and TODAY() functions	Chapter 3	Using Date and TIme Functions
3.3.2	Calculate dates by using the WEEKDAY() and WORKDAY() functions	Chapter 9 / Online	Using the NETWORKDAYS and TEXT Functions / Using the WEEKDAY() Function
3.4	**Perform data analysis**		
3.4.1	Summarize data from multiple ranges by using the Consolidate feature	Chapter 7	Consolidating Data by Position

MOS Excel 2019 Expert

MOS Obj #	MOS Objective	Your Office Chapter	Your Office Section Heading
3.4.2	Perform what-if analysis by using Goal Seek and Scenario Manager	Chapter 10	Use Goal Seek to Determine Values Needed to Achieve an Objective
			Using the Scenario Manager
3.4.3	Forecast data by using the AND(), IF(), and NPER() functions	Chapter 5	Constructing an IF Statement (and throughout the chapter)
		Chapter 11	Using the NPER Function
		Chapter 12	Calculating a Moving Average (and throughout the chapter)
3.4.4	Calculate financial data by using the PMT() function	Chapter 3	Using Financial Functions
3.5	**Troubleshoot formulas**		
3.5.1	Trace precedence and dependence	Chapter 8	Auditing Formulas with Trace Dependents and Trace Precedents
3.5.2	Monitor cells and formulas by using the Watch Window	Chapter 8	Opening and Using the Watch Window
3.5.3	Validate formulas by using error checking rules	Online	Validating Formulas by Using Error Checking
3.5.4	Evaluate formulas	Chapter 8	Using the Evaluate Formula Tool
3.6	**Create and modify simple macros**		
3.6.1	Record simple macros	Chapter 8	Creating an Absolute Macro Reference (and throughout the chapter)
3.6.2	Name simple macros	Chapter 14	Create Custom Functions with VBA
3.6.3	Edit simple macros	Chapter 14	Create Custom Functions with VBA
4.	**Manage Advanced Charts and Tables**		
4.1	**Create and modify advanced charts**		
4.1.1	Create and modify dual axis charts	Chapter 4	Creating Combination Charts
4.1.2	Create and modify charts including Box & Whisker, Combo, Funnel, Histogram, Map, Sunburst, and Waterfall charts	Chapter 12	Visualize Outliers with a Box and Whisker Chart
			Using a Histogram to Visualize Data in Bins
4.2	**Create and modify PivotTables**		
4.2.1	Create PivotTables	Chapter 6	Exploring PivotTable Variations
			Creating a PivotTable
			Summarizing Data with a PivotTable
4.2.2	Modify field selections and options	Chapter 6	Configuring PivotTable Options

MOS Excel 2019 Expert

MOS Obj #	MOS Objective	Your Office Chapter	Your Office Section Heading
4.2.3	Create slicers	Chapter 6	Adding a Slicer to the PivotTable
4.2.4	Group PivotTable data	Chapter 6	Summarizing Data with a PivotTable
4.2.5	Add calculated fields	Chapter 6	Configuring PivotTable Options
4.2.6	Format data	Chapter 6	Configuring PivotTable Options
4.3	**Create and modify PivotCharts**		
4.3.1	Create PivotCharts	Chapter 6	Adding a PivotChart
4.3.2	Manipulate options in existing PivotCharts	Chapter 6	Adding a PivotChart
4.3.3	Apply styles to PivotCharts	Chapter 6	Adding a PivotChart
4.3.4	Drill down into PivotCharts details	Online	Drill Down into PivotCharts Details

Glossary

3-D formula A formula that references the same cell or range of cells across multiple worksheets in a workbook.

3-D named range A named range that references the same cell or range of cells across multiple worksheets in a workbook.

3-D reference Allows formulas and functions to use data from cells and cell ranges across worksheets.

A1 reference style Refers to the way cell references are written. If letters appear for the column headings, the reference style for Excel is currently A1. In this mode, cells are referenced using a letter for the column and a number for the row.

A

ABS function Returns the absolute value of a number analyzed by the function.

Absolute cell reference The exact address of a cell when both the column and the row need to remain constant regardless of the position of the cell when the formula is copied to other cells.

Absolute macro reference A macro that affects the same cell reference each time the macro is run.

Active cell The cell that is the recipient of an action, such as clicking, typing, entering a calculation, or pasting; identified by the thick green border. Only the active cell can have data entered into it. Also, the currently selected cell.

Active worksheet The worksheet that is visible in the Excel application window. The active worksheet tab has a white background with bold letters and a thick bottom border.

Add-in An application with specific functionality geared toward accomplishing a specific goal.

Add-ins for Office Apps that enhance office and run in the side pane to provide extra features such as web search, dictionary, and maps.

Advanced Filter A way to filter data where the filtering criteria are set up on the spreadsheet; the filtering criteria must be set up as rows above the data table with field headings that are identical to the data set; criteria can be set up in one or more cells below the field names.

Aggregate To consolidate or summarize data with functions like SUM, COUNT, or AVERAGE.

Amortization schedule A table that calculates the interest and principal payments along with the remaining balance of the loan for each period.

Amortize Pay off the balance of a loan over a period of time in multiple installments or payments.

AND function A function that returns TRUE if all logical tests supplied are true; otherwise, it returns FALSE.

Annuity A recurring amount paid or received at specified intervals.

Any value validation A type of data validation that utilizes the input message to communicate rules to enter data in a cell.

Application Start screen The first screen seen when a program is opened but an existing program file is not open. In the screen, you can select a blank document, workbook, presentation, database, or one of many application-specific templates.

Area chart A chart that emphasizes the magnitude of change over time and visually depicts trends.

Argument A variable or value a function requires in order to calculate a solution.

Array function A function that can perform multiple calculations on one or more items in an array. Array functions look different from other functions because curly brackets { } are required for the function to calculate correctly.

Auto Fill A feature that copies information from one cell or a series in contiguous cells into contiguous cells.

AutoRecovery A feature that will attempt to recover any changes made to a document since your last save if something goes wrong.

AutoSave A feature that will attempt to recover any changes made to a document since your last save if something goes wrong, but this should never be relied upon as a substitute for saving your work manually.

AVERAGE function A function that returns an average or mean from a specified range of cells.

AVERAGEIF function Averages the cells that meet the specified criteria.

AVERAGEIFS function Averages a range of data, selecting data to average based on criteria specified; allowing multiple criteria to determine the subset of data.

B

Bar chart A chart that displays data horizontally and is used for comparison among individual items.

Base value A calculated field that resolves to a value as part of a KPI.

Bidirectional KPI A KPI in which the value becomes worse the farther it deviates from the target value in either direction, such as the temperature for storing a particular product; damage could occur if the temperature gets too cold or too hot.

Binding constraint A constraint is binding if changing it also changes the optimal solution.

Binomial distribution A discrete probability distribution that is used to model the number of successful trials based on the total number of trials and the rate of success.

Bins Intervals into which you want to group your data.

Bootcamp Mac software that allows the user to decide which operating system—Mac operating system or Windows—to run.

Break-even analysis Used to calculate the break-even point in sales volume or dollars, estimate profit or loss at any level of sales volume, and help in setting prices.

Break-even point The sales level at which revenue equals total costs; at the break-even point, there is neither a profit nor a loss.

Built-in cell style   Predefined and named combination of cell and content formatting properties that can be applied to a cell or range of cells to define several formatting properties at once.

Built-in function   A function included in Excel that can be categorized as financial, statistical, mathematical, date and time, text, or so on.

Business intelligence (BI)   A variety of software applications that are used to analyze an organization's data to provide management with the tools necessary to improve decision making, cut costs, and identify new opportunities.

C

CALCULATE function   Evaluates an expression based on the specified filters—similar to COUNTIFS or SUMIFS in Excel.

Calculated Table   A table created from a function that populates the data in the new table.

CALENDAR function   Creates a new table with one field named Date and populates the field with dates automatically based on a given start and end date.

Capital budgeting   The planning procedure used to evaluate whether an organization's long-term investments are worth pursuing.

Cash flow   The movement of cash into and out of a business.

Cell   The intersection of a row and column.

Cell alignment   Allows cell content to be left-aligned, centered, and right-aligned on the horizontal axis as well as top-aligned, middle-aligned, and bottom-aligned on the vertical axis.

Cell range   The cells in the worksheet that have been selected.

Cell reference   A reference to a cell or cell range within a formula or function instead of a value.

Central tendency   The way in which data tends to cluster around some value.

Changing cell   The various data cells whose values can differ in each scenario.

Chart gridlines   Lines that go across charts to help gauge the size of the bars, columns, or data lines.

Chart sheet   A special worksheet that is dedicated to displaying chart objects.

Circular reference   An error in a worksheet indicating a single formula that references itself or multiple formulas that reference each other.

CLEAN   A text function that removes any nonprinting characters from a text string.

Cleansing text   Removing unwanted characters, rearranging data in a cell, or correcting erroneous data.

Clipboard   A temporary storage location where information that was cut or copied is stored until you paste or clear the information.

Close   Closes a file; also, exits the program if no other files are open for that program.

Cloud computing   Computing resources, either hardware or software, on remote servers being used by a local computer over the Internet.

Co-authoring   Allows two or more users to open and work on an Excel workbook at the same time.

Code window   The window where VBA code is typed and where VBA that is generated by a recorded macro can be viewed and edited.

Codification scheme   Rules that combine data values in specific formats and locations to generate a new data value.

Codified data value   A value created by following a system of rules in which the position of information is tied to its content.

Collaboration   Allows workbooks to be shared among different users.

Column   A vertical set of cells that encompasses all the rows in a worksheet.

Column chart   A chart that is used to compare data across categories and show change, sometimes over time.

Combination chart   A chart that displays two different types of data by using multiple chart types in a single chart object.

Competitive advantage   A strategic advantage that a business has over its competition. Attaining a competitive advantage strengthens and positions a business better within the business environment.

CONCAT   A text function used to join strings of text together using up to 254 individual arguments.

Conditional formatting   Applies custom formatting to highlight or emphasize values that meet specific criteria. It is called "conditional" because the formatting occurs when a particular condition is met. Allows the specification of rules that apply formatting to a cell as determined by the rule outcome.

Consolidate by category   Aggregates data in cells with matching row and/or column labels. Data does not need to be in the same relative position to create a summary sheet.

Consolidate by position   Aggregates data in the same position in multiple worksheets. A summary sheet can be created but only when the source worksheets have an identical structure.

Constant   A number that never changes.

Constraint   A rule that you establish when formulating your Solver model.

Contextual tab   A ribbon tab that contains commands related to selected objects so that you can manipulate, edit, and format the objects. A contextual tab does not appear unless the object is selected.

Contiguous cell range   A range consisting of multiple selected cells, all directly adjacent to one another.

Continuous variable   Can contain an infinite number of different values within a range.

Convert Text to Columns Wizard   A special wizard that is used for separating simple data in Excel.

Convert to Range   An option used to convert a data table back to a range of data; the formatting remains, but the functionality of tables, such as adding new columns or rows, will no longer automatically be added or updated to the named ranges, and formulas would need to be manually copied down a column.

Correlation coefficient   A unitless value that describes the strength and direction of a relationship between two variables. A correlation coefficient of −1 is said to have a perfect negative relationship; a coefficient of 1 is considered to have a perfect positive relationship; a coefficient of 0 is said to have no relationship. The closeness of the value to −1 or 1 describes the strength of the relationship.

Cost-volume-profit (CVP) analysis   The study of how cost and volume are related and the effect their relationship has on profit.

Count   The count of all values in the sample.

COUNT function   A function that returns the number of cells in a cell range that contain numbers.

COUNTA function   Returns the number of cells within a range that contain any type of data.

COUNTIF function Counts the number of cells that meet specified criteria.

COUNTIFS function Allows for multiple criteria in multiple ranges to be evaluated and counted.

Coupon The interest rate that a bond pays.

Covariance A formula that can calculate the relationship between two variables, such as age and dollars spent, as well as the direction of the relationship. If one variable increases and the other variable also increases, then the relationship is considered positive. If one variable increases and the other variable decreases, then the relationship is considered negative.

CUMIPMT function A function used to calculate the amount of interest paid over a specific number of periods, such as quarterly or annually.

CUMPRINC function A function used to calculate the amount of principal paid over a specific number of periods, such as quarterly or annually.

Cumulative distribution function The probability of a value being less than or equal to the value of x.

Current yield Considers the current market price of a bond, which may differ from the par value, and gives a different yield rate on that basis.

Custom validation A more complex type of data validation that allows the user to apply multiple criteria simultaneously by using formulas.

D

Data The values that describe an attribute of an object or an event.

Data bar Graphical components that are overlaid onto data in worksheet cells.

Data cleansing The process of fixing obvious errors in data and converting the data into a useful format.

Data model A collection of tables and their relationships that reflect the real-world relationships between business functions and processes.

Data point An individual data value in a data series.

Data series A group of related data values to be charted.

Data set A collection of related data consisting of observational units, variables, and organized data, which includes fields and data that have context and meaning.

Data table A what-if analysis tool that takes sets of input values, determines possible results, and displays all the results in one table on one worksheet.

Data validation Rules that determine what can and cannot be entered in specific cells.

Data verification The process of validating that the data is correct and accurate.

Data view The view where calculations can be added and data can be seen.

Data visualization The graphical presentation of data with a focus on qualitative understanding.

Database functions Designed to easily aggregate and retrieve data from a database where specified criteria are met.

DATE A function that returns the sequential serial number that represents a particular date.

Date and time functions Used for entering the current day and time into a worksheet as well as for calculating the intervals between dates.

Date data Data recognized by Excel as a date; takes the form of a serial number, with the number 1 representing January 1, 1900.

Date validation A type of data validation that specifies only a date can be entered into a cell.

DATEDIF function Enables you to calculate the time between two dates.

DATEVALUE A function that converts a date in a text format into a serial number.

DB function A function used to calculate the depreciation of an asset for a specified period using the fixed declining balance method.

DDB function A function used to calculate the depreciation of an asset for a specified period using the double declining balance method.

Decimal validation A type of data validation that restricts users to enter only data that contains digits and allows decimal places.

Decision tree A diagramming tool that allows you to break down potential decisions in a logical, structured format.

Default A setting that is automatically in place unless you specify otherwise.

Delimiter A way of indicating the beginning and end of a text data segment.

Dependent cell A cell whose value depends on the value in the active cell for its result.

Depreciation schedule Records the date when the asset was placed into service, a calculation for each year's depreciation, and the accumulated depreciation.

Descriptive statistics The process of deriving meaningful information from raw data.

Destination cell The cell that received the result of an operation such as Paste or an AutoSum function. Also, the location cell to be modified by a move or paste operation.

Developer tab A tab that contains the buttons needed to create, edit, and run macros.

Dialog Box Launcher An icon in a group that opens a corresponding dialog box or options.

Digital dashboard A mechanism that delivers business intelligence in graphical form. Dashboards provide management with a big picture view of the business, usually from multiple perspectives, using various charts and other graphical representations.

Discrete variable A variable that can have only a finite number of values and all possible values are known.

Do...Until loop Loops through code until a specified condition is true.

Do...While loop Loops through code while a specified condition is true.

Document A document can be a letter, memo, report, brochure, resume, or flyer.

Drilling down A method for accessing the detailed records used in a PivotTable to get some aggregated data.

E

Economic risk The risk that a chosen act or activity will not generate sufficient revenues to cover operating costs and to repay debt obligations.

Elastic Responsive to change; a small change in price is accompanied by a large change in the quantity demanded.

Embedded chart An object located on the same worksheet with the data.

Encryption A method of protecting a workbook by assigning a password that unscrambles the code once it has been opened.

Error Alert   A message that informs a user when entered data violates validation constraints.

Evaluate Formula   A tool that breaks down a formula into its individual pieces and evaluates each part separately so you can see how the formula works.

Event   An action initiated either by a user or by VBA code.

Evolutionary method   The Solver method used when a worksheet model is nonlinear and nonsmooth. It typically uses functions such as VLOOKUP, PMT, IF, and SUMIF to derive values based on or derived from the variable cells or changing cells.

Excel Online   A web-based Excel application that can be used to view, edit, and collaborate on Excel workbooks.

Explicit calculated field   A field that is created when a formula is typed in the Calculation Area of the Power Pivot window. Explicit calculated fields can use a wide variety of functions beyond general aggregation and can be used in any PivotTable, PivotChart, or Power View report. They can also be extended to become a KPI.

Exponential distribution   A continuous probability distribution that is used to model the time in between events.

Exponential smoothing algorithm   When older data is given progressively less relative weight or importance whereas newer data is given progressively greater weight in making a forecast.

External data   Any data not stored locally or not in an Excel format (.xls or .xlsx).

F

Factor   An argument for the rate at which the balance declines. If factor is omitted, Excel assumes the value to be 2.

Field   An item of information in a worksheet column that is associated with something of interest.

FIELDS pane   Where you can access and see all of the table and fields available for use.

File extension   Letters that come after the period in the name of a file that is assigned by the Office program to indicate the file type.

File path   The physical location of the file starting with a letter that represents the drive and separating folders with a "\".

Fill Across Worksheets   A command that can be used to copy cell contents, formats, or both contents and formats to worksheets in a group.

Fill color   The background color of a cell.

Fill handle   A feature that allows the user to extend—fill—a series of numbers, dates, or text to a desired number of cells.

Filtering   A process of showing only the records that meet specified criteria in a data set. Filtering enables a user to examine and analyze, if desired, a subset of records.

Financial functions   Used for common financial calculations such as interest rates, payments, and analyzing loans.

FIND   A function that searches for a specified string of text in a larger string of text and returns the position number where the specified text begins.

Fixed cost   An expense that never changes regardless of how much product is sold or how many services are rendered.

Flash Fill   A feature that recognizes patterns in data as you type and automatically fills in values for text and numeric data.

Font   The way the letters in words look, including the size, weight, and style.

For...Each loop   Loops through an object collection or an array.

For loop   Loops through code until a specified number of loops have been completed.

FORECAST.ETS function   A function that can help you predict things like future sales, inventory requirements, or consumer trends.

Foreign key   A shared field that is not a primary key but serves as a link to another table in which the same field is a primary key. Also, a field in a data set that stores a value that is the primary key in another data set. It is called foreign because it does not identify a record in this data set; it identifies a record in another—foreign—data set. A foreign key can appear in the same data set many times.

Form control   An object that can be placed into an Excel worksheet, providing the functionality to interact with your models.

Format Painter   A tool that copies the format of objects, such as text or pictures, to other objects and selections.

Formula   A mathematical equation that produces a result and may contain numbers, operators, text, and/or functions. Also, performs a mathematical calculation (or calculations) using information in the active worksheet and other worksheets to calculate new values; it can contain cell references, constants, functions, and mathematical operators.

Formula bar   A tool bar at the top of the Excel spreadsheet window that can be used to enter, edit, or copy text, data, or formulas.

Function   A built-in program that performs a task, such as calculating a sum or average, and/or performs operations on data.

Function Arguments dialog box   A dialog box that provides additional information and previews the results of a function being constructed.

Function procedure   A group of VBA statements that performs a calculation and returns a single value.

fv   An argument used for the future value of the loan balance you reach after the last payment has been made.

FV function   A function used to calculate the value of an investment with a fixed interest rate, term, and periodic payment over a specific period of time.

G

Gallery   A set of menu options that appears when you click the arrow next to a button.

Gauge visualization   Shows how a current value relates to a minimum, target, and maximum value.

Get & Transform   A powerful business intelligence tool that is used to discover data, connect it to your workbook, and transform the data into a more useful state. Also, a business intelligence tool within Excel that enables Excel to connect to a wide variety of data sources and perform a series of recorded steps to combine and refine data for use.

Goal Seek   A scenario tool that maximizes Excel's cell-referencing capabilities and enables you to find the input values needed to achieve a goal or objective.

Graphical format   The presentation of information in charts, graphs, and pictures.

GRG Nonlinear method   A Solver method used when the worksheet model is nonlinear and smooth; it is the default method used. A nonlinear model is one in which just one of the constraint lines breaks the linearity of the model. You may have several constraints that are linear but one constraint line that breaks the linearity of the model.

Gridlines   The vertical and horizontal lines on a worksheet that help define a cell's boundaries.

Grouping   Selecting multiple worksheets at a time.

Grouping variable   A field that could be used to categorize or group for the purpose of comparison.

Groups   Logical groupings of related commands on the ribbon.

Guess   An argument used when you want to guess what the interest rate will be. If nothing is entered, Excel assumes that the guess is 10 percent.

H

Help   Microsoft Help is a window opened via the Help button or the F1 key. Help can give you additional information about a feature or steps for how to perform a new task.

Histogram   A statistical graph that summarizes the distribution of data and how the data fits into defined bins.

HLOOKUP function   Helps retrieve values located in another location and is used when your comparison values are located in a row—horizontally—above the data that you want to retrieve.

Horizontal multiples   Multiples that expand across the available space in the container; if additional space is needed, a horizontal scroll bar is added.

HTML   Short for Hypertext Markup Language, the language that defines how web page content is displayed in a browser.

Hypergeometric distribution   A discrete population distribution that calculates the probability of drawing a specific number of target items from a collection.

Hyperlink   A link that opens another page or file when you click on it.

I

IF function   A logical function that returns one of two values depending upon whether the supplied logical test being evaluated is true or false.

IFERROR function   A function used for detecting an error and displaying something more user-friendly than the error message.

IFS function   A function that allows you to test up to 127 different conditions, specifying a value if true for each with the option to also specify a default value to return if none of the conditions returns true.

Implicit calculated field   A field that is created when you drag a field such as Sales or Quantity Sold into the Values area of a PivotTable. The calculation takes place, but a new calculated field is not being created. Implicit calculated fields can use only standard aggregate functions such as AVERAGE, SUM, COUNT, MAX, etc.

INDEX function   Works in conjunction with the MATCH function; returns the value of an element in a table or array selected by the row and column number indices.

INDIRECT function   A function that can change a text string within a cell to a cell reference.

Inelastic   Not responsive to change; a large change in price is accompanied by a small amount of change in demand.

Inferential statistics   The process of taking data from a sample of the population and making predictions about the entire population.

Information   Data that have context, meaning, and relevance and thus value to the user.

Input box   An effective way of using VBA code to increase the interactivity of a dashboard by prompting the user for information and storing that information in a variable to be used later.

Input Message   The message that appears when a user makes a validated cell active and prompts a user before data is entered with information about data constraints.

Insights   An Excel feature that quickly analyzes data and produces useful visuals in an Insights task pane.

INT function   Rounds down any decimal values to the nearest whole integer.

Intercept coefficient   Part of a regression analysis; the value at which a regression line will cross the y-axis, which is used in the slope intercept formula to predict values.

Interquartile range   The difference between the third and first quartiles of data.

Interval data   Measures the size of the difference between values.

IPMT function   A financial function that calculates how much of a specific periodic payment is going toward the interest that has accrued on the loan.

IRR function   A function used to indicate the profitability of an investment. It is commonly used in business in choosing between investments.

Iteration   A process that repeatedly enters new values in the variable cell or cells to find a solution to the problem.

K

Keyboard shortcut   Keyboard equivalents of software commands that allow you to keep your hands on the keyboard instead of reaching for the mouse to make ribbon selections.

Key performance indicator (KPI)   A quantifiable measure that helps managers define progress toward both short-term and long-term goals.

KeyTip   A form of keyboard shortcuts. Pressing (Alt) will display KeyTips (or keyboard shortcuts) for items on the ribbon and Quick Access Toolbar.

Kurtosis   Characterizes the peakedness or flatness of a distribution compared to the normal distribution.

L

Landscape orientation   For page layout and printing purposes, landscape indicates that the page is wider than it is tall.

LEFT   A text function that returns the characters in a text string based on the number of characters you specify, starting with the far left character in the string.

Legend   An index within a chart that provides information about the data.

LEN   A text function that calculates the length of a specified string by returning the total number of characters in a string.

Line chart   A chart that is used to convey change in data over a period of time; good for showing trends.

Linear programming   A mathematical method for determining how to attain the best outcome in a given mathematical model.

List validation   A type of data validation that presents the user with a list of data values that the user can choose from.

Live Preview   Shows the results that would occur in your document if you were to click that particular option.

Local templates   Templates that are stored in the default Templates folder on your hard drive.

Logical function   A function that returns a result, or output, based upon evaluating whether a logical test is true or false.

Logical operator   Used to create logical tests and includes <, >, <=, >=, and <>.

Logical test   Also known as a logical expression, an equation with a comparison operator that can be evaluated as either true or false.

Lookup and reference functions   Functions that look up matching values in a table of data.

Loop   Used in VBA to execute a series of statements multiple times.

LOWER   A text function that converts all uppercase characters in a text string to lowercase.

M

Macro   A program using VBA that records keystrokes and plays them back when the macro is run.

Map visualization   Allows you to represent locational data such as country, state, zip code, or geological coordinates on a map.

Markup language   A language that uses special sequences of characters or "markup" indicators called "tags" inserted in the document to indicate how the document should look when it is displayed or printed.

MATCH function   Looks for a value within a range and returns the position of that value within the range.

Mathematical operator   Parentheses ( ), exponentiation ^, division /, multiplication *, addition +, or subtraction –.

Maturity   The length of time before par value is returned to the bondholder.

MAX function   A function that examines all numeric values in a specified range and returns the maximum value.

Maximize   The button located in the top-right corner of the title bar.

Maximum   The largest value in the sample.

Mean   The average of all the variables in a sample, often referred to as the arithmetic mean.

Measure in Power BI   Calculates a result from an expression formula and then is available under the FIELDS pane to use in visualizations.

Median   Describes the value falls in the middle when all the values of the sample are sorted in ascending order.

Merge & Center   A feature that combines selected cells into a single cell and then centers the text within that single cell.

Message box   A dialog box object created in VBA and used to display informative messages to the user that includes buttons the user can interact with.

Metadata   Data about data. It describes the content and context of the data.

Method   An action that an object is able to perform.

Microsoft Query   A special tool to help users import individual data fields into their Excel applications and keep the worksheet data synchronized with the data in the external sources.

MID   A text function that returns a specific number of characters from the middle of a text string, starting at the position you specify, based on the number of characters you specify.

MIN function   A function that examines all numeric values in a specified range and returns the minimum value.

Mini toolbar   A toolbar that appears after text has been selected and contains buttons for the most commonly used formatting commands, such as font, font size, font color, center alignment, indents, bold, italic, and underline.

Minimize   Hides a window so it is visible only on the taskbar.

Minimum   The smallest value in the sample.

Mixed cell reference   Using a combination of absolute cell referencing and relative cell references. In a mixed cell reference, the column or row portion of the reference is absolute, and the corresponding row or column is relative.

Mixed cost   A cost that contains a variable component and a fixed component.

Mode   The value that appears most often in a sample.

Module   A container for VBA code.

Most Recently Used list   A list maintained by Office of your most recently modified files: documents, spreadsheets, databases, and presentations.

Moving average   Calculates the average of values over time on the basis of specified intervals.

Multiples   A series of identical charts that have the same x- and y-axes but contain different values.

N

Name Manager   Used to create, edit, delete, or troubleshoot named ranges in a workbook.

Named range   A cell or group of cells that have been given a name, other than the default column and row cell address reference, that can then be used within a formula or function.

Negative KPI   A KPI in which the greater the value, the worse the KPI, such as the number of sick days in a specific time period.

Nested IF function   A function that uses IF functions as arguments within another IF function and increases the number of logical outcomes that can be expressed.

Net book value   The original cost of an asset minus depreciation and amortization.

NETWORKDAYS   A function that calculates the number of available work days between two given dates and will omit holidays if specified.

Nominal data   Uses numbers for categorical or classification purposes only.

Nominal yield   Information provided when a bond is purchased; considered the least helpful when it comes to analyzing the true value of a bond.

Nonbinding constraint   A less severe constraint that does not affect the optimum solution.

Noncontiguous cell range   A range consisting of multiple selected cells with at least one cell not directly adjacent to one another.

Normal distribution   One of the most important distributions in statistics. When charted, it takes on the shape of a bell and is often referred to as the "bell-shaped curve," in which 98% of all values occur within three standard deviations from the mean.

Normal view   The default view in Excel. Only the cells in the worksheet are visible; print-specific features such as margins, headers, footers, and page breaks are not displayed.

NOT function   A function that returns the reverse of the logical value to which the expression evaluates. For example, if the logical expression evaluates to TRUE, the function will return FALSE.

Note   A text box, like a sticky note, that is attached to a cell in a worksheet in which you can enter information or give instructions.

NOW function   Inserts the current date and time in a cell.

nper   An argument used for the total number of payments that will be made to pay the loan in full.

NPER function   A function used to calculate the number of payment periods for an investment or loan if you know the loan amount, interest rate, and payment amount.

NPV function   A function used to determine the value of an investment by analyzing a series of future incoming and outgoing cash flows expected to occur over the life of the investment.

Numeric data   Can consist of numbers (0–9) in any form not combined with letters and special characters such as the period (decimal) and/or hyphen (to indicate negative values).

O

Object   A combination of data and code that is treated as a single unit, including workbooks, worksheets, charts, PivotTables, and even Excel itself.

Object collection   A group of objects that are also considered an object, such as sheets and workbooks.

Object model   A hierarchical collection of objects, consisting of properties, methods, and events that can be manipulated by using VBA.

Objective cell   A cell that contains the formula that creates a value that you want to optimize: maximize, minimize, or set to a specific value.

Object-oriented programming (OOP)   Uses a hierarchy of objects, also called classes, as the focus of the programming.

Observational unit   A person, object, or event about which data is collected.

Office Background   An artistic design in the upper-right area of the title bar in Office.

Office Backstage   Provides access to the file-level commands, such as saving a file, creating a new file, opening an existing file, printing a file, and closing a file, as well as program options and account settings.

Office Theme   A color scheme used by Office.

OneDrive   Microsoft's cloud storage solution that offers a certain amount of storage space free and is fully integrated into File Explorer and Backstage. Also, Microsoft's online file hosting service, which allows users to store, retrieve, edit, and share files.

One-variable data table   A data table that can help you analyze how different values of one variable in one or more formulas will change the results of those formulas.

Online templates   Templates that are stored online that can be downloaded to your hard drive.

Optimize   To find the best way to do something.

OR function   A function that returns TRUE if any one logical test supplied is true; otherwise, it returns FALSE.

Order of operations   The order in which Excel processes calculations in a formula that contains more than one operator.

Ordinal data   Uses numbers to rank data as first, second, third, and so on based on some scale.

Outliers   Values that are abnormally different from the other values in a random sample.

P

Page Break Preview   A view that shows page margins, print headers and footers, and page breaks.

Page Layout view   A view that does not show page margins, headers, or footers.

Par value   How much the bondholder will receive at maturity.

Parameter   A term generally used to describe a value included for calculation or comparison purposes that is stored in a single location (a worksheet cell, for example) so that it can be used many times but be edited in a single location. Also, a special kind of variable used in VBA to refer to one of the pieces of data provided in a method.

Per   An argument that is represented as a number that must be between 1 and nper and is the specific period for which a loan payment is being applied.

Pie chart   A chart that displays a comparison of each value to a total.

PivotChart   A built-in analysis tool that allows for graphical representations of data with the added filtering capabilities of PivotTables.

PivotTable   Interactive table that extracts, organizes, and summarizes source data.

PMT function   A function used to calculate a payment amount based on constant payments and a constant interest rate.

Poisson distribution   A discrete probability function that has wide business applications such as demand for a product or service.

Population   Any entire collection of people, animals, plants, or whatever on which you may collect data.

Portable Document Format (PDF)   A file type that preserves most formatting attributes of a source document regardless of the software in which the document was created. A pdf ensures the document will look the same on someone else's computer.

Portrait orientation   For page layout and printing purposes, portrait indicates the page is taller than it is wide.

Positive KPI   A KPI in which the greater the value, the better the KPI, such as a company's profit.

Power BI Desktop   A free tool for analysts to develop powerful visualizations, models, reports, and analytics made for content developers.

Power BI service   An online, paid service that allows the analyst to share these reports in an interactive form—made for content consumers.

Power View   An interactive data visualization, exploration, and presentation experience that encourages the creation of ad hoc reports.

PPMT function   A financial function that calculates how much of a specific periodic payment is going toward the principal amount of a loan.

Precedent cell   A cell that supplies a value to the formula in the active cell.

Presentation   An oral performance aid that uses slides or a stand-alone presentation such as those at kiosks.

PREVIOUSYEAR function   Returns the date of the previous year from the current data being evaluated.

Primary key   A field that uniquely identifies the record and can only occur once.

Principal   The unpaid balance amount of the loan.

Print Preview   Backstage view of how a document, workbook, presentation, table, or other object will appear when printed.

Probability   The likelihood that some event will occur based on what is already known.

Probability density function   The probability of a value being equal to the value of x.

Probability distribution   Describes all the possible values and likelihoods that a given variable can be within a specific range; can be in the form of a graph, table, or formula.

Project Explorer window   A window that contains a hierarchical list of all the objects available in open workbooks including macros, modules, and worksheets.

PROPER   A text function that will capitalize only the first letter of each word in the text string while changing the other characters to lowercase.

Properties window   A window that contains a list of all the properties of a selected object, such as name, size, and color.

Property   An attribute of an object that can be referred to or manipulated by using VBA.

Protected View   The file contents can be seen and read, but you cannot edit, save, or print the contents until you enable editing. By default, Office will open files from email or a web browser in this view.

pv   The present value of an investment or loan.

PV function   A function used to calculate the present or current value of a series of future payments on an investment.

Q

Quartile   A descriptive statistic that divides data into four equal groups.

Query   A question that you would ask a database.

Quick Access Toolbar   Located at the top-left corner of the Office window, it can be customized to display commonly used commands.

Quick Analysis   A contextual tool that appears when you select data in a worksheet and offers single-click access to formatting, charts, PivotTables, and sparklines.

R

R1C1 reference style   This refers to the way cell references are written. If numbers appear for the column headings, the reference style for Excel is currently R1C1.

Random sample   A subset of a population that has been selected by using unpredictable methods in which each element of the population has an equal chance of being selected.

Range   The difference between the highest and lowest value in the data set.

rate   An argument in several financial functions that notes the periodic interest rate of the loan. Also, the periodic interest rate used for calculating interest accrued.

RATE function   A function used to calculate the interest rate for an investment or loan, given that you know the loan or present value, payment, and number of payment periods.

Ratio data   Similar to interval data except that the differences between the data can be quantified and proportions can be specified.

Raw data   Elements or raw facts—numeric or text—that may or may not have meaning or relevance.

Recommended Charts   A feature that quickly analyzes a selection in a worksheet and recommends chart types that best fit the data.

Record   All of the categories of data that pertain to one person, place, thing, event, or idea and that are formatted as a row in a worksheet.

Regression analysis   A method used to predict future values by analyzing the relationships between two or more variables.

RELATED function   A function that pulls a value from a field in a different table using the relationships defined in the data model.

Relational data   Data about a person, place, or event that is stored in multiple tables.

Relational database   A collection of tables linked together by shared fields. Each table consists of rows and columns, each row being uniquely identified by a primary key field. Also, a three-dimensional database software— because it is able to connect data in separate tables, allowing you to make the most efficient storage of your data.

Relationship   How the data in one data set connects to another data set through common fields known as keys.

Relationships view   This view shows all of the tables and how they are related to one another.

Relative cell reference   Default cell reference in a formula to a cell address position that will automatically adjust when the formula is copied or extended to other cells; the cell being referenced changes relative to the placement of the formula.

Relative macro reference   A macro that identifies cells relative to the location of the active cell when the macro was recorded.

Remove Duplicates   A tool in Excel for removing duplicate entries in data.

Report view   The default view where you build visualizations.

Required rate of return (RRR)   The minimum annual percentage that an investment must earn before a company chooses to invest.

Restore Down   When the window is at its maximum size, the button will restore the window to a previous, smaller size. When a window is in the Restore Down mode, the button expands the window to its full size.

Return on investment (ROI)   The ratio of the amount of money gained or lost from an investment relative to the initial amount invested.

Ribbon Display Options   Has three options: Auto-Hide Ribbon, Show Tabs, and Show Tabs and Commands.

Ribbon   The row of tabs with buttons across the top of the application where you will find most of the commands for the application. The ribbon differs from program to program, but each program has two tabs in common, the File tab and the Home tab.

RIGHT   A text function that returns the characters in a text string on the basis of the number of characters you specify, starting from the far-right character position.

Roaming settings   A group of settings that offer easy remotely synced user-specific data that affect the Office experience.

ROUND function   Used to round a number to a specific number of digits.

Row   A horizontal set of cells that encompasses all the columns in a worksheet.

R-squared   Part of a regression analysis; calculated by squaring the correlation coefficient. This provides a more conservative estimate of the independent variable's ability to predict the value of the dependent variable.

Run-time error   Occurs when VBA code containing improper logic is executed, displaying a description of the error.

S

Salvage value   What an asset is estimated to be worth at the end of its useful life.

Sample population   A subset of a population.

Scatter chart   A chart that shows the relationship between numeric variables.

Scenario   Allows you to build a what-if analysis model that includes variable cells linked by one or more formulas or functions.

Scenario Manager   Allows you to manage scenarios by adding, deleting, editing, and viewing scenarios and to create scenario reports.

Scenario PivotTable report   Summarizes the results of various scenarios side by side in a PivotTable format.

Scenario Summary report   Lists the results of scenarios side by side, allowing the outcomes to be easily compared.

Scenario tool   A tool that enables a user to calculate numerous outputs in other cells by referencing the target cell in formulas and functions.

ScreenTip   Provides a name or other information about the object to which you are pointing.

Scroll bar   A form control that is linked to a specific cell. As the scroll bar slides left to right or up and down, the value in the linked cell increases or decreases accordingly. Also, a form control used in what-if analyses that allows you to change a number in a target cell location in single-unit increments.

Security   A legal document that can be bought and sold and holds some financial value.

Separator   Indicates the distinction between the object container and the member of that container.

SharePoint   A document management and collaboration service developed by Microsoft used as a content management system for internal purposes.

Shortcut menu   A list of commands related to a selection that appears when you right-click.

Silverlight   A powerful tool for creating interactive user experiences. It is a free plug-in powered by the .NET framework and is compatible with multiple browsers, devices, applications, and operating systems.

Simplex LP method   A linear model in which the variables are not raised to any powers and no transcendent functions such as sine or cosine are used. A linear model can be charted as straight lines.

Skewness   Characterization of the degree of asymmetry of a distribution around its mean.

Slicer   A visual control that allows you to quickly and easily filter your data in an interactive way; can replace filter icons in PivotCharts. Also, a visual control that provides the user with buttons that can be used to quickly filter data in a table, PivotChart, or PivotTable.

SLN function   A function used to calculate the depreciation of an asset for a specified period using the fixed declining balance method.

Solver   An add-in that helps to optimize a problem by manipulating the values for several variables with constraints that you determine.

Solver Answer Report   A report that lists the target cell and the changing cells with their corresponding original values, final values for the problem, input variables, and constraints. In addition, the formulas, binding status, and slacks are given for each constraint.

Solver Limits Report   A report that displays the achieved optimal value and all the input variables of the model with the optimal values. Additionally, the report displays the upper and lower bounds for the optimal value.

Solver Population Report   A report that displays various statistical characteristics about the given model, such as how many variables and rows it contains.

Solver Sensitivity Report   A report that provides information about how sensitive the solution is to small changes in the formula for the target cell. This report displays the shadow prices for the constraint—the amount that the objective function value changes per unit change in the constraint. This report can be created only if your Excel model does not contain integer or Boolean—the values 0 and 1—constraints.

Source cell(s)   The cell(s) that contain the data supplied to a function.

Sparkline   Small charts embedded into cells on a spreadsheet, providing a way to graphically summarize a row or column of data in a single cell with a miniature chart.

Spin button   A form control that is linked to a specific cell. As the up and down arrows on the button are clicked, the value in the linked cell increases and decreases accordingly.

Spreadsheet   A collection of data that is organized in a row and column format. Also, a two-dimensional grid that can be used to model quantitative data and perform accurate and rapid calculations with results ranging from simple budgets to financial and statistical analyses.

Stacked bar chart   A chart that is useful when you want to see how the individual parts add up to create the entire length of each bar.

Standard deviation   The most commonly used method for determining the average spread of a data set from the mean. Mathematically, the standard deviation is calculated by taking the square root of the variance.

Standard error   Used to determine how accurately the sample mean predicts the population mean by dividing the standard deviation by the square root of the sample size.

Standard filter   Displays the values in the field that can be toggled on and off using check boxes.

Statistics   The practice of collecting, analyzing, and interpreting data.

Status threshold   Defined by the range between a high value and a low value as part of a KPI.

Structured reference   A formula that refers to table columns by names generated when the table was created.

Sub procedure   A VBA procedure that performs an action on your project or workbook.

SUBTOTAL function   A function specific to the filtering mechanism that will only run calculations on the data that is in the subset when a filter is applied. Also, a function that can return any of 11 different values including all of the AutoSum functions, the product, standard deviation, and variance.

Sum   The sum of all values in the sample.

SUM function   A function that adds of all numeric information in a specified range, list of numbers, list of cells, or any combination.

SUMIF function   Sums cells that meet specified criteria.

SUMIFS function   Sums a range of data, selecting data to total based on the multiple criteria specified.

Summary variable   Data that are not categorical in nature and can be aggregated by summing, counting, or averaging, such as gross revenue, quantity, or price; would likely be used for summarization.

Sunburst chart   A chart used to display hierarchical data.

Syntax   The structure and order of the function and the arguments needed for Excel to run a function.

T

Table   Typically contains related data organized into rows and columns that have been formatted as a table, using Excel's table tools helping to provide context to the user by organizing the data in a meaningful way.

Tabular format   The presentation of information such as text and numbers in tables—essentially organized in labeled columns and numbered rows.

Target value   A value that can be either another calculated field that resolves to a value or an absolute value as part of a KPI.

T-chart   A common method for dividing up the logic into outcomes and conditions.

Tell me what you want to do   A help tool on the title bar in Office applications that can launch commands in addition to accessing traditional help.

Template A workbook that provides a starting point for building other similar workbooks.

TEXT A text function that allows you to display numeric data as text in addition to using special formatting strings to display the text.

Text data Can contain any combination of printable characters, including letters, numbers, and special characters available on any standard keyboard.

Text file A simple container of text data that is structured by the use of delimiters.

Text function A function that manages, manipulates, and formats text data.

Text length validation A type of data validation used to limit the number of characters that can be entered into a cell.

TEXTJOIN A function in Excel that concatenates text and can include a delimiter between each string of text.

Text-to-speech A feature that reads the values of text back to you. Headphones or speakers are required for this feature to work properly.

Theme A collection of fonts, styles, colors, and effects associated with a theme name that enables you to create professional, color-coordinated documents quickly.

Tiles A dynamic navigation strip in Power View that allows you to navigate through a series of charts based on a particular value.

Time data Data recognized by Excel as representing time; represented as a decimal value, where .1 is 144 minutes, .01 is 14.4 minutes, and so on.

Time Intelligence Calculations that allow you to easily compare time hierarchy in years, quarters, months, and days.

Time validation A type of data validation that restricts only time values to be entered into a cell.

TODAY function Inserts the current date into a cell.

Toggle button A type of button where one click turns the feature on and a second click turns the feature off.

TOTALYTD function Calculates an expression from the first day of the year to the specified date.

Touch mode Applies to touch screen devices; the ribbon and shortcut menus are enlarged to make selecting commands with your fingertip easier.

Trace dependents A tool that automatically draws arrows from the active cell to its dependent cells.

Trace precedents A tool that automatically draws arrows from the precedent cells to the active cell.

Transformation The process of converting data from one format to another; can range from separating strings of text, to calculating the difference between dates, to appending sets of data from different sources together.

Treemap visualization Represents hierarchical data in the form of a rectangle with smaller rectangles inside where the size of the rectangles represents the value.

Trendline A line that uses current data to show a trend or general direction of the data.

TRIM A text function that removes all spaces from text except for single spaces between words.

Trusted Location A folder that has been identified in the Microsoft Office Trust Center as a safe location from which to open files that contain active code, including macros.

Two-variable data table A data table that can help you to analyze how changing the value of two variables affects the results of a formula.

Type An argument to indicate when the payments are due either at the beginning (1) or the end of a period (0). If type is omitted (because it is an optional argument), Excel assumes that the value is 0.

U

UPPER A text function that converts all characters in a string to uppercase.

USB drive A small and portable storage device, popular for moving files back and forth between a lab, office, and/or home computer.

V

Validation criteria Constraints that limit what users are allowed to enter into a particular cell.

Variable A value stored in a cell and used in a formula or function. The value can be changed to see how the change affects other values. Also, space in a computer's memory that is given a name and is used to store a value of a specified data type.

Variable cost A cost that changes based on how many products are sold or services are rendered.

Variance A calculation used in statistics to determine how far the data set varies from the mean.

Vertical multiples Multiples that expand across the width of the container and wrap down the container in the available space. If all multiples do not fit in the available space, a vertical scroll bar is also added.

Virtualization Software that mimics Windows in order to run Office on a Mac.

Visual Basic Editor (VBE) The tool built into Microsoft Office that is used for creating and editing VBA.

Visual Basic for Applications (VBA) A computer programming language that is part of most Microsoft Office products that users can use to implement a wide variety of enhancements to Microsoft Office applications.

Visualizations Many different kinds of connected visual content, for example a table, map, line, column, waterfall, and many more.

VISUALIZATIONS pane Where you create, configure, and format the visualizations—such as a map.

VLOOKUP function A function that matches a provided value in a table of data and returns a value from a subsequent column; also helps to retrieve values located in another location and is used when your comparison values are located in a column (vertically) to the left of the data you want to find.

W

Watch Window A feature that makes it possible to monitor cells the user considers important in a separate window.

Web query A method for importing data into a spreadsheet directly from a web page.

What-if analysis Allows one to examine the outcome of the changes to values in a worksheet; changing values in spreadsheet cells to investigate the effects on calculated values of interest. An analysis that changes values in a spreadsheet to explore all the various results.

White space   Space in a document or worksheet that does not contain data of any kind, allowing the user's eyes to rest.

Whole number validation   A type of data validation that requires only integers, or whole numbers, be entered in a cell.

Workbook   An Excel file that contains one or more worksheets.

Worksheet   A single spreadsheet; a grid of columns and rows in which data is entered.

X

XIRR function   A function used to analyze a series of cash flows that are irregular or not periodic.

XML   An acronym for Extensible Markup Language, which allows users to define their own tags in order to define the content of the document. Used for web documents and transmitting data between systems.

XML element   Includes the start and stop tags and everything in between them.

XML map   The same as an XML schema in that it describes the structure of an XML document. Excel either creates an XML map on the basis of an existing schema or creates a default map.

XML schema   Describes the structure of an XML document in terms of what XML elements it will contain and their sequence.

XNPV function   A function to determine the value of an investment or business by analyzing an irregular time series of incoming and outgoing cash flows.

Y

Yield   The amount of annual interest, expressed as a percentage of the par value; determines how much investors will receive on their investment.

Yield to maturity (YTM)   A yield calculation that takes into account the current market price and the time to maturity and assumes that coupon payments are reinvested at the bond's coupon rate.

Index

Page numbers in **bold** denote pages where key terms are defined or introduced.

Data (continued)
   relational, 712
   retrieving using lookup and reference functions, 293–314
   rounding, 178–179
   separating, 524–527, 531–534
   separating using wizards, 533–534
   storage in Excel, 497
   summarizing with PivotTable, 352–356
   text, 60, 508–511, 518–519
   time, 60
   transformation, 497
   using text functions to separate, 524–527, 531–534
   verification, 518
   XML, 503–508
Data analysis
   conditional formatting for, 557–558
   with data tables, 559–564
   developing questions for, 329
Data Analysis add-in
   adding, 660–661, 661 (fig.)
   correlation matrix creation, 683–684, 684 (fig.)
   creating a regression analysis using, 685–687
   descriptive statistics generated using, 661–662, 662 (fig.)
   enabling, 715–716, 716 (fig.)
Data Analysis Descriptive Statistics tool, 661–663
Data Analysis eXpressions (DAX), 721, 724, 832
Data bars, **246,** 246–247, 247 (fig.)
Data cleansing, **518,** 518–523
   data-related data, 537–538
   with Flash Fill, 518–520, 519 (fig.)–520 (fig.)
   nonprintable characters, 522
   with text functions, 521–523, 523 (fig.)
Data labels, 215, 216, 219, 234–235, 235 (fig.), 250
Data modeling, 359
Data models, **712**
   adding a table to, 719
   building using an Access database, 714–715, 715 (fig.)
   creating advanced using Power Pivot, 719–729
   relationships in, 720–721, 721 (fig.)
Data point, **214**
Data series, **214,** 215
Data sets, **323, 649**
   central tendency of, 653–654
   dates in, 511–513
   dispersion of, 655–656, 656 (fig.)
   filtering, 330
   importance of external, 497–502
   summarizing with the SUBTOTAL function, 339–341, 340 (fig.)
Data table, **559**
   automatic updating, 561
   hiding formulas in, 560
   one-variable, 559–561, 559 (fig.)–561 (fig.)
   two-variable, 562–564, 562 (fig.), 564 (fig.)
Data types in VBA, 785
Data validation, **436,** 436–450
   any value validation, 444
   codification schemes, 446–447, 447 (fig.)
   controlling data entry with, 436–437
   criteria, 436
   custom, 445–446, 445 (fig.)
   date, 440–441, 441 (fig.)
   error alerts, 437

   list validation, 437–439, 438 (fig.)
   text length validation, 443–444, 444 (fig.)
   text-to-speech for, 448–450, 449 (fig.)
   time, 441–442, 442 (fig.)
   when not to use, 446
   whole number validation, 442–443, 443 (fig.)
Data verification, **518**
Data view, **828**
Data visualization, **213**
   Map Charts for, 743–745
Database. *See also* Access
   connecting to, 513–515
   Excel, 342
   importing data from, 515–517
   Microsoft Query retrieval of data from, 515–517
   relational, 514
Database functions, **341**
   arguments, 342
   list and descriptions of, 343 (table)
   naming format, 342
   using, 342–347, 344 (fig.)–346 (fig.)
Database management system (DBMS), 341
Databases
   launching and connecting Power BI Desktop to, 824–828, 825 (fig.)–828 (fig.)
Date and time functions, **183,** 183–186, 184 (table)
Date data, **60**
   cleansing, 537–538
   formatting, 109–110
DATE function, **540,** 540–542
Date functions, 540–542
Date measures, 839–840, 847–848
Date validation, **440,** 440–441, 441 (fig.)
DATEDIF function, 184 (table), **185,** 185–186, 185 (table), 186
Dates
   creating with date functions, 540
   as numeric values in Excel, 539
   reconstructing dates Text to Columns wizard, 539–540, 540 (fig.)
   transforming using Get & Transform, 511–513
DATEVALUE function, **538,** 538 (fig.), 541
DAVERAGE function, 343 (table)
DAX functions, 724
DAY function, 184 (table), 541
DB function, **637,** 637–638, 638 (fig.)
DBMS (database management system), 341
DCOUNT function, 343 (table)
DCOUNTA function, 343 (table)
DDB function, **639,** 639–640, 640 (fig.)
Debugging VBA, 782–783, 783 (fig.)
Decimal validation, **439,** 439–440
Decision making
   creating information for, 121–140
   "machine," 140
   using conditional formatting to assist in, 131–136
Decision trees, **279,** 279 (fig.), 280
Declining balance depreciation (DB), 634, 637–638, 638 (fig.)
Default, **111**
Define Name, 173, 176
Delete dialog box, 67, 67 (fig.)
Deleting
   cells and cell ranges, 66–67
   chart elements, 241